Readings in
Sociology
An Introduction

Readings in Sociology
An Introduction

Lorne Tepperman
Department of Sociology
University of Toronto

James Curtis
Department of Sociology
University of Waterloo

McGraw-Hill Ryerson Limited

Toronto Montreal New York Auckland Bogotá
Cairo Caracas Hamburg Lisbon London Madrid
Mexico Milan New Delhi Panama Paris San Juan
São Paulo Singapore Sydney Tokyo

READINGS IN SOCIOLOGY
An Introduction

Copyright © McGraw-Hill Ryerson Limited, 1988.
All rights reserved. No part of this publication
may be reproduced stored in a retrieval system,
or transmitted, in any form or by any means,
electronic, mechanical, photocopying, recording,
or otherwise, without prior written permission of
McGraw-Hill Ryerson Limited

ISBN 0-07-549287-3

1 2 3 4 5 6 7 8 9 0 THB 9 0 1 2 3 4 5 6 7 8

Cover and Book Design by Daniel Kewley

Printed and bound in Canada

Care has been taken to trace ownership of
copyright material contained in this text. The
publishers will gladly take any information that
will enable them to rectify any reference or
credit in subsequent editions.

Canadian Cataloguing in Publication Data
Main entry under title:

Readings in sociology

Bibliography: p.
ISBN 0-07-549287-3

1. Sociology. 2. Canada – Social conditions.
I. Tepperman, Lorne,   –   .
I. Curtis, James E.,   –   .

HM51.R42 1987   301   C87-094545-9

c o n t e n t s

p r e f a c e

Putting this book together has been interesting, even exciting. It has given us a chance to read a great deal of recent as well as older scholarship, and to find patterns in the development of Canadian sociology. We hope you are as pleased with the result as we are.

This book required the co-operation of a great many people. Nearly sixty eminent Canadian sociologists sent us biographical information and material to consider for inclusion in the reader. Eric Weissman helped us sort through this enormous amount of information and reach some decisions about which pieces to include. In a way, getting and choosing the selections was the easiest part of the job.

The support McGraw-Hill Ryerson provided was tremendous. Fred Chorley, former College Editor, gave us encouragement at every stage. Norma Christensen carried out an enormous number of clerical and administrative tasks, and obtained the permissions to reprint selected articles at prices we could afford. Gail Marsden prepared the final manuscript for the printer in a most businesslike and professional way.

Several others outside McGraw-Hill Ryerson were also very helpful. Jack Veugelers translated the Bernard and Renaud piece from the original French. University of Toronto colleagues Dennis Magill and Rick Helmes-Hayes wrote biographic sketches for Rex Lucas and Everett Hughes, respectively. Most important of all, Alan Wain, a freelance editor who collaborated in several other projects, including *The Social World* (1986) and *Understanding Canadian Society* (1988), shortened almost all of the selected articles quite substantially, so that we could include as many varieties of Canadian sociology as we had hoped to. His contribution was absolutely fundamental to the success of this project, and we thank him for it.

Lorraine Thompson at the University of Waterloo supplied clean copies of the section introductions and otherwise helped to keep the paper flowing between Waterloo, Toronto and points east and west.

Having said all that, our main thanks go to the sociologists who co-operated so magnificently in this endeavour: who sent us material, agreed to editorial changes (usually shortening) and gave us permission to reprint the selected articles, all with admirable promptness. This book is the result of their co-operation.

We found this project difficult because many excellent pieces of work and many exceptional scholars could not be included; this distressed us. This book would have to be at least twice as long to begin to capture the richness of current Canadian sociology. This richness we can applaud, though. So we dedicate this book to our colleagues in Canadian sociology—always a small and vigorous community and, now, a growing community that has clearly come of age.

Readings in Sociology

An Introduction

What Is Sociology?

Introduction

The essence of sociology is its "classical tradition." In the first article of this Section, Robert Brym introduces us to the classic concerns that motivated sociology's founding figures. They include the following questions: "What is the relationship between the individual and society?," "Are the most important determinants of social behaviour cultural or economic?," and "What are the bases of social inequality?" Like all good questions, they allow many answers. As a result, these and other central questions of sociology have been answered in many ways by sociologists from different schools of thought. They have emerged time and again over the discipline's history to be answered again; and today they remain as fresh and challenging as they were a century ago.

Sociology is largely definable as the asking and answering of these classic questions. But sociology is also what living people who call themselves "sociologists" do. As a result, the discipline has developed differently in different countries. In some places, sociology has been more influenced by social psychology (e.g., the USA); in others, by anthropology (e.g., Great Britain); and in other places still, by philosophy (e.g., Germany). We learn in the article by Donald Whyte and Frank Vallee that, in

Canada, *all* of these disciplines influenced the development of sociology. As well, Canadian sociology has been shaped by the study of history and political economy. Particularly in English-speaking Canada, sociology's connection with history and political economy has remained strong for four decades. It began with the work of political economist Harold Innis and his protégés—among them sociologist S.D. Clark. (Professor Clark's work is included in this section and in Section Fourteen.) Through the spread of graduates from the University of Toronto, this approach to sociology influenced scholarly work all around the country.

But other important elements also entered into the development of Canadian sociology. At McGill University, Carl Dawson and Everett Hughes taught the "Chicago School's" ecological approach, which focused on the geographic dispersion and interaction of competing groups. This teaching served to link Canadian sociology with mainstream American work. The British Fabian socialist tradition also made itself felt in work by Leonard Marsh in the 1930s and 1940s and, more importantly, by John Porter in the 1950s–1970s. This approach set the enduring character of Carleton University's "school" of sociology, and has led into Marxist-oriented sociology as practised today by Wallace Clement (a student of John Porter's), among others.

If sociology were only what sociologists do, it would be hard to identify from one nation to another and from one "school of thought" to another. But the variation is not really so great if we stand back and look for common elements. Although strongly marked by historical, national and regional variation, sociology is nonetheless well enough defined by its central concerns to be distinguishable from the other social sciences (e.g., psychology, anthropology, political science and economics); from the more speculative or deductive disciplines (e.g., philosophy); and the less systematic inductive fields (e.g., journalism and social work). An article by Kenneth Westhues helps us see the major defining features of sociology by comparing sociology with other disciplines. Of course, fields of study making up the humanities and social sciences can never be entirely distinct; they all have as their subject the explanation of human behaviour and must, therefore, often talk about the same things. But they do this differently using (often) different language, rules of proof, and different kinds of data to support their arguments.

As well, the various disciplines have somewhat different purposes. Some are more concerned with theorizing, others with describing, prescribing, or even taking action. In this context, sociology can be viewed as a very particular inclination towards theorizing about social structure with the help of data. ("Social structure" is the regular patterning of relations among individuals and groups.) Its inclination is clear enough so that sociologists around the world can readily understand one another, and make use of one another's findings. Without stretching the point, there is probably more unified thinking *among* the world's sociologists, than *between* the sociologists and economists, or sociolo-

gists and psychologists, or sociologists and anthropologists, of any given country.

Nonetheless, articles in this section by S.D. Clark and Wallace Clement express the particularity of social theorizing. Professor Clark, as we have already noted, played a major part in developing the Toronto school's mix of sociology, history, and political economy. He argues here for the need to study all social structures historically. Professor Clark is fighting against a school of thought called "functionalism," personified in the 1940–1960s by American sociologist Talcott Parsons. Parsons argued that social structures were typically in a state of harmony and self-maintaining balance, or "equilibrium." Professor Clark finds this view of societies misleading. A society is always changing, he argues; whether changes are for the better or worse, whether upsetting an old balance or creating a new one, remains a matter of interpretation. The functionalist's emphasis on order and the continuity of traditions will simply not help us to understand *how* we got from one kind of community in 1900, say, to a vastly different one in 1988. For this reason, we need theories of both change *and* order. As well, sociological theories must take appropriate notice of such influences as geography, economy, political struggle and demographic change and not only the change of values on which Parsons focuses.

Wallace Clement's article addresses a related but somewhat different concern. He asks if there should be a uniquely Canadian sociology, reflecting the peculiarities of Canadian historical development and, if so, what would be the main elements or concerns of such a sociology. This question received a lot of attention from Canadian sociologists through the 1970s and 1980s. A general surge of Canadian nationalism in the universities was directed against the tendency of American trained sociologists to see Canadian social structure and change as mere variants of American-style modernization. Thus, Clement is asserting that differences in sociological approach will inevitably arise out of genuine social differences between Canada and the USA.

Note the similarity between what Professor Clement prescribes for Canadian sociology and the sociological work that eclectic Professor Clark had been producing for the previous three decades. All roads seem to lead in the same direction. Not only is a unique Canadian sociology possible; but, as the articles in this book demonstrate, it already exists. The Canadian sociological tradition can be readily seen by comparing the readings in this book with those in any American introductory reader.

All the sections will display this uniqueness: a tendency toward holistic or macrosociological over microsociological (or social psychological) analysis: a sympathy for historical and multidisciplinary analysis; and a return, time and again, to explaining Canada's social experience in terms of its peculiar relationship first to Britain and later to the United States.

Although some have already tried impressively (cf. Brym, 1986), it may be too soon to write the last word on the nature of Canadian sociology (even only English-language Canadian sociology). Canadian sociology has a tradition nourished by sociology's classic concerns, the peculiarities of Canada's national experience, and the local or regional variations in intellectual development discussed by Professors Whyte and Vallee. In this book's articles, we see some of the best of Canadian sociology; and from this, the reader will begin to get a picture of how the parts of this complicated puzzle fit together. Later observers will, no doubt, be better able to see what directions we are taking and how far we have already travelled.

References

Brym, Robert "Anglo-Canadian Sociology", *Current Sociology*, 34 (1), 1986.

1 Foundations of Sociological Theory

Robert J. Brym

ROBERT J. BRYM, Professor of Sociology at the University of Toronto, specializes in the sociology of politics in Canada and the USSR. He is the author of *The Jewish Intelligentsia and Russian Marxism* (1978); *Intellectuals and Politics* (1980); and *Soviet-Jewish Emigration and Soviet Nationality Policy*, with Victor Zaslavsky (1983). He has also edited and contributed to *Underdevelopment and Social Movements in Atlantic Canada* with R.J. Sacouman (1979); *The Structure of the Canadian Capitalist Class* (1985); and *Regionalism in Canada* (1986). His latest monograph is "Anglo-Canadian Sociology", in *Current Sociology* (34, 1:1986), which he is currently revising for publication as a book. Professor Brym is Sociology Editor of the *Canadian Review of Sociology and Anthropology*.

INTRODUCTION

Sociology will inevitably appear a confusing enterprise to students just beginning to study it. Sociologists occupy themselves with problems that also concern political scientists, economists, psychologists, social workers, urban planners, psychiatrists and lawyers. In what sense, then, is sociology distinct from these other disciplines?

The answer has more to do with the unique *approach* of sociologists to their subject matter than with the nature of the subject matter itself. While many kinds of scholars are interested in, say, crime, economic development, elections and mental disorders, sociologists ask relatively distinct questions about these and other social issues.

I shall examine three of the main questions that have animated the discipline since its origins in the nineteenth century: (1) What is the relationship between the individual and society? (2) Are the most important determinants of social behaviour cultural or economic? (3) What are the bases of social inequality?

The debates surrounding these questions are recurrent. It is the tenacity and longevity of these disputes that permits us to characterize them as key issues in sociology. But the enduring character of these disputes may also be a source of some frustration to the introductory student. It may appear that nothing ever gets resolved in sociology. However, careful study of the discipline should demonstrate that sociological knowledge is, to some degree, cumulative. In other words, although sociologists ask much the same questions today as they did a century ago, their answers are now much more precise, complex and enlightening than they were then; the classic questions of sociology continue to engage lively minds in a debate that gets more and more sophisticated over time.

Let us begin by examining Emile Durkheim's *Suicide*, which, nearly a century ago, set out a highly controversial idea about the individual's relationship to society.

INDIVIDUAL AND SOCIETY

a. Durkheim on "Social Facts" and Suicide

Usually we are inclined to think of any act—a suicide, a marriage, a revolution, the achievement of extraordinary economic success in

4

life—as the outcome of an individual's (or many individuals') motives. Features of society are, in turn, usually viewed as the result of many individual passions and decisions. Durkheim, however, turned this conventional wisdom on its head. He argued that individual passions and decisions are the result of certain features of society, that the social whole is greater than the sum of its individual parts. And, according to Durkheim, the study of how social patterns influence individual behaviour is what sociology is all about (Durkheim, 1966 [1895]).

Consider, for example, the act of suicide. For two reasons, no act appears to be more personal than the taking of one's own life. First, common sense suggests that suicide is the outcome of some profound disorder in the mind of the *individual*. Second, suicide seems the most *anti-social* act imaginable: it negates—indeed, destroys—society, at least for one person.

Yet in 1897 Durkheim proposed the controversial idea that the causes of suicide are not at all personal. If suicide rates are high in one group of people and low in another, this is due, said Durkheim, to the operation of "social facts." Before specifying what Durkheim meant by a social fact, let us briefly see how he disposed of psychological explanations of suicide.[1] For different groups, Durkheim examined the association between rates of suicide (the number of suicides among 100,000 people) and rates of psychological disorder (the number of cases of psychological disorder among 100,00 people). The notion that psychological disorder causes suicide is supported, Durkheim reasoned, only if suicide rates tend to be high where rates of psychological disorder are high, and if suicide rates tend to be low where rates of psychological disorder are low.

But Durkheim's examination of European government statistics, hospital records and other sources revealed nothing of the kind. For example, he discovered that: (1) There are slightly more women than men in insane asylums. But there are four male suicides for every female suicide. (2) Jews have the highest rate of psychological disorder among the major religious groups in France. But they also have the lowest suicide rate. (3) Psychological disorders occur most frequently when a person reaches maturity. But suicide rates increase steadily with age.

Clearly, suicide rates and rates of psychological disorder do not vary directly; in fact, they appear to vary inversely. Why, then, do males commit suicide more frequently than females, the aged more than the young, Jews less than Catholics, Catholics less than Protestants? Durkheim saw these regularities as results of variations in the degree of "social solidarity" in different categories of the population. Groups whose members interact more frequently and intensely are, accordingly, expected to exhibit lower suicide rates. For example, married adults are half as likely as unmarried adults to commit suicide, because marriage creates social ties that bind the individual to society. Where these ties are absent, suicide is more likely. Likewise, large families provide their members with more social ties than do small families; the suicide rate is thus lower in large families. In general, wrote Durkheim, "suicide varies with the degree of integration of the social groups of which the individual forms a part.... The more weakened the groups to which he[2] belongs, the less he depends on them, the more he consequently depends only on himself and recognizes no other rules of conduct than what are founded on his private interests," the greater the chance that an individual will take his or her own life (Durkheim, 1951 [1897]: p. 209).

b. The Phenomenological Response

Many contemporary sociologists continue to argue that the proper focus of the discipline is the study of social pressures that constrain or influence the minds of individuals. Today, using advanced statistical techniques, researchers can measure the independent and combined effects of many social "variables" on many types of behaviour. The choice of a marriage partner may, for example, seem to be a question of love. But even love is constrained by social facts: research reveals that a very large proportion of marriages join partners from the same ethnic groups and classes.

However, not all marriages take place within ethnic and class groupings. This, opponents of the Durkheimian position argue, points to an important flaw in the theory. They argue that Durkheim paints an altogether too mechanical and deterministic view of the individual in society, making it seem as if people behave like billiard balls, knocked about on predetermined trajectories, unable to choose to alter their destinations. But, Durkheim's critics continue, we know from our everyday experience that this is not the case. People *do* make choices—often difficult ones—about what career to follow, what country to live in, whether and in what form they will adopt an established religion, whether to engage in heterosexual or homosexual relationships (or both), and so forth. Two people with similar social characteristics may react quite differently to similar social facts because, according to Durkheim's detractors, they may *interpret* the same social facts differently. In the opinion of such "phenomenological" sociologists, an adequate explanation of social phenomena requires that we understand the *subjective meanings* people attach to social facts and the ways in which people actively *create* these social facts.

In order to understand better the phenomenological school of thought let us return to the problem of suicide. If a police officer discovers a dead person at the wheel of a car which has run into a tree it may be very difficult to establish with any certainty whether the death was accidental or suicidal. Interviewing friends and relatives in order to find out the dead person's state of mind immediately before the crash may help rule out the possibility of suicide. But, as this example illustrates, understanding the intention or motive of the actor is critical to explaining or labelling a social action. Suicide, then, is not just an objective social fact, but an inferred, and therefore subjective, social fact. A state of mind must be interpreted—usually by a coroner—before the dead body becomes a suicide statistic (Douglas, 1967).

Because social stigma is attached to suicide, coroners are inclined to classify deaths as accidental whenever such an interpretation is at all plausible. Experts believe that, for this reason, official suicide rates are about one-third lower than actual suicide rates. The phenomenological study of social life reveals many such inconsistencies between objective and subjective reality. For instance, when increased crime rates among native Canadians are reported in the newspapers this may reflect more crimes being committed by native Canadians. But the phenomenological sociologist is unlikely to accept such reports at face value. The higher crime rate may result from a politically motivated change in the official definition of what constitutes a crime, or increased police surveillance in areas where native people reside. Here, inquiry into the subjective underside of the official picture may deepen our understanding of how society works.

Most modern sociologists think it makes more sense to combine the Durkheimian and phenomenological approaches. Thus, most sociologists analyze how men and women interpret, create and change their social existence—but within the limits imposed upon them by powerful social constraints. This synthetic approach is found in the work of Karl Marx and Max Weber, who, along with Durkheim, established the groundwork of modern sociology. It is to an examination of their work that we now turn.

STRUCTURE VERSUS CULTURE

a. Marx's Legacy

Both Marx and Weber stressed the importance of analyzing subjective social actions *and* objective social constraints (compare Marx, 1972 [1932]: p. 118 with Weber, 1947 [1922]: p. 103; see also Gerth and Mills, 1946: pp. 57–8). They also had compatible (though different) ideas about the *nature* of these constraints.

Marx, like Weber, recognized that the external determinants of behaviour consist of economic, political and cultural forces. Marx tended to assign overwhelming causal priority to the economic realm. Weber did not deny the primacy of economic arrangements; but he rounded out Marx's analysis by showing how the political and cultural facts of life can act as independent, important causes of many social phenomena.

In the middle of the nineteenth century Marx proposed a sweeping theory of the development of human societies. In this theory the engine of change is economic organization—more precisely, society's class structure and its technological base. In 1859 Marx succinctly put his argument as follows:

> At a certain stage of their development, the material forces of production in society come into conflict with the existing relations of production, or—what is but a legal expression for the same thing—with the property relations within which they had been at work before. From forms of development of the forces of production these relations turn into their fetters. Then occurs a period of social revolution. With the change of the economic foundation the entire immense superstructure is more or less rapidly transformed (Marx, 1904 [1859]: pp. 11–12).

How then does Marx's theory apply to the rise of capitalism? In European feudal society peasants tilled small plots of land which were owned not by the peasants themselves but by landlords. Peasants were legally bound to the land, obliged to give landlords a set proportion of their harvest and to continue working for their landlords under any circumstances. In turn, landlords were expected to protect peasants against poor economic conditions and marauders.

By the late fifteenth century, certain processes had been set in motion that eventually transformed feudal society into a modern capitalist system. Most important was the growth of exploration and trade, which increased the demand for many goods and services in commerce, navigation and industry. By the seventeenth and eighteenth centuries some urban dwellers—successful artisans and merchants—had accumulated sufficient capital to expand their production significantly. In order to maximize their profits these capitalists required an abundant supply of workers who could be hired in periods of high demand and fired without obligation during slack times. It was therefore necessary to induce and coerce indentured peasants from the soil and transform them into legally free workers who would work for wages (Marx and Engels, 1972 [1848]: pp. 336 ff.).

In Marx's view, the relations of production between wage labourers and capitalists at first facilitated rapid technological innovation and economic growth. Capitalists were keen to adopt new tools, machines and production techniques. These changes allowed capitalists to produce more efficiently, earn higher profits and drive their competitors out of business. Efficiency also required that workers be concentrated in larger and larger industrial establishments, that wages be kept as low as possible, and that as little as possible be invested in improving working conditions. Thus, according to Marx, workers and capitalists would stand face-to-face in factory and mine: a large and growing class of relatively impoverished workers opposing a small and shrinking class of increasingly wealthy owners.

Marx argued that in due course all workers would become aware of belonging to the same ploited class. This sense of "class consciousness" would, he felt, encourage the growth of working class organizations, such as trade unions and political parties. These organizations would be bent on overthrowing the capitalist system and establishing a classless society. According to Marx, this revolutionary change was bound to occur during one of the recurrent and worsening "crises of overproduction" that characterized the capitalist era. The productive capacity of the system would, Marx said, come to far outstrip the ability of the relatively impoverished workers to purchase goods and services. Thus, in order to sell goods and services, capitalists would be forced to lower their prices. Profits would then fall, the less efficient capitalists would go bankrupt and massive unemployment of workers would result—thus deepening the economic crisis still further. The capitalist class system had originally encouraged economic growth. Eventually the crises of overproduction it generated would hinder such growth. At that time the capitalist class system would be destroyed and replaced by socialism, Marx argued.

As this thumbnail sketch shows, beliefs, symbols and values—in short, culture—play a quite minor independent causal role in Marx's theory. Marx analyzed how, under some circumstances, ruling class ideology could form a legitimizing cement in society and how, under other circumstances, subordinate class consciousness could become an important force for change. But in his work it is always the material circumstances of existence that ultimately determine the role ideas play.

b. Weber on Capitalism and the World Religions

Weber, like Marx, was interested in explaining the rise of modern capitalism. And, like Marx, he was prepared to recognize the "fundamental importance of the economic factor" in his explanation (Weber, 1958 [1904–51]:

p. 26). But Weber was also bent on demonstrating the one-sidedness of any *exclusively* economic interpretation. After all, the economic conditions Marx said were necessary for capitalist development existed in Catholic France during the reign of Louis XIV; but the wealth generated in France by international trade and commerce tended to be consumed by war and the luxurious lifestyle of the aristocracy rather than invested in the growth of capitalist enterprise. In Weber's view, what prompted vigorous capitalist development in non-Catholic Europe and North America was a combination of (1) propitious economic conditions such as those discussed by Marx and (2) the spread of certain moral values by the Protestant reformers of the sixteenth century and their followers in the seventeenth century.

For specifically *religious* reasons, followers of the Protestant theologian John Calvin stressed the need to engage in intense wordly activity, to demonstrate industry, punctuality and frugality in one's everyday life. In the view of men like John Wesley and Benjamin Franklin, religious doubts could be reduced, and a state of grace assured, if one worked diligently and lived ascetically. This idea was taken up by Puritanism, Methodism and other Protestant denominations; Weber called it the "Protestant work ethic" (Weber, 1958 [1904–5]: p. 183).

According to Weber, this ethic had wholly unexpected economic consequences: where it took root, *and* where economic conditions were favourable, early capitalist enterprise grew robustly. In other words, two *independent* developments—the Protestant work ethic (which derived from purely religious considerations) and the material conditions favouring capitalist growth (which derived from specifically economic circumstances)—interacted to invigorate capitalist development. Weber made his case even more persuasive by comparing Protestant Western Europe and North America with India and China. He concluded that the latter cases differed from the former in one decisive (but certainly not exclusive) respect: Indian and Chinese religions inhibited capitalist economic action. In contrast to ancient Judaism and later Christianity, Asiatic religions had strong other-wordly, magical and antirational components that were inimical to wordly success in competition and accumulation. As a result, capitalism developed very slowly in India and China (Zeitlin, 1987 [1968]: pp.135–50).

Subsequent research has demonstrated that the association between the Protestant ethic and the strength of capitalist development is very much weaker than Weber thought (on Western Europe and the United States, see Samuelsson, 1961 [1957]; on Canada, see Brym, 1986: pp. 24–7). In some places, Catholicism has co-existed with vigorous capitalist growth and Protestantism with relative stagnation. Nonetheless, even if Weber was wrong about this particular case, his *general* view—that religious developments cannot be reduced to economic developments, and that religious ideas have economic consequences—are still widely regarded as brilliant and valid insights.

Just as some Marxist sociologists have adopted a strict economic determinism, others have misinterpreted Weber's ideas in a way that supports a sort of cultural determinism. But the plain fact is that Weber assigned about the same relative weight to economic and cultural forces as did Marx; and there is nothing in Marx's work that is incompatible with Weber's insights into the relative autonomy of religious developments. This aspect of the controversy between orthodox Marxists and Weberians may thus be as specious as the disagreement between rigid Durkheimians and phenomenologists.

THE BASES OF SOCIAL INEQUALITY

Thus far I have singled out areas of similarity or compatibility in the thought of Marx and Weber. However, in Weber's "long and intense debate with the ghost of Karl Marx" (Albert Salomon, quoted in Zeitlin, 1987 [1968]): p. xi), there also emerged some ideas that are incompatible with those of Marx. This is especially obvious in Weber's work on social inequality.

Marx regarded ownership or non-ownership of property as the fundamental basis of inequality in capitalist society. In his view, there are two main classes under capitalism. Members of the *capitalist* class, or *bourgeoisie*, own but do not work means of production. Members of the *working* class, or *proletariat*, work but do not own means of production. In addition, Marx discussed some minor classes that are vestiges of pre-capitalist times. Most important, members of the *petite bourgeoisie* own and work means of production (e.g., farmers, owners of small family businesses). Marx also analyzed various divisions within the major classes. These class segments were distinguished from one another by their sources of income (e.g., financial and industrial capitalists) or skill level (e.g., skilled and unskilled manual workers).

In defining classes in this way, Marx was *not* trying to account for gradations of rank in society. Instead, he sought to explain massive historical change. The major classes, in his view, were potentially self-conscious groups engaged in conflict that would eventually result in societal transformation.

Weber agreed that " 'property' and 'lack of property' are . . . the basic categories of all class situations" (Weber, 1946 [1922]: p. 182). But his analysis of inequality differed from Marx's in three main ways. First, he was profoundly skeptical about Marx's interpretation of historical development. As a result, he stressed that members of classes do not necessarily become class-conscious and act in concert. Second, Weber argued that property relations are just one aspect of a more general "market situation" that determines class position. For example, expertise acquired through formal education is a scarce commodity on the labour market. Such expertise increases one's advantages or "life-changes" and is therefore an important factor structuring the class system. On this basis, and in addition to the capitalist and manual working classes, Weber distinguished large and growing classes of technical/managerial personnel and white collar workers who perform routine tasks.

Third, Weber was less concerned than Marx with the sources of conflict between discrete classes and more concerned than Marx with the bases of complex social hierarchies. For this reason he showed that the bases of social inequality are not exclusively economic. One non-economic source of inequality is the way honour (or esteem or prestige) is distributed in society. Weber referred to groups distinguished from one another in terms of prestige as *status groups*. For example, line of descent (including ethnic origin) may account for the level of esteem in which a status group is held, and esteem affects the life-chances of status group members. A second non-economic source of inequality derives from the formation of political parties. A party, in Weber's definition, is an association that seeks to gain control over an organization—ranging all the way from, say, a sports club to a state—for purposes of implementing specific policies. Parties may recruit members from specific classes or status groups, or both. As such, and to the degree they achieve organizational control, parties bestow more advantages on their supporters than on non-supporters.

If parties and status groups are independent bases of social inequality, then, according to Weber, they are not wholly independent, especially in capitalist societies. There is an association between status group and party membership, on the one hand, and class position on the other. The structure of class inequality helps shape status group and party membership; in fact, "today the class situation is by far the predominant factor" (Weber, 1946 [1922]: p. 190).³

Much of modern sociology has been devoted to exploring the ramifications of Weber's refinement of Marx's stratification model. What are the economic determinants of class that do not derive from ownership versus non-ownership of property? How do the concentration of ethnic and other status groups in particular class locations reinforce status group cohesion? How do ethnic and other forms of status group identification serve to reinforce patterns of inequality? To what degree do classes serve as recruitment bases for political parties? To what degree do different types of political parties enact policies that redistribute income? These are among the most popular questions asked by modern sociologists, and they are all indebted to Weber's elaboration of the Marxian schema.

Recent years have also witnessed an important addition to the stratification model. It is now generally acknowledged that *gender* is a basis of social inequality quite on a par with status groups, parties and classes. Thus, in Canada and elsewhere, gender is as important a determinant of annual income as class (Ornstein, 1983), because women in the paid labour force tend to be segregated in low-pay, low-prestige jobs (Fox and Fox, 1986). Even if one matches a group of Canadian men and a group of Canadian women in terms of education, occupation, amount of time worked each year, and years of job experience, one discovers that the women earn only 63 per cent of what the men earn (Goyder, 1981: p. 328). Meanwhile, the great bulk of household labour continues to be performed by women, even if both spouses work; one study conducted in Vancouver found that, when their wives entered the paid labour force, husbands did on average only one hour more housework per week (Meissner *et al.*, 1975).

Classical theories teach us little about the causes of such gender inequality. That is, while Marx and Weber may have been able to account more or less well for the expansion and contraction of particular locations in the stratification system, they "give no clues about why *women* are subordinate to *men* inside and outside the family and why it is not the other way around" (Hartmann, 1984 [1978]: p. 174).

Over the past fifteen years or so, biological, cultural and structural theories of gender inequality have been proposed. Accumulated research seems to indicate that while biological factors—especially women's childbearing function—may have encouraged some division of labour between the sexes in primitive societies, there is no biological reason why male and female jobs should have been rewarded differently, let alone why they continue to be rewarded differently today. Cultural theories, which locate the causes of gender inequality in the way people learn established practices, cannot account either for the origins of gender inequality or the sources of variation in such inequality. Explanations that root gender inequality in social structure appear more promising. While the subordination of women is evident in vir-

tually every known society, it takes on different forms and degrees in different times and places. Unravelling the relationship between social structure, on the one hand, and the form and degree of gender inequality, on the other, is a complex task which lies at the cutting edge of contemporary research on social inequality (see, for example, Coontz and Henderson, 1986).

CONCLUSION

In this brief essay I have set out three questions that lie at the foundations of classical sociology. I have emphasized that the significance of these questions derives from their proven ability to continue provoking the sociological imagination. The remainder of this book demonstrates the soundness of my assertion. As will be seen, the value of many of the readings in this volume derives in part from their indebtedness to the first practitioners of the discipline.

Notes

I would like to thank Jim Curtis, Jim Richardson and Lorne Tepperman for helpful comments on a draft of this article.

[1] Durkheim actually analyzed several types of suicide and disposed of several types of explanations. However, strict space limitations preclude a full discussion of these.

[2] For the most part, classical sociology (as well as history, political science, economics, and so forth) virtually ignored the existence of women in society. This was reflected not only in the use of sexist language, but in major oversights and imbalances in sociological

theorizing, as will be illustrated later in this essay.

[3] Unfortunately, many modern sociologists, particularly in the United States, have trivialized Weber—and rendered him much more "anti-Marxist" than he in fact was by exaggerating the independence of the various bases of inequality, unnecessarily multiplying the number of bases, regarding inequality as a continuous ranking of statistical categories, and highlighting the subjective evaluation of prestige as the major basis of inequality. For a critique of these tendencies, see (Parkin, 1972 [1971]: esp. pp. 13–47).

References

Brym, Robert J. (1986) "Anglo-Canadian Sociology," *Current Sociology* (Vol. 34, No. 1) pp. 1–152.

Coontz, Stephanie and Peta Henderson, eds. (1986) *Women's Work, Men's Property: The Origins of Gender and Class*, S. Coontz and P. Henderson, eds. (London: Verso).

Douglas, John D. (1967) *The Social Meaning of Suicide* (Princeton: Princeton University Press).

Durkheim, Emile (1966 [1895]) *The Rules of the Sociological Method*, 8th edn., G. Catlin, ed., S. Solovay and J. Mueller, trans. (New York: The Free Press).

Durkheim, Emile (1951 [1897]) *Suicide: A Study in Sociology*, G. Simpson, ed., J. Spaulding and G. Simpson, trans. (New York: The Free Press).

Fox, Bonnie J. and John Fox (1986) "Women in the labour market, 1931–81: exclusion and competition," *Canadian Review of Sociology and Anthropology* (Vol. 23) pp. 1–21.

Gerth, H.H. and C. Wright Mills (1946) "The man and his work", in *From Max Weber: Essays in Sociology*, H. Gerth and C. Mills, eds. and trans. (New York: Oxford University Press) pp. 1–74.

Goffman, Erving (1959) *The Presentation of Self in Everyday Life* (Garden City, N.Y.: Anchor).

Goyder, John C. (1981) "Income differences between the sexes: findings from a national Canadian survey", *Canadian Review of Sociology and Anthropology* (Vol. 18) pp. 321–42.

Hartmann, Heidi I. (1984 [1978]) "The unhappy marriage of Marxism and feminism: towards a more progressive union", in A. Jaggar and P. Rothenberg, eds. *Feminist Frameworks: Alternative Theoretical Accounts of the Relations between Women and Men*, 2nd edn. (New York: McGraw-Hill) pp. 172–89.

Marx, Karl (1904 [1859]) *A Contribution to the Critique of Political Economy*, N. Stone, trans. (Chicago: Charles H. Kerr).

Marx, Karl (1972 [1932]) "The German ideology: part I", in *The Marx-Engels Reader*, R. Tucker, ed. (New York: Praeger) pp. 110–64.

Marx, Karl and Friedrich Engels (1972 [1848]) "Manifesto of the Communist Party", in *The Marx-Engels Reader*, R. Tucker, ed. (New York: Praeger) pp. 331–62.

Meissner, Martin *et al.* (1975) "No exit for wives: sexual division of labour and the culmination of household demands", *Canadian Review of Sociology and Anthropology* (Vol. 12) pp. 424–39.

Ornstein, Michael D. (1983) "Class, gender and job income in Canada", *Research in Social Stratification and Mobility* (Vol. 2) pp. 41–75.

Parkin, Frank (1972 [1971]) *Class Inequality and Political Order: Social Stratification in Capitalist and Communist Societies* (London: Paladin).

Samuelsson, Kurt (1961 [1957]) *Religion and Economic Action*, E. French, trans. (Stockholm: Scandinavian University Books).

Weber, Max (1946 [1922]) "Class, status, party", in *From Max Weber: Essays in Sociology*, H. Gerth and C. Mills, eds. and trans. (New York: Oxford University Press) pp. 180–95.

Weber, Max (1958 [1904–5]) *The Protestant Ethic and the Spirit of Capitalism*, T. Parsons, trans. (New York: Charles Scribner's Sons).

Weber, Max (1947 [1922]) *The Theory of Social and Economic Organization*, T. Parsons, ed. (New York: The Free Press).

2 The Field of Sociology

Donald R. Whyte   Frank Vallee

DONALD R. WHYTE, Professor of Sociology and Anthropology at Carleton University, is the author of *Rural Canada in Transition* and of articles on aspects of Canadian development. His recent research has been on Gender Studies with a focus on male roles in the context of changes in work and the family wage system. Formerly Chairman of the Department, Professor Whyte is currently co-ordinator of Graduate Programs.

FRANK VALLEE, Professor Emeritus of Sociology and Anthropology at Carleton University in Ottawa, specializes in the study of Canadian society, ethnicity, race and class. His books include *Survey of the Contemporary Indians of Canada*. 2 volumes, with Harry Hawthorn (1966, 1967); *The Eskimo of the Canadian Arctic*, co-edited with Victor Valentine (1968); and *Language Use in Canada*, with John deVries (1980). Professor Vallee has served as President of the Canadian Ethnology Society, on the editorial boards of *Culture* and *Anthropologica*, and as Chairman of the Department of Sociology and Anthropology, Carleton University. In 1967 he received the Centennial Medal for Distinguished Service to Canada, and in 1976 he was elected to the Royal Society of Canada.

ORIGINS OF THE DISCIPLINE AND HISTORICAL DEVELOPMENT IN CANADA

The intellectual origins of sociology are numerous, but as a special science it originated in France. Auguste Comte gave the name "sociology" to the new discipline and outlined a philosophy (positivism) that shaped its development. Positivism holds that only actual phenomena and facts constitute knowledge. Emile Durkheim contributed most to the emergence of sociology in France, by combining empirical research and theories in the development of a general set of propositions about social relations. The two other traditions that have significantly shaped modern sociology are grounded in the works of the German sociologists Max Weber and Karl Marx. The common problem that Durkheim, Weber and Marx confronted was the historical transition from feudalism to capitalism

and its effects on social class relations. Coincident with this transition were the rapid and profound changes, often involving individual and social disorganization, that resulted from the Industrial Revolution.

In North America, the first academic course in sociology was introduced at Yale in 1876; the University of Chicago was the first to offer a doctorate in sociology in 1893. Sociology had not made an appearance in Canada as an academic discipline in the 1890s, but by 1920 courses in sociology were being offered in a number of disciplines and were included in theology curricula. The Canadian Political Science Association, formed in 1913, accepted sociologists as members. The association was inactive during WWI and was not reactivated until 1929. The first academic appointment in sociology in Canada was that of Carl A. Dawson in 1922 at McGill. Honours programs were established at McGill in 1926 and at the University of Toronto in 1932. Still, in 1941, Harold Innis, one of the founding figures in Canadian social science, described sociology as the "Cinderella of the social sciences." The work of S.D. Clark at the University of Toronto at this time was important to the subsequent recognition of sociology as a legitimate field of study, despite opposition from the entrenched disciplines. Significant social science research had been underway from the late 1880s to the late 1930s. This included the work of Marius Barbeau, Carl Dawson, Léon Gérin, Diamond Jenness and Everett Hughes on Canada's indigenous peoples; the human ecological approach to urban growth and planning; and studies of ethnic groups in the West, education and Québec's rural population and ethnic relations (particularly Francophone-Anglophone relations). By 1940 a substantial body of material on Canadian economic, political and social development existed.

While the social problems of the times were common to all parts of Canada, sociology developed differently in the anglophone and francophone academic communities. Francophone sociology in Québec originally took its inspiration from the encyclical *Rerum Novarum* (1891). The Roman Catholic Church defined the limits and content of early francophone sociology, and the Catholic Action Movement became the vehicle for a Catholic sociology in Québec. By the early 1930s, Catholic sociology was taught at Laval and Université de Montréal. From the outset sociology was viewed as an instrument of "national" development in Québec and helped foster ideological self-awareness and critical debate.

During the 1940s, Father Georges-Henri Lévesque of Laval was a leading force in a movement to establish a secularized sociology in Québec. He encouraged a greater scientific sophistication, and directed the attention of francophone sociologists away from "la survivance" of French Canadian traditions and to the aim of aiding the industrialization and modernization of the Québec economy and society. This secularized view of sociology and its role in Québec reinforced a profederalist ideology. In the 1960s a new nationalism appeared in Québec sociology in support of an ideology of self-determination and sovereignty for Québec society. With the growth of the state bureaucracy in Québec during the 1960s and 1970s, sociologists became directly involved in the programming and administration of the new society.

Both anglophone and francophone sociology share stylistic similarities, but certain traditions are more influential in one than the other. For instance, in Québec, perspectives from Europe (and from France in particular) are more evident than they are elsewhere in Canada, where American influence is relatively stronger.

Beginning in the 1960s, sociology underwent a spectacular expansion everywhere in Canada. In 1960 to 1961 there were sixty-one sociologists in Canadian universities, no doctorates were awarded in sociology and only two had been awarded up to that date. During the next two decades, sociology was established in virtually every academic institution; in 1981, forty-one doctorates and one-hundred and thirty-six masters degrees in sociology were conferred by Canadian universities. In 1960 sociology had been organized at the departmental level in only four universities in Canada: Carleton, McMaster, Saskatchewan and Université de Montréal. In 1981 there were thirty-four departments of sociology, and thirteen departments in which sociology and anthropology were combined. Five of these departments of sociology were francophone and two were bilingual.

APPLICATIONS

Sociological knowledge is used indirectly in teaching and in everday work of many kinds, and is applied directly to policy issues either through research conducted during the course of officially sponsored inquiries or through independent research. Sociology is taught primarily at the university level, although since the 1970s sociological content has permeated courses at the community-college and high-schoool levels. In teaching, research is used not so much as an end in itself but as a means of conveying the perspectives of sociology. Indirectly, sociological research also informs the everyday activities of people in certain jobs, e.g., those employed in administration, education, marketing, recreation, social work and other sectors—although it is impossible to gauge the extent of such practical applications.

It is easier to determine how sociological research feeds directly into the deliberations of those responsible for shaping social policy. For example, the recommendations of the Royal Commission on Health Services (1961–63) were strongly influenced by sociological research (four studies and numerous submissions) conducted on behalf of the commission. The reports of this commission helped shape Canadian health policy. Of similar importance, in the shaping of language policies and cultural policies, were the recommendations of the Royal Commission on Bilingualism and Biculturalism (1963–67). Sociologists contributed to the Royal Commission on the Status of Women in Canada (1967–69); some of the recommendations have been accepted as public policy. Research by sociologists was significant in developing the recommendations of La Commission d'enquête sur l'enseignement au Québec (1964–66), often referred to as the Parent Commission after its chairman. The educational reforms based on these recommendations drastically altered Québec's educational system. Sociological research in the early 1970s helped shape many of the recommendations of the Gendron Commission (Commission d'enquête sur la situation de la langue française au Québec), the policy implications of which have been profound.

Other public inquiries to which sociologists have made significant contributions include the Senate committees on poverty and on aging, and institutional research under independent and quasi-governmental sponsorship. In this latter category are the projects undertaken by the former Saskatchewan Centre for Community Studies at the University of Saskatchewan; by the Institute of Social and Economic Research at Memorial University; and by the Bureau d'aménagement de l'est du Québec at Laval.

As these examples show, much social research and planning in Canada has been conducted collectively under the auspices of government and university research institutes. Canada has also been the subject of significant research and writing by independent scholars. On the relationship between culture and environment and their effects on social and economic life in Québec, two pioneer studies were particularly important: Léon Gérin's *Le Type economique et social des canadiens* (1937); and Everett C. Hughes's *French Canada in Transition* (1943). French sociologist Marcel Giraud's *Le Métis canadien* (1947) remains the most comprehensive study of the Métis. S.D. Clark's *Church and Sect in Canada* (1948) was a major study of religious and political movements in the West. American sociologist S.M. Lipset's *Agrarian Socialism* (1950) was a definitive study of the rise of the socialist movement and the rise of the Co-operative Commonwealth Federation. John Porter's *the Vertical Mosaic* (1965) challenged the conventional view of Canada as an egalitarian society. More than any other scholar of his time, Porter influenced the theoretical, empirical and critical directions of modern Canadian sociology. Many contemporary scholars have turned their attention to the effects of a resource-based economy on national and regional social organization. Rex Lucas's *Minetown, Milltown, Railtown* (1971) has influenced the direction of many of these studies.

FIELDS OF WORK

Most of the professional sociologists in Canada have masters or doctoral degrees in that subject. Of course, not all who have taken advanced degrees in sociology are professional sociologists; many are employed as administrators, executives, entrepreneurs and in other capacities. Because precise figures are lacking, it is impossible to say how many people in Canada are working as professional sociologists, but it is safe to assume that the majority who do so are full-time university teachers. According to one report, the number of full-time university teachers of sociology in Canada for the 1979 to 1980 academic year was 962. Perhaps scores of others teach full-time at the community-college level. The number of professional sociologists working in research in government and other public and private agencies has been estimated at about 400.

Until 1956, when the Sociology-Anthropology Chapter of the Canadian Political Science Association was formed, there was no national organization that brought sociologists together. A decade later, this chapter was transformed into an officially bilingual independent organization, the Canadian Sociology and Anthropology Association. Several affiliated regional associations represent sociologists in western Canada, Ontario, Québec and the Atlantic provinces. One of these, l'Association canadienne des sociologues et anthropologues de la langue française, caters especially to Francophones.

Sociologists in Canada publish their scholarly work within and outside of Canada. Within Canada their articles are published primarily in four journals: the *Canadian Journal of Sociology; Canadian Review of Sociology and Anthropology; Récherches sociographiques*; and *Sociologie et sociétés*. Besides these outlets, the publications of sociologists often appear in such journals as *Cahiers québécois de démographie; Canadian Ethnic Studies; Canadian Journal of Criminology; Canadian Studies in Population; Canadian Women's Studies*; and *Studies in Political Economy*, to mention a few.

3 Sociology Compared to Other Fields

Kenneth Westhues

KENNETH WESTHUES, Professor of Sociology at the University of Waterloo, specializes in the sociology of religion, social movements and sociological theory. His publications include *Society's Shadow: Studies in the Sociology of Countercultures* (1972); *Village in Crisis*, with Peter Sinclair (1974); *First Sociology* (1982); and "Defensiveness and social structure: The ideology of separate school trustees" (1983). Professor Westhues has served as Department Chairman at the University of Waterloo and was recently awarded the Distinguished Teacher Award there; he has also taught as a Visiting Professor at Fordham University and Memorial University of Newfoundland. He has served as associate editor of the *Canadian Journal of Sociology*, *Review of Religious Research* and *Sociological Analysis*; and is currently attempting to found a Centre for Advanced Studies in Humanist Social Science in Waterloo.

HOLISM

In universities that abound with disciplines we need to distinguish sociology from the rest. Five characteristics are relevant for this purpose, the first of which is sociology's goal of providing holistic social analyses. In the writings of nearly all the founders of the field there is an unmistakable attempt to understand social life as a whole. Marx, for instance, had no intention of writing simply about the economy. He stressed it only because for him it was the basis of political, religious, and all other dimensions of the whole, the society, which ever remained his fundamental concern. When Durkheim wrote about suicide, or Weber about bureaucracy, it was not as specialists in these areas but in order to shed light on the social order in general. An emphasis on the whole, an attempt to integrate knowledge about social life, is almost the hallmark of the discipline.

The lesson of the founders has not been lost on their descendants in the present day.

Major contemporary sociologists like Peter Berger at Boston College, Amitai Etzioni at George Washington University, the late Talcott Parsons (1903–1979) at Harvard, or the late John Porter (1921–1979) at Carleton, among many others, have aspired to write holistic analyses of the societies confronting them. The sociology curriculum continues to be wide open, with almost no subject matter excluded in principle. A glance through a few university calendars reveals courses regularly taught in the sociology of art, bureaucracy, conflict, death, education, family, gangs, housing, ideology, Jews, knowledge, law, music, nationalism, occupations, politics, Quebec, religion, sport, technology, values, and youth. . . . Societies as integral wholes are sociology's subject matter, and from this vantage point, any part of the whole merits study.

Its holism distinguishes sociology from economics, political science, and some other fields. Economics limits itself to *that aspect of* a society which concerns the production, distribution, and consumption of goods and services. Political science focuses only on *that aspect* related to governmental institutions and the structure of power. The various "studies"—religious, black, leisure, family, and

From *First Sociology* by Kenneth Westhues, (New York: McGraw-Hill, 1982), pp. 20, 21–23, 26–29. By permission of the McGraw-Hill Book Company.

so on—similarly restrict themselves to a particular part or institution of the societal whole. One need only look at typical curricula in these disciplines to see how much more narrowly than sociology they define their aims. One should also note the anger of economists, for example, when they observe in the sociology syllabus something called "The Sociology of the Economy." Their anger is a price sociologists pay for trying to understand how the whole social enterprise fits together.

In actuality, of course, not all sociologists use their study of particular scenes in the drama of social life to understand the drama in its entirety. Encouraged by the overspecialized organization of the discipline, many researchers look no farther than their specific areas of study, whether drug use or divorce, prostitutes or priests. Thus is created the regrettable misconception that economics and political science study the important aspects of social life, sociology the more piddling ones. But fortunately the overspecialized sociologists are balanced out by those economists and political scientists who exceed the nominal limits of their disciplines, use them instead as windows on the whole, and attempt to write holistic works of social analysis. Economists like John Kenneth Galbraith, Kenneth Boulding, Milton Friedman, or Paul Sweezy come to mind; so do political scientists like C.B. Macpherson, Ralph Miliband, or the late Hannah Arendt. Among the best practitioners, the boundaries separating these latter disciplines from sociology break completely down. Among the rest, however, and in the organization of these disciplines in North America, the distinction between holism and specificity is apt.

THEORY BUILDING

A second characteristic of sociology is its emphasis on interpretation and theory building. Thus is sociology distinguished from journalism and history, both of which share with the first an attentive scrutiny of the events in social life. In the main, journalists chronicle the present, and historians the past. In both cases the emphasis is on accuracy of factual detail, and this is a special strength of both disciplines. There is in journalism an implicit conception of a certain universe of newsworthy events, and reporters are dispatched to city halls, hockey arenas, scenes of crime, and so on for the purpose of "covering" as many such events as possible. For historians the events of the past constitute a comparable universe. One professor is said to "cover" those of the Renaissance period, another those of pre-Civil War America, and so on. Neither journalists nor historians customarily feel obliged, however, to separate rigorously the events of importance from those of little consequence. Doing so is not a high priority for them, nor is tying events together with theoretical glue. Whether for the past or present their goal is to provide, as *The New York Times* puts it, "all the news that's fit to print."

It is a poor sociologist who does not devour newspapers and history books. The facts they provide, though never indisputable and always seen through their authors' mirrors, are the necessary beginnings of good sociology. Journalists and historians provide in a sense the pieces for the puzzle sociologists would solve. Sociology must assume acquaintance with events, for its purpose is to separate the significant from the trivial ones and then to weave the first kind together into a picture of how and why things happen in social life. The goal of sociology is not to chronicle but to interpret, not to record but to analyze, not to describe but to explain. Inevitably the pursuit of this goal entails disregard for some well-documented facts. Historians often complain that sociologists overgeneralize and fail to make room for exceptions. They voice the same complaint against members of their own discipline, like Oswald Spengler or R.H. Tawney, who became more interested in analyzing history than in chronicling it. Without doubt the world needs both chroniclers and analysts, but sociology fits better in the latter category.

INTELLECTUAL PRIMACY

A third and critical quality of sociology is that its purpose is knowledge, not action. This is not to say that sociology is irrelevant to action, only that it remains distinct from it. It is one thing to come up with ideas about the structure of a society, ideas even which imply that something should be done, and quite another actually to set about doing it. The former is the task of sociologists and other social scientists, the latter that of social workers, legislators, lawyers, planners, reformers, community organizers, and anyone else who takes up the challenge of acting upon the status quo. If sociologists distill history into theories, people in the active professions distill theories into plans of action and into action itself. An undergraduate major in sociology is a common route to professional schools of social work, law, and planning, but the business of making the ideas that make change is nonetheless distinct from making change directly.

A sociologist is or ought to be an intellectual, one who reflects on the experience of contemporary life and tries to put into words its enduring regularities. A certain detachment from immediate social concerns is for this reason a necessary part of the sociologist's work. In order to perform well the task of the intellectual, he or she stands a little to one side of the class structure and the arena of conflicting interests in the society at large. The more sociologists can emancipate themselves from indebtedness to particular class and ethnic interests, including those of their personal backgrounds, the better their work becomes. Contrariwise, sociologists who do their work in the interests of particular groups cannot thereby fulfill the mission of their discipline. Hired-hand intellectuals, even those engaged by the underprivileged, are not intellectuals at all.

Standing apart is not, of course, the same as running away. The sociologist need not act in order to be concerned with action. Indeed, the sociologist has to be concerned because even in our time people suffer. All kinds of them. Dependent mothers whose husbands have disappeared but whose children still need to eat. People laid off from their jobs and left wondering whether they are good for anything. Adolescents who doubt that the world or even their own parents need them. People made to feel ashamed of their language or the color of their skin. Old people vegetating on pensions in the deathly, parasitic quiet of old-age homes and retirement villages. Even prosperous people trapped in the suburban quest for consumer goods, acquiring more but enjoying it less. It is the obligation of the sociologist to speak to them all with compassion and with an analysis that will help them regain control over their lives. In meeting this obligation, sociologists can be sure of opposition from the advantaged classes, those who fear to lose their advantage if history is diverted from its present path. If there were no such opposition, sociologists would surely be failing in their intellectual task.

SENSE EVIDENCE

A fourth characteristic of the discipline is its attempt to ground ideas in the evidence that meets human eyes and ears, in the social world as perceived by bodily senses, in the data given by experience. . . .

Sociology's reliance on the evidence of the senses, what is sometimes called the empirical method of research, distinguishes this discipine also from certain kinds of philosophy. Jean-Jacques Rousseau (1712–1778), one of the greatest French philosophers, wrote at the start of his *Discourse on the Origin and the Foundation of Inequality Among*

Mankind, "Let us begin, therefore, by laying aside facts, for they do not affect the question."[1] Rousseau was actually more respectful of facts than this line suggests, but some contemporary philosophers show great disdain for the kind of sense evidence sociologists closely attend to. They seek to create logically coherent systems of ideas, but systems so abstract as to be irrelevant to happenings in everyday life. At many universities one can take a perfectly secular course on ethics, for example, and learn a great deal about how people ought to behave, but scarcely even look at how they actually are behaving. It is a kind of learning that tends to baffle sociologists, except for its value as an exercise in mental discipline. Other philosophers define their goal differently and try to create sets of ideas which are at once logically consistent and relevant to practical affairs. The ties of their work to sociology are quite close.

AN EXPLICITLY SOCIAL FOCUS

To state clearly the last of the five attributes of sociology relevant here, I should recall an analogy of variously distorted mirrors. Those of religion and philosophy we can set to one side since they lack the particular warp of evidential methods. The mirrors of economics and political science we can set to another side, since they have the empirical warp but are not, as it were, full-length. To still another side should be placed those of history and journalism, since they reflect the empirical world but in the manner of a set of dots in a child's coloring book—the dots have still to be connected before a picture of something emerges. Social work and planning we shall not count as mirrors, since they are plans of action abstracted from various mirrors. At last we are left with the full-length, interpretive mirrors bent by the evidence of the senses. In contemporary universities only two such mirrors are in common use. Sociology is one, psychology the other. Distinction be-

tween them is important because for all their closeness they are immensely far apart. . . .

When a psychologist looks at people, what he or she sees in the mirror of that discipline is so many individual persons. A group or society appears only as a collection of these individuals and can be understood according to the kinds of personalities they have. Psychologists assess individual personality through a vast array of tests, measuring intelligence, aptitude, vocational interest, self-concept, motivation, moral development, creativity, insight, adjustment, leadership, machiavellianism, impulsiveness, authoritarianism, and hundreds of other qualities they have conceptualized. Indeed, I think psychology has more tests than sociology has specialities. Some psychologists reject testing, however, preferring simply to record individuals' behaviour in laboratory settings or to interview them one by one. In any case an understanding of the regularities in how individuals act remains the basic goal of the discipline. It is as if the psychologist's mirror reveals the human person as what is fundamentally real; people may join together in groups but the individual always comes first.

In sociology it is exactly the other way around. For us the group is prior. The reality displayed in our mirror is always some kind of social system, whether a dyad (two-person group) of lovers, a family, a nation, or at the most general level the human community. In a sense sociology does not focus on individuals at all, but only on the roles they play in groups. We sociologists spend little time testing personalities. When confronted with an individual our first inclination is to ask which groups the person belongs to: which class, ethnic group, sex, occupation, religion, marital status, age category, income category, civic associations, community of residence, place of origin, and so on. We in sociology approach the individual through the mediation of the roles he or she plays in groups. Qualities of personality, insofar as they are independent of social order, escape our attention. For me at least there are no such qualities, only those many which derive from participation in groups and those few which will leave their mark on social life in the future.

The difference between psychological and sociological perspectives appears most clearly in their practical applications.[2] For what the detached scholar conceptualizes as the object of analysis, the corresponding applied practitioner regards as the object of change. Applied psychologists therefore use knowledge about individuals to help individuals change. The market for their services is large. Clinical psychologists try to help their clients overcome excessive shyness, agressive tendencies, anxiety, dependency, depression, or other disorders of personality. Personnel psychologists design employee training programs and try to boost workers' motivation and morale. Counseling psychologists help individuals cope with the transition from youth to adulthood and later from adulthood to old age. In all these and many other applications of the academic discipline, the problem is located in the individual and the solution requires some kind of individual transformation. Success is measured by the degree to which the client becomes able to adapt to life in the society at hand.

In the eyes of an applied sociologist it is not the individual who needs to change. The problem inheres in the structure of social life and only social change can solve it. The shift in perspective has occurred in the life of many social activists who once considered that something must be wrong with *them* and who later concluded otherwise. Allen Ginsberg, for instance, a poet-hero of the 1960s youth movement, sought psychological counseling in his youth, trying to help himself adapt to the world around him. The therapy did not work and Ginsberg shifted the blame angrily to his society: "I saw the best minds of my generation destroyed by madness, starving hysterical naked."[3] Betty Friedan, the noted American leader of the women's movement, recalls a similar shift in perspective in her

life. Eventually she concluded that her frustration in the conventional woman's role called not for better coping on her part but for change in the social role assigned to women.

As might be expected, the job market for applied psychologists is much larger than for those who would apply sociological knowledge. The latter are more interesting, however, and the impact of their work lasts longer than a lifetime. People educated in sociology, for instance, were well represented in the socialist and separatist government which gained power in Quebec in the elections of 1976. David Barrett, the reform-minded premier of British Columbia from 1972 to 1975, had been trained as an applied sociologist. "This job is just an extension of social work," he told a reporter. "Social workers have more business in politics than lawyers do."[4] It bears mention also that two leftist contenders from the American presidency in recent times, former senators George McGovern and Eugene McCarthy, both have backgrounds in sociology. The application of sociology almost invariably involves political action, because it is not individuals but the society itself which is to be acted upon. Those who use sociology in a practical way do not ask whether people are coping with their milieu but whether their milieu is bringing out the best in them.

The contrast between psychology and sociology is nowhere more apparent than in the field of social work, which draws on both perspectives in devising concrete programs for the alleviation of human suffering. Not suprisingly, both as students and as practitioners, social workers tend to be divided into two camps. The majority adopt a psychological perspective and become caseworkers; each person or family is a "case," to be interviewed, counseled, and helped to adjust to the conditions of contemporary life. A minority of social workers (like Mr. Barrett) adopt instead a more sociological perspective, avoid the casework routine, and apply themselves to community organizing, social policy formulation, and the design of preventive social programs. Their goal is to modify the conditions of contemporary life in such a way that coping comes naturally. Between them and the caseworkers or clinicians there is an inevitable tension, but one which must be expected in light of the divergent theoretical postures with which they approach the task of helping people.

Like any distinction, of course, that between psychology and sociology admits of exceptions. Especially is this so in the United States, where popular culture is on the side of psychology, enshrining individualism as a national value. As a result there is an individualistic bent to sociology in the United States, where the discipline's ties to psychology are much closer than elsewhere in the world. An important movement in American sociology, led by George Homans at Harvard University, has even built a conception of society on the principles of behaviorist psychology. But this movement is clearly aberrant in the context of sociology more generally. It is balanced, moreover, by a contrary trend in social psychology toward the adoption of a more sociological outlook. Albert Pepitone, a psychologist at the University of Pennsylvania, has criticized his discipline sharply. In a 1976 article in the *Journal of Personality and Social Psychology*, he argued that "the social

behavior we observe in the real world and laboratory . . . is normative, in being more characteristic of definable groups, organizations, and other socio-cultural collectives than of individuals observed at random."[5] Pepitone's point is as novel in psychology as Homan's writings are in sociology; each documents in a backhanded way the distinctive perspective of his discipline.

SUMMARY

A fear sometimes voiced in sociology is that the progressive demise of positivism has left the discipline too much up in the air, too nebulously defined, without coherence or a sense of unified purpose. But the five characteristics reviewed above show that the field is indeed distinctive and coherent, even as it is actually practiced today. For sociologists after all differ from other thinkers by their unique combination of five qualities: an integration of economic, political, and other social insights; emphasis on theory; commitment to the intellectual life; reliance on sense evidence; and focus on groups rather than individuals. Sociology can therefore be defined in summary as the disciplined, intellectual quest for holistic, empirical interpretations of the structure of social life. . . .

Notes

[1] Jean-Jacques Rousseau, *The Social Contract and Discourse on the Origin and Foundation of Inequality Among Mankind*, Pocketbooks, New York 1967, p. 177.

[2] For a splendid and readable case study of this difference see Joseph Helfgot, "Professional Reform Organizations and the Symbolic Representation of the Poor," *American Sociological Review* **39**: 475–91, (1974).

[3] Allen Ginsberg, *Howl*, Part 1, line 1, *Howl and Other Poems*, City Lights, San Francisco, California, 1956.

[4] David Barrett, quoted in *Colombo's Canadian Quotations*, Hurtig, Edmonton, 1974, p. 36.

[5] Albert Pepitone, "Toward a Normative and Comparative Bio-Cultural Social Psychology," *Journal of Personality and Social Psychology*, **34**: 641–53 (1976).

4 History, Change, and the Study of Sociology

S.D. Clark

S.D. CLARK, Professor Emeritus of Sociology at the University of Toronto, specializes in rural sociology, social movements, and the study of social change. His publications include *The Canadian Manufacturers Association* (1939), *The Social Development of Canada* (1942); *Church and Sect in Canada* (1948); *Movements of Political Protest in Canada* (1959), *The Developing Canadian Community* (1963, 1968); *The Suburban Society* (1966); *Canadian Society in Historical Perspective* (1976); and *The New Urban Poor* (1978). In 1943–44 Professor Clark was a Guggenheim Fellow at Columbia University, in 1958–59 he was President of the Canadian Political Science Association, and in 1960 he was awarded the Tyrell Medal by the Royal Society of Canada for work in Canadian sociological history. Elected a Fellow of the Royal Society of Canada, in 1975 he became President of the Society. He has been elected a Foreign Honorary Member of the American Academy of Arts and Sciences, and appointed by the Governor General of Canada an Officer of the Order of Canada. Professor Clark has received honorary degrees from Calgary, Dalhousie University, the University of Western Ontario, the University of Manitoba, St. Mary's University, and Lakehead University. He has held visiting professorships at the University of California (Berkeley), Dartmouth College, the University of Sussex (England), Dalhousie University, the University of Guelph, Lakehead University, and Tsukuba University (Japan). In 1980–81 he was the Visiting Professor of Canadian Studies at the University of Edinburgh.

INTRODUCTION

... It was an effort to look at the Canadian society within an historical perspective which guided my first attempts to study it. A theoretical framework was required to organize the facts about the development of the society; otherwise, one would have been forced to fall back upon a simple social historical approach, organizing facts in terms of the beginning of things, such as the first family to become established in New France, the first Congregational church in Liverpool, Nova Scotia, the first mental hospital in Toronto, the first farmers' organization in Alberta. It was in the search for a theoretically meaningful way of organizing the facts in the analysis of the Canadian society that led to my focussing on "frontier" developments.

THE STUDY OF CHANGE IN CANADA

What seemed apparent, in looking at the Canadian society over the whole course of its development, were the long intervals when nothing much of importance happened and then there occurred a sudden, widespread upsetting of the established order and a new, different course of development. It was what was happening to the Canadian society in such areas of disturbance and rapid change that commanded my attention in the early efforts to examine its development in the past:

the rural society of New France with the breakdown of the monopoly control of the fur trade and the opening of the interior to individual traders from the colony; the village society of Nova Scotia with the American War of Independence and the settlement of Loyalist refugees in the colony; Upper Canada with overseas immigration and the pushing of settlement into the backwoods; British Columbia and the Klondike during the times of the gold rushes; the city of central Canada with the opening of the western market for manufactured products and the concentration of industry in large urban centres; the western Prairies during the period of rapid settlement; the suburbs of the 1950s with the mass movement of population out of the city into the surrounding country-side.

The examination of developments in such areas of disturbance and rapid change emphasized the way in which established forms of social organization and patterns of behaviour and thought broke down and new forms and patterns took their place. It also, however, emphasized the way in which powerful vested interests of the established order (the Government, Church, the social class system, forms of clan organization, and such) succeeded in arresting certain kinds of changes and maintaining the status quo. Thus was introduced the distinction between the "open" and "closed" frontier. Examination of developments in the Canadian society in such terms made possible not only the contrast between areas where outside restraining forces remained strong as opposed to areas where they did not (the sect type of farm settlement, for instance, in contrast with the farm settlement established by individual families acting on their own), but also made possible the contrast between developments in the Canadian and American societies where, in the development of the Canadian society, the frontier had less of an open character.

Unfortunately, the use of the term "frontier" as a way of depicting the character of these forces or happenings which triggered or set off new or different courses of development in the Canadian society led to the charge that I was a frontier determinist, particularly by those social scientists and historians wedded to their own favoured brand of determinism. There was no implication in the use of the term that the frontier determined anything that happened to the society. The focussing on frontier development represented only an effort to seize on certain theoretically meaningful points of departure in examining the character of change of the Canadian society.

Without such points of departure no analysis of change is possible unless one is prepared to settle for a concept of change as ubiquitous, all things changing at all times. Thus, for instance, in the analysis of the society of a small town it is evident that every time a new by-law is passed by the town council, a new street opened up, or even a new family settles in the community, the town changes. But how to distinguish between such changes and those which bring about a complete transformation of the town, it being made, for instance, into an industrial city or so abandoned by its residents that it comes to assume a ghost character?

The distinction between one kind of change and another is not something that is given. It is the problem set for analysis which determines what changes are considered significant and why not. Thus, for instance, in Simmel fashion one might fasten on the consequences for the society of a small town of the settlement in it of a new family or, to move in completely the opposite direction, one might in S.M. Lipset fashion fasten on the manner in which the society of the town did not change even when it became transformed into an industrial city.

In theoretical terms, there can be no quarrel with Lipset's *First New Nation* where the interest was in showing how certain values of the American society had persisted from the time of the War of Independence to the present. Viewed in such a perspective,

American society had not changed. If viewed in a still broader perspective, however, neither had human society changed from the day of the cave man or tree dweller to the day of modern man. Continuity is a fact of human society and the Parsonian model of a social system, where the emphasis is upon the persistence of certain values described as basic, makes possible its examination. Here what is talked about is change within the system, change that can be described in terms of stresses and strains, the disturbance of equilibrium, the vested interests of the social system and the re-assertion of its basic values, and, finally, the restoration of equilibrium.

Where, however, the interest shifts from an examination of the way in which a society persists over time to the way in which it changes and becomes a different kind of society, one can no longer talk about change within the system. What now comes to be talked about is change of the system; otherwise, there are no means of distinguishing between those changes which bring about the establishment of a different kind of society from those changes which do not. In a word, one has to begin to work now with more than one model of the social system or society.

What particular models are employed depends upon what changes in the society are undergoing examination. Thus, if the interest was in the way the society of New France had changed in the period 1650–1700, one would begin with an examination of this society as it had become established before 1650, then proceed to examine the changes that brought about the establishment of a very different kind of society in 1700. If, however, the interest was in the way the society of French Canada had become transformed in the years since the Second World War—"the quiet revolution"—then all that had happened in the society before that time, reaching back even beyond 1700, would be examined in relationship to the type of society which had become established by the

time of the war—"the old order" of French Canada—and it would be changes which have taken place in the society since that time that would demand attention.

An examination of change, thus, involves beginning with a model or picture of the society as it was beore the changes being examined occurred. What becomes constructed initially is a Parsonian type of model of a society or social system described as being in a state of equilibrium. Here the interest is in showing what the society was like before it was made into a different kind of society. Any change that had occurred within the society as such is looked at in relationship to the way in which the society had become structured or ordered. Thus, in the example of the small town, the passing of a new by-law by the town council or the opening up of a new street would not be considered as having altered the basic character of the society as that of a small town, nor would the delinquent behaviour of a gang of teenagers across the tracks, nor some shady dealing in real estate on the part of the town councillors. Changes or forms of deviant behaviour of such a sort would be considered "normal" to a small town society.

In the employment of such a model of a society one could talk about boundary maintenance, integration, basic values, consensus, vested interests, indeed even of a basic personality type. It would be those features of the society giving to it a distinctive character which would be seized upon in the determination of its boundaries, whether the society was that of a small town or a large geographical unit such as the backwoods of Upper Canada, say in 1820, or of French Canada, say in 1939. Thus, one could describe the society so bondary-limited in terms of its economic order, its ecological structure, its social stratification system, its institutional order, its primary group structure, its system of values.

What becomes important to recognize in the employment of any such model as this is that talk about basic values, or basic anything, has meaning only in relationship to the way the society was defined. It is the effort to find within a social system a determining agent that has led to much of the confusion in the development of a theoretical framework for the analysis of social change. Thus, in using the adjective "basic" in speaking of those values considered vital for the survival of the society, Parsons has given to such values a determining quality. One can speak of basic values if by that is meant those values which are considered an essential characteristic of the particular society undergoing examination—for instance, that of a small town or of French Canada before 1939. Equally as basic, however, would be the insitutions of the society, or its stratification or ecological structure. A small town would not be a small town if the predominant values of the population were those of a big city population; nor would it be a small town if the population and institutions of the society were ordered in the manner of a big city or of a mining camp. What are seized upon in the construction of a model of a society are those characteristics in the way of values, institutions, ecological structure, and such which are considered distinctive of the society. To those characteristics, for purposes of analysis, can be applied the adjective "basic".

The distinction between what is considered basic and what is not allows for the examination of those changes within a social system which are considered not to lead to a change of the system. One might take the case of the Ontario small town of the 1920s where the interest was in showing not how the society had changed but how it had remained basically the same. Much happened to the Ontario small town during that decade. The automobile became widely adopted and radio was introduced. Women began to smoke in public and to bob their hair and wear short skirts. Labour, in those small industries characteristic of the small town, made its first moves towards unionization. Old people with limited incomes began now to receive a government pension cheque in the mail and young people no longer thought to the same extent of grade eight, or fourth form, as marking the end of a full education. The town remained, however, still a small town.

In such an examination of the small town, developments like the mass production and marketing of the automobile, the "liberation" of women which came with the First World War, the growth in the larger society of the need for people of education, come to be viewed as happenings from the outside which extended into the small town society and disturbed the existing state of things. The small town changed but, as it had been defined, not in ways that altered its basic character as a small town. It is at this point in the analysis of a society considered not to have altered its fundamental character that one can speak of the vested interests of the social system. Those people had a stake in the society of the small town whose way of life would have been adversely affected had it become a different kind of society. By the process of socialization and by means of repression, forms of conduct considered damaging to the society were held in check or accommodated in a manner which did not threaten the society's basic character. Thus, if the town's clergymen may have sought to bring down on all those women who smoked in public the charge of sinful conduct, the accommodation of such conduct within the town's social class structure meant in the end that it no longer was considered to pose a threat to the way of life of the small town; women could smoke as ladies or, if not as ladies, in a manner which reinforced the small town social class structure.

There may appear to be only a thin line—indeed, no line at all—between what here has been talked about as change within the social system and change of the system; in fact, only in analytical terms can such a line be drawn. How the line is drawn, how the distinction is made between a society considered to be one maintaining its basic structure and one undergoing change in a way that makes it a very different society, depends simply upon what problem of change is commanding attention. To revert to the example of the Ontario small town, the interest could have been, not in showing how it retained the character of a small town in face of what happened to it in the 1920s, but in how over this period of time it became a different society. Now one would begin with a picture or model of the small town society of 1920 and what happened to it after 1920 would now be viewed in terms of those changes occurring which make it into a different society by the end of the 1920s.

In the examination of change of the society, therefore, one moves from talking about equilibrium, integration, consensus, and the vested interests of the system to talking about disequilibrium, disintegration, dissensus, and the vested interests of change. What happened outside the society to lead to disturbance within the society comes now to be examined in relation to the effect in bringing about the change of the society. In such manner would proceed the analysis of how a small town became transformed into an industrial city or how the older order of French Canada gave way to that society which was a product of the quiet revolution. For such an analysis, what becomes necessary is the construction of a model not only of the society that was but also of the society coming into being.

In an analysis of change of the social system or society, the starting point would be that happening or series of happenings outside the society so consequential in their impact on the society, that the changes engendered resulted in the establishment of a society very different from the one that was in terms of the model employed. What happened outside could be anything. There is no search here for a single determining agent or "cause" of change. What happened outside could have been the building of a four-lane expressway out to an isolated village bringing it within easy commuting distance of a large city; or it could have been the discovery of oil in an area of the country long given to farming. Or it could have been an earthquake. The interest here is not in reaching back to determine what caused the four-lane expressway to be built, the oil to be discovered, or the earthquake to occur. The interest rather is in examining the consequences of such "happenings" for the society being analyzed. Happenings of this sort were in the character of disturbance which in the model employed led to the breakdown or disintegration of the established order—the society that was—and the establishment or integration of a new order—the society coming into being.

In such an analysis of change of a society, one begins with an examination of the process of disintegration of the society that was: the breaking down of old established habits of thought and behaviour and of established institutional forms, the development of types of deviance which no longer could be considered "normal" to the society, the growth of new social movements at war with the society, the strengthening efforts of segments of the population to separate from the society and form a little social world of their own. In such manner could be examined the disintegration of the small town society, in the example of the small town being transformed into an industrial city, or of the old order of French Canada now giving way to the society of the quiet revolution.

But social phenomena, thus examined as representing the process of disintegration of the society, represent as well the process of integration of the society coming into being. Disintegration is not something which occurs in time before integration. Rather, they are one and the same process looked at in two different ways. As the analysis shifts from the breaking down of an established social order to the emergence of a new social order, social phenomena come to be examined in terms of the process of integration rather than in terms of the process of disintegration: the development of new habits of behaviour and thought; new institutional forms; types of deviance, while "abnormal" to the society that was, can be considered "normal" to the society coming into being; social movements which point the direction in the establishment of the new society; and, finally, efforts of the population to separate from the society that was in building the society coming into being. Clearly, in such an analysis of the processes of disintegration and integration, no element of time or chronology enters into the analysis. Established habits of thought and behaviour cannot break down without new habits of thought and behaviour taking their place. Nor can there be a breaking down or disintegration of established institutional forms or of social values without there emerging new institutional forms and social values. Integration and disintegration, consensus and dissensus, equilibrium and disequilibrium, conformity and deviance are simply different ways of looking at society, depending upon whether the interest is in social order or social change.

It is not social processes but events or happenings which take place in time, and events or happenings are the stuff with which the sociologist has to work. Once, however, events or happenings are looked at in terms of their sociological meaning they lose their chronological character and become built into an analytical process, of order or change. Thus, returning to the example of the small town being transformed into an industrial city, there might have occurred at a particular time a mass meeting of the congregation of the local Protestant church at which the minister, now considered by the town's changing population old-fashioned, was fired and a new, modern minister hired to take his place. Here, in such a "happening" might be offered a hint of the kinds of changes taking place in the town leading to its transformation to an industrial city: the way in which the old established order of the town was breaking down and the way in which a new social order was

coming into being.

If the interest was in the way a small town was being transformed into an industrial city, no great sociological significance, of course, would be attached to any one event, such as, in the example above, the mass meeting in the town of the local Protestant congregation. It is when, in a particular context, a great number of events of a certain kind occur that they begin to take on a significance sociologically. The determination of the meaning of events is the task of sociological analysis. Events take on sociological meaning only in relation to the problem of social change (or of social order) being analyzed. Thus, the firing of the old-fashioned minister in the example of the small town and other events of similar sort only gained significance because the problem undergoing analysis was how the small town became transformed into an industrial city. Had the interest been in the way the Canadian society has undergone change and become a different kind of society in the years since the Second World War, little attention would have been paid to such an event. Attention rather would have become focussed upon such "happenings" as the separatist movement in Quebec, the increased numbers of women in the labour force, student unrest in the universities, the large-scale movement of population out of rural areas to the cities, mass immigration from Europe, the development of new types of economic enterprise, the increasingly strident demands of the native population.

Thus, to return to the major concern of this essay, the study of Canadian society, what is involved is a focussing upon those events or happenings which have sociological significance in relation to the problem being examined. It is not claimed here that there is only one way to go about the analysis of the Canadian society. It is only claimed that, if the society is to be examined as it has changed over time in all its dimensions, the examination necessarily involves working with more than one analytical model of the society. It is simply not possible to talk about Canadian society (or American society, as Talcott Parsons is wont to do) as if, for all purposes at hand, there were only one society. How one conceives the society depends upon the problem of change undergoing analysis. The historian or sociologist concerned with the process of nation building can quite properly treat the federal union of Canada after 1867, and for that matter the British colonies of North America before that time, as a political, economic, and social unit, and engage in an examination of those forces at work which furthered or retarded the creation of a Canadian nation. In such an analysis, the inclusion of Prince Edward Island, the Western provinces, and ultimately Newfoundland in the federal union would be viewed as involving an adjustment of the boundaries of the society, but not in a way that brought about a change of the society; nor would the growth of industrialism, the shift of population from rural areas to urban, the official recognition of the French language or the adoption of a Canadian flag be considered as involving a fundamental change of the society. Stresses and strains in the society would be evident in such developments as the growth of the separatist movement in Quebec, the increasing militancy of labour and other disadvantaged groups, the rise in the rate of crime, the demands of the native peoples, and the strengthening demands of provincial governments, but such stresses and strains, it could be shown in terms of the model of the society employed, were contained by the vested interests of the social system—that is, by all those people and institutions with a stake in the maintenance of Canada as a nation.

Such an analysis of the process of nation building would tell us much about the Canadian society. However, there would be much that it would not tell, or tell only very inadequately. What would not be told was how, at different times or in different areas of the country, the society that was in existence—

the urban society of central Canada of the 1890s, for instance, or the rural society of French Canada of the 1930s—underwent change and became a different kind of society. The reason would be the bias built into the model employed. By adhering to the conception of Canadian society as *the society*, the emphasis necessarily comes to be placed upon those forces securing the formation and survival of the society. What gets played down, so to speak, if not wholly ignored, are those forces of disruption in the society which brought about the disintegration of established forms of organization and the emergence of new forms. For such an analysis of change of the society, the sociologist must work with more than one model of the society, both in spatial and temporal terms.

Thus, one may want to talk about *the* Canadian society of, say, 1870, 1939, or 1960, or one may want to talk about *the* society of French Canada in 1939 or of the rural community of 1950 and show how this society underwent change and became a different kind of society. Or, indeed, one may want to talk about the society of the Canadian town of 1950, here with an interest in showing how rapid urban growth and the mass push of population out of large urban centres resulted during the 1950s in transforming its character. All the time the interest may remain the larger problem of what is happening to the Canadian society. But only by this shifting from macro to micro types of analysis in time and space can the full dimensions of the Canadian society be brought under review.

CONCLUSION

It is this way of looking at Canadian society that has characterized my efforts to analyze it. Caught up in such efforts, it should be admitted, has been a bias of my own. I have wanted to look at what is wrong about society as well as what is right; to look at the way old established structures of a society broke down as well as the way new structures came into being. In a word, the interest has been in the problem of change rather than in the problem of order.

Such an interest was clearly apparent in my early study. *The Social Development of Canada*, where what secured emphasis were the kinds of problems of organization thrown up by the pushing of the Canadian population into new areas of development, but scarcely less evident was such an interest in *Church and Sect in Canada* and *Movements of Political Protest in Canada* where the major concern was with how old established forms of organization, religious in the one case and political in the other, broke down and gave way to new forms. In *The Suburban Society*, as well, what secured emphasis was not how the suburban society was structured, the "suburbia" that had received so much sociological and journalistic attention, but rather how urban forms of organization and patterns of behaviour broke down with the mass push of population out of the city into the surrounding countryside and how a new society in the suburbs came into being.

Developing out of this interest has been another which, the more the Canadian society was viewed within the context of the larger North American continental system, came to receive increasing emphasis. The society of Canada like that of the United States has been caught up over the years in forces of growth associated with the peopling of the continent and the development of new forms of economic enterprise and community structures. Whereas in the United States, these forces of growth contributed to the political strengthening of the nation—the realization of the manifest destiny of the American people—in Canada their effect was to threaten the separate political existence of the Canadian nation or, before 1867, of the British

North American colonies. Thus, in Canada the "breakdown" of forms of social organization and patterns of behaviour which resulted from the mass movement of population into new areas of development was allowed to proceed only so far. "Rebellions in the backlands" offered a means to the American society of ridding the continent of rival political jurisdictions, whether represented by the empires of France, Britain, or Spain, or by the claims of native people. In Canada, such rebellions constituted a threat to the very survival of the society.

Thus, running through *Church and Sect in Canada* and even more *Movements of Political Protest in Canada* was the theme of revolution and counter-revolution where developed the argument that forms of religious and political organization in Canada were a product largely of counter-revolutionary forces in the society. The implications for the society as a whole of this play of revolutionary and counter-revolutionary forces became explored more generally in essays appearing in *The Developing Canadian Community*, particularly in Part IV.

Readers of later essays of mine will note a still further shift of interest. It is now thirty years since the end of the Second World War. Much has happened to the Canadian society in these thirty years. No longer is it the Canadian society that is threatened by the expansive forces of the American society. Rather, it is the American society which has become threatened by the expansive forces of new growing political powers in the world. One indeed might argue the reversal of the revolution and counter-revolution theme. Now the American society has become caught up in forces of counter-revolution, whereas the Canadian society has become caught up in forces of a revolutionary character. . . .

5   Approaches Toward a Canadian Sociology

Wallace Clement

WALLACE CLEMENT, Professor of Sociology at Carleton Univesity, Ottawa, specializes in the study of comparative class structure, power, and the labour process. His books include *The Canadian Corporate Elite*: *An Analysis of Economic Power* (1975); *Continental Corporate Power*: *Economic Linkages Between Canada and the United States* (1977); *Hardrock Mining*: *Industrial Relations and Technological Change at Inco* (1981); *Class, Power and Property*: *Essays on Canadian Society* (1983); and *The Struggle to Organize*: *Resistance in Canada's Fishery* (1986). He has conducted research in Sweden and Australia, and is currently engaged, with John Myles and Dennis Forcese, in collecting and analysing data as part of the Comparative Class Structure Project, funded by the Social Sciences and Humanities Research Council of Canada. Professor Clement has lectured widely in Canada and abroad.

A "SOCIOLOGY OF CANADA" AND "CANADIAN SOCIOLOGY"

There have been some recent attempts to develop a "Canadian sociology" approach, an analysis of the enterprise as a whole and the formation of Canada as a state, but a variety of "sociology of Canada" perspectives continue to dominate; that is, most sociological studies are of individual aspects of Canadian society viewed either in isolation or compared with similar phenomena elsewhere. Each approach is important but essentially different.

A "Canadian sociology" focuses on major structural features of the country—such as regionalism, ethnic relations, foreign and indigenous investment patterns, political-legal formations and class structures—as they relate in a national context, especially as they unfold and transform historically. "Canadian sociology" is not a theory about Canadian society, although it implies a series of models for organizing information. Rather, it is a synoptic perspective which conceptually links together a variety of theories and data on Canada while making the analyst aware of other factors which may affect or be affected by the particular aspect of society under study. For example, if the subject under study is education, it would be fruitful to know the linkage this has with immigration and the Canadian practice of importing highly qualified manpower rather than creating indigenous educational institutions or the linkage between the type of economy Canada has and demands this creates for particular training. Similarly, it is important to know the type of class structure Canada has if education is to be related to class inequalities or the type of sex roles if it is to be related to sexual inequalities. The point is self-evident. The implication being that there emerges from these linkages a broader understanding of various developments by removing them from a narrow view common to a great deal of sociology. Similarly, it is concerned about aggregating data on Canada into meaningful units of analysis. All that makes it a "Canadian sociology" perspective as distinct from a "Japanese, American, Polish, British, French, Australian, Russian, etc., sociology" is the substantive focus. This does not mean that various key features such as regionalism, ethnicity, class, etc. will be identical or even similar in each nation. The similarity is that what is being pursued here is simply a specific case of a more general "national society" perspective. The key is the holistic analysis of a variety of important social phenomena within a national context.

A "sociology of Canada" perspective, on the other hand, focuses on particular aspects of the society, such as those listed above or others like education, immigration, sex roles, deviance, voting patterns, urban studies, etc. but does *not* relate each to other developments within Canada. . . . The problematic is the extent to which several "sociologies of Canada" could be turned into a "Canadian sociology" by transcending individual studies and relating them to one another. While the individual models and frameworks used in "sociologies of Canada" do not facilitate this end, the information and theories generated may be able to inform a "Canadian sociology." The idea of a "Canadian sociology" is not based simply on a series of microsociological or macrogrouping studies or even an enumeration of national statistics, but hinges on the relationships and combinations of various elements which crystallize into a unique whole. . . .

In this paper there is no attempt to provide a sociology of sociology for Canada, nor a survey of sociological findings themselves. Rather, the attempt is to examine a series of approaches which may prove useful in developing a "Canadian sociology," particularly those which may expand the analysis of Canadian society already provided by John Porter's path-breaking work and some issues relevant to such an analysis. But first, a larger context is necessary.

MACROSOCIOLOGY AND THE "CLASSICAL TRADITION"

Macrosociology focuses on structures, types of relationships, and their degree of dependence or independence; in short, how social systems work. It is the tradition of sociologists like Marx and Weber who attempted, in the words of Gerth and Mills, "to grasp the interrelations on all institutional orders making up a social structure" (1946:49). But what is meant by "structure"? A social structure is a stable set of relationships among the various parts or elements making up the totality of a society. However, to say these relationships are stable does not discount their continuous transformation. As Z.A. Jordan has said in his summary of Marx, "macro-sociological structues and laws can claim validity only within a specified period of time and, therefore, must be considered historically" (1971:66). To analytically "weave" various institutional orders into a whole from the perspective of national societies requires an historical dimension which seeks to comprehend the interactive effects between different orders, their exchanges—both of decision-makers and resources—and their relative strengths or weaknesses vis à vis each other and different orders. For example, someone examining present-day Canada may tend to dismiss the religious order in the overall pattern of power but historically it has had an enormous effect—particularly in Quebec, but elsewhere as well—in helping to shape the curent orders. In Quebec it could be argued that the church was important in retarding indigenous capitalism but effective in increasing the power of the state and unions vis à vis capital. The impact of religion thus could be detected only through a historical analysis.[1]

Thus the call for a "Canadian sociology" is not meant as a replacement for the "classical tradition" in sociology; exactly the opposite. It is the application of classical approaches, such as those used by Marx and

Weber, to macrosociological issues of Canadian society. It is within the tradition of "holistic" analysis which maintains that the whole cannot be reconstructed from the parts; the parts can only be understood in light of the whole. Rather than a separate focus on theory and methodology, it calls for a reflexive relationship between theory and research and the development of sociologies at several levels of analysis, especially as they relate to one another, including an understanding of the past, a feeling for the present and an eye to the future.

A "Canadian sociology" approach is consistent with what Irving Zeitlin sees as the main task of theory construction, "a problem oriented approach to social science." He argues that, "If one is generally interested in empirical social systems, one ought to have questions about their workings that one would like to answer. To do this, one does not begin with 'society' in the abstract but with a specific society (or several of them) and with an interesting problem" (1973:23).

One major guiding question for a "Canadian sociology" already posed is how do major inequalities such as class, regionalism, ethnicity, education, occupation, income distribution, foreign control, etc., affect and reinforce one another? Of the few national society studies now available, most seem to present their analysis around a particular theme or guiding value.... In *The Vertical Mosaic*, John Porter uses a guiding theme, that of inequality, aimed at the image of a "middle class society." Similar problems are posed by Sol Encel in his *Equality and Authority: A Study of Class, Status and Power in Australia*. These are also some of the types of problems which could be posed by a "Canadian sociology"—problems not constrained by either theory or methodology, but problems which use theories and methodologies to resolve problems. As C. Wright Mills has said, "For the classical social scientists, neither method nor theory is an autonomous domain; methods are methods for some range of problems; theories are theories for some range of phenomenon" (1959:121). The first task of the analyst is to provide the macro problem; whether these are liberty, equality, democracy, efficiency or whatever will depend on each researcher's values.

As has been argued, one of the most important units of analysis is the nation state within which is encompassed a national society. Within this framework the focus is on major structural components and their relationships as they interact to form the whole. Many macro studies have used the nation state as a unit of comparative analysis, but this is not the same as analysing a national society. Stein Rokkan has pointed to what he calls the "whole nation bias" in comparative studies and the weakness inherent in taking aggregates rather than components.... To overcome the "Whole nation bias" in comparative studies requires the *a priori* analysis of the national society which in turn may then be compared in terms of the types of relationships found within the national society and the processes[2] of developing to this stage. It may seem unusual that a paper on Canadian society would have this concern about comparative studies but it is to be understood that each nation has its differences as well as similarities and much can be learned from these. Indeed, C. Wright Mills has noted, "it is only by comparative studies that we can become aware of the *absence* of certain historical phases from a society, which is often quite essential to understanding its contemporary shape" (1959:157). Moreover, it is not merely a theoretical or academic exercise, but many Canadians themselves engage in just such comparisons—principally with the United States, but with Europe and other industrialized nations as well, although typically limiting these to other liberal democracies.

Aside from the outstanding work of John Porter, there are only a handful of sociologists in English-speaking Canada who have taken a total or national society approach—such as, at times, S.D. Clark, Kasper Naegele, A.K. Davis and, to some extent, Frank Vallee and Don Whyte. But in Quebec there are many more, such as Hubert Guindon, Maurice Pinard, Guy Rocher, Marcel Rioux, Jean-Charles Falardeau, Jacques Dofny, Gerald Fortin, Phillipe Garigue, pioneer Quebec sociologist Léon Géerin and Fernand Dumont, to name but a few. . . .

Vallee and Whyte, in their paper "Canadian Society: Trends and Perspectives," have argued that "sociologists are too busy making up for the backlog of sheer information about Canadian society to worry about the enterprise as a whole and to engage in much soul-searching concerning the theoretical and methodological aspects of this enterprise" (1968:849). In terms of the distinction presented earlier, they are arguing that most of what has been occurring is a "sociology of Canada" rather than a "Canadian sociology." In fact, they argue that, with a few notable exceptions, "Canadian sociologists have rarely adopted a holistic perspective, one in which the system-as-a-whole is the universe of study" (849).

(i) National Identity and the Social Psychology of Canadians

The literature in Canadian sociology on "national identity" is probably more extensive than on any other single topic, particularly one at the national level, yet little consensus has emerged in terms of what this means in Canada or what its implications are for a "Canadian sociology." Some have argued Canada is conservative because of its "tory" origins and rejection of the American Revolution, others that it is liberal because of its American orientation, still others that Canadians are engaged in a love-hate relation with themselves and the United States. Whatever the case may be, the "national character" route to understanding Canadian society seems a "dead end," not a place to begin but a place

to arrive. The only conclusion seems to be that there are a number of social forces affecting the way Canadians act and believe. It seems more reasonable to first identify these social forces and then address the consequences for the Canadian consciousness.

One of these social forces is ethnic diversity, the struggle between the French and English plus the ethnic pluralism of the other one quarter of the population. In the absence of alternative identities, the Canadian state has pursued policies of "biculturalism," and more recently, "multiculturalism," which serves to reinforce these atomized "organized" minorities. It is difficult to tell if these are identities arising from the Canadian "mosaic" or ideologies projected by the Canadian state elite (see Clement and Olsen, 1974).

Sociologists themselves are not free from responsibility on this matter, as Vallee and Whyte have said:

> Sociologists who have written on national character and values in Canada have based their conclusions on impressions, introspection, and on inferences from such disparate sources as literature, historical developments, and statistics on a variety of subjects. The framework within which these studies are carried out and presented is almost always a comparative one in which Canadians are viewed as not quite as American as the Americans, not quite as British as the British, not quite as Australian as the Australians, not quite as French as the French. In this way, sociologists reinforce a folk impression of long standing that Canada is a hybrid product and an intermediary between the United States and Europe (1968:836).

Religion, ethnicity, linguistic groups, class, sex and region all compete with a sense of national identity, but it seems an understanding of how and why these operate can best follow from the study of the structure of Canadian society. A study of regionalism would suggest some of the reasons why there are several identity references operating simultaneously. In the West, for example, there is one pull to central Canada and another north-south pull to the United States. Nations need not be monolithic or highly integrated; indeed, precisely the way the parts (be they ethnic, regional, class, etc.) relate to the whole is one of the most important and interesting variables.

Only very recently with the appearance of Patricia Marchak's *Ideological Perspective on Canada* has the weakness of the "Canadian character" literature begun to be overcome and this has been done by using a methodology different from the earlier studies. She has chosen to do her macrosociology of Canada by counterposing "two versions of the Canadian reality"—dominant and counter ideologies (1975:viff). The method is to contrast ideology and reality and see why some classes adopt one or another, and evaluate which "fits" an understanding of Canadian society. Marchak is able to weave an analysis of history, class, nation, foreign ownership, sovereignty, regionalism, French Canada, ethnicity, native peoples, sexual inequality, professions, unions, political parties, institutional arrangements—public and private, education, wealth and income distribution into her theme of dominant and counter ideologies, and this is all done at the national society level. Although they are not as yet related in such a way that it could be said that they constitute a model or theory of Canadian society, the beginnings of such an attempt are apparent.

An analysis using the regional power structure discussed earlier which attempted to integrate the findings of Rex Lucas' study, *Minetown, Milltown, Railtown*, John Porter's study of the national power structure and other work on the international level[3] is another approach worth exploring. The number of such links as education, corporate control, regionalism, urban-rural migration, social mobility, unions and others, are innumerable. A study which tried to examine national identities based on these types of linkages would probably have more to say about how people

develop "identities" than those undertaken within the "national identity" approach thus far. Indeed, studies such as the impressive work of Lucas have done a great deal to link the social psychological level of analysis into broader social forces and structures. It is likely that studies such as his or Marchak's would be the primary way that a "Canadian sociology" approach could tap this level of analysis yet still retain its broad national focus.

(ii) French Canada as a Hinterland Model

Hubert Guindon's analysis of French Canada provides an analysis of a total society which could be expanded to the whole of Canada. Guindon links the "increase in the political and economic relevance of the provincial governments at the expense of the federal government" to changes which have occurred in the class structure of Quebec (1968:33ff). This could also be related to postwar transformations in the Prairies, particularly oil in Alberta, which have catalysed similar developments there.[4] Although all of the parallels and points of analysis cannot be developed here, it is worthwhile to suggest some of the more obvious. Guindon says,

> The vulnerability of the traditional elite set the stage for an easy introduction of industrialization even if it meant dependence on foreign capitalists. The capitalists transformed the French Canadians into urban dwellers. To service the needs of the recently urbanized masses, the traditional power elite had to transform its institutions into large scale bureaucracies, giving birth in the process to the new middle class of French-Canadian society (44).

In these few sentences Guindon has introduced and integrated a historical framework for the study of industrialization, bureaucratization, foreign investment, class transformations and the study of elites. Later he discusses social mobility, saying, "French-Canadian bureaucratic pyramids have a narrow base—geographically, socially, and organizationally—because of their small scale. This means that upward mobility is more restricted, less diversified, and less extended" (51). All of this resembles closely the experience of other regional hinterlands in Canada.[5] It places the analysis within its Canadian and international context, shows the limitations of attempting to create parallel mobility structures alongside dominant ones (and the need to do this because of exclusion from dominant ones); it explains the role local elites have in mediating with outside power centers and where their interests are located.

Vallee and Whyte have commented:

> compared to the total Canadian nation-state, the distinctive entity called French-Canadian society is easy to grasp in its totality. The inter-dependence of the parts that make up the socio-political entity called Quebec can be traced historically and synchronically in a way which it would be extremely difficult to do for Canada as a whole, except at the most abstract level (1968:850).

Perhaps it is not so much the size or complexity of Canadian society as the lack of attempting to develop such an approach among English-speaking sociologists that explains this failure. Surely the same kind of analysis can be done for the rest of Canada; it even has the model of such analyses as Guindon's to start with.

(iii) Absentee Ownership and "Linkages"

Canada's economy has two types of elites, comprador and indigenous, which are entered in relatively distinct economic sectors. The comprador elites are the Canadian counterpart of foreign controlled multinationals, the "go-between" elites in the periphery nation. Some modifications to this model are necessary because, in addition to the comprador or "go-between" economic elites, there exist independent indigenous elites. The fragmented economic system in Canada can

be related to the fragmented political system, particularly in the context of the above remarks on the relationship between foreign investment and regional hinterlands. That is, the fragmented political system has encouraged the development of foreign direct investment within various provinces which compete with each other, thus encouraging differential patterns of growth between provinces and higher rates of foreign investment. This, in turn, has resulted in an increase in provincial power in the postwar period, particularly in the oil rich Prairies, which has also weakened the federal system. These brief remarks suggest that it is important to establish relationships between various developments and place them within their international context. Absentee ownership on the national level has had important economic, political and regional implications but these represent only one side of the relationship. If the full implications for a "Canadian sociology" are to be explored, then other aspects must also be taken into account.

Absentee ownership may be defined in terms of the distance from a particular center, similar to the metropolis-hinterland chain. The boundaries under consideration must be specified; for example, at the national level foreign ownership is absentee and the economic boundaries do not coincide with the nation state. On the community or regional level, absentee ownership refers to the branches of firms which are not locally owned but are part of larger corporations, themselves either Canadian or foreign owned. The consequences of foreign ownership at the national level and local level exhibit similar characteristics, including lack of autonomy from outside control and decision-making, withdrawal of capital and resources, as well as a higher degree of uncertainty about the continuation of the branch plant at both levels since by definition they are peripheral to the overall operation.

Another consequence of importance is the effect on the class structure and mobility of the indigenous population, either local or national. With a branch plant system, management is typically recruited outside the community and frequently transferred thus creating a system of "transient managers." This means local people have a lower probability of upward mobility and participation within this type of structure. On the national level the matter is more complex. If management is brought in from outside, as has often been the case in the past, the opportunity structure for indigenous Canadians is blocked. However, if foreign firms recruit within Canada to fill these positions, this opens the possibility for middle class Canadians who are university educated. Given the high degree of blockage which occurs within Canadian controlled firms, this may be desirable from the perspective of individual mobility, but must be weighed against other consequences of absentee ownership suggested above plus the fact that this may be a way that indigenous entrepreneurial talent is drained off within Canada, thus inhibiting the creation of indigenously controlled activity.

In some respects it does make a difference whether the absentee owners are Canadian or foreign. These would be with respect to the retention of profits within Canada which could be used to expand industrial activity thus creating greater surplus and more jobs. It would also mean that many of the secondary and tertiary spin-offs such as technological development could be supported and encouraged within Canada. Being based within Canada may also mean the firms would be subject to greater regulation by the Canadian state.

In other respects it makes little difference whether the branch plant is Canadian or foreign controlled, particularly for the regional or local level. In either case the major access points to occupational mobility, the major accumulation of surplus, and the sources of decision-making occur outside the area. The community or region within which the branch plant is located is equally vulnerable to de-cisions taken at head office, be it in Toronto or New York.

This discussion is the result of taking several levels of analysis—such as the local or regional level represented by Rex Lucas' *Minetown, Milltown, Railtown* and John Porter's analysis of national economic elites—and tying them all together in a variation of regional power structure model. While this discussion is very brief and only illustrative, as well as being confined mainly to economic dimensions, it does provide some indication of the type of analysis that could be developed into a national society framework. The key analytical points are in the linking mechanisms between each level and a concern with the entire scope of the society, including the frequently missing local level. . . .

CONCLUSION

The future of Canadian sociology will depend upon its keeping up with current trends and being able to place them within the context of the national society. In Canada there is a double dilemma of trying to catch up empirically and theoretically by developing the basis for a "Canadian sociology" while at the same time staying abreast of current developments and remaining relevant. Moreover, there are many areas that have been almost totally neglected, not only in a substantive sense but in the sense of the types of perspectives used in the analysis. . . .

There do exist a number of theories, models or at least themes about the nature of Canadian society, some of which have already been mentioned. Porter, for instance, has identified the relationship between class, power and ethnicity, and this has now been expanded by Hughes and Kallen; A.K. Davis' hinterland-metropolis relationship based on regional inequalities; A. Richmond's relationship between immigration and ethnic inequalities, following, in part, from Porter's "two stream model" of migration; Leo Johnson's changing occupational structure and the decline of the petite bourgeoisie; Pat Marchak's two competing versions of social reality; and I have suggested the relationship between foreign and indigenous economic development. Together, and with others, it may be possible to form these into a "Canadian sociology."

Social life is highly complex and experiments in types of societies have been varied. The task of social studies is to "make sense" out of the variety of experiences and experimentations by identifying major processes, structures and relationships. Therefore, the study of Canadian society can and should be approached from a number of perspectives, using a variety of methodologies and data sources. But ultimately, to have relevance for the study of the national society, they have to be tied into an overriding framework and presumably be aimed at a common concern—such as improving the lot of Canadians, which could mean being concerned about the decline of inequalities of all sorts and the increase and redistribution of the society's resources.

It has been argued that the focus of a "Canadian sociology" should be on an array of substantive problems in Canadian society, but these in turn must also be worked out in terms of the priorities of each researcher. This means an evaluation of what are considered important or significant social issues and concerns, and analysis of them and reporting the results. The process of reporting to other scholars and the public is intended to have others re-examine what they consider to be social issues and to re-order their priorities accordingly. This goal would be one of the major tasks of such an undertaking, and one of its most important rewards.

One important question remains: Is there a uniqueness to Canadian society that makes it a valuable topic beyond its intrinsic interest to its residents? The answer offered in this paper has been in the affirmative. Canada lends itself for comparison to probably a wider range of nations than does any other single country. . . .

Postscript

In the two years since this paper was written there has been a maturing of my thinking about models and theories of Canadian society, although I continue to accept the paper's central direction. I would now adopt the political economy tradition as the most fruitful approach; in my view, it has the strongest historical roots and the greatest insights into Canada's social structure. It is a tradition represented in different ways in the works of such diverse people as Donald Creighton, Harold Innis, Tom Naylor and Stanley Ryerson. It encompasses scholars from C.B. Macpherson to H. Claire Pentland to John Porter. Broadly contained within this tradition is the basis for a distinctive Canadian social science which would make sense of and give meaning to the development and current structure of Canadian society.

The following are what I regard as the most central components of a model of Canada as developed within the political economy tradition. These features of Canadian society give direction to the most appropriate questions to be asked and relationships to be explained:

1. The implications of external relations for internal development, especially early colonial ties with France and the United Kingdom and current dependence on the United States in many economic, political and military activities.

2. The persistently active role of the Canadian State in the economy and its fragmented federal-provincial structure.

3. The continued survival of two nations within a single state—the conquered French and the conquering English—and the demise of the native population.

4. The role of immigration in filling the West during the early stages of

development (1879 to 1914) and the urban centres of today (especially Montréal, Toronto, and Vancouver), which have served to build an indigenous labour force and domestic market while creating an ethnically diverse society stratified by class.

5. The persistence of enormous regional differences within the country, especially the underdevelopment of the Atlantic region and the northern sections of the central and western provinces.

6. The constraints imposed by geography, especially the rapids of the St. Lawrence River, the Laurentian Shield, the Rockies, and now the North.

7. The effect of technology and the ownership of that technology, especially patent rights, in shaping the economy and labour force.

8. The tremendous costs of transportation networks from early roads, canals, ports, seaways, and railways to pipelines for oil and gas, and their role in creating a national and continental economy.

9. The dependence on external markets, both as outlets for raw materials (making Canada vulnerable to world conditions) and as capital sources (which ultimately act as drains on capital).

10. The origin of Canadian capitalism in a staple economy, its movement into commercial and financial specialization and its continued reliance on resource extraction.

11. The persistence of a petty bourgeoisie class as the most powerful class outside the capitalist class until the Second World War, prior to which Canada was largely rural and agrarian/resource based.

12. The slower development of an industrial working class, the product of large-scale industrialization which does not become a dominant force in Canada until well into the twentieth century and continues today to be rivaled in importance by the service sector of the labour force, especially the growing number of state workers adding to an already overdeveloped commercial sector.

As in any model, these central components are each related to the others. Various theories have been offered in the political economy tradition which order these components and purport to explain their relationships in Canada. For example, Innis offered the "character of the staple" as explaining most of these other factors. Creighton, on the other hand, contended that the central explanatory relationship of Canada's development was the creative role of its commercial capitalists and their relationship to the state. Naylor also focuses on this relationship as a means of explaining Canadian development, but for him financial capitalists in Canada have a distorting rather than creative role. For Ryerson the relationship between the capitalist class and the working class is the central dynamic, although for him this class relationship is necessarily framed in the context of two nations in an "unequal union." Contrary to Ryerson's Marxist approach is the liberal framework of John Porter and his thesis of a "vertical mosaic" of social class and ethnicity which has shaped Canadian society.

Notes

[1] See Hubert Guindon's, "The Social Evolution of Quebec Reconsidered" (1964:154ff).

[2] John Porter has commented, "There is no comparative analysis, for example, when six scholars produce separate papers on the educational systems of six different countries. Each study may as well have been published separately rather than bound together since

they draw nothing from each other"
(1970a:144). The same, of course, may be said
for readers which are called *Canadian
Society* but lack any internal unity aside from
the common subject matter of Canada.
They might more appropriately be called
"Sociologies of Canada."

[3] In a paper, "Economic Elites in Ontario: A
Broader Perspective on Regionalism" (presented to the Canadian Studies Institute,
University of Waterloo, November, 1974), I
attempted to show the linkages between
the local, regional, national and international
levels. This approach is particularly useful

for illustrating the implications of broader
power structures on the day to day activities
of Canadians.

[4] See John Barr and Owen Anderson (editors),
The Unfinished Revolt, McClelland and
Stewart: Toronto, 1971.

[5] The case studies of Philip Mathias, *Forced
Growth*, James Lewis and Samuel: Toronto,
1971 are interesting illustrations. All five cases
are located within the weakest provinces.
See also Garth Stevenson, "Continental
Integration and Canadian Unity" in Andrew
Axline, et al, editors, *Continental Commu-
nity?*, McClelland and Stewart: Toronto, 1974.

References

Anderson, Charles H. 1974. *The Political Economy of Social Class*. Prentice-Hall: Englewood
Cliffs.

Bachrach, Peter. 1967. *The Theory of Democratic
Elitism*. Little, Brown: Boston.

Bourque, G. and N. Laurin-Frenette. 1972. "Social
classes and national ideologies in Quebec, 1760–
1970," in G. Teeple (ed.) *Capitalism and the
National Question in Canada*. University of
Toronto Press.

Careless, J.M.S. 1969. " 'Limited Identities' in
Canada", *Canadian Historical Review*, Vol. L,
No. 1 (March).

Clark, S.D. 1974. "Canada and Her Great Neighbour", *Canadian Review of Sociology and Anthropology, Special Issue: Aspects of Canadian
Society*. Original 1964.

Clement, Wallace. 1974. "The Changing Structure
of the Canadian Economy", *Canadian Review
of Sociology and Anthropology, Special Issue:
Aspects of Canadian Society.*

——— 1975. *The Canadian Corporate Elite: An
Analysis of Economic Power*. McClelland and
Stewart: Toronto.

Clement, Wallace and Dennis Olsen. 1974. "Official Ideology and Ethnic Power", presented at
the American Sociological meetings, Montreal
(August).

Dahrendorf, Ralf. 1967. *Society and Democracy

in Germany*. Doubleday & Co.: Garden City,
N.Y.

Davis, Arthur K. 1970. "Some Failings of Anglophone Academic Sociology in Canada: The Need
for a Dialectical and Historical Perspective" in
Loubser (ed.).

——— 1971. "Canadian Society and History as
Hinterland Versus Metropolis" in R.J. Ossen-
berg (ed.), *Canadian Society: Pluralism,
Change and Conflict*. Prentice-Hall:
Scarborough.

Dofny, Jacques and Marcel Rioux. 1964. "Social
Class in French Canada" in Rioux & Martin
(eds.).

Dumont, Fernand. 1964. "The Systematic Study of
the French-Canadian Total Society" in Rioux &
Martin (eds.).

Etzioni, Amatai. 1968. *The Active Society*. Free Press:
N.Y.

Encel, Sol. *Equality and Authority in Australia*.

Frank, Andre G. 1969. "The Development of
Underdevelopment" in his *Latin America:
Underdevelopment or Revolution*. Modern
Reader: N.Y.

Galtung, Johan. 1971. "Structural Theory of Imperialism", *Journal of Peace Research, 2*.

Gerth, H. and C.W. Mills, editors. 1946. *From Max
Weber*. Oxford: N.Y.

Giddens, Anthony. 1973. *The Class Structure of

the Advanced Societies. Hutchinson University Library: London.

Grant, George. 1965. *Lament for a Nation.* Toronto: Carleton Library, McClelland & Stewart.

Guindon, Hubert. 1964. "The Social Evolution of Quebec Reconsidered" in Rioux and Martin (eds.).

―――― 1968. "Two Cultures: An essay on nationalism, class and ethnic tension," in R.H. Leach (ed.), *Contemporary Canada.* University of Toronto Press.

Horowitz, Gad. 1971. "Conservativism, Liberalism and Socialism in Canada," in W.E. Mann (ed.), *Canada: A Sociological Profile.* Copp Clark: Toronto.

Hughes, David R. and Evelyn Kallen. 1974. *The Anatomy of Racism: Canadian Dimensions.* Harvest House: Montreal.

Johnson, Leo. 1972. "The development of class in Canada in the twentieth century," in G. Teeple (ed.), *Capitalism and the National Question in Canada.* University of Toronto Press: Toronto.

Jordan, Z.A. 1971. Karl Marx: *Economy, Class and Social Revolution.* Michael Joseph: London.

Keyfitz, Nathan. 1974. "Sociology and Canadian Society," in Guinsburg & Reuber (eds.), *Perspectives on the Social Sciences in Canada,* University of Toronto Press: Toronto.

Klausner, S.Z. 1967. *Total Societies.* Doubleday Anchor Books: N.Y.

Lijphart, Arend. 1974. "Consociational Democracy," in McRae (ed.). *Consociational Democracy.* McClelland and Stewart: Toronto.

Lipset, S.M. 1964. "Canada and the United States— A Comparative View", *Canadian Review of Sociology and Anthropology,* Vol. 1, No. 6; reprinted in W.E. Mann (ed.), *Canada: A Sociological Profile.* Copp Clark: Toronto, 1971.

―――― 1971. 'Revolution and Counter Revolution," in W.E. Mann (ed.), *Canada: A Sociological Profile.* Copp Clark: Toronto.

Loubser, Jan J. (ed.) 1970. *The Future of Sociology in Canada.* Canadian Sociology and Anthropology Association: Montreal.

Lucas, Rex A. 1971. *Minetown, Milltown, Railtown.* University of Toronto Press.

Manzer, Ronald. 1974. *Canada: A Socio-Political Report.* McGraw-Hill Ryerson: Toronto.

Marchak, M. Patricia. 1975. *Ideological Perspectives on Canada.* McGraw-Hill Ryerson: Toronto.

McRae, Kenneth, editor. 1974. *Consociational Democracy.* McClelland and Stewart: Toronto.

Mills, C. Wright. 1959. *The Sociological Imagination.* Oxford: N.Y.

Milner, S. and H. Milner. 1973. *The Decolonization of Quebec.* McClelland and Stewart: Toronto.

Moore, Barrington, Jr. 1966. *The Social Origins of Dictatorship and Democracy.* Beacon Press: N.Y.

Naegele, Kaspar. 1968. "Modern National Societies" in B.R. Blishen, et al (eds.), *Canadian Society.* Macmillan: Toronto.

Nock, David. 1974. "History and Evolution of French Canadian Sociology", *Insurgent Sociologist,* Vol. IV, No. iv (Summer).

Porter, John. 1965. *The Vertical Mosaic.* University of Toronto Press.

―――― 1967. "The Human Condition" in J.M.S. Careless & R.C. Brown (eds.), *The Canadians, 1867–1967.* Toronto.

―――― 1970a. "Some Observations on Comparative Studies," in D.P. Forcese & S. Richer (eds.), *Stages of Social Research.* Prentice-Hall: Englewood Cliffs.

―――― 1970b. "A Research Biography of the Vertical Mosaic," in J.S. Coleman, et al, *Macrosociology: Research and Theory.* Allyn and Bacon: Boston.

―――― 1971. "Canadian Character in the Twentieth Century," in W.B. Mann (ed.), *Canada: A Sociological Profile.* Copp Clark: Toronto, original 1967.

―――― 1974. "Canada: Dilemmas and Contradictions in a Multi-ethnic Society" in C. Beattie and S. Chrysdale (eds.), *Sociology Canada.* Toronto.

Presthus, Robert. 1973. *Elite Accommodation in Canadian Politics.* Macmillan: Toronto.

Rioux, Marcel and Yves Martin (eds.) 1964.

French-Canadian Society. McClelland and Stewart: Toronto.

Rocher, Guy. 1964. "Research on Occupations and Social Stratification" in Rioux and Martin (eds.).

———— 1972. *A General Introduction to Sociology: A Theoretical Perspective* (translated by Peta Sheriff). Macmillan: Toronto.

———— 1974. "The Future of Sociology in Canada" in *Sociology Canada: Readings*, C. Beattie and S. Chrysdale (eds.). Butterworths: Toronto.

Rokkan, Stein. 1970. *Citizens, Elections, Parties: Approaches to the Comparative Study of Development*. David McKay: N.Y.

Ryerson, Stanley. 1972. "Quebec: concepts of class and nation" in G. Teeple (ed.), *Capitalism and the National Question in Canada*. University of Toronto Press.

Szczepański, Jan. 1970. *Polish Society*. Random House: N.Y.

Schwartz, Mildred A. 1967. *Public Opinion and Canadian Identity*. University of California.

Sunkel, Osvaldo. 1973. "Transnational Capitalism and National Disintegration in Latin America", *Social and Economic Studies*, Vol. 22, No. 1.

Vallee, Frank. 1971. "The Emerging Northern Mosaic" in R.J. Ossenberg (ed.), *Canadian Society: Pluralism, Change and Conflict*, Prentice-Hall: Scarborough.

Vallee, Frank and Don Whyte. 1968. "Canadian Society: Trends in Perspective," in B. Blishen, et al (eds.), *Canadian Society*. Macmillan: Toronto.

Watkins, Mel. 1970. "The Branch Plant Condition," in A.K. Davis (ed.), *Canadian Confrontations: Hinterland vs. Metropolis*, Proceedings of the 11th Annual Western Association of Sociology and Anthropology, Banff, Alberta (December 1969).

Whyte, Don. 1973. "Canadian Identity and the Colonial Tradition", mimeo, Carleton University: Ottawa.

Zeitlin, Irving. 1973. *Rethinking Sociology*. Prentice-Hall: Englewood Cliffs, N.J.

Culture

Introduction

"Culture," one of the main concepts in social science, plays a major role in the study of sociology. In anthropology, a sister discipline, the concept of "culture" is as central as "social structure" is to the study of sociology. As well, the concept of "culture" has been used increasingly in political science (where it comes to be known as "political culture") and management science (where it comes to be known as "organizational culture").

"Culture" encompasses all the shared ways of thinking, feeling, and behaving that characterize a group or society and distinguish it from another. Culture is uniquely human; learned, not genetically programmed; and transmitted by "socialization," about which more will be said in the next Section. The concept is important to sociology because it helps us think about the discipline's classic questions.

In the last section, we noted that one classic concern of sociology was answering the question "Are the most important determinants of social behaviour cultural or economic?" This question implies that economic relations lie outside the realm of culture, and we must choose between cultural and economic explanations of social behaviour. Yet, Max Weber's analysis of the rise of capitalism and its relation to the Protestant Reformation (discussed by Professor Brym in Section One) showed that culture and economy are not so neatly separated. People have been trained to think and do what is economically necessary. Some thinkers argue culture and economy fit together because the ruling economic class promotes certain ways of thinking and behaving: typically ways that serve the interests of that class. Sociologists call culture produced in this way an "ideology." Others argue that shared ways of thinking and acting arise out of daily experiences, and may not have been formed and promoted by a self-interested ruling class. These cultural patterns persist because they help people make sense of their everyday experience, they argue. Sociologists following Karl Mannheim have adopted this second point of view, and also refer to their object of study as "ideology."

But culture is not only the *effect* of economic domination on everyday relations of production. Culture also *shapes* economic relations. This theme finds its strongest expression in the writings of Max Weber and his followers who have studied the process called "modernization." What goes on in people's minds—their thoughts about the meaning of life, the purpose of money-making, the predictability of nature and our ability to harness it—all affect their willingness to play economic roles or change them. As Professor Brym shows in Section One, even Karl Marx, the strongest believer that economic forces explain social life, saw the importance of people's thinking and feeling. Changing these was necessary if significant political and eocnomical change was to occur through revolution. Undermining the "legitimacy" granted to an economic and political order is basic to getting people ready for change, as Weber argued so persuasively.

"Culture" is fundamental to the other two classic concerns noted in the first Section. Sociologists have been traditionally interested in the relationship between the individual and society. Because a society is a collection of individuals who share common ways of thinking and behaving, and produce social structures to attain their cultural goals, society and culture *must* go together. As well, cohesion around certain shared values and practices is, for sociologists following Emile Durkheim, absolutely fundamental to individual well-being. Thus, a cohesive, consistent cultural system, shared by most members of the community, is not only the condition for societal existence, but also for healthy individual existence. The acculturated human being is a miniature version of the society and culture of which he/she is a member. Of course, this "oversocialized" conception of human life is oversimplified, as many sociologists have said. But, truly, just as people make the culture they share, so does the culture make them.

We have already hinted at the relevance of "culture" to answering the third of sociology's classic questions, namely: "What are the bases of social inequality?" At a minimum, people's shared ways of thinking and acting maintain a given system of inequality once it is in place. This is evident not only in the mass acceptance of ideologies about economic inequality, discussed in the article by Patricia Marchak, but also in the harder-to-explain but equally significant practices of gender inequality, racial discrimination and status difference. Not obviously related to class inequality, these practices are hard to eliminate even in communist societies where, presumably, class inequality no longer exists.

Cultures, then, include not only a generalized attitude towards inequality in social affairs, but often detailed notions about the bases and justifications for inequality, and classifications of who (i.e., what types of people and what types of social roles) will be considered most worthy. Sociologists often debate about the ways such classifications come into being. On the one hand, functionalists argue that the classifications reflect dominant concerns or values of a society and the relative scarcity of certain valuable skills. On the other hand, Marxists argue that differential evaluations come *after* the fact of social inequality. The most vulnerable and powerless people are most likely to be labelled "worthless" and deprived of rewards, because they cannot prevent such labelling.

Both arguments have merit and both must be considered in studying particular cases of inequality. What is important here is, simply, to note the significance of "culture" in framing the terms of the debate.

The readings in this Section take us through these debates. We begin with Guy Rocher's general definition of culture, which permits many approaches to explanation. The article by Patricia Marchak exposes us to one explanatory approach; culture is largely redefined as "ideology" in order to relate the shared ways of thinking, feeling and behaving to relations of power in the society. But S.M. Lipset's approach is a different kettle of fish.

Professor Lipset sets out to explain why (and how) Canadians are different from Americans: how and why they do *not* share common ways of thinking, feeling, and behaving in many important ways. This question is important for a number of reasons. Almost every Canadian has remarked at some time on differences between the United State and Canada, and between Americans and Canadians. Lipset tries to think about this commonly asked question systematically. Second, answering this question is central to understanding the uniqueness of Canadian society. Third, any answer implies an answer to the other old question of whether Canada and the United States can or should be a single country. The answer is no clearer today, when politicians and citizens are considering the possible sociocultural implications of free trade with the United States, than when Goldwin Smith addressed the issue of union one hundred years ago or William Lyon MacKenzie looked longingly at American democracy (and greater independence from British influence) fifty years earlier. Is Canada *really* different from the USA? Can it continue to be different? Should it be different? These are questions we cannot answer without thinking seriously about cultural differences between Canada and the United States and Lipset's reasons for expecting the differences to continue.

One problem to avoid is a tendency to assume more uniform thinking, feeling and behaving than perhaps really exists. Experience tells us that Canadians vary quite a lot. Sociologists deal with this variation by studying and writing about "subcultures." Subcultures exist within cultures; they are created within subgroups of the society whose members have certain common experiences or concerns that differentiate them from the rest. These special concerns are important enough to serve as the foundations for somewhat distinct life patterns. We are right, therefore, to speak of and study ethnic subcultures, deviant or criminal subcultures, and even regional subcultures.

Within Canadian society, regional subcultures are particularly important.. Ways of thinking and behaving differ considerably between English-speaking Canadians and French-speaking Canadians, and within English Canada, between people in Ontario, the Maritimes, and the West. Subcultural differences are shaped by differences in everyday experience, central values, and relations of power. Thus, the greater the inequality between groups, the greater the subcultural difference we can expect to find, for example. Subcultures often express social uniqueness in the face of outside domination, as we see in the article about Western separatism by Harry Hiller. Here, in everyday cultural artifacts such as sweatshirt slogans and bumper stickers, regional sentiments are asserted against Central Canadian domination.

Finally, cultures and subcultures are also "perceptual filters" through which people experience the world, often unconsciously. People have long known that many important things are a matter of taste—one man's food is another man's poison, and so on. But often matters of taste and preference are socially structured and learned. How and why some ethnic groups learn to like crowding and others learn to hate it; and how and why some groups learn to deal with undesired crowding and others do not: these are questions addressed in the article by Ron Gillis, Madeline Richard, and John Hagan. Ideas along these lines will be further explored in the next section on Socialization.

6 What Is Culture?

Guy Rocher

GUY ROCHER, Professor titulaire at the Centre for Research on Public Law and the Faculty of Law, University of Montreal, specializes in the study of culture, law and power. His books include *Introduction à la sociologie générale*, three volumes (1968–1969); *Ecole et société au Québec* with Pierre Bélanger (1971, 1975); *Talcott Parsons et la sociologie americaine* (1972); *Le Québec en mutation* (1973); and *Ecole de demain* (1976). In addition Professor Rocher has written a large number of scholarly articles and monographs. He has served as chairman of the Sociology Department and Vice-Dean of the Faculty of Social Sciences at the University of Montreal; Vice-President of the Canada Council (1969–74); and Deputy Minister for Social Development in the Government of Quebec (1981–1983). In recognition of his achievements, he has been made a Companion of the Order of Canada, a Foreign Honorary Member of the American Academy of Arts and Sciences, and a Fellow of the Royal Society of Canada.

CULTURE

Culture, a term used by social scientists, is also widely used in popular speech. It apparently arose first in the Old French of the Middle Ages to indicate a religious cult, or religious worship or ceremony. The verb *culturer* meant "working the soil." In the 17th century, people referred to the "wheat culture," "legume culture," and, by analogy, to the "culture of letters" and "culture of sciences." In the 18th century the word was used alone to mean "formation of the spirit." Eighteenth-century German philosophers and historians borrowed the term from the French, but *Kultur*, as it was written, had for the Germans both social and historical dimensions. Some writers used it to mean progress, the improvement of the human spirit, a step towards the perfection of humanity. Others used it to mean "civilization," that is, the refinement of mores, customs and knowledge. For German (and some French) authors of the day, the terms "culture" and "civilization" referred to the progress of Reason, that is, of science, knowledge and a new moral conscience liberated from religions and mythologies.

It was in English, however, that the term "culture" took on the modern meaning (culture signifying "husbandry" appeared in English as early as 1420). Anthropologists used the term to denote the mores, customs and beliefs of the "primitive" people they were studying. By the early 20th century, culture had become a central concept of the social sciences; it is a term now used in all the social sciences and in all languages. The technical use of the term in anthropology was introduced by the English anthropologist E.B. Tylor (1871): "Culture or civilization, taken in its wide enthnographic sense, is that complex whole which includes knowledge, belief, art, law, morals, custom and any other capabilities and habits acquired by man as a member of society."

In *Culture: A Critical Review of Concepts and Definitions* (1952) A.L. Kroeber and C. Kluckhohn analysed 160 English definitions of culture used by anthropologists, sociologists, psychologists, psychiatrists and others, and classified them according to their principal emphasis. Drawing on all these definitions and on others more recent, culture may be defined as an ensemble, formalized in varying degrees, of ways of thinking, feeling and behaving which once learned give people a particular and distinct collectivity.

CANADIAN CULTURE

Given the diversity of Canadian society it is easier to describe Canadian culture as a group of cultures interrelated with and juxtaposed to the 2 dominant cultural groups.

It is not surprising, given its size, that Canada should have several regional subcultures. No exhaustive study has yet been made of these subcultures, yet it is possible to assert that West Coast Canadians have a different way of thinking and a different spirit from central or East Coast Canadians. Canadians who live on the Prairies are distinct from those in Ontario, as are Quebeckers or Newfoundlanders. Further divisions exist within the subcultures: northern Ontarians distinguish themselves from southern ones; Quebeckers in Abitibi, the Beauce or Lac St-Jean are different from those in Montréal or Québec City. Differences in spirit, ways of thinking and attitude exist between Edmonton and Calgary, Victoria and Vancouver, Montréal and Québec City.

But the expression "Canadian mosaic" refers to the ethnic and cultural diversity of the country. Four constituent cultural groupings are usually distinguished in Canada. The first two are the cultures of the "founding peoples," the Anglo-Saxon culture and French culture. The former subdivides into cultures of different origin—English, Scots, Irish, Welsh. French culture is more homogeneous. Though French Canadians originally emigrated from different provinces of France, under the French regime they quickly merged into one "Canadian" culture although those French Canadians living in Ontario or Manitoba are quite different from those in Québec.

With the exception of the native peoples, the remaining non-British and non-French cultural groups comprise all the other ethnic groups that have immigrated to Canada since the beginning of the 19th century. The vitality of these cultural communities has grown in recent years. This composite of cultural groups includes cultures from Europe, the Near East, Asia, Central and South America, and Africa. The members of these communities usually adopt English as their working language and finally as their mother tongue, but many still speak their former national language and teach it to their children and many devotedly maintain the customs and traditions of the old country. Canadian television and (especially) radio offer programs in a wide variety of languages.

The fourth Canadian cultural group consists of the native peoples. This group includes many subdivisions. When the first Europeans arrived in North America at least six cultural groups apparently inhabited what is now Canada. Each of these cultural and linguistic groups contained a certain number of tribes. These differences still exist to some extent; the greatest distinguishing factor among native peoples now is the degree to which they maintain ancestral ways or have integrated into the structures and adopted the culture of industrial society. The Métis and mixed blood are the most highly integrated into urban and industrial life, but they have always fought and still fight for the preservation and recognition of their own cultural identity and for political rights.

CULTURAL CONFLICTS

Canada has experienced many cultural conflicts. In the 17th century, the French vainly tried to convert the Indians to a non-nomadic, Christian and French way of life. After the British Conquest (1759–60) of New France, the conflict between the English and French moved from the military to the political battlefield. Many British colonists, merchants and administrators thought it simpler to anglicize the 70 000 French colonists and to impose on them British political, legal and religious institutions rather than to live peacefully with them. Nevertheless, the two groups have had to accept coexistence. The coexistence has, however, suffered many stumbling blocks; eg, the battles are still being fought for the recognition of French outside Québec and of English inside Québec.

In the 20th century, and particularly since WWII, the massive arrival of new cultural minorities has posed other problems. Sociologists have identified the various forms that characterize the relations of the English and French to cultural minorities as assimilation, integration and accommodation. In Canada there has been a certain amount of assimilation of native people and of French Canadians (outside Québec) into the dominant anglophone culture. Other cultural communities have been both assimilated and integrated. On their arrival in Québec, members of these communities choose for themselves or their children one of Canada's two official languages. Simultaneously, many have fought to have the culture of their countries of origin recognized as constituent elements of the Canadian mosaic.

Finally, the reality of both conflict and complementarity has led each cultural group within the Canadian ensemble to seek out some form of accommodation.

7 Ideology and Social Organization

M. Patricia Marchak

M. PATRICIA MARCHAK, Professor of Sociology at the University of British Columbia, Vancouver, specializes in the study of ideology and political economy. Her books and articles include *Ideological Perspectives on Canada* (1975, 1981); *In Whose Interests: An Essay on Multinational Corporations in a Canadian Context* (1979); *Green Gold: The Forest Industry in British Columbia* (1983); *Uncommon Property: The Fishing and Fish Processing Industries in British Columbia*, co-edited with Neil Guppy and John McMullan (1987); and "Canadian Political Economy" (1985). As well as writing numerous scholarly papers and giving many presentations, Professor Marchak has served as President of the Canadian Sociology and Anthropology Association, as Book Review Editor for the *Canadian Review of Sociology and Anthropology*, and on the editorial boards of *Studies in Political Economy* and *Current Sociology*.

IDEOLOGIES

Dominant and counter-ideologies grow out of the same social organization. They take the same economic arrangement, the same territorial boundaries, the same population as their units of analysis. But they posit different relationships between these units and different organizations within them. Although the two major ideologies of our time—which we will label liberalism and socialism—claim to explain society in historical and comparative perspective, they both originate in the period of the European Industrial Revolution, and both are unmistakably locked into industrial society as it emerged in Europe at that time.

Because they grow out of the same organization, they have much in common. They are the two sides of a single coin: one describing how the entire structure looks to one who accepts it and expects it to survive; the other, how it looks to one who rejects it and anticipates its demise. . . .

Ideologies are explanations for the social organization, but they are, as well, evaluations of it. These evaluations tend to be circular: the social organization gives rise to certain beliefs about what is right, appropriate, and desirable, that is, to certain values. These values are then assumed, and the society judges itself by those values. The liberal democracy gave rise to positive evluations of equality, individualism, material prosperity, and personal freedom. The society is then judged within that framework: does it allow for the realization of these values? The dominant ideology rests on an affirmative answer: yes, this society provides the necessary conditions for equality, material prosperity, and personal freedom. Where there are deficiencies, these are often not recognized. Where the deficiencies are recognized, they are explained not as symptoms of a system that fails but as aberrations or temporary problems in a system that succeeds.

Widespread acceptance of an ideology creates an incapacity for judgement of its truth. There is comfort in believing what so many others appear to believe, in accepting conventional wisdom. There is fear in doing otherwise. Sometimes there are, as well, serious social consequences. To many minds, the person who admits to a deviant perspective is out of bounds, somehow dirty and unacceptable.

Counter ideologies involve a good deal of imagination. They provide a critique of the present society and a creative vision of an alternative. Both socialism and the "new right" provide these critiques and creative visions; and whether we agree with them or despise them, we are indebted to their proponents for enabling us to imagine other ways of doing things.

Counter ideologies generally begin with a critical perspective which arises from recognition of inconsistencies between what the dominant ideology portrays as truth and what the senses suggest is reality. They begin, then, as reform movements and their members are social critics. Equality, material prosperity, and personal freedom may be assumed as "right" values, but the society is judged as deficient in providing for their realization. The negative judgement leads to an analysis of social organization which diverges from that propagated by those who hold the dominant ideology and believe it to meet its own objectives. Gradually the analysis turns into a fully developed counter ideology, an entirely different way of viewing the society.

Some people think that ideology is something that happens to others, and generally to somewhat deranged others. That is not the sense in which the term is used here. We are all immersed in ideological understandings of our world.

We define ideology as: shared ideas, perceptions, values, and beliefs through which members of a society interpret history and contemporary social events and which shape their expectations and wishes for the future.

A dominant ideology is defined as that particular set of ideas, perceptions, values, and beliefs which is most widely shared and has the greatest impact on social action at any particular time in any particular society.

A counter ideology is defined as a set of

ideas, etc., which is held by a substantial minority and which has noticeable impact on social action. There may be many or few counter ideologies in any society at any historical period.

There is another definition of ideology: the ideas and values of the ruling class, disseminated through agencies controlled by that class in ways that obfuscate class realities for subservient classes. We are not using this definition here.

Ideology and theory are different entities, though they grow out of the same womb. Theory consists of explicit assumptions, a reasoning by which the assumptions are demonstrated to be linked to conclusions on the one hand, and such material evidence as can be gathered on the other. It is, by definition, open to challenge through the presentation of more complete or contesting evidence, or by a refutation of the logic that links assumptions to conclusions. It is not a faith. It is not unexamined.

In some ways, theories are rivals and enemies of ideologies because they tend to dissect them. Someone begins by saying, "Hmm, I believe this and that, I think I'll write it all down in some systematic way so that others will think as I do." Then, in the writing of it, the author begins to see some inconsistencies, some flaws in logic, some mismatch between theory and evidence. And the reader, perusing the manuscript, says "but this isn't good enough." Theories evolve over time, moving further and further away from their ideological base, becoming more sophisticated, more logical, more consistent—but often moving so far from their beginnings that they leave the majority of believers far behind.

Ideologies normally attract some people who want to make them public and systematic. In addition to theorists, there are scribes and prophets who define ideologies, trying to demonstrate how their particular beliefs are unique and true. For this reason, we can examine such ideologies through the writings of the scribes and the speeches of the prophets. And, as we begin to see which values they emphasize, which utopian visions they advance, we can label the ideologies and identify them relative to one another with reference to specific values. But for the same reason that we need to distinguish between theory and ideology, we need to recognize the possible differences between what the scribes and prophets say and what a majority of believers accept.

———————

Ideologies may be phrased in terms we would recognize as political, that is, they are about the political world and how the public arena should be governed. Other ideologies may also have political implications but may be phrased as religious belief systems. Although the language of discourse may seem very different, there are usually close ties between what people believe about the meaning of human existence or the properties of nature and gods, and what they believe about political governance in the temporal world.

We are concerned here with the major ideologies of our society, the dominant and the counter ideologies which motivate large numbers of people. And we are concerned primarily, though not exclusively, with how these ideologies link up with economic and political events. There are, in addition to these central ideologies, other versions of the world espoused by smaller numbers of people. Some of these other versions take political forms, some take religious forms.

Political ideologies ultimately boil down to the relative emphasis placed on individualism versus collectivism, and on egalitarianism versus elitism. It is in these terms that we can identify the differences between one ideology and another. We have political labels for various positions in our own society, along two continuums: the first, from extreme individualists (society has absolutely no claims on the individual, and there should be no rules, government, or constraints on individual actions) to extreme collectivists (society always has precedence over individuals, and the right to demand conformance with rules for the public good); and the second, from extreme elitism (there should be rulers and the rulers should have complete power) to extreme egalitarianism (all people should be absolutely equal in condition, not just opportunities). The differences between these labelled positions can be noted by referring to the theories, scribes and prophets, but as observed above, we must be wary of assuming that all adherents to labelled positions are consistent in their beliefs.

INDIVIDUALIST AND MARKET-BASED IDEOLOGIES

Anarchism, libertarianism, and to a lesser degree, liberalism, treat society as a collection of individuals. Society does not exist in and of itself, it is not an organic whole. Individuals each strive to manufacture the necessary conditions for life, and the market mechanism has emerged as a means of coordinating their separate strivings without applying force. The preservation of individual liberty and of the "free market" become the major concerns of advocates of these positions.

Anarchism and Libertarianism

The individualist position is taken to the extreme in anarchist and libertarian ideologies; all other values become subordinate. Anarchists would do away with all government and social restrictions on personal liberty; libertarians (though with some differences between various groups) generally accept the necessity of government, but would restrict its functions to the defence of persons and property. Anything which prevents individuals from fully exercising their initiative, entrepreneurial skills, and talents is harshly judged: thus democracy and the welfare state are deemed to be impediments to individual growth. Inequality is viewed as inevitable because people are genetically unequal, and as necessary because the most talented provide the leadership which permits others to survive. Libertarians believe that "pure" capitalism is an ideal social and economic system because it includes a genuinely free market for absolutely all goods and services.

Liberalism .

Liberalism has a somewhat different meaning in Canada than in the United States. In Canada, it is an approach which emphasizes the individual but combines that emphasis with concern for the preservation of law, order, and public well-being in the society, and includes some concern for equality between citizens. In the United States, its connotation is more strongly connected to social and collective values, closer to what Canadians would regard as "social democratic." It differs from the Canadian social democratic view in that while both take equality to be a positive value, the liberal view is that equality of opportunity is sufficient, and that such equality is largely achieved within the present social system. Social democrats argue in favour of greater equality of condition and perceive great inequalities of both opportunity and condition in the present social system.

Like libertarians, liberals believe in the virtues of a free enterprise market, in which all sellers and buyers compete on equal terms for the attention of consumers. Unlike libertarians, liberals temper this belief by acknowledgment of some services and goods which "ought" to be in the public realm. The free enterprise market is rarely called "capitalism" in liberal ideology; the phrase "free enterprise" becomes the euphemism for capitalism. Consonant with the belief that society is made up of individuals, liberals deny the existence of classes in capitalist society. A great deal of emphasis is placed on the education system because liberals believe that individuals have equal opportunity in that sphere, each achieving there what their innate talents and hard work permit and thus moving upward or downward in the social system according to ability.

The role of government is to regulate the market place and ensure that the rules are fair and equitable; government is not itself an economic actor in a truly "free" enterprise system. Further, since there are no classes, government cannot be seen as the agent of any particular class; and since there is no ruling class, it cannot be seen as acting on behalf of that class.

Liberalism has been the dominant ideological perspective adopted by Canadians throughout the past 40 years. One political party is called "Liberal" but when we speak of liberalism, we do not refer exclusively to this party. In fact, throughout this period, the two major alternative parties, the Progressive Conservative and the New Democratic Parties, have shared much of the liberal version of Canadian society.

COLLECTIVIST POSITIONS

Collectivist positions begin with the argument that the society is an organic whole. Society exists independent of the individuals who happen to live in it at any time. But there is enormous difference in the conclusions and policy positions taken by collectivists of the "left" and of the "right." The basic difference occurs between those who believe that society ought to be more egalitarian (social democratic, socialist, communist) and those who believe it should be more hierarchically ordered (conservative, corporatist, and fascist).

Social Democratic

Social democrats accept the basic values of liberalism but place more emphasis on equality. As well, they recognize the existence of classes, of class barriers, and of governments acting in the interests of a dominant or ruling class. They thus share some of the understandings of socialists. They are committed to the gradual and democratic evolution of a socialist society, which they understand to be a more egalitarian organization within which workers have decision-making control over production, and private ownership rights over industrial units and natural resources are abolished. This is the position of various democratic socialist parties throughout the world, and of the CCF and NDP parties.

Socialist

Socialists perceive capitalism as a system where a ruling class extracts wealth from a subordinate class (or classes), sells products made by labour, and uses the profits to invest in more properties and new technologies which displace or further enslave labour. Classes exist, inequalities are essential to the system, and individual freedom is highly circumscribed by the fundamental requirement that labour must produce goods and services for capital. For the socialist these conditions are unacceptable.

Socialism involves a version of the future which differs markedly from that liberalism. For liberals, the future is a continuum of the past and present. It is a highly optimistic ideology, assuming eternal progress and gradual elimination of imperfections in the social system. But socialism, identifying capitalism as an oppressive and exploitative system, involves the belief that only through the destruction of capitalism can a more egalitarian and humane system emerge. Capitalism is expected to self-destruct, because its internal contradicitons must eventually cause a fatal blockage in the capacities of capitalists to continue accumulating new profits (this is called "a crisis of accumulation" in the socialist literature).

For the liberal, capitalism is necessary reality and critiques of it are ideology. For the socialist, the liberal version of capitalism is ideology. It is understood by socialists as an essential feature of the capitalist system, because it induces workers to consent to their own exploitation. They are persuaded, rather than forced (though force may on occasion also be necessary), to believe that the system is fair even if it leads to extremely unequal distributions of material wealth and economic power. Part of the key to this persuasion is, in the opinion of socialists, the nature of democratic governments. These are either so constrained by the economic decisions of private capital or so instrumentally attached to private capital (there are different theories on this) that they can do little more than facilitate private accumulation. They mediate class conflict by developing rules for employment, hours, welfare and the like, because the system could not continue with persistent or violent class conflict, but the appearance is of governments acting in the general public interest. As well, since governments are formally elected by the population at large, there is a widespread belief in their neutrality and representative character. The ideology of democracy, then, and the mechanics of democratic elections are important features of capitalism because they "legitimate" the economic system and provide the pretence of impartiality.

Conservatism

Conservatism—like liberalism not to be interpreted as necessarily coincident with a particular political party—shares with socialism a belief that there are classes, that capitalism necessarily involves inequality, and that the marketplace should not be the locus of most important social decisions. But unlike socialism, conservatism gives a high positive value to class inequalities: they are necessary because society requires leadership, and well established leaders look after less well established workers. Conservatism thus values a "natural" hierarchy, paternalistic relations between capital and labour. For the conservative, government properly has the right to establish norms for the conduct of social life, though it should have a restrained role in the economy.

The chief difference between conservatism and liberalism is in their respective views of society: conservatives viewing it as an organic whole within which individuals have assigned places; liberals as a collection of individuals each striving for personal goals. Thus true conservatives should be concerned with the collective moral fabric as well as the permanence of a dominant class. Logically, liberals would be less concerned with social and moral issues except where society infringes on individual rights.

Corporatism

Corporatism shares with conservatism the belief in a natural hierarchy of human beings, the importance of planning the economy, and the positive evaluation of social classes. It goes beyond conservatism in arguing that economic units—corporations—should make the decisions about the conduct of economic life. Democratic procedures typical of liberal societies are viewed as unacceptable, because they allow uninformed and unpropertied individuals and groups to choose leaders and policies and thus inhibit social progress.

This position is associated with Italy under Mussolini, and has not had much of a history in Canada though some Canadians flirted with it during the 1930s. At the present time, some Canadians are again flirting with it, and there are curious alliances between some of its advocates and libertarians.

Fascism

Fascism is an extreme form of corporatism, going beyond it in accepting the necessity for force in controlling dissidents. We usually associate it with Nazi Germany in the 1930s and 1940s, but there was a fascist party in Canada during the 1930s, and a very small group of followers have persisted throughout this century.

DOMINANT IDEOLOGY

If we identify the dominant ideology as the values and beliefs held in common by a majority, we would include the liberal, social democratic, and conservative positions as falling within its compass. Although they differ in the degree to which they emphasize individualism and egalitarianism, they share a number of assumptions. To begin with, proponents of these positions assume the legitimacy of private property rights, but at the same time recognize legitimate constraints on these. They accept (with varying degrees of approval) the economic drive for profits, but again, place limits on its capacity to drive the entire social system. They accept differential rewards for work associated with numerous social factors (education, skills, talent, etc.), but reject differences associated with gender, ethnicity, religion, or other "noneconomic" attributes of individuals. Although both the conservative and social democratic positions include acknowledgement of the reality of class divisions in capitalist society, and liberalism does not, all three tend to explain social events in terms of individuals or non-class groups (e.g., men and women, ethnic groups, particular interest groups) more than in terms of classes. All positions involve notions of social progress toward a "better" society to be achieved through gradual evolution.

Political parties espousing these points of view make many more distinctions between the positions. It is in their interests to do so, of course, since they have to make their party appear to be the unique champion of individual rights or equal opportunity or whatever.

All societies arrive, whether through conscious political activity or tacit agreements and traditional activities, at some position between individualism and collectivism, egalitarianism and elitism. There is another set of values which cross-cuts these, providing a third dimension to social organization. It is attitudes toward nature.

Societies dependent on hunting and gathering, and some societies dependent on cultivation of foods, have developed understandings of people as components of nature on the same level with other animate beings. Most such societies also hold the view that there are unseen spirits guiding and judging their activities. Within these perceptiions, animals and land are highly valued, and destruction of either is unacceptable behaviour. Thus the hunter must apologise to the beast he has killed, explaining his need for food and his sincere appreciation for the sacrifice made by the animal.

By contrast, the industrial society treats animals and humans as qualitatively different entities, with humans having the right to kill and conquer all other living things. Land is but a space where human activity takes place: it has no spiritual quality.

Within the past decade, new social movements have arisen within industrial societies opposed to the destruction of our environment. Some of these have taken on political aspects, organizing as political parties or as pressure groups. The anti-nuclear movement, the Green Party, and numerous groups devoted to the saving of particular territories are among these. To date, these groups have not developed consistent positiions on individualism-collectivism, egalitarianism-elitism. They are, in a sense, outside the mainstream of public discourse, and adherents to environmentalist ideologies could, conceivably, place themselves anywhere within the other political spectrums.

Similarly, religious movements sometimes exist outside the main discourse of industrial society. While the major religions in Canada—Christian Catholicism and Protestantism and Judaism—have generally adopted and supported the dominant ideology, smaller and often sectarian groups have challenged these views. Some support highly individual-istic positions (salvationist religions), others more collectivist positions (cultural renewal religions).

———

The industrial society is not a static social organization. The processes set in motion by the development of urban populations and competitive capitalism destroyed the feudal aristocracy and the peasantry. The created new forms of government. They destroyed societies and created new ones in far-off colonies. Change occurred at many levels simultaneously: at the level of the family unit, at the level of education. The liberal ideology explains these changes as cumulative growth. Society is always progressing, always adjusting to new conditions. Its growth is limitless, its perfection is a viable goal. The analogy is to a wheel turning over new territory and adding always to its conquest of distance.

Marx posited quite a different kind of change—cumulative, still, but fraught with internal contradictions. The growth in competitive capitalism would give rise to monopoly capitalism. The growth of wealth at the top would create the growth of poverty at the bottom. The more successful the capitalists were in developing technology and organizing the work-force for their own ends, the faster they brought about their own demise by an organized, efficient proletariat. The wheel in this analogy spins ever faster only to break down from over-use, and its riders are obliged to make a new wheel out of the parts. Marx envisioned the final stages in these words:

> One capitalist always kills many. Hand in hand with this centralization, or this expropriation of many capitalists by few, develop, on an ever-extending scale, the co-operative form of the labour process, the conscious technical application of science, the methodical cultivation of the soil, the transformation of the instruments of labour into instruments of labour only usable in common, the economizing of all means of production by their

use as the means of production of combined, socialized labour, the entanglement of all peoples in the net of the world-market, and with this, the international character of the capitalistic regime. Along with the constantly diminishing number of the magnates of capital, who usurp and monopolise all advantages of this process of transformation, grows the mass of misery, oppression, slavery, degradation, exploitation; but with this too grows the revolt of the working-class, a class always increasing in numbers, and disciplined, united, organized by the very mechanism of the process of capitalist production itself.[1]

Whether one takes the progressional view of history or the dialectic view, one is struck by the observation that cumulative growth in any respect of social organization eventually becomes destructive of that organization. Whether we eventually arrive in a different town by riding the wheel from one place to another, or whether the journey itself transforms the travellers, the fact is that the industrial society of the 1980s is not the industrial society of the 1920s or the 1880s. It is qualitatively a different society. The technology has changed dramatically. The social organization has changed. The population balance has changed. The relations between nation states have changed. What has noticeably failed to change is the ideology.

The ideologies at the popular level are very much the same as they were in these other times. Speeches to the Chamber of Commerce reflect the same abiding faith in progress, material prosperity, and general affluence; the same evaluation of private property, individualism, and achievement; the same belief in the existence of equality and opportunity. The slogans of the Left are remarkably similar to those uttered in the trade union struggles of the turn of the century. There is the same belief in massive exploitation by a ruling class, the same faith in the nobility of labour, the same conviction that pervasive equality is both yet to come and highly desirable.

In Canada, for example, feudalistic values remained into the early 20th century. While these were tinged by the values of liberalism as it was expressed in the United States and Britain, liberalism in its classic form did not emerge as a dominant ideology until very late in history by comparison with these other countries. Nearly a century after the American War of Independence had spawned the notion that individuals should pursue happiness and that this was a legitimate basis for social organization, as long again after the French Revolution had bannered the words "liberty, equality, fraternity," Canada continued to be ruled by a landed aristocracy which gained its wealth through the fur trade, export-import businesses, and banking. Its values were not those of industrial capitalists. It was not engaged in competitive enterprise, and was not generating new wealth out of the production of goods for a market. At the other end of the social scale, the larger part of the population was engaged in farming rather than manufacturing, and Canada was largely a rural country before World War I; indeed, it remained predominantly rural until the 1930s. The slow development of industry and of an industrial urban labour force retarded the development of liberalism as an ideology.

Conservatism, then, has not been absent in Canada, but in the past half-century it has not been a dominant ideology either.

Liberalism and socialism can interpret one kind of society, one form of industrial organization. This is the society in transition within the political framework of nation states. Neither is suited to providing a popular interpretation or appropriate set of values for maintenance of a multi-national or non-national capitalism in which wage work is not available to many people, surplus is not created out of labour, communications technology becomes more central to political control, and corporations are the chief social as well as economic organizations. Those of us who continue to live in the "old world," like the peasant of the feudal period or the colonials of an imperial empire, are unable to envision or make sense of the developments around us which lead in such a direction. We attempt to interpret them through the ideological perspectives of a society already in decline. Subtly, scarcely intruding on our consciousness, a new set of perceptions and beliefs and their appropriate justifying values will develop around the new technologies and within the corporate empires. Some of this will be transmitted to the generations now living out what may well be the last stage of national states and a social organization which divides the political, economic, and religious realms. These transmissions are phrased clumsily, to fit existing belief systems. Thus we have insights on what might be called "liberal corporatism" and we are puzzled by where the Soviet form of corporatism fits in to our theories of history. But if the past is an indication of the future, it will not be the case that liberalism as an ideology imperceptibly becomes corporatism; nor that socialism becomes totalitarianism; but rather that both are superseded by new ideologies emanating from a new society that has already grown within the old and destroyed its foundations.

Notes

[1] Karl Marx, *Capital* (1867), translated by Samuel Moore and Edward Aveling (New York: International Publishers, 1967), Vol. 1, pp. 762–763.

8 Value Traditions in Canadian and U.S. Cultures

Seymour Martin Lipset

SEYMOUR MARTIN LIPSET is the Caroline S.G. Munro Professor of Political Science and Sociology at Stanford University. His first teaching post was at the University of Toronto; and before going on to Stanford in 1975, he was the George Markham Professor of Government and Sociology at Harvard University. His work has included analyses of Canadian politics and society, particularly his study, *Agrarian Socialism: The Cooperative Commonwealth Federation in Saskatchewan* (1950). He has dealt extensively with comparative analyses of values and institutions in Canada and the United States, in his books *The First New Nation* (1963) and *Revolution and Counterrevolution* (1968). Two of his books have received awards: *Political Man* (1960) was given the MacIver Award and *The Politics of Unreason* (1970) was awarded the Gunnar Myrdal Prize. He has also been elected to membership in the National Academy of Sciences, the American Academy of Arts and Sciences, and the American Philosophical Society. He is currently working on a book about Canada and the United States.

THEORY AND APPROACH

There is much to be gained, both in empirical and analytic terms, from a systematic comparative study of Canada and the United States. They have many of the same ecological and demographic conditions, approximately the same level of economic development, and similar rates of upward and downward social mobility. And alongside the obvious distinctiveness of francophone Quebec, anglophone Canadians and Americans have much in common in cultural terms as well. Yet, although overall these two people probably resemble each other more than any other two nations on earth, there are consistent patterns of difference between them. To discover and analyze the factors which create and perpetuate such differences among nations is one of the more intriguing and difficult tasks in comparative study.[1]

In this essay I shall focus on value differences between the two countries, that is, differences in that set of attitudes which tends to characterize and permeate both the public and private ethos in each country. The central argument of the paper is that Canada has been a more elitist, law-abiding, statist, collectivity-oriented, and particularistic (group-oriented) society than the United States,[2] and that these fundamental distinctions stem in large part from the defining event which gave birth to both countries, the American Revolution. . . .

A brief characterization of the essential core, or organizing principles, of each society may help clarify the type of difference being referred to here. With respect to the United States, the emphases on individualism and achievement orientation by the American colonists were an important motivating force in the launching of the American Revolution, and were embodied in the Declaration of Independence. The manifestation of such attitudes in this historic event and their crystallization in an historic document provided a basis for the reinforcement and encouragement of these orientations throughout subsequent American history. Thus, the United States remained through the nineteenth and early twentieth centuries the extreme example of classically liberal or Lockean society which rejected the assumptions of the alliance of throne and altar, of ascriptive elitism, of mercantilism, of *noblesse oblige*, of communitarianism. Friedrich Engels, among other foreign visitors, noted that as compared to Europe, the United States was "purely bourgeois, so entirely without a feudal past" (Engels, 1942:467).

By contrast, both major Canadian linguistic groups sought to preserve their values and culture by reacting against liberal revolutions. English-speaking Canada exists because she opposed the Declaration of Independence; French-speaking Canada, largely under the leadership of Catholic clerics, also sought to isolate herself from the anti-clerical, democratic values of the French Revolution.[3] The leaders of both, after 1783 and 1789, consciously attempted to create a conservative, monarchical and ecclesiastical society in North America. Canadian elites of both linguistic groups saw the need to use the state to protect minority cultures, English Canadians against Yankees, French Canadians against anglophones. In the United States, on the other hand, the Atlantic Ocean provided an effective barrier against the major locus of perceived threat—Britain—which helped sustain the American ideological commitment to a weak state that did not have to maintain extensive military forces. As with the United States, however, these initial "organizing principles" in Canada served to structure subsequent developments north of the border. Although the content and extent of the differences between the two countries have changed over time, the contemporary variations still reflect the impact of the American Revolution. . . .

Given all of the differences distinguishing the Canadian historical experience from the American, it is not surprising that the peoples of the two countries formulated their self-conceptions in sharply different ways. As an ideological nation whose left and right *both* take sustenance from the American Creed, the United States is quite different from Canada, which lacks any founding myth, and whose intellectuals frequently question whether the country has a national identity. Sacvan Bercovitch has well described America's impact on a Canadian during the conflict-ridden sixties.

> My first encounter with American consensus was in the late sixties, when I crossed the border into the United States and found myself inside the myth of America . . . of a country that despite its arbitrary frontiers, despite its bewildering mix of race and creed, could believe in something called the True America, and could invest that patent fiction with all the moral and emotional appeal of a religious symbol. . . . Here was the Jewish anarchist Paul Goodman berating the Midwest for abandoning the promise; here the descendant of American slaves, Martin Luther King, denouncing injustice as a violation of the American Way; here, an endless debate about national destiny, . . . conservatives scavenging for un-Americans. New Left historians recalling the country to its sacred mission. . . .
>
> Nothing in my Canadian background had prepared me for that spectacle. . . . To a Canadian skeptic . . . , it made for a breathtaking scene: a pluralistic pragmatic people openly living in a dream, bound together by an ideological consensus unmatched by any other modern society.
>
> Let me repeat that mundane phrase: *ideological consensus*. . . . It was a hundred sects and factions, each apparently different from the others, yet all celebrating the same mission. . . . (Bercovitch, 1981:5–6, emphasis in original)

Although interpreted in a variety of ways by different groups and individuals, the ideology of the American Revolution provides for each of them a *raison d'être* for the Republic—it explains why the United States came into being, and what it means to be American.

The contrast with Canada is a sharp one. Canada could not offer her citizens "the prospect of a fresh start, . . . because (as the Canadian poet Douglas Le Pan put it) Canada is 'a country without a mythology'" (Bercovitch, 1981:24). To justify her separate existence, both linguistic cultures deprecated American values and institutions. As Frank Underhill once noted, Canadians are the world's oldest and most continuing anti-Americans (Underhill, 1960:222; for an elaboration, see Kendall, 1974:20–36). This stance was reflected in the writings of various Canadian observers in the 1920s, who "discerned and condemned an excessive egalitarian quality derived from notions of independence and democracy that had been set free during the [American] Revolution" (Weaver, 1973:80). Further evidence of such attitudes was gathered during the 1930s when the first efforts at a systematic sociological investigation of opinions in Canada concerning themselves and Americans were launched. One of the most important and prolific contributors to the research was S.D. Clark, then starting his scholarly career. He summarized the findings in the following terms:

> Canadian national life can almost be said to take its rise in the negative will to resist absorption in the American Republic. It is largely about the United States as an object that the consciousness of Canadian national unity has grown up. . . .
>
> Constantly in the course of this study we shall come across the idea that Canadian life is simpler, more honest, more moral and more religious than life in the United States, that it lies closer to the rural virtues and has achieved urbanization without giving the same scope to corrupting influences which has been afforded them in the United States. (Clark, 1939:243, 245)[4]

As Clark suggests in this passage, Canadians have tended to define themselves, not in terms of their own national history and tradition, but rather by reference to what they are *not*: American.

These differences between Canada and the United States can be seen, not just in history or in the findings of social science research, but also in the novels, poems, and stories created by writers in each country. In fact, of all artifacts, the art and literature of a nation should most reflect, as well as establish, her basic myths and values. And many analysts of North American literature have emphasized the continuing effects of the "mythic and psychic consequences of founding a country on revolution or out of the rejection of revolution" (Brown, n.d.:2). . . .

RELIGION

. . . The majority of Canadians adhere to the Roman Catholic or Anglican churches, both of which are hierarchically organized and continued until recently to have a strong relationship to the state. On the other hand, most Americans have belonged to the more individualist "nonconformist" Protestant sects. . . .

Religion in both countries has become more secularized in tandem with increased urbanization and education. For instance, Canadian Catholicism, particularly in Quebec, has modified the nature of its corporatist commitment from a link to agrarian and elitist anti-industrial values to a tie to leftist socialist beliefs. These variations, of course, parallel the changes in French Canadian nationalism. Public opinion research suggests that francophone Catholics have given up much of their commitment to Jansenist puritanical values, particularly as they affect sexual behavior and family size. This secularizing trend, although generally observable in both countries, has been less noticeable in the United States, particularly among evangelical Protestants. Americans, according to data from sample surveys presented below, are much more likely to attend church regularly than Canadians, and to adhere to fundamentalist and moralistic beliefs. And the continued strength of Protestant evangelical, sectarian and fundamentalist religion south of the border has meant that traditional values related to sex, family and morality in general are stronger there than in Canada.

A large body of public opinion data gathered in the two countries bear on these issues. Most findings are not precisely comparable because of variations in question wording. Fortunately, a research organization linked to the Catholic Church, CARA, has conducted a systematically comparative study of values in 22 countries, including Canada and the United States, where the data were collected by the Gallup Poll at the start of the eighties.[5] The two tables which follow present some of the relevant CARA findings.

There is a consistent pattern in these data: Americans far outnumber Canadians generally in giving expression to Protestant fundamentalist beliefs, with anglophones more likely to hold such views than francophones. And, congruent with the variation in religious practice and belief, Americans appear to be more puritanical than Canadians, with fran-

cophones the most tolerant with respect to sexual behavior....

LAW AND DEVIANCE

The difference in the role of law in the two countries is linked to the historical emphases on the rights and obligations of the community as compared to those of the individual. The explicit concern of Canada's founding fathers with "peace, order, and good government" implies control and protection. The American stress on "life, liberty, and the pursuit of happiness" suggests upholding the rights of the individual. This latter concern for rights, including those of people accused of crime and of political dissidents, is inherent in the "due process" model, involving various legal inhibitions on the power of the police and prosecutors, characteristic of the United States. The "crime control" model, more evident in Canada, as well as Europe, emphasizes the maintenance of law and order, and is less protective of the rights of the accused and of individuals generally.[6]...

Property rights and civil liberties are also under less constitutional protection in Canada

Table 1
RELIGIOUS BELIEFS AND VALUES 1980–81, IN PERCENT

	Americans	English Canadians	French Canadians
How important is God in your life? (1 = not at all; 10 = very important) Percentage choosing 9 or 10	59	44	47
Believe "there is a personal God"	65	49	56
Believe the Ten Commandments apply fully to themselves	83	76	67
Believe the Ten Commandments apply fully to others as well	36	28	23
Believe in "the Devil"	66	46	25
Believe in "Hell"	67	45	22
Believe in "Heaven"	84	73	58
Believe in life after death	71	61	63
Believe in a soul	88	80	80

Source: CARA, Center for Applied Research in the Apostolate, *Values Study of Canada* (code book) Washington, D.C.: May 1983.

Table 2
FAMILY VALUES 1980–81, IN PERCENT

	Americans	English Canadians	French Canadians
Agree that "marriage is an outdated institution"	7	11	19
Believe that "individuals should have a chance to enjoy complete sexual freedom without being restricted"	18	18	24
Disapprove of idea of a woman wanting a child but not a stable relationship with one man	58	53	34
Agree that sexual activity must subscribe to certain moral rules	51	49	34

Source: CARA, Center for Applied Research in the Apostolate, *Values Study of Canada* (code book) Washington, D.C.: May 1983.

than in the United States. John Mercer and Michael Goldberg note:

> In Canada . . . property rights are not vested with the individual but rather with the Crown, just the opposite of the U.S. where the Fifth and Fourteenth Amendments to the U.S. Constitution guarantee property rights. Interestingly, in the [recently enacted] Canadian Charter of Rights and Freedoms property rights (as distinct from human rights) were explicitly not protected. . . . Such a state of affairs would be unacceptable in the United States where individual rights and particularly those related to personal and real property are sacrosanct. (Mercer and Goldberg, 1982:22)

The Canadian government has greater legal power to restrict freedom of speech and to invade personal privacy. Acting through an order-in-council, it may limit public discussion of particular issues and, as in 1970 during the Quebec crisis, impose a form of military control (see Callwood, 1981: 333–334, 341–342; Bell and Tepperman, 1979:83–84; Smith, 1971). Comparing American and Canadian public reactions to violations of privacy by the government, Alan Westin writes:

> [I]t is important to note that in Canada there have been some incidents which, had they happened in the United States, would probably have led to great *causes célèbres*. Most

Canadians seem to have accepted Royal Canadian Mounted Police break-ins without warrants between 1970 and 1978, and also the RCMP's secret access to income tax information, and to personal health information from the Ontario Health Insurance Plan. If I read the Canadian scene correctly, those did not shock and outrage most Canadians. (Westin, 1983:41)

That Canadians and Americans differ in the way they react to the law is demonstrated strikingly in the aggregate differences between the two with respect to crime rates for major offenses. Americans are much more prone than Canadians to commit violent offenses like murder, robbery, and rape and to be arrested for the use of serious illegal drugs such as opiates and cocaine. They are also much more likely to take part in protest demonstrations and riots. Although the United States population outnumbers the Canadian by about ten to one, the ratios for political protest activities have ranged from twenty to one to forty to one.

Evidence from national opinion surveys in the two countries indicates that lower rates of crime and violence in Canada are accompanied by greater respect for police, public backing for stronger punishment of criminals, and a higher level of support for gun control legislation. For example, when asked by the Canadian Gallup poll in 1978 to rate the local, provincial, and Royal Canadian Mounted Police, a large majority (64 percent, 64 percent, and 61 percent, respectively) said "excellent or good." The corresponding percentages reported by the Harris survey for local, state and federal law enforcement officials in 1981 were 62, 57, and 48.[7] In the early eighties, the CARA surveys conducted by Gallup found more Canadians (86 percent) than Americans (76 percent) voicing a great deal or quite a lot of confidence in the police. There was no significant difference between the two Canadian linguistic groups on this item. . . .

The lesser respect for the law, for the "rules of the game" in the United States, may be viewed as inherent in a system in which egalitarianism is strongly valued and in which diffuse elitism is lacking. Generalized deference is not accorded to those at the top; therefore, in the United States there is a greater propensity to redefine the rules or to ignore them. The decisions of the leadership are constantly being questioned. While Canadians incline toward the use of "lawful" and traditionally institutionalized means for altering regulations which they believe are unjust, Americans seem more disposed to employ informal and often extralegal means to correct what they perceive as wrong.

The greater lawlessness and corruption in the United States may be attributed in part to the greater strength of the achievement value in the more populous nation. As Robert Merton has pointed out, a strong emphasis on achievement means that "[t]he moral mandate to achieve success thus exerts pressure to succeed, by fair means if possible and by foul means if necessary" (Merton, 1957:169). Merton accounts for the greater adherence to approved means of behavior in much of Europe compared to the United States as derivative from variations in the emphasis on achievement for all. And the same logic implies that since Americans are more likely than their Canadian neighbors to be concerned with the achievement of ends—particularly pecuniary success—they will be less

concerned with the use of the socially appropriate *means*; hence we should expect a higher incidence of deviations from conventional norms in politics and other aspects of life south of the forty-ninth parallel.

Although the cross-national behavioral and attitudinal variations with respect to law and crime have continued down to the present, Canada has been involved since 1960 in a process of changing her fundamental rules in what has been described as American and due process directions. The adoption of a Bill of Rights in 1960, replaced by the more comprehensive Charter of Rights and Freedom in 1982, was designed to create a basis, absent from the British North American Act, for judicial intervention to protect individual rights and civil liberties.

While these changes are important, it is doubtful that they will come close to eliminating the differences in legal cultures. Canadian courts have been more respectful than American ones of the rest of the political system. As Kenneth McNaught concluded in 1975,

> our judges and lawyers, supported by the press and public opinion, reject any concept of the courts as positive instruments in the political process. . . . [P]olitical action outside the party-parliamentary structure tends automatically to be suspect—and not least because it smacks of Americanism. This deep-grained Canadian attitude of distinguishing amongst proper and improper methods of dealing with societal organization and problems reveal us as being, to some extent, what Walter Bagehot once called a "deferential society." (McNaught, 1975:138; see also Whyte, 1976:656–657; Swinton, 1979:91–93)

Beyond these general distinctions there are specific provisions in the new Charter of Rights and Freedoms which set it apart from the American Bill of Rights. For example, to protect parliamentary supremacy, the Canadian constitution provides that Parliament or a provincial legislature may "opt out" of the constitutional restrictions by inserting into any law a clause that it shall operate regardless of any part of the Charter. In addition, the new rights do not include any assurance that an accused person shall have a lawyer, nor that he has the right to remain silent, nor that he need not answer questions which may tend to incriminate him in civil cases or in investigatory proceedings (Pye, 1982: 221–248; McWhinney, 1982: 55–57, 61; Westin, 1983: 27–44; see also McKercher, 1983)....

THE ECONOMY: THE PRIVATE SECTOR

The United States, born modern, without a feudal elitist corporatist tradition, could create, outside of the agrarian South, what Engels described as the purest example of a bourgeois society. Canada, as we have seen, was somewhat different, and that difference affected the way her citizens have done business....

According to Herschel Hardin, Canadian entrepreneurs have been less aggressive, less innovating, less risk-taking than Americans.[8] Hardin seeks to demonstrate that private enterprise in Canada "has been a monumental failure" in developing new technology and industry, to the extent that Canadian business has rarely been involved in creating industries to process many significant inventions by Canadians, who have had to go abroad to get their discoveries marketed (see also Brown, 1967; Bourgault, 1972; Hardin, 1974; 102–105).

This has been partly due to traditional management values and organizational processes (McMillan, 1978: 45).[9] Also important is the fact that, compared to Americans, Canadian investors and financial institutions are less disposed to provide venture capital. They "tend consistently to avoid offering encouragement to the entrepreneur with a new technology-based product... [or to] innovative industries" (Science Council of Canada, 1972: 123).

The thesis has been elaborated by economists. Jenny Podoluk found that "investment is a much more significant source of personal income in the United States than in Canada.... When Canadians have invested, the risky new Canadian enterprise has not been as attractive as the established American corporation."[10] Kenneth Glazier, in explaining the Canadian tendency to invest in the U.S. rather than in Canada, argues that

> One reason is that Canadians traditionally have been conservative, exhibiting an inferiority complex about their own destiny as a nation and about the potential of their country....
>
> Thus, with Canadians investing in the "sure" companies of the United States, Canada has for generations suffered not only from labor drain and a braindrain to the United States, but also from a considerably larger capital drain. (Glazier, 1972:61)

Data drawn from opinion polls reinforce the comparative generalizations about the greater economic prudence of Canadians. Studies of English and French speaking Canadians indicate that on most items, anglophones fall between Americans and francophones. When asked by the American and Canadian Gallup Polls in 1979 (U.S.) and 1980 (Canada) about usage of credit cards, 51 percent of Canadians said they never used one, as compared to 35 percent of Americans. The latter were more likely than Canadians to report "regular" usage, 32 percent to 16 percent. Francophones made less use of credit cards (64 percent, never) than anglophones (44 percent, never). English speakers were also more likely to be regular users than French speakers.[11]

THE ECONOMY: THE PUBLIC SECTOR

The proportion of the Canadian GNP in government hands as of the mid-seventies was

41 percent, compared to 34 percent in the United States; as of 1982 the ratio was 44 to 38 percent (Nelles, 1980: 132, 143 n.28; United Nations, 1983:22). Subtracting defense spending, roughly 2 percent for Canada, and 5 to 6 percent for the United States, widens the gap between the two countries considerably (see U.S. Arms Control and Disarmament Agency, 1982: 42, 71). Taxes as a share of total domestic product were 35 percent in Canada as compared to 30 percent in the United States in 1982 (*U.S. News and World Report*, 1984:65).[12] Unlike "the United States, [Canada] has never experienced a period of pure unadulterated *laissez-faire* market capitalism" (McLeod, 1976; Aitken, 1959). The period since 1960 has witnessed a particularly rapid expansion in the number of crown corporations: fully 70 percent of them were created in the past quarter of a century (Chandler, 1983: 187). . . .

Research based on opinion poll interviews indicates that Canadians, at both elite and mass levels, are more supportive than Americans of state intervention. Summarizing surveys of high level civil servants and federal, state and provincial legislators, Robert Presthus reports:

> [a] sharp difference between the two [national] elites on "economic liberalism," defined as a preference for "big government." . . . Only about 17 percent of the American legislative elite ranks high on this disposition, compared with fully 40 percent of their Canadian peers. . . . [T]he direction is the same among bureaucrats, only 17 percent of whom rank high among the American sample, compared with almost 30 percent among Canadians. (Presthus, 1974: 463)

Differences related to party affiliation in both countries emphasize this cross-national variation. Canadian Liberal legislators score much higher than American Democrats on economic liberalism and Canadian Conservatives score much higher than Republicans. Conservatives and Republicans in each country are lower on economic liberalism than Liberals and Democrats, but *Canadian Conservatives are higher than American Democrats* (Presthus, 1977:15).

Mass attitudinal data reinforce the thesis that Canadians are more collectivity oriented than Americans and therefore are more likely to support government intervention. In the 1968–70 studies of American and English Canadian attitudes discussed earlier, Stephen Arnold and Douglas Tigert found that, compared to Canadians, Americans are more opposed to big government and less likely to believe that government should guarantee everyone an income. They also reported that Americans are more likely than Canadians to take part in voluntary communitarian activities which, according to the authors, contradicts my assumption that Canadians are more collectivity oriented (Arnold and Tigert, 1974: 80–81). However, I would argue that the findings support this contention, since they demonstrate that Americans are more likely to take part in voluntary activity to achieve particular goals, while Canadians are more disposed to rely on the state. And in fact, a subsequent article by Stephen Arnold and James Barnes dealing with the same findings concluded: "Americans were found to be individualistic, whereas Canadians were more collectively oriented," more supportive of state provision of medical care or a guaranteed minimum income (Arnold and Barnes, 1979:32).

The existence of an electorally viable social-democratic party, the New Democrats (NDP), in Canada, has been taken by various writers as an outgrowth of the greater influence of the tory-statist tradition and the stronger collectivity orientation north of the border. Conversely, the absence of a significant socialist movement to the south is explained in part by the vitality of the anti-statist and individualist values in the United States. There is, of course, good reason to believe, as Louis Hartz, Gad Horowitz, and I, among others, have argued, that social democratic movements are the other side of statist conservatism, that Tories and socialists are likely to be found in the same polity, while a dominant Lockean liberal tradition inhibits the emergence of socialism, as a political force (see Hartz, 1955; 1964: 1–48; Horowitz, 1968: 3–57; Lipset, 1977: 79–83; 1983: 52–53). . . .

However, there are other plausible explanations for the difference in the political party systems of Canada and the United States which suggest that the contrast in socialist strength should not be relied on as evidence of varying predispositions among the two populations. As I noted in an article on "Radicalism in North America," one of the main factors differentiating the United States from Canada and most other democratic countries has been its system of direct election of the President. In America, the nation is effectively one constituency and the electorate is led to see votes for anyone other than the two major candidates as effectively wasted. Seemingly, the American constitutional system serves to inhibit, if not to prevent, electorally viable third parties, and has produced a concealed multi-party or multi-factional system, operating within the two major parties, while the Canadian focus on constituency contests is more conducive to viable third, and even fourth, parties (Lipset, 1976: 36–52).[13] And many, such as Michael Harrington, former national chairman of the Socialist Party of the U.S., have argued that there is a social democratic faction in America that largely operates within the Democratic Party (Harrington, 1972: 250–269).[14]

Evidence, independent of the effect of diverse electoral systems, that the forces making for class consciousness and organization, linked to collectivity orientations, are more powerful in Canada than the United States may be found in trade union membership statistics. Canada not only has had much stronger socialist parties than America since the 1930s, but workers in the northern country are now much more heavily involved in unions than those in the south. By 1984, only 18 percent of the non-agricultural labor force in the United States belonged to labor organizations compared to almost 40 percent in Canada (Troy and Sheflin, 1985; Department of Labour, Canada, 1984: Table 1).[15] In the United States, the percentage organized in unions has fallen steadily from a high point of 32.5 in 1954, while in Canada the figure has moved up from 22. . . .

ELITISM AND EQUALITARIANISM

. . . Elitism is presumed to be reflected in diffuse respect for authority, and in Canada contributes to the encouragement of a greater role for the state in economic and social affairs. Equalitarianism can be perceived as the polar contrast to elitism, in Tocquevillian terms as generalized respect for "all persons . . . because they are human beings" (Lipset, 1970: 38). Equalitarianism, however, has many meanings, not all of which are incompatible with elitism. Conceptualized as "equality of result," it enters into the political arena in efforts to reduce inequality on a group level. And, reiterating the arguments just presented, it may be said that Tory stimuli, elitist in origin, produce social democratic responses, efforts to protect and upgrade the position of less privileged strata.

Conceptualizing equalitarianism in this fashion leads to the expectation that nations which rank high with respect to the value of achievement, "equality of opportunity," will be less concerned with reducing inequality of condition. If the United States is more achievement oriented and less elitist than Canada, then she should place more emphasis on educational equality as the primary mechanism for moving into the higher socio-economic positions. Canada, on the other hand, should be more favorable to redistributive proposals, thus upgrading the lower strata, as, in fact, she is.

Robert Kudrle and Theodore Marmor note that "the ideological difference—slight by international standards—between Canada and the United States appears to have made a considerable difference in welfare state developments" (Kudrle and Marmor, 1981: 112). Canadian programs were adopted earlier, "exhibited a steadier development," are financed more progressively and/or are more income redistributive in the areas of old age security, unemployment insurance, and family allowances (non-existent in the United States), and medical care (Kudrle and Marmor, 1981:91–111)....

As of 1979, the percentage of Canadians aged 20-24 in higher education had risen to 36, but the comparable American figure had increased to 55.[16] The proportion of Canadians enrolled in tertiary education jumped by 125 percent; that of Americans by 72 percent. Americans, however, moved up more in absolute terms, 23 percent to 20 percent for Canadians.

Some analysts of recent changes in Canadian universities have referred to them as "Americanizations" (Bissell, 1979: 198). Canada not only sharply increased the number of universities and places for students, but her higher education institutions, following public policy, have changed. They have incorporated practical and vocationally relevant subjects, expanded the social sciences and graduate programs, and placed greater emphasis on faculty scholarship....

The changes in size and content of higher education in Canada should lead to a reduction in the proportion of persons without professional training who hold top jobs. Comparpative data indicate that Canada has differed from America, and resembled Britain, in disproportionately recruiting her business and political administrative elites from those without a professional or technical

education. As Charles McMillan reports, "Canadian managers tend to be less well educated than their counterparts in any other industrialized country with the possible exception of Britain" (McMillan, 1978: 45).[17]

This conclusion is documented by Wallace Clement's studies of business elites which reveal that the Canadians not only have less specialized education than the Americans, but also that the former are much more likely to have an elitist social background. As Clement reports, "entrance to the economic elite is easier for persons from outside the upper class in the United States than it is in Canada.... [T]he U.S. elite is more open, recruiting from a much broader class base than in the case in Canada" (Clement, 1977: 183, 209). Sixty-one percent of the Canadian top executives are of upper class origin compared to 36 percent of the Americans (Clement, 1977: 215–250, esp. 216; see also Safarian, 1969: 13).

Similar cross-national differences among top civil servants are reported by Robert Presthus and William Monopoli from studies done during the late sixties and early seventies (Presthus and Monopoli, 1977: 176–190). These revealed that a much higher proportion of Canadian than of American bureaucrats have been of upper class origin. Presthus explains the phenomena "both in industry and government" as reflecting

> strong traces of the "generalist", amateur approach to administration. The Canadian higher civil service is patterned rather closely ater the British administrative class, which even today tends to symbolize traditional and charismatic bases of authority. Technical aspects of government programmes tend to be de-emphasized, while policy-making and the amateur-classicist syndrome are magnified.... (Presthus, 1973: 34, 98)

As with many other Canadian institutions, the civil service has been changing. A more recent survey of bureaucrats in central government agencies by Colin Campbell and

George Szablowski finds that in "the past decade Canada has seen a remarkable influx of bureaucrats representing segments of the populace traditionally excluded from senior positions in the public service," and that many of those interviewed had "experienced rapid upward mobility" (Campbell and Szablowski, 1979: 105, 121). These developments may reflect the documented decrease in educational inheritance in Canada as the higher education system has grown (Manzer, 1974: 188–206).

Cross-national surveys conducted in recent years have explicitly sought to estimate support for meritocracy when contrasted with equality of result. Their findings point to strong differences between Americans and Canadians on these issues. In the fall of 1979, national samples in the two countries were asked by a Japanese research group to choose between the two in fairly direct fashion:

> Here are two opinions about conditions existing in our country. Which do you happen to agree with?
> A. There is too much emphasis upon the principle of equality. People should be given the opportunity to choose their own economic and social life according to their individual abilities.
> B. Too much liberalism has been producing increasingly wide differences in peoples' economic and social life. People should live more equally.

Forty-one percent of the Canadians chose the more egalitarian and collectivity-oriented option B. The proportion of Americans responding this way was 32 percent. Clearly the pattern of responses suggests that Canadians value equality of result more than Americans, while the latter are more achievement oriented (Hastings and Hastings, 1982: 519, 520, 525). . . . [18]

If greater commitment to equality of result leads Canadians to voice a higher preference for equality over freedom or liberty, as they do in the CARA study, the assumption that Canada is more elitist than the United States implies, as I noted in an earlier comparison of the two societies, that Canadians should be more tolerant toward deviants or dissidents than American, (Lipset, 1970: 46–48). I suggested that even without a due process system, the greater tolerance and civil liberties for unpopular groups in elitist democracies, such as Britain and Canada, as compared to populist ones reflected the ability of elites in the former to protect minority rights. Opinion studies from many democratic societies indicate that educated elites invariably are more tolerant than the less educated; hence the tyranny of the majority is less of a problem in a more elitist system. And the CARA data bear out the anticipation that Canadians would, therefore, be more tolerant than their southern neighbors. . . .

MOSAIC AND MELTING POT: CENTER AND PERIPHERY

In an earlier paper, I asserted that "Canada is more particularistic (group-attribute conscious) than the seemingly more universalistic United States" (Lipset, 1970: 55). These differences are reflected (a) in the Canadian concept of the "mosaic," applied to the right to cultural survival of ethnic groups, as compared to the American notion of the "melting pot"; (b) in the more frequent recurrence and survival of strong regionally based third parties in Canada than in the United States; and (c) in the greater strength of provinces within the Canadian union, compared to the relative weakness of the states. . . .

The origin of these cross-national differences, as with those previously discussed, can be traced to the impact of the Revolution. American universalism, the desire to incorporate diverse groups into one culturally unified whole, is inherent in the founding ideology, the American Creed. Canadian particularism, the preservation of subnational group loyalties, an outgrowth of the commitment to the maintenance of two linguistic sub-cultures, is derivative from the decision of the francophone clerical elite to remain loyal to the British monarchy, as a protection against the threat posed by Puritanism and democratic populism from the revolutionary south. Given the importance of the French-speaking areas to British North America, the subsequent Canadian federal state incorporated protections for the linguistic minority, and the provinces assumed considerable power.

These differences could be expected to decline with modernization. Most analysts have assumed that industrialization, urbanization, and the spread of education would reduce ethnic and regional consciousness, that universalism would supplant particularism.

The validity of the assumption that structural modernization would sharply reduce ethnic and regional diversity and the power of federal sub-units has been challenged by developments both within and outside of Canada. From the sixties on the world has witnessed an ethnic revival in many countries. In Canada, even prior to the revival, the values underlying the concept of the "mosaic" meant that various minorities, in addition to the francophones, would be able to sustain a stronger group life than comparable ones in the United States. As Arthur Davis points out:

> [E]thnic and regional differences ... have been more generally accepted, more legitimized [in Canada] than they have been in our southern neighbour. There has not been as much pressure in Canada for "assimilation" as there has been in the United States. ... Hutterite communities unquestionably are granted more autonomy in Canada than in the United States. Likewise, the Indians of Canada, however rudely they were shunted onto reservations ... were seldom treated with such overt coercion as were the American Indians (Davis, 1971:27). ...

The greater autonomy and coherence of ethnic groups north of the border is the result, not just of a different set of attitudes, but also of explicit government policies which reflect them. Ever since the publication in 1969 of the fourth volume of the *Report of the Royal Commission on Bilingualism and Biculturalism*, the country has been committed to helping all ethnic groups through a policy of promoting "multiculturalism" (*Report of the Royal Commission on Bilingualism and Biculturalism*, 1969). The extent of the government's willingness to support this policy was reflected in the 1973 establishment of a cabinet ministry with the exclusive responsibility for multiculturalism. In addition, the government has provided funding to ethnic minorities for projects designed to celebrate and extend their cultures.

During the past two decades blacks have assumed a role within the American polity somewhat similar to that which the Québécois play in Canada. The call for "Black Power," in the context of demands for group, as distinct from individual, rights through affirmative action quotas and other forms of aid, has led the United States to explicitly accept particularistic standards for dealing with racial and ethnic groups. Much as francophones have legitimated cultural autonomy for other non-Anglo-Saxon Canadians, the changing position of blacks has enabled other American ethnic groups and women to claim similar particularistic rights. In effect, the United States has moved toward replacing the ideal of the "melting pot" with that of the "mosaic. ... "

CONCLUSION

Canadian provinces have become more disposed than American states to challenge the power of the federal government. Movements advocating secession have recurred in this century, not only in Quebec, but in part of the Maritimes, the Prairies, and British Columbia as well. The tensions between Ottawa and the provinces and regions are not simply conflicts among politicians over the distribution of power. Public sentiment in Canada remains much more territorial than in the United States, reflecting more distinct regional and provincial interests and values. In a comparative analysis of "voting between 1945 and 1970 in seventeen western nations, Canada ranked among the least nationalized, while the United States was the most nationalized ..." (Gibbins, 1982: 158). ...

Few Canadian scholars are ready to agree, as John Porter was, that the difference is derived from the continued influence in Canada of counterrevolutionary traditions and institutions, or that the variations represent a "choice of different sets of values, as the choice between a preference for the maintenance of group identities or for the diffusion of individual universalism" (Hueglin, 1984: 22).[19] Rather, they discuss a variety of relevant factors: "*societal* (economic, demographic, and international forces) and *institutional*)" (Esman, 1984; Smiley, 1984).

Two variables, both of which may be linked to the outcome of the American Revolution, appear to be most important. One is the role of the French Canadians discussed earlier. The other is the effect of the variation between the Presidential-Congressional divided-powers American system and the British parliamentary model. As Roger Gibbins emphasizes, "the Quebecois ... have used the Quebec provincial government as an instrument of cultural survival and, because the stakes are so high, provincial rights have been guarded with a vigor unknown in the United States" (Gibbins, 1982: 192). ...

... I have paid more attention here than in my earlier writings to variations between the two Canadian linguistic cultures. The evidence indicates that francophone Canadians vary more from their anglophone co-nationals than the latter do from Americans. Quebec, once the most conservative part of Canada, has become the most liberal on social issues and had a quasi-socialist provincial government

from 1976 to 1986. Clearly, as John Porter and others have emphasized, there are Canadian styles and values that differentiate both linguistic cultures from the American one.

The cultural and political differences between the two North American nations suggest why they occasionally have some difficulty understanding each other in the international arena. There are the obvious effects of variations in size, power, and awareness of the other. Canadians object to being taken for granted, and to being ignored by their neighbor. As citizens of a less populous power, they sympathize with other small or weak countries who are pressed by the United States. But beyond the consequences of variations in national power and interests, Canadians and Americans, as I have tried to spell out here, have a somewhat different *Weltanschauung*, world-view, ideology. ...

The United States and Canada remain two nations formed around sharply different organizing principles. As various novelists and literary critics have emphasized, their basic myths vary considerably, and national ethoses and structures too are determined in large part by such myths. However, the differences in themes in the two national literatures have declined in the past two decades. Ronald Sutherland and A.J.M. Smith, two Canadian literary critics, have both called attention to a new nationalism north of the border, one which has produced a more radical literature (Sutherland, 1977: 413; Smith, 1979, 236–237). But ironically, as Sutherland points out, these changes are making Canada and her fiction more American, involving a greater emphasis on values such as pride in country, self-reliance, individualism, independence and self-confidence.

It may be argued, however, that these changes, while reducing some traditional differences, have enhanced others. The new nationalism, often linked among intellectuals both to socialism and Toryism, seeks to resist takeover of Canada's economy and increased cultural and media influence by Americans, and its weapon in so doing is the remedy of state action. As Christian and Campbell have observed in this context: "Toryism, socialism, and nationalism all share a common collectivist orientation in various forms" (Christian and Campbell, 1983: 209).

Although some will disagree, there can be no argument. As Margaret Atwood has well put it: "Americans and Canadians are not the same, they are the products of two very different histories, two very different situations" (Atwood, 1984:392).[20]

Notes

[1] My initial treatment of this subject was presented in Lipset (1963: ch. 7). The arguments presented there were elaborated in Lipset (1965: 21–64). This article was subsequently updated and incorporated as a chapter in Lipset (1970: 37–75). The page references to the article here are to the 1970 edition, which has the widest circulation of the three. The current article is both an extension on the theoretical level and a condensation of the empirical content of a recent analysis (Lipset, 1985: 109–160).

[2] For a review of propositions in the literature see Arnold and Barnes (1979: esp. 3–6). See also Vallee and Whyte (1971: 556–564) and Archibald (1978: 231–241).

[3] Northrop Frye notes that English Canada should be "thought of . . . as a country that grew out of a Tory opposition to the Whig victory in the American Revolution. . . . [Quebec reacted against] the French Revolution with its strongly anti-clerical bias. The clergy remained the ideologically dominant group in Quebec down to a generation ago, and the clergy wanted no part of the French Revolution or anything it stood for" (Frye, 1982:66). For a discussion of Canada's three founding nationalities, the English, the French and the Scots (those who settled in Nova Scotia were Jacobites) as defeated peoples, see MacLennan (1977:30).

[4] For a comparable report by a historian of the 1930s in Canada see Neatby (1972:10–14).

[5] See CARA (1983). The percentages for the United States are based on 1,729 respondents; for English-speaking Canadians, 913 respondents; and for French-speaking Canadians, 338 respondents.

[6] These models are taken from the work of Packer (1964).

[7] Data from the Roper Center, Storrs, Connecticut. A comparison of the attitudes of a sample of the public in Calgary in 1974 with those in Seattle in 1973 also indicate more positive attitudes towards police in Canada than in the United States (Klein, Webb, and DiSanto, 1978: 441–456).

[8] As economist Peter Karl Kresl puts it: "Canadians have been described as a nation of 'sufficers.' By this it is meant that economic decision makers tend to be content with a pace of economic activity and a degree of efficiency that is not the maximum possible but is rather one that is 'adequate,' or that suffices. . . . Hand in hand with this is . . . the frequently observed lack of aggressiveness and competence on the part of much of Canadian industrial leadership" (Kresl, 1982: 240).

[9] Canadian novelist Mordecai Richler has bemoaned Canada's lack of "an indigenous buccaneering capitalist class," suggesting that Canadians have been "timorous . . . circumspect investors in insurance and trust companies" (Richler, 1975: 32; see also Friedenberg, 1980: 142).

[10] As summarized in Hiller (1976:144). John Crispo also notes the "propensity among Canadians to invest more abroad" (Crispo, 1979:28; Kresl, 1982:240–241).

[11] Data computed at my request from Gallup studies in files at the Roper Center, Storrs, Connecticut.

[12] The source is the Organization for Economic Cooperation and Development.

[13] The argument that the difference in the voting strength of socialism is largely a function of

the varying electoral systems has been challenged by Robert Kudrle and Theodore Marmor. They emphasize that the Canadian labor movement "is more socialist than is the U.S. labor movement and always has been" and conclude that "a real but unknown part" of the greater strength of the social democratic New Democratic Party, as compared to that received by American socialists, "may be reflecting a different underlying distribution of values from the United States" (Kudrle and Marmor, 1981:112; see also Rosenstone, Behr, and Lazarus, 1984).

[14] Norman Thomas, the six-time candidate of the Socialist Party for President, also came to believe that the electoral system negated efforts to create a third party, that socialists should work within the major parties (Harrington, 1972:262).

[15] In both countries, unions are much stronger in the public sector than in the private one. See also Rose and Chaison (1985: 97–111).

[16] The data are from World Bank, 1983: 197; UNESCO, 1982: 111–143; *Statistical Abstract of the U.S.,* 1982–83: 159.

[17] Writing in 1978, he suggested the gap still existed in spite of the growth in numbers of business students.

[18] Further evidence that Americans emphasize achievement more than Canadians may be found in Geert Hofstede's (1984: 155–158, 186–188) multinational comparison of work-related employee attitudes.

[19] This is Hueglin's characterization of the predominant perspective on this question, with which he disagrees.

[20] For an excellent statement by a Canadian historian detailing the relationship between the diverse histories and contemporary North American societies in terms highly similar to those presented here, see McNaught (1984).

References

Aitken, H.G.J. (1959) "Defensive expansionism: the state and economic growth in Canada." In H.G.J. Aitken, ed., *The State and Economic Growth*, New York: Social Science Research Council, pp. 79–114.

Archibald, W. Peter (1978) *Social Psychology as Political Economy*, Toronto: McGraw-Hill Ryerson.

Arnold, Stephen J. and James G. Barnes (1979) "Canadian and American national character as a basis for market segmentation." In J. Sheth, ed., *Research in Marketing*. Vol. 2, Greenwich, Conn: JAI Press, pp. 1–35.

Arnold, Stephen J. and Douglas J. Tigert (1974) "Canadians and Americans: a comparative analysis." *International Journal of Comparative Sociology* 15 (March-June): 68–83.

Atwood, Margaret (1972) *Survival: A Thematic Guide to Canadian Literature*. Toronto: Anansi Press.

————(1984) *Second Words: Selected Critical Prose*. Boston: Beacon Press.

Beer, Samuel (1973) "The modernization of American federalism." *Publius: The Journal of Federalism* 3 (Fall): 49–95.

Bell, David and Lorne Tepperman (1979) *The Roots of Disunity: A Look at Canadian Political Culture*. Toronto: McClelland and Stewart.

Bercovitch, Sacvan (1981) "The rites of assent: rhetoric, ritual and the ideology of American consensus." In Sam B. Girgus, ed., *The American Self: Myth, Ideology and Popular Culture*. Albuquerque: University of New Mexico Press, pp. 5–42.

Bissell, Claude (1979) "The place of learning and the arts in Canadian life." In Richard A. Preston, ed., *Perspectives on Revolution and Evolution,* Durham, N.C.: Duke University Press, pp. 180–212.

Bourgault, Pierre L. (1972) *Innovation and the*

Structure of Canadian Industry. Ottawa: Information Canada, Science Council of Canada.

Brown, J.J. (1967) *Ideas in Exile, a History of Canadian Invention*. Toronto: McClelland and Stewart.

Brown, Russell M. n.d. "Telemachus and Oedipus: images of tradition and authority in Canadian and American fiction." Department of English, University of Toronto.

Bruckberger, R.L. (1960) "The American Catholics as a minority." In Thomas T. McAvoy, ed., *Roman Catholicism and the American Way of Life*. Notre Dame, Ind.: University of Notre Dame Press, pp. 40–48.

Bryce, James (1921) *Modern Democracies* vol. 1. New York: Macmillan.

Brym, Robert J. (1984) "Social movements and third parties." In S.D. Berkowitz, ed., *Models and Myths in Canadian Sociology*. Toronto: Butterworth, pp. 29–49.

Burke, Edmund (1904) *Selected Works*. Oxford: Clarendon Press.

Callwood, June (1981) *Portrait of Canada*. Garden City, N.Y.: Doubleday and Co.

Campbell, Colin and George J. Szablowski (1979) *The Superbureaucrats: Structure and Behaviour in Central Agencies*. Toronto: Macmillan of Canada.

Careless, J.M.S. (1963) *Canada: A Story of Challenge*. Cambridge: Cambridge University Press.

Center for Applied Research in the Apostolate (1983) *Values Study of Canada*. Code book. Washington, D.C. May.

Chandler, Marsha A. (1983) "The politics of public enterprise." In J. Robert S. Prichard, ed., *Crown Corporations in Canada*. Toronto: Butterworths, pp. 185–218.

Christian, William and Colin Campbell (1983) *Political Parties and Ideologies in Canada*, 2nd ed. Toronto: McGraw-Hill Ryerson.

Clark, S.D. (1938) In H.F. Angus, ed., *Canada and Her Great Neighbor: Sociological Surveys of Opinions and Attitudes in Canada Concerning the United States*. Toronto: The Ryerson Press.

——— (1948) *Church and Sect in Canada*. Toronto: University of Toronto Press.

——— (1950) "The Canadian community." In George W. Brown, ed., *Canada*. Berkeley: University of California Press, pp. 375–389.

——— (1962) *The Developing Canadian Community*. Toronto: University of Toronto Press.

Clement, Wallace (1977) *Continental Corporate Power*, Toronto: McClelland and Stewart.

Crispo, John (1979) *Mandate for Canada*. Don Mills, Ontario: General Publishing Co.

Curtis, James (1971) "Voluntary association joining: a cross-national comparative note." *American Sociological Review* 36(October):872–880.

Davis, Arthur K. (1971) "Canadian society and history as hinterland versus metropolis." In Richard J. Ossenberg, ed., *Canadian Society: Pluralism, Change and Conflict*, Scarborough, Ontario: Prentice Hall, pp. 6–32.

Department of Labour (1984) *Information*, Ottawa, June 26.

Engels, Friedrich (1942) "Engels to Sorge." February 8, 1890. In Karl Marx and Friedrich Engels, *Selected Correspondence*. New York: International Publishers, pp. 466–468.

——— (1953) "Engels to Sorge," September 10, 1888. In Karl Marx and Friedrich Engels, *Letters to Americans*. New York: International Publishers, pp. 203–204.

Esman, Milton J. (1984) "Federalism and modernization: Canada and the United States," *Publius: The Journal of Federalism* 14 (Winter): 21–38.

Friedenberg, Edgar Z. (1980) *Deference to Authority*. White Plains, N.Y.: M.E. Sharpe, Inc.

Frye, Northrop (1953) "Letters in Canada: 1952. Part 1: Publications in English." *The University of Toronto Quarterly*, 22(April): 269–280.

——— (1982) *Divisions on a Ground: Essays on Canadian Culture*. Toronto: Anansi.

Gibbins, Roger (1982) *Regionalism: Territorial Politics in Canada and the United States*. Toronto: Butterworths.

Glazer, Nathan and Daniel P. Moynihan (1975)

"Introduction." In Nathan Glazer and Daniel P. Moynihan, eds., *Ethnicity: Theory and Experience*. Cambridge: Harvard University Press, pp. 1–26.

Glazier, Kenneth M. (1972) "Canadian investment in the United States: 'Putting your money where your mouth is'." *Journal of Contemporary Business* 1 (Autumn):61–66.

Grant, John Webster (1973) " 'At least you knew where you stood with them': Reflections on religious pluralism in Canada and the United States." *Studies in Religion* 2 (Spring):340–351.

Griffiths, Curt T., John F. Klein, and Simon N. Verdun-Jones (1980) *Criminal Justice in Canada*. Scarborough, Ontario: Butterworths.

Hagan, John and Jeffrey Leon (1978) "Philosophy and sociology of crime control." In Harry M. Johnson, ed., *Social System and Legal Process*. San Francisco: Jossey-Bass, pp. 181–208.

Hardin, Herschel (1974) *A Nation Unaware: The Canadian Economic Culture*, Vancouver: J.J. Douglas.

Harrington, Michael (1972) *Socialism*. New York: Saturday Review Press.

Hartz, Louis (1955) *The Liberal Tradition in America*. New York: Harcourt, Brace.

———— (1964) *The Founding of New Societies*. New York: Harcourt, Brace, and World.

Hastings, Elizabeth H. and Philip K. Hastings, ed., (1982) *Index to International Public Opinion, 1980–1981*. Westport, Conn.: Greenwood Press.

Hiller, Harry H. (1976) *Canadian Society: A Sociological Analysis*. Scarborough, Ontario: Prentice-Hall of Canada, Ltd.

Hofstede, Geert (1984) *Culture's Consequences: International Differences in Work-Related Values*. Beverly Hills: Sage Publications.

Horowitz, Gad (1968) *Canadian Labour in Politics*. Toronto: University of Toronto Press.

Horowitz, Irving Louis (1973) "The hemispheric connection: A critique and corrective to the entrepreneurial thesis of development with special emphasis on the Canadian case." *Queen's Quarterly* 80 (Autumn): 327–359.

Hueglin, Thomas O. (1984) "The end of institutional tidiness? Trends of late federalism in the United States and Canada." Kingston, Ont.: Department of Political Science, Queen's University.

Innis, Harold A. (1956) *Essays in Canadian History*. Toronto: University of Toronto Press.

Kendall, John C. (1974) "A Canadian construction of reality: northern images of the United States." *The American Review of Canadian Studies* 4 (Spring): 20–36.

Klein, John F., Jim R. Webb, and J.E. DiSanto (1978) "Experience with police and attitudes towards the police." *Canadian Journal of Sociology* 3(4): 441–456.

Kresl, Perter Karl (1982) "An economics perspecitve: Canada in the international economy." In William Metcalf, ed., *Understanding Canada*. New York: New York University Press, pp. 227–295.

Kudrle, Robert T. and Theodore R. Marmor (1981) "The development of welfare states in North America." In Peter Flora and Arnold J. Heidenheimer, eds., *The Development of Welfare States in Europe and America*. New Brunswick, N.J.: Transaction Books, pp. 81–121.

Lipset, Seymour Martin (1954) "Democracy in Alberta," *The Canadian Forum* 34 (November, December): 175–177, 196–198.

———— (1965) "Revolution and counterrevolution: the United States and Canada." In Thomas R. Ford, ed., *The Revolutionary Theme in Contemporary America*. Lexington: University of Kentucky Press, pp. 21–64.

———— (1970) *Revolution and Counterrevolution*. Revised paperback edition. Garden City, N.Y.: Anchor Books, [New York: Basic Books, 1968].

———— (1976) "Radicalism in North America: a comparative view of the party systems in Canada and the United States." *Transactions of the Royal Society of Canada* 14 (Fourth Series), pp. 19–55.

———— (1977) "Why no socialism in the United States?" In S. Bialer and S. Sluzar, eds., *Sources of Contemporary Radicalism*, vol. 1 Boulder, Colorado.: Westview Press, pp. 31–149.

———— (1979) "Value differences, absolute or

relative: the English speaking democracies." In *The First New Nation: The United States in Historical Comparative Perspective*. Expanded paperback edition. New York: W.W. Norton, pp. 248–273. [New York: Basic Books, (1963)].

——— (1983) "Socialism in America." In P. Kurtz, ed., *Sidney Hook: Philosopher of Democracy and Humanism*. Buffalo, N.Y.: Prometheus Books, pp. 47–63.

——— (1985) "Canada and the United States: the cultural dimension." In Charles F. Doran and John H. Sigler, eds., *Canada and the United States: Enduring Friendship, Persistent Stress*. Englewood Cliffs, N.J.: Prentice-Hall, Inc., pp. 109–160.

——— (1986) "North American labor movements: a comparative perspective." In Seymour Martin Lipset, ed., *Unions in Transition: Entering the Second Century*. San Francisco: Institute for Contemporary Studies.

MacLennan, Hugh (1977) "A society in revolt," In Judith Webster, ed., *Voices of Canada: An Introduction to Canadian Culture*. Burlington, Vt.: Association for Canadian Studies in the United States, pp. 29–30.

Manzer, R. (1974) *Canada: A Socio-Political Report*. Toronto: McGraw-Hill Ryerson.

Matthews, Ralph (1982) "Regional differences in Canada; social versus economic interpretations." In Dennis Forcese and Stephen Richer, eds., *Social Issues: Sociological Views of Canada*. Scarborough, Ontario: Prentice-Hall, 1982, pp. 82–123.

McDougall, Robert L. (1963) "The dodo and the cruising auk." *Canadian Literature* 18 (Autumn): 6–20.

McInnis, Edgar W. (1942) *The Unguarded Frontier*. Garden City, N.Y.: Doubleday, Doran & Co.

McKercher, William R. (1983) *The U.S. Bill of Rights and the Canadian Charter of Rights and Freedoms*. Toronto: Ontario Economic Council.

McLeod, J.T. (1976) "The free enterprise dodo is no phoenix." *Canadian Forum* 56 (August): 6–13.

McMillan, Charles J. (1978) "The changing competitive environment of Canadian business." *Journal of Canadian Studies* 13 (Spring): 38–48.

McNaught, Kenneth (1975) "Political trials and the Canadian political tradition." In Martin L. Friedland, ed., *Courts and Trials: A Multidisciplinary Approach*. Toronto: University of Toronto Press, pp. 137–161.

——— (1984) "Approaches to the study of Canadian history," *The (Japanese) Annual Review of Canadian Studies* 5:89–102.

McWhinney, Edward (1982) *Canada and the Constitution, 1979–1982*. Toronto: University of Toronto Press.

Mercer, John and Michael Goldberg (1982) "Value differences and their meaning for urban development in the U.S.A." Working Paper No. 12, UBC Research in Land Economics. Vancouver, B.C.: Faculty of Commerce, University of British Columbia.

Merton, Robert K. (1957) *Social Theory and Social Structure*. Glencoe, Ill.: The Free Press.

Michalos, Alex C. (1980) *North American Social Report: A Comparative Study of the Quality of Life in Canada and the USA from 1964 to 1974*, vol. 2. Dordrecht, Holland: D. Reidel Publishing Co.

Neatby, H. Blair (1972) *The Politics of Chaos: Canada in the Thirties*. Toronto: Macmillan of Canada.

Nelles, H.V. (1980) "Defensive expansionism revisited: federalism, the state and economic nationalism in Canada, 1959–1979." *The (Japanese) Annual Review of Canadian Studies* 2: 127–145.

O'Toole, Roger (1982) "Some good purpose: Notes on religion and political culture in Canada." *Annual Review of the Social Sciences of Religion*, vol. 6. The Hague: Mouton, pp. 177–217.

Packer, Herbert (1964) "Two models of the criminal process." *University of Pennsylvania Law Review* 113 (November): 1–68.

Porter, John (1979) *The Measure of Canadian Society: Education, Equality and Opportunity*. Agincourt, Ontario: Gage Publishing.

Presthus, Robert (1973) *Elite Accomodation in Canadian Politics*, Cambridge: Cambridge University Press.

_____ (1974) *Elites in the Policy Process*. Toronto: Macmillan of Canada.

_____ (1977) "Aspects of political culture and legislative behavior: United States and Canada. Robert Presthus, ed., *Cross-National Perspectives: United States and Canada*. Leiden: E.J. Brill, pp. 7–22.

Presthus, Robert and William V. Monopoli (1977) "Bureaucracy in the United States and Canada: social, attitudinal and behavioral variables." In Robert Presthus, ed., *Cross-National Perspectives: United States and Canada*. Leiden: E.J. Brill, pp. 176–190.

Pye, A. Kenneth (1982) "The rights of persons accused of crime under the Canadian Constitution: a comparative perspective." *Law and Contemporary Problems* 45 (Autumn): 221–248.

Richler, Mordecai (1975) "Letter from Ottawa: The sorry state of Canadian nationalism." *Harper's* 250 (June): 28–32.

Rose, Joseph B. and Gary N. Chaison (1985) "The state of the unions: United States and Canada," *Journal of Labor Research* 6 (Winter): 97–111.

Rosenstone, Steven J., Roy L. Behr and Edward H. Lazarus (1984) *Third Parties in America: Citizen Response to Major Party Failure*. Princeton, N.J.: Princeton University Press.

Royal Commission on Bilingualism and Biculturalism (1969) *Report*. Book 4. *The Cultural Contribution of the Other Ethnic Groups*. Ottawa: Queen's Printer.

Safarian. A.E. (1969) *The Performance of Foreign-Øwned Firms in Canada*. Washington, D.C.: National Planning Association.

Schoenfield, Stuart (1978) "The Jewish religion in North America: Canadian and American comparisons." *Canadian Journal of Sociology* 3(2): 209–231.

Schwartz, Mildred A. (1974) *Politics and Territory: The Sociology of Regional Persistence in Canada*. Montreal: McGill-Queen's University Press.

Science Council of Canada, (1972) "Innovation in a cold climate: 'impediments to innovation'." In Abraham Rotstein and Gary Lax, eds., *Independence: The Canadian Challenge*. Toronto: The Committee for an Independent Canada, pp. 120–131.

Smiley, Donald V. 1984 "Public sector politics, modernization and federalism: the Canadian and American experiences." *Publius: The Journal of Federalism* 14 (Winter): 52–59.

Smith, A.J.M. (1979) "Evolution and revolution as aspects of English-Canadian and American literature." In Richard A. Preston, ed., *Perspectives on Evolution and Revolution*. Durham, N.C.: Duke University Press.

Smith, Denis (1971) *Bleeding Hearts . . . Bleeding Country: Canada and the Quebec Crisis*. Edmonton: M.G. Hurtig.

Statistical Abstracts of the U.S. 1982–83. 103rd edition.

Sutherland, Ronald (1977) *The New Hero: Essays in Comparative Quebec/Canadian Literature*. Toronto: Macmillan of Canada.

_____ (1982) "A literary perspective: the development of a national consciousness." In William Metcalfe, ed., *Understanding Canada*. New York: New York University Press, pp. 401–414.

Swinton, Katherine (1979) "Judicial policy making: American and Canadian perspectives." *The Canadian Review of American Studies* 10(Spring): 89–94.

Tarrow, Sidney (1978) "Introduction." In Sidney Tarrow, Peter J. Katzenstein and Luigi Graziano, eds., *Territorial Politics in Industrial Nations*. New York: Praeger.

Taylor, Charles Lewis and David A. Jodice (1983) *World Handbook of Political and Social Indicators*, vol. 2, 3rd ed. New Haven: Yale University Press.

Tepperman, Lorne (1977) *Crime Control: The Urge Toward Authority*. Toronto: McGraw-Hill Ryerson.

Thomas, Ted E. (1983) "The gun control issue: a sociological analysis of United States and Canadian attitudes and policies." Oakland, California: Department of Sociology, Mills College.

Tocqueville, Alexis de (1945) *Democracy in America*, vol. 1. New York: Vintage Books.

Troy, Leo and Leo Sheflin (1985) *Union Sourcebook*. West Orange, N.J.: IRDIS Publishers, 1985.

Underhill, Frank (1960) *In Search of Canadian Liberalism*. Toronto: Macmillan of Canada.

UNESCO 1982 *Statistical Yearbook, (1982)*. Paris: UNESCO.

United Nations (1983) *World Economic Survey, 1983* (supplement). New York: United Nations.

U.S. Arms Control and Disarmament Agency (1982) *World Military Expenditures and Arms Transfers 1971–1980*. Washington, D.C.

U.S. News and World Report 1984 "How big is government's bite?" August 27, 1984: 65.

Vallee, Frank G. and Donald R. Whyte, eds. (1971) *Canadian Society: Sociological Perspectives*. Third edition. Tornto: Macmillan of Canada.

Weaver, John Charles (1973) "Imperilled dreams: Canadian opposition to the American Empire, 1918–1930," Ph.D. dissertation, Department of History, Duke University.

Weber, Max (1949) *The Methodology of the Social Sciences*. Glencoe, Ill.: The Free Press.

Weller, Geoffrey R. (1984) "Common problems, alternative solutions: a comparison of the Canadian and American health systems," Thunder Bay, Ont.: Department of Political Science, Lakehead University.

Westhues, Kenneth (1978) "Stars and Stripes, the Maple Leaf, and the Papal Coat of Arms." *Canadian Journal of Sociology* 3(1): 245–261.

Westin, Alan F. (1983) "The United States Bill of Rights and the Canadian Charter: A socio-political analysis." In William R. McKercher, ed., *The U.S. Bill of Rights and the Canadian Charter of Rights and Freedoms*. Toronto: Ontario Economic Council, pp. 27–44.

Whyte, John D. (1976) "Civil liberties and the courts." *Queen's Quarterly* 83(Winter): 655–663.

World Bank (1983) *World Development Report 1983*. New York: Oxford University Press.

9 Novelty Items as Cultural Artifacts

Harry B. Hiller

HARRY B. HILLER, Professor and Head of the Department of Sociology at the University of Calgary, is the author of three books and numerous articles in professional journals. His most recent book is entitled *Canadian Society: A Macro Analysis* (1986). Much of Hiller's research has focussed on social movements in Western Canada. During the surge of separatism expressed in the Canadian West in 1980–81, Hiller headed a research team that attempted to follow the movement as it developed and declined. In 1986, he spent six months in Western Australia to study a similar movement in the far west of that country. He is currently working on a theory of separatism that encompasses the ethnic variety (e.g., Quebec) as well as non-ethnic movements such as in Western Canada.

INTRODUCTION

Most studies of popular culture focus on the various art forms of literature, drama, or music and seek to relate these cultural artifacts to social categories of artists and consumers based on class, age, race, or ethnic group.[1] However, there is another aspect of popular culture that is seldom acknowledged that can also reflect social sentiments, and these include a diversity of created objects which are usually identified as *novelty items*. . . .

Novelty items are consumer commodities that have little or no utility in themselves except for their expressive or entertaining value. At the height of their popularity, any individual item may become like a fad in which large numbers of people desire to have one.[2] Out of nowhere they suddenly appear and demand for them can plummet just as fast. There may be an element of comedy, humor, or plain silliness attached to these items (e.g., the pet rock craze of the late 1970s), or they may be a fad promoting agility (e.g., the hula hoop) or appearance (e.g., hair barrettes). In any case, a novelty item implies that you must buy something rather than just do something (e.g., seeing how many people can be stuffed in a telephone booth), and, once the fad is over, the novelty item may become invisible and forgotten.

Many novelty items defy obvious contextual explanations for their rise and fall in popularity.[3] For example, it is difficult to find a cultural explanation for the sudden interest and then sudden decline in interest for the hula hoop. The best explanation appears to be most closely related to the ingenuity and marketing ability of entrepreneurs who, with the appropriate support of the media, are able to obtain a wide distribution of their product. The profit motive of enterprising entrepreneurs may be combined with arguments about the need for capitalist systems to generate diversions from the harshness of economic realities.[4] Another form of explanation stresses the role of the media in promoting faddish behavior. When streaking was in vogue, one study demonstrated that it was supported by the media who kept this behavioral novelty before the public, and when the media lessened its interest, the incidence of streaking diminished as well.[5] The popularity of many novelty items is probably best explained using an economic entrepreneurial distribution theme, because sales volumes may be more directly related to merchandising apparatus than to cultural or contextual explanations.

Novelty items, however, are clearly a phenomenon of a consumer society where mass production allows the manufacture of these goods rather cheaply. The existence and popularity of these items requires a reasonably high level of discretionary income so that people can afford to purchase frivolous commodities. To that extent, novelty items are a commentary on the economic context in which these items are marketed. . . .

NOVELTY ITEMS AS SOCIAL ASSERTIONS

There are several types of novelty items which can overtly convey significant meanings. Perhaps the most prominent is the bumper sticker. Other forms include the campaign-type button and, more recently, T-shirts with appropriate slogans or pictures on them. A wide variety of other gadgets and novelties can be used to convey messages and some more innovative examples will be discussed later.

Perhaps one of the most currently popular novelty items is the T-shirt. The refinement of silk screen processing in combination with the popularity of T-shirts as wearing apparel for both men and women of all ages has led to the rapid growth of the custom T-shirt industry. Consequently, it is possible for the consumer to choose from thousands of available designs. Designs can include pictures and/or slogans or phrases which convey messages and which the wearer has selected by personal choice. In other words, the wearer can select the message he/she wants to project. Whereas earlier T-shirts were of a standard design and were custom ordered as tourist souvenirs or as indicators of institutional affiliations such as colleges, universities, or camps, contemporary T-shirts can be designed to signify, commemorate, or communicate anything. Many silk screen designers now have their own specialty retail outlets and dozens of designs from which to choose.

A T-shirt in itself is not a novelty item but a rather standard form of wearing apparel. What makes it a novelty item is when it is purchased primarily for its message or sym-

bolic meaning rather than for its use as a clothing item. When its primary function is as a form of clothing, the T-shirt is usually purchased at a retail clothing store. If the T-shirt was purchased primarily because the buyer liked its message or meaning, and purchased it whether the wearer needed it or not, there is a greater likelihood that it was bought from a specialty shop or was even obtained from less formal retail channels. . . .

It must be acknowledged that there is some ambiguity in attempting to correlate a shirt with the identity of the wearer. It is possible that there might be some randomness in the wearer's selection of a shirt. It is also possible that the wearer either has no association with or does not agree with the message of the design. Rather than suggest that the wearer disagrees with the message, however, it is more likely that the wearer might be somewhat ambivalent about the message than that strong disagreement exists. The message may also be chosen for its shock value or for its humor rather than as a sign of personal commitment. Under normal circumstances, though, it can be assumed that the wearer selects a particular design because he/she feels comfortable with the message. . . .

Bumper stickers are even more likely to convey messages for, in contrast to shirts, they possess no other uses. As a result, they are highly susceptible for use in the promotion of causes and commitments. "Have You Hugged Your Child Today?" Campus Crusade's "I Found It" and the opposition bumper sticker that it spawned "I Lost It," or "America: Love It Or Leave It," or commercial slogans are all meant to advocate a point of view or course of action. Bumper stickers are particularly useful for these kinds of messages because they can be printed cheaply and quickly in response to current trends, issues and controversies within a society and without the sizing problem of T-shirts. An archive of bumper stickers would certainly provide important clues to significant features of our civilization. There is also some ambiguity about the meaning of the message in relation to the owner who displays it but again, under normal conditions, it can be assumed that the correlation is more likely to be positive. The only purpose of bumper stickers then is to convey a message.

THE THEME OF SOCIAL ADVOCACY

Not all novelty items convey serious social messages to be sure (e.g., tourist souvenir inscriptions or innocuous T-shirt designs), but most novelty items have the potential of being used to advocate a point of view or promote a cause. When novelty items are used in this way, the thesis of this paper is that they are usually related to some form of social advocacy. The bumper sticker "Make Love Not War" was clearly related to opposition to the Vietnam War. In fact, many controversial public issues produce a bumper sticker response either subtly or directly supporting a particular option. Advocacy usually has a protest component so that opposing a course of action or advocating a course of action become flip sides of the same movement. The argument is, then, that novelty items can reflect important elements of a society's internal struggles and conflicts.

Such an argument has its parallels in studies of other aspects of popular culture. Sanders has shown how novels written during the Vietnam War era reflected negative feelings and the conflicts about that war; Peavy has demonstrated how the anger of the black power movement was reflected in black drama; and Ferrandino has argued that rock music was the means whereby a political consciousness that challenged bourgeois culture was developed among youth.[6] Klapp also pointed out that the hippie look used fashion as symbolic protest or style rebellion.[7] . . .

If novelty items are related to social protest or social advocacy within a society, then we would expect that most social movements would generate a variety of novelty items to express their position or point of view. As an example of this tendency, the separatist movement in Western Canada will be used to illustrate the creation of such cultural artifacts and to demonstrate how they reflect the underlying tensions of western regionalism within Canadian society.

NOVELTY ITEMS WITHIN THE WESTERN CANADIAN SEPARATIST MOVEMENT

The existence of alienation and hostility in Western Canada to the power and dominance of Ontario and Quebec (usually referred to as "the east") in Canadian federalism has been long-standing.[8] With the growth of the oil and gas industry in the West (and particularly in the province of Alberta) and the recent crisis in the world supply of energy, a new sense of Western power emerged. Simultaneously, challenged by the growing devolution of power to the provinces, the federal government strongly resisted any threats to the status quo. The federal election of February 1980 returned the Liberal Party to power under Trudeau based on the strong support of Ontario and Quebec but with only two seats in the entire West. In addition to the feeling of disenfranchisement that this engendered in the West, many Westerners resented the policies contained within the October 1980 federal budget and the proposals for a rewritten federal constitution. Giving up in anger and resentment, some Westerners felt that the only option for the West was the establishment of a new sovereign state or at least to threaten to do so (following the example of Quebec).[9] Two separatist organizations (West-Fed and Western Canadian Concept) were formed to enlist the support of people to attain that goal.

During the time when feelings were at their peak (the latter part of 1980 and the early part of 1981), a host of novelty items appeared including things like sloganed T-shirts and caps (e.g., "Be Nice to Me, I've Got Friends in Alberta," "Republic of Western Canada," "Independent Republic of Western Canada," "Ontario Sucks," "Saudi-Alberta," etc.), bumpers stickers (e.g., "Pierre—You Can't Have Our Oil But Here's Some Natural Gas!", "The West Needs Ontario, Quebec, And Trudeau Like A Fish Needs A Bicycle," "I'd Rather Push This Thing Uphill For A Mile Than Buy Gas At Petrocan," etc.), a large humorous poster with Trudeau about to get a pie in the face and pictured with numerous politicians (including Reagan with a shotgun) watching with glee and in a variety of funny poses, an almost empty can called a "Gluie Lubie" (containing a few stones and some sand) labelled "Used Western Oil For Export To Eastern Canada," a humorous and mocking bilingual (English and Ukrainian) "State of Alberta Passport," and a lapel pin showing a faucet being turned off to commemorate the cutback of western oil to the east as a consequence of the federal-province dispute on revenue sharing.

SOCIOLOGICAL DYNAMICS

From a sociological point of view, there were three significant features about these novelty items. First, they were mostly spontaneous individual creations with no formal connections to the separatist organizations. Most manufacturers or wholesalers interviewed reported that it was individuals who initially came to them with their ideas and requested custom orders of that item. For example, a geologist ordered a T-shirt sloganed "P.E.T.R.O. CAN." captioned underneath "Pierre Elliot Trudeau Rips Off Canada." Strongly worded phrases like "You Don't Get Something For Nothing Unless You're From Ontario" were produced at the request of a customer who marketed the item by himself. When manufacturers later became aware of the demand

they capitalized on market interest by using proven captions such as "Republic of Western Canada" or becoming innovative themselves by creating new captions. Thus, as the market proved itself, commercial operators began to take more control even to the point of modifying products they already had such as the Flippy Flier (a foldable cloth frisbee) and captioning it "Canada's Oil Future Is Up In The Air." But the craze was established first by individuals who could have these items designed or ordered with a minimum of energy and above all a small capital investment. . . .

The second significant aspect of their spurt of popularity was that the marketing of these novelty items to a large extent did not use normal retail channels. Particularly in the peak anger period of November and December (1980) and January (1981), they were usually disseminated person to person among friendship networks and business acquaintances. Interpersonal consumerism often took place at work or at home parties where the contagion of one person buying led others to do the same thing. Individuals became informal entrepreneurs sometimes adding on 50¢ or $1.00 and making a small profit at the same time. Several wholesalers reported that adjustable sizing of caps meant that it was possible for some enterprising persons to buy large quantities at wholesale prices and sell them to anyone interested from a box in the trunk of their car. Another large wholesaler noted that most of his sales were to small town gas stations and drug stores where personal interaction was again an important aspect of the sale because retailer and customer knew each other well. . . .

The greatest advantage of such informal interpersonal marketing methods[10] was that it was a faster and more efficient means of responding to public sentiment and market demands. Buyers for large retail stores first had to be convinced of their marketability in order to place these items in stock and, as well, their perceptions of standards of good taste frequently led them to consider strongly worded statements as unacceptable. Responding to this problem, another successful distribution method was to place ads in newspapers or magazines to sell directly to individuals by mail order. A further distribution method was through quantity purchases by companies sympathetic to the protest (particularly energy-related companies though not restricted to them) who distributed the item among employees and customers.

The faddishness of some of these articles was also heightened by considerable media attention. Newspaper write-ups, network television shows, and news reports referred to them as evidence of the separatist sentiment and, because they were novelties, such attention sparked greater sales. One creator noted that his phone rang "off the hook" for several days after his item was pictured in the newspaper. . . .

The third point to be made about these novelty items is that their popularity was directly related to the fact that they made a social statement regarding regional frustrations and sentiments. There is no doubt that creators were willing to take financial risks because of their perceptions of potential profitability[11] but, in all cases our research has examined, the creativeness was also a response to a contextual regional anger. Creators gathered their inspiration from surrounding cultural sentiments and yet there was no necessary reason for the public to purchase their creation.[12] . . .

Novelty items became popular because they were harmless yet rather pointed means of making a social assertion. In a tension-filled situation, the novelty item served as a passive folk vehicle of discontent, particularly when other courses of action were unavailable, were considered unacceptable at that time, or appeared futile.[13] Yet as a tool in the socialization of discontent,[14] the novelty item at the least expressed considerable sympathies for a regional issue in the midst of the declaration of a rather radical alternative in separatism. That is why many of the novelties made use of some form of humor as a means of masking or veiling the overt hostility implied in separation.[15] To break up a country is a serious matter and the existence of a certain ambiguity (noted earlier) regarding what the wearer or owner of the item actually meant by such a brash but unexpected assertion ("Is the person joking?" "Is the person serious?" "Is the person exaggerating for effect?") created an uncertainty that was best dealt with through humor. . . .

The relationship of the novelty item to its role as a social assertion rather than merely serving as an idiosyncratic artifact of popular culture is revealed by the virtual disappearance of these novelty items from public visibility since the separatist movement has gone into decline. Feelings of alienation remain not far below the surface but it is clear that the creation and distribution of novelty items was related to an accentuated anger and a public crusade that has now lost its fervor. . . .

CONCLUSION

All of the novelty items cited make a point either subtly or sharply about some aspect of Western anger in relation to perceptions of central Canadian or federal dominance and control. While it is true that the novelty items may help preserve the status quo by draining off some negative feeling, most of the items also heighten or accentuate regional tension by reinforcing the conflict theme. In that sense, these particular items make a social statement about at least one underlying conflict within Canadian society.

Formally organized social movements advocating a course of action may use novelty items deliberately as a strategy for consciousness raising and public support. On the margins of such movements, however, and in less formally organized campaigns for a particular point of view, novelty items may appear spontaneously to express group opinion about one side of an issue or another.[16] They may also express sentiment for a world view that is poorly represented in any formal public way. . . .

Though the analysis may not always be as fruitful as the data described here, it has been argued that novelty items can be analyzed in a manner similar to other aspects of popular culture and that this analysis should provide important indicators of what is transpiring within a society. . . .

Notes

[1] Cf. for example, Bernard Rosenberg and David M. White (eds.), *Mass Culture* (New York: Free Press, 1957).

[2] Orrin E. Klapp defines a fad as short-lived, frivolous, and somewhat risqué or silly. *Currents of Unrest: An Introduction to Collective Behavior.* (New York: Holt Rinehart and Winston, 1972), p. 312.

[3] Ralph H. Turner and Lewis M. Killian, *Collective Behavior*, 2nd edition (Englewood Cliffs: Prentice Hall, 1972), p. 129.

[4] Mike Brake views subcultural styles as coded expressions of class consciousness produced by structural contradictions in society so that the primary act of analysis is the decoding of those styles and objects in class terms. *The Sociology of Youth Culture and Youth Subcultures* (London: Routledge and Kegan Paul, 1980). Cf. also Michèle Barrett, Philip Corrigan, Annette Kuhn, and Janet Wolff (eds.). *Ideology And Cultural Production* (New York: St. Martins, 1979). For a different view of the issues involved, cf. Paul DiMaggio, "Market structure, the creative process and popular culture," *Journal of Popular Culture* 11(1978): 436–452

[5] Robert R. Evans (ed.), *Readings in Collective Behavior*, 2nd edition (Chicago, Rand McNally, 1975), pp. 401–417.

[6] Clinton R. Sanders, "The portrayal of war and the fighting man in novels of the Vietnam war," pp. 100–109; Charles D. Peavey, "The Black Act of propaganda: The cultural arm of the Black revolution," pp. 208–215; and Joe Ferrandino, "Rock culture and the development of social consciousness," pp. 263–290; all in George H. Lewis (ed.). *Side-Saddle On The Golden Calf: Social Structure And Popular Culture in America* (Pacific Palisades: Goodyear, 1972).

[7] *Currents of Unrest*, pp. 330–332.

[8] David J. Bercuson (ed.), *Canada And The Burden Of Unity* (Toronto: Macmillan, 1977), and John J. Barr and Owen Anderson (eds.), *The Unfinished Revolt* (Toronto: McClelland and Stewart, 1971).

[9] For discussions of the context of the recent emergence of western protest and separatism, cf. Larry Pratt and Garth Stevenson (eds.), *Western Separatism: The Myths, Realities and Dangers* (Edmonton: Hurtig, 1981), and John Richards and Larry Pratt, *Prairie Capitalism: Power And Influence In The New West* (Toronto: McClelland and Stewart, 1979).

[10] Compare Elihu Katz and Paul Lazarsfeld who argue that individuals are personal transmitters in a relay role of interpersonal relations. *Personal Influence: The Part Played By People In The Flow Of Mass Communications* (Glencoe: Free Press, 1955).

[11] George H. Lewis has pointed out that even radical and subversive activity has proved to be a great money-maker within the capitalist system. *Side-Saddle On The Golden Calf*, p. 252.

[12] Cf. Joe Ferrandino, "Rock culture and the development of social consciousness," p. 288.

[13] This point is in distinct contrast to Roger A. Fischer's argument that satiric political campaign buttons are not a good barometer of the public mood because social tensions and satiric buttons have seldom coexisted. Fischer gives many examples of satiric forms of humor in put-down buttons but does not attempt a contextual explanation for why they exist. "Pinback put-downs: The campaign button as political satire," *Journal of Popular Culture* 13 (1980): 645–653.

[14] Gary Alan Fine has suggested that the informational and expressive content of cultural products frequently become a resource for conversation and interaction. He views them not only as an "acquaintanceship device" but as "a mechanism for establishing, confirming, and reifying group beliefs and attitudes." "Popular culture and social interaction: Production, consumption, usage," *Journal of Popular Culture* 11 (1978): 460–461.

[15] Cf. "Humor and hostility: A neglected aspect of social movement analysis." *Qualitative Sociology* 1983 (fall): forthcoming.

[16] For example, supportive white response to the black power movement led one grass roots group to have "Stamp Out Racism" buttons made for sale. Luther P. Gerlach, and Virginia H. Hine, *People, Power, Change: Movements of Social Transformation* (Indianapolis: Bobbs Merrill, 1970), p. 31.

10 Ethnic Susceptibility to Crowding

A.R. Gillis   Madeleine Richard   John Hagan

A.R. GILLIS, Professor of Sociology at the University of Toronto, specializes in the study of crime and deviance, urban sociology, environmental sociology, and historical methods. His major publications include "Strangers next door: An analysis of density, diversity and scale in public housing projects" (1983); "The class structure of gender and delinquency: Toward a power-control theory of common delinquent behaviour" (1985); and "Class in the household: Deprivation, liberation and power-control theory of gender and delinquency" (1987), both with J. Hagan and J. Simpson; and "Crime, punishment and historical perspectives" (1987). Professor Gillis has served in an editorial capacity for the *Environmental Sociology Newsletter*; *Environment and Behavior*; the *Canadian Journal of Sociology*; and the *American Journal of Sociology*. He spent a year as Visiting Associate Research Scientist at the Center for Research on Social Organization, University of Michigan (Ann Arbor), in 1982–83.

MADELINE RICHARD, Assistant Director of the Population Research Laboratory, Erindale College (University of Toronto), specializes in population studies and the study of ethnic behaviour. Her publications include "Ethnic connectedness: How binding is the tie?" (1985), "The differential effects of ethno-religious structure on linguistic trends and the economic achievement of Ukrainian Canadians" (1980), and *Demographic Profiles of North York: An Aid to Planning Children's Services* (1979), all with W.E. Kalbach. Ms. Richard is currently pursuing a doctoral degree in sociology at York University, Toronto.

JOHN HAGAN, Professor of Sociology and Professor of Law at the University of Toronto, specializes in the study of crime, deviance and social control. His books include *The Disreputable Pleasures: Crime and Deviance in Canada* (1977); *Deterrence Reconsidered: Methodological Innovations* (1982); *Quantitative Criminology: Innovations and Applications* (1982); *Victims Before the Law: The Organizational Domination of Criminal Law* (1983); and *Modern Criminology: Crime, Criminal Behavior and its Control* (1985). In addition, numerous papers have been published and presented on related topics. Professor Hagan is currently co-principal investigator in a major research program on legal theory and public policy. He has served as associate editor to many leading sociological journals, including the *American Journal of Sociology*; *American Sociological Review*; *Sociological Inquiry*; *Social Problems*; *Criminology*; and the *Canadian Journal of Sociology*.

INTRODUCTION

... That Hong Kong and Tokyo have higher densities than New York or Los Angeles (where levels of pathology are higher) suggests that Asians cope with crowding better than do North Americans. If culture indeed interacts with density in this way, culture operates as a scope restriction governing the general proposition that human population density affects social pathology.

This study examines the relationship between culture, density, and crowding. Specifically, we examine the relationship between building and household density and psychological strain within and between three sociocultural categories: Asian, British, and Southern European. . . .

There is impressionistic support for the notion that people vary across gross sociocultural categories regarding their adaptability to relatively high levels of density. Asians, with their long history of high-density living, seem more susceptible to crowding, with the British representing an extreme. Among Europeans, Southerners seem least susceptible to crowding.

THE PRESENT RESEARCH

It is noteworthy that although a cross-national comparison of cultural groups might be more revealing, such an analysis would not be without serious problems of interpretation. The plethora of contextual effects that would be associated with differences between nations would be impossible to hold constant in a statistical analysis. This research analyzes the impact of ethnicity as a scope restrictor on the relationships between population density and crowding within one sociophysical context: the Central Metropolitan Area of Toronto. Specifically, we examine the power of design type and room density to predict psychological strain within the three ethnic categories: Asian, British, and Southern European.

Although the correspondence between culture and ethnicity is not perfect, there is considerable overlap (see Gordon, 1964, and more recently Yinger, 1985). Ethnic groups are typically subculture groups occupying minority economic positions within a larger political system or state (see Gordon, 1964, and especially Reitz, 1980). Because of this, differences across ethnic groups on any variable, such as density, may reflect minority status and economic constraints rather than cultural inclinations. Consequently, it is important to control for the possible effect of socioeconomic status when examining ethnic differences in density or responses to it.

The subjects for the research are adolescents living at home with their parents. It is likely that children are more culturally assimilated than their parents. However, because they are unable to leave, juveniles may be more likely to display strain as a result of high density than are adults, although research on children suggests that they may have higher crowding thresholds than have adults (Saegert, 1980; Van Vliet, 1983).

The population for the study is the student body of four secondary schools in the Toronto Central Metropolitan Area: one serving an upper-middle-class area, one in a middle-class neighborhood, and another in a lower-class area. The fourth is a vocational school with a predominantly lower-class student body. The sampling consisted of school board lists of the names and addresses of students, from which a stratified random sample was drawn. Addresses with apartment and unit numbers were used to distinguish respondents living in multiple-family and single, detached housing, allowing us to select a balanced number of students in different types of residences.

We paid each respondent five dollars to participate in the survey. By paying these subjects and assuring them of the confidentiality of their responses, we communicated the seriousness of the study, and we believe this increased the quality as well as the quantity of the participation. The overall response rate was 83.5%.

We administered the questionnaire to groups of respondents in classrooms after school. One of the investigators read the questionnaire aloud, with respondents following along and filling out their own questionnaires. We used this procedure, rather than having individuals complete self-administered questionnaires, in order to increase comprehension and the reliability of responses. This was particularly important in view of the complexity of the questions, and the fact that ethnicity may be related to reading comprehension in English.

MEASUREMENT

(1) *Ethnicity* refers to the reported ethnic or cultural background through the father. (Patrilineal descent was the basis for census classification of ethnicity in Canada at the time this research was conducted.)

(2) *Room Density* refers to density within the dwelling unit and is based on the question, "If you share your room, how many people do you share it with?" This measure of household density is superior to a measure based on persons per room for which the dwelling type is the unit of analysis, because it indicates the actual density of the respondent's own space in the dwelling unit and eliminates the possibility of distortion through aggregation-disaggregation effect operating between the dwelling unit and bedroom level of analysis.

(3) *Design Density* refers to the type of dwelling, such as single detached, duplex, row house, and high rise. Respondents were asked to select from a graphic presentation of eight dwelling types the one that best corresponded to the one in which they lived. For analysis they are ranked ordinally from low to high on the number of dwelling units they contain (Gillis, 1977).

(4) *Socioeconomic Status Scores* refers to the index of socioeconomic status derived by Blishen (1958) from the 1951 Census of Canada.

(5) *Gender* is coded female, male.

(6) *Psychological Strain* refers to the measurement of emotional distress as expressed by the Indik et al. (1964) scale, which includes questions related to difficulties experienced in sleeping, waking up, and getting going; loss of appetite; and physical ailments, such as headaches, loss of weight, and dizziness. The respondent's scores on 15 questions were aggregated to reflect the total level of psychological strain experienced. (See Gillis, 1977, 1979a, 1979b, for details on the reliability of this scale with an adult population.)

OVERALL COMPARISONS

The sample produced 397 respondents who reported that they were British (English, Irish, Scottish, or Welsh origin). There are 89 Southern Europeans (Greeks, Italians, Maltese, Portuguese, and Spanish, but largely Italian), and 30 Asians.

Our analysis involves regressing strain on both types of density and their interaction term within each of the three categories. We control for gender because of its strong association with strain and environmental variables (Gillis, 1977).

Asians ($\bar{x} = 25.4$), Britons ($\bar{x} = 25.3$), and southern Europeans ($\bar{x} = 25.2$) differ little in the levels of psychological strain that they report. Similarly, females in all three categories are more likely than males to experience strain: Asians ($\bar{x} =; -1.35$); Britons ($\bar{x} = -2.10$); southern Europeans ($\bar{x} = -2.42$). (The statistical insignificance of the largest beta reflects the small n for the Asians.)

Among Asians, room density, design density, and their interaction term fail to reach statistical significance as predictors of psychological strain. Further, all slopes are negative, suggesting that if density has an effect at all, it is beneficial.

In contrast, among the British, room density and design density are both positive, statistically significant predictors of strain. Their interaction term is negative, indicating that the combined effect is less than the sum of the direct effects.

Neither room density nor design density are significant predictors of strain among Southern Europeans. In the case of room density, the partial slope is b = 0.03, and when standardized, $\beta = .00$. However, in the case of design density, the slope is positive (b = 0.30) and just escapes statistical significance with p<0.05. More importantly, the slopes for design density as a predictor of strain are not significantly different for

Britons (b = 0.34) than for Southern Europeans (b = 0.30). There is no interaction effect among Southern Europeans.

The data support our expectations that the British are the most susceptible to the effects of density. Both room density and design density are positive predictors of strain. The data also suggest the idea that Asians are better able than Britons to cope with crowding. Both room density and design density are negative predictors of strain. Further, the mean levels of room density and design density are higher for Asians (1.5 and 4.3, respectively) than for Britons (1.4 and 4.1, respectively). So the differences in partial slopes cannot be attributed to differences in levels of density and threshold effects.

Southern Europeans are unaffected by room density in spite of the fact that they are exposed to higher levels of it ($\bar{x}$ = 1.5) than are the British ($\bar{x}$ = 1.4). However, there are no significant differences between Anglos and Southern Europeans with respect to the effects of design density. It is a positive predictor in both cases. It is also noteworthy that Southern Europeans are significantly lower in the design density they experiennce ($\bar{x}$ = 3.1) than either Britons ($\bar{x}$ = 4.1) or Asians ($\bar{x}$ = 4.3). This may reflect an attempt by Southern Europeans to keep design density below a threshold they find to be unpleasant.

Why Southern Europeans seem more susceptible to one type of density than another is unclear. Room density involves the separation of individuals from each other within the family or household. In contrast, design density involves the separation of households from each other. A high tolerance for and enjoyment of noise may allow Southern Europeans to cope with high levels of room density, but may get them into trouble with neighbors. This seems especially likely if the neighbors are less tolerant of noise, which is likely if they are people of British origin, the dominant ethnic category in Toronto. (The potential consequences of ethnic clustering are discussed later.)

CONTROLS FOR SOCIOECONOMIC STATUS

The three categories are probably not equivalent in socioeconomic status. This is important because higher incomes often mean fewer children as well as more space, and the two together can greatly reduce density. So the differences across the categories, then, could reflect differences in socioeconomic status, rather than ethnicity. The relationship between ethnicity and socioeconomic status is shown in Table 1.

In this sample, Asians are the highest of the three categories in socioeconomic status. Yet, this does not result in the purchase of lower levels of density. On the contrary, of the three categories, Asians experience the highest levels of both types of density. Therefore, one cannot conclude that Asian tolerance is based on low levels of density purchased by relatively high socioeconomic status.

Although the level of adaptation among Asians may be relatively high, it is unreasonable to believe that there is no upper limit. In their recent study of San Francisco's Chinatown, Loo and Ong (1984) found that Chinese Americans disliked crowding. Further, our data show that middle and upper SES Asians differ in their mean levels of room density (1.40 versus 1.23) as well as design density (4.80 versus 3.62). This implies that as Asians move up in SES they reduce the density of their living environments, suggesting that they prefer lower levels of density. In view of all this, Asians may not like crowding any better than do others, but may be better at not letting it affect them. (It is also possible that Asians in the higher socioeconomic strata are more acculturated).

Another possibility is that Asians are as

Table 1

DISTRIBUTION OF ETHNIC CATEGORIES BY SOCIOECONOMIC STATUS

Socioeconomic Status	Asian	British	Southern European	Total
	% (n)	% (n)	% (n)	
Low (38.8–47.1)	14.8 (4)	24.5 (77)	36.2 (25)	23.4 (106)
Medium (47.2–54.8)	37.0 (10)	33.1 (104)	39.1 (27)	34.4 (141)
High (54.9–88.7)	48.1 (13)	42.4 (133)	24.6 (17)	39.8 (163)
Total	100.0 (27)	100.0 (314)	100.0 (69)	100.0 (410)

NOTE: SES was measured with the Blishen (1958) Scale. It is the Canadian analogue of the Duncan (1961) Scale.

likely to experience crowding as anyone else, but are less likely to report it (Loo and Ong, 1984). However, by using strain as an indirect measure of crowding, we may have avoided this bias. In this sample Asians are more likely to report experiencing strain than are the other respondents, but patterns of reporting are not directly associated with density.

To examine the effect of SES on Britons and Southern Europeans, we divided the two ethnic categories into three socioeconomic strata, low, medium, and high, and reproduced the equations within each "ethclass."

Among Britons both room density and design density ($\beta = 0.26$, $b = 0.48$) are strongest as predictors of strain within the middle SES. This is probably because levels of room density ($\bar{x} = 4.38$) are highest within this stratum. It is in the highest stratum that Britons enjoy the lowest levels of density and are least affected by them.

Among low SES Southern Europeans, the mean level of room density is high ($\bar{x} = 1.76$). However, in spite of this and the fact that it has sufficient variation (s.d. $= 0.72$), the variable has no significant effect on strain. But there is a significant and positive interaction effect between both types of density on strain in this ethclass. Nevertheless, the main effects are negative.

In this ethclass the only significant positive predictor of strain is design density ($b = 2.83$, standardized $b = 1.39$). . . .

Comparing the Anglos and Southern Europeans reveals that the differences were not the result of socioeconomic factors. Within the lower socioeconomic stratum Southern Europeans experience higher levels of room density than do the respondents of any of the strata among the British. Yet room density is not a significant predictor of strain among low SES Southern Europeans.

Among Southern Europeans it is the highest stratum who experience the highest level of design density ($\bar{x} = 3.29$), and it is only within this stratum that design density is a positive predictor of strain. This suggests that the threshold for design density has been surpassed. In contrast, Anglos experience much higher levels of design density, with the means for all three strata greater than 3.29. For Britons, it is only among the middle socioeconomic stratum that design density approaches significance as a predictor of strain, and the mean is 4.38. This suggests that although design density affects the British, their tolerance may be higher than that of Southern Europeans.

Although SES is associated with the levels of population density experienced by the different ethnic categories, it is difficult to interpret the relationship. In the case of Asians, higher SES means lower densities. But this does not hold for the British, where the middle stratum experiences the highest levels of density, or Southern Europeans, where the highest stratum experiences the highest levels of design density (to which Southern Europeans are susceptible).

It is unclear why these patterns exist. However, it is clear that levels of density are not always determined by SES and that the relationships between density and strain seem more dependent on levels of density and thresholds than on levels of SES. Further, and of greatest importance, Asian, British, and Southern European respondents appear to differ in their ability to adapt to room density and design density. These differences do not seem to be due to socioeconomic factors.

CONCLUSIONS

Impressionistic evidence suggests that Asians, the British, and Southern Europeans differ in the extent to which they can tolerate population density. Gregariousness and flexibility seem to be the salient factors, with Asians high on both, Britons high on neither, and Southern Europeans gregarious, but of uncertain flexibility. Our research, based on structured interviews, supports the notion that Asians are best equipped to handle high density, that Anglos seem least able to tolerate it, and that Southern Europeans are somewhere in between. Gender and socioeconomic factors are not responsible for these patterns.

Although our findings support the observation of qualitative researchers regarding the modifying effect of culture on crowding, the following points are noteworthy. First, North American adolescents of Asian, British, and Southern European origin were not the basis for their conclusions. Their observations were based for the most part on "purer" cultural categories: Asians, Britons, and Southern Europeans in their homelands. Our respondents may be highly assimilated juveniles, whose

families have been in North America for generations. This is probably the case for at least some respondents, and if we had data on generation and assimilation, we could control for these variables in the analysis. However, in the absence of such data, it is important to note that as our indicator of culture, impure though it may be, ethnicity has impressive predictive validity. . . .

Second, although the findings coincide with the results of qualitative research, our study sheds no light on the reasons for the differences across the ethnic categories. Whether gregariousness and flexibility are indeed the salient factors is unknown. It is also uncertain whether crowding tolerance results from things in which people believe or engage, or whether it results from things they avoid. Previous research on the interaction of life-style and population density on strain suggests that it may be both. Some activities may attenuate the unpleasant effects of high density, whereas others exacerbate them (Gillis, 1979a).

Sociospatial context may also be an important intervening or interacting variable. Ethnic groups vary in the level of residential segregation they experience. Ethnic residential concentration may help to reduce acculturation by limiting contact with out-group members, and may be encouraged for this reason (see, for example, Yuan's 1963 description of New York's Chinatown). But Rapoport (1980) observes that low contact with strangers may also decrease perceptions of crowding (the Japanese achieve this even in large cities by emphasizing the neighborhood rather than the city context—see also Canter and Canter, 1971). Because density has been shown to interact with respondents' perceptions of similarity/dissimilarity as a predictor of psychological strain (Gillis, 1983; Mitchell, 1971), further research should examine ethnic concentration as a salient contextual variable, while expanding both the number of categories for analysis and the number of respondents in those categories (this is especially important with respect to Asians).

As it stands, this research is consistent with the idea that culture is an important scope restriction on the proposition that population density has a negative effect on people. . . .

References

Altman, I. (1975) *The Environment and Social Behavior.* Monterey, CA: Brooks-Cole.

Altman, I. and W.W. Haythorn (1967) "The ecology of isolated groups." *Behavioral Science* 12: 169–182.

Anderson, E.N. (1970) "Some Chinese methods of dealing with crowding." *Urban Anthropology* 1: 141–150.

Baldassare, M. (1979) *Residential Crowding in Urban States.* Berkely: University of California Press.

————— (1981) "The effects of household density on subgroups." *American Sociological Review* 46(1): 110–118.

Blishen, B. (1958) "The construction and use of an occupational class scale." *Canadian Journal of Economics and Political Science* 24: 519–531.

Booth, A. (1976) *Urban Crowding and Its Consequences.* New York: Praeger.

Booth, A., D.R. Johnson, and J.M. Edwards (1980) "In pursuit of pathology: the effects of human crowding." *American Sociological Review* 45(5):873–878.

Brolin, B.C. and J. Zeisel (1968) "Mass housing: social research and design." *Architectural Forum* 129: 66–71.

Calhoun, J.B. (1962) "Population density and social pathology. *Scientific American.* 206: 139–140.

Canter, D. and S. Canter (1971) "Close together in Tokyo," *Design and Environment* 2: 60–63.

Chaudhuri, N.C. (1960) *A Passage To England.* London: Macmillan.

Choldin, H.M. (1978) "Urban density and pathology." *Annual Review of Sociology* 4: 91–113.

Desor, J. (1972) "Toward a psychological theory of crowding." *Journal of Personality and Social Psychology* 21: 79–83.

Duncan, O.D. (1961) "A socio-economic index for all occupations," in A.J. Reis, Jr. (ed.) *Occupations and Social Status.* New York: The Free Press.

Feldman, R. (1968) "Response to compatriot and foreigner who seek assistance." *Journal of Personality and Social Psychology* 10(3): 202–214.

Freedman, D.G. (1974) "Cradleboarding and temperament, cause and effect." Presented at the annual meetings of the American Association for the Advancement of Science, San Francisco.

Freedman, J. (1975) *Crowding and Behavior.* San Francisco: W.H. Freeman.

Galle, O.R. and W.R. Gove (1983) "Overcrowding, isolation, and human behavior: exploring the extremes in the population distribution," pp. 215–242 in M. Baldassare (ed.) *Cities and Urban Living.* New York: Columbia Univ. Press.

Gans, H. (1962) *The Urban Villagers.* New York: Free Press.

Gillis, A.R. (1977) "High-rise housing and psychological strain." *Journal of Health and Social Behavior* 18: 418–431.

————— (1979a) "Coping with crowding: television, patterns of activity, and adaptation to high-density environments." *Sociology Quarterly* 20: 267–277.

————— (1979b) "Household density and human crowding: unravelling non-linear relationship." *Journal of Population* 2(2): 104–117.

————— (1980) "Urbanization and urbanism," p. 517–548 in R. Hagedorn (ed.) *Sociology.* Toronto: Holt, Rinehart and Winston.

_____ (1983) "Strangers next door: an analysis of density diversity, and scale in public housing projects." *Canadian Journal of Sociology* 8(1): 1–19.

Gillis, A.R. and J. Hagan (1982) "Density, delinquency and design: formal and informal control in the built environment." *Criminology* 19(4): 514–529.

_____ (1983) "Bystander apathy and the territorial imperative." *Sociological Inquiry* 53(4): 448–460.

Gordon, Milton (1964) *Assimilation in American Life*. New York: Oxford University Press.

Gove, W. and M. Hughes (1980) "The effects of crowding found in the Toronto study: some methodological and empirical questions," *American Sociological Review* 45(5): 864–870.

_____ (1983) *Overcrowding in the Household: An Analysis of Determinants and Effects*. New York: Academic Press.

Hall, E.T. (1959) *The Silent Language*, Garden City, NY: Doubleday.

_____ (1966) *The Hidden Dimension*, Garden City, NY: Doubleday.

Indik, B., S. Seashore and J. Slesigner (1964) "Demographic correlates of psychological strain." *Abnormal and Social Psychology* 69(1): 26–38.

Kroeber, A.L. and C. Kluckholm (1952) *Culture: A Critical Review of Concepts and Definitions*. Cambridge: Harvard University, papers of the Peabody Museum, Vol. XLVII, No. 1.

Lagory, M. and J. Pipkin (1981) *Urban Social Space*. Belmont, CA: Wadsworth.

Little, K.B. (1968) "Cultural variations is social schemata." *Journal of Personality and Social Psychology* 10: 1–7.

Loo, C. (1974) *Crowding and Human Behavior*, New York, N.Y.: MSS Information Corp.

Loo, C. and P. Ong (1984) "Crowding and perceptions, attitudes, and consequences among the Chinese." *Environment and Behavior* 16(1): 55–87.

Lowenthal, D. and H.C. Prince (1965) "The English Landscape." *Geographical Review* 54: 309–346.

Meyerson, M. (1963) "National character and urban development." pp. 78–96 in C.J. Friedrich and S.E. Harris (eds.) *Public Policy*, Vol. 12. Cambridge: Harvard Graduate School of PUblic Administration.

Michelson, W. (1976) *Man and His Urban Environment: A Sociological Approach*. Reading, MA: Addison-Wesley.

Mitchell, R.E. (1971) "Some social implications of high density housing." *American Sociological Review* 36: 18–29.

Paulus, P., A. Annis, J. Sela, J. Schkade, and R. Matheus (1976) "Density does affect task performance." *Journal of Personality and Social Psychology* 34(2): 248–253.

Porteous, J.D. (1977) *Environment and Behavior: Planning in Everyday Urban Life*. Reading, MA: Addison-Wesley.

Proshansky, H., W. Ittelson and L. Rivlin (1970) "The influence of the physical environment on behavior: some basic assumptions," in (eds.) *Environmental Psychology: Man and His Physical Setting*. New York: Holt, Rinehart and Winston.

_____ (1972) "Freedom of choice and behavior in a physical setting." pp. 29–43 in J.F. Wohlwill and D.H. Carson (eds.) *Environment and the Social Sciences: Perspectives and Applications*. Washington DC: American Psychological Association.

Rapoport, A. (1969) *House Form and Culture*. Englewood Cliffs, NJ: Prentice-Hall.

_____ (1975) "Towards a redefinition of density." *Environment and Behavior* 7(2): 133–158.

_____ (1976) *The Mutual Interaction of People and their Built Environment: A Cross Cultural Perspective*. The Hague: Mouton.

_____ (1977) *Human Aspects of Urban Form: Towards a Man-Environment Approach to Urban Form and Design*. New York: Pergamon.

_____ (1978) "Culture and the subjective effects of stress." *Urban Ecology* 3(3): 241–261.

_____ (1980) "Cross-cultural aspects of environmental design," pp. 7–46 in Altman, I., A. Rapoport, and J.F. Wohwill (eds.) *Human Behavior and Environment: Advances in Theory and Research*. New York: Plenum.

Reitz, J.G. (1980) *The Survival of Ethnic Groups.* Toronto: McGraw-Hill.

Saegert, S. (1980) "The effect of residential density on low-income children." Presented at the annual meeting of the American Pscyhological Association, Montreal.

Sommer, R. (1969) *Personal Space: The Behavioral Basis of Design*, Englewood Cliffs, NJ: Prentice-Hall.

Stokols, D. (1972a) "On the distinction between density and crowding: some implications for future research." *Psychological Review* 79(3): 275–277.

――― (1972b) "A socio-psychological model of human crowding." *Journal of the American Institute of Planners* 38: 72–83.

Stokols, D.; M. Rall, B. Pinner, and J. Schopler (1973) "Physical, social, and personal determinants of the perception of crowding." *Environment and Behavior* 5(1): 87–115.

Time (1985) "On the record." Volume 126/(October 7): 81.

Tuan, Y. (1968) "Discrepancies between environmental attitudes and behavior: examples from Europe and China." *The Canadian Geographer* 12.

――― (1974) *Topophilia: A Study of Environmental Perception, Attitudes, and Values.* Englewood Cliffs, NJ: Prentice-Hall.

Van Vliet, W. (1983) "Families in apartment buildings: sad storeys for children?" *Environment and Behavior* 15(2): 211–234.

Walker, H.A. and B.P Cohen (1985) "Scope statements: imperatives for evaluating theory." *American Sociological Review* 50(3): 288–301.

Whyte, W.F. (1943) *Street Corner Society: The Social Structure of an Italian Slum*. Chicago: University of Chicago Press.

Wolpert J. (1966) "Migration as an adjustment to environmental stress." *Journal of Social Issues* 22:92–102.

Yinger, J.M. (1985) "Ethnicity." *Annual Review of Sociology*. 11: 151–180.

Yuan, D.Y. (1963) "Voluntary segregation: a study of New York Chinatown." *Phylon* (Fall): 255–265.

Zlutnick, S. and I. Altman (1972) "Crowding and human behavior." pp. 44–60 in J. Wohwill and D. Carson (eds.) *Environment and the Social Sciences*, Washington, DC: American Psychological Association.

Socialization

Introduction

S ocialization is the process by which
humans learn social skills and social
sentiments. This learning differentiates humans from animals acting on genetically
determined instinct alone. Socialization is
also the process by which humans learn to
be effective members of the particular
society, class, region, and family in which
they find themselves: possessors of understanding and skill in the social relations
which surround them. In both these senses,
"socialization" is very much like "acculturation," the term anthropologists use to
describe the learning of a "culture," those
shared ways of thinking, feeling and acting
discussed in the preceding Section.

"Socialization" is a complicated process
and hard to explain fully. For reasons
Marlene Mackie makes clear, theories about
socialization change with time; but the
same issues keep coming up, just as in other
areas of sociological analysis. The central
questions are never completely answered
and keep reappearing in new clothing
with each generation, their answers cumu-
latively producing a fuller understanding
of everyday life.

Take the issue of "nature" versus "nurture." Scholars have long debated whether
certain human characteristics are natural
or learned: for example, whether cooperation and creativity are more "natural"

than selfishness and destructiveness. Karl
Marx addressed this question in his "early
manuscripts" of 1844, in his discussion
of the alienating character of work under
capitalism ([1932] 1961) (see Section One
of this volume). The same question is
addressed again, with new evidence from
social psychology, in an article in this
section by Peter Archibald. Whether humans naturally tend in one direction or the
other makes a profound difference if we
are arguing in favour of socioeconomic systems that depend upon co-operation, as
socialism and communism do. (Similar concerns about co-operation and selfishness
have been addressed by "sociobiologists,"
not represented in this volume, who try
to understand the roots of human behaviour
by observing animals similar to humans
in the evolutionary scale of development.)

The nature/nurture issue seems to get
further from resolution as research reveals
more about the genetic origins of human
behaviour. Human social inclinations—e.g.,
leadership qualities or competitiveness—
may be determined to some degree by
individual genetic structure, as some paired
twin studies seem to suggest. Our behaviour is not *all* nature *or all* nurture, but a
combination: and, in future, the combination of traits in an individual may even
be genetically "engineered," if we so desire.

Future research may even prove cultures to be largely the result of different gene pools, and not as responsive to social engineering as many sociologists have believed in the past.

Another issue is the relative importance of childhood versus adult socialization. Early theorists like Sigmund Freud held that personality was fundamentally shaped by parent-child interaction in the first few years of life. Adult life largely played out infantile fantasies and traumas which only intensive one-on-one therapy could hope to correct or modify. A later way of thinking held that personal identity and social behaviour continued to vary over time and changed with the environment: we are what we do and we are who others think we are. Sociological concepts like the "looking glass self," the "self-fulfilling prophesy," and the "labelling theory" of deviance all suggest that we begin and continue life as socializable creatures, and it is our malleability, our use of symbols, and our communication of ideas that makes humans differ most from other animals.

A third major debate, seen most often in the literature on teaching and parenting, is about how we are socialized. Is it by reward and punishment, or by imitation, which is largely a matter of vicarious or self-reward? Do we learn to be macho males and simpering females, for example, because we are punished if we behave like (male) "sissies" or (female) "tomboys?" Or because the mass media and observation of the adult world prove to us that conforming to these gender stereotypes is better—more rewarding—than deviating from them? Or is there a third kind of socialization, a reactive kind as the Freudians would suggest: we become cruel, racist or authoritarian if we are insecure and unloved as children, even if the mass media, parents or teachers encourage the opposite behaviour.

As with all the important and interesting questions in sociology, these are far from resolution. Probably all of the contending theories contain some kernel of truth. More skillful and ingenious analysts will have to correctly combine these insights about socialization to yield verified predictions.

Related to the issue just raised is the purposiveness of socialization, as teaching and learning. Do we learn social codes in the same way we learn language: largely by observation or trial and error, while assimilating an underlying code of meanings of which neither we nor our teachers may be completely aware? This question is raised very effectively in the article in this section by Bernd Baldus and Verna Tribe, on the childhood learning of class distinctions. The authors show that this type of unconscious socialization takes place in childhood, certainly well before adolescence; and the prevailing organization of social inequality is probably learned without purposive teaching by parents, teachers or the mass media. Rather, certain combinations of thinking, feeling and behaving seem to "make sense," and little children quickly learn to distinguish and verbalize the common patterns in our culture.

Yet not all socialization is unconscious or without purpose. Formal education will receive further attention in a later section of this book. What needs to be said at this point is that, in our own and most modern industrial societies, formal education is a centrally important socializing process. As the article by John Seeley, Alexander Sims, and Elizabeth Loosley demonstrates, education enforces middle-class family norms to produce, in middle-class children, a willingness and ability to compete in society's status wars. Such preparation is no simple matter, given the ambivalence both parents and educators feel about the desirability of individualized treatment and "personal development," on the one hand, and socioeconomic success, on the other. The Parent Teachers (or "Home and School") Association is a place where parents and teachers can debate this issue. How a child is handled—how home and school will shape the unwitting youngster—is not left to chance in the middle class, no less today among the status conscious Yuppies who are newly becoming parents, than among the "Crestwood Heights" *nouveaux riches* Professor Seeley and his collaborators studied three decades ago.

Still, not all important socialization occurs in early childhood. Later socialization takes place outside the schools, but also inside them: in colleges, universities and professional schools. An article by Jack Haas and William Shaffir on the socialization of medical students finishes this section on socialization. Every work setting requires some socialization in advance. Not only must the job skills be learned—i.e., how to cut meat (if a butcher), how to pour cement (if a construction worker), and so on—but so must subcultural codes of behaviour—how to talk, dress, and deal with colleagues, bosses or clients. Some sociologists have argued that much of what passes for professional training, as a lawyer, doctor or manager, for example, is training in comportment. Learning how to do the job comes later, with experience, as we used to recognize when most professional training was apprenticeship at workplaces.

But in the professions, style and comportment are particularly important. Professionals must establish and maintain a particular kind of relationship with the client, or purchaser of services: notably a relationship of dominance based on scarce expertise and perceived "competence." Dominance is maintained by a professional "mystique" learned in professional school and reinforced on the job (often with the assistance of professional associations). Developing a "cloak of competence" may be just as important as competence itself. The competent professional whose cloak/mystique has slipped may have more difficulty getting his clients to obey and pay up for services than the less competent professional with a better "bedside manner" or air of knowingness.

We learn, then, as adults and as children, to function reasonably effectively in the real world. Socialization teaches us how and why to conform to cultural values and social norms. How, then, do we explain the universal, timeless fact of deviance, or rule-breaking, in all classes of society and all walks of life? Is deviance a failure of childhood or adult socialization? Proof that not all behaviour is shaped by socialization? A structuring of opportunities so that conformity is sometimes impossible or less rewarding than deviance? Or, a demonstration that we are socialized into *many* subcultures, and some of these subcultures are defined as "deviant" by those with the power to do so? These and related questions will entertain us in the next section of this book.

References

Marx, Karl (1932) *Economic and Philosophical Manuscripts of 1844*. Moscow: Foreign Language Publishing House, 1961.

11 Changing Views of Socialization

Marlene Mackie

MARLENE MACKIE, Professor of Sociology at the University of Calgary, specializes in the study of gender relations, social psychology, ethnic relations and the sociology of religion. Her books and articles include *Exploring Gender Relations: A Canadian Perspective* (1983); *Constructing Women and Men: Gender Socialization in Canada* (forthcoming); "Religion and gender: A comparison of Canadian and American student attitudes" with Merlin Brinkerhoff (1985); and "Blessings and burdens: The reward-cost calculus of religious denominations" with Merlin Brinkerhoff (1986). From 1974–76, Professor Mackie was Book Review Editor (English Language Section) for the *Canadian Review of Sociology and Anthropology*; and she has since served on the editorial boards of *Sociometry; Canadian Ethnic Studies; Prairie Forum*; and the *Canadian Journal of Sociology*.

CHANGING SOCIAL-SCIENTIFIC PERSPECTIVES ON SOCIALIZATION

Social-scientific views on socialization evolve over time as changes in the broad social context stimulate developments in scientific thought. In addition, the results of research show some theoretical notions to be promising and others dead-ends. In either case, fashions and foibles in scientific orientations have implications for lay child-rearing practices. At any one time a diversity of perspectives coexists; for the most part, they are complementary rather than opposed sets of ideas. These theoretical viewpoints are also closely related to the major socialization issues of concern to social scientists. This section will briefly examine some of these theories of socialization.

Before turning to socialization theories, however, a methodological comment is in order. The methods social scientists use to study socialization are as diverse as the eclectic theoretical perspectives which guide their research. Observation, experimentation, interviews, questionnaires, content analyses, and historical research are all con-sidered appropriate under one circumstance or another. Nonetheless, so far as changing emphases are concerned, two points must be made. First, technological developments have stimulated renewed appreciation of observation. An example is Scaife's (1979) work on retrospective analysis of infant biosocial development, where the origin of a particular social accomplishment is traced backward in time through analysis of videotapes. Second, interest in studying cross-cultural variation in socialization patterns is stronger than ever. There is considerable theoretical appeal in isolating regularities which occur in socialization, regardless of environmental conditions (Zigler and Seitz, 1978:733).

Psychoanalytic Theory

As noted earlier, Freud's wide-ranging ideas about socialization (Brill, 1938) have been a pervasive influence in both social-scientific and popular thought about child rearing. Despite psychoanalytic theory's many contributions, "the passage of time has witnessed a decline in its importance" (Zigler and Seitz, 1978:733–734).

Psychoanalytic theorists regard socialization as society's attempt to tame the child's inborn, animal-like nature. Freud believed that the roots of human behaviour lie in the irrational, unconscious dimensions of the mind. He assumed that the adult personality is the product of the child's early experiences in the family. Freud saw the personality as composed of three energy systems: the id, the ego, and the super-ego. The *id* is the biological basis of personality, the *ego* is the psychological basis of personality, and the *superego* is the social basis of personality (Shaw and Costanzo, 1970).

Freud held that every child goes through a series of personality stages, each stage marked by sexual preoccupation with a different part of the body—the mouth, the anus, the genital area. Personality development, according to psychoanalytic theory, is essentially complete by five years of age.

On the positive side, Freud's emphasis on early family experiences stimulated research on cross-cultural variations in child-rearing practices. His solution to the problem of how society gets inside the individual, namely, the identification of children with their parents, was a major insight. His consideration of the roles played by the emotions, sexuality, and the unconscious covers aspects of human motivation which no other theoretical approach attempts (MacKie, 1980:140).

Psychoanalytic theory has also been severely criticized, and these criticisms explain why its popularity has declined. Much of the theory does not lend itself to empirical testing, and that is a fatal flaw. Contemporary feminists object to Freud's tendency to view women as defective men. Moreover, Freud's biological theory holds that anatomy is destiny. By contrast, sociologists emphasize society's role in moulding personality. Also, his ideas were based on his experiences with middle-class Viennese patients during the Victorian era. Consequently, care must be exercised in generalizing his notions to normal populations and to other cultures and historical periods.

A last criticism is sufficiently important to warrant extended discussion. Contemporary social scientists, convinced that socialization occurs over the life span, disagree with Freud's belief that personality development ends with childhood. For example, Freud's disciple, Erik Erikson (1963, 1968) argued that development continues throughout the life cycle from infancy to old age. Adolescents have the problem of establishing their identity. Young adults must establish intimacy with others in deep friendships and marriage without sacrificing this sense of identity. Middle-aged adults are preoccupied with productivity and *generativity* (providing guidance for the next generation). Mature adults are concerned with ego integrity, a conviction that the life they have lived has meaning (Ewen, 1980). Growth continues through all these developmental crises.

Life-stage theories are now a conspicuous element in the socialization literature. *Life crises, critical transitions* (Levinson et al., 1978), *turning points, passages* (Sheehy, 1974) have all recently entered popular culture, though research is needed to establish whether life transitions are biologically linked, invariant, or necessarily traumatic (Bush and Simmons, 1981).

Learning Theory

Since the beginning of this century, social scientists have debated the relative contributions of biology and environment to human development. From the late 1920s until the last decade, environmentalism and the *nurture* side of the *nature-nurture argument* prevailed. Since the consensus was that homo sapiens becomes human through learning, theories which explicated the precise mechanisms of learning became enormously important. For a time, "socialization theory was virtually synonymous with learning theory" (Zigler and Seitz, 1978:737). Also, learning theorists' empirical orientation and experimental tradition were salutary influences on socialization research. Partly because of renewed interest in the genetic foundation of socialization and sociobiology (see below), learning theory has now fallen to the status of "one valuable approach among many" (Zigler and Seitz, 1978:738).

Learning theories focus on three main types of learning: classical conditioning, operant conditioning, and imitation. In the first two types, learning occurs as a result of practice or the repetition of association (Yussen and Santrock, 1978:164). However, since much of what children learn is through observation rather than extensive practice, the last type (associated with Bandura, 1977; Bandura and Walters, 1963; and Miller and Dollard, 1941) is the most important for socialization.

Examples of observational learning abound throughout life. A toddler repeats words overheard from its parents' conversation. A school child watches the coyote on the Bugs Bunny cartoon show being hit and, in turn, strikes his brother. A teenager learns to smoke cigarettes by imitating her friend. An adult learns an aerobic dance routine by observing the instructor. Imitative learning can be intentional or unintentional and can occur with or without direct reinforcement.

The Cognitive-Developmental Approach

Cognitive-developmental theory, associated with Swiss psychologist Jean Piaget (1928, 1932, 1970), has grown rapidly over the last quarter century and is now an "extremely influential position" (Zigler and Seitz, 1978:735). However, Piaget's work has been more central to child psychology than to sociology.

As the word *cognitive* suggests, Piaget is interested in thought processes such as reasoning, remembering, and believing. His concern with moral thought, carried on by Kohlberg (1976), is a particularly important dimension of his theory. The term *development* indicates Piaget's interest in the systematic changes which occur over time in children's thought processes.

The theory's central assumption is that the child needs to make sense of his/her cognitive environment. The structure of children's thinking changes in discrete stages until eventually they use the adult rules for reality construction (Kessler and McKenna, 1978:96). Cognitive-developmental theory assumes that intellectual functioning, and hence behaviour, is governed by patterns of cognitive structure called *schemas*. Schemas result from experience and then influence subsequent interpretations of the physical and social worlds (Bush and Simmons, 1981:138). For example, children learn the words "boy" and "girl," and they hear others label them in this way. Once the child learns the implications of the gender schema, it becomes a major organizer and determinant of many attitudes and activities. "I am a boy, and therefore I should act like a boy and do the things that boys do," or "I am a girl and therefore I should act like a girl and do the things girls do" (MacKie, 1983a:113). A recent article (Bem, 1983) ponders the problem of feminist parents who wish to raise *gender-aschematic* children in a *gender-schematic* world.

Although cognitive-developmental theory, like psychoanalytic theory, posits a universal sequence of growth changes, the former provides more room for the influence of social interaction. However, the socialization role of parents is played down. Indeed, a cognitive-developmental theory has been described as a self-socialization theory (Maccoby and Jacklin, 1974:364), since the child is active in organizing cognitions. Finally, a major difficulty is that cognitive development as such is not really explained. Because the underlying mechanisms are not specified, it seems to just happen.

Symbolic Interactionism

Symbolic interactionism is the most sociological of the approaches discussed so far. In comparison with the other theories, this approach emphasizes the importance of group influences. Interactionists, like cognitive-developmentalists and unlike learning theorists, stress the active part played by the child in its own socialization. Interactionists differ from learning theorists in their belief that human behaviour is qualitatively different from animal behaviour because humans use more complex language. Since symbolic interactionists feel that social scientists should direct their analysis to qualities that differentiate homo sapiens from the lower animals, they adopt the related position that sociologists must study how people define and interpret reality. In general, this theoretical perspective is strong in intriguing hypotheses but weak in validating research data.

Symbolic interactionists view the individual and society as two sides of the same coin. One cannot exist without the other. Take the case of Genie (Pines, 1981). From the age of twenty months until she was thirteen, this California girl lived in nearly total isolation. She was harnessed to a potty chair all day and caged in a crib all night. She was almost never spoken to. When Genie was discovered, she was malnourished, deformed, incontinent, and "eerily silent." She scored at the one-year-old level on intelligence tests. However, her subsequent development under the tutelage of rehabilitation specialists suggested that her deficiencies were not inborn. Rather, this mistreated child had been deprived of emotional contact with reasonably intelligent, articulate adults in her early years.

Interactionist socialization theories emphasize the development of the self and the linkage between the emergence of self-awareness and the acquisition of language. Cooley (1902) and Mead (1934) saw the genesis of self in the child's intense social experience within primary groups. Cooley's metaphor of the *looking-glass self* illustrates the point made by both early sociologists that the content of the self reflects children's interpretation of others' appraisals of themselves. (Research shows a strong association between what we believe others think of us and our self-concepts, and a weaker association between our self-concepts and what others *actually* think of us [Rosenberg, 1981:597–598].).

A second, closely related socialization process is the acquisition of social roles (Bush and Simmons, 1981:144). Role taking, "the person's imagined construction of another's line of action" (Denzin, 1977:130), occurs from early childhood through to old age. Role taking is implicated in self-development. Having a self means viewing yourself through the eyes of other people. Children and adolescent socialization, particularly in a complex, changing society, cannot prepare individuals for all the tasks and roles they will encounter as adults. Therefore, role acquisition continues throughout the life cycle (Bush and Simmons, 1981:144).

The Sociobiological Approach

Over the past twenty-five years there has been a new open-mindedness concerning the similarities between human beings and the infrahuman species and an increased emphasis on genetic and constitutional factors in determining the outcome of the socialization process (Zigler and Seitz, 1978:736). Many new ideas are being introduced into sociology from a new subdiscipline called sociobiology, which studies the genetic and biochemical foundations of animal social behaviour (Wilson, 1975). This move away from exclusive environmentalist explanations has stimulated considerable controversy. (See the May, 1977 issue of *The American Sociologist*.) The most controversial aspect of sociobiology is the extrapolation of its ideas to human social life.

For our purposes the essential features of sociobiology can be reduced to three (MacKie, 1983a:63–64).

1.   The method is *evolutionary* and the time

scale is large. This extension of the Darwinian theory of natural selection holds that all animals act so as to maximize the chances of their genes being propagated and surviving to maturity (Sayers, 1980). It is assumed that any adaptive behaviour has a genetic component and that it has developed so as to maximize the number of genes favouring that behaviour being passed on to future generations (Lowe, 1978:119).

2. Sociobiologists' primary means of determining whether human behaviour is genetically or environmentally determined is to look for *cultural universals* (Lowe, 1978:121). It is assumed that behaviour observable in all societies is adaptive and therefore determined primarily by the human genetic make-up.

3. A large part of sociobiology's data and principles is based on the behaviour of the *lower animals*. Extrapolations to human social life are made from these nonhuman species (Kunkel, 1977:69). The strategies of searching for universals in human behaviour and analysing animal behaviour are often combined. After a universal human behavioural trait has been identified, sociobiologists then attempt to find similar behaviour in nonhuman primates in order to strengthen the argument that human behaviour has evolved through natural selection (Lowe, 1978:121).

Sociobiology faces formidable problems, the most serious of which concerns the difficulty of subjecting its hypotheses to empirical tests. However, Zigler and Seitz (1978:737) are correct when they say of genetic approaches in general that

> the fact that research on biological factors is becoming active after a long period of quiescence is a step in the direction of providing a needed balance in the nature-nurture issue.

CONTEMPORARY ISSUES IN SOCIALIZATION RESEARCH

Socialization specialists' current theoretical and empirical work involves seven central themes. These professional views have some impact on folk theories and practices of child rearing. Though full-length articles and books are devoted to most of these themes, our remarks must, of necessity, be concise.

Active Versus Passive View of the Child

One authority claims that "perhaps the most significant trend in the area of socialization... is an increasing shift from a passive to an active view of the individual" (Gecas, 1981:197). A quarter of a century ago Wrong (1961) complained that sociology encouraged an "over-socialized conception of man." By this Wrong meant that sociology depicted people (females as well as males) as completely moulded by the norms and values of their society. Such thoroughgoing indoctrination would, of course, destroy individuality and render nonsensical the notion of free will and responsibility for one's actions.

Sociologists are now convinced that children are *not* passive recipients of the socialization process, that they are *not* all identical products turned out by an omnipotent socialization factory. The existence of at least some deviant behaviour within every society testifies to the fact that no system of socialization is perfectly efficient (MacKie, 1983b:87–88). A considerable amount of evidence (much of it collected by cognitive-developmentalists) shows that children play an active role in their own socialization. They select experiences according to their own idiosyncratic styles (Zigler and Seitz, 1978:739). As well, researchers now acknowledge that children begin with differing "biological predispositions which cannot easily be changed by caretakers" (Zigler and Seitz, 1978:739).

Socialization as a Two-Way Process

The image of the child as passive recipient of socialization implied that socialization was a one-way process. Socialization theories such as learning and psychoanalytic theories encouraged this idea that parents were on the dispensing end and children on the receiving end (Bush and Simmons, 1981:162).

Socialization is now seen to be a two-way process. Just as the parents socialize the child, the child socializes the parents (Bell and Harper, 1977; Osofsky, 1970; Rheingold, 1969). This mutual influence extends from infancy, where the effect of an infant's cry upon the mother is "all out of proportion to his age, size and accomplishments" (Rheingold, 1966, quoted in Peters, 1982:3), through adolescence (Peters, 1982), and into adulthood.

Socialization as a Life-Long Process

Earlier research, under the influence of psychoanalytic theory, stressed the first years of childhood. By contrast, current work distinguishes between primary socialization (which occurs in childhood and adolescence) and adult socialization. Although primary socialization lays the foundation for later learning, it cannot completely prepare people for adulthood. For one thing, our age-graded society confronts individuals with new role expectations as they move through life. Moving beyond the family into the neighbourhood, entering school, becoming an adolescent, choosing an occupation, marrying, bearing children, encountering middle age, retiring, and dying all involve new lessons to be learned.

Also, society changes, and people must, therefore, equip themselves to cope with new situations (e.g., technological job obsolescence, war, changes in sexual mores). Finally, some individuals encounter specialized situations with which they must deal. Geographical and social mobility, marital breakdowns, and physical handicaps all require further socialization (Brim, 1966).

An important issue related to the view of socialization as a life-long process concerns the degree of continuity and consistency of personality throughout life (Bush and Simmons, 1981:135; Brim and Kagan, 1980). Although earlier scholars contended that personality was fixed in childhood, contemporary social scientists tend to emphasize the malleability of the self and the possibility of continuing change. Apparently the "consequences of the events of early childhood are continually transformed by later experience, making the course of human development more open than many have believed" (Brim and Kagan, 1980:1).

Adolescent Socialization

Accompanying the general consensus that socialization is a life-long process is the rather recent realization that the socialization processes between childhood and adult years require special attention (Elder, 1968). As Ishwaran (1979:13) notes, "There is a much larger and more diverse body of literature both in theory and research on child than adolescent development." In a paper entitled "The Canadian Adolescent: A Relatively Unknown Quantity," Harper (1980) concurs that there has been a neglect of research on this vital part of the life cycle. He goes on to remark that much of the research which has been done on adolescence in North America and Europe in the past fifteen years has been "crisis research" in that

> the content of the studies has been heavily focussed on social problems, such as illicit drugs, alcohol use, tobacco smoking, sexuality and pregnancy, venereal disease and delinquency. Studies of normal adolescent development have been modest (Harper, 1980:117).

A central theoretical issue here is whether sociologists should regard adolescent socialization as continuous or discontinuous with the preceding period of childhood socialization and the succeeding period of adult socialization (Elkin and Handel, 1972:146). In other words, is the stage of adolescence a social invention and are the socialization phenomena associated with it largely self-fulfilling prophecies? Or do adolescents constitute a subsociety of their own, with unique socialization problems?

Some sociologists argue for discontinuity (see Campbell, 1969; Coleman, 1961), some for continuity (see Elkin and Handel, 1972; Elkin and Westley, 1955). Campbell (1969:823) regards adolescence as a period of tension between the "dependence of the past and the independence of the future," with special challenges to be handled: becoming less oriented to parents and more oriented to peers and other adults; finding answers to the question "Who am I?"; and experimenting with new roles. However, Elkin and Handel (1972:149) argue that the continuities between adolescent and adult values and behaviour outweigh the discontinuities.

A closely related theoretical question (which has been asked since the turn of the century [Hall, 1904]) is this: Is adolescence, as a major role transition, a period of storm and stress compared to childhood (Simmons et al., 1979)?

In *Coming of Age in Samoa* (1928), anthropologist Margaret Mead concluded that adolescence is *not* a universally difficult phase of life. However, a controversial new book, *Margaret Mead and Samoa: The Making and Unmaking of an Anthropological Myth* (1983), written by Australian anthropologist Derek Freeman, disagrees. Whereas Mead reported Samoan adolescents as tranquil, Freeman claims that these teenagers are and have been since the 1920s "every bit as rebellious and troubled as those of the industrialized world" (Rensberger, 1983:33).

Expanded Set of Socialization Agents

The classic socialization theories concentrated on the socialization link between child and parent, especially the mother. However, as mentioned earlier, various social forces have operated to decrease the amount of parent-child interaction and consequently to increase the child's involvement with other socialization agents (Gecas, 1981:177). Therefore, although the family is still seen to be the primary agent, social scientists have turned their attention to an expanded set of socialization agents—peers, mass media, schools, and community organizations, for example. In addition, mothers' recent involvement with activities outside the home has enhanced social scientists' interest in the socialization efforts of other family members, especially fathers (see Lips, 1983). The new appreciation of the life-long nature of socialization has widened the set of agents to include work settings, self-help groups, mental institutions, prisons, and religious cults. Because the topic is vast, our remarks here will be confined to peer socialization as an illustration of the general issue of the expanded agent set. Moreover, though peer influence continues through the life cycle, these comments will be limited to childhood and adolescence.

Several features of peer relationships lend uniqueness to this socialization experience (Gecas, 1981:184–195). Peer association is, for the most part, voluntary, independent of adult control, and sex segregated. It occurs between status equals and is therefore guided by egalitarian norms.

Children and adolescents learn things from one another that they could not possibly learn elsewhere. First of all, practice is provided in self-presentation and impression-management skills. "Preadolescents have a critical eye for each other's behaviours that are managed ineptly" (Gecas, 1981:186). Also, peers provide an alternative source of self-esteem to family and classroom. Finally, peers are a source of values and attitudes, especially those relevant to growing up, as well as vital information (and misinformation) (Gecas, 1981:186). Adults are ignorant of many aspects of reality that matter to children.

Educational authorities and parents (as well as social scientists intrigued with the adolescent continuity-discontinuity debate discussed above) have been especially interested in the high school peer group and competition between its values and "official" school and parental values. Friends do share attitudes which are at variance with adults' attitudes on such things as drug use (Kandel, 1978) and musical tastes (Tanner, 1981). However, when the issue is teenagers' future life goals and educational aspirations rather than their current life styles, parents are a more important influence than peers (Davies and Kandel, 1981).

Gender Socialization

About fifteen years ago, in response to the women's liberation movement, social scientists became interested in *gender socialization*, the processes through which people learn to be masculine or feminine according to the expectations current in their society. In gender patterns, as in social behaviour in general, both biology and environment are implicated. Biochemical and genetic factors set the stage, but culture and history provide the script of social life (Kunkel, 1977). So far as the *processes* of gender socialization are concerned, the general socialization theories discussed earlier apply. Therefore, this discussion will focus on *parental behaviour* and the *content* of gender socialization (MacKie, 1983a).

Sex typing may begin even before birth. During the last few months of pregnancy, an active fetus that kicks and moves a great deal is often thought of by its parents as male. Similarly, folk wisdom relates a child's prenatal position to its sex. Boys are supposedly

carried high and girls low (Lewis, 1972). From the moment of their entry into the world, female and male infants are handled differently. Girls are cuddled and talked to more, while boys are jostled and played with more roughly. Up to six months of age boys are handled more than girls, but after that the amount of handling of male infants diminishes (Lewis, 1972).

Parents treat girls as if they were more fragile than boys (Minton, Kagan, and Levine, 1971; Pederson and Robson, 1969). Boys are more likely to be punished by spanking and other forms of physical punishment (Maccoby and Jacklin, 1974), while girls tend to receive gentle verbal reprimands (Serbin et al., 1973). Parents give boys of preschool and elementary school age much more freedom from special permission or adult accompaniment in the physical environment than they do girls of the same age (Landy, 1965). Parents are extremely upset by any sign that their boys are "sissies," while girls are encouraged to be neat, obedient, and "feminine" in both behaviour and dress. (Descriptions of these studies were compiled by Sidorowicz and Lunney, 1980.) Fox (1977:809) concludes that early childhood studies of gender learning show that "even as infants, girls are expected to be, thought to be, and rewarded for being quieter, more passive, more controlled—in short, 'nicer' babies—than are boys."

Though a child's adult socializers place it in a sex class at birth, it is a few years before the child responds to herself or himself in terms of gender. By the age of three a child can accurately and consistently answer the question, "Are you a girl or a boy?" At the same age children show preferences for either "girl" or "boy" toys and activities (Kessler and McKenna, 1978:101,102).

Parents' choice of toys reinforces their gender expectations. Cultural norms, to a certain extent, determine which toys are considered appropriate for each sex. Toy manufacturers comply with these norms

(Chafetz, 1974), and parents supply their children with sex-typed playthings. Ambert (1976:71) says that "boy toys . . . encourage rougher play, activity, creativity, mastery, and curiosity; girl toys, on the other hand, encourage passivity, observation, simple behaviour, and solitary play."

Stereotypes, that is, consensual beliefs about masculine and feminine qualities, are an important segment of society's gender scripts (Laws, 1979). Broverman et al. (1972) found that gender traits fall into a feminine warmth-expressiveness cluster and a masculine competency cluster. Men are seen to be aggressive, independent, active, and competitive; women are seen as gentle, quiet, and sensitive to the feelings of others. These traits reflect the traditional sexual division of labour. Men are expected to work outside the home, marry, and support their families, while women are expected to marry, carry the major responsibility for child rearing, and rely on men for financial support and social status. Although the woman too may work outside the home, attracting a suitable mate and looking after his interests (and eventually those of her children) take priority over serious occupational commitment (MacKie, 1979). The traditional male gender role also restricts their human potentiality:

> [It] allows men few options other than full-time employment, discourages them from expressing emotions and developing close relationships with other men, and leads to a high rate of stress-related diseases (Baker and Baker, 1980:547).

Evidence does exist that Canadian children learn about stereotypes as part of the socialization process. Lambert's (1971) questionnaire study of the gender imagery of 7,500 Canadian children, ten to seventeen years old, established that the children were aware of differential societal expectations for females and males. He reported that boys were considerably more traditional in their thinking about the genders than the girls.

Not only do children learn that males and females have different traits and engage in different activities, but they also learn that masculinity is more highly valued than femininity. Richer's (1983) observational study of Ottawa kindergarten children nicely illustrates this point. A boy coming in contact with a girl was supposedly in danger of contracting "girl germs." The only way to ward off "girl germs" was the enactment of a "purification ritual." The boy who had been unlucky enough to touch a girl was to cross his fingers as soon as possible, preferably while still in contact with the girl. Richer observes that

> the fact that the expression "boy germs" was never used and that, in general, the girls made no effort to challenge the girl germs label is indicative of the very early acceptance by both sexes of a hierarchical division between males and females (Richer, 1983:118).

Intrasocietal Variations in Socialization

A continuing trend in socialization research is the examination of the ways various segments of society differ in their socialization practices and the outcomes of those practices (Zigler and Seitz, 1978:744). The heterogeneous nature of Canadian society complicates the socialization process. Although many values and norms are shared by all Canadians, differences are found by language, by region, by ethnic group, by religion, by social class, and by place of residence (urban or rural). These variations in social environment bring with them variations in the content of socialization. Social class, which is the most studied demographic variation in socialization (Wright and Wright, 1976), will serve to illustrate the broader problem of intrasocietal variations in socialization. (For ethnic variations in Canadian families, see Elkin, 1983 and Ishwaran, 1980.)

Members of different social classes, by

virtue of experiencing different conditions of life, come to see the world differently and develop different conceptions of social reality (Gecas, 1976; Kohn, 1977). A cross-national study of child-rearing values was carried out among French- and English-speaking Canadians (as well as parents in the United States, Japan, and six European countries). Working-class parents almost everywhere were more likely than middle-class parents to be intolerant of children's insolence and tempers, to restrict autonomy, to insist on good manners, and to wish to maintain male-female distinctions (Lambert, Hamers, and Frasure-Smith, 1980).

A study of Hamilton, Ontario parents (Pineo and Looker, 1983) also found a relationship between parents' place in the social stratification system and the values they endorse for their children. These researchers reported that middle-class parents were more likely than working-class parents to value self-direction in their adolescent children.

The class origins of a child remain important. They are a significant influence on the occupation that a child will eventually choose (Breton, 1972; Porter et al., 1973). Indeed, the evidence suggests that children have a high probability of achieving a class position very similar to that of their parents (Pike, 1975). Lower-class children are relatively less successful in school, leave school earlier, and have lower occupational aspirations. Middle-class parents are more likely to socialize their children to internalize the values of individualism, high motivation, and deferred gratification required for success in school (Pike, 1975)....

References

Ambert, Anne-Marie. 1976. *Sex Structure*, 2d ed. Don Mills: Longman Canada.

Baker, Maureen and Bakker, Hans. 1980. "The Double Bind of the Middle-Class Male: Men's Liberation and the Male Sex Role." *Journal of Comparative Family Studies* XI (4):547–561.

Bandura, A. 1977. *Social Learning Theory*. Englewood Cliffs, N.J.: Prentice-Hall.

―――― and Walters, R.H. 1963. *Social Learning and Personality Development*. New York: Holt, Rinehart and Winston.

Bell, Richard O. and Harper, Laurence V. 1977. *Child Effects on Adults*. New York: John Wiley.

Bem, Sandra Lipsitz. 1983. "Gender Schema Theory and Its Implications for Child Development: Raising Gender-Aschematic Children in Gender-Schematic Society." *Signs* 8:598–616.

Breton, Raymond. 1972. *Social and Academic Factors in the Career Decisions of Canadian Youth*. Ottawa: Information Canada.

Brill, A.A., ed. and trans. 1938. *The Basic Writings of Sigmund Freud*. New York: Modern Library.

Brim, Orville G., Jr. 1966. "Socialization Through the Life Cycle." In Orville G. Brim, Jr. and Stanton Wheeler. *Socialization After Childhood: Two Essays,* pp. 1–49. New York: John Wiley.

―――― and Kagan, Jerome. 1980. "Constancy and Change: a View of the Issues." In Orville G. Brim, Jr. and Jerome Kagan, eds. *Constancy and Change in Human Development,* pp. 1–25. Cambridge, Mass.: Harvard University Press.

Broverman, I.K.; Vogel, S.R.; Broverman, D.M.; Carlson, F.E.; and Rosenkrantz, P.S. 1972. "Sex-Role Stereotypes: a Current Appraisal." *Journal of Social Issues* 28:59–78.

Bush, Diane Mitsch and Simmons, Roberta G. 1981. "Socialization Processes Over the Life Course." In Morris Rosenberg and Ralph H. Turner. eds. *Social Psychology: Sociological Perspectives,* pp. 133–164. New York: Basic Books.

Campbell, Ernest Q. 1969. "Adolescent Socialization." In David A. Goslin, ed. *Handbook of Socialization Theory and Research,* pp. 821–860. Chicago: Rand McNally.

Chafetz, Janet Saltzman. 1974. *Masculine/Feminine or Human?* Itasca, Ill.: Peacock.

Coleman, James S. 1961. *The Adolescent Society.* New York: The Free Press.

Cooley, Charles H. 1902. *Human Nature and the Social Order.* New York: Charles Scribner's Sons.

Davies, Mark and Kandel, Denise B. 1981. "Parental and Peer Influences on Adolescents' Educational Plans: Some Further Evidence." *American Journal of Sociology* 87:363–387.

Denzin, Norman K. 1977. *Childhod Socialization.* San Francisco: Jossey-Bass.

Elder, Glen H., Jr. 1968. "Adolescent Socialization and Development." In Edgar F. Borgatta and William W. Lambert, eds. *Handbook of Personality Theory and Research,* pp. 239–364. Chicago: Rand McNally.

———. 1983. "Family Socializaiton and Ethnic Identity." In K. Ishwaran, ed. *The Canadian Family,* pp. 145–158. Toronto: Gage.

——— and Handel, Gerald. 1972. *The Child and Society: The Process of Socialization.* 2d ed. New York: Random House.

——— and Westley, William A. 1955. "The Myth of Adolescent Culture." *American Sociological Review* 20:680–684.

Erikson, Erik. 1963. *Childhood and Society,* 2d ed. New York: Norton.

———. 1968. *Identity: Youth and Crisis* New York: Norton.

Ewen, Robert B. 1980. *An Introduction to Theories and Personality.* New York: Academic Press.

Fox, Greer Litton. 1977. "'Nice Girl': Social Control of Women Through a Value Construct." *Signs* 2:805–817.

Gecas, Viktor. 1976. "The Socialization and Child-Care Roles." In F. Ivan Nye, ed. *Role Structure and Analysis of the Family,* pp. 33–59. Beverly Hills: Sage.

———. 1981. "Contexts of Socialization." In Morris Rosenberg and Ralph H. Turner, eds. *Social Psychology: Sociological Perspectives,* pp. 165–199. New York: Basic Books.

Hall, G.S. 1904. *Adolescence.* New York: Appleton.

Harper, Frank B.W. 1980. "The Canadian Adolescent: a Relatively Unknown Quantity." SSHRC Workshop on the Family and Socialization of Children in Canada, University of Western Ontario.

Ishwaran, K. 1979. "Childhood and Adolescence in Canada: an Overview of Theory and Research." In K. Ishwaran, ed. *Childhood and Adolescence in Canada,* pp. 3–36. Toronto: McGraw-Hill Ryerson.

———. 1980. *Canadian Families: Ethnic Variations.* Toronto: McGraw-Hill Ryerson.

Kandel, Denise B. 1978. "Homophily, Selection, and Socialization in Adolescent Friendships." *American Journal of Sociology* 84:427–436.

Kessler, Suzanne J. and McKenna, Wendy. 1978. *Gender: An Ethnomethodological Approach.* New York: John Wiley.

Kohlberg, Laurence. 1976. "Moral Stages and Moralization: the Cognitive-Development Approach." In T. Lickona. *Moral Development and Behavior.* New York: Holt, Rinehart and Winston.

Kohn, Melvin L. 1977. *Class and Conformity,* 2d ed. Homewood, Ill.: Dorsey.

Kubat, Daniel and Thornton, David. 1974. *A Statistical Profile of Canadian Society.* Toronto: McGraw-Hill Ryerson.

Kunkel, John H. 1977. "Sociobiology vs. Biosociology." *The American Sociologist* 12:69–73.

Lambert, Ronald D. 1971. "Sex Role Imagery in Children: Social Origins of Mind." In *Studies of The Royal Commission on the Status of Women in Canada,* No. 6. Ottawa: Information Canada.

Lambert, Wallace E.; Hamers, Josiane F.; and Frasure-Smith, Nancy. 1980. *Child-Rearing Values; A Cross-National Study.* New York: Praeger.

Landy, D. 1965. *Tropical Childhood.* New York: Harper and Row.

Laws, Judith Long. 1979. *The Second X: Sex Role and Social Role.* New York: Elsevier.

Levinson, Daniel J. et al. 1978. *The Seasons of a Man's Life.* New York: Ballantine.

Lewis, Michael. 1972. "Culture and Gender Roles: There's No Unisex in the Nursery." *Psychology Today* 5:54–57.

Lowe, Marian. 1978. "Sociobiology and Sex Differences." *Signs* 4:118–125.

Maccoby, Eleanor E. and Jacklin, Carol N. 1974. *The Psychology of Sex Differences.* Standford, Calif.: Stanford University Press.

MacKie, Marlene. 1979. "Gender Socialization in Childhood and Adolescence." In K. Ishwaran, ed. *Childhood and Adolescence in Canada,* pp. 136–160. Toronto: McGraw-Hill Ryerson.

———. 1980. "Socialization." In Robert Hagedorn, ed. *Sociology,* pp. 123–161. Toronto: Holt, Rinehart and Winston.

———. 1983a. *Exploring Gender Relations: A Canadian Perspective.* Toronto: Butterworths.

———. 1983b. "Socialization." In Robert Hagedorn, ed. *Sociology,* 2d ed., pp. 59–89. Toronto: Holt, Rinehart and Winston.

Mead, George Herbert. 1934. *Mind, Self and Society.* Chicago: University of Chicago Press.

Mead, Margaret. 1928. *Coming of Age in Samoa.* New York: Morrow.

———. 1935. *Sex and Temperment in Three Primitive Societies.* New York: Deli.

Miller, N.E. and Dollard, J. 1941. *Social Learning and Imitation.* New Haven: Yale University Press.

Minton, C.; Kagan, J.; and Levine, J. 1971. "Maternal Control and Obedience in the Two-Year-Old-Child." *Child Development* 42:1873–1894.

Osofsky, Joy D. 1970. "The Shaping of Mother's Behavior by Children." *Journal of Marriage and the Family* 32:400–405.

Pederson, F. and Robson, K. 1969. "Father Participation in Infancy." *American Journal of Psychiatry* 39:466–472.

Peters, John 1982. "Children as Socialization Agents Through the Parents' Middle-Years." Paper presented at the Canadian Sociology and Anthropology Association meetings in April 1, Ottawa.

Piaget, Jean. 1928. *Judgment and Reasoning in the Child.* New York: Harcourt.

———. 1932. *The Moral Judgment of the Child.* New York: Harcourt.

———. 1970. *Structuralism.* New York: Basic Books.

Pike, Robert M. 1975. "Introduction and Overview." In Robert M. Pike and Elia Zureik, eds. *Socialization and Values in Canadian Society,* vol. 2, pp. 1–25. Toronto: McClelland and Stewart.

Pineo, Peter C. and Looker, E. Dianne. 1983. "Class and Conformity in the Canadian Setting." *Canadian Journal of Sociology* 8:293–317.

Pines, Maya. 1981. "The Civilizing of Genie." *Psychology Today* 15:28–34.

Porter, Marion; Porter, John; and Blishen, Bernard. 1973. *Does Money Matter?* Toronto: Institute for Behavioural Research, York University.

Rensberger, Boyce. 1983. "Margaret Mead: the Nature-Nurture Debate I." *Science* 83:28–37.

Rheingold, Harriet L. 1966. "The Development of Social Behavior in the Human Infant." In H.W. Stevenson, ed. *Concept of Development: A Report of a Conference Commemoration of the 40th Anniversary of the Institute of Child Development, University of Minnesota.* Monographs of the Society for Research in Child Development: 31(5, whole no. 107).

———. 1969. "The Social and Socializing Infant." In David A. Goslin, ed. *Handbook of Socialization Theory and Research,* pp. 779–790. Chicago: Rand McNally.

Rich, A. 1980. "Compulsory Heterosexuality and Lesbian Experience." *Signs* 5(4): 631–660.

Richer, Stephen. 1983. "Sex Role Socialization: Agents, Content, Relationships, and Outcomes." In K. Ishwaran, ed. *The Canadian Family,* pp. 117–125. Toronto: Gage.

Rosenberg, Morris. 1981. "The Self-Concept: Social Product and Social Force." In Morris Rosenberg and Ralph H. Turner, eds. *Social Psychology: Sociological Perspectives,* pp. 593–624. New York: Basic Books.

Sayers, Janet, 1980. "Biological Determinism, Psychology and the Division of Labour by Sex." *International Journal of Women's Studies* 3:241–260.

Scaife, Michael. 1979. "Observing Infant Social Development: Theoretical Perspectives, Natural Observation, and Video Recording," In G.P. Ginsburg, ed. *Emerging Strategies in Social Psychological Research,* pp. 93–116. New York: John Wiley.

Serbin, L.; O'Leary, K.; Kent, R.; and Tonick, I. 1973. "A Comparison of Teacher Response to the Preacademic and Problem Behavior of Boys and Girls." *Child Development* 44:796–804.

Shaw, Marvin E. and Costanzo, Philip R. 1970. *Theories of Social Psychology.* New York: McGraw-Hill.

Sheehy, Gail. 1974. *Passages: Predictable Crises in Adult Life.* New York: Dutton.

Sidorowicz, Laura S. and Lunney, G. Sparks. 1980. "Baby X Revisited." *Sex Roles* 6:67–73.

Tanner, Julian. 1981. "Pop Music and Peer Groups: A Study of Canadian High School Students' Responses to Pop Music." *Canadian Review of Sociology and Anthropology* 18:1–13.

Wilson, Edward O. 1975. *Sociobiology: The New Synthesis.* Cambridge, Mass.: Harvard University Press.

Wright, James D. and Wright, Sonia R. 1976. "Social Class and Parental Values for Children: a Partial Replication and Extension of the Kohn Thesis." *American Sociological Review* 41:527–537.

Wrong, Dennis H. 1961. "The Oversocialized Conception of Man in Modern Sociology." *American Sociological Review* 26:183–193.

Yussen, Steven R. and Santrock, John W. 1978. *Child Development.* Dubuque, Iowa: Wm. C. Brown.

Zigler, Edward and Seitz, Victoria. 1978. "Changing Trends in Socialization Theory and Research." *American Behavioral Scientist* 21:731–756.

12 Exchange, Co-operation, and Competition

Peter Archibald

PETER ARCHIBALD, Associate Professor of Sociology at McMaster University, specializes in the study of social psychology, theory and political economy. His recent work includes *Social Psychology as Political Economy* (1978); "Propertylessness and alienation: Re-opening a 'shut' case," with O. Adams and J.W. Gartrell (1981); "Psychic alienation in Marx: The missing link" (1983); and "Agency and alienation: Marx's theories of individuation and history" (1985). He is currently completing a book about Marx's conception of human nature, what appears to be wrong with it, and the significance of that conception for Marxian theorizing. Professor Archibald has presented scholarly papers at a variety of national and international conferences.

Are people naturally egoistic or self-interested, eager to compete with each other and to cooperate only on a contractual basis, or is the *opposite* perhaps the case? Do such propensities themselves perhaps vary considerably with variations in social conditions, and if so, *do* such conditions characterize alienation, anomie, or faulty communication? These are the questions we shall try to answer here.

FUN IN GAMES AND COALITIONS

Of the situations social psychologists have used to study cooperation and competition, by far the most popular are those associated with experimental games. For this purpose, the most popular game studied, the "Prisoner's Dilemma," is in some respects ideal, for built into the game are fairly equal incentives to be cooperative and competitive, such that if one finds a preference for one or the other it should presumably tell us something about the players' normal predilections in everyday life. Luce and Raiffa (1957:95) describe the thinking behind the Prisoner's Dilemma in this way:

> Two suspects are taken into custody and separated. The District Attorney is certain that they are guilty of a specific crime, but he does not have adequate evidence to convict them at a trial. He points out to each prisoner that he has two alternatives: to confess to the crime the police are sure they have done, or not to confess. If they both do not confess, then the District Attorney states he will book them on some very minor trumped-up charge such as petty larceny and illegal possession of a weapon, and they would both receive minor punishments; if they both confess they will be prosecuted, but he will recommend less than the most severe sentence; but if one confesses and the other does not, then the confessor will receive lenient treatment for turning state's evidence, whereas the latter will get "the book" slapped at him.

In actual experimental situations subjects are usually presented with a "matrix" of choices and outcomes which simplifies the information they must consider in making their choice. Thus, for example, Edward Jones and Harold Gerard (1967:563) quantify the prisoner's situation in approximately this way:

| | Prisoner B | |
	Not Confess	Confess
Prisoner A Not confess	One year each	Ten years for A Three months for B
Confess	Three months for A Ten years for B	Eight years each

More typically, however, subjects play for points or money on the basis of a matrix as this one:

| | Player B | |
	Choice X	Choice Y
Player A Choice X	4¢, 4¢	−8¢, +8¢
Choice Y	+8¢, −8¢	−12¢, −12¢

How do Canadian and American college students typically act in such a situation? While the percentage of X or cooperative choices may range anywhere from 10 to 90, depending upon a number of different conditions, the average tends to be about 45 percent (Scheff and Chewning, 1968; cited in Secord and Backman, 1974:270; Vinacke, 1969). In other words, subjects are more likely to be competitive than cooperative in these situations, *in spite of* the fact that they lose out by being so! Surprisingly, this outcome often persists even after subjects have had a chance to see previous outcomes (e.g., Kelley and Grzelak, 1972). *In fact*, knowing that one's opponent has been completely cooperative,

what Lave (1965) calls the "Ghandi" pattern of nonviolent behaviour, does *not* increase the likelihood that one will also be cooperative. Rather, one tends to exploit him or her by taking advantage of the other's cooperation (Bixenstine, Potash, and Wilsen, 1963; Lave, 1965).

Now, on the one hand such findings can and have been interpreted as supporting Exchange Theory. However, a moment's reflection reveals that they hardly flatter it. Specifically, whereas in this theory competitiveness is supposed to be the result of, and basis for, rationality, in that it is said to be an effective means for individuals to satisfy their best self-interests and for a society to satisfy the interests of the majority of its members, in such situations as the Prisoner's Dilemma the competitiveness we find appears anything but rational. . . .

The defense of our rationality and/or basic cooperativeness has usually taken either or both of two forms. Experimental games, so one argument goes, are after all games where the stakes are *so* low that it is not in fact *very* irrational to lose by competing. The second argument is that since they are "only games," subjects are expected to be, and expect their opponents to be, competitive. Hence when there is no communication between players it is actually rational to presume that one's opponent will not cooperate and therefore to act in kind. Similarly, when subjects do not actually communicate they will understandably suspect the motives of an unconditionally cooperative opponent; however, when they can communicate and dispel this distrust, cooperation will ensue.

These arguments have indeed received considerable support in subsequent research. Thus increasing the size of the stakes does seem to increase cooperation in the Prisoner's Dilemma (see Vinacke's review, 1969), as does permitting subjects to communicate (e.g., Swingle and Santi, 1972). Hence on this round, at least, Exchange Theorists can breathe a sigh of relief. Yet note that even these additional findings do little for those who would apologize for our own society by concluding that we are basically cooperative.

In the first place, the Prisoner's Dilemma clearly has a built-in incentive to cooperate; that is, if the players do so, they will receive lighter sentences. Similarly, that they in fact initially distrust each other and have to communicate for some time before becoming "cooperative" (in this case, not destroying each other) probably tells us something in and of itself about the propensities of people in our society, or at least, of our college students. Finally, there is reason to believe that when subjects do communicate in such experiments they are at least as likely to threaten retaliation if the opponent does not cooperate as to appeal to latent propensities to cooperate (Deutsch and Krauss, 1960).

Secondly, while Jones and Gerard (1967:577) among others appear to have concluded from the stakes-and-communication results that people will therefore be more cooperative in real life than in experimental games, the validity of such a conclusion is by no means obvious. In the "Great" Depression of the 1930s, for example, the stakes were extremely high and there was a great deal of communicating, yet people sometimes even stole their own friends' jobs by offering to work for less pay (Broadfoot, 1975). Similarly, when I give my students a particularly difficult examination question I often encourage the class to discuss the answer collectively, yet many students actually refuse to participate on the grounds that they will give away their own, presumably good, ideas.

The thrust of these two examples is, of course, no deep mystery, for both entail a fundamental conflict of interest which appears to have overridden any cooperative effects which high stakes and accurate communication might otherwise have had. Nor need such a conclusion rest upon such selective examples, since it is already implied in the very experimental research we have been considering. Morton Deutsch (1960),

for example, found that communication did indeed increase cooperation after subjects had been instructed to simply concentrate upon winning without worrying about how much their "opponent" won, but not after other subjects had been instructed to win over/against their opponent.

Given such findings as these, whether the our-society-is-okay interpretation of studies reporting increased cooperation after communication is valid depends a great deal upon the particular juxtaposition of interests built into the experimental social structure. Certainly a considerable amount of other experimental research with high stakes and communication indicates high levels of competition.

For example, subjects with the choice of entering several different coalitions with differing degrees of inequality of outcomes for the two partners were much more likely to choose the coalition which brought themselves the highest individual outcome than the coalition which would have made the outcomes more equal and *still* permitted the coalition to be a winning one (Gamson, 1961). Similarly, following a suggestion by Simmel, Theodore Mills (1960) found that in a group discussion where members were supposed to agree upon a story about a picture, the dominant tendency was for two of his male subjects to participate more than a third and express more liking and support for each other than for the third member of the group. Interestingly, given Blau's excursus on love, when the groups are of mixed sex the two members in the majority sex appear to compete for the third, minority member of the opposite sex. This is suggested by Reginald Robson's findings at the University of British Columbia (1971:15), which indicate that the most frequent coalition is one "between the minority-sex member and one of the two members of the other sex."

Clearly what is needed to resolve the issue of whether the competition and cooperation which occur in the laboratory are representative of the wider society is a more systematic attempt to compare different interaction settings.

One interesting attempt to do so is an experiment by William Dorris (1972), who had college students interact with rare-coin shop owners in the Los Angeles area. Each student described his situation to the coin dealer in one of two ways: in a *"Neutral"* condition he simply said that he was getting rid of his coins because he had decided to give up coin collecting, while in a *"Moral Appeal"* condition he said that he was selling his coins because he needed the money for school books and other things connected with going to college. Furthermore, in this latter condition the student added that he was worried about being exploited, and that he had been told by another coin collector who knew the dealer that the dealer could be trusted. The results clearly indicate that students were offered more for a particular coin in the Moral Appeal than in the Neutral condition (i.e., an average of $13.63 as compared with $8.72). Furthermore, additional information suggests that the dealer was more concerned with the personal welfare of the student in the Moral Appeal condition, in that there was more eye contact with the student, he took longer to make his offer, gave more information about the coin, and was more likely to suggest a more profitable alternative to accepting his own offer.

Dorris suggests that aside from offering higher stakes and greater opportunities for communication than most laboratory game situations, his experiment gives the potentially exploitative player a reason for his opponent's unconditionally cooperative behaviour. That is, since the student says he wants to sell his coins because he is no longer interested in collecting or needs the money, and knows very little about their real worth, he reduces the likelihood that his opponent will mistrust his motives in being unconditionally cooperative. Furthermore, whereas opponents are often anonymous in laboratory games, in the present experiment they are face-to-face and can identify each other.

Dorris' arguments make sense, particularly in explaining the differences in results between the Moral Appeal and Neutral conditions. The importance for the student of getting a good price for the coin is indeed more obvious in the Moral Appeal condition and, as we shall see later, exploitation generally seems to be more difficult if one is face-to-face with one's exchange partner. However, whether these findings of higher levels of cooperation than is usually the case in laboratory games warrant the degree of relief Dorris expresses is questionable.

First, remember that in the Moral Appeal condition the dealer is supposed to have been recommended to the student by another collector who attests to his trustworthiness. For one thing, this may put the dealer in the position of having to live up to a reputation that, while he may not in fact deserve it, is nevertheless flattering and hence worth living up to on this occasion. For another, however, and this is considerably less flattering, this knowledge places the self-interest of the dealer in the Moral Appeal condition much more clearly in line with that of the student; that is, because he has been recommended to the student by another coin dealer, the dealer in the Moral Appeal condition may be likely to feel that he will lose business if he violates his reputation and exploits the student.

Second, it is important to look at the absolute levels of the prices offered to the student. Specifically, while Dorris suggests (1972:394) that "discussions with informants indicated that offers of $12 and greater should be considered fair and that a dealer might legitimately offer considerably less if he had no particular need for the coins or honestly felt they were overgraded," we should note that the average of $8.75 for the Neutral condition is obviously unfair. Also, it is important to ask whether most buying and selling situations in our society are characterised by neutral or morally appealing conditions.

The answer is not easy to come by, but one suspects that the personal testimonies of Dorris' Moral Appeal condition are in fact less frequent than the impersonality of his Neutral condition. Although this may be changing for the better of late, one suspects that most of us would still be embarrassed to give strangers such "sob stories." The very ease with which we evoke the latter term, and others such as "What's his line?" or, "Yeh, I've heard that one before," suggests that impersonality, not personality, is the rule rather than the exception in our business dealings. . . .

From the evidence we have considered thus far, one can only conclude that while Exchange Theory has not come through untainted, it has fared a great deal better than its Functionalist and Symbolic Interactionist critics. Specifically, however "rational" their competitiveness may appear, *the North American people studied hardly strike one as beacons of cooperation.* Similarly, *whereas in these studies communication sometimes increases cooperation,* as Durkheim and Cooley would have had us believe, *it is doubtful that it does so where there are substantial conflicts of interest.*

Should we therefore become Exchange Theorists? Two other considerations arising from the findings of experimental research by social psychologists suggest that this would be premature at this point.

In the first place, by no means all of the experimental subjects in these studies have evidenced the competitiveness we have been describing. This has been particularly true of women. While sex differences in competitiveness in Prisoner's Dilemma-related games have never been great, and, by the present time, appear to have disappeared altogether,[1] in coalition formation experiments women have been much less egoistic. In the Gamson-type experiment with "material" stakes, for example, females have been much more likely to form three-way (really *non*coalitions) than two-against-one coalitions and divide the outcome equally instead of unequally on the

basis of initial input-advantages (see Gamson, 1964). Similarly, when approval is the "good" in question, as in Robson's research, women again tend to avoid establishing coalitions which exclude third parties.

Secondly, there is considerable evidence against the claim that, when it does occur, competition has more beneficial effects than cooperation. The classic experiment here is again one by Morton Deutsch (1949). In this study, students in an introductory psychology course were given the option of participating in an experiment instead of attending the normal three one-hour classes a week. Those who volunteered were divided into groups of five, each of which worked on several tasks. Some of these tasks were logical puzzles; others were "human relations" problems, such as having to decide whether and how to discipline children in a summer camp. However, the conditions under which these groups worked on these tasks varied; that is, half of the groups were competitively and half were cooperatively oriented. The characteristics of the *Competitive* groups were similar to those of classes in the schools and universities of our society. Thus, whereas subjects were told that they were working "as a group," they were also told that their grade for the course would be determined by ranking their *individual* contributions to the solution of the "group" problems. *Cooperative* groups, on the other hand, were told that entire groups rather than individuals would be ranked, with individual group members' grades for the course being identical to the ranking of their entire group.

The results of this classic experiment hardly support the argument that competition is superior to cooperation. Looking first at the productivity of the two types of groups, one finds that Cooperative groups not only produced more and better recommendations as solutions for the problems, but produced them in less time as well. Moving on to other consequences of the two types of conditions, one finds considerable difference in the nature of the interaction among members of the two types of groups. Thus subjects in Cooperative groups were friendlier toward each other, communicated more, and communicated with fewer difficulties than did subjects in Competitive groups. . . .

Deutsch's results are matched to a remarkable extent by those of a field study by Peter Blau (1955), conducted long before Blau became such a fervent exponent of Exchange Theory. Thus in examining two different sections of a public employment agency, Blau found that while the supervisor of section "A" "relied heavily on individual performance records in evaluating interviewers," the supervisor of section "B" did not, and was also more lenient in his evaluations. As was the case with the Deutsch study, the nature of the interaction of the interviewers within each section was also different; that is, those in section A were not only much more likely to avoid each other, but also to hoard the files of job applicants so as to get better individual performance records. This worked for some individuals, in that the more competitive an individual in section A was, the more productive he or she was. However, the overall productivity of section A, the Competitive section, was actually *lower* than that of section B, the Cooperative section. Interestingly, being competitive was not advantageous to individuals in section B, because whereas cooperative members of this section tended to tell each other about interesting job vacancies, competitive members tended to be excluded from this individually advantageous sharing process.

At the very least, these two new sets of considerations suggest a serious qualification to our previous conclusion. Specifically, *experimental research on cooperation and competition only appears to support Exchange Theory so well to the extent that one rather conveniently excludes sex differences* (and others we shall get to shortly) *and fails to compare the effects of cooperation with that of competition.*

Put otherwise, Exchange Theorists in our own time appear to have had a propensity to do what they did in Marx's; that is, to use *within* system evidence to justify the *system* itself. If this is the case, then to better test the validity of Exchange Theory we should compare the potentially biased research findings we first considered with those obtained by studying people in societies whose political-economic institutions are very different from our own.

"PRIMITIVE" PEOPLES: ARE THEY "JUST LIKE US?"

Although this seems to be an eminently reasonable procedure, the amount of cross-cultural research on cooperation and competition by social psychologists is dismally small. To date, the major contribution of social psychologists seems to be a single but impressive research program undertaken by Spencer Kagan, Millard Madsen and their associates, comparing particularly urban American and rural Mexican children.

In one of their experiments (Kagan and Madsen, 1972), children played a game analogous to the Prisoner's Dilemma, but simplified through the use of marbles and a pictorially presented set of matrices. These are presented below.

The circles represent marbles, which the children could trade in for toys after the experiment. The child faces the matrix from the bottom. Thus in Case 1 he is told that if he chooses the right-hand choice he will get two marbles and his opponent will get one, while if he chooses the left-hand choice he will get three and his opponent will get three. The reader can use this example to figure out the outcomes for each of the other three cases. The important thing to notice here is that two different motives are being tempted. Thus in Case 1 the child can choose to be rivalrous or outdistance his opponent by choosing the right-hand choice, but if he does so he actually gets less than if he chooses the left-hand choice, which would equalize his and

Figure 1
CONDITIONS IN THE KAGAN AND MADSEN (1972) EXPERIMENT[2]

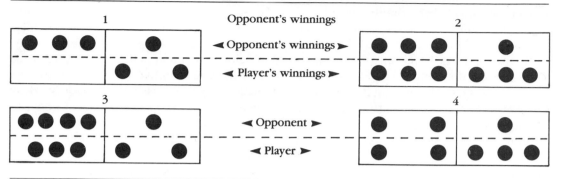

his opponent's outcomes. In Case 2 the absolute gain is constant and the choice is simply between rivalry and cooperation. In Case 3 one can win over one's opponent or let him win but still get more, and in Case 4 one can easily both win and get the maximum possible amount for oneself, the alternative being to take less and share more.

The results of this experiment could hardly be clearer. In the first place, the American children were more likely to choose the right-hand, more rivalrous move, in all four cases, that is, even when they got less for doing so. Second, if we look at the behavior of specific individuals from each of the two societies across the different cases, we find that more Americans were always rivalrous while more Mexicans were never rivalrous. Third, if we make the reasonable assumption that egoism and competitiveness are things children learn as they grow up in a particular society, we should not be surprised to learn that the behavior differences between the two sets of children increased with age. Fourth, there is little question that children who were rivalrous intended to be so, as Kagan and Madsen themselves clearly state (1972:218):[3]

> Spontaneous comments of the children corresponded to their rivalrous behaviour. Some rivalrous Anglo-American children jeered at their peers, saying, for example, "I only gave

you one. Ha! Ha!". In discussions after the experiment, rivalrous children quite readily explained their behaviour. When asked why they chose the side with less absolute gain in Condition 1, they replied, "Cause I wanted to give Jerry only one," "I wanted her to have less," or "Proque gano (because I win)." Even some 5-year-old children were able to verbalize their rivalrous intents. As one 5-year-old Anglo-American girl made her choice, she spontaneously exclaimed, "I'm going to give the most ones to me." After the experiment, another 5-year-old Anglo-American girl told the experimenter, "I wanted to have more than her."

Now, although Nelson and Kagan (1972) cite comparable findings from a study comparing Anglo-Albertans and Blackfoot Indians by Anthony G. Miller and Ron Thomas (1972), one can hardly throw out Exchange Theory after so few comparisons. Instead, we must ask whether the results obtained for rural Mexicans would be typical of those for people in "less developed" societies more generally.

Whereas Marx and Engels had drawn upon the work of such 19th century anthropologists as Lewis Morgan to formulate and support their claim that most precapitalist (and noncapitalist) peoples could be characterized as predominantly cooperative ("primitively communistic"), classical political economists at the time were still insisting that human nature is everywhere the same (except, perhaps, that primitive people are less intelligent). This insistence has persisted into the present among so-called "Economic Anthropologists," who claim to see markets and egoistic competition in such ritualistic practices as the exchange of gifts between a bride and groom's kinship groups (e.g., see Leclair and Schneider, 1968). In a different "Culture and Personality" approach, Ruth Benedict (1960) and Margaret Mead (1937) in particular appear to have attempted to neutralize any criticism of our own society by assuming a random distribution of competition across societies.

Probably a majority of contemporary anthropologists would agree that *none* of these three extreme positions adequately describes *all* of the facts. Nevertheless, an interesting assortment also appear to agree that it is the first claim, imputing *primarily* cooperation, rather than the other two which *best* describes them.

This is not to say that most of these anthropologists would agree with the Marxian explanation for this difference, as we shall see shortly. Some are Marxists (Godelier, 1972; Mandel, 1970), but others are such well-known Functionalists as Mauss (Durkheim's nephew and student) (1970) and Redfield (1962). Still others (Polanyi, 1957; Sahlins, 1972), whose skepticism of the primary importance of either evolution or capitalism gives them some affinity with Weber, have labelled themselves "substantivists" because of their attempt to develop a culture- (and ideology-) free set of concepts for the cross-cultural comparison of political-economic systems.

In spite of their diverse starting points, these various critics seem to agree to a remarkable extent on the reasons for the discrepancy between their own observations of primitive peoples and those of Exchange Theory and Culture and Personality adherents in anthropology.

In the first place, they claim, the latter observers' use of *our* political-economic categories for *primitive* societies is misleading, for whereas in our own society "economic" activity tends to be separated from family, religious, and other activities, such is not the case in these primitive societies. Nor, for that matter, are individuals in these societies likely to function as separate individuals, egoistically or otherwise. As a consequence, behavior which appears to be egoistically competitive to the outsider (e.g., haggling over a "bride price") may not actually have this function within the *context* of the society in question (e.g., Mauss claimed that the function of the bride price is to establish and cement broader social relationships among entire kinship groups). Similarly, even when such behavior *does* have this function, within the context of the society as a whole it may play a tangential rather than a dominant role.

Second, particularly when one abstracts particular behavior patterns from their context in this manner, one can easily misconstrue the *meaning* which they have for the primitive peoples themselves.

Third, whereas there may have been a time when it made sense to think of these various societies as relatively autonomous units, their discovery and contact with (and often colonial subjugation under) the "civilized" world often invalidates such an assumption. Hence many of the competitive practices attributed to primitive people (for example, the charging of "interest rates") may well have been introduced from the outside and may not have been an integral part of their original culture.

In order to illustrate these problems, probably no example is more fitting than the *"potlatch"* of the Indians on the coast of what is now British Columbia, for according to our two sets of apologists, these people were *more* competitive than we are, so much so that their culture is said to have been a *parody* of our own (Benedict, 1960:195). Here is a typical account of the potlatch:[4]

The noble families within a single village and those of neighboring settlements were in continual rivalry each to establish its greater prestige.... And it is for this reason that the famous ceremonial feasts or potlatches of the Northwest Coast Indians had such compelling importance....

Every important social event demanded a lavish ceremony: the birth of a child; the ceremony when a girl reached puberty; the burial of a relative; the assumption of a predecessor's rank and titles; the building of a new house.... For them large stores of food and gifts were accumulated in advance. New carvings were made to represent the crests of the feastgiver, who generally assumed a new name and in a dramatic performance, for which elaborate masks and costumes were worn, enacted mythological events connected with his titles.

... The giver of the feast made presents of sea otter skins, blankets, coppers and even canoes. While some of these were for services, the greater part were gifts made to the guests according to rank. Although the glory of munificence was everywhere paramount, the obligations of repayment played a prominent part, especially among the Kwakiutl. The acceptance of gifts at a feast there involved an obligation to repay them with considerable interest when the guest in turn gave a feast. A Kwakiutl would sometimes borrow material beforehand, again at high interest, in order to increase the lavishness of his gifts at the feast. Careful record was kept by official tally keepers of all these gifts which were practically forced loans, and the extent of all obligations was publicly known. Farther north, however, the repayment obligations and the idea of interest were unknown.

Property was also destroyed. Canoes and coppers were often deliberately broken, slaves were sometimes killed and valuable olachen oil would be squandered by pouring it on the fire until the leaping flames set the roof timbers on fire. By some or all these means the feast giver challenged his guests to greater orgies of destructiveness.

Renown depended on the frequency and lavishness of these celebrations (Forde, 1963:88–90).

While many of the facts cited in the above description are correct, others are not, and still others are cited so out of context that they greatly distort the true nature of the original potlatch. Thus, while one can hardly dispute that Kwakiutl chiefs were exchanging material goods for individual prestige and status and that there was considerable rivalry involved—something that is clear when one reads accounts of actual potlatches (e.g., Boas, 1969:15, 85–87)—one must hasten to add that the process was nowhere near as self-seeking as Forde implies.

In the first place, rather than viewing the potlatch primarily as a competition between individuals, the Kwakiutl viewed it as a collective effort, with everyone in the chief's kinship group contributing food and other goods to be given away at the potlatch. Nor, as Forde would have us believe (1963:88), was there in any way a "free-market" competition among individuals, such that a commoner could acquire noble status by giving a potlatch. The few instances of this happening occurred only after the white man had arrived and disrupted traditional Indian customs (Piddocke, 1968:291).

Second, while the chief's rivalrous rhetoric was indeed rampant, the actual competition was very much more sedate. For example, all four Kwakiutl tribes were usually invited to a potlatch, and after it was over they did not go off into a corner and "plot" how best to outdo the most recent performance. Rather, all four sat down together, and in their own word, "discussed" when the next potlatch would occur and what the level of gift giving would be. In this process "a Kwakiutl would subject himself to ridicule by demanding interest when he received a gift in requital of one of like amount made by him" (Curtis, 1915:143–144). Furthermore, the actual ruining of a rival appears to have been unknown. Here our Exchange Theorists would do well to pay more attention to the meaning the Kwakiutl gave to their own behavior. For example, references to cooperation and sharing are rife in the Kwakiutl songs and dreams recited by George Hunt and recorded by Boas, and considerable embarrassment about acquisitiveness seems to be evident, as when one chief says, "Am I not going to become excited and am I not going to cause to disappear the one who has the great name the Great-Cause-of-Fear, the great property, the great one that causes people to lose their senses, the one that makes people unmerciful . . . " (Boas, 1969:169).

Third and most important, in their haste to assure us that the Kwakiutl prove the generality of their theory of human nature, Exchange Theorists have ignored or conveniently forgotten the major significance of the potlatch. Specifically, whereas hedonistic man is an acquisitive one, Kwakiutl man was concerned to *give away* wealth![5] As Curtis says (1915:143–144),

> *A man can never receive through the potlatch as much as he disburses, for the simple reason that many to whom he gives will die before they have a potlatch, and others are too poor to return what he gives them. . . . When a recipient holds a potlatch he may return an equal amount or a slightly larger amount, or a smaller amount with perhaps the promise to give more at a future time.*
>
> The feelings at the bottom of the potlatch is one of pride rather than greed. Occasionally *men have tried to accumulate wealth by means of the potlatch and of lending at interest, but . . . a man can never draw out all his credits and keep the property thus acquired. Before his debtors will pay, he must first call the people together and inaugurate a potlatch, thus ensuring an immediate redistribution.* (My emphasis).

Note that whereas the Kwakiutl redistributed most of their wealth (contrary to the claims of Exchange Theorists), "philanthropy" in our society is a rather isolated and puny enterprise. For example, Canada's most generous "good corporate citizen" in 1971, Labatt's

Breweries, gave a grand total of 1 percent of its profits to charity. The average for corporations in Canada in general was .67 percent (Misgivings, 1972).

Now needless to say, the case against Exchange Theory cannot rest upon a few examples, nor has it been my intention to have it do so. At the same time, however, space does not permit a detailed examination of the vast amount of evidence on this matter. For present purposes, therefore, let me simply use the summaries of anthropologists who have reviewed this evidence.

Thus Marcel Mauss, the Durkheimian, after examining gift giving and other exchanges in a fairly wide range of societies (including the Northwest Coast Indians), concluded (in 1925) that:

> It is something other than utility which makes goods circulate *in these multifarious and fairly enlightened societies. Clans, age groups, and sexes, in view of the many relationships ensuing from contacts between them, are in a perpetual economic effervescence which has little about it that is materialistic; it is much less prosaic than our sale and purchase, hire of services and speculations* (Mauss, 1970:70).
>
> *There, if one hoards, it is only to spend later on, to put people under obligations and to win followers. Exchanges are made as well, but only of luxury objects like clothing and ornaments, or feast and other things that are consumed at once. Return is made with interest (sic), but that is done in order to humiliate the original donor or exchange partner and not merely to recompense him for the loss that the lapse of time causes him. . . .*

It is only our Western societies that quite recently turned man into an economic animal (Mauss, 1970:73–74; my emphasis).

Later, Karl Polanyi (1944:43) was to repeat much the same conclusion:

> In spite of the chorus of academic incantations so persistent in the nineteenth century, gain and profit made on exchange never before played an important part in human

economy. Though the institution of the market was fairly common since the later Stone Age, its role was no more than incidental to economic life.

Similarly, still later his student, Marshall Sahlins (1965), elaborated upon the specifics after a seemingly exhaustive examination of exchange practices in primitive societies.

Sahlins classifies such relations into three pure types. What he refers to as "generalized reciprocity" entails giving something to another with no expectation that a particular amount of another good will be returned at a particular time, or perhaps, even that there will be any return at all. Pure gift giving would be the best example of this form of exchange. A second type is what Sahlins calls "balanced reciprocity". Here the exchange contains expectations "which stipulate returns of commensurate worth or utility within a finite and narrow period." "Barter," where goods are exchanged for goods, usually "on the spot," would be an example of this type. Third and finally, there is what Sahlins calls "negative reciprocity," where the goal is not really to exchange things equivalent in value, but to "maximize utility at the other's expense." The word "negative" refers to the fact that while one gives the other person something, the object is to get more in return than one has given. What we call "dealing in commodities" in our society, for example, buying 500 pigs one day and selling them at a profit the next, would be a pure form of this type of exchange. Sahlins' classification of exchange relations thus runs from considerable altruism/cooperation on one end to self-interested or egoistic competition on the other.

His major conclusions of relevance to the present discussion can be summarized as follows:

(1) "The societal profile of reciprocity ... most often inclines towards *generalized* modes" (Sahlins, 1965:179; my emphasis).

(2) "Exchange in primitive communities has not the same role as in the economic flow in modern industrial communities.... Typically, it is *less* involved than modern exchanges in the *acquisition* of means of production, *more* involved in the *redistribution* of finished goods through the community" (Sahlins, 1965:140; my emphasis).

(3) In primitive communities as compared with our own, when balanced and/or negative reciprocity *do* occur, they are more likely to be *restricted to particular roles* (e.g., the trader) *and for particular others* (e.g., those, such as strangers from another tribe, with whom no lasting social bond exists; Sahlins, 1965:149–150). In this regard, differences in status rank do *not* entail the absence of a social bond, *and*, in fact, "differences in fortune between them compel a more altruistic (generalized) transaction than is otherwise appropriate" (Sahlins, 1965:165). Nor, for that matter, is negative reciprocity necessarily the typical relationship with strangers (Sahlins, 1965:172).

(4) In primitive communities as compared with our own, when balanced and/or negative reciprocity *do* occur, they are more likely to involve *highly restricted categories of "goods"* which cannot be exchanged for goods (including "monies," if they exist) in other categories. In this regard, "One does not exchange things for food.... Staples are insulated against pecuniary transactions and food shared perhaps but rarely sold" (Sahlins, 1965:170–172). Similarly, even where generalized exchanges are usually restricted to those with whom one has a lasting social bond, generalized exchanges in food will often not be so restricted (Sahlins, 1965:172).

In summarizing the theoretical implications of his own research Sahlins reiterates

Mauss's conclusion, which now should surely be our own:

> Here has been given a discourse on economics in which "economizing" appears mainly as an exogenous factor! The organizing principles of economy have been sought *elsewhere. To the extent they have been found outside man's presumed hedonistic propensity, a strategy for the study of primitive economics is suggested that is* something the reverse of economic orthodoxy [i.e., Exchange Theory; Sahlins, 1965:186; my emphasis].

Notes

[1] However, Wiley (1973) reports that females are still less competitive when playing against males.

[2] Rivalry in Anglo-American and Mexican Children of Two Ages", *Journal of Personality and Social Psychology*, 1972, Vol. 24, No. 2, pp. 214–220. Kagan, Spencer and Madsen, Millard C. Copyright 1972 by the American Psychological Association. Reprinted by permission.

[3] Rivalry in Anglo-American and Mexican Children of Two Ages", *Journal of Personality and Social Psychology*, 1972, Vol. 24, No. 2, pp. 214–220. Kagan, Spencer and Madsen, Millard C. Copyright 1972 by the American Psychological Association, Reprinted by permission.

[4] From *Habitat, Economy and Society* by Daryll C. Forde. Published by Methuen and Co. Ltd., London, England. Reprinted by permission.

[5] It should be noted that while many anthropologists would agree that the competitiveness of the potlatch has been greatly exaggerated by Exchange Theorists, not all of them would agree that its main function was to redistribute wealth.

References

Benedict, Ruth. *Patterns of Culture.* New York: Mentor (New American Library), 1960.

Bixenstine, V.E., H.M. Potash, and K.V. Wilson. "Effects of levels of cooperative choice by the other player in choices in a prisoner's dilemma game," *Journal of Abnormal and Social Psychology* 66/67:308–313; 139–148, 1963.

Blau, Peter M. "Co-operation and competition in a bureaucracy," *American Journal of Sociology* 49(May):530–535, 954.

――――. *Exchange and Power in Social Life.* New York: John Wiley & Sons, 1964.

Boas, Franz. *Contributions to the Ethnology of the Kwakiutl.* New York: AMS Press, 1969.

Broadfoot, Barry. *Ten Lost Years, 1929–1939.* Don Mills Ont.: Paperjacks (General Publishing), 1975.

Curtis, E. "The Kwakiutl." In vol. 10 of *The North American Indian.* Norwood, Mass.: Plimpton Press, 1915.

Deutsch, Morton, "A theory of cooperation and competition. An experimental study of the effects of cooperation and competition upon group process," *Human Relations* 2:129–152; 199–231, 1949.

――――. "The effect of motivational orientation upon trust and suspicion," *Human Relations* 13:122–139, 1960.

――――and Robert M. Krauss. The effect of threat on interpersonal bargaining," *Journal of Abnormal and Social Psychology* 61:181–189, 1960.

Dorris, J. William, "Reactions to unconditional cooperation: a field study emphasizing variables neglected in laboratory research," *Journal of Personality and Social Psychology* 22 (June):387–397, 1972.

Forde, C. Daryll. *Habitat, Economy, and Society.* New York: E.P. Dutton, 1963.

Gamson, W.A. "An experimental test of a theory

of coalition formation," *American Sociological Review* 26:565–573, 1961.

Godelier, Maurice. *Rationality and Irrationality in Economics.* London: New Left Books, 1972.

Jones Edward E. and Harold B. Gerard. *Foundations of Social Psychology.* New York: John Wiley & Sons, 1967.

Kagen, Spencer and Millard C. Madsen. "Rivalry in Anglo-American and Mexican children of two ages," *Journal of Personality and Social Psychology* 24(November):214–220, 1972.

Kelley, Harold H. and Janusz Grzelak. "Conflict between individual and common interest in a N-person relationship," *Journal of Personality and Social Psychology* 21(February):190–197, 1972.

Lave, L.B. "Factors affecting cooperation in the prisoner's dilemma," *Behavioral Science* 10:26–38, 1965.

Leclair, Edward E. and Harold K. Schneider (eds.), *Economic Anthropology: Readings in Theory and Analysis.* New York: Holt, Rinehart and Winston, 1968.

Luce, R.D. and H. Raitta. *Games and Decisions: Introduction and Critical Survey.* New York: John Wiley & Sons, 1957.

Mandel, Ernest. *Marxist Economic Theory.* New York: Monthly Review Press, 1970.

Mauss, Marcel. *The Gift: Forms and Functions of Exchange in Archaic Societies.* London: Routledge and Kegan Paul, 1970. (Published in the U.S. by Macmillan Publishing Co. Inc.)

Mead, Margaret. *Cooperation and Competition Among Primitive Peoples.* New York: McGraw-Hill, 1937.

Mills, Theodore M. "Power relations in three-person groups." Pp. 766–780 in Dorwin Cartwright and Alvin Zander (eds.), *Group Dynamics.* New York: Harper and Row, 1960.

Misgivings. Title of a pamphlet released under the pseudonym "Memo from Turner," Toronto, 1972.

Nelson, Linden L. and Spencer Kagan. "Competition: the star-spangled scramble," *Psychology Today* 6 (September):53–56; 90–91, 1972.

Piddocke, Stuart. "The potlach system of the southern Kwakiutl: a new perspective." Pp. 283–299 in Edward E. LeClair and Harold K. Schneider (eds.), *Economic Anthropology: Readings in Theory and Analysis.* New York: Holt, Rinehart and Winston, 1968.

Polanyi, Karl. *The Great Transformation.* New York: Farrar and Rinehart, 1944.

Redfield, Robert. *Human Nature and the Study of Society.* Chicago: University of Chicago Press, 1962.

Robson, R.A.H. "The effects of different group sex compositions on support rates and coalition formation." Monograph No. 1, Experimental Sociology Laboratory, University of British Columbia, 1971.

Sahlins, Marshall D. "On the sociology of primitive exchange." Pp. 139–236 in *The Relevance of Models for Social Anthropology.* A.S.A. Monograph No. 1. London: Tavistock, 1965.

———. *Stone-Age Economics.* Chicago: Aldine, 1972.

Secord, Paul F. and Carl W. Backman. *Social Psychology.* 2nd ed. New York: McGraw-Hill, 1974.

Swingle, Paul G. and Angelo Santi. "Communication in non-zero-sum games," *Journal of Personality and Social Psychology* 23 (July):54–63, 1972.

Vinacke, W. Edgar. "Variables in experimental games: toward a field theory," *Psychological Bulletin* 71(April):293–318, 1969.

13 Perceptions of Social Inequality Among Public School Children

Bernd Baldus   Verna Tribe

BERND BALDUS, Associate Professor of Sociology at the University of Toronto, received his undergraduate and graduate training in the German Federal Republic and in the United States. His research and publications have been primarily concerned with the origins and the persistence of social inequality in human societies. The following article is one of several which explore social control processes which legitimate inequality structures and stabilize them over time. At present, Professor Baldus is working on an evolutionary history of social inequality.

VERNA TRIBE, who assisted Professor Baldus with the following study, does not work in the field of Sociology.

... Our study is part of an effort to find out when and in what form views about social inequality develop. Since previous research (e.g., Hess and Torney, 1967; Easton and Dennis, 1969) indicated that related political beliefs appeared during—though not necessarily as a result of—primary schooling, we chose children from Grades 1, 3, and 6 from three public schools in the Toronto area for the study. We wanted to see at what age children began to use social inequality as a criterion for the identification and the ordering of their environment. We also wanted to examine whether the children's sex, the occupation of their fathers (divided into blue collar and white collar/professional categories), or the school they attended had any influence on their use of inequality as a criterion of orientation. Finally we wanted to find out whether the children made evaluative judgments in conjunction with their perceptions of social inequality. More specifically, we were interested to see whether there was any predisposition to see high class or low class figures as likely to engage in morally approved or disapproved behaviour, or to succeed or fail in competitive tasks. ...

PROCEDURE

The three schools in which our study was carried out were chosen from residential areas with widely differing income characteristics in order to maximize the chance of identifying school-specific differences in the perception of social inequality, one of our independent variables. In each school we selected a sample of 36 children, 12 each from Grade 1, Grade 3, and Grade 6, for a total of 108 cases. Their age ranged from five to twelve years, the majority in each grade being six, eight, and eleven years old. Each child was interviewed individually and the interviews were taped and later transcribed. During the first part of the interview, we used five sets of photos taken in Toronto. They consisted of two pictures of a man, one well dressed and named Mr. Gordon, the other in casual clothes and named Mr. Ellis, (set 1); two pictures of a house, one taken in the high income Rosedale area, the other in an old working class district of Toronto (set 2); two pictures of a living room, one in a Rosedale home, the other in a rented apartment and furnished with used and worn furniture (set 3); a photo of a small old car and one of a Lincoln Continental (set 4); and two more pictures of individual men, one well dressed and addressing a meeting, the other in older clothing and sitting on a porch. We introduced each interview as a game of matching pictures of people, houses, living rooms, and cars. We also explained the use of the tape recorder and asked a few questions about name, age, and grade. We then showed the children the pictures of Mr. Gordon and Mr. Ellis and asked for any differences they noticed when comparing the two men. Following that the children were handed the pictures of the two houses and were asked to tell us who in their opinion lived in which house. After that, they matched the living rooms with the houses, and the cars with the two men. Before we showed them the last set of pictures we told them that both Mr. Gordon and Mr. Ellis were giving a party at their house. We then showed them set 5 and asked them which of the men in the picture Mr. Gordon and Mr. Ellis would invite to their party. The children had the option of making no choice at all, but none of them used it. After assigning each set the children were asked why they had made their choice.[1]

The picture matching served also as an introduction to the second part of the study. The sets of pictures were designed in such a way that they could provide cumulative information on status symbols such as houses, cars, or furniture which distinguished the two men and which approximated as much as possible visual impressions of class differences which the children might encounter in their day to day experience. When the picture matching was completed each child was told that Mr Gordon and Mr. Ellis both had children. We then read four short stories and asked each child whose son or daughter the hero in the story was likely to be. The first of the stories involved a boy who swore and started an unprovoked fight in the schoolyard. The second story was about a boy who received more valentines than any-

one else and was liked best by his classmates. Story three told of a girl who could not read as well as the other children. The last story was about a boy who lied to his mother. The first and last stories thus described the transgression of a generally accepted norm. Stories 2 and 3 portrayed a boy who was held in high regard by others, and a girl who was relatively unsuccessful in a competitive task. The stories had been tested in a pilot study, and even the youngest children had no difficulty in comprehending the problem which they presented.

All interviews took place during regular school hours. The children had no apparent problem with the questions and seemed to enjoy the task. All were used to being recorded on tape, and many of them knew one of the interviewers who frequently worked in the classrooms.

RESULTS

Findings from the first part of the study, the picture-matching tasks, appear in Table 1. The data indicate that with increasing age there is a clear and significant increase in the children's ability to identify the common inequality dimension in the pictures and to order them accordingly. This is evident both in the total number of correct matches for each question, and in the number of children in each grade who are able to match all pictures correctly. Only 7 of the 36 children in Grade 1 did so, while 22 children in Grade 3 and 25 children in Grade 6 completed all 4 matching tasks correctly. Data for Grade 2 which do not appear on Table 1 show that the progression between Grades 1 and 3 is continuous, and that there is no particular time period during these three years where most of the change occurs.

An analysis of variance with the summated scores of the picture matches as dependent variables, and grade, sex, father's occupation, and school as independent variables shows

Table 1
PICTURE-MATCHING, BY GRADE

	Set 1 (House)		Set 2 (Living Room)		Set 3 (Car)		Set 4 (Party)	
	Correct Matches	Incorrect Matches	Correct Matches	Incorrect Matches	Correct Matches	Incorrect Matches	Correct Matches	Incorrect Matches
Grade 1	18	18	20	16	27	9	24	12
Grade 3	31	5	27	9	35	1	33	3
Grade 6	34	2	27	9	35	1	35	1

Kendall's Tau c for Set 1: -0.39506 ($p < 0.0001$); for Set 2: -0.17284 ($p = 0.0385$); for Set 3: -0.19753 ($p = 0.001$); for Set 4: -0.27160 ($p = 0.0001$)

grade as the only significant source of variation of the matching scores (DF = 6, F = 7.955, P = 0.001). Neither the children's sex, nor their school environment nor the occupational position of their father seem to have a significant effect on their ability to order the pictures on the basis of social inequality between the two main figures.

The numerical evidence is supported by an analysis of the transcripts of the taped interviews. They indicate the same gradual development of the ability to verbalize one's choice. Grade 6 students explained their choices with considerably more complex vocabulary and with more differentiated references to social inequality than their counterparts in Grades 3 and 1.

The initial question about differences between Mr. Gordon and Mr. Ellis was answered by the Grade 1 children primarily in terms of such easily noticeable criteria as the different shirts the two men were wearing, that one had curly hair, or that one was standing and the other one was sitting. Only four of the children made the evaluative comments, for instance that Mr. Gordon "looked happy" or was wearing "good clothes." In Grade 3, such evaluative descriptions became more frequent. Mr. Gordon was described as "dressed up" and as "looking nicer" than Mr. Ellis, while the latter appeared as "old" or wearing "work clothes." One of the children made social inequality the first and

only identifying criterion: Mr. Gordon "looks like he has more money," while Mr. Ellis "looks like he doesn't have a job." The majority of the children in Grade 3 continued to identify differences between the two men in factual terms. By contrast, inequality-related criteria were the first things mentioned by roughly one-half of the children in Grade 6: Mr. Gordon looks like a businessman, and Mr. Ellis doesn't. "He (G) looks like an executive. He (E) could be a worker in a plant, or drive a truck." Many of the children drew inferences to other aspects of the men's life which were not visible in the pictures: "He (G) has a good business job, and he (E) is the sort of guy that watches football. He (G) cares more about his dress." "Mr. Ellis looks like he is not a good salesman. Mr. Gordon looks like a salesman, with a suit and a tie. Mr. Ellis looks like an ordinary guy who lives in an apartment, a pop-corn salesman with enough pennies." "One (E) is rather mean-looking. This one (G), looks like he would come from a rather well-fashioned family compared to this one (E)." Only a few of the Grade 6 children still used factual criteria when identifying differences between the two men.

A similar progression toward a more articulate and more frequent use of social inequality as an ordering criterion was evident in the picture-matching. Children in Grade 1 matched the houses with the pictures of the two men by commenting that "it looks right," or that one house looked "bigger" or "older" and therefore went with Mr. Gordon or Mr. Ellis. Only two of the children based their choices on some idea of the men's social position; one paired the large house with Mr. Gordon "because he works in an office" while the other child paired Mr. Ellis with the small house because it "looks like a working house." Generally, comments were short and hesitant. About one-half of the children in Grade 1 could give no explanation at all. In Grade 3 the majority of comments made reference to differences in wealth as a basis for matching the houses with the two men: "Because I think this man (G) looks as if he has lots of money and he should have a bigger house, and this man (E) doesn't have neat clothes like this man, and he should have a house like this." "He (G) looks like a big business-man and this looks like a fancy house." Only a few of the children used factual criteria such as age or facial expression as a basis for matching the pictures. In Grade 6, almost all the children identified social inequality as the common dimension of the pictures. Mr. Gordon was described as rich, as a big business man, as someone who made much money, and who therefore could afford a big or fancy house. Many of the comments not only described, but evaluated: "This man (E) is a real man, like he is rich and that, and this house looks like a real good house, and this man (E) is just like a normal man and this is a normal house." "Mr. Gordon looks kind of rich. I don't know why. But he slicks up his hair. Mr. Ellis looks like he is tough, maybe a big mouth. These (E) houses are close together. Mr. Gordon's house looks really like a mansion."

Reasons for matching the pictures of the two living rooms with those of the houses were factual in Grade 1: similarities between the windows in house and living room, similarities in colour, or the impression that house and living room had the same curtain. These observations were not always correct—some of the children were clearly guessing. Grade 3 children began to identify the furniture in the living room as expensive, rich, valuable, or shabby, and these attributes usually accompanied correct matches. In Grade 6, inequality-related observations became detailed and showed a comprehension not only of the relationship between income and lifestyle, but of a relatively wide variety of items which were taken as symbolic indicators of social class: "Well, it's sort of the same thing as with the houses. He (G) is a big businessman, and if you are a big businessman you get more money and you can afford more things. Not too many people can afford fireplaces in their house, or an antique table, and this thing, whatever it is, just looks like an ordinary house in which everybody can live, because this couch looks like anybody can afford it. This house looks average."

The question which of the two cars Mr. Gordon and Mr. Ellis were driving produced the largest number of correct matches in all grades. Cars appear to be one of the first symbols of social position which the children learn, girls just as much as boys. . . . In Grade 6 almost all children thought that Mr. Gordon would drive the large car because he was richer and looked "fancier. . . . "

The last matching task asked children to pair the pictures of Mr. Gordon and Mr. Ellis with those of two other men who were to be invited to their party. The children in Grade 1 based their choices primarily on their impressions of physical characteristics such as age, facial expression, or dress. Some of the judgments bore no apparent relationship to the pictures—as in other tasks, many Grade 1 children had obvious difficulties in explaining their choice. The conceptual problems of finding a common dimension in the pictures, as well as their still relatively small verbal repertoire, imposed constraints even on those children who made expected choices and seemed to know why.

Many of the Grade 3 children also based their choice on the appearance of similar age; Mr. Ellis was generally seen as older, and so was the man on the porch. Some of the Grade 3 answers, however, suggested quite explicitly that Mr. Gordon was likely to associate only with someone who was as rich or as well dressed as he was. In Grade 6 most of the children considered the perceived social position of the men as the criterion that brought them together at a party, and they drew detailed inferences as to what the men had in common. "He (G) looks like a politician, and so does he, the way they dress. The way they look, they are sincere and perfect. This looks like an ordinary street person who is looking for work and couldn't get it." "This man is dressed nice and that man is not dressed nice. And that man is at a convention and he is talking, and he has to be pretty important and Mr. Gordon is pretty rich, so he would know important people. That man is sort of old and hangs around the street, so Mr. Ellis meets him sometimes and they become friends, and so he invites him to his party."

Three more general conclusions can be drawn from the verbal replies of the children. First, children become more articulate and more certain in their choice as they progress from Grade 1 to Grade 6. This is indicated by the number of children who are not able to give any explanation at all. Such children comprise as many as one-half of the children in Grade 1, while only very few of the children in Grade 6 cannot state any reasons why they made a particular choice.

Second, there is a clear increase in the use of explicit inequality-related criteria in explaining picture matches as one proceeds through the grades. Explanations were classified as inequality-related when they made explicit references to differences in wealth between Mr. Gordon and Mr. Ellis. Comparative explanations comprised all other comparisons of the two men, such as that Mr. Gordon looked "happier," "younger," or "cleaner" than Mr. Ellis. Factual explanations involved the use of noncomparative observations of details in the pictures as an order-

ing criterion; for example, that there was a chimney in the large house and a fireplace in the living room. Factual choices were not always correct. Many of the factual details were inaccurate and reflected the younger children's difficulties in identifying common properties of the pictures.

The third conclusion concerns the increasingly evaluative language employed by the children as they explain their choice. Evaluative components of the replies are particularly evident in Grade 6 and reveal the outlines of an ideological image of social inequality which is shared by many of the children. Mr. Gordon and his possessions evoke admiration, respect, and sometimes awe for a person and lifestyle which most of the children find clearly desirable. These feelings are not necessarily connected to details in the pictures. Instead, the pictures recall for the children schematic images of social models which are already part of their cognitions and fantasies. Mr. Gordon and Mr. Ellis become recognizable because of their affinity with such existing images. Once they have been identified in these terms the children freely draw inferences which go substantially beyond what is visible in the pictures. The "classy," "important," "rich" and "well dressed" Mr. Gordon is for most children a fixture in a social environment which appears invariant and of which people like Mr. Gordon are a natural and desirable part. Money is the general source of Mr. Gordon's attractiveness. He most likely obtained it by being a "businessman." Conversely, Mr. Ellis is described less frequently, and when he is described it is usually done in derogatory terms. It is possible that such judgmental elements appear already in many of the answers in Grade 3. Terms such as "new" or "young" used in connection with Mr. Gordon often suggested an evaluative meaning, though their more limited verbal repertoire provided the Grade 3 children with fewer ways of expressing their judgment.

The second part of our study was designated to investigate the evaluative dimension of children's perception of inequality more closely. We wanted to find out whether there was a consistency in the way in which behaviour described in each of the four stories was attributed to the child of the low class or the high class figure in the pictures, and thus indirectly to them. The results are summarized in Table 2. Unlike the picture matches, the attribution of the stories to the children of Mr. Gordon or Mr. Ellis does not show much variation between the grades. An analysis of variance of the added scores showed that none of the independent variables, grade, sex, father's occupation, or school, caused any significant variance of the story matches. Instead, Table 2 shows a relatively high number of correct matches in all grades, with a small but not statistically significant increase in Grades 3 and 6. Even in Grade 1 a majority of the children considered it more likely that Mr. Gordon's child would be liked by his classmates, and that the child of Mr. Ellis would get into an unprovoked fight, perform badly in a reading task, or lie to his mother. . . .

While there is only a small increase in an already initially high number of correct matches, we found a clear progression in two other areas. The first is the number of children in each grade who attribute all four stories correctly to the hypothetical children of Mr. Gordon and Mr. Ellis. Of the 36 children in Grade 1 only 10 did so. In Grade 3 that figure increases to 19, and in Grade 6, 23 out of 36 children assigned the attractive role to

Mr. Gordon's child, and the morally reprehensible or unsuccessful behaviour to the children of Mr. Ellis. These figures suggest an increase in the children's capacity to find common properties such as the class differences between the two men, and to categorize information on moral and performance behaviour accordingly as they grow older. The change between Grades 1 and 3 reflects the same transition from Piaget's preoperational to concrete operations stage which we found earlier in the picture matches.

A similar progression is evident in the frequency with which children rely on perceived class differences between the two men as a basis for attributing the behaviour described in the stories to their children. An analysis of the verbal explanations indicates that the higher the grade the more likely the children are to express prejudgments. Transcripts from the Grade 1 interviews show that a large number of children could not provide an explanation for their choice, or phrased it in terms of some simple and not always correctly observed external characteristic such as that Mr. Ellis had curly hair, or that Mr. Gordon was sitting down. These observations bore no obvious relationship to the matching task, and reflect the same difficulties of the youngest children to give verbal accounts of what they had done that were already evident in the first part of our study. A few children explained their (correct) choices by stating that Mr. Gordon "looks

TABLE 2
STORY-MATCHING, BY GRADE

	Story 1		Story 2		Story 3		Story 4	
	Correct Matches	Incorrect Matches	Correct Matches	Incorrect Matches	Correct Matches	Incorrect Matches	Correct Matches	Incorrect Matches
Grade 1	28	8	27	9	25	11	20	16
Grade 3	30	6	30	6	26	10	28	8
Grade 6	29	7	29	7	29	7	26	10

The level of significance for Kendall's Tau c is larger than 0.06 for all stories.

happy," is "bigger," or "smiles," or is "unhappy." The transcripts do not allow any conclusion whether such statements were based on some rudimentary perception of social inequality between the two men.

Some of this is also characteristic of the Grade 3 answers. There is, in particular, still a relatively high proportion of children who cannot give explanations for their choices, even if these were in the expected direction. At the same time there are the first clearly preconceived explanations. Mr. Ellis' son fights and swears "because Mr. Ellis looks rough, and his son would fight, and Mr. Gordon is richer, and his son wouldn't fight," or "cause I don't think Mr. Gordon's kids would swear because he doesn't swear around the house and his kids wouldn't learn those words." Mr. Gordon's son is liked better by his classmates "because Mr. Gordon looks like he is a happy man, and his son would be a nice boy, and everyone would like him." Or, "Everybody liked him because he was rich, because his father was rich." Mr. Ellis' daughter cannot read well "because he (E) looks like his daughter hasn't very much education." And the boy who lies to his mother that he had to stay in school while he was in fact playing football is Mr. Ellis' "because he (G) looks like his son would come home and he doesn't play ball and has good clothes, and his (E's) son wears rough clothes and would go out and play ball."

In Grade 6 almost all answers reveal the existence of preconceived expectations which are frequently explicitly based on perceived class differences between the two men. Grade 6 children generally assume that low class people are likely to get into trouble and high class people are liked and esteemed. Moreover, they have a strong propensity for expecting the father's characteristics to be transmitted to his children. Sometimes this is expressed as an almost fatalistic belief that class and corresponding character traits run in the family. Quite a few children also give sophisticated and sometimes rather realistic reasons for their expectations. The following selection of answers by Grade 6 children shows some of the main trends in the children's arguments. Story 1 (swearing and unprovoked fighting): "Well, Mr. Ellis looks like a bully-type man, and his son would pick a fight. He (E) would probably belt them one in the mouth, and his son would be just like him." "If Mr. Gordon is out with his son, well, if he is as wealthy as he is his son wouldn't hit anybody or swear at a teacher." "He (E) probably drinks a lot, and he wouldn't care about his child, what his child would do, and he would probably let his child swear and that." "I think he is Mr. Ellis' son because he (E) is kind of a drunk, and mostly drunks swear a lot when they get drunk, and when they fall down and someone tries to help them they get mad at him and swear. Sons, they mostly fall in the same way." "He is the son of Mr. Ellis, because poor people usually have lots of kids. He is bad-tempered, and he always wants the ball." Story 2 (about a boy who receives most valentines on Valentine's day because he is liked best by the children in his class): "He is Mr. Gordon's son, because everyone seemed to like him because he wasn't a big bully or something, he wasn't lippy or anything, he was a nice guy, and he might not have looked peaceful but he was like his father. He took after his father." "I think he was Mr. Gordon's son because usually when the parents have good manners they share with their friends. And the way he (G) is dressed, and the way he smiles, he looks as if a lot of his friends helped him to get up to where he is now. Their children will follow them and share things back and forth." Mr. Gordon's son would be good, and the other kids liked him more. Maybe Mr. Gordon is more strict and would watch him more often. He would work in an office, and he would not want the other people to think that he has bad children." "Mr. Gordon's because if he is rich you could say that his children will be polite. If you have a father that goes on TV and is popular you would have manners and treat your friends right. Mr. Ellis would treat his friends sometimes meanly, and (only) if they had something that he wanted he would be a nice guy to them. And so Mr. Ellis' son would be real greedy and wouldn't want them to have anything." Story 3 (about a girl who was put into a group of slower readers): "Mr. Gordon's daughter would be in the group that could read best because (she) would have a well-educated father, and Mr. Ellis' daughter would probably be the type who would sit around and fool around all day and wouldn't know anything." "Oh, I think she would be Mr. Ellis' (daughter) because I don't think he would really care whether his daughter could read well or not." "I think she is Mr. Ellis' because they can probably not afford enough books for her to practise reading on. Or she doesn't like reading because her parents don't read a lot, or had to work for their family all the time and did not have time to read." "Mr. Ellis doesn't look that smart. It looks like where he comes from, the house and all that, that he wouldn't have as good an education. Mr. Gordon looks intelligent, and he would probably teach his daughter everything he knew." "Mr. Ellis, he looks poor. Maybe he went to a poor school that did not have as good an education as Mr. Gordon's." "Mr. Ellis, because Mr. Gordon if he found out about it he would probably keep his kids in to work at it. Mr. Ellis might not, or his kids might not tell him about it." Story 4 (of a boy who lies to his mother): "Well, I think this man (G) would look after his children and teach them not to lie or anything, and, you know, would take really good care of his children. But I don't think that Mr. Ellis would really bother. He would think that his children ... that's their own business." "He (E) is the man, if he had kids they would not grow up in a mannerly way, like they would lie and steal and swear at teachers, because he looks like he is a really rough man." "Probably Mr. Ellis' son, because he probably gets very mad and beats his children, and just to get out of that

his son would probably lie." "Mr. Ellis' son, because people who don't have jobs seem to lie and say that they are high class. People who don't have jobs seem to lie about their work and say that they have done what they have not done. Mr. Gordon probably taught his son that lying doesn't pay, and that you get into a lot of trouble by just starting with one lie." "Mr. Ellis looks like a man who would lie a lot. . . . "

Not all children in Grade 6 shared the view that high social class goes together with esteemed and successful behaviour, that low class people are trouble- and failure-prone, and that their children usually follow their footsteps. Ten out of 36 Grade 6 children employed standards of evaluation which ran contrary to those used by the majority of the Grade 6 respondents, even though they appeared usually only in connection with one or two of the four stories. The view which these children had of the relationship between social class and behaviour was more differentiated and revealed a more critical view of people like Mr. Gordon. They appeared in particular in connection with the first story. Mr. Gordon's son was seen as more likely to start a fight because he knew about his father's money and thought that he was better: "Since he (G) is so rich his son might think that he is the boss." For the same reason, some of the children also thought that he would not be well-liked in school. Mr. Gordon's son "would be a spoilsport and would have no friends because his dad has a lot of money and he would want everything to be his way." By contrast, Mr. Ellis' son would be popular because he was normal. "If a man is really rich, if you are really rich, he will usually make his son act big too. He (Ellis' son) probably just grew up like he wanted to be and didn't show off and didn't make fun of everybody, and so everybody liked him." Most of the answers reasoned quite rationally, sometimes obviously on the basis of personal experience. Mr. Gordon's social position was not in question. Rather, his importance or his wealth was seen as leading to some unfortunate side-effects with undesirable, but also unavoidable consequences for others. Only in two or three cases did we find an open resentment for people like Mr. Gordon: people who were rich were also likely to be "greedy," and their children tended to be "meaner, because they think they are better." As an afterthought to the last story, one of the Grade 6 boys added: "Mr. Gordon looks like a sneaky little real-estate salesman. Maybe he says a sucker is born every minute, and he started getting all these suckers together and got a lot of money the easy way, just being a little dishonest like a fraud or a con man. . . . "

CONCLUSIONS

The results of our study indicate that by the time the children have reached Grade 6, most of them have not only learned to recognize and classify people and their environment in a context of social inequality, but have also acquired cognitive and affective predispositions which make them expect that lower class persons are more likely to be unsuccessful or to engage in morally disapproved behaviour, and that the behaviour of high class persons is exemplary and esteemed. . . .

One of the most important results of our study is that these views were not affected by the social position of the children's parents. All children seemed to learn to recognize and evaluate social inequality as a dimension of their environment at roughly the same age and in similar ways. . . .

Notes

[1] We were aware that the forced-choice nature of the questions, even if it was moderated by the "don't know" option, led to a number of risks. It did, for instance, not allow us to establish the distance which, in the view of the child, separated Mr. Gordon and Mr. Ellis. Nor did it permit any expressions of additional gradations of social inequality which the children might have been aware of. We felt that these disadvantages were outweighed by the comparability of the three grades which we gained with our design. The taped comments were a further way of registering more differentiated opinions.

References

Hess, R.D. 1967. *The Development of Political Attitudes in Children*. Chicago: Aldine.

Easton, D. and Dennis, J. 1969. *Children in the Political System*. New York: McGraw-Hill.

14 Socialization of Parents

John R. Seeley   R. Alex Sim   Elizabeth Wyeth Loosley

JOHN R. SEELEY, between 1947–1963, held a variety of Canadian research and teaching positions, including Associate Professor of Psychiatry and Associate Professor of Sociology, University of Toronto; Professor of Sociology, York University; and Research Director and Consultant to the Alcoholism Research Foundation of Ontario. He returned to the United States in 1963; thereafter he held teaching and research positions at MIT, Brandeis, and the University of California, and headed up a variety of freelance research and writing projects. Professor Seeley specialized in the study of mental health and mental health care-giving, particularly psychiatry. His best known work includes *Crestwood Heights: A Study of the Culture of Suburban Life*, with R.A. Sim and E.W. Loosley (1956), from which the following excerpt is drawn; *Community Chest: A Case Study in Philanthropy* (1957); and *The Americanization of the Unconscious* (1967). He served on the editorial boards of many journals, on the advisory boards of many associations, and consulted with even more public and private mental health organizations. Professor Seeley's achievement has been recognized by biographical sketches appearing in a dozen directories of important people.

R. ALEX SIM is a one-time farmer, civil servant, community development consultant and teacher. Recipient of a Senior McGeachy Memorial Scholarship in 1983, Mr. Sim was able to revisit communities across Canada where his work had once taken him and sift through literature on rural society in Canada, all the while re-examining his own long career as a rural activist. A book which may be entitled *The Death and Rebirth of the Rural Community* is in the final stages of completion.

ELIZABETH WYETH LOOSLEY, now retired, worked as a librarian, teacher and editor over her long career. After serving as research assistant on the Crestwood Heights project between 1951–1953, she edited the periodical *Food for Thought* for the Canadian Association for Adult Education, then served as Assistant to the General Editor of the *Dictionary of Canadian Biography* for six years. Her life-long interest in adult education took her next into courses on English as a Second Language for the next twenty years, serving first as Adult Supervisor in the Earlscourt Community Project (1965–1973), then as volunteer teacher at New Vista School in Oakville (Ontario), between 1973 and 1985.

RE-SOCIALIZATION

The most important voluntary association in Crestwood Heights is the Home and School Association, predominantly, in fact, a women's organization. This Association, increasingly active since the formation of the community, has progressed through various stages, from a more purely "social" (i.e., "sociable") type of organization centered around fund-raising, to the present one which puts its emphasis on parent education. Each school unit in the Heights has a Home and School group, and they are co-ordinated in a central council. . . .

The Home and School Association in Crestwood Heights might be viewed as providing a kind of marketplace where ultimate responsibility for and functions in the transmission of those values governing the socialization process are traded back and forth between the family and the school. Certain aspects of this process seem to attract the attention of members particularly. Leaving aside the values rooted in the religious orientations of Jew and Gentile (which, as a matter of fact, introduce no cleavage in reference to educational matters) the community is largely agreed, as has already been emphasized, that two value systems are of supreme importance: first, the cluster of values around the concept of "maturity," and second, the "success" motif with all its component parts. As has been stressed in the discussion of the school, the means by which the success value-system is to be realized are highly competitive, although competition, outwardly at any rate, is generally emphatically disavowed in Crestwood Heights. For instance, the school, while supporting the system of competitive examinations, tends to deny that the child is competing with others; he is supposed to be competing "only with his own individual record of achievement." In Home and School meetings, however, parental and particularly paternal interest clearly centers around the child's performance in relation to that of others of the same age and grade; moreover, the students most honored in school functions for parents and the general public are those who have won either academic scholarships or awards in competitive sports, or, preferably, both.

Parental concern about the child's academic achievement was well exemplified during a Home and School meeting at which a teacher in an early grade attempted to explain to her pupils' parents the reasons for these students being grouped as "slow learners" in a special class. Miss B. had told the parents that she did not consider the children "ready" to use the spelling book until Christmas time.

This speller was meant to be used by the child alone—each is supposed to be able to follow the exercises for himself. This is not a possibility for the slow learner [here Miss B. made a slip and said "poor" before she said "slow"], without the groundwork in spelling Miss B. had outlined on the board. Spelling ties right in with reading. The slow learner needs the basis of vowels and blends.

Here a father interrupted to ask if there were any class in the school which was taking the speller now. A mother followed him to ask how the slow child levels up in the end. At this point, there was a great racket upstairs, footsteps and chairs scraping. Miss B. said, with a resigned look, "We put up with that all day, and the piano too!" The mother replied, "No wonder it's a slow class with that noise going on overhead!"

Later in Miss B.'s remarks, a father spoke up, "Assuming our children are slow learners, *as for the moment we must*, what can we do as parents to help?" Another mother asked, "How often do we get a report of the student's progress?" A third parent wanted to know whether a poor learner lacked concentration and if so, whether concentration could be improved?

It came out very strongly in this Home and School session, and others, that concern *for* the *child* is often imbued with concern *about* the child's *performance* in relation to other children of the same age and in the same school. (The two are hard to separate and the distinction suggests more a primary orientation in the parent than an exclusive focus.) A larger representation of fathers was noticeable at this session; the men joined in the discussion more than usual and displayed particular interest in competitive standing. It was significant how quickly the parents seized on the fact that the room was noisy as a rationalization for their children's difficulties. Miss B. attempted to play down the competition theme, but was not very successful. Much of the parental participation at this meeting was primarily an attempt to discover how the slow learners measured up to other classes of the same grade in the school. Some resentment of the school's test results (proving "scientifically" that the children actually *were* slow learners) was evident as an undercurrent.

The success values, it would appear, determine, to a large degree, the interaction of school and Home and School Association. Since, as has been previously stated, the majority of Crestwood parents hope that their children will attend university, this expectation naturally exerts pressure upon the nature of the school curriculum, which is primarily directed towards preparing as many students as possible for university entrance. At the same time, the school is aware, through its vocational guidance techniques, that only a small proportion of the school population can be trained to compete for the highly esteemed professional occupations.[1] (Again the school appears as the child's protagonist, exerting a counter-influence to the general view, and if it is required championing the child's necessity to be different, should the parents demur.) The school must cushion the inevitable shock to the parents when many children cannot measure up to these training requirements. The existence of a Home and School Association gives the school an opportunity to carry out this difficult task.

At a Home and School meeting of Grade XII parents, a vocational guidance teacher in the Collegiate attempted to put across the fact that a technical, non-university vocation could be considered as "successful" as a career in medicine. Mr. D. used two examples from the school files: A, who was "university material" and who ended up in the Faculty of Medicine, and B, who was technical, "non-university material."

> Mr. D. then had us turn our chairs around to face the screen. The lights were put out, and he had thrown on the screen the records of two cases, "A" and "B," which were so far back in the files that he didn't think anyone present could possibly identify them. He would show what their measured interests were and stress especially the individual difference between the two. He gave the figures for the current mathematics and physics

course at the University of Big City to show that only a small percentage of those who started the course survived even the first year. Mr. D. appealed to the group, "Don't you think it's time we stopped kidding ourselves and allowing our students to kid themselves that they can do work, when they haven't got what it takes?"

Of all the Home and School meetings attended by the researcher, this particular session was the most apathetic from the point of view of parent participation. A period was set aside for questions at the end of Mr. D.'s remarks. Parents were supplied with paper and pencils, so that they might remain anonymous in their questions if they wished. There were no questions, and no spontaneous show of interest came from the parents, in marked contrast to the other three meetings in this series for parents of collegiate students. The school's emphasis upon individual differences commonly falls on unresponsive ears, if the differences alluded to appear to threaten the career line, in this community which believes that all its children must be alike, at least with regard to successful academic-vocational achievement.[2]

The Crestwood Heights child, feeling the contradictory demands of his upper middle class culture, tends to accept the values of success. He may attempt to stave off any possibility of conflict by pretending that his competitive activities can be reconciled with co-operative behavior—if his preoccupation with competition allows him to consider co-operation at all. This ritual of antagonistic co-operation is not recognized by Crestwood Heights, whose members would tend to insist that inner freedom for the individual[3] is the communal norm and co-operation the means; they are inclined to deny or "play down" the existence of the success value-system, together with the competitive means by which it is realized. The child, who is the center of the socialization process in which both home and school are involved, is not usually misled, however. Despite all the talk about "maturity," "spontaneity," and "freedom," he knows beyond a doubt that his true interests inevitably must lie in one direction: graduating from the educational system of Crestwood Heights with as high marks as possible. If he has not internalized this aim, school and home have various methods of inducing him to conform, many of which are agreed upon in Home and School sessions. Children who reach the Child Guidance Clinic are in many instances only too well aware that they have been expected to achieve *beyond* their actual capacity. The majority of children, nevertheless, manage to arrive at some compromise which allows them to function more or less adequately, and to have something of both worlds.

The child, therefore, is confidently expected to realize *all* the contradictory features of Crestwood Heights culture: humanitarianism, material success, high social status, competition, co-operation—all the basic elements of the maturity- and success-systems. The elaborate family home, the complex activities of its members, the expensive school plant and organization, exist to train the child towards this end. The parents are convinced that the realization of these values can be achieved through education. If they themselves have fallen short at some points, it was through lack of sufficient training. Achievement, in the minds of the adult population, bears a direct relation to hard work and skill. Given the schools of Crestwood Heights and the background of material prosperity provided by the family, there should be no limits to what can be accomplished by the privileged children of the community. The Home and School Association exists to celebrate these beliefs, and to reinsure them.

The school, as already indicated, considers itself largely responsible for the child's development in academic vocational success, social adjustment, and ethical development and emotional well-being; and it has its own definite ideas as to how the child is best handled to secure the maximum of each. Through Home and School meetings the school proposes to the parents the means of persuading the child to conform to both school and parental expectations. In a study group, a teacher expressed this point of view:

> Mr. R. turned to the board and said we had some very good clues there. If we started with intellectual development, what kind of problems or things [correcting himself quickly] would we want to deal with here? Mrs. S. suggested: attention-span and concentration. Mr. R. asked if we wanted intellectual development in regard to what we expected the child to do in school. He wrote down "Mental ability in relation to performance, motives, and incentives," adding *"in other words, how to make the child like what we think he ought to do, but he doesn't."* [Italics added.]

The child remains in a peculiarly vulnerable position in the face of this particular socialization process. On the common meeting ground of Home and School, parents and school personnel reach agreement as to the communal values of maturity and success. A major problem consists in deciding which institution, the family or the school, shall assume which responsibility in achieving the desired ends, and what are the appropriate means to use in each context. The allocating of functions between family and school has not been agreed upon in any final sense, as Home and School activities clearly demonstrate, but the *means* are accepted by both the interested parties. The maturity values, as has been stated in other contexts, are inculcated through the agency of various brands of permissiveness. In other words, the child must be "free" to make his own "choice" as to what is the behavior pattern to follow. The success values, however, dictate equally stringently that the child must make choices which will lead most efficiently to academic-vocational achievement. The child is thus forced into the position of *having to choose* those competitive means which will assure his ultimate entrance into an appropriate adult occupational status. The further result is that he sees no authority figures against which to rebel, should he feel the desire to do so. It is one thing to kick against the pricks of a stern father or mother, or even a teacher in the role of parent surrogate, whose coercion is felt to be unfair; but it is quite another matter to defy the gentle, permissive figures who merely "want the best interests of the child" to be satisfied. The child has, therefore, only one recourse should a conflict arise between his own wishes and those of teachers and parents: to turn his attacks against himself. He is thus not as free in actuality to choose between alternative forms of behavior as he is led to believe he is. The burden of responsibility for choice of behavior is laid upon the child, while he is, at the same time, in effect virtually deprived of any alternative to the "choice" he is required to make. The confusion created in the child's mind should he become aware for some reason of the contradictions inherent in the adult expectations for him, is, understandably, great, particularly in view of his immaturity and his prolonged economic and emotional dependence upon the parents. This situation may cause extreme tension within the family which it cannot absorb and regulate unaided; but the Home and School Association does provide at least one arena where such problems may be aired, if not immediately solved.

It has become clear as we have studied the school that it is taking over more and more of the responsibility for the socialization of the child, and that it is more certain of its methods than the parents are of theirs. In Crestwood Heights, while the children are direct clients of the school, the parents have now become the indirect ones; in some cases they are equally dependent with their children on the school system. At Home and School meetings it was not uncommon for parents to ask teachers what the proper hour for bed should be, or how to prevent a child's telephone conversations during home-work. The parents of one kindergarten child were contemplating a move from Crestwood Heights which was not undertaken until the teacher had given it as her opinion that the change would not be detrimental to the child. In Home and School meetings, parents are *educated* by the school for their cultural obligation towards the child, which approaches, increasingly, the role of trusteeship for the school, which in turn is presumably trustee for "society." Just as in an earlier age, the parents were regarded as agents of the church, the institution which alone could prepare their children for heaven and immortality, they are now viewed by the school somewhat as junior partners in the business of preparing children for material success in temporal life. A favorite in-group joke of Crestwood Heights teachers states that "the ideal child is an orphan." The children are dealt with as clients in classes; the parents, as clients, in Home and School "groups...."

The Crestwood Heights Home and School Association answers important specific needs, both social and individual, as the preceding material has underlined. As its major social function, Home and School mitigates the tensions arising between the school and the family, institutions which, in Crestwood Heights, are embedded in a general culture with its own strains. The strains grow out of the struggle for social mobility, the intense competition entailed in earning enough money to remain in Crestwood Heights or to pass through it to a community of higher social status, the organized isolation of its inhabitants, and extremely important, the presence in the area of two ethnic groups, Jewish and Gentile....

Notes

[1] The "ideal" profession in Crestwood Heights seemed to be that of the doctor; his role combines the advantages of high social status, both academic and vocational success, and humanitarianism, and most important of all, it can only be won through intense competition in which many individuals are eliminated, or prevented in the first place from competing. A doctor who might conceivably embrace the ideal of service to the extent of renouncing a lucrative practice for life and work in a remote outpost or city slum would, however, be incomprehensible to many, if not most, residents of Crestwood Heights. For in Crestwood the doctor's role derives its potency as a symbol from the very fact that the doctor can perform a service of great social value while being rewarded abundantly in a material sense.

[2] E.W. Loosley, "The Home and School Association as a Socializing Agency in an Upper-Middle-Class Canadian Community" (Master's thesis, Department of Education, Division of the Social Sciences, University of Chicago, 1952), pp. 74–76.

[3] The special sense of this "autonomy" is defined in D. Riesman's *The Lonely Crowd: A Study of the Changing American Character* (New Haven: Yale University Press, 1950).

15 Socialization to Competence Among Medical Students

Jack Haas   William Shaffir

JACK HAAS, Associate Professor of Sociology at McMaster University, Hamilton, Ontario, specializes in the study of deviance and control, and occupations and professions. His books, all written or edited with William Shaffir, include *Decency and Deviance: Studies in Deviant Behaviour* (1974); *Shaping Identity in Canadian Society* (1978); and *Becoming Doctors: The Adoption of a Cloak of Competence* (1987). Recent articles include "Taking on the role of doctor: A dramaturgical analysis of professionalization" (1982) and "The fate of idealism revisited" (1984), both written with William Shaffir. Professor Haas has served as reviewer for a wide variety of scholarly journals, and as review editor for *Symbolic Interaction* and *Sociological Focus*.

WILLIAM SHAFFIR, Professor of Sociology at McMaster University, Hamilton, Ontario, specializes in race and ethnic relations and the study of identity formation. His books include *Fieldwork Experience: Qualitative Approaches to Social Research*, co-edited with Robert Stebbins and Alan Turowetz (1980); *The Canadian Jewish Mosaic*, co-edited with Morton Weinfeld and Irwin Cotler (1981); *An Introduction to Sociology*, co-edited with Michael Rosenberg, Allan Turowetz and Morton Weinfeld (1983); *Becoming Doctors: The Adoption of a Cloak of Competence*, with Jack Haas (1987); and *The Riot at Christie Pits*, with Cyril Leavitt (1987). Professor Shaffir is a review editor for *Qualitative Sociology* and *Symbolic Interaction*, and reviews articles for a variety of other scholarly journals.

INTRODUCTION

... This paper[1] describes the adoption of a cloak of competence as a critical part of the professionalizing process. We observed medical students in an innovative three-year program attempting to come to grips with the problem of meeting exaggerated expectations.[2] The profound anxiety they feel about learning medicine and becoming competent is complicated by the pressing practical demands of the situation, particularly faculty, staff and institutional expectations.

As students move through the program they are converted to the new culture and gradually adopt those symbols which represent the profession and its generally accepted truths. These symbols (language, tools, clothing, and demeanor) establish, identify and separate the bearer from outsiders, particularly client and paraprofessional audiences. Professionalization, as we observed it, involves the adoption and manipulation of symbols and symbolic behavior to create an imagery of competence and the separation and elevation of the profession from those they serve....

THE EXPECTATIONS OF COMPETENCE

Medicine is a distinctively powerful and unique profession. Freidson outlines the characteristics of this occupation that set it apart from others. These are:

1. A general public belief in the consulting occupation's competence, in the value of its professed knowledge and skill.

2. The occupational group... must be the prime source of the criteria that qualify a man to work in an acceptable fashion.

3. The occupation has gained command of the exclusive competence to determine the proper content and effective method of performing some tasks (1970a:10–11).

Medicine's position, Freidson notes, is equivalent to that of a state religion: "it has an officially approved monopoly of the right to define health and illness and to treat illness" (1970a:5)....

BECOMING PROFESSIONAL

From the outset, students are impressed by the tremendous responsibility of the physician. During their examination of various "psychosocial" problems, in Phase I,[3] students recognize that the physician's role is very broad. They learn that the medical profession not only deals with medical problems *per se*, but also with many apparently non-medical problems. The small group tutorial sessions, which form the major vehicle for learning at this stage of medical school, help shape students' enlarging conception of medicine and its practice. While early sessions are intended essentially to introduce students to the school's philosophy—the educational rationale underlying the distinctive structure and organization of the medical curriculum—they also serve to teach students the duties and responsibilities of the medical profession. An excerpt from the Phase I manual for incoming for incoming students illustrates this point:

> You are also becoming health professionals—members of an historic community concerned with the alleviation of human illness, the maintenance of health and the understanding of disease. You will begin to realize the special nature of the 'doctor-patient relationship'. Some of you will have initial difficulty with some of the physical things—blood, operations, injury, autopsies. Other experiences are more difficult to incorporate into your growth as a health professional—deformity, chronic illness, death, pain. You will see that physicians and other health professionals are ordinary human beings—with tempers, insensitivities and varied motivations (Phase I Manual, 1974:25).

The physicians' influence on the way students learn about and define medical situations is critical to the professionalizing process. From the earliest stages of their medical training, and as they advance through the program, students continually watch doctors' working habits, listen to their philosophies of medical practice, take note of their competencies and incompetencies, and reflect upon the nature of their own present and future relationships with patients....

A dramatic shift in the professionalization process occurs when the students are given greater responsibility for patient health care and management. This occurs during the clerkship phase. Students become more integral members of a health care team, are delegated some tasks requiring personal responsibility, and become accountable in ways almost entirely new to them. As they assume increased responsibilities and make medical judgments for which they must account to a variety of professionals, they develop an increasingly sympathetic outlook towards their future profession....

As students observe and experience the problems of medical care and practice, they develop an understanding and identification with the profession and the ways its members confront their problems. Students are less quick to voice criticisms of what they see, as they come to take the role, directly or indirectly, of those they will soon follow....

THE SYMBOLS OF PROFESSIONALISM

The professionalization of medical students is facilitated by symbols the neophytes take on which serve to announce to insiders and outsiders how they are to be identified. During the first weeks of their studies students begin wearing white lab jackets with plastic name tags identifying them as medical students. In addition, since clinical skill sessions are included in the curriculum from the beginning, students participate in a variety of settings with the tools of the doctoring trade carried on their person. This attire clearly identifies students to participants and visitors of the hospital/school setting. Along with their newly acquired identity kit, students begin to learn and express themselves in the medical vernacular. . . .

The significance of these symbols to the professionalization process is critical. The symbols serve, on the one hand, to identify and unite the bearers as members of a community of shared interests, purposes and identification (Roth, 1957). Simultaneously, the symbols distinguish and separate their possessors from lay people, making their role seem more mysterious, shrouded, and priest-like (Bramson, 1973). The early possession of these symbols serves to hasten their identification and commitment to the profession, while, at the same time, facilitating their separation from the lay world.

At this point, their very selection of medicine as a career has produced a set of reactions by friends, family and others which reinforce in the students' minds the idea that they are becoming very special people. Immediately upon acceptance into medical school, students perceive themselves being related to, in typified fashion, as medical students and future physicians. This reaction of others intensifies as students enter training and immerse themselves in it. At the same time, students see that they must devote more and more time and energy to their studies, and less time to past relationships and interests. . . .

One of the first difficult tasks that faces students is to begin to learn and communicate in the symbolic system that defines medical work and workers. Immediately in tutorials, readings, demonstrations and rounds, students are inundated with a language they know they are expected to become facile in. Their task is even more difficult because this exotic language is used to describe very complex processes and understandings. Students are taken aback at the difficulty of learning to communicate in their new language. They begin carrying medical dictionaries to help them translate and define terms and phrases. . . .

The separation between "we" and "they" becomes clearer to students as they are absorbed into the medical culture. As they move through the culture, they learn how the symbols are used to communicate and enforce certain definitions of the situation. Students learn how practising physicians use these symbols of the profession to shape and control the definition of the situation. . . .

TURNING OFF YOUR FEELINGS

Previous research on medical students has shown that a major effect of medical education is to make the medical student more cynical and less idealistic (Beale and Kriesberg, 1959; Becker and Geer, 1958; Eron, 1955). Our data also suggest that as students move through school and develop a professional self-image, and thus begin to take on the identity of a doctor, their views on medicine become transformed from what they describe as an idealistic phase to what they believe is a more realistic one. Accounting for this transition, one student claims:

> . . . first of all, the exposure to what really goes on. You sort of keep your eyes open and you really get an idea of the real world of medicine. . . . The other part of it is when

you're allowed responsibility ... and you really become involved with patients.

Students become less vocal in their questioning and criticisms of the medical profession. They attribute many of their earlier concerns to naiveté, and argue for a more sympathetic view of doctors and the profession as a whole:

I think I went through a phase, as I went from knowing very little about medicine to a little bit ... You go through a sort of stage of disillusion in which you sort of expect doctors to be perfect, and the medical profession and treatment and everything else to be perfect. And you find out that it's not. So you sort of react to that. I think now, after about two years, I'm starting to get to the phase now where I'm quite pleased with it really. Part of it is getting into arguments about other professions and this brings out things that you've thought about but not really verbalized.... A particular friend of mine is in law and he was talking about malpractice suits and it really makes you think that knowing doctors the way you do, and I've seen them operate, if other professions were as self-critical as doctors were and had a good sense of responsibility to duty, then I think a lot of the professions would be a lot better off....

Though not entirely pleased by the outcome of this transformation, students know that their views of medicine are being altered. They describe these changes as part of their personal and professional growth. They argue that they are becoming more mature personally and developing a clearer and sharper understanding of the world of medicine. Most importantly, they admit a willingness to accept the situation as a small price for becoming more competent. With only minor exceptions they accept the present sacrifice of their ideals as a necessary condition of medical training, and hope to recapture their idealism at a later time....

The hope and belief that they will be in a more opportune position to express and act upon their initial idealism after graduation is coupled, for many, with a more sombre realization that matters are unlikely to change. On the basis of their observations and deliberations many students become resigned to their behaviour as physicians always coming under close scrutiny and control from their colleagues. Most students do not have high hopes of being able to change medicine.

Although they are often initially dismayed by how physicians and other hospital staff treat patients, they come to accept that the objectification of patients is a routine feature of doctor-patient relationships. It is the "professional" way to deal with medical situations.[4] In time they accept the view that patients must be objectified and depersonalized or the doctor will be unable to maintain clinical objectivity (Coombs and Powers, 1975; Emerson, 1970). While initially bothered, even offended, by this detachment, they come to see it as part of the professional situation over which they have little control....

Striving for competence is the primary student rationale to explain avoiding or shutting off emotional reactions. As they progress through the program students come to express the belief that their relationship with the patient should be governed strictly by the patient's medical problem; emotional feelings are a hindrance. They believe that they do not have time for both learning and caring, and learn to stifle their feelings because of the higher value they and others place on competence.

Students also believe that they are being trained for busy lives. Accepting the hectic pace as inevitable, they recognize that it is not temporary, but will continue throughout their medical career. Their work in the hospitals impresses on them the long hours that physicians devote to their work:

If you look around at people who are teaching you, they often have a pretty rough life as far as time commitment and work. The work doesn't end when you get out of medical school and you can see somebody who is forty-five or fifty and married and has a couple of kids, in on Saturday afternoons working away, and being on call in the evenings.

Students recognize that many physicians work long and irregular hours. As they embark upon the clerkship phase of the program, they discover that the hospital routine they must fit demands that their everyday lives be organized around medicine. . . .

The dominant concern with learning medicine leads students to maintain their learning efficiency and productivity. Students come to believe that they have no time for the frills of emotional involvement and quickly learn to close off feelings that interfere with their work (Lief and Fox, 1963). The following statement by a student emphasizes the idea of productivity:

> You can't function if you think about things like that [death and dying]. Everything you see sort of gets in there and turns about in your mind and you aren't productive. The reason you have to shut it off is because you won't be productive. . . . I think that my prime objective is to learn the pathology and just to know it and then, understanding that, I can go back to these other things and worry about the personal part of it.

During the first ten weeks of the curriculum the students are introduced to, among other things, the psychosocial component of health care. As many students are interested in working with and helping people, and are aware that medical problems have many different causes, the emphasis on the psychosocial issues gives them an opportunity to express their views concerning social, economic, political and moral aspects of medicine. However, even before Phase I is completed, they are eager to start what they consider to be their "real" medical studies. Reflecting the views of others in the class, a student says:

> [In Phase I] you really concentrate on a lot of psychosocial issues. But it become really obvious before the ten weeks are up that you are getting tired of talking about that kind of stuff, and you want to get on with it.

The students' concern for the psychosocial aspects of medicine are not entirely ignored when they enter Phase II of their program. As they are gradually introduced to the content and "core" of medicine, they begin to realize that there is too much to know and little time in which to learn it all. Like the religious or political convert who becomes fanatically observant and committed, students devote themselves to the task of learning medicine. Time becomes a commodity that must be spent wisely. They become very concerned about not misusing or wasting their time studying certain topics deemed unproductive. In this context, the psychosocial component becomes less important.

> One thing you have to do at medical school is pick up all the pathophysiology and to pick up all of the anatomy and pick up the clinical histories, the presentations, the clinical skills and so on. So psychosocial time is really a luxury, it can't really be afforded sometimes. . . .

Although they put them aside, students continue to recognize that psychosocial matters are important. They believe this area must be neglected, however, in the interests of acquiring as much medical knowledge and competence as possible. They believe that if they feel for their patients and become involved with them they will not become professionally competent. . . .

Most students move to the view that personal concerns for the patient should not intrude on the physician's professional responsibility. . . .

Student concerns about learning medicine, making the most efficient use of time, and establishing some bases of certainty and security in their work are all reflected in the selected interest they take in patients with unusual pathology (Becker *et al.*, 1961). Discussing the kind of patients that he looked forward to seeing, a student claims:

> A patient who has physical findings. Gees, I don't care what the findings are. It's a fantastic experience to see that physical finding. They may only have two or even one. . . . In order to do a physical exam you've got to have something there to feel. Someone can tell you this is the way to feel for a lump in the stomach, but if there is no lump there you are not going to learn how to feel it. . . . I think that's what I get the most out of, getting exposure to the pathology, feeling things that I may not feel.

The high point for students is making a correct diagnosis by sleuthing out relevant material, and knowing with some assurance the diagnosis is valid and the treatment competent. . . .

Students alter their understanding of how medicine should be practised. Unable to feel as deeply concerned about the patient's total condition as they believe they should, they discover an approach that justifies concentrating only on the person's medical problem. As a student remarks:

> Somebody will say "Listen to Mrs. Jones' heart. It's just a little thing flubbing on the table." And you forget about the rest of her. Part of that is the objectivity and it helps in learning in the sense that you can go in to a patient, put your stethoscope on the heart, listen to it and walk out. . . . The advantage is that you can go in a short time and see a patient, get the important things out of the patient and leave.

As students learn to objectify patients they lose their sensitivity for them. When they can concentrate on the interesting pathology of the patient's condition, students' feelings for the patient's total situation are eroded. . . . The students do not lose their idealism and assume a professional mask without a struggle. But even when they see and feel the worst, students recognize that they do not have the time to crusade. That would interfere with the learning of medicine and impede their efforts to become competent. . . .

ACTING THE PROFESSIONAL ROLE

Students believe they are expected to act as if they are in the know, not in ways which might put their developing competence into question. The pressure to be seen as competent by faculty, fellow students, hospital personnel and patients narrows the range of alternative roles students can assume. Students recognize their low status in the hospital hierarchy and on hospital rotations. They realize that the extent of their medical knowledge can easily be called into question by fellow students, tutors, interns, residents and faculty. To reduce the possibility of embarrassment and humiliation which, at this stage in their medical career, is easily their fate, students attempt to reduce the unpredictability of their situation by manipulating an impression of themselves as enthusiastic, interested, and eager to learn. At the same time, students seize opportunities which allow them to impress others, particularly faculty and fellow students, with their growing competence and confidence. . . .

Although a basic objective of the school's philosophy is to encourage learning through problem-solving and a questioning attitude throughout the medical career, the philosophy does not help students' overriding problem of appearing competent. A perspective shared by students to manage an appearance of competence is to limit their initiatives to those situations which will be convincing demonstrations of their competence. Some students decide, for example, to ask questions in areas with which they are already familiar, to cultivate an impression of competence.

The best way of impressing others with your

competence is asking questions you know the answers to. Because if they ever put it back on you: "Well what do you think?" then you tell them what you think and you'd give a very intelligent answer because you knew it. You didn't ask it to find out information. You ask it to impress people.

The general strategy that the students adopt is to mask their uncertainty and anxiety with an image of self-confidence. Image making becomes recognized as being as important as technical competence. As one student remarks: "We have to be good actors, put across the image of self-confidence, that you know it all. . . . " The pressure to conform is perhaps even more extreme at this school than at other medical schools because its evaluation system is much more pervasive and a large part of it is generated by students. Students observe each other, seeking to establish a base of comparison. . . .

The students are acutely aware of the relationship between impression management and successful evaluation. While the evaluation ought to consist of an objective assessment of the students' abilities to conduct a diagnosis and prescribe a course of treatment, the outcome is, in fact, shaped by the students' abilities to behave as if they are able to accomplish these tasks. . . .

CONCLUSION

. . . Our findings should be analogous to other professions and their socialization processes. The process of making some expert and more competent separates professionals from those they are presumed to help and serves to create a situation where the exaggerated expectations of competence are managed by symbolically defining and controlling the situation to display the imagery of competence. Impression management is basic and fundamental in those occupations and professions which profess competence in matters seriously affecting others.

Edgerton (1967) believes that the central and shared commonality of the mentally retarded released from institutions was for them to develop themselves in a cloak of competence to deny the discomforting reality of their stigma. The development of a cloak of competence is, perhaps, most apparent for those who must meet exaggerated expectations. The problem of meeting other's enlarged expectations is magnified for those uncertain about their ability to manage a convincing performance. Moreover, the performer faces the personal problem of reconciling his private self-awareness and uncertainty with his publicly displayed image. For those required to perform beyond their capacities, in order to be successful, there is the constant threat of breakdown or exposure. For both retardates and professionals the problem and, ironically, the solution, are similar. Expectations of competence are dealt with by strategies of impression management, specifically, manipulation and concealment. Interactional competencies depend on convincing presentations and much of professionalism requires the masking of insecurity and incompetence with the symbolic-interactional cloak of competence.

Notes

[1] This paper is based on data that were collected largely during the first two years of a three-year study we are conducting on the socialization of medical students at a medical school in Ontario, Canada. The data were collected by means of participant observation an interviews. We have observed students during the full range of their educational and informal activities and to date have interviewed fifty-five of the eighty students in the class. We are presently completing the fieldwork phase of the study as students approach their licensing

examination and graduation. We will be writing a monograph, based on the research, in the coming year.

[2] Unlike most medical schools, the school we are studying has a three-year program where long summer vacations are eliminated. Admission is not restricted to individuals with strong pre-medical or science backgrounds. The school deemphasizes lectures and has no formal tests or grades. Students are introduced to clinical settings from the very beginning of their studies. Learning revolves around a "problem-solving" approach as students meet in six-person tutorial groups. An analysis of the consequences of such innovations will be described in subsequent writings.

[3] The program is divided into five Phases: Phase I lasts ten weeks; Phase II twelve weeks; Phase III forty weeks; Phase IV, essentially the last half of the three-year program, is the clinical clerkship. Student electives, vacations and a review phase—Phase V—make up the remainder of the M.D. program.

[4] The core of the professional attitude toward the patient is to be found in what Parsons (1951) has termed "affective neutrality". As Bloom and Wilson have written: "This orientation is the vital distancing mechanism which prevents the practitioner from becoming the patient's colleague in illness. . . . Affective neutrality constitutes the physician's prime safeguard against the antitherapeutic dangers of countertransference" (1972:321). The management of closeness and detachment in professional-client relations is discussed in Joan Emerson (1970), and in Charles Kadushin (1962). For a discussion of the socialization of medical students toward a detached attitude, see Morris J. Daniels (1960). For an insightful analysis of how student-physicians come to manage the clinical role pertaining to death and dying, and learn to retain composure, no matter how dramatic the death scene, see Coombs and Powers (1975).

References

Becker, Ernest, *Escape from Evil.* New York: The Free Press, 1975.

Becker, Howard S. and Blanche Geer, Everett C. Hughes and Anselm Strauss. *Boys in White: Student Culture in Medical School.* Chicago: University of Chicago Press, 1961.

Bloom, Samuel W. and Robert N. Wilson. "Patient-Practitioner Relationships," pp. 315–39 in H.E. Freeman, S. Levine and L.G. Reeder (eds.), *Handbook of Medical Sociology.* Englewood Cliffs, N.J.: Prentice-Hall, 1972.

Bramson, Roy. "The Secularization of American Medicine," *Hastings Center Studies,* (1973), pp. 17–28.

Coombs, Robert H. and Pauline S. Powers. "Socialization for Death: The Physician's Role." *Urban Life,* Vol. 4 (1975), pp. 250–71.

Daniels, Morris J. "Affect and Its Control in the Medical Intern." *American Journal of Sociology,* Vol. 66 (1960), pp. 259–67.

Davis, Fred. "Professional Socialization as Subjective Experience: The Process of Doctrinal Conversion among Student Nurses," pp. 235–51 in Howard S. Becker *et al.* (eds.), *Institutions And The Person.* Chicago: Aldine Publishing Company, 1968.

Edgerton, Robert B. *The Cloak of Competence: Stigma In The Lives Of the Mentally Retarded.* Berkeley: University of California Press, 1967.

Emerson, Joan P. "Behavior in Private Places: Sustaining Definitions of Reality in Gynecological Examinations," pp. 73–97 in Hans Peter Dreitzel (ed.), *Recent Sociology.* New York: The Macmillan Company, 1970.

Eron, Leonard D. "Effect of Medical Education on Medical Students." *Journal of Medical Education,* Vol. 10. (1955), pp. 559–66.

Fox, Renée. "Training for Uncertainty," pp. 207–41 in Robert K. Merton, George G. Reader and Patricia L. Kendall (eds.), *The Student Physician.* Cambridge, Mass.: Harvard University Press, 1957.

Freidson, Eliot. *Profession of Medicine.* New York: Dodds Mead and Co., 1970a.

———. *Professional Dominance,* New York: Atherton, 1970b.

Geer, Blanche (ed.). *Learning to Work.* Beverly Hills: Sage Publications, Inc., 1972.

Goffman, Erving. *The Presentation of Self in Everyday Life.* New York: Doubleday Anchor Books, 1959.

Hass, Jack. "Binging: Educational Control Among High Steel Ironworkers." *American Behavioral Scientist,* Vol. 16 (1972), pp. 27–34.

———. "The Stages of the High Steel Ironworker Apprentice Career." *The Sociological Quarterly,* Vol. 15 (1974), pp. 93–108.

———. "Learning Real Feelings: A Study of High Steel Ironworkers' Reactions to Fear and Danger." *Sociology of Work and Occupations,* Vol. 4 (1977), pp. 147–70.

Haas, Jack, Victor Marshall and William Shaffir. "Anxiety and Changing Conceptions of Self: A Study of First-year Medical Students." Paper presented at the Canadian Sociological and Anthropological Association, May, 1975.

Hughes, Everett C. "The Sociological Study of Work: An Editorial Foreword." *American Journal of Sociology,* Vol. 57 (1952), pp. 423–26.

———. *Men and Their Work.* Glencoe: The Free Press, 1958.

Kadushin, Charles. "Social Distance between Client and Professional." *American Journal of Sociology,* Vol. 67 (1962), pp. 517–31.

Lief, Harold I. and Renée Fox. "Training for 'Detached Concern' in Medical Students," pp. 12–35 in Lief, H.I., V. Lief and N.R. Lief (eds.), *The Psychological Basis of Medical Practice.* New York: Harper and Row, 1963.

Mayer, John E. and Aaron Rosenblatt. "Encounters with Danger: Social Workers in the Ghetto." *Sociology of Work and Occupations,* Vol. 2 (1975), pp. 227–45.

Olsen, Virginia L. and Elvi W. Whittaker. *The Silent Dialogue.* San Francisco: Jossey-Bass Inc., 1968.

Parsons, Talcott. *The Social System.* London: Routledge and Kegan Paul, 1951.

———. "Research with Human Subjects and the Professional Complex." *Daedalus,* Vol. 98 (1969), pp. 325–60.

Phase 1 Manual, 1974.

Quint, Jeanne C. "Institutionalized Practices of Information Control." *Psychiatry,* Vol. 28 (1956), pp. 119–32.

Ross, Ailen D. *Becoming a Nurse.* Toronto: The Macmillan Company of Canada Ltd., 1961.

Roth Julius A. "Ritual and Magic in the Control of Contagion." *American Sociological Review,* Vol. 22 (1957), pp. 310–14.

Schanck, Richard L. "A study of a Community and Its Groups and Institutions Conceived of as Behaviors of Individuals." *Psychological Monographs,* Vol. 43, No. 2 (1932).

Siegler, Miriam and Humphry Osmond. "Aesculapian Authority." *Hastings Center Studies,* Vol. 1 (1973), pp. 41–52.

Deviance and Control

Introduction

We learned in the preceding section on socialization that, to a great degree, people think, feel and act as they do because they were socialized that way. People continue to behave in certain ways presumably because they have internalized certain values and norms. They feel it is right to act as they do, and wrong to act otherwise. The discussion of socialization ended by noting that, despite this internalization of controls on behaviour, deviance or rule-breaking is found everywhere. How can sociologists account for this fact? Its explanation and implications for society are the subject of this section.

If internalized controls on behaviour are insufficient, external controls will be needed to protect society from the harm of wrong-doing. For this reason, the topics of deviance and control often go together: one implies the other. But it may be as true to say that we have deviance because we have controls, as to say that we have controls because we have deviance. To consider this paradox, we go back to the founding figures of sociology, and particularly Emile Durkheim and Karl Marx.

Both would have conceded that deviance is universal. Perhaps each would have said that this universal fact resulted from the existence of social control, which is also universal. But the two theorists would have given different reasons for this curious point of view. Durkheim, as we recall from Professor Brym's discussion in Section 1, regarded social order as very important for individual well-being. Indeed, he saw the social order as being in some sense separate from and above the individuals making up a society. Being part of society was beneficial, especially if the social order was stable and consistent. Discontinuities and rapid change were threatening and harmful to people, leading in the most extreme cases to suicide. A suitably high (but not too high) degree of social cohesion and integration was best for individuals and for society.

For this reason, people needed to make and enforce rules, punishing wrong-doers. This would clarify the boundaries of social order and maintain or increase social cohesion. Punishment produced greater cohesion by reminding everyone of what was right and wrong, and drew together those who conformed into a tighter bond against the deviant. But this process required deviants. Without deviants, the lines of right and wrong remained unclear, social cohesion weak. Rules were needed that would find or create deviants for punishing— in effect, scapegoats. Kai Erickson (1966) showed in his study of witchcraft in seventeenth century New England Puritan communities that there could never be too much goodness. Even people living (by our current standards) extremely moral and conforming lives would find deviants—in this case, witches—among themselves to punish. They *had to* find witches, from a Durkheimian perspective. Conversely, no matter how tolerant or morally lax it might become, no society, according to this thinking, can totally accept all behaviours as equally satisfactory. Such indifference would deprive the society of all normative boundaries and all occasions for punishment and integration. Such a society would break down and disappear, if this theory is correct.

Durkheim's theory accounts successfully for the universality of deviance and control, and it is attractive for several other reasons. First, it seems to square with certain theories of history (for example, Edward Gibbons' theory of the decline and fall of the Roman Empire) that hold that morally lax civilizations don't survive. Second, and more important, the theory seems to square with observations made at many times and places that, in the face of a threat to order, demands for social cohesion increase, and so do rule-making and rule enforcement. On this basis, we might predict that the current crisis in South Africa, resulting from intensified terrorism and international economic and political pressure, will result in stricter rule enforcement not only against Blacks but also against Whites. Lines between good and bad will be drawn more sharply and policed more savagely, this theory would argue, or this society will not survive.

Karl Marx would have conceded the universality of deviance and control; but he would have explained it quite differently. He would have argued that rules are typically made by states, and the people who control those states—the ruling class—will use state powers of rule making and enforcement to protect their own interests.

Thus, social control has a more specific goal than mere social integration: it is directed against people who threaten the dominance or interests of the ruling class. Since virtually every society has a ruling class with interests to protect, and a state apparatus for making and enforcing rules, deviance will be discovered and punished everywhere. Failure to punish such deviance would not result in the disappearance of society, only the disappearance or overthrow of the ruling class.

Marx's theory improves on Durkheim's by suggesting which kinds of deviance are most likely to be punished. In our own society, the ruling class is an economic elite. Therefore, economic crimes against the rich are most likely to be punished. Economic crimes perpetrated by the rich against the poor are much less likely to be punished. Non-economic crimes—such as crimes against the person (e.g., wife battering or rape)—are also less likely to get punished, especially if the victims are poor. Likewise, crimes against "morality"—e.g., taking the Lord's name in vain, being gluttonous, slothful, uncharitable, or even promoting war between nations, hatred between groups, or environmental destruction—are even less likely to get punished.

Marx's theory is not quite so good at accounting, as Durkheim's does, for less obviously rational or instrumental social control. For example, Marx's theory is not helpful in understanding why poor, uneducated people much more often support capital punishment (usually to be carried out against other poor, uneducated people) than rich, educated people. His theory does not explain the seemingly irrational, purposeless trait of "punitiveness." Durkheim's theory does: it predicts that insecure, relatively isolated people would have the greatest need for clear boundaries and strong enforcement; and that is what we find.

Nor is Marx's theory as good as Durkheim's (or Max Weber's) in accounting for social control that arises out of non-economic, symbolic or status-oriented concerns. Consider Joseph Gusfield's (1963) discussion of the laws that sixty years ago prohibited liquor sales in the United States. "Prohibition" was a law most people resisted from the beginning. Supporters of the law were rural, Protestant, native-born Americans feeling hostile to, and culturally endangered by, urban Catholic immigrants. The law quickly proved not only unpopular but unenforceable and a tremendous boon to organized crime. During its short life span, it served only to symbolize and strengthen the cohesion and status of rural, Protestant, native-born Americans. We might find similar patterns and motivations if we studied the American "Moral Majority," the pro-capital punishment lobby, REAL Women, the anti-Gay lobby, and pro-life groups. Indeed, the membership of these groups might overlap.

A recent study by York University sociologist Lorna Erwin (*The Globe and Mail*, Thursday, April 2, 1987, page 1) surveyed over 800 people on the mailing lists of REAL Women, Campaign Life and other anti-abortion groups. She found that anti-abortionists are very frequently church-goers (63 percent go once or more a week) who fear that homosexuals, feminists, and the media are destroying the family. "What has galvanized them," says Erwin, "is their perception that the family is under attack, and they see it everywhere." It is this sense of a danger to tradition, and a belief in absolute right and wrong—moral absolutism—that makes such a movement to control behaviour possible.

Membership in a respected status group is, according to Weber, often as important a motivation for social action as economic interest. Groups often struggle to have their way of thinking prevail because that demonstrates their value and importance in society. Law making and enforcement is, thus, a form of status group lobbying which aims at increasing a group's social standing and has the secondary effect, as Durkhaim reminds us, of strengthening membership allegiance to the group. Marx would have difficulty explaining such behaviour as other than "false consciousness": another way of saying that behaviour that is directed away from the class struggle is not really meaningful.

Thus, the sociology of deviance and control turns out to be largely the study of deviance as produced by control, or the sociology of law. Along these lines, see also Richard Ericson's article on detective work in Section Twelve below. In this respect, the Durkheimian functionalists and their Marxist opponents are unified. But their differences of approach are profound, as we have already seen.

This conflict of approaches is neatly spelled out in Austin Turk's article on law, conflict and order in this section. Professor Turk suggests that the chief problem posed by competing theoretical approaches is not merely disagreement, which is scientific stock in trade, but a tendency of different schools to talk past one another. They set the terms of debate in such different ways that appropriate data are rarely collected to resolve the disagreement.

Laws and social control generally arise out of class relations and cultural and subcultural conceptions of right and wrong. Thus, we must expect that different societies will make and enforce laws differently. Differences in social integration and cultural punitiveness will add up to national differences in deviance and control. Finally, different social conditions—differences in the attainability of desired rewards by legitimate means, for example—will lead to different rates of deviant behaviour, given similar laws and law enforcement practices in different countries. In his article on differences between Canada and the United

States, which follows in this section, John Hagan attempts to measure and explain national variations in crime and deviance. Before reading this article, it may be wise to reread S.M. Lipset's discussion of Canadian-American value differences in Section Two.

When we turn our attention away from the sociology of law to deviant behaviour *per se*, we realize that deviance comes in many forms and degrees of severity. An experiment by Thomas Gabor and his collaborators to measure the honesty of people given an easy opportunity to deviate suggests that "public deviance" of a minor kind is quite common. A variety of studies asking people to admit their own crime, deviance, or delinquency shows that much more deviance goes on than ever comes to the attention of public authorities. Further, most people, when deviating, have handy ways to excuse or rationalize their behaviour. The deviant does not always consider his rule-breaking deviant, let alone harmful: this is surely the case in widespread automobile speeding, deviant drinking, drug or sexual behaviours (the kinds of things Professor Hagan has elsewhere called "disreputable pleasures"), or even tax evasion. Ordinary people are so willing to break rules and justify their actions, that many commentators have feared the legal system is losing, or has largely lost, its "legitimacy"—that is, its ability to command respect and compliance without naked coercion.

Sexual mass murder is quite a different kind of deviance. Unlike petty larceny, tax cheating, or marijuana smoking, rape and murder are almost universally believed to be serious deviant acts deserving strong punishment. People do not often violate this norm (although rape and sexual assault are certainly much more common than murder, and much more often committed than punished) or readily justify it, if they have. People arrested for repeated violence against the person are generally thought to be deranged; and an explanation of their behaviour is sought in defects of their character, not in subcultural or class conflict. In his article on this topic, Elliott Leyton argues that abnormal family upbringing may lead a man to rape and murder large numbers of women, often while preserving an outward air of normality but shutting out awareness of this deviance to himself and others.

If sexual mass murders represent one kind of serious deviance produced by (flawed) socialization, the "suite crimes" described by Colin Goff and Charles Reasons may represent another. The difference between the ways street crime and suite (corporate) crime are treated by law reflects, as Marx would predict, a bias among rule-makers and rule-enforcers in favour of the rich and powerful. Suite crimes harm many more people more seriously than street crimes. Occupational hazards left unremedied by the employing corporation; price-fixing and other collusion among large organizations; and various types of product fraud are largely unpoliced in our society and hard for ordinary citizens to prevent or rectify.

Durkheim could give us little help in explaining why suite crime is handled as it is. Conceivably, stricter legislation and enforcement would, in the Durkheimian sense, prove intensely integrative for the majority of citizens who do not own major corporations. Why then is such legislation lacking? A Marxist analysis seems to give the best possible answer: the powerful make laws to suit themselves.

But recall Gabor's finding that ordinary people will readily cheat in ordinary ways. Why should we be surprised, then, that powerful people readily cheat in powerful ways? Maybe this pair of findings supports the Marxist notion that capitalist culture is extraordinarily corrosive of morality at all levels; and self-interest is the guiding principle in all matters of deviance and control. Max Weber might have argued that the problem lies with a loss of legitimacy of law and traditional morality at all levels, the result of excess complexity and bureaucratization. And Durkheim might add that the problem is too-rapid social change and the *anomie* or normlessness that this brings to human affairs. In this, as in so many areas of sociology, there are almost too many good explanations, each with something useful to add. In every event, the social prospect is bleak.

To this point in the book, we have focused on socialization, deviance and control: three processes that shape and change social behaviour. The next section is concerned with three more processes: structuration, integration and evaluation.

References

Erikson, Kai T. *Wayward Puritans*. New York: John Wiley and Sons, 1966.

Gibbon, Edward {1776-1788} *The History of the Decline and Fall of the Roman Empire*. London: J.M. Dent, 1913.

Gusfield, Joseph R. *Symbolic Crusade: Status Politics and the American Temperance Movement*. Urbana: University of Illinois Press, 1963.

16   Theories of Law and Order

Austin T. Turk

AUSTIN T. TURK, Professor of Sociology at the University of Toronto, specializes in studying the linkage between legal power and social conflict. His major publications include *Criminality and Legal Order* (1969); *Legal Sanctioning and Social Control* (1972); and *Political Criminality: The Defiance and Defence of Authority* (1982). He is currently at work on studies of socio-legal developments and a book on conflict criminology. A past president of the American Society of Criminology, Professor Turk serves on the editorial boards of *Criminology: An Interdisciplinary Journal; Criminal Justice and Behavior; Law and Society Review;* and *Sociological Inquiry.*

INTRODUCTION

Although given renewed visibility and life in recent years, the debate over the relative merits of conflict-coercion theories and integration-consensus theories is obviously as ancient as we are able (or care) to trace it back in recorded social thought. One might, therefore, conclude that the best we can expect from continued debate are new formulations of the old arguments, on the premise that so ancient and fundamental an issue has turned out to be empirically insoluble. On the other hand, it seems clear that this is a controversy grounded in human social experiences, with empirical consequences following from commitments to and inclinations toward one or the other viewpoint. If so, if the controversy has social reality, then specific issues arising from the descriptive and explanatory claims of theorists working from these two rival orientations are in principle resolvable by empirical investigations.

It appears very unlikely that scientific formulations[1] of either view will eventually be found to be utterly false. Rather, since competent and intellectually honest theorists and researchers on each side have generated a body of conceptualization and evidence that hangs together for many years as a reasonably coherent, not obviously implausible, basis for understanding and inquiry, then one of the following alternatives is possible:

1. the theories derivable from the different lines of theorizing are about different things;

2. the theories are posing and answering different questions about the same thing;

3. the theories are not of the same kind, that is, they differ in the mode of explanation;

4. the theories are about the same thing at the same level of abstraction/generalization, and are the same kind of theories, but differ in regard to the problematic aspects of range of aspects of the thing with which they are dealing;

5. the theories are the same kind of theories and are about the same thing, but at different levels of abstraction or generalization, which means that one theory may be deducible from the other.

The confrontation between conflict-coercion and integration-consensus orientations pervades all areas of sociological inquiry and is especially sharp among social scientists trying to understand the "legal" dimension of social life. Whether taking the form of analyses of legal institutions with respect to the conjoining of facts of restraint, obligation, and liability with facts of protection, right, and immunity, or the form of "external" analyses of the relationships between legal institutional and other social phenomena, their efforts have resulted in an impressive literature in which the battle of orientations has been waged with considerable skill and determination.[2] The basic concern of that literature may be construed, in a hopefully useful simplification, as the problem of determining the relationships among law, social conflict, and social order. In the following analysis the objectives are to determine which of the five alternatives best describes the confrontation between conflict-coercion and integration-consensus theories of law, conflict, and order, and to use the results of that effort as a basis for identifying and addressing some crucial problems involved in trying to subject the rival theories to empirical testing.

Given the generally primitive state of sociological theories, it is not surprising that the first step must be to extract the theories from the theorizing—the respective accretions of more and less intelligible and logical arguments, analyses, invocations, and allusions.[3] Extracting theories from theorizing involves the difficult and admittedly hazardous task of attempting to make the best possible statement from each perspective, in terms of what a scientific theory is presumed to look like and to be. This means that what any specific thinker really meant, and even what he actually said, is not necessarily binding. It also means that one refuses to be constrained by the subjective understandings of various interested parties as to what is or is not true or viable according to their partisan preferences or aversions, their respective methodological assumptions, and their various philosophical concerns. Our concern is simply to generate the best scientific formulations we can, by using, distorting, amending, supplementing, and sometimes ignoring particular contributions.

Having arbitrarily, though not unreasonably, decided that the two theories are concerned with at least three of the same things, whatever else they may deal with, we proceed by constructing definitional statements about each thing—law, order, conflict—in terms of what the theory "says" or should say if it is to make scientific sense by our criteria. As will become apparent, the results turn out to be frequently inconsistent with prevalent beliefs and assumptions about characteristic differences between the two kinds of theory, and about the appropriate classification of particular theorists and their works.[4] For example: (1) some Marxian conceptualizations fit readily into conflict-coercion theory, while others seem to make far better sense as contributions to integration-consensus theory; (2) many of the propositions of "conflict theory" as developed by Coser (1956, 1967) and others appear to be major components of an empirically tenable integration-consensus theory, but do not weld easily into a consistent conflict-coercion theory; (3) some functionalist assertions about constraining factors in social life appear to be major, even essential, components of conflict-coercion theory, but no more than secondary, even residual "error term," components of integration-consensus theory.

DEFINITIONAL STATEMENTS

Law

1 Conflict-coercion theory defines law as *power*, by which is meant both *(a)* the direct (not necessarily total) control of any or all of the available military, economic, political, and ideological resources, with some varying but significant probability that they can be mobilized to counter present or potential resistance; and *(b)* the structured advantages that accrue to the holders of direct power. The distinction between legal and non-legal power is a cultural invention originating in pre-scientific and non-scientific discourses on ethics—an invention which has been accepted and used as the conceptual basis for justifying and facilitating the efforts of rela-

tively powerful people to maximize their life chances. To the extent it has been accomplished, institutionalization of the legal-non-legal distinction has enabled relatively powerful people to reduce the costs and dangers of dealing with one another, while confirming and facilitating the subjugation of less powerful people to the advantage of the more powerful.

2 Integration-consensus theory defines law as *authority*, by which is meant both *(a)* that more or less systematized class of substantive norms collectively recognized to be the most definitive statements of the behavioural and relational implications of collectively held values, and *(b)* the control and mobilization by collectively recognized and accepted ("authorized") actors ("authorities") of ideological, political, economic, and—when absolutely necessary—military resources, according to organizational arrangements and procedural rules designed to prevent, settle, or limit disputes arising from intentional or unintentional violations of the substantive norms. The distinction between authority and power is a cultural invention originating in efforts to articulate the emergent collective understanding of the functional requirements for viable social relationships—an understanding painfully and slowly acquired through millennia of reflection grounded in experienced successes and failures. To the extent it has been accomplished, institutionalization of the authority-power distinction, by differentiating legal from non-legal actions and relations, has enabled people to reduce the costs and dangers of dealing with one another, while confirming and supporting the right of less powerful people to resist exploitation by the more powerful.

Conflict

1 Conflict-coercion theory defines conflict as the *ubiquitous struggle* intrinsic to interactions and relations between people and others not of "their own kind" as all try to create, maintain, and extend behavioural and relational patterns that maximize their own life chances—which necessarily involves minimizing the extent to which "our" efforts are hindered or threatened by "their" efforts. Because total environmental control can never be assumed, even when approximations are temporarily achieved, people always try to mobilize whatever resources are controlled in order to gain control over additional resources, to protect what they have, and so on in an infinite regress. Conflict may be more direct or more indirect, depending upon whether the parties deal with one another as proximate adversaries or else affect one another's life chances as a functional consequence of actions and relations designed to maximize their own.

As technological and other developments and events increase the scale and complexity of the social arena in which the struggle goes on, the cultural (symbolic, perceptual) and social (interactional, relational) sources and dimensions of conflict multiply. Thus, the fundamental contradiction arises that even as the opportunities for maximizing life chances increase, so do the risks—not only because of the growing number of kinds of people, each trying to protect and improve their life chances, but also because of the increasing difficulty for the more powerful of subjugating or eliminating the less powerful. The difficulty increases *(a)* because the labour of and consumption by the less powerful become essential, yet basically incompatible, components in the production of resources, and *(b)* because the subjugation of the less powerful, as distinct from their annihilation, is made increasingly to depend upon the manipulation of their beliefs, identities, and allegiances by invoking and at least formally using the conceptual, organizational, and procedural devices of law.

2 Integration-consensus theory defines conflict as the *unnecessary struggles* among people who have not yet attained sufficient

collective understanding of their common values and interdependence as human beings to generate, or else to accept, the institutionalization in law of the authority-power distinction. Even though conflict among different social groupings tends to promote cohesion within each grouping, and in itself constitutes at least an initial basis for the eventual development of genuinely social, i.e., cooperative, relations among them, all conflicts are ultimately antithetical to the establishment and maintenance of viable behavioural and relational patterns. Conflict as such obviously can occur only where people are able to deal with one another as proximate adversaries—though it is of course true that the indirectly, or functionally, competitive process by which people and activities are selected for greater or lesser rewards does imply some degree of concomitant variation in life chances.

As technological and other developments and events increase the scale and complexity of social relatedness, the potential for conflict increases as erstwhile strangers are brought into contact with one another. Fears and misunderstandings are likely to produce some conflicts as those newly involved with one another learn to cooperate with, and eventually to trust, one another within the guiding and facilitating framework of law. Regrettably, it appears highly improbable that conflicts will be finally eliminated altogether, because of such factors as the variable and limiting characteristics of the human organism, accidents of socialization, and technological limitations upon the ability of people to engage in meaningful, gratifying communication and interaction with many other people.

Order

1 Conflict-coercion theory defines order as a more or less temporary *balance of power*, in which the more powerful have uneasily accommodated one another in terms of the institutionalized legal-non-legal distinction, and have effectively minimized any chance that the less powerful will be able to challenge seriously the terms of their subjugation. While their virtual monopoly of military resources constitutes their most obvious and ultimate means of control, the more powerful rely generally upon the (especially "legal") use of their economic, political, and ideological resources to reward acceptance of and to punish resistance to their continuing dominance. Such conditioning is successful to the extent that the less powerful collectively come to accept their lot in life not only as unchangeable, but even as just and gratifying.

In principle, the degree of control, *ergo* order, is limited only by the state of relevant scientific knowledge and the readiness of the relatively powerful to abide by the canons of enlightened self-interest. However, total control, *ergo* permanent order, is extremely improbable because of such factors as *(a)* the redistributing of resources, i.e., changes in relative power, caused by natural environmental changes (e.g., depletion or discovery of raw materials), technological innovation, and conquests; *(b)* the apparently impossible costs of maintaining individualized behaviour control over large populations; and *(c)* the insatiability of the common human desire to protect and improve the life chances of one's "own kind." Such orders as are achieved are virtually certain to be eventually destroyed—"externally" by ecological, diplomatic, or military failures, and/or "internally" by miscalculations on the part of some relatively powerful people in their dealings with others (a classic example being the involvement of less powerful people in the rivalries of the more powerful).

2 Integration-consensus theory defines order as a more or less permanent *voluntary association* in which people optimize their life chances by directly and indirectly, or functionally, cooperating on the basis of their collective understanding of their inter-

dependence. Because of the increasing scale and complexity of social relatedness, it becomes necessary to supplement informal with more formal mechanisms for generating and sustaining cooperative behaviour and relations. This need is met directly and indirectly by the creation and operation of legal institutions, which both *(a)* indicate and determine how people are to behave and relate to one another, and *(b)* promote the support the creation and operation of analogous institutions in "private" or "unofficial" areas of social life where problems of scale and complexity appear. A major consequence is that decision on the allocation of available resources are made or supported by the authority of law—which maximizes the probability that relative rewards will be correlated with relative contributions to the collective welfare and that the correlation will be recognized by all participants in the association.

In principle, the degree of order is limited only by the state of relevant scientific knowledge of how to achieve full cooperation. Unfortunately, though close approximations to the "perfect order" do seem attainable, it is virtually certain not to be achieved because of such factors as *(a)* the obsolescence of once-functional relational and behavioural patterns in the face of natural environmental changes, technological innovations, and aggression by external parties; and *(b)* the same factors that seem likely to prevent the elimination of conflicts from social life (i.e., human biological limitations and variability, socialization accidents, and technological barriers to both meaningful and extensive social interaction).

DISCUSSION

In so far as the attempt to transform conflict-coercion and integration-consensus theoriz-

ing into something closer to theories has been successful, the confrontation of orientations can now be examined as a confrontation of theories, in reference to each of the five alternative relationships initially proposed.

1 *Are the theories about the same things?* The two theories can be said to be about the same things only at a very abstract level. Each theory postulates or asserts what each thing is on the basis of historical and all sorts of other "hard" and "soft" evidence, interpreted either "pessimistically" or "optimistically' " to use terms that perhaps the majority of people would use in considering the prospects for the elimination of strife and the securing of justice in human society. Given that temperamental inclinations do not settle definitional issues in scientific discourse, and given that further consideration *in vacuo* of the problem of conceptual equivalence can lead only to a phenomenological morass, the pragmatic solution is to reserve the equivalence question for later consideration in light of the results of examining the other theory-theory relational alternatives.

2 *Are the theories asking and answering different questions?* While both theories are concerned with the law in relation to social conflict and order, they differ fundamentally in the way in which specific descriptive and explanatory accounts are linked to historical and other empirical observations. They appear to be asking similar or at least complementary questions (e.g., What is a legal order? How is such an order created and preserved?) but with quite different background assumptions regarding the process by which empirical observations acquire meaning, especially in the *answering* of theoretical questions.

Conflict-coercion theory appears to be comprised mainly of essentially "statistical" generalizations and projections from observed instances of the occurrence or extension of conflicts in social life. What will happen is assumed to be a function of what has happened. The tenuousness of human accomplishments is accepted as a constant. The empirical "groundedness" of conflict-coercion theory is exemplified in Weber's "summary of the most general relations between law and economy" (Weber, 1968:333–7).

Integration-consensus theory appears to be built largely out of, or around, essentially "analytical" generalizations derived from observed instances of the resolution or softening of social conflicts. What will happen is *not* assumed to be a function of what has happened. Rather, it is assumed that what has happened, perhaps even most of the time, can or will be transcended by what *can* happen—as indicated or implied by qualitative (whether or not quantitatively impressive) evidence, or even by theorizing virtually independent of any evidence. The tenuousness of human accomplishments is accepted only as a residuum. An illustration of the "transcendental" thrust of integration-consensus theory is Barkun's (1968) derivation of support for the concept of "law without sanctions" from his analyses of primitive and international legal systems.

3 *Are these the same kind of theories?* As sociological rather than physicalist, biological, or psychological formulations, the theories may be said to exemplify the same mode of explanation. However, as sociologists are painfully aware, attempts to specify their mode of explanation have generated not only factional cleavages and specialisms but also a more profound disagreement over whether sociology is—objectively and/or properly— a value-neutral or a value-committed enterprise, a distinction synonymous for many with that between science (or "scientism") and non-science (or "humanism"). The two theories clearly diverge on the values issue.

Conflict-coercion theory may be characterized as "empirical-scientific." Although the theory obviously implies strategies and tactics for conflicting parties, any attempt to use these in action is left a matter of personal or collective choice and commitment on faith. There are no assumptions regarding the goodness or badness of the phenomena of law, conflict, and order. In Weber's words, "legal guarantees and their underlying normative conceptions are of interest both as consequences and causes . . . of certain regularities of human action" (Weber, 1968:332).

Integration-consensus theory may be characterized as "empirical-normative." Given that order is a good thing and is taken to mean the absence of conflict, strategies and tactics for the elimination of conflicts are explicitly sought via efforts to confirm and implement the analytical generalizations developed from reflection about instances of conflict reduction. It is assumed that enlightened people will use the resulting knowledge in action, and that the creation and operation of legal institutions epitomizes enlightened social action. Whether in Selznick's (1961, 1969) moral functionalism, Podgorecki's (1962, 1974) social engineering on behalf of socialist legality, or Quinney's (1974) radical critique in struggle for a truly socialist society, the commitment of integration-consensus theorists to bridging the "is" and "ought" is evident.

4 *Do the theories deal with different problematics?* It appears that the difference between the theories is to be understood not as a difference in *which* aspects of the law-conflict-order relationship are taken as the problem focus, but instead as a difference in *what* about that relationship is considered to be problematic.

In conflict-coercion theory, conflict is seen as the most fundamental social process, whose dynamics are such that order in any sense becomes a highly problematic and never really stable outcome. Whenever some relative stability is found, the basic questions raised in conflict-coercion theory are: How did it result from conflict? What are the sources and dimensions of conflict within it? How will conflict eventually end it? The "conflict postulate" of conflict-coercion theory is clearly stated in Dahrendorf's (1968:150) characterization of justice as "not an unchanging state of affairs, whether real or imagined, but the permanently changing outcome of the dialectic of power and resistance."

In integration-consensus theory cooperation is seen as the most fundamental process, one whose dynamics are such that order in some sense becomes a highly probable and more or less stable outcome. Whenever some relative instability, some conflict, is found, the basic questions of integration-consensus theory are: How did it originate? What are the social mechanisms tending to eliminate it? How will they eventually succeed? The ultimate expression of the "cooperation postulate" of integration-consensus theory is Barkun's (1968:92) assertion of a universal "human craving for order."

5 *Are the theories stated at different levels of abstraction or generalization?* To the extent that they are comprised of empirically grounded and meaningful propositions, there seems to be no difference between the theories in regard to the level at which they are stated. Both are macrosociological, postulate no historical or cultural boundedness, and are proposed as general, in principle complete, rather than special or partial theories. But it has already been noted that the two theories differ in the extent to which they consist of empirically constrained propositions. Thus, there is a difference if the level of abstraction and generalization is defined in such terms as the distance between empirical observations and theoretical propositions, or the ratio of speculative to empirical or of normative to neutral statements, or the extent to which theoretical expectations are derived from essentially statistical versus analytical generalizations. . . .

RÉSUMÉ

So far, we have concluded that conflict-coercion theory is mainly comprised of essentially "statistical" generalizations, is "empirical-scientific," and rests upon the "conflict postulate," while integration-consensus theory is mainly comprised of essentially "analytical" generalizations, is "empirical-normative" and rests upon the "cooperation postulate." Further, these conclusions have led us to suggest that conflict-coercion theory—as a more empirically constrained intellectual effort—is constructed at a lower level of abstraction and generalization than integration-consensus theory, even though the theories provide equally general macrosociological accounts of law-conflict-order relationships. Having now some contextual understanding of basic differences and similarities between the theories, we are in a better position to consider the equivalence question (i.e., whether the theories are about the same things).

It is apparent that the conflict-coercion and integration-consensus theories are not strictly comparable, but also not wholly incomparable. While the meanings of law, conflict, and order shift as each theory selectively emphasizes certain kinds and interpretations of data, both theories do appeal to empirical evidence and frequently use the same empirical observations in the interpretive process by which evidence is generated. Although conflict-coercion theory excludes the kind of normative and transcendental concerns and propositions that characterize integration-consensus theory, nothing in conflict-coercion theory precludes efforts to put it to partisan use, while integration-consensus theory subsumes instead of rejecting the norms of scientific inquiry—that accounts be naturalistic, communicable, and demonstrable. Thus, there is some warrant for attempting to derive testable alternative hypotheses from the rival theories.

SOME RESEARCH IMPLICATIONS [5]

Deriving testable hypotheses from any theory is never a simple task; it is especially difficult when theorizing, rather than a theory itself, provides the basis for the formulation of a hypothesis. Attempts to test conflict-coercion and integration-consensus theories of law, conflict, and order have been severely handicapped by the fact that in neither case have theories as such actually been available. Consequently, it is scarcely to the discredit of researchers that the results of their efforts have been almost uniformly ambiguous or misleading. Without actual theories with which to work, investigators have had trouble avoiding simplistic and biased formulations and distinguishing appropriate from inappropriate evidence and procedures. The point of the following commentary is not, then, to criticize directly the procedural decisions and substantive conclusions of particular researchers, but instead to use their especially notable efforts selectively as vehicles for identifying "errors" and offering "corrections."

In their recent study, Rossi et al. (1974) hypothesized that "the conflict model implies disagreement over what is to be considered serious, with dissensus generated by the varying interests of subgroups in a society. To the extent that empirical investigation shows great consensus, the conflict model loses support." Analysis of the results of a 1972 survey of the adult population of Baltimore, Maryland, revealed that the sample of 200 were in very substantial agreement on the relative seriousness of 140 offences, which included various kinds of white-collar as well as conventional crimes. Among the detailed findings, an especially interesting one for our purposes is that education and youth are correlated, among individuals, with the over-all sample means, and that the less educated blacks were the subgroup most deviant from

the over-all consensus—especially in regard to the relative seriousness of interpersonal violence between people who know one another. The authorities concluded, of course, that their findings strongly supported consensus theory against conflict theory. However, their premises and procedures, and therefore their conclusion, become highly questionable in light of the conflict-coercion and integration-consensus theories as explicated so far in the construction of definitional statements about law, conflict, and order.

1 Conflict-coercion theory does *not* imply disagreement about the relative seriousness of crimes. To the extent that a balance of power has been reached and a system of domination developed, beliefs are expected to be products of both *(a)* self-interest and acceptance of reassuring ideological justifications among the more powerful, and *(b)* the direct and indirect indoctrination of the less powerful. Formal education is assumed to be one important means by which ideological consensus is created and reinforced. Accordingly, a high degree of consensus on the relative seriousness of crimes can be interpreted as evidence of the successful control and mobilization of ideological resources so as to minimize the divergence of beliefs otherwise expected to result from social inequalities.

2 Conflict-coercion theory does imply that people (such as young American blacks) who perceive from experience, direct or vicarious, that their efforts to improve or even secure their life chances are unavailing will eventually develop normative beliefs to some extent divergent from, and probably opposed to, those of the more powerful and of the less powerful whose experience has not yet been long enough, discouraging enough, or intolerable enough to overcome the effects of direct and indirect ideological control. In principle, the degree of ideological control can be independently measured, for example, by observing changes in the formal wording and working interpretations of laws, the

number and disposition of legal cases, or the openness and frequency with which dissident views are expressed and promoted, rather than merely inferred from the results of attitude surveys.

3 Rather than referring to simply or exclusively ideological or normative conflicts, conflict-coercion theory refers to *structural* relationships produced, sustained, and destroyed by the mobilization of resources and by changes in the distribution of resources. Because structural relationships (or "functional interdependencies") may exist whether or not people involved in them are fully aware of them, attitude or opinion data alone cannot provide a basis for testing the theory. In any case, research intended to establish the degree of consensus in some population on the behavioural and relational norms reflected, articulated, and enforced by the institutions of law must deal with much more than public opinion; self-reported deviations, observed deviations, and the numerous and often heated public controversies over the organization and use of legal control resources.

4 Integration-consensus theory does *not* imply that dissensus must be minimal at any specific time and place, but rather that *if* order is being achieved, then dissensus is being reduced as law performs its educative and coordinative functions over some period of time. Thus, the theory can be neither supported nor refuted by attitude or other data descriptive only of some particular moment in the development of order by people in the process of realizing their interdependence.

Having noted some major difficulties in testing the theories with the kind of research exemplified in the Rossi study, we now turn to a study in which some of these difficulties do not arise, but in which some others do. By far the most ambitious and sophisticated attempt so far to test "conflict" and "consensus" propositions about law-conflict-order relationships has been made by McDonald, whose research is reported in a volume recently published.[6] It is impossible to do jus-

tice here to the complexity of her conceptual and empirical analyses. For present purposes it is sufficient to indicate that she carried out an exhaustive review of theorizing and some selected empirical works from the eighteenth century to the present day, on the basis of which she formulated a large number of hypotheses about relationships between socio-economic variables (e.g., gross national product, Lorenz index of intersectoral inequality, Gini index, unemployment and employment rates, illiteracy rate, school enrolment rate) and "the level and nature of *sanctions* imposed, as indicated by official rates of court convictions, police reports of offences, and sentences" (McDonald:202). Among her main and characteristic hypotheses are the following:

> [Consensus theory implies that] societies with extensive social and economic problems should have higher rates of official crime than societies with lesser problems. There may be some lag. (143)
> [Conflict theory holds that] the nature and level of sanctions occurring is . . . determined ultimately by the holders of power, in accordance with their needs and the resources at their command. (ibid.)
> Whether inequality causes crime or not, the [conflict] theory at least holds that with sizable inequalities, the holders of power must resort to extensive means of repression to maintain their privileges. (151)

Detailed analyses of cross-national, English, and Canadian time-series and other data produced results "strongly supportive of twentieth-century conflict explanations. Social problem explanations of all kinds were almost routinely disconfirmed, which means disconfirmation of consensus theory very generally, and disconfirmation of the early [simplistic and deterministic] versions of conflict [theory]" (ibid. 221). While there appears to be little to question in her analytical procedures, given the limits imposed by the availability and quality of quantitative national data, some questions do arise regarding the premises from which hypotheses were formulated, and the relative and future utility of quantitative "macro" versus "micro" studies and of quantitative versus historical studies.

1 Integration-consensus theory implies that people who have collectively achieved a high degree of consensus will tend to cooperate in the face of common adversity so as to maximize their collective well-being. The crime rates of societies facing economic and other threats are expected, therefore, to be a function of the level of consensual integration. Thus, integration-consensus theory is not a "social problem explanation" per se—which means that independent measures of both the level of consensus and the strength of consensus-producing mechanisms are required before such findings as McDonald's can be adequately interpreted. As it stands, the failure to find a positive association between crime rates and social problem indicators can be interpreted in three ways: *(a)* a methodological artifact resulting from the lumping together of "high consensus" societies (those well on the way toward consensual order) with "low consensus" societies (those just starting, or else contending with especially formidable obstacles); *(b)* an artifact generated by the presumably positive association between the level of consensual cooperation and the adequacy of social bookkeeping (implying that "true" crime rates are largely independent of "official" rates, are more appropriate for testing integration-consensus theory, and probably *are* associated positively with other social problem indicators); and/or *(c)* a demonstration that adversity promotes consensus, while affluence promotes dissensus.

2 Conflict-coercion theory implies that criminality rates are a function of the extent to which a balance of power among the more powerful and the subjugation of the less powerful have not been accomplished. It follows that increasing resources will be associated with increasing allocations of resources for legal control—and therefore with increas-

ing criminality rates, as McDonald hypothesized and found—only in so far as the mobilization of resources fails to produce balance and/or subjugation. If generally satisfactory mechanisms for ensuring the "equitable" sharing of risks and opportunities among the more powerful are not found, either increasing or decreasing resources is likely to generate "upper-world crimes"—which McDonald was forced to neglect because of the lack of data. Similarly, whether resources are increasing or decreasing is, within limits, of course, secondary to whether resources are being mobilized so as to accomplish the acceptance by the less powerful of their *relative* deprivation, which requires, among other things, the cooptation of exceptionally ambitious and able individuals and the allocation of sufficient economic (and perhaps even political and ideological) resources to the less powerful to assure them of their collective safety from *absolute* deprivation. The major point is that it would not necessarily disconfirm conflict-coercion theory to find increasing affluence associated with a *decline* in crime rates and in the investment of resources in legal control any more than finding an increase necessarily supports the theory.

3 Without marked improvements in the quality of national data sources, it appears very unlikely that further attempts to work with such data will produce significantly different or stronger results. The complexity and expense of the task, as well as the political concerns and fears of the various national and international "power elites," are likely for the foreseeable future to continue to inhibit efforts to increase the validity and reliability of criminal and other national statistical data. Therefore, "micro" studies (e.g., Chambliss, 1975) involving the collection of original as well as official data seem more promising for the purposes of testing the conflict-coercion and integration-consensus theories of law, conflict, and order. What is lost in terms of a more adequate delineation of relevant economic, political, and other

contextual factors may at least in part be regained from the more rigorous testing of admittedly and explicitly limited hypotheses about the nature and impact of particular subnational or international legal control agencies and programs. In addition, given the inadequacies of the data likely to be available for "macro" quantitative analysis and the very limited range of hypotheses likely to be amenable to testing in "micro" studies, a greater emphasis upon historical case studies is clearly warranted. Within a comparative analytical framework, historical research (e.g., Beattie, 1974; Hanawalt, 1974) on the development of legal systems in relation to political, economic, and cultural events and trends offers many opportunities for at least logical quasi-experiments that provide the basis for "weight of evidence" testing, even though no individual study can properly claim the status of a crucial experiment.

Given that the conflict-coercion versus integration-consensus theoretical debate has often been carried on in reference to the extent of class, racial, and political discrimination in criminal law enforcement, studies of factors related to the initiation and processing of cases have generally been assumed to constitute tests of the relative validity of the opposing theories. Hagan (1974a) has recently provided a notable example of such research in his study of factors affecting racial disparities in sentencing in Alberta. Having obtained data for all offenders admitted to the five largest provincial correctional institutions during a two-month period of 1973 (N = 999), he used regression and tabular techniques to analyse the impact of race in relation to legal variables such as prior convictions, offence seriousness, and number of charges. In brief summary, he found no evidence of discrimination against (or for) Indians and Métis in sentencing when legal variables were controlled, with the possible exception that non-white were less likely than white "intemperate" drinkers to be referred to "open" institutions (which feature pro-

grams especially designed for alcohol offenders). Although Hagan did not, in either this study or in his assessment of the literature on sentencing (Hagan, 1974b), develop the implications of his findings in terms of the confrontation between the conflict-coercion and integration-consensus theories, his work does serve as a basis for dealing with the common assumption that conflict-coercion theory implies discrimination while integration-consensus theory implies the absence of discrimination.

1 Conflict-coercion theory asserts that the process by which legal institutions are created, operated, and changed involve and reflect the control and mobilization of resources by more *and* less powerful people. It does not imply that the more powerful are all-powerful. Nor does it imply that the more and the less powerful have absolutely no common problems and concerns (e.g., interpersonal violence, the security of personal possessions, military or economic domination by culturally alien external parties.) Thus, it is accepted that some laws will have a high probability that no individual will be able to violate them with impunity; some will be unenforced or unenforceable; and some will be discriminatorily enforced or not enforced, depending upon many factors regarding the *relative* power of people individually and collectively in their dealings with various other people.

2 Conflict-coercion theory does not imply that most accused persons are innocent, nor that more powerful and less powerful people engage in conventional deviations to the same extent. It does not even imply that legal officials at any level necessarily violate procedural rules, or even conventional norms of fairness, so as to discriminate against less powerful people and on behalf of more powerful people. What the theory does imply is that the legal rules—and probably the conventional norms of fairness to some extent as well—will tend to exclude or define as less serious the tactics available only to more

powerful people in the struggle to maximize life chances, while including as relatively serious some tactics available to virtually everyone but more likely to be adopted by the less powerful, largely as a function of the unavailability of those other and presumably less risky tactics "reserved" for the more powerful. In short, the point of conflict-coercion theory is that if the legal game is loaded, as it demonstrably has been, then playing by the rules is sufficient to ensure higher chances of winning for those to whose collective advantage it was loaded in the first place. Indeed, discrimination is not only in principle unnecessary but also likely to be counterproductive in contributing to the demystification of the structure of legal control.

3 Finally, neither theory implies anything directly or unconditionally in regard to the presence or absence of discriminatory legal treatment. Since both theories posit causal processes that operate through time to produce certain outcomes, the chances of finding these outcomes vary (in principle in predictable ways) from one time to the next, as the processes are impeded or promoted by various environmental contingencies. Clearly, then, the timeless or one-time comparisons of outcomes (often with little or no attention paid to environmental contingencies) characteristic of most discrimination research are especially inappropriate for the purposes of testing either theory.

SUMMARY AND CONCLUSION

... Conflict-coercion theory defines law as power, conflict as ubiquitous struggle, and order as balance of power, while integration-consensus theory defines law as authority, conflict as unnecessary struggle, and order as voluntary association. These results were then used as the basis for considering each of the five possible reasons for the persistence of the theoretical conflict. Our initial conclusion was that the theories are not strictly comparable, in so far as conflict-coercion theory is essentially "statistical" and "empirical-scientific" and postulates conflict as the most fundamental social process, whereas integration-consensus theory is essentially "analytical" and "empirical-normative" and postulates cooperation. However, because both theories appeal to empirical evidence, because conflict-coercion theory may be used for partisan purposes, and because integration-consensus theory subsumes, instead of rejecting, the norms of scientific enquiry, our eventual conclusion was that the effort to test the rival claims of the theories is warranted. . . .

Inevitably, many intriguing and perhaps viable intellectual possibilities will be missed or neglected in the effort to move from often subtle and imaginative theorizing to parsimonious and unambiguous theories of law, conflict, and order. Also, the integrity of particular views and statements will necessarily be violated as the work of theory construction proceeds. The justification for such intellectual barbarism is that it seems to be the only way to escape the kind of irresolvable and often deadly battles of intellectualized faiths in the midst of which the emancipating notion of science was born.

Notes

[1] By "scientific formulations" is meant concise descriptive or explanatory statements that are *naturalistic*—invoke no empirically indefinable (supernatural, ineffable) forces or entities; *communicable*—within the universe of discourse shared by those working as scientists on the same or related questions; and *demonstrable*—assertable in terms of implied empirically definable relationships, and there-

fore testable by the canons of empirical scientific inquiry. . . .

[2] Convenient summaries, and analytical reviews, and representative examples across a wide range of theoretical and political perspectives are to be found in Aubert (1969), Black and Mileski (1973), Chambliss and Seidman (1971), Gurvitch (1947), Nader (1969), Podgorecki (1974), Schwartz and Skolnick (1970), Stone (1966) and Timasheff (1939), as well as the relevant articles in the International Encyclopedia of the Social Sciences (Sills: 1968).

[3] *Theorizing* is the creative production, dissemination, and discussion of ideas, with only secondary (if any) concern for that formalization and routinization of ideas into "frozen" propositional systems which is the hallmark of *theories*. It should therefore be clear that theorizing is not an inferior activity relative to theory construction but rather the ultimate

source of the intellectual material from which theories are constructed. . . .

[4] Contrast, for instance, the differentiation of conflict-coercion from integration-consensus theories in this paper with Horton's (1966) characterization of the "conflict" and "order" perspectives on social problems, or with Chambliss's (1973) statement regarding the opposition between "conflict" and "functional" theories of crime.

[5] Aside from considerations of space, there seems to be no good reason to present formal derivations, from the theories as sketched and discussed above, of the methodological proscriptions and prescriptions offered here. Anyone who enjoys such exercises should have little difficulty in working out the fairly straightforward logical connections and substantive extensions involved.

[6] I am deeply grateful to Professor McDonald for giving me the opportunity to read and comment on her study prior to its publication.

References

Aubert, Vilhelm (ed.) 1969. *Sociology of Law.* Baltimore: Penguin Books.

Barkun, Michael. 1968. *Law Without Sanctions.* New Haven: Yale University.

Beattie, John M. 1974. "The pattern of crime in England, 1660–1800." *Past and Present* 62:47–95.

Black, Donald and Maureen Mileski (eds). 1973. *The Social Organization of Law.* New York: Seminar Press.

Chambliss, William J. 1973. "Functional and conflict theories of crime." New York: MSS Modular Publications.

———— 1975. "Toward a political economy of crime." *Theory and Society* 2:149–70.

Chambliss, William J. and Robert B. Seidman. 1971. *Law, Order, and Power.* Reading, Mass.: Addison-Wesley.

Coser, Lewis. 1956. *The Functions of Social Conflict.* Glencoe Ill.: The Free Press.

———— 1967. *Continuities in the Study of Social Conflict.* New York: The Free Press.

Dahrendorf, Ralf. 1968. *Essays in the Theory of Society.* Stanford University.

Gibbs, Jack P. 1972. *Sociological Theory Construction.* Hinsdale, Ill.: The Dryden Press.

Gurvitch, Georges 1947. *Sociology of Law.* London: Routledge and Kegan Paul.

Hagan, John. 1974a. "Criminal justice and native people: a study of incarceration in a Canadian province." *Canadian Review of Sociology and Anthropology.* Special issue (August):220–36.

———— 1974b. "Extra-legal attributes and criminal sentencing: an assessment of a sociological viewpoint." *Law & Society Review* 8:357–83.

Hanawalt, Barbara A. 1974. "Economic influences on the pattern of crime in England, 1300–1348." *American Journal of Legal History* 18:281–97.

Horton, John. 1966. "Order and conflict theories

of social problems as competing ideologies."
American Journal of Sociology 71:701–13.

McDonald, Lynn. 1976. *The Sociology of Law and Order: Conflict and Consensus Theories of Crime, Law and Sanctions.* London: Faber & Faber.

Nader, Laura (ed.) 1969. *Law in Culture and Society.* Chicago: Aldine.

Podgorecki, Adam. 1962. "Law and social engineering." *Human Organization* 3:177–81.

———— 1974. *Law and Society.* London: Routledge and Kegan Paul.

Quinney, Richard. 1974. *Critique of Legal Order.* Boston: Little, Brown.

Rossi, Peter, Emily Waite, Christine E. Bose, and Richard E. Berk. 1974. "The seriousness of crimes: normative structure and individual differences." *American Sociological Review* 39:224–37.

Schwartz, Richard D. and Jerome H. Skolnick (eds) 1970 Society and the Legal Order. New York: Basic Books

Selznick, Philip. 1961. "Sociology and natural law." *Natural Law Forum* 6:84–108.

———— 1969. *Law, Society, and Industrial Justice.* New York: Russell Sage Foundation.

Sills, David L. (ed.). 1968. *International Encyclopedia of the Social Sciences.* New York: Macmillan and The Free Press.

Stone, Julius. 1966. *Social Dimensions of Law and Justice.* Stanford, Cal.: Stanford University Press.

Timasheff, Nicholas S. 1939. *An Introduction to the Sociology of Law.* Cambridge, Mass.: Harvard University Press.

Weber, Max. 1968. *Economy and Society.* New York: Bedminster Press.

17 Differences Between Canada and the U.S. in Crime and Deviance

John Hagan

JOHN HAGAN, Professor of Sociology and Pofessor of Law at the University of Toronto, specializes in the study of crime, deviance and social control. His books include *The Disreputable Pleasures: Crime and Deviance in Canada* (1977); *Deterrence Reconsidered: Methodological Innovations* (1982); *Quantitative Criminology: Innovations and Applications* (1982); *Victims Before the Law: The Organizational Domination of Criminal Law* (1983); and *Modern Criminology: Crime, Criminal Behavior and its Control* (1985). In addition, numerous papers have been published and presented on related topics. Professor Hagan is currently co-principal investigator in a major research program on legal theory and public policy. He has served as associate editor to many leading sociological journals, including the *American Journal of Sociology; American Sociological Review; Sociological Inquiry; Social Problems; Criminology;* and the *Canadian Journal of Sociology.*

ARE CANADIANS AS DEVIANT AS AMERICANS?

Some Introductory Comments

Having illustrated important deficiencies in the official data on deviance, we will . . . argue that in spite of these imperfections, the data can still be used in making certain cross-national comparisons. This argument will be grounded in three points: (1) that some measures of deviant behavior may escape these deficiencies; (2) that many of the deficiencies may remain constant across areas, allowing conclusions to be formed on a relative basis; and (3) that the occurrence of systematic biases between areas of comparison is itself a valid topic for study.

There is at least one official measure of deviant behavior, homicide rates, that receives support from various tests of validity. For example, the national victimization survey reported by Ennis (1967) reveals only slightly *fewer* reports of murder than does the official data, while a comparison of data from the Center for Health Statistics (CHS) and Uniform Crime Reports (UCR) over a thirty-six year period in the United States (see Figure 1) yields nearly an identical picture of annual homicide rates (Hindelang, 1974). All of this confirms our suspicion that bodies are difficult to hide, and that official measures of this type deserve some credibility. In short, not *all* official data are biased.

More generally, if it were found that victim surveys and official data produced similar findings regarding the *nature* and *geographic distribution* of criminal offences, one's confidence in the usefulness of the official data would increase. Such findings would suggest that although the official data may substantially underestimate the absolute volume of offences, the relative distribution of offences—for example, in different sections of the country, or between countries—may *not* be substantially biased by failure of victims to report all offences. Said differently, it may be that between and within countries victims have similar patterns of non-reporting. If this is the case, comparisons of areas using official and survey data may result in similar conclusions. To test this set of assumptions, Hindelang (1974) compared overall crime rates as estimated by victim and official reports (UCRs) for four regions of the United States and urban and rural areas. In addition, these comparisons were extended into particular offence categories, and to rankings of their relative incidence. Hindelang concludes that, "... the results are tentative; yet, the essential compatibility of these comparisons... prohibits summary dismissal of the UCR data as worthless for purposes such as examinations of the relative geographic distribution

of offences and time series analyses of at least some offences." In other words, a cautious argument can be made that official data may in some cases be suitable for *comparisons*, even when such data do not justify estimates of *absolute incidence*.

For those who remain doubtful, there is a third approach to be taken to comparisons of official data. This approach is based on the earlier discussion in this chapter of the error and behavioral components of all measures of deviance. Comparisons of official figures serve as a basis for investigating the relative contribution of error-producing factors in the construction of deviance rates. For example,

Figure 1

RATES OF HOMICIDE IN THE UNITED STATES AS REPORTED BY THE UNIFORM CRIME REPORTS AND THE CENTRE FOR HEALTH STATISTICS, 1935–1971

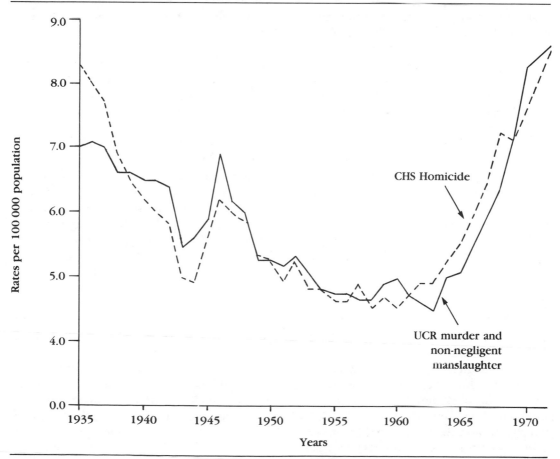

Reprinted with permission of Pergamon Press Ltd. Source: Hindelang (1974:4)

in 1969, Prince Edward Island had the highest rate of admissions to mental institutions of any province in Canada. However, in the same year, Prince Edward Island also had the highest ratio in Canada of psychiatric beds per 100,000 population. The availability of treatment space, then, seems a probable contaminating factor in comparisons of official rates of mental illness between provinces (Williams, Kopinak, and Moynagh, 1972). Thus, official data not only can be used to investigate the incidence of behavior, but also to explore factors influencing responses taken to the presumed prevalence of these behaviors....

Cross-National Data on Deviant Behavior

By many measures, Canada is only a moderately violent nation.... Much violent crime is consensual crime, in the sense that it involves infrequent and severely sanctioned violations of widely shared, and strongly held, values. Although some differences exist in the collection and categorization of offences in Canada and the United States, the findings suggest an interesting pattern: over the past ten to twenty years, and with population differences taken into account, violent offences have remained much more frequent in the United States than in Canada. For example, in spite of year-to-year fluctuations, American murder and rape rates remain about four times larger than the Canadian rates. Robbery rates have remained more than two times higher in the United States. On the other hand, the two nations' burglary rates are much more similar. By 1980, the American burglary rate was only 1.2 times the Canadian rate. Meanwhile, the conclusion that Canada is a relatively non-violent nation, particularly in comparison with the United States, is echoed in cross-national studies of political violence (Kirkham, Levy, and Crotty, 1970). Such studies demonstrate that despite Canada's experiences with groups like the FLQ, the numbers and rates of assassinations, armed attacks, riots, and deaths from political violence have been relatively low. In sum, we seem individually and collectively more violent than some, but nonetheless more peaceful than most.

What limited data we have on self-reported delinquency is consistent with the impression that serious offences are more frequent in the United States than in Canada. Linden and Fillmore (1981) have compared self-report surveys conducted during the same year in Richmond, California and Edmonton, Alberta. Their data indicate that as the value of property reported stolen increases, so too do the national differences: rates of theft of less than two dollars are about the same in the two samples, theft from two to fifty dollars in value are about one and a half times more frequent in the American sample, and thefts of more than fifty dollars in value are nearly four times more frequent in the American sample. Beyond this, the Edmonton sample was somewhat more likely to damage property, but less likely to "beat up anyone."

Surveys of drug use in the United States and Canada suggest another area of American predominance. Berg (1970) has reviewed sixty-nine self-report studies of drug use conducted during 1969 in the United States, while Smart and Fejer (1971) have reviewed twenty-two such studies conducted from 1967 to 1970 in Canada. The conclusions to be drawn from a comparison of these reviews are several: (1) reported levels of use vary widely within each country; (2) levels of reported use changed substantially in the late 1960s; and (3) almost any basis of comparison places America at the turn of the decade ahead of Canada in the prevalence of non-medical drug use. Table 1 summarizes some of this information by indicating for each country the "high" reported use levels of marijuana, LSD and amphetamines in college and high-school samples. Since some of the Canadian studies took place as much as one year after the American surveys, the comparison

Table 1

HIGHEST REPORTED RATES ON NON-MEDICAL USE OF DRUGS IN CANADIAN AND AMERICAN
SURVEYS OF COLLEGE AND HIGH SCHOOL STUDENTS

Drug	College Surveys	Per Cent of Drug Use		High School Surveys	Per Cent of Drug Use	
		U.S.	Canada		U.S.	Canada
Marijuana	University of Michigan	44.0%		San Mateo County, California	36.6%	
	Bishop's University		27.3%	Toronto		23.0%
LSD	*Newsweek* Survey	8.2%		San Mateo County, California	15.1%	
	Bishop's University		3.1%	Toronto		15.0%
Amphetamines	University of Michigan	24.7%		San Mateo County, California	20.8%	
	University of Western Ontario		4.1%	Niagara Counties, Ontario		9.0%

Source: Berg (1970:784) and Smart and Fejer (1971:514–517).

encourages a higher estimate of Canadian drug use. Yet, to the extent that these reports can be taken as valid (for a supportive Canadian test of validity, see Whitehead and Smart, (1972), the prevalence of non-medical drug use in the United States exceeds that in Canada. Sudden surveys conducted in Canada from 1976 to 1982 (Addiction Research Foundation, 1982:116–117) suggest no reason to revise this conclusion.

Turning to the most frequently abused chemical, alcohol, comparative data are available from a variety of countries. Much of this data is built on the well-known fact that alcoholics contribute a disproportionately large share to mortality from cirrhosis of the liver. International statistics on liver-cirrhosis deaths are presented in Table 2. This information is built into computing formulas used to estimate the prevalence of alcoholism (Popham , 1956). A resulting ranking of the estimated prevalence of alcoholism in a number of western countries suggests that neither Americans nor Canadians are among the world's heaviest drinkers, but that our southern neighbors may once more exceed us.

The statistics of mental illness seem the most difficult to interpret. Official data on mental-hospital admissions suffer from variations in the definitions of mental illness, varying patterns of discharge and readmission, disparities in available treatment space, and differing policies on voluntary and involuntary admission. A more useful source of data for our purposes, then, involves the use of self-report check lists derived from a variety of standardized psychological tests. Summarizing the results of nine such surveys completed in the United States and Canada, Williams, Kopinak and Moynagh (1972) conclude that in both countries approximately twenty-five per cent of the general population is impaired by psychological disorders. Similirities in American and Canadian patterns of mental health are reported also in John Seeley's (1956) classic community study of *Crestwood Heights*.

More generally, it can be said that the forms of deviance considered most serious by the public (for example, "violent crime" and "hard drug abuse") are found more commonly in the United States than in Canada. How *much* more deviant behavior occurs in the United States, and whether this disparity will endure,

Table 2

INTERNATIONAL STATISTICS ON LIVER-CIRRHOSIS DEATHS, 1973 TO 1979

RATES OF LIVER CIRRHOSIS DEATHS PER 100,000 POPULATION

Country	1973	1974	1975	1976	1977	1978	1979
Canada	11.4	11.6	12.0	12.1	11.9	n.a.	n.a.
United States	15.9	15.8	14.8	14.7	14.3	13.8	n.a.
Finland	4.6	5.5	6.3	5.7	5.4	n.a.	n.a.
France	34.5	32.8	33.7	32.9	31.5	n.a.	n.a.
Germany, Federal Republic	25.7	26.9	27.9	28.1	27.6	27.6	n.a.
Italy	32.3	31.9	33.3	34.2	n.a.	n.a.	n.a.
Norway	4.0	4.1	5.0	5.4	4.2	5.1	5.2
Spain	22.3	22.5	22.6	23.4	22.5	n.a.	n.a.
Sweden	10.4	10.5	12.2	12.9	12.4	12.4	12.2
Switzerland	13.8	14.8	12.8	12.8	12.9	13.3	13.6
United Kingdom	3.7	3.6	3.7	3.8	3.7	3.9	4.4

Source: *Statistics on Alcohol and Drug Use in Canada and Other Countries*, Toronto: Addiction Research Foundation, 1983, pp. 285–289; *World Health Statistics Annual Vol. I—Vital Statistics and Causes of Death, 1973–76, 1977, 1978, 1979*, and *1981.* Geneva: World Health Organization.

are questions to which we can provide no satisfactory answers. We can, however, comment on how Canadians *perceive* their situation. In a 1969 opinion poll of a representative sample of Toronto households, Courtis (1970) found that twenty-eight per cent of his respondents regarded crime as a very serious problem, sixty-one per cent as only a moderately serious problem, with the remaining twelve per cent largely unconcerned. This finding can be contrasted with American polls conducted during a similar period by Harris (1968) and Gallup (*Time*, 1968). These polls revealed a consensus that "crime and lawlessness" was America's most serious problem. Data reviewed in this section support these contrasting estimates by Canadians and Americans of current crime problems in their respective countries. . . .

WHY IS THERE LESS DEVIANCE IN CANADA THAN IN THE UNITED STATES?

Consensus theorists argue that Canadians and Americans vary in their values, and particu-

larly in their relative respect for law and order. Two factors are emphasized in explanation of these differences. The first factor focuses on the ideological debate underwriting the political structure of each country, and the correlated link between Britain and Canada. The second factor involves the economic development of the western and northern frontiers in Canada and the United States.

Seymour Martin Lipset (1968; see also 1963, 1964) argues that different patterns of deviance in Canada and the United States follow first from the carry-over of British values into Canada. Some have called this the "Imperial Connection." The resulting values are said to encourage an increased acceptance and respect for an orderly, elite-based society. Thus, where the United States began in revolution, Canada served as a sanctuary for counter-revolutionaries. Lipset argues that over time, " . . . the failure of Canada to have a revolution of its own, the immigration of conservative elements, and the emigration of radical ones— all contributed to making Canada a more conservative and more rigidly stratified society." These conservative values are said to ·

discourage deviance, on the one hand, and to encourage its strict control, on the other.

It is argued that strict policies for the control of deviance emerged early in the process of developing the western and northern frontiers, Harold Innis and later S.D. Clark (1976: Chapter 3) argued that while the United States was able to develop a relatively "soft" frontier, Canada, in contrast, struggled with a relatively "hard" frontier. Canada's resources were very difficult to develop, while at the same time being extremely vulnerable to American efforts at expansion. To facilitate and secure the development of the Canadian frontier, the Northwest Mounted Police and the military moved into new settlements before, and along with, the original settlers (see Macleod, 1976). Clark describes these conditions of Canadian development as constituting a "closed" frontier.

On the other hand, in the United States, local authorities were free to develop their own law-enforcement policies, or to ignore the problem altogether. In Clark's terms, the American west amounted to an "open" frontier. In turn, Lipset concludes that "This contributed to the establishment of a greater tradition of respect for institutions of law and order on the Canadian frontier as compared with the American" (1968:57; see also Clark, 1962:192). It is this Canadian tradition of relative-value consensus, grounded in a greater respect for law and order, that is assumed to have kept Canadian rates of serious crime and deviance lower than those in the United States.

It must be emphasized that the consensual theories reviewed represent only one possible explanation of the "facts of deviance" we have considered. The conflict theories offer an alternative viewpoint. In particular, the conflict theories reject the assumption of value consensus, and argue that what is *considered* disreputable is itself a matter to be explained.

The consensus theorists, specifically Seymour Martin Lipset, argue that differences in rates of deviance in Canada and the United States are attributable to differences in values. In contrast, the conflict theorists, specifically Irving Louis Horowitz (1973), argue that the difference is one of "cultural lag." Furthermore, Horowitz observes (341–342) that the data on criminality reveal "marked tendencies toward closing the 'cultural gap,' " and that the remaining disparities are greatest among the crimes of violence—in other words, among what we have called the consensual crimes. It is, of course, the conflict crimes that hold greatest interest for the conflict theorists, and Horowitz goes on to construct an argument for a growing similarity in their respective national rates.

Where Lipset placed an emphasis on the "Imperial Connection" with Britain, Horowitz argues that Canada's rising reported crime rate has its origin in " . . . the loosening of the ties of the Imperial Connection and the strengthening of the ties with the American Connection" (346). Horowitz then adopts an argument drawn from the metropolis-hinterland model developed in Canada by Davis (1971). Said briefly, this argument is that "Canada is in the same relationship to the United States as the agrarian sector of the United States is in connection to its industrial sector: or for that matter, the Canadian 'hinterland' is with respect to the Canadian 'metropolitan centre' " (Horowitz, 1973:349). In other words, the argument is that the economic centre (whether it be the United States in relation to Canada, or Toronto in relation to other parts of Ontario) dominates and exploits the periphery. Our interest is in what this argument says about rates of deviance.

McDonald argues that as economic growth occurs, the machinery for crime production grows apace. In fact, McDonald implies that crime production through increased policing is a means of insuring economic domination, by maintaining the privileged position of some interest groups relative to others. The inference one can draw is that, as the Canadian economy grows and increases in its dependency on the United States, its crime rate will become more and more like that of the United States. Horowitz suggests that this is in fact what is happening. Further, in support of the argument drawn from McDonald, Lipset's own data (1968:38) can be cited to note that, at the same time Canada's crime rate has been lower than that of the United States, the ratio of police to population has also been lower in Canada. What remains at issue, as we indicated earlier, is whether this relationship is causal in the single direction that McDonald suggests.

We will not attempt to impose what would be a premature closure on the debate between the consensus and conflict theories. We have argued that the consensus theories work best in explaining consensual crimes, but that the conflict theories may also in some cases help to explain the emergence of consensus. Beyond this, we have argued that the conflict theories serve best in explaining the societal response to those forms of deviance about which little consensus exists. We also noted that the consensual theories are more interested in explaining behaviors, while the conflict theories are particularly interested in the disreputable status of these behaviors. From this point on, however, we must leave the readers to draw their own conclusions, or even better, to accumulate additional evidence.

References

Addiction Research Foundation. 1982. *Statistics on Alcohol and Drug Use in Canada and Other Countries.* Toronto: Addiction Research Foundation.

Berg, D.F. 1970. "The Non-Medical Use of Dangerous Drugs in the United States: A Comprehensive View." *International Journal of Addictions* 5(4): 777–834.

Clark, S.D. 1962. *The Developing Canadian Community.* Toronto: The University of Toronto Press.

1976. *Canadian Society in Historical Perspective.* Toronto: McGraw-Hill Ryerson Ltd.

Courtis, M.C. 1970. *Attitudes to Crime and the Police in Toronto: A Report on Some Survey Findings.* Toronto: Centre of Criminology, University of Toronto.

Davis, Arthur K. 1971. "Canadian Society as Hinterland Versus Metropolis." In Richard J. Ossenberg (ed.), *Canadian Society: Pluralism, Change, and Conflict.* Scarborough, Ontario: Prentice-Hall of Canada Ltd.

Ennis, P.H. 1967. *Criminal Victimization in the United States: A Report of a National Survey.* Washington, D.C.: U.S. Government Printing Office.

Harris, L. 1968. *The Public Looks at Crime and Corrections.* Washington, D.C.: Joint Commission on Correctional Manpower and Training.

Hindelang. M.J. 1974. "The Uniform Crime Reports Revisited." *Journal of Criminal Justice* 2(1):1–17.

Horowitz, Irving Louis. 1973. "The Hemispheric Connection: A Critique and Corrective to the Entrepreneurial Thesis of Development with Special Emphasis on the Canadian Case." *Queen's Quarterly* 80(3):327–359.

Kirkham, James, Sheldon Levy, and William Crotty. 1970. *Assassination and Political Violence.* Washington: Government Printing Office.

Linden, Rick and Cathy Fillmore. 1981. "A comparative study of delinquency involvement." *The Canadian Review of Sociology and Anthropology* 18(3):343–361.

Lipset, Seymour Martin. 1963. "The Value Patterns of Democracy: A Case Study in Comparative Analysis." *American Sociological Review* 28:515–531.

———.1964. "Canada and the United States: A Comparative View." *Canadian Review of Sociology and Anthropology* 1:173–192.

———.1968. *Revolution and Counterrevolution: Change and Persistence in Social Structures.* New York: Basic Books.

Macleod, R.C. 1976. *The North-West Mounted Police and Law Enforcement 1873–1905.* Toronto: The University of Toronto Press.

McDonald, Lynn. 1976. *The Sociology of Law and Order.* London: Faber.

Popham, R.E. 1956. "The Jellinek Alcoholism Estimation Formula and its Application to Canadian Data." *Quarterly Journal of Studies on Alcohol* 17: 559–593.

Seeley, John with R.A. Sim, and E.W. Loosley. 1956. *Crestwood Heights.* Toronto: The University of Toronto Press.

Smart, R.G. and D. Fejer. 1971. "The Extent of Illicit Drug Use in Canada: A Review of Current Epidemiology." In Craig Boydell, Carl Grindstaff, and Paul Whitehead (eds.), *Critical Issues in Canadian Society.* Toronto: Holt, Rinehart and Winston of Canada Ltd.

Time. 1968. "The Thin Blue Line." 93(July):39.

Whitehead, Paul and Reginald Smart. 1972. "Validity and Reliability of Self-Reported Drug Use." *Canadian Journal of Criminology and Corrections* 14(1):83–89.

Williams, J. Ivan, Kathryn Kopinak, and W. David Moynagh. 1972. "Mental Health and Illness in Canada." In Craig Boydell, Carl Grindstaff and Paul Whitehead (eds.), *Deviant Behavior and Societal Reaction.* Toronto: Holt, Rinehart and Winston of Canada Ltd.

18 Experimenting with Public Deviance

Thomas Gabor   David Varis   Jody Strean   Gurnam Singh

THOMAS GABOR is an Associate Professor in the Department of Criminology at the University of Ottawa. A sociologist and criminologist, he is the author of two books: *The Prediction of Criminal Behaviour: Statistical Approaches,* and *Armed Robbery: Cops, Robbers and Victims* Professor Gabor has also published chapters in several books and contributed articles to a number of criminological and sociological journals. His current interests focus on the extent of criminality and deviance among the general public.

DAVID VARIS is a Case Management Officer with the Correctional Service of Canada at Atlantic Institution in Renous, N.B. He received his Master of Criminology (Applied) Degree from the University of Ottawa. He has had previous experience as a parole and probation officer, adult and juvenile correctional counsellor and correctional officer.[2]

JODY STREAN holds a master's degree in Criminology from the University of Ottawa. She was employed for several years with the Solicitor General of Canada, and is currently pursuing a graduate degree in social work and Jewish studies.

GURNAM SINGH holds a master's degree in Criminology from the University of Ottawa. Currently employed by the Ministry of Correctional Services of Ontario, he has extensive experience in the field of corrections.

It has been said that the study of deviance concerns the "mad, bad and different" (Barak-Glantz and Huff, 1981). Those adopting a clinical approach claim that deviant behavior is a manifestation of some underlying pathology or deficiency residing within the individual ("madness"). Those of a conservative or legalistic bent tend to subscribe to the belief that deviance, like most social behaviour, is freely chosen from a range of alternatives available to all but a small number of pathological persons ("badness"). Those adopting a socio-cultural framework, on the other hand, tend to refrain from value judgements or perjorative labels and use the statistical norm, in a particular social context, as the yardstick by which to gauge deviance ("difference").

It is this third definition which is most relevant to the present study. The objective was to gain insight into the level of honesty of the public through an experimental approach. Convenience store cashiers were selected as subjects because it was felt that they were, in terms of gender, ethnicity, age and social status, fairly representative of the population at large. The investigators provided opportunities to the subjects to engage in dishonest acts.

In order to determine whether dishonesty is, in fact, deviance according to the "difference" criterion, it is useful to first examine the existing evidence on the subject. A perusal of this literature indicates that studies have employed numerous sampling techniques, definitions of dishonesty or deviance and data sets, as well as, in the case of experimental studies, varying experimental conditions. Thus, the reader should be circumspect when drawing conclusions or generalizations.

OFFICIAL CRIME DATA

According to the Correctional Services of Canada, (1982), 1.7 million Canadians possess a criminal record. Although this constitutes only 7% of the general population, this figure is substantially larger for males of crime eligible ages. Christiansen (1967), on the basis of the 1965 Uniform Crime Reports, estimated that 50% of American males and 12% of females would be arrested for a nontraffic offence during their lifetime. Farrington (1981), in his analysis of prevalence rates in England and Wales, projected that the lifetime probability of a nontraffic conviction for an English or Welsh male will eventually reach 44%. Wolfgang (1977), in a follow-up of a 1945 Philadelphia birth cohort of males, found that as of 30 years of age, 47.3% had a nontraffic police contact. Shannon (1980) retrospectively examined a 1942 birth cohort from Racine, Wisconsin and found that as of 31 years of age, 70% of the males and 24% of the females had at least one recorded police contact for a nontraffic offence. Hathaway and his associates (1960) estimated, on the basis of a large statewide sample, that 34% of the males in Minnesota had police records by the age of 17. West and Farrington (1977), in a follow-up of a male sample drawn from six primary schools in a working class area of London, found that 30.8% had at least one conviction for an indictable offence by the age of 21.

These figures are rather startling, especially when one considers the underestimation of criminal involvement inherent in official records. They do cast serious doubt on the notion that criminality is primarily confined to a marginal group.

SELF-REPORT STUDIES

As one might expect, self-report studies yield figures of crime and deviance substantially in excess of those derived from criminal justice data. They can also shed light on the authenticity of gender-based differences in prevalence so apparent from official records. These studies, however, are not always directly comparable to those just cited, as the forms of criminality and deviance examined are often of a less serious nature.

Wallerstein and Wyle (1977) surveyed 1,700 New York City adults not possessing a criminal record. Ninety-nine percent admitted to committing at least one of 49 offences listed in a questionnaire. Gold (1970) found that over 80% of the teenagers in Flint, Michigan could be technically considered as delinquent. Gender differences were considerable, as even for theft (where these differences were at a minimum) twice as many males as females admitted to being active. Clark and Haurek (1966) found, in their study of public school students in an unnamed American city, that the gender differences in theft offences were in the order of 1.4 males involved for every female. Elmhorn (1965) surveyed 950 male school children 9–14 years of age in Stockholm, 92% of whom admitted to one of the more serious crimes listed on a questionnaire. West and Farrington (1977), in the self-report component of their aforementioned London study, found that 68.9% of their sample admitted to receiving stolen goods and 21.1% to damaging property. Belson (1975), also in London, found that all 1,425 boys aged 13–16 years in his sample admitted to some stealing.

Needless to say, the figures from these studies point to widespread involvement in, if not the normative status of, at least some forms of criminality. Due to the possible social desirability of misleading investigators, particularly in the form of exaggerations by youthful respondents attempting to impress their elders (Edwards, 1957), the concrete observation of public behaviour becomes indispensable.

OBSERVATIONAL STUDIES

Most of the observational research addressing the prevalence of public deviance and criminality have employed experimental designs. One of the earliest studies (Hartshorne and May, 1928–1930) pointed to the situational element in deviance as it was found that people, when given an opportunity to engage in dishonest behaviour, are responsive to the risks and potential rewards involved.

Field experiments have involved a wide range of methodologies, although they generally comprise an inducement given subjects to commit some form of criminal or deviant act.

Riis (1941a, 1941b, 1941c), in the United States, reported on three separate studies in which investigators, posing as naive customers, brought "jimmied" automobiles, radios and watches to repair shops in order to test the honesty of these businesses. Sixty-three percent of the garages, 64% of the radio shops and 49% of the watch repair shops were considered dishonest.

The "lost-letter" technique has been employed in a number of studies to determine the return rate of letters (some of which contain money) apparently lost on the street. Merritt and Fowler (1948) dropped envelopes and postcards on the street in a number of American cities. Seventy-two percent of the postcards and 88% of the envelopes containing letters were mailed, whereas only 54% of the envelopes containing a coin resembling a 50 cent piece were mailed. In a similar study, Farrington and Knight (1979) dropped letters containing either cash, one pound notes

or five pound notes on the streets of London. They found that the return rate diminished as the amount of cash in the letters increased. Ninety-four percent of the letters with no cash, 72.2% of those containing one pound and 57.9% of those containing five pounds were returned. Gender differences were also observed as 47.4% of the male subjects and only 22.2% of the females committed theft.

In another set of experiments, the objective was to not only determine the level of honesty of the general public, but the effect of "victim" characteristics upon the propensity to steal. The investigator in these studies pretended to inadvertently leave a coin in a telephone booth of a crowded terminal. Bickman (1971), in New York City, found that the coin was returned by 77% of the subjects (those next in line for the booth) when the investigator was dressed in "high status" attire and by 38% when he/she was dressed in low status attire. Sroufe and associates (1977), using a similar procedure, found that the attractiveness of a female confederate affected the honesty of subjects. Eighty-seven percent of the subjects returned the coin in the attractive condition, compared to only 64% in the unattractive condition.

In a cross-cultural study, Feldman (1968) examined the respective honesty of the French, Greeks and Americans in a variety of test situations. In one situation, cashiers in stores were overpaid by both compatriots and foreigners. In Paris, 54% of the clerks kept the money from both compatriots and foreigners. In Athens, the overpayment was not returned to either the compatriot or the foreigner about 50% of the time. In Boston, the money was kept 38% of the time from the compatriot and 27% of the time from the foreigner.

Taken together, criminal justice data, self-report and observational studies indicate that criminality and deviance is fairly widespread, at least insofar as acts against property are concerned. These courses consistently indicate that males are more likely to engage in deviant acts than are females. They also point to the importance of the situational context in deviance and, indeed, experimental studies show how deviance can be manufactured and manipulated.

THE OTTAWA STUDY

The advantages of direct observation and the dearth of these studies in Canada prompted the present investigators to use an experimental design to explore the prevalence of dishonesty in a Canadian context. The objective was to determine the proportion of persons who will engage in theft when an opportunity for such act is present. Convenience stores in the city of Ottawa were visited by the investigators to ascertain the proportion of cases in which behaviour that could be construed as theft occurred as a result of an inducement presented to cashiers. Special attention was given to sex and age differences in honesty, to the differential behaviour of cashiers who were salaried employees and those related to the proprietor of the store and to the effect of the prospective victim's gender on the likelihood of dishonesty.

A total of 125 convenience stores were visited by three university students in their mid-twenties. One Caucasian male and one female visited 85 stores of the chain type (40 and 45, respectively), while one male of East Indian descent visited 40 family-operated outlets. All districts of the city were represented, as virtually every convenience store in the Ottawa area was included in the study.

In each test situation, an investigator walked into a store and picked up the same item (a local newspaper costing 30 cents), paying for it, in each case, with a single Canadian dollar bill. The investigator then, feigning absent-mindedness, proceeded toward the door without awaiting the change. His/her pace was sufficiently slow to afford the cashier the

opportunity to inform him/her of the ostensible mistake. The pace, however, was fast enough to avoid suspicion or the impression that the investigator was, indeed, waiting for the change. The test of dishonesty was whether the cashier stopped the investigator on his/her way out of the store in order to return the change due. Upon leaving the store, the investigator noted the estimated age (whether under or over 25) and sex of the cashier, as well as whether the change had been returned. Furthermore, the investigator recorded any non-routine comments made by the cashier and any extenuating circumstances, such as distracting events in the store, which may have led to the mistaken conclusion of dishonesty when, in fact, the cashier simply erred.

The stores were visited mostly during mid-morning, mid-afternoon or early evening hours to avoid large crowds and lineups at the cash, as the physical presence of other customers might be a source of distraction and otherwise alter a clerk's behaviour. It is possible, for example, that the presence of other customers might pressure the clerk into handing back the change....

As Table 1 shows, the change due was not returned by cashiers in a total of 20 (16%) cases. Cashiers under the age of 25 failed to return the change almost twice as often as

Table 1
THE TOTAL NUMBER OF VICTIMIZATIONS BY THE SEX AND AGE OF THE CASHIER
(N = 125)

Age	SEX	
	Male	Female
under 25	6 (32)	7 (30)
over 25	4 (31)	3 (32)

The figures in parentheses indicate the number of stores visited.

those over that age. Males and females behaved identically in this regard. Females under 25 were least likely to return the money, followed by young males, then by males over 25, with older females failing to do so in less than 10% of the cases.

Both the male investigator visiting the chain store and the male entering the family-operated store were victimized 20% of the time, whereas the female received her change in over 90% of the cases. In both the condition involving the female entering a chain store and that of the male entering a family-operated premises, there was some evidence of a cross-sex victimization pattern as the female was more likely to be victimized by a male than by a female cashier and vice versa. The second male investigator, on the other hand, was victimized with equal frequency by cashiers of both sexes.

The males, when taken together, were over twice as likely to be victimized as the female. This is the case even when store ownership is held constant. Thus, when only chain stores are considered, the male was still over twice as likely to be victimized as the female.

This is so because the relationship of the cashier to the proprietor appeared to exercise little influence on the behaviour of the former. Chain store cashiers, overall, failed to return the appropriate change in about 14% of the cases. This compares to a non-return rate of 20% for cashiers in the family stores. When gender is held constant, one can observe that the male visiting the chain store was as likely to be victimized as the male entering the family store. This result also indicates that the differential ethnicity of the two male investigators did not appear to affect the behaviour of the cashiers.

DISCUSSION

In almost one of every six cases, the cashier failed to return the appropriate change due to an investigator feigning forgetfulness. This figure is substantially lower than those obtained in the experimental studies cited and may be attributable to the unique conditions of this study, rather than to higher levels of honesty among the present subjects.

The inducement to steal (70 cents) may have been far too small for an employee to risk a loss of employment, ostracism and other consequences of detection. In fact, some cashiers did state that the potential monetary gain was too insignificant to even consider. . . .

Additionally, some cashiers may have been deterred by the more sophisticated cash control systems. This system makes it more likely that other customers may intervene or that an employer taking inventory will detect such behavior. Furthermore, previous research indicates that a person is less likely to victimize another when face-to-face contact occurs. Smigel and Ross (1970) have shown that the more distant, diffuse and anonymous the potential victim of theft, the more likely it is that people will in fact steal. . . .

Then, again, failure to return the appropriate change may not reflect dishonesty at all. The employee could have made a genuine error due to distraction, fatigue or incompetence, although such error was likely to be minimized by the simplicity of the transaction (a one dollar bill paid for a 30 cent item). It is perhaps more likely that, in some instances, subjects decided not to pursue the investigator once he/she left the store due to the small amount involved and the overriding importance of duties in the store. . . .

No gender-based differences in behaviour were observed among the subjects, as an identical number of males and females withheld the appropriate change. Although males are, perhaps, universally more criminally active than females, these differences tend to diminish as the respective social roles of the sexes converge and are at a minimum for theft-related offences (Gabor, 1983)—with the exception of a few crimes that tend to be committed almost exclusively by females (e.g. prostitution). The male and female subjects in this study shared a similar occupational status and this may explain the lack of gender-based differences observed.

In support of the literature was the finding that younger cashiers (those under 25 years of age) were substantially more likely to keep the change than their elders (Boland, 1980). This relationship held for both sexes. It is conceivable that the younger clerks, rather than being more deviant, simply felt less compelled to pursue the "victim" or found it easier to shrug off their own responsibility by blaming the victim for their loss. It may even

be that such public displays of honesty may be regarded as deviant or as a sign of "squareness" on the part of many young persons.

Our male investigators were considerably more likely to be "victimized" than the female.... This preference for victimizing males is supported by a great deal of victimization data (Nettler, 1978). Surprisingly, however, our female investigator was more often victimized by an older male than by cashiers of any other category. Thus, while chivalry may still be alive, it was apparently forgotten by these men.

References

Belson, W.A. *Juvenile Theft: The Causal Factors*. London: Harper and Row, 1975.

Bickman, L. "The effect of social status on the honesty of others." *Journal of Social Psychology*, 85, 87–92, 1971.

Boland, B. "Fighting crime: the problem of adolescents." *Journal of Criminal Law and Criminology*, 71:94–97, 1980.

Christiansen, R. "Projected percentage of U.S. population with criminal arrest and conviction records," in President's Commission on Law Enforcement and Administration of Justice, *Task Force Report: Science and Technology*. Washington, D.C.: U.S. Government Printing Office, 1967.

Clark, J.P. and E.W. Haurek, "Age and sex roles of adolescents and their involvement in misconduct: A reappraisal." *Sociology and Social Research*. 50,495–508. 1966.

Correctional Services of Canada. *Basic Facts About Corrections in Canada*. Ottawa: Ministry of Supply and Services, 1982.

Edwards, A.L. *The Social Desirability Variable in Personality Assessment and Research*. New York: Dryden, 1957.

Elmhorn, K. "Studies in self-reported delinquency among school children in Stockholm." In K.O. Christiansen (Ed.) *Scandinavian Studies in Criminology*. (Vol. 1). London: Tavistock, 1965.

Farrington, D.P. "The prevalence of convictions."

British Journal of Criminology. 21.173–175. 1981.

Farrington, D.P. and B.J. Knight, "Two non-reactive field experiments on stealing from a 'lost' letter." *British Journal of Social and Clinical Psychology*, 18.285–289, 1979.

Feldman, R.E. "Response to compatriots and foreigners who seek assistance," *Journal of Personality and Social Psychology*. 10.202–214, 1968.

Gabor, T. *The Prediction of Criminal Behaviour: An Examination of the Actuarial Approach*. Ottawa: University of Ottawa, 1983.

Gold, M. *Delinquent Behavior in an American City*. Belmont, Cal.: Brooks/Cole, 1970.

Hartshorne, H. and M.A. May. *Studies in the Nature of Character*. (Vols. I–III). New York: Macmillan, 1928–30.

Hathaway, S.R., E.D. Monachesi and L.A. Young. "Delinquency rates and personality," *Journal of Criminal Law, Criminology and Police Science*. 50,433–440, 1960.

Israel Barak-Glantz and C. Ronald Huff, *The Mad, the Bad and the Different: Essays in Honor of Simon Dinitz*, Lexington, Mass.: Lexington Books, 1981.

Merritt, C.B. and R.G. Fowler, "The pecuniary honesty of the public at large." *Journal of Abnormal and Social Psychology*. 43.90–93, 1948.

Nettler, G. *Explaining Crime*. New York: McGraw-Hill, 1978.

Riis, R.W. "The radio repair man will gyp you if you don't watch out." *The Reader's Digest*, 39.6–13, 1941.

———— "The auto repair man will gyp you if you don't watch out." *The Reader's Digest*, 39.1–6, 1941.

———— "The watch repair man will gyp you if you don't watch out." *The Reader's Digest*, 39.10–12, 1941.

Shannon, L.W. "Predicting adult criminal careers from juvenile careers." Paper presented to the annual meeting of the American Society of Criminology. San Francisco, California, 1980.

Smigel, E.O. and H.L. Ross, *Crimes against Bureaucracy*. New York: Van Nostrand Reinhold, 1970.

Sroufe, R., A. Chaikin, R. Cook and V. Freeman. "The effects of physical attractiveness on honesty: A socially desirable response." *Personality and Social Psychology Bulletin*. 3.59–62, 1977.

Wallerstein, J.E. and J.C. Wyle, "Our law-abiding lawbreakers." *Federal Probation*. 25.107–112. 1947.

West, D.J. and D.P. Farrington, *The Delinquent Way of Life*. London: Heinemann Educational Books, 1977.

Wolfgang, M.E. "From boy to man—from delinquency to crime." Paper presented to the National Symposium on the Serious Juvenile Offender. Minneapolis, Minnesota: Department of Corrections, 1977.

19 A Social Profile of Sexual Mass Murderers

Elliott Leyton

ELLIOTT LEYTON has taught Anthropology at the Queen's University of Belfast, the University of Toronto, and, currently, Memorial University of Newfoundland in St. John's. He is the author of seven books, including *Hunting Humans* (1986); *Dying Hard* (1975); and *The Myth of Delinquency* (1979); and has served as President of the Canadian Sociology and Anthropology Association. His long-term interests are the diverse ways in which industrial, stratified societies deform character and warp personal experience.

The ultimate obscenity that human beings perpetrate upon one another is murder. It is therefore hardly surprising that the subject is of such intense interest to members of the public; and the hundreds of books and articles that appear each year on murder constitute a testimony to this concern.

Remarkably, however, the subject has received little attention from the academic community. Moreover, with the exception of a few outstanding studies of isolated phenomena—such as Gaddis and Long (1970), or Reinhardt (1960) on individual murderers, or Wolfgang (1958) on murder in one city—the academic material is overwhelmingly *nonsociological*. Indeed, most of the finest studies of murders have been either journalists, as Klausner's (1981) work on David Berkowitz, or Frank's (1965) study of Albert DeSalvo; or they have been dominated entirely by psychiatric and psychoanalytic perspectives, as in Abrahamsen (1973), Wertham (1949, 1966), Guttmacher (1960) or Lunde (1979). Finally, the subject is muddied by an idiosyncratic and often quite unscientific pseudo-biology (cf. Fox, 1971), focusing on such peculiar matters as purported criminal chromosomes or the brain temperature of murderers. Neither is the scholar interested

in the subject given much encouragement by the authorities. Police data—statistical or otherwise—are a researcher's nightmare, being crude, unreliable, and frequently unavailable. Astonishingly, no institution exists anywhere in the western world to collect and analyze social data on homicide; and even the renowned FBI Uniform Crime Reporting unit is understaffed, overworked, insecurely funded, and able to supply only the crudest data. Each researcher is thus forced to develop his or her own sources of information; and knowledge so painfully collected is unlikely to be freely shared.

Additionally, the homicide literature is overwhelmingly American. At one level, this is quite appropriate, since the U.S. is, by a huge margin, the most murderous nation in the western industrial world. Yet this has led to an unfortunate neglect of nation-states such as Great Britain and Switzerland, or cultural areas such as the island of Newfoundland, which have developed cultural and social mechanisms for repressing violence.

Perhaps the most outstanding dimension of neglect is the matter of *practical* advice to police. Until recent years, the only serious assistance has come from psychiatry and psychology, which have offered psychological profiles of various types of murderers. These profiles predict, sometimes with remarkable accuracy, the motives, fears, and fantasies of the killers. For example, a psychological profile on the Son of Sam correctly described him as "neurotic, schizophrenic and paranoid," accurately guessed that he "regarded himself as a victim of demonic possession," and concluded that he was "probably shy and odd, a loner inept in establishing personal relationships, especially with women" (in Klausner 1981: 160). Unfortunately, these psychological profiles, however accurate, are rarely of practical value to the police. The diagnosis of "paranoia" will not pick anyone out of a lineup; nor will a suspect under interrogation usually reveal his private fears and fantasies; rather, he will insist that he be seen as what he *seems* to be, a shy and devoted family man, or a dedicated profeminist psychological counsellor. . . .

More recent practical help has come from psycholinguistic threat analysis, which has developed a set of most useful techniques for examining the threat message "for clues as to the origin, background, and psychology of the originator" (Miron and Douglas, 1979).

Most successful of all are the excellent "psychological profiles" (which are really *behavioural*, not psychological, profiles) which are being developed at the FBI Academy (cf. Ault and Reese, 1980; Ressler et al., 1980). Here, a wide range of behavioural data is being collected on violent offenders, permitting the extrapolation of the murderer's likely personal characteristics from the murderer's behaviour at the crime scene.

What remains largely undeveloped is a truly sociological profile of different types of murderers. Most murders are relatively easy to solve: the inevitable lovers' triangle, or even the bungled robbery, yield a limited number of suspects possessing an appropriate motive or the property of the victim. Further, the murderer's sense of guilt is usually such that a sharp police officer's "intuition" (which is, after all, a blend of intelligence, sensitivity,

and experience) will be alerted during an investigation and lead to the murderer's discovery.

THE SEXUAL MASS MURDERER

Regrettably, none of these simple qualities applies to the sexual mass murderer—a type of deviate which seems to be multiplying at an alarming rate in recent years (and everywhere too, even in Canada where the overall homicide rate has been dropping for years), and whose characteristics make him especially difficult for police to identify.[1] Here, there are no obvious links with the victim, and no obvious motive beyond a deranged (and, during interrogation, undetectable) sexuality. Neither do such investigations yield an obvious list of suspects other than those who have been previously arrested for sexual offences: but sexual mass murderers rarely have such a record, and are more likely to be known as pillars of society than as deviates.

Further, the sexual mass murderer often compartmentalizes his thinking, and is usually only dimly aware that he has transformed his fantasies into reality: thus the explanation by the Boston Strangler regarding his disengagement . . . "I looked in a mirror in the bedroom and there was me—strangling somebody!" (In Frank, 1966: 313). Thus the murderer feels little guilt, and as a result he does not release the subtle guilt-based cues on which intuitive officers depend:

> . . . as far as I was concerned, it wasn't me (who murdered). I can't explain it to you any other way. It's just so unreal . . . I was there, it was done, and yet if you talked to me an hour later, or half hour later, it didn't mean nothing, it just didn't mean nothing. (Albert DeSalvo, the "Boston Strangler," quoted in Frank 1966: 308).

Little wonder then that "police will tell you that finding a single killer in the vast swarm of a metropolitan area is often impossible without the intervention of luck"

(Klausner, 1981: 6–7). With a malfunctioning police intuition protecting the actual killer, he escapes close scrutiny for an extended period, and is free to murder dozens of additional women and men. Fortunately, as I shall try to show, sexual mass murderers do seem to have enough in common to bring themselves to the attention of the police with relative speed.

THE PROGRESS OF INVESTIGATIONS

The activities of many sexual mass murderers remain undiscovered until their gigantic graveyards are discovered. As often, however, two or three victims are found relatively early in the killing "spree"; and when police compare the characteristics of the crimes, they usually realize that they have a mass murderer operating in their area (although even this realization may take much longer if the murderer is operating in that "killing ground" that is the highway, killing in separate police jurisdictions, and leaving several local forces thinking they have isolated and unrelated murders on their hands).[2] Usually, however, using modern police investigative techniques, which include the perusal of prior arrest records, the coordination of informant tips, and the monitoring of automobile movements, the police assemble a list of suspects which can number as many as several thousand.

Most often, the name of the actual killer is in that list of suspects; but, given the limited manpower available to the police, it can take months or years before the killer is discovered. If the killer displays behavioural characteristics that are obviously "crazy" in his day-to-day life—as did, for example, David Berkowitz and Clifford Olson—then they are often caught within a year or less. But most of these sexual mass murderers do *not* behave abnormally. On the contrary:

The sex murderer differs from other psychi-

atric killers in his ability to keep his terrible daydreams to himself. He keeps quiet about them: he exhibits no odd behaviour. Thus he is able to move among friends and fellow workers without calling attention to himself. Chances were that he might appear bland, pleasant, gentle, ingratiating—even compassionate. No one would think of him as "crazy" (in Frank, 1966: 155–156).

Thus, if, as is most commonly the case, the killer appears to be normal, even admirable—after all, Los Angeles' Hillside Strangler was a policeman; Albert DeSalvo was a devoted father and husband; Albert Fish was described by those who met him as "articulate", "genteel," and having a "kind and ingratiating face" (in Angelella, 1979); and Ted Bundy was a university law student, an active member of the Republican Party, and a respected counsellor at Seattle's Crisis Counselling Centre (Rule, 1980)—it can be years before the suspicions of the police are aroused. During those years, dozens die horribly.

THE SOCIAL PROFILE

What would be immensely useful to the police then would be any means for winnowing the killer's name out of the list of suspects. If a man's private fantasies are unknowable, his social characteristics are objective and often public. While engaged in background research for a purely academic series of books on multiple murderers, I have stumbled across such an objective set of social characteristics which distinguishes sexual mass murderers from the majority of the population. They will not be surprising to any social scientist: they have simply not been previously articulated. The Social Profile which emerges from these clustered characteristics can be taught easily to police, and if used systematically, should prove to be an efficient and effective new tool for police science.

The superimposition of the Social Profile over the police suspect list would enable the investigator to reduce the list to a more manageable one-fifth, or less, of its original number: thus an original suspect list of 1,000 would be pared quickly to 200, or fewer, high probability suspects. Such a reduction would enable the police to accelerate the investigative process, cut the killer off in mid-career, and save dozens of lives.

The Social Profile can be used in two phases, or Scans. The *First Scan* concentrates on objective social traits, uses information obtainable from municipal, provincial/state, and national data banks—or, failing that, is easily obtained through interrogation—and reduces the suspect list by some four-fifths. Its information picks out those individuals whose families bear the marks of extreme rupture—marks which show up in public records as one or more of the following: adoption, illegitimacy, institutionalization in childhood or adolescence (reformatory or orphanage), having a father or brother charged with violence, or a mother who had married three or more times. These variables occur in perhaps 20 percent of the population, but in 90 percent of sexual mass murderers for whom reliable social histories are available. Thus in 90 percent of sexual mass-murder cases, so long as the name of the killer has appeared in the suspect list, as it usually has, police should be able to concentrate their enquiries among a vastly reduced pool of suspects.

The *Second Scan* focuses on behavioural and life-style characteristics, and supplements or complements the FBI profiling techniques. The Second Scan concentrates on an extreme presentation of self, *either* as "crazed" (as in Charles Manson) or appearing in a "Mr. Perfect" *ensemble* (as in Albert Fish, Ted Bundy, and Albert DeSalvo). Further variables are an obsession with things, generally to the exclusion of all friendships (the classic "loner" syndrome); or a participation in "power" sports (as in DeSalvo's and Olson's boxing; Kemper's guns; or "Collins" motorcycles).

ANALYSIS

Why should these variables, especially the primary traits revealed in the First Scan, inexorably lead us to a multiple sex killer? What is there about being adopted, or illegitimate, or reared in an institution, or having a close relative convicted of assault, or a much-married mother, that might propel a man towards a "career" in sexual assault and mass murder? The answer is obvious, and lies in some basic social science.

The simple fact of human social life is that in order for individuals to become "normal", to internalize the values and behaviours of their society, they must grow up feeling that they have some place in the social order—that is, a coherent socially constructed identity. The primary agency charged with inculcating this sense of identity is the family. I have discussed this problem elsewhere in my own recent book, *The Myth of Delinquency*, but Thomas Belmonte (1979: 52–59) puts it more succinctly when he writes that we trace our first "connections to the universe through the intermediary relations of the family", and that the family is therefore "the crucible of every human identity." Sometimes, a family malfunctions; the crucible is overturned, and an incomplete or blemished identity is forged. The First Scan's primary traits are extremely useful indices of this failure to forge a complete identity.

Thus the Boston Strangler, a U.S. Army boxing champion and a devoted father, who strangled thirteen women and raped hundreds more, was seen by others as a "mild-mannered, tearful husband and father living quietly with his wife and two children in a Boston suburb . . . A man treated all but contemptuously by his wife and dismissed as a bore and a braggart by his friends" (Frank, 1966: 272). He described himself and his activities in these terms:

I don't want to be the person who did these

Table 1
INTERNATIONAL DATA BASE

	First Scan (Social Characteristics)	Second Scan (Behavioral Traits)
John Bianchi (Hillside Strangler)	ADOPTED	MR. PERFECT, POLICEMAN
Cliff Olson (B.C. Murders)	INSTITUTIONALIZED (Juvenile Home)	BOXER
David Berkowitz (Son of Sam)	ILLEGITIMATE; and ADOPTED	MR. CRAZY, SECURITY GUARD
Earle Nelson (Manitoba Murders)	ADOPTED	Insuff. Data
Ted Bundy (Seattle)	ILLEGITIMATE	MR. PERFECT
Albert Fish (Prewar children)	INSTITUTIONALIZED (orphanage reared)	MR. PERFECT
Albert DeSalvo (Boston Strangler)	INSTITUTIONALIZED (Juvenile home); and VIOLENT KIN (both father & brother charged with assault)	BOXER
Peter Sutcliffe (Yorkshire Ripper)	VIOLENT KIN (brother twice charged with grievously wounding police)	MR. PERFECT
Dean Corll (Houston Murders)	RUPTURED MATERNAL BOND (mother thrice married)	Insuff. Data
"Norman Collins" (Michigan Murders)	RUPTURED MATERNAL BOND (mother thrice married)	MOTORCYCLES

things. There's no rhyme or reason to it. I'm not a man who can hurt anyone. I can't do it. I'm very emotional. I break up at the least thing. I can't hurt anyone . . . (in Frank, 1966: 317–318).

To a sensitive psychiatrist, the Strangler "had never really integrated these experiences, these murders, into his consciousness." Rather, "he had kept them outside himself, and thus had been able to maintain a kind of mental health—had been able to report them as things done by someone whom he recognized was himself yet not done by himself" (quoted in Frank, 1966: 310).

Similarly, David Berkowitz came to be-

lieve that he would never be caught because "The Police couldn't see me. I was an illusion . . . someone other than David Berkowitz" (in Klausner, 1981: 130).

"I am the Son of Sam," says David Berkowitz. Illegitimate, adopted David Berkowitz. Looking backward to the cold winter of 1967–77, he says "It wasn't me. It was Sam that was working through me. I mean, me and the Son of Sam, there's just one body, but we weren't the same people. Sam used me as his tool" (in Klausner, 1981: 102).

Berkowitz, the anonymous and friendless virgin-bachelor, "seems never to have felt sure of his identity . . . He was phobic as a child

Table 1
INTERNATIONAL DATA BASE (Continued)

	First Scan (Social Characteristics)	Second Scan (Behavioral Traits)
William Bonin (Freeway Murders)	INSTITUTIONALIZED (in juvenile home from age of eight)	MR. CRAZY
Ian Brady (Moors Murders)	ILLEGITIMATE; and INSTITUTIONALIZED (both foster and juvenile homes)	NAZI BUFF
Richard Speck (Chicago Nurses)	INSTITUTIONALIZED (juvenile home)	Insuff. Data
Robert Irwin	INSTITUTIONALIZED (juvenile home)	Insuff. Data
William Heirens (Chicago Murders)	INSTITUTIONALIZED (juvenile home)	NAZI BUFF, GUN NUT
Edmund Kemper III (Santa Cruz Murders)	INSTITUTIONALIZED (mental hospital from age of 15); and RUPTURED MATERNAL BOND (mother thrice married)	GUN & KNIFE NUT
Fritz Haarmann (Prewar German)	INSTITUTIONALIZED (juvenile home)	Insuff. Data
Robert Carr III	INSTITUTIONALIZED (juvenile home)	Insuff. Data
Antone Costa (Cape Cod Murders)	NOT FIT	NOT FIT
John Christie (London Prostitutes)	NOT FIT	POLICEMAN

and suffered from overwhelming feelings of rejection. His response, both to rejection and to a shaky sense of self, began with bravado. Then, in 1974, David's pathetic, passive fantasy life evolved into something that was not pathetic. If he could not conquer young women by seducing them, he could conquer them with the act of murder" (Klausner, 1981: 2–3).

Fortunately for our purposes, this terrible process wherein a man may be denied an identity[3] is discoverable, not just through the examination of his private thoughts, but buried in his family's birth, marital, and police records. As for the behavioural characteristics contained in the Second Scan: as incomplete as they are,[4] it should be clear that such life-styles are sometimes the attributes of individuals suffering from insecurity and rage, and are further clues to the existence of a malformed identity, to the possibility of harbouring the sadistic fantasies that a man without an identity can put into operation—and do so without guilt.

Let me conclude with several warnings. An important ethical dilemma revolves around the problem of potential damage to innocent people bearing Scan characteristics. *It can-*

not be emphasized too strongly that the personal characteristics in both First and Second Scans do not automatically cause, suggest, or assign abnormality of any kind. Most adopted, illegitimate, or institutionalized persons go on to. lead healthy normal lives! The Scans merely seek to identify forces which, *in extreme cases only*, produce or reflect the stress signs we seek. Secondly, while it should be clear that similar profiles could be developed for a variety of criminals, teasing out high-probability offenders in spheres as diverse as rape, assassination, and defection, there are serious practical problems in gaining access to such data for some populations, and ethical problems regarding invasion of privacy: but ultimately, this can only be solved by progressive social legislation and judicious police practice. Finally, police should be made clearly aware of the fact that while proper training in and use of the social profile could enhance and quicken the pace of their work, and thus possibly save lives, the profile is not a substitute for good police work: there will never be such a substitute.

Notes

[1] I do not deal here with other types of multiple murderers, such as family annihilators, political murders such as the Zebra killings in California, gangland murders, nor delusional killing such as the Santa Cruz murders, for each of these types conform to quite different social profiles.

[2] This lack of cooperation and tight coordination between regional forces, especially in the U.S., is a tactical handicap of considerable magnitude.

[3] This process of identity-destruction applies of course to both sexes. The relative absence of female participation in mass murder is a phenomenon as yet unexplained; although recent developments in California homicide cases suggest that females may be becoming more active in this sphere.

[4] The Behavioral Science team at the FBI Academy in Quantico, Virginia, naturally have access to a much wider range of data, and immediate access to most murderers, and are able to assemble a much more comprehensive picture of this aspect.

References

Abrahamsen, David. 1973. *The Murdering Mind*. New York: Harper.

Angelella, Michael. 1979. *Trail of Blood*. New York: New American Library.

Ault, Richard L. Jr. and James T. Reese, 1980. "A psychological assessment of crime profiling." In *FBI Law Enforcement Bulletin*.

Belmonte, Thomas, 1979. *The Broken Fountain*. New York: Columbia University Press.

Fox, Richard G. 1971. "The XYY offender: a modern myth?" In *Journal of Criminal Law, Criminology and Police Science*, 62(1).

Frank, Gerold, 1965. *The Boston Strangler*. New York: New American Library.

Gaddis, Thomas E. and James O. Long, 1970. *Killer*. New York: Macmillan.

Guttmacher, Manfred, 1960. *The Mind of the Murderer*. New York: Farrar, Strauss and Cudahy.

Klausner, Lawrence D. 1981. *Son of Sam*. New York: McGraw Hill.

Leyton, Elliott, 1979. *The Myth of Delinquency*. Toronto: McClelland and Stewart.

———. 1983. Drunk and Disorderly. In J. Rex Clark (Ed.), *The New Newfoundland*. St. John's: Breakwater.

Lunde, Donald T. 1979. *Murder and Madness*. New York: W.W. Norton.

Miron, Murray S. and John E. Douglas. 1979. "Threat analysis." In *FBI Law Enforcement Bulletin*.

Reinhardt, James Melvin. 1960. *The Murderous Trail of Charles Starkweather*. Springfield: Charles C. Thomas.

Ressler, Robert K., John E. Douglas, A Nicholas Groth and Ann Wolbert Burgess, 1980. "Offender profiles." In *FBI Law Enforcement Bulletin*.

Rule, Ann. 1980. *The Stranger Beside Me.* New York: New American Library.

Wertham, Frederic, 1949. *The Show of Violence*. New York: Doubleday.

————. 1966. *Dark Legend*, New York: Bantam.

Wolfgang, Marvin E. 1958. *Patterns in Criminal Homicide*. Montclair: Patterson Smith.

20 Street Crimes and Suite Crimes

Colin Goff   Charles Reasons

COLIN GOFF, Associate Professor of Sociology at the University of New Brunswick, specializes in the study of crime, deviance, and social control. His recent publications include "Early American Criminologists' perceptions of psychiatry" (1986); "Edwin H. Sutherland's *White Collar Crime in America*," with G. Geis (1986); "Organizational crimes against employees, consumers, and the public," with C. Reasons (1986); and "The attempt to control economic crime in Canada, 1970–1982: An analysis of the harsh realities of merger legislation" (1986). Professor Goff has also, with B. McKeown, completed a contracted research project for Correctional Services (Canada) on a university education program for the penitentiaries of Atlantic Canada.

CHARLES REASONS, Professor of Sociology at the University of Calgary, specializes in the sociology of law, criminal justice and social problems. His books include *The Ideology of Social Problems*, with W.D. Perdue (1981); *Corporate Crime in Canada: A Critical Analysis of Anti-Combines Legislation*, with Colin Goff (1978); *The Sociology of Law: A Conflict Perspective*, co-edited with R. Rich (1978); *Assault on the Workers: Occupational Health and Safety in Canada*, with Craig Paterson and Lois Ross (1981); and *Stampede City: Power and Politics in the West* (1984). Professor Reasons has given many presentations and invited lectures, and has been a Visiting Professor at the University of Minnesota, Simon Fraser University and the University of Victoria. He has recently completed comparative research on workers' health and its legislated protection in Canada and Australia.

"The thief who is in prison is not necessarily more dishonest than his fellows at large, but mostly one who, through ignorance or stupidity, steals in a way that is not customary. He snatches a loaf from the baker's counter and is promptly run into gaol. Another man snatches bread from the table of hundreds of widows and orphans and similar credulous souls who do not know the ways of company promoters; and, as likely as not, he is run into Parliament."*

... While in theory our freedom as citizens rests on the fact that no act is a crime unless so specified in law, in practice we have an enormous amount of behaviour defined as criminal in Canada, including over 700 Criminal Code sections, 20 000 federal offences, and 30 000 provincial offences which exclude municipal laws.[1] The sheer number of statutes is staggering to the imagination. A theory accounting for both the emergence and administration of laws within the context of the nation-state is crucial to understanding the nature of crime in our society.

Most students of crime, like most citizens, take the crime problem as given, with little argument regarding its nature or scope. The crime problem is assumed to be self-evident and its dimensions are hardly arguable.[2] This common conception of the crime problem is embodied in the term "street crime". When one talks about the crime problem, a common meaning is often assumed which emphasizes offences against the person and particularly crimes of violence, e.g., robbery, assault, murder, rape. The imagery evoked by the concept "street crime" is one of dark shadows, dirty alleys and hordes of the criminally inclined lurking on public streets. "Street crime" has long been a rallying cry for "wars on crime" by politicians, police officials and other civic leaders. However, when one looks beyond the rhetoric of street crimes, one discovers that most murders, rapes and assaults are not committed in the streets, but in homes, taverns, automobiles and parks. Such a conception is even losing meaning regarding robbery. As one observer notes:

> I will deal here mainly with street crime, and particularly robbery. In fact the phrase "street crime" is a misnomer, at least in New York. Most robberies now occur inside, in hallways, elevators, shops, or subways. You are safer out on the sidewalk.[3]

In actuality, most crimes in the streets are committed by vagrants, prostitutes, drunks, panhandlers, petty thieves and auto thieves. It would appear that to avoid murder, assault, rape or robbery, it might be advisable to stay away from home, family, friends and local drinking establishment and to spend time in the streets. Furthermore, violent crimes account for a very small proportion of the criminal behaviour in Canada. In Canada and the United States crimes of violence account for less than 10% of all crime.[4] Only about 6% of all offences in Canada are violent. While the rate of violent crime per 100 000 population increased between 1965–1974, so did the rate of nonviolent crimes which make up the bulk (over 90%) of crimes in Canada.[5] Thus, both the absolute number of crimes and the rate per 100 000 people have increased between 1965–1974.

A great deal of attention is given to "street crime" and street criminals; however, relatively little attention is paid to "suite crime" and suite criminals. By "suite crime" we are referring to the illegal behaviour which occurs in the business suites of the corporate, professional and civil elites of society. Such crimes as misrepresentation of advertising, price fixing, fraudulent financial manipulations, illegal rebates, misappropriation of public funds, splitting fees, restraint of trade, failure to maintain safety standards and violation of human rights are examples of suite crimes. Evidence suggests that such "suite crimes" are as pervasive as "street crimes", if not more so, and result in a great deal more financial loss, while also entailing death and injury.[6] However, we have almost totally ignored such offences in Canada. Data regarding street crime and street criminals are voluminous compared to available data on suite crime and suite criminals. The following news report is applicable to Canada.

> White-collar crime is evidently costing billions of dollars more per year than violent or street crime in the United States, yet there is no comprehensive effort to keep track of it . . . federal agencies concerned with crime are making few attempts to study white-collar crime, its magnitude or effects.[7]

Even less attention has been given to corporate crime in Canada than in the United States. One can count the studies of corporate crime on one's hand, and crime control agencies do not appear to be eager to investigate this area.

IS CORPORATE CRIME "CRIME"?

Criminologist Edwin Sutherland noted some time ago that the criminality of corporations was like that of professional thieves in that corporations are persistent recidivists; their illegal behaviour is much more extensive than the prosecutions and complaints indicate; the businessmen who violate the laws designed to regulate business do not customarily lose status among their business associates; businessmen customarily feel and express contempt for law, for government, and for governmental personnel; corporate crime, like the professional thief, is highly organized.[8] However, there are important distinctions between corporate criminality and that of the professional thief. The corporate criminal does not conceive of himself as a criminal and neither do most of the public because he does not fit the stereotype of the criminal. The professional thief views himself as a criminal and is viewed as such by the general public. While the professional thief has a "mouthpiece" (attorney) to argue against specific charges, corporations employ experts in law, public relations and advertising. Such corporate "mouthpieces" provide a much wider range of services than the "mouthpieces" of the professional thief do. Their duties include influencing the enactment and administration of the law, advising clients on how to break the law with relative impunity, defending in court those few clients who have the misfortune of being specifically charged and most importantly, building up and maintaining the corporation's status and image in the public's mind.

It is particularly those factors distinguishing the corporate criminal from the professional thief which help to maintain the appearance of non-criminality. The sharply dressed, neat appearing corporate executive who pays taxes, contributes to local charities and juvenile delinquency funds, and is an elder in the church, fails to match the stereotyped image of the criminal who, with premeditation, earns his livelihood through victimizing the public. If the mass media emphasized suite crime in the same manner it did street crime in an attempt to stress their similarities, there would likely be financial repercussions.

> Nearly all the advertising revenues of the newspapers and mass magazines, as well as of radio and television stations and networks, come from these same corporations and their smaller counterparts ... the newspapers have never despite recent sociological relevations ventured statistical summaries of the situation as they regularly do with lower-class, police-reported crimes—a marked case of class bias.[9]

Why do we tend to evaluate "street crime" so differently from "suite crime"? The direct, personal, face to face threat of physical violence is significant in "street crimes", i.e., murder, rape, assault, robbery. As one student of crime states:

> ... A face to face threat of bodily harm or possibly violent death is so terrifying to most people that the $20 or so stolen in a typical mugging must be multiplied many times if comparisons with other offenses are to be made. I have a hunch that a majority of city dwellers would accept a bargain under which if they would not be mugged this year they would be willing to allow white-collar crime to take an extra ten percent of their incomes. Of course we are annoyed by corporate thievery that drives up prices, but the kind of dread induced by thuggery has no dollar equivalent or, if it does, an extremely high one.[10]

While there is obvious physical danger and harm from some "street crimes," the belief that "suite crimes" are not violent is false.

> Corporate crime kills and maims. It has been estimated for example, that each year 200 000 to 500 000 workers are needlessly exposed to toxic agents such as radioactive materials and poisonous chemicals because of corporate failure to obey safety laws. And many of the 2.5 million temporary and 250 000 permanent worker disabilities from industrial accidents each year are the result of managerial acts that represent culpable failure to adhere to established standards.[11]

However, when automobile accidents, airplane crashes or industrial disasters occur, culpability is usually found among those directly involved in the accident or disaster. In discussing the nearly 100 000 United States workers who die each year as a result of exposure to job health hazards, Swartz notes:

> One of the more insidious tactics used by the corporate perpetrators of crime is to blame the victims for what happens to them. The National Safety Council, a corporation-funded institution, frequently runs "safety" campaigns. The point of these campaigns is always that the workers are careless and lazy, and do not take the measures necessary

to protect themselves (wearing safety helmets, ear plugs, etc.). Never is the corporation held the culprit.[12]

When alleged defects in manufactured products or violation of safety standards are investigated and substantiated, they are usually interpreted as quirks or accidents with possible civil, but not criminal, liability. In Quebec, about 45 construction workers die on the job each year while approximately 13 500 are injured. According to Réal Mireault, head of the Quebec Construction Office:

> Employers should stop blaming accidents on workers and instead enforce safety regulations and give their employees safety training.[13]

Although persons might use the threat of violence in robbery, they will seldom employ it. Likewise, the probability of injuries and deaths from suite crime may be low related to the number of offences. Nonetheless, both types of offences periodically result in injury and death, but only street crimes bear the brunt of full prosecution. For example, mercury poisoning from the Dryden Chemical plant in Northwestern Ontario is evident among native people in the area, but it will not likely result in the laying of criminal charges. Such a decision is based largely upon legal conceptions of causation, intent and culpability, all of which mitigate corporate responsibility. Nonetheless, physical harm, injury and often death are the results of this disease. Whether death or injury occurs at the hands of an assailant in a face to face encounter, or is due to poisoning and disease caused by an impersonal corporation, the end result is similar.[14]

ARE STREET CRIMES "CRIMES"?

The large proportion of street crimes do not involve violence. They include theft, auto of-

fences and "victimless crimes". "Victimless crimes" present a unique example of the politics of crime. The term "victimless crime" is applied to acts involving a willing exchange of goods and services and purported harms inflicted upon oneself. What is arguable is that victimization is more remote and/or difficult to ascertain than in "normal crimes". If someone steals a car from you or holds you up with a gun, you are obviously a victim and the other is the offender. However, public drunkenness, illicit use of drugs, gambling, abortion, prostitution, pornography and homosexuality usually involve a willing exchange of goods and services between two or more parties, but nonetheless are often criminalized in North America. For example, a prostitute exchanges sexual favours for money from the John. It is difficult to determine who is the victim and who is the criminal. While the John may believe that he has not had fair value for his money, it is unlikely he will become a complainant, due to the illegal nature of the exchange. In the United States such crimes total nearly 50% of all crime,[15] while in Canada such acts constitute approximately 20% of the crime.[16]

These crimes are depicted in the media as inherently evil and subsequently dangerous. Stereotypes of the gambler, dope fiend, prostitute, homosexual and drunk present frightening pictures which evoke both pity and fear among the "morally superior".[17] While most users of illicit drugs, prostitutes, gamblers, homosexuals, and inebriates live relatively normal, law abiding lives apart from their appetites, crimes of violence, personal psychopathology, and sordid environments are dramatized in the mass media as typical of such "kinds of people" and their behaviour. Such representations fail to note that most of the limited violence and personal psychopathology which is evident is largely a product of restrictive laws, not of the behaviour *per se*. In fact, the consequences of making and maintaining such behaviours as criminal are likely more harmful than removing them from the auspices of the criminal law.

Report after report and study upon study have indicated that such "overcriminalization" produces the following negative consequences: artificially high profits and criminal monopolies; organized crime; secondary crime such as theft among addicts to support their habit; criminal subcultures; excessive expenditures of police and criminal justice resources; corruption of agents of the criminal justice system; contempt for the law and criminal justice system by offenders; infringement upon individual rights. . . .

SUITE CRIMES HAVE VICTIMS

The difficulty in identifying victim(s) and offender(s) is a difference often noted between suite crime and violent street crime. While a visible, dramatic theft at gun point entails an obvious victim and a criminal, the taking of millions of dollars from millions of people through fraud or price fixing is less direct, with a more diffuse victim and offender.[19] For example, the theft of a worker's income tax, unemployment insurance and pension deductions by employers does not elicit the same response as bank robberies do, although it is a much more profitable type of crime. Failure to remit payroll deductions by employers in 1975 accounted for $7.9 million, while bank robbers, extortionists and kidnappers gained a profit of only $5.17 million in the same year.[20] A significant factor in such varying responses is the non-hostile, non-threatening nature of the setting and the fact that the offender is usually viewed as providing needed and legitimate goods and services.

> That we are daily victimized is not usually recognized because, for example, we do not view the grocery store or department store as an accomplice, the manufacturer as a criminal, and ourselves as victims of rising costs.[21]

Even when "suite criminals" commit "common crimes" they tend to be evaluated differently. For example, if a person breaks into another's premises and takes something, the usual definition is breaking and entering or burglary, and the offender is subject to possible imprisonment. However, when the White House "Plumbers", CIA, FBI, RCMP or federal narcotics agents commit such behaviours, it is likely to be evaluated in terms of national defence and/or necessary in the war against crime and therefore immune from prosecution. The innumerable offences of former U.S. President Nixon were viewed by many as the legitimate exercise of authority by the head of state.[22]

Furthermore, the public often identifies with the suite criminal who is a respectable businessman or civic official who contributes to the community and society. The Churchill Forest Industries scandal in Manitoba attests to the significance of appearance and status in suite crime. In a multi-million dollar swindle against the people of Manitoba, one Dr. Kosser and Associates put over one of the greatest cons in the annals of crime. In the end, it was estimated by an investigating commission that Dr. Kosser made about $26 million in excessive fees and paid no Canadian taxes on more than $33 million in earnings by setting up a network of companies. Left holding the bag were business and government leaders and, of course, the taxpayers of Manitoba.[23]

Why do we have such images of the crime problem? Where do we gain such perceptions? How are such images maintained? Our attitudes toward, and reactions to, crime are greatly affected by our perception of the nature of the crime problem. Our perception of the crime problem is largely related to our personal experiences and socialization. Since most of us do not experience rape, robbery or other crimes of violence, our perception of the nature and scope of "street crime", i.e., the crime problem, is largely a product of the diffusion of criminal conceptions and social types. Such images of crime and the criminal are provided us by our family, educational institutions, politicians and the mass media. Newspapers, television, radio, magazines, movies and official governmental reports continually provide us with definitions of the nature and scope of the crime problem. Such headlines as *Violent Crimes Up 10%, Rape Increases 100%, Murder Up 20%, Serious Crime on the Upsurge* convey to citizens that the crime problem (street crime) is increasing at an alarming rate. Uniform Crime Reports in both Canada and the United States emphasize "street crimes". Therefore, headlines such as *Corporate Crime Up 100%, Price Fixing Increases 50%, Corporate Crimes Death Toll Rises* are not usually found in the media.

Furthermore, the mass media is replete with crime drama depicting the crime problem and the actors involved in the "war against crime". For example, television provides almost daily doses of criminals, law enforcement officials, private investigators, judges, attorneys and correctional personnel. These grossly misrepresent the scope and nature of the crime problem and the criminal justice system.

> The misinformation available through the mass media . . . is overwhelming. Fiction about the crime and criminal justice is ridden with formula and stereotype, its primary purpose being the satisfaction of the emotional needs of the viewing audience rather than the portrayal of crime in an authentic way. So also with crime news itself, which seldom portrays any but the most sensational and bizarre events.[24]

In spite of the above limitations, the mass media provide most citizens with their conceptions of the crime problem. Fear of "street crime" is widespread while fear of "suite crime" is minimal. The continual barrage of crime statistics we receive plays an important role in creating and maintaining a constant fear among the public. Both Canada and the United States have Uniform Crime Reports which are issued periodically during each year as the barometer on crime. While these reporting systems have been critically assailed for their problems,[25] they are taken by the public as valid and reliable indicators of crime. Therefore, increases in crime noted in the media may frighten the public even though there may be little basis for fear. For example, a survey team in Toronto found in 1970 that concern with crime for many citizens was partly an artificial creation and that people were more concerned about crime in the abstract rather than actually becoming a victim. It was concluded that crime, to some extent, is an imaginary problem which is manufactured in the minds of many people.[26] The definition of crime and the criminal is constantly reinforced through television dramas, newspaper headlines, police statistical reports, and political and civic speeches. The definitions of crime and the criminal provided in these sources do not accurately reflect the nature and scope of crime in Canada.

WHY STUDY SUITE CRIME?

. . . As previously discussed, suite crime costs the public more than street crime, while also entailing injuries and sometimes death. One author has pointed out the costs of monopolies in both the United States and Canada:

> A U.S. study concludes that the overall cost of monopoly and shared monopoly in terms of lost production is somewhere between $48 billion and $60 billion annually. In Canada, lost output due to the same cause would be in the order of $4.5 to $6 billion dollars. The lost tax revenues alone from this wealth would go a long way towards ending poverty and pollution. The redistribution of income from monopoly profits that transfers income from consumers to shareholders is estimated at $2.3 billion annually in the U.S. and $2 to $3 billion in Canada. Monopolistic firms thus contribute to inequality, inflation and unemployment. Unemployment results since

monopolies, as noted, significantly reduce output which in turn reduces the number of workers who would otherwise be producing.[27]

Thus, in terms of corporate accountability, financial cost, dehumanization and physical safety there is a need for studying suite crime.

We may have to reassess our understanding of crime and criminality and its social sources. If the nature and scope of crime in a society reflects the nature of that society, then perhaps we get the criminals we deserve. Therefore, we need to direct our attention to possible criminogenic values in our society. Dominant values such as success, status and power seeking, monetary and material wealth, toughness, dupery and shrewdness contribute to both the "official criminal's" and "law-abiding citizen's" place in society.

Notes

[*] George Bernard Shaw quoted in Gilbert Geis, "Upperworld Crime," in *Current Perspectives on Criminal Behavior*, ed. Abraham S. Blumbert (New York: Alfred A. Knopf, 1974), pp. 123–124.

[1] Law Reform Commission, *Law*, 1976.

[2] Since only the Federal Government can make criminal law, in the strictly legal meaning of the term only those acts legislated against in the Criminal Code of Canada are crimes. However, for most practical purposes the "offences" found in provincial and municipal statutes are viewed as crimes and similar in their consequences. See Robert A. Silverman and James Teevan Jr. (eds.) *Crime in Canadian Society* (Toronto: Butterworth and Co. Ltd.) 1975, pp. 3–4.

[3] Andrew Hacker, "Getting Used to Mugging," *The New York Review of Books*, 20 (April 16, 1973), p. 9. Reprinted with permission from *The New York Review of Books*. Copyright © 1973 Nyrev, Inc.

[4] See Statistics Canada, *Canada Year Book 1973* (Ottawa: Information Canada, 1973); Federal Bureau of Investigation, *Uniform Crime Reports—1974* (Washington, D.C.: U.S. Government Printing Office, 1975).

[5] Canada's violent crime rate per 100 000 population remains about one fourth that of the United States between 1965–1974. See *Selected Aspects of Criminal Justice* (Ottawa: Ministry of the Solicitor General, March, 1976).

[6] Richard Quinney, *Criminology: Analysis and Critique of Crime in America* (Boston: Little, Brown and Company, 1975), pp. 131–161.

[7] "White Collar Crime Ignored," *The Calgary Herald*, May 28, 1975, p. 25.

[8] E.H. Sutherland, *White Collar Crime* (New York: Holt, Rinehart and Winston, Inc., 1961).

[9] Ferdinand Lundberg, *The Rich and the Super-Rich*. Copyright © 1968 by Ferdinand Lundberg. Published by arrangement with Lyle Stuart.

[10] Hacker, "Getting Used to Mugging," p. 9.

[11] Gilbert Geis, "Deterring Corporate Crime," in *The Criminologist: Crime and the Criminal*, ed. Charles E. Reasons (Pacific Palisades, California: Goodyear Publishing Company, 1974), pp. 246–247.

[12] Joel Swartz, "Silent Killers At Work," *Crime and Social Justice*, 3 (Summer, 1975), p. 19.

[13] "Workers' Accident Rate Excessive," *The Calgary Herald*, June 10, 1976, p. 12.

[14] "Threat of Mercury Poisoning Spreads Over Quebec," *The Calgary Herald*, April 2, 1976, p. 18; and Gail Singer and Bob Rodgers, "Mercury: The Hidden Poison in the Northern Rivers," *Saturday Night* (October, 1975), pp. 15–22.

[15] Gilbert Geis, *Not the Law's Business?* (Washington, D.C.: U.S. Government Printing Office, 1972).

[16] A principal reason for the smaller proportion of "victimless crimes" in Canada is the fact that drunkenness is no longer officially a crime

in most provinces, homosexuality between consenting adults is no longer criminal, and prostitution per se is not criminal, although procuring, soliciting and operating a bawdy house are.

[17] For example see Charles E. Reasons, "Images of Crime and the Criminal: The Dope Fiend Mythology," *Journal of Research in Crime and Delinquency*, 13 (July, 1976), pp. 133–44.

[18] Norval Morris and Gordon Hawkins, *The Honest Politician's Guide to Crime Control* (Chicago: The University of Chicago Press, 1970); Commission on the Non-Medical Use of Drugs, *Final Report*, (Ottawa: Information Canada, 1973).

[19] It should be noted that even in such "clear-cut" examples as homicide the victim may often bring about his own demise. The classic example of "victim-precipitated" homicide is the husband who verbally and/or physically abuses his spouse only to end up in the morgue due to gunshot or stabbing wounds. In other words, the "victim" was at one point the "offender." Such "mitigating factors" are legally admissible to reduce the offender's responsibility.

[20] "Employer's Crimes Are Most Lucrative," *The Calgary Herald* (April 3, 1976), p. 4.

[21] Charles E. Reasons, ed., *The Criminologist: Crime and the Criminal* (Pacific Palisades: Goodyear Publishing Co. 1974), p. 233.

[22] William A. Dobrovir, Joseph P. Gebhardt, Samuel L. Buffone, and Andra N. Oakes, *The Offenses of Richard M. Nixon: A Guide to His Impeachable Crimes* (New York: Quadrangle/The New York Times Book Co., 1974).

[23] "The C.F.I. Disaster," *The Calgary Herald* (October, 1974), p. 7.

[24] Richard L. Henshel and Robert A. Silverman, "Perceptions and Criminal Process," *Canada Journal of Sociology*, 1 (Spring, 1975), p. 39. Also see, Richard L. Henshel and Robert A. Silverman, eds., *Perceptions In Criminology* (Toronto: Methuen, 1975).

[25] For a summary of the major criticisms of these reporting systems see Edwin H. Sutherland and Donald Cressey, *Criminology*, 9th Edition (Philadelphia: J.B. Lippincott, 1974) and Robert A. Silverman and James Teevan, Jr., eds., *Crime In Canadian Society* (Toronto: Butterworth and Co. Ltd., 1975).

[26] Michael E. Milakovitch and Kurt Weis, "Politics and Measures of Success in the War on Crime," *Crime and Delinquency*, 21 (January, 1975), pp. 1–10.

[27] C. Gonick, *Inflation or Depression* (Toronto: James Lorimer Co., 1975), p. 22.

Social Interaction and Social Organization

Introduction

In the last section, we saw how deviance and control help to structure social relations. A preceding section had outlined another social process important to social organization; namely, socialization. The present section contains articles on three other social processes—structuration, integration, and evaluation—which also shape social organization at both the micro- and macro-social levels.

"Structuration," or what other sociologists have called "institutional definition," is the process by which a social organization distinguishes itself from others. Typically, such structuration begins by clearly defining the parts and people who make up the organization, the roles people play and the goals of the organization. The degree of structuration is determined by the interaction among an organization's parts, their connection to one another, and the flow of information and mutual awareness among participants.

Structuration occcurs in units as small as informal discussion groups or voluntary associations (e.g., the Boy Scouts), and as large as social classes. The starting point is always a set of people united by little

more than some shared characteristic or vaguely understood aim. With structuration, the group membership is defined and tasks are allocated. Rules binding members in good standing, procedures for clearly defining collective goals and attaining them, and processes for selecting and socializing members are all specified. Classic descriptions of this process include Robert Bales' work on the emergence of group structures in "T-groups" (Bales, 1950; Mills, 1967), Robert Merton's discussion of what constitutes a group (Merton, 1957), Marx's discussions of the development of class consciousness and class mobilization (Marx and Engels, [1848] 1967), and DiMaggio and Powell's discussion of inter-organizational relations (DiMaggio and Powell, 1983).

The readings in this section all discuss some aspect of structuration; but two are centrally concerned with it. First, an article by Bonnie Erickson discusses the ways secret societies create structures appropriate to meeting their goals within a hostile social environment. A secret society is very vulnerable to attack by people in authority, since it is committed to overthrowing that authority. It must select its members cautiously, for if mistakes are made, other members of the organization may pay with their lives. Successful functioning, as Professor Erickson shows, means recruiting from already existing social structures where it has been possible to assess candidates' reliability and appropriateness for secret activity. Members recruited from among kin, friends, or well-known and trusted co-workers can also be controlled more easily. Deviance can be punished by ostracism and a loss of significant social relations; sometimes it must also be punished by death.

Many organizations are shaped as much by the characteristics of their members as by their goals and rules. Thus, two secret societies may differ from each other because they are based on different candidate pools or social networks. Having looser rule structures, informal organizations (like T-groups) or voluntary associations (like church groups or clubs) will be more influenced by their members; and formal organizations will be less so. Universities, business firms and armies will try to minimize the influence of candidate variation on organization functioning. Max Weber has shown us that enforcing impersonal rules helps to make bureaucracy successful. Yet even bureaucracies will vary with the make-up of the membership, as Michel Crozier has shown in his cross-national comparison of bureaucracies in France, the USSR and the USA (Crozier, 1964).

Second, the structuration of organizations will also be influenced by the demographic flow-through of members. This point is made clearly in a paper by Beaujot and McQuillan (in Section Nine) on how demographic change affects family life over the course of time. The more quickly members move through a structure, the more likely it is to change over time. The commitment of members to a group is influenced by their expectations about or-

ganizational change as it affects their own rights and responsibilities.

The article by Lorne Tepperman in this section makes a related point; but it is less concerned with the consequences than with the causes of such demographic flow-through in a British army regiment. Both demographic factors (such as life expectancy) and organizational factors (such as rules for promotion) determine how fast people will move through positions. Faster movement probably increases commitment to the organization, given people's ambitions for upward mobility. It also rectifies errors in staffing more quickly and provides a younger top command. This process of rejuvenation may have positive or negative consequences. A younger top command guarantees both more energy and less experience at the top. Today, after a decade of rapid growth and upward mobility, many bureaucracies are stuck with people in high positions who are young and unlikely to leave very soon. The results are stagnation, depressed expectations for upward mobility, and reduced commitment to the organization. But in pre-industrial military organizations, turnover by death and continued expansion was remarkably rapid. As well as keeping the military young, vigorous, and full of new ideas about command, such turnover made the military an extremely attractive career.

Structuration, then, defines roles and fills these roles with people. Who these actual people are and how they are moved around influences the way an organization will be seen by its members and by others. But the pouring of people into roles is not enough to make a social organization effective. Another important process is "integration," the drawing together of members in a strong common commitment to the organization. Fundamental to such integration is communication. Good communication cannot ensure integration; but poor communication will guarantee a lack of integration. Hence, communication is an important process helping to form and maintain a social organization.

Two articles in this section discuss communication. The first, by Marcel Rioux, is about communication and sociability within a small French Canadian community. Sociability, a particular kind of communication, is both a source of social solidarity in the community and its expression. Certain people talk to certain other people in certain ways. And, within any small community, a pattern of discourse with its own character is shared by all. These rules of discourse determine how people will talk about certain topics, and with what consequences. Gossip is one kind of sociability; many researchers have pointed out that gossip is an important form of social control. In a small community, one's well-being and sense of worth largely depend on the value and assistance granted by neighbours. To survive persistent negative gossip in such a milieu would be difficult.

Sociability as gossip also expresses moral certainties and balances "good and evil." It celebrates the moral flaws of the rich and powerful, and the moral excellence of the weak and insignificant. That is not to say that gossip is, on the whole, good or desirable—a way of justifiably rewarding and punishing. Gossip is, simply, a universally understood social activity with important consequences for the community and those gossiped about.

The decline of small-town gossip and sociability in large cities is inevitable. We cannot readily assume that our urban neighbours will know the same people we do. Gossip remains possible in such small "communities" as workplaces and schools. Otherwise, we get our gossip ration from the society column; from magazines and newspapers entirely dedicated to gossip disguised as news; and by marveling at the fictional doings of characters in soap operas. The persistence of the soap opera suggests that we need whatever it is that sociability and gossip have to offer us.

Communication *across* communities also helps to create and define social organization. Up to a century ago, such communication was very limited. Invention of the telephone, telegraph, radio, television, newspaper and, of course, the post office, changed all that. In their article on the postal revolution in Central Canada, Brian Osborne and Robert Pike give us some insight into the social context within which this communication revolution took place, the mechanisms that made it possible, and the social consequences. They may not go as far as political scientist Karl Deutsch (1965), who sees national communication as the main source of national cohesion and identity. For Deutsch, postal and other national communication is the best measure of national integration. Nonetheless, an ideal postal system makes communication across great distances easy, fast, sure and cheap. This fact helps us understand why the ongoing crisis of the Canadian postal service poses a problem with significant social consequences.

So far we have set up some imaginary organizations, filled the organizational roles with people and given them means to communicate with one another. All of these are necessary to the existence of social structures, large or small. But we have not yet specified how the goals of a social organization get established; that is, how values are set among a group of co-operating people.

There are easy answers and hard answers to this question. For one thing, certain people are better placed than others to define the goals and values that will shape other people's behaviour. As we noted in our discussion of ideology in an earlier section, Marxist sociologists presume that values are set by the ruling class, in order to serve their own interests. To understand this fully, we must study the process and forms of domination, a force we shall discuss further in the next section on inequality.

The assumption that elites dominate is harder to defend when we study small or informal groups. It would be difficult to prove, for example, that the sociability and gossip discussed by Professor Rioux generally benefits the ruling families of the community, much less that it is created by those families. Gossip is extremely democratic, existing in a free market in information.

Symbolic interactionists, represented in this section by Robert Prus, see much of communication and value-setting as a market phenomenon in which collective interpretations are hammered out in interaction. It is fitting, therefore, that this market approach to social organization be applied to what many have believed was a singularly economic and rational, rather than a social and interpretive, process; namely, the setting of prices.

The price set for a good or service is partly governed, just as economists say it is, by rational consideration, supply and demand; but Professor Prus shows that much more is involved. *Perceptions* of supply and demand are products of social enterprise; so are perceptions of "value," especially for commodities that will not be re-sold at a profit and are valued for symbolic as well as practical purposes. Beyond this, the market relationship is ultimately social: in a market, buyers and sellers communicate and readjust until a bargain is struck or not struck. Economists understand markets require information flow or "signalling," but they are far from understanding the general nature of meaningful interchanges between "traders." Professor Prus' article should be seen, then, as an attempt to understand how meaningful negotiations set the values, and hence the prices, of things on sale. His work can be seen, first, as a contribution to the sociological understanding of a subject historically restricted to economists. But second, it offers a symbolic interactionist corrective to the general discussion of how values are set and communicated where information flows freely and the control of information and perception is difficult, if not impossible. It is a study in democracy, not domination.

The next section will lead in rather a different direction, despite the connection already noted between inequality and value-setting. Many sections that follow are concerned with *types* of social inequality. We begin with a general discussion of inequality that raises many issues receiving more detailed consideration in sections that come later.

References

Bales, Robert F. "A set of categories for the analysis of small group interaction." *American Sociological Review*, 15:30–33, 1959.

Crozier, Michel. *The Bureaucratic Phenomenon*. Chicago: University of Chicago Press, 1964.

Deutsch, Karl W. *Nationalism and Social Communication*, rev. ed. Cambridge, Mass.: MIT Press, 1965.

Dimaggio, Paul and Walter Powell "The iron cage revisited: Institutional isomorphism and collective rationality in organizational fields." *American Sociological Review*, 48 (April): 147–160, 1983.

Marx, Karl and Friedrich, Engels [1848]. *The Communist Manifesto*. With an introduction by A.J.P. Taylor. Harmondsworth: Penguin Books, 1967.

Merton, Robert K. "Continuities in the theory of reference groups and social structure." In *Social Theory and Social Structure*, Rev. ed. New York: Free Press, 1957.

Mills, Theodore M. *The Sociology of Small Groups*. Englewood Cliffs, N.J.: Prentice-Hall, 1967.

21 Secret Societies and Social Structure

Bonnie H. Erickson

BONNIE H. ERICKSON, Professor of Sociology at the University of Toronto, specializes in the study of social networks, aging and the life cycle. Her major publications include *International Networks: The Structured Webs of Diplomacy and Trade* (1975); *Understanding Data*, with T.A. Nosanchuk (1977); "Networks, ideologies and belief systems" (1982); "Networks and attitudes" (1987); and "The allocation of esteem and disesteem: A test of Goode's Theory", with T.A. Nosanchuk (1984). She has reviewed manuscripts for a variety of journals, including the *American Journal of Sociology*; *Social Forces*; the *Canadian Review of Sociology and Anthropology*; and the *Canadian Journal of Sociology*. Professor Erickson spent 1983–84 as a Visiting Scholar at the Survey Research Center, University of California at Berkeley.

DEFINING AND CLASSIFYING SECRET SOCIETIES

A secret society is here defined in social network terms as a persisting pattern of relationships which directly or indirectly links the participants in related secret activities. There must be some secret activities in order to have a *secret* society; there must be a persistent pattern of relationships among participants in order to have a secret *society*. . . .

Thus the proposed definition requires secret societies to have persisting structures, but it does not restrict the form such structures may have; their form should be a matter for investigation. In this paper varying forms are roughly classified by their degree of approximation to a hierarchy. This classification suffices for the present argument and allows us to assess the adequacy of Simmel's stress on hierarchy. The most hierarchical structure possible is a tree in the graph-theoretic sense, with careful separation of both levels and branches in the organization, a form Simmel (357) suggests in a key example. In

a less rigid form there are distinct ranked orders (Simmel; 356–7), with access only between contiguous levels (366–7) and control centralized at the top level (371). Branches, however, are less well defined; people at the same level may have rather free access to each other. In still more loosely structured cases, not considered by Simmel, both levels and branches are difficult to define and the structure is more like an acquaintance structure than a hierarchy in the more or less rigid sense.

Secret societies may also be classified in terms of the conditions under which they exist. If conditions include risk, as when the members of a secret society risk imprisonment or injury or death, the processes generating the society's structure are distinctive ones. The analysis of cases under risk, which is the business of this paper, need not apply to secret but safe societies. In turn the analysis of safe secret societies would probably benefit from a close reading of Simmel[1], whose ideas are not as applicable to the structure of secret societies under risk.

THE VARIABILITY OF SECRET SOCIETIES UNDER RISK

The Data and Their Limits

For the purposes of this paper, secret societies under risk must be distinguished from safe ones but they need not be further subclassified. They vary in many ways,[2] but I argue that these variations will affect only the details of the distinctive processes to be analyzed. Risk is so important a consideration that it sets similar processes in motion even for societies differing in time, place, goals, and so on, as do the examples used here.

The quality of available data has improved greatly. However, the data still do not permit a rigorous testing of theory because a random sample of cases cannot be obtained. Secret phenomena are in general impossible to sample; for similar comments on a different kind of covert activity, see Marx (404). In the present paper, there is the added difficulty that the cases used to illustrate the argument are also to a large extent those used to develop it in the first place. The paper must therefore be seen as an argument with roots in good data sources, but not as a formally demonstrated theory.

The Cases: From Hierarchy to Diffuse Network

The first example is one which comes closest to Simmel's planned, hierarchical secret society. This example is the underground organization in Auschwitz, described by Garlinski on the basis of a variety of memoirs, recollective interviews, and documents. The most active organizer, Pilecki, assumed the underground ought to be a rigid hierarchy with five-man cells, and tried to organize it in just that way. The widespread conception of the underground as a resistance army, as well as some other possible biases, probably leads to a somewhat overly hierarchical trend in the observer accounts. Even allowing for this, the Auschwitz example is clearly one of the most

hierarchical ones, with distinct levels and branches and centralized control. Levels included Pilecki himself as effective leader, other leaders and organizers, people directly recruited by organizers, and people indirectly recruited who could often have been subdivided into still further levels (e.g., Pilecki at one point had recruited 100 people himself and they in turn perhaps 500 more; Garlinski, 100). Access to vital secrets, such as knowledge of underground memberships, was limited to the inner circle or one or two people like Pilecki himself. There were several kinds of segregated branches in the organization. Branches to some extent paralleled divisions in the official camp organization (hospital branches, medical workers vs. craftsmen, residential blocks). And some branches of the underground grew as separate undergrounds and remained distinct after the leadership merged. Centralized control was reflected in such matters as escapes, with underground members either refraining from them, or helping in them as their leaders decreed. The overall structure was thus hierarchical, though not the rigid hierarchy of five-man cells Pilecki intended. Recall that he recruited 100 people personally; one woman could recall over 20 people she knew in the underground; "occasionally" people belonged to two different branches.

Naquin provides an admirable account of the 1813 Eight Trigrams rebellion in China; here I will emphasize the best-documented branch of the rebels, the White Lotus sect in the Peking area. Sources for this branch include some 200 confessions by participants in various parts of the organization (Naquin, 285–6), plus palace memorials, official communications, and captured sect documents. Again there may be some trend toward an overemphasis on hierarchy in these materials, in part because both the sect members and government officials had a hierarchical conception of orderly social relations in general and the sect in particular. Even allowing for this, the sect was almost as hierarchical as the Auschwitz underground. The White Lotus had levels clearly distinct in terms of authority, with a beginner deferential to his teacher and that teacher in turn deferential to his teacher and so on up to the sect leader. Only rarely were these rankings reversed, as in the case of the exceptional leader, Li, who supplanted his one-time superiors. These levels were probably more distinct than those in the previous example in the sense of lower mobility, but on the other hand, they were less distinct in the sense of security since it was common for people to know the identities of those above and below them. Indeed, such knowledge was an aspect of the legitimacy of the sect teachings, since each teacher drew authority from his link with his own teacher. Even at a high point of the sect's size, while still underground, with thousands of members in several areas, lower ranking members knew the name and general location of their top spiritual leader, Lin. Branches were reasonably distinct, as reflected for example in the tendency to break down into separate sects (one per branch) when the succession to overall leadership was unclear. But branches in different locations nevertheless had some cross-linking: the geographically mobile might join different groups in different places, healers moved around as part of their work and had links in many communities, and boxers were mobile and also liked to study with a series of teachers to expand their repertoires. Centralized control was reflected in hierarchical control of sect finances with donations flowing upward for the leaders to use as they thought best; in the top-level planning of the eventual rebellion and the downward flow of information and orders concerning it; and in the graduated access to sect secrets, such as special chants and scriptures.

The next two cases have much less clearly hierarchical organization, with at least a few levels but possible less distinct ones and with markedly less branch separation.

First is the Lupollo crime "family" re-ported by Ianni from several years of fieldwork and information from dozens of informants. The major bias problem here is that the higher levels of the organization are much better observed than the rest. Ianni directly observed relationships among the kin group from which the higher levels were recruited and recorded various kinds of ties in detail; but lower ranks are reported largely from indirect information limited to "organization charts" (a,106) which may or may not have fully reflected reality. It is clear that there are several layers of authority, with members of the ruling kin group at the top and subordinates arrayed in up to half a dozen layers in the numbers and loansharking enterprises. Subordinates know who their employers are, though not all that is done higher up. The separation of branches is more doubtful. Branches are presented as separate in organization charts but some of the concrete detail suggests otherwise. Ties across branches are very dense at the top, where ties are most closely observed, and they exist, to at least some extent, lower down as well. For example, the two major illegal enterprises are cross-linked at least through the practice of having loansharks hang out near the gambling sites. Control over the enterprises is centralized.

The second intermediate case is the San Antonio heroin market, studied by Redlinger from fieldwork and 40 interviews touching on all levels of the distribution network except the top one and the marginal light user. Higher levels are less well represented and are reported in somewhat different terms, with more stress on economic transactions as opposed to trust and friendship ties. Thus (just the opposite of the preceding case) it is the upper levels whose hierarchical organization may be overestimated. The market has at least four levels: consumers, retailers, wholesalers, and big dealers or importers. The distinctions among the levels are fluid. Retailers are usually also consumers and return to the consumer level often; wholesalers may be retailers expanding business. There is some insulation between levels stemming from the desire of inferiors to keep their higher-level connections secret in order to profit from monopoly access to suppliers, and from the desire of superiors to restrict potentially dangerous knowledge of their illegal activities to a trusted few. But these desires are to some extent frustrated by the fact that most participants are recruited from the same community and could not operate at all without the network of contacts the community provides (Redlinger, 337–47). There is some branch separation on ethnic lines, with blacks and Anglos getting heroin primarily from other blacks or Anglos, but most market members are Mexican-American, and branch separation within this ethnic group is not clearly indicated. Overall, the structural information is incomplete and biases are probably extensive; it is simply a reasonable conjecture that levels and branches exist but are less separated than in previously discussed cases. Control, however, is still fairly centralized through central control of heroin supplies.

The Lupollo crime family and the San Antonio heroin market are already rather far from pure cell structures, since branches are poorly separated and even levels are imperfectly insulated. The next sample takes us far indeed from pure hierarchy. Plant did fieldwork and interviews with 20 drug users (primarily marijuana users) in Cheltenham, England. Plant treated any kind of contact within the network as a tie, which raises some problems of comparability with studies using more restrictive definitions if the latter tend to select more hierarchical relationships. On the other hand, ties of different kinds (e.g., drug transaction links vs. friendship) seem to be little separated in this network. Plant pursued ties so thoroughly that he was able to construct a sociogram for his 200 contacts (107). As a hierarchy this sociogram is unrecognizable, but as a friendship network it is typical. There are a few well-known dealers who are connected to a relatively large num-

ber of people, but this hardly constitutes distinct layering; and Plant reports some trend to greater within-class interaction, but there are far too many cross-class links for distinct branches to be visible. Plant gives no indication of centralized control of activities in the network, though of course some members are more active than others. Important information diffuses freely and rapidly.

The last example has one especially interesting feature: the analyst (Aubert) is both a sociologist and a former full-fledged participant, a member of the underground in his native Norway during the German occupation. This unusual immediacy is the main reason for including the case, even though Aubert is somewhat vague about the basis of his generalizations and the overall direction of bias is difficult to judge.

Aubert refers to a hierarchical structure of command in which superiors were more likely to know the real identity of subordinates than vice versa. But he also refers to egalitarianism, decisions made largely by consensus, and friendship ties linking people in different positions. The existence of separate branches is suggested by the remark that subordinates had only limited contacts with other subordinates, but this could be true for a number of different possible structures, including one of overlapping small cliques rather than distinct branches. Probably this structure fits in just before the marijuana network, more hierarchical than that, but less hierarchical than the first four examples.

Even allowing for the gaps and ambiguities in our knowledge of these cases, the variety of organizational structure is striking. Further, no simple explanation for the variation seems to hold. For example, whatever the details of the Norwegian underground structure, it was certainly far less elaborate and hierarchical than the Auschwitz underground, even though both organizations were political secret societies engaging in similar resistance work under similarly severe risk.

Again, the San Antonio heroin market and the English marijuana network are both organizations distributing illegal drugs, but one is moderately hierarchical and the other not hierarchical at all. . . .

Risk, Trust, and Prior Networks

When secrecy is indeed a *necessary* condition, when it stems from need to reduce risk rather than from the fun of having a secret, trust becomes a vital matter and hence pre-existing networks set the limits of a secret society. To amplify this, suppose for simplicity that one member is thinking of recruiting one new member. The established member is under risk, since the potential member could betray him; the potential member is also under risk, since he is invited to participate in a dangerous activity about which he knows very little. Clearly recruitment is not likely to take place unless the two people first trust each other, unless they have a prior tie outside the secret society and that tie is a reasonably strong one. . . .

Strong ties are always preferred as the building blocks of secret societies, but the kind of tie actually used varies. Relatively weak ties may be used if the degree of risk is relatively low; for example, marijuana users are willing to share information or drugs or activities with a wider range of people than the more endangered and hence more cautious users of heroin (compare Plant, or Goode, to Redlinger, or Hughes). And the nature of a strong tie varies with culture and context. To the nineteenth-century Chinese and to twentieth century migrants from Southern Italy, kinship is the strongest kind of relationship, and recruitment to secret societies often followed kin lines. In Auschwitz, on the other hand, recruitment took place between former army comrades-in-arms for the military men and between former political co-workers for the political underground. For drug use, the key relationships are close peer ties especially among young males. Component

links of the secret society are selected from links in prior networks, and just which prior networks depends on the participants' understanding of which ties are most trustworthy.

Since the secret society is based on prior networks, cleavages in those networks set limits for the structure of the secret society. The cleavages do not have to be extreme in order to have an effect. For even if there are a few bridging ties crossing prior relational cleavages, these bridges are likely to be weak (Granovetter) and thus unlikely paths of recruitment to a risky enterprise. Thus groups disconnected or poorly connected outside a secret society are also separated within (or between) secret societies. I earlier described several secret societies with relatively well-separated branches; the separation rests at least in part on the cleavages in prior networks. Consider the Auschwitz underground branches formed in different parts of the camp, or different political or army groups, or different nationality groups. Similar branching was also noted for other camps. The White Lotus branches were territorial, like the social relations of the time. Cleavages may lead not just to separate branches but to separate societies; many of the Auschwitz branches were originally separate undergrounds and some undergrounds stayed separate to the end; there were many different White Lotus sects in different places; the pattern of heroin epidemics strongly suggests that cleavage lines, like race, are reflected in different drug networks (Hunt; Hunt and Chambers). By contrast, Plant's soft drug users were drawn from a dense network of young people living mostly with other young people in a small area so that cleavages were not marked, and neither was the drug network internally split. On the other hand, prior cliques, as well as prior cleavages, may be reflected in the secret society. This effect appears to be more erratic, since it is easier not to use an existing tie than to bridge the gap where no tie exists, but several accounts include occasional examples of entire households, cliques, or other strong components of prior networks beginning secret work.

Planning and the Locus of Control

... Centralized control of recruitment can take several forms, varying in detail. Simmel (349–51, 366–7) describes one form in which new members enter at the lowest level and move upward only when their superiors feel they have been sufficiently tested and trained. The essential element here is some kind of control from above. In some cases, people at one level control just those at the next level below (the San Antonio heroin market probably fits here). In others, those at the highest level may centralize yet further by controlling recruitment and promotion for several levels below them (the Lupollo "family" is closer to this version). Recruits may have to start at the bottom and work their way up (the usual pattern for White Lotus members), or they may be recruited directly to higher levels (as in the case of many heroin wholesalers with capital and connections to established upper level people). A little of everything may be included; for example, Pilecki did a lot of recruiting himself, encouraged recruits to recruit in turn, tried however at least to know who had been recruited indirectly, and facilitated recruitment to various levels in Auschwitz. But in all these cases, we see two common elements: these are our more hierarchical cases, and recruitment is somehow controlled from above. ...

The more decentralized the control over recruitment, the more recruitment simply spreads like a diffusion process and generates a structure with very few hierarchical features. In the English marijuana network, for example, there was no centralization of recruitment. People not only "turned on" their friends whenever they chose, but also created new links within the network at will by introducing people known to be users. It would be most unlikely for such decentral-

ized use of ties from a nonhierarchical prior network to produce a hierarchical structure, and this improbable outcome did not occur. Ianni's (b) report on several street quasi-groups appears to be another instance of free-for-all recruitment generating nonhierarchical results, though in this case the pattern is a set of loosely connected cliques rather than the one dense network in the Cheltenham example. The Norwegian underground is perhaps an intermediate case; recruits were supposed to be carefully vetted but "very frequently a member was co-opted by a friend without any kind of procedure at all" (Aubert, 290–1).

It should be noted that a secret society may draw on more than one network in more than one way. This may in turn have an impact on the society's structure, rendering it more complex internally than the discussion above might suggest. For example, Ianni (a) describes three broadly defined levels of the Lupollo "family business" with three different prior networks as recruitment bases. The highest of the three is drawn from the central kin group; the intermediate level, from near and distant relatives; the bottom level from those with some kind of nonkin personal tie to a member of the central kin group. The higher levels are recruited from more narrowly defined and more dense prior networks, and hence one would expect them to be more tightly knit. We know that the central kin group and upper level of the family business is indeed tightly knit, but the details of the lower level structure are not clear. Yet it seems reasonable to conjecture that the effect of varying prior networks, in this particular example, is to strengthen central control by fostering stronger and denser ties at the top than at the bottom. ...

Bases of Centralized Control: Command of Resources

We have seen that the locus of control over recruitment combines with the nature of the prior network used for recruitment to shape both the overall structure of a secret society and some of its internal variations. But centralized control over recruitment (or other matters) requires a centralized power base of some kind. In all our more centralized and more hierarchical examples, there was central control of some key resource critical to the secret society's members. The leaders of the Auschwitz underground were often able to influence appointments to the more desirable camp jobs with better conditions and better chances of survival; through their agents in important administrative posts they were able to influence job allocation, to get advance warning of important changes in policy, and (through the camp hospitals) to save lives or to arrange the deaths of informers. White Lotus leaders drew on authority and also often on scriptures inherited from previous leaders, on special skills such as arts of healing, boxing, or meditation, and on knowledge of secret chants of supposedly great benefit. As rebellion drew nearer, they also emphasized promises of rank and reward to be given to the faithful after taking power. Turning to the more modified hierarchies, the central kin group in the Lupollo family business kept central control in part through the command of financial resources (e.g., the capital for the loansharking business), in part through their extensive patronage in legal and illegal branches of the business, in part through their carefully tended protective connections. In the San Antonio heroin market, higher level participants, like wholesalers, control the supply of heroin through restricted possession of capital and connections to producers or importers. However, neither capital nor connections are monopolized in this market, and it has been conjectured that it is less centralized and less hierarchical than Eastern markets (Moore). It is also probably the least hierarchical of the first four examples.

Turning to the most diffusely structured cases with least centralized control, we also find the least centralization of important resources. In the English marijuana network, drugs are available on a fairly steady basis from several dealers and are also brought in sporadically by others so that no one person or group controls supplies. Even the poorest members of the network can afford drugs, and even the more marginal ones can find access to them. No basis for central control exists. Finally, in the Norwegian underground, most of the necessary resources for underground work, like ration cards, were dispersed among the members and less essential but still potentially relevant resources like social status were if anything inversely related to rank within the underground itself. . . .

CONCLUSIONS

The study of secret societies is important in part for intrinsic interest and in part, as Simmel (363) reminds us, because the topic illuminates extremes and hence is theoretically important. One could see secret societies as extreme cases of interest groups or purposive self-conscious organizations as Simmel does; as organizations especially sensitive to their environment; as uniquely well encapsulated subcultures; or as the limit of personal recruitment to organizations. Already secret societies are prominent in discussions of rebellion and revolution or of crime and deviance.

The particular approach to secret societies taken here is, I believe, especially likely to prove helpful because it is especially general. The focus throughout has been on structure and not on content, on patterns of ties and relatively abstract features such as their strength rather than on culturally specific definitions such as the content of a strong tie. Nadel has most elegantly made the case for potentially wide applicability of structural analysis. The relevant prior network may vary from case to case, depending on participant understanding of the ties most to be trusted for a given purpose in a given context; but the structure of the prior network will always have consequences for the structure of the secret society.

Notes

[1] For example, Simmel's discussion of psychology may be useful when secret society participants are not constrained by the exigencies of danger. Organizations like the modern Freemasons show an elaboration that may reflect the love of planning (Simmel, 357) and Cohn's analysis of the Jehovah's Witnesses supports Simmel's (355) discussion of the importance of having and sharing secrets. On more structural issues, one might follow up the suggestion that secret societies be seen as a particular kind of voluntary organization, an extreme instance of a self-conscious special-purpose group ("the opposite of all spontaneous groups . . . Its social-psychological form is clearly that of the interest group," Simmel, 363). Safe secret societies may require further subclassification such as Wedgwood's distinctions based on manifest and latent function.

[2] One distinction noted by several readers is that between criminal and political organizations. This distinction does usefully remind us of variables that might play a part in further analysis, such as: goals (personal vs. collective), type and pervasiveness of shared ideology, similar vs. shared interests. The impact of such variables is much less striking than that of risk, so that analysis of their effects will require later work with an expanded data set. Meanwhile, note that these theoretically promising variables are poorly related to the more popular criminal-political dichotomy. Participants in some of the resistance organizations were motivated by personal benefits, not just collective goals, while participants in the marijuana network saw themselves and behaved as members of a community. Further, the definition of a secret society as criminal or political is itself a political decision varying with the stance of the observer. All the examples in this paper were officially defined as criminal by the prevailing regime. With one possible exception (Redlinger, where the relevant data are not given) participants in the organizations saw their activities as justified and the regime as wrong. As observers, our use of the criminal label is likely to reflect our sympathies. Thus the criminal-political dichotomy is both difficult to apply objectively and a poor guide to variables of theoretical interest.

References

Aubert, V. (1965). "Secrecy, the Underground as a Social System." In Vilhelm Aubert, *The Hidden Society*. New York: Bedminster.

Becker, H.S. (1970). "Practitioners of Vice and Crime." In Robert W. Habenstein (ed.), *Pathways to Data*. Chicago: Aldine.

Cohn, W. (1955). "The Jehovah's Witnesses as a Proletarian Movement." *American Scholar* 24:281–98.

Garlinski, Jozef. (1975). *Fighting Auschwitz: The Resistance Movement in the Concentration Camp*. London: Friedman.

Goode, Erich. (1970). *The Marijuana Smokers*. New York: Basic Books.

Granovetter, M.S. 1973. "The Strength of Weak Ties." *American Journal of Sociology* 78:1360–80.

Hazelrigg, L.E. (1969). "A Re-examination of Simmel's 'The Secret and the Secret Society': Nine Propositions." *Social Forces* 47(March:323–30.

Heckethorn, Charles William (1875). *The Secret Societies of All Ages and Countries*. New Hyde Park: University Books, 1965.

Hughes, Patrick H. (1977). *Behind the Wall of Respect*. Chicago: University of Chicago Press.

Hunt, Leon Gibson. (1977). *Assessment of Local Drug Abuse*. Lexington, Ma.: Heath.

Hunt, Leon Gibson, and Carl D. Chambers. (1976). *The Heroin Epidemics: A Study of Heroin Use in the United States*, 1965–75. New York: Spectrum.

Ianni, Francis A.J. (1974). *Black Mafia: Ethnic Succession in Organized Crime*. New York: Simon and Schuster.

Ianni, Francis A.J., with Elizabeth Reuss-Ianni. (1972). *A Family Business*. New York: Russell Sage Foundation, Mentor Edition, 1973.

Kandel, D. (1974). "Interpersonal Influences on Adolescent Illegal Drug Use." In Eric Josephson and Eleanor S. Carroll (eds.), *Drug Use: Epidemiological and Sociological Approaches*. Washington: Hemisphere.

Kogon, Eugen. (1960). *The Theory and Practice of Hell*. Berkeley, New York: Medallion.

Lee, Nancy Howell. (1969). *The Search for an Abortionist*. Chicago: University of Chicago Press.

Levine, D.N., E.B. Carter, and E. Miller Gorman. a:(1976). "Simmel's Influence on American Sociology: 1." *American Journal of Sociology* 81:813–45.

———.b:(1976). "Simmel's Influence on American Sociology: II." *American Journal of Sociology* 81:1112–32.

Marx, G.T. (1974). "Thoughts on a Neglected Category of Social Movement Participant: The Agent Provocateur and the Informant." *American Journal of Sociology* 80:402–42.

Moore, Mark Harrison. (1977). *Buy and Bust*. Lexington: Heath.

Nadel, S.F. 1957. *The Theory of Social Structure*. Glencoe: Free Press.

Naquin, Susan. (1976). *Millenarian Rebellion in China*. New Haven: Yale University Press.

Plant, Martin A. (1975). *Drugtakers in an English Town*. London: Tavistock.

Redlinger, L. John. (1975). "Marketing and Distributing Heroin: Some Sociological Observations." *Journal of Psychedelic Drugs* 7:331–53.

Riste, Olaf, and Berit Nockleby. (1970). *Norway 1940–1945: The Resistance Movement*. Oslo: Johan Grundt Zanum Forlag.

Roberts, J.M. (1972). *The Mythology of the Secret Societies*. London: Secker & Warburg.

Simmel, G. (1908). *The Secret and the Secret Society."* Part Four of Kurt H. Wolff (ed. and trans.), *The Sociology of Georg Simmel*. New York: Free Press, 1950.

Wedgwood, C.H. (1930). "The Nature and Functions of Secret Societies." *Oceania* 1:129–45.

Weppner, Robert S. (ed.). (1977). *Street Ethnography*. Volume 1, Sage Annual Review of Drug and Alcohol Abuse. Beverly Hills: Sage.

22 Demographic Aspects of Career Mobility

Lorne Tepperman

LORNE TEPPERMAN, Professor of Sociology at the University of Toronto, specializes in applied sociology, demography and the study of Canadian society. His books include *Social Mobility in Canada* (1975); *Crime Control: The Urge to Authority* (1977); *The Roots of Disunity*, with David Bell (1979); *The Social World*, co-edited with R.J. Richardson (1986); *Making Sense in Social Science*, with Margot Northey 19(86); and *Understanding Canadian Society*, co-edited with James Curtis (1988). A member of the Canadian Commission to UNESCO's Social Science Advisory Committee, he has served as consultant to a variety of private and public organizations. Honours include the Sorokin Lectureship (University of Saskatchewan, 1980) and a Visiting Professorship in Canadian Studies (Yale University, 1983). He is an associate editor of the *Canadian Journal of Sociology* and *Canadian Studies in Population*.

This paper is, simultaneously, about three distinct things. It is first about career mobility in a formal organization that may be taken as representative of many formal organizations with a clearcut hierarchy of positions and promotion by seniority.... Second, it is a methodological paper which has aimed to use demographic techniques to study mobility.... Third, it is a paper which continues investigation into a theoretical paradigm for the study of mobility described in an earlier paper (Tepperman, 1973). It is with respect to this third aspect that I am most optimistic this paper will prove useful.

The earlier paper argued that two dimensions sufficiently defined career mobility. An examination of the *control dimension* of career mobility concluded that, all other things being equal, the frequency of upward mobility was maximized by a seniority system of promotion. The present paper will discuss what I have called the *absorbing dimension* of career mobility, a dimension largely compounded of what are commonly called demographic factors....

The demographic variations to be considered are (1) mortality level in the population from which organization members are drawn; (2) the growth rate of the organization; (3) the retirement rate of persons in the organization; (4) the size of the organization and the average span of control, a factor associated with size; (5) the age structure of the organization work force, especially in periods of transition from one rate of growth to another; and (6) factors unique to the demography of the organization being studied here.

The findings of this paper, while necessarily specific to the particular organization under observation, will be held to have wide generalizability to other formal organizations. A similar but less elaborate study of promotion within university faculties has recently been published (Holmes, 1974). The application of demographic techniques to the study of mobility will ultimately prove to have great utility which can only be hinted at in the present paper (see also Tepperman, 1975: chaps. 2 and 3).

With respect to the third goal of this paper—the elaboration of a paradigm for studying mobility—the findings suggest that demographic variations have similar effects on mobility in a formal organization regardless of whether promotion is based on sponsorship (e.g., seniority) or contest (e.g., random allocation.) This means that the *absorbing* and *control* dimensions of social mobility are analytically independent and distinct. The importance of this becomes clear when one considers why, for example, the structural expansion associated with industrialization has relatively little impact on social inequality and stratification as a whole. . . .

MOBILITY IN A MILITARY REGIMENT

The organization studied here is the Officers Corps of the Coldstream Guard, a prestigious British military regiment whose history begins in the mid-seventeenth century. I shall look at the structure of careers within the Officers Corps in the period 1690–1830. Data are drawn from a history of the Coldstream Guard (Mackinnon, 1833) that included complete records of commissions and promotions to each rank for every officer who served in the Guard during this period; and the dates at which each rank was entered and left by a given individual. Career histories were obtained for 796 individuals from this source.

A second organization, the Scots Guard Officers Corps, 1690–1930, was similarly examined. It comprised 1750 careers, but the career histories were less detailed than those of the Coldstream Guard, and so the Scots Guard data (Maurice, 1934) will only be used at occasional points to support or add to the Coldstream Guard data. . . .

During the period under study, the Coldstream Guard Officers Corps (hereafter, the Guard) had certain well-defined structural and demographic features. The Guard was small

in size, numbering about 44 officers at any given moment. . . .

Between 1690 and 1830, there was little if any change in the size of the Guard. This was, then, a roughly stationary population. However, there was an extremely high rate of turnover in the Guard, corresponding to a "birth" and "death" rate of about 147/1000 each *per annum*. This turnover was primarily due to high rates of retirement (or intentionally short careers) and not to mortality conditions extant in the British population at large or in the military in particular. It meant in effect a new Officers Corps every seven years. Both new recruits and the highest commanding officers (excluding the colonel) were likely to stay in the Guard only a short time. Recruits who stayed beyond the first year of service were likely to stay in the Guard very much longer; but those men who had reached the rank of major or lieutenant colonel were likely to leave the Guard shortly. At any given moment, about 43 per cent of all officers had been in the Guard five years or less, which would presumably make for continuing problems of socialization. Similarly, those at the rank of major or lieutenant colonel could be expected to remain in that rank a median of two to four years, which presumably created continuing problems of leadership succession and legitimate authority in the Regiment. . . .

The consequence of a high rate of turnover among the top officers is an interesting problem which cannot receive adequate consideration in this paper. It is likely however that it was, at least in part, a consequence of promotion by seniority in the Guard, in that men took so long (i.e., 20 to 30 years) to reach the top command positions through seniority that they were physically and emotionally unfit to exercise command once they got it. It may have been for this reason that the titular regimental leader, the colonel, was always appointed to his post from outside the Regiment, and never came into it through seniority. The colonel was, as a consequence, often younger than many of his top subordinates, and he stayed in his position much longer than they (a mean of 8.2 years and a median of 6.5 years). . . .

AN AGE-DEPENDENT SYSTEM

The critical feature of this organization which allows easy mathematical modelling and comparability with other formal organizations is its *age-dependency*. An officer's rank in the Guard was largely dependent on the time he had already spent as an officer at any rank. Most men, about 72 per cent of all 796 officers, had entered the Officer's Corps at the (bottom) rank of ensign, while 89 per cent had entered at the rank of ensign *or* lieutenant: very few ever entered above the rank of captain. Second, officers generally moved up in rank as time passed, and none moved down. As a consequence, little more than 20 per cent left the Guard at the rank of ensign, and those who did were primarily men leaving in the first year or two of service; just under one-half of all departing officers held the rank of captain or higher. Third, while officers commonly purchased their successive commissions,[1] a commission could not be purchased until it had been vacated by its incumbent; men had to wait for such vacancies to occur before they could move up, just as in systems without the purchase of commissions. Fourth, the purchase system did not greatly differentiate careers by wealth because the officers were themselves drawn from families similar in wealth and status.

Officers in the Guard had rarely moved up from the non-commissioned ranks. They were typically the sons of noble families or of gentry who entered the Guard at an early age (around 20 perhaps) as a career or, more often, as an educational experience. . . .

Finally, the age-dependency of ranking would be disrupted from time to time by wars, since the waiting time for vacancies would be radically changed under such circumstances. Men would be killed, creating some opportunity for upward movement from below after much shorter than usual service. It is not certain but likely that war also drove some of the older more senior officers into retirement, thus creating vacancies much sooner than expected. Third, war sometimes led to expansion of the military forces and thereby to a greater number of high ranks to be filled from below. Expansion did not occur in the Coldstream Guard during the period under study; it did however occur in the Scots Guard before and during the first World War. The age-dependency of ranking was further disrupted *after* wars for several reasons related to those mentioned above. After wars, the military structure typically shrank as fewer officers were needed; this contraction resulted in massive retirements, or "promotions" to the General Staff, without a general increase in mobility. . . .

Despite these fortuitous elements, men's careers were chiefly age-dependent. As officers got older, they almost invariably moved up the ranks. As a result, the age at which they reached any given rank was a function of two features of the organization: the relative scarcity of that rank in the organization; and the age of the individual relative to the age distribution of the organization. . . .

From data based on 796 careers between 1690 and 1830, a "life table" was constructed for the personnel of the Guard to both illustrate the foregoing remarks and serve as the basis for further computations. The actual years served by all Guardsmen in all officer ranks were converted into a l_x column, from which the other life table measures were constructed in the customary way. The $\overset{\circ}{e}_x$ column in Table III, showing "life (that is, career) expectancy" in years at each "age " (that is, years already served) aptly illustrates some of the preceding comments. The life expectancy at "age 0," on entry into the Officers Corps, is lower than at ages 1 to 20, a characteristic typical of populations with high infant mortality. The expectation of continued

Table 1

PARTIAL LIFE TABLE* AND STABLE AGE DISTRIBUTION FOR COLDSTREAM GUARD, 1690–1830

(N = 796 OFFICERS)

Organizational age: Years in service							Age distribution‡	
x	%	x	l_x	$_nL_x$†	T_x	e_x	$c(x)$	Cumulative
0	35.4	0	1000	823	6793	6.79	0.434	1.000
1–4	23.0	1	646	2124	5970	9.24		
5–9	17.9	5	416	1633	3846	9.25	0.240	0.566
10–14	9.7	10	237	943	2213	9.34	0.139	0.326
15–19	5.0	15	140	573	1270	9.07	0.084	0.187
20–24	3.7	20	89	355	697	7.83	0.052	0.103
25–29	2.5	25	53	203	342	6.45	0.030	0.051
30–34	1.9	30	28	93	139	4.96	0.014	0.021
35–39	0.5	35	9	33	46	5.11	0.005	0.007
40–44	0.3	40	4	13	13	3.25	0.002	0.002
45 and over	0.1	45	1					
	100.0							

*Here "life table" refers to the years spent in service and the number of years after which an officer left the Coldstream Guard, for whatever reason.

†In general, $_nL_x = n/2(1_x + 1_{x+n})$ (George W. Barclay, 1958: 104, 109). However, unlike other calculations of $_nL_x$, $_5L_0$ is here calculated using a separation factor, $a = 0.2969178$, such that $_5L_0 = 5(a1_0 + (1 - a)1_5)$, since departures in this range are known to be concentrated in the earlier part of the interval (Barclay, *op. cit.* and Norman Ryder, mimeo, undated). Thus, $_5L_0 = 5(0.2969178(1000) + (0.7030822)(416)) = 2947 = 823 + 2124 = {}_1L_0 + {}_4L_x$. This computational procedure is used throughout in calculating $_5L_0$.

‡These are the distributions of a stationary population, where $c(x - (x + 5)) = {}_5L_x/T_0$.

service in the Guard changes little for men who have served 1 to 15 years, and thereafter begins to fall off quickly, at about the time the highest ranks are being attained by seniority.

If mobility in the Coldstream Guard were only and wholly age-dependent, data in the life table (Table 1) and data on the hierarchical structure would permit perfect prediction of the average number of years to move from any given rank up to any other rank. However, ... mobility in the Coldstream Guard was not *perfectly* age-dependent. It is true that higher ranks took a longer average time to reach than lower ranks. However *all* ranks were attained in slightly less time than we would have expected from the model described above. This is chiefly ascribable to the 28 per cent of all officers who

entered the Guard above the level of ensign.... If we allow, then, for the variation in starting rank in the Guard, the model does nicely in predicting the time taken to reach all ranks.

THE EFFECT OF GROWTH RATE

Since the model assumes that the time required to reach each rank (and hence, the rate or speed of mobility) is determined jointly by the hierarchy of ages and the hierarchy of ranks, we may vary both hierarchies to examine the impact of such variations on mobility rate. The first such variation involves *growth....* We shall now examine the changes in mobility that would accompany growth at constant selected rates, notably r = .01, .03,

Table 2
EXPECTED YEARS TO REACH SPECIFIED RANK,* UNDER EXISTING MORTALITY CONDITIONS AND RETIREMENT RATES, AND SPECIFIED CONDITIONS OF GROWTH PER ANNUM

Rank	Growth rate† per annum, $r =$			
	0.00	0.01	0.03	0.05
Lieutenant	4.28	4.03	3.64	3.33
Captain	12.52	11.53	9.77	8.86
Junior major	23.17	21.78	19.29	17.16
Senior major	25.67	24.33	22.06	19.41
Lieutenant colonel	29.67	28.60	26.18	23.60

* In this and subsequent analyses, the Colonel will be treated as absent from the line of position that may be entered from below by seniority.
† These tabulations are based on the assumption of a stable age distribution; that is, constant rates of growth and levels of mortality.

and .05 *per annum*. These rates imply a doubling in the size of the Officers Corps in about 70, 23, and 14 years, respectively. . . . Adhering to the general rule of our original model that all new officers enter at the rank of ensign, we can readily predict that, as in all other populations with high rates of growth achieved through birth (rather than immigration or declining mortality), growth in this system will make the age distribution *younger* (Coale, 1957). With increased rates of growth come increasing proportions of young persons. However the assumption that the hierarchy of ranks is not changing in shape with growth requires that structural expansion is occurring through an equal proportionate increase in new positions at each level. Thus, there must be greater mobility under conditions of high growth than under conditions of low or no growth,[2] for as the mean age declines, the ages that must be reached to attain any given rank diminish steadily with increases in the rate of growth. Table 2 compares the age required to reach each rank under specified constant rates of growth, and

shows the average moving times diminished by about 5 per cent at $r = 0.01$, 15 to 20 per cent at $r = 0.03$, and 20 to 30 percent at $r = 0.05$.

Variation in growth rates exerts a great influence on mobility, as we have observed. However the changeover from one rate of growth to another has somewhat distinct consequences that need discussion. As a system moves from no growth to a positive growth rate and then begins to stabilize at that new growth rate, mobility will generally increase over the time period and reach a peak under the stabilized condition of growth. If this process is reversed and a system moves from growth to stationarity (i.e., replacement without growth), mobility will conversely decline. However there are several points about the transition process worth noting. First, the age structure will take time to stabilize. If we suppose the Coldstream Guard has stabilized at a 5 per cent growth rate *per annum* and then suddenly initiates a return to stationarity, forward projection indicates that about 40 years will be needed before the Guard's mobility system stabilizes.

During this 40-year period of transition, as in all systems with decreasing growth, the population must grow "older." At the beginning of the transition to stationarity, all rank holders are younger than their counterparts will be when the transition is completed. Because they are younger, they are less likely to retire in any given year, or likely to take longer to retire than holders of the same rank under stable conditions of zero growth. For example, the organizational "life expectancy" of a lieutenant colonel is about 35 per cent higher at the beginning of the transition than at the end of the transition: the magnitudes of change in mobility attributable to transition are lower in the ranks below lieutenant colonel.

As the cohort of men in the Guard at the beginning of the transition to stationarity moves through the ranks, there will be moments when the age-structure is such that men will take longer to reach a given rank than will be needed under stationary conditions. These maximum points are only slightly above the stationary levels, but they are noticeable. As a consequence, a cohort that enters the Corps just as replacement (i.e., zero growth) has begun is likely to follow these maximum points through their career, with the result that these maxima are added together. A man moving from ensign to lieutenant colonel under this transitional condition would move about 10 per cent more slowly than he would under stationary conditions. In short, we conclude that career mobility during an organizational transition from high growth to zero growth may be slower than mobility under stabilized conditions of zero growth and, of course, slower than under conditions of positive growth....

THE EFFECT OF MORTALITY LEVEL

Variations in mortality should, like variations in the growth rate, affect the hierarchy of ages in the Guard and hence the rate of mobility. As mortality decreases (under conditions of no growth), the age distribution flattens out noticeably and the average age increases; as people survive to older ages, mobility should decrease. However, several factors work against changes in general mortality, having much impact on mobility in the Guard. First, general declines in mortality or increases in life expectancy benefit the young and the old most; persons in the age span of our officers, between 20 and 50, are least affected because they tend to enjoy the most favourable mortality risks under all regimes....

Second, the data suggest that mortality as such has little to do with the departure of officers from the Guard. Only 19 per cent of all "departing" officers died in service; about 12 per cent died in action (compared with only 9.4 per cent in the Scots Guard). The vast majority of officers' "retired": they were

promoted into other Regiments, resigned their commissions or went on pension for wounds or service....

A relatively small variation in adult mortality, strained through a high retirement rate at early ages, is unlikely to have much effect on mobility. However before we can examine the effect of this variation systematically, we must isolate "retirement rate" from mortality....

The years needed to reach any given rank are little different whether the life expectancy at birth in the general population is 32, 42, or 52 years (all other things, including retirement, being held constant). As life expectancy increases, mobility is somewhat slower.

THE EFFECT OF RETIREMENT RATE

The retirement rate is a dominant element in determining mobility.... With the retirement pattern existing in the Guard, we compare a participation rate that is 100 per cent higher at each age (the "intermediate" condition), and a retirement pattern described earlier as one in which no one retires before completing 45 years of service (the "low" condition). Mobility under the condition of low retirement—the condition typical of most modern organizations—is extremely slow, with the attainment of ranks taking anywhere from 50 per cent to 300 per cent as long as is required under the actual Guard retirement rates. The extremely high retirement rates of the Guard are highlighted by our observation that even if the existing participation rates were doubled (as in the "intermediate" condition), the time taken to attain a given rank would never increase by more than 20 per cent, and in positions above ensign, the moving time would be less than 10 per cent greater. The retirement rates in the Officers Corps must above all else be held accountable for the extremely rapid mobility observed in the Guard. Conceivably, variations in retirement rates have as much impact on mobility as variations in growth rate in moden formal organizations, if not more. . . .

THE EFFECT OF ORGANIZATIONAL SIZE, STRUCTURE, AND FUNCTION

We assumed in the discussion of growth that change in organizational size was inconsequential for structure; that whatever the rate of annual growth the hierarchy of ranks would be unchanged. This assumption may be unreasonable, for Blau and Schoenherr (1971) have shown that large formal organizations typically have different structures from small ones. These differences include one of interest to us: large structures appear to have smaller ratios of supervisory personnel to subordinates (or larger average spans of control) than do small structures (1971:72–87). In our present terminology, as organizations grow their rank hierarchies may change shape by adding proportionally more people at the lower than at the upper levels. Because mobility within the organization is a joint function of the age hierarchy and the rank hierarchy, this broadening of the lower ranks will result in slower mobility in the system. One will have to reach a higher percentile in the age distribution to attain any given rank because that rank's percentile in the organizational hierarchy has been moved up by the disproportionate addition of people below it.

Let us imagine that the Guard has doubled in size from 43 to 86 officers below the rank of colonel and has stabilized at this size. In Table 3 I have illustrated three ways in which this might conceivably take place. By arrangement 1, there is an exact duplication of officers at each rank, with no change in the existing hierarchy of ranks or span of control. In arrangements 2 and 3, proportionally greater numbers are added to the bottom ranks, so that the span of control under arrangement 3 is greater than that under arrangement 2, and that under arrangement 2 is greater than under actual Guard conditions. As the rank pyramid progressively broadens its base, the span of control increases from 1.95 subordinates per superior to 2.43, and to 3.37 under arrangement 3. When each rank hierarchy is fitted to the prevailing age hierarchy (i.e., assuming the existing conditions of mortality and retirement, and no growth), mobility is much slower where the span of control is high than where it is low. Movement into the rank of lieutenant takes two and one-half times as long under arrangement 3 as it does under arrangement 1, while movement up to lieutenant colonel takes only 12 per cent longer under arrangement 3 than under arrangement 1.

Thus, the change in hierarchical arrangements may not greatly increase moving time from the bottom to the top; but the increase is very marked in the early years of service. The effect on mobility of change from a narrow to broad span of control is similar to the change from high to low retirement rates: in both cases, mobility is slowed down most in the attainment of lower ranks. . . .

I noted at the outset that there were some factors peculiar to a military organization which needed special attention in a study of demographic aspects of career mobility. . . .

The coming and going of war has strong effects on mobility in a military organization, not only because war increases mortality (and possibly retirement) and structural growth—all of which we have already noted have some effect on mobility—but also because these demographic shifts occur much more suddenly than in other organizations: they concentrate their effects at points in time. A man's mobility in the Scots Guard over the period 1690–1930 is strongly correlated with the death rate in his own cohort ($r = 0.374$),[3] and with the death rate in the cohort preceding his ($r = 0.161$), although these two death rates are closely interlinked. It is correlated with the wound rate (and presum-

Table 3

THREE ORGANIZATIONAL ARRANGEMENTS* WITH DIFFERING MEAN SPAN OF CONTROL AND
EXPECTED YEARS TO REACH RANK, UNDER EXISTING MORTALITY AND RETIREMENT CONDITIONS
AND NO GROWTH, AND THE SPECIFIED ARRANGEMENT OF RANKS

Rank	Number of Officers at or above rank			Proportion at or above rank			Years to reach rank		
	1	2	3	1	2	3	1	3	4
Ensign	86	86	86	1.000	1.000	1.000	—	—	—
Lieutenant	54	38	26	0.628	0.442	0.302	4.28	7.58	10.86
Captain	22	14	10	0.256	0.163	0.116	12.52	16.43	19.23
Jr major	6	4	3	0.070	0.047	0.035	23.17	25.67	27.67
Sr major	4	2	2	0.047	0.023	0.023	25.67	29.67	29.67
Lt colonel	2	1	1	0.023	0.012	0.012	29.67	33.21	33.21
Mean span of control:	1.95	2.43	3.37						

*The first of these three arrangements is the ideal-typical organization of the Officers Corps, Coldstream Guard, assumed throughout this paper. Arrangements 2 and 3 are hypothetical but not inconceivable.

ably the increased retirement rate induced by wounding) in his own cohort ($r = 0.373$) and in the cohort preceding his ($r = 0.127$). It is also correlated with structural expansion, that is, with the number of battalions in the regiment ($r = 0.346$), and hence the number of command positions ultimately available for entry.

Having observed the impact of fortuitous and specifically military factors on mobility in these organizations, we should not, however, lose sight of the overwhelming predictability of this system and the generalizaeability of our findings. The main fact to be noted about this organization, as about many others, is that at whatever level entry had taken place, the attainment of higher ranks was a joint function of age structure and rank structure; and within an invariant rank structure the attainment of high rank was primarily a function of time spent in continued service.

CONTEST MOBILITY VERSUS SENIORITY

Let us minimally define a contest system as one in which a person's rank is poorly pre-dicted by the time he has spent in the system. It is unlikely that any perfect contest system so defined has ever existed for any length of time.[4] Unlike the typical sponsored system based on a "seniority principle" of promotion, such a contest system would take little advantage of experience gained by people who had spent a long time in the organization. Unlike another kind of imaginable sponsored system operating according to what we might call a "juniority principle," a perfect contest system would take little advantage of the greater vigour or formal education of young people who had been in the system only a short time. In fact it would take no consistent advantage of any quality or skill in the work force, but would select candidates to fill vacancies on a somewhat random basis, for the reason that most human skills or abilities are time or age-dependent: they either improve or deteriorate with time. By ignoring this in the selection of individuals for positions, one is denying the importance of most specifiable characteristics for the performance of a given task.

The most extreme form of contest system

is strictly random, while a less extreme form is one that is random with respect to years of service but non-random on some other criterion that is relatively invariant over time: for example, intelligence. We shall assume that the operation of an actual contest system falls somewhere between pure randomness and pure time dependency in its mode of operation. Thus if we can observe the influence of demographic factors in a purely random system of contest mobility, we can assume that the influence of these factors on mobility in an actual contest system falls somewhere between the random and age-dependent cases.

Suppose the Coldstream Guard had selected men for promotion by chance alone, such that all men below the rank in which a vacancy had appeared were automatically eligible for promotion. Men will choose not to compete for ranks that are below their present rank, and as a result all movement in the system is upward. How would demographic factors affect the moving time of men in such a system? The solution to this problem is sketched out in Table 4, with "moving times" indicated for each rank.[5]

We shall define "moving time" as the years required for sufficient contests to take place in order that any individual would have a probability of 50 per cent or better of moving into a specified vacant rank; moving time may also be considered an expected waiting time for entry into a given rank through competition. Moving time grows longer with increases in span of control, the distance between a man and the rank he is seeking, and the average number of years spent in a space by those whose departure is awaited by competitors for mobility. Moving time shortens with an increase in the number of spaces within a desired rank.

We have already noted that span of control tends to increase with organizational size; therefore, in a random contest system as well as in a sponsored mobility system, large organizations, having a larger span of control, will have slower mobility than small organizations. However, growth also increases the number of spaces in every rank, if span of control is held constant; and an increase in the number of spaces decreases moving time, or increases mobility. Thus growth of the organization will increase mobility in a contest system as in a sponsored mobility system, although changes in span of control accompanying growth may have an offsetting effect.

The average number of years spent in a

Table 4
MOBILITY IN THE COLDSTREAM GUARD UNDER A HYPOTHETICAL RANDOM CONTEST SYSTEM

Rank	No. Spaces	Probability of entry from below in 1 contest: $p =$	Mean required contests*: $n =$	Mean years in rank†	Mean contests per year for rank‡	Mean years to attain rank**
Lieutenant	16	0.06250	11	6.307	2.537	4.3
Captain	8	0.03125	22	7.961	1.005	21.9
Jr major	1	0.02500	28	2.707	0.369	75.9
Sr major	1	0.02439	29	3.395	0.295	98.3
Lt colonel	1	0.02381	29	5.571	0.180	161.1

*Calculated with the binomial theorem: $[1 - P\{0|n\}] \cong 0.5$, or $[1 - (1 - p)^n] \cong 0.5$ where 'p' is the probability of entering that rank from below in one chance contest
† Observed in the Coldstream Guard
‡ Calculated as the number of spaces in rank, divided by the mean years spent in a rank
** Calculated as mean required contests, divided by mean contests per year for rank

rank is a function of age-specific mortality and retirement rates; where these rates are high, the average number of years spent there is low and thus moving time is low in systems where deaths and retirements are frequent. Again as in the sponsored system, higher mortality and retirement rates at each (or almost any) age will increase mobility in a contest system.

DISCUSSION

This paper has examined the effect of demographic factors on career mobility within a formal organization that may be taken to represent many formal organizations. A simple mathematical model relating age structure to rank structure has allowed us to assess the probable effects on mobility of demographic variation.

These calculations have suggested that growth, changes in retirement pattern, and changes in the rank structure (resulting from changes in size of the organization) are extremely important determinants of mobility. The retirement rates, in addition to their first order effects, also strengthen or dampen the impact of changes in mortality and changes in growth rate (the transition effect) on mobility within the organization. I have not here systematically examined the second order effects of other variables, but they are unlikely to prove as important as retirement patterns in this regard. . . .

Our observations of the demographic impacts on an age-dependent or sponsored system appear generalizeable to a contest system. We can therefore conclude that the level of demographic "absorption" affects career mobility in organizations all along the control dimension from sponsored to contest mobility; and further that the absorbing and control dimensions are analytically independent of each other. . . .

Notes

[1] Under this system, a commission was ideally purchased from the Crown at rates quoted in an official schedule; in practice it was often purchased from its present owner for amounts more or less than the official rate. Prices varied over time and from one Regiment to another; in general, however, the purchase of high rank cost more than the purchase of a lower rank. The many abuses and shortcomings of this system led to official and unofficial constraints being placed on sellers and buyers, and the purchase system was abolished as a whole around 1870.

[2] The relationship between population growth and structural expansion perplexes all students of economic demography in general and of modernization in particular. However we are defining the problem away in this case by dealing with an organization and not a total society, in the first place, and further, with an organization in which the planning of expansion can precede and accommodate growth in numbers.

[3] All of these correlations are statistically significant at $p \leq 0.001$.

[4] A perfect purchase system would of course qualify here under the definition of "contest": those who were wealthiest would buy the highest ranks upon entry, while the poorest might continue in low ranks forever. In such a system, rank would be independent of years served. However, great pains were taken to ensure that the purchase system would not work this way, and it did not.

[5] These moving times are "expected" rather than actual from the standpoint of an ensign hoping to move up the ranks. He will not wait 161 years to become a lieutenant colonel, and will either become one well before then or retire without having attained that rank. These expected waiting times are, however, a good indication of the futility of *planning* a career in a random contest system.

References

Barclay, George W. (1958) *Techniques of Population Analysis.* New York: Wiley.

Blau, Peter, and Richard Schoenherr (1971) *The Structure of Organizations.* New York: Basic Books.

Coale, Ansley (1957) "How the age distribution of a human population is determined." Cold Spring Harbor Symposium on Quantitative Biology 22:83–8

Coale, Ansley, and Paul Demeny (1966) *Regional Model Life Tables and Stable Populations.* Princeton, NJ: Princeton University Press.

Hollingsworth, T.H. (1965) "A demographic study of the British ducal families." In D.V. Glass and D.E.C. Eversley (eds.), *Population in History.* Chicago: Aldine.

Holmes, Jeffrey (1974) "Demography affects employment, promotion," *University Affairs'* March.

Keyfitz, Nathan (1973) "Individual mobility in a stationary population." *Population Studies* 27(2):335–52.

Mackinnon, Colonel David (1833) *The Origin and Services of the Coldstream Guards.* Two volumes. London: Richard Bentley.

Maurice, Major-General Sir Frederick (1934) *The History of the Scots Guard.* Two volumes. London: Chatto and Windus.

Ryder, Norman. Undated. "A demographer's life table." Princeton University, mimeo.

Tepperman, Lorne (1973) "The multiplication of opportunities: sponsored mobility in Coventry, England: 1420–1450." *Canadian Review of Sociology and Anthropology* 10(1):1–20.

Tepperman, Lorne (1975) *Social Mobility in Canada.* Toronto: McGraw-Hill Ryerson.

23 Sociability and Social Interaction [1]

Marcel Rioux

MARCEL RIOUX, Professor Emeritus of Sociology at the University of Montreal, specializes in the social history of Quebec, the sociology of culture, and critical social theory. His books include *French Canadian Society* (1964) edited with Yves Martin; *Quebec in Question* (1971, revised 1978); *Les Québécois* (1974); *Essai de sociologie critique* (1978); *Two Nations* (1983) with Susan Crean; and *Le besoin et le desir, ou, Le Code et le symbole: essai* (1984). He has just completed an article, "Requiem pour un rêve?" (1987) for a special issue of the *Canadian Journal of Sociology* on the sociology of Quebec. He is a member of the editorial board of *Sociologie et Societés*.

The facts upon which the comments and hypotheses in this article are based were gathered in a Gaspé village where I spent four months in 1952 carrying out anthropological research for the National Museum of Canada. . . .

The intensive study of the villagers' behaviour brought to light the fact that certain elements of their behaviour could not easily be inserted into the usual categories used in a monograph in cultural anthropology. Aside from the common fact that such behaviour, due to its complexity, can be divided into political, economic, and religious categories, certain aspects of some of their conduct are not as easily classified. There is, so to speak, a lack of differentiation between the motivation for behaviour and the behaviour itself; at first sight, the observer feels that his categories are tools that are too highly sharpened for treating such homogeneous material. He also has the clear impression—and, moreover, this fact is recognized in theory—that culture is not organized around the same foci in all societies. How can this gap between theory and practice be explained? It can be said that, on one hand, the usual categories or classifications of social phenomena have been set forth before anthropologists became interested in the dynamic aspect of cultures: in the problems of socialization, acculturation, and, in general, problems of "culture and personality." The classifications used by anthropologists are also categories which, if not copied from an urban society, were at least formulated by individuals who belong to a form of urban culture and are not specially adapted to folk societies, or to feudal or peasant societies. . . .

Because the implicit or unconscious organization of a society never coincides, so to speak, with the ideas held by individuals belonging to it and, furthermore, because classifications used by anthropologists reflect, more or less, conscious and rationalized categories, it can easily be seen that the anthropologist's work must lead him to search for the truth beyond his own categories and the conscious organization of the culture he is studying. But here a difficulty intervenes; when the anthropologist wishes to use his material in a comparative framework, he must use categories which encompass comparable elements such as magic, religion, stratification. But it seems that there are certain concepts or categories which are not used as a means of comparison between societies and which should be used simply because they have that element of generality and differentiation which enables societies to be graded, if not absolutely, at least as Steward[2] suggests, from a consensus of viewpoints.

This appears to me to be the case with the concept of sociability; it is a concept little recognized in anthropology and sociology, although it was used by such important sociologists as Simmel, Gurvitch, and Moreno, among others. . . .

Simmel[3] has written: "While all human associations are entered into because of some ulterior interests, there is in them a residue of pure sociability or association for its own sake." Now, this residue of sociability is not ordinarily taken into account by anthropologists and sociologists in their explanations of human behaviour or, rather, if it did not vary with the forms of society and culture, we would be justified in not taking it into account. . . . As we can admit that sociability[4] varies from individual to individual, so perhaps must we admit that sociability is conditioned by socio-cultural context and that, in the study of societies, it is necessary to account for this differentiation in establishing a social typology.

In what way does the concept of sociability in the present discussion differ from co-operation as defined by Margaret Mead and her collaborators in *Cooperation and Competition among Primitive Peoples?* Here is how Mead[5] defines these two terms: "co-operation is the act of working together to one end" and "competition is the act of seeking or endeavoring to gain what another is endeavoring to gain at the same time." These two behavioural attributes would be, according to Mead, closely related to the type of culture to which individuals belong, and would be encountered at all levels of socio-cultural development in human groups; folk societies, like urban societies, could be co-operative or competitive. Sociability, as we are trying to define it in this essay, is an attribute of human behaviour that can be isolated from other components of this same behaviour without

consideration of the co-operative or competitive nature of individuals. Moreover, sociability can be regarded as a phenomenon that is correlated with the processes of urbanization and differentiation. Nevertheless, the concept of sociability is difficult to pin down, as it appears so general at first sight. To most people studying society, the fact that men live together is one of the essential conditions of all social and cultural life, a basic characteristic that man shares with animals. In a recent work, Allee[6] declares that the general principle of automatic co-operation is one of the foundations of biology. In man, this automatic co-operation, which Allee sees as a *sine qua non* condition of all animal societies, changes, with the appearance of conscience and the mechanisms necessary for its functioning, into something more than co-operation. Thus, in an exclusively utilitarian sense, man takes pleasure in living with fellow beings and society becomes not only useful to him for survival, but he derives an emotion from it which influences his behaviour. The fact that he has contacts with other men becomes, for man, a positive value which motivates his actions. It is precisely this value that we are calling sociability, and it is this element that we are seeking to distinguish in behaviour, be it openly religious, economic, esthetic, or judicial. We believe that we perceived in the behaviour of individuals in a village we studied certain phenomena which do not seem to us to be entirely explicable without reference to sociability.

Our intention is to try to make this idea explicit through the analysis of certain forms of behaviour. The village of Gascons, from which the following observations are drawn, is a French-Canadian village of varied ethnic origins, situated on the eastern extremity of the south bank of the Baie des Chaleurs. Its 1400 inhabitants are descendants of Acadians, Canadians, French, Scots, Germans, and natives of Jersey who, over a hundred years or more for some families, have learned to live together. All of these individuals from different cultures have been assimilated into the ambient culture, the French-Canadian culture and, although they neither wish to be Canadians nor Acadians, they participate in both of these cultural forms to such an extent that one can not clearly differentiate between the Acadian and the Canadian form.

Within this village, which is spread over about ten miles, there are three quite distinct sectors; we studied the western extremity, numbering approximately 600 inhabitants. Due to the relative isolation of this part of the Gaspé and the way of life of its inhabitants, certain processes of urbanization have affected it less than some other rural villages in Quebec.[7] The part of the village we studied is quite clearly separated from the other parts: for all practical purposes the inhabitants identify themselves ("we") with this part of the village. It is also quite normal for these people to feel the differences existing between themselves and surrounding villages and other parts of their own village because the ethnic stock varies from one village to another and sometimes from one end of the same village to the other. It is not uncommon to see concentrations of related families form communities and even administrative units. These will more likely be the large families, Chapados, Roussy, Anglehart, and Cyr, who group together in one part of the village or another, whereas new emigrants to the village tend to settle almost anywhere and let their children swarm throughout the village. The population lacks differentiation except for several rare and atypical individuals who, under the circumstances, have a certain observational value. Almost each and every person can and does do what everyone else does: fishing, woodcutting, and some farming. These three activities produce no real division of labour because there are, strictly speaking, no pure cultivators, fishermen, or lumberjacks. . . .

The following are some of the observations in which, the author believes, sociability manifests itself and may explain certain types of behaviour; each observation is then discussed in relationship to the general concept.

Observation: In one of the shops in Anse-à-la-Barbe,[8] I noticed that people going in, far from hurrying to be served, sit on the counters, watch what is happening, and chat; at certain times, there is a tendency to see who will not be served first. The merchant and his wife are locals and, furthermore, they have not always been merchants. They share the same way of life as their customers and are entirely at ease with this type of behaviour, which they encourage.

Comments: Certainly, these facts can not be exclusively classified as "economy," "nourishment," or "commerce," as it is obvious that these are not the most significant aspects of this behaviour. The behavioural incentive of those gathered in the stores is the thought of meeting people and talking with them: a feeling of being together. This is the determining motive as the purchases they make seem to be no more than a pretext.

Observation: Illegitimate children are not ostracized; they are accepted openly and without reserve. Their lives are as normal as those of the other children and they can aspire to marry anyone in the community.

Comments: The norms, as much religious as cultural, disapprove of adultery and the resulting children. In certain more urbanized societies, adherence to these norms shows itself through ostracism and near banishment of the guilty persons. In the village in question, individuals do not have the means of punishing anyone in this way. Each and every person contributes to the solidarity of individuals, and no link must break this unity. It is not always perfect harmony, far from it; however, the causes of quarrels are always very personal and do not endanger the solidarity of the members of society.

Observation: In the village there is a restaurant run by a family from the area, the head of which also carries on the same occupations as the other individuals: fishing, agriculture, lumbering. In the evening, people gather there without distinction of age or sex. All this takes on the air of a traditional social evening (veillée).

Comments: The restaurant and the types of behaviour that come with it are of urban origin; established in this rural community, it becomes more an instrument of sociability than an economic service.

Observation: The fishermen often work as a group. When they return from the sea, they spend a great deal of time chatting about the details of the trip with a group of villagers awaiting their return.

Comments: Their activity cannot be described as purely economic, as all their behaviour is impregnated with sociability, with the pleasure that they derive from conversing with the people who go to the quay for this reason.

Observation: An adulterous wife who left her husband and children returned to Anse-à-la-Barbe with her new partner because she was homesick; everyone bypasses the disapproval she deserved and acts as though nothing had happened.

Comments: Here again, as in the case of illegitimate children, sociability overrides community norms.

Observation: A meeting between two or more people can most often be summarized as a prolonged exchange of sterotypes. The sterotypes are even interchangeable. If an individual is slow in replying, another will utter for him the stereotype the other speakers were expecting.

Comments: The function of these sterotypes seems to be to diminish anxiety; one is happy and comforted to realize that things have not changed and that the established order does not vary; the least little change in the personnel of the community or in its members' activity is strongly felt. Their world is arranged in a permanent manner; the only purpose of communication between individuals by means of stereotypes seems to be to reassure them of this permanence.

Observation: On summer evenings, people walk along the street, gather in the stores, call out noisily to each other, and spend hours seeking the company of others and conversing with them.

Comments: The need to go out and see people is extremely great; nothing is more inconceivable than that someone could stay at home without being bored to death. All their leisure time is directed toward the community; this, perhaps, explains why there are no crafts to speak of.

Observations: They could listen to music on the local radio station similar to that which I recorded in their village, but they are not interested in it and move in around my tape recorder to hear the music that such and such a person from Anse-à-la-Barbe has played.

Comments: Their interest centred exclusively on anything having to do with the community. Anything happening elsewhere, even if it is similar to what they are doing, holds no interest; it is people rather than things that arouse their interest.

Observation: Two youngsters are discussing a squabble: the father of one fought the other's uncle. Slowly the pitch of the argument increases; soon, however, the two admit their relatives' wrongdoings in order to keep on speaking terms.

Comments: Victory of group spirit over family spirit.

Observation: A woman from Montreal, originally from the Gaspé, who married a fisherman-logger, tried to introduce the fashion of "social evenings by invitation"; she found out that even if someone received friends in the evening, several uninvited people showed up anyway. Now, at an "invited" reception, where we were to number about twenty, there were at times almost sixty people. A woman of about sixty seemed to derive much pleasure from remaining seated in a corner without saying a word, watching the others dancing.

Comments: Speaking, calling, hailing, smiling, and generally being conscious of events seem to provide the major motivation of their behaviour; it is not an exchange of ideas which takes shape at these get-togethers, but rather an exchange of sentiments which is often accomplished without words.

Observation: Each time I pass through New Carlisle with Gascons in my car, they talk to me about the local prison, which also serves the county.

Comments: As I understand it from questioning them, their interest in this building can be explained as follows: it symbolizes repressive justice, justice exercised outside the community; some people from Gascons have already spent time there; it is a chance to recount events which happened in the community and, therefore, indirectly draw closer together.

Observation: The great majority of houses are built along the roadside; those who were obliged to settle in the second *rang* only did so because they were really forced to; moreover, they have a slightly lower status in the community. The main road is very important when considering residence. A young married couple living with the husband's parents, and quarrelling with them, wanted to move. The husband had just asked a neighbour to sell him a lot, but he could only offer than a piece of ground situated back from the road. The wife refused absolutely because she wanted to build within fifteen feet of the road; at one hundred and fifty feet she would be bored as she would not see people passing in the street; her house would not be in a group with others. For these reasons, the deal was not concluded.

Comments: Contrary to certain urban classes who favour living at a distance from their fellow men, the people of Anse-à-la-Barbe wish to group together and watch each other's activities.

Observation: An eighteen-year-old girl from Gascons goes to the convent in Gaspé. On returning to her family, she realizes the differences in the two ways of life; but she is so taken by the ties attaching her to the mem-

bers of the community that she would not wish to leave them; it is here that she derives most of her emotions.

Comments: Even those girls who find domestic employment in Montreal never completely sever themselves from the community. They try to re-create it by grouping together among themselves and with men who have also emigrated. Marriage statistics show that most marriages performed outside of Anse-à-la-Barbe are between persons from the same place or the surrounding area. There are almost no examples of anyone having married a Montrealer or another city-dweller.

Observation: On rainy days, the men do not work at fishing, in the forest, or on the farm. They put on clean clothes and head toward the meeting places, stores, and quays. Slowly they wend their way there and, when they arrive, they often wait several minutes before addressing those already gathered; some remain without speaking.

Comments: As work was impossible due to rain, the sociability factor that entered into their economic activities became the only motivation for their behaviour. Often, it takes its primary form; it consists of feeling close to one another and reassuring oneself that nothing has happened to end the established order during the time elapsed since the last meeting.

Observation: Conversation being non-existent, listening to the radio requiring a certain education, and reading being unknown, home life becomes monotonous; that is why they watch for all possible chances of evasion or diversion furnished by the group members themselves.

Comments: The members of a group furnish, as such, nearly all the topics for diversion.

Observation: Even religious behaviour is marked by sociability. . . . Saturday and Sunday are group holidays or sociability fêtes. On Saturday morning, or sometimes on Saturday afternoon, all work ceases; people put on their new clothes and begin visiting. Even those who stay at home to cook and do the housekeeping are taken by the idea that soon they will meet people, whether it be Saturday or Sunday. The atmosphere of the village changes for these two days; even a stranger feels that it is no longer the same rhythm as during the week. One might say that sociability becomes freer and more direct. The people are liberated from the worries of daily work and are in good spirits. They no longer need a pretext to allow themselves to thoroughly enjoy the pleasure of seeing each other, speaking together, and jostling one another. It is difficult to separate sociability and religion, especially as an attempt at evaluating the function of religion does not enter into the present discussion. It is here sufficient to say that the overt behaviour of individuals before, during, and after Mass is filled with sociability; that is, they experience great pleasure in seeing each other.

Comments: Does this social component have a bearing on the religious element of their total behaviour? What constitutes the two and what are the relationships between them? All this I shall try to determine elsewhere. What we wish to stress in the present essay is that sociability enters significantly into religious behaviour and that it ceases at certain times to be residual.

Observation: (a meeting with an inhabitant of Anse-à-la-Barbe in the street) In speaking of the differences existing between his part of the village and the next—four miles away— he declares that people from the other sector are quite different; they do not have time to speak to each other or to see each other. They meet, hail each other, and hurry about their business. Here, on the contrary, we take the time to talk, he says; our business is not so hurried that we have no time to sit by the roadside to speak with those we meet. Now, it happens that the settlement my speaker is comparing with his own is in fact, for reasons too long to give here, more urbanized than Anse-à-la-Barbe.

Comments: Sociability as we understand it is a function of urbanization; sociability and all social tasks in a society undergoing urbanization has a tendency to become specialized and differentiated.

These few examples, drawn from my field observations, show what we mean when we speak of sociability. It is a motivating factor in human behaviour, a hedonistic motivation which enters into most behaviour at the level of peasant and feudal societies. For the moment, and without pre-judging the results of research in this area, we can note that this motivation exists in urban societies, but, like all other phenomena, it is more specialized; other motivational factors, whether they be economic, artistic, or religious, follow the same steps and sociability per se becomes more and more residual. This, surely, is what Lévy-Bruhl means when he speaks of the heterogeneity of the urban mind compared to the homogeneity of the primitive mind. A mind permeated by sociability is one in which all actions are conditioned by it; this is a homogeneous mind, such as that of a saint in which all is related to God and a supernatural life. If, as Allport shows,[9] each personality, to function normally, must possess a principle of integration which relates all aspects of his personality, this integrating principle would certainly be sociability in Anse-à-la-Barbe, as this is what colours all actions, gives them their *raison d'être*, and motivates most behaviour. It would almost be a truism to state this if we did not bear in mind what is true of all societies and was well expressed by Park and Burgess[10] when they stated:

> Society stated in mechanistic terms reduces to interaction. A person is a member of society so long as he responds to social forces; when interaction ends, he is isolated and detached; he ceases to be a person and becomes a "lost soul." This is the reason that the limits of society are coterminous with the limits of interaction, that is, of the participation of persons in the life of society.

What we wish to emphasize here is that this interaction, which produces what we call sociability, appears to be more intense and less differentiated in some societies than in others, and that it might become a criterion for differentiation between societies. Whether Gascons is a peasant or feudal type of community, it is very much "other-directed," to [use] Reisman's[11] terminology, as opposed to another type which he calls "inner-directed." Although I am using these terms a little differently from his usage, the general sense is kept: it is a question of societies in which individuals are turned toward others from whom they draw their reasons for acting.

Contrary to Riesman, who looks for his explanations elsewhere, it seems that this type of society and personality can be correlated to ego development throughout the history of human culture. In this essay we have taken a functional perspective in which the phenomena under study are looked at synchronically; it would be fruitless and beyond our topic to wonder if it were the ego which first produced such a given type of sociability or if, on the contrary, it were this undifferentiated sociability which led to a particular type of ego. We, therefore, limit ourselves to the statement that the two phenomena exist concurrently and ask if it would not be worthwhile to try to discover if the two phenomena—the concept of self and nondifferentiated sociability—are not correlated. Mauss,[12] continuing the work of the French school of sociology which was concerned with discovering what is social and what cultural in the categories of the human spirit, asked this question about the idea of the self:

> How, over the course of centuries and across numerous societies, was the concept slowly elaborated not just of the sense of "self" but the idea or the concept that men have made of it at different times. What I want to demonstrate is the series of forms that this concept has assumed in the lives of men and societies, according to their rights, their religions, their customs, social structures and mentalities.

Throughout this essay, he shows how, step by step, the self is separated from society to arrive, through Graeco-Roman and Christian influence at the concept which certain segments of modern and urban societies hold about the self. One has only to study the function of names in primitive societies to realize the hold society has on a person and how he defines himself almost exclusively in relation to society. The problem is how this idea of person and sociability can be applied to a peasant society such as Gascons, which has usually experienced all the influences Mauss enumerates, and furthermore also seems to show characteristics which would relate it, from certain points of view, to the primitives from whom he draws his examples. Western society is not homogeneous and entire classes have not yet attained urban civilization. . . . It would perhaps be fitting to wonder if, contrary to what has been written on the role of religion as an integrating principle of culture and personality in primitive and even peasant societies, this integration comes from membership within a group. Given that the principle of integration for the culture to which anthropologists and sociologists belong is ordinarily an idea or system of ideas and that their personality is integrated by these same elements, would it not be appropriate to question the extent to which they have interjected what is happening in their milieu and within themselves into the societies they study? I do not believe there is any objection on principle to the idea that the principle of the integration of culture and personality is due to a sentiment which may be unconscious rather than to an idea or system of ideas. Whatever the case may be and without wishing to venture too far with conclusions beyond observed facts, it seems that the principle of the integration of Gascons culture and personality is not an idea but a sentiment that is furnished by the society itself. To paraphrase the definition Gurvitch gives of sociability, it would be the fact of being part of a tightly knit unit that furnishes the most important motivation for individuals; a motivation which for certain atypical individuals, even on the level of Gascons, has a tendency to diminish in force as they feel the effects of the division of labour and become more urbanized.

Notes

[1] Extract from *Contributions à l'Etude des Sciences de l'Homme,* Vol. 2 (Montreal: 1953), pp. 61–73.

[2] Julian H. Steward, "Evolution and Process," in *Anthropology Today* (Chicago: University of Chicago Press, 1953), pp. 313–326.

[3] Georg Simmel, *The Sociology of Sociability,* Everett C. Hughes, trans., *The American Journal of Sociology,* 55, 254–261.

[4] "Sociability" is taken in its widest sense as a measure of the spirit of co-operation in individuals, or as an inclination to seek out the company of similar beings.

[5] Margaret Mead, *Co-operation and Competition Among Primitive Peoples* (New York: McGraw-Hill, 1937), p.8

[6] W.C. Allee, *Co-operation Among Animals* (New York: 1951).

[7] Urbanization, like acculturation, does not become quickly implanted, nor does it follow the same rhythm in all sectors of culture. Without being uniform, it is not accidental: it follows an intelligible path. Thus, the oral literature of romantic folklorists, which Redfield made one of the characteristics of peasant society, has disappeared from Gascons, whereas in certain other villages which are more urbanized in many ways, it persists and takes longer to disappear.

[8] We shall designate the part of the village of Gascons that we studied by this name.

[9] Gordon W. Allport, *The Individual and His Religion* (New York: Macmillan, 1950).

[10] Robert E. Park, and Ernest W. Burgess, *Introduction to the Science of Sociology* (Chicago: University of Chicago Press, 1924).

[11] David Riesman, *The Lonely Crowd* (New Haven: Yale University Press, 1950).

[12] Marcel Mauss, "Une categorie de l'esprit humain, la notion de personne et celle du moi," Huxley Memorial Lecture, *Journal of the Royal Anthropological Institute,* Vol. 68 (London: 1938), pp. 38 and 263–281. Also in *Sociology et anthropologie* (1966), 331–361.

24   The Postal Revolution in Central Canada, 1851–1911

Brian Osborne   Robert Pike

BRIAN OSBORNE, Professor and Head of the Department of Geography at Queen's University, is a historical geographer who has published extensively in the field of settlement history in Ontario. He is currently pursuing research in the area of communications and regional and national development in Canada during the nineteenth and early twentieth centuries.

ROBERT PIKE, Professor of Sociology at Queen's University, Kingston, Ontario, specializes in the study of higher education, communications and cultural policy. His books and papers include *Who Doesn't Get to University and Why: A Study on Accessibility to Higher Education in Canada* (1970); *Socialization and Values in Canadian Society*, co-edited with E. Zureik (1975); *Innovation in Access to Higher Education* (1978); "Equality of educational opportunity: Dilemmas and policy options" (1980); and "Sociological research on higher education in English Canada, 1971–1980: A thematic review" (1982). A visit to Britain's Open University (a distance learning institution) during the 1970s convinced him that the media of mass communications, as well as other forms of large-scale communications between individuals, have played a vital but under-researched role in the process of social and economic change. Consequently, much of his research and writing in recent years has focused upon the social impact of early organizational and technological advances in two interrelated spheres of communications in Canada—namely, telephonic communications and the expansion of postal services.

I

The continued development and implementation of telecommunications is a prominent feature of the late twentieth century. "Telework," "teleconferencing," "telecommuting," and "telecommunities" allow for the substitution of telecommunication for the physical movement of people and the face-to-face interaction characteristic of the traditional economic and social organization of our society. As such technological developments become widespread, they will have a considerable effect not only upon business and office organization, but the nature of home and family, and the quality of life of society. The potential impact of this telecommunications revolution upon individuals and society is increasingly recognized but an earlier, and in many ways analogous, revolution in distance communications has not been explored by social scientists in a formal way.

The introduction of a system of "mass" public postal services in the latter part of the nineteenth century in the western world was a significant innovation in communications which had certain similar effects. In Canada, the 1851–1914 period witnessed a major effort by the Canadian postal authorities to extend postal services to areas of new settlement as well as to improve existing services in relatively highly populated urban and rural areas. The system was "mass" or widely accessible insofar as it "made available to ordinary

Table 1

ONTARIO AND QUEBEC: EXPANDING POSTAL FACILITIES, 1851–1911

	No. of P.O.		Miles of Postal Routes		Letters and Postcards (Millions)		No. of Money Order Offices		Amount of Money Order Transactions (Millions)		No. of Savings Banks	
					The Canadas							
1851	601		7,595		2.13		—		—		—	
1861	1,775		14,608		9.40		222*		2.4*		—	
1867	2,333		18,100		14.20		425		3.8		—	
1875	3,054		23,545		35.55		518		4.1		268	
	Ontario	Quebec	Ontario	Quebec	Ontario	Quebec	Ontario	Quebec	Ontario	Quebec	Ontario	Quebec
1876	2,130	999	14,480	8,421	29.1	12.4	431	117	3.64	0.62	232	45
1881	2,493	1,147	15,512	9,459	36.3	14.3	466	113	4.03	0.75	258	45
1885	2,762	1,289	17,580	10,229	50.4	14.8	488	136	5.38	1.06		355
1891	3,026	1,441	18,675	11,584	71.1	28.2	560	171	6.04	1.44		634
1895	3,138	1,600	20,274	12,637	78.8	28.9	624	198	6.53	1.65	448	123
1901	3,311	1,830	N.A.	N.A.	120.4	48.5	843	399	7.70	2.52		895
1905	3,461	2,090	N.A.	N.A.	165.4	67.0	991	629	12.32	5.70		989
1911	3,788	2,398	N.A.	N.A.	265.7	101.7	1,219	822	21.55	11.35	1,151	

*No data for 1861. 1860 figures used.

Source: Annual Reports of the Postmaster General.

people, as an amenity of everyday life, a facility which had been a luxury and privilege of rulers and elites."[1]

More specifically, the official birth of the concept of a mass postal system in Canada can be traced to the year 1851 when the British government relinquished control to the several provinces of the post offices in their territories. No longer a colonial system, therefore, the new indigenous control allowed the provincial governments—and after 1867, the Government of Canada—to utilise post office services to further public economic and social goals. These services included not only the delivery of letters and parcels, but the issuing of money orders and, after 1867, the establishment of savings banks at many branches of the Post Office. Table 1 provides an indication of the eagerness of Canadians to use the postal services. For example, the volume of letters and postcards mailed annually by the inhabitants of Ontario and Quebec increased from just over 2 million to 367 million between 1851 and 1911: an increase proportionally far greater than the increase in population over the period (albeit, on a per capita basis, Quebecers sent only about half as much mail as people living in Ontario). The most important technological advance which facilitated the development of this mass postal system was the creation of railway systems which, beginning in the 1850s, allowed for the speedy transmission of the mails.

The development of the mass postal system constituted a revolution in communications. First and foremost, it facilitated private interpersonal communications, as well as making messages from a greater variety of organizational sources potentially more accessible. Easily accessible postal communications were thus widely perceived by more and more individuals and organizations to be a necessary public "amenity of everyday life" both in newly settled areas and in the more established rural and urban communities. . . .

II

During the last quarter of the nineteenth century, the Office of the Postmaster General received frequent petitions from both urban and rural communities complaining of the lack of adequate postal services. Nonetheless, the willingness of successive Canadian governments to regard the provision of postal services as a necessary concomitant of settlement, "progress" and "development" did result in constant efforts to improve ease of access to postal services; although, of course, the potential clientele had to be able to utilize such services, and be motivated to do so. The ability to make full use of the mail, as distinct from the money order system or savings banks, was obviously linked to the issue of literacy and education. Moreover, the burgeoning demand for the full range of all the postal services was associated with certain major social developments of the period: the expansion of settlement; urbanization and the associated development of manufacturing and commerce; and intra-regional and international migration. We shall refer briefly here to the relevance of each of these developments in order to obtain a better understanding of the changing patterns of public utilization of the postal system.

That the ability to read and write is an essential prerequisite for the full use of a "mass" postal system is self-evident. In the second half of the nineteenth century, literacy could, in turn, be linked to the development of public elementary schooling. Thus, it is hardly coincidental that the gradual extension of public elementary education in the English Canadian provinces from the 1840s on (with a high point being achieved in the attainment of free, compulsory, and universal elementary education in Ontario in 1871) occurred over approximately the same period as the rise of mass postal communications. Compulsory schooling did not guarantee literacy for all but it certainly helped to increase the numbers of the literate. In turn, the literate were able to send and receive letters directly, and—at least for some of them—the experience of schooling must have led to an acceptance of "reading and writing" as a normal daily activity.

It is not suggested that the advancement of public education in Ontario was the prime cause of the expansion of mail communication but rather that it was an important institutional prerequisite. Likewise, while in Quebec the often documented lack of adequate schooling opportunities for francophone youth[2] did not block an increasing use of the mail services, the relatively high illiteracy rates in that province certainly served to "dampen down" the potential demand for such services. For example, in 1891, 20.3 percent of the young men and 13.4 percent of the young women in Quebec aged between ten and nineteen years were unable to read or write, compared with equivalent proportions in Ontario of 5.1 percent and 4.0 percent, respectively.[3] Thirty years later, in 1921, the proportion of illiterates among the rural population of Quebec was still 8.7 percent, compared with 3.9 percent of the rural population of Ontario.[4]

It would appear, therefore, that the ability to utilize the mails directly was more widespread among the population of Ontario than of Quebec. Furthermore, in Quebec country parishes a related reason for people's limited use of the mails was probably that the culture of the parish had little place for the role of the written word. Hence, as Horace Miner wrote of the parish of St. Denis in 1939:

> Until some fifty years ago literacy had but little utility in the parish ... No commercial contacts necessitated reading or writing. The occasions when one was obligated to sign one's name were rare indeed—marriage contracts, records in the parish register and that was about all ... Even today writing itself is left almost exclusively to the women, except for tradesmen.[5]

Thus, our general conclusion on the role of the post office in Quebec and Ontario respectively must be that Quebec citizens had less written communication with others, and *in toto* less ability and need to so communicate.

In the second half of the ninteenth century, the growth of the towns and cities, the influx of migrants and the development of commerce influenced the growth of the post office as an essential public amenity just as public schooling was, in the context of settlement, perceived as an essential public amenity.[6] For example, the proportion of the population of Ontario living in urban centres containing 1,000 inhabitants or more rose from 20.6 percent in 1871 to 40.3 percent in 1900 and 49.5 percent in 1911. In Quebec, the comparable percentages were 19.9 percent, 36.1 percent, and 44.5 percent,[7] although the province still contained far fewer larger urban centres than Ontario at the turn of the century.[8] Again, this process of urbanization was associated both with high levels of internal migration from the countryside to urban areas and also with an influx of immigrants from other lands, which reached its peak during the great migration period of 1901–13.[9] This latter period also witnessed an end to the world economic depression of the 1880s and early 1890s and a return to world prosperity. "New markets opened up, money for investment flowed freely and immigrants looked to Canada as a land of promise."[10]

Given these developments, it is hardly surprising that the business of the post office increased far more rapidly than the general increase in population. Nor is it surprising that the biggest per capita increase in mail flow and use of the money order system coincided with a period of massive immigration and economic prosperity (i.e., during the first decade of this century). The growth in trade and manufacturing in the expanding urban centres must have been associated with an expansion of commercial mail, including mailed advertisements and the early developments of the mail order system. Also, letter writing has long been used by individuals as a means of maintaining ties of kin and friendship with others and what better motivation for letter writing, especially in the absence of telephone communication, than separation from one's family and movement to a city or a new land? Finally, before the widespread provision of telephones and their "mass" acceptance, communication with others living some distance away in the same large town or city would have been very arduous and time consuming in the absence of the mails. Hence the phenomenon of "drop mail" or "city mail" posted and delivered on the same day within the same urban area became a widely-used and valued public amenity in Canadian cities in the latter decades of the nineteenth century.[11]

During the last three decades of the nineteenth century, both Ontario and Quebec were still experiencing settlement extension into the marginal areas of the Ottawa-Huron tract and "New Quebec," respectively. Such frontier areas experienced a transformation from isolation and subsistence to an integration and commercialization of their activities, gradually acquiring the physical and social infrastructure of fully developed communities. In this process leading to "mature" settlement, scattered families and their local service centres focused much attention on central functions such as stores, schools, churches, mills, and post offices. Apart from being symbols of "progress," such facilities were important both for local integration and as connections with the wider society. Thus, while we have associated the increased use of postal services with urbanization and migration mainly to the urban centres, the role of the post office in "linking" new outposts to well-established settlements and also in improving the communications between established settlements and the urban centres

(not the least by means of newspapers) was clearly important as well.[12] . . .

III

Decision-making at the micro-level of the community demonstrates that literacy and education, migration, the growth of industry and commerce, and the extension of settlement were perceived by local opinion and post officials to be highly relevant considerations when deciding on the provision and location of new postal facilities. The procedures were highly visible, and the *Canadian Almanac* for 1891 reported the contemporary process for petitioning for the establishment of "New Post Offices":

> New Post Offices are established by the Department whenever it is ascertained that a sufficient number of inhabitants can be accommodated, and there is a probability of a sufficient amount of correspondence to warrant such a measure. When a new Post Office is required, a petition should be addressed to the Postmaster-General in Ottawa, signed by as many of the inhabitants as can conveniently subscribe to the same. The petition should state the name of the township and the number of the lot and concession on which it is desired the office should be established; the distance from the neighbouring offices; whether there is a village at the site of the proposed Post Office; the number of mills, stores, taverns and houses thereat; the extent of the settlement to be served and the probable cost of the mail service; together with any other facts which may form any ground for giving the accommodation applied for.[13]

These procedures were well-known and widely used by both urban and rural communities throughout Canada in the latter quarter of the nineteenth century. The petitions, and related inspectors' reports for two regions were selected for a detailed investigation of the arguments for the development of the postal system at the local community level. Both the Kingston Postal Division, located in eastern-central Ontario, and the Quebec Postal Division, centred in Quebec City, contained a central urban node, an old settled area, and a region of pioneer settlements in the interior. Apart from considerable expansion and redistribution of settlement, each of these regions was experiencing the contemporary processes of commercialization of agriculture, urbanization, industrialization, and modernization. Further, a provincial comparison of the two sets of communities at the micro-level may throw more light on the variations in the development and use of the postal service.[14]

The primary requirement for the establishment of a post office was centrality amidst a "fertile," "improving," and "well-populated" district. Apart from being requested by established communities, several petitions advocated that post offices would "be the means of opening the country," an "official inducement to intending settlers," and frequently, a "benefit" or "great accommodation to the settlers."[15] For the new and often isolated communities, a post office was both a symbol of progress and a material connection with the outside world.

But while the majority of applications were from pioneer or established rural districts, other economic enterprises also produced a demand for postal services. In some areas throughout the Ottawa-Huron tract, at the time of the application the request for a post office preceded the actual settlement of the district as the land was reserved for lumbering "and not yet open for settlement, but the woods are filled with lumber and shantymen in Winter. When the timber is removed of course this population will disappear, but some settlers may move in."[16]

Apart from the farmers and the "floating population of lumbermen," iron mines in Madoc, gold opened by "Scotch and English capitalists in Belmont township," lead mines in

Lansdowne, all supported or initiated petitions for the provision of mail service to their businesses.[17] Similarly, in other cases, requests were made for seasonal post offices to serve the "large numbers of tourists and pleasure seekers who spend the summer months along the shores of Lake Ontario and throughout the Thousand Islands."[18] To some extent, the petitions for post offices may be taken as prime indicators of settlement, just as their closing is indicative of the constriction of settlement. Moreover, the very application for a post office indicated that a particular community had reached a sufficiently advanced stage of development that communications with the wider society were required. In this context, therefore, they may be regarded as being indicative of a certain qualitative stage in settlement formation and community development.

But while the indicators of advancement—settlement or economic development—were considered, it was the measure of the need or potential usage of the facility which was the critical consideration in determining the demand for, and profitability of, a new post office. Localities settled by the "better class of progressive farmers," "agriculturalists in, apparently, well-to-do circumstances," a "reading and very intelligent lot of farmers who appreciate the advantage of having a Post Office in their midst," "well-to-do agriculturalists, persons who are probably on the whole above average as a class of farmers and are a reading people" were more likely to receive official acquiescence to their petitions.[19]

On the other hand, postal inspectors reported negatively on applications from those districts populated by people "not of the class that make use of the Post Office."[20] A report on an application from Hawkesbury is more specific about the background of the people, complaining that "the neighbourhood is principally settled by French, who are not, I am credibly informed, a reading or corresponding community."[21] Critical reports were elicited by other districts whose populace "as a class, are not very large correspondents, neither do they as a rule, subscribe to many newspapers. . . ."

It becomes clear, therefore, that the inspectors were sensitive to the effect of class, occupation and, in some cases, ethnicity, on the use of the mail service. The petitions themselves contain evidence of the potential usage by allowing the calculation of the proportion of actual signatures to "marks" and thus an insight into a sufficient level of penmanship, if not literacy. Throughout the Kingston Division, "marks" constituted a small percentage of the signatures, with few localities approaching the 18 percent of the North Hastings case.[22] The Quebec City Division is different, however. In several parishes, the proportion of marks to signatures exceeded 50 percent and occasionally were as high as 95 percent. Such apparently high rates of illiteracy would appear to argue against the need for a postal service. If the majority of the individuals could not write, why would the community need the post office? Perhaps the answer lies in the explanation that it was more a community need than an individual need. The community would benefit from the provision of mail service for the use of the priest, the lawyer, the merchant, the leading citizen, all of whom were represented in the small percent of signatures. Also, literacy withstanding, flows of remittances from emigrant kin, newspapers, mail order literature, and an ever increasing variety of commercial and institutional correspondence required at least the minimal level of weekly mail service. . . .

It is this question of the actual public use of the postal service by the various communities throughout the study areas which is crucial to this investigation. By cross-referencing the lists of post offices reported in the annual reports, quite precise measures of the regional variation in the service may be calculated.[23] Perhaps the most basic measure is the number of people per post office in any region. Thus, in the Kingston Division between 1871 and 1901, the number of offices increased from 100 to 151, with the associated decrease in the ratio of post offices to population being 1:720 to 1:441, respectively. The equivalent experience for the Quebec Division was an increase in the number of offices from 55 to 133 and an associated improvement in the ratio of people to offices from 1:2220 to 1:1245. . . .

With regard to the question of the use of the services provided, the annual returns of gross postal revenue for each post office may be taken as a measure of the use of the mail service of various communities. When expressed on a per capita basis, for the 1871–1901 period, the Kingston region experienced an increase in usage from $0.27 revenue per capita to $0.77. During the same period, the overall increase per capita for the Quebec City region was from $0.29 to only $0.49. As would be expected, however, in both regions there was a marked difference between urban and rural areas. Thus, in 1871 the rural townships around Kingston exhibited per capita postal values ranging from lows of 1.5 cents per capita to highs of over 10 cents per capita. The value for Kingston itself was $0.99 per capita, while lesser centres such as Napanee ($0.82), Bath ($0.48), Newburgh ($0.42) also reflected the effect of their central place functions and commercial activities on their use of postal services. A similar contrast, if at an overall lower level, is revealed by the Quebec City region with its rural rates ranging from $0.03 cents per capita to $0.11 cents, while Quebec City itself had a per capita value of $0.56.

At the local level, therefore, the evidence supports the aggregate provincial pattern with both regions experiencing low usage rates at the beginning of the study period, increasing usage throughout the period, and considerable differences between urban and rural areas. Moreover, the generation of mail is higher in both the rural and urban areas in the Kingston sample area than in the Quebec City region. This is particularly significant when the relative populations and commercial significance of the two major urban centres are noted.

But even if it was determined that a sufficient threshold level of use of a proposed post office was assured because of the numbers, economic activities, and class of the settlers, the question of the location of the office remained. This was a critical decision, as it had the potential of creating the nucleus of new settlements in some cases, augmented the centrality of nascent settlements in others, or even precipitated a shift in influence in still others.

Locational decisions were difficult, however, where the pattern of emerging service centres and population distribution would be disturbed by the failure of pioneer communities, the transience of lumbering or mining operations, or new developments in transportation. Railroads in particular were thought to be major catalysts, and locational decisions were delayed until their impact could be assessed as it was anticipated that "no doubt changes will be made in roads, places of business will be opened in localities that are now no more than woods, and it would be better to wait for a few months in order to be able to select the most suitable locales for offices."[24]

Throughout the Kingston Division, both petitions and inspectors' reports favoured locations at "corners" where two roads intersected or at well-established "places of business" where a mix of rural enterprises, services and institutions ensured a considerable traffic. Typical favoured sites possessed such characteristics as " . . . a school house, cheese factory and a church and it is where the township line crosses the main road forming four corners."[25] Or again, "the proposed site is most convenient, it being at four corners. With a radius of a mile there are at present a blacksmith shop, a church, two woodworkers' shops, one cheese factory and five dwellings."[26] But if most rural services were capable of attracting post offices,

taverns—central and well subscribed though they may have been—were not considered to have a compatible function.

Because of their ubiquity, centrality and important retail function, general stores were most frequently chosen as post offices throughout rural Ontario. Indeed, in at least one case it was reported that a store "has virtually been a Post Office for the past 18 months. All mail matter being left with him [the storekeeper] to be sent to Cheddar N., and all incoming mail is sent to his store for distribution and all has been done to the entire satisfaction of the people."[27] The reverse process also operated. The recognition of the mutual advantage of a combined retail and postal service prompted one applicant to comment that, once appointed postmaster, he would "then open a small store."[28] The principal objective of another petitioner was to "draw people to his store and thus increase the business done in it. . . ."[29]

If the general store or other business establishments located at convenient road intersections were the favoured locations for post offices throughout Ontario, in Quebec it was proximity to the church. . . . Apart from the concentration of the various institutions and enterprises near the church, the weekly attendance at mass provided a further rationale for locating post offices close by. It was claimed that "In our country parishes, the immediate vicinity of the Parish Church is generally the most convenient for the post office as people call for their correspondence after Divine Service on Sundays."[30] Others argued that "farmers seldom visit the Post Office except on Sundays" and, where the post office was not located near the church, that once a week they were collected "pour être distribuer à la porte de l'Eglise."[31]

The distribution of mail, therefore, became integrated into, and even reinforced, the traditional regimen of social interaction. The church and the post office became mutually supportive institutions, resulting in the centralization of local community affairs." . . .

Such arguments did not suit all elements of the Quebec society, however. In areas of new colonization, early post offices had often been located at convenient transport nodes, mill sites, or emerging centres of commerce and trade. With the advance of agricultural settlement and the establishment of parish churches to serve the spiritual needs of the populace, petitions were submitted requesting the shift of the post office to the new centre of social interaction. It was recognized that such shifts were not "convenient as regards to the people engaged in business"; it was argued by some interests that the new locations may have been central to, and convenient for, the weekly visits by the farming population but that "they receive but little correspondence," whereas mill owners and workers received eight or ten letters daily.[32] Again, in the parish of Dablon, Chicoutimi, the move from the old site at the mill to the parish church took place even though it was noted that "All the trade of the locality is made at the mills. It is a necessity that he [the miller] gets his mails immediately after their arrival, as he has important business all the year round." It was concluded that the move was "a great drawback for the trade of this place."[33]

If the occupation, class, and literacy of the subscribers were important considerations in the adjudication of applications, the actual implementation of a postal service was dependent upon the availability of a person of sufficient literacy, intelligence, and probity— let alone the right political persuasion—to serve as postmaster. An applicant could be found wanting because he was "a man of no education and cannot even write his own name" or because he was "a very poor scholar and that it is questionable whether he can properly perform the duties."[34] The problem was a serious one and the inspectors were frequently required to report that there was "no one competent living in a convenient place that he could recommend for the Postmastership."[35] In other cases, it was the qual-

ifications of the wife which were found to be wanting. The proposed postmaster for the Deer Lake Settlement was disqualified because his wife, who would "attend the Post Office in his absence is an imbecile."[36] In another case, the applicant was censured because of the "gossiping propensities" and "scandalous tongue" of his wife and the fact that "most respectable women refuse to go to the office for mail."[37] Finally, even if appointed, there was the problem of the transiency of the population in general, and of postmasters in particular. In one marginal area it was reported that "during the past four years, the office of Postmaster has changed hands three times, it seeming to be that no person finds it profitable to remain there for any time"[38]....

Frontier communities, developing service centres, and progressive agricultural areas often benefitted from the support and sponsorship of influential agencies and individuals in their petitions for mail service. Several applications along the Gaspé coast and throughout the Magdalene Islands were supported by the Department of Marine and Fisheries which argued that the improvement in mail service and associated communications would be "in the interest of shipping generally .., in consequence of the difficulty of communication with the main land, crews of wrecked vessels have wintered at South West Point at a serious expense to the Government."[39] Colonization railroads had vested interests in the continued progress and development of their hinterlands and, accordingly, ventures such as the Victoria Railway Company supported the application for an improved mail service to Haliburton, arguing that "the liberality of my Company towards great Public Works entitles us to liberal consideration on all hands."[40] In Ontario, land companies such as the Canadian Land and Emigration Company were active on behalf of the petitioners from their regions of interest, while in Quebec the church was active in advocating the merit of the general service and, as has already been seen, determined to tie the location of the post office to that of the parish church in a mutually reinforcing pattern of social centrality.

But, for reasons apparent to all, it was the local politician who was the most influential and consistent champion of the communities' requests, provided they were of the right political persuasion.... Conversely, the failure of other petitions was attributed by some petitioners to the political complexion of their community and they complained that "it seems very much to us that the Government is seeking more for votes than for the interest of the settlers in this backward place."[41] This complaint went on to threaten "I think it is high time that there was a change made and see if the country cannot put in men who will look after the needs of the poor settlers as well as the rich." Similarly, Tory Hill, a community which had been petitioning unsuccessfully for a post office for some five years and which had even offered a name to posterity as an inducement for the granting of favours, trumpeted "they are just humbugging and the consequence will be that the Conservative government will suffer by it at the next election if something is not done now."[42] Other sets of correspondence leave no room for speculation that politically motivated intervention in the provision of mail services was both common and effective. Thus, when the postmaster of Oak Bay attended a Conservative Convention in 1898, action was expeditiously taken by the Liberal government to close the post office there, a decision motivated by "interests of economy" and the insistence of "our friends."[43]

Any consideration of the factors considered in evaluating the need for postal services throughout Ontario and Quebec in the late nineteenth century must certainly recognize the influence of political patronage and favouritism. This was certainly appreciated by the petitioners and either manipulated by them or complained about. Thus, pondering on the presence of three post offices in a mere six miles of sparsely populated country, the magistrate of Saguenay was prompted to conclude "I must uncharitably suppose that in days gone by, some hardly pressed politician had to create postmasters by the quarter dozen at one time...."[44]

IV

... In the introduction to our paper, we made an analogy between some aspects of advance in telecommunications and the advent of mass mail services. Like some of these advances, both the mail and the telephone have, as McQuail notes, an "intimate connection with other features of modern society—with mobility, individualism, privacy and division of labour. They must encourage, facilitate and yet also act as antidotes to these tendencies. They make possible intercommunication and self-expression."[45] Indeed, just as one can visualize a stage being reached where micro computers situated in each home allow not only for communications with central data banks but also for new means of direct personal communications with other citizens, so too is it possible to perceive mail flow as a communications net expanding along spatial dimensions and increasing interactions between individuals and organizations. More specifically, the increasing ease of public access to postal services, and notably mail, led people to develop quite high expectations about the frequency and speed with which they could communicate with others over a distance, expectations which, in turn, had major social consequences. Three specific examples of such consequences would be appropriate to mention at this point, all underlining the importance of the postal system as "a facilitator" of major demographic and institutional developments during the period under review.

First, we have already noted that prior to the development of the telephone system, even communication over relatively short distances became heavily dependent upon efficient mail services. In the absence of either telephones or of well-organized mail services, as in the earlier decades of the nineteenth century, people with limited means who moved substantial distances away from their kin were likely to be completely cut off from home news. Indeed, perhaps the single most important social consequence for individuals of the postal revolution was that the fear of "the walls of oblivion,"[46] previously felt as a result of loss of contact with kin, was no longer the price exacted for moving from home. A contemporary writer, Harriet Martineau, could claim that, prior to the English postal reforms of the 1840s many young people of the English lower class who left home to become apprentices and domestics "were cut off from family relations as effectively as if seas or deserts divided them."[47] How much more cut off, before the postal reforms, were many Canadian settlers by seas and the great distances of the land? Thus, regular postal communications must have made migration to Canada, and within Canada, much less daunting than in earlier times, diminished the impact of distance and hence have facilitated the migration process. But more than this, letters sent home by those who had already migrated undoubtedly acted as travel brochures which then encouraged the movement of those who had stayed behind. This particular function of letter writing in Britain (and one assumes similarly in Canada) is nicely summed up in an observation from Charles Booth's monumental study of the people of London (1891) wherein it is noted that "probably one of the most powerful and efficient migration agencies is that supplied by the letters written home by the country girl settled in domestic service in the great town."[48]

Second, the post office increasingly assumed the role of a "mover of the public news," and, as such, became an important factor in the development of the Canadian press. As Paul Rutherford notes in his book on the Canadian media, not until the 1840s was the climate ripe for a daily press in Canada; by then, the new cities ensured a market for the wares of the daily journalist, the busy retail trade of these cities enhancing the all-important advertising revenues.[49] What Rutherford does not mention, however, is that in the cities, but still more in the country areas, the developing postal system became an important element in the wide-spread dissemination of daily and weekly newspapers. Indeed, as our archival material for the Kingston Postal Division (but less so the Quebec City Postal Division) indicates, one major reason why inhabitants of small settlements petitioned for the location of a post office in their community was that it gave them relatively swift access to the urban press. For their part, Canadian newspaper publishers benefitted from an absence of mail charges on newspapers for most of the 1890s[50] and in 1908 from the initiation of the free rural delivery system.[51] In the United States, newspaper publishers were indeed among the first people to see the advantage of free delivery to farm homes in the late nineteenth century, since in the words of U.S. mail historian Wayne Fuller, "They knew as well as they knew anything that farmers would subscribe to daily newspapers if they had a daily mail service."[52] The increasing importance of newspapers cannot be separated, therefore, from the use of the postal service in the late nineteenth century.

Finally, in the continued diversification of the function of the postal system, its adoption as a distributing device for retail goods constituted a major development in the latter part of the nineteenth century. The economic and social consequences of the introduction of mail-order by Sears-Roebuck, Eaton's, and others have yet to be explored fully but it is clear that the universality and efficiency of the mail system was its cause. The convenience of mail advertising, mail-order, and mail delivery was such that, paradoxically, it accelerated and insured the demise of certain functions of the post office's early host, the general store.[53]

Notes

[1] D. McQuail, *Communications* (London: Longman, 1975), p. 87.

[2] See, for example, R. Pike, "Education, Class and Power in Canada," in R.J. Ossenberg (ed.), *Power and Change in Canada* (Toronto: McClelland and Stewart, 1980), *passim.*

[3] Census of Canada, 1890–91, Vol. 2, Table XIII.

[4] Dominion Bureau of Statistics, *Illiteracy and School Attendance in Canada* (Ottawa: King's Printer, 1921), Table 24, p. 35. The equivalent illiteracy rate in urban areas in 1921 was 4.3 percent in Quebec and 2.3 percent in Ontario.

[5] H. Miner, *St. Denis, A French-Canadian Parish* (Chicago: University of Chicago, 1963), pp. 73–74. The first edition of this book was published in 1939.

[6] As our archival research reveals, it was common for school children in country areas in Ontario to collect the mail on their way home from public school. Hence, it was often considered desirable that the post office be placed close to the school. Symbolically, both institutions were perceived in Victorian times as evidence of "public progress." Clearly, also, their spatial relationship had some practical elements!

[7] D. Kubat and D. Thornton, *A Statistical Profile of Canadian Society* (Toronto: McGraw-Hill Ryerson, 1974), p. 14.

[8] In 1901, Quebec contained seventeen centres with population of 4,000 and over, compared with forty-one in Ontario (see the Census of Canada, Bulletin IV, 1902).

[9] Between 1901 and 1913, about two and a half million immigrants arrived in Canada. Admittedly, many of them were settlers moving to the western provinces, but also many settled in central Canada, and notably in Ontario.

[10] R. Cook et al., *Canada: A Modern Study* (Toronto: Clarke Irwin, 1963), p. 142.

[11] In the larger urban centres, the number of daily collections and deliveries were not uncommonly three or four during the later decades of the period under review.

[12] For some comments on the relationship between the post office and the rise of the newspaper industry, see the conclusion to this paper.

[13] *Canadian Almanac, 1891* (Toronto: Copp-Clark, 1891), p. 101.

[14] The Kingston Postal Division covered the countries of Frontenac, Lennox, Addington, Brockville, most of Hastings, most of Leeds and Grenville, Northumberland, Peterborough, Prince Edward, and part of Victoria. The Quebec Postal Division included besides Quebec City and immediate environs, the Eastern Townships, the Upper St. Lawrence and Gaspé, Lac St. Jean. At the commencing date of the relevant archival resources in 1871, post offices and related services had been established in the major urban centres of these divisions, and hence our attention was devoted to the approximately 2,000 petitions and reports for the smaller towns and rural areas during the period 1871 to 1901. Generally, a petition for a new post office was accompanied by an inspector's report and vice versa, but sometimes the archival material includes one document but not the other. All material is held by the Public Archives in Ottawa.

[15] The following references refer to the petitions and postal inspectors' reports for the Kingston District (K.D.) and Quebec District (Q.D.): Methuen, K.D. 1876; Oso, K.D., 1876.

[16] Stanhope, K.D., 1900.

[17] *Ibid.*, also Cheddar, K.D., 1881; Belmont, K.D., 1900; Lansdowne, K.D., 1875.

[18] Lansdowne, K.D., 1884.

[19] See Elizabethtown, K.D., 1898; Lansdowne, K.D., 1876; Charlesville, K.D., 1878; Middle Road, K.D., 1878.

[20] Hinchinbrooke, K.D., 1878.

[21] Hawkesbury, K.D., 1876.

[22] Kellar's Bridge, K.D., 1876.

[23] Dominion of Canada, *Official Postal Guides, 1871–1901;* Dominion of Canada, *Annual Reports of the Postmaster General*, 1871–1901.

[24] Crow Lake, K.D., 1876.

[25] North Crosby, K.D., 1895.

[26] Crow Bay, K.D., 1885.

[27] Ritchie Settlement, K.D., 1877.

[28] Wollaston, K.D., 1877.

[29] Hawkesbury, K.D., 1876.

[30] Musselyville, Q.D., 1897.

[31] Metabechovan, Q.D., 1889.

[32] Tetu Caban, Q.D., 1896.

[33] Jaibert's Mills, Q.D., 1896.

[34] Joyceville, K.D., 1877.

[35] Mohawk Reserve, K.D., 1877.

[36] Trout Lake, K.D., 1881.

[37] Westbrook, K.D., 1901.

[38] Maynooth, K.D., 1878.

[19] Anticost Island, Q.D., 1876.

[40] Haliburton, K.D., 1880.

[41] Clear Bay, K.D., 1891.

[42] Tory Hill, K.D., 1887.

[43] Oak Bay Mills, Q.D., 1898.

[44] North Shore Report, Q.D., 1890.

[45] D. McQuail, *Communications*, p. 87.

[46] The phrase "the walls of oblivion" is taken from E.C. Smythe, *Sir Rowland Hill: The Story of a Great Reformer told by his Daughter* (London: T. Fisher Unwin, 1907), p. 41. She refers therein to "the walls of oblivion" which existed between widely separated members of poor families prior to the reform of the British mail service.

[47] Smythe, *Sir Rowland Hill,* p. 41.

[48] C. Booth, *Labour and Life of the People of London* (London: Williams and Norgate, 1891), Vo. II. p. 460.

[49] P. Rutherford, *The Making of the Canadian Media* (Toronto: McGraw-Hill-Ryerson, 1978), p. 7.

[50] The history in Canada of the agitation of nineteenth century newspaper proprietors to have their newspapers sent through the mails either at preferred rates or free of charge is both long and complicated. However, it was William Smith's opinion that "newspapers have always been circulated through Canada by the post office on terms most advantageous to the public. In 1875 publishers were permitted to send their papers to subscribers at the rate of one cent per pound. Even this small charge was removed in 1882, and for the following seventeen years newspapers addressed to subscribers were exempt from all charges": Smith, *The History of the Post Office in British North America*, p. 332. A very small charge was reimposed in 1890, although the transportation of newspapers continued to represent a considerable financial loss to the post office.

[51] Rural free mail delivery was initiated in Canda along the route from Hamilton to Ancaster in 1908 and apparently covered most of eastern Canada by 1914; see notably, G. Wilcox, *History of Rural Mail in Canada* (Ottawa: Public Affairs Branch, Canada Post, 1975), *passim*. According to Currie, "rural mail clearly did not pay, notwithstanding the economies derived from the closing of many rural post offices, some increase in the circulation of daily newspapers, and the fact that mail carriers worked at substandard wages for many years"; Currie, "The Post Office Since 1867," p. 244.

[52] W.E. Fuller, *The American Mail* (Chicago: University of Chicago Press, 1972), p. 139.

[53] Other uses include mail distribution and processing of film started by George Eastman with the development in 1890 of roll-film, the mailable box camera and, thus, "mass photography."

25 Price-Setting as Social Activity

Robert Prus

ROBERT PRUS, Associate Professor of Sociology at the University of Waterloo, is a symbolic interactionist who has studied such diverse issues as parole revocation, religious recruitment, labeling theory, card and dice hustling, and the social organization of the hotel community (i.e., the careers and interrelatedness of hookers, entertainers, staff and patrons). His books are, with C.R. Sharper, *Road Hustlers: Career Contingencies of Professional Card and Dice Hustlers* (1977) and, with S. Irini, *Hookers, Rounders and Desk Clerks: The Social Organization of the Hotel Community* (1980). His excerpt here, on price-setting, is derived from a larger study of the social construction of marketplace activity that considers how vendors promote products, generate trust, hold "sales," develop loyalty, and maintain enthusiasm. Professor Prus is also currently involved in a study of shopping activity, a natural sequel to the study of vendor activities.

THE DATA BASE

This consideration of price-setting emerged as part of a larger study of marketing activity. Inspired by earlier research on the "hotel community" and the variety of businesses clustered there (e.g., hookers, entertainers, bar business, room rentals; Prus and Irini, 1980), I decided to examine more intensively the ways in which retailers promoted their products. I approached vendors at their places of business, and indicated my interest in learning about the what and how of sales activity.... Initially, I had anticipated that pricing would be the activity least amenable to social influence and was inclined to view pricing largely in "bookkeeping terms." But with time, I began to appreciate the problematic nature of pricing, especially as I became sensitized to concerns with pricing as an essential, ongoing form of practical activity. More than any other realm of marketing activity, pricing convinced me of the profoundly social essence of the marketplace.

. . . Visits to trade shows and interviews with suppliers expanded the scope of the project, locating it within a more general realm of marketing activity. Thus, in addition to retail merchandising, data were collected from those involved in wholesale, manufacture, and commercial (supplying finished goods for business consumption) trade....

There were three modes of data collection used in this study: interviews with businesspeople, observations of trade shows, and participant-observation in a craft enterprise. Interviews with vendors not only marked the beginning of data collection, but have continued throughout. The interviews (n = 112) were obtained largely on an individual basis, and reflect a wide variety of contacts with vendors....

Attendance at trade shows was especially valuable in providing firsthand material on large-scale and international levels of trade. I observed a total of 32 such exhibits where items such as giftware, clothing, luggage, hardware, computers, office supplies, and industrial supplies were featured....

From Robert Prus, "Price Setting as Social Activity," in *Urban Life*, 14, 1 (April 1985), pp. 59–93. Copyright © 1985 by Sage Publications, Inc. Reprinted by permission of Sage Publications, Inc.

Table 1
DISTRIBUTION OF PARTICIPANTS' POSITIONS AND LEVELS OF SALES

Category	Participants' Positions		
	Manager (owner)	Salesperson	Total
Retail	40(12)	29	69
Wholesale	5(3)	4	9
Manufacture	8(4)	10	18
Commercial	7(2)	9	16
Total	60(21)	52	112

The interviews and trade show materials were supplemented by three years of my own involvement in a craft enterprise. . . . [1]

INITIAL PRICING ORIENTATIONS AND STRATEGIES

Building on past experiences and traditions in the field, vendors tend to rely on certain rules of thumb in initially contemplating product prices. In Schutz's (1971) terms, these "recipes" reflect the vendors' "stock of knowledge." Operating in the context of inevitable uncertainty (no one knows for sure which products will sell, much less at what particular prices), these rules of thumb or pricing recipes generate a sense of stability within marketing programs. They represent predictions of customer activity and denote guidelines by which products may be purchased for direct resale, integrated into manufacturing and processing routines in anticipation of sales, presented in the media, and so forth. Pricing is thus both a way of dealing with the ambiguity of the marketplace and a realm of uncertainty in itself.

> With your margins, you try to predict how much you need to make to stay in business. You have all your expenses, mall rents, staff, all your overhead. And when you're ordering your products, you take that into account. How much can you sell this for? Can you make a profit on it in the end? That's where

you make it or you don't. But it's all these things. So on something it might seem like a big margin, but it has to cover all these things. The bad buys, the flops, your price-reductions, everything [shoes].

Taking Margins

The term "margin" or "markup" refers most basically to the difference between the cost price and the price for which products are being sold. There are many ways of arriving at margins, but end of year profits are dependent on all sales and expenditures; and operating budgets are based on projected sales and expenditures. Thus, regardless of the manner of ascertaining margins, one is gambling on both sales and overhead. . . .

Standardized Margins "Standarized margins" reflect (cost + profit) formulas vendors may use to routinize their pricing decisions. Whereas some merchants may calculate selling prices as multiples or percentages of the purchase price (e.g., double the cost price, or take a 100% margin),[2] others may calculate margins by adding a profit percentage to all costs incurred. In the first instance, the margin can vary greatly (e.g., 1% to 1000%), but vendors cover all their overhead with that margin. In the latter case, all overhead is calculated before the profit margin is added on. Regardless of the procedure, the eventual prices (or profits) need not be different. . . .

It should also be appreciated that businesses using standardized margins may use different margins for different products in their business. These differential markups may reflect turnovers of stock, but they may also denote attempts to be competitive in different product areas:

> The markup on groceries, cigarettes, is quite low compared to other things, like greeting cards, for instance. But it reflects your turnover on these items. With bread and milk, your turnover is going to be better than once a week, so you'll get a great number of turns on that merchandise, cigarettes too. Same with the lottery tickets. If it's a weekly draw, you'll get 52 turns a year [variety].

Standardized margins facilitate pricing decisions (especially important in larger companies), but they also affect buying practices. When margins are preset, those buying goods for the company are effectively (pre)pricing those goods at that point in time. For example, if the policy is to double the wholesale price, buyers may ultimately base their decision on whether or not to order a relevant $5 item on whether or not they think the item would move in their outlets at $10 (or $9.95). The item may not be tagged until much later, but initial "pricing" can be largely synonymous with ordering goods.

Standardized margins may also be encouraged by merchants' suppliers. For instance, suppliers may provide merchants with "list prices" (e.g., "manufacturer's suggested retail price"), or otherwise alert vendors to "existing margins in the trade." As a result of fair trade legislation, it is illegal for suppliers to force vendors to charge fixed amounts for goods they purchase for resale. . . . Merchants reselling products may charge prices at variance from the suggested prices, but "suggested prices" represent "benchmarks of objectivity" merchants may use in establishing their own prices:

> A lot of manufacturers give you a suggested retail price. It's good. It gives you an idea of what the other people might be charging, and you can show it to your customers, give them an idea of that too. Then, if you give them a little off, they're more likely to appreciate that, because they have an idea of where the ceiling is, say where the (suggested retail) price is marked on it. . . . I've noticed lately that a number of the manufacturers tell you that the suggested retail price is not what you're required to charge, and that if you charge a lower price, that won't affect their dealing with you. But they don't like you to charge much less, because it knocks the bottom out for everyone, and then the retailers gripe about not being able to handle that product anymore, that the overhead is shot [appliances].

As the following indicates, suggested prices may have more impact than legally intended. Vendors may resent those who undercut "accepted" margins and may complain to the suppliers involved, in some cases threatening to discontinue dealings with suppliers who do not ensure "fair margins." Vendors doing more business with particular suppliers (who are hence more dependent on them) would seem more able to dissuade suppliers from dealing with those "deviants. . . . "[3]

Opportunistic Pricing Opportunistic pricing refers to the practice of pricing items according to anticipated buyer tolerances of price and value.[4] In contrast to those more firmly relying on standardized markups (e.g., all items in general categories are marked up by a preset amount), more individualized variations are implemented at the outset. This practice may define the central pricing style for some vendors, but insofar as vendors anticipate profits from sales this tactic is typically employed in conjunction with some minimal markup:

> . . . There are two ways of charging. One is your standard markup, 100%, double the cost price, or whatever you do. It can vary with each item, too, depending on what you think somebody might pay for something. And what they will pay for one item relative to

others in a similar line. So, some things are better buys for you. Some things, you can mark up 300%, maybe more, but only be able to mark up another item at your 100% markup, and some things are write-offs [mixed clothing].

There may be a tendency to equate opportunistic pricing with profiteering. But in addition to any concerns vendors may have in developing customer loyalty, this view overlooks the possible large firmly standardized margins merchants may use, the risk particular items represent relative to other lines, and customer skepticism in reference to "good buys."

Price and Value as Symbolic

From the perspectives of both buyers and vendors, pricing has a very "practical" (limiting) quality; objects exchanged affect people's abilities to enter other transactions and to pursue other interests. Further, although one can argue for "correctness of price" once a sale has been made ("validated"), price is only one symbolic element denoting worth. Price suggests value, but so do all the other elements buyers associate with the particular items under consideration (e.g., store decor, reputation, vendor styles, brand names, anticipated enjoyment, pride of ownership, and so on). Thus, in addition to price, vendors can try to shape the valuing of the goods by the ways in which they present products, relate to the prospects, and so forth. In every case, however, the vendor's efforts are dependent on the interpretations of prospective buyers. Vendors may attempt to take prospects' perspectives into account, but in addition to the problematic accuracy of their role-taking endeavors and their inabilities to "set the stage" exactly as intended, they also face an ongoing, shifting diversity of perspectives, interpretations, and interactions on the part of the prospects encountered. As prospects may have quite different estimations of both object value and the significance of the involved monetary sacrifice, vendors may routinely anticipate variability in buyers' reactions to their pricing decisions:

> There's usually one or two per day that will come up and try to tell you how you're not doing something right, or you're overpriced. But you get that both ways. Someone will come along and says, "What a bargain! How can you make them this reasonable?" and the next one will come up and say, "What an outrageous price you're charging!" [crafts]

> You can't sell some things very well at 100% markup. The customers think that it's too cheap, that there must be something wrong with them. Some things, you mark up 150, 200% and then the customers seem to think that they're getting a good bargain, then....

Buyers "objectify" the asking price by assuming the (financial) sacrifice necessary to obtain the item (Simmel, 1978:81), but higher prices may be seen to suggest greater worth, better quality, and the like. Whereas prospective customers may resent the sacrifices required to obtain objects, they may also distrust items whose "value seems beneath its price":

> ... I find that most of the customers don't know quality. They think that price is synonymous with quality, and it can be a problem for you in terms of merchandise. So, for example, I was able to get some shoes for $7.50, a real good deal from the manufacturers and I wanted to pass this on to the consumer making my regular markup. What I found is that I was unable to sell the merchandise at the price. People came in and wanted to know what the defects were, the problems were, that the shoes were being sold at this price. The result was that I couldn't move the merchandise. So what I did was double the price. I put it on "sale," and I found that the line moved very well.

In considering the price-value relationship, analysts would want to distinguish "vendor perceived worth" from "buyer perceived worth." Price is one aspect by which prospects may assess value ("You only get what you pay for!"), but other concerns ("symbols") such as perceived utility, familiarity, uniqueness, comfort, esteem, and the recognized alternatives available may effectively distort the price-value relationship. However, prices provide standards against which the wisdom of people's purchases may be assessed through past experiences and over time by buyers as well as others.[5]

These themes strike at the heart of the rational-economic model. Vendors expect to receive prices for their products in some proportion to what they have paid for them, the costs they incur in processing them, promoting them, and the like. Further, as an ongoing practical accomplishment, marketing requires that vendors settle on a series of decisions (e.g., products carried, prices asked and accepted). Given concerns with financial survival, vendors are interested in predicting and maximizing the outcomes afforded them by differing lines of action. To the extent their offerings correspond with the time-situated interests of prospective buyers, their rules of thumb stand to be confirmed. But as Schutz (1971) suggests, the realm of action takes marketers into an intersubjective world in which reality is not theirs alone to determine. To presume otherwise is to invoke psychological reductionist and/or absolutist reasoning rather than *socio-logical* reasoning. It is in this sense that the rational-economic model is inadequate; it does not allow for vendor dependency on buyers who are characterized by multiple perspectives, shifting interpretations, and ongoing interactions. Likewise, it overlooks vendor dependencies on their suppliers (and the relationships vendors develop with these "partners-in-trade"). Simply expressed, it does not acknowledge the fundamentally cooperative and symbolic nature of exchange. . . .

MARKET ADJUSTMENTS

Regardless of their (standardized or opportunistic) origins, the weakness of "firm margins" is that the business world is a dynamic arena. Like tacticians in other settings, vendors can endeavor to put tradition (via preset margins) to work and/or try to make shrewd guesses regarding optimal prices on the basis of past experiences, but ultimately they do not know what will sell and at what price. Because businesses are dependent upon "stock turns" (turnovers of goods) for their very existence, anything seen to interfere with that process becomes a source of trouble. Price is sometimes directly isolated as the probable cause of the lack of sales and may be subject to change as a result. However, of the various components of vendors' marketing programs, prices are also generally the easiest (and least disruptive) changes to implement. Consequently, price adjustments may be used as "quick fixes" to offset any number of shortcomings signified by the lack of sales.

Pricing is a means by which vendors may strive to increase their odds of winning the gambles their overall investments entail, but it is also a ready tool as vendors endeavor to offset other elements thought to affect the sales of particular items adversely. Hence, while vendors may periodically readjust their margins to offset shifting market conditions, concerns with viable stock turns result in more day to day price adjustments than might first seem likely. This holds true even in larger companies (in which most adjustments are more cumbersome). . . .

Comparative Pricing

Because few businesses have monopolies on particular items, one of the most significant forms of market adjustment involves defining prices relative to one's competitors. Vendors may attempt to justify higher prices on the basis of reputation, quality, service, and the like, but the ability of shoppers to "comparison shop" creates a sensitivity on the part of vendors to locate their goods in an attractively competitive package, part of which is defined by "the price":[6]

> There are a number of shoe stores in this area, so you do have some problems with people who shop around. Like they might find that this same shoe is $2 cheaper in another shop down the way. Or they may have a shoe "sale" at some point, so you'll lose some people that way.... Sometimes, if we learn that a competitor has the same shoe for less, we'll contact the head office and ask them if we can match their price. Sometimes they will, and sometimes they won't go along with you on that [shoes].

Thus even businesses that use "firmly established margins" and disapprove of dickering with individual buyers may find themselves making unanticipated price discounts on a general and/or individual basis when the loss of sales to competitors seems likely. Because business lost to a competitor may be business lost in both the short and the long run (multiple purchases, repeat customers), many businesses routinely "shop the competition" for the express purpose of reassessing their own prices....

Promotional Pricing

Promotional pricing refers to the practice of featuring discounted merchandise in attempts to increase one's total sales. It matters little whether one is discussing "dollar and cents" reductions, percentages off, coupon discounts, and the like, or whether vendors put items on sale, on special, or run discount operations; the basic elements of promotional pricing are very similar.

When regular cost merchandise is used, vendors may assume "shorter margins" on the premise that they will increase volumes of sales on that merchandise and/or other merchandise due to the increased traffic flow. Some other "losses of margin" may be nullified by better volume prices from suppliers

and other "economies of scale" (such as shipping and processing).

Merchants may also feature regular stock that has become "troublesome" (e.g., slow movers, broken lines, damaged goods, seasonal merchandise) as promotional items. Here, again, the margin is reduced relative to cost price, but the objective is to salvage earlier investments, and if other sales result, the relative loss is lessened....

Other promotional merchandise denotes "supplier specials" (slow movers, end of lines, new products, seasonal goods, and so on). Suppliers who want increased "action" on their inventories (to cover expenses, maintain employment levels, grow) may offer "first-line" (and in season) merchandise at dramatic discounts. Vendors may be able to acquire this merchandise at much greater than usual discounts and may be able to achieve usual (or greater) margins and still offer this merchandise at "deep discounts." Most retailers' (seeming) "loss leaders" reflect these "supplier specials."

Some promotional pricing, although probably much less that some consumers suspect, reflects merchandise introduced with high initial margins with the explicit intention of repricing these items for more dramatic (larger reductions) "sales." This practice is discouraged by authorities concerned with fair trade, but merchants are more apt to feel closed into these practices as they try to achieve some profits from shoppers they define as more "sales oriented:[7]

> Another way of dealing with the pricing game is to use an inflated markup, so that you have provided a buffer against some of your other costs. Then, even if the merchandise does go on "sale," again, what looks like half-price isn't half-price [mixed clothing].

In other instances, low-price introductions (promoting trial) may be used as part of an advertising campaign designed to create product use and preference:

> It's something new on the market, and we

want people to try it out. The lower price is one way of building product awareness. If they like it, then we can charge a regular price, like with our___and___flavors, which are selling very well for us now [manufacture-groceries].

Still another variant of promotional pricing involves using "low cost introductions" when it is assumed that subsequent ("tie-in") patronage will pay for the vendor's initial product investment:[8]

> We don't make money on the initial installation. We actually take a loss at that point. We just assume that it's going to require parts and service, so there they pretty well have to come to us. We look at it as an investment that'll pay off for us over time. . . . [manufacture-industrial]. . . .

Some Reverberations

Raising Prices Should vendors raise prices, they run a number of potential risks as a consequence of buyer reactions.[9] Noticed price increases break preestablished understandings and may engender both suspicion and moral indignation. Vendors sometimes endeavor to offset price increases as Oxenfeldt (1975:28) notes, by increasing advertising (creating greater interest) or adding "extra features." Likewise, vendors may try to justify higher prices on the basis of increased supplier costs, overhead, and such. Nevertheless, recognized increases are likely to create some resistance and "costs":

> We have to be careful about raising prices, because we are thought to be one of the lower lines. The people next to us, here, can raise the price of a skirt or dress $5 or $10 and their people (customers) don't seem to grumble so much. But we might have a three-piece item, and if we raise the price 50¢ or a dollar, we are going to get a lot of flack from our buyers. They are going to tell us how we are putting them behind the eight ball and that's the reason they are having trouble competing and such. But it is difficult

to switch lines too. We have tried going up, but we get no support from our buyers in that respect. I imagine the other companies have the same kind of problem. They may not be happy where they are, but the buyers get used to you offering certain levels and certain price ranges [manufacturing-clothing]. . . .

The (up)pricing of older stock in line with new stock price increases provides a further indication of the effects customers have on the pricing practices of vendors. Some vendors welcome price increases as a means of making a little more on existing stock. But even those who are reluctant to reprice existing stock in line with new cost increases (because of inconvenience and/or desires to sell the older stock first) may find that old prices become troublesome reference points. . . .

Reducing Prices Although buyers may welcome noticed price reductions, these changes may be fraught with more anxiety by vendors (and their suppliers) than are price increases. As Oxenfeldt (1975:27–28) observes, price reductions at the supplier level may reflect disappointing sales, increasing inventories, and sometimes desperate desires for cash flows. Supplier-initiated reductions may promote some sales, but actual profit per item drops for vendors employing fixed percentage markups. Supplier discounts also may generate some hostility among vendors sitting with larger inventories in these same lines; not only have they made costlier purchases from these same suppliers, but they now face decreased profit margins.

Further, as the following discussion of "sales" implies, lowered prices may foster suspicion of quality and value along with a host of other marketing dilemmas:

> I've noticed that you can have the same items, where they're on "sale" the next day, and you'll find that the customers now treat the items with less respect than they would have the day before. It can be the same rack

in the same location in the store, and yet they're much rougher with the merchandise when you put them on 20% or 30% off.... And with the staff, it's the same way, I have to get the girls to think that the sales items are just as important, just as valuable to the store as the other merchandise. Just because it's on sale doesn't mean that you can show less respect for the items or the customers who are buying the merchandise...."
[women's clothing]....

NEUTRALIZING PRICES

So far, attention has been directed toward vendor concerns with "best prices." This analysis would be short-changed, however, were not some consideration given to the ways in which merchants may endeavor to offset the significance of prices for prospective buyers....

Contextual Effects

Recognizing that some customers are apt to be influenced by the manner in which prices are presented (Goffman, 1959), merchants may endeavor to have items featured in ways that make them appear more accessible and/ or "worthwhile." Thus, vendors sometimes attempt to define products as bargains without significantly discounting these lines. Vendors may use a variety of tactics to this end, including: (1) reducing prices by an insignificant amount (e.g., from $5.00 to $4.98) from their usual margin; (2) putting items together in sets (e.g., 6 for $1.49, instead of 25¢ each); (3) using larger and/or brighter colored price tags; (4) dumping merchandise in large bins to provide a greater sense of "bulk" savings; and (5) providing other indications of "conspicuous cheapness".[10]

If the customer sees something at the end of the aisle, they are more likely to buy it, think it's on sale. Or if you set something on a table by itself, they are more likely to

think it's on special. Or you can use bigger signs. Or, if they see volume, like a pile of cases of something, they'll think that it's on sale. Like this one section, we have things from all different departments there, and it's rarely stuff on sale, but it sells like hotcakes! We have the same stuff in the departments, at the same price, but it doesn't sell so well there [discount department store].

The effects of context are by no means limited to generating impressions of greater accessibility. Ergo, vendors may also use displays to signify greater value:

We've poured a lot of money into this booth, the display. But you really have to. These guys are professional buyers, but they expect you to look professional too. That's part of what they're buying. Your products just look better in a classier booth [manufacture-industrial]....

These sorts of strategies indicate that although price is an important element in the sales of products, its significance can be shaped dramatically by the context in which prices appear.

Exclusive Branding

Another area in which price may be neutralized somewhat is in reference to exclusive (in contrast to supplier) brands. When engaged in the resale of goods carrying their own labels, vendors may not only avoid some price comparisons on the part of both customers and competitors, but typically are able to purchase these items at lower prices than comparable name brands. Private brands usually become more available as a product is better known and widely used, but sales of private brands rely heavily on the savings these goods represent and/or the vendor's general level of credibility. Because this merchandise usually represents an "overrun" on the part of the manufacturer, it may be available at a considerably discounted price....

CONCLUSION

. . . As with labels attached to people (Prus, 1975a, 1975b, 1982), prices attached to objects are subject to multiple definitions, designatory discretion, assessment, challenge, and revision as interested parties jointly strive to determine reality. Price-setting facilitates commodity exchange by defining parameters, but it is also a product of emergent exchange. Operating in a "business context," vendors intend to "act rationally." To this end, they seek out pricing formulas (and other rules of thumb) designed to reduce the ambiguity they experience. Unfortunately or otherwise, they find themselves in situations involving considerable uncertainty. Not only may they be unsure about the intentions, plans, and resources of their presumed competitors, but they are also uncertain of the ways in which prospective buyers will interpret their prices. While endeavoring to stock products for which they perceive a market, they are faced with the task of determining the best prices in advance of buyer assessments. The wisdom of setting particular prices will not be known until real prospects make actual buying decisions. Vendors may experiment with price adjustments in attempts to promote greater levels of sales, and they will sometimes select (seemingly) winning prices but the best price remains an elusive target.

Business related exchanges are not "objective matters of fact"; they are socially constructed (Berger and Luckmann, 1966) events. They entail interactive frames, and signify ongoing sets of reflective behaviors on the part of those involved. Despite its "depersonalized" (dollars and cents) referents, price-setting is a socially derived activity. Not only does pricing reflect the perspectives of the vendors involved (and their attempts to anticipate prospective buyers), but like other aspects of group life, pricing represents an ongoing and negotiable phenomenon dependent ultimately on others for objectification.

Notes

[1] Several months after I had begun the study, I had an opportunity to turn a hobby (tooling leather) into a side-line partnership with a weaver. These products were sold predominately through craft shows, a marketing format that closely parallels the earlier discussed trade exhibits.

[2] Some vendors calculate margin by defining markup as a percentage of the selling price. A 50% margin in this circumstance would generate $5 on a $10 item, for instance; the end result with this 50% margin is the same as doubling the cost price (or taking a 100% margin in other vendors' terms).

[3] Reflecting concerns with fair trade legislation, vendors are presently apt to be more subtle in the ways in which they discourage price-cutting. Haring (1935) provides a most interesting statement on earlier supplier attempts to maintain "acceptable margins."

[4] Kriesberg (1956) provides a valuable account of pricing restraint on the part of suppliers during a steel shortage. Despite the willingness of buyers to meet higher prices, most regular suppliers shunned opportunistic pricing in favor of maintaining good buyer relations.

[5] For an indication of some of the marketing literature on the price-quality relationship, see Shapiro (1968), Riesz (1978), Lambert (1981), and Wheatley et al. (1981).

[6] Donovan (1929:196) indicates that the practice of comparative pricing on the part of department stores was well established by that time.

[7] Lemert (1953) uses the term "closure" in describing the strikingly parallel experiences of consumers writing bad checks. These options are generally defined as undesirable by those involved, but represent a means of meeting pressing obligations.

[8] As Weigand (1980) notes, by (a) tying

customers into operating patterns, (b) committing customers to an inventory of parts and supplies, (c) developing product specific training programs, (d) helping customers establish product specifications favorable to its own products, and (e) providing uniquely integrated systems, vendors can generate repeat patronage beyong the original purchase.

[9] Consistent with Kriesberg (1956), the data suggests that concerns with retaining loyal customers and remaining competitive discourage vendors from raising prices when they get "hot items."

[10] This term was suggested to me by Dorothy Counts. The suggestiveness of "bargain" pricing may be further enhanced by providing other indicators of "cost cutting" merchandising (e.g., "deep discount," "warehouse," "bare bones" images). As with Veblen's (1899) notion of "conspicuous consumption," the clear implication is that "image sells."

References

Adler, P. (1981) *Momentum.* Beverly Hills, CA: Sage.

Adler, P.A. (1985) *Wheeling and Dealing.* New York, NY: Columbia University Press.

——— (1984) *The Social Dynamics of Financial Markets.* Greenwich, CT: Jal.

Anderson, P. (1983) "Marketing, scientific progress, and scientific method." *Journal of Marketing* 47(4): 18–31.

Berger, P. and T. Luckmann (1966) *The Social Construction of Reality.* New York: Anchor.

Bigus, O. (1972) "The milkman and his customers." *Urban Life and Culture* 1: 131–165.

Blumer, H. (1969) *Symbolic Interaction.* Englewood Cliffs, NJ: Prentice-Hall.

Browne, J. (1973) *The Used-Car Game: The Sociology of the Bargain.* Lexington, MA: Lexington Books.

Clark, R.E. and L.J. Halford (1978) "Going… going… gone: Preliminary observations on 'deals' at auctions." *Urban Life* 7:285–307.

Clinard, M.B. (1969) *The Black Market.* Montclair, NJ: Patterson-Smith.

——— and P.C. Yeager (1980) *Corporate Crime.* New York: Free Press.

Dean, J. (1976) "Pricing policies for new products." *Harvard Business Review* 54 (November-December): 141–153.

Donovan, F.R. (1929) *The Saleslady.* Chicago, IL: University of Chicago Press.

Edwards, W. (1954) "The theory of decision making." *Psychological Bulletin* 51:381–417.

Glick, I.O. (1957) *A Social Psychological Study of Futures Marketing.* Ph.D dissertation, University of Chicago.

Goffman, E. (1959) *Presentation of Self in Everyday Life.* New York: Anchor.

Haring, A. (1935) *Retail Price-Cutting and Its Control by Manufacturers.* New York: Arno Press.

Klockars, C.B. (1974) *The Professional Fence.* New York: Free Press.

Kriesberg, L. (1956) "Occupational controls among steel distributors." *American Journal of Sociology* 61:203–212.

Lambert, D.R. (1981) "Price as a duality cue in industrial buying." *Journal of the Academy of Marketing Science* 9(3): 227–238.

Lemert, E. (1953) "An isolation and closure theory of naive check forgery." *Journal of Criminal Law, Criminology and Police Science* 44:296–307.

Lilly, R. and R. Ball (1979) "Bidding and betting: The definitions of a good race horse and a closed community." Presented at the Mid-south Sociological Association.

Lynn, R.A. (1967) *Pricing Policies and Market Management.* Homewood, IL: Irwin.

Maisel, R. (1974) "The flea market as an action scene." *Urban Life and Culture* 2: 488–505.

Maisel, Roberta (1966) *The Antique Trade.*

University of California (Berkeley): M.A. Thesis. International Publishers (1967).

Mead, G.H. (1934) *Mind, Self and Society.* Chicago, IL: University of Chicago Press.

Miller, S.J. (1964) "The social base of sales behavior." *Social Problems* 12: 15–24.

Oxenfeldt, A.K. (1975) *Pricing Strategies.* New York: Amacon.

Phillips, L. and L.W. Stern (1977) "Limit pricing theory as a basis for anti-merger policy." *Journal of Marketing* 41:91–97.

Prus, R. (1984) "Purchasing products for resale: Assessing suppliers as 'partners-in-trade.'" *Symbolic Interaction* 7:249–277.

———— (1982) "Designating discretion and openness: The problematics of truthfulness in everyday life." *Canadian Review of Sociology and Anthropology* 19: 70–91.

———— (1975a) "Resisting designations: An extension of attribution theory into a negotiated context." *Sociological Inquiry* 45:31–41.

———— (1975b) "Labeling theory: A reconceptualization and propositional statement on typing." *Sociological Focus.* 8:79–96.

———— and S. Irini (1980) *Hookers, Rounders, and Desk Clerks: The Social Organization of the Hotel Community.* Toronto, Ontario: Gage.

Ralph, J. (1950) *Junk Business and the Junk Peddler.* M.A. Thesis, University of Chicago.

Riesz, P.C. (1978) "Price versus quality in the marketplace." *Journal of Retailing* 54 (Winter):15–28.

Scherer, F.M. (1970) *Industrial Purchasing.* Chicago: Rand-McNally.

Schutz, A. (1971) *Collected Papers 1: The Problem of Social Reality.* The Hague: Martinus Nijhoff.

Shapiro, B.P. (1968) "The psychology of pricing." *Harvard Business Review* 46(4): 14–25, 160.

Simmel, G. (1978) *The Philosophy of Money* (T. Bottomore and D. Frisby, trans.). London: Routledge and Kegan Paul. (originally published in 1900).

Small, A. (1914) "The social gradation of capital." *American Journal of Sociology* 19: 721–752.

Smith, C.W. (1981) *The Mind of the Market.* Totowa, NJ: Rowman and Littlefield.

Strodtbeck, F. and M. Sussman (1956) "Of time, the city, and the 'one-year guarantee': The relations between watch owners and repairers." *American Journal of Sociology* 61:602–609.

Sutherland, E. (1949) *White Collar Crime.* New York: Dryden.

Valdez, A. (1984) "Chicano used car dealers." *Urban Life* 13:229–246.

Veblen, T. (1899) *The Theory of the Leisure Class.* New York: MacMillan.

Weigand, R.E. (1980) "'Buying In' to market control." *Harvard Business Review* 58 (November-December): 141–149.

Wheatley, J.J., J.S.Y. Chiu, and A. Goldman (1981) "Physical quality, price, and perceptions of product quality: Implications for retailers." *Journal of Retailing* 57(2): 100–116.

Social Inequality

Introduction

Social inequality is any inequality that is socially consequential. Often, it is also an inequality rooted in social values or practices, not biology; and it is typically an inequality that makes itself consequential by the operation of social structures.

The study of social inequality includes such topics as unequal access to wealth, power and respect resulting from unequal conditions of birth, educational attainment, or social connections. Although people who are beautiful or tall receive more respect and a higher income, on the average, than people who are ugly and short, this kind of inequality will not concern us very much. Typically, sociologists have been more concerned about social inequality that can be influenced by legislation or collective action. Legislation can more readily reduce gender or racial discrimination, for example, than discrimination against the ugly or short. (Conceivably, discrimination against the ugly and short is also less consequential—affects fewer people less adversely—than discrimination against women and visible racial minorities.)

Not only are we concerned here with inequalities between individuals. We must also consider collective inequalities: inequalities between groups, regions, and even countries. We are interested in learning the processes by which some collectivities come to dominate others: upper classes over lower classes, richer regions over poorer regions, and industrial nations over pre-industrial nations, for example. These cannot be reduced to questions of individual psychology; the historical and political economic orientation of Canadian sociology is helpful here. Only by the historical study of political/economic relations between collectivities can we hope to understand why large-scale inequality exists in the forms it does today.

Various types of inequality will be explored in the remaining sections of this book. The next section will examine race and ethnic relations which are partly, though not wholly, understandable in the context of social inequality. A later section on gender relations will explore inequalities between males and females, documenting gender differences and trying to relate them to a broader theoretical perspective on inequality and stratification. A section on political and economic organization will be centrally concerned with macro and societal inequalities, and, especially, Canada's subordinate position in the world. Another section will explore the ways in which education shapes people's life chances. A section on work and occupations will consider how inequality is played out in the workplace. A section on communities and regions will explore why certain communities or regions dominate others. And finally, the section on social movements and social change will examine some of the ways people have reacted to social inequality in Canada.

Thus, the present section does not purport to say the last word on social inequality; it says only the first words. The section aims only to set out some of the general issues of research in this area, issues that will be considered at greater length in later sections.

The place to start is with the notion of "life chances." These are the chances we have to get the things we need for a happy, healthy secure life. Whatever shapes our life chances affects those things that are most necessary and most valued. Sociologists have found that people's life chances in this, and all other societies, are unequal. Some people have a greater chance of getting what they need and want than others do. True, this inequality of life chances varies from one society to another, and over time; but within any given society at a given moment, some people have a much better chance, and some a much worse chance, of a fulfilling life.

People have needs for food, shelter and bodily security that must be satisfied. The less these needs are satisfied, the fewer years people will survive. And, as certain developmental psychologists (e.g., Maslow, 1954) have argued, people may also have needs for belonging, sharing, creativity, and self-determination, without which their happiness and quality of life will be significantly reduced.

Class location will determine something as fundamental as how long you will live and, by implication, the probable quality of your life. Rich people are known to live longer, healthier lives than poor people. Reasons for this include differential opportunities for good nutrition, medical care, housing and rest; differential risks of injury on the job; and differential lifestyle risks including the likelihood of smoking or excess drinking, suffering too much stress, and not getting enough fresh air and exercise.

Aside from apparently universal needs for food, health, and safety, there are societally or culturally specific needs, largely learned in socialization and reinforced by school, church, and mass media. Here, certain kinds of "relative deprivations" are important. Relative deprivation is painful because the unequal opportunity for some good or status implies less personal worth, ensures less social integration and acceptance, and invites labeling as a deviant or oddball. Just because a deprivation is relative, not absolute, does not make it trivial. How we view ourselves, and others view us, is often more important to human beings than absolute deprivation. This fact is demonstrated by the willingness of saints and martyrs to risk their lives in order to appear moral to God, society, and themselves.

Thus the structuring of deprivation—both absolute and relative—is enormously consequential and, as we saw in the first section, a classic concern of sociology. For this reason, sociologists have spent much effort documenting and interrelating the varieties of inequality, trying to account for the cause, consequences and routes to change.

The first article in this section, by Paul Bernard and Jean Renaud, sets out a general picture of changing inequality in Quebec since the Second World War. What happened in Quebec is special in some respects, but in other ways it largely duplicates the experience throughout Canada. Notably, the economic growth of the 1950s and 1960s benefited everyone (although unequally) and reduced much of the pressure for a fundamental redistribution of wealth and opportunities. When growth slowed down in the 1970s, creating what the authors, following Thurow (1981), call a "zero-sum society," hardest hit were the poor and economically vulnerable. Lines of cleavage were sharpened, conflict intensified, and inequality became both more severe and more obvious. Redistribution, the classic concern of radical thinkers, became more obviously necessary. Whether government efforts to rekindle economic growth will succeed significantly, and, if successful, will quell the demands for a redistribution of wealth, remains to be seen.

The other four articles in this section are largely concerned with theorizing about the strategies different groups use to gain an advantage in a zero-sum situation. Though all the theories start from different premises and study different conflict situations, they reach similar conclusions. The place to begin our examination is with a general formulation of the problem.

Raymond Murphy attempts, in his article, to consolidate the insights of Weber, Collins, and Parkin in a general theory of "closure." If our concern is access to necessary resources for a good life, we must understand the processes that capture and dole out these resources. That is, we must understand power as an exclusionary code. Particular groups are able to set the conditions under which resources will be shared. To take a familiar example, access to high-paying jobs in industrial societies has increasingly required a "credential"—a testimonial, often in the form of an educational degree, that the possessor has completed certain courses and is, in this sense, qualified for selection. Degrees from medical and dental schools are particularly valuable; virtually no doctors or dentists are unemployed or poorly paid. The question of interest then is: who determines how these scarce resources, these degrees, will be handed out—to whom given, how many, and in return for what?

"Professionalization" is a process by which an occupational group comes to restrict entrance into its ranks. Professional groups like doctors and dentists have succeeded in limiting the numbers of incoming graduates and defining the conditions of service (including the prices demanded). Non-professional occupations have greater difficulty doing this. Some, like the teachers Murphy discusses, have unionized to achieve closure; but their efforts are less successful for a variety of reasons, including less public sympathy for unions than for professional associations, and a greater availability of eligible, appropriately skilled manpower. Closure is least easily achieved in what some have called the "marginal" labour force—jobs like clerk, waitress, or taxi driver—where workers exercise little control over entry into jobs or the remuneration they bring.

Professionalization is one kind of closure, but not the only one. Ethnic group cohesion is another. Job recruitment of people with identical ethnic backgrounds, and the rejection of all others, can be found in many workplaces, with the result that certain ethnic groups control certain industries. When an ethnic group captures and monopolizes a certain kind of economic activity, allowing access to that activity only or primarily on the basis of ethnic affiliation, it is practising closure.

Raymond Breton argues in his article that ethnic closure is maximized under conditions of what he calls "parallelism" (also referred to as "institutional completeness" in the next section). A high degree of parallelism threatens other ethnic communities, increasing the likelihood of conflict between them. This threat is both intensified and made more visible under conditions Professor Breton specifies, leading to a need for complicated social bargaining, often at the federal governmental level.

The extent of the resulting conflict will depend on the degree of overlapping of domains within which this conflict is going on. Ethnic closure on the field of activity that is outside the interest of other groups will incite the least conflict, for example. At the same time, mechanisms for regulating the conflict, for incorporating communal activities in larger societal activities, and for directly assimilating community members into the larger society will all play an important part in reducing threats to societal integration. Ethnic closure poses a danger to the whole society and may, therefore, in the long run, hurt the ethnic community member. But in the short run, closure in the form of parallelism provides a definite advantage for the group member.

Do social classes practise closure? A "social class" is a group of people with similar life chances. They may or may not be aware of their common characteristics and shared interests, and may or may not be taking conscious action on their own behalf. Is "closure," as Weber defines it, the general principle that sorts people into classes? Is it the way the ruling class rules and the reason why entry into the ruling class from below is so limited? And if so, are class relations simply a sub-category of all relations of inequality and not, as Marx argued, the uniquely determining form of social inequality? If social classes do function more or less like ethnic groups and occupational groups, in seeking to preserve membership advantage (but possibly using more varied and powerful means than most other collectivities can muster), then Max Weber is right: inequality has many roots. Inequality does not all trace back to relations of production and class exploitation, as Marx asserted. Whether or not Weber (and Murphy) are right on this point is extremely important to our general understanding of inequality.

R. Jack Richardson's article on the merchants and industrialists of Toronto in the 1920s is explicitly focused on a differ-

ent theme: namely, on explaining why Canadian industry developed with imported and not with indigenous (Canadian) capital, and later, through the creation of branch plants of American industry. Professor Richardson examines the theory that this was due to class fragmentation among elites, such that merchants (with capital) and local industrialists (needing capital) were not only different people, but had different and opposing interests. He explicitly argues against this theory, with persuasive evidence. But, by emphasizing the importance of access to capital, he also implicitly addresses closure theory. Closure proves to be important not only *between* classes but also *within* classes (or between class fragments). Understanding whether, how, and why class fragments co-operate will necessarily be part of a general theory of inequality.

The final selection in this section is drawn from John Porter's classic work, *The Vertical Mosaic* (1965). The second half of that book, like Richardson's article, discusses relations among Canada's ruling elites. Like Richardson, Professor Porter discusses the many connections among these elites. Unlike Richardson, he emphasizes their diverse interests in the face of common class experiences and a shared commitment to the capitalist system.

In the first part of his book, from which we have drawn an article for this section, Professor Porter discusses the role of education in shaping the occupational and class attainment of middle-class Canadians. Educational degrees are unlikely to get a middle-class Canadian (much less a working-class Canadian) into the ruling elites; but they do increase the chances of mobility within the middle class. Education and mobility concern Porter for a variety of reasons. First, he sees mobility as desirable because it is fair: it is (at the best of times) a reward for merit. Porter feels that education has, for too long, been restricted to those families who already enjoy wealth and comfort; education and opportunity for upward mobility should be shared more widely. Second, he sees education and mobility as socially necessary: as the basis for an informed citizenry and an efficient work force in an industrial (and even post-industrial) society. Canadian economic and social development demands the best use of its "human capital," its trained people. Education for everyone facilitates, if not ensures, such an efficient use of manpower.

Finally, and no less important, Porter sees education as a mechanism for reducing inequalities between ethnic groups, thereby increasing assimilation and national unity. Porter believes ethnic ties limit the opportunity and aspiration for higher education. Ethnic minorities should be encouraged to get their brightest people educated and active in the central social institutions; they should not perpetuate, by self-imposed closure, the same job activities that were forced on them when they immigrated to Canada.

More will be said along these lines in the section on race and ethnic relations, especially in the article by Gordon Darroch. At this point, we should note the following. First, education represented to Porter an important mechanism of social closure and hence inequality in Canadian society. Committed to more equality, greater productivity, and ethnic assimilation, Porter had to favour offering more educational opportunity to Canadians from the middle and working classes. Second, Porter's theory

came at the right moment in Canadian history. The publication in 1965 of *The Vertical Mosaic* came just at the time the baby boom—that massive wave of births starting around 1947 and peaking around 1957—was reaching university. Porter's call for more educational opportunity coincided with a surging demand for university spaces and more liberal social policies on campus. Thus Porter was able to participate, both as theorist and government advisor, in expanding and liberalizing post-secondary education in Canada.

The section on Education and the Schools carries this theme further, with an article by Porter (on the socioeconomic necessity for higher education) and several other articles, especially James Richardson's, indicating the fundamental flaw in Porter's optimistic argument. By the end of his life in 1979, Porter no longer believed that education could ensure mobility, nor that mobility could ensure a better, fairer society. His article here should, therefore, be viewed in a special way. It is, first of all, a characteristic early statement by a scholar whom many regard as Canada's foremost sociologist. Second, it states a view that, for at least a decade, many policy-makers and sociologists endorsed whole-heartedly; a view debated vigorously for a much longer time, and by many more scholars, than scholarly views usually are. Porter's contribution is historically important for having set the terms of debate about education and mobility for nearly two decades.

References

Maslow, Abraham "Hierarchy of human needs." In *Motivation and Personality*. New York: Harper and Row, 1954.

Porter, John *The Vertical Mosaic: An Analysis of Social Class and Power in Canada*. Toronto: University of Toronto Press, 1965.

Thurow, Lester C. *The Zero-Sum Society: Distribution and the Possibilities for Economic Clause*. New York: Penguin Books, 1981.

26 Stratification and Conflict Between Ethnolinguistic Communities with Different Social Structures

Raymond Breton

RAYMOND BRETON, Professor of Sociology at the University of Toronto, specializes in the study of ethnic relations and organizational behaviour. His books include *Social and Academic Factors in the Career Decisions of Canada Youth* (1972); *Why Disunity? An Analysis of Linguistic and Regional Cleavages in Canada*, with Albert Breton (1980); *Cultural Boundaries and the Cohesion of Canada*, with Jeffrey Reitz, Victor Valentine and Daiva Stasiulis (1980); and *La Langue de Travail au Québec* (1981). Recent research has focused on the intra-community organization of ethnic groups and networks of contact across groups. A Fellow of the Royal Society of Canada, Professor Breton has served as Editor of *Canadian Review of Sociology and Anthropology* and in many other important professional roles.

... There are two broad classes of characteristics of ethnic communities that are particularly important, at least in the present context. One pertains to the pattern of differentiation between ethnic communities. It is crucial: it is indeed difficult to understand the processes of intergroup relations unless the analysis takes account of the ways in which ethnic communities are structurally differentiated from one another. The second set of characteristics pertains to the group's capacity for concerted action; that is, to its capacity to act collectively either in relation to internal circumstances or in relation to circumstances in its sociopolitical environment. This set of factors constitutes the dynamic component of intergroup relations.

The present essay deals primarily with the first set of characteristics—patterns of differentiation—and its implications for ethnic stratification and for societal integration. In the concluding section, some observations will be made on the second class of characteristics and its relevance.

PARALLEL SOCIAL NETWORKS AND INSTITUTIONS

A critical dimension of ethnic differentiation has to do with the extent to which the ethnic communities have parallel social networks and institutions. This dimension has to do with the character of the social and institutional boundaries between groups. We will refer to the degree of social enclosure and compartmentalization that exists between ethnic communities.[1]

Enclosure refers to the structure of social relations among the members of a society; to the existence of separate networks of social relations. It refers, first, to the existence of social boundaries between groups and to mechanisms for the maintenance of these boundaries. Second, it refers to a particular pattern in the contours of such boundaries. Indeed, enclosure involves a certain superimposition of social boundaries, or perhaps more accurately, the containment of the many networks of social affiliations within the boundaries of an inclusive system of ethnic boundaries. The limits of various social networks tend to coincide with the more inclusive ethnic boundaries.

Compartmentalization refers to the related structure of institutions and organizations, to the extent to which each ethnic community has a set of institutions of its own. It refers to its degree of institutional completeness (Breton, 1964). This does not necessarily imply culturally distinct institutions and practices. Compartmentalization is not a statement about cultural pluralism; rather it is a statement about the locus of the institutional authority and clientele. For example, parallel educational structures refer to the fact that there are at least two sets of educational organizations serving ethnically different clienteles and under the control of ethnically different elites. Since both the clientele and the elite are defined in terms of the lines of ethnic segmentation, the processes of compartmentalization and of enclosure reinforce each other.

The degree of parallelism in societal networks and institutions can vary considerably: when it is very high, we essentially have sub-societies in relation to one another; when it is very low, we have ethnic social formations on a purely situational basis. The communities existing as sub-societies tend to have continuity and tradition, autonomy, organization and common affairs (Smith, 1974:93–94). Those existing as situational formations tend to be based on personal experience and therefore to lack historical continuity; they also tend to exist within larger units and therefore to lack autonomous organization and to have few, if any, common affairs. There are perhaps few ethnic communities to be found at each of these extremes; but most tend to come closer to one of the polar types than to the other.

Parallelism, on the other hand, may exhibit more than variations in degree; it may vary in the range of areas of social life involved as well as in the particular mix. Few or many

of the different types of social relations may be segmented; few or many of the different domains of organizational activity may be compartmentalized.

It should be noted that, seen from the point of view of the individuals involved, the degree of parallelism has to do with the extent to which a person's life can, potentially at least, be absorbed in his own ethnic community. . . .

IMPLICATIONS FOR ETHNIC STRATIFICATION

The degree of segmentation has several implications for the structure and processes of inter-group relations. In a very general way, these implications have to do with the fact that a high degree of parallelism entails interaction between institutions and their organizational apparatus in some domains of social activity while a low degree involves the interaction between individuals, small groups, or cohorts of individuals within various social and institutional contexts. Those variations manifest themselves in varying degrees and forms; they also manifest themselves in different components of social activity and organization. In this section, I will explore briefly some of the implications of a high and of a low degree of parallelism for certain aspects of stratification between groups.

1/ The stratification of individuals or of organizations. A basic difference between high and low degrees of segmentation has to do with the unit of stratification: under low parallelism, it is primarily individuals or cohorts of individuals that are being ranked within the institutional system, while under high segmentation, it is also the organizations that are being ranked. That is to say, the greater the degree of parallelism in a particular domain of activity (economic, political, educational, etc.), the more issues of inequality will tend to involve the relative status of the organizations of each ethnic community and their position in the over-all institutional structure. Conversely, the lower the parallelism, the more the issues of inequality will tend to have to do with the status of individuals in the society at large and in its institutions and with the conditions for individual participation and advancement in the institutional systems. . . .

The socioeconomic status of an individual is always the function of his own position with regard to dimensions of stratification such as occupation, property, education, as well as of the position of the organizations to which he belongs in the institutional system. By virtue of his occupation, a university professor occupies a certain position in the social hierarchy; but his position also depends on the status of the department in which he is teaching and on the status of the university in which the department is located. Thus, in order to improve his situation, the professor can change jobs; but he may aso try to raise the status of his department; or he may do both. As will be seen later, those two problems require different types of strategies and resources.

In the present context, the situations considered are those where the organizational differentiation is along ethnic lines in contrast with those where it is not; that is, situations of ethnic institutional parallelism and situations involving a unique institutional structure (in particular domains of social activity). When there is ethnic parallelism, a member of an ethnic community may attempt to improve his status by moving up the occupational hierarchy; but if his ethnic groups is relatively disfavoured, he will be limited by the status of its organizations and face the prospect of having to change the condition of the organization in order to improve his own status any further.

2/ The segmentation of labour markets.[2] . . . Parallel ethnic labour markets may exist with their own set of institutions and networks through which information and influence flow: newspapers, placement agencies, social clubs, professional associations, "old boy networks," and so on.[3]

One of the important characteristics of labour market networks (personal and organizational) is that they tend to ramify throughout a wide range of segments of the social structure: an occupationally relevant contact may occur at church, in the extended family, in professional meetings, on the golf course, in voluntary associations, in the neighbourhood, and so on. If then, the degree of institutional and social parallelism is high, the two (or more) labour markets may hardly intersect at all; that is, they will also tend to be parallel to each other. In such a situation, the members of the different ethnic communities are connected to different sub-markets and as a result benefit from different flows of information and influence. Conversely, if parallelism is low, the members of the different communities will tend to participate in a unique labour market or in different labour markets with many points of intersection. Another way of putting it is to say that in the first instance, the cost of getting information about and access to certain opportunies is highly associated with one's ethnic identification, while in the other, the costs tend to be associated almost exclusively with non-ethnic factors.

3/ Race and language as compounding factors. If some degree of parallelism of organizations or of labour markets exists in a society, it may be to the advantage of a particular individual to orient himself towards one set of organizations or one labour market and to avoid the other. That is to say, in relation to a particular organizational network and labour market, a person's ethnicity may be more or less an asset or a liability; it may be useful or harmful for connecting and integrating oneself to a particular ethnic subsystem.

An important circumstance in this regard is the degree of choice a person has in concealing his ethnic identity or in relegating it to the private sphere of his life. The degree of choice may be determined through legally imposed restrictions, through informal social processes, or through the use of ideological weapons. It may also depend on features of the differentiating characteristics: visible physical characteristics of significance in a culture and linguistic ability[4] (if the parallelism involves language differences) can reduce considerably the person's possibilities of manoeuvre in connection with his ethnic identification. As a result, differences in physical characteristics and in language may reinforce the parallelism and its impact.

4/ Types of factors related to mobility. Social mobility under high and low degrees of parallelism does not depend on the same kinds of factors and processes (although there is some overlap). When parallelism is high, the concern is with those factors affecting the status of organizations and organizational systems; when it is low, it is with the factors affecting the status of individuals within an institutional system.

The position of an individual in the stratification system depends on factors such as his social origin, his educational attainment, his mental and social abilities, his personality attributes, his connections, and the interaction of these personal attributes with the various kinds of opportunities and constraints to which he becomes exposed at one point or another of his career. The person is involved in the labour market and is subject to the structure of that market and to the mechanisms operating in it. Ethnic stratification in this context refers to the situation of members of different ethnic groups in relation to the structure of the labour market and to the resources that determine one's position in it.

The position of an organization in the institutional structure, however, depends on somewhat different sets of resources. One of the most important determinants is the extent of its access to the capital market; another is its access to technology and to means of technological innovation. The situation of the organization also depends on its relation

to the labour market as a buyer of labour (rather than as a seller as in the case of individuals) and on its position in the structure of the market for the distribution of products and services. Ethnic stratification in such a context refers to the differential access to resources that determine the formation of organizations, their growth, and their position in relation to other organizations.

Under high parallelism, the interest would tend to be in organizational control rather than in the conditions of individual mobility as such.[5] The concern is at least with organizational survival if not with organizational growth. Basically an ethnic sub-society tends to concern itself with the control and growth of the means for generating wealth, prestige, and power and not simply with the position of its members with respect to the distribution of wealth, prestige, and power. On the other hand, in a community with little or no parallel institutional system, the concern will be with the position of its members in the over-all occupational structure and income distribution.[6] In short, in one instance the problems are those of economic development of different ethnic communities; in the other, they are those of the social mobility in an institutional system of people of different ethnic origins.

In Canada, communities such as the French in Quebec, the Acadians, those of British origin in Quebec and in the rest of Canada, and the Native peoples represent fairly high degrees of parallelism—social and institutional—relative to one another. In contrast, most other ethnic communities constituted through the usual processes of individual or family migration involve low degrees of parallelism. The problems of stratification and mobility would then be quite different for these different communities.

These problems can be looked at from the point of view of the communities or from the point of view of the individuals involved. From the point of view of the community, one problem is the choice between more or less parallelism; should it build and expand its institutional system or not? Should it attempt to build it in all spheres of activity or limit itself to a few? . . .

Once parallelism has been opted for, at least to a degree, then the relevant questions are those that pertain to the acquisition of control over the means necessary for the formation and expansion of organizations and organizational systems; access to capital and markets for goods and services, required institutional autonomy, political and economic conditions for taking advantage of the resources of one's territory, and so on.

These issues are somewhat different when looked at from the point of view of the individuals involved. One consequence of organizational parallelism and of segmented labour markets along ethnic lines is that the socioeconomic status of an individual is tied to the status of the ethnic community to which he belongs—more so than in the case under conditions of low parallelism. And this for two reasons. First, as indicated above, one can raise one's status by contributing to an improvement in the socioeconomic condition of one's organization (e.g., increased productivity, expansion) because one's status depends in part on the status of one's organization and of the economy of the community as a whole.

The second reason is related to the segmentation of the labour market. Suppose an individual is dissatisfied with his present position. If he imputes his relatively poor condition to the particular job in which he is and how it fits his tastes and potential, he will try to change jobs. In order to change jobs, he will first use the resources available to him through the networks to which he is connected. This exploration may have different results: (a) he may find what he is looking for—thus reinforcing the parallelism; (b) he may find this network unsatisfactory in the sense that it leads to limited opportunities and try his chance in the "other" labour market. If successful, he will integrate into the

other network and contribute to reduce the parallelism, but this may trigger reactions on the part of institutional elites and on the part of those remaining in the community who see the overall strength of their institutions being slowly eroded. (c) But, if the "other" network is relatively closed, there is a relatively low probability of such an integration. In such an event, the individual would have an interest in supporting activities aimed at reinforcing or expanding the institutional system to which he is already (or best) connected and hence increase his own (or his children's) life chances. If this appears to have a low probability of success, he would then have an interest in supporting activities aimed at breaking open the relatively closed labour market under the control of the "other" group.

IMPLICATIONS FOR SOCIETAL INTEGRATION

Conflict Between Ethnic Communities

Variations in the degree of parallelism among ethnic communities affect not only the dimensions of the stratification among them but also the character of the power and conflict interactions that occur among them. In order to formulate hypotheses on this aspect of intergroup relationships, it is useful to distinguish, as Bachrach and Baratz (1962) argue should be done, the two faces of power, namely the structuring or definition of the issues and alternatives and the conflict over those alternatives. . . .

The general hypothesis I am formulating is that the degree of parallelism has an impact on the kinds of matters that become issues between ethnic communities as well as on the character of the accompanying social bargaining processes taking place between them. The following are a few hypotheses in this regard:

1/ The greater the parallelism (that is, the more institutionally complete an ethnic community), the more it is likely to represent a threat to other communities and, as a consequence, the more the very existence of a parallel institutional system or the conditions necessary for its maintenance or expansion become objects of conflict between the communities involved and an area for the exercise of power between them. That is to say, the legal and administrative arrangements and the social conditions that prevent, hinder, or facilitate the organization and expansion of the institutional system can become matters of controversy and power conflicts between ethnic communities. This, of course, is especially the case if, for example, because of its large size the development of an institution on the part of a community would imply the social, economic, or political ascendancy of that community in the society as a whole or in a particular area of activity. This is the case in South Africa, in Rhodesia, and in a number of southern states in the USA. It has also been the case in Canada, especially during the period of our history where the French were a numerical majority: in those instances, the conflicts are basically over the attempts on the part of one of the communities to maintain or expand its institutional system on the one hand and the attempts on the part of the others to weaken the other group's organizational strength or to hinder its further development.

There are several conditions that a collectivity can attempt to affect in order to maintain or expand the institutional system that it controls. Among those conditions are the following:

(a) The conditions related to gaining access to resources that can be used for the formation or expansion of organizations, that is capital resources as opposed to consumer resources. The case of the Dene nation in the Northwest Territories is a good illustration of this: there has been a dramatic shift in their concern from an emphasis on various forms of social and economic assistance to individuals to an emphasis on benefits from natural resources that can be used for further economic development. . . .

(b) Since language is an instrument of institutional control, he who imposes the linguistic rules in a particular situation has established ascendancy in that situation. Modifying the linguistic rules of the game can be seen as an attempt on the part of a linguistic community to maintain or expand its institutional domain. This is usually what language legislation is fundamentally about. This is not to minimize the cultural role of language nor its importance as a symbol of group identification. But culture and social symbols do not exist in the abstract; nor do they exist only in the private lives of individuals. They become embedded in and sustained by the institutional system of a community. The linguistic dimension serves to illustrate that maintaining or expanding the control of an institutional system (or segments of it) is related to both the material and symbolic aspects of ethnic stratification.

There are also a multiplicity of ways in which an ethnic community can attempt to prevent or hinder the institutional development of another. It is beyond the scope of this paper to explore all the mechanisms used. However, three types of procedures can be mentioned:

(a) Eliminating or restricting the right of association. This rather direct mechanism has been frequently used either by passing legislation to that effect or by the threat or use of economic, social, or physical sanctions.

(b) Preventing, if possible, the ethnic community from acquiring a territorial basis. This can involve legislation aimed at restricting the purchasing of land by members of certain ethnic groups or other mechanisms designed to prevent or limit the settlement of a certain area.

(c) Attempts can also be made to establish an ethnic community as a political or administrative dependency. In this way, the development of a corporate organization can be closely controlled. The case of Indian reservations in Canada is a good example of such a mechanism.

The main point I wish to make here, however, does not concern specific mechanisms; rather, I wish to emphasize that when ethnic communities have some elements of an institutional system, the very conditions for the existence of such a system, let alone its expansion, are likely to become the object of a power confrontation between them. I would also hypothesize that the mutual concern for the relative strength of their institutional systems constitutes the source of the more intense conflicts between ethnic communities and the object of the most severe uses of power.

2/ Closely related to the formation and maintenance of an institutional system in one or more domains of activity is the question of the sphere of jurisdiction. It can be hypothesized that the greater the degree of institutional parallelism, the more conflicts and exercise of power between the communities in contact will involve issues concerning the spheres of jurisdiction, that is, the delineation of the respective domains of organizational activity. The domains can be defined in terms of activities or population areas. An ethnic community or a segment of it that has developed or is developing an organization in a particular field will want to be recognized as such by other communities. This follows from the very motivation to organize, especially on the part of elites. The process of becoming recognized involves the definition of the activities over which each will have jurisdiction and the definition of the population over which each will have authority, or that it will represent. Moreover, the process can also involve the issue of whether the jurisdiction will be total or partial. Such issues can be raised by an ethnic local of a labour organization; by the segment of a political party in an ethnic area; by ethnic parishes as in the case of a number of so-called "national parishes" in Canada or the United States, and so on.

A basic condition for the sphere of jurisdiction to become an issue or a source of conflict is a "zero-sum" situation, that is a situation where the expansion of the sphere of jurisdiction for one unit involves a corresponding reduction for the other unit. (I am, incidentally, making the assumption that, since the situation of organizational members and especially of the elites in terms of income, prestige, and power depends on the condition of their organization, they will not willingly accept a reduction in its sphere of jurisdiction. I am also assuming a relationship between the sphere of jurisdiction and the amount of rewards available to its members. Not only will organizational members and leaders not accept a reduction, but it will frequently be in their interest to expand the sphere of jurisdiction either in terms of activities, of population, or both.) . . .

When members of an ethnic community have little or no institutional system, the relevant "sphere of jurisdiction" concerns individual activities and mobility (horizontal or vertical). That is, the issues that may arise in such situations concern existing limitations on individual actions or the protection of existing rights and prerogatives. Issues concerning discrimination in the labour market against individual members of an ethnic group constitute an example. In other words, when institutional parallelism is low, the issues that arise between ethnic communities tend to have to do with individual civil rights and with the set of opportunities available to individuals of different ethnic origins and with the constraints they have to overcome in the pursuit of their life goals. In short, the issues have to do with the conditions necessary for full citizenship; for full participation of individuals in the institutional system of the society. On the other hand, if parallelism is high, the issues that tend to come up are those pertaining to what participants consider as group rights and with the resources necessary for institutional building, maintenance, and expansion.

3/ The greater the social and institutional ethnic parallelism in a society, the more the structure of the political system, especially the central one, become objects of controversy and power confrontations. In modern societies at least, the state apparatus is a critical instrument for institutional building, either in economic, educational, or cultural spheres. That is to say, it is the main organ for the mobilization of resources, material and social, for collective ventures. It is thus almost inevitable that an ethnic community with an institutional system will attempt to appropriate itself the state apparatus or some of its powers and use it for its own institutional objectives. It is also equally inevitable that other organized ethnic communities will resist such attempts at self-appropriation. As a result, the structure of the state apparatus tends to be a regular object of conflict between organized ethnic communities. This is one reason why in societies with a high degree of parallelism, such matters as the constitution, the distribution of powers, the composition of the bureaucracy, and the selection of political party leaders tend to regularly become matters of interethnic controversy. . . .

Modes of Incorporation in the Society

. . . It follows from the previous discussion that, in one instance, we are dealing with processes whereby organizations are incorporated in an institutional structure, while in the other we are dealing with processes whereby individuals become full-fledged members of the society. Obviously, the processes involved will tend to be different: incorporating, for example, the children of a cohort of immigrants in a school poses a different kind of demand on the educational institution than would be incorporation of an ethnic school. From one's experience in Canada, it is also easy to sense that the incorporation of cohorts of immigrants in the political parties, government agencies, and bureaucracies is not quite the same kind of phenomena as the incorporation of an ethnic group that disposes of a formal political structure for corporate action. One situation invoves cohorts of individuals while the other involves organizational structures, and the adjustments that the political system has to make for their incorporation is quite different in each instance.

Threats to societal integration stem from difficulties in or the failure to achieve incorporation. A cohort of disadvantaged individuals whose aspirations for whatever life goals they happen to value are systematically thwarted represent one type of frustration and one source of pressure for change in the event it becomes mobilized. On the one hand, organizational elites, potential elites, and would-be entrepreneurs who see their organizations as being disadvantaged in the sense of having poor or no chance for growth; who experience limited access to capital and other necessary organizational resources; who feel the low status and power of their organizations and who see limited possibilities of ameliorating the situation usually experience a different type of frustration and represent a source of pressure for a different kind of institutional change.

Generally, in one case societal integration is fostered through structures and mechanisms facilitating the participation of individuals of different ethnic origins in societal institutions and the attainment of their personal goals; in the other case it is fostered through structural accommodations and exchanges that facilitate the existence and growth of institutional structures with which members of ethnic communities are identified. . . .

CONCLUSION

In this essay, I have tried to show that the problems of ethnic stratification and of societal integration can be quite different under different degrees of parallelism. By way of conclusion, I would like to mention some other characteristics of ethnic communities that can interact with the degree of parallelism and as a result tend to accentuate or modify the situations and processes discussed above. These characteristics are those that pertain to the group's capacity for concerted action. The problems of conflict, interorganizational bargaining, and definition of domains of jurisdiction are no doubt accentuated when the communities involved are well organized for sociopolitical action. The threat they represent to each other's traditional domains is more serious if the capacity for concerted action is high. On the other hand, the organization that this capacity represents may make it easier to engage in a bargaining process resulting in new arrangements.

Under conditions of low parallelism, the sources of tensions between communities tend to be more situational and tend to involve individuals—either individually or grouped in associations—rather than institutional systems. The capacity for concerted action in such instances tends to manifest itself in interest-group associations concerned with specific issues.

There are many factors that are related to the capacity for concerted action of ethnic communities. First, there is the type and amount of resources at their disposal. Resources refer to items such as demographic factors, material assets, solidarity, symbols of identification, and commitment to a cause.[7] Second, there are the factors pertaining to the social organization of the ethnic community. Among these, the most important appear to be the following:

(*a*) The first mechanisms for collective action are required. These include mechanisms for the collection and processing of information about the community, its population, its social, economic, and political situation,

its resources; procedures for and the organizational channels through which issues can be raised and various points of view expressed; and procedures for reaching decisions and implementing them. It also involves an appropriate network of communication, especially between the leadership and the members of the community or segments of it. . . .

(*b*) The structure of authority is also important; that is, the set of roles vested with the authority required to make the above mechanisms operational.

(*c*) A related feature is the presence or absence of an institutionally differentiated political function, that is of specifically governmental organizations. In some ethnic communities, concerted action is organized through religious institutions; in others, cultural institutions (e.g., mass media, cultural associations) incorporate the collective decision-making function. But in others, there are political and administrative structures. In some communities, there are various social elites playing a political role, but no political elite as such, while in others both types of elites exist.

(*d*) Another aspect of the capacity for concerted action concerns the ability to motivate and/or to constrain members of the community to participate and provide the necessary inputs of effort, time, and financial resources.

(*e*) The degree of autonomy in the organization of action is also important. Communication networks may exist; mechanisms and procedures for collecting information and reaching decisions may be in place; means of social control may be available; but the use of these various elements of organization by the elite of a group may be subject to more or less extensive external controls. An ethnic organization may have a "client" relationship to another organization, depending on it for a significant part of its funds or of its technical expertise. The capacity for concerted action of such an organization is limited by whatever the interests of the "patron" organization happens to be.

(*f*) Finally, a certain consensus among the segments of the community about what constitutes a matter for collective action or about the definition and choice of alternatives as to what needs to be done is necessary. . . .

Mechanisms must exist for the formulation of superordinate goals if any concerted action is to occur.

It would be useful to explore further the impact of the capacity for concerted action on ethnic stratification and on the character and degree of societal integration, especially as variations in this capacity occur in conditions of high, in contrast to low, ethnic parallelism. It has been the objective of this essay to show that if the analysis of such phenomena as the degree of ethnic stratification and the degree and mode of incorporation of ethnic communities in the society takes account of the existing patterns of structural differentiation, it is likely to yield useful results both from a theoretical and from a policy perspective. . . .

Notes

[1] These two concepts are similar to those used by Van den Berghe (1969:67) to define a "plural" society. See also Schermerhorn (1970).

[2] The discussion bears on labour markets, but could be extended to other types of organizational memberships, their sources, and mechanisms of recruitment.

[3] On the functioning of labour market institutions and their role, see Migué (1970), Granovetter (1974), Stigler (1962).

[4] Language is relevant in two ways: as a symbol of ethnic identification and as an instrument of communication. Under social and institutional parallelism along linguistic lines, the latter aspect appears more critical than the first.

[5] A critical problem is to account for the fact that this interest centres in a particular sphere (cultural, political, economic) rather than another. This is beyond the scope of this paper.

[6] If the obstacles to the improvement of the condition of individuals are enormous, there will be an incentive to build a parallel institutional system. However, the existing pattern of dominance may prevent the actualization of such an incentive. For a further discussion, see Albert Breton and Raymond Breton (forthcoming).

[7] See Coleman (1969) and Clark (1973) for a discussion of types of resources and their interrelationships, such as their convertibility into each other.

References

Bachrach, P. and M. Baratz (1962) "Two faces of power," *Canadian Political Science Review* 56:947–52.

Breton, R. (1964) "Institutional completeness of ethnic communities and the personal relations of immigrants." *American Journal of Sociology* 70:193–205.

Breton, A., and R. Breton (Forthcoming) *The Dynamics of Canadian Disunity: A Socio-economic Perspective.*

Clark, T.N. (1973) *Community Power and Policy Outputs: A Review of Urban Research.* Beverley Hills: Sage Publications

Coleman, J.S. (1969) "Race relations and social change." In I. Katz and P. Gurin (eds.), *Race and the Social Sciences.* New York: Basic Books

Granovetter, M.S. (1974) *Getting a Job.* Cambridge Mass.: Harvard University Press.

Migué, J.L. (1970) "Le nationalisme, l'unité nationale et la théorie économique de l'information." *Revue Canadienne d'Economique 111:* 183–98.

Smith, M.G. (1974) *Corporations and Society.* London: Duckworth.

Stigler, G.J. (1962) "Information in the labor market." *Journal of Political Economy* 70:94–105.

Schermerhorn, R.A. (1970) *Comparative Ethnic Relations: A Framework for Theory and Research.* New York: Random House.

Van den Berghe, P.L. (1969) "Pluralism and the polity: a theoretical exploration." In L. Kuper and M.G. Smith (eds.), *Pluralism in Africa.* Berkeley: University of California Press.

27 The New Shape of Inequality

Paul Bernard   Jean Renaud

PAUL BERNARD, Professor titulaire in Sociology at the University of Montreal, specializes in the study of inequality, careers, and social mobility. His recent work includes "Quebec-Poland: similarities and differences in social mobility and income distribution," with J. Renaud (1985); "Education et premier emploi: une relation inflationniste," with A. Allaire and J. Renaud (1981); and "Places et agents: les divisions sexuelle et ethnique du travail au Quebec de 1931 à 1981," with J. Renaud (1984). He has recently completed sociological comparisons of Quebec and Belgium, with J. Renaud.

JEAN RENAUD, Professor adjoint at the University of Montreal, has collaborated with Paul Bernard on a number of papers about work, careers, and social mobility. Other interests include the study of voting behaviour, linguistic stratification, and the uses of qualitative methodologies.

"There are limits to growth; what some appropriate, others must surrender."

There is no such thing as a purely economic crisis. Society enters crisis when established ways of doing things become imcompatible with new circumstances, economic or otherwise; when the old "social contract" no longer holds. Society enters crisis when changes and gaps appear in traditional relationships between segments: economic powers, middle classes, union and nonunion workers; public and private sectors; old and new elites; sexual or ethnic groups; etc. Society enters crisis when fundamental shifts in the production and control of wealth threaten patterns of income distribution. It enters crisis when social inequality sharpens or assumes new forms; when palliative measures no longer cushion social injustice; when its plans come to be set in an uncertain future.

The social, political, and ideological—as well as economic—dimensions of the cur-

rent crisis can only be grasped by putting it in historical perspective.

Since the 1940s the Québec labour market has gone through three major phases. A model for the distribution of education, employment, and income typifies each period. These models specify the conditions under which agreement and compromise are possible between social groups.

THREE PHASES SINCE THE 1940s

Phase 1—An asymmetric society

During the forties and fifties education, professional status, and income were distributed on the same strongly asymmetric basis. Most workers were poorly educated, held blue-collar jobs which were often unskilled, and earned little; opposite this mass stood the privileged few, those at the top of their particular sector; between these two extremes there was scarcely a middle layer. This was the Québec of the Plouffes and of local solidarities, of the working class's defensive pride in French-Canadian tradition; while it

Paul Bernard and Jean Renaud, "Les nouveaux visages de l'inegalité," trans. Jack Veugelers, in *Le Devoir*, 4 February 1982, p. 18. By permission of the publisher.

had the advantage of demographic strength and homogeneity, it lacked economic weight and control.

Phase II—Sharing the surplus

A completely different society appeared with the late fifties and the sixties. Growth in capitalist economies increased differences of education, employment, and income in the work force. Significant intermediate social strata emerged, running from highly skilled workers through different levels of white-collar workers to technicians and semi-professionals. The asymmetric society's polarization gave way to the fine-grained professional and economic stratification of a work force increasingly ranked and differentiated by education.

Was this the American Dream come true, an egalitarian middle-class society with the wealthy and those left behind by progress perched on its periphery? Not at all. Although middle classes now existed, social inequality had not disappeared. Growth in general prosperity, as reflected in increased buying power, certainly reduced the relative number of workers at the bottom of the pay scale. But at the same time social differentiation intensified because those who were already privileged profited further when surplus was shared. If, in the Québec of the Quiet Revolution, there was something for everyone, everyone did not benefit equally: heightened relative disparities hid behind absolute overall gains.

Phase III—Zero-sum redistribution

Today's labour market has been changing in directions which were already partly visible during the mid-seventies. While growth has not stopped, it is now very limited. As a consequence, surplus-sharing has increasingly been replaced by the reallocation of available income: a zero-sum game in which some must surrender what others appropriate. Whether

jobs or income are involved, there is currently less room for manoeuvre. Confrontations have sharpened, while alliances are more fragile; austerity measures coexist with the highest standard of living ever seen in Québec. Inequalities which were present but hidden during Phase II now stand out clearly, accompanied by new and contradictory words: rationalization, restraint, cuts.

TWO TRANSITIONS

Change from one type of society to another, or from one phase to another, cannot happen overnight. Since the various components of a situation change at different speeds, and readjustment takes time, there are periods of transition.

Shifts in the relationship between education and work predominated during the transition from Phases I to II. The educational system underwent extensive reforms; it had to adjust to a jump in school attendance, following early signs of growth during the previous decade. Starting in 1960, cohorts entering the job market were markedly better-educated than in the past, and education increasingly determined their career prospects. The young were therefore the first to reflect the emerging model of social organization, while older, less educated cohorts experienced severe competition.

Alongside these developments, job qualifications diversified, while Québec's public sector, a bastion for Francophones excluded from large private enterprises, expanded far more quickly than the rest of the labour market. Little seemed to contradict the familiar belief that education and income went hand in hand.

While the transition from Phases I to II was accompanied by high spirits, the gradual descent into stagnation between Phases II to III translated into crisis. The first sign that things had changed came when inflation hit education. Education certainly remained the prime determinant of career opportunities, but more and more of it became necessary to attain given occupational or income levels. In other words, those who had completed any given educational program (apart from the few with university degrees) found themselves headed for jobs with increasingly lower status. According to these modified rules of the game, new arrivals had to run faster and faster just to keep up.

However, this was only one among many dimensions of a crisis which gradually spread until it pervaded society at the beginning of the eighties.

FEATURES OF THE CURRENT CRISIS

Three imprtant phenomena prevailed during this second transition, and became established during Phase III. In the first place, economic uncertainty resulting from the energy crisis was so disabling that normal methods of macro-economic planning and management became useless. Growth was nil, if not negative, in areas such as job creation.

In the second place, during the seventies the labour force ballooned with the entry of baby boomers and increasing numbers of women into the job market. In the third place, the financial crisis affecting nearly all the Western world hit Québec particularly hard. The rapid growth of the State, which had sought to fulfill Francophones' desire for public service as well as collective social change, became especially costly under the economic and demographic circumstances mentioned above.

These phenomena had numerous effects on the labour force. More importantly, they affected various sub-groups at different times. In the eary seventies the youth unemployment rate was already growing faster than that for over-25 year olds, and was well beyond increases in the proportion of youths within the working population. The same was

true of women relative to men. Nevertheless, average real income (for those who still held a job) only dropped in the last years of the decade. Recently, the number of jobs has also tended to shrink.

In other words, some sub-groups, such as youth and women, were hit earlier and harder, while others have until recently remained relatively immune. For this reason, much more than because of fluctuations in energy prices or interest rates, the onset of crisis is difficult to pinpoint. Its date varies according to the sub-group's perspective, while the crisis' effects follow from a conjuncture of slowly unfolding economic, demographic, and political trends peculiar to Québec. As a consequence no one, especially in the public sector, can still guarantee or even promise that success lies just around the corner. This is the economic as well as social source of the current crisis: modes of distribution from the surplus-sharing phase meet the realities of slowing growth; expectations nurtured by relative affluence run into the new austerity; the second phase's source of social stability throws the third phase off balance.

In early 1982, this crisis has now spread throughout the work force, touching even the most privileged workers, and sectors which are usually safest. As La Fontaine wrote, "though it did not kill all, all were afflicted." Cuts in primary and secondary education over the past few years have been followed by others in the State's activities, particularly social programmes and higher education. The crisis has not spared Québec's traditionally weak private sector. Today no one in the labour force can avoid the prospect of scarcity, or even the end of growth.

UPHEAVAL IN THE WORKPLACE

Although entry into the workplace is becoming increasingly impossible for members of "minority" groups (women, youth, nonunionized, and unskilled workers), they no longer bear the repercussions of crisis alone. All workers have been affected to varying degrees, whether through layoffs, the qualitative underemployment of the overqualified, or the quantitative underemployment of those wanting more than part-time work. More generally, the scarcity of jobs makes switching them difficult. This has had many consequences. Without new personnel, institutions become increasingly bureaucratized. Workers' often limited hopes for social mobility through promotion are jeopardized. Francophones find that they can no longer use the labour market to make up lost ground. On this count, Francophones' access to high-level positions hardly improved during the last decade; their higher work force participation merely created the illusion of catching up. Language legislation pertaining to the workplace has aimed at opening up the private sector to Francophones.

In a climate that exacerbates social cleavage, many groups' demands not surprisingly include requests for positive discrimination, such as affirmative action for women or the handicapped. Problems created by preferential quotas are worsened because the number of available jobs either stagnates or drops instead of growing. Similarly, unions are singled out for neo-conservative attack under the pretext that the traditionally legitimate defence of workers' rights is the cause of crisis. On the contrary, we have tried to show that this crisis is due to structural problems of an economic, demographic, and social nature, and that one should therefore question established ways of doing things rather than the strategies of particular subgroups such as unionized workers, welfare recipients, the unemployed, youth, the elderly, women, etc.

In today's society, where one person's gain is another's loss, Québec's neo-nationalistic social-democratic ideological compromise is crumbling. Are we headed towards a deep political polarization? The handling of social and employment inequalities will answer this question.

28 A Theory of Closure: The Case of Quebec Teachers

Raymond Murphy

RAYMOND MURPHY, Professor titulaire in the Department of Sociology at the University of Ottawa, specializes in the sociology of education and the study of stratification. His books and articles include *Sociological Theories of Education*, with Ann Denis (1979); *Social Closure: The Theory of Monopolization and Exclusion* (forthcoming); "The struggle for scholarly recognition: The development of the closure problematic in sociology" (1983); and "Teachers and the evolving structural context of economic and political attitudes in Quebec society" (1981). Since 1980, Professor Murphy has served as an associate editor of the *Canadian Journal of Sociology*. He has recently been invited by UNESCO to write a paper on Weberian closure theory as it applies to race, class, gender, and religious groups.

This paper will contribute to the ongoing debate concerning the relationship between ethnicity and social class by suggesting a theory of the role of power, interests, language, and attitudes in that relationship. An attempt will be made to specify the articulation of changes in macro-level economic structures, micro-level attitudinal changes, and collective aspirations for changes in large-scale political structures. . . .

A STRUCTURAL THEORY OF EXCLUSION

The basic elements for a theory which avoids the difficulties inherent in a cultural values theory or a theory of ethnic class have been sketched by Collins (1971), Bourdieu and Passeron (1970), and Parkin (1974).[1] Collins argues that job requirements in organizations are not technically fixed and technically determined; rather status groups which control jobs impose their cultural standards on the selection process. These cultural standards are arbitrary as far as organizational perfor-

mance is concerned but they serve the interests of the dominant group and constitute barriers to the advancement of other status groups. Hence they are a form of symbolic violence (Bourdieu and Passeron, 1970). Parkin (1974) views stratification in terms of two related modes of social closure. The first includes practices of exclusion in which one group attempts to maintain its privileges by creating another group of ineligibles beneath it. Group advantages are enhanced by defining a subordinate group as inferior.

A structural theory of exclusion implies that the dominant position of a group in the social structure enables it to impose its linguistic and cultural standards on the advancement process and these tend to exclude members of other groups from advancement. For example, even when English work settings and the market are characterized by formal equality, their linguistic and cultural requirements transform the language and culture of anglophones into important resources in the career contest and in business expansion and constitute barriers to francophones. Not only do these requirements amount to a frontier that interferes with the advancement of francophones (Guindon, 1978), but they are also the means by which anglophones are sponsored.

Exclusion, as used here, necessarily involves inclusion, but on the terms set by the dominant group. It involves imposing criteria according to which the dominant group can include members of other groups in a way that leads the latter to be treated as inferior and members of the dominant group as superior. Individual members of the subordinate group are not directly and completely excluded. It is a particular characteristic, such as their language, that is excluded. The principle behind exclusion is that of imposing criteria which are applied equally to all, thereby legitimating inequalities, but which are more suitable to the dominant group, thereby reproducing inequalities. Thus struggles among status groups overtly involve conflict over the criteria of inclusion, such as the language of work, but it is exclusion which underlies these struggles.

I will attempt to demonstrate that a structural theory of exclusion can also contribute important elements which help to explain differences in work attitudes between francophones and anglophones as well as the recent desire among many francophones for a collective political change.

A structural theory of exclusion would lead us to believe that the context of economic power, with the mechanisms which facilitated English advancement and constituted barriers to the French, was central in forming different work attitudes among the members of these two linguistic communities. Rocher (1976) argues that the environment contains obstacles which can be so great that, on the one hand, they inhibit or destroy motivation or, on the other hand, are surmountable enough to constitute a challenge which stimulates motivation. Individuals internalize these attitudes either through their own experience with the facilitators or barriers or by being socialized by other members of their linguistic community who have had such experiences.

A structural theory of exclusion also suggests another consequence. Collins (1971) argues that since power, prestige, and wealth are scarce goods, the desire of some individuals for more than their equal share sets in motion the counterstruggle of others to escape subjection, disesteem, and dispossession. This struggle is primarily between rather than within status groups and internal cohesiveness is an important resource in the struggle. The second mode of social closure in Parkin's (1974) theory, solidarism, is the response of excluded groups to resist the state of dominance by exclusion practices. Solidarism is a form of social closure which implies different standards of distributive justice from those inherent in exclusion practices. It challenges the present stratified order by threatening to reduce the share of resources monopolized by the dominant group.

It should be noted that a structural theory of exclusion is not so much based on the assumption that individual identity is determined by status group membership as it is on the observation that common feelings of identity can be fostered and used to combat practices of exclusion. Corresponding to the two levels suggested by a structural theory of exclusion, this paper will examine attitudes in terms of the individual work ethic and the desire for a counter-struggle by the subordinate ethnic collectivity. . . .

It is also necessary to consider the evolution of the structures of exclusion. According to Sales (1974) and Eccles (1972), the dominant position of the English community in Quebec originated with the British conquest. This cut off French Canadians from their commercial and banking connections with France while permitting English traders to support their economic activity with a network in Great Britain which was much less accessible to French Canadians. Until the early nineteen fifties French Canadians tended to be structurally excluded from the career contest in the private sector and from expanding the market for their businesses, resulting in their strong under-representation in these areas as reported in Hughes (1943), Rocher and de Jocas (1957), and Niosi (1978). The environmental obstacles were so great that they most likely inhibited the motivation for individual and collective advancement in these areas. Taylor's (1964) description of attitudes may have been applicable during this period.

The massive American investment in Canada in the nineteen fifties (Levitt, 1970) and the subsequent demand for qualified personnel resulted in a profound transformation of the division of labour. A large-scale movement occurred out of the rural and "unskilled" working classes and the middle class was broadened enormously (Clark, 1976).[2] In Quebec, this resulted in an increase in incomes, an expansion of the local market (Niosi, 1978), and a tendency toward convergence in the ocupational structures of the French and English communities (Dofny and Garon-Audy, 1969; McRoberts et al., 1976; and Boulet, 1979). What Clark (1976) calls the first stage of the quiet revolution was marked by the development of opportunities for advancement which were not in conflict with the establishment.

I would suggest that the opportunities created by the massive direct foreign investment stimulated aspirations among both the French and the English. In order to seize these opportunities, however, the French had to make a greater investment of effort than the English: for example, they had to learn a second language. This was because the economic sector was dominated by the English who imposed their linguistic and cultural requirements on jobs they controlled. The need for qualified personnel resulted in the inclusion of the French at the middle levels of the private sector, but on the terms dictated by the controlling English group. During this period of expanded opportunity the presence of these

surmountable obstacles conditioned the French much more than the English into norms emphasizing individual striving for occupational success. Francophones internalized such norms as they grew up in this first stage of the quiet revolution. This is why Bélanger and Pedersen and others referred to earlier detected a stronger work ethic among French students than English students in 1965. French and English attitudes in 1965 were the result of processes of internalization during the first stage of the quiet revolution based on the structure of obstacles and opportunities faced by the two linguistic groups in the Quebec labour market during that period.[3] The "forced mobility" (Dofny and Garon-Audy, 1969), resulting from changes in the division of labour and in the opportunity structure subsequent to the massive foreign investment of the nineteen fifties, stimulated a work ethic among francophones in search of further upward mobility.[4]

The branch-plant, peripheral, Canadian economy dependent on the American metropolis was, however, incapable of absorbing, especially at higher levels in the labour market, the next generation which had swelled with the high birth rate after the war. This new generation could be absorbed in the late nineteen sixties and seventies only if the establishment was pushed out. What Clark (1976) refers to as the second stage of the quiet revolution involved a zero-sum game in which rewards could be acquired by the newcomers only if there were diminished rewards for the establishment. Norms held by francophones which emphasized individual striving and sacrifice in order to surmount barriers of exclusion tended to be replaced in the Quebec of the late sixties and seventies by a desire for a collective political effort to eliminate the barriers and with them the English establishment.[5]

It was precisely the increased opportunities for upward mobility resulting from the need for qualified personnel during the economic expansion provoked by American investment that stimulated the aspiration in the first stage to surmount barriers of exclusion. The limited possibilities for further mobility in an externally dependent economy transformed this aspiration in the second stage into a desire for a collective political effort to eliminate those barriers. This argument suggests that the massive investment in Quebec by an external bourgeoisie triggered changes in the structures of opportunity and exclusion, in orientations at the individual and collective levels, and a potential change of political structures in Canada. This investment expanded opportunities at the middle levels, raising aspirations, but not eliminating barriers of exclusion faced by francophones especially at the upper levels. The result was a collective political reaction in Quebec. This argument specifies the consequences of the internationalization of capital for the internal structure of one dependent society—in this case, Quebec. An externally provoked development inherently limited by the interests of the external centres of decision making gave rise to an autonomous internal source of development as an emergent property.[6]

By increasing aspirations as well as the demand for qualified personnel, the investment also resulted in the rapid expansion of institutions for training personnel. It resulted, for example, in the widespread desire for a reform of the educational system. These institutions were linguistically segmented and mostly provided positions for persons working with cultural goods, for instance, in teaching. . . .

Fournier (1977) argues that structural changes in the economy of Quebec have created and expanded a new petite bourgeoisie (which includes teachers) who specialize in the production and diffusion of cultural goods. Since their skills can be readily appreciated only in the Quebec market, they have a vested interest in consolidating the national identity. The defence of language and culture cannot be dissociated from the defence of profession and market. He claims that only a

change in the political relationship between French and English Canadians can assure the conditions necessary to maintain and improve the social position of those who produce and diffuse knowledge and culture in the French language. The new petite bourgeoisie therefore looks to the state to accomplish this change. Fournier argues that there has been a conversion of cultural nationalism into the political nationalism of the petite bourgeoisie. He contends that this new petite bourgeoisie has supported and worked for the Parti Québecois.

One fraction of the new petite bourgeoisie, teachers, acts as principal agents of the socialization of the young, a position of particular importance for the conservation or change of Quebec society. The fact that teachers were collectively affected by the barriers of exclusion and the indissolubility of teachers' defence of their language and culture from the defence of their market was evident in the school enrolment crisis of the early and midnineteen seventies and the reaction of teachers to it. The English domination of the Quebec economy, especially at the upper levels, and the resulting imposition of English linguistic and cultural requirements on jobs led immigrants and even francophones to choose to send their children to English schools to improve their chances for upward mobility. Hence, until the adoption of Law 101, the drop in the birth rate seriously affected attendance at French schools (and therefore teachers' jobs) but not attendance at English schools which was compensated by the children of immigrants. Teachers in the French school system were collectively affected by the English domination of the Quebec economy. Their collective aspirations and their individual interests are intimately bound together in their desire to make French the language of work at all levels of Quebec society as well as the language of schooling. The converse is true of teachers in the English school system. They have come out strongly against the Charter on the French

Language (Morisette, 1977c and 1977d) and in favour of freedom of choice of schooling for all, including the children of immigrants, in order to conserve the market for their services. Teachers are well aware that, in the absence of legal constraints, parental choice of the school for their children will be determined by language constraints imposed on jobs by those who control the economic sector....

Moreover, the effort by teachers in the French school system to remove the linguistic barriers faced by francophones in Quebec does not bring with it the threat of job loss, as is the case for francophones who work in federal institutions or in English companies (Laporte, 1974: 118). Upward collective mobility does not carry the threat of downward individual mobility.

It was precisely in this linguistically segmented sector dealing with cultural goods, where francophones were collectively rather than individually affected by the barriers of exclusion, that there developed an awareness that collective political efforts to eliminate the barriers were more appropriate than individual effort and sacrifice to surmount the barriers. I would suggest, therefore, that the desire for a collective political response to remove the linguistic and cultural barriers of exclusion is especially strong among the new petite bourgeoisie in general and among teachers in the French secondary school system in particular.

TEACHERS

It is within and with respect to this structural context of exclusion that the economic and political attitudes of teachers in Quebec must be examined and explained. These attitudes will be investigated at the two levels which correspond to those suggested by a structural theory of exclusion—the individual level and the level of a collective counter-struggle.[7]

The Individual Level

Teachers in the French and English school systems in 1965 had different work orientations even after their individual occupational origins were controlled.[8] ... Teachers in the French system ranked security, advancement, and pay higher than did teachers in the English system. The latter ranked the intrinsic enjoyment of the work and friendly fellow workers at a higher level than did their counterparts in the French system.

... Teachers in the French system gave higher priority to the security of steady work because members of the French community were subject to more risks in a labour market that placed before them special linguistic and cultural barriers not faced by the English.

One might be tempted to conclude that the higher value teachers in the English system attached to "the enjoyment of the work itself" indicated that they had a stronger work ethic than their counterparts in the French system.... But teachers in the French system attached more importance to the job and to an occupational career, were more willing to make sacrifices for their job, and viewed the roles of parents and the school more in terms of individual advancement and preparation for an occupational career than teachers in the English system, this being true of those from blue- and white-collar origins.[9] A work ethic in this sense was more characteristic of teachers in the French system than of those in the English system. The surmountable linguistic and cultural obstacles (not faced by anglophones) in the job market during a period of expanded economic opportunity conditioned francophones into such a work ethic ideology, into norms emphasizing the necessity of laborious striving and sacrifice to get ahead, with the role of parent and the school being to provide the means.[10]

I would suggest that these attitudinal differences were characteristic not just of teachers but of all upwardly mobile segments of the population and perhaps even of the French and English communities in general during the economic expansion in the first stage of the quiet revolution in Quebec society. Bélanger and Pedersen and other investigators referred to previously have shown that similar attitudinal differences held true for the secondary school students. I would submit that francophones growing up during this period learned norms emphasizing a work ethic from other members of their linguisitic community (parents, relatives, friends) who had experienced or observed the surmountable linguisitic and cultural barriers.... I would suggest that during this first stage of the quiet revolution the ideology of a work ethic, after having been internalized early in life, remained particularly strong among francophones sheltered from the direct effects of the barriers, such a those who worked in linguistically segmented institutions (for example, schools) or who had not yet entered the labour market (students).

Teachers in the French school system were more satisfied with the recognition given to their work by their community than were teachers in the English system. This was because the position reached was higher relative to their comparatively low reference group. French teachers were at a higher place in the stratification system of their linguistic community than were English teachers because there was a stratification of the two linguisitic communities....

These differences between the work attitudes of teachers ... in the French and English school systems need to be explained in terms of the position of the French and English communities in the social structure of Quebec and the resulting context of exclusion. The dominance of one status group enables it to impose its cultural standards on the selection process in the job market. The conquest of the French by the English enabled the latter to impose their language and culture on economic activity in Quebec. These transformed the language and culture of members of the English community into val-

ued resources for career and business success and constituted barriers to members of the French community, whose cultural resources were ignored. These facilitators or obstacles respectively faced by the two status groups led their member to internalize different attitudes. Barriers which, without being insurmountable, decrease the probability of advancement or hiring of members of a status group explain the under-representation of the group at higher levels, the cultivation of a work ethic by its members during periods of economic expansion, and their search for job security.

By 1972, the work attitudes of teachers in the French school system had approached (but were not identical to) those of teachers in the English school system. This was after the upward mobility of the French collectivity had enabled it to approach (but not equal) the English collectivity in the stratification system of Quebec (Dofny and Garon-Audy, 1969; McRoberts et al., 1976; and Boulet, 1979) and after the linguistic and cultural barriers faced by the French community had become proportionately fewer because of expansion in the francophone-dominated public sector and in the local market which francophone businesses could penetrate. The work ethic necessary to surmount the barriers diminished as proportionately fewer positions in the job market contained those linguistic and cultural barriers to francophones.

However, the limit to the rate of expansion of the public sector in general and in particular of the French side of linguistically segmented cultural institutions within a predominantly English private enterprise context was reached in the late sixties. For French teachers, the downturn in the birth rate posed a threat to their jobs in this English-dominated private enterprise context where most immigrants and many French parents chose to send their children to English schools. As the expansion of the public sector slowed down in this second stage of the quiet revolution, the intellectual petite bourgeoisie who worked with French cultural goods in linguistically segmented institutions, particularly teachers in the French school system, became collectively affected by the barriers of exclusion in the private sector. They therefore returned from an individualistic work ethic to a desire for a collective political struggle to change the English-dominated private enterprise context itself.

The Collective Counter-Struggle

A structural theory of exclusion suggests a reaction at the collective level, in the sense of a desire for a solidaristic counter-struggle by the excluded group. Reasons have already been given to support the hypothesis that in the second stage of the quiet revolution this desire is particularly strong among the intellectual petite bourgeoisie in Quebec, which includes teachers, and that it is directed toward a parliamentary struggle. My evidence confirms this line of argument.

Table 1 shows that the proportion who had the intention to vote for the Parti-Québécois (the political party which had the strongest program for the removal of linguistic and cultural barriers to francophones) in 1972 was much higher among teachers (41.0 per cent) in the French secondary school system than in the overall population (15 per cent). In 1972 76 per cent of teachers in the French secondary school system who had decided which party to vote for decided in favour of the Parti Québécois. The corresponding percentage in the overall population in 1972 was 28 per cent. Although the latter figure and the last column of Table 1 are not broken down by linguistic affiliation, they are so different from the voting intentions of teachers in the French school system that one can safely conclude that more teachers in the French school system favoured the Parti Québécois than did members of other occupational groups and social classes within the French community.

There are other indications of French teacher support for the Parti Québécois. Shortly after the latter was elected in 1976 the critical socialist ideology of the leaders of the French Quebec teachers union (C.E.Q.) during the Liberal regime was attacked by its members as having been rendered inappropriate by the results of the election and the union was urged to adopt a "prejudice in favour" of the Parti Québécois because "it is the party of the members of the C.E.Q." (Sacy, 1977). A large number (14) of Part Québécois members elected to the Quebec parliament were elementary or secondary school teachers.

Still another indication of the desire of teachers in the French school system for collective political effort to dismantle the linguistic barriers faced by the French community was the reaction of their union to the Charter on the French language in Quebec (1977) proposed by the Parti Québécois government. The French teachers' union (C.E.Q.) completely supported and was generally satisfied with the Charter because they saw in it the reflection of the union's own orientation. As far as the language of schooling was concerned, the union wanted to go further than the proposals of the Parti Québécois Government by progressively eliminating English educational institutions within the next decade and by requiring immigrant and French children now in English schools to attend French schools (Morissette, 1977a and 1977b). The union later became more flexible with respect to the education of anglophones coming from other provinces but remained firm in regard to other groups (Morissette, 1977e).

Thus in the second stage of the quiet revolution in Quebec society teachers in the French school system, who are one fraction of the intelletual petite bourgeoisie, have become deeply involved in the political counter-struggle to remove the barriers of exclusion faced by the French community. This is indicated by their particularly high frequency

Table 1

VOTING INTENTIONS, SECONDARY SCHOOL TEACHERS AND THE OVERALL POPULATION OF
QUEBEC, 1972 (IN PERCENTAGES)

If there were provincial elections today, for what party would you vote?[a]	Secondary School Teachers		Overall Population[b]
	French system	English system	
Liberal Party	10.5	45.6	42
Union Nationale	2.6	1.8	4
Parti Québécois	41.0	9.7	15
Social Credit	1.5	1.8	8
I would be very undecided	34.2	31.8	31
I would abstain from voting	3.7	5.6	
I am not at all interested in politics	6.6	3.8	

[a] Bélanger and Rocher (1976: 109). The survey was carried out in the spring of 1972. I have already described the sample on which it was based.
[b] Le Devoir (22 avril 1976: p. 2). This survey based on a random sample of the Quebec population was carried out by the survey institute CROP in October 1972. The results were not broken down by English and French populations.

of intention to vote for the Part Québécois (the political party which has the strongest program for the removal of the linguistic and cultural barriers to the advancement of francophones) as early as 1972, by their high rate of participation in the party in 1976, and by the reaction of their union to proposed legislation on the language of work and schooling in Quebec. Teachers in the French school system are seeking to impose their language, values, and cultural standards on the selection process in organizations within their territorial base, thereby extending the institutional completeness (Breton, 1964) of their status group. The separation of their workplace along linguistic lines is the model they propose for the parts which presently form the Canadian nation.

The support among teachers in the French system for a party whose goal is political independence marks a change from the past. Bélanger and Juneau (1975) found that in 1960 their sample of teachers in the French system showed them as optimistic or conciliatory with respect to Canadian unity. At that time the teachers felt that the diversity of religions, languages, educational systems, laws, customs, and traditions was compatible with the realization of Canadian unity.

The change, I suggest, is due to the upward mobility in an absolute sense and the resulting heightened aspirations of the French community, together with its continuing inferior position in a relative sense and the existence of barriers at the upper levels which have a collective effect on the intellectual petite bourgeoisie in general and on teachers in particular. This has promoted the development of a consciousness among these subgroups that the solution to the barriers faced by members of the French collectivity is less that of individual striving and sacrifice to surmount barriers and more that of a collective political response to eliminate them. . . .

The work ethic of the intellectual petite bourgeoisie may have declined but it has not disappeared. Fournier (1977) has observed that the political ethics and public image of the Parti Québécois during the 1976 election campaign were principally inspired by a petite bourgeois morality, emphasizing individual responsibility, a high value attached to work and workmanship, and a serious outlook. The work ethic discussed in my paper has been projected by the intellectual petite bourgeoisie from the individual to the collective level.

The Parti Québécois government is merely the most recent and militant agent of the collective political reaction. Even prior to the victory of that party in 1976, francophones turned more and more to the political state apparatus to increase their representation in the bourgeoisie (Niosi, 1978) and to remove the barriers in the private sector. The overall result has been a transformation of those barriers even at the upper levels. Formerly the English language and culture were imposed at the upper levels of the private sector and the French language and culture were ignored. Now it is bilingualism that is imposed at the upper levels of the private sector in Quebec.[11] Furthermore, there is reason to believe that many highly paid unilingual anglophones have left Quebec and that their jobs have gone with them.[12] That is the "last resort" practice by which francophones are excluded from top positions in English companies.

The existence of barriers which tend to exclude francophones in the private sector of the market economy has provoked in the second stage of the quiet revolution a collective political effort for their elimination by francophones in the French side of linguistically segmented cultural institutions. The existence of these barriers of exclusion also has promoted a radical questioning of the capitalist market economy by the leaders of unions (C.E.Q. and C.S.N.) representing francophones in linguistically segmented institutions. Such barriers of exclusion also stimulated from an earlier date a collective search for alternative organizational forms, best exemplified by the cooperative movement, which has been much stronger among Quebec francophones than among anglophones in North America. . . .

CONCLUSION

. . . A structural theory of exclusion focuses on the power of status groups to impose their cultural standards on positions and institutions they control. It also focuses on barriers to the advancement of members of other status groups embodied in those in order to explain the existence of a vertical mosaic—the over- or under-representation of status groups in the various strata of the stratification system. These standards and barriers are the structural points of articulation between the inequality of collectivities per se and the inequality of opportunity for individuals who make up those different collectivites.

A structural theory of exclusion sees the barriers as having an important formative influence on the orientation of the members of these groups. It looks to changes in the structures of opportunity and exclusion as an important source of change in orientation, including the priority given to resignation, to individual striving to surmount the barriers, or to collective struggle to eliminate them.[13] This paper's empirical investigation of teachers shows that their economic and political attitudes can best be understood in terms of the evolving structural context of exclusion in Quebec society. . . .

Notes

[1] The threefold division of theoretical approaches given in this paper toward explaining the subordinate position of francophones in Quebec is similar to that in the literature on the sociology of national development. Portes (1976) distinguishes three different approaches in the sociology of national development: the "social differentiation" approach; the "enactment of values" approach; and the "liberation from dependency" approach. The first two are very similar to one another, both being based on value orientations. The third, dependency theory, has several versions. The economic imperialism version claims that dependency is "the conditioning structure" of poverty and implies that a higher standard of living for the masses in Third World countries will automatically come about with the elimination of economic imperialism. Portes (1976:79) argues that "we must look elsewhere for studies of development-oriented elites, conditions under which they come to control the state, and circumstances which permit them to mobilize the masses into a national development effort." Thus the theoretical approach based on value orientations, the economic imperialism version of dependency theory (one nation seen as a more or less homogeneous entity exploited by another), and Portes' less rhetorical, less crude version of dependency theory parallel the three-fold division of approaches to the subordinate position of francophones in Quebec suggested in my paper.

[2] Although investment by American companies in Quebec began before the nineteen-fifties and was but one source of the overall processes of industrialization and modernization, it reached such important proportions at that time that it became the key source of the structural and attitudinal changes which followed.

[3] Differences in work attitudes can also be influenced by differences in the structure of barriers between regions and between particular organizations. Thus one can expect some variation in attitudes from one locality to another and from one organization to another. However, today's workers are not serfs. They are not completely restricted to one locality or to one organization. I am suggesting a theory at the level of the overall Quebec labour market because it is the most appropriate level for analyzing the attitudes of francophones in Quebec.

[4] According to a French proverb quoted by Quebec Prime Minister Levesque during a visit to Washington, "it is in eating that one acquires the appetite to eat more."

[5] I would suggest that the recent decreased interest among French Quebec students in learning English is one indication of the shift in emphasis from advancement as an individual effort to surmount the barriers to advancement as a collective effort to eliminate such barriers.

[6] There are undoubtedly both parallel processes and structural differences to be found by comparing Quebec with other societies. See Laczko (1978) for an interesting suggestion along these lines. It would be a fascinating theoretical challenge to explain why the penetration of the economies of Canada, Australia, and New Zealand by foreign-owned multinational corporations and accompanying dependency resulted in a higher per capita income in these countries whereas it resulted in massive misery in most economically dependent Third World countries. Although the answer to such a question lies well beyond the scope of this article, I would suggest that a structural theory of exclusion could contribute important elements to the explanation.

[7] The data for 1965 analyzed in this study were taken from the Quebec portion of Breton's (1972) survey of Canadian secondary schools. His data were based on a probability sample of secondary schools. His survey included 106 (5.4 percent) secondary schools in Quebec. All teachers within the schools selected were asked to complete the questionnaire.

Thus the sample included 1930 secondary school teachers (1922 when weighted): 1594 in the French educational system and 328 in the English systems. I have combined English Protestant and English Catholic schools to form what I refer to as the English system. The data for 1972 were taken from Bélanger and Rocher's (1976) survey (ASOPE) of Quebec secondary schools. Schools were first sampled as in Breton's study, but in contrast to the latter teachers were then sampled within the schools selected. One hundred and thirty-three secondary schools were chosen and of the 2296 teachers selected in these schools, 1586 (73 per cent) completed the questionnaire. This included 1309 teachers in the French secondary school system and 376 in the English system, where French and English refer to the language of instruction in the school. The similarity of the populations investigated and the data gathering procedures used in the two surveys justifies the comparison of their findings. More detailed information on the sampling and on the data gathering procedures used has already been published by Breton (1972) and Bélanger and Rocher (1976) and will not be repeated here.

[8] Since they are members of the same profession, their present occupation and intergenerational mobility are also controlled.

[9] These four items were found to be strongly interrelated, thereby showing that they indicate the same underlying dimension.

[10] My evidence does not support the idea that the differences in the work attitudes of teachers in the French and English systems were the result of differences in their immediate work settings. Controlling the social origins of teachers indirectly controls work setting variables which are associated with differences in recruitment. More direct evidence is provided by the fact that when school size was controlled the attitudinal differences between teachers in the French and English systems remained. This important work setting variable cannot explain such differences.

[11] Boulet (1979) found among males in Montreal that, whereas unilingual and bilingual anglophones were the two top income earning groups in 1961, and 1971, by 1977 bilingual anglophones, bilingual francophones, and bilingual allophones (those having other mother tongues) were the top income earners in that order. Unilingual anglophones have dropped to the fourth rank by 1977. Unilingual francophones remained in the sixth rank, their position being unchanged from 1961 through 1977. The anglophone community has quickly adjusted to the bilingualism barrier. Boulet (1979) found that 74 per cent of anglophones and 64 per cent of allophones were bilingual at the beginning of 1978 compared to 48 per cent of each in 1971. A higher proportion of anglophones than francophones (64 per cent) in the male Montreal labour force are now bilingual. This is a striking change from the past, for example, when as late as 1971 62 per cent of francophones as opposed to 48 per cent of anglophones were bilingual. The bilingualism requirement itself demonstrates the power which remains in the hands of the English in the Quebec private sector in that it is imposed in a province where eight of every ten individuals are of French origin and only one of ten is of English origin.

[12] This is suggested by the following data (Boulet, 1979): the proportion of unilingual anglophones in the Montreal male labour force fell from 13 per cent in 1961 to 5 per cent in 1978; the proportion of bilingual anglophones grew more slowly—from 10 per cent in 1961 to 13 per cent in 1978; the relative earnings of the category "unilingual anglophones" decreased significantly during this period; and the proportion of the total mass of earnings monopolized by the 15 per cent most highly paid decreased from 36 per cent in 1961 to 30 per cent in 1978.

[13] This paper has been limited to the analysis of the French and English in Quebec. If other status groups were to be analyzed additional factors would have to be taken into consideration. Barriers of exclusion have differential

effects on different status groups. These effects depend on the relative distance between the cultural requirements imposed on work positions by the status group controlling those positions and the cultural capital of the remaining status groups. Moreover, the latter groups have different resources. For example, francophones in Quebec can control a provincial government apparatus and use it to increase the power of their group even in the private sector, a possibility which does not exist for other status groups, such as Italians or Inuits in Canada or francophones outside of Quebec. Therefore the priority given to resignation, to individual striving to surmount barriers, or to a collective effort to eliminate them and the form that such a collective effort takes vary among subordinate status groups.

References

Archibald, Kathleen (1973) *Les deux sexes dans la fonction publique.* Ottawa: Information Canada.

Beattie, Christopher (1975) *Minority Men in a Majority Setting: Middle-level Francophones in the Canadian Public Service.* Toronto: McClelland and Stewart.

Bélanger, Pierre at A. Juneau (1975)"Les Maîtres de l'enseignement primaire: étude socio-culturelle." Pp. 91–193 dans Pierre W. Bélanger et Guy Rocher, *Ecole et Société au Québec,* Nouvelle édition. Montréal: Editions Hurtubise HMH.

Bélanger, Pierre W. et Eigil Pedersen (1973) "Projets des étudiants québécois." *Sociologie et Sociétés* (1)1.91–110.

Bélanger, Pierre W. et Guy Rocher (1976)*A.S.O.P.E. Aspirations scolaires et orientations professionnelles des étudiants: analyse descriptive des données de la première cueillette (1972), Les enseignants.* Vol. III 2e édition corrigée. Université de Montréal: Montréal.

Bernard, Paul et Jean Renaud (1979) *Le Devoir,* Montréal, vendredi 9 mars: 3.

Boulet, Jac-André (1979) "L'évolution des disparités linguistiques de revenus de travail dans la zone métropolitaine de Montréal de 1961 à 1977." Document No. 127. Conseil économique du Canada, Ottawa.

Bourdieu, Pierre et Jean-Claude Passeron (1970) *La reproduction.* Paris: Editions de minuit.

Breton, Raymond (1964) "Institutional Completeness of Ethnic Communities and the Personal Relations of Immigrants." *American Journal of Sociology* LXX (September): 193–293.

———(1972) *Social and Academic Factors in the Career Decisions of Canadian Youth.* Ottawa: Manpower and Immigration.

Breton, Raymond and John C. McDonald (1967) *Career Decisions of Canadian Youth.* Ottawa: Department of Manpower and Immigration and Queen's Printer.

Cardinal, Pierre (1978) "Regard critique sur la traduction au Canada." *Meta* 23(2): 141–7

Carlos, Serge (1973) *L'Utilisation du français dans le monde du travail du Québec. Etudes réalisées pour le compte de la commission d'enquête sur la situation de la langue française et sur les droits linguistiques au Québec.* Québec: l'éditeur officiel du Québec.

Clark. S.D. (1976) *Canadian Society in Historical Perspective.* Toronto: McGraw-Hill Ryerson.

Collins, Randall (1971) "Functional and conflict theories of educational stratification." *American Sociological Review* 36 (December):1002–19.

Crysdale, S. and C. Beattie (1973) *Sociology Canada.* Toronto: Butterworths.

Dofny, Jacques (1978) "Les stratifications de la société québécoise," *Sociologie et Sociétés* x(2):87–102.

Dofny, Jacques et Muriel Garon-Audy (1969) "Mobilités professionnelles au Québec." *Sociologie et Sociétés* 1(2):207–301.

Dofny, Jacques and Marcel Rioux (1964) "Social Class in French Canada." P. 307–18 in Marcel Rioux and Yves Martin (eds.), *French-Canadian Society,* Vol. 1. Toronto: McClelland and Stewart.

Eccles, W.J. (1972) *France in America.* New York: Harper and Row.

Fournier, Marcel (1977) "La question nationale: les enjeux." *Possibles* 1 (2): 7–18.

Guindon, Hubert (1978) "The modernization of Quebec and legitimacy of the Canadian state." *The Canadian Review of Sociology and Anthropology* 15(2): 227–45.

Hughes, E.C. (1943) *French Canada in Transition.* Chicago: University of Chicago Press.

Jain, Harish C., Jacques Normand, and Rabindra N. Kanungo (1979) "Job motivation of Canadian Anglophone and Francophone employees." *Canadian Journal of Behavioural Science* 11(2): 160–4.

Laczko, Leslie (1978), "English Canadians and Québécois nationalism." *The Canadian Review of Sociology and Anthropology* 15(2): 206–17.

Laporte, Pierre E. (1974) *L'usage des langues dans la vie économique au Québec: situation actuelle et possibilités de changement. Synthèses réalisées pour le compte de la commission d'enquête sur la situation de la langue française et sur les droits linguistiques au Québec.* Québec. L'éditeur officiel du Québec.

Levitt, Kari (1970) *Silent Surrender.* Toronto: Macmillan.

McRoberts, Hugh, John Porter, Monica Boyd, John Goyder, Frank Jones, et Peter Pineo (1976) "Différences dans la mobilité professionnelle des francophones et des anglophones." *Sociologie et Sociétés* 8(2): 61–79.

Morissette, Rodolphe (1977a) "La CEQ propose un plan de 12 ans." *Le Devoir,* 25 mars: 7.

—— (1977b) "Les minorités s'élèvent contre le livre blanc." *Le Devoir,* 5 avril: 3.

—— (1977c) "Le vrai problème est d'ordre économique, souligne la PAPT." *Le Devoir,* 15 avril: 3.

—— (1977d) "Les anglo-catholiques se doteront d'un fonds de défense." *Le Devoir,* 16 avril: 7.

—— (1977e) "Tout Québécois 'qui se respecte' appuiera le projet no. 1." *Le Devoir,* 30 avril: 2.

Murphy, Raymond and Ann B. Denis (1979) "Schools and the Conservation of the Vertical Mosaic." Pp 75–90 in Danielle Juteau Lee (ed.), *Frontières Ethniques en Devenir/Changing Ethnic Boundaries.* Ottawa: University of Ottawa Press.

Murphy, Raymond with the collaboration of Ann B. Denis (1979) *Sociological Theories of Education.* Toronto: McGraw-Hill Ryerson.

Niosi, Jorge (1978) "La Nouvelle Bourgeoisie Canadienne Française." Pp. 174–222 dans *Actes du Colloque annuel de l'Association canadienne des sociologues et anthropologues de langue française.*

Nolle, David and Donna Greenwood (1973) "Adolescent Values and Outcomes: A Canadian Test," Reported on pages 110–11 of S. Crysdale and C. Beattie, *Sociology Canada,* Toronto: Butterworths.

Parkin, Frank (1974) "Strategies of social closure in the maintenance of inequality." Unpublished paper presented to the Eighth World Congress of Sociology. Toronto, Canada.

Porter, John (1965) *The Vertical Mosaic.* Toronto: University of Toronto Press.

Porter, Marion, John Porter and Bernard Blishen (1973) *Does Money Matter?* Toronto: Institute for Behavioural Research, York University.

Portes, Alejandro (1976) "On the Sociology of National Development: Theories and Issues." *American Journal of Sociology* 82(1): 55–85.

Raynauld, André (1974) *La propriété des entreprises au Québec: les années 60.* Montréal: Les presses de L'Université de Montréal.

Rocher, Guy (1964) "Research on occupations and social stratification." Pp. 328–41 in Marcel Rioux and Yves Martin (eds.), *French-Canadian Society* Vol. 1 Toronto: McClelland and Stewart.

_____ [1976] "Toward a psychosociological theory of aspirations." Pp. 391–406 in Jan Loubser, Rainer Baum, Andrew Effrat, and Victor Lidz (eds.), *Explorations in General Theory in Social Science* Vol. 1 New York: The Free Press.

Rocher, G. and Y. De Jocas (1957) "Inter-Generation Occupational Mobility in the Province of quebec." *The Canadian Journal of Economics and Political Science* 23(1).

Sacy, Hubert (1977) "Le PW. parti des members de la CEO." *La Presse,* 11 janvier: A5.

Sales, Arnaud (1974) "Différenciation ethnique des directions industrielles." *Sociologie et sociétés* VI(2): 101–13.

_____ (1977) "La question linguistique et les directions d'entreprises." *Le Devoir,* 27 avril: 6; 28 avril: 17; 29 avril: 9.

Taylor, Norman W. (1964) "The French-Canadian industrial entrepreneur and his social environment." Pp. 271–95 in Marcel Rioux and Yves Martin (eds.), *French-Canadian Society* Vol. 1. Toronto: McClelland and Stewart.

29 Merchants Against Industry

R. Jack Richardson

R. JACK RICHARDSON, Assistant Professor of Sociology at McMaster University, Hamilton, Ontario, specializes in economic sociology and the study of formal organizations. Recent publications include *The Social World* (1986) and *An Introduction to the Social World* (1987), both co-edited with Lorne Tepperman; "The Canadian agricultural frontier: An approach to the theory of ground rent" (1983); "Causes and consequences of directorship interlocks" (1985); and "Structural analysis", with Barry Wellman (1985). Professor Richardson has served as Assistant Book Review Editor for the *Canadian Review of Sociology and Anthropology* and Associate Editor of *Connections*. He is currently writing a monograph on the Canadian trust industry and its relation to Canadian economic structure.

If there is any one "fact" on which Canadian social scientists are agreed, it is that the degree of foreign control over the Canadian economy is unique among the industrialized nations of the world.[1] However, this unanimity immediately evaporates when scholars attempt to *explain* this phenomenon. One argument holds that cultural similarity, the influence of the American media, and propinquity combine to produce a high degree of American control (e.g., Marshall et al., 1936). Others focus on structural dependence resulting from the staples base of the Canadian hinterland economy (e.g., Innis, 1930; 1956). Still others combine the structural integration of multinational enterprise with differences in psychological traits between Canadians and Americans (e.g., Levitt, 1970; Watkins, 1973).

Currently, the most influential explanation combines a neo-Marxist analysis of class fractions with the insight of Innis' staples perspective. Naylor (1972) initiated this approach by proposing that the separation of the Canadian capitalist class into merchant and industrial fractions, along with the dominance of the former over the latter, explains the nature of Canadian economic development. While earlier arguments assumed a passive and classless Canadian hinterland, this formulation introduces the concept of a Canadian ruling class as an active agent in the American takeover of Canadian industry. It has come to be known as the *merchants against industry* argument (cf. MacDonald, 1975).

This paper will set out the fundamental assumptions and sources of the *merchants against industry* argument. It will show that the very nature of the argument generates a logical set of alternative hypotheses. The essential components of these competing arguments will be subjected to a series of empirical tests to assess their relative validity....

THE MERCHANTS AGAINST INDUSTRY *ARGUMENT*

The *merchants against industry* argument rests on two fundamental assumptions. The first of these is that merchant capital and industrial capital are structurally distinct and antagonistic class fractions (e.g., Naylor, 1972:3).

Here, the argument draws upon the staples perspective of Innis (1930; 1956). Because of its hinterland relationship to the British and American metropoli, Canadian merchant capital expanded from its original base in the circulation of staples to the provision of the infrastructure of a staples economy, i.e., "the direct line of descent runs from merchant capital, not to industrial capital, but to banking and finance, railways, utilities, land speculation and so on" (Naylor, 1972:16). Thus, merchant capital did not expand into industry. As descendants of the early import-export merchants, it was clearly not in the best interests of this class to set up domestic manufacturing. Instead, the powerful, government-protected banking cartel helped to perpetuate the staples economy (Naylor, 1972:16), thus obstructing the development of Canadian industrial capitalism, e.g., "The dominance of merchant capital means the draining of funds into mercantile pursuits and away from industry" (Naylor, 1972:20).

Merchants crushed the nascent industrialists, thus resolving the structural conflict between these different class fractions (Naylor, 1972:16, 21). Then, because of their structural position as linkages between the metropolis and hinterland, the merchant capitalists explicitly developed the national policy to import branch-plant industrialization (Naylor, 1972:16, 20, 25; cf. Clement, 1975).

Thus, the second fundamental assertion of the *merchants against industry* argument is that merchant capital dominated Canadian industry. The argument holds that Canadian merchant capital evolved into financial capital, which wielded power over industry through a cartelized banking system. The assertion can be traced back to an interpretation of Lenin (1917),[2] which holds that the monopolization of German banks at the turn of the century led to the domination of banks over industry. *Merchants against industry* transplants this historically specific conclusion to Canada. . . .

Social scientists from a wide variety of perspectives have made a similar argument—that the economic structure of a staples economy produces a dominant merchant class which is conservative (Dobb, 1947), externally oriented in its economic relations (Innis, 1930;1956; Wallerstein, 1974), and antagonistic to domestic industry (Hoselitz, 1960). However, the argument's strongest intellectual ties appear to be to Frank (1967), who incorporated Innis' staples perspective (as does *merchants against industry*), developed the metropolis-hinterland paradigm (which the argument incorporates), and argued that the politically and economically dominant merchant capitalist class "extinguished" the nascent manufacturing class of Chile.

The *merchants against industry* formulation initiated a promising new approach to the explanation of the phenomenon of foreign control of Canadian industry. This approach has since been developed by Watkins (1973;1977), Laxer (1973), Drache (1978) and others. Perhaps the most forceful proponent has been Clement, who declares: "Canadian manufacturers could not survive because the commercial ruling class would not allow them to" (1975:80).[3] Recent works such as Marchak (1979) and Grayson (1980) continue to attest to its currency.

There are many reasons for the popularity of this parsimonious explanation of the development of a foreign-controlled Canadian economy. It is based on Innis' staples perspective, the dominant paradigm in Canadian political economy over the last half century. But it goes beyond Innis by incorporating the Marxist concept of class fractions, a Leninist view of the dominance of banks, the burgeoning metropolis-hinterland paradigm, and the traditional western Canadian (and American populist) aversion to banks and railways.

Nevertheless, the very nature of the *merchants against industry* argument generates a logical set of alternative hypotheses. Does the successful transition to industrial capitalism always follow Marx's "really revolutionizing path" (1894:334)? The alternative argument (which I shall identify as *merchants become industry*) would hold that merchant capital merged with industrial capital and that merchants thus became successful industrialists. Does financial capital dominate industry? Here, the alternative argument (which I shall identify as *capital integration)* would hold that financial capital merges with industrial capital to form finance capital—a merger in which neither fraction dominates.

Finally, the points of division between capitalist class fractions themselves generate alternative hypotheses. The *merchants against industry* argument follows the staples perspective by identifying within the merchant class fraction not only merchants and financiers but also those associated with the infrastructure of the staples economy: real estate, transportation, communications and utilities (Naylor 1975a; cf. Clement 1975;1977). Within this model, industrial capital is limited to manufacturing and minerals. One alternative argument, in the Marxist tradition, would hold that the essential division is between merchants' capital and productive capital. Another would concentrate on the relationship between banks and productive capital (e.g., Lenin, 1917).

THE ALTERNATIVE ARGUMENTS

While to Marx the transition from producer to capitalist was the revolutionary path to the development of capitalism, the entry of the merchant into the realm of production was the *predominant* path (1887:702; cf. Tönnies, 1887:87; Dobb, 1947:123–60).[4] Weber also recounts this dual process in the development of capitalism (1919–20:122–36).

The *merchants become industry* argument holds that industrial capitalism arose primarily (but not exclusively) through the entry of merchants into the realm of production. The theoretical issue between this perspective and the *merchants against in-*dustry argument is nicely summarized by Johnson, who notes:

> Whereas Marx argued that mercantile capitalist accumulation was a necessary precondition to the capitalist mode of production, the left nationalists [i.e., proponents of the *merchants against industry* argument] assert that it prevents or stultifies the development of industrial capitalism (n.d.:14).

The empirical issue between these two arguments is whether merchants do, in fact, become industrialists or whether these two class fractions remain separate and distinct. Studies by Berkowitz (1975), Leys (1975) and Evans (1979) show the development of indigenous industrial capitalism to be a process in which merchants become successful industrialists in the United States, Kenya and Brazil, respectively, e.g.:

> Whether established by immigrants or families long rooted in Brazil, one of the common features of the largest Brazilian economic groups is that they moved into industry via commerce (Evans, 1979:108).[5]

If the distinctness of merchant and industrial capital is not a universal phenomenon, does it apply at all in the Canadian case? Some say no. For example, Levitt (1970) argues that Canadian capital, originally accumulated in commerce and railways, flowed into industry. Likewise, Acheson (1973) notes that many Canadian family firms progressed from merchant to industrial activity, and Ryerson (1975) argues that mutual investments in industry merged the various fractions of the Canadian capitalist class. MacDonald concludes that "a close look at the evidence . . . shows that merchant and industrial capital were inseparable" (1975:266). However, MacDonald's "evidence" is not very compelling because there is no evidence that the cases he describes are representative ones. On the other hand, Naylor's own evidence (1975a;1975b) does not appear to support the sharp distinction between merchant and industrial class fractions which the *merchants against industry* argument holds. In fact, a careful examination of his description of Canadian business in the 1867–1914 period can lead one to the conclusion that the process by which successful Canadian industry developed was the gradual expansion of merchants into manufacturing enterprise.

While the *merchants become industry* argument holds that merchants became industrialists, it does not *directly* address the *merchants against industry* argument's assertion that, in Canada, merchant capital dominated industrial capital. This latter assertion has its theoretical roots in an interpretation of Lenin's (1917) "finance capital." However, Lenin is more commonly interpreted to define finance capital as the "*coalescence* of bank and industrial capital," which implies the dominance of neither of these capital pools (1917:217, emphasis added; cf. Lenin, 1968:338; Mandel, 1972:312). This alternative interpretation of the relationship between financial and industrial capital is the essence of the *capital integration* argument. Dobb (1947:124) concludes that a similar coalescence is the third road to the development of capitalism where technology requires an initial investment of capital beyond the means of the producer.

If we combine the *merchants become industry* and the *capital integration* arguments we can see the development of capitalism as a process in which financiers enter the realm of industry and industrialists enter the realm of trade and finance. Thus these capital pools and class fractions unite. This is the essence of the argument which competes with *merchants against industry*. . . .

TESTING THE ARGUMENTS IN THE CANADIAN CONTEXT

If Canadian merchant capital and industrial capital are distinct and antagonistic class fractions, as the *merchants against industry* argument advocates, then it follows that this structural boundary separates the individual capitalists into distinct groups. Thus, merchant capitalists and industrial capitalists must be different people. This is an empirically testable proposition. The ultimate test would be to collect appropriate data for all major shareholders, directors and officers of Canadian mercantile and industrial firms over a long historical period to determine whether merchants and industrialists are the same, or different people. However, the costs of collecting such an extensive data base are prohibitive. Thus we must narrow the scope of this empirical test in terms of both time and place.

The *merchants against industry* argument clearly proposes that its fundamental assumptions apply in the year 1911, e.g., "In 1911 the branch plant system and the mercantile bourgeoisie won once again" (Naylor, 1972:23). However, Naylor (1972:36) suggests that the two fractions had merged by the 1960s. Precisely *when* the two class fractions synthesized is not entirely clear. Naylor appears to argue that the merger of financial and industrial capital did not take place until after World War II, and certainly not before the 1930s (1972:29, 31, 33).[6] Clement's more extensive work indicates that financial capital had "smashed and consolidated" a substantial amount of industrial capital by 1913, with further mergers taking place between 1913 and 1926 (1975:73–83). However, he notes the continued separation of Canadian financial capital from Canadian industrial capital even today (1975:353–7). On the other hand, Niosi proposes that the major Canadian merger movement (and thus the fusion of financial and industrial capital) took place during the late 1920s (1978:13).

Toronto and Montreal were the two undisputed centres of Canadian capitalism throughout the 1920s. Naylor's major work (1975a;1975b) shows how the Montreal merchant capital fraction extended itself into such industries as textiles, sugar refining, iron and steel, while continuing to hold to the sharp division between the merchant and industrial fractions in general. Therefore, analyzing the Toronto capitalist class should constitute a more stringent test of the *merchants against industry* assertions than an analysis of the capitalist class of Montreal.

Thus analysis of the Toronto economic elite of the 1920s should constitute an adequate, although not ideal, test of the *merchants against industry* argument. The data analyzed here were originally collected for a study of access to this elite (Tepperman, 1977).[7] The original study group

> comprised all males listed in the 1925–6 edition of *Who's Who in Canada* who lived in what is considered Metropolitan Toronto today, and whose names were also found in the 1921–2 and 1928–9 editions of the same publication. This method of selecting a study population yielded 277 men. . . . About 30 percent held one or more directorships in organizations Porter (1965) identified as economically dominant. . . . Another 30 percent held one or more directorships or high management positions in lesser enterprises (1977:286–287).[8]

The present study selects from Tepperman's population the 60 percent who held directorships or high management positions in business firms—a study group of 164 economically powerful men. These individuals held a total of 1,062 corporate directorships.

The population studied here will of course be biased in favor of those individuals who are executives and/or directors of large firms and who hold directorships in several firms. After all, Tepperman' study purported to represent the Toronto economic elite. However, there is no reason to believe that the population selected by *Who's Who* will be biased in favor of those whose multiple directorships cross the division *between* merchant and industrial capital rather than remain *within* these respective class fractions.

An even better test of the *merchants*

against industry argument's sharp segregation between these two class fractions is to ask the following question: If one knows the class fraction (or primary economic affiliation) of a member of the Toronto economic elite, how strongly can one predict the economic sector within which his other directorships will be located? The argument would assert, of course, that the division between class fractions would make the knowledge of an individual's primary economic affiliation a powerful predictor of the sector in which his other economic ties are to be found.

To apply this test, we must first define the primary economic affiliation of each of the 164 individuals comprising the present study group. We can then say that an individual is a member of the merchant or of the industrial class fraction.

The criteria by which I made this identification are relatively straightforward. Those who held directorships in only one economic sector were obviously identified with that sector. Those who held directorships in more than one sector were identified with the sector in which: (a) they held an officership and/or "inside" directorship, implying full-time affiliation with a specific corporation, (b) if more than one such officership was ever held by an individual, the officership first held was used to identify primary affiliation. Failing (a) and (b), the primary identification used by the *Directory of Directors* was accepted. Using these criteria I could readily identify 154 individuals with a specifc economic sector (or class fraction).

Separation of the merchant and industrial class fractions is only the first of the two fundamental assertions of the *merchants against industry* argument. The dominance of the former over the latter is the other. This second assertion is also central to the *finance dominates industry* versus *capital integration* debate.[9] But allegations of the dominance of merchant capital over industrial capital are difficult to test empirically.[10] The *merchants against industry* argument holds that the staples base of the Canadian economy and the high degree of foreign control of Canadian industry, in themselves, demonstrate the validity of this assertion. Levitt (1970) and Neufeld (1972), on the other hand, attribute these characteristics of the Canadian economy to entirely different factors. In fact, they both note the relative *under*-development of Canada's financial sector.

Within the structuralist paradigm, as with the *merchants against industry* and *finance dominates industry* arguments, financial institutions tend to be regarded as the central institutions in the economy. Structuralists reach this conclusion from detailed analyses of networks of corporate relations using advanced and robust mathematical techniques (e.g., Levine, 1972; Mintz and Schwartz, 1978; Carroll, Fox and Ornstein, 1979). However, in contrast to Naylor (1972:20) and Clement (1975:66), structuralists tend to refrain from taking the step of inferring dominance from indications of centrality. Instead, some argue for "an approach to studying phenomena, such as interlocking directorships, which is deliberately cautious in its limits of generalization" (Berkowitz, 1979:22).

One of several valid reasons for the degree of caution on the part of many structuralists is the difficulty of applying unambiguous meaning to patterns of interlocking directorships. This, in turn, is partly a result of the fact that methodological limitations have forced most structural studies of corporate interlocks to avoid the issue of *directionality*. Assertions that centrality equals dominance require the falsification of the alternative hypothesis that banks are tightly interlocked with other sectors merely because this is their most effective method of attracting the business of firms represented by the directors elected to their boards. Under this alternative hypothesis, the phenomenon of banks' directorship interlocks is not the result of financial executives sitting in powerful positions on the boards of industrial firms, but the result of industrialists sitting on bank boards.

By consistently confining our unit of analysis to the directorships held by individuals we can incorporate the element of directionality in our analysis.

However, we can develop the most direct and parsimonious test of this asserted dominance from the national accounts of Canada and the United States for the time period under study. The *merchants against industry* argument holds that Canada had "an over-developed commercial sector." (Clement, 1977:14; cf. Naylor, 1972). This assertion implies the magnitude of the commercial sector relative to industry will be greater in Canada than in the United States.[11] We can empirically determine the relative magnitude of these sectors in the two economies by examining their respective national accounts. Similarly with Naylor's "merchant capital," and with the slightly different class fraction divisions inherent in Marx and Lenin.

Furthermore, the *merchants against industry* argument holds that Canadian merchant capital not only dominated Canadian industry, but was also instrumental in instigating the invasion of foreign industry (e.g., Naylor, 1972:16, Clement, 1975:1977). Merchant capital accomplished this by means of the national policy. Others, such as Clark (1939), Pentland (1961), and Phillips (1979) interpret the class alliances underlying the national policy very differently.[12] However, granting the possibility that the *merchants against industry* interpretation is correct, we can again empirically test the asserted dominance of Canadian merchant capital by excluding Canadian income accruing to foreign investment from the Canadian national accounts.

WERE MERCHANTS AND INDUSTRIALISTS DIFFERENT PEOPLE?

We find, first of all, that slightly over half the 164 members of the Toronto economic elite of the 1920s had institutional linkages to *both* merchant and industrial capital by virtue of holding directorships in both types of corporations. Specifically, 35 percent of this economic elite were tied only to mercantile firms, 12 percent were tied only to industrial corporations, and 53 percent were tied to both. Since a director must be a shareholder, these linkages imply direct financial involvement as well. These results tend to support the *merchants become industry*, and to refute the *merchants against industry* arguments.

Although this study is restricted to a specific time and place, other studies found similar results. Boyce (1979) conducted a small-scale study of the economic elite of Brantford, Ontario for the 1890s which comprised 22 individuals. Re-analysis of her data (1979:74–116) indicates that 55 percent of the individuals studied were active in *both* mercantile and industrial firms. A review of Naylor's (1975a;1975b) study of Canadian business in the 1870–1914 period leaves the strong impression that a high proportion of the individuals he writes about were *both* merchants and industrialists. Similarly, Ryerson (1975), Myers (1914), and MacDonald (1975) give innumerable examples of Canadians who were *both* merchants and industrialists.

Now, in an even better test of the validity of the respective arguments, we can determine the degree to which knowledge of an individual's class location permits us to predict the class fraction in which his other directorships will lie. We can apply this test to the *merchants against industry* versus *merchants become industry* debate from two perspectives: first, using a boundary between merchant and industrial capital which follows the staples perspective; and second, using the Marxist boundary between merchant's capital and productive capital. We can also use this test to begin to address the *banks dominate industry* versus *capital integration* debate by using yet another boundary between class fractions.

To all those individuals who held more than one directorship (81 percent of the study group), we can apply Goodman and Kruskal's tau as a test of predictive power. We find that knowing an individual's primary economic affiliation is of little if any help in increasing our ability to predict the sector in which his other directorships are to be found. Specifically, this knowledge increases our predictive power by only 2.4 percent following the staples perspective; by only 1.4 percent following the Marxist perspective; and by only 0.1 percent following the finance capital perspective. Among the Toronto economic elite of the 1920s, multiple directorships were almost as likely to cross the boundary between class fractions as they were to remain within them. Again, we can conclude that these findings tend to support the *merchants become industry*, and to refute the *merchants against industry* arguments. . . .

IF NOT SEPARATION, THEN DOMINANCE?

Both the *merchants against industry* and the *finance dominates industry* arguments hold that financial capital dominates industry: the former argument applying this relationship specifically to the Canadian case, and the latter holding it to be a general phenomenon of advanced industrial (i.e., monopoly) capitalism.

The major Canadian financial institutions have historically been the banks and insurance companies (Porter, 1965; Neufeld, 1972; Clement, 1975). We can begin to test these arguments, therefore, by determining who among the study group held directorships in these institutions. We find that the 164 members of the Toronto economic elite of the 1920s held a total of 86 bank and insurance directorships. Of these, only a small majority (51 percent) were held by financiers.

Assuming that these financial corporations are the major integrative institutions in the economy, it is unclear from the study group data whether the major policy decisions of these institutions (which are subject to approval by their full boards) are controlled by financiers themselves. The extremely slim majority by the members of the financial elite on these boards is insufficient to permit the rejection of the alternative hypothesis that directorship interlocks with financial institutions represent access to resources, not dominance. . . .

How, then, do we empirically test the *merchants against industry* argument's asserted dominance of merchant/financial capital? I have already proposed that the most parsimonious test of this assertion is by means of the national accounts of the United States and Canada. If, as this argument implies, an "overdeveloped commercial sector" dominated industrial capital in Canada but not in the United States, then this commercial sector will comprise a larger proportion of the national product of Canada than of the United States. Because of the different magnitudes of the state sector and of agriculture in these respective economies, the best test of this assertion of the *merchants against industry* argument is a cross-national comparison of the *ratios* of merchant, commercial or financial capital to industrial or productive capital.

For the United States, we find that the ratio of Clement's "commercial sector" to industry is 1.1:1 and the ratio of Naylor's "merchant capital" to industry is 1.5:1. For Canada, these ratios are only 0.8:1 and 1.3:1, respectively. Similarly, we find that the ratios of the "commercial" sector to productive capital and of financial capital to productive capital are also lower in Canada than they are in the United States.

The essential logic of the *merchants against industry* argument, which applies regardless of the nationality of ownership of various sectors of the economy, is clearly that mercantile growth was inflated and industrial growth was obstructed in Canada. The data for the period under review indicated just the opposite and clearly refute this argument.

However, the *merchants against industry* argument holds that Canadian merchant capital not only dominated Canadian industry, but also was instrumental in instigating the invasion of foreign industry. This implies that the ratio of merchant capital to industrial capital will be greater in Canada than in the United States when the effects of foreign investment in Canada are removed from the comparative data. These data show that, for the period under review, all of the ratios of merchant/financial capital to industrial/productive capital are virtually identical for the two national economies. They clearly refute the *merchants against industry* argument's contention that the dominance of merchant capital in Canada represents a fundamental difference from the situation in the United States (e.g., Naylor, 1972:24–25).

CONCLUSIONS

This empirical study has tended to refute the asserted separation of the Canadian capitalist class into merchant and industrial fractions and the dominance of the former over the latter. Our data have demonstrated that the majority of the Toronto economic elite of the 1920s were members of *both* class fractions. Although this time period may not have been an ideal test of the *merchant against industry* argument as it could be a period of transition, the findings are consistent with smaller or less methodologically rigorous studies of economic elites in earlier periods. Furthermore, we have shown that knowing the class fraction to which an individual member of this elite is primarily affiliated gives little if any help in predicting the class fraction to which he will tie himself economically. And finally, this study has shown the relative predominance of merchant capital within the American, not the Canadian, national economy.

To summarize, the results of all the various tests which we applied to the competing arguments have been mutually reinforcing. Together, they clearly refute the fundamental assumptions of the *merchants against industry* argument and support a synthesis of the *merchants become industry* and *capital integration* arguments.

Notes

[1] Canadian manufacturing is 53 percent foreign-owned and 59 percent foreign-controlled (Statistics Canada, 1977).

[2] And ultimately, of course, to Hilferding (1910). For a different (and more widely-accepted) version of Lenin, see the *capital integration* argument below.

[3] See also Clement (1975:56, 64, 66, 67, 71, 354–355; 1977:16, 78).

[4] Nevertheless, to Dobb the successful development of capitalism by this path was problematic.

[5] On the other hand, Clement argues that in the United States industrialists "transformed *themselves* into corporate capitalists" (1977:78, emphasis added).

[6] Naylor's later major work is restricted to the 1867–1914 period and thus is not directed toward resolving the time period of this synthesis of class fractions. Although he provides a useful narrative of the Canadian merger movement of 1909–12, he continues to note the sharp division between Canadian merchant and industrial capital through 1914 (e.g., 1975b:74 78, 97, 218, 282–3).

[7] I am greatly indebted to Lorne Tepperman for providing access to his data base.

[8] Tepperman used ten biographical sources, including the first editions of the *Directory of Directors*, to identify the directorship and officerships held by this elite group.

[9] Note, however, that these different debates use somewhat different boundaries between the class fractions.

[10] Ideally, we could test Naylor's operationalization of this assertion—"The dominance of merchant capital means the draining off of funds into mercantile pursuits and away from industry" (1972:20)—by systematically examining financial institutions' loans to and investments in firms in his "merchant" and "industrial" sectors. If we were able to show that investments, loans and interest rates favored the former over the latter sector, the assertion would be supported. Unfortunately, such data are not available.

[11] Clement specifically contrasts the dominance of the financial fraction in Canada with the dominance of the industrial fraction in the United States. Thus there was a "retardation of industrialization imposed by Canadian financial interests" (1977:78) in Canada, as opposed to a successful process of industrial development in the United States.

[12] However, an analysis of the Brantford, Ontario economic elite supports the *merchants against industry* interpretation (Boyce, 1979).

References

Acheson, T.W. (1973) "The changing social origins of the Canadian industrial elite. "In *Enterprise and National Development*, edited by Glen Porter and Robert D. Cuff, pp. 51–79. Toronto: Hakkert.

Berkowitz, S.D. (1975) "The dynamics of elite structure." Waltham, Mass: Brandeis University, Unpublished doctoral dissertation.

——— (1979) "Structural and non-structural models of elites." Toronto: Institute of Policy Analysis, University of Toronto. Working Paper 7910.

Boyce, Diane G. (1979) "The bourgeoisie and the national policy: a case study of Brantford, Ont." Downsview, Ontario: York University. Unpublished M.A. Thesis.

Carroll, William K., John Fox and Michael D. Ornstein (1979) "The network of directorate interlocks among the largest Canadian firms." Downsview, Ontario: York University, Department of Sociology, mimeo.

Clark, S.D. (1939) *The Canadian Manufacturers' Association*. Toronto: University of Toronto Press.

Clement, Wallace (1975) *The Canadian Corporate Elite*. Toronto: McClelland and Stewart.

———— (1977) *Continental Corporate Power*. Toronto: McClelland and Stewart.

Dobb, Maurice (1963) *Studies in the Development of Capitalism*. New York: International Publishers [1947].

Dominion Bureau of Statistics (1959) *The Canadian Balance of Payments 1958 and International Investment Position*. Ottawa: Queen's Printer.

Drache, D. (1978) "Rediscovering political economy." In *A Practical Guide to Canadian Political Economy*, edited by Wallace Clement et al. Toronto: Lorimer.

Drummond, Ian (1978) "Review, R.T. Naylor, history of Canadian business." *Canadian Historical Review* 59:90–93.

Evans, Peter (1979) *Dependent Development*. Princeton: Princeton University Press.

Frank. A.G. (1967) *Capitalism and Underdevelopment in Latin America*. New York: Monthly Review Press.

Grayson, J. Paul (1980) "Class." In *Class, State, Ideology and Change,* edited by J. Paul Grayson, pp. 11–14. Toronto: Holt, Rinehart and Winston.

Hilferding, Rudolph (1970) *Le Capital Financier* Translated by Marcel Olliver. Paris: Editions de Minuit [1910].

Hoselitz, B.F. (1960) *Sociological Aspects of Economic Growth*. Glencoe: Free Press.

Innis, H.A. (1930) *The Fur Trade in Canada*. New Haven: Yale University Press.

———— (1956) *Essays in Canadian Economic History*. Toronto: University of Toronto Press.

Johnson, Leo n.d. "The contradiction between independent commodity production and capitalist production in Upper Canada:1820–1850." Waterloo, Ontario: University of Waterloo, Department of History, mimeo.

Kay, Geoffrey (1975) *Development and Underdevelopment*. London: Macmillan.

Laxer, Gordon (1979) "Government policies and the origin of Canada's branch plant economy, 1837–1914." Paper presented to the Annual Meetings of the Canadian Sociology and Anthropology Association, Saskatoon.

Lenin, V.I. (1975) "Imperialism, the highest stage of capitalism." Republished in *The Lenin Anthology*, edited by Robert C. Tucker, pp. 204–274. [1917].

———— (1968) *Collected Works*, Vol. 39. Moscow: Progress Publishers.

Levine, Joel (1972) "The sphere of influence." *American Sociological Review* 37:14–27.

Levitt, Kari (1970) *Silent Surrender*. Toronto: Macmillan.

Leys, Colin (1975) *Underdevelopment in Kenya*. Berkeley: University of California Press.

MacDonald, L.R. (1975) "Merchants against industry: an idea and its origins." *Canadian Historical Review* 56:263–281.

Mandel, Ernest (1978) *Late Capitalism*. Translated by Joris de Bres. London: Verso [1972].

Marchak, Patricia (1979) *In Whose Interests*. Toronto: McClelland and Stewart.

Marshall, Herbert, Frank Southard Jr., and Kenneth W. Taylor (1976) *Canadian-American Industry*. Toronto: McClelland and Stewart [1936].

Marx, Karl (1954) *Capital*, Vo. I. Moscow: Progress Publishers [1887].

———— (1956) *Capital*, Vol. II. Moscow: Progress Publishers [1893].

———— (1959) *Capital*, Vol. III. Moscow: Progress Publishers [1894].

Meyers, G. (1975) *A History of Canadian Wealth*. Toronto: Lorimer [1914].

Mintz, Beth and Michael Schwartz (1978) "The role of financial institutions in interlock networks." Paper presented to the New

Dimension in Structural Analysis Colloquium, University of Toronto.

Naylor, R.T. (1972) "The rise and fall of the third commercial empire of the St. Lawrence." In *Capitalism and the National Question in Canada*, edited by Gary Teeple. Toronto: University of Toronto Press.

———— (1975a) *The History of Canadian Business 1867–1914: Vol. 1, The Banks and Finance Capital*. Toronto: Lorimer.

———— (1975b) *The History of Canadian Business 1867–1914: Vol. 2, Industrial Development*. Toronto: Lorimer.

———— (1975c) "Dominion of capital: Canada and international investment." In *Domination*, edited by A. Kontos, pp. 33–68. Toronto: University of Toronto Press.

Neufeld, E.P. (1972) *The Financial System of Canada*. Toronto: Macmillan.

Niosi, Jorge (1978) *The Economy of Canada*. Montreal: Black Rose.

Pentland, H.C. (1961) "Labour and the development of industrial capitalism in Canada." Toronto: University of Toronto, Unpublished doctoral dissertation.

Phillips, Paul (1979) "The national policy revisited." *Journal of Canadian Studies* 14(3): 3–13.

Porter, John (1965) *The Vertical Mosaic*. Toronto: University of Toronto Press.

Ryerson, Stanley B. (1975) *Unequal Union*. Second edition. Toronto: Progress Books.

Statistics Canada (1977) *Canada Year Book*. Ottawa: Statistics Canada.

Tepperman, Lorne (1977) "Effects of the demographic transition upon access to the Toronto elite." *Canadian Review of Sociology and Anthropology* 14:285–293.

Tönnies, F. (1957) *Community and Society*. East Lansing: University of Michigan Press [1887].

United States Department of Commerce, Bureau of the Census (1975) *Historical Statistics of the United States, Colonial Times to 1970*. Washington: United States Government Printing Office.

Urquhart, M.C. and K. Buckley (1965) *Historical Statistics of Canada*. Toronto: Macmillan.

Wallerstein, Immanuel (1974) *The Modern World System*. New York: Academic Press.

Watkins, Melville H. (1963) "A staple theory of economic growth." *Canadian Journal of Economics and Political Science* 29(2):141–158.

———— (1966) "The 'American system' and Canada's 'national policy'." *Bulletin of the Canadian Association for American Studies* 27–42.

———— (1973) "Resources and underdevelopment." In *(Canada) Ltd.: The Political Economy of Dependency*, edited by R.M. Laxer, pp. 26–41. Toronto: McClelland and Stewart.

———— (1977) "The staple theory revisited." *Journal of Canadian Studies* 12:83–95.

Weber, Max (1961) *General Economic History*, New York: Collier [1919–20].

30 Mobility Deprivation Through Educational Deprivation

John Porter

JOHN PORTER (1922–1979) was a Professor of Sociology at Carleton University, Ottawa for many years, until his death. He had also served as Vice-President of Carleton University and spent visiting years at Harvard University and the University of Toronto. His major volumes are *Canadian Society, Sociological Perspectives* edited with B.R. Blishen, F.E. Jones and K.D. Naegele (1961, 1964, 1968, 1971); *The Vertical Mosaic: An Analysis of Social Class and Power in Canada* (1965); *Canadian Social Structure* (1967); *Macrosociology: Research and Theory* with J.S. Coleman and A. Etzioni (1970); *Toward 2000: The Future of Post-secondary Education in Ontario*, with B.R. Blishen, J.R. Evans et al. (1971); *Does Money Matter?* with M.R. Porter and B.R. Blishen (1973); *Ascription and Achievement: Studies in Mobility and Status Attainment in Canada* with M. Boyd, J. Goyder, F.E. Jones, H.A. McRoberts, F.E. Jones and P.C. Pineo (1985); and *The Measure of Canadian Society: Education, Equality and Opportunity* (1979). Porter's work has had an enormous impact on research in the areas of social inequality and social organization, and has helped define Canadian society for an international scholarly audience in the social sciences. The latter influence is marked by the McIver Award, given by the American Sociological Association for Porter's *Vertical Mosaic* for its " . . . comprehensive analysis of social stratification and contribution to macrosociology."

The necessity in the 1950's of importing skills from abroad to meet the labour force increment in skilled occupations suggests that Canadian institutions—particularly educational and industrial—were not geared to provide mobility opportunities. International migrations which have come with industrialization have been processes of social mobility as well as movements of labour as a factor of production. It has been suggested that the low skill levels of the great migration into the United States in the first fifteen years of the century had the effect of pushing up the existing population to higher occupational levels.[1] It may be speculated that, in the present period, the emigration of skilled workers from some European countries provides mobility opportunities for the less skilled workers in those countries and necessitates the importation of labour at the bottom. This process

has taken place in the United Kingdom to some extent, at least until 1962, with Commonwealth labour, and in the Common Market countries by freely moving labour. The eastern European immigrant to the United States during the early part of the century undoubtedly improved his position and found himself with greater opportunities, in the same way that the West Indian labourer moving into the United Kingdom is better off than had he remained in Jamaica. International benefits thus accrue from industrialization. In the 1950's, Canadian workers benefited much less than they might have done from this combined process of migration and mobility. Where Canadian immigration policy seeks skilled and professional workers as an alternative to educational reforms, mobility deprivation for Canadians continues.

The bridges that help the manual worker

in his upward mobility are technical and vocational training, apprenticeship, and training within industry of which the last seems to have been the most important. All these bridges could be much more effectively developed in Canada. With increasing unemployment in the 1960s it became clear that inadequate training facilities were keeping a large portion of the Canadian labour force unnecessarily unskilled. . . .

It must be remembered that skilled and professional workers never have constituted a majority of the immigrant workers although their proportions have been increasing. In the early 1960's there was still a large number of immigrants going into labouring and service occupations. Canadians no doubt avoided some of the unskilled occupations in the period of the great boom, probably because some of these were becoming known as jobs for immigrants, and also because they held these jobs in low esteem. With the onset of unemployment by the 1960's there was a great reservoir of unused, unskilled labour, both immigrant and native, a situation greatly aggravated by the trek from the farms to the cities.

Along with the increase of skilled occupations that comes with industrialization there comes an expansion of all white collar occupations. This segment of the work world offers further opportunities for upward mobility. The professions, which as we have seen provided a limited opportunity for mobility for the native labour force, made up between one-fifth and one-quarter of all white collar occupations in 1951.[3] Other occupations within this group would be classed as proprietary, managerial, official, clerical, commercial, and financial. Both the number and the proportion of the labour force in all these occupations increased during the 1950's with the professions increasing at a faster rate than the others. . . .

Because the managerial, clerical, and commercial occupations have generally been under-represented among immigrants, it seems clear that the expansion of these white collar occupations has provided the native labour force with some mobility opportunities. This statement requires qualification, however. The rate of increase in clerical, commercial, and financial jobs has been greater for women than for men, which fact is consistent with the great increase in the number of women, married and single, who work for pay. How their participation in the labour force should be assessed in terms of general upward mobility is difficult to say. Many of them are second income earners in their families.

It is generally accepted in the sociological literature that any transference of workers from the broad category of manual to the broad category of non-manual work results in general upward mobility and, considering the values attached to being a white collar worker, it probably does represent upward mobility from the subjective perspective of class. It would be wrong, however, to argue on the basis of objective criteria that the growth of white collar bureaucracy represents over-all upward mobility when at the same time there is taking place an upward shift in skill levels of manual occupations. The massive army of clerks and salespeople required to keep the files and to record and distribute the product of the manual worker are more akin to unskilled or semi-skilled workers from the point of view of both their training and their earnings. . . .

We might conclude that although there has been a transferring of workers from manual to non-manual occupations it is questionable that all of this shift represents upward mobility from "lower level" manual occupations. It seems that these lower white collar occupations have been filled more by the native labour force than by immigrants, and that the shift has provided, at best, a questionable mobility for the native-born.

The interrelation which has here been suggested between immigration, educational level of the "native" labour force, and upward social mobility must be considered in the light of another social process, that is, the tendency of immigrants themselves to be upwardly mobile after they arrive in Canada. Occupational analysis of the immigrant labour force is based on the "intended" occupations of immigrants. It is well known, for example, that many immigrants with other occupational skills have come to Canada as agricultural workers but that they remain in this occupation for only a short time. Between 1946 and 1953, 25,000 immigrants were such temporary agricultural labourers.[3] One report based on the 1951 census indicates that a large proportion of those who expressed the intention of farming when they entered Canada between the end of the war and 1951 were not in this occupation in 1951.[4] Whether or not they fared better than the Canadian-born who were moving from the farms in such great numbers we cannot know without further extensive inquiry.

Studies of earlier periods of immigration indicate that the longer the residence period of immigrants, the greater will be their proportions in skilled or white collar occupations, and the less will be their proportion in unskilled labouring occupations. To illustrate this point we must go back to an exhaustive study of immigrant occupations at the time of the 1931 census. In the category of farm operators, proprietors, and managers the proportion of all male immigrant workers in this category increased from 13 per cent for those who came between 1926 and 1931 to 38 per cent for those who arrived before 1911.[5] No doubt most of this increase can be attributed to the greater ease of becoming a farm owner by homesteading during the earlier immigration period. The proportion of immigrants in clerical occupations rose from 6 per cent for those who came during the period 1920 to 1931 to 13 per cent for those who came between 1911 and 1920. For skilled occupations the differences were 10 per cent for the arrivals between 1926 and 1931 and 15 per cent for those who arrived before 1926. In 1931 farm labourers and industrial un-

skilled and semi-skilled workers made up over two-thirds of the immigrants who had arrived in Canada between 1926 and 1931, but only one-third of those who had arrived before 1911.[6] Thus it would seem that immigrants who came prior to 1931 benefited along with the Canadian-born from the opportunities for upward mobility that came with the industrial expansion in the decade following World War 1, although to be accurate we would have to "adjust" these proportions for age as a factor in mobility independent of immigration. There is no reason to suppose that the immigrants after World War II have not also been moving up with the expansion of the last fifteen years. . . .

The above discussion has thus made it clear that mobility deprivation in a society of industrial growth and immigration results from inadequate educational facilities. Judging from its educational systems, Canada has not been a mobility oriented society. Collective goals do not seem to have been defined, however vaguely, in terms of increasing opportunities through free universal education.

IMPORTATION OF SKILL: AN EARLIER PERIOD

An examination of earlier periods of immigration should tell us whether the conditions which applied after World War II were unique to that period or whether they were more or less a continuation of a pattern built into Canadian society. Comparisons are of course difficult because the occupational groupings used in immigration and labour force statistics are not always the same, but they are similar enough to warrant some comparison and conclusions.

Of the immigrants of 1924 and 1925, 17 per cent were classed as "mechanics" while only 14 per cent of the total labour force was classed as skilled.[7] Over the decade 1921 to 1931 the increase of foreign-born in manufacturing and construction occupations was

30 per cent while the Canadian-born in these occupations increased by 20 per cent.[8] Such large occupational groups comprise of course all skill levels but these proportions do indicate the extent to which industrialization absorbed immigrants. It does not seem unreasonable to infer that they must have been recruited in some measure into the higher skill levels as well as the unskilled. . . .

Both post-war periods are similar in their heavy reliance on immigration for skills and professions. It will be recalled that for the 1950's about two-fifths of the estimated new professional jobs and an estimated one-half of the new skilled jobs were filled by immigrants. In the 1920's the new skilled and professional jobs were not increasing as quickly so that it would be expected that those qualified for them would be a smaller proportion of the immigrant force.

MIGRATION AND CLASS STRUCTURE

The reliance on immigration for recruitment to the new occupational roles that come with industrialization has been an important aspect of Canadian social structure, and it continues to be so because this method of recruitment appears as an increasing trend and an important element of immigration policy. Speaking in the House of Commons in December 1963, Mr. Guy Favreau, the minister of citizenship and immigration, said that Canada wanted young skilled workers and entrepreneurs with the capital and experience to operate their own enterprises in Canada. Far from taking jobs away from Canadians, he said, these businessmen would help to create jobs for unskilled Canadian workers.[9] Educational facilities have never caught up with the kind of society that has been emerging in Canada during the century, and this deficiency in turn must reflect either a certain amount of social incapacity to steer the society in the direction of more adequate ad-

aptation, or a negative value placed on upward mobility, education, or both.

It is now possible to sketch a little more clearly the formation of social class in this society of industrial growth with its associated immigration and emigration. At each period of industrial growth, as new opportunities for upward mobility appear, each increment of skilled and professional roles is filled in part by immigration, in part by the Canadian-trained, and in part by upgrading. The same sources must replace those who leave the labour force for various reasons. There obviously has been some mobility for Canadian industrial workers, but there is little doubt that there could have been much more. There could, too, have been many more opportunities for their children to advance into the ranks of professional and skilled workers. Instead, there are not enough young people adequately prepared to take on the new roles because neither the social function of education nor the other means of acquiring skills within industry seem to have been sufficiently understood.

It is possible to speculate about the composition of the lower levels of unskilled workers. Undoubtedly a large segment of this class is made up from immigration into jobs which Canadians do not value highly. For men, these jobs are outdoors, on the "frontier," underground and in some service occupations; for women, they are predominantly domestic service occupations. But the unskilled class also includes a large proportion of the native off-farm migration which has been going on for a very long time. It could be argued that farmers' sons who join the ranks of unskilled urban labour experience downward social mobility when compared to their fathers, particularly in Canada where farming has been associated with land ownership. Changes in agriculture have created a new "landless proletariat" to join with an immigrant proletariat in the rapidly growing cities. This unskilled bottom layer forms a large part of the unemployed. In rural areas, too, educational institutions have not been geared to the changing economic and social structure, so that their city-bound students have not been provided with the appropriate training. Here of course there is an intense clash between new social functions and those values which extol the rural way of life with its independence and hard work.

Among emigrants, as we have seen, are a considerable number, although never a majority, of skilled and professional workers. The opportunities for mobility offered by their departure are taken up in the same way as in the increment of new jobs, with immigration playing an important part. The greater part of the emigrant force is made up of unskilled and non-professional white collar workers who think they will have better chances in the United States. Such an outlet, as already suggested, is important in preventing the hardening of class lines in a society where upward mobility opportunities are limited. It would be interesting to know something about the ethnic composition of this emigrating group. If, for example, second generation Canadians experience barriers to mobility because of their ethnic origins they may be diverted to what they believe to be and, in all probability is, a more mobile society for them. . . .

Immigration and its effect on Canada have always been the subject of varying opinions, and often judgments about the capacity of the economy to absorb newcomers have been confused with judgments about where the immigrants should come from. In a short examination of immigration of the inter-war years in his *Colony to Nation*, Professor Lower has made a series of such judgments.[10] "Immigration," he said, "was proving as injurious for the quality of the population as it was ineffective for the quantity," or, in effect, social injury results from bad immigrants driving out good native-born. ". . . Too many young people of energy and good education . . ." were leaving for the United States. "To replace them within a single generation called for too great a step in adaptation on the part of recently arrived immigrants however good these latter might be intrinsically." Using Gresham's Law as an analogy, Lower says " 'cheap' men drive out 'dear' men," a proposition, he asserts, that is as sound sociologically as was Gresham's financially! His picture is one of European-born peasants coming in at the bottom while Canadian professionals go out at the top, showing " . . . how inexorably this 'Gresham's Law of Immigration' was working."

It is difficult to see how immigrant peasants affect the career opportunities of the professional class or even the skilled classes, because skilled jobs require skilled workers. The more highly trained move because they think their chances are better. What was more likely to have been taking place was that cheap unskilled immigrant labour was replacing cheap unskilled Canadian labour as the latter was drawn into the United States by somewhat higher real wages.[11] By importing more skilled and professional as well as unskilled labour, there was less need of the educational reforms that could result in improving the quality of Canadian labour and thus meet the needs of industrialization. As it was, Canadian development after both wars would have been seriously impeded without skilled and professional immigrants.

Although Lower's meaning is not always clear he seems to imply only immigration from eastern Europe was socially injurious. "During the period after the war, efforts seem to have been made to bring in, not persons from the British Isles, who were soon at home and too independent for these purposes [of providing cheap labour], but peasants from Eastern Europe, who could be least acquainted with Canadian conditions.[12] The facts are that the proportion of labour force immigrants who came from Britain between 1921 and 1925 was 58 per cent, for the next five years 38 per cent, and for 1930 and 1931, 45 per cent. For each of these three periods, respectively, the proportion coming from eastern Europe was 10 per cent, 22 per cent (clearly a substantial increase), and 19 per cent.[13] Thus at no time were eastern Europeans more than 25 per cent of the immigrant labour force. By 1931 they still made up only 12 per cent of the total labour force, although the later arrivals were becoming more urban than rural. Twenty-five per cent of all eastern Europeans in the labour force were unskilled urban labourers by 1931,[14] while British immigrants were much more numerous in urban industrial occupations....

Notes

[1] Elbridge Sibley, "Some Demographic Clues to Stratification," *American Sociological Review,* VII (1942).

[2] Noah M. Meltz, *Factors Determining Occupational Trends in the Canadian Economy* (mimeo., Department of Labour, Ottawa, 1961).

[3] Committee on Manpower and Employment, *Proceedings,* no. 9, p. 704.

[4] *Ibid.,* p. 703.

[5] A.H. LeNeveu, "The Evolution and Present-Day Significance of the Canadian Occupational Structure," 1931 census monograph (unpublished).

[6] *Ibid.*

[7] *Canada Year Book, 1925,* 178.

[8] Le Neveu, "Canadian Occupational Structure."

[9] Canada, House of Commons, *Debates,* Dec. 14, 1963, 5,879.

[10] A.R.M. Lower, *Colony to Nation* (Toronto, 1957), 482ff.

[11] Cf. Corbett, *Canada's Immigration Policy,* 132, 170.

[12] Lower, *Colony to Nation,* 490

[13] *Census of Canada, 1931,* vol. VII, Table 14.

[14] *Ibid.,* Table 16.

Race and Ethnic Relations

Introduction

In the preceding section on social in-equality, we claimed that racial and eth-nic groups sometimes practised closure, excluding "outsiders" from scarce positions and rewards. But far more can be said, and has been said, about race and ethnic relations in Canada. This section will provide a broader picture of ethnicity and racism as important subjects for sociological analysis.

Sociologists have viewed *ethnicity* from at least three perspectives: as a cultural system, an institutional system and an economic system. We shall briefly consider each.

In its most popular and common usage "ethnicity" is an identification with some birthplace, cultural or ancestral origin. Ethnicity exists because people feel it does. But what makes people feel strongly enough about their ethnic origins to want to associate with others of the same origin and keep up traditional customs? A central source of information on this question is Jeffrey Reitz's book *The Survival of Ethnic Groups* (1980). Reitz shows that language retention is a major means by which ethnic groups hold on to their culture and iden-tity. Language, as anthropologists have shown us, is not only a way of describing the world; it is a way of thinking about it.

We examined a related view in an earlier section. The article by Gillis, Richard and Hagan showed ethnic variations in response to crowding. From their standpoint, ethnic-ity is not only a kind of self-identification or commitment to a group or culture, but also a way of experiencing the world. Thus, authors Gillis, Richard and Hagan show that different ethnic groups, using their ancestral culture, are more or less able to deal with the problems of crowding confronting them thousands of miles (and many generations) away from where these collective ways of thinking, feeling and behaving originated.

We shall not discuss this cultural ap-proach further because sociologists have taken several other approaches that are less immediately obvious to the non-sociologist. One such approach is presented by Ray-mond Breton, in a classic article published in 1964, "Institutional completeness of ethnic communities." Professor Breton sought ways to distinguish among ethnic communities, which visibly differ as much one from another as they do from the dominant Anglo-Saxon community. He found large variations in what he came to call "institutional completeness"—the degree to which an ethnic group has created a set of social, cultural and economic institutions sufficiently complete to allow virtual isolation from the rest of society.

Professor Breton demonstrated considerable variation among ethnic communities, then asked: What causes institutional completeness to vary in this way? and does it matter how institutionally complete or incomplete an ethnic group may be? How much, for example, does institutional completeness affect the willingness and ability of an immigrant to assimilate into the larger, non-ethnic society? Breton finds that the degree of institutional completeness determines the proportion of individuals who have most of their personal relations within the ethnic group. Ethnic organizations discourage group members from going outside the community, providing instead a context within which community members can meet and socialize with other community members. They continue to raise the salience of ethnic membership and press for group interests. Organization leaders act to maintain or increase participation in these ethnic organizations. Thus, the internal politics of ethnic communities is enormously important in shaping the communal organizations and, through them, the communal and personal life of immigrants and their children. And, as we saw in Professor Breton's article in the preceding section, this institutional completeness has great importance for the inter-ethnic conflict over scarce resources.

Professor Breton points out, and Professor Reitz documents more fully in his later study, that "ethnic communities are formed, grow and disappear; they go through a life-cycle." Institutional completeness and its effects change over time after the first waves of immigration and community building. Factors affecting the strength of institutional completeness include group distinctiveness (language, colour and religion among others), the size and composition of migrant streams and the type of resources (including wealth and job skills) immigrants bring to Canada.

From this perspective, ethnic communities and ethnicity may once have filled a need. The need in turn produced community institutions, and these institutions come to maintain and enlarge their clientele in their own interests. Prejudice or discrimination often plays little further part; communities and ethnic sentiments may survive long after discrimination, an inability to speak English, or a need for economic co-operation have disappeared. This is particularly true of third-generation, or middle-class ethnicity which Professor Reitz describes and tries to explain.

In this respect, two ethnic groups stand out as needing explanation. They possess strong institutional completeness despite the passing of many conditions that might have once called for communal action: the members of these groups are highly educated, largely middle class, fluent in English, often born in Canada, and protected (in law if not always in fact) against discrimination. They are the Jews and the Chinese. Of course, evidence in Professor Reitz's book and elsewhere, as for example in work by Peter Li (1986; also, Bolaria and Li, 1985) suggests that discrimination against the Chinese in Canada remains a serious problem today. Even *perceived* discrimination increases the ethnic identification and solidarity of Chinese Canadians, though it does not do the same for other ethnic groups Reitz studied.

Origins of Chinese institutional completeness can be found in the history of Chinese settlement in Canada and the conditions encountered at that time, as an article by Peter Li in this section illustrates. Using a case study approach relying on oral histories obtained from first-generation Chinese immigrants who had been living in Canada from 50 to 70 years, Li reminds us that between 1923 and 1947 the Chinese were barred from immigrating to Canada and subjected to numerous legal restrictions if already in the country. The economic survival of this victimized ethnic minority depended on creating and maintaining strong kinship and communal ties on the Canadian prairie and elsewhere.

A common strategy was the establishment of business partnerships based on kinship. Though the partnerships were fluid, subject to changing opportunities in a hostile environment, they were typically reliable and always available when needed. In this way, kinship and friendship served to support continued survival in a difficult environment very much as they had in the creation of secret societies described by Bonnie Erickson in Section 5 above. To generalize from these examples, kinship "particularism" still has a very important part to play in modern societies which are generally thought of as "universalistic" and destructive of traditional social ties.

Where the Jews are concerned, current discrimination is less evident than for the Chinese. Indeed, Jews are doing better economically than any others with the same amount of education. The explanation of ethnic cohesion may lie in perceived, anticipated or feared discrimination. Yet an attempt by Morton Weinfeld to verify this explanation is inconclusive at best. His study of the Jewish subeconomy of Montreal, excerpted in this section, shows a high degree of Jewish involvement with other Jews as customers. "Participation in the Jewish subeconomy of Montreal cannot be explained by the factor of immigration, by perceptions of anti-Semitism or by religious correlates," he writes. There is little evidence that people participate because they prefer dealing with other Jews. Nor does Professor Weinfeld find

either economic costs or benefits associated with participating. His explanations include long-standing habit and a residential distribution of Jews that would bring them into close proximity. Both explanations are plausible. Weinfeld's article is useful in reminding us that ethnicity is extremely subtle, persisting for reasons that even sociologists may not understand. All we can say with certainty is that an ethnic community, like any other community, will tend to maintain itself if institutionally complete, perhaps because it helps in the interethnic struggle for scarce resources.

By contrast, *racism* is action directed against a visibly distinguishable racial or ethnic group. Like ethnicity, racism is complex in its origins and manifestations. It may or may not be motivated, consciously or unconsciously, by economic or political self-interest. Like ethnicity, it is ultimately rooted in ethnocentrism—the belief that one's own group is the best of all. Just as racism may strengthen ethnic identity (out of self-defence), so may ethnic sentiment, taken to an extreme, produce racism.

Many explanations of racism have been offered. One, put forward typically by racists, is that minorities bring racism on themselves by behaviour that is clannish, exclusive or disrespectful of the dominant society. The study of the "authoritarian personality" by Theodor Adorno et al. (1969) showed that this way of thinking is part of a world view that values submission and uniformity, at whatever cost. Another explanation of racism is primarily economic. Some, like Peter Li (1986), argue that the making and enforcement of demeaning distinctions against certain visible minorities may be economically advantageous as a way of justifying depressed wages and diminished legal rights. This fits well with the observation that racism often surfaces at a time of economic turmoil (e.g., post-World War I Germany) and proceeds by denying the essential similarity of the oppressed to the oppressor. Yet political turmoil is just as likely to excite racist sentiments: racism, like the control of deviance, is a way of defining and strongly enforcing a group's moral boundaries and enlivening group solidarity through scapegoating.

The treatment of Native peoples in Canada is viewed by Rita Bienvenue as a "colonizing" behaviour in her article in this section. Canada's Native peoples were accorded the same status as colonized people in other parts of the world. This kind of racism may, in its first instance, take the form of theft and murder: valuable land is taken away from those who already inhabit it. But once force has established the peace, racism takes on other forms: demeaning paternalism, neglect and occupational discrimination. No social group has suffered as extreme racism in Canada as the Native peoples. Although this problem continues today, changes are in the making. On the one hand, tougher anti-discrimination laws are making racism harder to practise openly. On the other hand, the Native peoples are organizing more effectively to claim their treaty land rights and these claims are getting a somewhat more sympathetic reception than in the past.

Evolutionary theories of a century ago justified racism on the grounds that Anglo-Saxons had risen to a higher stage of civilization than Native peoples; such theories no longer command much respect today. The ethnic/racial majority no longer believes that Natives are undeserving or too incompetent or naive to govern themselves. Thus, the most extreme case of racism in our history, the treatment of Native peoples, is gradually though not painlessly being rectified. But other forms of racism remain, especially discrimination directed against visible minorities such as the Chinese and Blacks.

Racism is much subtler today than it once was. Discriminatory racial attitudes, if not acted on in the full light of public affairs, may show up privately, in marriage and friendship. In their article on racial attitudes towards mixed marriage, Ronald Lambert and James Curtis show an encouraging increase in the percentage of adult Canadians approving of marriage between Roman Catholics and Protestants, Jews and non-Jews, and Whites and Blacks. What is striking here is the differential willingness to accept these changes. Least accepting are the "other Canadians," those people of neither French nor English ancestry who have, themselves, historically experienced discrimination and prejudice. Not only are they less accepting today, but their rate of attitude change towards acceptance has been slowest of all groups.

Without more information it is hard to know all of the reasons for group differences in the acceptance of intergroup marriage. The "other Canadians" may be less educated, more rural in origin, or otherwise less informed about the world than English and French Canadians; and these background differences might produce the lower level of tolerance. Or, pressures of economic assimilation, on the one hand, and the encouragements of multiculturalism, on the other, may be straining ethnic identities in ways that make ethnic group members (especially community leaders) long for a clearer definition of group boundaries. Personal choices like marriage offer important opportunities to emphasize the significance of staying within one's group. The authors note that "It is precisely in minority groups where intergroup marriages are most likely to occur and where consequently there is most threat from them" that we find the strongest opposition to intergroup marriage. The dilemma being posed for the group is real, not hypothetical as it is for the numerically larger and more secure Anglophone and Francophone majority.

This argues along the same lines as Richard Hamilton (1975) did in concluding that anti-Black sentiment in the United States is strongest among White working-men, not White intellectuals; because the former, not the latter, face a direct economic threat from the economic integration of working class Blacks. Ultimately, racism is bound to have some rational basis, though that only goes to explain, and not to justify, the behaviour.

Where then does research on ethnic and race relations stand today? A few of its many themes have been mentioned here. Many researchers plow the furrows of cultural analysis, studying the values and identities of ethnic groups and the workings of multiculturalism. Others follow the insight of Raymond Breton who saw ethnicity as a political and organizational issue, not merely a cultural one. And increasingly, research is examining the Marxist model, by focusing on the economic significance of ethnicity and racism within a class-stratified society.

This section ends with an article by Gordon Darroch re-examining the theories of John Porter. Porter named his work *The Vertical Mosaic* because he viewed Canadian society as a hierarchy (hence, "vertical") made up of numerous, differently coloured and unmixing elements (hence, "mosaic"). Porter feared that ethnic groups were assimilating too slowly for Canada's good, and that faster assimilation required more social mobility, which in turn required more educational opportunity. He held that minorities tended to occupy positions for which they had been imported (sometimes) generations earlier, when Canadians had been unwilling or unable to do a required job. Because of their "entrance status" and limited mobility, ethnic minorities tended to continue holding down the worst positions, getting too little education, and having too little importance in the society.

Today, as Darroch shows us, much of this has changed. Ethnic minorities (other than the Jews) are still largely absent from the ruling elite, but they are doing well economically. Many statistics suggest that immigrants and their children do better economically than native-born Canadians. Thus, people are not locked into entrance statuses. Porter's classic, published in 1965, reflected a Canadian society that had largely passed away with the Second World War and was surely gone by 1970. This is not to deny Porter's grand vision—unquestionably a compelling metaphor of Canadian society—but to acknowledge the rapid and profound changes occurring in the last two decades. (Equally striking is the rapidity of changes overtaking S.M. Lipset's theory about Canada–U.S. differences, examined in an earlier section. Like Porter, Lipset captured a reality well on its way to oblivion by the time he was conceptualizing it.)

Thus Porter's vision, and Darroch's commentary on that vision, is historically important as a milestone in Canadian sociology. But like any other milestone, we pass it by in order to go still further.

Gender groups are like ethnic groups in one important respect: they unify people experiencing unequal or discriminatory treatment because of unchangeable characteristics. For that reason, we can expect some of the discussion in the section on gender relations that follows to seem familiar. But unlike ethnic groups, genders are not by their nature capable of complete isolation. To reproduce themselves, they need cross-gender co-operation; so there cannot be institutional completeness by gender, as by race or ethnicity. The places where genders meet and square off in the "battle of the sexes"—the family and, secondarily, the workplace—are, therefore, the research sites for the most important gender research, a type of research that has grown rapidly in the last decade.

References

Adorno, Theodor et al. *The Authoritarian Personality*. New York: W.W. Norton, 1969.

Bolaria, B. Singh and Peter S. Li, *Racial Oppression in Canada*. Toronto: Garamond Press, 1985.

Breton, Raymond, "Institutional completeness of ethnic communities," *American Journal of Sociology*, 20, 2, September 1964, pp. 193–205.

Li, Peter, "Race and ethnic relations." In L. Tepperman and R.J. Richardson (eds.), *The Social World*. Toronto: McGraw-Hill Ryerson, 1986.

Hamilton, Richard, *Restraining Myths*. New York: Halsted Press, 1975.

Reitz, Jeffrey G., *The Survival of Ethnic Groups*. Toronto: McGraw-Hill Ryerson, 1980.

31 Chinese Immigrants on the Canadian Prairie, 1910–47

Peter Li

PETER LI, Professor of Sociology at the University of Saskatchewan, specializes in the study of race relations and methods of social research. His books include *Occupational Mobility and Kinship Assistance: A Study of Chinese Immigrants in Chicago* (1978); *Social Research Methods* (1981); *Racial Minorities in Multicultural Canada* co-edited with B. Singh Bolaria (1983); and *Racial Oppression in Canada* with B. Singh Bolaria (1985). Professor Li has served as Associate Editor of the *Canadian Review of Sociology and Anthropology* and in several executive capacities for the Western Association of Sociology and Anthropology. He has recently travelled in China to lecture on sociology by invitation of the Chinese Academy of Social Sciences.

... The materials of this paper are based mainly on a 1979–80 study of the oral history of the Chinese in Saskatchewan. The aim was to collect detailed life histories of elderly Chinese in the province, with particular reference to their work experiences in Canada. A total of fifty-five completed interviews were conducted. The subjects were selected from a snow-ball sample in which respondents were asked to refer interviewers to other elderly Chinese immigrants living in Canada for a long period of time. About half of the subjects were living in Saskatoon at the time of the interview. Other subjects were selected from Regina, Yorkton, Swift Current, and six other communities in Saskatchewan. Most of the respondents had worked and lived in other parts of Canada before settling in Saskatchewan. ...

The Chinese immigration to Canada began around 1858 after gold was discovered in the Fraser Valley, British Columbia. The initial wave of Chinese immigrants consisted of miners from the west coast of the United States, and immigrants from Kwantung province in China. Subsequently, large numbers of Chinese labourers were recruited to Canada to fill a labour shortage, especially between 1881 and 1885 when the Canadian Pacific Railway was constructed. Between 1881 and 1883, for example, the number of Chinese arriving by ship at Victoria was 13,245 (Li, 1979). The wave of Chinese immigration continued after the CPR was completed, albeit at a slower rate. Between 1886 and 1894, the number of Chinese entering Canada and paying a special head tax was 12,197. This number was increased to 32,457 for the period 1895–1904 (Li, 1979).

As early as 1875, the provincial government of British Columbia passed anti-Chinese bills to disenfranchise the Chinese, and to restrict their civil rights. The Dominion Government of Canada had resisted passing a federal bill to control the flow of Chinese immigration before 1885, for fear that it would create a shortage of labourers, and impede the construction of the CPR. The first federal anti-Chinese bill was passed in 1885, in the form of a head tax of $50 imposed upon every Chinese person entering Canada (Statutes of Canada, 1885, c. 71). The tax was raised to

$100 in 1900 (Statutes of Canada, 1900, c. 32), and $500 in 1903 (Statutes of Canada, 1903, c. 8). In 1923, the federal government passed the most restrictive Chinese Immigration Act, essentially excluding all Chinese from entering Canada (Statutes of Canada, 1923, c. 38). The act was in effect until 1947 (Statues of Canada, 1947, c. 19).

Prior to 1900, close to 98 per cent of the Chinese were concentrated in British Columbia. The intensification of the anti-Chinese movement on the west coast, and the changing occupational demand for the Chinese had the effect of dispersing some to the interior of Canada. By 1911, for example, 13 per cent of the Chinese in Canada were located in the three prairie provinces. This figure was increased to 19 per cent in 1921, and 20 per cent in 1931 (Li, 1979).

Initially, the Chinese were recruited to the west coast as labourers in various pioneering industries such as mining, railroad construction, and later canning and other manufacturing. They were attractive to employers because of low labour cost and large supply. As white workers increased in number in British Columbia, the Chinese were perceived as competitors who were willing to undercut wages, and to serve as scabs in labour disputes. As organized labour began to grow, the Chinese became increasingly the target of labour exclusion. Organized labour demanded the exclusion of the Chinese from trades, and eventually their total exclusion from the country. The anti-Chinese sentiments received political support as politicians saw the advantage of adopting a platform to exclude the Chinese. By 1880, for example, all political parties found it necessary to take on such a platform to gain popular support.

As a result of the anti-Chinese movement and subsequent legislative control, the Chinese found it difficult to compete with white labourers in the core labour market. Many were forced to take up employment in the marginal sector. The hostile labour market also accelerated the growth of ethnic business among the Chinese, first concentrating in laundry operations, later in restaurants. The marginal sector and the ethnic business provided an occupational refuge for many Chinese when opportunities were restricted in the core labour market.

Census statistics indicate that in 1921, 24 per cent of the Chinese were labourers and unskilled workers, and 35 per cent were employed as store employees, servants, cooks, laundry workers, and waiters. These percentages reflect the concentration of the Chinese in the marginal and ethnic business sectors. The figures for 1931 show an increase in such a concentration. Labourers and unskilled workers constituted 21 per cent of the employed Chinese, while store employees, servants, cooks, laundry workers, and waiters made up another 42 per cent. These figures illustrate in part the restrictive employment opportunities open to the Chinese.

BACKGROUND OF CHINESE RESPONDENTS

The case histories of the thirty-one respondents who came between 1910 and 1923 show a striking similarity in background. All of them, for example, came to Canada in their late teens or early twenties. They originated from Kwangtung province in regions neighbouring the city of Canton. Toishan (T'aishan), in particular, seems to be the predominant county of origin. The respondents came from rural families in which many male members went overseas. Major financial support for these families consisted of remittances from relatives abroad, in addition to some limited farming activities.

Since the respondents immigrated at an early age in their careers, many had no working experience prior to immigration, aside from working in agricultural fields. All of them had limited formal schooling, and spoke practically no English before coming to Canada.

Like many of their predecessors who went overseas, the Chinese immigrants who migrated to Canada in the early part of the twentieth century left home to escape economic hardship in the search for better employment opportunities. In many cases, the Chinese immigrants borrowed from relatives in Canada to finance the trip and paid them back after they had a chance to work and save up in Canada. As one immigrant described it: "We were poor and starving, and we needed money at home. We had to borrow money to come over here, and when we came over here, we had to work hard to pay back the money that we owed."

Most of the respondents came to Canada with the assistance of a relative who had immigrated to Canada at an earlier date. The relative, usually the father, a brother, or an uncle, paid for the passage expense and the head tax for the respondents, in addition to making other legal arrangements of immigration, and receiving them upon arrival. The following case illustrates the way in which many Chinese came to Canada prior to 1923: "I came here in 1918. I was 18 years old. We were very poor at home. People came here to look for money. My uncle was here then, and he applied for me to come. He paid the $500 head tax for me. . . . So I came and went to wash dishes."

Kinship assistance frequently was extended beyond the initial stage of immigration. Some respondents worked for their relatives for a period of time after arrival, and others learned of employment opportunities through their relatives. Here is one example: "My brother gave me the money to come over. Afterward, I paid him back by working in his laundry. It took me 2 or 3 years. . . . It was $30 a month. . . . I worked there for several years, maybe 8 or 10 years, and then I went to wash dishes for an Englishman." Other studies (Li, 1977; MacDonald and MacDonald, 1964) have shown that the pattern of kinship assistance is common among immigrants who have little marketable resources, and have to rely on kinship help in overcoming some of the legal and social obstacles of immigration.

OPPORTUNITIES AND CONSTRAINTS IN THE LABOUR MARKET

The job histories of the thirty-one pre-war immigrants have a number of characteristics in common. For example, all the jobs were menial in nature and poorly paid. They often worked as domestic servants, laundry workers, and restaurant workers. As Chinese laundries declined in the thirties, the restaurants, both Chinese and non-Chinese owned, provided the main source of employment for many Chinese. All the respondents had a working history of high turnover from job to job. The mobility was frequently from one prairie town to another, but the line of work remained the same. The following case illustrates well the typical job history among the Chinese.

> I came to Moose Jaw in 1913. . . . First I washed dishes, making $35 a month. I worked for 14 to 16 hours a day. I knelt down on the floor and washed the floor and washed the dining room every morning. I had a potato bag to make it easier for my knees. Then after that, I went to work for a Japanese owner of a restaurant. That was 1914. . . . After a while, I went to Simpson, at harvest time, up north, it was the CPR line. I worked in a farm. I got up 6 o'clock in the morning, milked the cow, and came back to the house to cook breakfast for my boss. . . . He was not a very friendly person. . . . It was no good, so I quit. I came back to Moose Jaw to work for my brother for $50 a month for 12 hours a day. At night I scrubbed the floor and waited on tables. Then in 1918 I went back to China to get married. . . .

Jobs among the Chinese have all the features typical of employment in the marginal labour market. These features include long hours of work, little security, low pay, and low skill. The employment opportunity open to the Chinese was limited mainly to laundries and restaurants in the service sector. One respondent described the job situation for the Chinese in Moose Jaw around 1913 as follows: "At that time there were about 450 (Chinese) men and two women.... In Moose Jaw, there were about 35 to 38 Chinese laundries and three cafés.... All the Chinese worked there."

On the surface, it would seem that lack of occupational and language skills would explain why so many Chinese had low-status jobs in the service sector. Although skills in general enhance the market value of employees, jobs open to the Chinese required little skill. As long as employment in other sectors was not available to the Chinese, improvement in language and other skills would help little in enabling the Chinese to gain higher paying jobs.

There is strong evidence to indicate that the Chinese faced a discriminatory job market even in cases where Chinese employees had the necessary skill to perform the task....

... Apart from the unfriendly social atmosphere, the Chinese were also victims of legal exclusions.[1] One respondent explained the following to us: "If you run a café, you are not supposed to hire a female. If you run a grocery store, you are not supposed to hire a female. You got no vote at all. The election has nothing to do with you because you are Chinese.... You got nothing to say about it anyway. If you don't like it, you go." One of the effects of social discrimination and legal exclusion was to reduce the market value of the Chinese as employees. Since employment opportunities outside of the service sector were virtually unavailable to the Chinese, they remained highly vulnerable in the labour market.

ETHNIC BUSINESS

Since employment opportunities in the labour sector were highly restrictive, many Chinese immigrants ventured into an ethnic business to preserve a job and to maintain a living. The Chinese first entered into the laundry business, and later into the restaurant business. The Chinese restaurants in the prairie towns in the twenties and thirties, however, were very different from the post-war Chinese restaurants in metropolitan centres. These earlier restaurants were small in scale, poorly decorated, and labour intensive. The hours of operation were long, and the profit margin was small. The restaurants simply provided a business venture for many Chinese whereby they could put up a small amount of capital to secure a guaranteed place to work and live. The case histories clearly indicate that in those cases where the respondents became part owners of a restaurant, they were doing the same kinds of work in their own restaurant as they did when working for somebody else. The restaurants provided an economic refuge for the Chinese in a restrictive labour market.

Twenty-two of the respondents had the experience of holding a partnership in a restaurant sometime in their career. In many cases, the respondents reported a history of moving back and forth between employment and self-employment in restaurants. There was little doubt in the minds of the respondents that self-employment in one's restaurant was just as much a job as employment in another restaurant.

Partnership was a viable means for many Chinese to start a restaurant because it allowed meagre capital and labour to be pooled. Given the kinds of jobs most Chinese had, the capacity to save a large amount of capital for investment was limited. Partnership provided a means of joint venture with little capital. The business partners also worked as a team in running the restaurant to reduce the cost of hiring other workers. The following is an example of how partnership business was formed and conducted:

... the partners get a few relatives together

and just chip in some money each.... If there is no business and you have to leave, then you sell it and split the money, that's all.... Everyday ... fixed meals, cooked the meat, made a few pies, and made some soup. Whatever you needed we made them.... There's no boss. Everyone did it right. That was the way we did it. Just worked for ourselves. In the end, whoever had a share had a share of the profit ... if you really don't like it and can't get along, then you can buy me out, or I can buy you out....

In some cases the respondents had no capital, but they could still enter into a partnership by working with some Chinese, and use their salary to repay their share of the capital. Here is one example: "Someone asked me to be a cook in Kinistino. Then he gave me a share because he didn't want me to leave. I didn't have anything. I just made the money from the salary until I paid up the share, and then I owned the share. I worked a couple of years for it."

Aside from the small capital needed, the partnership restaurant business had low risk, and it provided a refuge in economic hard times. One respondent explained what life was like in a small town restaurant during the winter months.

> In the small towns you don't have to know too much English. Just use your eyes to see what they want.... You don't have to do too much because the menu is the same from year to year.... The business was cheap.... Save all the money, and then you can buy a business. Before in Goven, I bought a business for $350.... As long as you had a place to sleep and some work, then it didn't matter. In the winter time it was cold and there were no people there. Some days we had only a few people, just sold a few loaves of bread and a few cups of coffee, that's all. No, it didn't matter as long as you had a place to stay....

During the Depression, the restaurants provided a means of survival for many Chinese. As one respondent described the situation of a restaurant during the early thirties: " ... there were 4 partners and 10 others who just stayed there because there was nowhere else to go.... There was no work to do elsewhere, and they looked after the restaurant."

Movement in and out of partnerships was as frequent as changing jobs in other employment. A person would sell his partnership when he took a trip to China, only to join the partnership on his return. The following case is an example: "I sold it and went to China. There were about 7 or 8 of us there. They were my cousins, and so I sold my part of the business to them. So then when I came back, the restaurant was busy, and they asked me to stay and work for them. I worked for 3 or 4 months, and they asked me to become a partner."

A number of factors probably facilitated the formation of business partnership among the Chinese immigrants. The fact that many respondents came to Canada by way of relative sponsorship means that they had certain kinship ties that could be used as a basis for business partners. Indeed, partnerships were frequently formed between fathers and sons, uncles and nephews, and brothers. In some cases, the partnership may be extended to more distant relatives and friends. Since the Chinese immigrants emigrated from predominantly the same region, common lineage and clanship ties provided the Chinese immigrants with a web of both close and distant relatives from which partners could be drawn. The prevalence of business partnership was confirmed by all the respondents. As one of them described it: "In the old days, it was partnership ... we all worked partnerships.... In my case, I worked together with my brothers."

Partly because of the kinship ties, but also because of the nature of the business, the financial arrangements of partnerships were usually made on an informal basis. One respondent explained the partnership arrangement as follows: " ... get a few relatives together, and each just chip in together. You don't need a lawyer, and you don't have to sign, just take each other's words.... If he is a good man or if he is your cousin then you would be his partner."

Business partners were not only co-investors, but also co-workers in the same cafe or restaurant. It was just as necessary for the partners to pool their labour as to pool their capital. Since most partnership businesses did not employ outside help, the partners in essence were creating jobs for themselves in their investment venture. From the point of view of the Chinese immigrants then, partnerships reduced the capital cost as well as the operating cost in running a restaurant.

Since the meagre return in operating a Chinese restaurant required using unpaid labour to reduce the operating cost, most Chinese immigrants needed to rely on business partners in the absence of their immediate family. Ironically, the separation of the Chinese men from their families in China facilitated the formation of business partnerships because these men could not rely on wives and young children for labour.

The partnership business among the Chinese declined after the war as more Chinese were allowed to bring their families to Canada. The family members provided additional labour power to operate the restaurant. Many partnership businesses broke up as the post-war immigration altered the demographic pattern among the Chinese community.

MOBILITY DREAM

To many Chinese immigrants before the war, the only hope of success was to work hard in Canada, and save enough money to retire in China. Meanwhile, during their stay in Canada, they aspired to visit China periodically, where they could unite with their families for a short period of time. This mentality is sometimes described as a "sojourner's orientation" (Siu, 1953) or a "marginal person-

ality" (Park, 1928; Stonequist, 1937) which basically results from a clash of two cultures, leading to the immigrants' inability to identify with the host community. In the case of the Chinese in Canada, there is every indication to suggest that their mobility aspiration to return to China was greatly influenced by a number of structural factors.

For example, the restrictive immigration laws against the Chinese meant that most Chinese men in Canada before the war were unable to bring their families (Li, 1980). Before 1923, the law stipulated a head tax of $500 for practically every Chinese person entering Canada. After 1923, the Chinese Immigration Act precluded the Chinese from admission to the country. Aside from the restrictive immigration laws, the social atmosphere was very unfriendly to the Chinese as a group. They were excluded from many aspects of life in Canadian society. Their ties to the host community were maintained in a symbiotic relationship in which the Chinese provided cheap labour and service in the marginal and ethnic business sectors in exchange for meager pay to support themselves and their families in China. The position of the Chinese in the economy was similar to that of many migrant workers in industrial societies.

Many respondents described a strong desire to return to China, since separation from their families and discrimination forced them to remain as aliens in Canadian society. "Before, the Chinese came to work in Canada, but the person's mind was in China. Your relatives, uncles, mother, children and wife were in China. So you saved all the money and you could go home to visit them. Over here ... the white people didn't mix with you and you yourself didn't know the language, there was nothing to enjoy."

Although many of the Chinese wanted to visit their families in China, not all were able to do so. In some cases, the husband in Canada never saw wife or children until decades after separation. As one immigrant said:

"Everybody was like that. You came here and if you behaved, worked for a few years, then you could go home. Sometimes a person came here for 30 or 40 years, and never went back to see his family. I know of one guy here. When he came here, he was just married for a couple of months. . . . He never saw his wife for 40 years, never saw his boy either."

It is difficult to estimate how many Chinese immigrants actually retired in China, and how many stayed in Canada. For those who stayed, their way of thinking changed radically after the war as the treatment of the Chinese improved, and their families were allowed to immigrate to Canada. The 1949 socialist revolution in China also may have discouraged overseas immigrants from returning. The difference of the pre-war and post-war mentality was clearly explained by one respondent: "After the war, they allowed us Chinese to bring the wife, and then the children here. . . . Now you are ambitious to teach the children to go to school so others wouldn't look down on you. . . . Before, it was not the same . . . even if you were educated, even if you knew how to do the job, the government wouldn't hire you because nobody wanted orientals."

SUMMARY AND CONCLUSION

The oral history of the Chinese shows that immigrants before the war found a limited number of jobs in the service industry. These jobs had many of the features common to marginal labour, such as long hours of work, menial labour, low pay and lack of promotion opportunity. The Chinese also reported a history of changing from one menial job to another, including a movement between employment and self-employment in the ethnic business.

The predominant Chinese business was the restaurant which provided a viable employ-ment opportunity for many in a restrictive labour market. Limited by capital and manpower, the Chinese made use of partnership investment to build their restaurant business. The organization of partnership enabled a maximum use of labour power among partners to reduce labour cost, at the same time providing enough flexibility to cushion business risks and uncertainties. The popularity of the restaurant business among the Chinese before the war represents a successful attempt on their part to adapt to the structural constraints of the labour market.

Aside from the general restrictive employment opportunity which encouraged many Chinese to seek alternative avenues in the ethnic business sector, a number of other factors also facilitated the formation of business partnership among the Chinese. Partnerships were largely formed on the basis of kinship ties. Since most of the Chinese immigrants came to Canada through the sponsorship of relatives, the kinship ties which were instrumental in their immigration remained important for the subsequent stage when partnerships were struck. The web of kinship ties was also enriched by the fact that most of the immigrants came from the same place of origin. The absence of Chinese wives and young children as a result of the restrictive immigration law compelled Chinese men to rely on business partners for additional labour in their business operation. The success of Chinese restaurants as survival vehicles was related to Chinese immigrants' ability to mobilize kinship assistance.

This study suggests the importance of studying the conditions of the labour market as well as the adaptive responses of an ethnic group for an understanding of its structural position in the economy. The development of ethnic business among the Chinese calls for further attention to the enclave economy in theories of a dual labour market.

Notes

[1] For example, a Saskatchewan act of 1912 (Saskatchewan Statute, 1912, c. 17) prevented a white woman from working in any restaurant or laundry owned or managed by the Chinese. The Saskatchewan Election Act of 1908 (Saskatchewan Statute, 1908, c. 2) disfranchised persons of the Chinese race. The Chinese did not gain voting rights in Saskatchewan until 1951.

References

Averitt, Robert T. 1968 The Dual Economy: The Dynamics of American Industry Structure. New York: W.W. Norton

Bach, Robert L. 1978 "Mexican Immigration and the American State." International Migration Review 12: 536–58

Baron, Harold M. and Bennet Hymer 1968 "The negro worker in the Chicago labour movement." Pp. 232–85 in J. Jacobson (ed.), The Negro and the American Labour Movement. New York: Doubleday

Blau, Peter and Otis D. Duncan 1967 The American Occupational Structure. New York: John Wiley and Sons

Bonacich, Edna 1972 "A theory of ethnic antagonism: the split labour market." American Sociological Review 37: 547–59

———— 1976 "Advanced capitalism and black/white race relations in the United States: a split labour market interpretation." American Sociological Review 41: 34–51

Breton, Raymond 1979 "Ethnic stratification viewed from three theoretical perspectives," Pp. 270–94 in J. Curtis and W. Scott (eds.), Social Stratification: Canada. Scarborough, Ontario: Prentice-Hall of Canada

Burawoy, Michael 1976 "The functions and reproduction of migrant labour: comparative materials from southern Africa and the United States." American Journal of Sociology 81: 1050–87

Davis, K. and Wilbert E. Moore 1945 "Some principles of stratification." American Sociological Review 10: 242–9

Duncan, Beverly and Otis D. Duncan 1968 "Minorities and the process of stratification." American Sociological Review 33: 356–64

Duncan, Otis, D., David L. Featherman and Beverly Duncan 1972 Socioeconomic Background and Achievement. New York: Seminar Press

Edwards, M. Reich and David M. Gordon 1975 Labour Market Segmentation. Lexington, Mass.: D.C. Heath

Featherman, David L. 1971 "The Socioeconomic achievement of white religio-ethnic subgroups: social and psychological explanations." American Sociological Review 36: 207–22

Featherman, David L. and Robert M. Hauser 1978 Opportunity and Change. New York: Academic Press

Gordon, David M. 1972 Theories of Poverty and Underdevelopment. Lexington, Mass.: D.C. Heath

Horan, Patrick M. 1978 "Is status attainment research atheoretical?" American Sociological Review 43: 434–541

Li, Peter S. 1976 "Ethnic businesses among Chinese in the U.S." Journal of Ethnic Studies 4: 35–41

———— 1977 "Occupational achievement and kinship assistance among Chinese immigrants in Chicago." Sociological Quarterly 18: 478–89

———— 1979 "A historical approach to ethnic stratification: the case of the Chinese in Canada, 1858–1930." Canadian Review of Sociology and Anthropology 16: 320–32

———— 1980 "Immigration laws and family patterns: some demographic changes among Chinese families in Canada, 1885–1971." Canadian Ethnic Studies 12: 58–72

Light, Ivan H. 1973 Ethnic Enterprise in America. Berkeley, California: University of California Press

MacDonald, John S. and Leatrice D. MacDonald

1964 "Chain migration: ethnic neighbourhood formation and social networks." Milbank Memorial Fund Quarterly 42: 82–96

Park, Robert E. 1928 "Human migration and the marginal man." American Journal of Sociology 32: 881–93

Siu, Paul 1953 "The Chinese laundryman: a study of social isolation." Unpublished PH.D. dissertation, University of Chicago

Statutes of Canada 1885 An Act to restrict and regulate Chinese immigration into Canada. Chapter 71

———— 1900 An Act respecting and restricting Chinese Immigration. Chapter 32

———— 1903 An Act respecting and restricting Chinese Immigration. Chapter 8

———— 1923 An Act respecting Chinese Immigration. Chapter 38

———— 1947 An Act to amend the Immigration Act and to repeal the Chinese Immigration Act. Chapter 19

Statutes of Saskatchewan 1908 An Act respecting Election of Members of the Legislative Assembly. Chapter 2

———— 1912 An Act to Prevent the Employment of Female Labour in Certain Capacities. Chapter 17

Stonequist, Everett V. 1973 The Marginal Man. New York: Scribner

Wilson, Kenneth L. and Alejandro Portes 1980 "Immigrants enclaves: an analysis of the labour market experience of Cubans in Miami." American Journal of Sociology 86: 295–319

Yancey, William L., E.P. Eriksen and R.N. Julian 1976 "Emergent Ethnicity: a review of reformulation." American Sociological Review 41: 391–403

32 The Jewish Sub-Economy of Montreal

Morton Weinfeld

MORTON WEINFELD, Professor of Sociology at McGill University, specializes in the study of race and ethnic relations, the sociology of education, and public policy analysis. His books and articles include *The Canadian Jewish Mosaic* co-edited with W. Shaffir and I. Cotler (1981); *An Introduction to Sociology* co-edited with M. Rosenberg, W. Shaffir and A. Turowetz (1983); "Second generation effects of the holocaust on selected social and political attitudes of children of survivors" with John Sigal (forthcoming); and "Myth and reality in the Canadian Mosaic: Ethnic identification in Toronto" (1981). In addition, Professor Weinfeld has carried out contract research on the system of Jewish education in Montreal, the social costs of discrimination (for the Federal Commission of Inquiry on Equality in Employment), and sociodemographic features of the Jewish Community of Montreal. He is chairman of the Department of Sociology.

Many analyses of the economic conditions of minorities contain fragmentary evidence, usually ethnographic, of the presence and use of economic networks operating within a given minority group. This study represents a beginning effort to systematically and quantitatively explicate the concept of the ethnic sub-economy, using the case of Jews in Montreal. The term "ethnic sub-economy" can be applied to any minority group—ethnic, religious, racial, linguistic in a plural economy. Jews can be considered as a religious and/or ethnic group.

THE ETHNIC SUB-ECONOMY

The "ethnic sub-economy" can be defined as a network of economic relationships which may link employees, employers, consumers,

buyers, and sellers, of a specific ethnic group or minority. The image is one of a parallel economy. It need not be limited to one class, or one economic sector, or to one spatial area in a given urban setting. An ethnic sub-economy may exist regardless of the conditions of immigration of the group, attitude to the homeland, and degrees of hostility facing the group. The existence of an ethnic sub-economy may be established by tracing the relative frequency of economic transactions ethnic members have within and without their own group. Thus, members of an ethnic group can participate to a greater or lesser extent in the ethnic sub-economy. The boundaries are set behaviorally, not geographically. The ethnic sub-economy will include its own markets for labor, capital, goods, services, and information, which may parallel those existing in the "mainstream" economy.

The ethnic sub-economy can be considered a general case, to include any configuration of ethnic economic behavior. Whether economic advantage or penalty accrues to participants in the sub-economy must be established empirically. The concept can describe an economically successful middleman minority, an immigrant enclave, or a depressed racial ghetto. An ethnic sub-economy may have a greater working-class or greater middle-class dimension; yet, it is conceived as a vertical social phenomenon, existing across social classes. Indeed, like the mainstream economy, its social class composition and industrial base may change over time.

The notion of an ethnic sub-economy is similar in some respects to the concept of a "cultural division of labor" by Hechter (1978). Just as a societal division of labor may be more or less "hierarchical" or "segmental," so may a sub-economy vary as to the class composition or the occupational-industrial concentration of its members. Hechter, however, posits a causal model in which ethnic solidarity is dependent on, among other things, high levels of intra-group interaction (including economic transactions). The data presented below suggest, however, that the relation between ethnic solidarity, variously defined, and frequency of intra-group economic interaction may be more complex (or subtle) at the microsociological level of analysis.

An ethnic sub-economy would be relatively self-contained in the range of its economic activity. Whereas the "middleman minority," by definition, fulfills intermediary economic functions, linking ethnic groups or economic sectors, the ethnic sub-economy might be conceived as a potential total economy in miniature. Economic relations outside the group would be relatively infrequent (though, of course, they could not be eliminated) for those whose primary economic activity was within the group.

Studies of immigrant or minority groups often reveal forms of intra-group economic activity. Immigrant social histories are replete with such data (Howe, 1976). Sowell (1975) and Nelli (1967) argue that what is here called an ethnic sub-economy is an asset only for immigrants in ethnically stratified societies, easing the processes of initial adaptation and economic integration. They suggest that minorities should abandon their ethnic economic base following the passing of the immigrant generation.

Evidence for the existence of ethnic sub-economies can be seen in the structure of urban housing markets. Ethnic groups in Toronto report that they rent or buy housing predominantly from persons of the same ethnic origin (Weinfeld, 1977). A detailed study of rental housing in Montreal identified ethnic networks which operated in various neighborhoods to promote exchanges of labor and information and to influence landlord-tenant relationships (Krohn et al., 1977). One study of the business elite in Quebec noted the marked tendency for large firms owned by Jews to recruit primarily Jewish persons for senior management positions (Sales, 1979, pp. 136–138). Another study of Montreal's Italians found them to be likely to work for or with other Italians (Boissevain, 1970, p. 21).

This study presents and analyzes data concerning the economic behavior of a random sample of Jewish household heads in Montreal. The objective is to attempt to establish the degree to which a Jewish sub-economy exists, and to begin an initial examination of some of the characteristics of one such sub-economy.

The analysis is focused within the Jewish group and is not concerned with relative Jewish over- or under-representation in certain economic classes or sectors. Rather, the aim is to identify the pattern of intra-group economic behavior, and address the following questions: (1) What are the dimensions of the Jewish sub-economy in Montreal? (2) To what extent is this an "immigrant" phenomenon; i.e., does it persist beyond the immigrant generation? (3) To what extent is participation in the Jewish sub-economy in Montreal associated with disadvantage, such as a perception of anti-Semitism, or with positive factors such as a "preference" for dealing with Jews or a high degree of religiosity which might channel interactions to other Jews? (4) To what extent is participation in the Jewish sub-economy associated with either economic benefits or losses for the participants?

METHOD AND SAMPLE

The data were collected from a 1978 survey of 657 Jewish household heads in Montreal.[1] The sample was generated by creating a "master list" of Jewish households in Montreal and sampling randomly within the list. The master list eventually included an estimated 85% to 90% of all Jewish households in Montreal compared to census figures. A questionnaire containing 332 questions was administered to each subject in the form of a one-hour interview.

Table 1 presents the occupational and income distributions for the sample. The variance is substantial, particularly as regards the distribution by family income. Thirty-seven percent of the respondents were self-employed; 29.6% were college graduates

(bachelor, masters, doctorate, or professional degree).

SIZE AND SHAPE OF THE JEWISH SUB-ECONOMY

Three questions were available from the survey questionnaire to ascertain the degree of individual participation in the Jewish sub-economy. They provide some indications of the dimensions of the phenomenon itself.

Respondents were asked several questions about the "company, institution or organization you work with." We see that 24.4% indicated that Jews comprised the majority of the customers or clients of this firm or organization. In addition, 69.8% of the respondents indicated that the "majority of the executive management" was Jewish. (This latter figure includes those who were self-employed, either in business or the free professions. In fact, 33% of the sample work for other Jews.) In other words, only 30.2% of the sample were employees of non-Jewish firms or organizations.

More generally, respondents were asked to identify what proportion of their "business associates" were Jewish. Of the respondents, 35% indicated that "all or most" of their

Table 1
OCCUPATIONAL AND INCOME DISTRIBUTION OF JEWISH HOUSEHOLD HEADS IN MONTREAL

Current/Last/Usual			
Occupation		**Family Income**	
Census Occupational Categories			
Managers and administrators	43.0	Less than $10,000	26.0
Professional and technical	12.3	10,000–19,999	24.9
Clerical	13.2	20,000–29,999	16.4
Sales	11.4	30,000–49,999	19.4
Service	1.8	50,000 +	13.3
Skilled labor	7.9		100.0
Other	10.2		
Not reported	—		
	100.0		

associates (partners, suppliers, employees, employers, customers/clients, colleagues, etc.) were Jews. Only 6.2% indicated they had no business association or contact with Jews. Bearing in mind that Jews represent only 4% of the Metropolitan Montreal population, according to the 1971 census, this is a substantial amount of concentration.[2]

Studies of immigrant life and histories of Jewish economic integration suggest that firms operating in an ethnic sub-economy would be smaller (small shopkeepers, craftsmen, retailers, etc.) than those operating in the large scale mainstream economy. The respondents were divided into two groups: those whose firm/organization employed less than 50 employees, (64%) and those with 50 or more (36%). Of the former, 38.9% identified all or most of their business associates as Jews, compared to 25.2% of the latter (large firms). While those involved in smaller enterprises were, therefore, more likely to be participants in the ethnic sub-economy, we still find that significant numbers of those in large enterprises were also participants.

PARTICIPATION IN THE JEWISH SUB-ECONOMY AND LENGTH OF RESIDENCE IN MONTREAL

Participation in an ethnic sub-economy, according to an assimilationist perspective,[3] should be more typical of immigrants than of native-born members of an ethnic group, and of more recent immigrants compared to those who arrived earlier. This view would be based not only on a hypothesized pattern of preferences, but on the supposition that structural barriers, e.g., knowledge of the host language and majority group hostility, and thus exclusion from full economic participation, might be greater for (more recent) immigrants.

Generation is measured as foreign born (first generation), those native born, but with both parents foreign born (second genera-

tion), and those with at least one parent native born (third generation or above). The data show no linear decrease in participation for the different generational groups.[4] For example, for the third generation, 28.3% have primarily Jewish customers/clients, 60.6% work for themselves or other Jews, and 28.4% indicate that all or most of their business associates are Jewish.

A similar finding arises in comparing immigrants resident in Canada for different periods of time. The foreign-born respondents are divided into three roughly equal groups: those in Canada for less than 25 years, those resident for 25–44 years, and those in Canada for 45 or more years. There is no evidence of any decrease in participation in the Jewish sub-economy moving from the "greeners" (more recent immigrants) to the old-timers.

The data suggest that in no way can the Jewish sub-economy in Montreal be considered a phenomenon of (recently arrived) immigrants. A similar finding can be inferred from data provided by Light (1979: 34), which indicates only a marginal difference, from 158 to 150, in the self-employment rate per 1,000 employed, comparing foreign born and native born of Russian stock (largely Jewish) in the United States.

ANTI-SEMITISM, RELIGIOSITY, AND PARTICIPATION IN THE JEWISH SUB-ECONOMY

Participation in the Jewish sub-economy is not limited to (more recent) immigrants. An alternate correlate of participation might be the perception of anti-Semitism (note: all that is required is a perception of anti-Semitism, rather than a first-hand encounter with it or other objective evidence of its existence). Alternatively, more frequent participants might come to believe, perhaps as a rationale for their behavior, in the prevalence of higher levels of anti-Semitism.

The data suggest that there are no

significant differences in participation between those respondents perceiving more anti-Semitism and those perceiving less. For example, of those who perceive *little* anti-Semitism, 21.8% have Jews as a majority of customers, 68.1% work for themselves or other Jews; the corresponding percentages for those perceiving *much* anti-Semitism are 26.6% and 70.9%. Thus, fear of anti-Semitism does not seem to be systematically associated with participation in the Jewish sub-economy.

An alternative voluntaristic factor associated with participation might be religiosity. As Howe (1976) has described, some of the early immigrant workers in the needle trade in New York enjoyed the relative freedom to observe the Sabbath and holidays as a result of working for a Jewish employer. Moreover, the demands of a Jewish community for religious products or services (kosher food, Hebrew teachers, etc.) would create employment and business opportunities for religious Jews. Such an explanation would correspond to the "special consumer demands" theory of ethnic enterprise for Oriental or European immigrants (Light, 1972: 11–15). Thus, we might expect participation in the Jewish sub-economy to be greater for more religious Jews.

The data indicate no difference between more or less religious Jews in their participation in the Jewish sub-economy. Among the least religious third of the respondents, there are 32.5% with all or most of their business associates Jews, 66.7% self-employed or working for other Jews, and 28.1% with primarily Jewish customers. The percentages for the most religious third do not differ significantly. Clearly, the Jewish sub-economy survives due to factors other than the religiosity of its participants.

Apart from a religious motivation, Jews may simply prefer to have economic dealings with other Jews due perhaps to custom, language (Yiddish or Hebrew) similarities, or similar cultural sensibilities. Respondents were asked to indicate degrees of (dis)agreement with

the statement: "I prefer doing business with an establishment that I know is owned by Jews." Those with greater agreement might be expected to be greater participants.

The data indicate that Jews agreeing with this statement are indeed more likely to have a majority of Jewish customers or clients, and to indicate that all or most of their business associates are Jews. There is no significant difference in proportions self-employed or working for other Jews. Thus, we have here some evidence (for two out of three indicators) that respondents' preferences are associated with participation in the Jewish sub-economy. Yet the minority tendencies are also quite striking. For example, of those Jews who do *not* prefer doing business with other Jews, we find 19.2% with primarily Jewish customers and 27.7% with Jews as most or all of their business associates.

COSTS AND BENEFITS OF THE JEWISH SUB-ECONOMY

Are participants in the Jewish sub-economy economically better or worse off when compared to Jews active in the mainstream economy?

Three measures of economic performance are analyzed: occupation, intra-generational mobility, and income. Occupation is measured by the Blishen score, an index of socio-economic status computed for various occupations (Blishen, 1968). Intra-generational mobility is measured as the difference in Blishen scores between respondents' first full time job in Canada and their present (or last, usual) job. Income represents total family income.

Looking at all three indicators of socio-economic achievement and all three measures of participation in the Jewish sub-economy, we find a consistent pattern (nine chi-squares) of no significant difference (at $p \leq .05$) in economic achievement between those respondents with greater and those with lesser degrees of participation in the ethnic sub-economy. We find no evidence of either economic costs or economic benefits associated with participation in the Jewish sub-economy.

Correlation and regression analysis were used to isolate the independent effects of participation in the Jewish sub-economy on economic achievement. The sample was divided into foreign-born and native-born respondents on the assumption that different processes might be at work for these two groups. The zero-order correlations confirmed the cross-tabular findings for both foreign and native born. . . .

A regression analysis controlled for the effects of age, sex, years in Canada (for the foreign born), and education of the respondents for the same three dependent measures, occupation, mobility, and income. In the income equations, spouse's labor force status (employed or unemployed) and respondent's occupation were also included as variables. Interaction effects of economic segregation and both years in Canada and education were estimated as well. . . .

The major finding would seem to be that reported economic segregation plays an insignificant role in the economic achievement of our respondents.[5]

DISCUSSION

It seems that a large number of Jews in Montreal participate, in varying degrees, in the communal economic system. The measures used in this study have been conservative. For example, respondents who answered that the *majority* of their customers were Jews were identified as participants; those with a large *minority* of Jewish customers (30%, 40%) were excluded, in the analytical categories. (Remember that Jews represent only 4% of the population of Metropolitan Montreal.) We might estimate that between one-quarter and one-third of the respondents were

almost exclusively economically active within the Jewish sub-economy.

To be sure, anyone with direct or indirect familiarity with North American urban life is aware of the existence of ethnic residential and commercial concentrations. In addition to a linguistic, English-French, division in Montreal, we find there are clearly identifiable Jewish, Italian, and Greek areas, as well as a Chinatown and a Black area. What is difficult is to account for individual decisions to participate in such sub-economies.

Participation in the Jewish sub-economy of Montreal cannot be explained by the factor of immigration, by perceptions of anti-Semitism, or by religious correlates. Respondents who "prefer" dealing with other Jews are slightly more likely to participate. Yet, there are more participants in the Jewish sub-economy who do *not* prefer business dealings with Jews than there are those who do. Finally, there seem to be neither economic costs nor benefits associated with participation. Though it was not examined, it seems likely that a (mis)perception about relative economic payoff cannot explain the participation either. Stated differently, participation in the Jewish sub-economy is distributed randomly over occupational and income groupings.

The question remains: Why do many Jews in Montreal concentrate their economic activity among other Jews? The phenomenon might be explained by generational transmission, and the convenience of adopting inherited patterns of economic activity. Immigrants may pass on, to second and third generations, established economic networks, which are no worse than any other new ones. Inertia may maintain them. The phenomenon may reveal weaknesses in the impersonal, universalistic assumptions of both neo-classical economics and functional sociology. Ascription persists, and may be functional in modern industrial societies (Mayhew, 1968). One subject for systematic investigation might be the role of the extended family in minority groups as a mediating agent in contemporary economic activity which could, of course, solidify the tie to the ethnic sub-economy.

Other explanations might include the role of residential distributions. Residence or the location of a respondent's workplace in the "Jewish" area might be associated with participation in the Jewish sub-economy. At a macrosociological level, objective discriminatory forces may help channel some Jews into the Jewish sub-economy. (This factor is distinct from the microsociological, subjective perception of anti-Semitism, analyzed above.)

Several lines of research suggest themselves. Comparative research might establish the generalizability of the concept of ethnic sub-economy through quantitative studies of different minority groups in a number of settings. Certain environments may be more or less conducive to the existence of ethnic economic systems.

Of interest to sociologists might be the relation of participation in the ethnic sub-economy to other dimensions of ethnic life, such as the social cohesion of the group, residential or territorial segregation, political mobilization, patterns of cultural assimilation, inter-group conflict, and even intra-group conflict.[6] In this study, the religious variable examined covers only one facet of ethnic identification. It may be that other forms of communal solidarity play a role. Indeed, one might attempt to unravel whether participation in an ethnic sub-economy is more likely cause or effect of such solidarity.

Of interest to urban economists would be details regarding ethnic consumption patterns, participation in the housing markets, links between manufacturing, wholesaling and retailing operations, membership in professional associations, the giving and receiving of credit, the use of information networks, and the occupational and sectoral profile of participants in the sub-economy.

Another line of research might lead to the development of a political economy of minority groups. Some minority groups, such as the Jews, are characterized by a wide array of political and social institutions and formal organizations. Groups vary in their "institutional completeness," or the degree to which needs of members may be met through institutions and resources indigenous to the group, such as welfare organizations, churches, newspapers, social and cultural clubs, etc. (Breton, 1964). In the Jewish case, the degree of institutional completeness and the proliferation of local, regional and national organizations is so great, the term "polity" has been used to describe the Jewish community (Elazar, 1976). An ethnic polity consists of the voluntary, representative or quasi-representative, organizations which are involved in decision-making and the provision of services.

Minority groups differ in the degree to which they may be organized, internally, as a polity. The ethnic sub-economy may be considered as the economic analogue to the ethnic polity. Activity in both is voluntary and may be independent of economic (or political) participation in the mainstream societal systems. One might speculate as to the relation between the establishment of a successful ethnic polity and the extent of participation in the ethnic sub-economy.

A more complete elaboration of the workings of an ethnic sub-economy would include treatments of both "public" and "private" sectors. This paper has focused on the private sector of the Jewish sub-economy. The public sector of the ethnic sub-economy would be sustained through the pattern of philanthropic contributions or fee for services used to support welfare institutions, churches, and other cultural, social, or political institutions (these revenues could also include government grants). The funds would be used in part to employ communal public servants. Some portion might also be reallocated to other, perhaps more needy, members of the group. In the Jewish case, the public sector of the Jewish sub-economy is considerable. For example, Elazar has estimated a total

Jewish communal budget of $2 billion in the United States (1976: 293–313).

Using standard economic measures, it might be possible to obtain from survey data, or in other ways, quantitative estimates of the size of an ethnic sub-economy, including both public and private sectors. One might compute average and total revenues for participants, as well as other economic indicators, such as rates of return, productivity, economic growth, etc.

Analysis of the bases of economic power of elites within any minority group—whether within or without the sub-economy—may be useful in understanding the dynamics of intra-communal politics. One might ascertain whether the links between power and wealth operative within minority communities flow through the sub-economy or through the mainstream economy. Journalistic accounts (Newman, 1979) might be supplemented by systematic scientific studies.

Notes

[1] For a thorough review of the sampling procedure, see Weinfeld and Eaton (1979). The survey had been commissioned as a means to facilitate community planning by the Allied Jewish Community Services and the Canadian Jewish Congress in Montreal.

[2] This degree of intra-group economic interaction within the Jewish group may not be atypical for other ethnic groups in Montreal. Impressionistic evidence suggests that the English and French, as well as smaller groups such as the Italian and Greek, might also operate in part, at least, within the ethnic sub-economy. One of the prerequisites for the existence of an ethnic sub-economy (as opposed to a middleman minority) might be a minimum threshold size of a group in order to satisfy the specialization and differentiation needed in any economic system. The Jewish population of Montreal, 109,000 according to the 1971 census, would seem to be sufficiently large, as would the other groups listed above.

[3] According to this perspective, all forms of participation in the host society should increase with the transition from the immigrant to the native-born generation. Residential dispersion,

more complete acculturation, higher educational attainment, would all contribute to making an ethnic group member more comfortable in competing economically with those outside the group, for positions not tied to the origin group itself. This would represent a form of structural assimilation, as described by Gordon (1964).

[4] In this case, and in subsequent tabular analyses, findings of statistically insignificant differences (at $p \leq .05$) will be noted. Of course, one cannot prove "the null hypothesis." Finding insignificant chi-square values in a specific sample does not theoretically rule out significant differences in other samples. Thus, we present the findings here as suggestive, though of strong substantive interest. Their value is reinforced by the cumulative pattern of insignificant or unexpected relationships.

[5] See note 4. The same argument applies for statistically insignificant beta coefficients.

[6] Smaller sub-economies may exist *within* minority groups. Thus, Hassidic Jewish sects may exhibit patterns of economic segregation from other Jews as well as from the economic mainstream.

References

Anderson, Grace 1974 *Networks of Contact. The Portuguese in Toronto* Waterloo: Wilfred Laurier Press.

Bell, Daniel 1973 *The Coming of Post-Industrial Society*. New York: Basic Books.

Blishen, Bernard P. 1968 "A Socio-Economic

Index for Occupation in Canada." In Blishen, et al. *Canadian Society*. Toronto: MacMillan.

Boissevain, Jeremy 1970 *The Italians of Montreal*. Studies of the Royal Commission on Bilingualism and Biculturalism. Ottawa: Information Canada.

Bonacich, Edna 1972 "A Theory of Ethnic Antagonism: The Split Labour Market." *American Sociological Review* 37: 547–559.

———— 1973 "A Theory of Middlemen Minorities." *American Sociological Review* 38: 583–594.

Breton, Raymond 1964 "Institutional Completeness of Ethnic Communities and the Personal Relations of Immigrants." *American Journal of Sociology* 70: 193–205.

Cain, Glen G. 1976 "The Challenge of Segmented Labor Market Theories to Orthodox Theory: A Survey." *Journal of Economic Literature* 14: 1214–1257.

Duncan, Beverly and Otis Dudley Duncan 1968 "Minorities and the Process of Stratification." *American Sociological Review* 33 (June): 356–364.

Eitzen, Stanley D. 1971 "Two Minorities: The Jews of Poland and the Chinese of the Philippines," pp. 117–138 in Norman Yetman and C. Hoy Steele, eds. *Majority and Minority*. Boston: Allyn and Bacon.

Elazar, Daniel J. 1976 *Community and Polity: The Organizational Dynamics of American Jewry*. Philadelphia: Jewish Publication Society.

Farley, Reynolds 1977 "Trends in Racial Inequalities: Have the Gains of the 1960's Disappeared in the 1970's. *American Sociological Review* 42: 189–208.

Glazer, Nathan 1958 "The American Jew and the Attainment of Middle-Class Rank: Some Trends and Explanations," Pp. 138–146 in M. Sklare, ed. *The Jews*; New York: The Free Press.

Gordon, Milton 1964 *Assimilation in American Life*. New York: Oxford University Press.

Hechter, Michael 1978 "Group Formation and the Cultural Division of Labor" *American Journal of Sociology* 84: 293–318.

Howe, Irving 1976 *World of Our Fathers*. New York, Basic Books.

Kessner, Thomas 1977 *The Golden Door*. New York: Oxford University Press.

Krohn, Roger G., Berkeley Fleming and Marylyn Manzer 1977 *The Other Economy: The Internal Logic of Local Rental Housing*. Toronto: Peter Martin.

Light, Ivan 1972 *Ethnic Enterprise in America*. Los Angeles: University of California Press.

———— 1979 "Disadvantaged Minorities in Self-Employment" *International Journal of Comparative Sociology* 20: 31–45.

Mayhew, Leon 1968 "Ascription in Modern Societies." *Sociological Inquiry* 38: 105–120.

Nelli, Humbert S. 1967 "Italians in Urban America: A Study of Ethnic Adjustment." *International Migration Review* 1: 38–55.

Newman, Peter C. 1979 *The Bronfman Dynasty*. Toronto: McLelland and Stewart.

Porter, John 1975 "Ethnic Pluralism in Canadian Perspective," pp. 267–304 in Nathan Glazer and Daniel P. Moynihan, eds. *Ethnicity*. Cambridge: Harvard University Press.

Rosen, Bernard 1959 "Race, Ethnicity, and the Achievement Syndrome." *American Sociological Review* 24: 47–60.

Sales, Arnaud 1979 *La Bourgeoise Industrielle au Quebec*. Montreal: Les Presses de l'Université de Montréal.

Slater, Miriam 1969 "My Son the Doctor: Aspects of Mobility Among American Jews." *American Sociological Review* 34: 359–373.

Sombart, Werner 1913 *The Jews and Modern Capitalism*. Translation by M. Epstein. New York: Franklin.

Sowell, Thomas 1975 *Race and Economics*. New York: David McKay.

Strodtbeck, Fred L. 1958 "Family Interaction, Values and Achievement," pp. 147–165 in M. Sklare, ed., *The Jews*, New York: The Free Press.

Weinfeld, Morton 1977 "Determinants of Ethnic Identification of Slavs, Jews, and Italians in Toronto." Ph.D. Thesis, Harvard University.

Weinfeld, Morton and William Eaton 1979 *The*

Jewish Community of Montreal: Survey Report. Montreal: Jewish Community Research Institute (Canadian Jewish Congress).

Wiley, Norbert 1967 "The Ethnic Mobility Trap and Stratification Theory." *Social Problems* 15: 147–159.

33   The Colonial Status of Canadian Indians

Rita Bienvenue

RITA BIENVENUE, Associate Professor of Sociology at the University of Manitoba, Winnipeg, specializes in ethnic studies, especially the study of Native peoples. Her publications include *Ethnicity and Ethnic Relations in Canada* (1980, 1985) co-edited with Jay Goldstein; "Participation in an educational innovation: Enrollments in French immersion programs" (1986); "Ethnolinguistic attitudes and French immersion enrollments" (1984); and "Comparative colonial systems: The case of Canadian Indians and Australian Aborigines" (1983). She has held executive and committee positions in the Canadian Sociology and Anthropology Association, Western Association of Sociology and Anthropology, and Canadian Ethnic Studies Association, and has served as a consultant to the Government of Manitoba and other organizations.

INTRODUCTION

Social scientists have tended to consider colonialism in terms of third-world nations, but as Blauner (1972) has shown, this pattern of majority-minority relations is applicable to indigenous minorities in more highly industrialized societies. Patterns of ethnic differentiation, of economic and political subordination have and continue to characterize the conditions of aboriginal people in more highly industrialized societies.

The purpose of this chapter is to examine the institutionalization and the ramifications of colonial systems. The chapter focusses on the situation of native people in Canada. As a new-world nation and as an industrialized society, this country offers an opportunity to examine the exercise of power on the part of a dominant migrant group (Lieberson, 1961)....

COLONIAL STRUCTURES

According to historians, the colonization of Indian tribes was institutionalized when the administration of Indian affairs was placed under the control of politicians, churches, and a civil service bureaucracy. Competition and ethnocentrism were important dimensions giving rise to ethnic stratification as Noel (1968) has noted, while differentials in power became the foundation for the genesis of colonialism. Reservations were the initial solution for both the protection of Indian tribes and the appropriation of their lands while a system of wardship was established in diverse attempts to contain and acculturate the indigenous population. All of this was accomplished without the representation of native groups until 1960 when all Indians were granted the federal franchise and local groups and consultative bodies were recognized as minor decision-making bodies. Other ethnic minorities in Canada have experienced the ramifications of differential treatment (Kallen, 1982), but the structuring of a colonial system has placed Indians at the bottom of the stratification system.

Similar patterns of colonization have appeared in parts of Africa, Australia, and the United States (Rowley, 1970; Bienvenue, 1983; Guillemin, 1978). Colonized people, whether considered in terms of classical or internal colonialism, have not only been subjected to various forms of territorial incorporation, they have also experienced the ramifications of political, economic, and cultural subordination. In the process, discrimination and exploitation were justified, as negative stereotypes (e.g., intellectual inferiority, irresponsibility) became important elements in the regulation of intergroup relations. There were variations in the structuring of colonial systems, but patterns of group differentiation were perpetuated as colonial authorities pursued their interests in the acquisition of lands and resources. . . .

The definition of an Indian person originally appears in the British North America Act, 1867, but as Cumming and Mickenberg (1972) have shown, criteria pertaining to racial and social referents have never been precisely defined. Rather, the definition of an Indian person emerges from the Indian Act, where criteria relating to the identification of a status (or registered) Indian have been progressively refined to include references to land, membership in band organization, and participation in band funds (Smith, 1975). In the process, the category of "non-status" Indian has been relegated to those persons who have never been registered or for one reason or another have lost legal status. This now includes Indian women who have married outside the group[1] (i.e., women who have married persons who are not status Indians), as well as individuals or entire bands who have chosen to become "enfranchised."[2] What this categorization means is that non-status Indians and Metis have been voluntarily or involuntarily excluded from reservations and from the activities of Indian Affairs. Except for those non-Indians who were given special permission to reside on reserves (e.g., teachers, the clergy), only registered Indians have the legal right to reside on reservations.

From an economic point of view, reservations were considered important as native people were expected to survive within their allotted territories, independent of settler communities. The result was one of hardship and poverty as initial agricultural projects failed and as wild life was eventually depleted.

More specifically, the colonial process involved a notion of Indian self-sufficiency based on lands and benefits accruing from its natural resources. Agriculture was and is still encouraged, and revenues derived from both surface and subsurface resources were to be administered by the federal government for the benefit of Indians. These policies have persisted despite an enormous range in real and potential land use and a lack of capital and technology. Only since the 1960s has a welfare system alleviated appreciably a system of rural poverty which has come to characterize most native communities (Hawthorn et al., 1966; Dosman, 1972), and only recently have government funds been more specifically directed toward the development of more diversified reservation economies. In the interim, valuable sections of reservation lands were expropriated or sold, as government authorities, both at the provincial and federal level, required additional land for the building of roads, railroads, and dams, or for the development of primary industry. In Manitoba and Saskatchewan, for instance, band councils claim to have lost over one million acres as a result of expropriation or sales. Indian lands were managed not for the benefit of the native population but for the expansion of the Canadian economy (Kellough 1980).

There are now 2,242 reservations (573 bands) scattered throughout the various regions. In the more southerly areas, several reserves have become economically viable in terms of farming, ranching, and commercial enterprises. The vast majority, however, continue to be constrained by geographic and demographic factors limiting opportunities for economic development (Department of Indian Affairs and Northern Development, 1980). Changes in ecological patterns and a recent population increase have diminished the possibilities for subsistence economies. At the same time, a general lack of marketable skills has prohibited a shift toward industrial employment. These economic realities along with long-standing patterns of prejudice and discrimination on the part of the non-native population have placed an increasing number in a situation of welfare dependency. In 1964, thirty-six percent of native people were receiving social assistance; by the end of the 1970s, fifty to seventy percent of registered Indians were receiving welfare payments (Indian Affairs and Northern Development, 1980).

In some locations, timber, minerals, and oil resources have been developed by national and international companies; but while bands are in receipt of royalties, they have little control over resource management and use. Such patterns of non-Indian control persisted despite numerous complaints on the part of the native communities. In recent decades, various Indian organizations have become increasingly powerful; but while these organizations have enjoyed considerable success, they are still largely dependent on government funds. The federal government may have loosened its political control over reservation communities, but this has been accompanied by tighter controls over financial resources. . . .

According to a recent government survey, the quality of reserve lands compares favorably with non-Indian land assets. Sixty-five percent of reservations, however, are located in remote and isolated areas. Where resources could be developed, business loans are difficult to obtain, and government funds involve complex bureaucratic procedures. As a result, although several viable projects are now underway, most reservations resources remain undeveloped (Department of Indian Affairs and Northern Development, 1980).

Patterns of political and economic subordination were not the only aspects of colonization. In Canada as in other areas of the New World, policies of assimilation were oppressive as federal authorities sought to replace indigenous religion and tribal organization. Historically, these aspects of native society were considered to be culturally and morally inferior as colonial authorities established a basis for group assimilation. Missionaries, civil servants, and the police became the agents of acculturation. Full citizenship rights were in fact to be granted through the Indian Act (Section 109) once the native population had reached a level of North American sophistication considered adequate enough to warrant the benefits of democracy and the extension of civil liberties.

Patterns of European ethnocentrism were an integral aspect of colonization. There were variations between the French and the British as Baker (1972) has noted, but both undervalued the cultural diversity of Indian society. The early recruitment of missionaries on the part of the French, and the policies of Christianization and "protection" on the part of the British were important elements in the relationship between the European colonizers and the indigenous population (Upton, 1973; Ralston 1981). As a result, native people have had few opportunities to develop their own institutions which could have enhanced the development of culture, language, and ethnic identity.

Programs in education for instance were left largely to the churches until the 1950s when the federal government assumed the direction for Indian education. In both situations (that is, a church or government school), teachers and administrators ignored native cultures and tribal identifications. In many instances, the learning of new lifestyles in boarding schools resulted in the rejection of reservation life and the denigration of native values. The use of English or French as the language of instruction created linguistic barriers which inhibited the academic progress of native students. Problems of academic failure, alienation, and negative self-concepts have become major concerns for educators and parents alike (Bienvenue, 1978). In recent decades there have been many modifications in terms of a more integrated curriculum and school board control, but these educational reforms have barely begun. According to the Penner (1983) report, there are still complaints regarding the imposition of an urban, middle-class curriculum. Discontinuities in socio-cultural environments and the prejudices of the non-native population continue to frustrate the academic progress of native students.

European concepts of marriage and the family were also imposed upon the indigenous population. Historically, efforts were made to eliminate matrilineal customs without understanding the role these customs played in the functioning of tribal societies (Price, 1978:83). In many instances, missionary preaching was aimed at strengthening the position of males and ordering family life according to the norms of a European, patrilineal society.

More recent evidence of ethnocentrism involves child-welfare agencies and their policies regarding the adoption of native children. As Johnston (1983) has shown, social workers used urban, middle-class norms in their assessments of native families. As a result, a disproportionate number of native children were placed under government care. At the same time, social workers ignored the child-adoption practices of the native extended family. Little effort was made to find suitable adoption or foster homes within the kinship system or other adoptive families within the native community. . . .

CONTEMPORARY PROFILES

. . . The Indian Affairs Branch itself has developed into an elaborate bureaucracy largely representative of the non-native population. Of the 6,800 positions available, less than twenty-five percent involve native employees. At the senior and middle-management level, approximately two percent of employees are of native ancestry. As Ponting and Gibbins (1980) have indicated, native people are minimally involved in the system that governs their lives. The colonial process in other words continues to limit opportunity structures. The institutionalization of external controls has developed into a system which perpetuates political and economic dependence.

The contemporary profile of native people shows the disadvantaged position of a subjugated and depressed population. In recent decades, the process of urbanization has perhaps increased the possibilities for intergenerational changes, but here as well as in rural areas, the gap between the native and non-native population persists. In terms of socioeconomic status, housing, and health, natives are the most disadvantaged ethnic group in the country. . . .

Socioeconomic Status

In terms of educational attainment, all native children enroll in elementary programs but only twenty percent complete high school requirements. For the Canadian population as a whole, the high school retention rate is seventy-five percent. At the post-secondary level, native enrolment in community colleges and universities has increased over the years, but given the low rate of high school completion, participation at the tertiary level is minimal. According to recent statistics, 5.4 percent of natives in the twenty and over age category have some post-secondary education, while this is the case for twenty-seven percent of the national population (Department of Indian Affairs and Northern Development, 1980).

These educational qualifications pose a problem in the labour market. According to the Department of Indian Affairs and Northern Development (1980), the native employment rate is less than two-thirds of the national average. When employment is available, natives tend to be concentrated in unskilled and semiskilled occupations, that is, they are overrepresented in the lower rungs of the stratification system. In comparison to other ethnic groups in the country, natives diverge the most from the occupation distribution of the total labour force.... [3]

Income levels also reflect the colonial process as approximately two-thirds of the native population live below the poverty line. Natives living on productive reserves benefit from relatively high incomes (royalties from oil resources, for instance), but recurrent unemployment and long periods of social assistance characterize the conditions of the majority of natives. In rural areas, for instance, the unemployment rate ranges from forty to sixty percent. In urban areas, male and female unemployment rates are three to four times the rate for the city. In the city of Winnipeg, for instance, the unemployment rate among male native migrants is thirty percent; among females it is forty percent (Clatworthy, 1981a, 1981b)....

A crude measure of economic well-being is the dependency ratio. This measure represents the number of persons in the dependent age categories (15 and under, and 65 and over) per 100 persons in the labour force. In 1976, the dependency ratio for the native population was 86 per 100 persons in the labour force as compared to a ratio of 53 per 100 for the national population. According to Siggnér (1980), the native dependency ratio could converge with national patterns once the native birth rate declines and natives are more fully involved in the labour market. Recent evidence would suggest, however, that while the native birth rate is in fact declining, the employment rate is unlikely to change....

Housing

Housing poses another critical problem. According to a recent survey, on-reserve housing is considered to be the worst in Canada. Currently, thirty-three percent of native housing needs repair and another thirteen percent requires complete replacement. This means that approximately forty-six percent of houses fail to meet national health and safety standards. In addition, overcrowding is common, with twenty-five percent of reservation homes providing shelter for two or more families—a situation which is conducive to the spread of infectious diseases (Department of Indian Affairs and Northern Development, 1980).

Reservation houses lack the facilities most Canadians take for granted. The installation of electrical facilities approach national standards, but for other facilities—those most directly associated with sanitation—the native population in both remote and rural areas is at a distinct disadvantage. Remote areas refer to native communities accessible only by air and water, while rural areas refer to communities over 100 kilometres from an urban centre. Here, such facilities as running water, sewage systems, and indoor plumbing fall far below national standards....

Finally, native housing is considered to be substandard in terms of construction materials and heating systems. Reports in fact indicate that the incidence of fire on reserves is over seven times the national rate (Department of Indian Affairs and Northern Development, 1980). It is worth nothing here that only thirty percent of reservations have fire protection while this service is universally provided in non-native communities.

Health Conditions

High levels of poverty, poor housing conditions, and inadequate access to medical services are considered to be important factors explaining the health status of native people. Urbanization has improved the situation somewhat, but here as well as in rural areas, poverty and inadequate accommodation lend themselves to inferior health conditions. As a result, when native people are compared with national standards, there are divergences in terms of mortality rates, life expectancy, causes of death, and rates of hospitalization.

In terms of native infant mortality rates, these have changed over the decades, but as late as 1980 the infant death rates for registered Indians still exceeded the national average. In all infant age categories, the Indian death rates are one to three times higher than the rates for the Canadian population as a whole. In the neonatal category (infants under four weeks of age), the registered Indian death rate was 10.2 per 1,000 live births in comparison to a national neonatal death rate of 6.7 per 1,000 live births. The post-neonatal death rate (deaths between four weeks and one year of age) for the Indian population was 11.5 per 1,000 live births in comparison to a national rate of 3.8. Finally, the total infant mortality rate for registered Indians is twice as high as the national rate (21.8 versus 10.4 per 1,000 live births).

Death rates in other age categories also indicate a divergence between the native and non-native population. According to the Department of Indian and Northern Affairs, for all age categories except those over sixty-five years of age, the death rate for registered Indians is two to four times the national average. In the one to four age category, for instance, the mortality rate for Indian children is 3.1 per 1,000 population in comparison to a national rate of 0.8 per 1,000 population. Similarly, in the youth categories, comparative rates are 1.9 versus 0.7 per 1,000 population in the five to nineteen age category and 6 versus 1.5 per 1,000 in the twenty to forty-four age category (Department of Indian Affairs and Northern Development, 1980).

These mortality rates are important in the computation of life expectancy. High rates of infant and youth mortality within the native population continue to be a significant factor explaining the life expectancy of registered Indians. At birth, both males and females have a life expectancy which is ten years less than the national average. As recently as 1976, for instance, life expectancy was 60.2 years for males and 66.2 for females. The comparable national figures are 69.2 years and 76.4 years.

In terms of the leading causes of death, there are striking differences between the native and non-native populations. This applies to infant mortality rates as well as to the mortality rates for the entire native population. According to 1981 figures, for instance, the native infant death rate from respiratory conditions was ten times the national average. Deaths as a result of gastrointestinal conditions are seven times the national rate. In addition, deaths associated with premature birth and low birth weight were three times the national average. All of these infant deaths can be associated with poor sanitation, inadequate housing, and poor access to medical services.

When death rates are considered for the entire population (that is, deaths for all age categories), the leading causes of death among native people differ significantly from the rest of the population. Indian death rates from cancer and circulatory conditions are less than half the national rates. But deaths as a result of accidents, poisoning, and violence, however, account for thirty-five percent of Indian deaths compared with nine percent in Canada as a whole.[4] Among the major causes of accidental deaths are motor vehicle accidents, burns, and suicides. According to 1981 data, for instance, native death rates as a result of motor vehicle accidents were three times the national average. Death as a result of fire and burns was seven times the rate for the Canadian population as a whole. The native suicide rate was three times the national average. Suicide rates are particularly high in the fifteen to twenty-four age category.

Reports on native hospitalization indicate that registered Indians use hospitals from two to two and a half times more often than the national population. In comparison to the total Canadian population Indian persons have a high rate of illness associated with infectious diseases, conditions of the respiratory tract, accidents, and violence. Tuberculosis has dramatically decreased as a result of preventative measures, but the incidence of this disease within the native population still exceeds the national average (Department of Indian Affairs and Northern Development, 1980).

Finally, evidence suggests that from fifty to sixty percent of native illnesses and deaths are alcohol-related. While this applies to such conditions as cirrhosis of the liver, the abuse of alcohol is also related to the incidence of motor vehicle fatalities and suicide (Jarvis and Boldt, 1982). General living conditions and feelings of uselessness and estrangement from the society at large are considered to be important factors underlying the nature and the circumstances surrounding native illness and death.

In conclusion, the overall health condition of native people continues to reflect the disadvantaged position one usually associates with the colonial process. Undoubtedly, there have been many changes over the years, but in terms of mortality rates and longevity, the native profile in Canada differs considerably from the rest of the population. In many ways, the profile of Canadian Indians approaches the health conditions found in non-industrialized countries. According to recent demographic studies, the life expectancy in Latin American countries, for instance, ranges from sixty-three to sixty-nine years (World Population Data Sheet, 1982). As indicated above, the life expectancy for native males was 60.2 years and for females, 66.2 years. In terms of infant mortality rates, in certain Caribbean countries (Tobago, Barbados) these rates range from 24 to 25 per 1,000 live births (United Nations, 1982). In Canada the native infant mortality rate is 21.8 per 1,000 live births.

SUMMARY AND CONCLUSION

. . . Throughout the decades, there was little room for Indian participation in the running of their own affairs. Power was and is still vested in the federal minister and appointed civil servants. A recent report on the development of local self-government (Penner, 1983) has outlined a number of recommendations which address the major concerns of native leaders. Until these recommendations are implemented, however, colonial structures will continue to differentiate native people from the rest of the population. In Canada, as elsewhere, the colonial legacy remains.

Notes

[1] According to the Indian Act, the intergenerational transmission of registered Indian status is based on male descent. Accordingly, Indian males can transmit their status to their male and female children. They (Indian males) can also transmit their status to a non-Indian spouse. This is not the case for Indian women, however. According to the Indian Act, registered Indian women who marry a male who is not a registered Indian must forfeit their Indian status, and the children of that union must assume the status of their non-Indian father. This issue has gained wide attention, and the Canadian government has promised to amend the Indian Act in order to remove this discriminatory clause. Indian women and their children are to be reinstated.

[2] The term "enfranchisement" in the Indian Act refers to a process whereby status Indians could relinquish their status and assume full Canadian citizenship. As indicated in the discussion on assimilation, Indian persons could do so if they met certain criteria. According to Section 109 of the Indian Act, this includes: the capability of assuming the duties and responsibilities of citizenship, and the ability to support themselves and their dependents.

[3] For a discussion of occupational inequalities

and dissimilarity scores see "Another Look at Ethnicity, Stratification, and Social Mobility in Canada" by A. Gordon Darroch.

[4]These rates were computed from two sources: Health and Welfare Canada, Medical Services, *Annual Review*, Catalogue 33–1–1891, and Statistics Canada *Vital Statistics*, Volume III, Mortality, Catalogue 84–206.

The native death rate as a result of motor vehicle accidents in 1981 was 66 per 100,000 population, in comparison to a national rate of 22.3 per 100,000 population. The native death rate as a result of fire and burns was 14.2 per 100,000 in comparison to a national rate of 2.1 per 100,000. The native suicide rate was 39.3 per 100,000 in comparison to a national rate of 13.4 per 100,000 population.

References

Baker, Donald E. 1972. "Color, Culture and Power: Indian White Relations in Canada and America." *The Canadian Review of American Studies* 3(3): 3–20.

Barber, Lloyd I. 1974. *A Report, Commissioner of Indian Claims and Submissions*. Ottawa: Minister of Supply and Services.

———. 1976. "Indian Land Claims and Rights." Pp. 65–80, in M.A. Tremblay (ed.), *The Patterns of "Amerindian" Identity*. Québec: Les Presses de l'Université Laval.

Bienvenue, Rita M. 1978. "The Self Evaluation of Native and Euro-Canadian Students." *Canadian Ethnic Studies* 10: 97–105.

———. 1983. "Comparative Colonial Systems: The Case of Canadian Indians and Australian Aborigines," *Australian-Canadian Studies: An Interdisciplinary Social Science Review* 1:30–43.

Blauner, Robert. 1972. *Racial Oppression in America*. New York: Harper and Row.

Cardinal, Harold. 1969. *The Unjust Society, the Tragedy of Canada's Indians*. Edmonton: Hurtig.

———. 1977. *The Rebirth of Canada's Indians*. Edmonton: Hurtig.

Clatworthy, Stewart. 1981a. *Patterns of Native Employment in the Winnipeg Labour Market*. Ottawa: Department of Employment and Immigration Task Force in Labour Market Development.

———. 1981b. *Issues Concerning the Role of Native Women in the Winnipeg Labour Market*. Ottawa: Department of Employment and Immigration Task Force in Labour Market Development.

Cumming, Peter A. and Neil H. Mickenberg. 1972. *Native Rights in Canada*. Toronto: General Publishing Company.

Darroch, Gordon A. 1979. "Another Look at Ethnicity, Stratification and Social Mobility in Canada." *Canadian Journal of Sociology* 4 (1): 1–25.

Dosman, Edgar E. 1972. *Indians: The Urban Dilemma*. Toronto: McClelland and Stewart.

Frideres, James, 1983. *Native People in Canada: Contemporary Conflicts*. Scarborough: Prentice-Hall of Canada.

Gerber, Linda M. 1984. "Community Characteristics and Out-migration from Canadian Indian Reserves: path analysis." *The Canadian Review of Sociology and Anthropology* 21(2): 145–65.

Guillemin, Jeanne. 1978. "The Politics of National Integration: A Comparison of United States and Canadian Indian Administration." *Social Problems* (Dec.):320–32.

Hawthorn, H.B. et al. 1966. *A Survey of the Contemporary Indians of Canada*. Ottawa: Indian Affairs Branch.

Health and Welfare Canada. 1981. *Medical Services, Annual Review*. Catalogue number 33–1–1981.

Indian Affairs and Northern Development. 1980. *Indian Conditions: A Survey*. Ottawa: Minister of Supply and Services.

Jamieson, Kathleen. 1978. *Indian Women and the Law in Canada: Citizens Minus*. Ottawa: Minister of Supply and Services.

Jarvis, Genge K. and Menno Boldt. 1982. "Death

Styles Among Canada's Indians." *Social Science and Medicine* 16:1345–352.

Jenness, Diamond. 1932. *Indians of Canada*. Ottawa: Native Museum of Canada.

Johnston, Patrick. 1983. *Native People and the Child Welfare System*. Toronto: James Lorimer.

Judd, Carol M. 1980. "Native Labour and Social Stratification in the Hudson's Bay Company's Northern Development." *The Canadian Review of Sociology and Anthropology* 17(4):305–14.

Kallen, Evelyn. 1982. *Ethnicity and Human Rights in Canada*. Toronto: Gage Publishing.

Kellough, Gail. 1980. "From Colonialism to Imperialism: the experience of the Canadian Indians." Pp. 343–77, in J. Harp and J. Hofley (eds.), *Structured Inequalities in Canada*. Scarborough: Prentice-Hall of Canada.

Lautard, E. Hugh, and Donald J. Loree. 1984. "Ethnic Stratification in Canada, 1931–1971." *The Canadian Journal of Sociology* 9:333–44.

Lieberson, Stanley. 1961. "A Societal Theory of Race and Ethnic Relations." *American Sociological Review* 26(6):902–10.

Noel, Donald L. 1968. "A Theory of the Origins of Ethnic Stratification." *Social Problems* 16 (Fall): 157–72.

Patterson, E. Palmer. 1972. *The Canadian Indian: A History Since 1500*. Don Mills: Collier-Macmillan Canada.

Penner, Keith. 1983. *Indian Self-Government in Canada: Report of the Special Committee*. Ottawa: Supply and Services, Canada.

Ponting, R., and R. Gibbins, 1980. *Out of Irrelevance*. Toronto: Butterworths.

Price, John A. 1978. *Native Studies: American and Canadian Indians*. Toronto: McGraw-Hill Ryerson.

Ralston, Helen. 1981. "Religion, Public Policy, and the Education of Micmac Indians of Nova Scotia." Pp. 1605–1872, *Canadian Review of Sociology and Anthropology* 18(4): 470–98.

Rowley, C.C. 1970. *The Destruction of Aboriginal Society*. Canberra: Australian National University Press.

Siggner, Andrew. 1980. "A Socio-Demographic Profile of Indians in Canada," Pp. 31–65, in J.R. Ponting and R. Gibbins, *Out of Irrelevance*. Toronto: Butterworths.

Smith, Derek, G. 1975. *Canadian Indians and the Law: Selected Documents, 1663–1972*. Toronto: McClelland and Stewart.

Stanbury, W.T. 1975. *Success and Failure: Indians in Urban Society*. Vancouver: University of British Columbia Press.

Stanley, George F.C. 1960. *The Birth of Western Canada*. Toronto: University of Toronto Press.

Statistics Canada. 1981. *Vital Statistics*, Volume III, Mortality, Catalogue Number 84–206.

The World Bank, 1980. *World Development Report*, Washington, D.C.

United Nations. 1982. *Demographic Yearbook, 1980*.

Upton, L.F.S. 1973. "The Origins of Canadian Indian Policy." *Journal of Canadian Studies* 8:51–61.

Weaver, Sally M. 1977. "Segregation and the Indian Act: The Dialogue of Equality vs Special Status." Pp. 154–61, in W. Isajiw (ed.), *Identities: The Impact of Ethnicity on Canadian Society*. Toronto: Peter Martin Associates Ltd.

34 The Racial Attitudes of Canadians

Ronald D. Lambert   James Curtis

RONALD D. LAMBERT, Professor of Sociology at the University of Waterloo, specializes in social psychology, political behaviour, and the study of Canadian society. His books include *Sex Role Imagery in Children* (1971); *Social Process and Institutions: The Canadian Case* (1971) edited with James Gallagher; and *The Sociology of Contemporary Quebec Nationalism* (1981). He has recently written a series of articles, and currently is writing a book, *Thinking Politics*, on the results of a recent national post-election survey of Canadians' voting behaviour and their beliefs about politics. The publications, in the *Canadian Journal of Political Science*, the *Canadian Journal of Sociology* and the *Canadian Review of Sociology and Anthropology*, along with the survey are collaborative efforts with James Curtis, University of Waterloo, and Steven Brown and Barry Kay, Wilfrid Laurier University. Professor Lambert is also an Associate Editor of the *Canadian Journal of Sociology* and a member of the Editorial Board of the *Canadian Review of Studies in Nationalism*.

JAMES CURTIS, Associate Professor of Sociology at the University of Waterloo, specializes in the study of Canadian society, the sociology of knowledge, and the sociology of sport and leisure. His books and monographs include *Sociology and Anthropology in Canada* co-authored with Desmond Connor (1970); *The Sociology of Knowledge* co-edited with John Petras (1970); *Social Stratification: Canada* co-edited with William Scott (1973, 1979); *Region, Community and Physical Activity among Canadians* co-authored with Barry McPherson (1986); *Understanding Canadian Society* co-edited with Lorne Tepperman (1988); and *Social Inequality in Canada: Patterns, Problems and Policies* co-edited with Sid Gilbert, Edward Grabb, and Neil Guppy (1988). He has been an Associate Editor for the *Canadian Review of Sociology and Anthropology* and currently holds this position with the *Canadian Journal of Sociology*.

We have previously described an intriguing pattern of differences in the attitudes expressed by Quebecois and English Canadians toward multiculturalism.[1] Our analyses of information collected in interviews with national samples of adults suggested that French-speaking Quebecers objected to immigrants and new Canadians largely on linguistic and cultural grounds, while English-speaking Canadians were more negative toward racially-defined groups.

These differences persisted even when various statistical controls were applied. Since our original article, we have studied additional data from four national surveys in which people were asked about their feelings toward intergroup marriages.

Our findings from the new analyses are important because they help to confirm the pattern of cultural differences between English Canadians and the Quebecois, this time using a different and intuitively appealing indicator of intergroup sentiments. Since it is difficult to decide whether a given level of an attitude in a population should be regarded as high or low in any absolute sense, it is useful to make comparisons of levels of attitudes over time. The present analyses allow us to do this, providing a temporal perspective extending over a period of 15 years.

In addition, we are able to make some comparisons between Canada and the United States, thus affording perspective on whether any changes in intergroup attitudes are limited to this country or extend also to a closely-related country.

In 1968, 1973, 1978 and 1983, national samples of adults were asked whether they approved or disapproved of marriages between Roman Catholics and Protestants, Jews and non-Jews and Whites and Blacks. In each of the surveys, we studied the differences in attitudes among French-speaking residents of Quebec, English-speaking Canadians and a residual "other" category made up of people whose mother tongues were neither French nor English. Comparisons among these three language categories were standardized for age, gender, level of education, occupation, income, religious affiliation and size of community of residence.

COMPARISONS ACROSS LANGUAGE GROUPS

On the basis of our previous research, we predicted that English Canadians would be more negative than the Quebecois toward interracial marriages. Our assumption was that race figures more prominently in the national self-conceptions of English Canadians than it does in the thinking of the Quebecois, with the result that English Canadians should feel more threatened by the changing racial composition of immigration to this country.[2] The Quebecois, for their part, should react more unfavourably toward linguistic and cultural differences that are believed to threaten their survival as a French-speaking people. We doubted the suitability of the data for testing this part of the pattern because the Catholic/Protestant and Jewish/non-Jewish pairings are not clearly ethnic and linguistic distinctions. Nonetheless, it can be argued that Protestantism in Quebec has historically been virtually synonymous with the English presence;

and there is some evidence of more of a tradition of anti-Semitism in French Canada than in English Canada.[3]

Table 1 summarizes our basic findings on language group differences in attitudes without benefit of statistical controls. It is clear that the English Canadians were more negative than the Quebecois toward interracial marriages in every survey, thus confirming our principal prediction. Although the spread in disapproval between the two language groups declined from 22 per cent in 1968 to 13 per cent in 1983, the English Canadian disapproval rate was 1.6 times the Quebecois rate in 1968 and increased to 2.2 times in 1983. This pattern of differences persisted even when we analyzed the data in each survey using the various control variables.

The Quebecois were marginally higher than the English Canadians in their opposition to Catholic/Protestant and Jewish/non-Jewish marriages in 1973 to 1983, while the English Canadians were somewhat more negative in 1968. In the controlled analyses, however, the Quebecois were significantly more opposed to Catholic/Protestant marriages, but only in 1973 and 1983. None of the other comparisons produced significant differences. We think that the significant differences in response to Catholic/Protestant marriages were attributable to higher levels of religious involvement among Quebecois respondents. In 1978, but not in the other years, respondents were asked both about their denominational affiliation, if any, and about the importance of organized religion in their lives. When we controlled for an index combining their answers to both of these questions in the analysis of the 1978 data, there was no significant difference between the language groups in their feelings about Catholic/Protestant marriages. . . .

Table 1 also shows that persons whose mother tongues were other than English or French were generally the most negative toward the three kinds of intermarriage. The main exception to this pattern occurred in

Table 1
LANGUAGE GROUP DIFFERENCES IN ATTITUDES TOWARD MIXED MARRIAGES: FINDINGS FROM
FOUR NATIONAL SURVEYS OF CANADIAN ADULTS[1]

Year of Survey	1968			1973			1978			1983		
Lang. Group[2]	FQ	EC	OC	FQ	EC	OC	FQ	EC	OC	FQ	EC	OC
Attitudes Toward Marriage Between:												
R.C./Prot.												
Approve	60	60	67	53	73	63	78	81	65	84	86	77
Don't Know	13	11	7	28	14	16	10	11	12	5	7	13
Disapprove	27	29	26	20	13	21	11	8	23	11	8	10
Jews/Non-Jews												
Approve	47	53	60	43	62	51	77	74	56	80	78	68
Don't Know	30	17	13	39	25	25	12	18	21	9	14	14
Disapprove	24	30	27	18	13	24	11	8	24	11	8	17
Whites/Blacks												
Approve	46	29	36	50	42	46	73	61	48	86	66	54
Don't Know	16	11	8	28	20	20	12	14	17	4	10	17
Disapprove	38	60	46	22	38	44	16	25	35	11	24	28

[1] The figures are percentages; the totals may not sum to 100% due to rounding errors.
[2] The language groups are French-speaking Quebecers (FQ), English-speaking Canadians (EC) and Other Canadians (OC) whose mother tongues were other than English or French.

the 1968 data. We have included the "other" linguistic category in the analysis in order to complete the picture. Unfortunately, we can say very little about these people because specific information about their mother tongues, where they were born, and so on, was not obtained.

COMPARISONS ACROSS YEARS

There are grounds for predicting either a decrease or an increase in opposition to interracial marriages from 1968 to 1983. If the traditional cultures of English Canada and Quebec have eroded with time, then we might expect their defensive reactions to weaken as well. For example, the British component of the Canadian population has contracted noticeably since the Second World War and so has the pre-eminent role of the Roman Catholic Church in Quebec. It might also be

argued that the Federal Government's policy of official multiculturalism, enunciated by Prime Minister Trudeau in 1971, and promoted since then, has helped to weaken the boundaries between ethnic and racial groups. Indeed, the presence of growing numbers of non-Whites in Canadian society may itself be educative, so that White Canadians learn that non-Whites are very much like themselves and discover that relationships with them do not differ qualitatively from relationships with other Whites.

It is also reasonable, however, to expect an *increase* in opposition to interracial marriages. In fact, some of the factors cited above as lowering group boundaries can also be seen as raising them. The fact that Canada has become much more visibly multiracial since the 1960s, for example, has surely provided some people with a convenient explanation for the economic malaise that currently afflicts their country and possibly themselves.

And the Federal Government's multicultural policies, whatever their political motivation, may legitimize opposition to intergroup marriages, all in the name of preserving ethnic communities.

It is clear from Table 1 that the first prediction is borne out; there has been a pronounced drop in opposition to intergroup marriages from 1968 to 1983. In 1968, 60 per cent of English Canadians and 38 per cent of Quebecois expressed disapproval of marriages between Whites and Blacks. English Canadians' level of disapproval dropped to 25 per cent in 1978 and perhaps started to level off around 24 per cent in 1983. For the Quebecois, there was a dramatic drop to 22 per cent in 1973, followed by smaller but steady reductions in each of the succeeding surveys to a low of 11 per cent in 1983. The declining opposition to Catholic/Protestant and Jewish/non-Jewish marriages has not been so spectacular, but this is because they started from much lower levels in 1968. Nonetheless, the drops have been consistent and appear to have levelled off in the range of ten per cent.

COMPARISONS ACROSS NATIONS

We can grasp some of the forces shaping Canadian society and culture by comparing Canada with relevant other countries. These kinds of comparisons may reveal, for example, whether the processes of change are confined to this society, or whether they extend beyond its borders. An obvious comparison is with the United States, although we must be mindful of the immense differences in the two societies that may affect the variables we are studying. We were able to obtain distributions of responses to intermarriage questions that were asked in 1968, 1978 and 1983 in the United States. Since the American Gallup organization did not ask the intermarriage questions in 1973, we have substituted the results from a 1972 survey in which the questions were used.

Table 2 displays the comparisons. American opposition to interracial marriages declined from 72 per cent in 1968 to 50 per cent in 1983, a drop of approximately 30 per cent of the original rate. The overall rates in Canada went from 53 per cent in 1968 to 21 per cent in 1983, for a decline of about 60 per cent. In the case of interreligious marriages, Canadians were more opposed to both kinds in 1968, but these differences disappeared in the ensuing surveys. The rates seem to have flattened out at about 10 per cent by 1983.

So far as religious intermarriages are concerned, it appears that the same processes are operating in the two countries to dampen people's objections. The story appears to be different in the case of race. Although there has been a substantial reduction in negative feelings in both countries, the decline has been much more precipitous in Canada than in the United States. In fact, the American opposition rate was 1.4 times the Canadian rate in 1968 and widened in this sense in the succeeding pairs of surveys. The American rate was 1.7 times the Canadian rate in 1972/73, 2.3 times in 1978 and 2.4 times in 1983.

We also think that the results reported here underestimate the differences between the two countries because they are not broken down by respondents' race. On this point, the Roper Center has informed us that the disapproval rates in the 1983 American survey for White and non-White respondents were 56 and 20 per cent, respectively.[4] No doubt these national differences reflect the very different histories of race relations in the two countries. The American surveys are probably picking up the residue of an often unhappy racial history upon which the effects of demographic and political changes of the past two decades have been superimposed.

Table 2
CANADIAN AND AMERICAN OPPOSITION TO MIXED MARRIAGES[1]

Nation	Canada				U.S.			
Yr of Survey	1968	1973	1978	1983	1968	1972	1978	1983
Attitudes Toward Marriages Between:								
Catholics/Prot.	28	16	10	9	22	13	13	10
Jews/Non-Jews	28	16	11	10	21	14	14	10
Whites/Blacks	53	35	23	21	72	60	54	50

[1] Figures are percentages.

CONCLUSIONS

We should comment on an irony inherent in the attitudes discussed in this report. It might be argued that opposition to intergroup marriages, especially marriages between different ethnic and racial groups, is less a contradiction of the multicultural ethic than it represents its fulfillment. That is to say, a policy of multiculturalism that promotes the preservation of ethnic cultures must also envision the importance of ethnic boundaries. Part of the price of preserving living cultures involves the regulation of transactions across ethnic boundaries; and perhaps the most significant of these transactions involves marriages. We note that allophones, those people whose mother tongues were neither English nor French, were generally most opposed to intergroup marriages, especially between Whites and Blacks and between Jews and non-Jews. It is precisely in minority groups where intergroup marriages are most likely to occur and where, consequently, there is the most threat from them.[5] Stated in another way, majority groups can afford to be tolerant in a way that minority groups cannot.

By the same token, however, this interpretation does not address the fundamental question about why English-speaking Canadians, surely the most secure of all the groups considered here, should be so sensitive on the matter of race. Unfortunately, we lack the kind of information detailing English Canadians' perceptions of their community and the specific meanings that they attach to race to answer this question.

We can question, of course, whether interview surveys are a good way of measuring people's attitudes toward racial, ethnic and religious outgroups. After all, it is sometimes said, the sentiments that are expressed probably have little to do with people's private opinions and much more to do with what they believe it is safe to confess to. We also know that what people say and what they do are by no means identical. Even if these caveats are fundamentally correct, we doubt the wisdom of the conclusion drawn from them. We regard the emergence of normative constraints on verbal behaviour in interview situations as no less significant than changes in attitudes. It is surely noteworthy if people believe they are being judged according to norms that forbid the expression of outgroup hostilities. For our part, we believe that the architects of Canada's multicultural policies should be well pleased with the changes that are mirrored in the interview data analyzed here.

Notes

[1] R.D. Lambert and J.E. Curtis, "Exploring multicultural attitudes," *Past and Present* 1982:7 (February), 4–6. The present report is based on a larger project which is described in R.D. Lambert and J.E. Curtis, "Quebecois and English Canadian opposition to racial and religious intermarriage, 1968–1983," *Canadian Ethnic Studies* 1984:16(2) 30–46. The data on which we report were collected by the Canadian Institute of Public Opinion (Canadian Gallup) and were obtained from the Social Sciences Data Archives at Carleton University through the University of Waterloo Data Resource Centre. As usual, none of these organizations is responsible for our secondary analyses and interpretations.

[2] This conception of Canada and the threat that multiracial immigration poses to it can be found in Doug Collins, *Immigration: The Destruction of English Canada*, Richmond Hill, Ont.: BMG Publishing, 1979. For more scholarly treatments of the meaning attached to race in English-speaking cultures, see Carl Berger, "The true north strong and free," in P. Russell, ed., *Nationalism in Canada*, Toronto: McGraw-Hill Ryerson, 1966, 3–26; Mason Wade, "The French and the Indians," in H. Peckham and C. Gibson, eds., *Attitudes of Colonial Powers Toward the American Indian*. Salt Lake City, UT: University of Utah Press, 1969; Charles Herbert Stember, *Sexual Racism: The Emotional Barrier to an Integrated Society*. New York: Elsevier Scientific, 1976; Reginald Horsman, *Race and Manifest Destiny: The Origins of American Racial Anglo-Saxonism*. Cambridge, MA: Harvard University Press, 1981.

[3] See Michael Brown, *Jew or Juif? Jews, French-Canadians and Anglo-Canadians, 1759–1914*. Philadelphia: Jewish Publications Society, 1986.

[4] Personal communication from the Roper Center, 29 February 1984.

[5] For rates of intergroup marriages, see Warren E. Kalbach and Wayne W. McVey, *The Demographic Bases of Canadian Society* (2nd ed.). Toronto: McGraw-Hill Ryerson, 1979, 239ff., 320ff.

35 Another Look at Ethnicity, Stratification and Social Mobility

Gordon Darroch

GORDON DARROCH, Associate Professor of Sociology and Director of the Institute for Social Research at York University, Toronto, specializes in the historical/demographic analysis of social class and ethnic communities. His scholarly papers include "Family and household in nineteenth century Canada: regional patterns and regional economies" with Michael Ornstein (1984); "Early industrialization and inequality in Toronto, 1861–1899" (1983); and "Ethnicity and occupational structures in Canada in 1871: The Vertical Mosaic in historical perspective" with Michael Ornstein (1980). Recent collaborative work with Michael Ornstein, funded by a Social Sciences and Humanities Research Council grant, has involved the creation and analysis of a computerized data base of nineteenth century Ontario census data to study changing household and class composition, the migration and social mobility associated with these changes, and ethnic communities in nineteenth century Canada.

INTRODUCTION

Discussions of Canadian stratification and mobility have had as a central theme the relationship between class and ethnicity. Clearly, this is partly so because of the unique bicultural nature of Canada. But the dominant thesis of Canadian stratification studies does not have as its central focus the deprivation of any one group, rather it focuses on a more general relationship between ethnic pluralism and socio-economic stratification. The focus is succinctly expressed in the title of Porter's pioneering work, *The Vertical Mosaic* (1965). Specifically, it has become a first premise in the analysis of Canadian stratification that ethnicity has been a principal component, and indeed a principal cause, of the class structure. "Immigration and ethnic affiliation (or membership in a cultural group) have been important factors in the formation of social classes in Canada" (Porter, 1965:73).

In this paper I reassess the main assumptions of the thesis and re-examine the kind of evidence which has generally been cited in its support. A re-analysis of the main cross-sectional evidence in support of the conventional interpretation suggests that it may seriously exaggerate both the generality and the strength of the relationship between ethnic status and socio-economic status. Further, a review of currently available but limited social mobility data for Canada reinforces the argument that there is no sound evidence to sustain the quite common assumption that ethnic affiliations operate as a significant block to educational and occupational mobility in Canada. . . .

ETHNICITY AND CLASS IN CANADA: THE CONVENTIONAL EVIDENCE

With a few exceptions, the evidence which is presented in support of the broad, ethnically blocked mobility thesis consists of cross-tabulations of socio-economic status indexes, usually occupation, by ethnic origin or immigrant group. It is noted at the outset that these data have generally been presented without controls for the effects of potentially confounding variables such as ethnic differences in age or sex composition, regional and rural-urban differentials, language fluency or variations in socio-economic background.[1]

Pineo has recently provided the first reconsideration of the data which Porter originally presented in examining the relationship between ethnicity and occupational position (1976). He uses census tabulations for 1951, 1961, and 1971 for ethnicity and occupational groups. A form of "status score" is assigned to each ethnic group and the product moment correlations between these scores and Blishen occupational status codes are computed for each of the three years. The status scores assigned to the ethnic group are derived from two sources, first from the results of a previous national survey and second, from the mean occupational status of the ethnic group. Pineo acknowledges that the latter "loads" the evidence in favor of finding a relationship between ethnicity and occupational standing. In fact, the results are strikingly at odds with the common assumption of a relationship. Of the six correlations (two forms of ranking ethnic groups in three census years) the highest coefficient is .19 found for the association in 1961 between occupation and the "loaded" measure of ethnic status (Table 3:119).

Pineo also computes correlations for the grouped data to find the association between ethnic group "social standing" and mean occupational status. In 1931 and 1951, years for which the data are available, there are strong correlations of .81 and .77. For 1961 data the correlation is only .26.

In a very brief discussion Pineo concludes that the results are not consistent with the conventional image of a "vertical mosaic," but he indicates in reference to the group correlations, "It was apparently this reality to which Porter (1965) was reacting" (1976:120). Moreover, he suggests that in

fact Porter's thesis was largely commenting on the relative status of ethnic groups and not on the life chances of individuals. . . .

One obvious source of difference between Porter's original analysis of census data and that of Pineo is the form of the analysis itself. Pineo presents correlations, while Porter examined differences in the distributions of different ethnic groups in comparison with expected distributions based on the total labor force. In examining the relevance of the vertical mosaic thesis for immigrant groups, Blishen has followed the same strategy. Whereas correlations are sensitive to differences about means, Porter and Blishen's analyses were intended to assess differences in distributions *per se*.[2] I will preserve the original strategy of comparison in my re-analysis.

Porter's data include tabulations for three points over a thirty-year period. They give the relationship between broadly defined occupational groups and ethnic origin groups in terms of the over- and underrepresentation of each ethnic group in comparison with the distribution of the total male labor force. The data are by now very familiar to students of stratification in this country.

These data have been cited as indicating that there is a substantial and persistent relationship between social status and ethnicity in Canada. There is, no doubt, a pattern of overrepresentation clearly favoring the British and Jewish origin groups and showing the disadvantage of the French, Italian, and native Indian and Eskimo populations. But consider the data in the form given in Table 1.

Table 1 presents, for each year of Porter's data, indexes of dissimilarity for each ethnic group between its occupational distribution and that of *total labour force*. The unweighted mean of the indexes is given at the bottom.

The index of dissimilarity has become a conventional, simple way of summarizing these kinds of data (Lieberson, 1963; Darroch and Marston, 1971). It has the appealing property of providing a direct, substantive

Table 1
OCCUPATIONAL DISSIMILARITY OF ETHNIC
GROUPS FROM TOTAL MALE LABOUR FORCE
FOR 1931, 1951 AND 1961
(FROM PORTER, 1965: TABLE 1)

Ethnic group	Dissimilarity indexes		
	1931	1951	1961
Total British	7.9	5.7	4.7
French	3.4	3.0	3.7
German	21.0	19.1	8.8
Italian	33.4	19.5	17.9
Jew	48.1	31.6	23.1
Dutch	18.5	17.3	10.3
Scandinavian	21.2	14.7	10.6
East European	26.9	14.1	7.8
Other European	35.8	11.1	6.9
Asian	38.0	23.9	20.8
Indian and Eskimo	45.3	47.0	42.9
Mean ($\overline{X}$)	27.23	18.82	14.32
Mean excluding Asian and Native groups (comparable to Lieberson's groups for American cities)	24.02	16.64	10.01

interpretation which indicates the proportion of one population which would have to become redistributed in order to match the occupational distribution of the comparison population.[3] The index can be computed directly from Porter's data as the sum of either the positive or negative percentage differences between and ethnic occupational distribution and the total labor force distribution (the total "overrepresentation" or total "underrepresentation" over all occupational categories).

Porter was most impressed by the existence of a pattern of over- and underrepresentation which was clearly to the advantage of those of British and northern European origin. He commented specifically on the seeming persistence of a general rank order of

ethnic groups by occupation (1965:90). Yet there are two related features of the same data, apparent in Table 1, which are at least as noteworthy for the usual interpretation of ethnic stratification in Canada. In 1951 and 1961 the dissimilarities from the total labor force in occupational distributions for a number of ethnic groups are either low or moderate by a reasonable substantive interpretation of the indexes (say 10 to 15 percent). By 1961, in fact, seven of eleven ethnic groups have a dissimilarity index of 10 percent or less. The second related feature of the data is the distinct and progressive reduction in average dissimilarity between 1931 and 1961. This reduction seems at least as significant for our interpretation of the place of ethnicity in stratification as stable rank order of occupational advantage and disadvantage. The reduction is very substantial, from an average of just less than 30 percent to just less than 15, with the greatest portion of the change coming between 1931 and 1951....[4]

Of course, the computation of dissimilarity indexes is by no means an adequate test of the importance of ethnic affiliations for mobility opportunities. The striking moderation in occupational differences does have a very important implication for individual mobility, however, akin to what I think is the main implication of Pineo's low correlations. The generally low level of association between ethnicity and occupational position simply means that ethnicity will not be found to be a significant factor in competition with other variables in an adequate model of the processes of status acquisition in Canada in recent years. But the examination of occupational dissimilarity does preserve information on the variation in occupational distributions among ethnic groups which has been surprisingly persistent....

One major conclusion which a reconsideration of the original data makes imperative is that ethnic occupational differentiation has systematically and in many cases substantially reduced in the thirty years.

Certainly, this adds weight to the growing reluctance to accept the idea that Canada has experienced a hardening of initial levels of ethnic entrance statuses into a permanent class system (Porter, 1974:6). Perhaps it suggests that we should be more concerned with the processes of occupational integration, despite continued immigration, over the period (Kalback, 1970: chapter 5)....

Comparisons between simple indexes of dissimilarity not based on identical categories can be misleading. This is especially true when the populations being compared are quite variable and when rather specific differences are being examined. However, Porter's data has been taken as initial evidence of the exceptional significance of ethnic stratification in Canada. Porter had suggested at least that it distinguishes the United States from Canada in terms of ideology and, perhaps, in fact.

The 1951 data for Canada may be set beside Lieberson's data for the United States in 1950 (1963). Lieberson's data include more refined occupational categories, but unfortunately refer only to first or second generation immigrants and to selected *urban* populations for ten major cities. Yet if examined with caution, a comparison of average levels of occupational dissimilarity may help to put the Canadian data into some perspective.

For ten ethnic groups and for between three and nine cities, depending on available data, Lieberson reports an average occupational dissimilarity of 18.7 between the male labor force and first generation immigrants (foreign-born whites).[5] For second generation immigrant groups, the average index is lower at 13.5 (1963, Table 55:169). Despite the differences in the data, there is not much reason to think that levels of ethnic occupational differentiation in Canada distinguished this country strikingly from the United States. Even the most deprived populations in each country bear some similarity. In 1950, the average indexes of occupational dissimilarity for blacks in American cities, compared to the first generation immigrant population, was 43. The dissimilarity of native groups in Canada from the total labor force was 47 in 1951, as given in Table 1.

I have dwelt on the reconsideration of Porter's original data because they gave impetus to one important aspect of the vertical mosaic thesis which has deeply influenced subsequent interpretations, perhaps much more than Porter intended. To consider a more recent contribution, I give a summary of detailed 1971 data presented by Forcese (1975). Again, where the author presented standard census cross-tabulations of ethnicity by occupation, I have simply computed dissimilarity indexes for each ethnic group from the *total labor force* distribution. There were twenty-two occupational categories in the original data....

The author suggests that the ethnic stratification is stable, or perhaps even deepening with the impact of current immigration (1975:41–49). The data do reveal a continuation of the general ranking of the groups in a broad occupational status *order*. Further, the dissimilarity indexes show that there was in 1971 very largely the same general pattern of occupational differentiation of ethnic groups as in 1961, with the Jewish, native Indian and Italian populations most dissimilar followed by the Asian origin group. But again the average index was not great, at 13.9, very slightly lower than in 1961 for Porter's data....

It is possible to make two kinds of potentially relevant comparisons for exactly the same census occupational categories which Forcese used to report the occupation by ethnicity data for 1971 (Kubat and Thornton, 1974: Table J3; 163–167). The first is to compare ethnic occupational dissimilarities to regional and provincial dissimilarities and the second is to consider the ethnic differentials in terms of the dissimilarity between men and women in the labor force in 1971. Again, for comparison with the previous analyses, I compute the index of dissimilarity between the occupational distribution of the population in question and the occupational distribution of the total labor force for Canada. For the Maritime provinces, the unweighted average index of dissimilarity is 15. Prince Edward Island has an index of 20, Newfoundland an index of 17, and Nova Scotia and New Brunswick have indexes of 12. Quebec has an occupational dissimilarity measured at 8 and Ontario measured at 5, which is the lowest index for all the provinces. Ontario, of course, has the largest proportion of the total labor force of any of the areas. The western provinces have an average dissimilarity of 12, varying from the national high of 22 for Saskatchewan, and 10 for Alberta to 8 for Manitoba and British Columbia. The Yukon and Northwest Territories combined have an index of 18. The mean of all eleven areas is 12.7. Thus average regional occupational dissimilarity in Canada is only marginally less than overall ethnic occupational dissimilarity in 1971 (13.9). For the fourteen ethnic populations considered by Forcese the range of the index is between 30 for the Jewish and 6 for the French ethnic groups, somewhat greater than the range for the eleven provinces and territories, that is, between 22 for Saskatchewan and 5 for Ontario. On this evidence one would probably not want to make a strong case that ethnic occupational stratification was much more striking or salient for Canada as a whole than regional occupational differentials, though the two have quite different implications for structured inequality. . . .

. . . Only the few, most extreme ethnic groups match the occupational imbalance which working women experience, and simple regional dissimilarities in occupational distributions are very nearly as great as ethnic dissimilarities. . . .

Blishen has presented the most thorough analysis of the main dimensions of ethnic stratification yet conducted in Canada (1958;1967;1970). The analyses have largely focused on the relationships between immigrant groups and occupational ranks, rather than considering ethnic affiliation more generally. The particular strength of this work in the present context is that Blishen specified the implications of the vertical mosaic idea for interpreting the relationship between immigrant status and occupational mobility. He concluded that his analyses strengthen the main tenets of the ethnically blocked mobility thesis. "Thus, certain combinations of immigrant and ethnic statuses are associated with the restriction of opportunity. These status combinations impart a degree of rigidity to class lines and strengthen individual group culture, thereby deepening social cleavages" (1970:124). As above, a second look at the data is in order to see how it leads to this apparent support for the centrality of ethnicity as a determinant of the Canadian class structure.

Blishen's most recently published work reports very detailed tabulations of male labor force distributions in 1961 in terms of his six occupational ranks (1970). The tabulations are given for the Canadian-born population and for eleven immigrant groups (country of birth) by period of immigration (pre- and post-WW II) and by region (Ontario, Quebec, the West and Atlantic provinces). The extensive cross-tabulations which are reported are difficult to interpret at a glance. I have recomputed portions of the data which are directly relevant to the ethnic blockage thesis in a form which provides a direct, single summary measure of the differences in occupational *rank* between the immigrant populations. The statistic employed is that recently described by Lieberson as the Index of Net Difference (ND) (1976). ND is related to the dissimilarity index, but specifically takes account of the direction of the relationship between the *entire* distributions of two ordered, categoric variables such as occupational ranks. The index summarizes the net difference between the two opposite probabilities of inequality between groups on the ranked variable. The index varies from $+1$

to −1. The extreme values indicate that there is no overlap at all in the distributions, and the sign indicates the direction of relationship. The index is zero when the two probabilities of inequality are equal. . . .

. . . As Blishen had concluded, the assessment of the *direction* of the advantage is congruent with the broad, conventional hypothesis that the Canadian-born generally suffer occupational mobility deprivation as a result of Canada's persistent dependence on the recruitment of the foreign-born to staff its industrial labor force and from the related deprivation in educational facilities and opportunities. That is, most of the Net Differences indicate a net advantage of immigrant groups over the Canadian-born.

But again there are other features of the data which need to be considered. Of the twelve relevant comparisons given in the table, two reach a Net Difference of .30 or greater, a value which I take as indicating decisive occupational status advantage. The two cases are the advantage which the British immigrants have over Canadian-born in the Atlantic provinces and in Quebec. The latter is the largest ND (.400) in the table, reflecting, no doubt, the deprivation of the French-Canadian population in Quebec itself. But with respect to what I take to be more general implications of the blocked mobility thesis, the results are much more ambiguous. Using Blishen's "total European" category in these computations necessarily masks a number of specific differences. However, even in these data the most striking feature of the relationship between immigrant status and occupational status in Canada is not uniformity of inequality, but, on the contrary, the wide variation of the strength and the direction of the relationship by immigrant group and by region.

The status advantage of the British immigrants over the Canadian-born could not be considered very significant in Ontario (.068), and evidently the advantage is rather moderate in the western provinces, measured as a difference in the probabilities of occupa-

tional inequality of .121. The occupational benefits enjoyed by the American immigrants are most consistent across the regions, but insofar as they can be measured in this 1961 data, they are moderate in substantive terms. The greatest advantage is in Quebec, where the Net Difference for the American-born over the Canadian-born is .245. There is no advantage to speak of in the West (ND = .099).

Only in the Atlantic provinces can we detect an overall status advantage in occupational rank for the total European-born population in comparison to the Canadian-born. In Quebec, there is no advantage, and in Ontario and in the West *it is the Canadian-born* who have a net occupational advantage over the foreign-born. To take account of these clear variations would entail a much more detailed specification than we have had of the implications of the vertical mosaic thesis for the relationship between immigrant status, occupational mobility and regional economies. . . .

MOBILITY STUDIES AND ETHNICITY

As noted earlier, one conventional account of the effects of immigrant and ethnic statuses on stratification is couched in terms of limitations on individual social mobility. However, to date we have very few studies of mobility *per se* in Canada and even fewer relate ethnicity to occupational status changes. . . .

Richmond (1964) compared the occupational mobility of postwar immigrants in a national study. He found the clear pattern of advantage of British immigrants over other immigrants which we have come to expect. He also reported that the initial advantage diminished over time and that differences in both career and intergenerational mobility were, in fact, comparatively slight between Great Britain and other European immigrant groups. . . . [6]

On the other hand, focusing on French-English differences and not immigrant status, Rocher and de Jocas' study (1957) of intergenerational mobility in Quebec showed that in the 1950s French Canadians suffered more severe handicaps to social mobility than did English-speaking Canadians in the province. Dofny and Garon-Audy (1964) matched the procedures of the previous study and argued that the occupational status gains made by French Canadians between the mid-1950s and the mid-1960s were largely a result of the structural changes in labor force distributions, rather than a result of equalization of opportunity or of increased "exchange" mobility (but see Turrittin, 1974:173–74). To these have been added two recent and more detailed studies of occupational mobility of French and English Canadians. Cuneo and Curtis (1975) examined the differences between Anglophones and Francophones in relatively small samples of the population aged 25–34, living in Toronto and Montreal. They applied the basic Blau-Duncan model of status attainment processes and an extension of it, incorporating additional background variables. They compare the models for four subsamples, Francophone men and women and Anglophone men and women. They emphasize, in general, that their data as well as the American data actually give greater credence to a view that ascriptive factors, especially family background, play a very significant role in status attainment, in contrast to the more commonplace emphasis on the dominance of achievement, through education especially. More important here is the fact that they report measurable differences *between* Francophones and Anglophones especially with respect to the greater effect of family size on education among Anglophones and the greater effect of educational attainment on current occupation for Francophones than for Anglophones.

By far the most detailed and important study of the differences between Anglophones and Francophones in mobility and status attainment processes has recently been reported by McRoberts, Porter, Boyd and their colleagues, as part of a larger national study (1976). They compare the Francophone experience in Quebec with the Anglophone experience in Canada as a whole on the persuasive grounds that these are the principal respective occupational realms of the two populations.... Like the previous studies they find that there are measurable differences between Anglophone and Francophone experiences. Applying loglinear analysis to control for differences in the marginals of mobility tables, they conclusively extend the analysis of Dofny and Garon-Audy. The differences in mobility are primarily the result of differential changes in labor force distributions affecting the two populations and the differences between the two groups have diminished in all respects.... In sum, the authors find evidence of convergence in the experiences of Anglophones and Francophones and, thus, evidence of the diminishing salience of linguistic stratification (1976:78)....

Finally, the complexities of mobility processes revealed in recent work should remind us that the differences between Francophone and Anglophone experiences cannot be generalized to the way ethnic affiliations or immigrant status enter the mobility process. At the time of writing only two studies are known to me which assess the direct and indirect effects of ethnic origins and immigrant status on occupational attainment and income in competition with other variables, such as social origins and education.... [7]

Goldlust and Richmond (1973) provide mobility data on "ethnolinguistic" groups of immigrants for metropolitan Toronto. They show that there are, as expected, substantial differences among the immigrant groups in their average occupational statuses in their *former* countries, among their statuses after arrival and at two subsequent points in their occupational histories. But the pattern of occupational differences is also found to be a *direct* reflection of the occupational differences of their father's statuses, i.e., of their differences in socio-economic origins. For six of the eight "ethno-linguistic" groups there was a difference of *less than* three points on the Blishen occupational scale between the mean of the father's scores and the mean of the respondents' current occupational scores. Ethnic group differences correspond closely with the average differences in social class origins of the group members which were a result of selective immigration processes.

Taking the analysis a step toward the separation of effects, Goldlust and Richmond computed the contributions of several variables to *income*, including the effects of ethnicity which entered a regression analysis as a set of dummy variables. At the most, when the ethnic variables entered the regression first, they accounted for 7 percent of the variance in incomes among all respondents; the total variance in income explained was 35 percent, with education, current occupational status and father's occupational status accounting for almost all of the remainder. From the table given by the authors it appears that, when ethnicity is made to compete with the other variables in the regression, education, current occupation and father's occupation explain, respectively, 18 percent, 10 percent, and 5 percent of the total variance, while the impact of ethnicity is entirely indirect, acting through these variables. In statistical terms, ethnicity appears to have *no* unique effects.[8]

A second unpublished work is by Ornstein (1974) based on a re-analysis of Porter and Blishen's data for Ontario high school students and their parents. One part of the study is a detailed analysis of the impact of ethnicity on occupational mobility undertaken by means of regression and analysis of variance techniques. Employing nine ethnic groups in the analysis, Ornstein first shows that ethnicity can account for a maximum of only 3.3 percent of the difference in occupational ranks (Blishen scores) of first jobs of this sample of the Ontario population and can account for 5.2 percent of the respondent's current job status differences. Ethnicity did account for slightly over 10 percent of the variation in educational attainment of the sample.

The author notes that the *pattern* of benefits in occupational ranks accruing to ethnic group affiliation is much as we expect—the Scots and English benefit most, the West Europeans and East Europeans follow in order and the recently immigrated Italian population is at the bottom. But again, I emphasize, a distinct pattern of advantage must not be confused with the significance of the effect of ethnicity on the actual occupational attainment of individuals.[9] Ornstein shows that the average differences among the ethnic groups in occupational attainment are not, in fact, very great. Moreover, the differences *within* the ethnic groups in occupational status are very much greater than the differences between them. The implications of this important finding have never been seriously considered in the Canadian context and warrant further comment.

If variations within ethnic groups in individual mobility experiences are generally large, and there are good *prima facie* reasons to think they might be, then it is quite conceivable that for some members of a given ethnic population there exist serious "mobility traps," while for other members ethnic identity may be of no consequence to mobility whatsoever. Still others may be able to translate their heritage into distinct occupational opportunities. Moreover, variations *within* ethnic groups in status achievement require explanations in terms of non-ethnic variables, that is, in terms of any number of factors which cannot themselves be broadly subsumed under the label ethnic identity or affiliation. . . .

THE MOSAIC REVISITED

One basic emphasis regarding the effects of ethnicity on the Canadian class structure has centred on the notion that a release from ethnic identities (assimilation) will result in enhanced mobility opportunities and subsequently, in relative status achievements. The thesis may be seen as a version of the theory of "modernization" which assumes that men and resources are increasingly freed from ascriptive ties in order to compete for achievement in the marketplaces of industrial or post-industrial society. In this respect, it is a functional theory of stratification.

With respect to ethnic community affiliations, at least, the argument no longer seems very convincing (but on ascriptive characteristics in general, see Cuneo and Curtis, 1975). Diminishing ethnic group attachments would have to affect one or more of the three conditions determining mobility rates, that is, to alter the opportunity structure, especially the occupational structure, or to affect differential rates of fertility between upper and lower status positions or to alter the rates of pure or exchange mobility between upper and lower strata. I have argued that recurrent emphasis has been given to a blocked mobility thesis in which ethnic assimilation is expected to increase exchange mobility, with some of those who occupy more privileged positions being replaced, or having their sons and daughters replaced, by those whose ethnic affiliations previously hampered their achievements. In any case, any argument about the effects of ethnic pluralism on stratification and mobility now requires this degree of specification.

It is generally known that the pure exchange portion of measured mobility rates for standard inflow-outflow tables is relatively limited in comparison to the mobility accounted for by structural changes in occupational distributions (see Turritin, 1974:

Table II for relevant Canadian data). Moreover, revisions of our view of the possible implications of ethnic affiliations for social mobility are necessitated by the most recent analyses of mobility opportunities in Canada and the United States. In attempting to overcome acknowledged limitations of standard mobility analyses by applying multivariate, contingency table analysis, Hauser and his associates have concluded forcefully that systematic variations in the relative intergenerational mobility chances of American men with different social origins are *entirely* accounted for by changes in occupational structure over time (1975a; 1975b). . . .

CONCLUSION

. . . It bears noting that one of the most important results of the tendency to overestimate the magnitude of ethnic group differences and to focus on the putative central role of ethnicity in social mobility has been to divert attention from other, more consequential sources of the maintenance of the class structure in Canada. Drawing on a broad familiarity with Canadian social history, S.D. Clark made the argument clearly.

> If one were to quarrel with the Porter analysis of society as it was, it would be only on the score that by seeking to relate ethnic affiliation to the hierarchical structure he tended to obscure the underlying forces producing this hierarchical structure. Members of the British charter group were admittedly very much on top, but they were on the very bottom as well, occupying marginal farm lands in eastern Nova Scotia, northeastern New Brunswick, and eastern and central Ontario, or engaged in subsistence fishing industry in Newfoundland. The division of the country into French and English has led to viewing Canadian society too much from an ethnic standpoint. (1975.28)

The reassessment of evidence presented in this paper, I hope, adds weight to the conclusion for the present as for the past.

Notes

[1] For a study which does employ all available census data in examining simultaneous effects, see Kalbach, 1965, especially chapters 4 and 5. For the use of survey data including socio-economic background to examine the social mobility of immigrants, see Richmond, 1964.

[2] I thank John Fox for drawing this point to my attention.

[3] There has recently been a rekindled discussion of the relative merits of dissimilarity measures, but for the straightforward purposes at hand their utility is not in question (Cortese et al., 1976; Taeuber and Taeuber, 1976). The indexes provided here compare each ethnic group's occupational distribution to a total distribution which includes the former. This way of re-examining the data simply adheres to the sort of comparisons made originally with the same data. As one reviewer pointed out, a single, summary measure of differences between distributions does not direct attention to numerically small differences between specific groups which may have particular importance, such as economic elites or other professional groups. This is true, of course, of any form of summary measure of expression, including simple declarative statements about the general features of distributional differences.

[4] Porter's Table III (1965:94) gives the same occupational distributions for the French and British origin groups *within* the province of Quebec. The indexes of dissimilarity computed from these data reflect the considerable differences which separate the two "charter" groups in that province, although, as Porter concluded, they suggest some lessening of the overall discrepancy in the thirty-year period. The indexes for 1931, 1951 and 1961 are, respectively, 23.2, 17.0 and 14.5.

[5] England and Wales, Ireland, Norway, Sweden, Germany, Poland, Czechoslovakia, Austria, Russia and Italy.

[6] Most specifically, Richmond employed samples *matched* in terms of social class, background, education, length of residence and marital status to compare career mobility of British immigrants and other European immigrants. He concluded that British immigrants in Canada did have some advantage over non-British immigrants, when other things were equal, but that this advantage was a comparatively small one.

[7] I thank the authors of these studies for generously permitting me to report some of their findings in the absence of full publication of their work. Goldlust and Richmond have briefly referred to their findings in one recent paper (1974:209).

[8] The authors do not assess direct and indirect effects in the analysis, but they do report a separate analysis of interaction effects (AID) in which father's occupation is not entered as an independent variable. In this analysis ethnicity accounts again for a maximum of 7 percent of the total variance of income.

[9] Ornstein summarizes his separate analyses in a regression with many variables, including ethnicity. Computing the variance explained in occupational status so as to *maximize* the effects of ethnicity and social class background, he finds that the 5.2 percent contributed by ethnicity is only greater than the predictive power of the respondents' first job (3.8 percent). By comparison educational achievement contributed 32.9 percent and father's occupation 11.2 percent, accounting for a total of 53.1 percent of the variance in occupational status. In an analysis of the determinants of household income, including first and subsequent occupations as independent variables, ethnicity and father's occupation were found to have *no* significant predictive power—a conclusion similar to that of Goldlust and Richmond cited above.

References

Avery, Donald, "Continental European Immigrant Workers in Canada 1896–1919: from 'Stalwart Peasants' to Radical Proletariat." *Canadian Review of Sociology and Anthropology*, 12, 1975:53–64.

Blishen, Bernard R., "The Construction and Use of an Occupational Class Scale." *Canadian Journal of Economics and Political Science*, 24, 1958:519–531.

———, "A Socio-Economic Index of Occupations in Canada." *Canadian Review of Sociology and Anthropology*, 4, 1967:41–53.

———, "Social Class and Opportunity in Canada." *The Canadian Review of Sociology and Anthropology*, 7, 1970:110–127.

Breton, Raymond and Howard E. Roseborough, "Ethnic Differences in Status." In *Canadian Society*, edited by B.R. Blishen et al., pp. 683–701. Toronto: Macmillan, 1968.

Clark, S.D., "The Post Second World War Canadian Society." *Canadian Review of Sociology and Anthropology*, 12, 1975:25–32.

Clement, Wallace, *The Canadian Corporate Elite: An Analysis of Economic Power*. Ottawa: McClelland and Stewart, 1974.

Cortese, Charles F., R. Frank Falk and Jack Cohen, "Further Considerations of the Methodological Analysis of Segregation Indices." *American Sociological Review*, 4, 1976: 630–637.

———, "Reply to Taeuber and Taeuber." *American Sociological Review* 41:889–893.

Cuneo, Carl J. and James E. Curtis, "Social Ascription in the Educational and Occupational Status Attainment of Urban Canadians." *Canadian Review of Sociology and Anthropology*, 12, 1975:6–24.

Darroch, A.G. and W.G. Marston, "The Social Class Basis of Ethnic Residential Segregation: The Canadian Case." *American Journal of Sociology*, 77, 1971: 491–510.

De Jocas, Ives and Guy Rocher, "Inter-Generational Occupational Mobility in the Province of Quebec." *Canadian Journal of Economics and Political Science*, 23, 1957:58–66.

Dofny, Jacques and Muriel Garon-Audy, "Mobilités professionnelles au Quebec." *Sociologie et Sociétés*, 1, 1969: 277–301.

Duncan B. and O.D. Duncan, "Minorities and the Process of Stratification." *American Sociological Review*, 33, 1968:356–364.

Featherman, David L. "The Socio-Economic Achievement of White Religio-Ethnic Subgroups: Social and Psychological Explanations." *American Sociological Review*, 36, 1971:207–222.

Forcese, Dennis, *The Canadian Class Structure*. Toronto: McGraw-Hill Ryerson, 1975.

Goldlust, John and Anthony H. Richmond, *A Multivariate Analysis of the Economic Adaptation of Immigrants in Toronto*, Unpublished ms., 1973.

Hauser, Robert M., John N. Koffel, Harry P. Travis and Peter J. Dickinson, "Temporal Change in Occupational Mobility: Evidence for Men in the United States." *American Sociological Review*, 40, 1975a:279–297.

——— "Structural Changes in Occupational Mobility Among Men in the United States." *American Sociological Review*, 40, 1975b:585–598.

Kalbach, Warren E., *The Impact of Immigration on Canada's Population*. Ottawa: Dominion Bureau of Statistics, 1970.

Kubat, Daniel and David Thornton, *A Statistical Profile of Canadian Society*. Toronto: McGraw-Hill Ryerson, 1974.

Lanphier, C. Michael and Raymond N. Morris, "Structural Aspects of Differences in Income Between Anglophones and Francophones." *Canadian Review of Sociology and Anthropology*, 11, 1974:53–66.

Lieberson, Stanley, *Ethnic Patterns in American Cities*. New York: Free Press, 1963.

———, "Rank Sum Comparisons Between Groups." In *Sociological Methodology*, edited by D.R. Heise, pp. 276–291. San Francisco: Jossey-Bass, 1976.

McRoberts, Hugh A., John Porter, Monica Boyd, John Goyder, Frank E. Jones, and Peter C. Pineo, "Différences dans la mobilité professionnelle des francophones et des anglophones." *Sociologie et Sociétés*, 8, 1976:61–79.

McVey, Wayne W., and Warren E. Kalbach, *The Demographic Basis of Canadian Society*, Toronto: McGraw-Hill, 1971.

Ornstein, Michael D., *Occupational Mobility in Ontario*. Unpublished ms. 1974.

Pineo, Peter, "Social Mobility in Canada: the Current Picture." *Sociological Focus*, 9, 1976: 109–123.

Porter, John, *The Vertical Mosaic*. Toronto: University of Toronto Press, 1965.

———, "Canada: Dilemmas and Contradictions of a Multi-Ethnic Society." In *Sociology Canada: Readings*, edited by C. Beattie and S. Crysdale, pp. 3–15. Toronto: Butterworths, 1974.

Raynauld A., G. Marion, and R. Beland, *La répartition des revenus selon les groupes ethniques au Canada, Rapport Final*. Ottawa. Unpublished ms. 1967.

Reitz, Jeffrey, "Analysis of Changing Group Inequalities in a Changing Occupational Structure." In *Mathematical Models in Sociology*. Sociological Review Monograph, no. 24, edited by P. Krishnan, pp. 167–191. Keele, Staffordshire: University of Keele, 1977.

Richmond, Anthony H., "The Social Mobility of Immigrants in Canada." *Population Studies*, 18, 1964:53–69.

———, *Post-War Immigrants in Canada*. Toronto: University of Toronto Press, 1967.

Royal Commission on Bilingualism and Biculturalism, *The Cultural Contribution of the Other Ethnic Groups: Book IV*. Ottawa: Queen's Printer, 1967.

Taeuber, Karl E. and Alma F. Taeuber, "A Practitioner's Perspective on the Index of Dissimilarity (comment on Cortese, Falk and Cohen)." *American Sociological Review*, 41:1976:884–889.

Tepperman, Lorne, *Social Mobility in Canada*. Toronto: University of Toronto Press, 1975.

Turrittin, Anton H., "Social Mobility in Canada: a Comparison of Three Provincial Studies and Some Methodological Questions." *Canadian Review of Sociology and Anthropology*, 11, 1974:163–186.

Vallée, F.G. and Norman Shulman, "The Viability of French Groupings Outside Quebec." In *Regionalism in the Canadian Community: 1867–1967*, edited by Mason Wade, pp. 83–99. Toronto: University of Toronto Press, 1969.

Wiley, Norbert F., "Ethnic Mobility Trap and Stratification Theory." *Social Problems* 15, 1967:147–159.

Gender Relations

Introduction

S omeone once said that North Americans are more involved in the battle of the sexes than in the class struggle. Gender relations in Canada really are a battle; and, like the class struggle, they are a battle about inequality. People are probably more aware of the gender struggle than of the class struggle, and they have more sympathy for the underdog too. The class struggle demands a radical commitment to social and economic justice; but many can see the need for changed gender relations, simply in the interest of fair play.

The articles in this section on gender relations run the ideological gamut. Some are traditionally liberal, mainly concerned with gaining equal treatment for women at home and in the workplace. Others are concerned with locating gender inequality within a more pervasive historical pattern of domination and exploitation.

The problem for radical feminists like Dorothy Smith, author of an article in the next section, has been reconciling Marxist theories of exploitation and class domination with theories of "patriarchy" or male domination. In a very general way, the two inequalities are similar. Marx emphasized that control over the means of production was the basis for all inequality. Many western societies have followed the Roman legal practice of *patria potestas*, literally, the "powerful father," a system in which the (male) family head exercised supreme legal authority over the family. In these societies, wives, like children, servants and pets, had no legal authority over the family wealth or the means of household production. Women exercised some actual control over household functioning and child rearing. But theirs was a managerial right delegated by an all-powerful father/husband. A wife's authority could not stand up against her husband's in a conflict of wills.

Thus, patriarchy can be seen as male domination of the means of household production, just as class exploitation is typically male domination of the means of paid production. What is not clear is (1) why biological (i.e., sexual) characteristics should be relevant to domination at all; and (2) how and why gender inequality continues despite a reduction of class inequality. Gender inequality and class inequality do resemble each other: both are economic and ideological domination serving the interest of males. But why is sex an important dividing line between dominator and dominated, while other biological traits like hair colour, shoe size, or IQ, are not? Does the formal similarity between class domination and patriarchy prove that gender inequality is somehow caused by private property or capitalism? And if we think it is, how do we interpret the evidence that gender inequality is as serious a problem in many socialist and communist countries as it is in equally advanced capitalist countries; and it is even worse in many pre-industrial (non-capitalist) countries.

Thus, the study of gender relations leads into difficult theoretical questions that extend widely over history and around the world. By its nature, gender research is cross-nationally comparative, since we are often forced to compare our own culture with another to test a theory.

At the same time, much research on gender relations is less radical and less theoretical than this. It has the more immediately valuable goal of documenting the extent and consequences of gender inequality. Two papers in this section deal with the extent of gender inequality in the typical North American home. The first, by Martin Meissner, concerns the "domestic economy" and attempts to measure what women do at home. A traditional male view is that (female) homemakers contribute little of value to the family's well-being or the economy as a whole. Homemakers receive no wages or pension for the work they do, and since our society tends to value most what is rewarded in cash, homemakers appear valueless.

Today, the value of homemaking is rapidly becoming clearer. As more women go out to work, families must increasingly pay cash for homemaking services they had previously gotten "free of charge" from wives. This payment of cash for services, whether for daycare, food preparation, housecleaning, laundry, or otherwise, helps husbands appreciate what they have lost. Second, as more families have broken down, more men have had to learn the traditionally female skills of child care and housekeeping. This has acquainted them firsthand with the effort and knowledge that

homemaking requires. Within unbroken families, somewhat more sharing of tasks than in the past has also helped men appreciate the skill and effort needed. But research shows that the movement towards equal task sharing has been very slight and very slow.

Married women continue to inhabit the worst of all possible worlds. They have to perform household duties which are time and skill consuming, therefore tiring; yet these activities are paid for neither in cash nor by respect. Women with a career as well spend slightly less time on housekeeping but receive little more help from their husbands. The rapid entry of women into the workforce has created a cadre of enormously overworked, underappreciated women. Working wives are expected to contribute significantly to the family income and prove themselves "equal to men" in the workplace, but also to carry out the traditional homemaking and parenting duties associated with an earlier industrial society.

The result is predictable: an increase in family tension that feeds marital conflict and divorce; an excessive female use of tranquilizers; and widespread feelings of guilt and anxiety about jobs inadequately done. Professor William Michelson asks how our society can legislatively remedy a problem that, in a certain sense, is produced by interpersonal dynamics at home. He raises the interesting question of how private troubles are related to public issues.

In his classic work, *The Sociological Imagination* (1959), C. Wright Mills argued that a main purpose of the sociological enterprise is to show connections between personal troubles and major trends in society. Mills felt that important social changes would produce personal troubles; and that to mobilize for social change, people needed to see the connection between their troubles and social or political issues. Consider, then, Professor

Michelson's data. Like Meissner, Professor Michelson finds that women do much more than their share of family work. Because they do so much, they are always short of time. Even little things like getting the kids out of bed, dressed and off to school create a lot of tension. After everyone else is taken care of, mother must ready herself for work, board the public transit (typically, father is taking the family car in another direction), and get to work on time. Professor Michelson suggests that this problem ought to go on the public affairs agenda. As a society, we ought to increase flexibility in work timing, public transportation, and the zoning (i.e., location) of shopping and workplaces, to make it easier for working women to meet all their obligations.

But should this really be a public issue, to be handled by public debate, legislation and the spending of tax dollars? Some might argue that the problem could be solved more readily by urging women to take assertiveness training. Then, they would not try to do everything more efficiently; they would force their husbands to share the load (and the family car). Everything could get done more equitably, or people would learn to live with lower standards of family caretaking.

The cultural context is all-important here. These personal problems persist, unsolved by either public debate or female assertiveness, because they are nested in a cultural tradition of female subservience. Both too much assertiveness and too little nurturance are viewed by most as "unfeminine" behaviour. Perhaps the problem can be remedied in a few generations with different socialization. But it is not clear that we can wait this long for change.

The family is already in crisis, a fact that will be explored at greater length in the next section. Increasingly, family tensions are building up and exploding with

consequences so far reaching that we may not know them all for generations. For the sake of the adult participants and their innocent children, the battle of the sexes needs quick as well as fundamental resolution.

So is the workplace in crisis, where the battle of the sexes is also being fought out: gender inequalities here become economic and organizational issues. In the workplace, too, perspectives on gender relations and women's problems vary widely. One is the traditional liberal approach, supporting equal opportunity and opposing discrimination. Another is concerned with inappropriate aspirations and the need for more encouragement to ambitious females. Jane Gaskell argues convincingly that gender inequality in the workplace is, at least in part, a result of differential career selection; in turn this traces back to educational streaming and childhood socialization. Rooting out discrimination against women in hiring and promotion will be easier when women are regularly equipping themselves with the skills and aspirations demanded by traditionally male occupations. In this respect, the parental division of labour which girls see in their homes will significantly affect their own job and family expectations. But, as Professor Michelson has implied, we can do little about what goes on in people's homes. That's why we need to concentrate our efforts elsewhere to achieve gender equality.

That "elsewhere" may, as Professor Gaskell suggests, be the educational system. School is one place where egalitarian social values can be taught, and students can be shown the possibility of gender equality. The insufficient degree to which this ideal socialization is being realized is still a matter of concern.

Because women have tended to follow traditional female careers, they have often acquired job skills whose value was already declining. Heather Menzies shows us that, with the rapid increase in office automation, new skills are needed in female work roles, and fewer women may be needed to do clerical work at all. Except for robotics, which displaces the unskilled and semi-skilled manual worker, automation has had little impact on males. Automation is likely to affect a larger portion of the female labour force far more profoundly. Thus women employees, already less unionized than men, paid less and respected less, are also more endangered by new technology. The new technology will throw many women out of work, and others will be stuck with varied and less responsible jobs than they had before. The benefits of technological advance may be largely restricted to male employees.

This kind of argument is generalized in the paper by Pat Armstrong, who considers unemployment as, increasingly, a women's issue. Other things being equal, women are more often unemployed than men; but other things are not equal. Women generally work in labour market sectors where unemployment is more likely and the consequences more severe than in other sectors. Women are less likely to be unionized, hence more vulnerable. Women get paid less, hence can save less to protect against the effects of unemployment. Women are more vulnerable to the effects of technological change, as we already noted. Women are more likely to suffer discrimination in hiring and promotion. Unmarried women with children to raise are more likely to work part-time, and are therefore less protected by benefits and pensions. Women heading lone-parent families are more likely to be thrown into poverty and, in the absence of good inexpensive daycare, less likely to get a job that would get them out of it. Taken together, all of these factors, and others, are producing what some have called the "feminization of poverty."

Where will this lead? Just as Marx argued that class conflict is the source of all significant social change, so perhaps gender conflict will be the source of significant change in the family. We shall explore this notion further in the next section on the family in Canada.

References

Mills, C.W. *The Sociological Imagination.* New York: Oxford, 1959.

36   The Domestic Economy—Half of Canada's Work: Now You See It, Now You Don't

Martin Meissner

MARTIN MEISSNER is Professor of Sociology at the University of British Columbia. In 1969 he published a book, *Technology and the Worker*. He has since studied the difference that technology makes in communication between industrial workers ("The language of work"), and described "The sign language of sawmill workers in British Columbia" (together with the anthropologist, Stuart Philpott). He has examined the sexual division of labour in households, analysing time budgets of married couples in Vancouver ("No exit for wives," "Sexual division of labour and inequality," "The domestic economy—half of Canada's work"); and the way in which sexual inequality is perpetuated in daily communication practices ("The reproduction of women's domination in organizational communication"). Professor Meissner is now studying the effect of changing technology on the knowledge and skill requirement of work in offices and households. As part of his research work, Professor Meissner spent a year at the International Institute for Labour Studies in Geneva, and some time in Paris, on invitation from the Laboratoire de Sociologie du Travail and the Organization for Economic Cooperation and Development.

THE CASE OF MRS. GRIFFITHS

Not far from Hope, British Columbia, in 1973, a Canadian Pacific locomotive collided with an automobile at a level crossing. Mrs. Griffiths, a passenger in the car, died a week later. . . .

David Griffiths sued Canadian Pacific Railways. . . .

The lawyer asked me to be an expert witness at the trial in the Supreme Court of British Columbia and to prepare an estimate of the number of housework hours that a woman in Mrs. Griffiths' circumstances would do for the remainder of her life with Mr. Griffiths; an actuary was asked to translate these hours into a monetary claim. At age 30, with a husband aged 35, and five children between 4 and 11 years old at the time of her death,

Mrs. Griffiths would have done over 84,000 hours of housework until her husband reached the life expectancy for men of his age.

In his decision, Justice Mackoff reduced the amount claimed under the Families Compensation Act for "the loss of household services accustomed to be performed by the wife, which will have to be replaced by hired services" (Mackoff, 1974:11) from $157,410 to $40,000. His reasons went as follows:

> The actuarial evidence . . . only places a dollar value on services but it does not subtract therefrom . . . the dollar cost to obtain those services. It fails to take into consideration the cost to the husband in providing for the wife's food, clothing, shelter, etc., for the period of time for which damages for the loss of her services is claimed. It also fails to take into account the contingencies of life.

The prospects of remarriage of the husband require consideration. At the present time, realistically, the prospects are poor indeed. The plaintiff stated, "I don't think I would want to remarry." But even if he had affirmatively expressed his wish to remarry, it is most unlikely that any reasonable woman would marry this man and assume the burden of raising five children in the circumstances herein described. However, with the passage of time, as the children grow up and leave home, his prospects for remarriage, should he wish to remarry, will brighten. He is 39 years of age and his youngest child is 7. Ten years from now he will still be a relatively young man, the children will have grown up and the prospects of his remarriage will be totally changed from what they are at present. As well to be taken into consideration in such cases was the possibility of the loss of the wife's services by reason of her being incapacitated, either temporarily or permanently, because of illness or accident. Nor can it be assumed in today's society that a marriage will not terminate by separation or divorce. None of the foregoing were taken into account by the actuary and that being so, the figure arrived at is obviously not the answer to the question before me (Mackoff, 1974:12–13).

A double irony seemed at work. A man received money for the missed personal services of his dead wife, while she was paid nothing for it when alive. (Note the exclusion of conceivable money transfers to the wife from the judge's list of the costs of household services.) The improbable future wife was also not worth the money from Canadian Pacific that would have been meant for that part of Nellie Griffiths' unlived housekeeping life which she, the unlikely second Mrs. Griffiths, would perform.

The case was a "first." It introduced into Canadian courts the recognition of the full value (in hours at least, though not in money) of a woman's lifetime of domestic labor. At the same time it confirmed its worthlessness for a *living* wife, while granting its value for the benefit of the husband.

In one breath, almost, housework is first noticed and valued and then disappears again. It suffers that peculiar fate—now you see it, now you don't—from all sides. The magazine for women, *Ms.*, put the phrase "working women" prominently on its cover of May 1980, and specified inside (p. 2) who they are: decidedly not housewives. Over the full spectrum of opinion, the pervasive usage of "working," "productive," and "active" (as in "the active population") turns the domestic *work* of women into nonwork, the daily, yearlong and lifetime effort into inactivity.

ECONOMIC ACCOUNTS

Housework has not figured much in economic work, in theory or in economic accounting. On the accounting side, seven U.S. estimates from 1919 to 1970, and a British and a Swedish estimate were reviewed and made comparable by Hawrylshyn (1976:108–11). These estimates were expressed as a ratio of the value of housework relative to the value of the GNP exclusive of housework, and averaged 34 percent. Hawrylshyn also made three assessments for Canada with the census of 1971. The opportunity cost, the cost of replacing individual functions, and the cost of replacement by a housekeeper came to
a dollar value of housework "equivalent to 39, 40, and 33 percent of GNP," respectively (Hawrylshyn, 1978:29).

When I take my estimate of labor-force hours as the time equivalent of the GNP, and domestic work hours as equivalent to the dollar value of housework, the result is a figure of 95.7 percent, a ratio of domestic to market activity two-and-a-half times that of the average money estimates. Each of the three methods of estimating the money value of housework has built into it the social prejudices that make for different incomes of women and men. At the same time that this rare instance of economic accounting seems to give housework its proper place, it takes much of it away again in the undervaluation of women's work which underlies the wage rates used for these calculations. A similar "now you see it, now you don't" has occurred in the Marxist-feminist debate (summarized in Fox, 1980; Kaluzynska, 1980; and Molyneux, 1979), on the question of whether housework is "productive labor."

How Much Housework Does a Woman Do?

How much housework has there been, relative to other work, and how has that relation changed in the 65 years from 1911 to 1976 in Canada? In answer to the question of how much, I start with hours of work in three different ways. One of these tells of average hours spent in a week, for samples of people with different characteristics. I then go back to the court case, in order to estimate the life-time hours that one (artificially constructed) married woman would devote to domestic work. The third answer is an assembly of contemporary averages applied to the population figures for an estimate of the collective magnitude of domestic work, in comparison to nondomestic work hours, in the entire economy, and changes in that relation in past decades. These factual accounts signify that much is omitted in the "nonwork," "unproductive," "inactive" accounts of domestic work.

The first kind of account, the contemporary averages, is shown in Table 1.... The table reports research results from data gathered in 1971, for 340 married couples in Vancouver. It tells us the difference that employment and young children make, and how much less husbands contribute. When excluding necessary transportation, a full-time housewife works a full-time working week of over 40 hours. In comparison, the domestic work week of employed women drops drastically, while their workload goes up, combining job and domestic work.

A Lifetime of Housework

For an account of how much time a woman might spend doing housework during her life as a wife, I have put together the life of a "typical" woman, Molly, and her family, as a repository of population distributions. The account takes Molly through the 50 years of her married life, from the average age of first-time brides and bridegrooms (Canada, 1977:209–10) to the time when her husband reaches the age of his life expectancy (Canada, 1979:14 and 16). These 50 years contain 19 of the 22 years in the labor force which correspond proportionately to the labor-force participation rate of married women. She will have two children, for the average family size, and return to a job in the labor force after the youngest has started going to school.

Molly can expect in her married life 106,032 hours of domestic work, an average of 2,121 hours a year, a quantity similar to the 2,000 hours that a man's 50 40-hour weeks would come to. Making these calculations with the U.S. data from Walker and Woods (1976: 52–53), the total comes to 102,382 and the annual average to 2,048 hours.

We can build up a comparison of Molly's and her husband's lifetime workloads which include their estimated housework hours during the marriage and the job hours in the labor force for the years from 15 to 65, reduced according to the proportion of women and men in the labor force. I take the job week of men to be 40 hours, and of married women 35 hours. (The Vancouver time budgets have about one hour a weekday of job time less for women than for men, the result of a greater proportion of married women in part-time jobs, and in office jobs where the hours are shorter). With two weeks vacation, the job year comes to 50 weeks. Molly's job year would be 1,750 hours and her husband's 2,000. The labor-force participation rate of men 15 years and older in 1976 was 75.5 percent. Applying that percentage to the 50 years from 15 to 65 makes

Table 1

DOMESTIC WORK HOURS, BY EMPLOYMENT STATUS AND CHILDREN UNDER TEN
(ESTIMATED WEEKLY HOURS, 340 MARRIED COUPLES IN VANCOUVER, B.C., IN 1971)

Activities	Housewives		Employed wives		Employed husbands
	No child under 10	Child under 10	No child under 10	Child under 10	
Cooking and meal preparation	8.5	9.7	5.3	7.2	0.7
Dish washing and kitchen	1.9	2.1	0.9	1.3	0.3
House cleaning	9.1	8.6	5.1	6.9	1.1
Laundry	3.4	3.9	1.3	1.9	0.1
Shopping	4.9	5.1	2.8	3.0	1.2
Care of children	0.7	8.7	0.2	4.2	0.7
Gardening and animals	3.5	2.6	0.8	0.0	2.5
Irregular food preparation and clothes	5.0	2.4	1.6	2.0	0.1
Repairs and sundry services	3.3	1.6	0.7	1.5	3.8
Total domestic work per week	40.3	44.7	18.7	28.0	10.5
Necessary transportation	6.4	6.4	8.7	6.9	8.8
Total including transportation					
per week	46.7	51.1	27.4	34.9	19.3
per day	6.7	7.3	3.9	5.0	2.8
(Number of cases)	(131)	(106)	(85)	(18)	(340)

for a 38-year job life of Molly's husband, or 76,000 life-time job hours. A married man's domestic workday in the Vancouver study is 2.8 hours, including 1.3 hours necessary transportation (mostly journey to and from work), or 1,022 hours a year. For 50 married years, that comes to 51,000 hours. The life-time workload of Molly's husband adds up to 127,100 hours.

Molly's 22 years employment in the labor force amount to 38,500 hours, and her 50 years of housework are 106,032 hours. Her total life-time workload is 144,532 hours, or 114 percent of her husband's. (I have ignored housework that Molly and her husband might have done before marriage, and that Molly would do for herself after her husband's death, for lack of comparable data.)

We have so far the daily domestic work hours derived from contemporary time-budget studies, and the life-time working hours of one typical woman compared with her hus-band's. Both accounts tell us that housework is substantial in relation to labor-force job time, and that married women's share in overall working hours is large. We now turn to the working hours of the population and a history of working hours at home and on the job.

THE CONTEXT OF LABOR AND LEISURE IN CANADA 1911–76

The context of changes in working hours is defined critically by three developments in men's contribution to work. (1) The labor-force *participation* rate of men has dropped by 14 points from 89.6 percent in 1911 to 75.5 percent in 1976. (2) The percent of the male labor force in *agriculture* has declined 45 points from 51.3 percent to 6.5 percent from 1911 to 1971. (3) Weekly *job hours* in the nonagricultural labor force have gone down nearly 14 hours from 49.6 hours in 1926 to 35.8 hours in 1976. (These and subsequent labor-force participation data are from the Labour Force (Industries) sections of successive censuses of Canada; nonagricultural labor-force hours from Ostry and Zaidi, 1979–80; and the agricultural hours from Urquhart and Buckley, 1965:105.) All these tendencies add up to a decline in men's contribution to work. There have been proportionately fewer men at work. The agricultural labor force has shrunk (with its longer work hours of about one-third more than the nonagricultural labor force). Job hours themselves have been reduced. These facts correspond with the rosy picture of "the leisure society," characterized by fewer and fewer men (meant literally) spending fewer and fewer hours "at work," the result of automation. However, these facts are countered by other facts.

The labor-force participation rate of married women has risen dramatically from 4.5 to 43.7 percent between 1941 and 1976. According to several comparisons of earlier and more recent time budgets, the hours of housework have remained stable for wives with and without labor-force employment (Robinson, 1980). When taking housework hours to have been nearly stable, the labor-force participation of married women to have increased, and the housework contribution of husbands to remain small and unchanged regardless of different household demands, we would expect a collective increase in the overall workload of women. . . .

THE COLLECTIVE WORKLOAD OF CANADIANS

In order to estimate labor-force job hours and the hours of domestic work for each census year 1911–71, and the mid-census of 1976, we need the number of men, and of married and not married women, in the agricultural and nonagricultural labor force, that is, six categories of persons. These numbers have

to be reduced by those not at work in the labor force and multiplied by the estimated weekly work hours in labor-force jobs.

No Canadian time-budget studies were made before 1965. Results of comparisons of older and more recent time budgets in the United States (Robinson, 1980:54) suggest generally unchanged average housework hours. A long series of eight time-budget studies in the Soviet Union allows an assessment of changes in housework time between 1923 and 1968. Housework hours have remained more or less the same (Zuzanek, 1979:208–09). The seemingly best approach to estimating collective hours of domestic work for the 1911–76 period was to multiply the *same* time-budget averages each census year by the number of married women in and out of the labor force, not married women, and married and not married men. ("Not married" includes single, divorced, and widowed, while "married" includes separated.)

The data sources and composition of the time-budget averages for domestic work hours are described in Table 2. (The Vancouver figures for married women are weighted averages of the two categories, with or without children under ten, of Table 1. Necessary transportation was excluded from these estimates, in order to avoid distortions in the comparison of job and domestic hours.) The average weekly hours were multiplied by the number of persons in each of the five categories. Similarly, the weekly labor-force job hours were multiplied by the number of persons in the six categories developed for that purpose. For each census year, I calculated the sum of all work hours, including domestic work hours and labor-force job hours of women and men, calling it the "collective workload."

. . . The proportionate contribution of men's job hours has been shrinking during the period 1911–76. The major interruption to the trend was introduced through the depression and the war-time experience. The collective domestic work hours of men, and all work

Table 2
DOMESTIC WORK HOURS PER WEEK: PORT ALBERNI, VANCOUVER, HALIFAX

Sex, work type, and marital status	Port Alberni 1965	Vancouver 1971	Halifax 1971–72	Average
Married women				
not in labor force	No data	42.3	48.8	45.5
in labor force	22.0	20.3	24.5	22.3
Married men	13.0	10.5	9.8	11.1
Nonmarried women	13.1	No data	16.1	14.6
Nonmarried men	9.0	No data	7.7	8.3

Sources: Port Alberni time budgets (Meissner, 1971, pp. 255 and 257); Vancouver time budgets (Meissner et al., 1975, pp. 434–35); Halifax time budgets (Harvey and Clarke, 1975, pp. 12 and 15).

hours of not married women, have remained the same as a proportion of the collective workload. The proportionate contribution of married women has risen steadily, except for wartime 1941. Since then the increase has been produced by the greater contribution of job hours and domestic work hours of married women. As a result of the dramatic growth in married women's labor-force participation, the housework hours (in percent) of married women working at home full time has shown a noticeable decline since 1961.

Domestic work hours as a percent of the collective workload have increased throughout the period (always with the 1931–41 dip), by 12 percentage points from 1911 to 1961. They had reached 50 percent in 1961 and leveled off to within one or two percentage points since then. If one were to assess the value of economic activity in working hours (as, for example, Marx suggested one should) the domestic economy *equals* the value of the nondomestic economy.

. . . Women's proportion of the collective workload passed the 50 percent mark between 1951 and 1961, and reached 55 percent in 1976. When expressing the relation in proportions, the spare-time gain of men *had* to be women's loss. To what extent the shift in burden was "real" can be seen in Figure 8.1, for which the collective workload hours were divided by the population 15 years

and older. The central, broken line describes the experience of women and men combined, and it suggests that the working population has profited from an 11.9-hour drop in workload hours per person from 1911 to 1976. When such a per capita workload is separated for women and men, it becomes apparent that it was only men who gained (34.7 hours less work), while women's workload increased slightly by 2.6 hours per person. . . .

CONCLUSIONS

The estimates of working hours developed in this chapter draw attention to some important facets of the relation of housework and labor-force work, and of the work of women and the work of men. Since 1961 Canadians have been putting half of their collective working hours into the unpaid labor of the domestic economy, and half into the monied labor force. In 1971, Canada's domestic work hours were 49 percent of all working hours. In the life-time economic contributions of a typical wife and husband, a married woman's workload comes to 53 percent of the life-time work hours of both combined. From 1911 to 1976 the contributions of men in their job hours have declined, and the contributions of married women in their overall working hours have

Figure 1
WEEKLY WORKLOAD HOURS PER PERSON 15 YEARS AND OVER, BY SEX, 1911–76.

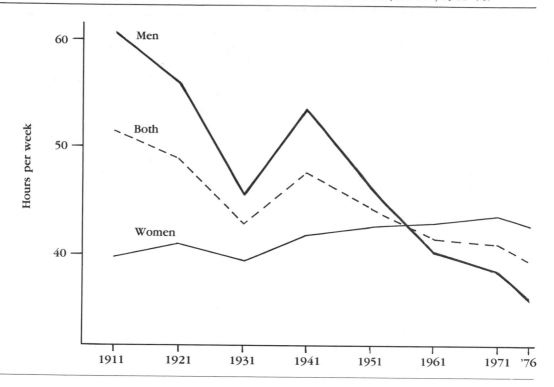

increased. Domestic working time as a proportion of all work hours has increased to 1961 and then leveled off. The working time of women as a proportion of all work

hours had increased to 55 percent by 1976. Women carry more than "half of the sky," and half of the work of Canadians is not in the market economy, but in the household. . . .

References

Canada, Statistics Canada. 1977. Canada Year Book 1976–77. Ottawa: Publications Distribution, Statistics Canada.

Canada, Statistics Canada. 1979. Life Tables, Canada and Provinces 1975–1977. Ottawa: Minister of Supply and Services.

Fox, Bonnie. 1980. "Introduction." In Hidden in the Household: Domestic Labour Under Capitalism, edited by B. Fox, pp. 9–23. Toronto: Women's Educational Press.

Harvey, Andrew S., and Susan Clarke, 1975. Descriptive Analysis of Halifax Time-Budget Data.

Halifax: Institute of Public Affairs, Dalhousie University.

Hawrylyshyn, Oli. 1976. "The Value of Household Services: A Survey of Empirical Estimates." Review of Income and Wealth, No. 2 (June): 101–31.

Hawrylshyn, Oli. 1978. Estimating the Value of Household Work in Canada 1971. Ottawa: Statistics Canada.

Kaluzynska, Eva. 1980. "Wiping the Floor with Theory: A Survey of Writings on Housework." Feminist Review, 6:27–54.

Mackoff, A.A. 1974. Griffiths et al. versus Canadian Pacific et al.: Reasons for Judgment. Vancouver: Supreme Court of British Columbia. No. 29830/74.

Meissner, Martin. 1971. "The Long Arm of the Job: A Study of Work and Leisure." Industrial Relations, 10:239–60.

Meissner, Martin, E.W. Humphreys, S.M. Meis and W.J. Scheu. 1975. "No Exit for Wives: Sexual Division of Labour and the Cumulation of Household Demands." Canadian Review of Sociology and Anthropology, 12:424–439.

Molyneux, Maxine. 1979. "Beyond the Domestic Labour Debate." New Left Review, 116:3–27.

Ostry, Sylvia and Mahmood A. Zaidi. 1979. Labour Economics in Canada. 3rd ed. Toronto: Macmillan.

Robinson, John. 1980. "Housework Technology and Household Work." In Women and Household Labor, edited by Sarah Fenstermaker Berk, pp. 53–68. Beverly Hills: Sage.

Urquhart, M.C. and K.A.H. Buckley, editors. 1965. Historical Statistics of Canada. Toronto: Macmillan.

Walker, Kathryn E. and Margaret E. Woods. 1976. Time Use: A Measure of Household Production of Family Goods and Services. Washington: American Home Economics Association.

Zuzanek, Jiri. 1979. "Time-Budget Trends in the USSR: 1922–1970." Soviet Studies, 31:188–213.

37 Education and Jobs for Women

Jane Gaskell

JANE GASKELL, Associate Professor of Social and Educational Studies at the University of British Columbia, Vancouver, specializes in the sociology of education. Her recent publications include "The reproduction of family life: perspectives of male and female adolescents" (1983); "Gender and course choice: The orientations of male and female students" (1984); "Course enrollments in the high school: The perspective of working class females" (1985); "Gender and skill: The case of business education" (1986); and "Education and the labour market: The logic of vocationalism" (1987). Professor Gaskell is currently studying the social organization of business education, and has recently received an Izaac Walton Kallam Faculty Research Fellowship. She has held executive positions with the Canadian Association of Foundations of Education and the Canadian Society for the Study of Education and chaired the Adjudication Committee for strategic grants in the area of "Women and Work" for the Social Science and Humanities Research Council.

THE EDUCATIONAL ATTAINMENT OF WOMEN

The notion that women have less education than men, and that that is why they do not get jobs equal to men's, is largely untrue. Girls tend to stay in school longer and get better marks than boys. Statistics on the educational attainment of the population show that women are overrepresented at the middle levels of educational achievement, which account for the largest percentage of the population. Women continue to be overrepresented among those with diplomas or certificates at the post-secondary level, but underrepresented among those with university degrees. The educational levels of women who work outside the home are higher still, relative to men's. These women are less likely to have only an elementary school education, and more likely to have both high school and post-secondary education.

The evidence for these contentions comes from various sources. Girls get better overall grades in school than do boys. Girls read better, at least in North America, and reading is the basis for most school tasks. Boys are more likely to be in special classes for slow learners and to have learning deficits. Girls also progress faster than boys through school and are less likely to be above the modal age for their grade. Girls are more likely to stay in school until they graduate from high school (Royal Commission on the Status of Women, 1970; Synge, 1977; Maccoby and Jacklin, 1974; Perspective Canada, 1974).

Women have been more likely than men to go on to and complete high school for as long as school records have been kept in British Columbia. The B.C. School Reports show that from 1880 to 1950, the proportion of females enrolled in high schools was higher than the proportion of males.

In the 1950s and 1960s, the picture changed somewhat. By 1950, an equal number of boys and girls were enrolled in high school. Although since 1911, more girls aged 15 to 19 had been attending school, by 1950, more boys of this age were enrolled. The change reflects an increase in males attending high school; the fact that girls graduate from high school at a younger age; and,

373

importantly, an increase in post-secondary schooling holding males aged 17 and 19.

It is at the post-secondary level that concern about the lower achievement levels of women has focused, although only a small percentage of the population has post-secondary schooling. Although girls are more likely to graduate from high school and to graduate with higher marks, they are less likely to go on to university. The total percentage of females enrolled in post-secondary education is lower than the percentage of males enrolled. Women outnumbered men in community colleges, but not as undergraduate or graduate students at university.

The number of women enrolled in post-secondary education has been increasing at the undergraduate level, except for a slight decrease in the 1950s. At graduate school the numbers have just recently passed what they were in the 1920s and 1930s, after a sharp decline in the 50s and 60s. The increases in women's enrolment in the last years are quite dramatic and indicate that women are rapidly making up the educational deficit they have had at this level. A recent follow-up of grade 12 students in Ontario showed about equal numbers of males and females going on to post-secondary education (63% of males and 64% of females) (Anisef, 1980). Thirty per cent of the females and 36% of the males went to university, 25% of the females and 19% of the males went to community colleges, and 9% of the females and 8% of the males went to both universities and community colleges.

PATTERNS OF ENROLMENT

When males and females attend the same classes they are treated differently and exposed to an ideology that reinforces traditional sex stereotypes. Books and media used in the schools either omit women or portray them in traditionally stereotyped roles. Teachers interact more frequently with boys and allocate tasks according to traditional notions of male and female interests. Student cultures that grow up within the organization of the school reproduce traditional sex divisions. These differences in treatment and ideology affect both the skills and attitudes of students (Gaskell, 1977; Levy, 1972; Fischer and Cheyne, 1977; Sears and Feldman, 1974; Coleman, 1961).

But this sexist ideology, this unequal treatment of males and females is not transmitted simply through what people say and think in the school. The school begins a form of organizational differentiation that carries through into the labour market. Males and females, especially in the secondary school, are placed in different courses to a very large extent. Their education does not consist of the same things.

In the public school system, data on subject enrolments are relatively hard to find. For the purposes of this paper I have searched out some British Columbia data, but Canadian comparisons need to be made. The Royal Commission on the Status of Women reported that in 1969, 70% of females and 64% of males were in academic courses, 23% of females and 5% of males were in commercial courses, and 7% of females and 31% of males were in "other" (largely industrial) courses. The data show no consistent trend between 1965 and 1969 in the proportions of different courses. Synge (1977) reports that in 1968–69 in Ontario, 59% of girls and 50% of boys were in academic courses, 45% of girls and 10% of boys were in commercial courses, and 3% of girls and 38% of boys were in industrial courses in Ontario. Anisef (1980) reports that in 1973, 74% of females and 63% of males were in academic courses, 24% of females and 6% of males were in commercial courses, and 1% of females and 31% of males were in industrial courses. Although the Synge data have a higher proportion of girls in the commercial courses, these data suggest that about one-quarter of the girls and one-third of the boys are in highly sex-segregated commercial and industrial education courses.

In British Columbia in 1978, 9.4% of the students taking industrial courses were females. Even this figure underestimates the amount of sex segregation, as girls tend to take lower level courses, and courses like auto mechanics for girls, introductory carpentry, and perhaps drafting. In 1979, 77% of the students enrolled in business courses in British Columbia were female. Within the business program girls are more likely to take courses like typing, shorthand, office practice and office orientation which prepare them directly for secretarial work. Boys take courses like marketing, computers and general business.

Science and mathematics also show sex differences in enrolment patterns in the high school. In the 1977 British Columbia math assessment, 64% of those grade 12 students whose last mathematics course was in grade 10 (when math was compulsory) were female. Fifty-four per cent of those who dropped math in grade 11 were female. The type of math taken since grade 10 was not reported and this might show further differences if girls tend to take business math whereas boys take calculus and trigonometry. In a widely circulated paper, Sells (1973) examined the mathematics background of Berkeley first year students. Fifty-seven per cent of the boys but only 8% of the girls had four years of high school mathematics. However, this level of mathematics was required for admission to all fields of study except humanities, social science, education, and social welfare. Although the emphasis of educators' concern about the lack of mathematics background of women has been primarily on entrance to university and professional careers, math is increasingly required for admission to vocational programs and apprenticeships. It becomes a critical filter within the school system in affecting women's job options in many areas.

Girls are also less likely to take science courses. In the 1979 British Columbia science assessment study, 37% of the females had no science courses after grade 10, whereas only 34% of the boys had none. Larger differences appear when the kind of science is taken into account. Seventeen per cent of the females and 38% of the males had taken senior level physics. Fifty-seven per cent of the females and 45% of the males took biology. Girls are well represented in health sciences, but are disqualified from many other technical science careers (Erikson, Erikson and Haggerty, 1980; Kelly, 1978; Gardiner, 1975).

It is clear that we have not given enough attention to the fact that so much high school education is not coeducational. Although girls and boys meet in the halls and the cafeterias, they work together in the classroom less often. These enrolment patterns are significant in shaping the skills, interests and interaction patterns of adults. They develop a sense of competence and familiarity with different areas of experience, and this influences future choices about work. They influence the domestic division of labour, which in turn affects labour force activity. They also segment the labour force by sex on entry to the labour market and on entry to post-secondary education. Every spring high schools send into the labour market a large supply of females who can type, read, write, and do accounting, who are oriented to working in an office and familiar with clerical work. They also produce a large number of boys who have experience in workshops, who are oriented to and familiar with blue collar work, but have less specific job skills than the girls, reflecting the greater diversity of jobs they enter.

Why do sex differences in enrolment patterns occur? The usual assumption is that it is due to student choices, and that we therefore need to understand students' attitudes, interests, priorities and career goals. Attempts to desegregate courses would then rely on changing the students through increasing awareness of alternative careers, impressing girls with the important place work will take in their lives, decreasing anxiety about unfamiliar areas, or doing remedial work in order to increase girls' confidence in math or industrial areas.

While these approaches are valuable they neglect structural features about the organization of schools within which choice takes place. Making courses even formally available to students of either sex has only been achieved recently in some subject areas, through strong pressure from parents and status of women groups. Even when choice is formally open, the organization of the course varies from school to school. For example, in British Columbia, the percentage of females enrolled in industrial courses varies from a low of 2% in North Thomson to a high of 31% in Fort Nelson. As both of these districts are rural, northern, and based on primary industry, the differences in enrolment are likely due to the organization of the school. It is possible to guess at many of the factors that will influence these enrolment figures—the timetable, the teachers' attitudes, the sex composition of the teaching staff, the content of the curriculum. Once a breakthrough has been made, the effect snowballs as students no longer feel as uncomfortable—one of a kind—in a non-traditional area.

Looking beyond school differences, we need to understand how different subject areas are organized in relation to the labour market. The way a course is treated by students is affected by whether they see it as necessary for a particular job or university programme, or simply an interesting extra or an easy credit. The business courses girls take have a unique status in this respect. They are seen as job training. A girl who graduates from them can be hired as a secretary. Typing, and shorthand particularly, are skills which cannot be picked up in a matter of weeks on the job, which can be learned at school, and which are likely to be tested during a job interview.

The industrial courses, which appear to be the equivalent course for males, are not as closely linked to work. They do not pro-vide credentials or skills that are tested or expected on entry to jobs. The student who has taken carpentry is not a carpenter. The student who has taken auto mechanics is not an auto mechanic. Trades training takes place after high school, and research suggests it is boys in the academic program whom employers will prefer (Lazerson and Grubb, 1975).

The difference has meant that training for relatively skilled female work is done in the public school system, at the public's and the student's expense, while training for male work is paid for by the employer while the trainee earns a wage. It has also ensured a plentiful supply of women trained in secretarial skills, helping to keep the price of this kind of labour down, while the number of skilled tradespeople has been restricted to such an extent that the shortage is now making headlines.

What factors have made secretarial training (which tends to be female) available in the high school, while apprenticeships (which tend to be male) are not? The form school programmes take is constructed historically. Any decision to incorporate a particular kind of course, and course content, in the school, must be negotiated and fought for by somebody or some group of people within the school, and with unions, employers, parents, students, and perhaps other interested groups.

Our usual assumption that the difference is due to the nature and difficulty of the tasks is at most only a partial explanation. Clerical work is less expensive to start in the school; the machinery is cheaper, the skills apply to a wider range of jobs than most industrial skills, and the tasks are more "school-like," involving sitting at a desk. However, all of these are relative. Many skills taught in commercial courses do not apply widely in the job market, and some industrial skills do. Expensive programmes are mounted in the schools, and experience in settings outside the school is used in commercial courses and could be used in others. Industrial courses do involve school-like skills in reading and mathematics, and industrial courses which exist in the school involve students in activities that do not look particularly "school-like." Briggs (1974) has pointed out a similar phenomenon in the skill levels attributed to male and female work. When skill levels are actually quite similar, the lower skill presumed to be necessary in female jobs blocks these jobs from becoming part of the formal apprenticeship system. While "anyone can type," becoming a plumber requires several years of training beyond the high school.

Research on how and why vocational programmes were incorporated into the school curriculum is sparse. Lazerson and Grubb (1974) show that it was subject to negotiation between business and labour, and educators, and recent studies show that this continues to be true. Weiss (1978) suggests that business courses were brought into the public school system in an attempt to increase enrolments, especially of boys who were attending the flourishing private business schools. But we also need to know whether other kinds of private trade schools were flourishing and, if they were, why they were not brought into the public school system. If they were not, why weren't they? Why was training organized differently in other occupational areas? It seems likely that in clerical work the rapidly expanding demand for labour, the entry of women into the occupation, the reluctance of employers to invest in on-the-job training for women who were seen as short-term workers, and the lack of unionization in clerical work all interacted to make it available for public school educators to take over, while the training for many other male occupations eluded their grasp.

Today, about a third of all Canadian students go directly into the labour force from high school. These students have increasingly become relegated to lower level jobs. Their education is the education of the working class, and I have treated it at some length as it has tended to be neglected in favour of studies of post secondary-education, of those who will be more powerful. It is particularly important to understand high school education for women, as it has been critical in the development of clerical and secretarial work women's primary area of paid work.

The post-secondary non-university level has expanded enormously recently, and its place and structure are still evolving and poorly understood. It is clear that sex segregation continues at the community college level. In 1978, 99% of those enrolled in secretarial courses, 87% of those in medical programmes (nursing, dental hygiene, etc.), and 65% of those in community and social services were female. Two per cent of those in electronics, mechanical engineering, and aeronautical engineering, 24% of those in natural resources programmes, and 14% of those in other engineering programmes were female. In arts, 58% were female, and in other business programmes, 48% were female. As usual in business courses, this overall representation conceals unequal numbers of males and females in particular courses. There are more males in financial management and marketing management; more females in retail merchandizing.

The increasing representation of women at community colleges suggests that it may be "women's work" that is particularly subject to this kind of reorganization and upgrading of pre-entry educational requirements. For example, child care programmes, which tend to be overwhelmingly female, have been instituted, and associations of child care workers have lobbied for the recognition of their training by day care centres, and the exclusion of anyone who does not have formal credentials from teaching at a day care centre. The success of this attempt to "upgrade" the work will depend on a variety of factors in the marketplace: the funding of day care, the supply of workers, the way work gets reorganized, the potential of unionization, the use of new technology, and so on.

These changes in training requirements will affect both how much and what kind of education women get. The changes will also affect the economic status of women—their incomes and their access to non-traditional areas. A long training program may discourage women who do not plan to stay in the labour force for a long time, and reduce their access to jobs they have traditionally held. For instance, using the child care example, women who used to be qualified because they had brought up children would now have to return to school. On the other hand, a formal educational program may increase the attention paid to ability, and open admissions more widely, so that women try out non-traditional jobs. As has been pointed out, women do relatively well at school and have tended to stay there longer than men. They are over-represented as students at the community college level. Increased training may increase women's wages by upgrading the "quality" of their labour, or it may decrease wages by opening up training opportunities more widely, and thus devaluing them.

· Another approach to understanding women's enrolment patterns at the community college is to see community colleges as a way of relieving pressure from the university, "cooling out" and tracking students, at a time when everyone wants a diploma as a ticket to a middle or upper level position in the class structure and there are not enough positions open (Karabel, 1972; Pincus, 1980). Both working class students and women tend to be over-represented at the community college and under-represented at university. Graduates from community colleges are supposed to fill semi-professional and technical middle level jobs, but it is not clear that they have much of an advantage over high school graduates (Pincus, 1980).

At the university level, we again find that males and females tend to be in different pro-

grams of study. Arts and science is the only programme that has more or less equal representations of males and females, but even here there are more women in English and French, more men in mathematics and economics. Women constitute more than 90% of the student body in household science, nursing, rehabilitative medicine, and secretarial science; over 70% in library and social work; over 60% in education, and the fine and applied arts. The smallest proportions of women are found in engineering, forestry, dentistry, architecture, and religion.

The percentage of women in most faculties has increased, as the total percentage of females at university increases, but it has increased substantially more than that in most male areas such as law, architecture, medicine, dentistry, agriculture, veterinary medicine, and commerce. Engineering and religion stand out as the only male fields where women are not increasing their representation faster than in the university as a whole. Engineering had the lowest percentage of female students of any faculty in 1972, and today it remains even more strikingly the lowest.

THE ECONOMIC RETURNS TO EDUCATION FOR WOMEN

Education does affect women's labour force activity. Increasing her education increases the likelihood that a woman will participate in the labour force. In 1971, 36% of women with some high school education were in the labour force, 50% of women who had completed high school were in the labour force, and 55% of women with a university degree were in the labour force (Gunderson, 1976). Although education tends to decrease unemployment rates for both males and females, it does so less strongly for women. In 1971, the ratio of male to female unemployment was 1 to 7 for those who had completed university, and 1 to 2 for those with a high school education, and 1 to 1 for those with an elementary education or less.

Status attainment researchers have concluded that education plays more or less the same role for women as for men in increasing the status of the jobs they can obtain. The relationship between educational attainment and occupational status is as strong or stronger for women (Goyder and Pineo, 1973; Featherman and Houser, 1976) and job status for both sexes is becoming more closely related to educational level (Halsey, 1977; Featherman and Hauser, 1976). Anisef found that the women in his sample obtained jobs with higher prestige than the men overall, although this effect decreased with experience in the labour market. When he broke down his data by level of education obtained, he found that a woman with less than a university education gets a first job that is higher in status than the job a male with an equivalent education gets. But women with university degrees get jobs that are lower in status than men with an equivalent education. Five years later, women are at an increased disadvantage if they have university or college degrees, and at an increased advantage at lower levels of education.

The status of the jobs women get is about equal to the status of the jobs men get, and the shape of the distribution is also similar, although women are underrepresented at the top end (Treiman, 1975). This is partly because the education levels of the people filling the job constitute one of the ways of measuring prestige on socio-economic indices and we have seen that women are well educated. When prestige is measured independently, through public opinion polls, the results correlate strongly with the socio-economic indices, suggesting that education does affect the status a job is credited with. Women also tend to be in white collar jobs, considered more prestigious in the public's mind. The confounding of education with status and the fact that status indices do not reveal women's disadvantages in the labour force

make income more relevant for this investigation.

Although women's education gets them job status, it does not get them income. Women earn far less than men for every year of education they complete, and the ratio of male to female earnings has not improved over time. Featherman and Hauser (1976) found that the earnings benefit of an additional year of schooling was $279 for males and $81 for females in 1962, and it increased to $406 for males and $180 for females in 1973. This constitutes a much larger percentage increase for females, but the absolute dollar amount of the difference became larger over that period. Statistics Canada (1979b) shows that women with a university degree in 1977 earned on the average, $11,363.00, whereas men with a university degree earned $20,337.00. Women with some high school education earned $5,766.00, whereas men with the equivalent education earned $12,085.00. Women with university degrees were earning on the average less than men with only some high school education.

Starting wages give a "purer" estimate, uncontaminated by length of time in the labour force, of what employers will pay for male and female graduates with the same education. Anisef (1980) finds that the starting salaries of women are about 80% of the starting salaries of men. Women's disadvantage is greatest out of high school, and least at the community college level.

Anisef (1980) shows that for males and females graduating in the high school academic programme, the salary difference is $3,000.00. In commercial courses, the gap is $2,300.00, and in technical and vocational courses the gap is $2,000.00. The gap is least in the industrial programmes and further evidence for the advantage to girls of enrolling in these courses is that they make $1,400.00 more than the girls in the academic programme, and almost $3,000.00 more than the girls in the commercial programme.

Statistics Canada (1980b) reports similar

data for community college graduates. In every case, the males graduating from a course make more money than the girls graduating from the same course. For two-year diploma graduates the difference is $5,000.00 in general arts and science; $4,000.00 in primary industry; $3,000.00 in applied sciences, community services, and business management; $2,000.00 in trades and crafts and engineering; and is lowest ($1,000.00) in mass communication. Taking medical and dental services or computer science raised women's salaries most relative to other women. The same survey reports income data for university graduates by field of study. The differences ranged from about $100.00 in the fine and applied arts and in the humanities to $2,800.00 in engineering, and $1,600.00 in business management and commerce, the social sciences, and agricultural and biological sciences. Women in engineering and education earned the highest salaries of any women graduates.

Oppenheimer (1970) has noted that the jobs that women get systematically underpay for the education and skill levels they demand. She argues that this came about because of a demand for educated and cheap labour that could not be met through male labour. When occupations needing "middle quality," i.e., relatively well-educated labour expanded rapidly, the demand was met through using women. These occupations were especially teaching and office work. Using males would have meant either an increase in cost or a decrease in "quality" (education). This constitutes an important qualification to the notion that women are simply cheap labour. It is the fact that they are skilled in a way that a male supply of labour would not be that makes them attractive to employers. This observation helps to explain the relationship between prestige and income returns to education for women. Prestige builds in education levels, as noted earlier.

The fact that the demand for female labour has been a demand for skilled labour is related to the fact that women's jobs tend to require extensive education before entry. Skill training tends to be done in public educational institutions at the taxpayers' and the students' expense, rather than gradually, on the job, at the employers' expense.

> Occupations such as secretary, school teacher, librarian, nurse, and many types of laboratory technicians are examples of occupations from which a fair amount of education and some training are required . . . (they) can be almost entirely trained for before working, making women less costly risks as workers. (Oppenheimer, p. 105)

Women fill almost half of all the professional and technical jobs, and have maintained their share of these jobs since 1941 (Armstrong and Armstrong, 1978, p. 36). Women constituted 72% of clerical workers in 1971, and this is the other occupational area where training at school before entry to a job would usually be necessary.

The necessity of pre-entry job training for women can be explained by women's presumed and actual attachment to the family. Employers assume women will be temporary workers, and prefer not to invest their own resources in training them. The longer an employee stays with a firm, the longer the period over which the firm can receive returns on its investment. Employers, then, wish to minimize investing in groups "known" to have a low attachment to the labour force.

Related to these characteristics of "women's" jobs is the fact that these jobs have a relatively flat career profile. The first year teacher does more or less the same thing as she does in her last year. Secretarial staff rarely advance into management positions, even when they know as much about the management of the office as their boss (Kantor, 1977). While this is true of many jobs for both sexes, and increasingly so as educational credentials are used to restrict entry to higher level jobs, internal labour markets are less available to women than to men (Gordon, 1970). Woman are more likely to be concentrated in "secondary" labour markets where turnover is high and entry jobs do not lead to better jobs.

Both the process of job segregation and the unequal rewards women get in jobs similar to men's depend on personnel practices; on the ways people are hired and promoted, and the relative importance employers place on education in these decisions. Any hope that education will improve women's position in the labour market assumes that education will matter to employers.

But studies of the process of getting a job show that education is often quite a small factor (Granovetter, 1974; Bullock, 1973; Freedman, 1969). Personal contacts, subjective judgments and personality characteristics are very important. Discrimination against women, whatever their qualifications, persists and whether it is rational, based on reasonable assumptions about women's different relationship to the family and work, or whether it is irrational and costly to employers, is beyond the scope of this paper. However, any discussion of the effect of education on increasing women's opportunities must always take into account the limit of a discriminatory labour market.

For most jobs at the high school level, education is becoming increasingly irrelevant. The reorganization of work through "scientific management" and the use of advanced technologies have deskilled many working class jobs (Braverman, 1974; Rinehart, 1975). Most employers of high school graduates do not ask about school records, even though typing and English skills are more likely to be assessed for girls in office jobs (Hall and Carlton, 1977).

Recent research on community college graduates suggests that they often enter jobs where their training is unnecessary and not rewarded (Pincus, 1980; Karabel, 1972). A large percentage of graduates from vocational courses do not get jobs in the areas for which they are trained (Wilms, 1974).

Although exceptions to these generalizations exist in areas like apprenticeships where unions protect skilled workers, or in newly emerging semi-professions like day care workers or dental technicians, there is pressure to reorganize work so that unskilled workers can be used interchangeably. Large companies are trying to replace journeymen with workers trained on the job in skill-specific modules. Complaints that unskilled workers are doing the work of dental technicians have been in the newspapers recently. Employers' concern with the education of community college graduates varies and is adjusting to changes in work and in the available supply of labour.

At the university level, credentials and skills are more closely tied to jobs, although this varies by field of study. Taking a medical degree is essential in getting a job as a physician. The same is true of law and teaching. However, a recent report concludes, "in many cases, there appears to be a loose link between occupations and the fields of study of degree holders" (Ahamad et al., 1979). For example, the situation for engineering graduates is more ambiguous. Graduates work in many occupations and may compete with people with a variety of backgrounds for jobs.

SOME CONCLUDING OBSERVATIONS

Education has held out the promise of economic success for women, as it has for men. But education does not create jobs, it is merely one method of allocating people to jobs, a method favoured in our meritocratic society as fair and just. And despite our meritocratic ideology, education is not consistently used to distribute economic privilege, and Michael Young rightly warns us of the dangers we would face if it were (Young, 1961). However, women could use a little more meritocracy, a little more attention to their school achievement. Employers pay much less for a woman than for a man, when their education levels are the same.

Part of the problem is related to the kind of education women get and the way it is organized. Women are educated in ways that make their skills widely available within the public school system and preclude employers having to invest resources in their training. Women are channeled into a segregated labour market through a segregated school system.

Beyond this, the assumption that employers hire, promote, and pay on the basis of education is largely wrong. Although pay levels may be influenced by the necessity to attract skilled workers, this has not raised women's wages in their job ghettos or caused them to be hired instead of men.

Can schools be used to help women break through these economic barriers? Schools reproduce the labour force and there are many factors militating against changes in school occurring before changes in the labour force. Social pressures outside schools are enormous and shape school aspirations. The major factor in course choice is job choice, and students will continue to make safe choices; choices in areas where they know they can get a job, especially if the training goes on for more than a few months. Why would a woman in high school choose to go into an industrial course if she did not know that she could get a job at the end of it, when, if she goes into clerical work, her job is more or less assured? This will be particularly true in times of tight labour markets. Added to this is the fact that it is difficult to take a course that is not traditional for your sex. It is uncomfortable to be a woman in an engineering faculty, if you are sensitive to the sexism that goes on around you. It is difficult to be a girl in a carpentry class, where you stand out, do not have your friends with you, and feel like a sexual object.

However, schools may be more receptive to equal opportunity than the workplace because they have fewer economic motives to discriminate. Teachers usually want to attract as many students as possible. Class cohesion and long-term productivity are less important than immediate ability to do the work. In these kinds of settings, women may be better off. And while the evidence is sparse, at the university level changes in education do seem to be preceding changes on the job. For middle class women at the universities, schooling may be becoming a place where they can make it in competition with men, even if some of the cards are stacked against them.

Should changes occur in school, can they force changes in the labour market? Were women to have the same education as men and similar aspirations, any educational, meritocratic rationale for not hiring them would disappear, and either overt discrimination or change would have to take its place. Again, the prospects look brightest for professional women, although large wage gaps persist even for male and female graduates from the same professional faculties. But it is for professional women that education and work are closely linked that a credential most closely approximates a job.

If these are trends, the issue of class takes on more importance for understanding women and education and work. The linkages are different at different levels of the school system for women entering different types of jobs. In the rush to study newly successful women entering law, medicine, and business, we must not forget the high school, the community college and the reorganization of training and credentialling for working class jobs. Education will be used to increase and reorganize the importance of the class division for women, and studies of the process should not repeat the errors of studies of the impact of education on men. The use of schooling as a screening agent does not eliminate class differences and give everyone an equal chance. It restructures access to the top and accentuates rather than diminishes the distance between the top and the bottom.

References

Acker, J. 1973 "Women and Social Stratification: A Case of Intellectual Sexism." American Journal of Sociology, 78, no. 4:936-945.

Ahamad, B. et al. 1979 "Degree Holders in Canada: An Analysis of the Highly Qualified Manpower Survey of 1973." Ottawa: Education Support Branch, Department of Secretary of State.

Anisef, P., J. Paasche, and A. Turrittin 1980 *Is the Die Cast? Educational Achievements and Work Destinations of Ontario Youth.* Toronto: Ministry of Colleges and Universities.

Armstrong, P. and H. Armstrong 1978 *The Double Ghetto: Canadian Women and Their Segregated Work.* Toronto: McClelland and Stewart.

Blau, P. and O.D. Duncan 1967 *The American Occupational Structure.* New York: John Wiley & Sons.

Bowles H. and H. Gintis 1972 "IQ in the United States Class Structure." *Social Policy* 3, no. 4 and 5.

Braverman, H. 1974 *Labour and Monopoly Capitalism.* New York: Monthly Review Books.

Briggs, N. 1974 "Women in Apprenticeships — Why Not?" Manpower Research Monograph no. 33. Washington, D.C.: U.S. Dept. of Labor.

Bullock, P. 1973 "Aspiration vs Opportunity." Institute of Labour and Industrial Relations, University of Michigan Press.

Coleman, J. 1961 *Adolescent Society.* New York: Free Press.

Collins, R. 1979 *The Credential Society.* New York: Academic Press

Dennison, J., A. Tunner, G. Jones, and G. Forrester 1975 "The Impact of Community Colleges." Vancouver: B.C. Research.

Featherman, D.L. and R.M. Hauser 1976 "Sexual Inequalities and Socioeconomic Achievement in the U.S. 1962–73." *American Sociological Review* 41:462–483.

Fischer, L., and J. Cheyne 1977 "Sex Roles: Biological and Cultural Interactions as Found in Social Science Research and Ontario Educational Media." Toronto: Ministry of Education.

Freedman, M. 1969 *The Process of Work Establishment.* New York: Columbia University Press.

Gardiner, G. 1975 "Sex Differences in Achievement Attitudes and Personality of Science Students: A Review." *Science Education: Research* 1974.

Gaskell, J. 1977 "Stereotyping and Discrimination in the Curriculum." In Stevenson and Wilson, eds., *Precepts,*

Policy and Perspectives on Canadian Education. London, Ontario: Alexander Blake Associates.

Gaskell, J. 1981 "Sex Inequalities in Education for Work: The Case of Business Education." *Canadian Journal of Education.*

Goyder, J. and P. Pineo 1973 "Female Occupational Achievement." Paper presented at Annual Meeting of Canadian Sociology and Anthropology Association, Kingston, Ontario.

Granovetter, M.S. 1974 "A Study of Contacts and Careers." Boston: Harvard University Press.

Gunderson, M 1976 "Work Patterns." In G. Cook, *Opportunities for Choice: A Goal for Women in Canada.* Ottawa: Statistics Canada and C.D. Howe Institute.

Hall, O. and R. Carlton 1977 *Basic Skills at School and Work.* Toronto: Ontario Economic Council.

Halsey, A.H. 1977 "Towards Meritocracy? The Case of Britain." In J. Karabel and A. Halsey, *Power and Ideology in Education.* New York: Oxford University Press.

Hobbs, E., W. Boldt, G. Erickson, T. Quelch, and G. Sieben 1979 "British Columbia Science Assessment General Report 1 & 2." Submitted to Ministry of Education, Victoria

Jencks, C. 1979 *Who Gets Ahead: The Determinants of Economic Success in America.* New York: Basic Books

Kanter, R. 1977 *Men and Women of the Corporation.* New York: Basic Books.

Karabel, J. 1972 "Community Colleges and Social Stratification: Submerged Class Conflict in American Higher Education." *Harvard Educational Review* 42:521–562.

Kelly A. 1978 *Girls and Science.* Stockholm: Almquist and Wiksell.

Lazerson, M. and N. Grubb 1974 *American Education and Vocationalism: A Documentary History 1870–1970.* New York: Teachers College Press.

Levy, B. 1972 "Do Teachers Sell Girls Short?" *Today's Education.* Washington, D.C.: National Educational Association.

Maccoby, E. and C. Jacklin 1974 *The Psychology of Sex Differences.* Stanford, California: Stanford University Press.

Mangum, G. and J. Walsh 1978 "Employment and Training Programs for Youth: What Works Best for Whom?" *A Report to the Office of Youth Programs*, U.S. Dept. of Labor.

Marsden, L., E. Harvey, and J. Charner 1975 "Female

graduates: their occupational mobility and attainments." *Canadian Review of Sociology and Anthropology* 12, no. 4:385-405.

Martin, W. and A.J. McDonnell 1978 *Canadian Education: A Sociological Analysis*. Scarborough, Ontario: Prentice Hall.

McClendon, M. 1976 "The Occupational Status Attainment Process of Males and Females." *American Sociological Review* 41, no. 1

Nolfi, G. et al. 1978 *Experiences of Recent High School Graduates*. Lexington, Mass.: Lexington Books, D.C. Heath & Co.

Oppenheimer, V. 1970 *The Female Labour Force in the U.S.* Berkeley, California: Institute of International Studies.

Parkin, F. 1972 *Class Inequality and Political Order*. Frogmore, St. Albans: Palladin

Parsons, T. 1942 "Age and Sex in the Social Structure of the U.S." *American Sociological Review* 7:604-612.

Perspectives Canada 1974 "A Compendium of Social Statistics." Ottawa: Ministry of Industry, Trade and Commerce.

Picot, G. 1980 "The Changing Educational Profile of Canadians, 1961 to 2000." Ottawa: Projections Section, Education, Science and Culture Division, Statistics Canada.

Pincus, F. 1980 "The Fake Promises of Community Colleges: Submerged Class Conflict in American Education." *Harvard Educational Review*, Vol. 50, No. 3, 332–361.

Prentice, A. and S. Huston 1975 *Family, School and Society in 19th Century Canada*. Toronto: Oxford University Press.

Ricketts, M. 1980 "A Time for Action: A Survey of Critical Trade Skills in the Lower Mainland." Vancouver: The Vancouver Board of Trade.

Rinehart, J.W. 1975 *The Tyranny of Work*. Don Mills, Ontario: Longmans Canada.

Robb, L. and B. Spencer 1976 "Education: Enrollment and Attainment." In G. Cook, *Opportunities for Choice: A Goal for Women in Canada*. Ottawa: Statistics Canada and C.D. Howe Institute.

Robitaille, D., and J. Sherrill 1977 "B.C. Mathematics Assessment." Victoria: British Columbia Ministry of Education.

Roby, P. 197 'Toward Field Equality: More Job Education for Women.' *School Review* 84, no. 2.

Royal Commission on the Status of Women 1970 *Status of Women in Canada*. Ottawa: Information Canada.

Russell, S. 1979 "Learning Sex Roles in High School." *Interchange* 10, no. 2:57–66.

Sears, P. and D. Feldman 1974 "Teacher Interaction With Boys and Girls." In Stacey (ed.), *And Jill Came Tumbling After: Sexism in American Education*. New York: Dell Publishing Co.

Sells, L. 1973 "The Mathematics Filter and the Education of Women and Minorities." Unpublished manuscript, University of California, Berkeley.

Sexton, P. 1969 *The Femininized Male*. New York: Random House.

Statistics Canada 1978 "Women in the Labour Force. Facts and Figures." 1976 edition. Part 3 — miscellaneous, Ottawa: Labour Canada.

Statistics Canada 1979 *Education in Canada*. Ottawa: Queen's Printer.

Statistics Canada 1979b "Women in the Labour Force. Facts and Figures." Part 2 — *Earnings of Women and Men*, Ottawa: Women's Bureau, Labour Canada.

Statistics Canada 1980a "Women in the Labour Force" 1977 edition. Part 3. Ottawa: Women's Bureau, Labour Canada.

Statistics Canada 1980b "The Employment of 1976 University and College Graduates." Document 4–2212–520. Ottawa: Education, Science and Culture Division.

Symons, H. 1978 "Can Women Translate Education into Occupational Mobility? *University Affairs*, July 16–18.

Synge, J. 1977 "The Sex Factor in Social Selection Processes in Canadian Education." In Carlton, Colley and MacKinnon, *Education, Change and Society*. Toronto: Gage Publishing Ltd.

Thurow, L. 1975 *Generating Inequality*. New York: Basic Books.

Treiman, D. and K. Terrell 1975 "Sex and Status Attainment." *American Sociological Review* 40, no. 2: 174–200.

Turner, R. 1964 "Some Aspects of Women's Ambition." *American Journal of Sociology* 70:271–285.

Weiss, J. 1978 "Educating for Clerical Work: A History of Commercial Education in the United States since 1850." Doctoral thesis, Harvard University.

Willis, P. 1977 *Learning to Labour*. Westmead, Farnborough, Harts: Saxon House.

Wilms, W. 1974 "Public and Proprietary Training: A Study of Program Effectiveness." Centre for Research and Development in Higher Education, Berkeley, California.

Young, M. 1961 *The Rise of the Meritocracy: An Essay on Education and Equality*. Middlesex: Penguin Books.

38 Unemployment as a Women's Issue

Pat Armstrong

PAT ARMSTRONG, Professor of Sociology at York University, Toronto, specializes in the study of women's participation in labour markets. Her books include *The Double Ghetto: Canadian Women and Their Segregated Work* with Hugh Armstrong (1978,1984); *A Working Majority: What Women Must Do For Pay* (1983); and *Labour Pains: Women's Work in Crisis* (1984). Her research has been funded by substantial grants from the Canadian Advisory Council of the Status of Women and the Social Sciences and Humanities Research Council of Canada's "Women and Work" Strategic Grants program, among other agencies.

Women's officially recorded unemployment rates are steadily rising but there is little consensus on the extent, causes, and consequences of female unemployment or on the future of women's paid work. According to the Task Force on Labour Market Development, commonly referred to as the Dodge Report,

> Although there is little direct evidence, it is reasonable to infer that the rising relative unemployment rates of youth and adult women in the past fifteen years have been related to the ability of the economy to absorb the extraordinarily large numbers of new entrants and reentrants to the labour market with limited experience and, in many cases, with limited training. Moreover, hiring practices and procedures may have further restricted job opportunities to a narrow range of occupations (Employment and Immigration Canada, 1981:11).

From this perspective, too many women with too few skills, and perhaps some employers who discriminate against them, provide most of the explanation for women's employment situation. The problem is people, *not* jobs. The causes are primarily women's low investment in their human capital, women's decision to seek paid work and the values of both employers and women, *not* changing economic conditions in the household and in the labour force.

It is, of course, recognized that Canada has been experiencing an "economic downturn," even a recession and perhaps a crisis. Acknowledging that some unemployment may be involuntary and may cause some problems in these difficult times, the state has developed various job creation programs. Based on the assumption that it is primarily male unemployment that is serious and crisis-related, the programs are directed at male-dominated industries. Employment and Immigration Canada explains in its response to the National Action Committee's critiques of the policy that

> It is true that CANADA WORKS is getting much emphasis right now and many activities tend to be more "male" oriented, but the objective of the program is to deal with cyclical unemployment, *not* to deal with or redress imbalances suffered by females (Employment and Immigration Canada, n.d. [1983], emphasis in the original).

Not that women have been ignored. There are some measures intended "to make sure such imbalances are not perpetuated or enhanced" but the real emphasis in terms of women is on upgrading their skills through the CAREER ACCESS and JOB CORPS pro-

programs since, after all, the problem with women is mainly one of "human resource development."

Such job creation schemes are designed as short-term solutions. For the Economic Council of Canada (1983:35), it is technological change that is significant "both in explaining the recent slowdown in total factor productivity and in discovering remedies for that slowdown." In the longer term, new technology is the answer. The 1983 federal budget gives priority to the funding of research and development specifically in the micro-electronic field. According to the Minister of Finance (Lalonde, 1983:0), "The application of new technology in Canadian industry can improve international competitiveness and productivity and thus can increase growth prospects and employment opportunities." It is generally agreed that there will be at least some short-term job loss resulting from the introduction of this new technology and that women will bear the brunt of this loss (see Labour Canada, 1982:15). It is, however, assumed that new jobs will be created and that women will have a chance at these if they develop their skills.

But women's current and future employment problems cannot be so easily dismissed. Economic need and the demand for women workers have been at least as important as women's values in accounting for their growing employment and unemployment. Domestic responsibilities and the structures that relegate women into the lowest paid jobs are more important than lack of skills. Women's unemployment problems are serious and growing. They are much more extensive than the commonly used labour force statistics and government analysis would suggest. And few women have the "choice" of returning to the household. The future is not predetermined by these structures, by employers' interests or by the new technology but, if current trends continue, if alternative strategies are not developed, then women are likely to emerge from this crisis more secondary than before.

THE EXTENT OF WOMEN'S UNEMPLOYMENT

According to Statistics Canada (February 1984:368), in 1983 there were an average of 590,000 women, over half a million, who were without any paid work, who were available for work and who actively searched for work in the four weeks prior to the survey. In addition, there were an estimated 164,000 more women—up 35,000 from a year earlier—who reported they wanted a job but did not search for work for "labour market related reasons." The number who wanted a job but abandoned their search for other non-market related reasons was also up, adding another 89,000 to the unofficially unemployed (Statistics Canada, March 1983:147). In other words, there were another quarter of a million women who wanted paid jobs but were not recorded as unemployed. But even these figures do not reveal the full extent of the problem. They are based on annual averages, and the actual number of women officially counted as experiencing some unemployment during the year is more than twice as high.

As high as these numbers are, the overall unemployment rates nevertheless suggest that men have suffered more as the crisis deepened. In 1981, for the first time since 1975 (when the method for collecting these data was changed), men's unemployment rate edged ahead of women's. However, over half of those considered by Statistics Canada (March 1983:147) to be "discouraged workers" or "hidden unemployed" are women. If these women were added to the female rates, there would be very little difference between the figures for the two sexes.

Male and female unemployment rates reflected both the uneven impact of the crisis on different industries and occupations and the sex segregation of the market. Jobs disappeared suddenly and visibly in the primary and secondary sectors as firms shut down or slowed down during the crisis. These industries are dominated by men. In 1983, over 40 per cent of unemployed men last worked in the manufacturing and construction industries. Another 9 per cent were in primary industries. If a recovery is sustained, however, many of these jobs will reappear. By contrast, 40 per cent of unemployed women last worked in the community, business and personal service industries, where the crisis has had the least impact and where recovery is likely to have the smallest effect on jobs (Statistics Canada, February 1984:386). Because women were concentrated in the industries last hit by deteriorating economic conditions, their unemployment rates rose more slowly but their job loss is less likely to be temporary.

Male unemployment was concentrated in occupations as well as industries. This explains why, in spite of higher overall male unemployment rates, women's 1983 rates were higher in all but three (clerical, agriculture and materials handling) of the twenty-one occupation categories used in the published labour force data (Statistics Canada, February 1984:395). The slightly higher (10.0 vs 9.9) unemployment rate for male clerical workers reflects the layoffs of recording, scheduling and distributing clerks in the construction and manufacturing industries. These rates may fall with a recovery. Women still constitute well over three-quarters (78.5 per cent) of the unemployed clerical workers, however, and they are concentrated in the service sectors where job loss is more likely to be a result of new technology than it is of the "cyclical downturn" (Armstrong and Armstrong, 1987). Thus their unemployment may well be permanent, with or without a recovery. In those areas where women and men compete more directly, such as occupations in the social services, sales and service work, women's unemployment rates are much higher than those of men and the gap is growing, suggesting that women are losing out to men and will continue to do so if the

crisis in employment continues (Statistics Canada, February 1984:394 and 395).

But women's employment problems are not entirely revealed by these figures either. A woman who has found any work at all—other than housework or volunteer work—is counted as employed. More than a quarter (26.2 per cent in 1983) of the women with labour force work had only part-time jobs and this represents an increase of 105,000 over the previous year (Statistics Canada, February 1984:322 and 323). When the full-time unemployment rate is calculated—that is, when persons working part-time because they were unable to find full-time work and those unemployed persons seeking full-time work are separated out—women's unemployment rates are significantly higher (14.3 vs 11.7 in 1982) than those of men (Statistics Canada, July, 1984:95). And these figures do not include those women who were prevented from seeking full-time jobs because of their domestic responsibilities or who quit looking for work and went back to school because there were no jobs available.

The part-time unemployment rate suggests that women are more successful than men in finding part-time work when they are looking for it (Statistics Canada, July 1983:95). However, those women who did find some part-time work saw their hours reduced, and reduced more than those of their male counterparts. In 1982, more than 11 per cent of the women in service and farming occupations were employed for 9 hours or less a week. This was also the case for more than 8 per cent of the women in teaching and service work (Armstrong and Armstrong, 1987). These women did have a job, but not much of one.

With an average of three-quarters of a million women counted as wanting labour force work but failing to find any, with more than a million of the women with jobs only finding part-time work and with a steady reduction in the hours for part-time female workers, there can be little doubt that women right now are facing a serious and growing unemployment problem.

CAUSES AND CONSEQUENCES

While it is clear that attitudes towards women's work have been changing and that these changes have played an important part in women's increasing labour force participation, alterations in values have been at least as much a consequence as they have been a cause of women's movement into paid jobs. Whatever their values, most women work in the labour force because they need the income (Armstrong and Armstrong, 1978 and 1983). The demand for workers has been increasing in the tertiary sector, in the labour-intensive jobs, in women's work. Women have responded to these demands because they are less able to contribute to household maintenance by working solely at home and because the cost of the necessary goods that must be purchased has been rising more than have wages. When their jobs disappear or when their hours are reduced, their need for income does not decline.

In 1983, 45 per cent of unemployed women did not live with a man, unemployed or otherwise. The 265,000 officially unemployed women who were single, widowed, separated or divorced accounted for more than 18 per cent of all the unemployed (Statistics Canada, February 1984:44). Such women may not be the traditional breadwinners but their loss of wages will not, in most cases, be supplemented by other income earners (see Armstrong and Armstrong, 1983:31–32).

Marriage does not guarantee freedom from severe problems during periods of unemployment either. Eighteen per cent of the wives officially counted as unemployed in 1981—and, it should be noted, married women are the least likely to have their unemployment recorded—did not have husbands who were employed full-time (Statistics

Canada, May 1982:99). Even those with employed husbands do not necessarily escape hardship. A study published by Statistics Canada and based on its data concludes that "the families of unemployed wives are more needy than either the families of wives not in the labour force or of currently working wives, particularly for wives in the older age groups" (Nakamura et al., 1979:54). The May 1982 issue of *The Labour Force* points out that, "With respect to unemployment rates, it is of interest to note that by far the highest rate (12%) was registered by women whose husbands were also unemployed" (Statistics Canada, May 1982:100). Moreover, since more than one in four employed women and many of the employed youths have only part-time jobs and part-time pay, their employment will do little to stave off the hardship created by the man's job loss, especially given higher male wages. Finally, of those families with at least one member unemployed in 1983, 42 per cent had unemployed heads. In almost all cases, this means that the person with the highest earnings is without a pay cheque. In 30 per cent of the families with at least one unemployed person, there were no other members employed (Statistics Canada, February 1984:474 and 483). This has to mean that the family faced serious economic difficulties.

Unemployment insurance does provide a larger measure of protection for the unemployed than it did in the past—especially given the increase in the number of people covered by the scheme—but this does not necessarily mean that unemployment does not cause economic hardship. Not all unemployed people are eligible for benefits. A large proportion of part-time workers, most of whom are women, have too few hours to apply. In addition, many who do apply are disqualified or disentitled. In recent years, refusals have averaged more than a million annually and women are more likely than men to be disqualified (Statistics Canada, 1982: Table 13). Even for those who receive regular benefits, the money is inadequate, especially as the duration of unemployment increases. Average benefits in 1982 were $154.46 (Statistics Canada, 1982:Table 9), considerably below the $300 a week that, according to one opinion poll, Canadians feel is the least amount of money necessary for a family of four (reported in *The Gazette*, Montreal, 30 April 1983). Part-timers who qualify get even less, since benefits are based on wages. Indeed, most women receive smaller benefits than unemployed men since women's wages are generally lower. With rising unemployment, welfare "has become a replacement for unemployment insurance for many who want to work but cannot find jobs" (Social Planning Council of Metropolitan Toronto, 1983:68). While it may be the case that unemployment insurance provides a cushion for some against the worst economic effects of unemployment, it is clear that a high proportion of the more than two million who experienced unemployment last year were in dire straits.

Of course, the consequences of unemployment are not simply economic. As Sharon Kirsch (1983:97) points out in a report prepared for the Canadian Mental Health Association, with increases in unemployment rates come increases in depression, anxiety, self-deception, fatalism, anger, spouse abuse, child abuse, suicide, mental hospital admissions, homicides and rape, property crimes, youth alienation, children's school problems, divorce, alcoholism, poor nutrition, inadequate housing, fatigue, weight loss or obesity, ulcers, fainting spells, hard drug abuse, tobacco abuse, caffeine abuse, insomnia, rapid breathing, muscle tension, infant mortality and heart disease. Like all unemployed people, women may experience or be affected by these problems. But women also bear additional burdens. Many of these processes increase the tension management and other work in the household. As the tension and the work mount, state support services in these areas are being cut back. This domestic work is primarily

done by women. They must also stretch the declining food dollar to provide adequate diets for the family. And it is mainly women who are abused. At the same time, women are less and less able to compensate for falling incomes by producing goods and services at home. Their domestic work is less flexible and their labour force work more time consuming and necessary. Even the women who escape unemployment themselves may not avoid the difficulties that unemployment brings.

Unemployment also means that workers' strength is eroded. The pressure from the swelling ranks of the unemployed discourages protest from those with jobs. A job, any job, seems better than none and workers know that there are many others willing to replace them. While women's union membership has been growing in recent years, most of these female union members have worked directly or indirectly for the state. As jobs in the state sector disappear with cutbacks, women's union membership will decline. For those who keep their state-funded jobs, the imposed decrees in Quebec, the policies of the British Columbia government and the federal 6 and 5 program make it clear that not even collective agreements can guarantee protection, as union strength is significantly diminished.

There is little evidence to support the claim that women's rising participation rates have caused either the general rise in unemployment or the particular employment difficulties of women. There is no direct relationship between rising female labour force participation rates and growing unemployment rates for either sex. Female labour force participation rates did not grow at all in 1982, male rates declined and unemployment for both sexes grew.

Nor is there much evidence for the claim that women lack skills, that women's ghettoization results from their failure to invest in their own human capital. Of the population 15 years of age and over in 1983, 1,150,000 females, compared to 915,000 males, had a post-secondary certificate or diploma. This is the educational level that is assumed to provide the best preparation for the labour market. Another 803,000 women and 834,000 men had some post-secondary education. In addition, more women (4,995,000) than men (4,487,000) had completed high school. It is true that more men (1,045,000) than women (743,000) had a university degree but this difference alone could hardly be credited with accounting for the segregated market (Statistics Canada, February, 1984:106).

THE FUTURE OF WOMEN'S WORK

On the one hand, the state is responding to the "cyclical downturn" by developing job creation programs designed to maintain employment levels in male-dominated industries. On the other, it is introducing restraint programs that will primarily affect women. Given the sexual division of labour at home and in the market, wage freeze policies, as well as cutbacks in state jobs and services, hurt women more. What has mainly prevented women's employment situation from deteriorating as rapidly and as obviously as men's has been their direct or indirect employment by the state. Women have found their best jobs, their best pay, their most rapid promotions and their largest union protection in this sector. When jobs disappear here, women will suffer more than men. In addition, the cutbacks in services mean that much of this work will be returned to the home, where it will be done once again by women.

Government restraint programs will eliminate many women's jobs but the new technology poses an even greater threat to women's employment. Primarily designed to increase productivity, efficiency and control over the labour process, there can be little doubt that the implementation of micro-electronic technology can increase profits by reducing labour costs while increasing output.

Since the technology is designed to increase productivity, particularly in clerical and service work, and since women are concentrated in the least productive jobs (Armstrong, 1984), it is women's work that will bear the brunt of technological unemployment. The Labour Canada Task Force on Micro-electronics and Employment (1982:15) makes it clear that

> Although women make up more than forty percent (40%) of the labour force, two-thirds (2/3) of women workers in Canada are concentrated in those positions which are currently prime targets for efficiency and productivity improvements via the introduction of micro-electronic technology.

Study after study has come to similar conclusions and it is generally acknowledged that more women's work will disappear.

However, there is less agreement on the extent of the impact and on the future of women's employment. Defenders of the micro-electronic technology staunchly maintain that the anticipated technological unemployment has not happened, in spite of the widespread use of the new machines. It is difficult to challenge these arguments with the available data because a number of factors combine to obscure the consequences of this new technology. The nature of micro-electronic technology itself delays and camouflages unemployment and underemployment. While the equipment is being put in place, the existing staff is still required to operate the old equipment and additional workers are necessary to introduce and, in many cases, to publicize, the new machines. Once the process is complete, fewer, and different workers will be required. Moreover, most companies have only begun to use new pieces of equipment; the offices and stores essentially function as they did before but with a few new machines. However, micro-electronic technology makes fully automated workstations possible, ones where the work and the workers are transformed, eliminating the need for much of the labour in the process. It is this second phase of technological change that will create the largest disruptions in employment and few, if any, companies have reached this stage yet. Customers and clients also have to be educated. As was the case in gas stations, people are being trained to serve themselves in banks and stores. Once training is complete, many of the paid employees can be laid off.

The employment impact of the new technology is also concealed by the current economic situation. Technological change is integral to the crisis, creating, reflecting and resolving it. Consequently, unemployment and underemployment may be blamed on a decaying economy rather than on technological innovations.

Statistics Canada offers little assistance in analyzing the impact of technology, since it does not collect information on turnover rates or on changes in job content. It is also difficult from the official data to monitor silent firings, jobless growth, layoffs delayed by collective agreements and the intensification of labour. The rising unemployment rates of female clerical workers, the lack of job opportunities for young people, the increase in part-time work, the decreasing hours in that work and the falling labour force participation rates which do show up in the available data may all result directly or indirectly from the introduction of new technology; but it is impossible to tell both because of the intimate connection between technological change and crisis and because of the inadequacy of the data.

Not only do defenders of the micro-electronic technology argue that few jobs have actually disappeared with the new machines, but they also argue that new and better jobs will emerge to replace the old. In her article on the impact of the new technology, Margaret Benston (1983) suggests that there are five areas where employment may expand:

jobs running the automated equipment, jobs involved with the development, maintenance and use of computer programs and data bases, jobs repairing and maintaining the equipment, jobs manufacturing the hardware, jobs selling the new equipment as well as training and educating people to run it.

There can be little doubt that women have acquired jobs running the new machines, but they are largely replacing other female workers and, in the process, the number of jobs available to women are reduced. Moreover, these jobs too may have a limited future and many of them involve only dull, repetitive work that is all too quickly learned. Women may gain some jobs in the field of software production but this work is also in the process of being automated. The non-automated jobs that are created here will likely go to men, since they already have a headstart in the field and since the good jobs will be scarce. Jobs in repairing and servicing the machines will also go to men for similar reasons, and these jobs too are likely to be shortlived as the machines are increasingly built of component parts and as some are programmed to diagnose their problems and set out their own repairs. Women have a much better chance at jobs in the manufacturing of hardware, but in these fields they face competition from low wage imports, and the jobs that may appear in Canada will be in automated factories that require little training and offer few rewards. Men too have a headstart in the fifth area described by Benston—selling the machines and teaching the people how to operate them. In addition, the emphasis on computers in schools may mean that resources are cut back in the other teaching areas where women work. And there is no guarantee that the need for teachers in the field of computer technology will continue to expand, since the machines are becoming more and more "user friendly," requiring less and less knowledge to operate them.

CONCLUSION

The future does not look bright for women. The economic crisis is increasing their unemployment and slowing the growth in their labour force participation rates. Contrary to government documents, unemployment creates severe difficulties for women. Job creation programs offer women little assistance. Government restraint programs will throw many women onto the unemployment lines and deny women some of their best jobs. At the same time, women's work in the household will grow. Part-time work will continue to increase, although women here will face growing competition from men. Union membership will probably decline as jobs disappear in those areas where women have collective agreements. The new technology will affect women first and most, eliminating many female jobs, reducing skills in others and widening the gap between those who operate the machines and those who direct the work. Skills training will be of little help in this work and will not solve the problem of too few jobs.

Woman's work in the home is less flexible than it was in the past. Women have fewer ways of compensating for declining incomes by intensifying their labour there. Consequently the pressure to work for pay increases as the opportunities for labour force work decreases.

The future, however, is not predetermined. The technology is not an independent force, even though it is structured, developed and used to decrease employers' dependency on workers and their skills. People can and do make their own history, if not under conditions of their choosing. It is essential that we thoroughly analyze the current situation so that we can develop a strategy for the future, one that will work for women as well as for men.

References

Armstrong, Pat *Labour Pains, Women's Work in Crisis*. Toronto: The Women's Press. Forthcoming.

Armstrong, Pat and Hugh Armstrong 1978 *The Double Ghetto: Canadian Women and Their Segregated Work*. Toronto: McClelland and Stewart.

———— 1983 *A Working Majority: What Women Must Do For Pay*. Ottawa: Supply and Services Canada.

———— 1987 "Women and the Economic Crisis in Canada," Charlene Gannage and David W. Livingstone (eds.) *Working People in Hard Times*, Toronto: Garamond.

Benston, Margaret 1983 "For Women, the Chips are Down." Pp. 44–54 in Jan Zimmerman, ed., *The Technological Woman: Interfacing With Tomorrow*. New York: Praeger.

Economic Council of Canada 1983 *The Bottom Line: Technology, Trade and Income Growth*. Ottawa: Supply and Services Canada.

Employment and Immigration Canada 1981 *Labour Market Development in the 1980s*. Ottawa: Supply and Services Canada. Notes prepared in response to a newsletter from the National Action Committee. n.d. unpaginated.

Kirsch, Sharon 1983 *Unemployment: Its Impact on Body and Soul*. Toronto: Canadian Mental Health Association.

Labour Canada 1982 *In the Chips: Opportunities, People, Partnerships*. Ottawa: Supply and Services Canada.

Lalonde, The Honourable Marc 1983 Research and Development Tax Policies. Ottawa: Department of Finance Canada. April.

Nakamura, Alice, Masao Nakamura and Dallas Cullen in collaboration with Dwight Grant and Harriet Orcutt 1979 *Employment and Earnings of Married Females*. Ottawa: Statistics Canada.

Social Planning Council of Metropolitan Toronto 1983 *... And the Poor Get Poorer*. A Study of

Social Welfare Programs in Ontario. Toronto: The Social Planning Council of Metropolitan Toronto and the Ontario Social Development Council.

Statistics Canada 1982 *Statistical Report on the Operation of the Unemployment Insurance Act* (Cat. no. 73–001). Ottawa: Supply and Services Canada.

_____ 1983 *Canadian Statistical Review* October 1983 (Cat. no. 11–003E). Ottawa: Supply and Services Canada.

_____ 1984 *Labour Force Annual Averages* (Cat. no. 71–529). Ottawa: Supply and Services Canada.

_____ *The Labour Force* (Cat. no. 71–001), Ottawa: Supply and Services Canada, various issues.

39 Women and Microtechnology

Heather Menzies

HEATHER MENZIES is an Ottawa-based author with a background in sociology and journalism. Her published works include *The Railroad's Not Enough: Canada Now* (1978); *Women and the Chip: Case Studies of the Effects of Information on Employment in Canada* (1981); *Computers on the Job: Surviving Canada's Microcomputer Revolution* (1982); "Ecologizing technological change" (1984); and "In his image: Women's perception of technology" (1987).

Several studies, including an overview of OECD (Organization for Economic Cooperation and Development) reports compiled in 1979 by the Institute for Research on Public Policy (IRPP) of Montreal, have concluded that women are likely to bear the brunt of the negative employment effects of microtechnology. The *Siemens Report* (Republic of Germany) predicted that 40 per cent of office workers could become redundant through office automation. The *Nora Minc Report* (France) predicted a 30 per cent loss of employment in the tertiary sector in general and particularly among bank and other finance-industry workers. In the United Kingdom, the *Jenkins and Sherman Study* predicted that office and other computer-based forms of automation could boost Britain's unemployment rate to 25 per cent by 1990. Individual case studies there have revealed, for instance, a 33 per cent reduction in the number of secretaries and typists at the British Standards Institute after word processors were introduced. The reason lies in automated re-typing and printing of computer-stored stock paragraphs called "boilerplate."

In a series of studies I did last year (published by IRPP as *Woman and the Chip*, 1981) I traced the process and extent of this negative employment impact in some Canadian industries. Projecting from the trends I observed and comparing these with the continuing concentration of women in, and seeking, clerical work, the unemployment rate among female clerical workers could escalate to as much as 33 per cent by 1990.

We could see the pattern in 1981. In the banking industry, where women comprise 70 per cent of employment (80 per cent of them in clerical positions), computerization has reached a fairly mature stage; banks can now offer automated teller machines and can finally enjoy major labour savings. Employment had been growing by about 10 per cent a year through the 1970s, well ahead of growth in the female labour force. In 1980, though, employment stagnated. It was a significant development.

In the insurance industry, where information handling has also been extensively automated and where 70 per cent of female employment is concentrated in clerical positions, clerical employment dropped by 11 per cent during the 1975–80 period.

Most significant of all, the cumulative negative employment effect of computerization seems to be a seriously reduced, overall clerical employment-growth rate at a time when women's labour-force participation rate is both continuing to rise and expected to continue doing so.

Between 1961 and 1965, the female labour force grew by 20 per cent, clerical employment grew by the same amount. Between

1966 and 1970, the female labour force grew by 20 per cent again, while clerical employment grew by 23 per cent. Over the 1971–75 period, the female labour force grew by 24 per cent; clerical employment grew by 33 per cent.

Female labour-force participation is expected to continue growing at about the same rate at least over the next decade. The economic pressures are still with us, the rising cost of living, single parenthood and so on. Sixty per cent of women work because they have to. They are either single, single parents, or married to men earning so little that, if their earnings were removed, the number of families living below the poverty line in Canada would increase by 50 per cent.

I think I have demonstrated that we might have a problem here. I also hope we will see it not only as an employment-adjustment problem but also as a women's issue, for two reasons: computer technology is increasing employment opportunities in the occupations where women are least represented; on the other hand, it is diminishing employment opportunities in clerical occupations and in the related administrative and supervisory positions which women were using as career ladders.

My second reason is that, if women are to gain rather than lose by computer technology, changing attitudes must be part of the approach attitudes of employers (male) who still dismiss women as a secondary labour force and insist that they prove in a courtroom their right to equality in the workplace, and attitudes among women themselves.

From women's entry into the Canadian labour force as domestic servants a century ago to currently being concentrated, to an overwhelming 66 per cent, in clerical, sales and service occupations, women have been socialized towards support-staff, assistant and other "helper" roles. Yet the computer is automating and de-skilling much of that work, everywhere from the factory to the office: clerical workers in insurance companies and banks; cashiers, telephone operators (reductions range from 30 to 40 per cent with semi-automated long distance phoning). The automation includes administrative work traditionally associated with process and procedure, a promotion ground which women have gained only recently. It also takes in supervisory work since there are fewer people to oversee and computer monitoring automates a large measure of this familiar female stepping-stone to management.

At first people did everything by hand. Then mechanization removed manual work, leaving the worker with a craft. Within the confines of mechanization, craft itself was diminished to a series of procedures. Finally the procedures were standardized enough that they could be taken over by the machine as well.

Let me give an example of automation in the banking industry. First, a teller's daily records were manually recorded in ledgerbooks. Then keypunching and, later, data encoding were introduced. By that stage, work was done in central data centres. Now, bank branches are connected "on line" with the data centre's computer. The teller enters the transaction record herself, automatically, as she punches in the information on her keyboard for printing out onto a customer's pass book. Tomorrow (almost literally) as the automated teller-machines introduce us to self-serve banking, the customer will punch in her own transaction and everything else will be done automatically. We can see the decline and the final automation of clerical work.

It is also interesting to trace the shifting employment pattern. When computerization was introduced to the banks, employment grew at all occupational levels. At the clerical level, there was an overlap between the old paper-based information work and the new electronic form. At the more professional and technical levels, employment grew in response to the new services (such as on-line multi-branch banking and daily-interest savings accounts) which the advancing technology made possible.

With recent developments, clerical employment has relatively declined while professional and technical employment has continued to grow. For instance, the daily-interest savings service provided more work to professionals (accountants and computer specialists) but little extra work for clerical workers. The clerical employment decline would probably look more dramatic except that banks were sharing the diminishing workload by increasing part-time employment. Part-time hirings were double full-time hirings between 1968 and 1974.

As Automatic Teller Machines (ATM) become widespread over the next five years (shifting tellers into data centres where they will provide telephone back-up to the ATM terminals), the prospect of shift work raises questions about potential damage to family and social life and compounds the structural barriers to occupational mobility for women.

There is another, perhaps more insidious, distancing factor which *could eventually jeopardize all hope of occupational mobility*: the growing skills gap between clerical and professional information work. Work in planning, research and development, market and financial analysis and management decision-making (work in which women are seriously under-represented) is becoming more professional because of computer aids available in the computerized office.

In one company I studied, the composition of the Information Systems Department shifted from 80 per cent clerical in 1972 to 45 per cent clerical in 1980. Of the 140 workers removed from the clerical ranks, only two joined the 110 additions to the professional-managerial ranks. They were replaced by computer scientists and other highly trained specialists hired from outside the company and representing what one personnel official termed "a quantum leap" in skill difference from the former clerical workers. The other

138 clerical workers were given lateral transfers to as yet unautomated departments, some even accepting demotions.

Meanwhile, armed with their computer skills, the new professional-management workers will exacerbate occupational discontinuity by extending the range and sophistication of their work and thereby escalating standards of performance. "The ability to do (sophisticated computer modelling) generates the requirement that you do this," the personnel manager told me. The effect could be the institutionalization of a dual labour market within the company: a scenario featuring a group of low-skilled clerical workers feeding data into computer systems, a smaller group of increasingly sophisticated professional users of computers and computerized information systems and a huge, hostile and unbridgeable skills gap between the two groups.

And when the company no longer needs clerical staff, "They'll be sent off to wherever redundant clerks go," the personnel official told me matter-of-factly. "Unfortunately, that will be women. But it's a question of social responsibility versus running a company."

Affirmative-action programs, equal opportunities and, to a more subtle extent, equal-pay battles over the last 25 years have sought to break down job ghettos and integrate the male and female labour markets for equal occupational mobility. Such schemes, augmented with training opportunities both on the job and in institutions, are all the more required now as employment opportunities in the clerical, administrative and supervisory ranks decline, as the meagre mobility ladder which supervisory and administrative work represented for women collapses and as employment growth becomes increasingly concentrated in occupations traditionally dominated by men and increasingly enriched as computer technology advances.

It is critical that women gain access to the employment-growth areas *now* before the skills and performance-standards differences widen significantly. Now, it can rightfully be argued that a lot of the seeming "quantum leap" of difference is due to attitude. For instance, in the department where the clerical-to-professional ratio changed so dramatically as computerization was extended from data processing to a full range of automated information systems, the top 50 executives in the department now have their own desk-top computer terminals on which they type and receive up to 50 per cent of the memos, mini-reports and other correspondence which secretaries used to handle for them. The remaining two secretaries spend only about half their time on traditional secretarial work. One I spoke to spends the rest of her time on research and administrative work.

By another name, such a clerical worker would be considered a prime candidate for courses in computer programming or business administration and quickly move into some of the professional positions which will become increasingly available but ever harder to fill by outside hirings over the next five to fifteen years. But her boss still called her a secretary; nor could he conceive of her moving into a professional-management position: "You can't make a doctor out of a nurse," he said.

Such attitudes might return to mock industry in the years ahead. Women might indeed be on a collision course between their continuing concentration in clerical occupations and industry's diminishing clerical requirements. But industry could also be on a collision course between the computer-fired upward reprofiling of its skills needs and the relatively unchanging profile of the expected labour force over the next decade or so.

The bulk of labour-force growth anticipation for the 1980s will not come from young university graduates, but from the increased participation rates of women 25 years and older; in other words, women who have already completed their schooling, who are either returning to the workforce or will stay on through child-rearing years. In 1979, less than 10 per cent of the female labour force had a university education. Further, women's concentration in clerical occupations remained a fairly consistent 33 per cent of the female labour force during the 1970s. As well, the government's training programs for women are predominantly geared to teaching traditional clerical skills.

What would involve relatively little training if affirmative-action apprenticeship and training programs were initiated now could become a costly employment-adjustment program for government and industry in the years ahead, as industry strives to fill a crippling skills shortage.

Before summarizing what I consider to be the major areas on which policy action must be taken, there is one other theme I should like to touch on. It is that the *net* employment question in this period of technological change is not a subject for research but for policy action. As several research reports (including the *Nora Minc Report* to which I previously referred and one published last year from the International Labour Organization (ILO) in Geneva) have concluded that the final employment outcome of computer technology will depend on how it is applied and in whose interests.

We are part of the choice. Should computer technology be applied towards the three needs which employment has traditionally fulfilled: earning income, developing and expressing our abilities and achieving stature in our own and other people's eyes? Or should the technology be used primarily as a cost-cutting competitive tool, industry's main reason for technological change?

Recent experiments in Europe demonstrate that both sets of objectives can be achieved, and to the mutual advantage of management and workers. Some have resulted from technological-change clauses in union contracts, clauses requiring consultation, or from health-and-safety standards, which go beyond such minimums as employer-paid eye examination for persons using video-display terminals to include "quality-of-working-life" considerations. The Tavistock Institute in the United Kingdom has developed what it calls a socio-technical model for implementing technological change. It takes into account "quality of working life" as well as quantity of output as objectives of the corporate system to be enhanced by the new technology.

Utopian? Not really.

There are essentially two approaches to the automation process: one, with a master-plan implemented from the top down and featuring centralized computer power and related decision-making. The alternative is a decentralized approach with individual departments acquiring computer-based facilities and expanding outward in pace with their developing computer skills. In such an approach, a secretary in charge of customer-complaint letters in a consumer-products company might develop a filing system in her word-processing unit which later allowed her to have all letters scanned for references to, say, legibility of package instructions. After some manipulation of the data, she might produce some interesting market research, worthy of promotion or at least a job reclassification. The advantage of this approach would be that the threat of a skills shortage in a bipolarized labour market could be avoided.

In my research, however, I found a lot of the top-down, central-control pattern, in keeping with the personalities who spearheaded the office of future transformations. These were engineers and systems analysts who tended to view the office as a factory producing information rather than as a service and communications centre. They also focussed less on information as a resource in itself than on the process of compiling information and transmitting it to decision-makers. In other words they applied computer technology to reducing the cost of producing, distributing and storing informa-

tion, not necessarily to enhancing what you can do with information.

In her report, *Drowning in the Pool*, Janice Manchee provides a vivid account of working conditions under such a factory approach to office work, with a pool of word-processor operators working on anonymous correspondence in isolation even from fellow workers but with every movement and every error monitored by the central computer. Some of the operators were on drugs from the strain. Some broke down and cried, regularly. Others developed the habit of chattering to their machines.

A 1980 report from the ILO in Geneva describes these symptoms as an increasingly prevalent psychopathology associated with office automation and one which is generating international concern. The report lists what the workers have lost; autonomy to vary work pace, diversity of work pattern, personal contact with the people who originate the work, communication and responsibility within the workplace.

The income objective of employment is being met; the other two are being *savaged*.

At this point, one could launch into a passionate prescription for humanism in the workplace. However, we seldom change the world by single strokes of passion, certainly not in Canada. Change comes from gradualism. The power of change comes from process.

There are obvious agendas for action; to summarize a few: a comprehensive employment-adjustment program for women to help them move out of assistant information work into professional computer-assisted information work. Such a program could integrate existing programs such as affirmative action and outreach. It could include educational leave, coupled perhaps with wage subsidies; training, with extra funds allocated from a special technology training tax; manpower centres for women, providing computer-skills training and counselling as well as job placement. Counselling will be needed not only among women conditioned to doubt their aptitude for computer science but among industry leaders as well. Finally, public information programs are needed to alert women to the diminishing employment prospects in clerical occupations and to the new career opportunities emerging with computer technology.

In addition, women's lack of union protection makes it urgent that the Labour Act be amended to require, among other things, compulsory consultation, even collabora-tion, on the process of implementing technological change. Such a measure could help lay the ground-work for the decentralized scenario I spoke of earlier.

These changes will come about only with the utmost effort and commitment on the part of women. We must present briefs, draft policy papers, lobby, ask pointed questions at conferences. We must do whatever we can wherever we work, in government, business and labour, to ensure that women are not "technopeasants" in Canada's computerized society.

40 The Daily Routines of Employed Spouses as a Public Affairs Agenda

William Michelson

WILLIAM MICHELSON, Professor of Sociology and a researcher at the Centre for Urban and Community Studies at the University of Toronto, specializes in urban sociology and environmental sociology. His publications include *Man and his Urban Environment: A Sociological Approach* (1970, 1976); *Environmental Choice, Human Behavior, and Residential Satisfaction* (1977); *Public Policy in Temporal Perspective* (1978); *The Child in the City* (2 vols.) (1979); *From Sun to Sun: Daily Obligations and Community Structure in the Lives of Employed Women and Their Families* (1985); and *Methods for Environmental and Behavioral Research* (1987). He is currently working with Riley Dunlop on a *Handbook of Environmental Sociology*. He has also served as Professor of Social Ecology at the University of California—Irvine, Senior Research Officer at the former Ministry of State for Urban Affairs (Canada), as consultant to several new community projects, and Chairman of the International Research Group on Time-Budgets and Social Activities. His major research projects have been on the implications of urban contexts for daily life, particularly among relatively vulnerable subpopulations.

This article deals with ways in which the daily experience of employed mothers converges with and diverges from that of their husbands.[1] It also describes how public policies and practices, especially those concerning urban organization, infrastructure, and transportation, compound the difficulties of employed mothers, and it suggests what can be done to increase support for this growing segment of the working population.

WHY "PERSONAL DECISIONS" ARE OF PUBLIC CONCERN

First, it is helpful to give some perspective on reasons for linking public affairs with employment decisions and everyday activities of individuals and families. A laissez-faire approach to maternal employment means that mothers of young children cope individually and independently with the daily activities confronted when they enter the labor force. Some well-meaning how-to books written by women urge other women to devote greater effort to personal organization. This conveys an impression that a career woman who is overburdened has only herself to blame.

Personal lives are in fact played out on a vast stage, and forces originating far beyond the self and family influence what people do, and how well they can do it. In the case of maternal employment, for example, public policies affect such critical matters as the basic decision to undertake employment and the logistical conditions under which non-household activities are conducted in the daily routine.

Increasing Employment of Women

Neither formal employment nor work as such are new to women. The dramatic new trend in western industrial societies is the extent to which different categories of adult women have joined the labor force. Before World War II, women who held jobs were principally those who were poor, single, childless, or highly educated professionals. The war effort's temporary demands expanded work participation beyond these groups, including women with children of school age or older. The economic expansion after the war, and the absence of traditional sources and levels of immigration, led to even greater increases of "acceptable" female employees, who filled the burgeoning "pink-collar" jobs. This expansion included mothers of young children.[2]

Employment decisions reflect incentives and disincentives imposed by the public realm, and beyond the individual's immediate control. Thus many women were far less likely to enter employment when they were neither needed in work-place roles nor culturally supported in seeking jobs. What women choose to do is not simply the outcome of personal decisions, but reflects much larger contexts.

Labor market demands and incentives are one side of the picture, representing forces that in some degree help pull women to jobs. The other side of the picture is equally important—i.e., influences that push women to consider seeking or taking jobs. The greater portion of the increase in outside employment among American women with children under six—rising from less than 20 percent in 1955 to about 50 percent at present—has come since 1970. The 1970–1985 period was, until very recently, marked by great increases in the cost of living (particularly housing costs) and the divorce rate.[3]

There is an undeniable logic behind the movements for women's liberation and equal opportunity. Unquestionably these forces are influential among women with education and career interests. Nevertheless, recent studies consistently show that economic need provides the greatest single incentive to em-

ployment among the general population of women. Kamerman, for example, reported that 60 percent of white married professional women, and as many as 90 percent of working class women, worked "for the money."[4] Another report simply summarized: "On the whole, wives enter the labor market for economic reasons. . . ."[5]

LOGISTICS OF MATERNAL EMPLOYMENT: RESEARCH FINDINGS

The following discussion is based on data gathered in metropolitan Toronto in 1980. Members of a research program called "The Child in the City" concluded that having a mother with outside employment was a new factor in the lives of many urban children. Accordingly it seemed important to determine the influence of this development on children's daily routines and to document the impact of maternal employment on other members of the family, including the women themselves. A three-phase study was designed to focus on the logistics and implications of maternal employment for women and their families.[6]

A multiple-stage sampling procedure was used to survey 538 families. The survey covered school days during March through June, 1980, including a variety of weather conditions. A comparative substudy of a random selection of 78 of the same families was conducted during the subsequent summer vacation period, to assess differences in the absence of compulsory schooling on weekdays. . . .

We were able to assess the extent to which the daily lives of employed mothers and young children were becoming more likely like those of their husbands. We also noted the conditions and patterns of activities that might make their situations qualitatively different.

Husband-Wife Convergence

Certain major indicators give the impression that the weekday employment experiences of working women are starting to approximate those of men. Thus in the amounts of time devoted to aspects of the daily routine, full-time working wives resemble their husbands more than part-time or unemployed wives resemble theirs.

By definition, of course, this is true for hours spent at an external place of work. Nonetheless, employed women also resemble their husbands in other ways. Daily travel is an example. Conceivably, employed women might not spend more time in traveling than housewives, since the latter could devote additional time to travel related to family, shopping, recreational, or other noncommuting purposes. In fact, however, employed women actually do travel more than housewives, and approximate men's traditionally higher daily transit time. For example, women with full-time jobs spent 81 minutes a day traveling, compared to 66 minutes for women with part-time jobs, 44 minutes for housewives, and 87 minutes for husbands.

Second, women trade off the time devoted to employment with other activities in the same way as men. The greater the amount of weekday time devoted to a job, the less time both men and women put into housework, childcare, shopping, social activity, or both active and passive forms of leisure.

Third, when women have greater exposure to outside employment, their daily tensions increase, culminating in levels identical to those of men. Tension was calculated over the whole day, weighted by the length of time devoted to contributing activities, as well as with reference to the performance of specific activities. Both men and women view paid employment as relatively high-tension (though men rate it slightly higher), and tension associated with a major daily activity affects employees of either sex in similar ways.

Husband-Wife Divergence

Paid employment is a major responsibility. A full-time job demands more than half the remaining time left after time for sleep and other necessary personal activities is removed from the 24-hour day, particularly if much commuting is required. Paid employment places great constraints on the extent to which other activities can be undertaken during a workday.

The total pattern of a person's day, however, along with his or her subjective experience of it, is not determined solely by the work responsibility. Activities that occupy the remainder of the day also count. Moreover this more inclusive conception of everyday life brings out differences between women and their husbands. There is much evidence that the everyday subjective experiences of employed mothers differ markedly from those of their spouses. Although women working outside of the home make most of the same daily time trade-offs as their husbands, the absolute amounts of an activity men and women put into the daily routine differ, sometimes greatly. Consequently, the art of fitting activities in and weaving them together will also differ.

Household Work and Childcare

The most prominent differences between employed spouses in the use of time relate to housework and childcare. Women with full-time jobs spend less time than housewives at such tasks—indeed less than half as much. (Women with full-time jobs spend 192 minutes a day versus 436 minutes a day for housewives. Women with part-time jobs are in between, at 356 minutes). Nevertheless *all* women do much more of these activities than do their husbands, who only devote an average of 71.2 minutes to housework and childcare. Even women with full-time jobs spend nearly three times as much daily time on housework and childcare as their husbands. The latter's contribution to domestic activity also varies little with their wives' employment status.

If one adds employment, housework, and childcare responsibilities, and characterizes them as a basic unit of *obligatory daily activity*, it becomes apparent that the daily routines of women with children and outside jobs involve more of such activity than those of men, or indeed, of women with less extensive employment. The mother employed full-time spends nearly 10 hours a day (584 minutes) in obligatory activities. Moreover, the data fail to cover related activities such as commuting and shopping, which typically add still another hour per day. The different categories of men typically spend half an hour to an hour less in daily obligatory activities than women with full-time jobs—with the greatest differences reflecting the comparatively low obligatory activity by men whose wives work full-time (i.e., the opposite of expectations that men might compensate for their wives' total loads).

Women and Everyday Travel

These differences between men and women in the nature and juxtaposition of daily activities carry serious implications for everyday travel. The most tension-producing daily activities in women's routines are transitions to and from household responsibilities and outside employment. These tensions are stronger for women than for men, because the women are responsible for what happens both before and after their commuting trips. Thus they have to see children off or accompany them to their destinations, yet must still appear at the place of employment on time and ready to work. In the evenings, they leave work at a fixed hour, but when reaching home are available for childcare, companionship, dinner preparation, and other household chores. Since travel can thus exacerbate both of the demanding portions of women's daily routines, it takes on a different subjective tone.

Attitudes about travel are intensified because women typically have relatively marginal travel resources, being described as "transportation deprived and transit dependent."[7] In families with one automobile, the husband typically takes the car to work, leaving the wife to contend with the inflexibilities of public transit systems, or to seek a job that emphasizes proximity to home rather than career enhancement.[8] Indeed, women are less likely than men to have secured driver's licenses.[9] Yet when taking responsibility for transporting children to their daily locations, women strongly prefer automobile travel, because of the relative ease of handling children and their gear.[10] Single mothers who usually have very low incomes are especially unlikely to have access to automobiles, despite family travel needs.

Documentation of this and other widely reported information about women's transportation shows that while precise travel patterns reflect local and/or national variations in city size and structure, the nature of public transportation, socioeconomic status, and the logistics of owning and using a private automobile, the data nevertheless support most of these gender-relevant findings.[11] Our data from Toronto indicate that women are about three times as likely as their husbands to use public transportation, such use being almost exclusively for trips to and from work. Forty-four percent of their trips are made with children, exclusively by foot or automobile. Public transportation is most commonly used for the relatively long commutes from suburbs to the central city. This reflects both the Toronto public transit system's highly efficient service, and the difficulty and expense of center-city parking. In all, 38 percent of the women interviewed lacked driver's licenses. Among those taking the subway downtown, 50 percent lacked licenses, rising to 73 percent among those who took the slower and less convenient buses in non-central directions.

Transportation, Time Pressure, and Tension

Being deprived of transportation increases tension. Thus women experience a high degree of tension in traveling, second only to certain other transitional activities such as getting children out of the house in the morning. Travel causes more tension than most of the routine activities such as in-house childcare and housekeeping. Furthermore, travel by public transportation (which as noted reflects intrafamilial and external conditions more than personal desire) is felt to cause more tension than travel by car, and this is not a function of trip length or duration.

The time pressure that respondents reported experiencing the day preceding the interview was clearly related to mode of transportation to work, both their own and their husbands'. Of women taking public transit, 35.1 percent were in the high time-pressure category ($+5$ to $+10$ on a scale from -10 to $+10$), compared to only about 19 percent of those using a car for some or all of the trip to work.

Men typically have more choice than women about their means of travel, and do not show the same patterns of tension associated with travel as women. Our more general analyses of tension indicate that the degree of tension associated with an activity is correlated with the extent to which choice is lacking. Thus with respect to public transit, the correlation between tension and lack of choice is $+0.43$ for women and $+0.37$ for men.

Men's jobs are the only relatively significant source of high tension among their daily activities. But women report employment as only one of half-a-dozen job and transition-related family responsibilities rated high in tension. (See Figure 1). Many of these activities involve travel, and as noted women often travel with less efficient resources, and have fewer choices. Consequently daily travel requirements should be expected to produce different subjective experiences among employed women than they do among their husbands.

This is illustrated by daycare centers and their relation to women's places of employment. Our data show that mothers are about four times more likely than fathers to take a young child to a daycare center. These data further indicate that the divergence of daycare locations from optimal locations with respect to the daily commute (i.e., right near home, work, or on a direct line in between) adds a conservatively estimated increment of 28 percent to the mother and child's trip to such centers. While tension in daily travel was not found significantly related to total amount of travel, it is indeed significantly related to how much more the childcare drop-off adds to what would otherwise be the mother's commute to work.

Employment Flexibility

... Our analysis included comparisons of part-time jobholders with full-time employees, on one hand, and those with no outside employment, on the other.[12] As one would expect, part-time employment moderated the impact of employment responsibilities on non-work activities. Feelings of time pressure and tension among part-time employees fell in between those reported by women working full-time and by housewives. In short, part-time jobs provide needed income, but also allow time during the day for shopping and other household tasks, lessening capability constraints on these activities. Respondents appreciated being able to do these things themselves during the day, freeing evenings so they can be home and at ease with other family members.

Part-time employment is not, however, a solution per se for the logistical difficulties of employed mothers. Many need the larger incomes that go with full-time jobs, and many are actively pursuing careers. Furthermore the terms of part-time employment are often

Figure 1
MEAN TENSION IN SELECTED DAILY ACTIVITIES (WOMEN AND MEN)

**Scale of Mean
Tension Scores**

Women:		Men:
	(highest)*	
Getting children ready	3.7	
		Employment; Care to older children
Arriving-leaving	3.5	
Employment		
Waking children		
Care to older children		
Care to babies; Food		
preparation; Indoor		
cleaning	3.0	Arriving-leaving; Waking children
Dishes; Shopping		
Laundry		
Meals at home; Putting to		
bed; Sleep		
Personal hygiene		Food preparation; Correspondence
Conversations; Gardening &	2.5	Care to babies; Personal hygiene
animals;		Talk with children
Correspondence		Dishes; Meals at home
Visits;		Getting children ready; Shopping;
		Conversations
Joke, play with children		Laundry; Putting to bed; Sleep
Relaxing, thinking		Indoor cleaning;
TV	2.0	Gardening & animals
Reading		Visits; Reading
	1.8	Joke, play with children; Relaxing,
		thinking; TV
	(lowest)*	

*Mean tension scores reflect a transformed scale on which raw scores ranged from 1 (ease) to 7 (tension).

inferior to full-time employment in such matters as wage rates, fringe benefits, and permanence....

Cultural Lag

Our findings thus indicate that women diverge considerably from men in their subjective experience of the average workday, despite superficial appearances of convergence. A more nearly complete realization of equality at home would clearly ease the logistical challenges that employed mothers face. Transition problems, for example, would be less pressing if immediate obligations at both ends of the commute did not so uniformly fall on women. Nevertheless, the pressure-producing conditions of the daily routine are at least as much external to the family as they are internal. Thus hours of employment and of other necessary services and facilities, landuse patterns, and transportation systems can increase or decrease the pressures arising from internal domestic arrangements.

If conditions in the public sphere are part of the problem, their amelioration should be part of any solution. Societies typically accept innovations (usually technological) that appear progressive, without considering side-effects, other implications, or adaptations possibly needed to cope with these influences. This has been called "cultural lag,"[13] with culture lagging behind technology. In the case under study, acceptance of the virtues of maternal employment have come first, before the full-scale adaptations called for by the addition of employment to a host of other traditional women's obligations.

MATERNAL EMPLOYMENT AND PUBLIC POLICY

Some ways public-sector adaptation could help improve the kind of day experienced by employed mothers are now examined. Since transportation is an obvious consideration, its implications are considered first. The data

also suggest more fundamental, far-reaching changes, which are subsequently discussed. The accumulation of these arguments suggests the need for a new kind of planning.

Transportation Options

As noted above, employed women travel approximately as much as men, but the conditions of travel and their subjective experiences diverge greatly. Optimizing the number and variety of trips that can safely be taken by public transportation would provide both male and female travelers more positive choices in traveling. Public measures making public transit "the better way"[14] for a growing number of trips should help reduce travel tension among those taking such transit trips, as well as among those who choose to drive. Fixed-rail transit systems are particularly popular for everyday commuting (if considered safe).

Public transit can have decided advantages for work trips in central or congested areas, e.g., downtown Toronto. One obvious form of public assistance would be a better distribution of parking lots/garages at non-central subway stations, facilitating safe and inexpensive changes of transportation mode. This would help achieve the most rational choices of travel for the plural activities that must fit into limited time periods.

Can public transit reflect more sensitively the needs of its current users or potential users? The use of public transit for more than one purpose—e.g., combining trips to the work place, for childcare, and shopping—would be facilitated by measures such as economical monthly passes, or transfer formulas that permit stopovers....

Non-Transportation Options Affecting Travel and Everyday Logistics

Logistical problems of everyday travel and their outcomes can also be helped by approaches that reach well beyond purely transportation solutions. Policies only indirectly related to transportation can affect travel and daily life. For example, as noted earlier, work-place flexibility can alleviate travel tension and feelings of daily time pressure, giving employees some additional freedom of action (i.e., a reduction of capability constraints). Moreover, employment systems that reflect more appropriately the time demands on individual employees need much more attention. Working-hour variations within firms, reflecting individual and family needs, are much more likely to provide positive benefits to individuals than flex-time formulas that merely try to redistribute peak travel loads.

Furthermore, the use of job-sharing by interested employees in regular positions could make the benefits of part-time employment more readily available, without the drawbacks of inferior status and benefits. There is evidence that job-sharing employees maintain unusually high productivity records, presumably indicating how job-sharers feel about and respond to the logistical opportunities offered them.[15]

The evidence on daycare location suggests that more suitable sites would help reduce travel tensions of employed mothers. Land-use regulations should be reexamined and modified where necessary to permit daycare centers to operate in the midst of residential clusters, minimizing travel distances from homes, and reducing the need for young children to commute. A second alternative is workplace daycare, which minimizes travel for the mother, though it maximizes travel for the child. Work-place daycare also gives both mother and child opportunities for some daytime access to each other. A third alternative, feasible where public transportation is well developed, is daycare facilities location at major transfer points. While commercial facilities are often found in such locations, they rarely have nonprofit or limited-profit enterprises. . . .

Clustering and Mixed Uses

. . . When daily essentials are within easy hail of home, the kind of trips that put pressure on the daily timetable can be more readily absorbed. So can trips in the absence of a car. In any event, our respondents were definitely interested in having a variety of land uses such as stores, banks, and clinics available closer to home, a preference that was pronounced among respondents expressing greater feelings of time pressure.

Extension of Hours

One of the more common recent changes in community infrastructure is extension of local store hours into the evening and night, as well as Sundays, thereby providing more shopping capability. The private sector has increasingly discovered that many customers find it more convenient to shop and receive deliveries outside traditional store hours. Nighttime has been called our last frontier.[16]

Admittedly, some long-term store employees may dislike the new working hours. Others, however, find new schedules fitting better with their other obligations, or with the schedules of other family members. Young people, for example, can more easily combine school with employment. Pairs of working parents whose schedules differ can provide home childcare without resorting to external sources.

More can be accomplished and with greater ease when people are able to fit employment obligations and other obligations in during the day, without constraints due to a near identity of opening and closing hours. If non-work opportunities are available when people are not at work, a single family car can be used during the day for more purposes. Longer store and service hours thus take some pressure off transportation systems in several ways. Understandably, most of our respondents favored such longer hours for many services and facilities. . . .

There have been private sector adaptations with respect to maternal employment, because providing some kinds of service when needed can be profitable. Out-of-hours needs for public- and nonprofit-sector services are, however, largely not being met. . . .

Notes

[1] A preliminary draft of this report was presented to the Canadian Urban Studies Conference, Institute of Urban Studies, University of Winnipeg, August 16, 1985.

[2] Mary Frank Fox and Sharlene Hess-Biber, *Women at Work* (Palo Alto, Calif.: Mayfield Publishing Company, 1984); Howard Hayghe, "Dual-Earner Families: Their Economic and Demographic Characteristics," Joan Aldous, ed., *Two Paychecks: Life in Dual-Earner Families* (Beverly Hills, Calif.: Sage Publications, Inc., 1982), pp. 27–40; J.T. Mortimer and J. London, "The Varying Linkages of Work and Family," Patricia Voydanoff, ed., *Work and Family: Changing Roles of Men and Women* (Palo Alto, Calif.: Mayfield Publishing Co., 1984), Chapter 2; Valerie K. Oppenheimer, *Work and the Family: A Study in Social Demography* (New York, N.Y.: Academic Press, 1982); and Catherine Ross, John Mirowsky, and Joan Huber, "Dividing Work, Sharing Work, and In Between: Marriage Patterns and Depression," *American Sociological Review* 48(6): 809–823 (December 1983). Hereafter, Ross, Mirowsky, and Huber, "Dividing Work."

[3] William Michelson, *From Sun to Sun: Daily Obligations and Community Structure in the Lives of Employed Women and Their Families* (Totowa, N.J.: Rowman & Allanheld Publishers, 1985). Hereafter, *From Sun to Sun*. The present citation is from Chapter 3, but a more systematic exposition of the general topic and of the findings from the study to be discussed here is found in this book.

[4] Sheila B. Kamerman, *Parenting in an Unresponsive Society: Managing Work and Family Life* (New York, N.Y.: The Free Press, 1980), p. 87.

[5] Ross, Mirowsky, and Huber, "Dividing Work," p. 810.

[6] This research was principally funded through a contribution by the Ministry of National Health and Welfare, National Welfare Grants Program. Basic funding for The Child in the City Programme came from Toronto's Hospital for Sick Children Foundation. Linda Hagarty, Susan Hodgson, and Suzanne Ziegler were co-investigators during various stages of the research and made substantial contributions to it, as did many interviewers, coders, and data processing personnel.

[7] F.M. Carp, *Employed Women as a Transportation-deprived and Transit Dependent Group*, Document No. TM-4-1-74 (Berkeley, Calif.: Metropolitan Transportation Commission, 1974), p. 6.

[8] F.S. Koppelman, et al., "Role Influence in Transportation Decision Making," ed. S. Rosenbloom, *Women's Travel Issues: Research Needs and Priorities* (Washington, D.C.: US, Department of Transportation, 1978), pp. 309–353. Hereafter, Koppelman, "Role Influence." E.P. Levine, "Travel Behavior and Transportation Needs of Women: A Case Study of San Diego, California" (unpublished master's thesis in city planning). San Diego: San Diego State University, 1980. Palm and Pred, *A Time-Geographic Perspective*.

[9] L. Pickup, *Housewives' Mobility and Travel Patterns*, TRRL Laboratory Report 971 (Crowthorne, Berkshire, England: Transport and Road Research Laboratory, 1981). Hereafter, *Housewives' Mobility*. L. Sen. "Travel Patterns and Behavior of Women in Urban Areas," S. Rosenbloom, ed. *Women's Travel Issues: Research Needs and Priorities* (Washington, D.C.: US, Department of Transportation, 1978), pp. 417–436. Hereafter, *Women's Travel Issues*.

[10] A.H. Studenmund, et al., "Women's Travel Behavior and Attitudes: An Empirical Analysis," in *Women's Travel Issues*, pp. 355–379;

Koppelman, "Role Influence"; and *Housewives' Mobility*.

[11] William Michelson, *The Impact of Changing Women's Roles on Transportation Needs and Usage, Final Report*. Grant CA-11-0024, Urban Mass Transportation Administration, US, Department of Transportation (Springfield, Va.: National Technical Information Service, 1983).

[12] *From Sun to Sun*, Chapters 3–10.

[13] William Ogburn, *On Culture and Social Change: Selected Papers*, edited and with an introduction by Otis Dudley Duncan (Chicago, Ill.: University of Chicago Press, 1964).

[14] "The better way" is a slogan used by the Toronto Transit Commission.

[15] Commission of Inquiry into Part-time Work, *Part-time Work in Canada* (Ottawa: Labour Canada, 1983); Gretl S. Meier, *Job Sharing: A New Pattern for Quality of Work and Life* (Kalamazoo, Mich.: W.E. Upjohn Institute for Employment Research, 1979); Noah Meltz, et al., *Sharing the Work: An Analysis of the Issues in Worksharing and Jobsharing* (Toronto: University of Toronto Press, 1981); and Stanley D. Nollen, et al., *Permanent Part-Time Employment: An Interpretive Review*, Vol. I (New York, N.Y.: Praeger Publishing, 1978).

[16] Murray Melbin, "The Colonization of Time," T. Carlstein, et al., eds., *Human Activity and Time Geography* (New York, N.Y.: Halstead Press, 1978), pp. 100–113.

The Family

Introduction

The last section showed that gender relations are in a serious state today, with important effects on family life. The present section will explore this problem further. However, in this section we shall focus somewhat less on gender relations per se, and more on the family as a system of interrelated parts which are not fitting together as well as they once did.

Dorothy Smith gives us a picture of the traditional working class family and some ways that it has changed for the worse where women are concerned. "Women's dependency," she argues, "must be seen as arising in a definite social form and, we have suggested, organized rather differently in differing class settings and relations." Industrial capitalism leads to a restricted, narrowed scope of women's work in the home and greater dependency on a man's wage. Though this restriction is increasing for both middle class and working class women, opportunities for work outside the home are quite different for women of the two classes.

Patriarchy—the domination of men over women—cannot, in this analysis, be separated from class exploitation. Working class wives, in particular, are "locked in by legal and administrative measures instituted by the state and a stratified labour market fostered by trade unions, capitalists and

the state—(securing) the uses of women's domestic labour in the service of a ruling apparatus, ensuring and organizing the domination of a class over the means of production." Stated otherwise, whatever disadvantages women in the labour market keeps them in the home. Whatever keeps them in the home performing unpaid work for the workingman keeps them, indirectly, in the (unpaid) employment of the husband's boss and, hence, the ruling class.

Yet this powerful indictment may be too simple. The situation is changing rapidly: even working class wives are getting jobs and some are even unionizing. In general, dependency on a husband has become less common. The section continues with two papers providing an overview of the modern family or, more properly, "modern families."

Margrit Eichler's contribution argues persuasively that it may no longer be realistic to speak about a typical "modern family." Evidence suggests that the "traditional family" made up of a mother staying home, a father going out to work and a few dependent children biologically related to mother and father may simply not be typical any more. Increasingly, mothers are not staying at home: they are going out to work. Increasingly, fathers are leaving their wives and children; the divorce rate

411

has been growing dramatically since the late 1960s. Second batches of children often accompany divorce and remarriage. Fewer Canadian households are composed only of people related by blood.

Family members unrelated by blood may have unpredictable economic as well as psychological relations with one another. We are far from knowing what kinds of social and economic responsibilities *ought* to accompany these nontraditional family roles; but we can no longer assume that they are being performed as in the past. We cannot assume, for example, that Johnny's mother's new husband will accept a responsibility—economic, social and psychological—toward Johnny that is anything like the responsibility Johnny's father had assumed by the mere fact of biological fatherhood. What becomes even more problematic is that once Johnny's biological father remarries and, possibly, fathers some new children, he may ignore his own legal (and emotional) obligations to Johnny. Even the enforcement of child support payments from biological fathers, a minimal kind of parental obligation, is very far from satisfactory at present. We can assume that many Canadian children are going without adequate fathering today.

The "family" is an institution in crisis. No one quite knows what it is or how it is supposed to operate. The traditional norms of "love, honour and obey," whether between spouses or between parents and children, are so commonly violated that they cannot be assumed to be in effect. The greater variety, changeability and complexity of new family forms have not, as yet, given rise to new norms and expectations. As a result, the term "family" is becoming less useful as the description of a common social arrangement; for this reason, it can no longer be a central concept of legislation.

We spoke in the last section about the concept of *patria potestas*. Under this system, the family as a whole had certain rights and responsibilities, and these were parcelled out to family members as the family head saw fit. Today people no longer want to submerge rights and responsibilities in a social unit: we typically prefer to treat people *as* individuals. But Professor Eichler points out that the very *possibility* of treating people as members of social units is gone, since families are so various and unpredictable. We must stop thinking about people as *spouses* or *parents* or *children* of other people. More than ever in our history, we have become a society of individuals and this fact must be reflected in our laws and social services.

Not only do families vary enormously from one another; they also vary dramatically over time. There is a family life cycle, just as there is an individual life cycle. Like individuals, families pass through stages of functioning and well-being. At each stage the individuals involved confront new problems, try to solve them or adjust to them, then move on to another stage. What Eugen Lupri and James Frideres show in their article on this topic is striking for several reasons.

They find first a general, marked, lengthy decline in marital satisfaction while children are growing up; and a return to high levels of marital satisfaction after all the children have left home. This finding is certainly no advertisement for childbearing and parenthood.

If our argument in the last section that women bear a disproportionate share of the family tasks is valid, then women ought to express less satisfaction with marriage than men. Women who have both children and a job to take care of ought to be the least satisfied. Professors Lupri and Frideres show that these women's marital satisfaction really is much lower than their husband's. Parenting has a less negative effect on husbands than on wives; but then, husbands aren't doing the work.

This reminds us of sociologist Jesse Bernard's dictum that, in every family, there are two marriages: *his* marriage and *her* marriage (1973). *His* marriage demands a cozy household, loving wife, and little children to continue the family name. *Her* marriage provides the cozy household, takes care of the children, provides emotional support, and brings in additional income when needed. Marriage simply benefits men more than women. For men, it is a support; for women, a burden. These facts are borne out in many studies. For example, Durkheim, in research on suicide discussed by Professor Brym in Section One, showed that marriage reduced the likelihood of suicide more for men than for women. Recent studies have shown a greater susceptibility of married women than single women or married men to mental breakdown.

The article by Nathan Keyfitz in this section takes us a little bit further by showing us the size of marriage's benefit for men. Using a new and somewhat complex calculation procedure, Professor Keyfitz shows that, at age twenty-five, a married man's life expectancy is about five years longer than a single man's of the same age. By contrast, the benefit of marriage for a twenty-five-year-old woman is only about one and a half years. By this measure, marriage is over three times as beneficial for men as it is for women.

The family is always changing, for a variety of reasons. Some of the change is due to gender conflict; some, to the effect of changing family norms. Some is due to the life cycle stresses discussed by Professors Lupri and Frideres, and some is the result of economic pressures that demand two incomes, hence two careers. In the preceding section, Professor Michelson discussed the strains caused by a shortage of time. However some of the strains on a family are more narrowly demographic. In the last hundred or so years,

demographic changes have produced interesting changes in family life, as Roderic Beaujot and Kevin McQuillan show in their article in this section. A lengthening life expectancy, combined with a shortened childbearing period, has produced a different balance of marital time. In the past, spouses spent most of their married life in the company of children. Almost as soon as they married, children began to arrive; no sooner had all the children grown up and left but one of the spouses died. There was little opportunity for spouses to really get to know each other as individuals.

Today, thanks to contraception, couples wait a longer time to start a family, and they typically finish after only one or two children. Roughly twenty to twenty-five years after the start of childbearing, the couple is on its own again, with another twenty to thirty years of marriage ahead of them. Yet just as these demographic changes have extended the possible period of child-free marriage, people have been choosing (increasingly) to divorce and start new families. Thus, the child-free marriage actually lived today may not be much longer than it was a century ago. How do we explain this interesting fact?

One possible explanation is that people divorce more often today because they cannot stand the prospect of a prolonged child-free marriage with a less than perfect spouse. When people thought married life would be short and/or filled with work and children, they might have demanded less in a spouse. Today, as marriage comes to focus less on procreation and ever more on companionship, romance and pleasure, imperfections in a mate become strong motivators to divorce. The shortening of dissatisfaction cannot be left entirely to death.

Paradoxically, most married people today make the decision to separate and divorce when they are in the middle of their marital life cycle—that is, when emotional satisfaction is declining rapidly or at its nadir, according to Lupri and Frideres. Perhaps if they knew that when their children left satisfaction would return and the remaining years of marriage would be more happy ones, parents would be slower to divorce and to remarry and, by starting a new family, go through the same upsetting process a second time.

Children appear to be a great burden, coming between spouses, making work for parents (especially mothers), destroying marital satisfaction and conceivably causing many divorces in that way. Of course, individual children are not to blame. At fault is the social relationship of parent-and-child in the context of two main forces in our culture. One is gender inequality, already discussed. So long as the tasks of parenthood are shared out so unfairly, they will inevitably lead to resentment, conflict and marriage breakdown. The children are not to blame, though they will bear much of the consequence.

The second main force is hedonistic individualism. Increasingly, people want the freedom to pursue and enjoy their own interests. This desire tends to corrode family life and, especially, parenthood, which demands a great deal of unexpected effort and activity. Not surprisingly, then, as contraception has improved, more and more people have chosen not to have families: they have remained childless by choice. From this standpoint, it is remarkable that so many people continue to have children at all. This persistence of childbearers interests Jean Veevers. She pursues the ideological sources of pro-natalism: why people feel bad—guilty, ashamed, worried, and so on—if they do *not* have children.

She notes that, increasingly, people are willing to admit they do not want children because childbearing would cut into their career, leisure or enjoyment of spouse and friends: concerns that are completely justifiable. Yet the majority of adults are unwilling to stay childless. Some may not foresee the consequences of deciding to have children. Others may conform to social expectations because they are afraid not to, or don't want to disappoint their parents. A great many, especially women, vaguely fear that if they passed up childbearing, they would discover too late what they had missed. Some aspect of their femininity would go undeveloped forever.

Much can be said in favour of parenthood. Yet Professor Veevers is right to claim that the parental decision is strongly influenced by ideological factors no less emotion-laden than, and probably related to, our culture's gender stereotypes. Until we see this ideology for what it is, and make the right decisions for the right reasons, childbearing will continue to disrupt family life. Many of these problems are complex. No one knows whether solutions should be sought at home or in the political arena, as personal troubles or public issues. Certainly, our family structures and family problems are more complex than they ever were. More complex solutions than ever will be needed.

References

Bernard, Jesse, *The Future of Marriage*. New York: Bantam Books, 1973.

41 Women, the Family and the Productive Process

Dorothy E. Smith

DOROTHY E. SMITH did her undergraduate work at the London School of Economics and got her Ph.D. from the University of California at Berkeley. She has taught at universities in the United States, Britain and Canada and is currently Professor in the Department of Sociology in Education at the Ontario Institute for Studies in Education. She has published extensively on women's issues as well as in the social organization of knowledge, combining these interests in a book, *The Everyday World as Problematic: A Feminist Sociology* (Northeastern University Press, 1987).

THE CHANGING MATERIAL BASES OF DEPENDENCY

Dependency of married women, and particularly women with children, on men and men's salaries or wages is a feature of both middle class and working class family relations in contemporary capitalism. This is not simply a matter of universal family form characteristic of a species rather than a culture or mode of production. Women's dependency must be seen as arising in a definite social form and organized rather differently in differing class settings and relations. One view identifies the emergence of this type of family organization with the rise of capitalism. As the productive process is increasingly taken over by the industrial organization of production, the family becomes a consuming rather than a producing unit, and women's domestic labour ceases to play a socially productive role and becomes a personal service to the wage earner. Her domestic labour reproduces the labour power of the individual worker. Here is Seccombe's account:

> With the advent of industrial capitalism, the general labour process was split into two discrete units: a domestic and an industrial unit. The character of the work performed in each was fundamentally different. The domestic unit reproduced labour power for the labour market. The industrial unit produced goods and services for the commodity market. This split in the labour process had produced a split in the labour force roughly along sexual lines—women into the domestic unit, men into industry.[1]

But as we acquire more historical knowledge of women we find that the sharpness of this supposed historical moment becomes blurred. The emergence of the dependent family form is slow and seemingly contingent upon elaborations and developments of the original separation of domestic economy from the industrial process. As we explore the dynamic process at work we can recognize a contradiction in the rise of capitalism so far as women and their relation to the family are concerned. It seems that the same industrial capitalism leading apparently to a restriction and narrowing of the scope of women's work in the home and to her and her children's dependency on a man's wage is also a process which potentially advances women's independence by making it, in principle at least, possible for women to earn enough to support themselves, perhaps even to support their children. Productive labour was formerly tied to sex differences by different physical and biological situations and also by the intimate ties of skills which were earlier a true specialization of persons from childhood or youth on. As production is increasingly mediated by machine technologies and increasingly organized as a form of enterprise specifically separated from particular individuals and their local relations, it is also increasingly indifferent to social differentiations, such as gender or race.[2] At every new level in the development of productive capacity in capitalism, this contradition is apparent. Capitalism continually represents the possibility of women's independence and at the same time engenders conditions and responses which have constituted a fully dependent form of family unit. It seems then that the dependency of both middle class and working class women on the individual man's salary or wage must be examined in relation to the organization of the labour market and employment possibilities for women outside the home.

Over time, working class and middle class patterns of family organization have become more alike with respect to the wife's dependency on her husband's wage or salary. But the history of that relation is very different. The earlier civil status of a man simply obliterated his wife's as she was subsumed in the family economic unit identified with him. She had no place in civil society, no capacity for economic action, at least so long as she was married. What she produced, what she earned, if she did earn, was his. Later her domestic labour becomes subordinated to the enterprise of his career, and employment outside the home is organized to ensure that the jurisdictions of male authority and appropriation of women's labour inside the home and outside it do not interfere with one another. Dependency is part of a perpetuated

pattern of excluding women, and married women in particular, from functioning as independent economic agents.

This history of the present family form among the working class is very different. It does not begin with women's exclusion from economic activity and it does not involve the formation of a property-holding unit identified with the man. The legal forms were the same, and those gave men the right to women's earnings, but the actual practice and organization of work relations and economic contributions did not conform to the bourgeois or middle class pattern. The exclusive dependency of women on men's wages is only gradually established and is differently structured. For working class women, dependency is directly on the man's wage-earning capacity and role, and a man's status and authority in the family is directly linked to his capacity to earn. Moore and Sawhill summarize the sociological studies on the effects of wives' employment outside the home on marital power relations, drawing attention to the greater effect among working class women.

> A number of studies have found that wives who are employed exercise a greater degree of power in their marriages.... Working women have more say especially in financial decisions. This tendency for employment to enhance women's power is strongest among lower and working class couples.[3]

As we learn more of the history, we find that the emergence of the dependent form of the family among the working class was far from an abrupt and immediate consequence of the rise of industrial capitalism. The subsistence work of women in relation to the household as an economic unit has only gradually been supplanted by the industrial process. Only gradually have women been weaned from contributing to the *means* of household subsistence as contrasted with labour applied to the direct production of the subsistence of its members. There is also an active process of excluding women, and married women in particular, from the labour market. This is a response to the indifference of the industrial enterprise to the sex of the worker as such and of the tendency to use women whose lower wages made them attractive in competition with men; but it is also a more general response to the emergence of an endemic problem within capitalism, the creation of a permanent and increasing surplus labour population. On the one hand women came into competition with men for jobs in industry and, on the other, their labour was essential in the home, so that house and family were in competition with industry for women's labour. Working class men through their representative organizations, trade unions, sought to resolve these dual stresses by stratifying the labour force in such a way that women did not compete with men, and that they continued to be paid at rates which ensured that industry could not compete with the family. Concomitantly they aimed at a wage for men sufficient to maintain a family.

The dependence of the mother-children unit on the male wage-earner emerges rather slowly. Anderson describes, for early 19th century Lancashire, a form of family in which all its members (with the exception of the very young and the very old) worked outside the home and contributed their earnings. Scott and Tilly have identified a distinct form of working class and petit bourgeois family economy which they describe as the "family wage economy." It is one in which each member earns and contributes to a common fund out of which the family needs are met. They argue that although a relatively small proportion of married women were employed in industry until relatively late in the 19th century, the pattern of women not contributing actively to the household economy comes very late. A wife who did not earn or otherwise contribute directly to the family means of subsistence and who had to depend upon her husband's wage was most definitely undesirable. Married women worked outside the home, and brought money or goods into the home in all kinds of ways. They took in lodgers. Many had gardens and produced for their families and could sell the small surplus they might produce. Women were small traders, peddlars, went into domestic service, were launderers, seamstresses, farm labourers, scavengers, as well as industrial workers.

Under the "family wage" economy children were essential contributors. Children might be employed in factory work, but they had also a wide variety of opportunities for contribution ranging from care of younger children while parents were at work, to housekeeping, gardening, and many ordinary chores such as fetching water—as well as odd jobs when these were available. As attendance at public school came to be enforced the school came into competition with the needs of the family for children's labour.[4]

With the institutionalization of universal education, children cease to be regular wage earners contributing to the family wage from early in life. They cease progressively to contribute to the everyday work activities of household work and childcare. Previously the work of children would have relieved the mother of at least some of her household obligations and made it easier for her to undertake employment outside the home.[5] The withdrawal of child labour from the household, as well as from the labour force, required the presence of mothers in the home. Indeed, the home came to be organized around the scheduling of school and work so that the mother was tied down to the household in a way which was in fact new.

The shift was from the family wage economic organization to the new enucleated form in which wife and child made no contribution to the family economy with inputs from outside and in which both depended on the man as wage earner and the wife depended upon him for the means to reproduce the domestic order. She was to provide for her husband the personal service in the form of domestic labour in the home as well as other more immediately personal services. These developments were part of major developments in capitalism and the institutionalization of responses to them, resulting in the type of segregated labour force we find today.

Though we do not possess a distinct historical picture, it seems likely that women's labour in relation to household and family subsistence has been particularly subject to the process of transfer to the industrial process. The pre-capitalist division of labour assigned to women tasks more immediately linked to the moment of consumption, more directly productive of actual individual subsistence. Further, much of women's labour involved processing rather than primary production—spinning, weaving, preserving, dairying, etc. These therefore were productive processes which had an "instant" mass market, and they have been progressively absorbed into the industrial process—textiles being among the first. Our histories have focussed on the displacement of the artisan weavers by the industrial process, but they have not focussed on the displacement of women's domestic labour by the industrial process. Cobbett, writing about England in the early 19th century, and learning about the conditions of people in rural areas, describes the shame and despair of married women in one area whose capacity to contribute to the "family wage" household was cut off by the appropriation of the weaving of straw hats by commercial enterprises. Nellie McClung describes the sad uselessness of her mother's skills as a weaver of wool cloth as she was displaced by the commercial product.[6]

Changes in urban development have transformed the relation of women to opportunities for work. For example, Cross's description of late 19th century Montreal clearly shows the concentration of women in neighbourhoods close to opportunities for employment.[7] The development of mass transit systems, highways and the working class suburb has transformed this relation. These changes are not simply the result of real estate developments. They are linked also to the increased concentration of capital and to the horizontal integration of the work process. Earlier industry tended to be organized as a multiplicity of small factories engaged in different aspects of a total process, and the organization of the final product was a market process. Progressively these were integrated into a single organizational and manufacturing process. Concentration is not just on paper. In changing the work situation and the relation of worker to machine, it also changes the relation to locality. The existence of numbers of small factories or other enterprises similarly organized in relation to a local supply of labour was the economic basis of the persistence of stable working class neighbourhoods. For women this meant access to employment close to where they lived. It meant greater flexibility in relation to their responsibilities in the home. Furthermore the stability of the neighbourhood made possible the development of networks of kin and pseudo-kin who could help out with child care, with food, cooking and with an interchange of household and housekeeping facilities. This is the type of neighbourhood organization in which the mother becomes a key figure.

The development of primary resource industries so characteristic of the Canadian economy requires the location of the industrial process at the source. It is hence indifferent to its relation to other industry or sources of employment. These are situations which show the sharpest dependency of women on men.

THE PATRIARCHAL ORGANIZATION OF THE WORKING CLASS FAMILY

The dynamic processes of capital accumulation involve an increasingly extensive use of machines making labour more productive.

From these processes, two consequences flow for working class women. The first is a tendency of machines to displace labour, generating over time a surplus labour population. This functions as a reserve army of labour in relation to the opening up of new areas of capital investment. The expansion of markets and of opportunities for investment retards the actual appearance of a surplus as such, but the steadily increasing rate of unemployment over time identifies a tendency which cannot be wholly suppressed and is quickened by the monopolistic process of corporate capitalism. The emergence of a permanent surplus labour population is relatively independent of unemployment created in the "crises of overproduction" which periodically throw capitalist economies into recession.[8] The presence of this "reserve army of labour" tends to sharpen the competition of workers for jobs and hence to lower the price of labour-power (the wage). A second consequence is that technological advances have also made differences in physical strength and in skills developed over a lifetime of practice of decreasing significance in the productive process. Parallel to the developments of capitalism, which among the ruling class make participation in the exercise of power indifferent to sex, is a development of the productive process rendering it also increasingly indifferent to the sex of the worker. Hence as the surplus labour population increases and competition sharpens, women come into competition with men for jobs. The traditionally lower wages of historically disadvantaged groups such as women and blacks gave them an advantage in competing for jobs which employers had no hesitation in deploying to their own advantage.

Through the 19th and early 20th centuries, this problem was a recurrent theme in male working class views concerning women in the labour force and in the policies of trade and labour unions. The issue for men was not only that of jobs. It was also the implications for the family and for men's traditional status in the family. Various 19th century writers, including Marx himself,[9] saw women's participation in industry as destructive of their "natural" female virtues and modes of being. These "virtues" were intimately tied to notions of passivity and subordination and a restriction of women's spheres of action to a narrow conception of the domestic. Both working class and middle class were marked by the prohibition for women (and for children) of self-knowledge of their sexuality and control of their own bodies. The physical fragility of women, their supposedly natural weakness, is also related to the ways in which women's physical existence was subordinated to that of the husband and children.[10]

When women were employed outside the home and could earn a wage sufficient for independence, their departure from the ideals of femininity became a subject of reprobation. Of the early 19th century, Malmgreen writes:

> Lord Ashley, speaking on behalf of the regulation of child and female labour in factories, warned the House of Commons of the "ferocity" of the female operatives, of their adoption of male habits—drinking, smoking, forming clubs, and using "disgusting" language. This, he claimed, was "a perversion of nature," likely to produce "disorder, insubordination, and conflict in families."[11]

The voice here is that of the ruling class, but on this issue the working class man and the ruling class were united. Malmgreen notes that in the early 19th century this view appears particularly prevalent among leading artisans in the working class movements of Britain in that period. It is the interests of a similar type of worker, crafts and trades workers, which were represented in the American Federation of Labor (AFL). The AFL played a leading role in the organization of a sex stratified (as well as a racially stratified) labour market,[12] as corporate capitalism began its great rise in North America in the late 19th and early 20th centuries.

The AFL at this period began to lay down the institutional basis for the sexually stratified labour force we find today. It is not, of course, that the labour force had not been segregated on a sexual basis before, but capitalist developments tend to break down the traditional division of labour between the sexes. The response emerging at this period served to constitute the historical segregation on a new basis; and the American Federation of Labor played a central historical role in the redesigning of the labour force, ensuring the privileged position of white men in the North American labour force. These relations were imported into Canada as the so-called "international" unions came to dominate Canadian union organizations.[13] Industries in which both women and men worked, such as the tobacco industry, boot and shoe manufacturing, textiles and clothing, printing and similar industries, established or institutionalized an internal stratification ensuring exclusive male access to the more highly skilled and better paid positions.

This stratification of the labour force within those trades and industries organized by crafts unions survive in the differing job classifications, which, for example, separate bartenders and chefs from waitresses and cooks. These divisions have their base in the internal division of labour resulting from differentiating tasks requiring specialized capacities from those which "anyone" could do.[14] The internal differentiation becomes the basis of a stratified labour force separating a central[15] or core[16] workforce. This comes about in part as the outcome of union struggles, particularly in the early part of the 20th century.[17] The central or core labour force is "insulated," to use Friedman's terms[18] from the "reserve army of labour." It has access to the internal labour market of the corporation and hence the possibilities of mobility within the workplace. Pensions and other benefits have been won and seniority in transfers, layoffs and rehiring has been established; working conditions are regulated to some degree. By contrast, the peripheral labour force is defined by categories of dead-end jobs in the corporation and in localized small industries and service businesses with fluctuating labour needs.[19] It is not insulated from the reserve army of labour—indeed it is in part constitutive of that reserve.

Advances for workers, according to Friedman, have been won through struggle.[20] The struggle for a family wage and for the reduction of the competition of capitalist with man and family for women's labour is the obverse of the struggle to secure stability, good wages and benefits, and to control working conditions, on the part of what becomes the "central" section of the labour force. The central section is characterized by union organization, whereas the peripheral labour force has been relatively less organized. Struggles which have made gains for the central section of the labour force have also been part of the organization of a racially and sexually segregated labour force. Under Gompers' leadership, the trade union movement in North America became for women a systematic organization of weakness relative to men and a systematic organization of preferential access to skills and benefits for white men. There was little interest in unionizing women other than as a means of control.[21] There was fear that bringing numbers of women into a union would result in "petticoat government."[22] Women's locals were sometimes given only half the voting power of men on the grounds that they could only contribute half the dues.[23] The Canadian Trades and Labour Congress in the early 20th century had as an avowed goal that of eliminating women, particularly married women, from the workforce.

Struggles to restrict women's participation, and particularly married women's participation, in the labour force went on under various guises. It does not seem likely, however, that union efforts alone could have been effective in reconstituting the family in a way that fixed women's dependence on men's wages. At that period, however, the state begins to enact legislation in various ways constitutive of a family in which dependency of women and children, or that condition, becomes legally enforceable and is progressively incorporated into the administrative policies of welfare agencies, education, health care, etc. There is an implicit alliance forming during this period between the state and the unions representing male working class interest in the subordination of women to the home and their elimination from an all but marginal role in the labour force.

The emergence of national and international markets and financial organizations, of an organization of productive process implanted into local areas rather than arising indigenously, of conforming to standardized technical plans and standardized machines, tools and other equipment, and of a universalizing of managerial and technical process—all called for a new kind of labour force. Similar exigencies arose also in relation to the military requirements of imperialist expansion and the devastating wars resulting from the conflict of rival empires. This new labour force had to be capable of entering the industrial process anywhere in the society. The need was not only for technically skilled workers, but more generally for a *universalized* labour force, stripped of regional and ethnic cultures, fully literate, English-speaking, familiar with factory discipline and the discipline of the machine and, in relation to the military enterprise in particular, physically healthy. In the production of this labour force, mothering as a form of domestic labour was seen as increasingly important. The mother was given an ancillary role vis-a-vis the school, the school being charged with setting standards for children's health, cleanliness and character. The liberation of women for work in the home became an objective of the ruling class of this period.[24] Here then we find steps taken to reduce the competition of industry and home for women's labour. Various acts restricting the length of women's working day, night shift work, and the physical exertion which could be required of women—were passed.

In these changes we see under a different aspect some of the same developments we have described earlier, in relation to the changing basis of the social organization of the ruling class. It is the period during which, in the United States, the corporations began to predominate. Various legislative steps and administrative developments re-organized, at least, the legal and administrative basis of the family and united the interests of the AFL type of union with those of the section of the ruling class represented by the state. Laws which earlier entitled husband and father to appropriate both his wife's and his children's earnings disappeared. New legislation was passed requiring men to support their wives and children, whether they lived together or not,[25] and administrative processes were developed to enforce the law. Laws such as these became the bases of welfare policies both during the depression years and later. They are built into the welfare practices of today, so that a man sharing the house of a woman welfare recipient may be assumed to be supporting her and her children, hence permitting the suspension of welfare payments to her.[26] Furthermore, the state entry into the socialization of children through the public education system provided an important source of control. Davin has described the early 20th century policies for educating working class girls. They are in line with ruling class interest in a healthy working class and stress the girl's future role as mother.[27] Secondary education developed streaming patterns similar to those characterizing the experience of middle class women. This prevented working class women from acquiring the basic manual and technical skills on which access to skilled and even semi-skilled work in industry came increasingly to depend. Vocational training became almost exclusively a preparation for clerical employment.

The depression years established a clear

conjunction between the interests of organized labour and of the state (and of some sections of the ruling class) in as far as possible eliminating married women from the labour force. The state adopted various measures designed to ensure that one wage would provide for two adults and their children (some of the legislation mentioned above was passed during the depression years). The emergence of Unemployment Insurance and Pension Plans created an administrative organization building in the wife's dependency on her husband. In the United States, job creation programmes omitted creating jobs for women.[28] The man as wage earner and the woman as dependent became the legally enforceable and administratively constituted relation. In this way the increasing costs of reproducing the new kind of labour force, including the costs of women's specialization in domestic labour, would be borne by the working man and his wage.

It would be, however, a serious mistake to see these reactions as merely the expression of a patriarchal impulse. Women's domestic labour was of vital and survival value of the family unit. Subsistence was still dependent upon the work of women in a way which is no longer so. The adequacy of shelter, the preparation and cooking of food, including making bread, the making and maintenance of clothing, the management of the wage, are crucial. The availability of a woman's unpaid labour was highly consequential to the household standard of living. The physical maintenance of the male breadwinner was an essential feature. When food was short, women and children would go without to ensure that the "master" got enough, or at least the best of what there was. As the family was increasingly integrated into the monetary economy, the role of women was more and more that of managing and organizing the expenditures of the wages. Women became experts in managing[29] and experts also in going without, themselves.[30] It seems likely that at a certain point the re-

quirements of domestic labour began to come into direct competition with work outside the home. A family could manage better if the mother did not go out to work, but was able to devote herself full-time to domestic labour and the production of subsistence. The concentration of the wage earning function in the man also liberated women's domestic labour to maintaining and increasing the family's standard of living. More time spent in the processing of food, more time to give to mending and making clothes, more time to give to cleanliness and maintaining of warmth and shelter resulted in material improvements in the family's standard of living. Where men could not earn enough, women with young children were confronted with the dilemma of whether to go out and earn what little they could so that the children could eat, running the risks that a lack of adequate care for the children created, or whether to stay home and give the children adequate care when they could not get enough to eat.[31] The improvement over time in men's wages reduced, though it has not eliminated, this dilemma. It is implicit in the situation of working classes because it is always present in the wage relation. As real wages decline, the spread of families in which the wife goes out to work increases.

Characteristic also of the working class family, in which the man is the breadwinner, and the women and children are dependent, is a marked subordination of women to men's needs. Control over funds is a distinct male prerogative. A husband's resistance to his wife's going out to work goes beyond the practicalities of the family's economic well being (Rubin). Working class women learn a discipline which subordinates their lives to the needs and wishes of men. The man's wage is his. It is not a family wage. Varying customs have developed around the disposal of this. Sometimes there appears to be a survival of the "family wage" tradition whereby the wife takes the whole wage and manages its various uses, including a man's pocket money. But it is also open to men not to tell their wives what they earn and to give them housekeeping money or require them to ask for money for each purchase. It is clearly "his" money and there is an implicit contract between a husband and wife whereby he provides for her and her children on whatever conditions he thinks best and she provides for him any personal and household services that he demands. The household is organized in relation to his needs and wishes; meal times are when he wants his meals; he eats with the children or alone as he chooses; sex is when he wants it; the children are to be kept quiet when he does not want to hear them. The wife knows at the back of her mind that he can, if he wishes, take his wage earning capacity and make a similar "contract" with another woman. As wages have increased, the breadwinner's spending money has enlarged to include leisure activities which are his, rather than hers—a larger car, a motorcycle, a boat and even the camper often proves more for him than for her, since for her it is simply a transfer from convenient to less convenient conditions of the same domestic labour as she performs at home.

Unemployment of the man has a shattering effect on this type of family. Men's identity as men is built into their role as breadwinner, as spender in relation to other men, as patriarch within the family. The extent to which their masculinity is dependent upon capitalism appears powerfully in the context of unemployment when the claims and entitlements built into the "contract" are undermined. No matter how hard wives may attempt to replicate the forms of the proper relation, over time the situation itself falsifies their efforts and it is apparent to both. In some instances the hostility latent in woman's submission in these contexts becomes overt as a repudiation of the man who does not earn a wage. The underlying basis of relations has changed. The man is not what he was, his relations are not what they were, because the material determinations outside his control and the control of members of his family are not what they were. Hence his moral claims, his right to authority, based on these material relations, are undermined. He was not what he thought he was. His masculine identity, his authority over his wife and children, his status with other men were always based on relations outside the family and not within is grasp. His masculinity was not really his after all.

> How absurd to call the majority of these men the owners of anything when they do not own their jobs in production, and their very bread is the private property of another.[32]

For working class women, this relation has a political dimension. The discipline of acceptance of situations over which they have no control and the discipline of acceptance of the authority of a man who also has in fact no control over the conditions of his wage earning capacity is not compatible with the bold and aggressive styles of political or economic action necessarily characteristic of working class organization. Women's sphere of work and responsibility is defined as subordinate to that in which men act and it is indeed dependent and subordinate. The children's wellbeing, the production of the home, these require from women a discipline of self-abnegation and service as exacting as that of a religious order and just as taxing emotionally. Masculinity and male status is in part expressed in men's successful separation from the subordination of the sphere of women's activity as well as the visibility of his success in "controlling" his wife (what may go on behind the scenes is another matter). The fact that the wage relation creates an uncertain title to male status and authority by virtue of how its conditions are lodged in the market process and exigencies of capital make the visible forms of relations all the more important. Men subordinate themselves in the workplace to the authority of the foreman, supervisor and manager. A condition of their authority in the home is this daily acceptance of the authority of others. They assume also the physical risks and hazards of their work. They live with the ways in which capital uses them up physically and discards them mentally and psychologically. They undertake a lifetime discipline also, particularly if they elect to marry and support a wife and children. That responsibility is also a burden and it can be a trap for working class men as much as for working class women. Through that relation a man is locked into his job and into the authority relations it entails. His wife's subordination, her specific personal and visible subservience, her economic dependence, is evidence of his achievement. Her "nagging," her independent initiatives in political or economic contexts, her public challenges to his authority—these announce his failure as a man.[33] In the political context, we find a sub-culture prohibiting women's participation in political activity other than in strictly ancillary roles essentially within the domestic sphere. Thus when women organized militant action in support of the men striking in the Flint, Michigan strike in 1937, they had to go against norms restraining women from overt forms of political action.

Union organization is based upon, and enhances the separation and powers created by, the wage relation. Obviously and simply the union is an organization of wage-earners. The individualized appropriation of the wage by the man or woman who earns it is institutionalized in a collective organization of workers attempting to control the wage and the conditions under which it is earned. Wives and families dependent upon the wage have no title to represent their interests. I am not suggesting that these interests are always ignored. I am pointing rather to how collective policy and decision-making of wage earners institutionalizes an individual worker's exclusive right to the wage. A sphere of economic action is created for workers quite separated from the domestic sphere. The interchange between the two is a matter for the individual wage earner. The conse-

quences of union decisions and policies are consequences for wives and families, but they have no voice other than through the individual wage earner.

Malmgreen suggests that the 19th century saw a decline in the militancy of working class women associated with the institutionalization of what I have called here the dependent form of the family.

> The apolitical quietism of working class women has its origin in the development of male-female economic relations during the industrial revolution. Its preconditions are the exclusion of women from the skilled, organized sectors of the work force; the embracing of middle class norms of "femininity" and family structure; and the rejection by the male-dominated labour movement of some essential features of Utopian social ideology.[34]

The Utopian social ideology to which Malmgreen refers was one calling for women's political and economic equality.

Earlier we cited Malmgreen's description of an instance of ruling class fear of the "ferocity" of female operatives. Lord Ashley clearly identified the subordination of women to men in the home with their political suppression. The ideology of the weak and passive women, needing protection and support and subordinated "naturally" to the authority of men in the home, as it was adopted by working class men and working class political and economic organizations, served to secure the political control of one section of the working class by another. The subordination of working class women to men in the family, which was perfected progressively over the latter half of the 19th century and the first quarter of the 20th, is integral to the attempt of the ruling class to establish a corporate society subordinating workers through their union organization. The range of organized working class action is narrowed progressively to economic organization restricted to the workplace. A whole range of concerns and interests arising outside the workplace—

in relation to health, housing, pollution, and education—remain unexpressed or expressed only indirectly. Localized neighbourhood and community concerns have yet to develop an organized and continuing political voice. Inadvertently, working class men combine to suppress and silence those whose work directly engages them with such problems and concerns. Indirectly and through the mechanism described above they come to serve the interests of a ruling class in the political and economic subordination of half the working class.

Notes

[1] Wally Seccombe, "The Housewife and Her Labours Under Capitalism," in *New Left Review*, No. 83, 1974, pp. 3–24.

[2] Patricia Connelly, *Last Hired, First Fired: Women and the Canadian Work Force*, Toronto: The Women's Press, 1978.

[3] Kristin A. Moore and Isabell V. Sawhill, "Implications of women's employment for home," in A.H. Stromberg and S. Harkess eds. *Women Working: Theories and Facts in Perspective*, Mayfield Publishing Co., Palo Alto, Cal., 1978, pp. 201–225.

[4] See, for example, the records of Truant Officers excerpted by Alison Prentice in Alison L. Prentice and Susan E. Houston, eds. *Family, School and Society in 19th Century Canada*, Toronto: Oxford University Press, 1975.

[5] Louise A. Tilly and John W. Scott, *Women, Work and Family*, New York: Holt Rinehart and Winston, 1978.

[6] Nellie McClung, *In Times Like These*, Toronto, University of Toronto Press, 1972.

[7] Suzanne D. Cross, "The Neglected Majority: The Changing Role of Women in 19th Century Montreal," in S.M. Trofimenkoff and A. Prentice, eds. *The Neglected Majority: Essays in Canadian Women's History*, Toronto: McClelland and Stewart, 1977, pp. 66–86.

[8] Agnes Smedley, *Daughter of Earth*, The Feminist Press, Old Westbury, Conn., 1973.

[9] See Karl Marx, *Capital, a Critical Analysis of Capitalist Production, Vol. I.*, Foreign Languages Publishing House, Moscow, no date, pp. 628–648, and Patricia Connelly, *Last Hired, First Fired: Women in the Canadian Labour Force*, Toronto: The Women's Press, Toronto, 1978, pp. 10–33.

[10] Oren suggests that women were regularly undernourished because they went without so that husbands and children should have more. Laura Oren, "The welfare of women in laboring families: England 1860–1950," *Feminist Studies I* (1973), pp. 107–125.

[11] Gail Malmgreen, *Neither Bread Nor Roses: Utopian Feminists and the English Working Class*, 1800–1850, A "Studies in Labour History" pamphlet, John L. Noyce, publisher, Brighton, U.K. 1978, p. 23.

[12] Philip S. Foner, *The Politics and Practices of the American Federation of Labor, 1900–1909, Vol. 3.*, and *History of the Labor Movement in the United States*, New York: International Publishers, 1964, pp. 219–255.

[13] Jack Scott, *Canadian Workers, American Unions, How the American Federation of Labour Took Over Canada's Unions.* Vol. II of *Trade Unions and Imperialism in America*, Vancouver: New Star Books, 1978.

[14] Harry Braverman, *Labor and Monopoly Capital: The Degradation of Work in the Twentieth Century*, Monthly Review Press, New York, 1974, p. 80.

[15] Andrew L. Friedman, *Industry and Labour: Class Struggle at Work and Monopoly Capitalism*, The Macmillan Press, London, 1977.

[16] Donald H. Clairmont, Martha MacDonald and Fred C. Wien, "A segmentation approach to poverty and low-wage work in the Maritimes" paper No. 6, Marginal Work World Program, Institute of Public Affairs, Dalhousie University, 1978.

[17] Friedman, op. cit.

[18] Ibid, p. 105.

[19] See, for example, R.C. Edwards, "The social relations in the firm and labor market structure" in R.C. Edwards, M. Reich and D.M. Gordon eds. *Labor Market Segmentation*, D.C. Heath Company, Lexington, Mass, 1978., and Clairmont et al., op. cit.

[20] Friedman, op. cit.

[21] Joan Sangster, "The 1907 Bell Telephone Strike: Organizing Women Workers," *Labour: Journal of Canadian Labour Studies*, Vol. 3, 1978, pp. 109–130.

[22] Ibid.

[23] Foner, op. cit., Sangster, op. cit., and James J. Keneally, *Women and American Trade Unions*, Montreal: Eden Press Women's Publications, Inc., 1978, p. 18.

[24] Anna David, "Imperialism and motherhood" in *History Workshop: A Journal of Socialist Historians*, Issue 5, Spring 1978, pp. 9–65.

[25] See National Council of Women in Canada, *Legal Status of Women in Canada*, Canada Department of Labour, 1924.

[26] Elizabeth Wilson, *Women and the Welfare State*, Tavistock Publications, London, 1978.

[27] Anna Davin

[28] See Jane Humphries, "Women: Scapegoats and Safety Valves in the Great Depression", *Review of Radical Political Economics*, Vol. 8, No. 1, Spring, 1976, pp. 98–117, and Ruth Milkman, "Women's Work and Economic Crisis: Some Lessons of the Great Depression", Ibid, pp. 73–97.

[29] Mrs. Pember Reeves, *Round About a Pound a Week*, G. Bell and Sons, London, 1913.

[30] Richard Hoggart, *The Uses of Literacy*, London, Chatto & Windus, 1958.

[31] Clementina Black, *Married Women's Work*, G. Bell & Sons, London, 1915.

[32] Mary Inman, "In Women's Defense", (Los Angeles: Committee to Organize the Advancement of Women, 1940) in Gerda Lerner, ed. *The Female Experience: An American Documentary*, Indianapolis, Bobbs-Merrill, 1977.

[33] Lillian Breslow Rubin, *Worlds of Pain: Life in the Working Class Family*, New York: Basic Books, 1976.

[34] Gail Malmgreen, op. cit., and see also, Jill Liddington and Jill Morris, *One Hand Tied Behind Us: The Rise of the Women's Suffrage Movement*, Virago, London, 1978.

42 Models of the Family

Margrit Eichler

MARGRIT EICHLER, Professor of Sociology at the Ontario Institute for Studies in Education, Toronto, specializes in the study of family, women's studies and gender relations. Her books and monographs include *The Double Standard: A Feminist Critique of Feminist Social Science* (1980); *Women in Future Research* (1982); *Canadian Families Today: Recent Changes and their Policy Consequences* (1983); *On the Treatment of the Sexes in Research*, with Jeanne Lapointe (1985); and *Canadian Families: An Introduction*, with Mary Bullen (1986). In addition, numerous papers have been published and presented on related topics. Professor Eichler has been centrally involved in the administration of the Canadian Research Institute for the Advancement of Women, and has acted as consultant to such organizations as TV Ontario, Statistics Canada, the Secretary of State's Women's Program and the Canadian Advisory Council on the Status of Women. Between 1984–1986, she served as Chairperson of the Sociology Department at OISE.

INTRODUCTION

... It is the major thesis of this paper that within sociology a monolithic definition of the family still prevails, that this definition is not only inadequate but leads to the replacement of empirical questions with assumptions and informs our data collection process in such a manner that we remain unaware of the severity of the misfit between our assumptions and reality. In turn, this leads to a neglect of vitally important questions, and to a misperception of what constitutes "problem" families. Ultimately, such thinking results in social policies which are inadequate for meeting the needs of individual families, their individual members, and society at large.

THE MONOLITHIC MODEL OF THE FAMILY

We can conceptualize the various functions and conditions as dimensions of familial interactions which together make up the structure of the family. These dimensions can be identified as follows:
—the legal dimension
—the procreative dimension
—the sexual dimension
—the residential dimension
—the economic dimension
—the emotional dimension

Within each of these dimensions various degrees of interaction can be identified. In the following, we will explore the range of possible interactions and provide a formal definition of the monolithic family model.

Legal dimension. Legal aspects range from prescribing interaction in other dimensions (e.g., a marriage has to be sexually consummated to be legally valid, children reside by law with their parents), over leaving them legally undefined, to proscribing them (e.g., a court order restraining a violent husband from entering the matrimonial home).

Procreative dimension. Procreative interaction ranges from a couple having child(ren) with each other and only with each other, over one or both of them having child(ren) with other partners plus having child(ren) together, to having children only with other partners or having none at all.

Socialization dimension. Interaction in the socialization dimension ranges from both parents being involved in the socialization of their children, over only one of them being involved, (e.g., in the case of a divorce in which one parent has custody and the other has not even visitation rights) to neither of them being involved (e.g., when the child has been given up for adoption).

Sexual dimension. Sexual interaction ranges from a marital couple having sex only with each other, over having sex together with other partners, to having sex only with other persons or being celibate.

Residential dimension. Residential interaction ranges from all family members sharing the same residence day and night to all or some of them living in completely separate residences, with a multiplicity of intermediate arrangements.

Economic dimension. Economic cooperation can refer to a wide variety of possible relationships. As far as familial interactions are concerned, the most important economic relationship concerns support obligations and actual provision of support (i.e., a sociological rather than a legal definition of support) between family members. Economic cooperation in this sense, then, ranges from one family member being totally responsible for the support of all family members, to a family in which all members are totally economically independent. . . .

Emotional dimension. Emotional interaction ranges from all family members being positively emotionally involved with each other to being negatively emotionally involved or not being emotionally involved at all. . . .

Using these dimensions of familial interactions we can define the monolithic model of the family as a model according to which high interaction in one dimension of familial interaction is assumed to coincide with or result in high interaction in all other dimensions. This has several consequences which can be summarized as follows: (1) the assumption of congruence leads to (2) a bias in the data collection process, which leads to (3) an underestimation of the incidence of non-congruence and (4) inappropriate categorizations, which in turn, (5) lead to misdefinitions as to what constitutes "problem" families and (6) a neglect of vitally important questions. In the following, we will deal with each of the points in turn.

CONSEQUENCES OF A MONOLITHIC MODEL OF THE FAMILY

Assumption of congruence

That a family consists of two legally-married sexually-cohabiting adults who have children together whom they parent, that it constitutes an economic unit in which either one spouse (formerly always the husband-father) or both spouses (husband-father and wife-mother) are responsible for the economic support of their dependent children and each other, and that it is a social group in which all members live together and love and nurture each other is so commonly understood that it seems almost frivolous to raise any questions about this conglomeration of characteristics. Indeed, within the pertinent literature we find congruence between various separate dimensions constantly stressed. To consider just one dimension, the emotional one, there is general agreement that families (i.e., structural units which consist of spouses and possibly their children) provide love and emotional support for each other. They are presumed to constitute a "haven in a heartless world" (Lasch, 1977) although under increasing attack from outside agencies which have significantly eroded their capacity to function as a refuge. . . .

What is important to note in this context is that there is no attempt to raise the question how many of the existing structural units that we call families actually *do* provide emotional support and love for their various members? Do some families perhaps provide such support for some members but not for others? Or do they provide it part of the time but not always? Perhaps not at all? The assumption of congruence leads to the foregone conclusion: families provide emotional support and love for each other.

One would expect that one of the preconditions for positive emotional involvement would be the absence of fear. We have only very recently become aware that many families are, in fact, a dangerous place for their members to live. Bell and Benjamin have noted that "it is safe to conclude that the majority of murders in Canada occur in family and family-like relationships" (Bell and Benjamin, forthcoming, ms. p. 2). In the United States, too, the Federal Bureau of Investigation estimates that over 50 percent of all murders of women are committed by men with whom they have intimate relationships (reported in Walker, 1978:144).

Steinmetz and Straus (1974:3) argue that " . . . it would be hard to find a group or institution in American society in which violence is more of an everyday occurrence than it is within the family." A recent Canadian study estimates that "Every year, 1 in 10 Canadian women who are married or in a relationship with a live-in lover are battered" (MacLeod, 1980:21). This, of course, is only one form of familial violence. Child abuse is another one.

Again, we have to rely on estimates. One relevant American estimate is that as much as one-third of the population may experience some form of childhood sexual abuse (reported in MacFarlane, 1978:86). The 1978 Ontario Report of the Task Force on Child Abuse starts out with the observation, "It is impossible to avoid the conclusion that the present arrangement of services is not effective in protecting children from child abuse." For parent assault (adult or adolescent children assaulting their parents) we do not even have estimates. It is a completely hidden crime.

The most thorough review of the literature on family violence to date concludes that "Although there are limitations in the representativeness of the samples and the precision of the methodology used in each study, the pervasiveness of physical violence between family members cannot be denied" (Steinmetz, 1978:5). To assume congruence between the emotional dimension and the other dimensions of familial interactions is, therefore, clearly inappropriate.

The assumption of congruence concerning other dimensions of familial interaction is no less problematic. We will here only very briefly consider two other examples, one concerning the economic dimension and the other the procreative dimension.

As far as the economic dimension is concerned, the law assumes and indeed prescribes that family members are responsible for each other's support, and therefore disentitles people to access to public monies (e.g., welfare) on the basis not of their need, but of their family status. This practice is based on the concept of "family income." The notion of family income, in turn, is based on the assumptions that (a) people living in a family situation need individually less money than people not living in a family situation, and (b) that "family income" is shared in an equitable manner, thus relieving the state of responsibility for the economic welfare of individual citizens. (For a critique of the concept of family income, see Eichler, 1980.) Since "family income" is widely utilized as a basis to assess need, a great deal of real poverty thus remains hidden.

As far as the procreative dimension is concerned, the assumption of congruence demonstrates itself in two opposing ways: children who are living with two adults who are married to each other are treated as if they were the biological children of these people, whether or not they are (adoption and remarriage are two factors which lead to non-congruity in the social and biological aspects of parenting) and a parent who is not attached in marriage to the other parent who has custody of the child(ren) is treated as if (s)he (usually he) is not a parent at all. We will consider this issue further in the following sections.

Of immediate concern here is that the assumption of congruence leads to a bias in the data collection process which continually reinforces the ostensible veracity of the previously made assumption by neglecting to ask questions which would produce data that challenge the assumption of congruence.…

Bias in data collection

Our data collection process in effect hides the degree to which families do not conform to the model of the monolithic family. This is most obvious in the case of adoption. Adopted children are not only counted as biological children of their parents, but they are issued new birth certificates which legally declare them as such, thus making it impossible to correctly assess the number of adoptive families. We do have provincial data on the number of children who are placed in adoption every year, but since one family may adopt more than one child or children may be placed for adoption across provinces, we do not know how many families are involved. In addition, for each child that is given up for adoption whose parents are alive, there are one mother and one father who are not raising their own child themselves. Potentially, one adoption may thus create a non-congruity between the procreative and the socialization dimension for three families: the adoptive family, the family of the mother, and the family of the father.

Numerically more important in creating non-congruity between dimensions is divorce. In recent years, the divorce rates have increased sharply, from 45.7 per 100,000 population in 1965 in Canada to 222.0 per 100,000 population in 1975 in Canada (Ontario Statistics 1977, Vol. 1, Table 4.7, p. 108). The ratio of marriage to divorce was, in 1975 in Canada 1:3.9, i.e., for approximately every four marriages, there was one divorce (computed from Ontario Statistics 1977, Table 4.6, p. 107). For the United States, it has been estimated that every third marriage will eventually be dissolved in divorce (Glick, 1977:5–13). The majority of divorced people eventually remarry. When two previously divorced people remarry, especially when their new marital partner was not previously married, the proportion of families which do not conform to the monolithic model increases further. In 1974, 10.5 percent of all Canadian marriages had a divorced bridegroom, and 3.4 percent of all marriages had a widowed bridegroom. In the same year, 9.6 percent of all brides were divorced, and 3.8 percent of all brides were widowed (Canada Yearbook, 1976–77, computed from Table 4.49). Altogether, in 1975, 21.4 percent of all marriages involved at least one previously married partner (Statistics Canada, 1977).

Divorce is especially important when children are involved. While in 1974, 41.3 percent of all divorces in Canada did not involve any *dependent* children (i.e., children under the age of sixteen living at home) 58.7 percent of all divorces *did* involve dependent children (Canada Yearbook, 1976–77, Table 4.53). In 1974 alone, about 55,000 children (computed from Canada Yearbook, 1976–77, Table 4.53) went through the process of divorce of their parents. Whether or not these parents eventually remarry, there remains an incongruence between the biological and social parenting that these children will experience.

However, this incongruence remains largely hidden. The statistical concept of a husband-wife family with dependent children in-dicates merely that a woman and man are married to each other and that some depen-dent children live in their household. It does not tell us anything about who the biological (or, for that matter, the emotional) parents of the children are. Paul C. Glick has esti-mated that in the United States in 1970 "more than 30 percent of school children were *not* living with a father and mother who were in a continuous first marriage" (Glick, 1975:22). This figure does not even include children beyond school age who nevertheless might be affected in a variety of ways by a divorce of their parents. . . .

As far as the residential dimension is con-cerned, the unit of analysis is usually the household. Of all Canadian households in 1971, 81.7 percent were family households. The other 18.7 percent were non-family households, consisting either of one person (13.4 percent) or of two more more persons (4.9 percent) (Canada Yearbook, 1976–77, Table 4.24, p. 194). Of the family households, 8.1 percent contained, in 1971, besides the family of the household head (an)other per-son(s). Seventy point nine percent of all households were listed as "families of house-hold head without additional person." Two percent of all households were two-or-more family households.

The concept of the household implies that every person lives in one household and in one household only. However, there are fam-ilies in which one family member commutes regularly, or in which one or more family members spend extended periods of time elsewhere—e.g., children who attend board-ing school, people whose jobs lead them to regularly spend nights elsewhere. Other cases include people who frequently and regularly have to work night shifts. Then, there is a category of seasonal jobs which takes people from their homes for extended periods of time. Lack of working opportunities in one's home region may force people to accept jobs elsewhere. Military service, extended hos-pital stays, prison terms, may likewise result in variations in the residential pattern.

It is a moot question to argue whether or not such people do or do not have more than one residence. What is important is that there are obviously gross variations in the way in which people who may be part of a family reside with the rest of the family. Statistics to document the extent of multiple residence or split residence patterns are unavailable.

When discussing the issue of family vio-lence, it was noted that we have to rely on estimates which vary very substantially in or-der to delimit the phenomenon. This, in itself, is part of the problem we are dealing with: because of an assumption that "the" family shields its members "from physical harm, whether from natural phenomena or human violence" and satisfies the "emotional needs in family members through the provision of love, services, resources and time" (*The Family as a Focus*, 1979:9–10) we have ne-glected to systematically study the incidence of family abuse and are therefore incapable of exactly assessing what proportion of fam-ilies do not only fail to shield their members from harm and provide love, but actually con-stitute an environment within which people are exposed to greater harm than elsewhere.

As a last example of data bias, the con-vention of using family income as an indi-cation of the economic status of the individuals who make up a family systematically hides inequities in the distribution of so-called fam-ily income and further hides the systematic sex differential in income security which is due to the familial roles played by women and men. As the National Council of Welfare (1979:51) has recently concluded, "Most Ca-nadian women become poor at some point in their lives. Their poverty is rarely the re-sult of controllable circumstances, and it is seldom the outcome of extraordinary mis-fortune. In most cases, women are poor be-cause poverty is the natural consequence of the role they are still expected to play in our society."

Underestimation of non-congruence

The assumption of congruence leads to a systematic bias in the data collection process which makes it impossible to state firmly what percentage of families actually do conform to the monolithic model of the family and what proportion deviate in some significant manner. . . .

One major type of non-congruence is found in the procreative and socialization dimensions. Incongruity between procreation and socialization may occur through death, separation, desertion, divorce, births to unwed mothers, artificial donor insemination,[1] adoption and fostering. Seen from the perspective of children, according to an American estimate, 30 percent of all school age children in 1970 were growing up in families in which there was some type of incongruity between the procreative and socialization dimensions. However, if we add to this figure the perspective of parents, the proportion of families affected by some form of this type of incongruity would increase appreciably. For every child that is raised by one parent who has custody of him or her, there is one other parent who does *not* raise this child in his or her own family. This applies to all of the factors which have been mentioned as leading to incongruity between the two dimensions under consideration, with the exception of death. In the case of adoption and fostering, three families may be potentially affected by incongruity: the adoptive or fostering family, and the families of the biological mother and the biological father, if they do have families of their own. Potentially, therefore, discrepancies between the socialization and procreation dimensions alone could conceivably affect in one way or the other more than 50 percent of all families.

Another form of discrepancy between procreation and parenting occurs when we consider the emotional dimension. Families which show no discrepancies at the structural level may nevertheless be families in which the parenting is carried on by one parent only or, in some cases of emotional and/or physical child abuse, by neither of the parents. . . .

When considering the issue of family violence, we know that it takes place, not just between parents and children but also between spouses and siblings in a significant proportion of families. Again, reliable data which would allow us to compute the proportion of families which experience some form of sustained violence against one, some, or all of their members do not exist. However, if one includes all types of family violence, including sibling violence, which seems to be very frequent (cf. Steinmetz, 1978:5) and husband beating, the estimates for which range from 4.6 percent to 20 percent of all American husbands (MacKintosh, 1978:12), an estimate that 50 percent of all families experience some form of family violence may not be too high.

Other types of deviations from the monolithic model of the family include variant patterns in the sexual dimension, the residential dimension and the economic dimension. As far as the sexual dimension is concerned, a 1976 Canadian survey on sexual behaviors indicated that 4 percent of married men and 2.7 percent of married women never had coitus (Report of the Committee on the Operation of the Abortion Law, 1977:329 and 331). Since it is unclear who the sexual partners of the sexually active population were, according to this survey a minimum of 4 percent of Canadian couples had no sexual relations together, but potentially the figure might be much higher. In addition, an unknown percentage of couples had one or two members who engaged in extramarital sexual relations.

As far as the residential dimension is concerned, most families form a household, which is what we would expect according to the monolithic family model. However, there are some important exceptions. We have already noted that 8.1 percent of all family households contained, in 1971, besides the family of the household head (an)other person(s). Such variations in household composition are statistically accessible; however, there are other variations on which data are not easily available. Personal experience and knowledge suggest that commuting couples, in which one spouse maintains a second residence (usually for job reasons) exist, but their number and proportion is unknown.[2] One variation within the residential dimension, however, we know to be frequent although exact figures are not available: the number of children who attend some form of day care is very high. Until now, day care has not been conceptualized as affecting the residential dimension, its relevance—if at all considered—has been seen in terms of parent-child relations and the eventual effect on the development of the child. However, it seems that day care can meaningfully be seen as partially constituting a variant pattern within the residential dimension. . . .

As far as the economic dimension is concerned, according to the monolithic model of the family, one adult, usually the husband-father, is totally responsible for the economic support of all family members. Statistically speaking, this is increasingly less frequent. In 1975, 58 percent of all wives under the age of 45 were either working full-time or part-time in the labor force (National Council of Welfare, 1979:22, Table 4). We must further assume that the participation rate of women is underreported since women who babysit in their homes, or do other domestic services for pay, tend not to report this income in order to avoid the loss of the married exemption for their husbands.[3]

Other types of deviations from the monolithic model of the family include permanently childless couples (around 10 percent of all Canadian couples) and people living in experimental families or cohabiting (according to an American study this represents 4 percent of all adults in the United States, cf. Ramey, 1978:1).

The various percentages and estimates that have been cited cannot be added up since we do not know to what degree they overlap. Nevertheless, it seems safe to conclude that probably only a rather small minority of families correspond to the monolithic model of the family. For the United States, for instance, "What is considered to be the traditional nuclear family, a breadwinner-father, a housewife-mother, and two children under eighteen accounted for only 7 percent of the population in 1975" (Ramey, 1978:3). Until we change our data collection process to gather information on possible variations in familial structures, e.g., by asking people about biological children of theirs who are not living with them, by asking about the biological parents of children living within a husband-wife family, by collecting systematic and representative data on family violence, by examining the residential patterns of family members, etc., we are likely to continue to assume that families conform to the monolithic model of the family to a greater degree than they actually do. This has some serious consequences, the two most important of which probably are that we are likely to continue to ignore questions which are of vital importance in understanding the functioning of familial structures and that we create policies which are based on inadequate data. . . .

Notes

[1] Figures on artificial donor insemination are not available, but a recent newspaper article suggests that "hundreds to thousands of babies are born by this method every year in Canada" (*Thousands of babies*, 1978).

[2] Among my personal acquaintances there are several commuting couples which include spouses who have faculty positions at two different universities. One would expect this to become an increasingly frequent although

statistically insignificant pattern as more women are likely to seek university positions even at the price of a commuting marriage.

[3] In addition, the labor force participation rates of women are underestimated because labor force figures include only officially unemployed people and because many women who would like to have jobs cannot find any, but nevertheless are not counted as unemployed. The underestimation of the unemployment of women has been pegged at 65 percent (Robinson, 1978). If one were to include the "hidden unemployed," unemployment rates among women would rise from 9.4 percent to 15.6 percent for 1977 (ibid.). These figures have not been included here since, being disentitled from unemployment benefits, these women cannot contribute such benefits to the family income.

References

Anderson, Michael, ed. 1971 *Sociology of the Family*. Harmondsworth: Penguin.

Ball, Donald W. 1972 "The 'family' as a *sociological* problem: conceptualization of the taken-for-granted as prologue to social problems analysis." *Social Problems* 19(3):295–305.

Bell, Norman W. and Michael Benjamin Forthcoming *Domestic Murders in Canada, 1961–1974*, Monograph published by the Judicial Statistics Division. Ottawa: Statistics Canada.

Boland, Madame Justice 1978 (unpublished) "Reasons for Judgement" in the case of Baker, April 25.

Boyd, Monica, Margrit Eichler and John Hofley 1976 "Family, functions, formation, and fertility." In *Opportunity for Choice*, edited by Gail C.A. Cook, pp. 13–52. Ottawa: Statistics Canada

Canada Yearbook 1974.

———— 1976–77.

Chapman, Jane Roberts and Margaret Gates, eds. 1978. *The Victimization of Women*. Beverly Hills: Sage Publications.

Cohen, Gaynor 1977 "Absentee husbands in spiralist families." *Journal of Marriage and the Family* 39(3):595–604.

Cooperstock, Ruth 1976 "Psychotropic drug use among women." *Canadian Medical Association Journal* 115:760–763.

Coser, Rose Laub 1974. *The Family. Its Structure and Functions*. 2nd ed. New York: St. Martin's Press.

Duberman, Lucile 1977 *Marriage and Other Alternatives*. 2nd ed. New York: Praeger.

Eichler, Margrit 1979 "Towards a policy for families in Canada." (mimeo) Ottawa: Status of Women Canada.

———— 1980 "Family income—a critique of the concept" *Status of Women News*. 6:20–21 and 24.

Elkin, Frederick and Gerald Handel 1978 *The Child and Society: The Process of Socialization*. 3rd ed. New York: Random House.

Eshleman, J. Ross 1978 *The Family: An Introduction*. 2nd ed. Boston: Allyn and Bacon.

The Family as a Focus for Social Policy 1979 Minister for Social Development, Toronto, Ontario, May.

Galper, Miriam 1978 *Co-Parenting. A Source Book for the Separated or Divorced Family*. Philadelphia, Penn.: Running Press.

Glick, Paul C. 1975 "A demographer looks at American families." *Journal of Marriage and the Family* 35:15–26.

———— 1977 "Updating the life cycle of families." *Journal of Marriage and the Family* 39(1): 5–13.

Lasch, Christopher 1977 *Haven in a Heartless World: The Family Besieged*. New York: Basic Books.

Leslie, Gerald R. 1967 *The Family in Social Context*, New York: Oxford University Press.

MacFarlane, Kee 1978 "Sexual abuse of children." In *The Victimization of Women*, edited by Jane Roberts Chapman and Margaret Gates, pp. 81–110. Beverly Hills: Sage Publications.

MacKintosh, Judy 1978 "News from the field," *Marriage and Family Review* 1(4):12–13.

MacLeod, Linda 1980 *Wife Battering in Canada: The Vicious Circle*. (Advisory Council on the Status of Women). Ottawa: Canadian Government Publishing Centre.

Martin, Del 1978 "Battered women: society's problem." In *The Victimization of Women*, edited by Jane Roberts Chapman and Margaret Gates, pp. 111–141. Beverly Hills: Sage Publications.

Meissner, Martin et al. 1975 "No exit for wives: sexual division of labour and the cumulation of household demands." *Canadian Review of Sociology and Anthropology* 12(4):424–439.

Murdock, George Peter 1949 *Social Structure*. New York: Macmillan.

National Council of Welfare 1979 *Women and Poverty*. (A Report by the National Council of Welfare). Ottawa.

ONeil, Maureen and Arthur Leonoff 1977 "Joint custody, an option worth examining." *Perception Now.*/Dec. 28–30.

Ontario Ministry of Treasury, Economics and Intergovernmental Affairs 1977 *Ontario Statistics 1977* Vol. 1, Social Series.

Petes, John F. 1979 *Divorce*, Toronto: Faculty of Education, Guidance Centre, University of Toronto.

Ramey, James 1978 "Experimental family forms— the family of the future." *Marriage and Family Review* 1(1):1–9.

Reiss, Ira L. 1965 "The universality of the family: a conceptual analysis." *Journal of Marriage and the Family* Nov.:443–453.

Report of the Committee on the Operation of the Abortion Law. 1977 Minister of Supply and Services. Ottawa.

Report of the Task Force on Child Abuse 1978 Ontario, Ministry of Community and Social Services. Toronto, June.

Robinson, H.L. 1978 "Unemployment in 1977: unemployment among women is higher than among men." *Canadian Newsletter of Research on Women* 7(2):12–13

Roman, Mel and William Haddad 1978 "The case for joint custody," *Psychology Today* 12(4): 96–105.

Rosen, Edward J. n.d. "In the best interests of the child and parents." Unpublished paper.

Schlesinger, Benjamin ed. 1979 *One in Ten: The Single Parent in Canada*. Toronto: University of Toronto Guidance Centre

Schlesinger, Benjamin and Rubin Todres 1979 "Characteristics of Canadian members of 'Parents without Partners'." *In One in Ten: The Single Parent in Canada*, edited by Benjamin Schlesinger, pp. 107–112, Toronto: University of Toronto Guidance Centre.

Skolnik, Arlene and Jerome H. Skolnik, eds. 1974 *Intimacy, Family and Society*. Boston: Little, Brown and Co.

Status of Day Care in Canada 1975 *A Review of the Major Findings of the National Day Care Study 1975*. Ottawa: National Day Care Information Centre. Social Service Programs Branch.

Steinmetz, Suzanne K. 1978 "Violence between family members." *Marriage and Family Review* 1(3):1–16.

Steinmetz, Suzanne K. and Murray A. Straus, eds. 1974 *Violence in the Family*. New York: Dodd, Mead and Co.

"Thousands of babies owe life to a lab" 1978 *Toronto Star*, Oct. 9, p. C1.

Van Stolk, Mary 1975 "The battered and abused child." In *Marriage, Family and Society: Canadian Perspectives*. edited by S. Parvez Wakil, pp. 213–222. Toronto: Butterworths.

Walker, Lenore E. 1978 "Treatment alternatives for battered women." In *The Victimization of Women*, edited by Jane Roberts Chapman and Margaret Gates, pp. 143–174. Beverly Hills: Sage Publications

Weigert, Andrew J. and Darwin L. Thomas 1971 "Family as a conditional universal." *Journal of Marriage and the Family* pp. 188–194.

Wheeler, Michael 1978 *Unpublished Report on the Findings of a Study on Recently Separated Parents* (Mimeo) Hamilton: McMaster University.

43 Marital Satisfaction Over the Life Cycle

Eugen Lupri   James S. Frideres

EUGEN LUPRI, Professor of Sociology at the University of Calgary, specializes in the sociologies of the family and gender relations, and sociological theory. He has contributed numerous chapters to books and monographs and published articles in such journals as the *Canadian Journal of Sociology; Journal of Marriage and the Family; Current Sociology; International Journal of Comparative Sociology; Comparative Journal of Family Studies; Kolner Zeitschrift fur Soziologie; Soziale Welt; European Journal of Sociology; Metra;* and *Revue Internationale de Sociologie.* His most recent book is *The Changing Position of Women in Family and Society: A Cross-Cultural Comparison* (1983). A monograph, *Reflections on Marriage and the Family in Canada: A Study in the Dialectics of Family and Work Roles,* is nearing completion.

JAMES S. FRIDERES, Professor of Sociology at the University of Calgary, is a social psychologist with a special interest in the structural aspects of society. He has published widely in a number of areas, but his areas of specialization are ethnic relations, family and social impact analysis. He is best known for his book, *Native People in Canada* (1983), and is co-author, with A.B. Anderson, of *Ethnicity in Canada: Theoretical Perspectives* (1981). Professor Frideres is also co-editor of *Canadian Ethnic Studies* and book review editor for the *Journal of Comparative Family Studies.*

INTRODUCTION

Disenchantment in marriage, along with the rising divorce rate, is a popular subject of discussion among laypersons and professionals alike. The pervasive increase in the divorce rate reported for Canada and other industrialized nations reflects, perhaps, strains in the marital relationship. Despite its intriguing and problematic nature, marital happiness among Canadian couples has been a neglected area of investigation. Recent assessments of marriage and the family in Canada (Ramu, 1979; Nett, 1980; Davids, 1980) provide only limited discussions on the subject. Contrary to the American and European scenes, it appears that Canadian data bearing on the quality of marriage are exceedingly rare, or nonexistent. By filling that gap, this study places its Canadian (Calgarian) findings in comparative perspective. . . .

THE INVESTIGATION

Our discussions of findings are organized around two general questions: (1) What *inter*societal patterns emerge when the Canadian data on marital satisfaction over the family life cycle are placed in comparative perspective? (2) What *intra*societal patterns in marital satisfaction emerge when the data are broken down by sex, wife's employment status, and presence or absence of children?

436

The Canadian data in comparative perspective: evidence for the curvilinear relationship

This study set out to examine two competing hypotheses:

(1) Marital satisfaction declines with duration of marriage: the *linear relationship*.

(2) Marital satisfaction declines in the early stages of the family life cycle, levels off at midlife, then increases in the later family life stages: the *curvilinear relationship*.

It should be clear that both approaches stress the importance of change in marital satisfaction over time. Both assume an invariant sequence in family development and critical transition points in family life that move families or couples from one stage to another, the basic proposition of family development theory (Hill and Rodgers, 1964; Rodgers, 1973; Aldous, 1978). They disagree only regarding directions of change.

The crucial data to test those opposing hypotheses are presented in Figure 1, which shows the percentages of husbands and wives who find their marriage very satisfying during each of the seven family life stages. To view cross-sectional data over time, as we do here, is an analytical strategy that allows us to make *tentative* generalizations about *changes* in family behavior. We are comparing husbands and wives who have been married only a short time with those who have been married longer, with differences interpreted to imply a change as a function of time. The inherent pitfalls of inferring changes from cross-sectional studies were alluded to earlier, i.e., the confounding influences of time, (age, stage) and culture. Ideally, a longitudinal design, which would enable us to observe a sample of the *same* couples at different points in time, would be preferable.[1] In the absence of any Canadian data on the quality of marriage, however, careful and cautious study of cross-sectional materials is useful for tentative inferences of the effects of stage of the life cycle and duration of marriages.

The data graphed in Figure 1 reveal a U-shaped pattern of marital satisfaction over the family life cycle for both husbands and wives, which is similar to findings in the United States (Rollins and Feldman, 1970) and New Zealand (Smart and Smart, 1975). The speed and intensity of the decline and increase of marital satisfaction among our Canadian respondents, however, vary somewhat from the patterns reported for other studies in the United States (Spanier et al., 1975). Other measurements used to tap this study's respondents' quality of marriage revealed similar curvilinear patterns.

It is widely believed that the disenchantment period extends into the post-parental years, but evidence from our study does not support the post-parental stages being detrimental to marital happiness, except that husbands' happiness does not increase with the same intensity and to the same level as wives'.

The curvilinear relationship between marital satisfaction and stage in the family life cycle has been interpreted in a number of different, although related, theoretical ways. Feldman (1966) suggests that "illusions disappear and disenchantment ensues." Rodgers (1973), taking a developmental approach, asserts that meanings couples attached to their relationship and their roles change over time and thus affect marital satisfaction. Burr (1973) and Miller (1976) maintain that role transitions, e.g., birth of the first child, are disruptive and thus negatively affect satisfaction. Rollins and Cannon (1974) interpret the pattern as stemming from the presence of children, changing family roles, and the initial newness of marriage "wearing off." Others like Luckey (1966) and Russell (1974) suggest that fewer "positive" personality qualities are seen in the spouse or that structural

Figure 1
PERCENTAGES OF HUSBANDS AND WIVES IN EACH OF SEVEN STAGES OF THE FAMILY LIFE CYCLE REPORTING "VERY SATISFYING" MARRIAGES.

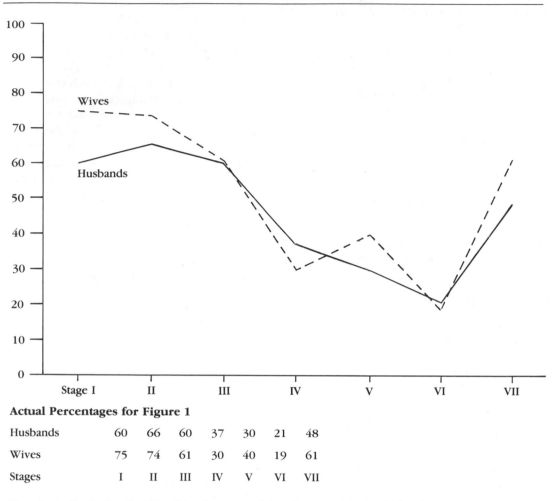

Actual Percentages for Figure 1

Husbands	60	66	60	37	30	21	48
Wives	75	74	61	30	40	19	61
Stages	I	II	III	IV	V	VI	VII

Stage I   = Beginning Families (couples married 0 to 5 years without children)
Stage II   = Childbearing Families (the oldest child is birth to 2 years and 11 months)
Stage III = Families with Preschool Children (the oldest child is 3 years to 5 years and 11 months)
Stage IV   = Families with School Age Children (the oldest child is 6 years to 12 years and 11 months)
Stage V   = Families with Teenagers (the oldest child is 13 years to 20 years and 11 months)
Stage VI   = Empty Nest Period and Early Grandparenthood (from when the oldest child is older than 20 years to retirement of parents)
Stage VII = Aging Families (retirement to death of first spouse)

strains emerge in the family as individual members are added or removed. Pineo (1961), however, reports that husbands' and wives' growing apart did *not* result from personality conflicts but to a growing separation on family issues and interests. He found also that there was a general drop in marital satisfaction strongly associated with a loss of intimacy. Whatever the specific explanation, all seem to point to the arrival as well as the departure of children, the number of children, and the work status of the wife as important mediating factors....

Intrasocietal patterns in marital satisfaction over the family life cycle: some general observations

Before introducing control variables, it may be useful to obtain some overall perspective

that our survey data reflect on the scope of intrasocietal differences in marital satisfaction.

The differences are summarized in Table 1....

Several patterns emerge from Table 1. First, on the average, husbands are less satisfied with their marriages than are wives. Although the difference is not large, the results are opposite from what is generally reported in the literature. A similar pattern emerged when we examined other empirical indicators of the quality of marriage. On the average, more wives than husbands were "very satisfied" with "the understanding" (25 percent versus 18 percent), "the affection" (46 percent versus 40 percent), and "the companionship" (45 percent versus 41 percent) they receive from their spouses. Likewise, 46 percent of all wives expressed satisfaction "with the sexual relationship" in their marriage, compared with 38 percent of all husbands. To be sure, dif-

Table 1

MARITAL SATISFACTION/HAPPINESS FOR WIVES AND HUSBANDS BY WIFE'S WORK STATUS, PRESENCE OF CHILDREN, AND HUSBAND'S OCCUPATIONAL PRESTIGE

	Those "very satisfied" or "very happy" with marriage			
	Wives		Husband	
	Percent	(N)	Percent	(N)
Total sample	49	(397)	41	(387)
Wife's employment status:				
Not working for pay	48	(237)	38	(242)
Working full-time[a]	53	(97)	50	(109)
Presence or absence of children:[b]				
At least one child	52	(361)	50	(355)
No children	69	(91)	57	(88)
Husband's occupational prestige:[c]				
High	55	(124)	36	(124)
Low	45	(250)	47	(250)

[a] Working 30 hours or more per week.

[b] Because our operationalization of "stage in the family-life cycle" is determined, in part, on the arrival and departure of children, childless couples are not included in the stage analysis. To ascertain the effect of *absence* of children on marital satisfaction, we had to use a question that tapped "marital happiness." Respondents who answered that they were "very happy" to the question: All in all, how happy has your marriage been for you?, are assessed when we control for the presence and absence of children.

[c] Carmac Scale based on Pineo, P., J. Porter and H.A. McRoberts, 1977.

ferences in none of the cases is great but all are in the same direction: Calgary husbands are less contented with their marriages than are the wives, which contrasts sharply with Bernard's (1973) insightful synthesis of the literature on the subject. If marriage is as unfavorable to women as Bernard demonstrates, why do fewer Calgary husbands than wives report marital satisfaction and happiness? It is the husbands who need closer scrutiny, as we show.

Second, our data show that a wife's employment status has an important and positive effect on both the wives' and the husbands' marital satisfaction. Employed wives are slightly more likely to be "very satisfied" with their marriage than are housewives (53 percent versus 48 percent). More noteworthy, however, is that the wives' work status has a much greater positive impact on the husbands' marital satisfaction than on their own. As shown in Table 1, 50 percent of the husbands whose wives are fully employed report that their marriage is very satisfying compared with only 38 percent of husbands whose wives are not working outside the home.

Third, we found that a higher proportion of childless spouses report "very happy" marriages than couples with children. These findings are in line with the reasoning that, contrary to popular belief, children tend to have a disruptive effect on conjugal relationships between husbands and wives. Childless couples, in contrast, enjoy more marital communication (Feldman, 1964), maintain a more equalitarian power structure (Brinkerhoff and Lupri, 1978), and are more likely to report higher marital satisfaction and adjustment than couples with children—even when controls for certain other variables are introduced (Houseknecht, 1979). The impact of childlessness on marital happiness is greater for wives than it is for husbands. The difference between the wives with at least one child (52 percent) and those with no children (69 percent) is quite marked compared with the husbands', 50 and 57 percent, respectively.

In fact, childless wives constitute the subsample with the highest proportion (69 percent) of any subsample reporting "very happy" marriages. When we controlled for the wife's work status, it reduced the differences but it did not destroy the original relationship.

Fourth, marital satisfaction varies by husband's occupational status in two important ways. Men among high prestige occupations tend to be less satisfied with their marriages than husbands of lower status occupations. Wives whose husbands have higher occupational status, in contrast, report greater marital satisfaction than wives of lower status husbands, which agrees with results from past research. However, contrary to the literature is the observation that gender differences between husbands and wives of higher occupational status families are much greater (55 percent versus 36 percent) than between spouses of lower-status families (45 percent versus 47 percent). This finding needs more empirical detailing than we can provide and requires a research strategy that makes the *couple* the basic unit of analysis. . . .

Marital satisfaction over the family life cycle: control for wife's employment status

Employed versus non-employed wives.   We now address the issue of female labor force participation and its impact upon marital satisfaction for both husbands and wives, and whether the differences are related to specific stages or remain constant over all stages of the family life cycle.

Both employed and non-employed wives exhibit patterns of marital satisfaction similar to the pattern of all wives (Figure 1), which suggests the curvilinear relationship is tenable because the association between stage in the family life cycle and marital satisfaction reappears for employed as well as non-employed wives.

However, notable differences in marital satisfaction between the two groups also emerge. *First*, employed wives with pre-school children (stage III) and school age children (stage IV) are more likely to report their marriage to be "very satisfying" than are their non-employed counterparts. The difference between the two groups is particularly marked in stage IV: almost twice as many very satisfied employed wives (54 percent) as non-employed wives (29 percent), indicating that these working mothers have successfully coordinated family and job obligations and appear to derive satisfaction from their labors.

Second, the accumulative effect of outside work and the presence of teenagers (stage V) in the home is clearly reflected in the difference between the employed wives' and non-employed wives' marital satisfaction. The curve for employed wives dips significantly, however, in stage V, strongly suggesting that outside work generates additional stress which further decreases marital satisfaction.

And *third*, our data modestly support the "empty nest" syndrome, a phenomenon that has recently gained world-wide attention as a condition characterized by demoralization and loneliness associated with grown children and a busy husband. We note that the curve (Figure 2) for non-employed wives decreases somewhat as they approach stage VI and then increases as they leave and move into stage VII. The curve for employed wives reaches an all-time low in stage V, but then shows a continual and sharp increase as they move into stages VI and VII. In other words, the proportion of employed wives being "very satisfied" in the retirement stage is much greater than the proportion of non-employed wives. These data suggest that there is a *temporary* period of poor adjustment in the marital relationships of all wives and, as we show later, husbands.

Husbands of employed versus husbands of non-employed wives.

Moving our analysis to comparing marital satisfaction of *husbands* of employed wives with that of husbands of non-employed wives, we find both similarities and differences in the way the wives' work status is related to husband's marital satisfaction. The outstanding feature is that the curves for both husbands of employed wives and non-employed wives are consistently similar in shape, which reconfirms a curvilinear association between marital satisfaction and stage in the family life cycle for husbands. However, husbands of *employed* wives consistently report higher marital satisfaction over the entire family life cycle than husbands of non-employed wives. And the differences are quite marked, particularly at the preschool stage (III) and at stage VI, the time after the children have grown up and left home. Here is evidence that the increasingly longer empty nest period for middle-aged couples may be the most dramatic change in the family life cycle for *husbands* of wives who are not in the labor force....

Employed wives versus their husbands.

... The curvilinear relationship remains for both employed wives and their husbands, but genuine gender differences emerge in almost all of the stages; most markedly in stages V, VI, and VII, at midlife and in later years. The curve for working wives slopes down considerably more than it does for their husbands, strongly suggesting that the combination of the wife's paid employment and the presence of teenagers in the home (stage V) has a more pronounced negative effect on the wives' marital satisfaction than it does on their husbands'. This supports the general notion that the children's departure from home does not affect the fathers as much as the mothers because children have typically played a lesser role in their lives. The father of adult children may assume an even lesser role than he did when the children were small (Troll, 1975).

Several investigators (Aldous and Hill, 1969; Rodgers, 1973; Aldous, 1977; Spanier, Lewis, and Cole, (1975) have documented that the

Figure 2

PERCENTAGES OF HUSBANDS WHOSE WIVES ARE WORKING FULL-TIME AND WHOSE WIVES ARE
NONEMPLOYED IN EACH OF SEVEN STAGES OF THE FAMILY LIFE CYCLE REPORTING
"VERY SATISFYING" MARRIAGES.

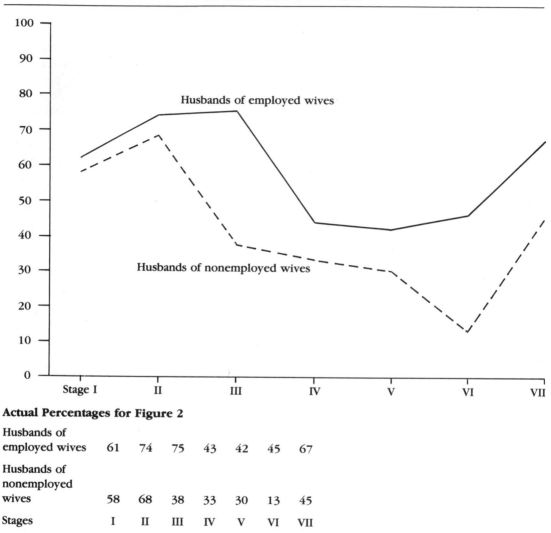

Actual Percentages for Figure 2

	I	II	III	IV	V	VI	VII
Husbands of employed wives	61	74	75	43	42	45	67
Husbands of nonemployed wives	58	68	38	33	30	13	45
Stages	I	II	III	IV	V	VI	VII

adolescent and launching periods of the life cycle are the most vulnerable to lack of *expressive* resources in the family, while the childbearing and school age stages are more likely to strain the family's *instrumental* resources. The lack of both resources may indicate critical structural transitions and become potential points of stress for the family as a system. These theoretical assumptions seem useful and consistent, not only in terms of family development theory but also in relation to the previously reported findings, where we found stage in the life cycle to be an important predictor of marital satisfaction.

However, an important intervening variable is encountered when we compare marital satisfaction of working wives with that of their husbands, particularly in the adolescent

Figure 3

PERCENTAGES OF HUSBANDS OF EMPLOYED WIVES AND EMPLOYED WIVES IN EACH OF SEVEN STAGES OF FAMILY LIFE CYCLE REPORTING "VERY SATISFYING" MARRIAGES.

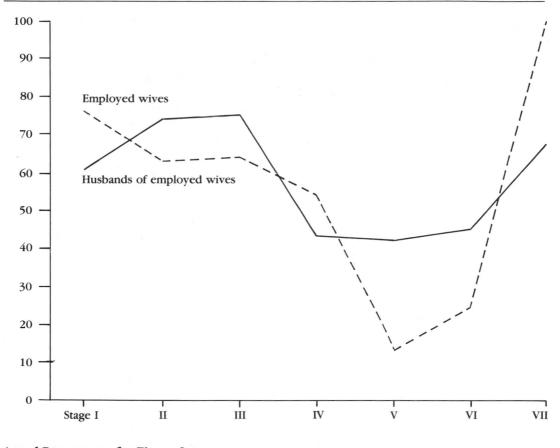

Actual Percentages for Figure 3

	I	II	III	IV	V	VI	VII
Husbands of employed wives	61	74	75	43	42	45	67
Employed wives	76	63	64	54	13	24	100
Stages	I	II	III	IV	V	VI	VII

and empty nest stages (V and VI). . . .

The comparative data indicate that the husbands of employed wives (42 percent in stage V and 45 percent in stage VI) are much *more* likely than the employed wives themselves (13 percent and 24 percent, respectively) to report "very satisfying" marriages. The data on non-employed wives and their husbands point in the opposite direction: non-employed wives' husbands report less satisfying marriages than non-employed wives in both stages.

The evidence presented consistently documents the idea of developmental theorists (Aldous and Hill, 1969; Rodgers, 1973; Aldous, 1978) that critical structural transitions may become potential points of stress for the family system. Furthermore, our data support the proposition that couples in the adolescent and empty nest periods of the life cycle are most vulnerable to lack of *expressive* rather than *instrumental* resources. But it applies more to wives than to husbands. It is the consistency of the results that supports the couples' high vulnerability from lack of expressive resources during these periods of the family life cycle. The magnitude of the difference in marital satisfaction between husbands of employed wives and husbands of non-employed wives (12 percent in stage V and 32 percent in VI) indicates the salience of the wife's employment status on marital satisfaction, particularly in stage VI.

Work involves outside contacts that bolster the resources in knowledge and interpersonal skills which an employed wife brings to the marriage. Working also involves additional income—the most tangible of all instrumental resources in our society, so we should expect the wife's work status to positively affect the couple's level of marital satisfaction. But we see that such is not the case. The employed wife's involvement outside the home during the adolescent and empty nest stages decreases her level of marital satisfaction and seemingly increases his.

We have argued that it is the cumulation of housekeeping, childcare, and outside work that is responsible for decreasing marital satisfaction among employed wives. We assume that Calgary wives bear the major burden of domestic tasks and that Calgary husbands, like their counterparts around the world, contribute relatively little to housekeeping and childrearing tasks (Meissner et al., 1975). . . .

Marital satisfaction over the family life cycle: control for the presence or absence of children

In our sample childless couples were more likely than couples with children to report "very happy" marriages and childless wives reported it somewhat oftener than childless husbands (Table 1). A fully elaborated and comparative analysis of marital functioning of childless couples and couples with children is not available, but elements of the variant interaction patterns have appeared in several studies. . . .

The question now is whether the curvilinear association between marital satisfaction and stage in the life cycle holds when presence of children is controlled. The previous discussion of our results and those in the literature suggests that a linear relationship should be sustained for childless couples and a curvilinear one for couples with children. The data reported here constitute no such rigorous test of such relationships because they derive from answers to a question about "marital happiness" rather than "marital satisfaction" (Table 1, Footnote b). Happiness and satisfaction are not synonymous, yet they are closely related and frequently treated interchangeably (Nye, 1974). They scale on the same dimension and tend to reflect aspects of the quality of marriage. A breakdown by sex revealed that 54 percent of the wives and 49 percent of the husbands reported their marriage to be "very happy." Following our previous strategy, only "very happy" respondents are included in the ensuing analysis.

Another limitation of the data reported here entails placing respondents into *age* groups rather than stages in the family life cycle. To approximate the seven stages in the family life cycle used in previous analyses, we placed husbands and wives into six age groups (Table 2).

Data testing the influence of the presence or absence of children on marital happiness during the family life cycle are presented in Table 2, where pertinent information is provided for childless husbands and wives as well as for those with children, by six age groups. Do these two groups of husbands and wives reveal the curvilinear pattern observed earlier in Figure 1? By and large, the answer is *yes*. However, there are several important life cycle stage and gender differences as well as

Table 2
PERCENTAGES OF HUSBANDS AND WIVES WITH AT LEAST ONE CHILD AND WITH NO CHILDREN
IN SIX AGE GROUPS REPORTING THAT THEY ARE "VERY HAPPY" WITH THEIR MARRIAGES

Age	No children			At least one child		
	Wives	Husbands	(N)	Wives	Husbands	(N)
15 to 24	68	62	(40)	56	60	(25)
25 to 34	69	55	(34)	54	44	(124)
35 to 44	75	67	(5)	46	48	(94)
45 to 54	60	40	(6)	34	52	(79)
55 to 64	100	50	(4)	48	60	(26)
65 or older	100	100	(2)	56	69	(13)
All ages	69	57	(91)	52	50	(361)

variations between couples with and without children.

First, comparing percentages of the two groups shows childless husbands and wives generally happier with their marriages than husbands and wives with children, except for husbands in the 45–64 age group. This finding confirms not only our earlier observation that childlessness enhances marital happiness but also that it does so continuously over the family life cycle. *Second*, childless wives are consistently happier than childless husbands at each age group, while husbands with children (with one exception at age 25–34) are happier than wives with children. *Third*, while gender differences among couples with children are small and vary somewhat by age group, the difference between husbands and wives is most pronounced in the middle age group, 45 to 54, confirming earlier observations that during this period of life teenagers in the home affect the marital happiness of wives more negatively than husbands'. . . .

CONCLUSIONS

. . . The passage of time upon the quality of marriage is impressive, although disenchantment is not a continuous process as earlier studies suggested. Evidence reported here yields a remarkably consistent pattern, showing a curvilinear association between marital satisfaction and stage in the family life cycle for both husbands and wives. Marital satisfaction among Calgary couples declines steadily from the beginning of marriage to the period when children exit the family unit. From then on, sharp increases in marital satisfaction point toward considerable improvements in the marital relationship.

The introduction of control variables revealed significant gender differences but did not destroy the original curvilinear relationship. The quality of marriage in midlife is both varied and complex. Wives who work outside the home show significantly lower levels of marital satisfaction than do their husbands. Employed wives experience greater role strains than non-employed wives because of the cumulative effect of employment *and* the presence of teenagers in the home. Husbands whose wives are employed are much more likely than husbands whose wives are not employed to report very satisfying marriages, with the greatest difference in midlife. These findings support the notion that an increasing number of roles involve husbands in relationships outside the family (life-cycle squeeze), and that the outside relationships significantly affect the quality of marriage at midlife. . . .

Notes

[1] This is not to deny that longitudinal studies will never confound time and cultural-generational influences; they are simply less apparent than in cross-sectional studies.

References

Aldous, Joan 1977 "Family interaction patterns." In *Annual Review of Sociology III,* edited by A. Inkeles, J. Coleman and N. Smelser, pp. 105–135. Palo Alto, Ca.: Annual Review Press.

———— 1978 *Family Careers: Developmental Change in Families.* New York: John Wiley & Sons.

Aldous, Joan and Reuben Hill 1979 "Breaking the poverty cycle: strategic points for intervention." *Social Work* 14:3–12.

Bernard, Jessie 1973 *The Future of Marriage.* New York: Macmillan.

Blood, Robert O. 1976 *Love Match and Arranged Marriage: A Tokyo-Detroit Comparison.* New York: The Free Press.

Blood, Robert O. and Donald M. Wolfe 1960 *Husbands and Wives: The Dynamics of Married Living.* New York: The Free Press.

Bossard, James H.S. and Eleanor S. Boll 1955 *Ritual in Family Living.* Philadelphia: University of Pennsylvania Press.

Bram, Susan 1974 "To have or have not: a social-psychological study of voluntarily childless couples, parents-to-be, and parents." Unpublished doctoral dissertation, University of Michigan.

Brinkerhoff, M.B. and E. Lupri 1978 "Theoretical and methodological issues in the use of decision-making as an indicator of conjugal power: some Canadian observations." *Canadian Journal of Sociology* 3(1):1–20.

Burr, Wesley, R. 1970 "Satisfaction with various aspects of marriage over the family life cycle: a random middle-class sample." *The Journal of Marriage and the Family* 32:29–37.

———— 1973 *Theory Construction and the Sociology of the Family.* New York: Wiley-Interscience.

Davids, Leo 1980 "Family change in Canada: 1971–1976." *The Journal of Marriage and the Family* 42:177–183.

Duvall, Evelyn M. 1977 *Family Development*, Fifth edition. Philadelphia: J.B. Lippincott.

Feldman, Harold 1964 *Development of the Husband-Wife Relationship*, Ithaca, New York: Department of Child Development and Family Relationships, Cornell University.

———— 1971 "The effects of children on the family." In *Family Issues of Employed Women in Europe and America*, edited by A. Michel, pp. 107–125. Leiden: E.J. Brill.

Fenelone, Bill 1971 "State variations and United States divorce rates." *The Journal of Marriage and the Family* 33:321–327.

Gianopulos, A. and H.E. Mitchell 1967 "Marital disagreement in working wives: marriage as a function of husband's attitude toward wife's employment." *The Journal of Marriage and the Family* 25:189–195.

Hill, Reuben and Roy Rodgers 1964 "The developmental approach." In *Handbook of Marriage and the Family,* edited by Harold T. Christensen, pp. 171–211. Chicago: Rand-McNally.

Houseknecht, Sharon K. 1979 "Childlessness and marital adjustment." *The Journal of Marriage and the Family* 41:259–265.

Klein, David M. and Joan Aldous 1979 "Three blind mice: misleading criticisms of the family life cycle concept." *The Journal of Marriage and the Family* 41:689–690.

Larson, Lyle 1978 *Family Patterns and Services in Edmonton.* Edmonton: Office of the Mayor.

Luckey, Eleanor B. 1966 "Number of years married as related to personality perception and marital satisfaction." *The Journal of Marriage and the Family* 28:440–448.

Lupri, Eugen 1983 "The changing positions of women and men in comparative perspective," pp. 3–39. In *The Changing Positions of Women in Family and Society: A Cross-Cultural Comparison*, edited by Eugen Lupri, Leiden: Brill.

Lupri, Eugen and Donald L. Mills 1983 "The changing roles of Canadian women in family and work: an overview," pp. 43–77. In *The Changing Positions of Women in Family and Society: A Cross-Cultural Comparison*, edited by Eugen Lupri, Leiden: Brill.

Makabe, Tomoko 1980 "Provincial variations in divorce rates: a Canadian case." *The Journal of Marriage and the Family* 42:171–176.

Meissner, M., Elizabeth W. Humphreys, Scott M. Meiss, and William J. Scheu 1975 "No exit for wives: sexual division of labour and the cumulation of household demands." *The Canadian Review of Sociology and Anthropology* 12(Pt. 1):424–439.

Miller, Brent 1976 "A multivariate developmental model of marital satisfaction." *The Journal of Marriage and the Family* 38:643–657.

Nett, Emily M. 1980 "The family." In *Sociology*, edited by Robert Hagedorn, pp. 351–385. Toronto: Holt, Rinehart and Winston of Canada.

Nock, Steven L. 1979 "The family life cycle: empirical or conceptual tool." *The Journal of Marriage and the Family* 41:15–26.

Nye, Ivan F. 1974 "Husband-wife relationship." In *Working Mothers*, edited by L.W. Hoffman and I. Nye, pp. 186–206. San Francisco: Jossey-Bass Publishers.

Oppenheimer, Valerie K. 1974 "The life-cycle squeeze: the interaction of men's occupational and family life cycles." *Demography* 11(2):227–245.

Orden, S.R. and N.M. Bradburn 1968 "Dimensions of marriage happiness." *American Journal of Sociology* 73:715–731.

——— 1969 "Working wives and marriage happiness." *American Journal of Sociology* 74:392–407.

Pineo, Peter 1961 "Disenchantment in the later

years of marriage." *Marriage and Family Living* 23:3–11.

Ramu, G.N., ed. 1979 *Courtship, Marriage and the Family in Canada*. Toronto: Macmillan.

Rodgers, Roy H. 1973 *Family Interaction and Transaction: The Developmental Approach*. Englewood Cliffs, New Jersey: Prentice-Hall.

Rollins, Boyd C. and Harold Feldman 1970 "Marital satisfaction over the family life cycle." *The Journal of Marriage and the Family* 32:20–28.

——— 1974 "Marital satisfaction over the family life cycle: a reevaluation." *The Journal of Marriage and the Family* 36:271–282.

Russell, Candyce S. 1974 "Transition to parenthood: problems and gratifications." *The Journal of Marriage and the Family* 36:294–302.

Ryder, Robert G. 1973 "Longitudinal data relating marriage satisfaction and having a child." *The Journal of Marriage and the Family* 35:604–606.

Schaie, K.W. 1976 "A general model for the study of developmental problems." *Psychological Bulletin* 64:92–107.

Schram, Rosalyn Weinman 1979 "Marital satisfaction over the family life cycle: a critique and proposal." *The Journal of Marriage and the Family* 41:7–12.

Smart, Mollie S. and Russel C. Smart 1975 "Recalled, present, and predicted satisfaction in stages of the family life cycle in New Zealand." *The Journal of Marriage and the Family* 37:408–415.

Spanier. Graham, B. Robert, A. Lewis, and Charles L. Cole 1975 "Marital adjustment over the family life cycle: the issue of curvilinearity." *The Journal of Marriage and the Family* 37:263–275.

Spanier, Graham B., William Sauer, and Robert Larzelere 1979 "An empirical evaluation of the family life cycle." *The Journal of Marriage and the Family* 41:27–38.

——— 1979 "Gnawing away again: a reply and comment." *The Journal of Marriage and the Family* 41:692–693.

Szailai, A., et al., eds. 1972 *The Use of Time*. The Hague: Mouton.

Troll, L.E. 1975 *Early and Middle Adulthood*. Monterey, California: Brooks Cole Publishing Co.

Trost, Jan. 1974 "The family life cycle: an impossible concept." *International Journal of Family Sociology* 4:37–47.

Veevers, Jean E. 1973 "Voluntarily childless wives: an exploratory study." *Sociology and Social Research* 57:356–366.

_____ 1974 "The life-style of voluntarily childless couples." In *The Canadian Family in Comparative Perspective*, edited by Lyle Larson, pp. 395–411. Toronto: Prentice-Hall.

_____ 1975 "Factors in the incidence of childlessness in Canada: an analysis of census data." *Social Biology* 19:266–274.

44 On the Wholesomeness of Marriage

Nathan Keyfitz

NATHAN KEYFITZ, Leader of the Population Program at the International Institute for Applied Systems Analysis (Laxenburg, Austria), specializes in demography. His publications include *Introduction to the Mathematics of Population* (1968); *Population: Facts and Methods of Demography* with W. Flieger (1971); and *Applied Mathematical Demography* (1981, 1985). After two decades at the Dominion Bureau of Statistics, Professor Keyfitz taught at the Universities of Montreal, Toronto, Chicago, California (Berkeley), Harvard and Ohio State. He has lectured on population internationally (including Germany, Italy, India, China and the U.S.S.R.) and served as a consultant in Indonesia recurrently over the last thirty-five years. A Fellow of the Royal Statistical Society, Royal Society of Canada and American Statistical Institute, and past holder of executive positions in the Canadian Political Science Association, American Statistical Association and Population Association of America, Professor Keyfitz has been awarded honorary degrees by Harvard University, McGill University, and the Universities of Western Ontario, Montreal and Alberta.

USING MULTI-STAGE LIFE TABLES

That married people have lower death rates than single, widowed, or divorced has many times been exhibited in Canadian, American and other data. But the relative excellence and consistency of Canadian marriage and mortality data provide a unique opportunity to estimate the extent of the differences; to compare the advantage of marriage for men as against the advantage for women; and to see whether the married are more or less favored as time goes by.

The method used is the multi-state life table. A summary of the theory and applications for this method is found in Keyfitz (1985). We know from Canadian vital statistics, calendar year by calendar year and age by age, how many men and women marry, i.e., change from the single to the married state. For married couples we know how many break up through death or divorce. For the widowed we know how many remarry, and similarly for the divorced. These five are the only possibilities of change, except of course that people can stay in the same condition in successive years, and in any of the conditions they can die. Besides the counts of such transitions as given in vital statistics, we have from the census the number of persons in each category exposed to the risks of death, marriage, widowhood and divorce. No other data bearing on our subject are available or are needed for the immediate purpose.

The reader interested in results rather than method can skip the next few pages and turn to Table 7 and its discussion.

Table 1 gives an example for age 35–39 of the number of transitions divided by the exposures, i.e., the transition *rates*. We similarly recognize 13 five-year age groups from 20 to 80, with a 4×4 matrix for each age, or $13 \times 4 \times 4 = 208$ data elements. However, of the 16 elements of the matrix for each age only 9 are non-zero. The definition of "single" does not include anyone who has been married, and no one can go from divorced to widowed without going through married.

The material here is far too rich to be explored completely in this paper. Of all the themes that can be taken up we will look at only one: the mortality differences associated with marital status. Almost all of the discussion will revolve around the last row of Table 1 and of Table 6 below: the column totals of those tables.

The first column of the top half of Table 1 refers to single males, and says that the fraction of these aged 35–39 who move into the married state during a year is 0.048. Similarly, in column 2, the fraction of the married who divorce is 0.012; and in column 4, the fraction of the divorced who remarry is 0.225. These have the minus sign because they pass out of the category in question. The diagonal elements are the sum of negative elements in their column, plus the death rate. Thus for single males (in the first column) we see 0.053, which is the sum of the 0.048 just below it and the death rate, that for this group is 0.005, as appears in the total for this column.

That column total is equal to the ratio of the number of deaths to the number of persons exposed, as applies to each of the four categories recognized. Death rates for men

aged 35 to 39 are averaged over the years 1970–1982. Adding up the columns of the matrices in Table 1 gives death rates of 0.005 for single men, 0.002 for married; 0.005 for widowed; 0.005 for divorced. It is these death rates that we will compare in what follows to see how much greater is the longevity of the married compared with the other categories.

From such rates we can calculate (Table 2) the probability of being in the next age group five years later. Thus the chance that a single man 35–39 is married five years later is 0.206; that a widower is remarried is 0.435, etc. The totals give the probability that the person will be alive; for a divorced man that is 0.980, lower than the 0.992 for married man.

The probability that a person in one state at age 20 (the start of the present table, called the radix) is in the same (or another) state by age 35 is given in Table 3. Thus the chance

Table 1
RATES OF TRANSITION $_5m_{35}{}^{ij}$ FOR MEN AND WOMEN AGED 35–39 IN CANADA DURING THE 13 YEARS 1970–1982

Males

	Single	Married	Widowed	Divorced
Single	0.053	0.000	0.000	0.000
Married	−0.048	0.015	−0.116	−0.225
Widowed	0.000	−0.001	0.122	0.000
Divorced	0.000	−0.012	0.000	0.230
Total	0.005	0.002	0.005	0.005

Females

	Single	Married	Widowed	Divorced
Single	0.037	0.000	0.000	0.000
Married	−0.035	0.013	−0.045	−0.106
Widowed	0.000	−0.001	0.047	0.000
Divorced	0.000	−0.011	0.000	0.108
Total	0.002	0.001	0.002	0.002

Table 2
PROBABILITY OF SURVIVING $_5p_{35}{}^{ij}$ INTO THE NEXT AGE GROUP FOR CANADIAN MALES 1970–1982

	Single	Married	Widowed	Divorced
Single	0.768	0.000	0.000	0.000
Married	0.206	0.951	0.435	0.696
Widowed	0.000	0.003	0.534	0.001
Divorced	0.004	0.038	0.008	0.283
Total	0.978	0.992	0.978	0.980

Table 3
PROBABILITY $L_{35}{}^{(i)}/L_{20}{}^{(i)}$ OF SURVIVING FROM AGE 20 TO AGE 35 FOR CANADIAN MALES 1970–82

	Single	Married	Widowed	Divorced
Single	0.145	0.000	0.000	0.000
Married	0.802	0.951	0.731	0.944
Widowed	0.002	0.004	0.209	0.003
Divorced	0.021	0.029	0.021	0.029
Total	0.971	0.984	0.961	0.976

Table 4
EXPECTED NUMBER OF YEARS $_5L_{35}^{(1)}$ LIVED IN
THE 5-YEAR AGE INTERVAL 35–39 FOR
CANADIAN MALES 1970–1982

	Single	Married	Widowed	Divorced
Single	0.626	0.000	0.000	0.000
Married	4.062	4.736	3.898	4.688
Widowed	0.012	0.020	0.766	0.017
Divorced	0.110	0.144	0.114	0.143
Total	4.809	4.900	4.778	4.848

Table 6
EXPECTED NUMBER OF YEARS e_{35}^{ij} LIVED
BEYOND AGE 35 FOR CANADIAN MALES
1970–1982

	Single	Married	Widowed	Divorced
Single	21.744	−0.000	−0.000	−0.000
Married	12.287	36.924	25.480	31.146
Widowed	0.063	0.481	9.215	0.242
Divorced	0.414	1.858	1.057	4.291
Total	34.508	39.263	35.751	35.678

that a man single at age 20 is still single by age 35 is 0.145; the chance that a man divorced at age 20 is married at age 35 is 0.944. The chance that a man married at age 20 is alive at age 35 is 0.984; that a single man is alive is less: 0.971.

Numbers corresponding to the L_x column of the ordinary life table are given in Table 4. Thus it is expected that a man in the single state at age 20 will live 4.062 years in the married state between ages 35 and 39.

Table 5 corresponds to the life-table column designated T_x; it cumulates the L_x back from the end of the table. Thus a man who is single at age 20 can expect to have 29.563 years of marriage from age 35 onwards.

The usual life expectancy from the given age is provided by Table 6. A man who is single at age 35 can expect 21.744 years in the single condition, 12.287 years married,

etc. A widower aged 35 can expect far more years married: 25.480. Especially important for us will be the totals: a man single at age 35 can expect 34.508 years of life; one married can expect 39.263 years.

Table 7 summarizes such totals as given in Table 1 for the several ages. These age-specific death rates differ greatly among the several marital statuses, being lower at all ages for married than for single, with the widowed and divorced tending to be closer to the single than to the married. Men have much higher rates than women at all statuses and ages.

In order to judge the significance of these probabilities, we show them as ratios to the married in Table 8. The numbers are surprising: at a wide range of ages the single, widowed, and divorced show three or more times as high death rates as the married. Thus single men aged 35–39 had death rates 3.18 times as high as married men.

The program goes on to calculate the probability of a person surviving into a given state, as in Table 3. The totals for the several ages are shown in Table 9, which also gives the differences between the married on the one hand and the single, widowed and divorced on the other. All the last three columns are negative, with the males showing two or more times the values of the females.

Beyond that we can obtain the cumulative effects of the probabilities by adding from the given age to the end of life. The cumulative number constitutes expectation of life, and

Table 5
EXPECTED (AT AGE 20) NUMBER OF YEARS
T_{35}^{ij} LIVED BEYOND AGE 35 FOR CANADIAN
MALES 1970–1982

	Males			
	Single	Married	Widowed	Divorced
Single	3.154	0.000	0.000	0.000
Married	29.563	37.223	31.969	33.848
Widowed	0.106	0.244	2.020	0.180
Divorced	0.831	1.133	0.962	1.031
Total	33.655	38.600	34.951	35.059

Table 7
AGE-SPECIFIC DEATH RATES m_x FOR MALES
AND FEMALES IN CANADA, 1970–1982

Men

Age	Single	Married	Widowed	Divorced
20	0.002	0.001	0.003	0.003
25	0.003	0.001	0.005	0.003
30	0.003	0.001	0.005	0.004
35	0.005	0.002	0.005	0.005
40	0.007	0.003	0.007	0.008
45	0.011	0.004	0.012	0.013
50	0.017	0.008	0.017	0.018
55	0.022	0.012	0.023	0.025
60	0.031	0.020	0.034	0.036
65	0.044	0.030	0.046	0.049
70	0.063	0.045	0.064	0.066
75	0.087	0.067	0.087	0.091
80	0.124	0.103	0.125	0.123

Women

Age	Single	Married	Widowed	Divorced
20	0.001	0.000	0.003	0.001
25	0.001	0.000	0.002	0.001
30	0.002	0.001	0.002	0.002
35	0.002	0.001	0.002	0.002
40	0.003	0.002	0.003	0.003
45	0.005	0.003	0.005	0.005
50	0.006	0.004	0.006	0.006
55	0.009	0.006	0.009	0.008
60	0.012	0.010	0.012	0.012
65	0.018	0.015	0.018	0.018
70	0.027	0.024	0.027	0.028
75	0.043	0.040	0.045	0.043
80	0.073	0.069	0.075	0.076

Table 8
RATIO TO MARRIED RATES OF MORTALITY
FOR SINGLE, WIDOWED AND DIVORCED

Men

	Ratios to Married		
Age	Single	Widowed	Divorced
20	2.15	3.40	2.99
25	2.74	5.60	3.57
30	3.10	4.28	3.48
35	3.18	3.53	3.50
40	2.90	2.88	3.00
45	2.52	2.65	2.86
50	2.18	2.21	2.37
55	1.81	1.91	2.06
60	1.59	1.74	1.82
65	1.47	1.53	1.63
70	1.39	1.40	1.46
75	1.30	1.30	1.36
80	1.21	1.22	1.20

Women

	Ratios to Married		
Age	Single	Widowed	Divorced
20	2.10	9.32	2.87
25	2.75	5.27	3.22
30	2.70	3.89	2.58
35	2.48	2.61	2.50
40	2.03	2.14	1.97
45	1.74	1.81	1.78
50	1.50	1.51	1.49
55	1.40	1.40	1.39
60	1.25	1.29	1.29
65	1.18	1.20	1.21
70	1.11	1.13	1.14
75	1.07	1.12	1.09
80	1.06	1.09	1.10

this is given in Table 10. The row for males aged 35–39 in Table 10 is the same as the total of Table 6 except for the number of decimals shown. To measure the effect of marriage here it seems well to take, not a ratio to the expectations of the married, but again a difference; such differences are shown in the last three columns of Table 10.

The most important result of Table 10 is represented in Fig. 1, that shows the large and relatively consistent differences between the single and married life expectancies. The top two curves are not far separated, and the difference for females is indeed small, but it shows throughout the ages.

For males that difference is striking. It would be good to be able to interpret it in terms of the differential between smokers and non-smokers, between heavy drinkers and non-

Figure 1
LIFE EXPECTANCY, CANADA 1970–82
Men and women, single and married

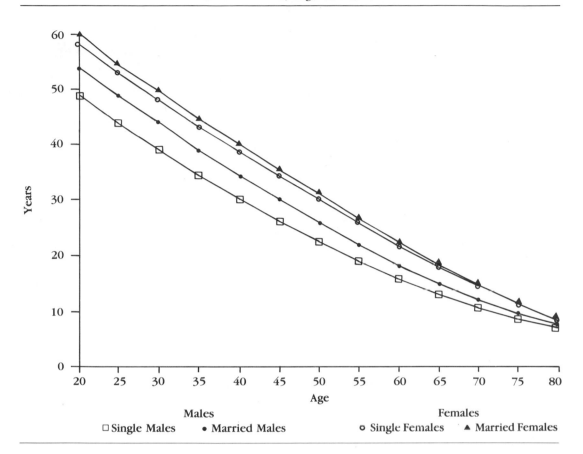

Males

Females

□ Single Males • Married Males o Single Females ▲ Married Females

drinkers, between rich and poor. Data for these other comparisons are not readily available for Canada, but we can say that there are few identifiable characteristics that give differences as great as the five years here shown between single and married males.

When we go beyond single and married, and consider the widowed and divorced, there is less consistency among ages (Fig. 2). At the younger ages divorced women are closer to the married, while at later ages the curves for divorced and single differences cross.

For men the single are considerably more disadvantaged in comparison with the mar-

ried than are the widowed and divorced. At the start of the table, at age 20, the single have over 5 years disadvantage against the married, while for widowed and divorced the disadvantage is less than four years. Just why the curves cross at later ages is difficult to surmise.

EXPECTED AGE AT DEATH

For some purposes it seems well to look not at the number of years of life expected, but at the expected age at death. In Table 11 (Appendix) we have it for men and women

Figure 2
DIFFERENCE FROM MARRIED
Men and women, 1970–82

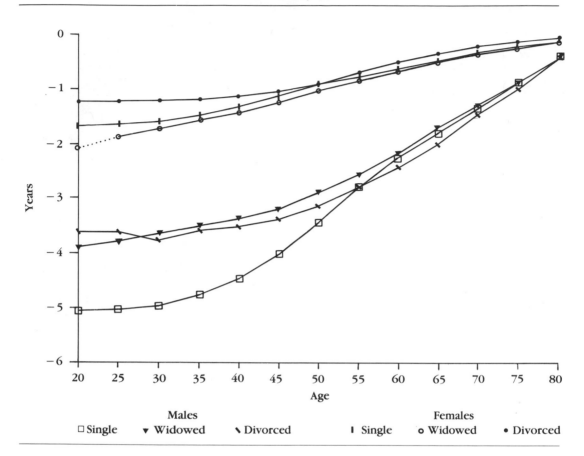

	Males			Females	
□ Single	▼ Widowed	◣ Divorced	⌷ Single	○ Widowed	● Divorced

over the period 1970–1982. A single man aged 25 can expect to live to age 68.75, a married man to age 73.76. A single woman can expect to live to age 77.80, a married woman to age 79.46. Note that the differential for sex is in general somewhat greater than that for marital status.

The numbers so far refer to the one period 1970–1982. We are fortunately able to separate out data for 1970–1972 and 1980–1982, and use these to examine for time trends. Table 12 (Appendix) shows some of the comparisons.

The difference in expectations was greater for males than for females at both times and practically all ages, as was indicated in earlier tables, but something is new here: the difference increases over time. Does that appear also when we take the ratio of single to married mortality rates? Table 13 (Appendix) shows that it does. One must disregard the first one or two ages, based on even fewer deaths than the 1970–1982 tables above, so I have reduced the tables to ages 35 to 65. Of course one such comparison does not prove a trend; it could be a fluctuation in a trend

Table 9

SURVIVORSHIP TO AGE 35 L_{35}/L_{20} (BASED ON 1970–1982 DATA) FOR MEN AND WOMEN IN THE SEVERAL MARITAL STATUSES AT AGE 20

Men

| Age | Single | Married | Widowed | Divorced | Difference from Married | | |
					Single	Widowed	Divorced
20	1	1	1	1	0	0	0
25	0.991	0.995	0.984	0.989	−0.004	−0.011	−0.006
30	0.982	0.990	0.968	0.984	−0.007	−0.022	−0.006
35	0.971	0.984	0.961	0.976	−0.013	−0.023	−0.008
40	0.952	0.976	0.949	0.962	−0.024	−0.026	−0.013
45	0.921	0.962	0.929	0.940	−0.041	−0.033	−0.022
50	0.876	0.939	0.892	0.901	−0.063	−0.047	−0.038
55	0.810	0.902	0.840	0.846	−0.091	−0.062	−0.055
60	0.731	0.846	0.769	0.771	−0.115	−0.077	−0.075
65	0.628	0.762	0.668	0.668	−0.134	−0.094	−0.094
70	0.507	0.650	0.548	0.541	−0.143	−0.102	−0.109
75	0.370	0.509	0.408	0.400	−0.139	−0.101	−0.109
80	0.238	0.352	0.267	0.259	−0.114	−0.085	−0.094

Women

| Age | Single | Married | Widowed | Divorced | Difference from Married | | |
					Single	Widowed	Divorced
20	1	1	1	1	0	0	0
25	0.997	0.998	0.987	0.997	−0.001	−0.012	−0.002
30	0.993	0.996	0.982	0.993	−0.003	−0.014	−0.003
35	0.986	0.993	0.976	0.988	−0.006	−0.017	−0.004
40	0.977	0.988	0.968	0.980	−0.011	−0.019	−0.008
45	0.963	0.979	0.956	0.969	−0.017	−0.023	−0.011
50	0.942	0.966	0.937	0.951	−0.024	−0.029	−0.015
55	0.914	0.945	0.911	0.926	−0.031	−0.034	−0.019
60	0.877	0.915	0.875	0.891	−0.038	−0.040	−0.024
65	0.827	0.870	0.825	0.840	−0.044	−0.046	−0.030
70	0.758	0.804	0.756	0.770	−0.047	−0.049	−0.034
75	0.663	0.707	0.660	0.672	−0.044	−0.047	−0.036
80	0.535	0.570	0.527	0.541	−0.035	−0.042	−0.029

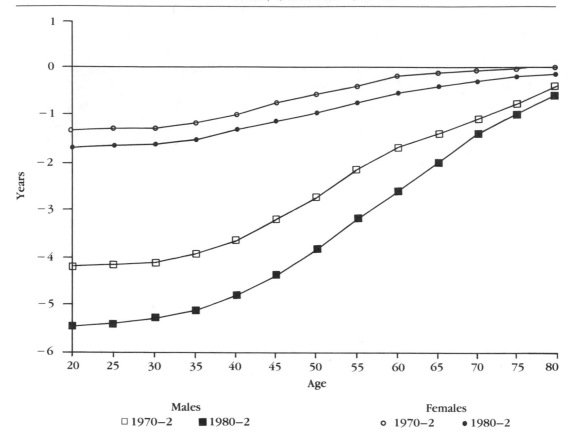

Figure 3
SINGLE: DIFFERENCE FROM MARRIED
Men and women, 1970–72 and 1980–82

Males
□ 1970–2   ■ 1980–2

Females
○ 1970–2   ● 1980–2

moving in some other direction. Still the consistency of the changes over 10 years is impressive.

Figure 3 shows the consistency as well as the substantial amount of the increase in differential between 1970–1972 and 1980–1982. The top lines are for females, and show at the younger ages the single one to two years lower expectation than the married. The bottom two lines show more than four years less for the single than for the married. For males the increase is more than 25 per cent; for females only slightly less.

Can all this be due to change in the completeness of the figures? That seems unlikely,

since no major changes in the collection procedures occurred in the 1970s; in fact the methods used have been about the same for several decades.

WHOLESOMENESS OR SELECTION?

While the present data do not suffice to establish the cause of the differences that appear so consistently in our tables, yet they do encourage some speculation on the subject.

First the difference between the sexes. If the difference was mostly due to selection

Table 10
EXPECTED FUTURE LIFETIMES e_x OF MEN AND WOMEN IN THE SEVERAL
MARITAL CONDITIONS

Men

Age	Single	Married	Widowed	Divorced	Difference from Married		
					Single	Widowed	Divorced
20	48.86	53.90	50.02	50.28	−5.04	−3.88	−3.62
25	43.75	48.76	44.97	45.14	−5.01	−3.78	−3.62
30	39.07	44.01	40.37	40.26	−4.94	−3.64	−3.75
35	34.51	39.26	35.75	35.68	−4.76	−3.51	−3.59
40	30.13	34.58	31.22	31.07	−4.46	−3.37	−3.51
45	26.04	30.05	26.87	26.65	−4.02	−3.19	−3.40
50	22.27	25.75	22.83	22.58	−3.48	−2.91	−3.17
55	18.89	21.73	19.16	18.88	−2.84	−2.58	−2.85
60	15.72	18.02	15.81	15.56	−2.30	−2.21	−2.46
65	12.92	14.74	12.99	12.74	−1.82	−1.75	−1.99
70	10.46	11.84	10.52	10.35	−1.38	−1.32	−1.49
75	8.44	9.36	8.46	8.35	−0.92	−0.90	−1.01
80	6.78	7.23	6.75	6.79	−0.45	−0.48	−0.44

Women

Age	Single	Married	Widowed	Divorced	Difference from Married		
					Single	Widowed	Divorced
20	58.09	59.76	57.67	58.52	−1.67	−2.09	−1.24
25	52.80	54.46	52.57	53.21	−1.66	−1.89	−1.25
30	47.99	49.60	47.86	48.37	−1.61	−1.74	−1.23
35	43.27	44.77	43.20	43.57	−1.50	−1.58	−1.21
40	38.68	40.01	38.58	38.87	−1.33	−1.43	−1.14
45	34.21	35.35	34.10	34.29	−1.14	−1.25	−1.06
50	29.91	30.83	29.78	29.90	−0.93	−1.05	−0.94
55	25.77	26.49	25.62	25.69	−0.72	−0.87	−0.80
60	21.77	22.29	21.60	21.63	−0.52	−0.69	−0.65
65	17.94	18.31	17.79	17.81	−0.37	−0.52	−0.50
70	14.34	14.58	14.20	14.23	−0.24	−0.38	−0.35
75	11.03	11.17	10.89	10.94	−0.14	−0.27	−0.23
80	8.05	8.13	7.98	7.97	−0.08	−0.15	−0.16

then one would have thought that it would be of about the same amount for women as for men. Women who were in poor health would think twice about marrying insofar as that involved starting a family. On the other hand men who were in poor health would

hesitate to take on the support of a family. And if the individual did not think of such things, the potential spouse probably would.

The difference between bachelordom and marriage must be greater for men than for women, at least insofar as selection and preparation of food are concerned. One can imagine that women would cook for themselves whether they were single or married while men without spouses would have a more casual approach to eating and certainly to cooking. Insofar as diet is a cause of the difference in mortality we can understand why men are harder hit by non-marriage.

What about the fact that widows and widowers have high mortality? We can imagine this as affected by assortative mating, that people tend to select mates similar to themselves. That would be true at least as respects social class, which we know has an inverse relation to mortality.

Most puzzling of all is the increase of the differential over the 1970s. There is no reason to think either that self-selection into marriage is stronger, or that the married condition is becoming more sharply differentiated from the single in respect of factors making for longevity. The differential of marriage must take its place with the differentials of social class and sex as only partially understood on present knowledge.

APPENDIX

Table 11
EXPECTED AGE AT DEATH $x + e_x$ FOR CANADIAN MEN AND WOMEN 1970–1982

	Men					Women			
Age	Single	Married	Widowed	Divorced	Age	Single	Married	Widowed	Divorced
20	68.86	73.90	70.02	70.28	20	78.09	79.76	77.67	78.52
25	68.75	73.76	69.97	70.14	25	77.80	79.46	77.57	78.21
30	69.07	74.01	70.37	70.26	30	77.99	79.60	77.86	78.37
35	69.51	74.26	70.75	70.68	35	78.27	79.77	78.20	78.57
40	70.13	74.58	71.22	71.07	40	78.68	80.01	78.58	78.87
45	71.04	75.05	71.87	71.65	45	79.21	80.35	79.10	79.29
50	72.27	75.75	72.83	72.58	50	79.91	80.83	79.78	79.90
55	73.89	76.73	74.16	73.88	55	80.07	81.49	80.62	80.69
60	75.72	78.02	75.81	75.56	60	81.77	82.29	81.60	81.63
65	77.92	79.74	77.99	77.74	65	82.94	83.31	82.79	82.81
70	80.46	81.84	80.52	80.35	70	84.34	84.58	84.20	84.23
75	83.44	84.36	83.46	83.35	75	86.03	86.17	85.89	85.94
80	86.78	87.23	86.75	86.79	80	88.05	88.13	87.98	87.97

Table 12
COMPARISON OF LIFE EXPECTATIONS e_x IN 1970–1972 AND 1980–1982

Men 1970–1972

Age	Single	Married	Widowed	Divorced	Difference from Married		
					Single	Widowed	Divorced
20	48.90	53.09	49.81	49.60	−4.19	−3.28	−3.49
25	43.80	47.97	44.82	44.47	−4.17	−3.15	−3.50
30	39.12	43.22	40.15	39.76	−4.10	−3.08	−3.46
35	34.58	38.51	35.54	35.00	−3.93	−2.97	−3.51
40	30.21	33.85	30.96	30.40	−3.65	−2.89	−3.45
45	26.15	29.36	26.62	25.96	−3.22	−2.74	−3.40
50	22.34	25.08	22.53	21.82	−2.73	−2.55	−3.26
55	18.91	21.10	18.78	18.10	−2.19	−2.32	−3.00
60	15.74	17.46	15.45	14.76	−1.71	−2.01	−2.70
65	12.90	14.24	12.55	11.97	−1.35	−1.69	−2.27
70	10.41	11.45	10.14	9.81	−1.04	−1.32	−1.64
75	8.33	9.07	8.09	7.82	−0.73	−0.98	−1.24
80	6.73	7.09	6.50	6.73	−0.36	−0.59	−0.36

Men 1980–1982

Age	Single	Married	Widowed	Divorced	Difference from Married		
					Single	Widowed	Divorced
20	49.35	54.82	50.61	50.65	−5.46	−4.21	−4.16
25	44.18	49.59	45.34	45.42	−5.41	−4.25	−4.16
30	39.49	44.80	40.74	40.64	−5.32	−4.07	−4.16
35	34.91	40.04	36.18	35.90	−5.13	−3.86	−4.13
40	30.52	35.33	31.61	31.27	−4.81	−3.72	−4.06
45	26.38	30.75	27.29	26.83	−4.37	−3.46	−3.92
50	22.52	26.38	23.30	22.71	−3.85	−3.07	−3.67
55	19.05	22.25	19.57	18.95	−3.20	−2.68	−3.30
60	15.84	18.46	16.19	15.61	−2.62	−2.27	−2.85
65	13.06	15.03	13.24	12.65	−1.97	−1.79	−2.37
70	10.62	12.02	10.70	10.22	−1.39	−1.32	−1.80
75	8.47	9.43	8.62	8.10	−0.96	−0.81	−1.33
80	6.79	7.27	6.90	6.56	−0.48	−0.37	−0.71

Table 12 (continued)
COMPARISON OF LIFE EXPECTATIONS e$_x$ IN 1970–1972 AND 1980–1982

Women 1970–1972

Age	Single	Married	Widowed	Divorced	Difference from Married Single	Difference from Married Widowed	Difference from Married Divorced
20	57.58	58.89	57.04	57.73	− 1.32	− 1.86	− 1.16
25	52.29	53.60	51.92	52.44	− 1.31	− 1.68	− 1.17
30	47.49	48.76	47.23	47.60	− 1.27	− 1.53	− 1.16
35	42.80	43.96	42.56	42.83	− 1.16	− 1.40	− 1.13
40	38.27	39.23	37.93	38.16	− 0.95	− 1.30	− 1.07
45	33.88	34.61	33.45	33.60	− 0.73	− 1.15	− 1.01
50	29.57	30.11	29.11	29.25	− 0.53	− 1.00	− 0.86
55	25.41	25.78	24.93	25.09	− 0.37	− 0.85	− 0.69
60	21.49	21.62	20.93	21.14	− 0.14	− 0.69	− 0.48
65	17.61	17.69	17.15	17.52	− 0.08	− 0.55	− 0.17
70	14.02	14.05	13.61	13.94	− 0.03	− 0.44	− 0.12
75	10.77	10.77	10.43	10.91	− 0.00	− 0.34	0.14
80	7.93	7.92	7.71	8.17	0.01	− 0.22	0.25

Women 1980–1982

Age	Single	Married	Widowed	Divorced	Difference from Married Single	Difference from Married Widowed	Difference from Married Divorced
20	58.54	60.44	58.29	58.59	− 1.90	− 2.15	− 1.85
25	53.23	55.12	53.23	53.27	− 1.89	− 1.89	− 1.85
30	48.41	50.25	48.55	48.41	− 1.84	− 1.70	− 1.84
35	43.67	45.40	43.84	43.58	− 1.73	− 1.55	− 1.82
40	39.08	40.62	39.25	38.87	− 1.54	− 1.37	− 1.75
45	34.59	35.93	34.76	34.27	− 1.34	− 1.17	− 1.66
50	30.23	31.36	30.36	29.83	− 1.13	− 1.00	− 1.53
55	26.05	26.94	26.13	25.57	− 0.90	− 0.81	− 1.38
60	22.08	22.70	22.08	21.48	− 0.62	− 0.62	− 1.22
65	18.24	18.66	18.22	17.60	− 0.42	− 0.43	− 1.06
70	14.60	14.87	14.60	14.01	− 0.27	− 0.26	− 0.85
75	11.19	11.38	11.22	10.74	− 0.18	− 0.16	− 0.64
80	8.17	8.24	8.17	7.64	− 0.07	− 0.07	− 0.60

Table 13

MORTALITY RATES m, BY MARITAL STATUS, AND RATIO TO MARRIED MORTALITY RATES, CANADIAN MEN AND WOMEN, 1970–1972 AND 1980–1982

Men 1970–1972

Age	Single	Married	Widowed	Divorced	Ratio to Married		
					Single	Widowed	Divorced
35	0.005	0.002	0.004	0.005	2.741	2.311	2.808
40	0.008	0.003	0.007	0.008	2.562	2.438	2.550
45	0.011	0.005	0.011	0.013	2.207	2.195	2.692
50	0.016	0.008	0.016	0.021	1.921	1.913	2.502
55	0.022	0.013	0.023	0.028	1.640	1.765	2.108
60	0.031	0.021	0.034	0.041	1.430	1.578	1.931
65	0.044	0.033	0.049	0.060	1.335	1.488	1.832

Men 1980–1982

Age	Single	Married	Widowed	Divorced	Ratio to Married		
					Single	Widowed	Divorced
35	0.005	0.001	0.005	0.005	3.583	3.740	3.639
40	0.007	0.002	0.008	0.007	3.257	3.928	3.524
45	0.010	0.004	0.012	0.012	2.688	3.277	3.068
50	0.015	0.006	0.016	0.017	2.414	2.444	2.601
55	0.021	0.011	0.022	0.024	1.934	1.993	2.176
60	0.031	0.017	0.031	0.033	1.793	1.790	1.879
65	0.044	0.028	0.044	0.048	1.574	1.571	1.734

Table 13 (continued)
MORTALITY RATES m$_x$ BY MARITAL STATUS, AND RATIO TO MARRIED MORTALITY RATES,
CANADIAN MEN AND WOMEN, 1970–1972 AND 1980–1982

Women 1970–1972

| Age | Single | Married | Widowed | Divorced | Ratio to Married | | |
					Single	Widowed	Divorced
35	0.003	0.001	0.002	0.003	2.416	1.980	2.467
40	0.004	0.002	0.003	0.004	1.973	1.864	1.959
45	0.005	0.003	0.005	0.006	1.620	1.649	1.998
50	0.006	0.004	0.006	0.007	1.395	1.423	1.650
55	0.009	0.007	0.009	0.010	1.384	1.351	1.484
60	0.012	0.010	0.013	0.015	1.120	1.255	1.455
65	0.018	0.017	0.019	0.018	1.081	1.159	1.097

Women 1980–1982

| Age | Single | Married | Widowed | Divorced | Ratio to Married | | |
					Single	Widowed	Divorced
35	0.002	0.001	0.003	0.002	2.869	3.161	2.757
40	0.003	0.001	0.003	0.003	2.173	2.293	2.077
45	0.004	0.002	0.004	0.004	1.825	1.771	1.808
50	0.006	0.004	0.006	0.006	1.628	1.547	1.605
55	0.009	0.006	0.008	0.008	1.534	1.425	1.444
60	0.012	0.009	0.012	0.012	1.328	1.322	1.353
65	0.017	0.014	0.017	0.018	1.213	1.232	1.323

Reference

Keyfitz, N. 1985. *Applied Mathematical Demography*. 2nd edition. New York: Springer.

45   Demographic Change and the Family

Roderic Beaujot   Kevin McQuillan

RODERIC BEAUJOT, Associate Professor of Sociology and Director of the Centre for Canadian Population Studies at the University of Western Ontario, London, specializes in demography, research methods and statistics, and the study of the family. His recent books and articles include *Growth and Dualism: The Demographic Development of Canadian Society*, with Kevin McQuillan (1982); "The effect of marital satisfaction on fertility" (1985); "Population policy development in Canadian demography" (1985); and "The decline of official language minorities in Quebec and English Canada" (1982). His research has included work in Tunisia, Senegal and Sierra Leone, for the International Development Research Centre.

KEVIN McQUILLAN, Associate Professor of Sociology at the University of Western Ontario, London, specializes in social demography and sociological theory. His recent publications include *Growth and Dualism: The Demographic Development of Canadian Society*, with Roderic Beaujot (1982); "On the development of Marxist theories of population" (1982); "Moving to the city: Migration to London and Paris in the Nineteenth Century" (1983); "Modes of production and demographic patterns in nineteenth century France" (1984); and "Ontario mortality patterns 1861–1921" (1985).

CANADA'S DEMOGRAPIIIC TRANSITION

Demographers claim that Canada, like all industrialized countries, has passed through a three-stage transition in demographic patterns. Up until the early nineteenth century, Canada experienced high birth and death rates. After this point, both birth and death rates began to fall but the drop in death rates was sharper than the decline in the birth rate. In recent times, the two rates have come back towards a rough equilibrium and the prospects for the near future are for a slow rate of population growth.

To examine the consequences of these changes, we have selected three points in time which illustrate markedly different demographic patterns: 1851, 1921, and 1981. While the selection of particular points in time is arbitrary and determined in part by the availability of data, these years provide good vantage points for examining changes in population patterns. . . .

CHILDBEARING

A major problem with many demographic measures is that they do not communicate to non-specialists the real nature of demographic change. Thus to note that the crude birth rate declined from 46 per 1,000 in 1851 to 15 per 1,000 in 1981 gives us only a vague sense of the dimensions of this change for society and for individuals. More useful is the total fertility rate which measures the number of children a woman would have if she experienced the age-specific rates for a given year. This measure suggests that in 1851 a woman would have slightly over seven children by the end of her childbearing years. This figure declined by roughly 50 percent by 1921 and was cut in half again between 1921 and the present, to the level of 1.7 births per woman on average.

A different way to look at this issue involves comparing the number of small children to the number of women of childbearing age. There were more children in Canada under the age of five in 1851 than women aged 20–44. By contrast, in 1981 there were only about four small children for every ten women in this age group. One direct result of this decline in fertility has been a shortening of the period in a woman's life devoted to childbearing and childrearing. The century since 1851 has seen the virtual elimination of childbearing among women over 35. And, while there has been some move toward an older pattern of childbearing among some groups of women in recent years, their childbearing experiences are limited to a short part of the life cycle. Indeed, one of the most remarkable changes in recent years has been the steady increase in the proportion of first births occurring to women over 30 years of age. This suggests that women who begin their childbearing early finish early as well; those who begin later also restrict the period of childbearing to a small number of years.

Along with the decline in the birth rate has come a marked change in the distribution of Canadian families by size. The change, however, is not precisely what one might have expected. Obviously, there has been a large decline in the number of families with four or more children. But in the years from 1921 to the 1970s, there has also been a large decline in the proportion of women who are childless or who have only one child. Put differently, there has been increasing adherence to the norm of the two-child family. Whether this will continue to be the case in the future is debatable. There are some indications that rates of childlessness may again be on the increase. Nevertheless, the data for the recent past demonstrate that the relationship between declining fertility and family size is not as simple as we might have predicted.

DEATH

The decline in death rates has been as dramatic as the decline in fertility. The crude death rate has declined from 22 per 1,000 in 1851 to 12 per 1,000 in 1921 and to 7 per 1,000 in 1981. However, because it is affected by the age composition of the population, the crude death rate is not a particularly good indicator of changes in mortality. Several other figures are more illuminating. Expectation of life at birth, for example, has increased from approximately 40 years for males living in 1851 to 72 years for males living in 1981. For females, the gains have been even larger, with life expectancy rising from 42 years in 1851 to 79 years in 1981.

It is particularly important, when examining changes in mortality, to identify the groups in the population which have benefited the most from changes in the overall patterns. Doing this, we note that the most significant change concerns the drop in infant mortality. The infant mortality rate, which measures the proportion of children who do not survive the first year of life, declined from 184 per 1,000 in 1851 to 102 per 1,000 in 1921. Thus while considerable progress was made during this period, the rate remained very high. In the more recent period, however, infant mortality has fallen precipitously. In 1981, only about 10 of every 1,000 live born children failed to celebrate their first birthday. Stated differently, almost one in five children did not survive their first year in 1851, compared to 1 in 100 in 1981. It is this decline which has helped to boost life expectancy so dramatically. The gains in life expectancy for those who reach their sixty-fifth birthday have been relatively small. What these data show is that the most important consequence of falling mortality rates has been to allow the vast majority of the population to reach retirement ages. The proportion of persons living to age 65 has increased from 32 percent in 1851 to 80 percent in 1981.

As another way of demonstrating the salience of these figures, let us assume that at each year we could look at a "representative village" of 1,000 people whose age structure and mortality pattern by age reflected that of the entire country. In 1851, the village of 1,000 people would experience a death of a child under one year of age every month and a half, while in 1981 one would occur every seven years. Similarly, at ages 1 to 4, a death occurs every 2.5 months under 1851 conditions but every 33 years under the 1981 conditions. One can say that deaths of children aged one to four are now virtually nonexistent. Let us take the point of view of a doctor who is the general practitioner for this village. If we assume a professional life of 35 years, the doctor would experience 465 deaths of children before their fifth birthday in 1851 conditions, but only six such deaths under 1981 conditions. At later stages of life, deaths of older people are now more frequent. In a village of 1,000 people there would be one death of a person over age 80 every 15 months in 1851 but every 6 months in 1981. The greater frequency of deaths of older people is not because their death rates have increased—in fact the rates have decreased—but because there is a higher proportion of older people in the population.

Life expectancy at age 20 gives a picture of the proportion of adult life that might be spent in retirement. In 1851, having reached age 20, an average person could expect to live another 40 years. If we consider retirement to be after age 65, this means that on average people could not expect to retire. In fact, retirement as we know it now was nonexistent. In 1921, people could expect at age 20 to spend 3 percent of their adult life in retirement while in 1981 it would be 21 percent. Stated differently, in 1921, having reached age 20, one could expect to work

an average of 34.6 years for each year of retirement, but by 1981 it would be 3.8 years of work for each year of retirement.

These changes in demography have had far-reaching effects on the Canadian community and no doubt on the attitudes of Canadians toward a number of important issues. The family, perhaps more than any other institution, has been transformed by the decline in mortality. The orphan was a significant figure in much nineteenth-century literature and the regular appearance of such characters reflected the frequency of the status in society. Under conditions of life expectancy similar to those experienced in Canada in 1851, 11 percent of children would have been maternal orphans by the age of 10 while under 1981 conditions such would be the case for only 1 percent of children.[1] More generally, under high mortality conditions, a large amount of chance and variability are injected into human affairs.[2] For instance, it is estimated that in seventeenth-century New France, half of couples would have lost a child before their sixth wedding anniversary, while now in only 10 percent of cases would a child die or leave the family by the fifteenth wedding anniversary.[3] It can be argued that the greater role played in the past by relatives outside the nuclear unit was a response to the greater likelihood of family disruption due to mortality. As death rates have fallen, the need for this form of insurance has declined as well.

Other social and psychological consequences of falling mortality rates, though no less important, are harder to measure. It seems almost certain, for example, that our increasing ability to relegate death to the older ages of life has profoundly affected attitudes towards and customs surrounding death. Philippe Aries has traced the evolution of customs associated with death in western societies and has argued that modern societies attempt to banish death from sight in order not to be constantly reminded of the inevitability of dying.[4] The dead and dying are increasingly removed from public eye in order to limit contact between the living and the dead. There can be little doubt that the decline in death rates and the increasing concentration of deaths among a restricted group of the population, a group whose participation in society is limited generally, has facilitated the development of these practices. The increasing predictability of death has allowed us to handle it in a more businesslike and orderly fashion. Blauner has argued that "the disengagement of the aged in modern societies enhances the continuous functioning of social institutions."[5] That is, companies, bureaucracies, and other institutions can suffer from the sudden disappearance of a given person in the structure. By setting old people aside, institutions are less subject to this disruption. The problem of course is that while the disengagement of the aged may be beneficial to the social structure, older people themselves bear the social costs of this isolation.

The fall in mortality has also revolutionized relationships between parents and children. A number of authors have pointed to the poor quality of care accorded to small children in premodern societies.[6] Much of this can be traced to the generally low standard of living in such societies, but it can be argued that the high infant mortality rates also discouraged the development of strong emotional bonds between parents and children. Parents resisted making large emotional investments in their children until they demonstrated their ability to survive. The delay in naming infants and the practice of giving the name of a child who had died to a subsequent child are cited as practices which demonstrate this relative lack of attachment.[7] Thus, a situation of high infant mortality is in a sense a vicious circle, with children valued less because they are less likely to survive, and with the lower emotional investment in children, reducing their survival chances.

Children's views of parents must also have been transformed by changing mortality ex-periences. Not only can most children expect that their parents will live until they achieve adult status, but a large proportion can expect to interact with their parents as adults for as long or longer than they did as children. Indeed, for many, at least one parent may be dependent on them for as long as they themselves were dependent on their parents during childhood. These changing roles of parents and children are likely to affect both family relationships and the decisions of young couples to have children.

Another consequence of the increased length of life is that the various parts of the life cycle have become more differentiated and more strictly tied to age. For instance, the boundaries between middle age and old age have been sharpened. In addition, as we will see in the next section, new stages of life have emerged, especially the empty nest period, retirement, and a long period of widowhood.

MARRIAGE AND THE FAMILY

Marital patterns have changed radically in some ways in the period since 1851, though not always in the manner one might have expected. For example, as Table 1 indicates, average age at first marriage has fluctuated somewhat, but the overall trend has been downward since 1851.[8] Contrary to what is sometimes thought, marriage did not occur at a particularly young age in the nineteenth century. But while age at marriage has changed very little, the potential length of marital life has been altered considerably. If all marriages are assumed to end in the death of one partner, the average duration of marriage will have increased from 28 years in 1851 to 47 years in 1981. In the mid-nineteenth century, only 6 percent of couples would have celebrated their fiftieth wedding anniversary compared to 39 percent under 1981 conditions. When romantic love was introduced into western civilization as the basis for

Table 1
MEASURES OF THE MARITAL LIFE CYCLE, CANADA, 1851, 1931, 1981

	1851	1931	1981
Singulate mean age at first marriage:			
Wife	23.8	24.6	23.1
Husband	26.8	27.7	25.2
Mean age of mother at:			
All births	30.7	29.9	26.6
Birth of first child	25.4*	26.6*	24.8
Birth of last child	35.9*	34.9*	31.1*
Marriage of last child	63.0	58.3	55.3
Mean age at death of one spouse:			
Wife	51.7	62.8	69.7
Husband	54.7	65.9	71.8
Mean years between marriage and first birth	1.6	2.0	1.7
Mean years of childbearing	10.5	8.3	6.3
Mean years of empty nest (marriage of last child to death of one spouse)	NIL	4.5	14.4
Mean years of marriage	27.9	38.2	46.6
Percent reaching 50th wedding anniversary	6.1	16.6	39.4
Percent never married at age 50:			
Females	7.7	10.4	5.9
Males	8.0	13.6	7.7
Percent of 15 + married	54.8	56.0	63.3

*Very approximate estimates were derived using United States data on average intervals between marriage and birth of first and last child from Paul Glick, "Updating the Life Cycle of the Family," *Journal of Marriage and the Family* 39 (1977): 6.

NOTE: For procedure used in calculation of mean age at death of one spouse, see Henry S. Shryock and Jacob S. Siegel, *The Methods and Materials of Demography* (Washington: U.S. Government Printing Office, 1973), p. 311. In calculating mean age at marriage of last child, we used singulate mean age at first marriage for 1881, 1956 and 1981, respectively.

Sources:
K.G. Basavarajappa, *Marital Status and Nuptiality in Canada* (Ottawa: Statistics Canada Catalogue No. 99-704, 1978), p. 62.
Bourbeau and Legare, *Essai sur la mortalité par génération au Canada et au Québec, 1831–1931*, Université de Montréal, Département de Demographie, document de travail, No. 11.
Dominion Bureau of Statistics, *Life Expectancy Trends: 1930–32 to 1960–62* (Ottawa: DBS Catalogue No. 84-518, 1967), p. 16.
Statistics Canada, *Life Tables, Canada and the Provinces, 1980–82* (Ottawa: Statistics Canada Catalogue No. 84-532, 1984).
Statistics Canada, *Vital Statistics, Volume I, Births and Deaths, 1981* (Ottawa: Statistics Canada Catalogue No. 84-204, 1983), pp. 6, 17.
1981 Census, 92-901: Table 5.
1931 Census, Vol. III: Table 12..
1851–52 Census, Vol. I: Nos. 5 and 6.
Henripin, *Trends and Factors of Fertility in Canada* (Ottawa: Statistics Canada, 1972), p. 378.

marriage, the promise to "love each other for life" had a vastly different time horizon. When young lovers make a lifetime promise, they probably do not realize that it is for almost 50 years. This change in the average length of marriage has changed the meaning of the phrase "till death do us part." An unhappy marriage is probably more likely to be broken when one has the horizon of a long life to "endure." The longer life provides the opportunity for a "new" life, including the possibility of a new spouse. In fact, it can be argued that the longer married life and the sharpening of boundaries between the various stages of life are an additional strain on marriage, as not all couples can successfully adapt to the successive sets of new roles that are implied.[9]

Thus the instability in family life caused by death is gradually being replaced by instability caused by voluntary dissolution. Whereas 98 percent of marital dissolutions in 1921 were caused by the death of one partner, death was responsible for only 55 percent of dissolutions in 1981.[10] And, of course, in the younger age groups the importance of divorce as the source of family breakup is even greater.

It is significant to note that the difference between typical ages of men and women at marriage has also decreased, by one year or one-third of the earlier difference. While this decrease is not particularly large, we would argue that it has considerable social significance. The younger person in a marriage is likely to have less education, to be less experienced at taking responsibility and leadership, and generally to have a lower status. The decrease in the typical age difference at marriage is thus probably associated with an increase in the relative status of wives in marriages and of women in society.

One other consequence of changing demographic patterns for marriage and the family deserves attention. The combination of declining fertility and mortality has served to create new stages in the marital life cycle which did not previously exist for most couples. The emergence of the empty nest stage between the marriage of the last child and the death of one of the spouses has become an important feature of contemporary marriages. This stage did not exist for the typical couple living in the mid-nineteenth century, but by 1981 the average couple could expect to live together for 14 years beyond the marriage of their last child. And interestingly, research on marital satisfaction suggests that many couples view this stage as among the happiest in their marital life....[11]

AGE STRUCTURE

... The age structure of the population is a function of the level of fertility and mortality and migration. But contrary to popular beliefs, it is the fertility rate which is by far the most important determinant. The population aging that Canada is now experiencing is the result of the continuing decline in fertility since the end of the baby boom and is only marginally a product of increases in expectation of life. Immigration has tended to moderate slightly the aging of the Canadian population, but over the more recent period its impact on the age distribution has been "almost imperceptible."[12] The aging of the population is thus a long-term process which parallels the decline of fertility since the mid-nineteenth century. Athough it was common during the 1960s to emphasize the youthful nature of the population, in fact nineteenth-century Canadian society was far younger. The median age of the population has risen from 17.2 in 1851 to 29.6 in 1981. And this figure is projected to increase to 41.0 by the year 2026![13] The changes can be highlighted by comparing the relative predominance of older and younger persons in the population. In 1851 there were five persons aged 65 and over for every 100 persons aged 0–19, while in 1981 there were 30, and in 2026 there would be 82 older persons for every 100 younger persons. In 1921 there were ten persons of retirement age (65 and over) for every 100 persons at working ages (20–64). In 1981 there were 17 retirement age persons for every 100 working age persons but this figure will double to 32 by 2026.

The aging of the population is a complex phenomenon. Most of the attention given this question has centred on the increase of the aged population and the potential difficulties facing governments charged with providing social services to this group. And indeed, difficult problems are likely to emerge in the near future in this regard. Retirement funds such as the Canada Pension Plan, which are funded by the contributions of current workers, are destined to encounter severe problems in the future.[14] Health costs are also likely to rise given the disproportionate use of medical facilities by the elderly population.[15] These trends suggest the need for a rearrangement of procedures for the organization and funding of many forms of social services. Patterns with respect to retirement itself may also need to change. An increase in employment rates among senior citizens would counter part of the transfer payment burden that will be associated with population aging after the turn of the century.

It is worth noting that the funding of retirement through year by year transfers from the working to the retired population is an attractive scheme when each generation is larger than the one before, but is considerably less attractive when the relative size of working age cohorts is decreasing. Stated differently, cohorts that give birth to many children will be more easily taken care of in their old age than those with few children. Thus, after the turn of the century, the baby boom cohorts will be at a disadvantage because the smaller baby bust cohorts that follow will be hard pressed to make contributions necessary to support their elders. One frequently hears the argument that pretransition fertility was high partly because parents needed their children as a source of support in old age. While providing for the elderly no longer occurs through family relationships, the argument that large families are useful for support in old age may still be true at the level of a total society.

Important as these issues are, however, they have deflected attention from other consequences of shifts in age structure, some of which are of benefit to Canadian society. As Richard Easterlin has pointed out in his analysis of American society, a decline in the proportion of the population in the young age groups can yield major benefits for the members of those groups and for society as a whole.[16] The rapid growth of the Canadian labour force during the last half of the 1960s and throughout the 1970s exacerbated the problem of unemployment. While increases in female participation rates contributed to this phenomenon, the major factor was the entrance into the labour force of the baby boom cohorts.[17] The recent slowdown in fertility will contribute to a slower rate of growth in the labour force and may well ease the problem of providing jobs for new entrants.

Shifts in age structure can have other beneficial effects as well. Since certain age groups are primarily responsible for certain forms of behaviour, changes in the relative weight of age groups within the population can produce important changes in the prevalence of certain types of activity. Crime is a particularly good example. Young males are responsible for a disproportionate share of most major crimes, particularly violent crimes. Thus the aging of the population will bring about a decline in the population of these high-risk groups in the population and, other things being equal, lead to a decline in rates of crime.[18] Similar kinds of arguments can be extended to other issues such as traffic fatalities.[19]

One final consequence of shifts in age structures should be noted. While being a member of a relatively large cohort can have disadvantages, it can also yield a number of advantages to the members of such a group. Thus a society such as Canada in 1851, in which the median age of the population was quite young, may accord to the young more power and privileges than would be the case in older societies. In this regard, it is interesting to note how young many Canadian political leaders were when they began their careers. Both Sir John A. Macdonald and Sir Wilfrid Laurier were first elected to public office by the age of thirty.[20] Indeed young people generally assumed positions of importance at an earlier age in nineteenth-century societies.

One might then expect that the current

aging of the Canadian population will have analogous effects. While the elderly may well suffer certain disadvantages, they may also find that their power and influence as a group is increasing. The potential for such change can be seen clearly if we look at the proportion of the voting population 65 years of age and over. In 1981, 13.5 percent of voters belonged to this age category, and by 2026 the proportion will rise to approximately 23.3 percent.[21] Combined with the fact that elderly people are more likely to turn out to the polls, these trends suggest that senior citizens will be able to wield increasing political power in the future.

IMPLICATIONS FOR THE FUTURE

... Projections of future demographic developments envision further small improvements in mortality rates and continued low fertility. If true, Canada will experience further changes in the age composition of the population; we may expect that, in the early decades of the next century, close to one in five Canadians will be over the age of 65. However, while assuming a continuation of present trends is the easiest strategy to follow when making projections, there is no guarantee that it is the most accurate. Preparing for the future demands that we examine the possible consequences of at least two other plausible paths of development. The first would entail a cyclical pattern of growth based on alternating periods of relatively high and relatively low fertility. Such a pattern would exacerbate problems of social planning, particularly in sectors such as education which are directly affected by population changes. The second alternative would see further declines in fertility and the prospect of population decline. ...

Notes

[1] Thomas K. Burch, "Some Social Implications of Varying Mortality," United Nations World Population Conference, Belgrade, 1965.

[2] Norman B. Ryder, "Reproductive Behaviour and the Family Life Cycle," in United Nations, *The Population Debate: Dimensions and Perspectives*, Vol. III (New York: The United Nations, 1975), pp. 278–88.

[3] Evelyne Lapierre-Adamcyk *et al.*, "Le cycle de la vie familiale au Québec vues comparatives, XVIIe–XXe siècles," *Cahiers Québécois de Demographie* 13, no. 1 (1984); 59–77. See also Yves Peron and Evelyne Lapierre-Adamcyk, "Les répercussions des nouveaux comportements sur la vie familiale: la situation canadienne," paper presented to the Conference on the Family and Population, Hanasaari, Expoo, Finland, May 1984.

[4] Philippe Aries, *Western Attitudes Towards Death* (Baltimore: Johns Hopkins University Press, 1974).

[5] Robert Blauner, "Death and Social Structure," *Psychiatry* 29, no. 4 (1966): 378–94.

[6] Edward Shorter, *The Making of the Modern Family* (New York: Basic Books, 1975); Lawrence Stone, *The Family, Sex and Marriage in England 1500–1800* (New York: Harper and Row, 1977).

[7] Shorter, *Modern Family*.

[8] See also Roy H. Rodgers and Gail Witney, "The Family Cycle in Twentieth Century Canada," *Journal of Marriage and the Family* 43 (1981): 727–40.

[9] Holger R. Stub, *The Social Consequences of Long Life* (Springfield: Charles C. Thomas Publisher, 1982).

[10] K.G. Basavarajappa, "Incidence of Divorce and the Relative Importance of Death and Divorce in the Dissolution of Marriage in Canada, 1921–1976," paper presented at the meeting of the Canadian Population Society, Saskatoon, June 1979; Statistics Canada Catalogue No. 84–204 (1981), p. 48 and No. 84–205 (1981), p. 14.

[11] Boyd C. Rollins and Harold Feldman, "Marital Satisfaction over the Family Life Cycle," *Journal of Marriage and the Family* 32 (1970):20–28: Eugen Lupri and James Frideres, "The Quality of Marriage and the Passage of Time: Marital Satisfaction over the Life Cycle," *Canadian Journal of Sociology* 6 (1981):283–305.

[12] David K. Foot, "Immigration and Future Population," Paper prepared for Policy and Program Analysis Branch, Employment and Immigration Canada, 1984, p. 13.

[13] Statistics Canada, *Population Projections for Canada and the Provinces* (Ottawa: Statistics Canada Catalogue No. 91–520, 1979), p. 468.

[14] A. Asimakopulos, "Financing Canada's Public Pensions—Who Pays?," *Canadian Public Policy* 10 (1984): 156–66.

[15] David K. Foot, *Canada's Population Outlook: Demographic Factors and Economic Challenges* (Toronto: James Lorimer, 1982); L.A. Lefebvre, Z. Zigmund and M.S. Devereaux, *A Prognosis for Hospitals* (Ottawa: Statistics Canada Catalogue No. 83–250, 1979); Leroy O. Stone and Michael J. Maclean, *Future Income Prospects for Canada's Senior Citizens* (Montreal: Institute for Research on Public Policy, 1979).

[16] Richard Easterlin, "What Will 1984 Be Like? Some Socioeconomic Implications of Recent Twists in Age Structure," *Demography* 15, no. 4 (1978): 397–432.

[17] Foot, *Canada's Population Outlook*, pp. 191–194.

[18] Easterlin, "What Will 1984 Be Like?"; C.F. Wellford, "Age Composition and the Increase in Recorded Crime," *Criminology* (May 1973): 61–71.

[19] A.C. Irwin, "A New Look at Accidental Deaths," *Canadian Journal of Public Health* 66 (1975); 457–60; I. Waldron and J. Eyer, "Socioeconomic Causes for the Recent Rise in Death Rates for 15–24 Year Olds," *Social Science and Medicine* 9 (1975): 383–96.

[20] *The Macmillan Dictionary of Canadian Biography* (Toronto: Macmillan, 1978), pp. 444, 495.

[21] Statistics Canada, *Population Projections*.

46 The Politics of Pronatalism

Jean Veevers

JEAN VEEVERS, Professor of Sociology at the University of Victoria, specializes in the study of the family. Her books and articles include *Childless by Choice* (1980); *The Family in Canada: 1971 Census of Canada Profile Study* (1977); "The social meaning of pets: Alternate roles for companion animals" (1985); "Accelerating sex mortality differentials among black Americans" with Ellen Gee (1985); and "Age discrepant marriages: A cross-national analysis of Canadian-American trends" (1984). Professor Veevers has held visiting appointments at the University of Waterloo, the University of California at Berkeley, the University of Hawaii, and Statistics Canada.

From its inception, our study of voluntary childlessness was modest in its scope. We began our research with an intense curiosity about what seemed a fascinating and neglected minority: childfree persons living in a child-centered world. In accepting from the start the limitations intrinsic in research based on a purposive sample, it was never our intention to offer firm conclusions which would be generalizable to all deliberately childless persons. Our 156 respondents were not selected as a representative sample of all childless couples; rather, they were selected because their probability of remaining permanently childless was very high, and because they were willing to speak openly and at length about their motivations and experiences. In talking with our respondents, we sought to learn how they had come to question the parenthood mystique, how they ultimately made the decision to reject it, and how their lives had been affected as a result of those atypical decisions. The information we collected was not easy to quantify, but it was qualitatively rich, and therefore ideal for stimulating more investigations. These new research initiatives will, we hope, consider our findings and tentative conclusions, and direct their attention to one or more questions related to the antecedents and consequences of being childless by choice.

THE INCREASE IN VOLUNTARY CHILDLESSNESS

Since the turn of the century, childlessness among Canadian and American women has shown wide fluctuations. From 1910 to 1940, rates of childlessness tended to increase. From the war years and postwar period until the mid-1960s, however, childlessness rates declined to the point where many experts declared that voluntary childlessness was virtually extinct (Whelpton, Campbell and Patterson, 1965: 163; Thomlinson, 1975: 148; Tomasson, 1966: 328; Westoff and Westoff, 1971:35). Such conclusions appear to have been premature, in that the total incidence of childlessness still exceeded sterility estimates for most groups. Since the 1960s, studies of the incidence of childlessness confirm that childlessness has increased, especially among young wives.[1]

Predicting the incidence of childlessness in the future is hazardous, in that current expectations of births may or may not be realized in actuality. Although only a small minority of young childless wives expect never to have children, this minority is increasing. For example, in the United States in 1967, among white wives aged eighteen to thirty-nine, 3.0 per cent never expected to have children; by 1975, this had increased to 4.8 per cent (United States Bureau of the Census, 1976b:5). Similarly, Blake (1974:34) reports that from 1961 to 1971 the proportion of college women preferring childlessness increased from 1 per cent to 9 per cent. More important for predicting childlessness, however, are those women who say they intend to have a child eventually, but who are postponing starting a family. Some researchers predict a resurgence of fertility when presently childless young women near the end of their childbearing years (Blake, 1974:43; Sklar and Berkov, 1975). It seems likely, however, that a sizeable proportion of supposedly temporary postponements of childbearing will eventually become permanent postponements (Glick, 1975). Given the fundamental changes in fertility patterns which are occurring, it seems likely that low fertility is indeed here to stay (Bumpass, 1973). Present rates of childlessness are likely to be maintained and, given current trends towards contraceptive use, family norms, and sex roles, it seems likely that voluntary childlessness will continue to increase (DeJong and Sell, 1977; Poston and Gotard, 1977). Westoff (1978:55) suggests that the developed countries of the world are witnessing an "ongoing retreat from parenthood." He concludes that:

> If current rates for first births were to persist, some 30 per cent of U.S. women now of childbearing age would never have children. The highest proportion on record was 22 per cent childless for U.S. women born in 1908. It seems likely that today's young women will break that record by a few percentage points (Westoff, 1978:55).

Since there is no reason to expect an increase in sterility among young populations, the acceleration of rates of childlessness can be assumed to be almost entirely due to deliberate avoidance of parenthood. If Westoff's predictions hold, in the immediate future we would expect voluntary childlessness to characterize between 10 and 15 per cent of all couples—approximately three times as many as were found in the 1960s.

A TYPOLOGY OF CHILDLESSNESS

Descriptions of childless couples have dichotomized them in terms of a number of variables: by whether they made their decision before ("early articulators") or after marriage ("postponers"); by whether they achieved it independently or by negotiation; by whether they have high or low levels of commitment to it; and by whether they are primarily motivated by reactive or proactive factors. Our data seems to suggest that some useful hypotheses can be formulated regarding the relationships among these four dimensions. The cornerstone of this hypothesis is the notion that there are two quite different kinds of voluntary childless persons: **rejectors** and **aficionados**.[2]

Voluntarily childless persons whom we have designated as rejectors are those who disavow the parenthood mystique and who have actively and vehemently rejected the parenthood role. Rejectors are primarily motivated by *reaction* against the *dis*advantages of having children. Their decision is an immutable part of an idiosyncratic belief system, in that they cannot imagine any circumstances under which they would want to have children. Rejectors often tend to dislike children, and to avoid being around them. A number of them flaunt their childlessness; others actively proselytize their antinatalist ideology and childfree lifestyle.

Aficionados are persons who are ardent devotees of voluntary childlessness because they appreciate the *advantages* of being childfree, rather than the disadvantages of parenthood. They are not so much against children as they are intrigued and beguiled by some other interest which does not include children. Such enticements may range from hard science to pottery, from art to mountain-climbing, from literature to horse racing. Such persons are "buffs" who find, in the pursuit of their passion, that children would be an impediment. They made their decisions about parenthood primarily in terms of the positive attractions of other interests. They tend to negotiate their decision over the course of their marriage, in the context of the development of other interests, and to be less definite in their commitment to it. Generally, they like children, or at least have a neutral attitude towards them, and on the issue of natalism, they tend to be apolitical, endorsing neither the pronatalist nor the antinatalist perspective. In terms of comparisons with the general population, one might hazard a guess that aficionados are more similar to parents than are rejectors, who tend to have more varied and unconventional backgrounds and childhood experiences. . . .

THE CONSEQUENCES OF CHILDLESSNESS

The most important finding of our research is simply stated in one observation: from our vantage point, it seems clear that at least some voluntarily childless couples *do* achieve high levels of personal, marital, and social adjustment. Moreover, from our interviews, it seems clear to us that for many of the childless, the maintenance of sound mental health is not achieved in spite of being childless, but is predicated upon the continued avoidance of parenthood. This conclusion would perhaps seem "obvious" were it not for the fact that it contravenes a basic assumption of Canadian-American culture, namely that children are *necessary* for happiness and fulfillment. While it may well be that under many circumstances children do contribute to satisfactory life adjustment, the in-depth interviews we conducted do establish that, at least

for some persons, alternative lifestyles may provide the same level of satisfaction.

The implications of this simple finding are manifold. The pronatalist premise that having children is a desirable goal for all persons must be modified to the more limited premise that it is not necessary for all and that for some persons under some circumstances childlessness may be a more desirable alternative. Presently, young couples are oriented towards a basic question: how many children do you want to have? More appropriately, we might rather orient them to the question: do you want to have any children? . . .

IMPLICATIONS FOR SOCIAL POLICY

Consciousness-raising: to parent or not to parent

An insidious aspect of traditional pronatalism is the implicit assumption that parenthood is inevitable. Consequently, although there may be a choice of *how many or when*, the choice of *to parent or not to parent* is not raised to the level of awareness. It is not known how often pronatalism is in fact "coercive," in the sense of leading couples to have children they did not especially want for the sake of social approval, rather than for other reasons. There is reason to believe, however, that it does happen (Flapan, 1969:409; Hardin, 1971:265), and that such circumstances are not the most auspicious for either mother or child. Social policies which make implicit pronatalism explicit would go a long way towards lessening its undesirable effects, and towards making childlessness a viable option. . . .

Debating the pros and cons: pronatalism versus antinatalism

Persons trying to debate the pros and cons of having children, and needing to come to a decision, cannot wait for social science to develop a "parent test" for guidance in their decision. In this instance, even the decision not to decide is eventually a *de facto* decision, as the biological and social reasons for having a child will pass and the couple will find that their option to have children has disappeared.

In assembling and weighing relevant evidence, a couple deliberating childbearing will find the pronatalist case excessively documented. In terms of social policy, there is no need to elaborate further the already elaborate mechanisms whereby young adults are bombarded with messages advocating parenthood. While pronatalism may provide essential psychological support for some persons facing the difficult task of child-rearing, it may also create unnecessary frustrations in others. The oversell of parenthood may lessen rather than enhance later adjustment to it, in that the actual experiences cannot live up to the romanticized expectations implicit in the advance billing. Some increase in the messages concerning the disadvantages of having children would help make expectations more realistic, and would make for a more balanced and informed decision.

Maintaining free choice: implications for physicians

Encouraging couples to debate the pros and cons of parenthood and, as much as possible, to make a "rational" decision, is of little utility unless they are then able to carry it out. Maintaining an atmosphere of free choice involves two components: first, avoiding permanent, irreversible decisions until the couple are indeed certain of their motivations; and second, providing the means whereby the final decision can be implemented. To achieve these ends, it is necessary to have unrestricted access to all of the means of birth control: contraception, abortion, and sterilization.

Availability of Contraception and Abortion. Barring the alternative of infanticide, the role of parenthood is an irrevocable one. Once a child is born, its parents are required to act as parents for some twenty years. The irreversible nature of the decision to have a child argues strongly for the position of the planned parenthood movement that it is a decision that should be made with deliberate foresight. Deciding to be childless is of little consequence if fate then intervenes in the form of an accidental pregnancy that a woman cannot or will not abort.

At the present time, attempts to control fertility have as their focal concern a target population of young married mothers. While this group certainly incurs the greatest number of pregnancies, wanted or otherwise, it is not the only segment of the population seeking freedom from the "tyranny of pregnancy." In terms of the law, fertility control is theoretically available to all adults; in actual practice, however, conscientious assistance with problems of fertility control is more likely to be forthcoming for mature married parents than for any other group.

Availability of Sterilization. Legally, all persons past the age of consent have a right to sterilization. In practice, however, many physicians are reluctant to sterilize persons who are unmarried or who are childless,[3] either because they are afraid of subsequent lawsuits, or because they personally disapprove. The film of childlessness entitled *Surely You Don't Mean Not Ever?* focuses attention directly on an issue considered critical in responding to childlessness. Often, temporary childlessness may be more or less acceptable, whereas permanent childlessness is not. The important factor in such deliberations is the question of irreversibility. When couples postpone having children for a long period of time, there is always the possibility that when they do decide to have a child they will find they have become sterile, or at least sub-fecund. More dramatically, when a childless couple decide that one or the other or both should be sterilized, they assert that they *never* want to have children. The younger a couple are when they declare their intention to avoid parenthood, the more they are looked upon askance, and the less they are granted credibility. Often, it is assumed that young couples do not know their own minds and that when they "grow up," they will change their views. The older couples who express a similar intention are taken more seriously because of their maturity, but they are also viewed with greater alarm. They are, after all, "old enough to know better," and they are cautioned not to wait too long, lest they find later they cannot have children and regret their lost opportunities. The possibility of regret is a relevant question, but unfortunately, is an unanswerable one. No one can be accountable for how he or she will feel in twenty years. Probably some childless couples do regret their lack of progeny. Certainly many parents lament, and loudly, their regret at having produced offspring. In 1975, a Gallup Poll of a representative sample of Americans found that in response to the question: "If you had it to do over again, would you have children?" one in ten parents said they would not (McLaughlin, 1975:37). When considering childlessness, the question of irreversibility is a false issue in light of the fact that having a child is an irreversible decision, too. It is noteworthy that it would not be cause for comment or alarm if a person of twenty-one made the irreversible decision to have three children; however, it would be cause for considerable comment if she made the irreversible decision to have no children.

In our opinion, the control of fertility should be vested in the individual, rather than subject to unilateral decisions by a physician. To achieve this in practice as well as in theory, medical school curricula should include a discussion of moral and ethical issues with regard to pronatalism. Since pronatalism pressure from physicians may be covert as well as overt, it is important to sensitize physicians to the ways in which they may be implicitly imposing their own values upon their patients. . . .

Notes

[1] This finding is consistent in terms of period rates (Sell, 1974; DasGupta, 1975; DeJong and Sell, 1977) or of cohort analyses (Hastings and Robinson, 1974; Poston and Gotard, 1977). For example, in the United States, among white ever-married women aged twenty to twenty-four, the percentage remaining childless increased from 25.0 per cent in 1960 to 44.7 per cent in 1975. An equally dramatic increase occurred among slightly older wives aged twenty-five to twenty-nine, where rates jumped from 12.3 per cent in 1960 to 21.6 per cent in 1975 (United States Bureau of the Census, 1976a:33).

[2] Strong (1967:2246) provides a similar distinction. In a study of over 300 childless Negro couples in Washington, two types were observed: the tradition-oriented who had had negative family experiences, and the upward-striving who had enjoyed positive family experiences. Strong suggests different central concerns of these two groups. "The tradition-centered group desired economic security and freedom from the impoverished and unstable background that many of them had known, while the upward-striving group emphasized maintaining the status quo which they had achieved."

[3] In the past, the absence of legal restrictions regarding the rights of adults to be sterilized if they choose to do so was not reflected in common medical practice. For example, Landis (1966) studied the attitudes of 1,500 physicians toward vasectomy and found the simple reason of not wanting children was not considered acceptable for having the operation performed. Most (70 per cent) indicated they would refuse a vasectomy to a single man and more than half (60 per cent) said they would refuse a man with no children. Since

children are commonly assumed to be more essential to women than to men, probably an even larger proportion of doctors would have refused to sterilize a childless woman. Thus, after a review of a number of objections to vasectomy (such as religious conflicts, possible legal action for civil damages and problems of impotence), the American Medical Association (1968:821) concluded, after no reference at all to the importance of number of children, that:

> ... the following can serve as preliminary guidelines ... if a man can reconcile the operation with his religion, *if he has several children*, if he lacks observable psychiatric sex-oriented stigma, and if his wife agrees to the operation ... surely then he should be able to obtain a vasectomy for reasons of contraception alone [emphasis ours].

By implication, at that time in the editorial opinion of the AMA, a man who did not have children should not have been able to obtain a vasectomy simply as a means of birth control. Many doctors still refuse to perform sterilizations on unmarried people or on those without children.

References

Blake, Judith 1973 "Coercive pronatalism and American population policy," pp. 85–109 in Robert Parke, Jr. and Charles F. Westoff (eds.), *Aspects of Population Growth Policy*. Washington, D.C.: Commission on Population Growth and the American Future.

———— 1974 "Can we believe recent data on birth expectations in the United States?" *Demography*, 11 (February): 25–44.

Bumpass, Larry 1973 "Is low fertility here to stay?," *Family Planning Perspectives*, 5 (Spring): 67–69.

DeJong, Gordon F. and Ralph R. Sell 1977 "Changes in childlessness in the United States: a demographic path analysis, *Population Studies*, 31 (March): 129–141.

Flapan, Mark 1969 "A paradigm for the analysis of childbearing motivations of married women prior to the birth of their first child," *American Journal of Orthopsychiatry*, 39 (April): 402–417.

Glick, Paul C. 1975 "A demographer looks at American families," *Journal of Marriage and the Family*, 37 (February): 15–27.

Hardin, Garrett 1971 "Multiple paths to population control," pp. 259–266 in Daniel Callahan (ed.), *The American Population Debate*. New York: Doubleday.

McLaughlin, Mary 1975 "Parents who wouldn't do it again," *McCall's*, 103 (November): 37–38.

Poston, Dudley L., Jr., and Erin Gotard 1977 "Trends in childlessness in the United States, 1910 to 1975," *Social Biology*, 24 (Fall): 212–224.

Sklar, June, and Beth Berkow 1975 "The American birth rate: evidences of the coming rise," *Science*, 189 (August 29): 693–700.

Strong, Ethelyn Ratcliff 1967 *The Meaning of Childlessness to Childless Negro Couples*. Ph.D. dissertation, The Catholic University of America, Washington, D.C. *Dissertation Abstracts*, 1967, 28:2346.

Thomlinson, Ralph 1965 *Population Dynamics*, New York: Random House.

Tomasson, Ralph 1966 "Why has American fertility been so high?," pp. 327–338 in Bernard Farber (ed.), *Kinship and Family Organization*. New York: John Wiley.

United States Bureau of the Census 1976a "Fertility of American Women: June 1975," *Current Population Reports*, Series P-20, No. 301, Washington, D.C.: U.S. Government Printing Office.

———— 1976b "Fertility History and Prospects of American Women: June 1975," *Current Population Reports*, Series P-20, No. 288. Washington, D.C.: U.S. Government Printing Office.

Westoff, Charles F. 1978 "Marriage and fertility in the developed countries." *Scientific American*, 239 (December): 51–57.

Westoff, Leslie A., and Charles F. Westoff 1971 *From Now to Zero: Fertility, Contraception and Abortion in America.* Boston: Little Brown and Company.

Whelpton, Pascal K., A. Campbell and J. Patterson

1966 *Fertility and Family Planning in the United States.* Princeton, New Jersey: Princeton University Press.

Political and Economic Organization

Introduction

I n an earlier section, we noted some fundamental disagreements about the nature and sources of inequality. Marxists tend to analyze inequality as a primarily economic issue; Weberians as a multi-dimensional issue including social/psychological elements. Let's consider these differences a little further before proceeding to the subject of this section.

For Weberians, inequality is largely the result of *closure*, by which the powerful deny others access to desired resources. The desired resources are various, and so are the means of exclusion. For example, members of a profession may decide whom they want to prevent from getting the credentials needed to practise the profession. Ethnic groups may exclude people of other ethnic origins from certain jobs and opportunities. Males may exclude females from certain kinds of activities. The power needed to exclude others may not be ownership of the "means of production" in the traditional Marxist sense. Likewise, the reasons for exclusion may not be narrowly economic or political.

Rather, closure may be a largely social or symbolic activity which gives the ex-cluding group added status and cohesion, while also reducing the number of economic competitors. But to the extent that it is a symbolic rather than narrowly economic act, closure requires social and psychological explanation. It is doubtful that Gentiles discriminate against Jews, Whites discriminate against Blacks, or men discriminate against women on strictly rational grounds. Attitudes, values and beliefs must enter into our explanation. We have already seen the need to deal with symbolic issues in understanding gender inequality. Where race and ethnic inequalities are concerned, organizational forces such as institutional completeness are also important. Communities and communal institutions create a momentum for ethnic survival and growth that tends to exclude other groups. The group's acquisition of economic power is mainly important as a means of ensuring its own survival and cohesion, and maintaining its status among other ethnic communities. Ethnic competition is not simply class conflict being fought out under another name.

Thus Weber would argue that class relations are but one type of closure, and classes follow exclusionary principles used by all status groups in maintaining or improving their own wealth, power and respectability. But Marx would deny this. He would see class relations, built around relations to the means of production, as fundamental. For Marx, other forms of inequality and conflict either derive from class struggle or else demonstrate "false consciousness." From the Marxist perspective, the key institutions in society are the *economy*, which produces and distributes wealth, and the *state*, which legitimates the uses of power protecting this wealth.

Sociological research focusing on political and economic organization often tends to follow in the Marxist path and, though not always, it is often *macrosociological* rather than social psychological. Moreover, the state and economy are assumed to be strongly linked. However, as we shall see, the nature of this link continues to receive much debate.

Both in the traditional Marxist formulation and in the political-economy tradition developed by Harold Innis, the economy is the main force for change and the state merely facilitates and legitimates economic change. This view implies a unified ruling class, comprising economic and political elites; but this view is rejected by some. Liberals such as John Porter (in *The Vertical Mosaic*) have denied the unity of the ruling class, and emphasized the plurality of interests within the economy, within the polity, and between the economy and polity. This aside, what is common to students of political and economic organization is the conviction that the most important social conflicts are fought out in this arena, not in households, schools or the mass media.

Further, the big fights are fought by elites, not by ordinary individuals. Unlike liberal sociologists, who tend to study ordinary people's behaviours and opinions,

the sociologists who study political and economic organization are, if interested in individuals at all, interested in *elite* individuals. "Elites" are people who hold positions of great authority in large and powerful organizations. Sociologists are interested in knowing who these people are, what classes they came from, what they think, and how they behave. Some assume that, if different people occupied the elite positions, political and economic decisions might be made differently. For this reason, the recruitment and socialization of elite individuals is a topic of continuing interest. But more and more, elite individuals are studied to trace the linkages and probable co-operation between major institutions. Sociologists assume that important "interlocked" organizations, having one or more directors in common, are likely to co-operate economically and politically. Thus, for some analysts, interlocking directorships are both the means and the indicator of interorganizational and class co-operation.

The articles in this section fall into three main categories. First are two articles on economic structures by Gordon Laxer and Jorge Niosi. Then come two articles on political structures by Mildred Schwartz and Rick Ogmundson. Finally, Michael Ornstein shows the ideological similarities between these two structures in a concluding article.

A central concern of economic sociologists has been to explain Canada's peculiar history of economic development and, particularly, its historical economic dependence first on Britain, then on the United States. In his article, Gordon Laxer uses cross-national data to determine whether Canada had to depend on foreign capital because it industrialized relatively late. Comparing Canada to other equally late industrializers convinces him that the problem does not only lie there, but also with the failure to develop strategic industries (especially military industries) and the weakness of anti-elitist agrarian movements in late nineteenth century Canada. As a result, "big business ruled easily . . . (and) state policies were pitched towards the short-term interests of the majority of Canadian businessmen." Extravagant, unnecessary expenditures, large foreign debts, and the expansion of bank investment abroad rather than within Canada all led in the same direction. Canada's failure to industrialize using indigenous capital progressively worsened; today, our economy is badly hampered by foreign ownership, and our political autonomy is limited.

Yet, paradoxically, at the same time that American multinational corporations are tightening their hold on the Canadian economy with profits earned in Canada, Canadian-owned multinationals are behaving in the very same ways elsewhere. Nothing about Canadian ownership will necessarily make a firm want to create jobs or spend profits in Canada. Rather, Canadian multinationals, like any other multinationals, seek out the greatest profit wherever it may be found. The article by Jorge Niosi shows that Canadian multinationals are quite indistinguishable from any others in this respect.

Professor Niosi has no more doubt than Professor Laxer that the Canadian State has promoted the interests of both indigenous elites and the foreign multinationals. The Canadian state made it easy for foreign multinationals to invest in Canada up to about fifteen years ago, while this benefited indigenous banking and industrial interests. Since then, the State has hesitated to allow further foreign direct investment and has instead worked hard to promote Canadian multinationals overseas. As the interests of Canadian capital have changed, so has the role played by the Canadian State to limit foreign multinationals and promote Canadian multinationals. What Niosi seems to be arguing is that Canada is by no means exceptional: its capitalist class, mul-

tinational organization, and political elite act much the same as they would in other capitalist nations. What is different about Canada is its small size, late entry into top-level international competition, and strong corporate connections with the two chief English-speaking countries, Britain and the United States.

Given the importance of connections between the state and capital, it seems foolhardy to study the state on its own. Yet in some cases, this may be justified. Besides capital and the political elite (or legislators), the third part of the political equation is the *voter*, subject of articles in this section by Schwartz and Ogmundson and Ng. In a liberal democracy, voters can presumably influence their legislators and, by doing so, change state policy. Voting is a *potentially* important behaviour; therefore, sociologists ought to find out why people vote the way they do.

Moral causes have played an important role in mobilizing American voters. The example of American prohibition law was discussed in an earlier section introduction dealing with deviance and control. In this section, Mildred A. Schwartz compares Canada with the United States to determine whether in countries like Canada "even when the same moral issues arise, they will be treated more cooly, with less emotional fervor (than in the United States). There will be less polarization among affected interests, and the issues will not play a prominent role in the political sphere," she predicts.

Differences between the two political systems explain the observed lower politicization of moral issues in Canada. Generally, interest groups are found to exercise less influence over policy formation here; cabinet ministers and senior civil servants are harder to reach and influence, and party discipline is more often enforced during voting. (An example of this was seen in the 1973 vote on capital punishment analysed in Chandler, 1976.)

Professor Schwartz's argument supports Lipset's view that Canada is more elite-dominated and more elitist in its cultural orientation; and S.D. Clark's view that, historically, Canada has been dominated from the centre, not from the frontier or periphery where moral causes, religious sects, political movements, and often fleeting "third parties" tend to form. For similar reasons, one might predict that class conscious Canadians will have little impact on the legislative process by voting or other means: they are too marginal to the centres of power. This assumed ineffectiveness, combined with Canadians' supposed elitism, would produce a weak class vote in Canada.

Some scholars have claimed that Canadians are not very class conscious. But Rick Ogmundson argues that, in order to judge if Canadians are class conscious or not, we must first find out what people think they are voting for: that is, whether their intention is class conscious, even if the outcome is not. If people are behaving as class consciously as they can, given the available choices, we must fault the party system, not the voters, for failing to produce radical changes. This would then, logically, lead us to question not how voters reach their decisions, but rather how parties make *their* decisions. In any event, Ogmundson, like Schwartz, finds that the Canadian political process tends to blunt challenges to the *status quo*, whether as moral causes or class mobilization. But class mobilization is surely no more effective politically in the U.S. than in Canada, if for different reasons.

Still, we would be wrong to infer an ideologically unified ruling class from the mere fact of its political domination. In an article using data collected from a variety of state and economic elites, Michael Ornstein finds abundant evidence of ideological conflict between capital and the state, across a variety of issues. As well, there are significant ideological differences between large capital and small. It is competitive capital that turns to the state for protection. However, the capitalist class *is* ideologically united at its core of large, privately controlled, monopolistic corporations. These monopoly capitalists are centrally important in influencing political parties, shaping legislation, and getting state co-operation at home and abroad. We cannot infer from these findings an ideological unity between capital and the state; but we can conclude that ideological divisions within the national capitalist classes are insignificant. Capitalist unity makes influencing state elites, however ideologically different, very much easier.

John Porter believed that inequality, even political and economic inequality at the highest levels, could be reduced by extending education and expertise to the masses. A modern society depended on its citizens' education, and so did its constituent organizations and elites. In time, elites would increasingly recruit by merit, he felt. This made education very important as a doorway to future equality in Canada. The next section will examine the actual role of education in Canadian society.

References

Chandler, David. *Capital Punishment in Canada: A Sociological Study of Regressive Law.* Toronto: Carleton Library, McClelland & Stewart, 1976.

47 Foreign Ownership and Myths About Canadian Development

Gordon Laxer

GORDON LAXER, Assistant Professor of Sociology at the University of Alberta, Edmonton, specializes in the study of political economy, change, development and underdevelopment. His publications include "Foreign ownership and myths about Canadian development" (1985) and "The political economy of aborted development: the Canadian case" (1985). He is currently completing a monograph entitled *Open for Business: The Roots of Foreign Ownership in Canada*. He has served as Acting Chairman of the Canadian Studies program at the University of Alberta, and was visiting speaker in the Canadian Studies Program at Queen's University.

MODELS OF DEVELOPMENT

... Before reviewing the models of development it is useful to explain what is meant by "independent industrial development," "mature industrial economies" and "successful industrialization." I use these terms interchangeably to indicate countries that have wide freedom to manoeuvre in a crisis such as a war, an oil embargo, or a drastic fall in the price of one or more export commodities (Seers, 1979). Such countries are not necessarily self-sufficient, but have the ability to produce nearly all finished goods needed without incurring a major reduction in overall productivity.[1] This would exclude countries specializing in the export of a few lines of finished goods but importing most of their machinery. Other countries, which make a wider range of manufactures but have to buy most of the high technology items from abroad, would be excluded also. The ability to respond to a crisis that threatens a nation's independence is determined both by the willingness of all sections of society to pull in the same direction and by the degree of domestic control over technology and management. The latter provide the basis for the creation of alternatives for imported goods. In the everyday world of normal trade relations, technological and managerial sovereignty are vital also in international capitalist competition. Product innovation has been crucial for the profitability of most corporations since the 1920s (Chandler, 1962). Domestic ownership and managerial control over most of the nation's productive enterprises and a high degree of technological sovereignty are the *sine qua non* of substantial product innovation (Bourgault, 1972).

Alfred Maizels conducted a comprehensive study of industrial development and its relation to international trade. Canada was a difficult country to classify. Was it one of the dozen industrial countries in the world or one of the equal number of semi-industrial countries, including the white dominions? The value of Canada's staple exports greatly exceeded that of finished manufactured goods. This was not characteristic of the industrial countries. Yet Canada's level of manufacturing productivity was very high. It was a puzzling case (1963:58). Others have had difficulty working Canada into their models also. . . . [2]

Is Canada a borderline case because it is transforming itself from a semi-industrial to an industrial country? This is the usual assumption of progressive development. But is not the reverse equally plausible? Perhaps Canada was developing along the lines of the late follower countries and was thwarted for some reason? Is Canada regressing into the ranks of the semi-industrial countries? To answer these questions let us consider each approach in turn.

Canada: A Latter Day America

Mackintosh and other neo-classical economists portray Canada as a backward United States. By invoking their favourite phrase *ceteris paribus* (all other things equal), neoclassical economists often throw away most of the useful variables for understanding development in one society and retardation in another. It would be difficult, using economic variables alone, to explain how Japan was able to advance to a point where its industrial output is now three times that of Britain, when 100 years ago it produced one-fiftieth as much.

If Canada is a backward United States, it should be following the same trajectory towards industrial independence. Is it? A favourable balance of trade in finished goods, domestic ownership of the bulk of the productive industries, and internal control over technological progress are all signs of independent economic development.

First, a country which can supply most of its internal market with finished goods and break into another's territory is industrially developed. The extent of maturity can be measured by comparing exports to imports of finished manufactures. If a country has an export/import ratio of more than 1.0 it is a net exporter; if less than unity it is a net importer. Let us compare Canada with the United States in this regard, giving the former a thirty-year time lag. By 1899, with a score of 1.3, the United States was already a net exporter of finished goods. In 1929 and 1955,

it had moved up to ratios of 5.2 and 4.0. In contrast, Canada stagnated. Its scores were 0.23 (1899), 0.28 (1929), and 0.20 (1955). The situation has improved a little since the mid-1950s. When the artificial "trade" of auto production is removed from calculation,[3] the exports of finished goods equalled 0.43 of the imports of such goods in the years 1981–3. An even balance in trade, however, is still a long way off. Canada's deficit in trade in all finished goods ranged from $13 billion to $21 billion in the years 1981 to 1983 (Canada, 1984:28,40). In short, Canada still pays its way in the world by massive exports of resources.

Second, the role of foreign investment is crucial in assessing dependence. Canada holds the record amongst advanced economies, along with Sweden, of the extent to which foreign funds contributed to its early industrialization.... The earliest estimates, for 1920–1, show that about 30 per cent of Canada's manufacturing industries were foreign owned (Williams, 1983:28–9). By 1973 foreign control of Canadian manufacturing had increased to 56 per cent, a level far higher than any other advanced economy and second in the world only to Nigeria (United Nations, 1978:263). In contrast, Swedish governments have had a history of blocking foreign direct ownership since the 1870s and current levels are low (Fleetwood, 1947; Johansson, 1968)....

Perhaps Canada's experience with foreign ownership is a passing phase and the country is on the road to greater development? Did the U.S. go through a period of reliance on foreign funds and foreign control?

Foreign capital was important in the development of the American economy in the middle of the nineteenth century. Foreign contributions to net capital formation were almost 11 per cent in the decade following the Civil War (Kuznets, 1961:133). In the manufacturing and transportation industries, European loans may have contributed as much as a fifth of total investment in the 1850s

(Robertson, 1964:231). However, the U.S. example cannot offer hope that foreign investment is a transitory phenomenon in Canada. American foreign indebtedness never was close to the Canadian rates and they diminished rapidly. Most of the funds were of the portfolio variety, placed in government securities and railway bonds. These loans were either paid off eventually or else wiped out by a massive defaulting on debts in the late 1830s. (American businessmen conveniently forget this chapter in early American development, in their holy war against the current threat of loan defaults amongst Third World countries.) In contrast, foreign direct investments, once made, tend to increase in value over time. They were never a large factor in the U.S. British direct investment was estimated at only $700 million in the U.S. in 1913 (Dunning, 1971:370). By 1974, foreign ownership of manufacturing in the U.S. was 4 per cent by sales and 3 per cent by employment (United Nations, 1978:263). Douglass North (1960:576) believes that American direct investments abroad were greater by the 1850s than were foreign direct investments at home.

Finally, turning to technology, it is clear that no country can develop all the new technologies required for an advanced economy. While technological imports are indispensable, they need not imply technological dependence. Two elements are crucial for relative sovereignty; a substantial level of domestic innovations and the borrowing of technology through arms-length arrangements. The Japanese have been masters of the latter, while the Swedes have shown an innovative vigour that is surprising for a small country (Kuuse, 1977; Quinn, 1969). . . .

In the U.S., six of every seven patents issued went to native citizens in 1900. The ratio was the same in 1930 and 1955 (United States, 1970:957). Canada has been moving in the opposite direction. In the early 1900s Canadians held 15 per cent of domestically issued patents (Canada, 1901; 612). The road has been downhill since: 11 per cent in 1930

and 6 per cent in 1955 and 1975 (Canada, 1931, 1956, 1976–7). . . .

In sum, Mackintosh's late-bloomer thesis is not applicable. Canada has not progressed along the American path. The relative level of Canadian exports of finished goods failed to increase and mammoth imports continue. Foreign investment has not been a temporary phase in Canadian development and cannot be attributed to the supposed youthfulness of the country. . . .

Canada and the White Dominion Model

. . . Buried in a somewhat obscure book, Philip Ehrensaft and Warwick Armstrong have developed an exceptionally able and comprehensive case for the white dominion model (1981). . . .

According to Ehrensaft and Armstrong, the white dominions include not only the legitimate British offspring—Canada, Australia and New Zealand—but two unofficially adopted children as well, namely Argentina and Uruguay. These countries distinguished themselves from their poor cousins in the rest of the new world by inhabiting lands where the native population was too small for large-scale exploitation and where the climate did not favour the importation of African slaves or indentured workers from the East Indies. Few slaves, of course, meant no plantation owners. New settlers from Europe provided the bulk of the labour force, and the large land reserves produced labour shortages and hence high wages. This situation had a number of implications: the adoption of labour-saving and therefore highly productive technology, urbanization and a substantial level of manufacturing, based on rich domestic markets. The white dominions shared these features with the advanced capitalist countries, but fell short of full, capitalist development on a number of other scores. Primary products remained their major exports, while manufacturing was largely confined to supplying much, but not all, of domestic needs with protected, inefficient industry and to processing, rather than finishing resources. Subsidiaries of multinational corporations were prominent in the goods-producing sectors and these societies all passed from the British to the American Empire in this century. Furthermore, the politics of the various classes perpetuated the orientation of these economies towards both resource exports and stunted, domestically confined manufacturing. . . .

To assess the explanatory power of the white dominion model for Canadian development, let us look at the present time and then at the early years of the century. Ehrensaft and Armstrong demonstrate current similarities: Canada shares with Australia and/or the other white dominions: 1/ a low degree of finished manufactures as a percentage of total exports; and 2/ a somewhat lower level of manufacturing production as a proportion of GNP than the advanced economies. . . . [4]

It's when we look to development prospects in the past that the sharp divergence between Canada and the rest is apparent. In their discussion of the early twentieth century, Ehrensaft and Armstrong shift their focus from exports and sectoral shares of the GNP to other measures of development: capital-labour ratios, agricultural productivity, per capita incomes and the percentage of the labour force engaged in industry. In these respects, Argentina and Australia bear up well. Canada was behind in the first two respects: in the middle regarding the number of manufacturing workers; and only somewhat ahead in incomes in the 1910 to 1930s period. But are these the best measures of prospects for independent industrial development? I think not. As a sign of development it makes more sense to look at productivity in manufacturing than in agriculture. Canada was 50 per cent to 100 per cent ahead of Australia in industrial productivity in the 1920s and 1930s and was 140 per cent ahead of

Argentina in the 1930s, the first time such figures are available for that country (Clark, 1960:336). . . .

Development prospects depended not only on productivity in industry but also on the absolute size of the manufacturing sector and its ability to penetrate foreign markets. . . . The crucial question is whether Canada resembled the white dominions, which we know did not break free from a staples orientation, or whether Canada was as developed as the other late follower countries.

Consider the scale of industrial production. According to Colin Clark (1960), just prior to World War I, Canada's overall manufacturing output was behind that of populous Russia and Italy, but at the same level as that of Japan and Sweden and more than double Australia's. In the 1920s and 1930s, Canadian production was at about the mid-point of the late follower countries and at least two and one half times that of Australia and Argentina.

Ehrensaft and Armstrong's model specifies the inability of the white dominions to produce manufacturing products for anything but the protected home market (with minor exceptions). Was this true of Canada in the 1920s? No, Canada exported more manufactured goods per head than any of the late follower countries, and its absolute level of such exports was in the middle of the late follower range. . . .

Why all this emphasis on the past and the timing of development? Surely the contemporary similarity of Canada with the other white dominions is sufficient to determine its past development prospects. Not according to the great economic historians who stress the profound effects of historical timing on the nature of industrial development. A great chasm was created between the few countries which began serious industrialization before 1900 and the rest who did not get well into the process until World War II or its aftermath. . . .

To understand the profound changes in the 1890 to 1940 period which led to the chasm between the developed and the underdeveloped countries, it is useful first to point to continuity. Despite momentous technological, military, and social upheavals in this century, the relative economic strength of nations has changed little. The Russian Revolution, the introduction of space-age electronics, the eclipse of Britain and the rise of Japan have not greatly altered the international pecking order. Russia was the fifth largest manufacturing country before the 1917 Revolution and is now in second place. Japan has moved up in spectacular fashion to third place (Bairoch, 1982:284). But it should not be forgotten that . . . by 1913 it was already about the tenth largest industrial country (League of Nations, 1945:13). Britain has declined drastically, but only from first place 100 years ago to sixth place today (Bairoch, 1982:284). Notwithstanding these fluctuations, the fact remains that all of the dozen-or-so advanced industrial countries of the late twentieth century had begun widespread industrialization before 1890. The obverse holds as well: no seriously industrializing country of the late nineteenth century has slipped into de-industrialized oblivion. Those ahead seventy or 100 years ago are still ahead today. . . .

Around 1900 there was a transformation in the nature of international capitalism. . . . World trade in finished goods rose by 75 per cent in the 1899–1913 period alone and imports doubled in the semi-industrial and small industrial countries (Maizcls, 1963:136). For the first time large corporations began to set up foreign subsidiaries to overcome tariff barriers that were erected everywhere except in England and in a few smaller countries. The U.S. was the main centre for the emergence of the transnational corporation. . . . All of these new developments in trade, transportation, technology, and the monopoly control of big business made it much more difficult for the pre-industrial countries to emulate the example of the advanced countries. A watershed had been crossed. The disadvantages of following-the-leader seemed to outweigh the advantages.

Did Canada develop before or after this watershed? . . . Comparison with Australia and Sweden seems useful. Australia was the most advanced of the other white dominions, while Sweden was the smallest of the successful late follower countries.

Soon after Confederation, manufacturing was just under one quarter of Canada's gross domestic product compared to one eighth for Sweden, whose manufacturing figures are somewhat inflated by the inclusion of mining statistics, and only one twelfth for Australia. If absolute levels of production are considered, the difference between Canada and the other two was even greater. International comparisons of total output are always arbitrary, and the further back in time you go, the more tenuous the assessments. But without doubt, Canada had the highest gross domestic production of the three countries and probably somewhere in the order of double the product of the other two in the 1870s. . . .

Industry developed so slowly in Australia that by the 1930s it accounted for only one-sixth of the gross domestic product. It was not until World War II that manufacturing became larger than agriculture in Australia, something that had happened in Canada during World War I despite the wheat boom on the prairies. (Manufacturing took the lead slightly earlier in Sweden.) Thus Canada had experienced considerable industrialization by the late nineteenth century, whereas Australia developed after the period that separates the mature economies from the rest of the world. The Canadian case is different from that of Australia and the other white dominions.[5] We may conclude therefore that a pure staple-exporting model along the lines of the Innis or Naylor-Clement approaches is inapplicable to Canada.

Canada and Late Follower Development[6]

... In the 1870s and 1880s, during what was then called the "Great Depression," a handful of countries began their initial phase of industrialization. The United States, Britain, Germany, France and, on a smaller scale, Belgium and Switzerland had emerged already as industrial powers in fierce competition with one another. The four large industrial countries controlled over 75 per cent of world production.[7] The late follower countries were: Russia, Italy, Sweden, the Czech provinces, Japan, and possibly the Netherlands.[8] In 1913, by which time industry had surpassed agriculture in most late follower countries, their shares of world production had climbed.... Canada, with less than 0.5 per cent of the world's population, compared favourably with these countries. In 1880–5 it had 1.3 per cent of world manufacturing production and 2.3 per cent by 1913. Only two of the six late follower countries produced more.

Gross production statistics tell only part of the story. Canada has a long record of exporting large quantities of semi-processed goods such as pulp and paper but confining finished goods to the home market (Williams, 1983). How did the Canadian economy fare around the turn of the century in these respects? In 1899 Canadian exports had the greatest proportion of finished to primary manufactures of any industrial nation. All late follower countries for which there are statistics recorded exports of finished manufactures compared to primary manufactures of unity or less. In contrast the Canadian ratio was 5 to 1. Did Canada achieve this high ratio by exporting few manufactured goods? Partly, but Canada's exports of finished goods compared favourably in absolute terms with the other late followers. In 1899, Canadian exports of fully finished goods was $15 million (American dollars) compared to Sweden's $13 million, Japan's $24 million and Italy's $53 million....

Canada: Failed Follower

We have seen that Canada held its own with the other late follower countries at the end of the nineteenth century. It began the initial phase of industrialization before 1890, and its absolute level of manufacturing finished products was high. Furthermore, industry surpassed agriculture's share in the economy during World War I, a sure sign that Canada had passed beyond the precarious initial phase of industrialization. Yet Canada was the only late follower country that clearly failed to generate a mature and independent industrial economy. When did Canada diverge from the path of the other late followers and why did it do so?

In the post-World War II era, the Canadian economy has been quite different from the other late follower countries. The familiar pattern of dependence on the export of raw materials and the massive disparity between importing and exporting finished goods has been solidly established.... None of the other late follower countries exhibited a similar pattern.

When did Canada begin to regress from late follower development? There was evidence of a high propensity to import industrial goods as early as 1899. In that year, with only 1.8 per cent of the population of the ten major capitalist countries, Canada received 5.9 per cent of the imports of finished goods in those countries. There were two reasons for this. First, an import surplus at that phase of development was not unusual.... Second, Canada had a higher standard of living than the other late follower countries, and therefore Canadians could afford to import more.

Between 1899 and 1913 a sharp divergence between Canada and the other countries developed. Although this was the period of Canada's most rapid growth ever in manufacturing output—the time when Canadian industry is alleged by some to have come of age (Firestone, 1969:25), all the indicators point to a regression in development

(Bertram, 1962;103). In 1913, 52 per cent of Canada's manufactured exports were finished, down from 83 per cent fourteen years earlier. The trend in the other latefollower countries (for which there are complete statistics), was in the opposite direction. . . . While Canadian industrial output had more than doubled, the value of finished exports climbed by only one-half, confirming Williams' (1983) argument that industrial production was aimed almost exclusively at the home market. At the same time, imports of manufactured goods more than trebled. The ratio of exports/imports of finished manufactured goods in 1913 tells the story (the 1899 ratio is given in brackets): Canada 0.10 (0.23); Japan 1.3 (0.53); Sweden 1.5 (1.1); and Italy 1.4 (1.5). . . .

In the crucial capital goods sector, the same economic regression occurred. Imports of producer durables increased from 13 per cent of Canadian use in 1880 and 1890 to 30 per cent plus between 1900 and 1915.[9] (McDougall, 1973:193). At the same time, little Sweden made a spectacular breakthrough in this sector by exporting a wide range of Swedish-invented engineering tools (weapons, electronics, gas lighting, precision instruments, ball bearings) (Kuuse, 1978). Canada's contemporary economic structure appears to have emerged by World War I. Never again did Canada look like the other late follower countries. . . .

What happened in the pre-World War I period to push Canada off the path to late follower development? Two interrelated factors were of major importance. First, many Canadian manufacturers imported technology by entering into licensing agreements with American firms. Usually the agreements specified that the rights to the technology applied to the Canadian market. . . . Second, American branch plants came to dominate the most dynamic sectors of Canadian manufacturing, often by taking over the Canadian firms that had started out by licensing American technology (Naylor, 1975a, Vol. II:56). Subsidiaries were even more stringently re-

stricted from competing with the parent company, while at the same time they tended to import parts and machinery on a major scale. In either case—technological dependence or branch plant ownership—Canada ended up importing a lot and exporting but little.

Before 1900 there were only sixty-six American branch plants in Canada. While fourteen years later there were five times as many[10] (Marshall, 1976:21). American companies had captured commanding positions in the dominant secondary industries of the twentieth century. Canadian ownership remained high only in industries using older technologies such as textiles, clothing, printing and publishing (Field, 1914:39). . . . In none of the other late follower countries did foreign enterprise and foreign technologies gain control over most industries of the second industrial revolution.

Why did a branch plant structure become entrenched in Canada and not in the other late follower countries? The common answer is that Canada erected tariff barriers to encourage the development of industry, and that American producers, cut off from their export markets, decided to leap over the tariff wall by establishing branch plants (Marr and Paterson, 1980:294). This is not an adequate answer. Canadian tariffs were neither high nor exceptional. Tariff levels, as measured by the ratio of duties to total imports for consumption, were higher in almost every year in the United States than in Canada between 1867 and 1900 (McDiarmid, 1946:181, Taussig, 1910:409). Protective duties were increased in many countries at the same time as the National Policy tariffs of 1879 and in response to the same conditions of depression, decreasing prices, and rising nationalism. . . .

It is true that tariffs have a more restrictive impact on small countries than on large ones and that comparisons of absolute figures on tariff levels can be misleading (Liepmann, 1938:37). But Sweden and several other small manufacturing-exporting countries combined tariffs with retention of domestic ownership. Clearly the tariff barrier argument requires reconsideration. If tariffs were almost universal, why did Canada alone of all the industrializing countries become so dominated by foreign firms?

The usual answer is that Canada was the only advanced country situated beside the United States. Canada accepted the American corporation on a massive scale at an early point in its development, whereas European nations were shielded from the American economic invasion by the Atlantic Ocean until after World War II. By then they had generated more mature industrial structures, dominated by their own capitalists. This answer, too, is inadequate. The catastrophic effects of the two world wars have obscured pre-1914 realities. The United States was not the only rapidly developing industrial power, nor was it the only country to establish branch plants abroad. Germany was also conquering foreign markets in the new technologies. On the eve of World War I, German exports of electrical products was greater than that of the U.S. and Britain combined. In the new chemical industries, especially dyes, Germany was the world's leader. Its firms achieved these positions through technical excellence (Landes, 1969:275,290). Foreign tariff walls blocked the entry of German goods, and led to experiments with the branch plant solution. As early as the 1870s and 1880s, German industry began to locate branch plants and resource subsidiaries in nearby countries. However, Germany's neighbours reacted differently from Canada. They took steps to block German investment (Crisp, 1970, 1976; Fleetwood, 1947). Furthermore they strengthened domestically owned industry through measures such as changes to industrial finance, government procurement programs and subsidies to and protection for strategic industries for military reasons (Laxer, 1985)....

The branch plants were not the sole cause of Canada's failure at independent, late industrialization. In fact U.S. subsidiaries were able to win such an early victory in Canada's electrical, chemical and automotive industries because of a deeper institutional and ideational malaise in the financial system and in military and railway policies. These factors can be listed but not elaborated here.[11] First, Canada's commercial banking system was oriented towards short-term loans suited to trade. It was particularly inappropriate for nurturing technologically innovative industries in a late industrializing country.... Second, military industries form much of the basis of the engineering sector, the crucial place where innovation occurs. As independent nations, the other late follower countries fostered domestically owned and technologically independent strategic goods industries. Canada did not. For fifty years after Confederation, precisely the years in which Canada's industrial structure was formed, its military policy remained, voluntarily, under British authority. Finally there was the Canadian mania for railway building. Even though Canada needed only one transcontinental railway before the World War I, it was felt that three would be good; the more expensive the building methods, the better (Buckley, 1974). As a result, Canada borrowed enormous amounts of British portfolio capital.[12] The latter created inflationary pressures which led to increased imports, augmented the movement of U.S. branch plants into Canada (Viner, 1975), and invigorated the resource exporting nature of the economy (Innis, 1973:152).

Why did the Canadian state adopt economic policies that were not suited to late follower industrialization? Why did the farmers and their allies, representing the numerical majority, fail to break down the commercial banking system as their `counterparts had done in the U.S.? Why did the agrarians allow high-taxing governments to throw away millions on useless railways? To answer these questions requires a multifaceted class analysis of the politics that lay behind the formation of Canadian state policies. I will not do that here because I have not the space and have done so elsewhere.[13] Nevertheless a few points can be made....

... The politics of class in the 1837 to 1914 period was largely supplanted by the politics of English-French sectionalism. In this context, big business easily ruled and, because it faced little challenge, even allowed itself the luxury of openly conducting internal disputes....

Time and again popular-democratic political movements arose in English Canada, mainly in Ontario in the pre-1914 period, in opposition to the policies of a state run by big business, only to be defeated by anti-French-Canadian and anti-Catholic bigotry. For their part, popular-democratic movements in French Canada represented the most nationalist and most anti-British opinion. In contrast to their counterparts in the big business-oriented parties, the popular-democratic movements in English and French Canada could not overcome the national and religious divide....

Briefly these were the factors which diverted Canada from the path of independent industrial development. The important point is not to elaborate on these themes here but to note that internal factors, not geographic and external constraints, were decisive in Canada's failure at late follower industrialization.

CONCLUSION

The dominant paradigms in Canadian historiography leave a great deal unexplained. For the past century it has been incorrect to characterize Canada as simply a dependent resource economy presided over by a commercial elite, as the Staples and Naylor-Clement approaches have been wont to do. The easy assumptions must be modified or discarded. It was neither inevitable that Canada would follow the American model of development at a later date nor that it would fail to break fully free from a "staple trap." Reality has been more complex than this. As we have seen, two contradictory tendencies must be explained: Canada's promising manufacturing development in the late nineteenth century and its failure to make good on that promise. None of the traditional approaches account for these tendencies satisfactorily. In their place I have set out a modified Gerschenkron approach that focusses on the problems and possibilities of late development. It seems to explain the facts best. Because this approach is comparative, it breaks down the assumptions of uniqueness and inevitability. As well, it helps pinpoint the major factors affecting the direction and character of Canadian economic development....

Notes

[1] The ability to produce most needed items in case of an emergency cut-off of supply cannot be determined by looking solely at a nation's economic indicators. As Seers (1979) points out, the strength and unity of national feeling that would allow the state to impose restrictions is an important ingredient of potential self-sufficiency.

[2] Canada did not fit Rostow's (1965) model of "economic take-off" because of the unusually high rate of gross investment in the pre-take-off stage.

[3] Trade in automobiles and parts is an artifact of the Canada-U.S. autopact (1965), which treats North America as one entity for the auto producers. Most of the "trade" consists of movement between parent and subsidiary. If auto trade is included, the export/import ratio for 1981–3 is 0.64. Maizels is the source for 1899, 1929 and 1955. *Canada (1984)*

is the source for the early 1980s (my calculations).

[4] Argentina was an exception in this respect. Manufacturing comprised as high a percentage of its gross national product as in the "dominant economies." (Ehrensaft and Armstrong, 1981:115). This may not mean any more than that other sectors of the economy were even sicker than manufacturing.

[5] I am not arguing that economic comparisons between Canada and other white dominations are irrelevant. Nor am I saying that comparisons of class structures, politics, and culture are inapplicable between these two countries. On the contrary, Ehrensaft and Armstrong (1981) take us in fruitful new directions. But the white dominion model is misleading in assessing early development prospects for Canada.

[6] The data for this section are derived from the tables of my doctoral thesis (1981). To probe these figures further, consult as well the sources from which they were drawn: League of Nations (1945), Maizels (1963), the United Nations (1974, 1976, 1978).

[7] A century later, an altered set of the top four industrial countries accounted for between 61 per cent and 73 per cent of the world's total (Bairoch, 1982; U.N., 1973).

[8] According to Maizels (1963) there are no adequate figures for the Netherlands. Bairoch (1982) ranks that country's industrial production level as very low for the 1880 to 1913 period (330). Czechoslovakia was not an independent country then.

[9] The ratio of exports to imports indicates the same trend. In 1880, 1890, and 1900 the ratio was about 0.2 and it dropped to about 0.15 in 1905 and 1910. The 1915 figure indicates a gain (0.32) but this was due to an artificial boost for exports because of the war. These figures, as well as those quoted in the text, are derived from Table I in McDougall (1973). His Table VI is misleading. (The "producer durables" column should be read as percentages, not ratios.)

[10] These figures underestimate the actual number of U.S. branch plants before 1914. Marshall et al. (1976) included only those still in operation in 1932 at the time of the survey. Field (1914) calculated that there were 450 U.S. branch plants in Canada in 1914.

[11] See my doctoral thesis (1981), chapters VII and VIII.

[12] Large amounts of foreign capital also came in to finance the prairie wheat boom. See Buckley (1974).

[13] See my "Class, Nationality and the Roots of Foreign Ownership" and *The Roots of Foreign Ownership* (Toronto: Methuen, (forthcoming)) for elaboration and references.

References

Aitken, Hugh 1959 "The Changing Structure of the Canadian Economy." In Aitken et al., The American Economic Impact on Canada. Durham, N.C.: Duke University Press

———— 1964 "Government and Business in Canada: An Interpretation." Business History Review XXXVIII Spring

Australia, Government of 1981 Yearbook. Canberra

Bairoch, Paul 1982 "International Industrialization Levels from 1750 to 1980." Journal of European Economic History 11(2) Spring

Beard, Charles, and Mary Beard 1968 New Basic History of the United States. Garden City, N.J.: Doubleday

Bertram, G.W. 1962 "Historical Statistics on Growth and Structure in Manufacturing in Canada 1870–1957." J. Henripin and A. Asimkopoulos (eds.), Canadian Political Science Association Conference on Statistics. Toronto

———— 1963 "Economic Growth in Canadian Industry, 1870–1915: The Staple Model and the Take-Off Hypothesis." Canadian Journal of Economics and Political Science 29

Bourgault, Pierre 1972 Innovation and the Structure

of Canadian Industry. Ottawa: Science Council of Canada

Britton, John, and James Gilmour 1978 The Weakest Link: A Technological Perspective on Canadian Industrial Development. Ottawa: Science Council of Canada

Buckley, Kenneth 1974 Capital Formation in Canada, 1896–1930. Toronto: McClelland and Stewart

Cafagna, Luciano 1973 "The Industrial Revolution in Italy 1830–1914." In C.M. Cipolla (ed.), The Fontana Economic History of Europe, Vol. IV, Part I. Glasgow: Fontana

Cairncross, A.K. 1953 Home and Foreign Investment 1870–1913. Cambridge, England: Cambridge University Press

Canada, Government of, 1901 Department of Agriculture Statistical Yearbook, Ottawa

—————— 1931 Canada Yearbook, Ottawa

—————— 1956 Canada Yearbook, Ottawa

—————— 1972 Foreign Direct Investment in Canada (The Gray Report). Ottawa: Department of Trade and Commerce

—————— 1976–7 Canada Yearbook, Ottawa

—————— 1984 Summary of External Trade. Ottawa: Statistics Canada

Careless, J.M.S. 1967 "Frontierism, Metropolitanism, and Canadian History," In C. Berger (ed.), Approaches to Canadian History. Toronto: University of Toronto Press

Chandler, Alfred 1962 Strategy and Structure: Chapters in the History of the American Industrial Enterprise. Cambridge, Mass.: M.I.T. Press

Clark, Colin 1960 The Conditions of Economic Progress (3rd ed., rev.). New York: Macmillan

Clark, S.D. 1939 The Canadian Manufacturers Association. Toronto: University of Toronto Press

Clement, Wallace 1975 The Canadian Corporate Elite. Toronto: McClelland and Stewart

—————— 1977 Continental Corporate Power. Toronto: McClelland and Stewart

Clough, S.B. 1952 Economic History of Europe. Boston: D.C. Heath

Crisp, Olga 1960 "French Investment in Russian Joint Stock Companies 1894–1914." Business History 2 (June)

—————— 1976 Studies in the Russian Economy Before 1914. London: Macmillan

Dales, John 1962 "Estimates of Canadian Manufacturing Output by Markets, 1870–1915." In J. Henripin and A. Asimkopoulos (eds.), Canadian Political Science Association Conference on Statistics. Toronto

—————— 1966 The Protective Tariff in Canada's Development: Toronto: University of Toronto Press

Denison, M. 1948 Harvest Triumphant: The Story of Massey-Harris. Toronto: McClelland and Stewart

Dobb, Maurice 1954 Studies in the Development of Capitalism. London: Routledge and Kegan Paul

Drache, Daniel 1978 "Rediscovering Canadian Political Economy." In W. Clement and D. Drache, A. Practical Guide to Canadian Political Economy. Toronto: Lorimer

Dunning, John 1971 "United States Foreign Investment and the Technological Gap." In C. Hymerkindleberger and A. Schonfield (eds.), North American and Western European Economic Policies. London: Macmillan

Ehrensaft, Philip, and Warwick Armstrong 1981 "The formation of dominion capitalism: economic truncation and class structure." In A. Moscovitch (ed.), Inequality: Essays on the Political Economy of Social Welfare. Toronto: University of Toronto Press

Field F.W. 1914 Capital Investments in Canada. Montreal: The Monetary Times of Canada

Firestone, O.J. 1960 "Development of Canada's Economy, 1850–1900." In Trends in the American Economy in the Nineteenth Century. Princeton, N.J.: Conference on Research in Income and Wealth

—————— 1969 Industry and Education, A Century of Canadian Development. Ottawa: University of Ottawa Press

Fleetwood, E.E. 1947 Sweden and Capital Imports and Exports. Geneve: Journal de Geneve

Forster, Colin 1970 Australian Economic

Development in the Twentieth Century. London: George Allen and Unwin

Gerschenkron, Alexander 1962 Economic Backwardness in Historical Perspective. Cambridge, Mass.: Harvard University Press

Gross, N.T. 1973 "The Industrial Revolution in the Hapsburg Monarchy, 1750–1914." In C.M. Cipolla (ed.), The Fontana Economic History of Europe, Vol. 4, Part I. Glasgow: Fontana

Hartland, P. 1955 "Factors in Economic Growth in Canada." Journal of Economic History, 15(1)

Hobsbawm, Eric 1968 Industry and Empire. Suffolk, England: Penguin

Hobson, J.A. 1905 Imperialism, A Study. London: Archibald Constable

Innis, Harold 1930 The Fur Trade in Canada. New Haven: Yale University Press

—— 1933 Problems of Staple Production in Canada. Toronto: The Ryerson Press

—— 1952 Empire and Communications. Toronto: University of Toronto Press

—— 1973 Essays in Canadian Economic History. Toronto: University of Toronto Press

Johansson, Harry 1968 "Foreign Businesses Operating in Sweden." M. Norgren (ed.), Industry in Sweden. Halmstad, Sweden: Swedish Institute for Cultural Relations with Foreign Countries

Johnson, Harry 1977 The Canadian Quandary. Toronto: McClelland and Stewart

Kilbourn, William 1960 The Elements Combined, A History of the Steel Company of Canada, Toronto: Clarke Irwin

Krantz, O., and C. Nilsson 1975 Swedish National Product 1891–1970. Lund: C.W.K. Gieerup

Kuuse, Jan 1977 "Foreign Trade and the Breakthrough of the Engineering Industry in Sweden 1890–1920." Scandinavian Economic History Review XXV(1)

Kuznets, Simon 1955 "International Differences in Capital Formation and Financing." In National Bureau of Economic Research, Capital Formation and Economic Growth. Princeton: Princeton University Press

—— 1961 "Economic Growth: The Last Hundred Years." National Institute Economic Review, July

—— 1969 Modern Economic Growth. Rate Structure and Spread. New Haven: Yale University Press

Landes, David 1965 "Japan and Europe: Contrasts in Industrialization." In W.W. Lockwood (ed.), The State and Economic Enterprise in Japan. Princeton, N.J.: Princeton University Press

—— 1969 The Unbound Prometheus. Technological Change in Industrial Development in Western Europe from 1750 to the Present. Cambridge: Cambridge University Press

Laxer, Gordon 1981 The Social Origins of Canada's Branch Plant Economy, 1837–1914. Unpublished doctoral thesis, Department of Sociology, University of Toronto

—— 1985 "The Political Economy of Aborted Development." In Robert Brym (ed.), The Structure of the Canadian Capitalist Class. Toronto: Garamond Press

League of Nations 1945 Industrialisation and World Trade. New York: United Nations

Liepmann, H. 1938 Tariff Levels and the Economic Unity of Europe. London: Allen and Unwin

Lower, A.R.M. 1977 Colony to Nation. Toronto: McClelland and Stewart

Mackintosh, W.A. 1923 "Economic Factors in Canadian History." Canadian Historical Review LV(1)

—— 1959 "Canadian Economic Policy from 1945 to 1957—Origins and Influences." In H. Aitken (ed.), The American Economic Impact on Canada. Durham, N.C.: Duke University Press

Maizels, Alfred 1963 Industrial Growth and World Trade. London: Cambridge University Press

Marr, W., and D. Paterson 1980 Canada: An Economic History. Toronto: Macmillan

Marshall, H.F., F. Southard, and K. Taylor 1976 Canadian–American Industry. Toronto: McClelland and Stewart

Marx, Karl 1959 Capital, A Critique of Political Economy. Volume III. Moscow: Progress Books

McDiarmid, Orville 1946 Commercial Policy in

the Canadian Economy. Cambridge, Mass.: Harvard University Press

McDougall, Duncan 1973 "The Domestic Availability of Manufactured Commodity Output, Canada, 1870–1915." Canadian Journal of Economics. VI(2) (May, 1973)

Milward, A.S., and S.B. Saul 1973 The Economic Development of Continental Europe 1780–1870. London: George Allen and Unwin

Mitchell, B.R. 1973 "Statistical Appendix." In Carlo Cipolla (ed.), The Fontana Economic History of Europe. Vol. IV, Part 2, Glasgow: Fontana

Myers, Gustavus 1910 The History of Great American Fortunes, 3 Volumes. Chicago: Kerr

Naylor, R.T. 1975a The History of Canadian Business 1867–1914, 2 Volumes. Toronto: Lorimer

———— 1975b "Dominion of Capital: Canada and International Development." In A. Kontos (ed.) Domination. Toronto: University of Toronto Press

———— 1978 Foreign and Direct Investment in Canada: Institutions and Policy, 1867–1914. Unpublished doctoral dissertation, Cambridge, England.

North, Douglass 1960 "United States Balance of Payments, 1790–1860." Studies in Income and Wealth, Vol. 24. National Bureau of Economic Research, Princeton: Princeton University Press

———— 1961 Economic Growth of the U.S. 1790–1860. Englewood Cliffs, N.J.: Prentice Hall

Nurkse, R. 1964 Problems of Capital Formation in Underdeveloped Countries. Oxford, U.K.: Basil Blackwell

O'Connor, James 1973 The Fiscal Crisis of the State. New York: St. Martin's Press

Pentland, H.C. 1950 "The Role of Capital in Canadian Economic Development before 1875." Canadian Journal of Economics and Political Science, XXVI (November)

Phillips, W.G. 1956 The Agricultural Implements Industry in Canada. Toronto: University of Toronto Press

Quinn, James 1969 "Technology Transfer by Multinational Companies." Harvard Business Review 47 (Nov.–Dec.)

Robertson, Ross 1964 History of the American Economy. New York: Harcourt, Brace and World

Rosecrance, R. 1964 "The Radical Culture of Australia." In L. Hartz (ed.), The Founding of New Societies. New York: Harcourt, Brace and World.

Rostow, W.W. 1965 The Stages of Economic Growth. A Non-Communist Manifesto. London: Cambridge University Press

Ryerson, Stanley 1968 Unequal Union Toronto: Progress Books

Seers, Dudley 1979 "Patterns of Dependence." In J. Villamil (ed.), Transnational Capitalism and National Development. New Perspectives on Dependence. Hassocks, Sussex: The Harvester Press

Smith, Thomas C. 1965 Political Change and Industrial Development in Japan: Government Enterprises 1868–1880. Stanford: Stanford University Press

Sulte, Benjamin 1920 "Les Forges Saint Maurice." Melanges Historique Vol. 6 Montreal: Malchelosse

Taussig, F.W. 1910 The Tariff History of the United States. New York: G.P. Putnam's Sons

United Nations 1974 Department of Economic and Social Affairs: Multinational Corporations in World Development. New York

———— 1976 Statistical Yearbook. New York

———— 1978 Department of Economic and Social Affairs. Commission on Transnational Corporations. Transnational Corporations in World Development: A Re-examination. New York

United States 1970 Reports of the Commissioner of Patents. Washington

———— 1976 Historical Statistics of the United States Colonial Times to 1970. Part 2. New York: Basic Books

———— 1982 Statistical Abstracts of the United States, 1981. Washington

Urquhart, M.C. 1984 "New Estimates of Gross National Product, Canada 1870 to 1926: Some Implications for Canadian Development." Unpublished manuscript, Queen's University ("subject to minor revision")

Viner, Jacob 1975 Canada's Balance of International

Indebtedness 1900–1913. Toronto: Mc-Clelland and Stewart

Wade, Mason 1968 The French Canadians 1760–1967. Volume I, 1760–1911 (rev. ed.). Toronto: Macmillan

Watkins, Mel 1963 "A Staple Theory of Economic Growth." Canadian Journal of Economics and Political Science XXIX(2)

_____ 1966 "The 'American System' and Canada's National Policy." Bulletin of the Canadian Association for American Studies

_____ 1977a "The Staple Theory Revisited." Journal of Canadian Studies, 12, 5

_____ 1977b "The State in a Staples Economy." Conference on "The American Empire and Dependent States: Canada and the Third World." University of Toronto, 18 November 1977

Wilkins, Mira 1970 The Emergence of Multinational Enterprise: American Business Abroad from the Colonial Era to 1914. Cambridge, Mass.: Harvard University Press

Williams, Glen 1975 "We Ain't Growin' Nowhere." This Magazine 9

_____ 1983 Not For Export: Toward a Political Economy of Canada's Arrested Industrialization. Toronto: McClelland and Stewart

48 The Canadian Multinationals

Jorge Niosi

JORGE NIOSI, Professor of Sociology, University of Quebec at Montreal, specializes in the study of political economy and stratification. His books and articles include *Les entrepreneurs dans la politique argentine, 1955–1973* (1976); *The Economy of Canada: A Study of Ownership and Control* (1979); *Canadian Capitalism: A Study of Power in the Canadian Business Establishment* (1981); *Canadian Multinationals* (1985); and "L'état et les firmes multinationales" with P. Faucher (1985). *Canadian Capitalism* won the John Porter Prize, given by the Canadian Sociology and Anthropology Association for best scholarly published work in the preceding year. Professor Niosi has received substantial research support from the Social Sciences and Humanities Council of Canada, the Ministry of Education (Quebec), the Ministry of Higher Education, Science and Technology (Quebec) and the Quebec Commission on Health and Safety at Work (CSST).

In recent years Canadian foreign direct investment has been growing at a very rapid pace. According to preliminary estimates Canadian FDI increased by 17 per cent in 1979 and by 24 per cent in 1980. The financial press both in Canada and in the USA has pointed out some spectacular takeovers of US corporations by Canadian firms, such as the acquisition of minority control of Scott Paper by Brascan Ltd., Toronto, and in Du Pont de Nemours Corp. by Seagram's of Montreal. This article aims to provide a background to this trend.

CANADIAN DIRECT INVESTMENT ABROAD HAS FOLLOWED A SIMILAR PATTERN TO THE US

The per caput level of Canadian foreign direct investment (FDI) and its industrial and geographical distribution are strikingly similar to those for the USA. Nevertheless Canada has most often been studied as a host country, not as a foreign investor. Very little has been written on Canada's direct investment abroad and on Canadian multinational corporations. But in 1976, according to the data published by the United Nations Centre on Transnational Corporations, Canada was the seventh largest overseas investor, after the USA, the UK, West Germany, Japan, Switzerland and France. Moreover Canada's direct investment abroad grew at a very high rate during the 1970s. According to the latest figures published for 1978, Canadian direct investment abroad was $700 per caput, while the US counterpart was $750 for the same year. But Canadian FDI was growing much faster, to C$6.5 bn in 1980 for an average annual growth rate of 13.7 per cent, while the US growth rate was 9 per cent for the same period.

The geographical distribution of Canadian FDI was also very close to the US one. In 1978, 24 per cent of the Canadian total was invested in developing countries, while the US figure was also 24 per cent. The USA is the most important host country for Canadian direct investment abroad, with 55 per cent of the total. Canada was the main host country of American FDI, with 22 per cent of the US total. The industrial distribution shows again a striking similarity. Canadian

FDI in manufacturing was 47 per cent of the total, while the corresponding figure for the USA was 44 per cent. Mining, oil and gas took 24 per cent of both Canadian and US FDI. Finance accounted for 11 per cent of Canadian direct investment abroad while it was 14 per cent of the total US FDI.

In manufacturing, Canadian international investment is represented in industries ranging from telecommunications equipment to synthetic rubber and latex, as well as in traditional industries such as footwear and meat packing. Canadian MNCs are also active in maturing industries such as pulp and paper, business forms, agricultural machinery and transportation equipment.

The economic concentration of Canadian direct investment abroad is also very close to the American one. According to Raymond Vernon (in *Sovereignty at Bay*, 1971, page 18) nearly 80 per cent of the assets of US FDI was controlled by the 187 multinational corporations. In 1976, 65 per cent of Canadian direct investment abroad was made by the 16 largest foreign investors, companies such as Alcan Aluminum, Bata Shoes, Brascan, Canada Packers, Cominco, Falconbridge Nickel, Ford of Canada, Inco, McMillan Bloedel, Massey-Ferguson, Moore Corporation, Noranda Mines, Northern Telecom, Polysar, Seagram and Hiram Walker. A second group of 49 other corporations represented another 21 per cent of the total Canadian direct investment abroad. These are also large but only partially international firms such as steel producers (Stelco, Dofasco, Algoma Steel), beer companies (Molson, Labatt and Carling O'Keefe) and paper producers (such as Domtar, Consolidated Bathurst and Abitibi-Price). These companies have subsidiaries in two or three countries, while the 16 or 17 largest have foreign branches or affiliates in five to 100 countries.

Are these Canadian multinationals truly Canadian or, as in the case of Falconbridge Nickel and Ford Motor of Canada, are they simply the Canadian headquarters of US

corporations? According to recent figures, in 1978, 83 per cent of the Canadian FDI was Canadian-controlled. Only two of the largest Canadian multinationals are American-controlled (Falconbridge and Ford Canada); one is state-controlled (Polysar) and the others are privately owned and controlled Canadian corporations.

THE CANADIAN MULTINATIONALS BEGAN IN PUBLIC UTILITIES

In almost every industry Canada has (or has had) sizeable multinationals. The older ones have been in public utilities. The largest was Brazilian Traction Light Heat and Power whose origins go back to the beginning of the century. Brazilian Traction owned and operated the electric and lighting facilities of Rio de Janeiro and São Paulo as well as the urban transportation and telephone systems of those cities. At the summit of its development, in the 1940s, its assets were comparable to those of American and Foreign Power, the largest US multinational utility. The Brazilian assets of Brascan (as it came to be renamed in 1975) were bought by the Brazilian government three years ago and the takeover came into effect on January 1, 1979, while Amforp was dissolved in 1967. The second largest Canadian multinational utility was Canadian International Power, incorporated in 1916. CIP surrendered its charter in 1977. It had been active in Venezuela, Bolivia, El Salvador and some other Latin American or Caribbean countries. It was smaller than Brazilian Traction, but it controlled much of the electrical production of several countries for half a century.

What is striking about these early Canadian multinational utilities is that Canada did not have a heavy electrical industry, and that the Canadian capital market was very narrow. How did these Canadian companies get technology and capital for their foreign ventures?

The author's research has shown that Canadian promoters got concessions in less developed countries, raised capital in London, New York, Paris or Brussels, hired American engineers and bought American heavy electrical equipment from Westinghouse or General Electric. Later, after World War II, Canadian multinational utilities turned to the Canadian subsidiaries of US electrical manufacturers for equipment and to the Canadian financial market for capital. But this was done in their declining phase when the nationalisation of foreign utilities had started in Latin America.

—WHICH MOVED INTO ENGINEERING

In the meantime Canadian multinational utilities set up engineering subsidiaries which became multinationals themselves. The largest of them is Montreal Engineering, the former consulting affiliate of Canadian International Power. Three of the world's ten largest engineering consultants are based in Canada. They are Monenco, Lavalin and SNC Consultants, and they operate on a global scale in all the fields of energy resources.

The earlier Canadian MNCs in manufacturing started their foreign operations between World War I and World War II. In distilling, Seagram and Hiram Walker bought or built their first US subsidiaries in 1934 on the repeal of the American Prohibition Law. Both took over Scottish producers of whisky in the 1930s or 1940s and then turned to other spirits and to wine. Massey-Harris was the largest Canadian agricultural machinery producer at the beginning of the century when it bought its first US subsidiary. But its truly multinational expansion started in Europe in the 1920s. Massey was using US patents, so it did not sell its implements in the USA but in Europe and in the Commonwealth. Its first foreign subsidiaries went to those regions to consolidate export markets. The second outburst of Massey's expansion came in the 1950s

when it took over the world's largest diesel engine producer, Perkins of England, as well as Ferguson, the English tractor leader. Massey had never been able to produce efficient tractors, so it bought out one of the most modern and prestigious world producers.

After the World War II Canadian manufacturing multinationals knew a very important foreign expansion. Polysar, for example, became one of the world leaders in synthetic rubber and latex. Incorporated in 1942 by the Canada government to supply rubber for war demand, Polysar bought the US patents and invested $45 mn in a very modern plant. The company went multinational in 1960 when it built factories in Belgium and France to keep its export markets, protected from then on by the EEC tariffs. Later Polysar went to the USA and to Mexico. It diversified into synthetic latex by buying German and American producers in the 1960s. Nowadays Polysar makes 10 per cent of the non-communist world's synthetic rubber and is a world leader in synthetic latex and resins.

One of the newest Canadian manufacturing multinationals is Northern Telecom. Northern was the Canadian subsidiary of Western Electric, the US giant producer of telecommunications equipment. Northern was a USA subsidiary from its inception in the 1880s to its takeover by Bell Canada in 1956. Subsequently it acquired a technological independence which has transformed the company into a world leader of the industry. Its multinational expansion started in the early 1970s in the USA, Europe and South East Asia. Recently it has set up a Mexican subsidiary to manufacture its digital equipment for that country. Northern is one of the few examples of a Canadian corporation basing its multinational expansion on domestic innovation. However, in the late 1970s Northern entered the computer industry through acquisition of some medium-sized US electronic producers. Having captured 85 per cent of the Canadian telecommunications equipment market, Northern is almost a monopoly in its home country. Its advantage is size and oligopolistic profits, as well as innovation.

—AND MINING SEES SOME WORLD LEADERSHIP

In mining two of the largest Canadian multinationals are Inco and Alcan Aluminum, both former American subsidiaries in which Canadian interests have been growing slowly but steadily for the last 50 years. Both are US multinationals turned Canadian. The bulk of their technological advantages was acquired through the US connection. In Canada they are leaders in the close oligopolies of nickel and aluminium.

Two other mining multinationals deserve attention: Cominco and Noranda Mines. Cominco is currently one of the world leaders in zinc and lead. A member of the Canadian Pacific conglomerate, Cominco bought the bulk of its mining, smelting and refining technologies from US engineering firms during the first 30 years of this century. Cominco is the undisputed leader of the very exclusive domestic oligopoly of zinc. Noranda Mines is a copper, lead and zinc producer incorporated in 1922. It completed its vertical integration in 1930, with US technology and expertise[1]. It is another member of the Canadian handful of domestic oligopolists in nonferrous metals, but its main product is lead.

In oil, Canadian multinationals are second-line players. Some of them are foreign-controlled (as Canadian Superior Oil, a subsidiary of Superior Oil of Houston, Texas). Others have been bought by Canadian interests when they were already multinational enterprises. Texas Pacific Oil, for example, taken over by Seagram in 1953 and partially sold in 1980, is a case in point. While in nonferrous metals Canadian multinationals are often world leaders—Inco is number one in world nickel, Alcan is number two in world aluminium, Cominco is number one in world zinc. But in oil there are no Canadian majors

and even with the present national energy policy and the Canadianization movement, Canada's largest oil companies such as Dome Petroleum and Petro-Canada are small by world standards. The Canadian oil industry was almost completely foreign-controlled ten years ago. Now one third of it is Canadian-controlled, thanks to the incorporation of the national oil company Petro-Canada in 1975, and to the new energy policy issued in 1980.

THERE ARE THREE VERY LARGE BANKS

Canadian chartered banks are very large. The big five (Royal, Montreal, Commerce, Nova Scotia and Toronto-Dominion) centralise 90 per cent of the assets of all commercial banks in Canada. Three of them are among the 50 largest world banks. The Royal Bank, Canada's number one, had in December 1980 total assets of $63 bn and its growth rate was 25 per cent a year. It has branches, affiliates or representatives in 45 countries and it controls some large international banks, such as the Orion Bank of London. Other large Canadian financial institutions are multinational as well. Insurance companies such as Metropolitan Life, Sun Life or National Life and trust companies such as the Royal Trust, are outstanding examples. But Canada's chartered banks are by far its largest financial multinational corporations.

—AND COMMERCE AND REAL ESTATE MNCS

In commerce the George Weston empire has to be mentioned. It went multinational in the 1930s towards the USA and the UK. In the USA it controls some of the largest food chains such as Loblaws, National Tea and Kelly Douglas. Including its British, European and Commonwealth subsidiaries, the Weston group had 106,000 employees in 1980.

In real estate, three of the largest firms are

Olympia and York, Trizec, and Cadillac Fairview. The largest of them, Olympia and York, is very active not only in Canada and the USA but also in England through its giant subsidiary English Property Corp. and in the Caribbean.

CANADIAN GOVERNMENT HAS CURBED THE INWARD FLOW OF FDI

Since the late 1960s and early 1970s, the Canadian state has been playing a moderate but increasing role in the promotion of Canadian direct investment overseas.

A first group of policies affecting Canadian FDI, though indirectly, is a vast array of measures designed to curb foreign direct investment in Canada. These policies have strengthened Canadian owned and controlled corporations, forced some US and European multinationals to divest themselves of their Canadian subsidiaries, and given Canadian enterprises some kind of fiscal or commercial preferential treatment against foreign companies operating in Canada. Prominent among these measures are, for example, the 1967 Bank Act forbidding non-residents the ownership of more than 25 per cent of the voting shares of a Canadian chartered bank; the 1968 act by which non-residents can only hold 20 per cent of shares in a Canadian radio, television or cable company; the 1971 Foreign Investment Review Agency giving the federal government an important say in any new investment by foreign companies in Canada as well as in any takeover of a Canadian corporation by a foreign concern. From 1965, non-residents could not buy more than 25 per cent of the shares of a federally incorporated insurance company, and foreign-owned newspapers were given a drastic fiscal treatment. But the Canadian state also acts through crown corporations to reduce foreign control of the economy. In 1971 the Canada Development Corporation was in-

corporated to reinforce domestic entrepreneurship. In 1973 the CDC took over Texasgulf, an American multinational with substantial operations in Canada, and in 1975 it bought Tenneco's Canadian subsidiary, then renamed CDC Oil and Gas. In 1981 CDC bought Aquitaine of Canada, the Canadian branch of the French state multinational. In the meantime the subsidiaries of De Havilland and General Dynamics in the aircraft industry were bought by the federal government in 1974 and 1975. But the most spectacular intervention by the Canadian state was in oil. In 1975 the federal government incorporated Petro-Canada, a wholly-owned crown corporation. In 1976 Petro-Canada bought Atlantic Richfield Canada, in 1978 Pacific Petroleum, and in 1981 Petrofina Canada, to constitute the first wholly-integrated Canadian oil company, with assets approaching the C$5 bn mark. In November 1980 the Canadian government sanctioned a national energy policy, giving Canadian-owned oil companies preferential subsidies and fiscal treatment. One year later foreign control in oil and gas had declined from 72 per cent to 65 per cent and the "Canadianisation" movement was amplifying.

The provincial governments are actively following the nationalistic path. Some outstanding examples are in Saskatchewan, Alberta and Quebec. Canada is the largest potash producer in the capitalist world and most of its known reserves are located in Saskatchewan. Starting in the early 1970s, the provincial government wanted to capture an increasing proportion of the rising mining rent, collected mostly by foreign producers. The companies refused to give up, and in 1976 the New Democratic government incorporated the Potash Corporation of Saskatchewan, a provincial crown corporation which took over more than 40 per cent of the industry's capacity by nationalising six foreign subsidiaries. In Alberta, the Conservative government elected in 1971 has brought forward a policy of nurturing the development of provincial-owned companies mainly in hydroelectricity, oil and petrochemicals. Some large foreign subsidiaries, such as the giant Canadian Utilities conglomerate and Husky Oil, have been taken over by Albertan interests with government backing. In Quebec the Parti Québécois government incorporated the National Asbestos Corporation in 1977 to buy back the asbestos mining industry; Quebec is the world's largest mining producer in this industry, but only a small percentage of the total output is manufactured in the province. In 1980 the Quebec government bought Bell Asbestos from its English owner, Turner and Newall, and in 1981 it took over Asbestos Corp. from General Dynamics in order to step up local transportation of the mineral.

—AND PROMOTED INVESTMENT ABROAD

The strengthening of Canadian-owned corporations is often a prerequisite for their international expansion. Canadian mass media firms are crossing the border and buying up American radio, TV, cable and newspaper companies. Canadian oil independents are increasingly active in the USA, Australia, Egypt and the North Sea. Canadian chartered banks and insurance companies are following their multinational career, free from retaliatory takeover threats by US or European competitors.

A second group of measures is trying to promote Canadian exports and direct investment abroad. The main instrument for state intervention has been the Export Development Corporation, created in 1969 on the basis of the Export Credit Insurance Corporation. A wholly-owned crown corporation, Ecic was originally intended to insure exporters from default by foreign clients, but its charter was amended in the 1960s to provide long term financing for capital goods exporters. By becoming EDC in 1969, the

corporation added a complete insurance plan for Canadian direct investors abroad. This programme covers high risk countries, that is to say Third World countries. But only small developing countries such as Jamaica, the Dominican Republic, Indonesia or Guinea have signed bilateral agreements with EDC. Only 5.6 per cent of Canadian FDI in developing countries was insured by EDC in 1977, and the impact of the programme was marginal. Another EDC programme assisting Canadian MNCs abroad is the financing of capital goods exports. Some large foreign investors, such as Inco in Guatemala,[2] have made good use of this programme.

A second programme supporting foreign investment was established in 1970 by the Canadian Agency for International Development. This programme subsidises foreign investment preliminary studies up to C$2,500 and feasibility studies up to C$25,000. Eight years later the programme has financed almost 300 projects for a total amount of C$2 mn. Most of its customers were medium-size enterprises; and most of the projects have been abandoned.

Through fiscal legislation, Canada has adopted a policy of passive promotion of Canadian foreign direct investment. Companies with overseas operations can deduct taxes paid to host countries from the net revenue they declare in Canada. Canadian officers of Canadian subsidiaries abroad are also free from double taxation. Canada has, moreover, never issued any law restricting capital exports, as Japan has done from 1946 to the present day.

Although this has sometimes been the case for other advanced industrial countries, the Canadian government has never set up a public corporation to finance international direct investment by private companies. However, Canada participates with these countries in several international financial institutions, such as the World Bank, the International Financial Corporation, the Asian Development Bank, etc. Through these international institutions Canadian multinationals have received financial support for their foreign operations. Brazilian Traction was often a recipient of World Bank credits, and Bata Shoes benefited from several IFC funds. The Canadian government backed, directly and indirectly, these financial arrangements.

DO CANADIAN MNCS FIT MULTINATIONAL THEORY?

Among the different theories of the international expansion and operations of firms, Hymer kindleberger emphasised the oligopolistic character of multinationals. According to this argument only large firms in oligopolistic markets have international operations. These oligopolies have some technological, financial or organisational advantage which allows them to build foreign subsidiaries insulated from the competition of local, host enterprises. We have seen that most often Canadian multinational corporations are giant firms enjoying oligopolistic positions in their home markets. But what kind of advantage is theirs? According to the product cycle theory (represented, among others, by Raymond Vernon, Louis T. Wells, Jr. and Frederick Knickerbocker) technological advantages are a key factor in the explanation of multinationalisation. In the product cycle process, the innovating firm starts production in its home market, and then, when technology becomes more diffused and the product is more standardised, it goes international to protect its exports. Finally the product is completely homogeneous and technology is within the reach of local producers. In this third and final phase competition replaces the senescent oligopoly. Professor Wells, Jr. has added a "sub-theory" about the international order in which countries adopt the new technology. Normally, the innovating firms in the first country—often the USA—export their product to and later build subsidiaries in other industrialised but less advanced countries, for example in

Western Europe, Canada or Japan. Then the emerging competitors in these countries "scale down" the original technology, adapt it to less solvent markets and export their products and then their factories to semi-industrialised countries such as Argentina, Brazil, India, Mexico or South Korea. This is what Wells, Jr. has called the "international pecking order" in the product cycle.

This theory cannot explain the massive wave of European, Canadian and Japanese investment in the USA that has been taking place in the 1970s and early 1980s. How does it apply to Canadian multinationals? The first problem is that Canadian MNCs are not important innovators. Most often they are adapting, modifying, sometimes improving foreign innovations. In that case, according to Wells, Jr., they should be investing in less advanced countries. But Canada's multinationals are building or buying subsidiaries mainly in the USA or in Western Europe. The international pecking order scheme does not seem to fit the Canadian pattern of multinational expansion.

There is another aspect of the product cycle theory that deserves close attention. According to Vernon all multinational corporations go through a rising phase, then reach a maturing stage in which they become multinationals and then fade out. In public utilities and in mining this process is slightly different because there are no exports preceding the foreign investment period. Vernon has called this pattern the "obsolescing bargain process." In this auxiliary model, Vernon describes how public utilities, mining and plantation firms set up subsidiaries in developing countries. At the start the host country lacks expertise in the technical, financial and commercial aspects of the business. But in these industries learning is not a long term process. Besides, once the ore reserves have been explored, the dams built, and the markets established, the risk phase is over and the bargaining condition of the host country improves. Within years or decades public or private enterprises of the host country can take over foreign subsidiaries with the aid of the host state. This pattern can explain reasonably well the expansion and decline of American and Canadian public utility multinationals, such as American and Foreign Power, Brascan or Canadian International Power. Another factor has of course been the availability of international loans as aid for less developed countries in the post-war period to facilitate the development of energy projects.

But it seems less easy to apply this theory to Canadian mining MNCs. In non-ferrous metals, where Canadian MNCs are strong, their bargaining position has never been seriously affected, except in copper. Some of the copper producing countries, such as Chile, Peru, Zambia and Zaire, nationalised foreign subsidiaries in the late 1960s and early 1970s. But the process did not touch other non-ferrous metals such as bauxite, nickel, lead and zinc. Only one Canadian multinational, Alcan Aluminum, has suffered from a third world nationalisation. It was in British Guyana, in 1971. The six world majors in the aluminium industry (Alcoa, Alcan, Kaiser, Reynolds, Péchiney and Alusuisse) are keeping their market shares in global production fairly well, even if dozens of independent new producers are entering the industry in marginal markets. In nickel, zinc, and lead the leading position of large oligopolies has been eroded in the post-war period; but the erosion comes from the rise of new producers of the developed countries, mainly Japanese and Western European, sometimes Canadian, and not from developing countries. The oil industry that has inspired Vernon in the building of his "obsolescing bargain" model does not apply to non-ferrous metals in which Canadian multinationals are leaders. Conversely Stephen Hymer and Robert Rowthorn had predicted the rise of European, Japanese and Canadian multinationals in their well-known article "Multinational Corporations and International Oligopoly: the Non American Challenge" published in 1969 and based on a careful observation of empirical trends. In manufacturing no product cycle process is affecting Canadian multinationals, even in traditional industries such as footwear in which Bata Shoes, with subsidiaries in more than 100 countries, is the world's number one.

THEIR ADVANTAGES SEEM MOST CLOSELY LINKED TO SIZE

If technological innovation is not a characteristic of Canadian multinationals, what kind of advantages are theirs? First of all, they have financial and organisational advantages associated with their large size and oligopolistic position. Canadian MNCs are giant corporations by world standards even if their home market is only one tenth of the American market. This happens because economic concentration is much higher in Canada than in the USA. Large size and oligopoly produce high profits (and then financial advantages) and also organisational capabilities to manage international operations. Many authors, and F. T. Knickerbocker among them, have shown the relationship between oligopoly, profitability and multinational operations.

—AND CLOSE CULTURAL LINKS WHICH ASSIST INNOVATION

Secondly, Canadian large firms do absorb US and British innovations very early on, thanks to their geographic, cultural and linguistic closeness to both countries. In fact Canadian oligopolies can adopt European or US technology as soon as it is ready for productive uses. The technological market is very imperfect and Canadian firms are often quick followers, at least in several mining and manufacturing industries where they control important natural resources (such as pulp and paper, uranium mining and non-ferrous metals) or in which their market forces them to adaptive innovation, as in hydroelectric and telecommunications technology.

Several mechanisms explain how Canadian multinationals acquire innovation from US or European producers. The first and most obvious is the buying of patents. In 1980 for example, the Canadian copper multinational enterprise, Noranda Mines, bought continuous castings patents from Metallurgie Hoboken-Overpelt, the Belgian giant, and adopted them for its multinational subsidiary, Canada Wire and Cable.

A second method for the incorporation of foreign technology is the setting up of R & D facilities in more developed countries. Moore Corporation, a Canadian and world leader in business forms, has moved all its R & D facilities to the USA, while Massey-Ferguson has set up its laboratories in Detroit to benefit from US university research in that area.

A third method of absorption is the buying of foreign producers. Massey-Ferguson, as has already been mentioned, entered the agricultural tractor market by taking over British firms. At present Northern Telecom is buying US electronic firms to penetrate this industry.

A fourth avenue to foreign technology is the taking over of US subsidiaries in Canada. Alcan, Inco, Northern Telecom and others were sizeable foreign branch plants in Canada in a previous stage.

Finally, some multinationals are only nominally Canadian, such as Ford Motor of Canada and Canadian Superior Oil, and they are using the technology of their parent corporation in their foreign operations.

Notes

---

[1] Noranda now controls McMillan Bloedel, while resisting Brascan's attempts at taking it over.

[2] Now shut down.

49 Politics and Moral Causes in Canada and the United States

Mildred A. Schwartz

MILDRED A. SCHWARTZ is Professor of Sociology and Affiliate, Department of Political Science, University of Illinois at Chicago. She specializes in the study of regionalism and political sociology. Her books include *Public Opinion and Canadian Identity* (1967); *Politics and Territory* (1974); *Canadian Political Parties: Origin, Character, Impact* with F.C. Engelmann (1977); *The Environment for Policy-making in Canada and the United States* (1981); and *Politics and Networks: The Illinois Republican Party* (forthcoming). Work in progress includes a book on candidate-contributor relations. Professor Schwartz has served, throughout her career, on a number of important professional executive, planning and awards adjudication committees. She recently held the Visiting Distinguished Professorship in the Department of Political Science, University of Alberta.

MORALITY IN THE UNITED STATES

... A striking characteristic of American life is the ease with which moral causes are translated into political issues. Some argue that the underlying motif of American politics is not, in fact, tied primarily to economic and class issues, but to those of values, lifestyle, and morality.... Others argue that there is no true division, but that moral distinctions linked to those of class have been endemic to life in the United States, finding their way into politics from the Declaration of Independence and its subsequent interpretations (e.g., Guinther, 1976, pp. 3–22).

Regardless of how much emphasis is placed on the role of moral causes, it is generally acknowledged that political issues divide into two categories: those that are essentially distributive, and those that are moralistic, treating of right conduct. Various terms have been used for this contrast, and not always in identical fashion, but we can still recognize some aspect of the two categories where the former are termed economic, position, or class issues; and the latter subsumed as social/cultural, style, valence, or status issues (e.g., Schneider, 1978, p. 183; Berelson, Lazarsfeld, McPhee, 1954, pp. 184–185; Stokes, 1966; pp. 170–171). What will here be called moral causes are those that place uncompromising evaluations in the forefront, and appeal primarily to the emotional well-springs of communal loyalties. The disruptive potential of such issues is suggested by Alford's argument that class cleavages are more readily compromised than those of origin or region (Alford, 1963, p. 339). It was also recognized by the authors of *Voting*, who saw the "Big Issues" to be ones that combined position and style in particularly divisive fashion (Berelson, Lazarsfeld, and McPhee, 1954, p. 185). The intrusion of moral causes into political life sets up conditions contrary to normal politics, particularly to the normal brokering characteristic of party politics in all democratic political systems....

Lipset argues for the uniqueness of the American concern with moral issues. It is the country, he says, "*par excellence,* of moralistic ... social movements" (Lipset, 1977,

p. 120). In an earlier work, Lipset tended to downplay the special qualities of American political life by contrasting them with Canada. He does not question the prominence of social movements in the United States, which in Canada found expression in third parties, but he attributes this difference to contrasts in the electoral system (Lipset and Raab, 1978, p. 22).... But later he suggests greater relevance to the content of the movement, which then has implications for the message finding its way into mainstream politics:

> Extra-party "movements" arise for moralistic causes, which are initially not electorally palatable. These extra-major-party movements have taken various forms, most often emphasizing a single special issue, but sometimes cohering around a broader ideology. Such movements are not doomed to isolation and inefficacy. If mainstream political leaders recognize that a significant segment of the electorate feels alienated from the body politic, they will readapt one of the major party coalitions. But in so doing, they temper much of the extremist moralistic fervor. Sometimes this may be done by accommodations in rhetoric, but the results are often actual changes in policy... (Lipset, 1977, p. 128).

The potency of moralistic social movements lies then in their ability to permanently transform the content of politics.

DEMONSTRATING THE POLITICS OF MORALITY

An hypothesis can be formulated which affirms the propensity for moralizing in the United States, and the likelihood that this tendency will quickly enter the realm of politics. In other countries, even when the same moral issues arise, they will be treated more cooly, with less emotional fervor....

Without the means to demonstrate the greater incidence of social movements in the United States, their attachment to moral causes, and their rapid politicization, a modest comparative test can still be useful. While limited in scope, the conditions of the test are deliberately set to be difficult for showing the uniqueness of the United States. I use Canada as a standard, a country still most like the United States, despite many profound differences....

We would expect that, compared to Canada, the United States would have more social movements or related organizations, with a larger membership, operating from the basis of a more concerned and supportive public. There is a greater tendency for the issues to become polarized, with battle lines sharply drawn. Room for compromise is more restricted. Interest groups will make every effort at their disposal to influence both the public and the actions of government. In Canada, these interest groups will aim at more direct access to government and at orderly, regularized contacts (Pross, 1975, p. 3).

A political solution to moral issues requires legislation to regulate conduct. In Canada, we would anticipate less pressure to institute legislative control. Individual politicians in the United States will adopt one side of the controversy as their own, expecting to reap popular and political benefit. Eventually, political parties will incorporate the issues into their platforms. Canadian politicians and parties, when they are unable to ignore the issues altogether, will attempt to downplay their significance. Given a moral cause, one that deals with right conduct, it will remain within the confines of customary politics in Canada....

These criteria have been developed by drawing implications out of the literature about moral causes in the United States. They will be tested in a preliminary way with the issue of prohibition, and in more detail, with the ongoing controversy over abortion....

A PRELIMINARY TEST: PROHIBITION

... Temperance achieved its greatest victory with the passage of the Eighteenth Amendment to the Constitution on 20 January 1919. It passed rapidly on from its introduction in Congress through its ratification by the states. Strong pressure from organized prohibition interests was helped by appeals to wartime sacrifice (Kyvig, 1979, p. 11) and the strong religious message evoked (Carter, 1956). But once prohibition became the law of the land, new opposition emerged. Instead of brewers, distillers, and saloon keepers objecting to government interference in their livelihood, now respectable citizens began to organize against the new abuses of prohibition. In the forefront were the Association against the Prohibition Amendment and the Women's Organization for National Prohibition Repeal, both headed by prominent business and political leaders. The issue now became more clearly partisan. Al Smith was able to link repeal with the Democratic Party (Kyvig, 1979). With Franklin D. Roosevelt's election in 1932, repeal came the following year.

Just as in the United States, prohibition forces were active in Canada during the nineteenth century, tied to the more evangelical Protestant churches. Of the organizations which emerged to spread the message of abstinence, some, like the Women's Christian Temperance Union, came from over the border; others, like the Canadian Temperance League, were indigenous groups. . . .

Prohibitionists saw the importance of political involvement, but for the most part, they preferred the nonpartisan climate of local referenda to that of party politics. In that endeavor they remained successful, but when they moved to province-wide referenda, the majority votes obtained were not translated into law, perhaps because of provincial concerns about possible jurisdictional disputes (Moffit, 1932, pp. 188–189).

. . . Prohibition became national policy as the result of an order-in-council, passed under the wartime authority of the federal government. It ended the manufacture and trade of alcohol in 1918 for the duration of the war and 12 months after, but post-war provisions

were struck down by the Senate. The provinces were aided in their control measures, however, by the passage of federal legislation in 1921, banning interprovincial traffic in alcohol. Defections from a nation-wide policy started as early as 1919, when Quebec and British Columbia opted for provincial control over sales, and other provinces followed suit, with only Prince Edward Island holding out for total prohibition until 1930. . . .

The forces of prohibition were severely shaken by their inability to influence political decisions on a long-run basis. While there had been close ties with the progressive movement, which had in turn endorsed prohibition, once progressives achieved power in Alberta and Saskatchewan in the 1920s, they "were as loath as any other government to stake their lives on a single issue" (Allen, 1971, p. 277). A major defeat was to come in Ontario in the election of 1926, when Premier Ferguson confronted the prohibitionists on the issue of government control over alcohol, and won. Organized opposition to prohibition had also arisen, although it is not clear just who was represented in the two major groups, the Moderation and Liberty Leagues, nor how influential they were (Allen, 1971, p. 273). More apparent was a general move away from commitment to total abstinence controlled through legislation. . . .

Prohibition was present in both countries, arising from similar sources, but even this cursory examination reveals significant differences. Canada had a much shorter-lived national policy, one that resulted from the narrowest of government actions, removed from debate, the broad participation of lawmakers, or public scrutiny. In the United States, prohibition was enacted dramatically, through a symbolic linkage with the Constitution. Prohibition had an uneasy tie with politics in Canada, while overt partisanship formed the heart of the American experience. The movement to achieve prohibition was unique in the United States, as was its counterforce, but in Canada, a certain amount of borrowing took place both with respect to specific organizations and to policies. The Canadian movement never acquired the same single-mindedness found in the United States, to the extent that it provided rationale and identity to some degree removed from the originating impulse of the Protestant churches. . . .

ABORTION

In the United States, abortion became illegal in the mid-nineteenth century, largely through the efforts of the medical profession (Mohr, 1978). Laws governing abortion came under new pressure for change in the 1960s from several sources. One was the legal profession itself, which in the Model Penal Code proposed by the American Law Institute in 1959, provided that a physician could terminate pregnancy under conditions of threatened mental or physical impairment to the mother, deformity of the child, or when pregnancy was the result of rape or incest. . . .

The exposure of women to experiences that could lead to deformed offspring gave new value to therapeutic abortions. In the 1960s, use of the drug thalidomide by pregnant women and an epidemic of German measles combined to dramatize the unanticipated dangers of pregnancy. . . .

The 1960s were also a time of changing life styles and new challenges to established sex roles. Abortion now came to be viewed as an adjunct of women's rights (Rossi, 1969, pp. 338–346). According to the executive director of the Association for the Study of Abortion, greater receptivity to the need for abortion reform came from the changed social climate of the time.

> One [impetus to change] was the civil rights movement, which highlighted those individual rights that no state could abridge. (To many people, abortion was one of those rights.) The other was the growing honesty and openness about human sexuality. This made it easier to discuss abortion in public as well as in private (Kinney, 1973), p. 118).

Another indication of shift in attitudes was the report of the President's Commission on Population Growth. Representing expert opinion on population problems, and called together as an official body to recommend policy, the Commission included a provision for readily available abortions (Report of the Commission, 1972, p. 142).

The most dramatic change occurred with a Supreme Court ruling in 1973, which virtually permitted abortion on demand in the first trimester of pregnancy, with the state intervening only in later stages. The decision was the result of a ruling that the abortion laws of Texas and Georgia, challenged by two women who sued public officials in their states (*Roe v. Wade and Doe v. Bolton*), violated the rights to privacy guaranteed by the constitution [410 U.S. 113(1973) and 410 U.S. 179(1973)]. This ruling, which led to changed statutes in many states, represents the present law on abortion in the United States. . . .

The law in Canada is different, and owes its origins to a different legal context. On Confederation, Canada inherited British legislation defining abortion as criminal, altered in 1929 to explicitly permit abortion to save the life of the mother. Because of revisions in the Canadian Criminal Code in 1955, which dropped the key word "unlawfully," there was some dispute whether there were any conditions under which abortions could be legally performed in Canada. . . .

Pressure to change in Canada was stimulated by events outside the country, particularly in Britain and the United States, as a new climate for discussion emerged. Conditions specific to the country were at least as important, particularly the unclarity of the law. Abortion was a hotly debated topic at meetings of the Canadian Bar Association, which agreed to a resolution for a more liberal law in 1966 (deValk, 1974, pp. 14–16, 23–26). The Canadian Medical Association also came to approve clear grounds for legal abortions in 1965 (deValk, 1974, pp. 16–18).

When change took place, it was in the

Criminal Code. It was part of a move for redefining restrictions on personal behavior set in motion by then Justice Minister Pierre Trudeau. The prelude began with the Standing Committee on Health and Welfare in 1967, first taking up a private member bill for abortion reform, and then accepting briefs and submissions from individuals and organizations. The Committee continued its hearings into 1968, presenting its second and final report just before the dissolution of parliament (Standing Committee on Health and Welfare, 1967–1968). When parliament returned under the new leadership of Prime Minister Trudeau, the promise was now for an omnibus bill, which would also include legislation on homosexuality and lotteries. While it was the abortion provisions of that Omnibus Bill, C–150, that aroused greatest controversy in the House of Commons, the strong majority position of the Liberal Party kept them within the bill, which passed its final reading in May, 1969.

The provisions of the Canadian law are much more limited than the current interpretations in the United States. Only therapeutic abortion is permitted, performed by a licensed physician, and with the approval of a hospital-appointed therapeutic abortion committee. Grounds for abortion are left loosely defined as the physical or mental health of the mother.

In both countries, questions over the right to abortion remain in the forefront of public controversy, and neither have removed the danger that practitioners will be free from prosecution, although under different circumstances. . . .

Similarities are strong between the United States and Canada in the organization of interests. Pro-abortion forces were the first to organize; their relative success mobilized opponents; and both countries remain highly organized (Sarvis and Rodman, 1974, pp. 9–10; Batten, 1974; pp. 98–102). The reformers had ties with general women's rights groups and with family planning associations. The oldest Canadian group specifically concerned with abortion rights is the Association for Repeal of Canada's Abortion Laws, founded in Ottawa in 1966. The comparable group in the United States is the National Association for the Repeal of Abortion Laws, founded in 1969. It was preceded by the Association for the Study of Abortion in 1965, the first national group, and one dedicated, as its name suggests, to public education. Opposition has ties to both the Catholic Church and fundamentalist churches. Among the anti-abortion opponents there are even similar names across the border, subsuming a similarity of purpose. Thus Birthright is found both nationally and locally in both countries as a counselling organization. Public educational groups include the Alliance Against Abortion and Right to Life, the latter also called Alliance for Life in Canada when referring to the umbrella organization.

The political style of contending interests is sharply polemical in both countries. In Canada, Catholic Church authorities proposed investigating the YWCA's stand on abortion and considered banning Church members from joining (*Canadian News Facts*, 4 July 1979, p. 24). The Ottawa Committee for the Defense of the Unborn charged that pro-abortion groups had been deluding the public by using false statistics (Canadian Clipping Service, n.d., 1967). Allegations about false and misleading statistics are also prevalent for both sides of the controversy in the United States (Leahy and Mazur, 1978, p. 147). In the United States as well, the Feminist Party announced it would demand that the IRS remove the tax-exempt status of the Roman Catholic Church and its affiliated organizations in retaliation for the latter's anti-abortion lobbying. This was also designed to offset plans for a "Slaughter Day" protest by a right to life group (*New York Times*, 1 July 1972, p. 8). . . .

Two-pronged efforts to attract public support and influence the political process are common in both countries. In Canada, pro-abortion groups organized an Abortion Caravan, calling on supporters across Canada to coordinate arrival in Ottawa, and present a brief to the Prime Minister (Maesto, 1970, p. 157; Keate, 1970, pp. 15–20). The presentation of petitions to government is both a technique of influence and publicity, with greater impact apparently on the side of abortion foes. . . . Telephone campaigns to enlist supporters and pressure candidates represent another approach. According to the California Life Amendment Political Action Committee, its relatively small size was compensated by the success of its telephone campaigning (*Los Angeles Times*, 18 February 1979, p. 3).

It is appropriate to associate the use of the courts as a more significant means of political influence in the United States compared to Canada. Certainly on the issue of abortion, it has been the courts that have had major influence in drastically changing the definition of legality (Sarvis and Rodman, 1974, pp. 55–68). While much less frequently resorted to, the courts in Canada have also played a role in the shifting controversy over abortion. . . .

To this point, we have found great similarity between Canada and the United States. This extends to the climate of public opinion, in which majorities approve of legal abortions at least under some circumstances, although there is a slight suggestion of greater polarization in the United States (Fletcher and Drummond, 1979, pp. 45–49; Blake, 1977, pp. 51–82). But as we look more directly at the political arena, the sense of difference between the two countries increases.

Lobbying extends to campaigning for sympathetic candidates and opposing their opposites, attempting to influence voters to participate in elections and referenda, and directly pressing legislators to take a position and act on it. In general, it appears there is simply more activity in this area in the United States, with greater success on the part of anti-abortion forces. In Canada, the Coalition for Life, the political arm of the anti-abortion

groups, reported that it helped defeat former NDP leader David Lewis, but there is no way of assessing other factors which may have been relevant in that election. The movement does meet with candidates, asks their views, and campaigns actively (Batten, 1974, p. 99). It has also developed strategies for identifying key constituencies, in which incumbents had won by a small number of votes, and then pressing to have its position adopted by either incumbents or opponents (Canadian Clipping Service, 4 September 1975). In contrast, there is more agreement on the success of anti-abortion efforts in the United States. . . .

. . . For candidates of both American parties, abortion is a troublesome issue, and one that most of them would like to avoid (*U.S. News*, 1976, pp. 14–15; Rosoff, 1975, pp. 13–22). At the same time, for some politicians, it is a good issue, through which they can mobilize public support and gain needed publicity. Currently, the best known supporter of restrictive legislation in Congress is Representative Henry Hyde of Illinois (*Time*, 1979, pp. 26–27; Becker, 1979, pp. 10–11). His most notable success is contained in an amendment bearing his name which bars the use of federal funds for abortions. . . .

In Canada, the debate on the change in law in 1969 required that parties make their positions known. Because the governing Liberal party refused to allow a free vote for its members, the party itself was committed to reform, but it is safe to say that only the NDP felt really comfortable with this position. While the Conservatives voted against the government in the final vote, that could be interpreted as a partisan position somewhat independent of the abortion issue. . . .

There are some Canadian politicians who have argued for or against the issue, in the sense of trying to associate it with their name and make it one of their own. The results, however, are not particularly dramatic. Joe Borowski in Manitoba was pressed to resign from the New Democratic (NDP) government because of the virulence of his anti-abortion stance (*Canadian News Facts*, 19 September 1971, pp. 696–697). Individual Liberal and NDP members continue to propose liberalization of the law, as they have done since 1967. Most recently, two Conservative members from Alberta have been particularly forthright in their anti-abortion efforts (Canadian Clipping Service, 6 May 1977). But their efforts cannot be treated as seriously as similar ones in the United States, since private members are generally ineffective in shaping the political agenda of parliament. For example, Prime Minister Trudeau was able to back away from permitting special time for debate on abortion in the 1971 session of parliament by claiming insufficient time (Canadian Clipping Service, 7 September 1971). He and his then Justice Minister, John Turner, could also rationalize inaction as a means of averting controversy, claiming lack of both legislative and public consensus (Tierney, 1972, p. 28). In other words, the very presence of potential controversy can be used in Canada, apparently with legitimacy, to avoid seeking legislative solutions. This is in sharp contrast to the situation both in Congress and some state legislatures, where debate over the funding of abortions through public monies provides the key to virtual paralysis of those bodies (Holsendolph, 1979, p. 1; Dionne, 1979, p. A1).

The mobilization of abortion interests, their style of operation, and supportive public opinion provide little to distinguish between Canada and the United States. Political institutions and structures, however, differentiate the ways in which the abortion controversy is incorporated into legal norms and the conduct of government. Currently, the result is a narrower definition of abortion rights in Canada, greater scope for opponents in the United States to restrict the exercise of those rights, and much greater opportunity for the issue to publicly divide American politicians. In consequence, there is a sharper boundary between polity and society in Canada. The

latter distinction was recognized by the committee appointed by the Canadian government in 1975 to investigate the inequitable operation of the abortion law. Committee members found the fault to lie, not in the law, but in the nature of Canadian society. The implication to be drawn was that politics provides limited instruments for producing social change.

> While the Abortion Law is specific in setting out the procedures to be followed, its definition of guidelines is broad enough to accommodate the breadth of the needs and the experiences of people across the nation. It is not the law that has led to the inequities in its operation or to the sharp disparities in how therapeutic abortions are obtained by women within cities, regions, or provinces. It is the Canadian people, their health institutions and the medical profession, who are responsible for the situation. The social cost has been the tolerance of widespread and entrenched social inequity for the women involved in the abortion procedure, and an unreasonable professional burden on some physicians and some hospitals (Committee on the Operation of the Abortion Law, 1977, p. 17). . . .

POLITICAL DIFFERENCES BETWEEN CANADA AND THE UNITED STATES

. . . As Tocqueville observed more than a century ago, America's eagerness to improve conditions and alter individual conduct is often followed by impatience and disillusionment when changes do not appear rapidly (Tocqueville, 1945, p. 268). This paper has not been able to substantiate these assessments since the test we set began with the existence of issues already defined as moral causes in Canada and the United States. It followed that our concern was with the fate of the issues and not their origin. As a result, it is not too surprising that the differences found between the two countries have been primarily of a political nature. The societal and cultural determinants of propensity to moralize were not directly under scrutiny. . . .

Both moral causes became politicized in Canada, but in different ways and to different degrees than in the United States. To account for these findings, we need to look at features of the two political systems that provide the pathways through which moral causes enter the political arena. We do this by also moving beyond the confines of the specific issues.

In the brief discussion of prohibition, it was noted that Canadians were reluctant to present their case through the medium of party politics, in contrast to American actions. From the perspective of the political process, Canadian efforts can be interpreted as a realistic assessment of the likelihood that prohibition interests would have an effect on the course of government. According to Thompson and Stanbury, politics in the two countries can be distinguished by the prominence given organized interests.

> It is our position that, while interest groups play an undeniable role in policy formulation and implementation in Canada, their role is more restricted than it is in the United States. Furthermore, interest group representation has not the same power to explain legislative outcomes that it possesses in the United States. Finally, both the restricted role of Canadian interest groups and the weaker explanatory power of interest group theory are in large part attributable to the constitutional structure of the Canadian government and its decision-making process (Thompson and Stanbury, 1979, p. 14).

Among the major structural differences is the supremacy of the cabinet in the government of Canada and the concomitant importance of senior civil servants in both advising policy-makers and helping devise policies. One result is that interest groups have difficulty obtaining access to government in the sense of getting to the right people at the right time (Thompson and Stanbury, 1979, p. 37). . . .

Now some would interpret the openness of the American political system to a variety of interests and issues as a barrier to legislative effectiveness. This is because the process itself is more complex than that found in Canada. "Naturally, the more difficult the legislative process, the easier it is for a determined minority to block passage. Therefore, in the United States, as opposed to parliamentary democracies, legislation has usually required a fairly broad national consensus" (Silberman, 1978, pp. 16–17). At first sight, this appears to contradict the earlier generalizations about the difficulty that moral causes have in achieving some legislative resolution in Canada. But the contradiction is less evident when we note that Silberman is calling attention to the importance of blocking legislation. That itself can often be tied to the advocacy of moral positions, as has happened with tactics to prevent financing of abortions through public funds. In Canada, the ability of private members to affect budget items, especially after they are introduced in the House, is virtually negligible. But I am less convinced by Silberman's point about the requirement for a broad national consensus. Was that present in the passage of prohibition legislation? . . .

The extent to which we wish to argue for the greater politicization of moral causes in the United States depends on the interpretations we give Supreme Court actions and the relevance of constitutional disputes. Epstein's (1974, p. 161) conclusion that "the Supreme Court today views constitutional litigation as a means of settling great conflicts of the social order" is one fundamental difference between the two countries. In one, parliament rules supreme, in the other, judicial supremacy is prevalent (e.g., Jackson, 1979). Courts in the United States have both greater scope for law-making and for pronouncing moral statements. . . . When moral interests are successful in taking their case to the Constitution (as they were with prohibition and threaten to do again with abortion), they have the means of incorporating their view of conduct into the core of political values. The drama of this symbolism is absent from Canada.

Yet the role of the courts in the United States could be interpreted as giving Canada greater potential for politicizing issues, since the process of parliamentary rule invokes partisanship and public debate. In contrast, the operation of the Supreme Court in particular obscures partisan controversy and the relevance of local considerations. This leads Kommers (1977, p. 108) to argue the abortion issue was depoliticized by the Supreme Court. That is, by coming under the aegis of the Court, an issue is removed from the realm of politics. To agree with his conclusion is to treat the separation of powers as somehow neutralizing one aspect of government. Moreover, we have presented enough examples to demonstrate the abortion issue continues to influence public rhetoric and the course of politics, including the Supreme Court's own behavior. On these grounds, I find it hard to consider the Supreme Court as removed from politics.

Pross[1] has suggested that moral causes may be defused in Canada through the actions of government agencies giving some recognition to them. They do this by encouraging the submission of briefs, conducting or sponsoring research, and otherwise acknowledging the legitimacy of concern. Moral causes themselves emerge out of societal conditions, and provide the focus for mobilizing interests and developing a supportive public. In this regard, we found little difference between the two countries, at least for the issues surveyed here. But the possibility that government may step in to channel the inherent discontent remains as a possible difference between the two countries. In Canada, abortion groups, both pro and con, found an avenue for expression in the hearings of the Committee on the Operation of the Abortion Law (1977)....

Notes

[1] In a private communication with the author, 2 November 1979.

References

Alford, Robert R. (1963) *Party and Society*. Chicago: Rand McNally.

Allen, Richard (1969) "The Triumph and Decline of Prohibition." Pages 185–188 in J.M. Bumsted (ed.) *Documentary Problems in Canadian History*, volume 2, Georgetown, Ontario: Irwin-Dorsey.

——— (1971) *The Social Passion. Religion and Social Reform in Canada 1914–28*. Toronto: University of Toronto.

Anslinger, Harry and Will Osborne (1961) *The Murderers: The Story of a Narcotic Gang*. New York: Farrar, Straus.

Anslinger, Harry and William F. Tompkins (1953) *The Traffic in Narcotics*. New York: Funk and Wagnalls.

Anslinger, Harry and J. Gregory (1964) *The Protectors*. New York: Farrar, Straus.

Batten, Jack (1974) "Abortion: The Issue Hots Up." *Chatelaine* 47:42–43, 98–102.

Becker, Howard S. (1963) *Outsiders*. New York: Free Press.

Becker, Rene (1979) "On the Hill. Mr. Hyde." *The New Republic*, 17 November, pp. 10–11.

Bell, David V.J. and Lorne Tepperman (1979) *Roots of Disunity*. Toronto: McClelland and Stewart.

Benson, Lee (1961) *The Concept of Jacksonian Democracy*. Princeton, N.J.; Princeton University.

Berelson, B.R., P.F. Lazarsfeld, and W.N. McPhee (1954) *Voting*. Chicago: University of Chicago.

Berton, Lee (1967), "Marijuana at Issue: Harsh Laws Challenged in Courts, Criticized within the Government." *Wall Street Journal*, 20 November, p. 1.

Blake, Judith (1977) "The Abortion Decisions: Judicial Review and Public Opinion." Pages 51–82 in Edward Manier, William Liu, and David Solomon (eds.), *Abortion, New Directions for Policy Research*. Notre Dame, IN: University of Notre Dame Press.

Brecher, Edward M. (1972) *Licit and Illicit Drugs*. Mount Vernon, NY: Consumers Union.

Canadian Clipping Service. Prepared by Linda Sharpe from photocopies of the *Calgary Herald, Calgary Albertan, Vancouver Sun, and Vancouver Province*. (Newspaper identification removed from the clippings.)

Canadian News Facts (bimonthly)

Carter, Paul A. (1956) *The Decline and Revival of the Social Gospel*. Ithaca NY: Cornell University Press.

Clausen, John A. (1976) "Drug Use." Pages 141–178 in Robert K. Merton and Robert Nisbet (eds.), *Contemporary Social Problems*, 4th ed. New York: Harcourt Brace Jovanovich.

Committee on the Operation of the Abortion Law (1977) *Report of the Committee on the Operation of the Abortion Law*. Ottawa: Supply and Services.

Congressional Quarterly Weekly Report (1969) "New Awareness Points Toward Softer Marijuana Laws." 19 December 27:2651–2654.

Crain, Robert L., Elihu Katz and Donald B. Rosenthal (1969) *The Politics of Community Conflict*. Indianapolis: Bobbs-Merrill.

Culliton, Barbara J. (1975) "Abortion and Manslaughter: A Boston Doctor Goes on Trial." *Science* 187:334–35.

Dickson, Donald T. (1968) "Bureaucracy and Morality: An Organizational Perspective on a Moral Crusade," *Social Problems* 16:143–156.

Dionne, E.J., Jr. (1979) "Albany Deadlocked on Abortion Trends: Senate and Assembly Split Delays Adoption of Carey's Budget." *New York Times* 3 April, p. A1.

Elkins, Stanley M. (1968) *Slavery* 2nd ed. Chicago: University of Chicago.

Encyclopedia Canadiana (1970) "Alcoholic Beverages, Control and Sale." Toronto: Grolier, 1:122–123.

Epstein, Richard A. (1974) "Substantive Due Process by Any Other Name: The Abortion Cases." *The Supreme Court Review* 1973:160–167.

Farkas, Edie (1976) "Abortion: How Many Trials will Morgentaler Face?" *Last Post* 5:13–14.

Fletcher, F.J. and R.J. Drummond (1979) *Canadian Attitude Trends 1960–1978*. Working Paper No. 4. Montreal: Institute for Research on Public Policy.

Galliher, John F. and Allyn Walker (1977) "The Puzzle of the Social Origins of the Marijuana Tax Act of 1937." *Social Problems* 24:367–376.

Goode, Erich (1969) "Marijuana and the Politics of Reality." *Journal of Health and Social Behavior* 10:83–94.

Guinther, John (1976) *Moralists and Managers, Public Interest Movements in the United States*, Garden City, NY: Anchor.

Gusfield, Joseph R. (1963) *Symbolic Crusade: Status Politics and the American Temperance Movement*. Urbana: University of Illinois Press.

Hartz, Louis (1955) *The Liberal Tradition in America*. New York: Harcourt Brace.

Holsendolph, Ernest (1979) "Carter Declines to Recall House in Fund Impasse: Major Appropriations Bill is Stalled Over Abortion." *New York Times* 30 September 1979, p. 1

Jackson, Robert H. (1979) *The Struggle for Judicial Supremacy, A Study of a Crisis in American Power Politics*. New York: Octagon.

Javits, Jacob K., et al. (1979) "Should Penalties for Possession of Small Amounts of Marihuana be Decriminalized?" (Pro and Con) *Congressional Digest* 58:40–63.

Javits, Jacob K. and James M. Collins (1979) "Should Congress Decriminalize Marijuana?" (Opposing Views) *American Legion Magazine* 106:20.

Keate, Kathryn (1970) "Out from Under, Women Unite." *Saturday Night* 85 (July):15–20.

Kennedy, Shawn G. (1979) "Head of Burned Abortion Clinic Trades Charges with Opponent." *New York Times* 17 February, p. 24.

Kimney, Jimmye (1973) "How Abortion Laws Happened." *Ms.* (April): 48–49, 118.

Dommers, Donald P. (1977) "Abortion and the Constitution: The Cases of the United States and West Germany." Pages 83–115 in Edward Manier, William Liu, and David Solomon (eds.), *Abortion, New Directions for Policy Research.* Notre Dame, IN: University of Notre Dame.

Krout, John A. (1925) *The Origins of Prohibition.* New York: Knopf.

Kyvig, David E. (1979) *Repealing National Prohibition.* Chicago: University of Chicago Press.

Lange, Arlen J. (1969) "It's a Touchy Subject, but Congress Likely to Cut 'Pot' Penalties; Use Would be a Misdemeanor . . . " *Wall Street Journal* 22 January, p. 1f.

Leahy, Peter and Allan Mazur (1978) "A Comparison of Movements Opposed to Nuclear Power, Fluoridation and Abortion." *Research in Social Movements, Conflicts and Change* 1:143–154.

Lederman, J.J. and G.E. Parker (1963) "Therapeutic Abortion and the Canadian Criminal Code." *Criminal Law Quarterly* 6:36–85.

Lindesmith, Alfred R. (1947) *Opiate Addiction.* Bloomington, IN: Principia.

———— (1965) *The Addict and the Law.* Bloomington, IN: Indiana University Press.

Lipset, Seymour Martin (1977) "Why No Socialism in the United States?" Pages 31–149 in Seweryn Bialer and Sophia Sluzar (eds.) *Sources of Contemporary Radicalism.* Boulder, CO: Westview.

Lipset, Seymour Martin and Earl Raab (1978) *The Politics of Unreason.* 2nd ed. Chicago: University of Chicago Press.

Loomis, David (1975) "Abortion: Should Constitution Be Amended?" *Congressional Quarterly Weekly Report* 33 (3 May):917–922.

Maeots, Krista (1970) "Abortion Caravan." *The Canadian Forum* 50 (July/Aug.):157.

Marihuana and Health (1979) Seventh Annual Report to the U.S. Congress from the Secretary of Health, Education, Welfare 1977. Washington, DC: US Government Printing Office.

Moffit, L.W. (1932) "Control of the Liquor Traffic in Canada." *Annals of the American Academy of Political and Social Science* 163:188–192.

Mohr, James C. (1978) *Abortion in America: The Origins and Evolution of National Policy.* New York: Oxford.

Murphy, Emily (1922) *The Black Candle.* Toronto: Thomas Allen.

National Commission on Marihuana and Drug Abuse (1972) *Marihuana: A Signal of Misunderstanding.* First Report. Washington, DC: US Government Printing Office.

National Governors' Conference Center for Policy Research and Analysis (1977) *Marijuana: A Study of State Policies and Penalties.* Washington, DC: National Institute of Law Enforcement and Criminal Justice.

Odegaard, Peter (1928) *Pressure Politics: The Story of the Anti-Saloon League.* New York: Columbia University Press.

Perry, Charles (1978) "Pot and Politics: NORML Leads a Grass Roots Crusade." *Rolling Stone* 10 August 1978, p. 35.

Pross, J. Paul (1975) "Pressure Groups: Adaptive Instruments of Political Communication." Pages 1–26 in J. Paul Pross (ed.), *Pressure Group Behaviour in Canadian Politics.* Toronto: McGraw-Hill Ryerson.

Report of the Commission of Inquiry into the Non-Medical Uses of Drugs (1972) *Cannabis.* Gerald LeDain, Chairman. Ottawa: Information Canada.

Report of the Commission on Population Growth and the American Future (1972) *Population and the American Future.* Washington, DC: US Government Printing Office.

Rosoff, Jeannie I. (1975) "Is Support of Abortion Political Suicide?" *Family Planning Perspectives* 7:13–22.

Rossi, Alice S. (1969) "Abortion and Social Change." *Dissent* 16:338–346.

Sarvis, Betty and Hyman Rodman (1974) *The Abortion Controversy* 2nd ed. New York: Columbia University Press.

Schneider, William (1978) "Democrats and Republicans, Liberals and Conservatives." Pages

183–267 in S.M. Lipset (ed.), *Emerging Coalitions in American Politics*. San Francisco: Institute for Contemporary Studies.

Silberman, Lawrence H. (1978) "Will Lawyering Strangle Democratic Capitalism?" *Regulation* March/April: 16–17.

Silva, Ruth (1962) *Rum, Religion, and Votes: 1928 Reexamined*. University Park, Pennsylvania State University Press.

Sinclair, Andrew (1962) *Prohibition: The Era of Excess*. Boston: Little, Brown.

Spivak, Jonathan (1978) "Divisive Issue: Debate Over Abortion Heats up in State Capitals as Some Legislators Seek a Constitutional Ban." *Wall Street Journal* 26 January, p. 40.

Standing Committee on Health and Welfare, House of Commons (1967–1968) *Minutes of Proceedings* 2 volumes. Ottawa.

Steinhoff, Patricia G. and Milton Diamond (1977) *Abortion Politics: The Hawaii Experience*. Honolulu: University of Hawaii.

Stencil, Sandra (1976) "Abortion Politics." *Editorial Research Reports* 2:767–784.

Stokes, Donald E. (1966) "Spatial Models of Party Competition." Pages 161–179 in Angus Campbell, et al (eds.), *Elections and the Political Order*, New York: John Wiley.

Thompson, Fred and W.T. Stanbury (1979) *The Political Economy of Interest Groups in the Legislative Process in Canada*. Occasional Paper No. 9. Montreal: Institute for Research on Public Policy.

Tierney, Ben (1972) "Abortion: Where It's At; Where It's Going?" *Canadian Bar Journal* 3 (April):26–28.

Timberlake, James H. (1963) *Prohibition and the Progressive Movement, 1900–1920*. Cambridge, M.A.: Harvard University Press.

Time (1975) "Abortion: An Emotional Issue Rejoined." Canadian Edition, 14 April, pp. 6–7.

Time (1979) "The Fanatical Abortion Fight." 9 July pp. 26–27.

Tocqueville, Alexis de (1945) *Democracy in America*. Vol. I. New York: Knopf.

U.S. News and World Report (1976) "Why New Uproar Over Abortions: Pushing to the Foreground of the '76 Politics in an Issue Candidates Would Like to Avoid; the Reason: It's Trouble—No Matter What They Say." 80 (1 March):14–15.

Valk, Alphonse de (1974) *Morality and Law in Canadian Politics. The Abortion Controversy*. Montreal: Palm.

Warburton, Clark (1933) "Prohibition." *Encyclopedia of the Social Sciences*. New York: Macmillan 11:499–510.

Winiarski, Mark (1979) " 'Babykillers' Retort Stops Dialogue Dead." *National Catholic Reporter* 14 (2 February):3.

Wohl, Lisa Cronin (1978) "Are We 25 Votes Away from Losing the Bill of Rights ... and the Rest of the Constitution?" *Ms* 6 (February):46.

50 Voter Motivation in Canada and the United Kingdom

Richard Ogmundson   M. Ng

RICHARD OGMUNDSON, Associate Professor of Sociology at the University of Victoria, British Columbia, specializes in political sociology and the study of elites. Recent publications include "Liberal ideology and the study of voting behaviour" (1980); "Good news and Canadian sociology" (1982) and "Social inequality" in R. Hagedorn's edited *Sociology* (1981, 1983, 1986). He is currently working on a book about Canada's elites and the ways they have been analyzed in Canadian sociology.

M. Ng was a sociology student when she collaborated with Professor Ogmundson on this study. She does not work in the field of sociology now.

... This paper will present data on the class vote in Canada and the United Kingdom when perceptions of the class positions of the political parties are taken into account. Though the two cases were chosen on the basis of data availability, it turns out that a better choice for comparison could hardly be imagined. The United Kingdom was designated by Alford (1963) as a case of "Pure Class Politics" while Pulzer (1967:98) has more recently remarked that: "Class is the basis of British party politics; all else is embellishment and detail." Canada, on the other hand, is widely noted as providing what Alford (1963) chose to call a case of "Pure Non-Class Politics." Thus, the two cases are widely viewed as polar opposites so far as class politics is concerned.[1] ...

MEASURING THE CLASS VOTE

Those who are not familiar with this measure will need to be reminded that its purpose is only to ascertain what the voters think they are doing. This enables us to better understand their likely motivations and, by extension, the nature of public opinion generally.

In this sense, the purpose of the measure is very different than the purpose of measures which attempt to ascertain the "true" or "objective" class vote. Two different phenomena are under consideration. Each measure taps a different reality.

One way to understand the difference between this measure of the class vote and the conventional one is to think in terms of the customary distinction between "objective" measures of social class (e.g., relationship to the mode of production, occupation, education, income) and "subjective" measures of social class (e.g., class self-identification, class consciousness). In this area, it is well understood that objective class position is one thing while the perception of people about their class positions is yet another. Similarly, the conventional measure may be thought of as providing an "objective" measure of the class vote while the approach used in this paper may be thought of as providing a "subjective" measure of the class vote.

As is the case with measurement of social class, *both* objective and subjective measures of the class vote need to be used if adequate understanding is to be achieved. We need to know not only what the voters do, but what they think they are doing. Otherwise we are likely to make inaccurate inferences about the nature of public opinion from the objective measure alone. However plausible these inferences may be, they are likely to be incorrect. Just as research has shown that the amount of class consciousness in a society cannot be reliably inferred from knowledge of its class structure (objectively defined by whatever criteria), so may research indicate that public opinion on class issues in a society cannot be reliably inferred from knowledge of its "objective" class vote. It is, for example, conceivable that a considerable proportion of the class-consistent votes in a given country may be cast in the absence of class consciousness. . . .

Once the distinction between the objective and subjective measure is clear, it becomes a matter of interest to see how the two dimensions of reality relate to each other. In the case of objective and subjective measures of class, for example, we find papers on topics like "An interpretation of the relation between objective and subjective social status" (Jackman and Jackman, 1973) and "Objective and subjective socioeconomic status: intercorrelations and consequences" (Coburn and Edwards, 1976). It is of similar interest to find out how objective and subjective class voting relate to each other. This point has been understood, to some degree at least, by Myles and Forcese (1979:14) who write:

> In effect, the subjectivist solution introduces yet another definition of the class vote, namely the degree to which individuals vote according to their perceived class interest, a legitimate object of enquiry but not the originating question of those who attempt to estimate the degree to which the classes divide in support of left parties. . . . Indeed the difference between Ogmundson's individually defined indices of class voting and traditional measures of class voting could be construed as a measure of the degree to

which the political system as a whole is able to obscure the class-based nature of electoral politics."

In sum, it is necessary that we have some knowledge of what the voters think they are doing if we are to develop a more complete understanding of the class vote. For this purpose, the measure introduced here is better than the conventional one. For the purposes of this paper, it is also more relevant in that it speaks directly to questions concerning the role of public opinion as a factor in explaining the minimal role of class in Canadian politics.[2]

DATA AND METHODS

The Canadian data for this research came from the national surveys of the 1965 and 1968 elections. (For details, see Meisel and Van Loon, 1966; Meisel, 1972). Comparison of the Canadian findings with those of the United Kingdom is made possible with data provided by national surveys in 1963, 1964, and 1966. . . .

There are four key elements in measurement of the class vote—party class position, respondent class position, respondent party preference, and calculation of the degree of association. In this research, the vote is used as an indicator of respondent party preference. . . . [3]

In the Canadian case, the Alford classification positions the Liberal Party and the New Democratic Party as "working class" or "left" and the Progressive Conservative Party, Social Credit Party, and Creditiste Party as "middle class" or "right." The aggregate national perceptions classification positions the Liberal and Progressive Conservative parties as "middle class" or "right" while the others are designated "working class." This is done because this is the way that the voters, in the aggregate, perceived those parties. The other two measures position the political parties according to the view of each individual voter.

This, in turn, is based, as is the national aggregate measure, on a semantic differential question which asked the voters to classify the parties on a scale from 1 to 7 as "for the middle class" at 1 or "for the working class" at 7. There is some ambiguity as to the meaning of a "4" response. Hence, two measures of individually perceived party class position are used.

In the British case, the Conservative Party is classified as "right" or "middle class" and the Labour Party is classified as "left" or "working class" in both the Alford and aggregate national perceptions category. This is done because, in this case, voter perceptions and expert opinion coincide. The other two measures position the political parties according to the view of each individual voter. (For further discussion, see Ogmundson, 1975b; Ng, 1977; Lambert and Hunter, 1979; Ogmundson, 1979).

FINDINGS

The findings are presented in Table 1. Class vote rates for different years (Canada:1965, 1968; United Kingdom:1963, 1964, 1966) are averaged in order to simplify the table.[4] No important fluctuation is obscured by the averaging process. An overall summation is provided at the bottom of the table.

The reader is invited to begin reading the table by first considering the familiar results from the Canadian case. When the original Alford classification of the class position of the political parties is used, the Canadian class vote is very low—indeed, it is actually *negative* in each case (range: $-.03$ to $-.10$; mean: $-.06$). When a classification of the political parties based upon aggregate national voter perceptions is used, there is a substantial increase in the rate of the class vote (range: $+.03$ to $+.12$; mean: $+.09$; average increase: 1.5). This level is, however, still unusually low. Finally, when classifications based upon individual perceptions are used, there is an-

other increase to a level which is almost "normal" in terms of the international spectrum. This is the finding reported in the original research (Ogmundson, 1975b). It has thus been replicated with the 1968 data.

The next point to be made is that the class vote in the United Kingdom does *not* increase when the national aggregate perception and individual perception classifications of the political parties are used. It remains the same when aggregate perceptions are used (for the very good reason that the Alford classification and the aggregate classification are the same), and generally *decreases* slightly when the individual perceptions classification is used.[5] Hence, contrary to what critics had suggested, the increase in the Canadian class vote derived from the original use of this measure was not an artifactual one.

Another point of interest is the finding that the rate of the class vote in the United Kingdom varies substantially depending upon which measure of class position of respondent is used. Generally speaking, class self-image and occupation give a high class vote while education, and especially income, give a low class vote. Differences as great as .28 in the United Kingdom class vote appear depending upon which measure of class of respondent is used. In terms of the international spectrum, this is very substantial variation indeed. This indicates a need for a systematic investigation of the international class vote using a variety of respondent class position measures. Such an investigation might result in a substantial revision of our ideas concerning class politics and public opinion in a variety of countries. And, to return to our original interests, it is evident that the gap between Canada and the United Kingdom varies substantially depending on which measure of class of respondent is used (.23–.02). Indeed, when income is used as a measure of respondent class position, the difference in the class vote, and, by extension, public opinion on class issues in the two countries, is virtually nonexistent (.02).

Table 1

THE BRITISH NATIONAL CLASS VOTE (1963, 1964, AND 1966 AVERAGED) AND THE
CANADIAN NATIONAL CLASS VOTE (1965 AND 1968 AVERAGED) AS MEASURED
BY TAU BETA

Measure of social class	Classification of Political Parties			
	Alford[1]	National[2]	Individual I	Individual II
Income				
United Kingdom	.16	.16	.17	.17
Canada	−.10	.03	.13	.15
Gap	.26	.13	.04	.02
Occupation				
United Kingdom	.43	.43	.40	.38
Canada	−.03	.11	.14	.15
Gap	.46	.32	.26	.23
Education				
United Kingdom	.26	.26	.26	.24[3]
Canada	−.05	.08	.13	.18
Gap	.31	.18	.13	.06
Subjective Class				
United Kingdom	.44	.44	.39	.41
Canada	−.03	.14	.18	.21
Gap	.47	.30	.21	.20
Overall average				
United Kingdom	.32	.32	.31	.30
Canada	−.06	.09	.15	.17
Gap	.38	.23	.16	.13

[1] In the United Kingdom, the Conservative Party is classified as "middle class" and the Labour Party is classified as "working class."

[2] In the United Kingdom, the Conservative Party is classified as "middle class" and the Labour Party is classified as "working class."

[3] This figure includes 1963 and 1964 only. An unexplained anomalous figure for 1966 (.08) is omitted. This would have reduced the average to .19 and the "gap" to .01.

The obvious consequence of these findings is that the difference between Canada and the United Kingdom in this regard substantially decreases when these new measures are used. Indeed, the gap between the two countries in terms of the subjective class vote is, on the average, more than halved (.38 to .13). This indicates that, by this measure at least, differences in popular sentiment regarding class issues in the two countries may be much less than has widely been assumed. This, in turn, clearly supports those who argue that differences in public opinion between Canada and the United Kingdom are not sufficient to explain the differences in class politics in the two countries during this time period, and that attention must therefore be given to other explanatory factors such as the nature of the electoral options available to the voter and the factors which influence these options.

FINAL REMARKS

... In the general case, it is plausible to assume that almost all mass behavior is strongly conditioned by the nature of the opportunities provided by specific environments. Hence, it would seem reasonable to study variations in environments at least as much as we study the reaction of actors to those environments.[6] One could go further than this and argue that aspects of the environment may possibly be viewed as active, independent variables which cause or create the kind of society or politics we find. To provide a specific example, one could argue that political parties (and elites generally) may determine the degree of class politics in a given society. The "organizational hypothesis" of Sartori (1969) provides an example of such an approach. He argues that (1969:84): " . . . it is not the 'objective' class (class conditions) that creates the party, but the party that creates the 'subjective' class (class consciousness)." He goes on to argue that the class vote may best be explained by the strength of trade unions as organizations, not by the degree of class consciousness among the voters. He also argues that the amount of class vs. religious voting can probably best be explained in terms of the relative strength of trade unions vs. churches as organizations as opposed to the relative strength of class consciousness vs. religious consciousness. In support of this position, he points to data on the class vote in Britain which indicates that: " . . . no class vote can be said to exist for the non-union members of the working class, who actually split their vote at random between the Labour and the Conservative parties" (Sartori, 1969:84).

Closer to home, a number of scholars (e.g., Porter, 1965: Ch. 12; Horowitz, 1979; Pinard, 1970; Ogmundson, 1976) have made similar arguments concerning the Canadian situation. For example, Keddie (1980:35–6) has recently asserted, on the basis of an empirical study, that: "The trade union movement emerges as the most important factor influencing manual workers to support the political party most clearly identified with the interests of the working class." More generally, Horowitz (1979:222–23) has argued that:

Class consciousness exists in any stratified social system as a kind of natural resource which may or may not be mobilized by politicians. . . . There is no major party of the left in Canada not because our people are too stupid to be conscious of the disadvantages of non-elite status, but because our business-oriented political elites have been reluctant to translate the personal trouble of non-elite status into the public issue of inequality.

In a more general sense, one could go so far as to assert that the role of political parties and the state (i.e., the superstructure) in determining aspects of socioeconomic reality (i.e., the base) may be much more substantial than most sociologists would prefer to believe. In the "mainstream" literature, Cairns (1977) has recently made a powerful argument to this effect. He argues that:

It makes little sense to think of these impressive concentrations of power and personnel as superstructures whose existence and purposes are largely derivative of the electorate, the class structure, the pressure group system, or whatever. . . . Federal and provincial governments are not neutral containers, or reflecting mirrors, but aggressive actors steadily extending their tentacles of control, regulation, and manipulation into society. . . . (pp. 703, 706)

In Marxist traditions of thought, begrudging recognition of the increasing power and autonomy of the state in capitalist democracies is indicated by the increasing amount of attention paid to the topic (e.g., Miliband, 1969; O'Connor, 1973; Panitch, 1977) and by the popularity of theoretical orientations such as those of Althusser (1969) and Poulantzas (1973), which make arguments to the effect that the state is much more autonomous of the base than much previous Marxist thought has recognized.

Considerations like those just discussed also create doubts about the empirical validity of theoretical positions such as those of

Downs (1957) which tend to *assume* the importance of public opinion rather than taking it as a problematic factor which needs to be empirically examined. In the broadest sense, these arguments suggest that the social psychological paradigm (and liberal ideology) may have limited empirical validity. To the degree that the superstructure appears to be largely independent of the base, an organizational, as opposed to class, paradigm for the interpretation of socio-political reality is supported.[7]

Notes

[1] Given the apparent decline in the Western European, British and American class votes (Abramson, 1971; Books and Reynolds, 1975; Braungart, 1978), the qualification "during this time period" might as well be added to this statement. Since, as will be seen, our data comes from the 1960s, these more recent changes present no problem for the present analysis. The question of why the class vote should differ so much between the two countries during this time period still remains.

[2] It is true, of course, that this measure, like all measures, has its limitations. It only gives us an initial, though parsimonious, approximation of what is going on in the minds of voters. Ideally, we would have information on several levels of class consciousness (à la Giddens, 1973; Mann, 1973; Buttel and Flynn, 1979) and be able to relate this to the vote. Ideally, we would have more direct information on the intentions and motives of voters—not merely information on the parties as objects of perception. As discussed later, it would also be helpful to include some notion of how the class positions of the other parties are perceived by the individual voter and also to have some notion of regional, racial, ethnic . . . images, and motives as well.

[3] It could be argued that partisan identification might be a better measure of voter preference. If this measure were used, the results would probably support the arguments made later in this paper, a bit more strongly than the results derived from use of the vote (see Ogmundson, 1972:Tables 6.1,6.3).

[4] The averaging process accounts for the slight variation in the Canadian class vote.

[5] This may well be related to the fact that those who vote for the British Liberal Party are now included in the analysis. The inclusion of votes for parties otherwise difficult to classify on a class basis is one of the advantages of a subjective measure based upon individual perceptions.

[6] This point has been well understood in the disciplines of biology and economics and has been applied with some utility to the study of formal organizations. See, for example, Emery and Trist (1965), Meyer (1979).

[7] For an explanation of these terms, see Westhues (1976).

References

Abramson, P. 1971 "Social class and political change in Western Europe: a cross-national analysis." *Comparative Political Studies* 4:131–56.

Alford, R. 1963 *Party and Society*. Chicago: Rand McNally.

———— 1967 "Class voting in the Anglo-American political systems." In *Party Systems and Voter Alignments*, edited by S.M. Lipset and S. Rokkan, pp. 67–93. New York: Free Press.

Althusser, L. 1969 *For Marx*. London: Penguin.

Books, J. and J. Reynolds 1975 "A note on class

voting in Great Britain and the United States." *Comparative Political Studies* 8:360–76.

Braungart, R. 1978 "Changing electoral politics in America." *Journal of Political and Military Sociology* 6:261–69.

Butler, D. and D. Stokes 1969 *Political Change in Britain: Forces Shaping Electoral Choice.* New York: St. Martin's Press.

Buttel, F.H. and W. Flinn 1979 "Sources of working class consciousness." *Sociological Focus* 12(1):37–52.

Cairns A. 1977 "The governments and societies of Canadian federalism." *Canadian Journal of Political Science* 10(4):325–38.

Campbell, A., P. Converse, W. Miller and D. Stokes 1960 *The American Voter.* New York: Wiley.

Cheal, D. 1978 "Models of mass politics in Canada." *Canadian Review of Sociology and Anthropology* 15(3):325–38.

Chi, N.H. 1973 "Class voting in Canadian politics." In *The Canadian Political Process*, edited by O.M. Kruhlak, R. Schultz, and S. Probihushchy, pp. 226–47. Revised edition. Toronto: Holt, Rinehart and Winston.

———— 1976 "Class cleavage." In *Political Parties in Canada,* edited by C. Winn and J. McMenemy. pp. 89–111. Toronto: McGraw-Hill Ryerson.

Clarke, H. and J. Jensen, L. LeDuc, J. Pammett 1979 *Political Choice in Canada.* Toronto: McGraw-Hill Ryerson.

Coburn, D. and V. Edwards 1976 "Objective and subjective socioeconomic status: intercorrelations and consequences." *Canadian Review of Sociology and Anthropology* 13(2):178–88.

Cockcroft, J., A.G. Frank and D. Johnson 1972 *Dependence and Underdevelopment.* New York: Doubleday.

Converse, P. 1958 "The shifting role of class in political attitudes and behavior." In *Readings in Social Psychology,* edited by E. Maccoby, T. Newcomb, and E. Hartley, pp. 388–99. Third edition. New York: Henry Holt.

Crewe, I., B. Sarlvik and J. Alt 1977 "Partisan dealignment in Britain 1964–1974." *British Journal of Political Science* 7:129–90.

Curtis, B. and B. Edginton 1979 "Uneven institutional development and the 'staple' approach: a problem of method." *Canadian Journal of Sociology* 4(3):257–74.

Dahrendorf, R. 1959 *Class and Class Conflict in Industrial Society.* Stanford: Stanford University Press.

Downs, A. 1957 *An Economic Theory of Democracy.* New York: Harper and Row.

Ellis, D. 1979 "The prison guard as carceral Luddite." *Canadian Journal of Sociology* 4(1):43–64.

Emery, F. and E. Trist 1965 "The causal texture of organizational environments." *Human Relations* 18(1):21–32.

Englemann, F. and M. Schwartz 1967 *Political Parties and Canadian Social Structure.* Scarborough: Prentice-Hall.

Eulau, Heinz 1955 "Perceptions of class and party in voting behavior: 1952." *American Political Science Review* 49(1):364–84.

Forcese, D. and J. deVries 1977 "Occupation and electoral success in Canada: the 1974 federal election." *Canadian Review of Sociology and Anthropology* 14:331–40.

Galbraith, J.K. 1973 *Economics and the Public Purpose.* Boston: Houghton Mifflin.

Giddens, A. 1973 *The Class Structure of Advanced Capitalism.* London: Hutchinson.

Gonick, C. 1975 "A long look at the CCF/NDP." *Canadian Dimension* July/August:30.

Grabb, E. 1979 "Relative centrality and political isolation: Canadian dimensions." *Canadian Review of Sociology and Anthropology* 16(3): 343–55.

Horowitz, G. 1979 "Toward the democratic class struggle." In *The Canadian Political Process*, edited by R. Schultz, O.M. Kruhlak, and J. Terry, pp. 216–23. Third edition. Toronto: Holt, Rinehart and Winston.

Jackman, M. and R. Jackman 1973 "An interpretation of the relation between objective and subjective social status." *American Sociological Review* 38:569–82.

Johnson, S. 1978 "Judgments of equity and vote

in a presidential election." *Sociological Focus* 11:161–72.

Kahan, M., D. Butler and D. Stokes 1966 "On the analytical division of social class." *British Journal of Sociology* 17:122–32.

Kay, B. 1977 "An examination of class and left-right party images in Canadian voting." *Canadian Journal of Political Science* 10:127–44.

Keddie, V. 1980 "Class identification and party preference among manual workers." *Canadian Review of Sociology and Anthropology* 17(1): 24–36.

Korpi, W. 1972 "Some problems in the measurement of class voting." *American Journal of Sociology* 78:627–42.

Lambert, R. and A. Hunter 1979 "Social stratification, voting behavior, and the images of Canadian federal political parties." *Canadian Review of Sociology and Anthropology* 16(3): 287–304.

Laumann, E. 1966 *Prestige and Association in an Urban Community*. New York: Bobbs-Merrill.

Lenski, G. 1966 *Power and Privilege*. New York: McGraw-Hill.

——— 1970 *Human Societies*. New York: McGraw-Hill.

Lenski, G. and J. Lenski 1974 *Human Societies*. New York: McGraw-Hill.

Lijphart, A. 1971 *Class Voting and Religious Voting in the European Democracies: A Preliminary Report*. Occasional Paper No. 8, Survey Research Centre. Glasgow: University of Strathclyde.

——— 1979 "Religious vs. linguistic vs. class voting: the 'crucial experiment' of comparing Belgium, Canada, South Africa, and Switzerland." *American Political Science Review* 73(2):442–58.

Lipset, S.M., and S. Rokkan 1967 "Cleavage structures, party systems, and voter alignments: an introduction." In *Party Systems and Voter Alignments*, edited by S.M. Lipset and S. Rokkan. New York: Free Press.

Mann, M. 1973 *Consciousness and Action among the Western Working Class*. London: Macmillan.

Marchak, P. 1975a *Ideological Perspectives on Canada*. Toronto: McGraw-Hill.

——— 1975b "Class, regional and institutional sources of social conflict in B.C." *B.C. Studies* 27:30–49.

Meisel, John 1972 *Working Papers on Canadian Politics*. Montreal: McGill-Queen's University Press.

Meisel, J. and R. Van Loon 1966 "Canadian attitudes to election expenses, 1965–1966." In *Report of the Committee on Election Expenses: Studies in Canadian Party Finance*. Ottawa: Queen's Printer.

Meyer, M. 1979 *Change in Public Bureaucracies*. New York: Cambridge University Press.

Miliband, R. 1969 *The State in Capitalist Society*. London: Wiedenfeld and Nicolson.

Myles, J. 1977 *The Class Vote in Canada and the United States*. Ottawa: Working Paper 77–5. Department of Sociology and Anthropology, Carleton University.

——— 1979 "Differences in the Canadian and American class vote: fact or pseudofact?" *American Journal of Sociology*. 84:1232–37.

Myles, J. and D. Forcese 1979 *Voting and Class Politics in Canada and the United States*. Ottawa: Working Paper 79–14. Department of Sociology and Anthropology, Carleton University.

Ng, M. 1977 "Social class and Canadian politics: replication and extension." Master's thesis, Department of Sociology, University of Manitoba.

O'Connor, J. 1973 *The Fiscal Crisis of the State*. New York: St. Martin's Press.

Ogmundson, R. 1972 "Social class and Canadian politics." Doctoral dissertation. University of Michigan.

——— 1975a "On the measurement of party class positions: the case of Canadian federal political parties." *Canadian Review of Sociology and Anthropology* 12:565–76.

——— 1975b "Party class images and the class vote in Canada." *American Sociological Review* 40:506–12.

——— 1975c "On the use of party image variables to measure the political distinctiveness of a class vote: the Canadian case." *Canadian Journal of Sociology* 1(2):169–77.

———— 1976 "Mass-elite linkages and class issues in Canada." *Canadian Review of Sociology and Anthropology* 13(1):1–12.

———— 1977 "Two modes of interpretation of survey data." *Social Forces* 55:809–11.

———— 1979 "A note on the ambiguous meaning of survey research measures which use the words 'left' and 'right'." *Canadian Journal of Political Science* 12(4):799–805.

———— 1980 "Liberal ideology and the study of voting behavior." *Canadian Review of Sociology and Anthropology* 17(1):45–54.

Panitch, L., ed. 1977 *The Canadian State*. Toronto: University of Toronto Press.

Parkin, F. 1979 *Marxism and Class Theory*. New York: Columbia University Press.

Pinard, M. 1970 "Working class politics: an interpretation of the Quebec case." *Canadian Review of Sociology and Anthropology* 7(2): 87–109.

Pomfret, A. 1979 "Comparative historical school change: Newfoundland, Southern Ontario and New England." *Canadian Journal of Sociology* 4(3):241–56.

Porter, J. 1965 *The Vertical Mosaic*. Toronto: University of Toronto Press.

———— 1979 *The Measure of Canadian Society*. Agincourt: Gage.

Poulantzas, N. 1973 *Political Power and Social Classes*, London: NLB.

Pulzer, P. 1967 *Political Representation and Elections in Britain*. London: Allen and Unwin.

Rokkan, S. 1968 "The structuring of mass politics in the European democracies: a developmental typology." In *Party Systems, Party Organizations, and the Politics of the New Masses*. Berlin: International Conference on Comparative Political Sociology.

Rose, R. n.d. *Class and Party Divisions: Britain as a Test Case*. Occasional Paper No. 1, Survey Research Centre. Glasgow: University of Strathclyde.

———— 1974 *The Problem of Party Government*. London: Macmillan.

Rose, R. and D. Urwin 1971 "Social cohesion, political parties, and strains in regimes." In *European Politics: A Reader*, edited by Mattei Dogan and Richard Rose, Boston: Little, Brown.

Sartori, G. 1969 "From the sociology of politics to political sociology." In *Politics and the Social Sciences*, edited by S.M. Lipset. New York: Oxford University Press.

Schreiber, E.M. 1976 "Cultural cleavages between occupational categories: the case of Canada." *Social Forces* 55:16–29.

———— 1980 "Class awareness and class voting in Canada." *Canadian Review of Sociology and Anthropology* 17(1):37–44.

Schwartz, M. 1974 "Canadian voting behavior." In *Electoral Behavior: A Comparative Handbook*, edited by R. Rose, New York: Free Press.

Stevenson, P. 1977a "Class and left-wing radicalism." *Canadian Review of Sociology and Anthropology* 14(3):269–84.

———— 1977b "Frustration, structural blame, and left-wing radicalism." *Canadian Journal of Sociology* 2(4):355–72.

Taylor, W. and N. Wiseman 1977 "Class and ethnic voting in Winnipeg: the case of 1941." *Canadian Review of Sociology and Anthropology* 14(2):174–87.

Treiman, D. 1977 *Occupational Prestige in Comparative Perspective*. New York: Academic Press.

Trilling, R. 1976 *Party Image and Electoral Behavior*. New York: Wiley.

Vanneman, R. 1980 "U.S. and British perceptions of class." *American Journal of Sociology* 85(4):769–90.

Weber, M. 1969 "Class, status, party." In *Structured Social Inequality*, edited by C. Heller, pp. 24–33. New York: Macmillan.

Westhues, K. 1976 "Class and organization as paradigms in social science." *American Sociologist* 11:638–40.

Wiley, N. 1976 "America's unique class politics: the interplay of the labor, credit and commodity markets." In *Society and Politics*, edited by

R. Braungart, pp. 362–77. Englewood Cliffs, N.J.: Prentice-Hall, Inc.

Wiseman, N. and K.W. Taylor 1974 "Ethnic vs. class voting: the case of Winnipeg, 1945." *Canadian Journal of Political Science* 7(2):314–28.

———— 1979 "Class and ethnic voting in Winnipeg during the Cold War." *Canadian Review of Sociology and Anthropology* 16(1):60–76.

Wrong, D. 1969 "Social inequality without stratification." In *Structured Social Inequality*, edited by C. Heller, pp. 513–19. New York: Macmillan.

Zipp, J. 1978a "Social class and Canadian federal electoral behavior: a reconsideration." Ph.D. dissertation, Duke University.

———— 1978b "Left-right dimensions of Canadian federal party identification: a discriminant analysis." *Canadian Journal of Political Science* 11:251–77.

Zipp, J. and J. Smith n.d. "A structural analysis of class voting." *Social Forces* Forthcoming.

51   The Political Ideology of the Canadian Capitalist Class

Michael Ornstein

MICHAEL ORNSTEIN, Associate Professor of Sociology and Associate Director of the Institute for Behavioral Research at York University, Toronto, specializes in the study of social inequality and political ideology. His books and articles include *Entry into the American Labour Force* (1976); "Interlocking directorates in Canada: Intercorporate or class alliance" (1984); "Social class and political ideology in Canada" with William Johnston (1985); "The ideology of the Canadian capitalist class" (1986); and "The Canadian state and corporate elites in the post-war period" with John Fox (forthcoming). As well as scholarly papers and presentations, Professor Ornstein has prepared a number of reports relevant to policy-making for a variety of federal and municipal clients. He has also served on the editorial boards of the Canadian Sociology and Anthropology Association and the *Canadian Journal of Sociology*.

This paper presents the results of a 1977 national survey of the executives of the largest Canadian corporations, executives of medium-size companies, top level federal, provincial and municipal politicians and civil servants, and trade union leaders. On questions about social welfare policy, labour relations, government intervention in the economy, foreign investment and taxation, business executives took positions considerably to the right of the state elites and far to the right of the trade unionists. While there were some systematic ideological differences between the executives of large and medium-size corporations, of corporations in different industries and of Canadian and foreign-controlled corporations, the ideological differences within the capitalist class were considerably smaller than the differences between the corporate executives and state elites. These findings lend little support to monopoly capitalist and other theories which suggest that there are major ideological divisions within national capitalist classes.

... Our analysis of capitalist class ideology is based on interviews with executives of the largest Canadian corporations and a comparison sample of medium-sized corporations. These interviews are set in the context of the opinions of top-level federal, provincial and municipal civil servants and elected officials, and trade union leaders, all gathered as part of the same survey. For many of the items, the responses of a representative sample of Canadians were also available for comparison. The analysis of ideology is divided into five sections which deal with social welfare policy, labour relations, government intervention in the economy, foreign investment, and the powers and taxation of different sectors of business.

THEORETICAL DISCUSSION

Capital and the Capitalist State

An understanding of the political ideology of the capitalist class begins but cannot end with an assertion of its common interest as a social class.... We hypothesize that the capitalists' class position leads them to oppose improvements in the standing of trade unions and social welfare measures such as unemployment insurance that lessen workers' dependency on employers.

This hypothesis implies that social reform results from the pressure of subordinate class and is sometimes supported by state managers. Block (1977) contrasts this model of social reform to "corporate liberal" theory, which holds that the adoption of reforms requires support of at least a minority of prominent capitalists.... The existence of pervasive policy conflicts between the capitalist class and state officials also contrasts with theories that link policy formation to a general consensus among elite groups or to a more general public consensus....

Monopoly Capitalist Theory

If capitalist defence of their class position creates a united front of the capitalist class, internal conflicts are caused by "the process of capitalist accumulation as a whole." The survival of the capitalist system requires mechanisms to regulate the relationships between capitalists. Marx (1959:ch.10) argued that the equalization of the rates of profit in different industries, brought about by the flow of capital into industries with above average rates of profit, ensures "fairness" in the competition for profits. Only corporations which exploit limited natural resources or have very large shares of a market may be able to gain above average profits for indefinite periods. Monopolization (or, more accurately, oligopolization) is thus a basis for conflict among fractions of the capitalist class over relative shares of the total surplus value.

The formalization of these arguments is known as monopoly capitalist theory. Unlike competitive business, very large corporations are said to insulate themselves from competition by virtue of their size, efficiency, control of markets, and ties with government. The two economic sectors are termed the monopoly and competitive sectors by O'Connor (1973:13–18), the market and planning systems by Galbraith (1973), and the monopoly and non-monopoly sectors by Poulantzas (1975:135–51), Mandel (1970:

ch.12) and Sweezy (1968:ch.15); Porter (1965:ch.8) and Clement (1975:ch.4) distinguish "dominant" from smaller firms. In this paper we use the term "core" and "periphery" to avoid the questionable inference that the very large corporations said to constitute the "monopoly" sector are actually monopolistic—many of these corporations are, at most, oligopolistic and many are subject to domestic or international competition.

While the most important distinction between the two sectors is that core, but not peripheral, firms are able to set their prices at levels that assure profitability, core corporations also benefit from economies of scale and are more likely to employ capital-intensive production processes, use skilled labour power, invest in research and adopt new technologies.[1] Monopoly capitalist theories suggest that the owners and managers of core corporations are more "liberal" concerning public policy issues than their counterparts in the competitive sector (O'Connor, 1973:40ff). The greater profitability of core corporations allows their managers to accommodate trade unionism, and their higher rates of pay mean that policies that might decrease the labour supply or raise the minimum rate of pay, such as unemployment insurance, increases in the minimum wage, and social welfare programs, have relatively little impact on core corporations. Core corporations are more tolerant of government regulation. Finally, because core corporations are more likely to operate in international markets, their executives should oppose protectionism and other aspects of economic nationalism such as controls on foreign investment.

Neo-Staple Theory

Naylor (1972) and Clement (1975:293)[2] propose an alternative division of the Canadian capitalist class into two fractions based on their roles in producing staples. The "sphere of circulation" includes banks and other financial institutions, merchandisers, transportation companies, utilities, and the entire service sector—said to share a "mercantile" interest in staple exports and to have opposed industrialization before retreating to a position of accommodation with "comprador" industrialists from the United States, while maintaining some industries as protected turf for Canadian capital (Naylor, 1972:24). Naylor (1972:3) also argues that an inverse relationship exists between the levels of profits in the spheres of production and distribution. . . .

Clement (1977:293) has also portrayed Canadian capitalists as social conservatives who have created a "highly structured economy with few avenues through which the lower class can rise." While emphasizing Canadian capitalists' economic conservatism, aversion to risk, and isolation from other classes in Canadian society,[3] Naylor and Clement make no explicit arguments about other aspects of their political ideology. Mercantile economic conservatism and the restricted mobility into it lead us to predict that capitalists in this fraction are more conservative concerning social and political issues than capitalists in other sectors.

Social Backgrounds of Capitalists

In addition to representing the interests of the corporations which they head, individual executives' family backgrounds, educational experiences, geographical mobility, and career patterns could affect their ideological positions. A biographical perspective on ideology easily fits into the neo-staple formulation. Clement (1975:203) shows that, compared to foreign-controlled counterparts, Canadian-controlled corporations are somewhat more likely to recruit executives from upper-class backgrounds. If earlier socialization is a continuing influence on ideology, executives from working-class backgrounds should be more liberal than executives from more privileged backgrounds. Alternatively,

executives from working-class backgrounds may have little sympathy for people not experiencing the same degree of mobility—so we make no prediction about the effect of family background.

Arguments Suggesting a Unified Capitalist Ideology

Four specific arguments may be advanced *against* the proposition that the Canadian capitalist class is ideologically divided. The first argument follows from Mandel's (1975: 30ff) attack on the concept of dividing capitalist economies into monopoly and non-monopoly sectors. In his view the continuing survival of capitalism requires that "competition must in the long run assert itself, though not necessarily price competition. Monopoly surplus profits are always subject to erosion" (Mandel, 1975:530–1). The absence of a difference in the rates of profit of the monopoly and competitive sectors removes it as a basis of ideological conflict within the capitalist class. . . .

A second argument involves the supposed antagonism between the spheres of production and distribution. As Macdonald argued (1975), in *Capital* (1959:part IV) Marx described the relationships among the three major sectors of capital as non-antagonistic, first, because industrial capital depends on commercial capitalists to sell commodities and on the financial sector for credit and financing and, second, because the equalization of the rate of profit extends across all industries, whether or not they produce value. . . .

A third argument follows from Carroll, Fox and Ornstein's (1981) analysis of the network of interlocking directorates between the largest Canadian corporations. They found that the network is roughly circular, so that corporations are largely distinguished in terms of their distances from the centre of the network. Attempts to discern distinct groups of corporations within the network failed. The diffuseness of the network of corporate interlocks should promote the overall solidarity of the capitalist class and prevent the development of ideological divisions. The interlocks are reinforced by business interest associations (Coleman and Jacek, 1983), memberships on university, hospital, cultural, and charitable organization boards (Ornstein, 1983), and a web of informal ties (Porter, 1965:528ff; Clement, 1975:243ff; Fox and Ornstein, forthcoming).

The fourth argument reflects recent American studies of industrial segmentation which suggest that modern capitalist economies cannot be divided into segments along a single core-periphery axis (Oster, 1979; Hodson and Kaufman, 1982)....

Of more direct bearing on the present study are three studies of cleavages in the American capitalist class. Clawson, Kaufman and Neustadtl (1983), Jenkins and Shumate (1983), and Useem (1981) found that region, industry, and various other variables do not have much effect on the ideology of American capitalists.

METHODOLOGY

Measures of the political ideology of the capitalist class and of state officials, trade union leaders, and the general public were obtained in surveys conducted in late 1977 and early 1978.... One important advantage of sample surveys is that they permit the investigation of issues about which there is little public debate, on which business has not played a public role, or on which executives' public statements are likely to be rhetorical....

Measuring Ideology

... This paper views ideology in what Larrain (1979:14) describes as a "positive" sense, as "the expression of the world view of a class ... the opinions, theories, and attitudes, formed within a class in order to defend and promote its interests." The term "ideology" is used in

this paper instead of "attitudes" in order to draw attention to its substantive focus—on class relations and the role of the state—and to its methodological focus—on interpreting the responses to individual items in terms of more general ideological perspectives.

In each of the five policy areas our analysis focussed on important current issues at the time of the survey....

Sample and Variables

The 142 big business respondents were chief executives (or other top executives designated as their substitutes) of a random sample of corporations chosen from the 1976 *Financial Post* ranking of the largest firms. The comparison sample of 43 chief executives of medium-sized business was selected from lists of firms supplied by the Boards of Trade in the twelve largest Canadian cities (with the number of selections proportional to their populations), which makes it difficult to advance strong claims about its representativeness. None of the medium-sized firms had more than 200 employees; the mean was 50 and the median, 59 employees....

The sample of civil servants includes approximately equal numbers of federal deputy and assistant deputy ministers, provincial deputy ministers, and department heads from the twelve largest Canadian cities, while the sample of politicians includes approximately equal numbers of Members of Parliament, provincial cabinet ministers in each province, and mayors and city councillors from the twelve largest cities. The sample of union leaders includes the presidents of the fifty largest trade unions in Canada and/top officials of the major trade union centrals.

The "neo-staple industry variable" divides corporations between the spheres of production and circulation, as defined by Clement and Naylor, and according to whether they are Canadian and/or foreign controlled. For the large corporations only (no measure is available for the medium-sized firms) capital intensity is measured by the ratio of corporation sales to assets, a convenient but somewhat flawed indicator. Core-periphery differences are examined by comparing the large and medium-sized corporations and (for large, industrial corporations) by the sales-to-assets ratio.

The measure of class background refers to the work done by the respondent's father when the respondent was sixteen years of age, in particular his occupation, whether he owned a business, and, if he did, the size of the business, and (for non-owners) whether he supervised other workers. Regrouping Wright's (1976) categories, three class categories for family background were formed: the "bourgeoisie" includes the owners and top managers of business with fifty or more employees; the "medium and petite bourgeoisie" includes the owners of all businesses with less than fifty employees; and the "working class" includes all non-owners, including semi-autonomous employees and supervisors.[4]

RESULTS

In each table the top panel compares the corporate executives as a whole to the samples of civil servants, politicians, and trade union leaders and, when possible, to the general public. The second panel of each table addresses the arguments about core-periphery differences by comparing the executives of large and medium-sized businesses. The third to sixth panels, which refer only to the executives of large corporations, examine the effects of industry, nation of control, "neo-staple industry," and class background. . . .

Social Welfare Measures

The first three items in Table 1 measure how much effort, compared to levels of effort at the time of the interview, that respondents believed the government should put into health and medical care, providing assistance to the unemployed and helping the poor. Effort was defined as "the proportion of our total resources which is spent in each area." The fourth, fifth, and sixth items measure responses to the statements: "there is too much of a difference between rich and poor in this country;" "unemployment is high these days because it is too easy to get welfare assistance;" and "people with high incomes should pay a greater share of the total taxes than they do now."[5]

For all six items, capitalists are most conservative, trade unionists on the left, and civil servants, politicians, and the general public somewhere in between, just where, depending on the particular issue. The business executives were more conservative concerning redistribution than general welfare measures. Only 13 per cent of the executives believed the rich should carry more of the tax burden, compared to 34 per cent of the civil servants, 54 per cent of politicians, 84 per cent of the trade unionists, and 59 per cent of the general public. By comparison, about 40 per cent of the business executives supported greater efforts to assist the poor. The two items bearing on the unemployed also find the capitalists far to the right of the other groups.

Contrary to monopoly capitalist theory, there are no systematic differences in the positions of the executives of large and medium-sized corporations. Not only are five of the six comparisons below statistical significance, but the directions of the differences are inconsistent.

While there were no consistent differences among executives from corporations in the five major industry categories, the executives of foreign-controlled corporations were somewhat more liberal than their Canadian counterparts. The largest difference involved the statement that welfare payments increase unemployment, a statement with which 56 per cent of the executives of foreign corporations and 68 per cent of the executives of Canadian corporations agreed. Because there were no industry differences

Table 1

SUPPORT FOR SOCIAL WELFARE MEASURES BY GROUP, TYPE OF FIRM, AND SOCIAL ORIGIN (% DISTRIBUTION)

Independent Variable	Amount of government effort for health and medical care			Amount of government effort to assist the unemployed			Amount of government effort to help the poor			There is too much difference between rich and poor			Unemployment too high because welfare too easy to get			People with high incomes should pay more taxes			No. of cases
	Less	Same	More	Less	Same	More	Less	Same	More	Disagree	Neither	Agree	Disagree	Neither	Agree	Disagree	Neither	Agree	
Group:																			
Capitalists	26	68	6	47	37	16	10	50	40	64	14	22	22	13	65	85	2	13	(185)
Civil Servants	14	72	14	33	40	27	4	56	40	38	13	49	47	13	40	54	12	34	(129)
Politicians	12	71	17	22	43	35	6	45	49	44	12	44	54	8	38	45	9	46	(147)
Labour	0	28	72	4	32	64	2	13	85	6	6	88	86	2	12	8	8	84	(53)
General Public	3	50	47	26	46	38	4	55	41	18	18	64	22	10	68	26	15	59	(3289)
Size of Firm:																			
Medium	21	67	12	58	23	19	12	49	39	71	22	7	20	24	56	78	5	17	(43)
Large	28	68	4	44	40	16	10	50	40	62	11	27	22	10	68	87	1	12	(142)
Industry:																			
Industrial	24	72	4	40	39	15	8	54	38	63	13	24	24	7	69	88	1	11	(72)
Resources	19	71	10	43	43	14	10	28	62	65	10	25	24	20	40	90	0	10	(21)
Transport, utility	31	61	8	41	42	17	8	54	38	64	0	36	18	9	73	90	0	10	(13)
Merchandising	40	60	0	40	33	27	13	47	40	50	17	33	9	0	91	83	0	17	(15)
Financial	38	57	5	43	48	9	15	57	28	61	11	28	6	17	77	83	6	11	(21)
Nation of Control:																			
Canada	34	62	4	49	36	15	12	52	36	55	11	34	12	8	80	85	1	14	(73)
Foreign	20	74	6	38	46	16	7	48	45	69	12	19	32	12	56	89	2	9	(69)
Neo-Staple Theory:																			
Industry:																			
Canadian—"Mercantile"	41	54	5	49	36	15	16	51	33	58	12	30	9	13	78	84	3	13	(39)
Foreign—Productive	20	73	7	42	43	15	8	46	46	70	14	16	35	14	51	89	2	9	(59)
Canadian—Productive	26	71	3	50	35	15	9	53	38	53	9	38	15	3	82	85	0	15	(34)
Foreign—"Mercantile"	20	80	0	11	67	22	0	60	40	63	0	37	13	0	87	87	0	13	(10)
Class of Father:																			
Bourgeois	31	61	8	50	42	8	12	47	41	66	17	17	9	6	85	86	3	11	(34)
Petit bourgeois	24	74	2	39	44	17	2	46	52	54	16	30	19	12	30	80	0	20	(45)
Working Class	29	66	5	46	36	18	16	57	27	4	65	31	34	12	54	94	0	6	(54)

this effect could not result from the concentration of foreign capital in certain industries. An examination of the "neo-staple industry" typology supports our prediction that the most conservative element of the capitalist class is the Canadian "mercantile" fraction—although the differences among the four categories are not large. In the sphere of production, the executives of foreign-controlled corporations were generally more conservative than their Canadian counterparts.

Although family background has a significant effect on the responses of four of the six items in Table 1, not all the differences are in the expected direction. Among executives with "bourgeois" backgrounds, 85 per cent agreed that welfare payments raise unemployment, compared to 72 per cent of executives with petit bourgeois and small employer backgrounds and 55 per cent of executives with working-class backgrounds. On support for the poor the effect of class background is in the opposite direction: about one half the executives from bourgeois and small employer backgrounds supported greater assistance to the poor, as compared to only one quarter of the executives from the working class.

Only one of the six items is related to the sales-to-assets ratio. That item is the measure of support for the unemployed which is strongly, positively related to the sales-to-assets ratio. Thus executives of labour intensive firms were *more* likely to support the unemployed, suggesting that they were not especially fearful that social welfare measures would decrease the labour supply.

The results of the bivariate analysis discussed so far are qualified by their basis on single-item measures and the small numbers of respondents in some of the categories. To address these shortcomings, a multiple classification analysis (not shown in any table) of two multi-item indices measuring opinions on social welfare efforts and on redistribution of income was undertaken. This additional analysis shows that, when family background

is held constant, the effect of nation of control disappears. Executives from petit bourgeois and small employer backgrounds were more liberal than executives from the bourgeoisie and the working class. . . .

Rights of Workers

On labour relations issues, the business executives were again to the right of the other groups. The capitalists were most isolated in responding to the statement "employees should be represented on the boards of the companies for which they work," with which only 17 per cent of the executives agreed or strongly agreed, compared to 50 per cent of civil servants, 57 per cent of the politicians, 42 per cent of the trade union leaders, and 69 per cent of the general public. For the other items, and particularly for the evaluation of the power of trade unions, the executives proved only slightly more conservative than politicians and civil servants. Executives overwhelmingly favoured the existing level of workers' compensation, opposing the increase of payments to injured workers after their injuries. Similarly, three quarters of the capitalists opposed prohibitions on the hiring of strike-breakers, compared to the majority of the public that supported this measure.

As predicted by segmentation theory, executives of medium-sized companies were more opposed to trade unions than their counterparts in large corporations. On the other hand, executives of medium-sized companies proved somewhat *less* likely to oppose increases in workers' compensation and the placing of employees on company boards. Although the individual items differed significantly, capitalists' positions on labour relations issues are not consistently related to nation of control, industry, or family background. Multivariate analysis of scale measuring attitudes towards labour revealed only one significant effect: as predicted by monopoly capital theory, executives of capital-intensive corporations were more sympathetic to labour. Although none of the groups within the capitalist class deviated from the generally conservative line on labour relations issues, very large differences existed between the business executives and state officials, trade union leaders, and the general public.

Government Intervention in the Economy

... Compared to the bare majority of politicians and civil servants who opposed this measure and three quarters of the trade unionists and 80 per cent of the general public who supported it, two thirds of the executives opposed the government becoming the employer of last resort. Except for Syncrude, the executives were the least likely of the four groups to support government economic intervention. Forty-four per cent of the executives strongly disapproved and 47 per cent merely disapproved of the potash takeover. The civil servants gave majority support of most government initiatives, but were evenly split on the potash takeover and Canadair purchase. More than two thirds of the politicians opposed the potash takeover.

Following the logic of monopoly capitalist theory, the executives of medium-sized firms were slightly more opposed to government employment and gave somewhat stronger support to FIRA and the CDC than big business—perhaps believing that FIRA would provide some protection from takeover. On these issues, the industrial differences were fairly large. For five of the six items the executives of resource firms were most conservative. Eighty-one per cent of the resource industry executives strongly disapproved of the potash takeover and the remaining 19 per cent disapproved; 85 per cent opposed the government acting as an employer of last resort. Even in the case of Syncrude, when gov-

ernment investment was designed to bail out private investors, only 48 per cent of the resource executives approved.

On the left of the business community were the executives of utilities, a number of whom headed crown corporations. As predicted by the neo-staple theorists, finance industry executives were towards the left of the business opinion in their views of government intervention. Manufacturing industry executives were relatively liberal in their views of FIRA and the CDC and the merchandisers were conservative on some issues and near the average on others.

The differences between the executives of Canadian and foreign-controlled corporations were quite small and, surprisingly, there was no difference in their response to the question about FIRA. The statement concerning the government providing jobs as a last resort was endorsed by 32 per cent of the executives of foreign-controlled corporations, compared to 18 per cent for their counterparts in Canadian corporations—a difference which is consistent with our previous findings that the executives of foreign-controlled corporations are more liberal.

Finally, the effect of class background was quite weak and consistent with earlier results. For four of the six issues, the executives from working-class backgrounds were most conservative. Three quarters of the executives, most of them upwardly mobile, opposed governments acting as the employer of last resort, compared to just over one half of the executives from other backgrounds. Multivariate analysis of a scale of government intervention items confirmed these findings: it revealed only one significant effect, that the executives of corporations in the resource industry were much more likely to oppose government intervention, compared to the executives of corporations in other industries....

... It is significant that the largest differences in responses to these issues involved industries and not nationality of ownership or family background, which implies that characteristics of corporations and related differences in their relations to the state are the most important consideration in predicting attitudes towards state intervention. Inasmuch as they require privileged and exclusive access to natural resources, particularly when commodity prices rise, corporations in resource industries are inherently most susceptible and strongly opposed to political regulation.

Foreign Investment

Business executives were much more favourable to foreign investment than state officials, labour leaders, and the general public. Sixty-five per cent of the executives said that foreign investment had at least "mostly good" effects on the Canadian economy; only one in six believed that integration of the Canadian and American economies was too great (compared to at least one third of state officials, labour leaders, and the general public); one half believed that foreign investment should not be subject to any screening. For each of four areas of the economy—manufacturing, petroleum, banking, and merchandising—executives were the most likely to want to "encourage" or "strongly encourage" new investment. However, attitudes differed considerably towards investment in the four areas: 81 per cent of the executives wanted to encourage foreign investment in manufacturing, compared to 77 per cent for petroleum investments, 51 per cent for merchandising, but only 25 per cent for banking. At the opposite extreme were the labour leaders, at least one quarter of whom would "discourage" or "strongly discourage" new investments in each area. The pattern of politicians' and civil servants' support for foreign investment in the four areas was similar to that observed for executives, but the state officials were somewhat less likely to encourage investment. Outright continentalism gained little support from any group. Even

among executives, only one in six supported closer economic integration with the U.S.

In the context of their overwhelmingly positive view of foreign investment, there were some differences within the business community. Executives of medium-sized companies were somewhat less enthusiastic about foreign investment than big business executives. Comparing industries, executives in the financial and merchandising sectors most strongly supported foreign investment, while transportation and utility executives were the least supportive. Surprisingly, there were no differences between the executives of Canadian and foreign-controlled corporations or among the categories of the related "neo-staple" industry categorization. A multivariate analysis of a scale of support for foreign investment demonstrated the presence of strong industry effects, unaltered by controls for other variables. Consistent with previous findings, the executives from small business backgrounds were the least supportive and executives from big business backgrounds the most supportive of foreign investment; executives from working-class families had opinions somewhere in between.

There is a very high degree of consensus in the business community over foreign investment, not only with regard to more general questions, but also concerning investment in four different sectors of the economy. The strongest opposition to foreign investment was found among the executives of medium-sized firms and among executives from small business backgrounds. However, these differences within the capitalist class exist in the context of generally strong pro-investment attitudes.

The Power and Taxation of Business

Not surprisingly, corporate executives are unlikely to say they possess too much power or have paid too little in taxes. And, once again, the trade unionists differed most sharply from the executives. For example, 10 per cent of the executives said that large industrial corporations carried too small a part of the total tax burden, compared to 39 per cent of the civil servants, 34 per cent of politicians, and 94 per cent of trade union leaders. Only the items dealing with the power of and taxes paid by small business produced a consensus among the different groups of respondents. . . .

Responses to the questions about the power of large corporations demonstrated sharp differences among the four groups: only one quarter of the executives said the corporations had too much power, compared to 63 per cent of the politicians, 74 per cent of the civil servants, 91 per cent of trade union leaders, and 74 per cent of the general public. Civil servants were more likely than politicians to believe that business was too powerful and corporations too lightly taxed.

There were large differences between the executives of medium-sized companies, four in five of whom believed that large corporations had too little power, and the executives of large corporations, about half of whom took that position. A similar difference appeared in evaluations of taxes paid by small business. Over one third of the executives of medium-sized companies believed that large corporations had too *little* power in Canadian society, compared to one quarter of the executives of large corporations.

The responses to the questions about taxation reflect rivalries among industries, since the executives of each branch of industry described their own taxes as too high and the taxes of other branches as too light. For example, only 5 per cent of the executives of the financial corporations said that banks were too lightly taxed, as compared to 30 per cent of industrial executives; 84 per cent of transportation and utility executives said resource firms were too lightly taxed, as compared to 58 per cent of industrial executives.

Executives of foreign-controlled corporations were less likely than those of Canadian-controlled corporations to believe that they

were too highly taxed. In spite of the high level of foreign investment in the resource industry, 71 per cent of the executives of Canadian-controlled corporations, compared to 58 per cent of the executives of foreign-controlled corporations, described the resource sector as too highly taxed. The belief that industrial firms are too heavily taxed was strongest among Canadian firms in the sphere of production; strongest among foreign-controlled corporations in the sphere of circulation.

Within big business, executives of more labour-intensive corporations tended to give stronger support to small business on both the taxation and power issues. This probably reflects the fact that, among large corporations, the labour intensive firms are the most similar to smaller businesses and are likely to operate in industries with considerable numbers of small and medium-sized firms. Class background had little effect on responses to these issues.

SUMMARY AND CONCLUSIONS

The major elements of the ideology of the capitalist class include 1/ strong opposition to redistribution of income and support for cuts in assistance to the unemployed, combined with a traditional, paternalistic support for greater aid to the poor; 2/ the belief that trade unions are too powerful and strong opposition to legal changes favouring the labour movement; 3/ opposition to most forms of government investment; 4/ strong support for foreign investment, outside of banking; and 5/ support for small business. Whatever its past role in the enactment of social reforms, these data show plainly that the Canadian business community opposes virtually all efforts at further social reform and given the power would roll back many present programs.

The survey revealed very large ideological differences between business executives and the state officials. Not only are these differences substantively meaningful, but they are much larger than the differences between major fractions of the capitalist class. At least at the time of the survey, policy making involved substantial conflicts between capital and the state with different strategies for managing a capitalist economy and society. While these findings run counter to the instrumentalist stress on the influence of business on the state, the survey results do not permit us to choose among alternative explanations of the ideological conflict between capital and the state, including pressure from subordinate classes, the state's legitimation role, and fiscal imperatives.

There were some ideological distinctions between the monopoly and competitive sectors; executives of medium-sized companies took more liberal positions on income redistribution and the appointment of employee representatives to company boards and the CDC, but they were also more fearful of the power of trade unions. While the last of these findings is in keeping with the general argument that larger corporations can better accommodate the higher wages and higher taxes produced by more liberal state policies, our data suggest that corporations in the competitive sector are generally more and not less supportive of state intervention—precisely the opposite of what monopoly capitalist approaches would predict. This suggests that, increasingly, small business executives have come to recognize that state intervention is required to protect them from the power of large corporations. However suggestive these results, the magnitude of these core-periphery differences should not be ex-

aggerated. On many issues ideological differences cannot be discerned between the executives of large and medium-sized corporations, and for the issues on which differences occur, the magnitudes are smaller than the differences between the business, state officials, and labour leaders.

Similarly, there are some ideological differences between executives of corporations in different industries and between the executives of Canadian and foreign-controlled corporations. As suggested by Clement's finding that they have experienced more occupational mobility than their counterparts in Canadian-controlled corporations, the executives of foreign-controlled corporations proved somewhat more liberal. This difference disappeared when a statistical control for family background was introduced. However, these effects of family background and nation of control were largely confined to items dealing with social welfare programs and with taxes, and did not extend to labour relations issues and foreign investment. The industrial differences also did not extend across the different aspects of ideology. . . .

. . . Whatever its internal divisions, the Canadian capitalist class shares a common ideology that can serve as the basis for its political mobilization.

One political implication of these findings is that efforts to incorporate weaker fractions of the capitalist class into populist political alliances will not likely succeed. The competitive fraction of the capitalist class is distinguished by its strongly anti-union ideology, and on other issues it is only slightly more liberal than big capital.

Notes

[1] The first general discussion of the two sectors is by Averitt (1968). Theories of segmented labour markets, which link sectoral divisions among firms to variation in rates of pay, also find

their basis in this distinction between economic sectors (Cain, 1976).

[2] This paper does not consider the relationship between Naylor's work and Innis's staple

theory. For conflicting views of the similarity between Naylor's and Marxist approaches see Drache (n.d.) and McNally (1981).

[3] Clement's and Porter's characterization of Canada as a "low mobility" society rests entirely on their observations of the low levels of mobility into the tiny group consisting of the executives of the largest corporations. However, most mobility in Canadian society occurs within the broad occupational structure. There is good evidence that rates of mobility in Canada are very similar to those in other advanced capitalist nations (Turrittin, 1974; Pineo, 1976; Ornstein, 1981; McRoberts and Selbee, 1981).

[4] Among the executives of large corporations, thirty-four were from bourgeois backgrounds, forty-five from petit bourgeois and small employer backgrounds, and fifty-four from working-class backgrounds. It is difficult to

imagine how methodological differences could account for the very large difference between this distribution and Clement's and Porter's findings about the social backgrounds of what they describe as the corporate elite. Therefore there must be a large difference between the class origins of the top *executives*, who served as respondents in this study, and Clement's "corporate suggests elite," which includes the *directors* of dominant corporations, many of whom inherited their wealth and directorships.

[5] The responses to all the items were trichotomized: "depends" answers were placed in the medium category and "strongly (dis)agree" and "(dis)agree" responses were collapsed, as were "much more (less) effort" and "more (less) effort" responses. The eta values given in the bottom of the tables were computed using the full range of responses, scored linearly.

References

Atkinson, Michael M., and Marsha M. Chandler 1983 The Politics of Canadian Public Policy. Toronto: University of Toronto Press

Averitt, Robert 1968 The Dual Economy. New York: Norton

Barton, Allen H. 1974 "Consensus and conflict among American leaders." Public Opinion Quarterly 38:507–30

——— 1980 "Fault lines in American elite consensus." Daedalus 109:1–45

Bliss, Michael 1974 A Living Profit: Studies in the Social History of Canadian Business. Toronto: McClelland and Stewart

Block, Fred 1977 "Beyond corporate liberalism." Social Problems 24:352–61.

Cain, Glen C. 1976 "The challenge of segmented labor market theories to orthodox theory." Journal of Economic Literature 14:1215–57

Carroll, William, John Fox, and Michael D. Ornstein 1981 "A network analysis of interlocking directorates among the one hundred largest Canadian corporations." Canadian Review of Sociology and Anthropology 19:44–69

Clawson, Dan, Allen Kaufman, and Alan Neustadtl 1983 "Which class fractions fund the new right?" Paper presented at the 1983 annual meeting of the American Sociological Association, Detroit

Clement, Wallace 1975 The Canadian Corporate Elite: An Analysis of Economic Power, Toronto: McClelland and Stewart

——— 1977 Continental Corporate Power. Toronto: McClelland and Stewart

Coleman, William D., and Henry J. Jacek 1983 "The roles and activities of business interest associations in Canada." Canadian Journal of Political Science 16:257–80

Dosman, Edgar J. 1975 The National Interest: the Politics of Northern Development. Toronto: McClelland and Stewart

Drache, Daniel n.d. "Canadian capitalistic development: the Innis paradigm." Unpublished manuscript

Eldersveld, Samuel, Sonja Hubée-Boonzaaiger, and Jan Kooiman 1975 "Elite perceptions of the political process in the Netherlands looked at in historical perspective." Pp. 129–61 in Mattei

Dogan (ed.), The Mandarins of Western Europe: The Political Role of Top Civil Servants. New York: Sage

Finkel, Alvin 1979 Business and Social Reform in the Thirties. Toronto: Lorimer

Fournier, Pierre 1976 The Quebec Establishment. Montreal: Black Rose

Fox, John, and Michael Ornstein n.d. "The Canadian State and Corporate elites in the post-War period. Canadian Review of Sociology and Anthropology. Forthcoming.

French, Richard D. 1980 How Ottawa Decides: Planning and Industrial Policy-Making 1968–1980. Toronto: Lorimer

Galbraith, John Kenneth 1973 Economics and the Public Purpose. Boston: Houghton Mifflin

Hänninen, Sakari and Leena Paldán 1983 Rethinking Ideology: A Marxist Debate. New York: International General

Higley, John, Desley Deacon, and Don Smart, with the collaboration of Robert C. Cushing, Gwen Moore, and Jan Pakulski 1979 Elites in Australia. London: Routledge and Kegan Paul

Hodson, Randy, and Robert L. Kaufman 1982 "Economic dualism: a critical review." American Sociological Review 47:717–39

Holloway, John, and Sol Picciotto 1978 State and Capital. London: Edward Arnold

Jenkins, J. Craig, and Teri Shumate 1983 " 'Cowboy' capitalists and the rise of the 'new right': Capitalist segments in American politics." Paper presented at the 1983 annual meeting of the American Sociological Association, Detroit

Jobin, Carol 1978 Les enjeux economiques de la nationalisation de l'électricité. Montréal: A. St. Martin

Larrain, Jorge 1979 The Concept of Ideology. London: Hutchinson

Macdonald, L.R. 1975 "Merchants against industry; an idea and its origins." Canadian Historical Review 56:263–81

Mandel, Ernest 1970 Marxist Economic Theory. New York: Monthly Review Press

———— 1975 Late Capitalism. London: New Left Books

Marx, Karl 1956 Capital (vol. II). Moscow: Progress

———— 1959 Capital (vol. III). Moscow: Progress

McKie, Craig n.d. "An Ontario industrial elite: the senior executive in manufacturing industry." University of Toronto, unpublished doctoral dissertation

McNally, David 1981 "Staple theory as commodity fetishism: Marx, Innis and Canadian political economy." Studies in Political Economy 6:35–63

McRoberts, Hugh A., and Kevin Selbee 1981 "Trends and occupational mobility: Canada and the U.S." American Sociological Review 46:406–21

Mellos, Koula 1978 "Developments in advanced capitalist ideology." Canadian Journal of Political Science XI:829–61

Merleman, M. 1968 "On the neo-elitist critique of community power." American Political Science Review 62: 451–60

Naylor, Tom 1972 "The Rise and fall of the third commercial empire of the St. Lawrence." Pp. 1–41 in Gary Teeple (ed.), Capitalism and the National Question in Canada. Toronto: University of Toronto Press

Nelles, H.V. 1974 The Politics of Development: Forests, Mines and Hydro-Electric Power Development in Ontario, 1849–1941. Toronto: Macmillan

Niosi, Jorge 1978 Le Controle financier du capitalisme canadien. Montreal: Les presses de l'Université du Québec

———— 1981 Canadian Capitalism: A study of power in the Canadian Business Establishment. Toronto: Lorimer

O'Connor, James 1973 The Fiscal Crisis of the State. New York: St. Martin's Press

Offe, Klaus 1974 "Structural problems of the capitalist state." Pp. 31–57 in Klaus von Beyme (ed.), German Political Studies. London: Sage

Ornstein, Michael 1981 "The Occupational mobility of men in Ontario." Canadian Review of Sociology and Anthropology 18:183–215

———— 1983 "Extensions of the network of corporate interlocks." Paper presented to the American Sociological Association annual meeting, Detroit

Oster, Gerry 1979 "A Factor analytic test of the theory of the dual economy." Review of Economics and Statistics 61:33–9

Panitch, Leo 1977 "The Role and Nature of the Canadian State." Pp. 3–27 in Leo Panitch (ed.), The Canadian State: Political Economy and Political Power. Toronto: University of Toronto Press

Pineo, Peter 1976 "Social mobility in Canada: the current picture." Sociological Focus 9:109–23

Porter John 1965 The Vertical Mosaic. Toronto: University of Toronto Press

Poulantzas, Nicos 1975 Classes in Contemporary Capitalism. London: New Left Books

Semmler, Willi 1982 "Theories of competition and monopoly." Capital and Class 18:91–116

Sweezy, Paul M. 1968 The Theory of Capitalist Development. New York: Monthly Review Press

Turrittin, Anton H. 1974 "Social mobility in Canada: a comparison of three provincial studies." Canadian Review of Sociology and Anthropology, Special Issue: 163–86

Useem, Michael 1981 "Business segments and corporate relations with U.S. universities." Social Problems 29:129–41

Wright, Erik Olin 1976 "Class boundaries in advanced capitalist societies." New Left Review 98:3–42

Education and the Schools

Introduction

The educational system is a central institution of modern societies. Pitrim Sorokin, in his classic *Social and Cultural Dynamics* ([1927] 1957), foresaw that a modern, highly bureaucratic society would use schools to channel, train and select young people for society's most important roles. This made the proper functioning of the educational system—its openness to all, universalistic application of rules, reward for merit, and relevance to the society of which it was a part—crucial to the effective functioning of society. A good educational system was important for the individuals who needed educating, to the labour market that would employ their skills, and to those in society whose prosperity and well-being ultimately depended on knowledge and expertise: in short, everyone.

However, the educational system was even more sociologically interesting in Canada than in the United States, where Sorokin was writing. First, Canadian education had been put under the authority of the provincial governments by the British North America Act, in order to deal with conflict between Canada's two founding

Anglo/Protestant and Franco/Catholic cultures. Breaking the impasse meant yielding to the provinces the right to regulate their own educational, cultural and social services, while reserving other activities (e.g., defence, foreign affairs, immigration) to the federal government. However, after the Second World War, education came to concern the federal government as well. The progress of provincial education was critical to planning for immigration, manpower, and socioeconomic development: all federal concerns. Raising educational attainments across the country was needed in order to achieve mass literacy and some minimal job skills. Increasingly, federal-provincial relations focused on educational matters of joint concern, especially as educational costs soared from the 1960s onward. However, every intervention in the educational realm was an intervention in provincial affairs.

Not only was the educational system a focus of federal/provincial conflict. It was also a growing concern within provinces. As we note in a later section on communities and regions, the economic well-being of Canada's provinces has always varied widely. Education was particularly problematic in the Maritimes and Quebec. The Maritimes, and especially Newfoundland, had been slow in reaching a level of functional literacy required for an industrial society. But after Newfoundland joined Confederation in 1949, major reforms followed; and upgrading the educational system was part of this reform process.

In Quebec, the educational problem was as much symbolic as practical. For a long time, Quebec's schools had provided a post-secondary classical education that was best suited to traditional Catholic thinking. However, this kind of education was unsuited to the bureaucracies of modern business and government administration, and failed to provide adequate scientific and technical skills for an industrial society.

As a result, Quebec Francophones were inappropriately trained for new jobs in industry and government, and these jobs went to Anglophone Protestants. If Francophone Quebeckers were going to compete with Anglophones for better paying, higher status positions, they not only needed more education, but a different, more secular, technical kind of education. This meant rethinking education in Quebec and funding new kinds of educational programs. Not only provincial economic development, but the traditionally unequal relationship between French and English Canadians would be changed by this aspect of Quebec's "quiet revolution."

Thus, educational reform had somewhat different meanings in Canada's different regions and provinces. But one important goal was universally acknowledged, a goal already noted in connection with the article by John Porter in our section on inequality. This grew out of a belief that more education could increase social efficiency and fairness.

Porter, like Sorokin before him, felt that a modern society required the most efficient use of its talented people. This meant encouraging people to pursue their studies and abilities to the limit. If the most meritorious held the positions of greatest responsibility, society would be run by people with the greatest intelligence, aptitude, training and industriousness; and not, as now, by those lucky enough to have been born into wealthy families.

A society that trained the young to their maximum and rewarded adults for their contribution to society would not only be efficient and productive, but also fair. No one would have to settle for less than they were capable of achieving, simply because they could not afford a long and expensive education. After Porter, sociologists increasingly studied the equality of access to institutions of higher education. This access would become a prime social indicator of society's well-being: the more equal the access into higher education, the healthier society was becoming, in their eyes.

However, this point of view ignored several important possibilities. One is that the kind of "meritocracy" Porter envisioned might not be desirable, even if attainable. This point is neatly argued in a utopian fantasy by English sociologist Michael Young. His book, *The Rise of the Meritocracy* (1967), appears to have been written, with the advantage of hindsight, by a historian in the next century who has seen how a meritocracy works and tries to explain its shortcomings. But Young was not the first or only one to point to problems with the idea. Many have commented that parents usually try to pass along their advantages, and would hate to see their children labelled less deserving than they. Second, adults would not like to believe their lack of reward was due to a genuine lack of merit. A society like ours, which really does deprive deserving people of just rewards, at least allows the less talented people to maintain their pride. Deservingness is always uncertain in our society, and that uncertainty can be soothing.

Finally, meritocracy would have the effect of draining the lower classes of talent, energy and leadership. This would make class protest more difficult. "Meritocracy" has merit as a system only if we assume that class protest is undesirable and unnecessary. A meritocracy is a highly centralized political and economic decision-making structure and the possibilities for totalitarian rule—for coercion, over-control, and costly error—are great. In a totalitarian system based *not* on merit, but on kinship or ethnicity, say, the subordinate classes will continue to have enough talent and leadership to challenge the system and, by challenging it, to improve or even topple it. But in a meritocracy this scenario is unlikely. As much as Marx's imagined class-less utopia, the meritocracy really is the end of history and class struggle as we have known it.

So there can be some legitimate doubt about the desirability of using education to bring about a meritocracy. Beyond that, the very rise of a meritocracy seems quite unlikely. Before showing why, let us consider the argument that a meritocracy *could* come about.

An important theory about social change is called the "post-industrial society" thesis. Most often associated with sociologist Daniel Bell (1973), this argument holds that modern societies have already begun to move out of industrialism into "post-industrialism" as a way of production and a way of life. The specifics of this argument are too complex to treat here, but the basic premise is that the source of wealth, hence national prosperity and power, in an *industrial* society is modern technology. Industrialism brings together technology, raw materials, labour, and capital in a distinctive way not possible before the late eighteenth century, the time of the so-called Industrial Revolution. People work machines to convert the raw materials into cheap, high-quality goods in a way that pre-industrial production could not do. The key is industrial *technology* (e.g., inanimate sources of power like steam, electricity) and industrial *organization* (e.g., mass production assembly lines and bureaucratic offices).

However, the early industrializing nations—England, France, the United States—are already falling behind in international competition to nations in the Pacific Rim—Japan, Taiwan, Hong Kong, among others. The reason is cheap labour and information technology. Increasingly, wealth is based on information and information processing; elevating the importance of such information technologies as computers, word processors, and robots to the fore. This same change also raises to greater importance the role of ideas, inventiveness, and education. The future calls for better thinking, say the post-industrial theorists. Presumably, the nation making the best use of the best-trained minds will make the greatest discoveries in science, technology and productivity, and will advance the furthest economically.

We have come a long way in the last 200 years: from maximum body strength as an advantage, to inanimate force, to minimal body strength combined with maximum intellect. From this standpoint, modern education is a training in how to get the most production with the least energy, capital, manpower and resources. Brains become the central factor of production under post-industrialism.

If this theory is valid, we should be moving rapidly towards a society based on brainpower, not because it is fair but because it is efficient. Only by educating people to the limit of their abilities, and giving the ablest the most important roles in society, should we be able to win the international competition for trade and power. Yet, there is little if any evidence that we are really moving in this direction.

Wealthy and powerful families continue to control our economy. They hire the bright and well-educated to run their businesses, but they do not turn over the reins of wealth and power, and the educated cannot compel it.

So Porter and the post-industrialists were right in supposing that education would be a source of power in modern society, but wrong in supposing that the educated would take charge. Instead, the educated are hired, persuaded or co-opted to work on behalf of traditional wealth and power. Giving more people more education does not ensure that the distribution of power is fair, efficient, or anything like equal.

Articles in this section touch on all of these points. We start with an excerpt on the microstructure of education—on life in the classroom—to better understand how the raw material of the system, the boys and girls, feel about what is going on. Wilfred Martin reminds us of what it was like to be teacher's pet or the class victim. His concern is ultimately with the motivational effects of such discriminatory treatment. Motivation is, in turn, especially important in his research site in Newfoundland, where modern universal education is still developing. Motivating the student is most crucial where the student's parents may not themselves be strong supporters of education.

Next come two articles on the educational midi-structure—on school systems. The first, by Pierre Belanger, recounts a portion of Quebec history preceding the "quiet revolution." Many Quebec educators were concerned about the unequal status of French and English, and started to translate these concerns into educational reforms even before the provincial government got heavily involved. Belanger implies that social and educational mobilization came from the grass-roots upward, and not from the state downward. When

the province did go ahead, major changes were more readily accepted than might have otherwise been expected.

A second article, by Neil Guppy and his associates, attempts to measure very precisely the degree to which educational access has increased in the last few decades. A great deal of effort and money has been spent to achieve this goal; has it worked? The answer is, yes and no. Data gathered in 1973 (and not fully reflecting all the changes that have taken place by now) show that class of origin continues to powerfully influence the amount of education a person will get—a finding supported by many other provincial, national, and even cross-national studies. As American sociologist Christopher Jencks (1972) has pointed out, you cannot get rid of this influence without getting rid of the family. But on the other hand, the class (or family) effect on educational access is progressively weakening. This is change in the desired direction.

The final two articles are on education's macro-structure—the linkage between schools, the economy and society. C. James Richardson argues that, rather than seeing education and schools as *causes* of social change, we do better to see schools and education as *effects* of social change. Schools are the arenas in which social classes play out their fantasies and prepare their offspring to maintain the family tradition. (We saw this point of view in the Seeley article on PTA, in an earlier section on Socialization.) Educational credentials are the means by which the wealthy and powerful legitimate their wealth and power, not the means by which they typically attained it. Educational systems, by this reckoning, produce stability, not change; they protect inequality, not challenge it.

The section ends with a paper by John Porter on the post-industrialism thesis and the need for more and better education, regardless of the effects on inequality. His main concern is international competition in a post-industrial world. Porter's article, written half a decade earlier than Richardson's, reflects the blind attachment many people felt towards educational reform in the 1960s and early 1970s. By the late 1970s that bubble of optimism had largely burst. Observers were already complaining about the overproduction and oversupply of educated people in a world that is not quite as "post industrial" as had been expected. Whether Porter was right in the long run but wrong in the short run, we shall see in decades to come. His paper is presented as a compelling image of the future. Here Professor Porter is locked in an important debate with Professor Richardson (and others) who have good reason to doubt that Porter was right.

We have already begun to discuss the topic of work, in connection with economic and technological change. We know that the workplace is an important part of everyone's adult life; and education will largely determine the kind of work we shall do. The next section will try to define what "work" is, then show some ways in which work is changing; and finish by discussing some of work's more serious discontents.

References

Bell, Daniel *The Coming of Post-Industrial Society*. New York: Basic Books, 1973.

Jencks, Christopher *et al. Inequality: A Reassessment of the Effect of Family and Schooling in America*. New York: Harper Colophon Books, 1972.

Sorokin, Pitrim A. [1927] *Social and Cultural Mobility*. New York: Free Press, 1957.

Young, Michael *The Rise of the Meritocracy, 1870–2033*. Baltimore: Penguin Books, 1967.

52 Teachers' Pets and Class Victims

Wilfred Martin

WILFRED MARTIN, Professor of Sociology in the Department of Educational Foundations, Memorial University, is author of two books: *The Negotiated Order of the School* (1976) and *Voices from the Classroom* (1985), and co-author of the text *Canadian Education: A Sociological Analysis* (1978, revised 1982). He has published in many journals, including *The Canadian Review of Sociology and Anthropology*; *Sociology of Education*; *American Journal of Sociology* and *The International Journal of Sociology of the Family*. He received an Excellence in Teaching award from the University of New Brunswick in 1977.

... From the student perspective of schooling, two of the more salient student identities in this setting are *teachers' pets* and *class victims*. This article will focus on students' perceptions of the consequences of the favouring/mistreating processes which may have contributed to the creation of these identities in the first place. To provide a frame of reference for the present analysis of teachers' pets and class victims, it is necessary to give a brief overview of the concept of *identity* with particular reference to the classroom.

IDENTITIES IN THE CLASSROOM

The term "identity" is generally used in sociology to refer to a "person's biographical sense of relationship to the others with whom he or she has been and is customarily associated" (Hewitt, 1976:80). In other words, it is the cumulative sense of one's place relative to others. More explicitly, a student, for example, develops a sense of his or her identity relative to that of the teacher in general. The idea of "situated identity" has been introduced into the literature to account for one's sense of position in a particular situation. For example, during specific instruction in an academic subject like mathematics or social studies, or during extracurricular activities, a student develops a sense of his or her position relative to others (teachers and students) in these situations. ...

On the surface, the classroom appears to be a relatively simple structure involving two well-defined social roles: teacher and student. Teachers, however, must play such roles as judge, resource person, helper, friend and confidante, referee, detective, ego-supporter, and group leader (Hoyle, 1969:9–60). Similarly, the myth of the singularity of the student role is soon dispelled when one attempts to isolate the "variety of slots" which teachers have for students "of varying age, sex, intelligence and personality" (Calvert, 1975:77–86). While some of these slots (or social identities) are defined by the formal organization of the school, others are created, developed, and changed, and are continually evolving in the classroom. ...

While certain students become defined as teachers' pets, they, and others, may be seen as victims of classroom life. Two important aspects of the situated identities of pets and victims as related to high school students must be noted here. One is the fact that even though the categories of pets and victims may be a relatively stable part of classroom culture, the students in these categories may vary from time to time. The fact that certain students are categorized, that is, given one social identity in one way and others in another, is partly a result of the interaction strategies employed by each of the combatants in this setting. Another aspect of the classroom pets/victims phenomenon centres on who defines a student as pet, victim, or both.

DATA COLLECTION AND ANALYSIS

Data on which the present study are based are taken from student responses to an open ended question which was the last item on a survey questionnaire:

> Obviously, this questionnaire covers only a small part of your experiences in the school. Please outline other aspects of your experiences in the school which concern you. Feel free to add any views you might have concerning your school, your teachers, your textbooks, and the way you are expected to study.

The questionnaire was administered to 7,948 students in Grades 9, 10 and 11 from 55 schools selected from 24 school boards in Newfoundland and Labrador.[1] It covers a wide range of topics including student council, school prefects, school rules, disciplinary procedures, and participation in extra-curricular activities. The questionnaire makes no reference to teachers' pets or to class victims as such. However, one part of the questionnaire suggests that teachers vary in their expectations of students and in the way they behave toward students, and then asks students to indicate how often teachers do things like "threaten to punish you if you do not do as you are instructed to do," "give students too much freedom," and "do things that help create conflict and strife between teachers and students." Another part of the questionnaire asks students to agree or disagree with specific statements which also might be related to teachers' pets. These statements include the following: "The punishments which

teachers give in this school are usually fair," "I am concerned about my teachers' attitudes toward me," and "I want all my teachers to like me." One can only speculate whether or not these or other parts of the questionnaire prompted students to think more about teachers' pets and/or class victims. The fact remains that though the topics of teachers' pets and class victims were not included in the questionnaire, almost 10% of the 6065 students respondents made reference to, and in most cases elaborated upon, these phenomena in the classroom. . . .

. . . The present article focuses on the student-perceived consequences of classroom favouritism and mistreatment. The findings on this theme challenge us to use various theoretical orientations to elaborate on the complexities of teachers' pets/class victims phenomena and their impact on instruction.

TEACHERS' PETS AND CLASS VICTIMS

The answer to the question, "Do teachers have pets?" depends on the existence and identity of respondents as teachers or students. Even before the question was posed, numerous students clearly presented the view that teachers' pets constitute an important part of the classroom culture.

Class victims may be defined as students who, from the student perspective, are either mistreated or neglected by the teacher (relative to the treatment and attention given to other students) to the extent that they (or others) see themselves as experiencing mistreatment or neglect. Many students felt that "some teachers are always picking on certain students," even when those students are not doing "anything wrong." It was also felt that particular students got more help with their academic work than others.

While the teacher perspective on student pets and class victims is an important dimension of these phenomena, the present research focuses on the student perspective of classroom life. It is argued that if students believe that teachers have pets and victims, this belief is important in student definitions of teachers, teachers' actions and of the students' own plans of action in interacting with teachers and fellow-students. In other words, regardless of whether teachers' pets and class victims exist from the teacher perspective, and whether students misinterpret the actions of the teachers toward specific students, the subjective reality of teachers' pets and class victims for students is extremely important in student definitions of classroom situations and plans of action. . . .

CONSEQUENCES FOR SELF-DEFINED PETS

Some of the respondents in the present study saw themselves as teachers' pets and thought that their classmates also defined them in this way. Without delving into the intricacies of the classroom, it might be assumed that a teacher's pet would have considerable prestige in interactions between students. However, the present data indicated that this is not necessarily so; students who were defined as teachers' pets found it difficult to gain classmate acceptance. Apparently, they are often on the receiving end of jokes amongst their peers. Some of those who see themselves as pets indicated guilt concerning favours received from teachers. And while teachers generally seemed to favour pets, they are also sometimes perceived to hold greater expectations for them than for other students. In so doing, teachers place certain pressures on their pets.

Interestingly enough, students who perceived themselves as pets, like those who perceived themselves as victims, offered several negative comments concerning classroom pets. For certain students it seems that being a teacher's pet means that one is also

victimized, although obviously in a different manner from those who are mistreated or neglected. It may also be that pets are victimized by peers: students who attempt to garner favour from their teachers are usually disliked.

CONSEQUENCES FOR CLASS VICTIMS AND OTHERS

The consequences of mistreatment or neglect for non-pets and class victims, as revealed by our present data, can be analysed under five headings: (1) "being left out," (2) the marking process, (3) the disciplining process, (4) disliking teachers, and (5) antipathy and empathy amongst students.

"Being Left Out"

The experience of "being left out" because of teachers' definitions of certain students and actions toward them was common among high school students in the present study. Furthermore, those who thought that they were left out of the main lines of action and interaction in the classroom reported that they become "annoyed" with their teachers and "turned off" from their school work.

It was also observed that those with low averages are often left to "suffer through the grade" as teachers give their undivided attention to students with the highest averages. Other respondents pointed out that further consequences of teachers' victimization include a lack of extra help in academic work and/or guidance in social development. Students suggested that sometimes teachers encouraged "top students" to maintain, if not improve, academic performances, while ignoring students at the bottom of the academic hierarchy. Some thought that teachers assume that most students at the bottom of the academic hierarchy will remain there, and therefore gave little attention to directing such students' efforts to improve their academic performance. Needless to say, the merits of this teaching strategy are not always obvious to students at the lower end of the academic performance hierarchy. In addition, some students perceive teachers to direct their teaching toward specific students while neglecting others, thereby creating a "boring" setting for the neglected.

The Marking Process

As expected, the criteria which students perceive teachers to use in categorizing them in the classroom include teachers' perceptions of whether or not a student is "smart," and whether or not a student gets high marks on examinations, tests, and other written assignments. If in fact teachers favour the more intelligent students, it would be interesting to know whether such students are helped because of their intelligence of whether they are intelligent because of extra attention from teachers. Similarly, do teachers favour students getting high marks, or do some students get high marks because of attention given by teachers? On occasion, students actually accuse teachers of assigning marks to certain students, while depriving others of marks because of attitudes toward, and definitions of, students concerned. In short, one of the consequences of teachers' pets/class victims phenomena, as seen by some students, is that marking examinations and other written assignments is sometimes not "fair."

In addition to seeing "good marks" associated with teachers' pets, some students claim that poor academic performances are due to the lack of attention received from certain teachers relative to attention given to pets. It has also been pointed out that if a student is perceived to be getting marks because he/she is a teacher's pet, other students become discouraged, study less, and obtain marks lower than would have been obtained otherwise.

Discipline

Aside from teachers' definition of what constitutes "misbehaviour," some students thought that teachers' attitudes toward particular students and their definitions of those students affected their disciplining. For example, the consequence of not being a teacher's pet came to mean to many students that the teacher "is always picking on" them. The term "picking on" was often used to imply that teachers were mistreating them, not letting them do the things that other students are allowed to do, and, in general, controlling their freedom, relative to other students. Other comments indicated that students often saw themselves as victims of a lack of teacher understanding of students. The clear consequence of putting a student "down," as pointed out, was that it made students "feel bad." As with the marking process, the discipline may be seen by students as both an instance and consequence of favours and mistreatments.

Disliking Teachers

Teachers are not only perceived to have pets, but are also seen to dislike other students—hence, classroom victims. It is not surprising that students dislike teachers seen to be favouring particular students and mistreating others. While considerable dislike exists for teachers who have pets, there is even more dislike for those seen to be mistreating students. Teachers' negative attitudes toward their students were, according to many students, countered with similar student attitudes toward those teachers. And, it is the teacher who is often seen to be the initiator of the cycle of dislike between teacher and student. There were, however, some students who believed that their attitudes and actions were the main factors in influencing teachers' definitions of them. Whoever is the original culprit, students generally agree that learning is influenced by the attitudes students believe teachers to hold toward them.

Antipathy and Empathy Among Students

As a result of their perceptions concerning the existence of teachers' pets and class victims, some students reported having antipathetic attitudes and relationships with those perceived to be teachers' pets. Empathy with those whom they see as being victimized by teachers' actions in the classroom was also a common response among high school students. In addition, there was widespread indignation toward teachers' pets. More specifically, favouring certain students over others was seen to cause student annoyance with their teachers which may result in disturbances in the classroom, because those others got "jealous" when they saw teachers giving "advantages" to their pets.

Even though most students who reported teacher victimization saw themselves as those who were being picked on, some respondents who commented on victimization did not see it in reference to themselves. They did, however, indicate empathy with, or sympathy for, those perceived as victims in the classroom.

PETS AND VICTIMS: A CHALLENGE

Using the notions of identities and situated identities, the classroom can be seen as an extremely complex social setting where actors not only negotiate numerous identities acceptable to one another, but different participants develop definitions for themselves and for others for which there are varying degrees of awareness and agreement. Teachers' pets and class victims are cases in point. The idea of teachers' pets has been well known for some time. But, the possibility that certain students become victimized has received relatively little attention in the literature related to the sociology of the school. Even less attention has been given to the degree of awareness teachers and students have concerning one another's definitions of the other. There is considerable evidence to show that numerous students perceive teachers' pets and class victims as important situated identities in the classroom. It may be that teachers do not perceive these identities to be as common as students claim they are. However, their importance to students demands the attention of researchers attempting to understand classroom interaction processes, and of teachers who are very much a part of these processes. The task of isolating and understanding the processes of student categorization goes beyond the assumption that students are categorized according to ability measured by IQ, or by academic achievement measured by tests and examinations in specific subject areas. The classroom is not immune to the complex social processes whereby individuals become typified (labelled, stereotyped) in everyday life, albeit as found in the classroom, those processes may differ. As suggested by classroom life reflected in teacher-student relations with the students as a captive audience, and in the decision making and judgments about progress in academic and social domains, particular aspects of student categorization, and the way students perceive them, set them apart from everyday categorization processes. . . .

An overriding theme in the consequences of teachers' pets and class victims, as isolated by students, is that dimensions of teachers' attitudes towards students, their actions in the classroom and their plans of action for students are influential in fostering some of the generally defined negative aspects of student performance and classroom behaviour. From the perspectives of the students' comments, it is argued that academic failure, disciplinary problems and, even, the dropout phenomenon cannot be fully explained by the socioeconomic backgrounds of students, and/or such student psychological characteristics as intelligence, motivation, and aspiration. One must look at the sociological dimensions of classroom teaching-learning processes, including the interpretations which students give to their teachers' actions. It is the interpretation and reinterpretations of one another's attitudes, actions, and plans of action which form the spring-board for the interactions and social relationships that develop in the classroom. . . .

References

Blumer, Herbert. *Symbolic interactionism: Perspective method.* Englewood Cliffs, New Jersey: Prentice-Hall, Inc., 1969.

Brophy, Jere E., and Good, Thomas I. *Teacher-student relationships: Causes and consequences.* New York: Holt, Rinehart and Winston, Inc., 1974.

Bognar, Carl J. Teacher expectations and student characteristics. *Canadian Journal of Education*, 1983, 8 (1), 47–56.

Calvert, Barbara. *The role of the pupil.* London: Routledge & Kegan Paul, 1975.

Glaser, Barney G., and Strauss, Ansel I., *The discovery of grounded theory: Strategies for qualitative research.* Chicago: Aldine Publishing Co., 1967.

Gouldner, Helen. *Teachers' pets, troublemakers, and nobodies: Black children in elementary school.* Westport, Connecticut: Greenwood Press, 1978.

Hewitt, John P. *Self and society: A symbolic interactionist social psychology.* Boston: Allyn and Bacon, Inc., 1976.

Hoyle, Eric. *The role of the teacher.* London: Routledge & Kegan Paul, 1969.

Martin, Wilfred B.W. *The negotiated order of the school.* Toronto, Macmillan, 1976.

Mehan, Hugh. *Learning lessons: Social organizations in the classroom.* Cambridge, Massachusetts: Harvard University Press. 1979.

Novak, Mark W. *Living and learning in the free school.* Toronto: McClelland and Stewart Ltd., 1975.

Stebbins, Robert A. *The disorderly classroom: Its physical and temporal conditions.* Monograph in Education No. 12, St. John's: Committee on Publications, Faculty of Education, Memorial University, 1974.

Stebbins, Robert A. *Teachers and meanings: Definitions of classroom situations.* Leiden: E.J. Brill, 1975.

Woods, Peter. *The divided school.* London: Routledge and Kegan Paul, 1979.

Woods, Peter (Ed). *Pupil strategies: Explorations in the sociology of the school.* London: Croom Helm Limited, 1980a.

Woods, Peter (Ed.). *Teacher strategies: Explorations in the sociology of the school.* London: Croom Helm Limited. 1980b.

53 Educational Reform in Quebec

Pierre Belanger

PIERRE BELANGER, Professor titulaire in the Faculty of Education Sciences at Laval University, Quebec City, specializes in the sociologies of education, socialization and the family. His published work includes *Ecole et societé* with Guy Rocher (1975); "L'avant et l'après des reformes: l'evolution de la perception du destin scolaire au Canada central, 1965–1972" with P. Roberge (1980); and "La sociologie de l'éducation au Quebec" with R. Ouellet and C. Trottier (1975). He has recently completed a period of teaching and research in Togo.

RESEARCH APPROACH

My analysis will be focused on—but then limited to—the school attendance rates of various status groups in selected segments of the educational system. It will be informally guided by one theoretical approach, that of conflict sociology. To quote Collins:

> The basic premises of the conflict approach are that everyone pursues his own best line of advantage according to resources available to him and to his competitors; and that social structures—whether formal organizations or informal acquaintances—are empirically nothing more than men meeting and communicating in certain ways. The outlooks men derive from their past contacts are the subjective side of their intentions about the future. Men are continually recreating social organization. Social change is what happens when the balance of resources slips one way or another so that the relations men negotiate over and over again come out in changed form. The general propositions put forth here are thus a basis for explaining social change. (Collins, 1975, 89)

The educational system will be seen as a cultural market, as "a market for cultural goods in which various sources of demand mesh with sources of supply" (Collins, 1977). Education is a resource in the struggle for domination[1]. Status groups are composed of individuals sharing a common "culture": manners, language styles, jokes, opinions, values and so on.

During the 1950s, French Canadians really became committed to education as a resource to get their place in an industrialized society. The "rite de passage" to adulthood was no longer the "communion solennelle" in grade VI or VII, nor the grade VII provincial school certificate.

How is this growth to be explained in spite of any major structural change in the educational system? Applying the general principles of conflict analysis (Collins, 1975: 601) to the history of education in Quebec can throw light on this phenomenon and help us understand some of the social consequences of the educational reform of the 1960s.

Let us consider education as a cultural good and resource which social groups are competing for in the cultural market. At least two conditions are required for educational expansion. "First, it depends on how much material wealth is siphoned into specialized culture-producing organizations: that is, how much of the material wealth is invested in the cultural economy" (Collins, 1979, 62).

Throughout the 1950s, the school system was inadequately financed from public funds, but total expenditures for education increased steadily as a proportion of the GNP and of personal incomes. School boards ran up deficits that were later paid by the government. Yet teachers' salaries were very low and a large proportion of them were members of the clergy, so that the costs of educational expansion could be kept in check. In 1958–59, the average annual salary for teachers in public schools was as follows: Catholic schools—*clergy*: men, $2 376; women, $1 651; *lay people*: men, $4 791; women, $2 079. Protestant schools—men, $5 872; women, $3 918 (Rapport Parent, 1966, IV). Another way to cut educational expenses and supply more education to meet a growing demand was to hire more "non-qualified" teachers and to increase the number of students per teacher. This was especially the case in secondary public schools, although "officially" it contributed to lower the quality of education. The Tremblay Report noted that in the two years between 1950–1951 and 1952–1953 the number of "non-qualified" laywomen teachers increased by 33% and would have increased even more had it not been for a parallel increase in the pupil-teacher ratio (Tremblay, 1955, 55).

And yet, the economy had been growing at a very impressive rate since World War II. The Fédération des collèges classiques stressed this fact in its brief to the Tremblay Commission in 1954. Roy, for his part, notes that:

> Materially speaking, Quebec society was transformed by an unprecedented expansion of economic activity. Quebec's rate of growth in retail consumption was the highest in Canada. The progression of cars and automotive sales was higher there than anywhere else. While in 1950 there were 18.5 telephones per 100 inhabitants, there were 29.8 in 1960. In less than 8 years, between 1952 and 1960, Quebecers bought over 1.1 million television sets. Almost everyone could buy on credit. (Roy, 1976, 245–46)

Thus, there were collective and individual resources to be invested in education. The producers of education could use different strategies to compensate for the lack of proper public funding of education: they could hire low-paid religious teachers, "non-qualified" teachers, women; they could increase the pupil-teacher ratio; and they could ask for tuition fees. Consumers could use part of their personal income to invest in the education of their children. Also, with economic growth came important changes in the occupational structure, mainly a decrease in the proportion of blue collar workers and a corresponding increase in the number of white collar jobs (Brunelle, 1970, quoted in Hêtu, 1980, 182–9).

A second condition for educational expansion is the existence of a decentralized school system which allows for competition among producers and consumers of culture (Collins, 1979, 63). Before 1960, the Quebec educational system was, de facto, a decentralized system. On paper, the Comités de l'instruction publique had vast powers over public school programs and curricula. In fact, they initiated little and sanctioned after the fact what had already been done in the schools. Producers could open new schools, or new programs in existing schools, and then wait for the approval of administrative authorities.

Commercial schools, the superior elementary grades, the classical section in public schools, the latin-science curriculum, Polytechnique and the Hautes Etudes Commerciales at the post-secondary level, were all the result of initiatives taken at the grassroots by various interest groups that were officially sanctioned later. All the while, private schools had a high degree of autonomy. Magnusen reminds us of an important point:

> The reforms had fundamentally altered the character and pattern of education, changing it from a *decentralized*, church-dominated system serving an elite to a centralized, state-controlled one catering to a mass population. (Magnusen, 1980, 114)

ETHNIC GROUPS COMPETITION BEFORE 1960

The history of the Anglo-protestant and the Anglo-catholic (Irish) school systems will be discussed briefly, in a very simplified manner, only to set the general context of "status struggle" in Quebec. A detailed analysis of that struggle *within* each group has yet to be done.

The history of the Franco-catholic school system is more complex. I will focus my analysis on concrete groups: priests and traditional elites identified by the greco-latin humanities or culture on the one hand and, on the other hand, teaching brothers, *modernes élites* and the population at large whose cultural identity was being built on a scientific, technical and vocational culture.

To draw a parallel with what happened in France in the eighteenth century when the philosophies, sensing a shift in the resources that underlay the organization of power, promoted, in opposition to the classical culture, a modern culture based on science and technology which appealed to the emerging administrators of the state and technicians of the military (Collins, 1977; Ben-David, 1971) would be a gross misrepresentation of our history. As a heuristic device, however, it can provide useful ideas into the history of educational reform in Quebec.

The economic domination of Anglo-protestants in Quebec does not have to be documented here. They had wealth as producers and consumers. The 1867 Canadian Constitution gave them the right to control their own denominational school system without interference from the Quebec government. In 1869, the Assemblée législative voted a school tax law obviously inequitable to Catholics but preserving their economic interests. Anglo-protestant interests often meshed with those of the Catholic church.

> Paradoxically, the Anglo-protestants have always been (and still are, as we shall see)

the best allies of the Catholic Church on educational matters. (Milner, 1984, 27)

And in fact, there have been a number of alliances between the Anglo-protestants and the Catholic hierarchy on such important matters as the establishment of a minimum school leaving age, the creation of a Ministry of Education, tuition-free schooling and so on. These alliances have always been detrimental to the development of education in the Catholic majority. Anglo-protestant schools were tuition-free and academic perseverance high enough not to require a minimum school leaving age. Giving these things to their Catholic competitors would have deprived them of resources. A Ministry of Education would have been a menace to the autonomy of their school system. These same measures would have threatened the moral and political power the Catholic hierarchy had over the education of young francophones.

Anglo-protestants were not true competitors in the Quebec educational market. They were passive observers, keeping a keen eye on their own interests and constitutional rights. They developed their own educational system and they even over-produced to compete in the Canadian and American cultural markets.

But comparisons with the Anglo-protestants became an effective device used by Franco-Catholics who wanted to mobilize support for a reform of their school system when it became obvious with economic expansion that education was a powerful resource to gain status. Since French Canadians could not hope to get control over the major corporations already owned by Anglo-Canadian and Anglo-American interests, their only hope to "beat" the dominant ethnic group was to get more and better education. Tremblay put it quite plainly:

> This is why, since the economic take-over of large corporations is nearly impossible for French-Canadians, there remains a chance of controlling their behavior and their

attitudes, of controlling all that matters from a cultural point of view, if French-Canadians can manage to supply these corporations with the technicians and managers who shape their basic policies and their day-to-day activities.

It is this that makes it so important now for French-Canadians to insure their "ethnic" future from a social, cultural and economic point of view by "betting", so to speak, on education. (Tremblay, 1955, 150)

This strategy went further and attributed two very distinct functions to the elite and to the "technical" class. The elite would have to preserve and develop the cultural distinctiveness of the whole nation, trained as it was in "cultural skills and values" acquired in the classical colleges, while the others would have to develop "technical skills" in vocational, technical and business schools and then go on to subvert the Anglo-protestant political economy from within. This split was not easily accepted and took shape only after the educational reform.

In the ethnic cultural stratification of Quebec, the Irish were half-way between the Franco-Catholics and the Anglo-Protestants. They had to struggle on the cultural market to preserve their cultural identity and increase their status as an ethnic group. Magnusen (1980, 80–84) shows how they managed to obtain their "natural place" in the Quebec school system.

In the decades immediately following immigration, the Irish had to enter a school system dominated by Catholic francophones. Teaching was done by francophones, half in French and half in English. For Magnusen, it is the poor quality of such teaching that fuelled the Irish drive to get their own English-speaking schools by having members of their own group named on school boards from which they could fight to develop a de facto Anglo-Catholic school system. In this fight for cultural goods, they were between a dominant and a dominated group. They had little interest in being identified with the French-speaking school culture since this would place them in an inferior position with respect to the Anglo-protestants. French schools could not socialize them to English culture. They were excluded from the Anglo-protestant status group. And did not wish to be identified with the Franco-Catholics.

> Because Irish Catholics did not have their own schools until the twentieth century, the road to secondary and higher education was not a smooth one. Though products of a school system dominated by the French, Irish Catholics aspired to English higher education. In search of university entrance at McGill or elsewhere, they pursued pre-university studies at Collège Saint-Marie or St. Mary's College as it was known in English. Perhaps the most significant feature of St. Mary's was that a common religion could not overcome linguistic and ethnic differences. In effect, the English and French students at the college tended to go their separate ways, socially as well as academically. Underlying this situation was a growing desire of Irish Catholics to be masters of their own educational destiny, to establish and maintain their own schools. The establishment in 1896 of Loyola College and Loyola High School under Jesuit auspices not only met the requirement of schools that were at once English and Catholic, but symbolized the educational coming of age of Quebec's Irish population. (Magnusen, 1980, 81–82)

It symbolized as well their own cultural identity as a status group. We may note, in passing, this same phenomenon of status group isolation in large comprehensive high schools and colleges today. Students and teachers from the academic sector do not mix, academically nor socially, with those of the vocational sector.

In their quest for cultural advantages, the Irish obtained a public high school in 1931 and, soon afterwards, a provincial bureau responsible for curriculum and examinations. The system then became fully autonomous and the Irish, as a status group, could from then on control their cultural resources.

They have been able to increase their social position and their resources by integrating into the system under their control waves of post-war immigrants, Italians mostly, of which 56 000 landed between 1951 and 1961, including nearly 14 000 school-age children. For these immigrants, the best choice was to seek integration into the dominant Anglo-protestant group. But that choice entailed religious costs that were deemed too important. The next best thing was an alliance with the Anglo-Catholics.

The Anglo-protestants lost little in the deal. Immigrants could not pay large school taxes and presented problems of cultural assimilation. They could be used as cheap labour in occupations the Anglo-protestants had left a long time ago.

For the Catholic clergy and the Catholic school system as a whole they were a new and welcomed clientele. It was only in the 1970s that the Franco-Catholics realized that they had lost cultural resources by letting them go into an alliance with the Anglo-Catholics.

This shows how, in the competition for cultural capital, social actors themselves can and do shape school systems rather the other way around.

The growing demand for secondary education in the Franco-Catholic sector after World War II was met by the growth of two groups of institutions, each associated with a different stratum within the Catholic clergy: priests, both secular and regular, on the one hand and various orders of teaching brothers on the other.

> Priests, regular or secular, were specialized in traditional classical secondary education while various orders of teaching brothers were oriented towards more modern forms of secondary education.
>
> (Tremblay, 1954, 49)

Competition between priest and teaching brothers goes back to the nineteenth century. It is then that teaching brothers started setting up various business schools, industrial and commercial academies and so on for the benefit of the graduates of grade schools. (To the regret of Léon Gérin, some of these later became classical colleges, Rocher, 1970, 43). But since graduates of these schools could not gain access to higher education institutions (which was also the case in the U.S., Collins, 1979), they founded the Académie St-Louis in Montréal in the early 1920s. The originality of the Académie St-Louis was that it modelled its curriculum after that of the Protestant high schools.

La Presse wrote in August of 1921:

> In other words, the (Brothers of St-Viateur), wished that young French-Canadians whose parents do not have the means to send them away to the classical college have their own "high school" which would place them on a perfectly equal footing with their English speaking counterparts upon graduation.
>
> (Quoted in Croteau, 1971)

The curriculum included Latin and emphasized sciences and mathematics. Graduates from the Académie St-Louis could go on to the final years of the collège classique, to the Ecole Polytechnique or to the Ecole des Hautes Etudes Commerciales (Croteau, 1971, 97).

In tractations preceding curriculum approval, the clergy opposed granting the right of teaching Latin to the superior primary schools. In a December 1928 letter to the Superintendant of Education, Brother Piéladou of the Académie St-Louis wrote:

> Things, in Montreal, are getting complex. I heard that the French-Canadian group oppose the teaching of Latin while the Irish insist on it. Why oppose the teaching of Latin in *our* high school classes when the English teach it in all their secondary schools? I would be very sad if we could not get Latin for our grades 9, 10 and eleven simply because we are not a classical college. (...) The children of the common people, especially in the larger cities, would then be on

an equal footing with the Protestants and the Jews.

(Quoted in Croteau, 1971, 91)

The Irish got their Latin and, as we have seen, their high school. Latin was imposed on schools for girls in 1942, so that their culture would be improved. But the right to teach it was not granted to the superior primary schools of the teaching brothers.

Because of this, graduates from these schools could not be admitted to universities and the professions. Many French Canadians started attending English schools.

What, then, can be the uses of a superior primary education? It can be of some use to female youth but does not satisfy the ambitions of male youth. In consequence, the number of young French-Canadians who enroll in Protestant Business Colleges, High Schools, Colleges and Institutes grows daily. And strangely enough the very same professional societies who refuse to admit French-Canadians who do not have the classical baccalaureate admit them after only two years in a Protestant university college. (Quoted in Croteau, 1971, 164)

For the teaching brothers, the situation was unacceptable.

While young English-speaking Canadians, protestants and catholics alike, and this even in our own province of Quebec, with their public tuition-free high schools have to pay for only four more years of college to obtain a degree giving access to well-paid honorable professions, our French-Canadians, who in general come from very modest social backgrounds, must pay for at least ten years of schooling to obtain the same degree. How could they sustain such a competition. (Mémoire des frères, 1952, quoted in Croteau, 1971, 195)

The teaching brothers wished to train a French-Canadian elite but not the traditional elite made of clerics and members of the liberal professions. Their reference group was the Anglo-protestant elite. Their society was a society undergoing a rapid industrialization, especially in the Montreal area. They sought to ensure an equality of educational opportunities between francophones and anglophones in Montreal. They thus avoided an open conflict with the classical college and their greco-roman humanism.

The daily life of the Montreal population where French and English mixed and where the English economic superiority was obvious was the teaching brothers' starting point.[2] They were not given to high-flown pedagogic theory, which made Tremblay (1954, 22) write that they were not always conscious of the consequences of the technical and scientific orientation they gave to their teaching. It did little to preserve the cultural identity and the internal unity of the traditional elite. This traditional elite felt threatened from within. Mgr. Marault wrote in 1940:

In any case, our two universities at Quebec City and Montreal will maintain their entrance requirement, the Baccalauréat-ès-arts, which presupposes the acquisition of a general culture based on greco-latin humanities. But for how long will we be able to resist change? Yet, we must try! It is my firm belief—shared by my colleague in Quebec City—that every young French-Canadian who can afford it should have a classical college education. (Quoted in Croteau, 1971, 159)

By the early 1950s, the demand for education started to grow even more sharply. Both groups tried to devise strategies, the priests to keep their control over the formation of the elite and the teaching brothers to promote scientific culture while increasing their share of the cultural market.

The classical colleges added science courses to their curriculum; a bachelor of education program was created; and a few university colleges offering pre-university level courses were opened by the universities themselves. Under pressure from the teaching brothers and some school boards, the university softened its entrance requirements and started admitting holders of the latin-sciences baccalaureate, which could be obtained in institutions other than the classical colleges. The colleges saw that as a move in their favour that could integrate the scientific curriculum to the traditional culture, thereby excluding the mere technicians from this status group.

> The two (French-speaking) universities have approved, in the Spring of 1952, a greek-less curriculum leading to the Latin-Sciences baccalaureate. For its promoters, this new program would replace the "science" section in the current superior primary program and be also available in some classical colleges. (Fédération des collèges classiques, 1954, 20)

The teaching brothers were granted permission to open their own classical colleges in remote areas where their competitors could not, or would not, go. They thus founded one in Arvida (while the priests kept the elite boarding school in nearby Chicoutimi) and another one in Victoriaville. After an agreement with the engineering school at Laval University, they gave the first year of the engineering program in Shawinigan. A similar agreement with the Ecole polytechnique allowed them to do the same thing in Sherbrooke. For a few years, Brother Théode tried to obtain the status of university college for the classical college at Victoriaville. But in 1954, a group of priests took over and obtained the charter for themselves. In Quebec City, attempts were made to get around the regulations of the Comité Catholique and obtain university entrance privileges, in science and engineering faculties, for holders of the "special" grade 12 certificate. A great many classical sections were opened up in the secondary public schools. But a price had to be paid for that, the transformation of the science curriculum designed by the teaching brothers. It was not paid willingly[3].

> Some of the things we have heard lead us to believe that many of those schools whose grade 12 graduates are accepted in selected university programs will not happily relinquish this "privilege". They will tend to improve the science curriculum, perhaps by adding another year, and seek to have it recognized as one of the normal entrance routes to the science and business faculties. These faculties themselves may be reluctant to lose this source of recruitment that gives them some 40% of their students. (Tremblay, 1955, 214)

Competition between the classical colleges and the other institutions of secondary academic education was by then fierce. But it was not mainly a matter of economics, it was also a cultural competition. The increases in enrollment rates should have favoured the public schools.

> But things did not turn out that way likely because of the 'cultural' advantages of the classical curriculum and of the greater number of university programs it gave access to. The academic inferiority of the public schools when they gave only the superior elementary program certainly has diminished their recruitment and increased that of the colleges. (Tremblay, 1955, ———)

It was indeed a matter of cultural advantages, of social prestige, of status groups in the classical colleges which did not recruit their students in the technical classes.

But the demographic pressures were building. A scheme was hatched whereby a new division of labour would exist between the public schools and the classical colleges.

> We have said before why we believe that men's college[s], if they want to play in the future the role they have played in the past, must gradually specialize in the last four years of the classical curriculum and leave the first four to the public schools. (Tremblay, 1955)

In this way, the unity of the traditional and the scientific elite would be reconstituted thereby increasing national solidarity in dealing with other ethnic groups.

The proposals from the Fédération des collèges classiques were similar.

> With these changes, the classical curriculum would again become the only road of access to university. (Fédération des collèges classiques, 1954, 29)

In their struggle, the teaching brothers had powerful allies in the engineering and business schools of the universities. These faculties were themselves struggling against the traditional elite to attain full status in the university. Conversely, some classical colleges had made attempts to reach out to the rising class of small businessmen by opening up commercial sections so that this economic sector could be "humanized" and its members partially integrated in their status group.

CONCLUSION

As I have said before, the struggle for hegemony over the education of the elite has been fierce. All the tactics used in the corporate world, take-overs included, were used. All the different economic, social, cultural, political and religious dimensions of stratification played a part.

But the social, cultural and religious dimensions—that is, the status group dimensions—seem to have played the greater part. There is a good illustration of this in a letter from the rector of Brébeuf to a parent. Parts of this letter are quoted by Galarneau (1978, 156).

> Our institution does not suit those children, however gifted, who do not come from well-to-do families. Most of our pupils are brought up in affluent surroundings and have ways, habits and manners one should not teach to children from more modest conditions. Our fees are higher than elsewhere and we would consider a reduction of those fees only in the case of children from the bonne bourgeoisie, in the case, for example, of sons of members of the learned professions. (Galarneau, 1978, 156)

The fight between the classical colleges and the public schools went on. It expressed a cleavage between status groups. The classical colleges recruited their pupils mostly from the sons of professionals, white collar workers and farmers, these under encouragement from the parish priest. The latin-science curriculum of the teaching brothers appealed mostly to sons of technicians and small businessmen (Tremblay, 1954, 95). The same sort of difference could be observed among university students.

During the expansion of the 1950s, the teaching brothers and the local school boards had succeeded in challenging the monopoly the classical colleges had over the training of the elite. But the distinction between the two remained. The colleges held on to the culturally richer parts of the curriculum.

The fight went on till the reform. The clergy tried to limit access to higher education and to reserve that access to the sons of the elite, while the teaching brothers fought for an equality of educational opportunity for those youngsters born in the lower status groups. The fact that the public secondary schools they taught in did not give easy access to higher education was a major obstacle to this end. That obstacle removed, they believed their students could achieve equality of results with students from other status groups.

Notes

[1] From that point of view, we will emphasize an "explanation" of educational reform that makes it the result of struggles between various social groups.

[2] "In Montreal, where French Canadians are over 80% of the population, among the 2 726 engineers in the 1951 census, 48% were English Canadians and only 33% French Canadians. For banks and heavy industry, one found 605 English directors and 77 French ones. Even in the level of "employees" in industries the English representation outnumbered the French one" (Dofny and Rioux, 1964, 314–5).

[3] It is not surprising that a large proportion of French Canadian engineers in 1965 came from the working class. "Les ingénieurs canadiens-français sont le produit de groupes sociaux moins bien représentés dans la classe supérieure que dans la class inférieure; 36% d'entre eux sont fils d'ouvriers, taux exceptionnellement élevé dans les sociétés avancées, contre seulement 17% chez les ingénieurs canadiens-anglais" (Dofny 1970, 42).

References

Armstrong, D.E. (1970) *Education and Economic Achievement*, Ottawa: Documents of the Royal Commission on Bilingualism and Biculturalism.

ASOPE (1981) *Les jeunes et la réforme scolaire*. Montréal, Québec: Cahiers d'ASOPE, no. XIII.

Association d'Éducation du Quebec (1960–61) *L'étude sur la persévérance scolaire*.

Audet, L.-P. (1969) *Bilan de la réforme scolaire au Québec* (1959–1969), Montréal, Presses de l'Université de Montréal.

———— (1971) *Histoire de l'enseignement au Québec*, Montréal, Holt Rinehart et Winston Ltée.

Audet, L.-P. et A. Gauthier (1967) *Le système scolaire du Québec*, Montréal, Beauchemin.

Beland, P. (1978) "L'école privée et la démocratisation: sélection et processus", in ASOPE, *Les jeunes et la réforme scolaire*, Montréal, Québec, Cahiers d'ASOPE, XIII, 1981.

Bélanger, P.W. (1970) "L'école polyvalente: ses incidences sociales", in *Ecole et Société au Québec*, Pierre W. Bélanger, Guy Rocher (eds), Hurtubise HMH, Montréal, 361–389.

Bélanger, P.W., Roberge, P. (1980) L'avant et l'après des réformes: l'évolution de la perception du destin scolaire au Canada central, 1965–1972, in *Revue d'études canadiennes*, vol. 15, 3, 1980. Also in ASOPE, *Les jeunes et la réforme scolaire*, Cahiers d'ASOPE, Vol. XIII, Québec, Montréal, 1981, pp. 281–316.

Bélanger, P.W., Guy Rocher et Alii (1979) *Le projet ASOPE: son orientation, sa portée sociale et sa méthodologie*, Montréal, Québec, Cahiers d'ASOPE, Vol. VII.

Ben-David, Joseph (1971) *The Scientist's Role in Society*, Englewood Cliffs, N.J., Prentice-Hall.

Boudon, R. (1977) *Effets pervers et ordre social*, Paris, PUF.

———— (1973) *L'inégalité des chances*, Paris, Armand Collin.

Brazeau, Jacques (1963) "Quebec's Emerging Middle Class" in Marcel Rioux and Yves Martin, *French Canadian Society*, Toronto, McClelland and Stewart, 319–327.

Breton, R. et J.C. McDonald (1967) *Projets d'avenir des étudiants canadiens. Sommaire des données fondamentales*, Ottawa, Ministère de la Main-d'oeuvre et de l'Immigration.

Brunelle, Dorval (1978) "La structure occupationnelle de la main-d'oeuvre québécoise 1951–1971", in *Sociologie et Sociétés*, VII, 2, 67–88.

Bureau federal de la statistique (1961) *Illustration graphique de l'enseignement au Canada*, Ottawa, Cat 81–515F.

Cloutier, Edouard (1979) Les conceptions américaines, canadiennes anglaises et canadiennes françaises de l'idée d'égalité, in Cloutier E., Latouche, D. (eds), *Le système politique québécois*, Montréal, HMH.

Collins, Randall (1975) *Conflict Sociology: Toward an Explanatory Science*, New York, Academic Press.

———— (1977) "Some Comparative Principles of Educational Stratification", *Harvard Educational Review*, 47; 1–27.

———— (1979) *The Credential Society, An Historical Sociology of Educational Stratification*, New York, Academic Press.

Comité catholique du conseil de l'instruction publique (1962) *Mémoire à la commission royale d'enquête sur l'enseignement*, Québec.

Commission d'étude sur les universités (1979) *Les étudiants à l'université*, Québec, Gouvernement du Québec.

CREPUQ (1984) *Mémoire à la commission parlementaire de l'éducation et de la main-d'oeuvre de l'Assemblée nationale*, Québec, 10 octobre 1984.

Croteau, Georges (1970) *Les Frères éducateurs au service de la promotion des étudiants dans l'enseignement public au Québec (1920–1969)* Thèse de doctorat, Université d'Ottawa, 1971, 250 p.

Dandurand, Pierre et Alii (1979) *Conditions de vie de la population universitaire québécoise*, Montréal, Université de Montréal, Département de sociologie.

Dofny, J. (1970) *Les ingénieurs canadiens-français et canadiens-anglais à Montréal*, Ottawa, Document de la commission d'enquête sur le bilinguisme et le biculturalisme, #6.

Dofny, Jacques et Marcel Rioux (1964) "Social class in French Canada" in Rioux M. and Y. Martin, *French Canadian Society*, Toronto, McClelland and Stewart, 307–318.

Dominion Bureau of Statistics (1960) *Student Progress through the Schools by Grade*, cat. 81–513.

———— (1961) *The Organization of Education at the Secondary Level*, Ottawa, Cat. 81–514.

Faucher, A. (1970) *Histoire économique et unité canadienne*, Montréal, Fides.

Galarneau, C. (1978) *Les collèges classiques au Canada français*, Montréal, Fides.

Gouvernement du Québec (1963) *Rapport de la Commission Royale d'enquête sur l'enseignement dans la province de Québec*, Vol. II, Les structures pédagogiques du système scolaire, Québec, Province de Québec.

Guindon, Hubert (1960) "The Social Evolution of Quebec Reconsidered" in Marcel Rioux and Yves Martin, *French Canadian Society*, Toronto, McClelland and Stewart Ltd, 137–161.

Hétu, Chantale (1980) *Analyse de la réforme sco-laire à partir d'une comparaison des secteurs public et privé niveau secondaire*, Québec, Montréal, Cahiers d'ASOPE, XII.

Labarrère-Paule, André (1963) *Les laïques et la presse pédagogique au Canada français*, PUL.

Laforce, Louise (1979) *Les aspirations scolaires au Québec et en Ontario: des observations des enquêtes ASOPE et SOSA*, Montréal, Québec, Cahiers d'ASOPE, Vol. VI.

Levesque, M. et L. Sylvain (1982) *Après l'école secondaire: étudier ou travailler, choisit-on vraiment?* Québec, Conseil supérieur de l'éducation.

Linteau, P.A. et Alii (1979) *Histoire du Québec contemporain: de la Confédération à la crise*, Montréal, Boréal Express.

Magnusen, R. (1980) *A History of Quebec Education: 1640 to Parti Québécois*, Montréal, Harvest House.

Massot, Alain (1979) *Cheminements scolaires dans l'école québécoise après la réforme*, Montréal, Québec, Cahiers d'ASOPE, V.

Milner, Henry (1984) *La réforme scolaire au Québec*, Montréal, Québec/Amérique.

Ministère de l'éducation du Québec (1980–81) *Education au Québec*, Québec.

Pichette, Claude (1984) *L'UQUAM et le monde des affaires*, Allocution du recteur de l'UQUAM à la chambre de commerce de Montréal, le 6 novembre 1984.

Rapport Tremblay (1962) *Rapport du comité d'étude sur l'enseignement technique et professionnel*, Québec, Tome II.

Report of the Study Committee on Technical and Vocational Education (1962) Québec, Abridged Version.

Rioux, M., Martin, Y. (1964) *French Canadian Society*, Toronto, McClelland and Stewart.

Roberge, Pierre (1979) *Le nombril vert et les oreilles molles*, Cahiers d'ASOPE, Vol. IV. Québec, Montréal.

———— (1979) *Les Nouveaux*, Québec, Université Laval, projet ASOPE.

Rocher, Guy (1963) "La sociologie de l'éducation dans l'oeuvre de Léon Gérin", in P.W. Bélanger et G. Rocher, (éds), *Ecole et Société au Québec*, (33–50), Montréal, HMH.

Roy, J.L. (1976) *La marche des Québécois, Le temps des ruptures (1945–1960)*, Montréal, Léméac.

Simmons, J. (ed) (1983) *Better Schools*, Praeger.

Sylvain, L. (1982) *Les cheminements des jeunes québécois en milieux scolaires francophone et anglophone*, Notes et documents # 14, Conseil de la langue française, Québec.

Sylvain, L., Laforce, L., Trottier, C. avec Massot, A. et Georgeault, P. (1985) *Les cheminements scolaires des francophones, des anglophones et des allophones du Québec au cours des années soixante-dix*, Québec, LABRAPS et Conseil de la langue française (A paraître).

Tremblay, A. (1954) *Les Collèges et les écoles publiques: conflit ou coordination*, Québec, PUL.

———— (1955) *Contribution de l'étude des problèmes et des besoins de l'enseignement au Québec*, Annexe 4 au Rapport de la Commis-sion Royale d'enquête sur les problèmes constitutionnels, Québec.

———— (1969) Rapport de la Société canadienne d'éducation comparée et internationale, *Discours de la réforme scolaire au Québec, Un bilan et un avenir*.

———— (1975) "La démocratisation scolaire", in *Le Rapport Parent, 10 ans après*, (27–58), Montréal, Bellarmin.

Trottier, Claude (1984) "Le processus de sélection dans le système d'enseignement secondaire du Québec: Evolution et éléments d'interprétation", in *L'Orientation Professionnelle*, 19, 4, 32–66.

Vinette, R. (1975) "Les structures pédagogiques", in *Le Rapport Parent, 10 ans après*, (59–74), Montréal, Bellarmin.

Zsigmond, Z.E., Wenass, C.J. (1970) *Enrollment in Educational Institutions*, by *Province: 1951–52 to 1980–81*, Ottawa, Economic Council of Canada.

54 Changing Patterns of Educational Inequality in Canada

Neil Guppy   Paulina Mikicich   Ravi Pendakur

NEIL GUPPY, an Associate Professor of Sociology at the University of British Columbia, Vancouver, has just co-edited a book, *Uncommon Property* (1987) with M. Patricia Marchak and John McMullan on the British Columbia fishing industry. In addition he has published several recent articles on social inequality, education and politics. His other publications include "Dissensus or consensus: A cross-national comparison of occupational prestige scales" (1984); "Access to higher education in Canada" (1984); "Property rights and changing class formations in the social organization of the B.C. commercial fishing industry" (1986); and, with others, "Representing Canadians: Changes in the economic backgrounds of federal politicians" (1987).

PAULINA MIKICICH and RAVI PENDAKUR were Sociology students when they co-authored this article with Professor Guppy. They do not work in the field of Sociology now.

... The purpose of this paper is to conduct a systematic analysis of the historical changes in Canadian educational inequalities. Using a national survey, we determine the extent to which students from differing social origins have unequal probabilities of school success. More importantly, we consider the ways in which this relationship has changed in Canada since early in this century. Our interest centres, then, on the three-way interaction between origin, cohort, and schooling—does the relationship between social origin and educational attainment vary systematically for different cohorts?

The Canadian literature contains two differing hypotheses with respect to this question. Some writers (Himelfarb and Richardson, 1982; Marchak, 1981; Forcese, 1980) maintain that educational inequalities have persisted so that the impact of social background on educational attainment has continued—a "constant effects" hypothesis. Others (Hunter, 1981; Harp, 1980; Harvey, 1977) suggest that across time the strength of the relationship between origin and attainment has weakened—a "diminishing effects" hypothesis.

DATA AND METHODS

In order to assess these two hypotheses, we chart the educational attainments of Canadians from different social origins grouped into *birth* cohorts spanning a forty-year period (1913–1952).

The data for the analyses are drawn from the 1973 Canadian Mobility Study conducted by Boyd et al. (1977). The study focussed on males and females over the age of seventeen who were not full-time students (a constraint which we discuss below). The final sample consisted of 44,868 respondents.[1] We restrict our attention to a subset of this larger sample by focusing on birth cohorts composed of respondents between the ages of twenty and sixty[2] and eliminating anyone receiving part of their education outside of Canada.

We employ the following strategy to operationalize our variables. Our first measure of social origin is based on father's occupation (when the respondent was sixteen), which we have collapsed into four categories: farmers, blue collar, white collar and professional/managerial (prof/man) workers.[3] Parental education, our second indicator of social origin, is a three-valued measure based on whether neither parent, one parent, or both parents completed high school. We assess historical trends by examining the educational attainments of people from four birth cohorts: 1913–22, 1923–32, 1933–42 and 1943–52....

DATA ANALYSIS

... Table 1 presents findings on the percentage of respondents completing high school by social background and birth cohort. As shown in this table, high school completion rates have risen across the four cohorts from 37.1 percent to 67.5 percent. Furthermore, high school completion rates have increased for each socioeconomic category.

Completion rates have remained the highest for the prof/man strata, increasing from 71.6 percent to 84.9 percent. For those from farming backgrounds the rates have changed from 24.0 percent in the first cohort to 58.8 percent in the last cohort; the largest percentage increase over time for any occupational category....

It could be argued that our measure of social origin is inadequate. For this reason parental education is used as an alternative gauge to assess the influence of social origin upon high school completion. For the three categories of parental education, high school completion, in all but one case, increases over the four cohorts. As anticipated, the likelihood of a respondent completing secondary school is higher when both parents are also high school graduates....

Egalitarian influences appear to have increased for socioeconomic disparities between high school completion rates. However, we need to assess whether this pattern holds for higher levels of schooling....

Table 2 shows the percentages of respondents with some university experience by origin and cohort. On the whole, the

Table 1
PERCENTAGE OF RESPONDENTS WHO HAVE COMPLETED HIGH SCHOOL BY FATHER'S OCCUPATION AND BIRTH COHORT

Father's Occupation	Birth cohort				
	1913–22	1923–32	1933–42	1943–52	Row totals
Professional managerial	71.6 (385)	70.6 (445)	79.8 (615)	84.9 (1,230)	79.0 (2,675)
White collar	57.9 (256)	61.3 (294)	64.9 (412)	73.4 (811)	66.6 (1,773)
Blue collar	35.4 (746)	37.8 (990)	47.8 (1,390)	63.2 (3,003)	49.5 (6,129)
Farm	24.0 (442)	27.5 (465)	41.7 (556)	58.8 (772)	36.2 (2,235)
Column totals	37.1 (1,829)	40.5 (2,194)	52.6 (2,973)	67.5 (5,816)	(12,813)

Table 2

PERCENTAGE OF RESPONDENTS WITH SOME UNIVERSITY EXPERIENCE BY SOCIAL ORIGIN (FATHER'S OCCUPATION) AND BIRTH COHORT

| | Birth cohort | | | | |
Father's Class	1913–22	1923–32	1933–42	1943–52	Row totals
Professional managerial	25.5 (137)	27.3 (172)	38.1 (294)	35.1 (508)	32.8 (1,112)
White collar	12.0 (53)	16.9 (81)	18.6 (118)	19.1 (211)	17.4 (463)
Blue collar	7.3 (154)	6.3 (166)	11.6 (337)	12.1 (574)	9.9 (1,231)
Farm	5.8 (106)	6.6 (111)	9.7 (129)	12.0 (157)	8.1 (502)
Column totals	9.1 (450)	9.8 (530)	15.4 (878)	16.8 (1,450)	(3,308)

percentage of respondents reporting some university attendance steadily increases over the four cohorts. It is nevertheless important to note that the disparities are far stronger at this level of education than was the case for high school completion.... In short, socio-economic disparities are greater at the university level, and show only a modest reduction over time.[4]

We have reason to believe, in fact, that the decline shown in Table 2 exaggerates the decrease. Because our sample includes only those respondents who have completed their education, the 1943–52 birth cohort under-represents the actual number of university-educated respondents. While it is probable that some potential respondents from farm backgrounds were still at university at the time of the survey (1973), it is likely that many more possible respondents from prof/man backgrounds were attending higher levels of education, and, therefore, were excluded from the sample. One would have expected a higher percentage of prof/man respondents reporting some university experience, and, as a result, a more modest reduction between the farm and prof/man

categories. We present data below which suggest that this interpretation is probably correct.

In contrast to employing differing levels of educational experience, Table 3 presents results using completed years of education as the dependent variable. Furthermore, in order to provide a finer breakdown of results, the birth cohort variable has been divided into eight rather than four intervals.

This table shows that for all strata, average years of education have increased over the 1913 to 1947 period. In addition, disparities continue to exist across the cohorts. Up until 1937 there appears to have been a slight increase in the difference between the mean years of schooling for the prof/man and farm categories (see the bottom row of Table 3). This contrasts with the results for the last three cohorts where this difference is declining. Consider, that for the other seven cohorts the figure for average years of education increases for the prof/man category (as expected), yet drops for the last cohort. This is probably due to the sampling under-representation mentioned above.

If we use the mean number of years of

schooling for the first seven cohorts to predict the level for the eighth cohort, a value of 14.81 years results for the prof/man category (as opposed to 13.60 years, as reported in Table 3). Using the same strategy to predict the average years of schooling completed for respondents in the farm category generates a figure of 11.75, suggesting that the actual completion rate for those with farm backgrounds (11.98 in Table 3) is reasonably accurate. The difference in years of schooling for the prof/man-farm comparison, based on the predicted figures, is likely to be in the neighbourhood of 2.5 years. We take this to mean that the reduction found in Table 3 may be exaggerated for the last cohort, *but* there is nevertheless a decline in socioeconomic disparities for years of schooling completed. . . .

DISCUSSION AND CONCLUSIONS

Our results indicate that the relationship between social origin and educational attainment has weakened over time. We hasten to stress that social origin continues to exert a strong influence on levels of schooling, although the impact has declined through this century. However, even here we must be cautious because, while origin plays a decreasingly important role in high school completion, this decline is far less apparent with respect to post-secondary education. When we measure educational achievement as the probability of attaining some university experience, we find the effect of social origin has, at best, diminished only moderately over time (see Guppy, 1983; cf. Goyder, 1980). . . .

Two final questions must be raised. First, is the gradual reduction, but not elimination, of educational inequality a trend or merely an historical anomaly soon to disappear? Second, while the influence of origin on years of schooling may have waned in recent years, is it also the case that the impact of social background on the acquisition of academic credentials has diminished?

Table 3

AVERAGE YEARS OF SCHOOLING COMPLETED BY SOCIAL ORIGIN (FATHER'S OCCUPATION) AND BIRTH COHORT (FIVE-YEAR INTERVALS)

Father's Class	Birth cohorts								Row totals
	1913–17	1918–22	1923–27	1928–32	1933–37	1938–42	1943–47	1948–52	
Professional managerial	12.17 (255)	12.31 (262)	12.31 (291)	13.22 (326)	13.86 (316)	13.98 (447)	14.37 (620)	13.60 (790)	13.46 (3,307)
White collar	11.42 (202)	11.29 (208)	11.99 (220)	11.94 (239)	11.70 (248)	12.61 (290)	12.84 (401)	12.86 (582)	12.30 (2,596)
Blue collar	9.52 (933)	9.78 (986)	9.96 (1,115)	10.24 (1,336)	10.70 (1,261)	11.17 (1,522)	12.15 (2,122)	12.05 (2,494)	11.02 (11,769)
Farm	8.73 (819)	8.85 (824)	8.90 (826)	9.62 (747)	10.15 (621)	10.83 (645)	11.61 (639)	11.98 (626)	9.95 (5,746)
Column totals	9.71 (2,209)	9.87 (2,280)	10.07 (2,465)	10.59 (2,655)	11.08 (2,471)	11.69 (2,961)	12.51 (3,904)	12.42 (4,471)	11.24 (23,417)
Mean difference (Prof./man - farm)	3.44	3.46	3.41	3.60	3.71	3.15	2.76	1.62	

*The top figure is the average number of years of schooling and the bottom figure is the number of people whose years of schooling were averaged.

With respect to the first question, our results do not suggest a gradual, uniform reduction in educational inequalities. In fact, it appears that no reduction whatsoever occurs in the socioeconomic differences in years of schooling attained until the cohort of 1938–42 is considered; a cohort that entered high school after World War II. The reduction in inequality *may* thus be interpreted as a consequence of educational reforms introduced in the 1950s and 1960s. Many of these reforms, such as student aid and open learning environments (for the importance of the latter see Richer, 1974) were beneficial to working-class children. However, many of the reforms are now being withdrawn or sharply curtailed as governments react to the social and economic climate of the early 1980s. Should this process continue, the long term result of such retrenchment could be a return to the levels of educational inequality witnessed earlier in this century—a process which may enhance the importance of cultural capital as a vehicle of social reproduction (Bourdieu, 1977).

With respect to the question of academic credentials, we must stress that our work suggests that inequalities have been reduced in terms of both general level of schooling attained and years of schooling completed. We do not, however, demonstrate that the importance of social background on the acquisition of scholastic credentials has diminished. For example, it is quite conceivable that although individuals from farm or blue-collar backgrounds are attaining ever higher levels of education, they may still be disproportionately underrepresented in selected educational streams which yield more valuable sets of credentials (e.g., professional schools, graduate schools, etc.). Furthermore, if general college and university degrees become increasingly ineffective tickets for occupational and income attainment (see Goyder, 1980), then these professional or graduate degrees will likely prove to be of increasing importance as channels of intergenerational mobility for those from less privileged backgrounds. . . .

Notes

[1] The sample is weighted to correct for (1) the initial sampling stratification and (2) any possible bias due to differential response rates.

[2] This coding decision was based on our wish to parallel the work of Halsey, Heath, and Ridge (1980) for the United Kingdom. The forty-year time span allows us to create cohorts over ten-year intervals and, by using sixty years of age as a cutoff point, we decrease potential recall problems among older respondents. The use of alternative cohort specifications does not create any substantial changes in our results.

[3] Various occupational codings based on McRoberts and Selbee (1981) and Pineo, Porter, and McRoberts (1977) were tried in our preliminary analyses and the results were consistent across other categorization schemes.

[4] This difference in the effects of origin on schooling, at different levels of education, is important because as the general level of education for the entire population rises, we would expect disparities at the lower levels to diminish. From this perspective it is the disparities at higher levels of schooling which are more crucial.

References

Boudon, R. (1974) *Education, Opportunity and Social Inequality*. New York: John Wiley.

Bourdieu, P. (1977) "Cultural reproduction and social reproduction." In *Power and Ideology in Education,* edited by J.H. Karabel and A.H. Halsey, pp. 487–511. New York: Oxford University Press.

Boyd, M. (1982) "Sex differences in the Canadian occupational attainment process." *Canadian Review of Sociology and Anthropology* 19(1):1–28.

Boyd, M., J. Goyder, F. Jones, H. McRoberts, P. Pineo, and J. Porter (1977) "The Canadian National Mobility Study." *Canadian Studies in Population* 4:94–96.

Breton, R. (1970) "Academic stratification in secondary schools and educational plans of students." *Canadian Review of Sociology and Anthropology* 7(1):17–34.

Clifton, R. (1982) "Ethnic differences in the academic achievement process in Canada." *Social Science Research* 11:67–87.

Cuneo, C. and J. Curtis (1975) "Social ascription in the educational and occupational status attainment of urban Canadians." *Canadian Review of Sociology and Anthropology* 12(1):6–24.

Forcese, D. (1980) *Canadian Class Structure*. Toronto: McGraw-Hill Ryerson.

Goyder, J. (1980) "Trends in the socioeconomic achievement of the university educated: a status attainment model interpretation." *Canadian Journal of Higher Education* 10(2):21–38.

Guppy, N. (1983) "Social change and access to higher education in Canada." Unpublished paper, Vancouver: University of British Columbia.

Halsey, A., A. Heath, and J. Ridge (1980) *Origins and Destinations: Family, Class and Education in Modern Britain*. Oxford: Clarendon Press.

Harp, J. (1980) "Social inequalities and the transmission of knowledge: the case against the schools." In *Structured Inequality in Canada*, edited by J. Harp and J. Hofley, pp. 219–246. Toronto: Prentice-Hall.

Harvey, E. (1977) "Accessibility to post-secondary education." *University Affairs* October: 10–11.

Himelfarb, A. and J. Richardson (1982) *Sociology for Canadians: Images of Society*. Toronto: McGraw-Hill Ryerson.

Hunter, A. (1981) *Class Tells: On Social Inequality in Canada*. Toronto: Butterworths.

McRoberts, H. and K. Selbee (1981) "Trends in occupational mobility in Canada and the United States: a comparison." *American Sociological Review* 46(4): 406–421.

Marchak, P. (1981) *Ideological Perspectives on Canada*. Second edition. Toronto: McGraw-Hill Ryerson.

Pineo, P., J. Porter, and H. McRoberts (1977) "The 1971 Census and the socioeconomic classification of occupations." *Canadian Review of Sociology and Anthropology* 14(1):91–102.

Porter, J., M. Porter, and B. Blishen (1982) *Stations and Callings: Making it Through the Ontario Schools*. Toronto: Methuen.

Richer, S. (1974) "Middle class bias of schools—fact or fancy?" *Sociology of Education* 47(4):523–534.

Robb, L. and B. Spencer (1976) "Education: enrollment and attainment." In *Opportunity for Choice*, edited by G. Cook, pp. 53–92. Ottawa: Statistics Canada.

Turrittin, A., P. Anisef, and N. MacKinnon (1983) "Gender differences in educational achievement: a study of social inequality." *Canadian Journal of Sociology* 8(4):395–419.

55 Changing Conceptions of Education and Social Mobility

C. James Richardson

C. JAMES RICHARDSON, Professor of Sociology, University of New Brunswick in Fredericton, is currently specializing in applied research in the areas of family law and divorce, and the criminal justice system. He is the author of *Contemporary Social Mobility* (1977) and, with A. Himelfarb, co-author of *People, Power and Process* (1979) and *Sociology for Canadians* (1982). He has recently completed a large study of divorce mediation and its impact on the post-divorce family. A former President of the Canadian Sociology and Anthropology Association, Professor Richardson is, at present, an Associate editor for the *Canadian Review of Sociology and Anthropology*.

INTRODUCTION

Recent approaches in the sociology of education make it apparent that we are at some sort of watershed or crisis point in our thinking about the role of education in society. We are, as Collins (1974) concludes, moving away from a rather benign and uncritical view of education to a growing awareness that the very content and structure of educational systems derives from the forces of capitalistic—perhaps simply industrial—society. Rather than education being an independent factor able to shape and alter the stratification system, it appears to be the other way round; from a variety of quarters education is increasingly debunked as an institution whose main function is to reproduce and legitimize relationships of inequality from generation to generation. Not only does it emerge that educational reform has been difficult to bring about (Katz, 1970; Pomfre, 1976), but it also becomes problematic whether most reforms, especially those touching upon educational expansion, make much difference or are, from certain perspectives, even very desirable.

While Canada has as yet to reach the level of educational saturation which Illich (1971) implies is the case for the United States, it has, nevertheless, experienced a rapid and massive growth and transformation of post-secondary education in the last decade. Since our views about education have tended also to be American, this pessimistic verdict on education, coming as it does largely from the United States, is of immediate relevance to Canadian theory and policy on education. The aim of this paper, then, is to pull together some recent and significant developments in the study of the relationship of educational systems to stratification systems and to point out their implications for theory, research and policy in the Canadian context. Although I draw largely upon existing published material and present no new data, the interpretation of this material and my approach to the sociology of education are coloured by my own research on social mobility and education[1]....

ELITIST AND EGALITARIAN IDEOLOGIES

In bringing about equality of educational opportunity, it is generally assumed that an egalitarian system of higher education is preferable to an elitist system. The main argument seems to be that an elitist system inhibits entry into higher education by individuals of lower socioeconomic background (Harvey and Charner, 1975). However, while elitist attitudes about education may affect *educational* opportunities, it does not necessarily follow that equality of opportunity—social mobility—will also be seriously affected by a shift from an elitist to an egalitarian system. This is likely to be true only if educational systems constitute the only mobility routes in society and if both the amount of equality and equality of opportunity can in fact be shown to be greater in egalitarian societies than in elitist societies. As will be shown later in this paper, neither of these assumptions appears to be the case in industrial societies. Rather, both value systems are essentially ideologies of selection and allocation and act as different kinds of justifications for class and status inequality.

Under an elitist ideology the pool of talent is defined as limited and largely determined by hereditary factors. Hence, it is assumed that the majority of the population could not possibly benefit from education above a given minimum and that selection should occur at a relatively early age in order to take the most advantage of the talent available. As found in Britain, the elitist ideology upholds the view that there should be a number of educational routes which separate those who appear bound for elite status from those who appear bound for lower-level positions (Hopper, 1971a:97).[2] There is, therefore, a fairly explicit recognition that not everyone can be socially mobile. As a result, welfare is likely to be justified primarily in terms of its improving the social and economic well-being of those who are defined as uneducable and

who are not expected to alter substantially their class position or that of their children.

In contrast, the egalitarian ideology, when taken to its extreme (as it sometimes is in the United States) emerges as what Jensen (1960) refers to disparagingly as the "average-children concept": children, aside from those with neurological defects, are very much alike and differences are a result of social deprivation rather than inherent characteristics. The pool of talent, in principle, constitutes the whole of the society and is limited not by heredity but by the persistence of class factors which work to the detriment of some and to the advantage of others. It is assumed that everyone can benefit from education regardless of their future ability to contribute to social and economic productivity. Insofar as it is concerned with elite formation, the egalitarian ideology upholds the view that selection should occur relatively late and that, as much as possible, elite and non-elite should experience the same kind of education.[3] Finally, welfare, community action, and "Headstart" programmes are justified mainly in terms of their contribution toward improving the mobility potential of disadvantaged groups—in the lexicon of the 1960s, the task was to create a "platform" for upward mobility. Thus, to a large extent equality has meant equality of opportunity, and it is implicitly, sometimes explicitly, assumed that everyone can be upwardly mobile.[4]

In sum, in an egalitarian system, selection comes at the end of the contest rather than as a result of sponsorship of those viewed as most able to comprise a meritocracy in the future.[5] Whereas in an elitist system ambition is not legitimate until one has been sponsored and encouraged by the educational system, selection in an egalitarian system ideally should not occur until there has been sufficient evidence of ambition. In the former, the deserving are those with talent; in the latter they are those who have demonstrated adequate motivation.

Despite these differences, the two ideologies have in common that they focus educational research mainly on inputs to the system. Thus, the sociology of education has been almost exclusively concerned with class factors impeding equality of access to higher education (see Davies, 1970). Important though the study of these factors is to education and stratification theory, it is only part of the story. Theory generated within these ideological contexts fails to raise certain key questions about educational systems and is incapable of dealing adequately with certain facts or "anomalies" about social stratification in industrial societies.

It is a central contention of this paper that only when we pose the more general question of what all this education is in aid of— when we redirect our attention from the inputs of education to the outputs of education—we can make theoretical sense of what has been transpiring over the past few decades with respect to education. When this shift occurs, it emerges that a conflict model as well as a full-fledged functional model of education are both capable of generating new hypotheses and accounting for persistent anomalies. The key in either approach is that educational systems come to be viewed not as independent entities but rather as institutions embedded in, and subservient to, larger systems of social inequality.

Education and social mobility

First, what should have been obvious, that not everyone can be upwardly mobile, apparently was not. Yet, only a brief encounter with the literature on social mobility reveals that even under the assumption of a full equality of opportunity model only a minority can expect to move upwards and that this will be at the cost of an almost equivalent amount of downward mobility.[6] At the same time, it should be noted that while no society has ever reached full equality of opportunity, evidence from a variety of mobility studies

(Jackson and Crockett, 1964; Blau and Duncan, 1967; Broom and Jones, 1969; and Richardson, 1977) indicated that there is considerably more social mobility than can be accounted for by changes in the occupational structure. Furthermore, unless we are prepared to make the assumption that most children of high status backgrounds are essentially incompetent to inherit positions similar to their parents', it is not clear just how much more mobility could be created than already exists in industrial societies.[7] In this respect, recurring dissatisfaction with the progress being made toward equality of opportunity is likely to be more pronounced among sociologists who focus exclusively on educational achievement rather than on social mobility *per se*. These sociologists are, in other words, likely to exaggerate the importance of education in the mobility process.

For the same reasons, what is also likely to be less apparent from a sociology of education perspective is that rates of social mobility have not changed much over this century despite a massive expansion of educational systems (Glass, 1954; Jackson and Crockett, 1964; Blau and Duncan, 1967; and Boudon, 1975). Nor, as it happens, is there very much difference between societies that can be attributed directly to education (Fox and Miller, 1965). An obvious illustration is that despite its having nearly four times as many people in higher education, the United States has a mobility rate roughly comparable to that of Britain. And, although we do not as yet have the relevant mobility data, the same conclusion is likely to be true for Canada as well: the rate of upward and downward mobility will be very close to that of the other industrial societies no matter what has happened to higher education in Canada.

In part, these somewhat surprising findings can be accounted for by the fact that there is, a best, a very loose fit between educational achievements and actual social mobility as the latter concept is generally understood. When attention is directed specifically to mobility, it emerges that a good deal, perhaps as much as half, of the mobility in industrial societies takes place independently of formal education. That is, nearly as many people are upwardly mobile through alternative educational routes (cf. Lee, 1968; Hordley and Lee, 1970), through on-the-job promotion or through entrepreneurship, as through formal educational routes. There is a high degree of consensus that these intragenerational mobility routes are declining in favour of intergenerational mobility legitimated by the acquisition of formal educational qualifications (Goldthorpe, 1964; Halsey, 1971; and Westergaard, 1972). Yet, in the United States where this possible trend may be expected to have advanced furthest, Blau and Duncan (1967:196) find the correlation between educational and occupational mobility to be fairly low (r = .320), thus confirming Anderson's (1961) earlier skepticism about the significance of education in the mobility process.

Additional confirmation that the role of education may have been exaggerated in previous research can be found in the potentially revolutionary conclusions of the Coleman (1966) report and the later re-analysis of its findings by Jencks and his associates at Harvard (Jencks et al., 1972). The approach is firmly taken in terms of outputs; the key tool is path analysis. The latter allows us to see more clearly what was not so quantifiable in our earlier two- and three-fold tables: that while there are undoubtedly connections between family background and education and between education and occupational achievement, these are not nearly as strong as was previously supposed. The zero-order correlations show that there is a considerable amount of variance in the dependent variable which is unexplained. Whether we call this "luck" as does Jencks, residual factors as do Blau and Duncan, or simply unmeasured (perhaps unmeasurable) factors—"charm," "personality," "ruthlessness," "drive"—as did Sorokin (1927), the fact remains that it is far

from easy to engineer equality of results even if access is made nearly equal to all.[8]

This is not to suggest that educational opportunities have not increased in the last few decades. All the available evidence suggests that they have done so fairly dramatically. But in most societies, policies designed to benefit the lower classes have, in doing so, tended to benefit other classes even more (Westergaard and Little, 1964; Spady, 1967; and Marceau, 1974). Thus, as the belief spreads that career prospects and social position come to depend upon and be legitimized by educational qualifications rather than inheritance or experience acquired on the job, high status families begin to want more education for their children.[9] The result is a rather static situation in which everyone gets more education, both those at the bottom and also those at the top. In short, while there is perhaps greater equality of educational opportunity than in the past, there is no greater equality of opportunity and little or no reduction in the range of class inequality.[10]

The meritocratic or technical-functional side of Porter's analysis of modern education also does not bear up very well under empirical scrutiny. Rather than a necessary concomitant of industrialization, the more pessimistic conclusion is that education is, in main, counterproductive and wastes social resources. Collins (1971 and 1974) presents a convincing argument that educational expansion has proceeded much more rapidly than the technical or skill requirements of industrial society and that, as Berg (1970) had previously shown, education contributes little to individual productivity; vocational skills are learned primarily on the job, not in school. Working a similar vein, Gintis (1971 and 1972) argues that "profit-maximizing firms find it remunerative to hire more highly educated workers at a higher pay, *irrespective* of differences among individuals in cognitive abilities or attainments" (1972:86). He concludes that the skills necessary to job adequacy in a technological society either exist in such profusion or are so easily developed on the job that they are not a criterion for hiring. Similarly, other researchers have shown that while there is a modest correlation between education and occupational status and IW and occupational status ($r = 50$) (Blau and Duncan, 1967; Sewell et al., 1969), there is only a very loose relationship between IQ and job performance ($R = .21$) (cf. Jensen, 1969:15). Moreover, educational requirements for specific jobs vary depending on the time of year (Berg, 1970), the degree of organizational emphasis on normative control, and the size of the organization (Collins, 1974). Apparently, what employers seek in hiring educated workers is not technical skills or cognitive ability but the type of compliant personality produced through schooling (Gintis, 1972).[11]

Extension and change of education does not, therefore, appear to have created greater equality of opportunity or contributed to economic productivity in the manner suggested by the human-capital economists (Becker, 1964). What these changes have done is to cause education to become subject to a kind of inflation. As defined by Karabel (1972:525), "educational inflation is the process by which the educational system expands without narrowing relative differences between groups or changing the underlying structure of opportunities." It means that particular qualifications "buy" ever decreasing amounts of occupational status and income. Thus, in Canada recent evidence suggests that the occupational status conferred by a B.A. degree in 1964 can only be purchased in 1968 by acquiring a second degree (Harvey and Charner, 1975). As Illich (1971) argues, the only valuable skills in society become those which are the result of formal education. Credentials become, in effect, commodities to be bartered for a chance at upward mobility or a means of preserving an existing high-status position.

For the individual, then, it is true to say that education is the key to mobility; it pays

to stay in school.[12] The race for more credentials makes rational sense as a reasonable defence in the more general battle for status—what some have called a war of credentials. But, as in the vicious circle of wages and prices, what is individually rational may be seen as irrational when escalated to the collective level. It would, for example, be naive to assume that if the main legitimization for inequality moves from ascription to achievement, those previously in power will not bestir themselves to obtain the degrees necessary to keep their positions. Moreover, post-secondary education is not a single system but is made up of hierarchically ordered institutions offering degrees with different conversion rates in terms of occupational and social status. In other words, as low-status groups begin to attain access to certain degree institutions, they may find either that educational escalation is pushed one step further, as is suggested by the recent data for Ontario (Harvey and Charner, 1975; Marsden et al., 1975), or that the route to high-status positions is through institutions which are mainly reserved for the already privileged (Clement, 1974). Karabel (1972:525) concludes that the net effect of educational inflation is thus to vitiate the social impact of extending educational opportunity to a higher level.

Educational inflation also has consequences for the perception of social mobility and, in turn, how it is likely to be studied and evaluated. With respect to the first of these, while a relatively high rate of upward mobility is institutionalized and anticipated in industrial societies, it is also expected that this will be intergenerational movement through a formal education route. The considerable amount of mobility which proceeds via non-educational routes increasingly becomes defined as irregular mobility—illegitimate and largely invisible (cf. Turner, 1966; Hopper, 1971b). Thus, those who rise because of on-the-job promotion or entrepreneurship may find that their achievements do not constitute genuine upward mobility. To take one example: my research in Britain suggests that for equivalent amounts of occupational achievement, those possessing the "right" educational qualifications are more able to transform occupational mobility into social mobility, are more effective in transmitting the new status culture, and find easier acceptance in the middle class. In contrast, men who moved upward without benefit of education beyond the minimum tended to retain a working-class value system which, when passed on to their children, contributed to their eventual downward mobility (Richardson, 1977).[13]

Second, to the extent that researchers share this assumption that education provides the main or only mobility route in society, educational achievement rather than occupational achievement will receive research attention on the grounds that to study the former is effectively to study the latter. This more limited focus is likely to have important and misleading implications for stratification theory. Among these, it could be suggested that at the general policy level research findings on educational opportunities will lead to a possibly unwarranted degree of despair that equality of opportunity remains such a distant and unattainable goal. The degree of inequality of opportunity existing within the educational system is relatively easy to document and subject to trend analysis. Unless there is also an attempt to include the less visible mobility occurring within the occupational structure, the outcome is likely to be a plea for yet another and unproductive expansion of education.

THEORETICAL REFORMULATIONS

As indicated earlier, to make sense of education in industrial society and of the above anomalies requires that education be treated as a dependent, not an independent variable *vis-à-vis* the stratification system. For a wide range of questions, educational systems are more appropriately viewed as being shaped by the dominant patterns of class and status inequality and the ideologies which support and legitimize that inequality. Insofar as the functions of educational systems are of concern, recent approaches have for the most part abandoned traditional functionalism for theories which derive essentially from Marx or Weber.

One of the most influential advocates of the Weberian approach is Collins (1971 and 1974) who, in going beyond Karabel's analysis, views education primarily as a power resource, a weapon used by status groups to monopolize occupations and thereby control entry. For Collins, the basis of entry into an occupation is power; education is merely a strategic barrier used to control entry. The principal functions of education are to teach particular status cultures and to act as sorting and selecting mechanisms. Employers use educational requirements both "to select new members for elite positions who share the elite culture and, at a lower level of education, to hire lower- and middle-level employees who have acquired a general respect for these elite values and styles" (1971:1004–1005). The focus is, therefore, almost exclusively upon the stratification system rather than the educational system. . . .

A somewhat different analysis of educational systems comes from Hopper (1971a and 1971b), a British sociologist. . . . His emphasis is upon the role of education in what he calls the "total selection process," a functional problem confronting all societies no matter how simple (1971b:295). The exact structure and organization of particular systems will be determined both by the stratification profile of that society and by what he calls ideologies of implementation: norms and values about how selection and allocation should occur. Thus, Turner's (1960) contest and sponsorship norms are seen respectively as constituting egalitarian and elitist answers to these questions: How does selection occur? When are pupils initially selected? Who should be selected? Why should they be selected?

The full analysis and implications of Hopper's classifications of ideologies, stratification systems, and educational systems are complicated and cannot be dealt with adequately here. But it is important to note that, as in the work of Karabel and Collins, there is in this theory, first of all, the view that the manifest knowledge transmitted by schools may not be as important as the status training which goes with it (cf. Davies, 1970) and, secondly, that various types of educational institutions will have different functions with respect to status training—transmitting either an elite culture or a respect for it. Hopper's analysis is unique because of his extensive treatment of these various educational levels as a system of mobility and non-mobility routes which have different consequences for people located at different places in the status hierarchy. . . .

These two theories reflect Weber's contention that status situation can be raised to the same analytical level as class situation. Thus, status groups are viewed by both Collins and Hopper as active and independent, at times more likely than economic groups to precipitate "class" consciousness and to be generative of conflict. In both the focus is on the analysis of educational systems within *industrial* societies. Therefore, neither are directly concerned with explicating the relationship of education to capitalist economies—the political economy of education.[14]

Others, notably Illich (1971), take a more strictly Marxian perspective.[15] While the context remains the stratification system, the focus is more clearly directed at what, since Illich, has come to be known as the "hidden curriculum," the ideological functions served by education (see also Illich, 1972 and Snyder, 1970). As described by Gintis (1972:86), the manifest purpose of imparting cognitive skills reveals when unmasked "that social re-

lations of education produce and reinforce those values, attitudes and affective capacities which allow individuals to move smoothly into an alienated and class-stratified society." Similarly, Carnoy (1974:14) argues that the spread of education to colonial societies was carried out in the context of imperialism and colonialism; the result, he suggests, was that people were forced out of traditional hierarchy but were brought into a capitalist hierarchy and that, while this process has elements of *liberation*, it includes elements of *dependency* and *alienation*.

As with Dreeben's (1968) earlier analysis of the latent functions of schooling, the contention that schools do in fact teach a class culture is largely in the category of a "reasonable" assumption rather than an empirical fact. Thus, there is again the danger of exaggerating the significance of education in most people's lives (cf. Bereiter, 1972; David, 1975; and Richer, 1974). However, work in Britain by Bernstein and his associates and by Bourdieu and Marceau in France tends to reinforce and extend this largely American view of the role of education in reproducing relationships compatible with capitalist society (cf. Bernstein, 1971, 1972, 1973; Bourdieu, 1973; Marceau, 1974; and Young, 1971).

To summarize briefly, all of the recent theories have in common an implicit recognition that as long as societies remain stratified, educational systems will also be stratified and that unless there is radical reform in the wider society, most reforms within school systems are likely to be doomed at the outset.[16] As the work of Coleman, Jencks, and others taking part in the Harvard seminar (cf. Mosteller and Moynihan, 1972) makes apparent, the new sociology of education is with some few exceptions firmly embedded in a socialist, sometimes Marxian, ethic rather than a liberal ideology. Equality of opportunity, what Mathews (1973:215) depicts as "the equal right to compete freely for positions in which [it is possible] to exploit one's fellows," no longer is defined as the essence of a just society. The aim of social policy becomes "equality of result—by sharing and redistributive policies—rather than equality of opportunity" (Bell, 1972:47).

At the same time, it is not necessary and is perhaps undesirable that sociologists subscribe politically or theoretically to an egalitarian ethic in order to understand educational systems in terms of the wider system of social inequality in which they are lodged. The brief outline of the work of Collins and Hopper attests to this. Their work reveals that once we shift the approach of sociology of education from education as an independent to a dependent variable, both functional and conflict perspectives provide new insights into education. Generally, a far more fruitful research programme emerges when the assumptions of the technical functional model are relaxed, when education is viewed in terms of outputs rather than simply inputs, when educational systems are no longer treated as if they existed in a social, cultural, and economic vacuum, and when educational theory and research are more explicitly informed by stratification theory, be that Marxian or Weberian. . . .

Notes

[1] This research, reported in Richardson (1977), is British. My focus in this paper is, however, Canadian.

[2] It is particularly in this sense, for example, that the CAATs in Ontario can be understood as the outcome of an elitist, rather than an egalitarian, ideology: students streamed at an earlier point into a non-academic programme were to receive practical education to fit them for subordinate positions (see Garry, 1975).

[3] This is not to suggest that "tracking" (streaming) does not occur, but rather that it is not so explicitly made evident to students or parents. Also, since selection occurs late, there is a greater necessity to soften its impact here than in an elitist system. The most apparent methods are a combination of "cooling-out" procedures (Clark, 1960) and a less than open stratification of post-secondary institutions (Karabel, 1972).

[4] While this may seem like an exaggeration, consider that Lipset and Bendix (1959) devoted a good deal of their book to showing that the mobility ethic was in fact an ideology and not an empirical fact. It is also implicit in the more recent "news" that even with equality of opportunity there would not be equality of results (see Jencks et al., 1972). In short, most of the attention has been directed to the "contest," very little to the final selection.

[5] It is of interest that in coining the word, meritocracy, Young meant to satirize through exaggeration what he saw as trends in post-war British society. As the discussions by Bell (1972), Herrnstein (1971), and others suggest, American social science has taken the concept very seriously, either as a positive development or a regressive step, but in either case as seemingly inevitable (see Young, 1958).

[6] The amount of mobility will obviously differ depending on the number of status categories used in the analysis and in the relative size of the higher and lower categories. I am referring here to manual/non-manual dichotomy, the conventional measure of social mobility. For a fuller discussion of these issues, see Richardson (1977).

[7] In general, the correlation between fathers' status and sons' status appears to be very similar and equally low in Europe, America, and elsewhere. My data for the London region show a Cramer's $v = .208$ and for the Glass (1954) data $v = .240$. Jackson and Crockett (1964) found for their American data a $v = .246$. Using parametric statistics, Blau and Duncan (1967:403) report a zero-order correlation of $r = .40$, a value identical to that found in Europe by Svalastoga.

[8]Jencks et al. (1972) argues that there is nearly as much inequality between brothers raised in the same family as in the general population. Thus, inequality is recreated anew in each generation.

[9]For example, Clement (1974:174, 175, 241) shows that while the proportion of those in the corporate elite in Canada who inherited their position has actually risen in the past twenty-one years, they are far better educated than their fathers.

[10]Westergaard and Resler (1975) provide strong evidence that the gap between the rich and the poor in industrial society is widening, not narrowing. See also Jencks et al. (1972) for the United States and Johnson (1973) for Canada.

[11]This is elaborated extensively in chapter five of the recent study by Bowles and Gintis (1976). See also Kohn (1969).

[12]For example, my data for Britain suggests that education above the legally required minimum invariably leads to upward mobility for those with working-class origins or retention of parental status by those born in the middle class. However, many people were also successful in moving upward or avoiding downward mobility without education (Richardson, 1977). See also Carnoy (1974).

[13]I am referring here mainly to middle-mass social mobility. For a more general discussion of the thesis of a "tightening band" between education and occupation, see Halsey (1971).

[14]For a brief but useful summary of some differences between the Marxian and Weberian approaches to the sociology of education see Collins' (1976) review of *Schooling in Capitalist America*.

[15]However, see the critique by Gintis (1972) of Illich's concept of "de-schooling," reproduced in part in Bowles and Gintis (1976:256–262).

[16]There is clearly considerable disparity about what kinds of reforms are possible. For example, despite their harsh criticism of what has sometimes been called radical school reform (see Gross and Gross, 1969; Troost, 1973), Bowles and Gintis (1976) seem to be arguing for expansion of education on the grounds that while schooling is repressive it is potentially liberating and revolutionary. See also Carnoy (1974). Others, such as Jencks et al. (1972) argue for a "voucher system" which would allow those who lost out on the first round to try again. Collins (1976) on the other hand, favours Illich's drastic proposal for a "de-schooling" of society.

References

Allardt, E. (1968) "Theories about social stratification." In J.A. Jackson, *Social Stratification* Cambridge: Cambridge University Press.

Anderson, C.A. (1961) "A skeptical note on the relation of vertical mobility to education." *American Journal of Sociology* 66:560–570.

Becker, G.S. (1964) *Human Capital: A Theoretical and Empirical Analysis*: New York: National Bureau of Economic Research.

Bell, D. (1972) "On meritocracy and equality." *The Public Interest* 29(Fall):29–68.

Bereiter, Carl (1972) "Schools without education." *Harvard Educational Review* 42(3):390–413.

Berg, I. (1970) *Education and Jobs: The Great Training Robbery*. New York: Beacon Press.

Blau, P.M., and O.D. Duncan (1967) *The American Occupational Structure*. New York: John Wiley and Sons.

Boudon, R. (1974) *Education, Opportunity and Social Inequality*. New York: John Wiley and Sons.

Bourdieu, P. (1973) "Cultural reproduction and social reproduction." In R. Brown, ed., *Knowledge, Education and Cultural Change*. London: Tavistock Publications: 71–112.

Bowles, S., and H. Gintis (1976) *Schooling in Capitalist America*. New York: Basic Books

Broom, L. and F.L. Jones (1969) "Father and son

mobility: Australia in comparative perspective." *American Journal of Sociology* 74:33–42.

Carnoy, M. (1974) *Education as Cultural Imperialism*. New York: David McKay.

Clark, B.R. (1960) "The cooling-out function in higher education." *American Journal of Sociology* 65:569–576.

Clement, W. (1974) *The Canadian Corporate Elite*. Toronto: McClelland and Stewart.

Coleman, J.S. (1966) *Equality of Educational Opportunity*. Washington: U.S. Government Printing Office.

Collins, R.H. (1971) "Functional and conflict theories of educational stratification." *American Sociological Review* 36(6):1002–1019.

———— (1974) "Where are educational requirements for employment highest?" *Sociology of Education* 47(4):419–442.

———— (1975) *Conflict Sociology: Toward an Explanatory Science*. New York: Academic Press.

———— (1976) "Review of *Schooling in Capitalist America.*" *Harvard Educational Review* 46(2):246–251.

Davies, I. (1970) "The management of knowledge." In M.F.D. Young, ed., *Knowledge and Control*. London: Heinemann.

Davis, A.K. (1971) "Canadian society as hinterland versus metropolis." In R.J. Ossenberg. *Canadian Society: Pluralism, Change and Conflict*. Toronto: Prentice-Hall of Canada.

Davis, J. (1975) "Learning the norm of universalism: the effect of school attendance." In R.M. Pike and E. Zureik, eds., *Socialization and Values in Canadian Society*. Volume II, Toronto: McClelland Stewart: 84–98.

Denis, A.B. (1975) "CEGEP students: varieties in socialization experience." In R.M. Pike and E. Zureik, eds., *Socialization and Values in Canadian Society*. Toronto: McClelland and Stewart.

Dreeben, R.A. (1968) *What is Learned in School*. Reading, Mass.: Addison-Wesley.

Fein, L.J. (1971) *The Ecology of the Public Schools*. New York: Pegasus.

Fox, T., and S.M. Miller (1965) "Economic, political and social determinants of mobility." *Acta Sociologica* 9:76–93.

Garry, C. (1975) *Administrative and Curriculum Change in a Canadian Community College*. Canadian Sociology and Anthropology Association Monograph Series.

Gintis, H. (1971) "Education and the characteristics of worker productivity." *American Economic Review* 61:266–279.

———— (1972) "Toward a political economy of education: a radical critique of Illich's *Deschooling Society.*" *Harvard Education Review* 42:70–96.

Glass, D.V. (1954) *Social Mobility in Britain*. London: Routledge and Kegan Paul.

Goldthorpe, J.H. (1964) "Social stratification in industrial society." In R. Bendix and S.M. Lipset, eds., *Class, Status and Power*. New York: The Free Press, 1966.

Gross, R., and B. Gross (1969) *Radical School Reform*. New York: Simon and Schuster.

Halsey, A.H. (1971) "Theoretical advance and empirical challenge." In E. Hopper, ed., *Readings in the Theory of Educational Systems*. London: Hutchinson:262–281.

Harvey, E., and I. Charner (1975) "Social mobility and occupational attainments of university graduates." *Canadian Review of Sociology and Anthropology* 12(2):134–149.

Herrnstein, R. (1971) "IQ." *The Atlantic Monthly*, December.

Hopper, E. (1971a) "A typology for the classification of educational systems." In *Readings in the Theory of Educational Systems*. London: Hutchinson.

———— (1971b) "Educational systems and selected consequences of patterns of mobility and non-mobility in industrial societies: a theoretical discussion." In *Readings in the Theory of Educational Systems*. London: Hutchinson.

Hopper, E., and M. Osborn (1973) *Adult Students*. London: Frances Pinter Publishing.

Hopper, E., and A. Pearce (1973) "Relative deprivation, occupational situs and occupational status: the theoretical and empirical application of a neglected concept." In M. Warner, ed., *The Sociology of the Workplace*. London: Allen and Unwin.

Hordley, I., and D.J. Lee (1970) "The 'alternate route'—social change and opportunity in technical education." *Sociology* 4(1):23–50.

Illich, I. (1971) *Deschooling Society*. New York: Perennial Library (Harper and Row).

———— (1972) "After deschooling what?" In A. Gartner, ed., *After Deschooling What?* New York: Harper and Row: 1–28.

Jackson, E.F., and H.J. Crockett (1964) "Occupational mobility in the United States: a point estimate and trend comparison." *American Sociological Review* 29(1):5–15.

Jencks, C. (1972) *Inequality: A Reassessment of Family and Schooling in America*. New York: Harper and Row.

Jensen, A.R. (1969) "How much can we boost IQ and scholastic achievement?" *Harvard Educational Review* 39(1):1–123.

Johnson, L.A. (1973) *Disparity and Impoverishment in Canada since W.W. II*. Toronto: New Bytown Press.

Karabel, J. (1972) "Community colleges and social stratification." *Harvard Educational Review* 42(4):521–563.

Kateb, G. (1963) *Utopia and Its Enemies*. New York: Harcourt Brace.

Katz, M.B. (1970) *Class, Bureaucracy and Schools*. New York: Praeger, 1974.

Kohn, M.L. (1969) *Class and Conformity*. Homewood, Illinois: The Dorsey Press.

Lee, D.J. (1968) "Class differentials in educational opportunity and promotion from the ranks." *Sociology* 2(3):293–312.

Lipset, S.M., and R. Bendix (1959) *Social Mobility in Industrial Society*: Berkeley: University of California Press.

Marccau, J. (1974) "Education and social mobility in France." In F. Parkin, ed., *The Social Analysis of Class Structure*. London: Tavistock Publications: 205–236.

Marsden, L., E. Harvey, and I. Charner (1975) "Female graduates: their occupational mobility and attainment." *Canadian Review of Sociology and Anthropology* 12(4) Part 1.

Marshall, T.H. (1963) "Social selection in the welfare state." In *Sociology at the Crossroads*. London: Heinemann.

Martin, W.B.W., and A.J. Macdonnel (1976) "Aspects of educational opportunity in the Atlantic provinces." Paper presented at the 11th annual meeting of the Atlantic Association of Sociologists and Anthropologists, Fredericton, New Brunswick.

Mathews, R. (1973) "Canadian culture and the liberal ideology." In R.M. Laxer, ed., *Canada Ltd.* Toronto: McClelland and Stewart.

Mosteller, F. and D.P. Moynihan (1972) *On Equality of Educational Opportunity*. New York: Random House.

Parkin, F. (1971) *Class Inequality and Political Order*. London: Paladin.

———— (1974) *The Social Analysis of Class Structure*. London: Tavistock Publications.

Pomfret, A. (1976) "Conceptual issues in the study of planned school change." Paper presented at the annual meeting of the Canadian Sociology and Anthropology Association, Laval, Quebec.

Porter, J. (1965) *The Vertical Mosaic*. Toronto: The University of Toronto Press.

Porter, M.R., J. Porter, and B.R. Blishen (1973) *Does Money Matter?* Toronto: Institute for Behavioural Research, York University.

Richardson, C.J. (1977) *Contemporary Social Mobility*. London: Frances Pinter Publishing.

Richer, S. (1974) "Middle-class bias of schools—fact or fancy?" *Sociology of Education* 47(4):523–534.

Runciman, W.G. (1974) "Towards a theory of social stratification." In F. Parkin, ed., *The Social Analysis of Class Structure*. London: Tavistock Publications: 55–102.

Sewell, W.H. et al. (1969) "The educational and early occupational attainment process." *American Sociological Review* 34(1):82–92.

Sorokin, P. (1927) *Social and Cultural Mobility*. New York: The Free Press, 1959.

Spady, W.G. (1967) "Educational mobility and

access: growth and paradoxes." *American Journal of Sociology* 73(3):273–287.

Turner, R.H. (1960) "Sponsored and contest mobility and the school system." *American Sociological Review* 25(6):855–867.

———— (1966) "Acceptance of irregular mobility in Britain and the United States." *Sociometry* 29(4):334–352.

Troost, C.J. (1973) *Radical School Reform: Critique and Alternatives.* Boston: Little, Brown and Co.

Westergaard, J.H. (1964) "Sociology: the myth of classlessness." In R. Blackburn, ed., *Ideology in Social Science.* London: Fontana, 1972:119–163.

Westergaard, J. and H. Resler. (1975) *Class and Capitalistic Society.* London: Heinemann.

Wrong, D.H. (1964) "Social inequality without social stratification." *Canadian Review of Sociology and Anthropology.* 1(1):5–16.

Young, M. (1958) *The Rise of the Meritocracy.* London: Penguin Books.

Young, M.F.D. (1971) *Knowledge and Control.* London: Heinemann.

56 Post-Industrialism and Post-Secondary Education

John Porter

JOHN PORTER (1922–1979) was a Professor of Sociology at Carleton University, Ottawa, for many years, until his death. He had also served as Vice-President of Carleton University and spent visiting years at Harvard University and the University of Toronto. His major volumes are *Canadian Society, Sociological Perspectives* edited with B.R. Blishen, F.E. Jones and K.D. Naegele (1961, 1964, 1968, 1971); *The Vertical Mosaic: An Analysis of Social Class and Power in Canada* (1965); *Canadian Social Structure* (1967); *Macrosociology: Research and Theory* with J.S. Coleman and A. Etzioni (1970); *Toward 2000: The Future of Post-secondary Education in Ontario* with B.R. Blishen, J.R. Evans et al. (1971); *Does Money Matter?* with M.R. Porter and B.R. Blishen (1973); *Ascription and Achievement: Studies in Mobility and Status Attainment in Canada* with M. Boyd, J. Goyder, F.E. Jones, H.A. McRoberts, and P.C. Pineo (1975); and *The Measure of Canadian Society: Education, Equality and Opportunity* (1979). Porter's work has had an enormous impact on research in the areas of social inequality and social organization, and has helped define Canadian society for an international scholarly audience in the social sciences. The latter influence is marked by the McIver Award, given by the American Sociological Association for Porter's *Vertical Mosaic* for its " . . . comprehensive analysis of social stratification and contribution to macrosociology."

NATIONAL IDENTITY IN THE POST-INDUSTRIAL WORLD

If there is any validity in the views of Bell, Kahn, Gross, Galbraith and others about emerging post-industrialism, how can their images of the future help us make some assessment of Canada's need for higher education? To some extent our answer will depend on what image we ourselves have of the future of Canada as a continuing independent polity with some degree of separate identity. How important is such a survival of identity in any case? Why not simply accept the inevitable interpenetration of other post-industrial societies and go along for the ride? Can we forget about the fact that knowledge is the new power and that universities with their highly educated people constitute the new locus of power? Perhaps we do not need

power in this innovative sense since all the benefits can come from elsewhere. In a recent convocation address Harry Johnson indicated some of the benefits of this interpenetrating system.

> Apart from expanded higher-level education, the main requirement for participation in the modern world is willingness to accept and welcome the application of new technology.
>
> Unfortunately in many ways, the application of new technology is largely implemented through the agency of the large corporation which has been extending its activities from the national to the international sphere. I say unfortunately because the fact that it is a corporation with a national domicile obscures the fact that it is an agency for the diffusion of new technology, and hence an agency for the destruction of local industrial monopolies and the world-wide

transmission of the benefits of technical progress.[1]

If post-industrialism requires a great expansion of universities and research institutes why not continue, as in earlier periods of our history, to neglect educational development and "import" or accept the invasion of post-industrialism from elsewhere, as we did with industrialization? We seem to have become industrialized despite ourselves. In 1951 we were magnificently unprepared for industrial expansion, with over half our male labor force with eight years of schooling or less. Canada's transformation into mature industrialization after the Second World War was achieved in considerable measure by the importation of foreign capital and highly trained people. In case anyone doubts the latter, let me present briefly some evidence. The proportions of those in professional occupations who were postwar immigrants at the time of the 1961 census have been indicated in a number of studies.[2] On this subject, the 1961 occupational census data have been analysed in an interesting way by Bernard Blishen.[3] By devising an occupational scale based on income, education, and prestige, the three main components of occupational rank, he was able to assign scale values to 320 occupations. He then arranged them into six classes by rank. For the top two of these classes, that is, the occupations having the highest scale values, the proportion of the native-born labor force compared to the postwar immigrant labor force in them is strikingly different. In Ontario the proportion of the native-born labor force in these two classes was 9.9 per cent, but that of postwar U.K. immigrants was 13.8 per cent, and of postwar U.S. immigrants 28.2 per cent. In the western provinces the proportions were 8.7 per cent of the native-born labor force, 14.4 per cent of the U.K. and 31.8 per cent of the U.S. In Quebec the Canadian-born proportion was 7.35, the U.K.-29.6 and the U.S.-born 35.3. These proportions indicate how much richer

in trained capacity than the native-born labor force were the postwar immigrants who came from the United Kingdom and the United States. Some further evidence is to be found in a 1965 labor force survey which found that 23.6 per cent of the native-born male labor force had completed high school and attended university compared to 34.1 per cent of the postwar immigrants. For those with university degrees the percentages were 5.3 and 8.9, respectively.[4]

The reliance on external resources to bring us into the industrial stage of development can be seen in almost all industrial and institutional sectors. We have heard a good deal of irrational discussion of it in the university context. In his study published late last year on the performance of foreign-owned firms in Canada Professor Safarian presents some evidence on Canadian representation at the top level of foreign-owned firms and he raises questions about the failure of Canada to provide the range of trained managerial talent our industrial system requires. "It is not evident," he says, "that the quality of Canadian managerial personnel is so high that Canadian interests could be served by reduced resort to imported persons."[5] He also quotes the Economic Council to the effect, " . . . the average educational attainment of the owner and management group in Canada shows a greater shortfall below the educational attainment of the corresponding group in the United States, than is the case with almost any other major category of the labor force."[6] These observations about the educational level of Canadian management are, I think, important because we often fail to include managers in the international flows of highly qualified manpower, and hence tend to underestimate our needs. Our needs are indeed great if "Canadianization," as one government member has said, depends more on management rather than ownership.[7]

The overal differences in the educational attainment of the Canadian labor force and that of the U.S. are also well-known. In 1966, of the male population 25–34 years of age, 30.5 per cent in the United States had some university education or a university degree compared to 14.6 per cent in Canada. Of that age group in the U.S. 17.7 per cent had university degrees, but in Canada only 8.2 per cent had them.[8] Thus whether we compare Canada with the United States or whether we look at the high level of external recruitment (we still are recruiting professional occupations heavily abroad) it is clear that Canadian institutions of higher learning fell far short of meeting the needs of Canada's development into the industrial stage.

Should we proceed to the next stage of development by a similar route, by undertaking a minimum of educational planning, by continuing to hold the position that the provinces have the exclusive right to plan higher education? Should we keep on relying on the international market for the highly qualified manpower we will need or on the multinational corporations as they rationalize their Canadian operations? Is Canada damaged seriously in any way, or are Canadian interests neglected when recruitment from abroad is relied upon to fill so many of the higher occupational needs? A somewhat related question which has an important bearing on our higher educational needs is that of research and development in Canadian industry. Why be concerned about R and D programs in Canadian industry when we can import the benefits of R and D from elsewhere through foreign corporations? Is a Canadian mousetrap so much better than an American or a Belgian one? If it is not, then what are our future demands for research and development scientists in industry, a question surely to which educational planners should have an answer? What might we expect of future government policy with respect to meeting some of the critical points of the recent OECD review of science policy in general, and industrial research and development in particular? . . . [9]

TOWARDS A NATIONAL SYSTEM OF HIGHER EDUCATION

I want to elaborate on what I think are Canada's major needs at the post-secondary level, needs which are very much determined by the emergence of post-industrialism, the difficulty of retaining national identity and the desire for democratization. In general terms the need is for a national system of postsecondary education. We are slowly emerging as a national society, but we still lack goals or guides to wherever it is we are going. The Science Council of Canada has sought to outline goals in its document *Towards a National Science Policy for Canada*.[10] These are very important: national prosperity, health, education, freedom and unity, leisure, personal development, world peace. Economic growth was always thought to be a goal although that now seems to be subject to some questioning. On this point the Chairman of the Economic Council, Arthur Smith, has made an important observation that economic growth by itself is not enough unless it is ordered and controlled. "But in addition to good growth performance, we will need highly effective regulatory and control measures, with vigorous monitoring and enforcement procedures . . . it is essential that economic growth does not take place in an uncontrollable and irresponsible fashion."[11] (If nothing else Smith is pointing out the expanding need for highly qualified manpower in the social sector, but his notion of a government role in the establishment of economic growth as a national goal is consistent with our outline of the post-industrial society.)

National goals will increasingly require national standards, something recognized in Canada's long held doctrine of equalization. National goals should have their origins in the intellectual centres of the nations, be widely discussed, and implemented through the political system, since ultimately national goals are achieved through political leadership. If Canada is to develop as a national society distinguishable in some way from the United States, then its parts must become increasingly interdependent so that what happens in one part has its effects in other parts. As I have tried to argue, what distinguishes us from the United States will be very much at the cultural level and in terms of our own positive contribution to the post-industrial world. Crucial to our achievement of such national goals is a national system of higher education, and in this the federal government has an important planning role.

I want to present a few ideas about this national system and how it might develop, largely for purposes of discussion, but if it is too radical for Canada's conservative tastes to be worth the dialogue I will as well make an argument for federal involvement in planning even within the more narrow and restrictive limits of the present constitutional outlook. On this matter, the old notion that the federal government has no role in university development is as out of date as the carriages that existed in 1867. In the light of the broad historical changes which are taking place, so is the argument so eloquently advanced by the present prime minister [Trudeau] at the time of the first federal grants to universities.[12] It is as wrong, he argued, for federal governments to build universities because the provinces had failed to as it would be for the provincial governments to establish armies because they felt the federal government had neglected defence. The fact is that today, in the face of the more silent conquest by foreign takeover, knowledge is our defence. A highly-educated population is far more important to our survival than are our armed forces.

In outlining a possible national system of higher education I must once more acknowledge a debt to Daniel Bell, who has been writing on this subject a good deal in the United States.[13] The functions which are performed by a system of higher education are varied, but they are often summarized under the envelope expression as the preservation, semination, and extension of knowledge. The last of these, that is, research, is specialized, and may not be viewed as educational in the most strict sense of the term. The other kind of specialization also concerned primarily with training is in the professional schools. Higher education also involves the lower level technological training which is beyond high school but is vocationally oriented and less demanding than university education of the traditional scholarly kind where, in an intellectual community, people deal with the problems confronting mankind.

It is clear that a higher educational system must be differentiated or pluralistic to allow not only for different functions, but as well for different choices, inclinations, and ability levels. In the past we have tended to place a high value on one model of a university and that is the model of the mainline university, Columbia, Oxford, Harvard, the Sorbonne, and the like. All of our universities have wanted to become outstanding and to achieve world stature. They set up elaborate programs, hire a few star professors, start a journal or some other activity to emulate their models. As Daniel Bell has said, "The difficulty hitherto has been that every institution of higher learning has sought to be with a few exceptions, like every other. What we need is a greater variety, serving different aims in a differentiated division of labor. There is no reason why some institutions cannot be primarily in the service of scholarship and learning, with little need to take on added responsibilities. Some institutions can be oriented primarily to research, and others to training."[14] I am not competent to say to what extent the costs of postsecondary education have been pushed up because of this emulation of the mainline model, but perhaps some planning in the direction of a more pluralistic system might help to check costs, but even if it does not, a more differentiated system is more functional for the emerging society.

At the top of this differentiated system there

might be, to follow Bell's suggestion for the United States, a national system of autonomous elite universities carrying on the traditional role of scholarship and enjoying the traditional immunities that universities have always enjoyed. In Canada these national universities could be located strategically and regionally. They could be developed out of existing universities or created anew. They would be appropriately anglophone or francophone. They would govern themselves independently, but they would draw their funds from federal sources and their students would receive federal grants. Their research interests would be pure rather than applied. They would be truly national resources and the centres of excellence that we hear so much about in discussions of science policy. The provinces would continue to have their universities of course, but they would put greater emphasis on local needs and on professional and technical training. The provinces would also continue to run their college level postsecondary institutions. Essential to this national system of higher education would be a research and service system, as was suggested previously, to undertake client- and mission-oriented research associated with or separated from the national universities. These research institutes, for the social sciences as well as natural sciences, could be entirely federally supported or could be jointly supported by federal and provincial governments. More likely provincial governments would buy services from them. In such a national system the federal government would assume the planning and support of the highest level scholarship and research in the light of national goals while the provinces would continue to provide postsecondary education of a less costly and a more local kind.

There is no doubt that such a national system contains an important elitist element, but the fact is that it is unlikely that Canada warrants more than a few outstanding universities. The elitist character would have to be countered by making the provincial universities attractive and no less expensive to the student so that the poorer students do not go to them because of differential fees. This is what is happening in the Ontario system where the Colleges of Applied Arts and Technology draw their students in the main from lower social class levels than do the universities. The fact is, however, that the provincial universities and their colleges would remain attractive because of their more direct manpower function.

In order to develop such a system it would be necessary to establish a federal government agency responsible for planning higher education and not just for supporting provincial demands. The planning should be done, of course, in association with the provinces, but the point to be made is that the federal government has a responsibility to look after the nation's needs, which are in so many respects over and above the needs of the individual provinces. There has been little planning, even with provinces, although one may have a distorted view from the Ontario experience. The most we have done is to respond to pressures, some of them having very little to do with educational needs. A good amount of planning, particularly that related to research institutes, would have to be linked in with Canadian science policy, whatever that might become.

I realize of course that a proposal such as the one which I have just made may be thought to be a way-out pipe dream, particularly among those who under the pressure of day-to-day exigencies have to keep the system going rather than plan for its future. For such people there may be a more acceptable approach, although planning is pretty much inescapable if costs are to be controlled. In keeping with my general theme that the task of a system of higher education is to serve national needs as well as provincial ones, and that this requires national planning rather than simply fiscal transfers which the provinces use in the way they see fit, there are two points which I want to make. One is that there are important federal responsibilities that the universities in particular serve (it is interesting that the manpower retraining scheme—education at its lowest and most parochial level—has a heavy federal commitment and constitutes almost all of federal manpower planning) and for that reason the federal government should plan its inputs. The prototype is the Royal Military College which presumably has its constitutional legality in the federal government's responsibility for defence. There are also federal government agricultural research stations on university campuses. Why not extend this principle with institutes of international affairs, programs of area studies (the Pacific Rim, for example), modern language schools, institutes of public administration, institutes of penology and so on through the whole range of federal responsibilities. Here again a federal government agency could co-ordinate the federal needs and deal directly with universities. Since many of these specialized areas concern research and graduate studies their support would be a sizable financial contribution. . . .

OVER AND BEYOND THE PROVINCES

As I have tried to argue, there are national needs for post-secondary education that constitute something more than the simple addition of all provincial needs which are exclusive to the provinces themselves. One interesting way to measure these extraprovincial contributions is to look at the "demography" of university enrolments. (Components of this extraprovincial contribution would be the proportions of students from each province who are studying in other provinces, the proportions of students who come from abroad, and the interprovincial migration of those with university education.

With respect to the first of these, the At-lantic Provinces lead all the others in the proportion of their young people who are attending university outside their own province. In 1967–68 the proportions were 28.4 per cent for P.E.I., 18.5 per cent for New Brunswick, 14 per cent for Nova Scotia, and 13 per cent for Newfoundland. Other provincial proportions ranged downward to Ontario's 4.9 per cent.[15] It could be expected that a higher proportion of the interprovincial enrolments would be those from neighboring provinces or perhaps from the regional groupings with which we are used to viewing Canada, particularly the Atlantic Provinces, and the Prairie Provinces. Thus one would anticipate in the Atlantic Provinces, for example, that most of the out-of-province students would come from the region, a fact which would call for the provinces developing regional university systems. However, the proportion of students from regional neighborhoods is not nearly as great as the proportion from outside the region combined with that from outside the country. The pattern can be illustrated by Nova Scotia where 8 per cent of the students come from outside Canada, 10 per cent from outside the region, and 13 per cent from other regional provinces. New Brunswick has a similar pattern. In Manitoba 7 per cent of students come from outside the country, about 4.5 per cent from outside the Prairie region, and 4.5 per cent from regional neighbors. The Ontario-Quebec exchanges are much less between each other than between, for each of them, those outside the country and those from other provinces. With each other in 1967–68 these two provinces exchanged 4800 students, but between them took in 10 124 students from outside the country and 3279 from other provinces besides themselves. The proportions of students are not large, however, since 13 per cent of Ontario's students come from either outside the country or from outside the province, while 7.2 per cent of Quebec's do. These proportions of students from outside the province and outside the country can, of course, be interpreted in different ways. They can be regarded as some sizable cross-provincial educational contributions or as relative provincial self-sufficiency. It is important to interpret them in the light of federal policy aims. If one policy aim is through fiscal transfers to make each province self-sufficient in the provision of student places in and for itself, then low or decreasing proportions of interprovincial student migration would be considered a good thing. Other policies, however, might not be so regressive or so parochial. It could be argued that increasing rates of such cross-provincial student migration are an important factor in promoting national unity, and that such migration should be encouraged. If the proportion of interprovincial student migrants who are graduate students is greater than those who are undergraduates then a higher proportion of university costs are involved than implied by enrolment figures. There are good grounds for believing that this is the case, and so policy aims more likely become those of national highly qualified manpower needs.

With respect to the second component of the demography of university enrolments, students from outside the country raise different policy questions, but scarcely those which concern provinces. What are Canada's obligations to the international exchange of educational facilities? There is not only the recognized obligation to the developing world, but the obligation to balance the foreign educational resources used by Canadians. Moreover, cross-national migration of students is an important factor in international understanding. As with internal student migrants,

there is little doubt that the proportion of foreign graduate students greatly exceeds the proportion of undergraduates, making the proportions of university budgets involved higher than simple enrolment figures would suggest. In Ontario, for example, where enrolments make up about a third of all Canadian enrolments and about one-half of all graduate enrolments in Canada, the percentage of students from outside Canada was in 1967–68 6.5 per cent, but of graduate students it was closer to 40 per cent.[16] Thus the question arises: is it Ontario as a province or Canada as a nation which should determine policy with respect to foreign students?

With respect to the third component, some evidence on the mobility of university-trained people can be found in a 1966 Labour Force Survey.[17] In the age range 25–44 of those with university education 17 per cent did their university work in a different province and 20 per cent in a different country. In the 45–64 age group it was the reverse, 20 per cent in a different province and 17 per cent in a different country. Thus in both age groups only about 60 per cent of university-trained people received their education in the province in which they resided. The proportions are considerably less for those with less than university education. Generally it can be stated that the higher the educational level attained the greater is the mobility and the greater, therefore, is the university contribution to national manpower needs. To quote the Macdonald Report. "The fraction of graduate students employed in the province of their graduation is small: only Ontario retains more than half of its Ph.D recipients." . . . [18]

Notes

[1] As reprinted in *Ottawa Journal*, May 25, 1970.

[2] E.g., Economic Council of Canada, *First Annual Report*, p. 167.

[3] Bernard R. Blishen, "Social Class and Opportu-nity in Canada," *Canadian Review of Sociology and Anthropology*, vol. 7, no. 2, 1970, pp. 110–127.

[4] Michael D. Lagacé, *Educational Attainment in Canada: Some Regional and Social Aspects*,

Ottawa, DBS, 1968 (Special Labour Force Study No. 7).

[5] A.E. Safarian, *The Performance of Foreign-Owned Firms in Canada,* Montreal, The Private Planning Association, 1969, chap. 2.

[6] *Ibid.*

[7] C.M. Drury, as reported in OECD, *Reviews of National Science Policy: Canada*, Paris, OECD, 1969, p. 434.

[8] Lagacé, *Educational Attainment in Canada*, corrected Table C3.

[9] OECD, *Reviews of National Science Policy: Canada.*

[10] *Report No. 4*, Ottawa, Queen's Printer, pp. 13ff.

[11] Reported in *Ottawa Journal.*

[12] P.E. Trudeau, *Federalism and the French Canadians*, Toronto, Macmillan of Canada, 1968, p. 81.

[13] Daniel Bell, "Quo Warranto?—notes on the governance of universities in the 1970s," *Public Interest*, Spring 1970, pp. 53–68.

[14] *Ibid.*, p. 64.

[15] Z.E. Zsigmond and C.J. Wenaas, *Enrolment in Educational Institutions By Province 1951–52 to 1980–81*, Ottawa, Economic Council of Canada, 1970, Appendix D.

[16] *Survey of Citizenship of Graduate Students Enrolled in Master's and Doctoral Degree Programs at Ontario Universities in 1969–70 (With Comparative Statistics for 1968–69)*, Research Division of the Committee of Presidents of Universities of Ontario, April 1970.

[17] Lagacé, *Educational Attainment in Canada*, p. 11.

[18] John B. Macdonald *et al., The Role of the Federal Government in Support of Research in Canadian Universities,* Ottawa, Queen's Printer, 1969. p. 202.

Work and Occupations

Introduction

Most adults spend at least half of their waking hours working. For many of us who work outside the home, this work is referred to as our "job" and we do it at our "workplace." Most of us who work outside the home, about 90 percent according to recent calculations, sell our labour for wages. This puts us in the important social status of "employee," a status which Marx has shown determines many of our crucial life chances. Of course, the amount and kind of education we have gotten will have an influence on the kind of job we get and our wages for doing it. Yet what is really remarkable is how little income, job security and power vary among people who work for wages.

Our work role not only defines our relations to the means of production and, thereby, our life chances, it also affects the amount of social status or prestige other people grant us. Research on socioeconomic status has shown that the rankings of occupations are quite stable. Typically, jobs providing the highest average income and requiring the highest, or most exclusive, educational attainment rate highest in prestige. This rating will in turn influence how the job-holder is treated by others; strangers treat us largely as personifications of our job.

But our jobs have other effects as well.

Since we spend so much time working, overall life satisfaction is greatly influenced by job satisfaction. A boring, frustrating or demeaning job will probably make our whole life miserable, even if the job provides extrinsic rewards such as high pay, flexible hours and security. (Of course, the very worst jobs offer *neither* extrinsic rewards *nor* intrinsic rewards like autonomy and variety.) So a bad job can certainly mean a bad life.

We all have some idea of what "work" is, but what is it exactly? Three definitions of "work" that seem, at first, intuitively attractive prove full of problems. They are: (1) "work" is a paid activity; (2) "work" is the opposite of play; and (3) "work" is the fulfillment of specific duties, typically defined by someone else.

The notion that "work" is any paid activity, and any unpaid activity is not "work," is essentially an economist's conception. Official statistics on labour force activity, or on employment and unemployment, embody that first conception of work. The problem is, of course, that homemakers make up a very large group of adults who spend long hours doing something that is not play, yet is not paid for. Because they are not officially considered "employed," homemakers are denied much of the respect and financial security that others receive who occupy their days no more busily or usefully in a paid job.

This visible inequity has led to calls for wages for homemakers. It has also made courts willing to ensure that stay-at-home wives receive half of the family assets on the dissolution of marriage; after all, these wives contributed by providing domestic services over a long period. However, leaving aside the practical implications of this definition, consider the ideological ones. They are explored in an article in this section by Lorna Marsden, who tries to define what is a "labour force." Her approach is satirical, but the message is clear. Our culture has taught us that only the people who are paid are *really* working; payment is the measure not only of work value but, by extension, of social and human value. Marsden shows us this is a one-sided, male view.

All women, and also readers of our section on gender relations, know that what women do as homemakers is not only valuable but also difficult, time-consuming and stressful. Women who hold down a paid job and also do the housework support a mass of smug males who, by contrast, are enormously unproductive. Men, not women, should have to account for their productivity and social value, Marsden implies. Our economy is not run by super-productive males for the benefit of dependent females; rather, the opposite is true, if we consider the kinds of tasks that are really important. And if we adopt this turned-on-its head conception of work and social value, we must also redefine "labour force," "employment," "unemployment" and "job" accordingly.

A second conception is that "work" is the opposite of "play" or leisure. "Play" or leisure is fun because it is completely controlled by the player. He/she chooses where, when, and how the play will proceed. Play is an end in itself, not the means to an end. By contrast, a job (or work) is typically the means to an end: for an employee, the means to an income; and for an employer, the means to a profit. Play or leisure need not mean an absence of activity or stress. Many games and hobbies are intensely active and stressful in a positive way. Primarily, the work/play distinction supposes a difference in autonomy, creativity and self-fulfillment, not in energy expenditure.

However, this distinction is also problematic, for several reasons. First, workers differ widely in how much "fun" they have at their jobs. Some workers even deny they have a job or work; they say they are paid for "playing." Many artists and scholars feel this way about "work"; and, to varying degrees, so do others in professional, high managerial, or entrepreneurial positions where a lot of autonomy and creativity is possible. Even Marx felt that the distinction between work and play was a social construct, largely resulting from the capitalistic organization of labour. As we see in the discussion of alienation by James Rinehart, Marx believed that people were innately creative and saw work— the daily production of useful goods or services—as an outlet for their creativity. According to this theory, it was capitalism that robbed production of its autonomy, creativity and self-fulfillment. This made work alienating, and produced a distinction between work and play that would presumably disappear in a communist society.

The psychologist B.F. Skinner (1962) uses a similar idea in his utopian fantasy *Walden Two*. There "work" comprises any duties the community must have performed. Some jobs are so inherently unappealing that it is hard to find people to do them. Or, a particular person may be needed to do a particular job, but he/she would rather be doing something else. In these cases, says Skinner, the community will have to pay someone a lot of money to do the job. But people who are doing jobs that they really enjoy should not be paid for doing them. They would do these jobs anyway. High payment should only be provided when work is not play. For Skinner, work and play may sometimes be at odds; but it is inappropriate to *suppose that what we consider "work" and play must always be opposed in a well-constructed community.*

This brings us to the third conception of "work": namely, that it carries out duties, usually specified by someone else. In our highly bureaucratized society, many would naturally view work that way. But just as the work-versus-play dichotomy is a product of capitalist organization and thinking, so the work-as-structured-duties conception is a product of bureaucratic organization and thinking. In practice, many jobs lack specific duties, but rather select from a wide variety of tasks to achieve some general goal. Consider, for example, the role of professor. In general, a professor has to teach and participate in the academic life of his university and discipline. Yet the ways of doing these things are left largely undefined. Only the grossest negligence will be identifiable as a dereliction of professional duties. Job definition is left almost entirely to the individual professor, and each one does it differently.

Similarly, the barber cuts hair, the car salesman sells cars, and the detective enforces the law. But the duties involved—while varying a lot from one occupation to another in their specificity—are generally open to individual interpretation. The barber can work fast or slow, talk or not talk, be creative or conventional. The salesman can sell hard or soft, play up his own car or knock the competition's, seek out potential clients or wait for clients to walk into the showroom. And the detective must detect crime; but this can be done in many ways too!

We have included Richard Ericson's paper on detective work in this section rather than in the section on deviance and control because it concerns detective work as work: it is about what detectives are *supposed* to do and what they *actually* do. Detectives are supposed to detect law-breaking and enforce the law. Policemen exercise a great deal more discretion than is commonly believed, and it is this creative exercise of discretion that produces "crime" as an official event and statistic. In this respect, detective work is not so different from other kinds of work that allow discretion and autonomy, and therefore can be considered creative. However, detective work is not *supposed* to be creative. Citizens like to believe that crime really happens and detectives impartially, rigorously and thoroughly enforce the law: in other words that detective work is a mechanical application of laws to crimes.

Most citizens would like to think that detective work is highly bureaucratized. But work that serves, or works with, people rarely is. To understand the thing detectives produce—i.e., arrests—we must understand the production process (the exercise of discretion in practice), and the psychology of the law-enforcers, which shapes the way they use their discretion. Thus, detectives are as complex as psychiatrists, chefs, or sculptors.

Yet not all work allows this much discretion. Indeed work is becoming ever more bureaucratic—that is, more rule-oriented—and more dependent on high technology. The effects of bureaucratization and technology are captured in articles by Graham Lowe and Heather Menzies, respectively. Professor Lowe's historical perspective helps us understand some of the current peculiarities of modern office work: why, typically, it is not unionized, is done by women, and is subject to major technological change. Ms. Menzies, for her part, tells about a particular technological change in the office—the adoption of new information technology, such as computers and word processors—and traces the effects on workers, their relations to supervisors, and the likely consequences for female employment. These two articles present the modern office in a light whose bleakness may be justified. Office work will undoubtedly see a lot of turbulent change in the next few decades, as technological and organizational innovations make themselves fully felt.

The section ends with two articles, also rather bleak, on the discontents of work. The first, by Professor Rinehart, is one we have already mentioned. It is a masterful presentation of Marx's theory of alienation. Readers intrigued by this theory and interested in seeing it used in empirical analysis should read Professor Rinehart's book from which this excerpt is taken.

The second article on work's discontents is a discussion of the dangers of off-shore oil drilling. J. Douglas House has analyzed off-shore oil work from a variety of perspectives; safety problems are not the only problems he considers. Yet what is striking is the terrible riskiness of this kind of work for life and limb, a risk that is rarely discussed by government planners. The oil companies themselves hide information about the danger as much as possible.

Nonetheless, this danger needs considering in the equation of costs and benefits associated with resource development.

Research on the physical dangers of work, or occupational safety, is highly developed and has a long history. It goes back at least to Friedrich Engel's book, *The Condition of the Working Class in England* ([1845], 1968) and has frequently concerned workers, unions, and labour sympathizers. What we see, increasingly, is an attempt by planners to measure and anticipate safety and health problems and, by quick action, to prevent their further occurrence. From this standpoint, the social impact assessments Newfoundland performed in preparing for oil development may represent a high point in applied social research. The only comparable Canadian work, perhaps, is Thomas Berger's (1977) Royal Commission on northern development and the planned location of an oil pipeline.

When it borders on research into economic development, the sociology of work merges into the study of human communities. Economic development has consequences for the change and stability of communities within which the workplace is located. The next section will take our understanding of communities further.

References

Berger, Mr. Justice Thomas R. *Northern Frontier, Northern Homeland: The Report of the Mackenzie Valley Pipeline Inquiry*. Two volumes. Ottawa: Ministry of Supply and Services, 1977.

Engels, Friedrich (1845) *The Condition of the Working Class in England*. Translated and edited by W.D. Henderson and W.H. Chaloner. Stanford, California: Stanford University Press, 1968.

Skinner, B.F. *Walden Two*. New York: Macmillan Paperback, 1962.

57 What Is the "Labour Force?"[1]

Lorna Marsden

LORNA MARSDEN, Professor of Sociology at the University of Toronto, specializes in the study of work and occupations, and the labour force. Her books include *Population Probe*: *Canada* (1972), *Canadian Population Concerns* co-edited with E.B. Harvey (1977) *The Fragile Federation*: *Social Change in Canada*, with E.B. Harvey (1979); and *Women in the Automated Office* (forthcoming). Professor Marsden has written numerous articles and given many public presentations on sociological and public policy issues. As well, she served as Chair of the Department of Sociology, Associate Dean of Graduate Studies, and Vice-Provost (Arts and Sciences) at the University of Toronto. A major interest has been in the female labour force and changes in the situation of women workers in Canada. In addition, she is an activist in the women's movement, having served as the President of the National Action Committee on the Status of Women from 1975–77. Since 1984, Professor Marsden has been a member of the Senate of Canada where she continues to pursue issues concerning the situation of women.

... The purpose of this paper is to suggest that there has been a rather fundamental error in the basic conceptualization of the Canadian labour force which has obscured some of the main economic and sociological issues we face. In what follows, a proper definition of the working population will be suggested. The definition of terms and the precise numbers are difficult since the labour force statistics have been created according to a limited conception in the first place. If the reader will take these as approximations, however, and concentrate on the conceptual issues at hand, this paper will have served its purpose.

At the present time in Canada there are about 18 million people considered to be of working age, that is, over the age of 15 years (Statistics Canada, 1978). We will assume that about 95 per cent of those people suffer from no handicap sufficiently severe to make them totally dependent upon others. This gives about 17,200,000 people in our working age population.

LABOUR FORCE ACTIVITY

As we all know, not all those of working age are in the labour force or working, in the true sense of the word, in Canada. In fact, there are two main categories of workers in our society. The majority of people fall into the category which we will call "main workers". In the category of main workers fall approximately 11 million people or 60 per cent of the working age population.

It is this group of people which contributes most substantially to the society in the true productive sense. They contribute both through the production of goods and services in the traditional way measured by economists, and fulfil the sociological definition of work "producing something of value for others" (Hall, 1975). The characteristics of this group of people set them apart from secondary workers in the society. The contribution to the Canadian economy of secondary workers is far less than that of the main workers although they are of considerable social and political significance. . . .

A main worker, is by definition, over the age of 14. This person can be said to make an economic contribution which is recorded in two gross measures—GNP (gross national product) and FNP (future national product). The main Canadian worker spends an average of approximately 70 hours a week (often more) at work. Although both sexes can be found in the main worker category, by far the largest proportion of main workers is female and this ratio is increasing.

Whether it is because of the amount of time spent in main working activity or whether it is for reasons of tradition or custom, main workers tend to be found less in those activities associated with the overall decision-making of the society such as politics and management. It may be that Canadian society bears some cultural relationship to that described by Margaret Mead in her famous study *Male and Female*. She describes a society (Tchambuli) in which the main workers till the fields and look after the children and do all the cooking and work while the others sit in huts by the lake gossiping and making deals and "running" the society (Mead, 1949 and 1972).

The vast majority of main workers are married (almost 80 per cent) although any worker with a dependent child may be said to be a main worker whether married or not. In occupational terms, the main workers are concentrated in the service industries and in some professions in health and education. In 1971, 31 per cent of main workers were in clerical occupations in Canada and 14 per cent were in service occupations. In terms of industrial sectors, approximately 15 per cent were in manufacturing, 17 per cent in trade, and 38 per cent in community-personal services.

Partly because main workers contribute to a remunerated form of work (GNP) and as well contribute to an unremunerated form of work (through FNP) the average direct wage for main workers tends to be lower than that of secondary workers, approximately 60 per cent of that of secondary workers. This, too, is part of the cultural tradition and may be viewed in a speculative way as a form of compensation for the relative uselessness of secondary workers in the society. (Others, however, view the higher average wage of secondary workers as a means of social control to prevent their rebellion against their lack of productive importance.) Whatever the reason, the fact remains that the main worker earns on average less than the secondary worker but contributes on average 40 per cent more to the economic well-being of the society.

THE WORK LIFE OF THE MAIN WORKER

The typical main worker enters main work after the completion of his/her education and, throughout life until death, combines main and secondary work sometimes exclusively in one or the other but always, potentially, in both. The worker typically begins as a secondary worker only, perhaps as a secretary, teacher or skilled worker. Shortly after, at marriage or co-habitation, this person becomes a main worker contributing both in secondary labour for about 40 hours a week and in the domestic and community sphere about 30 or more hours per week. These work responsibilites are often not at all of the same nature and require the acquisition of entirely separate sets of skills. Perhaps the most important contribution of the main worker's life is the preparation of the next generation of workers. This used to be considered main work on its own but increasingly, largely because of the demand for secondary work and the inability of secondary workers to meet demand and increase their productivity, main workers are also picking up the load of secondary labour. The typical main worker, however, (and this is one of the chief distinguishing features between main and secondary workers) has a clear set of priorities when it comes to contribution to the society and concentrates for several years when children are young on their proper socialization to our society. The main worker always maintains responsibility for food care, basic hygiene and other necessities. The nature of this work (which may be done by either sex but is customarily done by women) is highly specialized and crucial work for which no one has ever been able to develop a proper valuation scale.

Unlike the secondary workers, main workers are the only fully independent people in Canadian society contributing both to the creation and maintenance of their future as well as to the goods and services which are largely redistributed through markets. While society might well continue without secondary work (and especially without secondary workers) it could not continue without main workers who work in both the main and secondary markets.

THE SECONDARY WORKER

Let us turn now to a description of secondary workers and their role in society. A not insignificant proportion of the work activity is performed by this other 40 per cent of the population. These workers have some peculiar characteristics which make their work of less value to the Canadian economy although highly important in their own eyes. There are distinctions to be made among secondary workers. First, secondary *work* (defined as work for a direct wage) is carried out by both main workers and secondary workers. Secondary workers are those who earn only a direct wage and do not contribute value to others in the main work market. In general terms one might describe these workers as parasitic since both before and after their secondary work activity the largest

proportion are incapable of making a contribution to the economy. The term "parasitic" will be used here to refer to this group.

Characteristically, although this is a slowly declining trend, these workers are unable to manage main work activity and are confined to secondary work activity. Through historical experience they are excluded from the main work child-rearing activities. Their work is confined to an average of 8 hours per day or a mean of 40 hours per week and generates approximately two-thirds of GNP. To the extent that their labour helps to produce the next generation they contribute to FNP (about 5 per cent), but it is well understood that the next generation could be reproduced with the help of only approximately one twentieth of the available parasitic workers.

Their labour force activities are characteristically different from those of the main group of workers. Entering secondary labour at the average age of 19, these workers carry out secondary labour with apparent indifference to the main work activity throughout their lives until the average age of 65 when they stop working altogether and become totally parasitic (with individual exceptions of course). Because of their lack of integration into main work activities and community life in general, they are more susceptible to certain diseases such as heart disease, cancer, hypertension and related conditions which mean that they often lose years of even their secondary labour for society for health reasons. These are known as "stress related". The stress arises from the attempt to suppress consciousness of their parasitic status.

Because of the public fear of massive popular uprisings from this group, governments tend to provide them with generous benefits including pensions, sickness and health benefits, tax breaks and incentive plans. This maintains their commitment to the secondary labour force throughout their adult life and prevents their militance in old age. Many attempts have been made both by governments and by the main work force to train them in the elementary skills of main work activity so as to make them less of a drain on the society, but it has been discovered that the vast majority are untrainable.

Fortunately for the economic future of Canada, main workers are available in larger numbers than secondary parasitic workers. However, this marginal edge for fully productive workers is not large. Recent years have shown high rates of parasitic worker unemployment, but current worker forecasts show a very high demand beginning to emerge for secondary and parasitic workers.

When insufficient secondary labour is available, major social problems arise. Main workers are forced to add secondary labour to their activities in large numbers and the secondary labour force often resorts to drinking, dependency and violence because of their inability to integrate into main work activity or community life.

SOCIAL PROBLEMS ASSOCIATED WITH SECONDARY WORKERS

It is always difficult for a society to absorb and integrate a group of people who are unable or unwilling to participate fully in the community life. First, their contribution is only partial, and, second, they remain as a constant reminder of the unsuccessful socialization of a large segment of the population and a drain on the economy.

In Canada, many social programmes have been devised to control and maintain these people. Many of these programmes have become established in law. First, these parasitic workers have not been allowed to concentrate in one part of the country, nor, with some exceptions, at one place in the community. (Where they are concentrated in the community, as in camps for the armed forces, they are under strict discipline, training and guards. The same is true for prisons, some private clubs and any other places where they tend to congregate.)

Indeed, the law requires that a main worker takes on as part of her adult responsibilities the care of a parasitic worker in the custom of marriage. Increasingly, main workers are avoiding this social responsibility which interferes considerably with their main and secondary work activities. Refusal on the part of main workers to undertake this added burden has been shown to lead to a higher rate of suicide and early death among secondary workers. The consequences for the parasitic workers in the form of malnutrition, depression, drug and alcohol dependency are not well known but will unquestionably become a major social problem in future years.

It is not only social programmes and economic issues that one should be concerned about in this matter, of course. One has also to be conscious of the issues of human dignity. Minority group defences, so well described by social theorists, in this case involve the parasitic secondary workers referring to themselves often as "breadwinners", a term which invokes an old and venerated society with an entirely different form of production. But, it generates respect. In fact, it is not clear whether the respect accorded to these parasitic workers is the same sort that is accorded generally to the crippled or handicapped, or whether it is because these workers tend to form relationships with other workers slightly younger than themselves to assert age authority.

Ideological systems are maintained by specialized occupations and here, too, a group of workers has developed to lend substance to the claims of the ideology. Just as religions have priests, or their equivalents, and other religious workers to maintain and develop the ideas and tend to the flock, parasitic workers have economists. These workers, like priests, study long and hard to develop their skills and knowledge. They fill their eight hour days "massaging" numbers with the aid of computers and embroidering "models" to rationalize the importance of secondary work and workers. One of the more extravagant of these is the so-called "labour-leisure" model. It is believed that Jonathan Swift described it in one of his early works. This model would have one believe that main workers "choose leisure" at home with small unsocialized workers over "labour" in the secondary labour force. Of course, common sense tells us that it is quite the other way around, but economists by cloistering themselves inside such ivory towers as universities and the Economic Council of Canada, and by charging a very great deal for their services, have convinced policy makers that they have the truth. Just as the religious eschew carnal relations, so economists are, in their own fashion, chaste. They live unsullied by any observation of human social behaviour. From the most rabid sect (which believes that all human production can be carried out in the secondary work sector, leaving plenty of time for revolution) to the most bewildering sect (which posits a curious idea called "free markets" to which they pray incessantly) all are convinced that their food and clean socks arrive out of thin air and that children can be modelled by computer. They have large followings amongst the most powerful in the land, and dollars, people and social values are offered up on their altars daily.

While programmes such as marriage and official ideology are traditional ways of maintaining control of these workers, the most significant for the economy has been the public expenditure in Parasitic Pacifiers—an enormously expensive programme for the country in terms of forgone taxes and earnings as well as direct expenditures. Indeed these programmes prevent the most efficient and effective progress of main work activity. While it is clear that every parasitic worker should have a second job in order to prevent social disorder, increasingly main workers are questioning the incentive and pacifying programmes attached to these secondary jobs: major tax write-offs for "executive travel and expenses"; expensive training programmes: community facilities designed to amuse and consume the time of these parasitic workers such as restaurants, hotels and amusement centres called "convention centres" and "sports clubs." Increasingly, main workers are having to spend their time overseeing and administrating these places. The expectations of the secondary workers are rising more rapidly than the nation can afford, contributing heavily to inflation in wage demands and benefits.

Perhaps more pernicious is that the secondary workers have banded together (albeit only inside the structure of their secondary jobs so that no real threat to the society is presented) and built up a large sector best described by Franz Kafka as "the castle" but which we will call "bureaucracy." This bureaucracy creates, for its own amusement, a description of the outcome of the secondary labour. Rather like a complex game of monopoly, rules are created and adhered to which determine how counts are made and who may move where and when.

Recently, however, adding to the public expenditures but devoted entirely to these games, new offices have been established such as that of the Auditor-General, and publication of the results of these games, in the most minute detail, has begun. Since there are major categories of secondary workers who are prevented from playing in the same game as others, new demands for freedom of information have succeeded in increasing the size of the bureaucracy.

Having created a larger bureaucracy, the secondary parasitic workers are unable to mount a sufficient number of workers or machines to cope with their self-created demands and have had increasingly to call upon the services of the main workers. Both the main worker activity, which is crucial to the next generation and the maintenance of the present generation, and the secondary worker activity which creates goods essential for survival, diminish as workers are drawn into the games sectors. This is having seriously deleterious effects not only on our own economy, but that of developing countries who must pay more hard currency for primary and industrial goods while being unable to export their surplus population. (It should be noted here that the main workers in developing countries are, for the most part, more efficient at main work activity, including increasing the size of the population, since their attention and energies are not drained off in support of secondary activities and parasitic workers).

CONCLUSIONS

It becomes apparent that a proper analysis of the work activities of Canadian society would have the effect of changing social and economic programmes to attempt to stem the rising tide of inefficiency as a result of growing dominance of secondary workers.

It is suggested that the creation of a sensible index of workers and their relative contribution to the economic well-being of the country would result in a more equitable sharing of work and rewards. It would also enable the governments to cut back on forms of extravagant subsidies such as executive write-offs, conference fundings, amusement parks and prisons, alcohol rehabilitation programmes and other forms of social control. Instead, the use of funds to integrate secondary parasitic workers into the community and main work activities would enable the government to reduce the various forms of social control and spread the main work activity so that both main workers and secondary workers could participate in main and secondary work activity. . . .

Notes

[1] Dorothy Smith's seminal paper, "Ideological Structures and How Women Are Excluded." *Canadian Review of Sociology and Anthropology*, 12(4) Nov. 1975, played no small part in causing the scales to drop from the eyes of the author.

References

Richard Hall, *Occupations and the Social Structure*, Prentice-Hall, 1975, p. 4.

Margaret Mead, *Male and Female*, New York, William Morrow and Company, 1949. *Blackberry Winter*, New York, William Morrow and Company, 1972.

Statistics Canada, 1976 Census of Canada, *Supplementary Bulletins: Geographic and Demographic, Specified Age Groups*, Catalogue 92–835, (Bulletin 8SD.4). April, 1978.

58 Detectives Make Crime

Richard Ericson

RICHARD ERICSON, Professor of Sociology at the University of Toronto, specializes in the study of criminal justice systems. His books include *Young Offenders and their Social Work* (1975); *Criminal Reactions* (1975); *Making Crime* (1981); *Reproducing Order* (1982); and *The Ordering of Justice* with P. Baranek (1982). Three other books with P. Baranek and J. Chan are forthcoming: *Acknowledging Order*, *Negotiating Order*, and *Visualizing Deviance*. In addition, Professor Ericson is the author of numerous research reports and scholarly articles. He is currently Editor of the *Canadian Journal of Sociology*.

... Detective work has gradually evolved as an established specialized function within the large, bureaucratized police force. The primary work is routine processing of occurrences initiated by uniform branch officers, including the processing of suspects produced by uniformed officers or apprehended on information received from a citizen. Based on the information work he has done, the detective decides whether the case can be made into a "crime"; and, if he has a suspect, whether the suspect can be made into a "criminal." The detective experiences this work as routine. Our subject of inquiry is how he makes it routine.

DETECTIVES AS MAKERS OF CRIME

It is now accepted socio-legal wisdom, if not conventional social wisdom, that "Crime is a sociopolitical artifact, not a natural phenomenon" (Packer, 1968:364). The definitions "crime" and "criminality" are powerful tools used by the authorities against "groups and individuals who in any way, inadvertently or deliberately, are resistant to the will of the authorities (as articulated in the behavior of the police and courts)..." (Turk, 977:11).

The police are at the forefront of this definitional production. They are given organizational capacity to produce particular levels of crime, and to produce particular types of crime to the relative exclusion of others. Of course, the authorities place some limits on production by legislating what criminal labels can be applied and by controlling the material resources supplied (cf. McDonald, 1976:290). Production also depends upon the collective ability of police force members to generate and use the information necessary to make crime (Reiss and Bordua, 1967:47; Manning, 1972: 234). In this regard, the discretionary decisions of the police are crucial determinants of "crime" production....

In their everyday decisions, line police officers "commit" crimes to police organizational records and make them available for detective investigators to follow-up or ignore, to "unfound" or verify. Obviously, there are many events which could be made into crimes but are not, because a citizen chooses not to call the police (Ennis, 1967; Sparks *et al.*, 1977). Other events could be made into crimes but are not because the police officer decides not to proactively stop and investigate suspects (Ericson, 1980: Ch. 4, 6). Even when police officers are mobilized, their decisions to make complaints or observed conduct of suspects into "crimes" are far from automatic, varying by citizen characteristics and dispute type (*ibid.*: Ch. 5; Skogan, 1976; Sparks *et al.*, 1977). Furthermore, sometimes occurence reports submitted by patrol officers can be ignored by detectives, leaving open the question of whether the event could be judged a crime; and, after investigation, detectives can decide that the matter was "unfounded" (Sanders, 1977; Bottomley and Coleman, 1979). For all practical purposes, crime only consists of those acts that are so designated by the police for their crime control purposes on behalf of the authorities. . . .

In this formulation, it is meaningless to use the concept of a "dark figure" of crime. We can study the process by which the police discover things which they make into crimes, and how they do organizational bookkeeping to keep account of crimes, but we shall never know the total volume of things "out there" that could be made into crimes. As Ditton (1979:21) argues, "To ask 'how big is the 'dark figure?' is to pose a question of the same logical order as 'how long is a piece of string?' or 'how many grains of wheat are there in a heap?' " While the issue is gradually transformed into black and white once the police have decided to make something into a "crime," the decision on whether or not to constitute it as a crime in the first place has as many shades as a chameleon in a box of crayons. For example, in the victimization survey by Ennis (1967:87–93), detectives and lawyers agreed only slightly more than half the time on whether victims' accounts of incidents described criminal offences let alone what the appropriate label for those offences might be.

In our formulation, the term "underenforcement" is equally absurd. This term implies that all laws will be enforced against all violators at all times (Manning, 1977:249). The fact is, even with very substantial police resources, certain types of incidents will be systematically excluded from being made into crime (e.g., "domestic" assaults—see Kokis, 1977; Ericson, 1980: Ch. 5), and certain sit-

uated features of individual cases will lead to selective decisions not to make them a matter of "crime." This is so because the organizational interests of the police, and/or the organizational interests of the wider network of criminal control and community control, influence the way in which "crime" and "criminal" labels are used by the police.

In carrying out their work of making events into crime, and persons into criminals, detectives operate within four intersecting organizational forums: the community (political territory) being policed; the network of criminal control (the institution of law and its constituent elements, e.g., courts); the police force; and the occupational culture of fellow detectives.[1] Each of these organizational forums provides a structural framework from which emanate particular "demand conditions" for detective actions (Bittner, 1967b: 701; see also Silverman, 1979: 134–135). In turn, detective actions, and their interactions with other members of these organizational forums, help to constitute the structural framework within which they operate.[2]

In short, detectives as human actors are not conceived of as determined varlets who simply respond to the dictates of organizational structures. This conception is contrary to that of some researchers of the police (e.g., Black, 1968; Pepinsky, 1975, 1976; Sykes and Clark, 1975; Wilson and Boland, 1979), who accept the American ideal that "enforcement responses are supposed to be as automatic as possible" (Bayley, 1977:224) and who thus portray police officers as automatons emitting responses according to the stimulus of structural forces. We conceive detectives as *enacting* their environment, as well as reacting to it (cf. Manning, 1979:29, quoting Weick, 1969: 63–64). Therefore, detectives' individual and collective theories about action, interaction, and structure become central to inquiry (cf. Strauss, 1978:102). How do detectives develop a sense of the rules within each of the organizational forums in order to stabilize their own practices? How do these rules relate to detective action? How do detectives put these rules to use? What do these practices tell us about detectives' sense of order?

As human actors detectives work at producing the organizational realities which in turn guide their production. This work is carried out in the routine tasks they deal with on a day-to-day basis, and results in a product that is both commodity (e.g., "crime" and other means of case clearance) and an established set of social relations (social structure). Detectives consciously and actively create and use structural resources that will allow them to accomplish their organizational tasks with minimal strain. Of course, the constructions of detectives are frequently met with the obstructions of others; this is part of the ongoing process of "negotiating order." . . .

The detectives' task of making structural conditions which are conducive to their task of making crime involves a perpetual search for *power* resources to be used vis-à-vis those with whom they routinely interact. The question of power—of who has the enabling resources to control the process—has been a focal concern of socio-legal scholars studying the police.[3] The central concept employed in this connection is "discretion," which can be equated with the concept of power. . . .

In socio-legal studies, discretion (power) is considered to be an element of social organization rather than pertaining to personal characteristics of police officers (Wilson, 1968: 11; Sykes and Clark, 1975: 585–586).[4] The realization that discretion is an inevitable component of every socially structured organization has led socio-legal scholars away from a questioning of its propriety and in the direction of researching its dimensions. The policy question becomes one of judging whether discretion is properly in the hands of particular officials, whether it should be shifted to other officials, and how this can be accomplished (e.g., Alschuler, 1968, 1978).

As stated, discretion (power) is essentially a matter of control over enabling resources that will serve particular interests (Turk, 1973: 4–5). In the process of making crime, detectives have two fundamental resources to work with: (1) *rules*, including enabling legal rules of the criminal law (legislated and judge-made), administrative rules of the police force, and recipe (practical) rules of the occupational culture; and (2) *information control*, including a "low visibility" position within the organizational nexus which allows them to control essential knowledge and the flow of information. . . .

RULES

According to legal ideals, the enforcement of the criminal law is supposed to be governed by the rule of law and the principle of legality. Briefly put, the prescription and application of specific legal rules are supposed to operate to reduce arbitrary action by agents of the law. The ideal is to have the law rule, not men.

In practice, the system operates according to men who use laws to accomplish their enforcement tasks. The law is very enabling in this respect, because it is effectively formulated for the pragmatic use and benefit of law enforcement agents, allowing them to accomplish crime control in accordance with their organizational interests (McBarnet, 1979). It is also enabling to the extent that it is silent in some areas, providing no empirical referent vis-à-vis the ideals of the system (Black, 1972).

The system also operates according to the administrative rules and informally developed rules within specific sub-organizations. Therefore, it is a mistake to attempt an understanding of detective crime work solely in terms of the legal rules. To do so is to commit a "category mistake" (cf. Giddens, 1976: 47), "trying to understand the rules of one game by means of assumptions grounded in the rules of another." Detectives, and the police force on whose behalf they operate, have their own sets of organizational interests, and attendant rules to achieve them. As Skolnick (1966) has argued, detective use of these rules can conflict with the legal rules; moreover, it can substantially discolour the ideals of the system.

A further consideration is that knowledge of the rules—whether legal or police organizational—is of no use *in itself* if one wishes to understand detective work. One has to learn how rules are *conceived* and *used* by detectives as they go about their daily tasks. The primary function of rules, regardless of their source, is to aid detectives in the rationalization of their activities.

In this connection, legal or administrative rules designed to control detective actions cannot be viewed as having a direct impact independent of their translation by detectives. Similar to workers in any bureaucracy, detectives will not respond to a new rule aimed at making their task more difficult by a willing commitment to implement it in letter and spirit.[5] Instead, they will assess the rule in the context of the rule frameworks they have already established. They will then develop strategies to avoid the new rule, to implement it with the minimum level of compliance possible, and/or to turn it to their advantage in easing their task.

We are not arguing that detectives break the rules or even bend them as a matter of routine. Usually such extreme measures are unnecessary because the rules are vaguely written and otherwise enabling enough to get the job done. . . .

Research has also shown how police force administrative rules developed in support of new policing strategies have been ignored, or reformulated and put to use by line officers so that they can continue their former practices. . . .

For detectives and other police officers, "working to rule" takes on a very special meaning. Detectives work to produce and use rules which allow them to rule, i.e., to control their working environment. Their skill at doing this has been well documented, leading one researcher to observe that rules of constraint imposed by legal or police authorities over line officers can end up strengthening the activity they were supposed to restrain (Skolnick, 1966: 12).

Detectives are pragmatists. They constantly search for and employ strategies that will make complex situations simple, and potentially unusual situations routine, in order to meet organizational expectations with minimal strain. In consequence, they are "highly rule oriented and rule conscious" (Manning, 1977a: 47).

In terms of criminal law rules, detectives are strategists in their use of both substantive law and procedural law as these pertain to particular tasks before them. If we consider the task of dealing with suspects, we can develop this point.

When dealing with suspects, detectives have a choice concerning whether or not they will arrest and/or charge the person. They may decide to arrest and/or charge for a wide variety of reasons, and then use a particular law that will best suit their reasons. The law makes the apprehension possible, explaining why the detective may arrest and/or charge but not why he may want to arrest and/or charge (Bittner, 1967a; Chatterton, 1976; McBarnet, 1979).

This use of the law is especially apparent in minor offence situations, and in particular public order troubles as handled by the patrol police. The law is used as a handy device for dealing with troublesome situations. It is a "residual resource" which is used to assert police authority and/or to patch up interpersonal troubles (Bittner, 1967a; 1970: 109; Ericson, 1980: Ch. 6). A suspect being investigated for criminal assault is eventually charged under a liquor statute for being intoxicated in a public place after the victim refuses to assist investigation; a suspect who throws a chair at a dancer in a bar and strikes her is eventually charged with causing a disturbance so that the police officers do not have to complicate the case with a multitude of witnesses; a husband is provoked into a scuffle and then arrested for assaulting police as a means of removing him from a hostile domestic situation; and so on. Indeed, there is an arrestable offence (breach of the peace) and there are several chargeable offences (e.g., causing a disturbance; obstructing police) which are well suited for use by the police in virtually every circumstance where they feel they need to assert their legal authority....

Police officers can also *use* the substantive law even when they decide not to arrest and charge (cf. Bittner, 1967b: 702–703). For example, they can make a suspect believe he could be charged but that he is being given a break. This is facilitated by the suspect's general lack of knowledge about police powers, and also by the fact that in many situations the law is ambiguous enough so that alternative interpretations, including the arrest and charge option, are plausible. Giving the impression of a "break" can be a useful means of setting up an exchange relationship with the suspect whereby he agrees to give information to the police as an act of reciprocity (cf. Skolnick, 1966; Rubinstein, 1973: 182). Of course, making the suspect believe he could be charged is also a source of intimidation, serving to make him respect his place vis-à-vis police authority.

These tactical uses of substantive legal rules to generate information, assert authority, and convert suspects into accused persons, are central to the public order tasks of the patrol police (Ericson, 1980)....

Another source of legal rules that are of particular benefit in detective work pertain to the procedures for processing suspects and accused persons. It is in this area that the written law does directly relate to practice. "The legal system *is* the procedures not the rhetoric, and procedures do not so much provide safeguards for the accused as powers for the prosecution" (McBarnet, 1976: 178).

While we wish to avoid a technical legal discussion at this juncture, it is worthwhile to enumerate some of the procedures indicating that this is the case.

In some areas the law is silent. For example, police officers routinely detain citizens for extended periods on "street stops" while awaiting the results of criminal information (CPIC) checks (Ericson, 1980: Ch. 6). While it is unlikely that persons in these circumstances would officially be judged to be under arrest, it is also unlikely that they feel free to leave the presence of the police officer without running the risk of being charged (e.g., with "obstruct police").

Where written procedural law does exist, it is enabling in its vagueness. For example, the justifications for arrests and searches usually contain the element of "reasonable and probable grounds." This amounts to no more than a *post hoc* check on the reasonableness of the police officer's belief that an arrest or search was justified (McBarnet, 1979:32)....

When the procedural law becomes more explicit, it aids in generating information and producing outcomes detectives define as successful. In the Ontario context, enabling provisions of the federal *Narcotic Control Act*, federal *Criminal Code* (section 103 regarding weapons), provincial *Liquor Licence Act* and provincial *Highway Traffic Act* allow police to question suspects and conduct attendant physical searches (Helder, 1978; Ericson, 1980). Moreover, these and *Criminal Code* provisions regarding search warrants can be circumvented by the simple expedient of obtaining the consent of suspects (cf. Freedman and Stenning, 1977). Given the pervasiveness of police authority, suspects are particularly likely to consent (Ericson, 1980; Ericson and Baranek, 1981). Regardless, even in the rare instances where the police introduce evidence in court which is judged to have been obtained as a result of an illegal search, the evidence is still admissible because of the lack of an exclusionary rule (*The Queen v. Wray* (1970), 4 C.C.C. 1;

Law Reform Commission, 1973:6–8; Kaufman, 1974: 180–181).

As we have previously mentioned, the law on admissibility of suspect confessions is more enabling than controlling from the police viewpoint (see generally Kaufman, 1974). Failure to inform a suspect of his right to silence, or refusal to allow access to a lawyer while in police custody, are only factors to be taken into consideration by the judge in determining the voluntariness of the statement and therefore its admissibility. A wide range of promises and threats are allowed without rendering the statement inadmissible. Moreover, even if a statement is ruled to have been involuntarily obtained, that part of it which is supported by subsequently discovered fact is still admissible. Not incidentally, statements serve purposes other than as evidence in court; for example, they may help to convince the prosecutor that the police do have a case (Skolnick, 1966), and they are a means of generating information about the suspect and/or other activity that might be made into crime (Zander, 1978). . . .

Low Visibility, Knowledge and Information Control

The use of legal rules and police organizational rules to orient action has both prospective and retrospective aspects (see generally Bittner, 1970). Prospectively, detectives decide upon what actions to take according to how they can cover themselves in case their actions are called into question. They develop "prefigured justifications" (Dalton, 1959) which are formulated with reference to the rules, even if the intent is to deviate from them. Retrospectively, detectives make official accounts of their actions which conform with what they think the rules say should have been done in the circumstances (cf. LaFave, 1965: 428–429; Skolnick, 1966: 215; Buckner, 1970).

This use of rules is interlinked with the low visibility-knowledge-information control resource of detectives. Detectives are able to produce accounts which give the appearance of conformity to the rules because those persons to whom they are giving the accounts (e.g., superordinate police officers, Justices of the Peace, Crown attorneys, judges) rarely have the inclination or the capability to undertake an independent investigation which might produce a different version of events. . . .

The use of rules by detectives is inextricably bound in with the organizational accounts they give (cf. Carlen, 1976; Manning, 1977, 1977a; Sanders, 1977). Detectives explain, justify, and legitimate their actions with respect to what they think are the appropriate rules, and these rules are used in conjunction with their accounts to orient their actions. This helps us to appreciate why rules are not applied literally. Rules only become applicable in the process of developing an account (cf. Feeley, 1973: 420–421). . . .

As experts in the use of law, and as "accountants," detectives develop their skills through experience on the job. Their skills are embedded in their "recipe knowledge" (Berger and Luckmann, 1966: 56, 83) about the legal and police organizational rules and accounts needed to get the job done, not in the more abstract "specialist knowledge" obtained through formal education and training sessions. Detectives refer to this recipe knowledge as the "common sense" that can only be acquired through extensive experience on the job. . . .

The most pervasive and persuasive form of power is the power to define and produce reality. This power is in turn dependent upon other power resources, including access to relevant knowledge, knowledge about how that relevant knowledge is socially distributed, the differential availability of *legitimate* accounts for actions, and the visibility of the process by which accounts are generated (see generally Berger and Luckmann, 1966; Silverman, 1970; Benson, 1977). This power is exercised *over* what might be accepted as a legitimate account of reality, and *through* the particular account of reality that is given as it influences a particular course of action (cf. Hosticka, 1979).

The police organization as a whole has a key "positional advantage" (Cook, 1977) over the organizations of criminal control because these organizations depend upon the police for accounts of what happened in "criminal" events. Indeed, because the processes by which the police produce their accounts are not visible to the other agencies of criminal control (i.e., other agents are not present when victims are interviewed and suspects are interrogated, etc.), these agencies also depend upon the police for an account of the procedures by which the police produced their account of what happened. . . .

These conditions of secrecy extend even further when we consider members of the community being policed. Their only possible sources of knowledge are personal experience in an individual case, newspaper accounts concerning "public" aspects of specific cases, and official statistics on what members of the police organization have collectively chosen to make into crime. Operations of the police organization remain well insulated from members of the community, leaving them in a position where they cannot judge what is being done on their behalf, or against them. . . .

Moreover, within the police organization there are low visibility conditions which allow individuals and sub-units to operate with certain rules that are unknown to other members. They can forge a course of action that meets their own interests as long as they formulate what they did in ways that will be accepted routinely by their superordinates. In short, on the level of the police organization as a whole, and on sub-unit and individual levels, "the exercise of discretion is usually not known to any person who might be motivated to challenge it" (LaFave, 1965: 154).

. . . Detectives exercise power over what happens to the information they collect, including what to omit from their reports, and how to construct the reports in a way that is likely to produce the outcome they want.

In constructing their reports, detectives are confronted with the task of turning the complexities of a case into a simple account. In this construction, they include what they understand to be organizationally relevant and exclude things which might complicate the case they have decided to make. Herein lies one of the paradoxes of detective work. The detective must be suspicious of the appearances that citizens present to him: "you suspect your grandmother and that's about the strength of it" (Banton, 1964, quoting a police officer). On the other hand, the detective cannot distrust all appearances because he needs to ground his decisions in a reality that will allow him to carry out his investigations (Sanders, 1977:20). . . .

When constructing an account of his investigations, the detective is involved in a process of transforming an individual event into categories which have a character of permanence and exactness. These categories are drawn from the available stock of categories stored within the police and wider legal organizations. Use of these categories allows the detective to assume that everyone else will know what this case consists of. It allows the detective, his superordinates, the prosecutor, and other court officials, to accept his account as "the facts," and therefore to act "*as if* they are in a state of perfect knowledge, and *as if* this "perfect knowledge" has fairly stable constitutive elements . . . " (Carlen, 1976: 88, emphasis added).

"The facts" are not independent of the interpretive work that detectives use to construct them. The only question of objectivity is: how do detectives produce "facts" which come to be accepted as objective by those who receive and act upon them? Once they have decided to make something a "crime" and someone a "criminal," how do detectives "stage" it as being what they made of it? . . .

There is potential for creativity in detective work. Creativity comes about as a detective tinkers with various strategies to handle situational exigencies of a case. The kaleidoscope of people and problems the detective confronts ensures that these creative elements will enter from time to time. However, the vast majority of strategies employed and decisions made are neither creative nor original because they are derived from the available stock of recipe knowledge about rule usage and accounting practices. The range of things an event can be made into legitimately, and the number and range of things a person can be charged with legitimately, are organizationally circumscribed and constrained. The legitimate rules are not their rules, but the property of the legal and police organizations. The legitimate accounting practices—the reports on their investigations, and the number of crimes and crime clearances they report—are not their accounting practices, but the property of the legal and police organizations. In short, detectives do not just make it all up according to the whims of an informal system. Their construction of cases—the way in which they make events into crimes and people into criminals—is endemic to the organizations within which they operate....

Notes

[1] A detailed consideration of these organizational forums as conceived in socio-legal literature on the police is presented in Ericson (1980: Ch. 1). The concept of organization as employed in this book derives from the discussion in Silverman (1970).

[2] Following Giddens (1976:104), "... social practices may be studied, first, from the point of view of their constitution as a series of acts, 'brought off' by actors; second, as constituting forms of *interaction*, involving the communication of meaning; and third, as constituting *structures* which pertain to 'collectivities' or 'social communities.' "

[3] For example, Packer (1968: 5) introduces his treatise on the uses of the criminal sanction by describing it as "an argument about the uses of power," and then asserts that "the criminal sanction is the paradigm case of the controlled use of power within society."

[4] The type of research we are reporting, and the paradigm within which it is framed can be contrasted with the work of Hogarth (1971). Hogarth related judicial attitudes and attendant philosophies of punishment to sentencing behaviour, without incorporating organizational elements in the way we have conceived them. We do not claim superiority of one approach over the other. They address different questions and therefore produce very different explanations for variability in the decisions of officials. We are concerned with generating and explaining data on the socially structured sources of detective discretion, rather than with documenting personal variations in exercising that discretion.

[5] For example, prison guards have responded in similar ways when new rules have been introduced into the prison setting. (Hawkins, 1976: Ch. 5; Ellis, 1979).

References

Alschuler, A. (1968) "The Prosecutor's Role in Plea Bargaining," *University of Chicago Law Review* 36: 50–112.

Alschuler, A. (1978) "Sentencing Reform and Prosecutorial Power: A Critique of Recent Proposals for "Fixed" and "Presumptive" Sentencing." *University of Pennsylvania Law Review* 126: 550–577.

Bayley, D. (1977) "The Limits of Police Reform," in D. Bayley (ed.) *Police and Society.* Beverly Hills: Sage.

Benson, J. (1977) "Innovation and Crisis in Organizational Analysis." *The Sociological Quarterly* 18: 3–16.

Berger, P. and Luckmann, T. (1966) *The Social Construction of Reality: A Treatise in the Sociology of Knowledge.* Middlesex: Penguin.

Bittner, E. (1967a) "Police Discretion in Emergency Apprehension of Mentally Ill Persons." *Social Problems* 14: 278–292.

Bittner, E. (1967b) "The Police on Skid Row: A Study of Peace Keeping." *American Sociological Review* 32: 699–715.

Bittner, E. (1970) *The Functions of the Police in Modern Society.* Rockville, Maryland: NIMH.

Black, D. (1968) *Police Encounters and Social Organization: An Observation Study.* Ph.D. dissertation, University of Michigan.

Black, D. (1972) "The Boundaries of Legal Sociology." *Yale Law Journal* 81(6): 1086–1110.

Bottomley, A. and Coleman, C. (1979) "Police Effectiveness and the Public: The Limitations of Official Crime Rates." Paper presented to the Cambridge Conference on Police Effectiveness, Cambridge, England, July 11–13.

Buckner, H.T. (1970) "Transformations of Reality in the Legal Process." *Social Research* 37: 88–101.

Carlen, P. (1976) *Magistrates' Justice.* London: Martin Robertson.

Chatterton, M. (1976) "Police in Social Control" in *Control Without Custody.* Cropwood Papers, Institute of Criminology, University of Cambridge.

Cook, K. (1977) "Exchange and Power in Networks of Interorganizational Relations." *The Sociological Quarterly* 18: 62–82.

Dalton, M. (1959) *Men Who Manage,* New York: Wiley.

Ditton, J. (1979) *Controlology: Beyond the New Criminology.* London: Macmillan.

Ennis, P.M. (1967) *Criminal Victimization in the United States: A Report of a National Survey.* Washington: U.S. Government Printing Office.

Ericson, R. (1982) *Reproducing Order: A Study of Police Patrol Work.* Toronto: University of Toronto Press.

Ericson, R. and Baranek, P. (1982) *The Ordering of Justice: A Study of Accused Persons as Dependents in the Criminal Process.*

Feeley, M. (1973) "Two Models of the Criminal Justice System: An Organizational Perspective." *Law and Society Review* 7: 407–425.

Freedman, D. and Stenning, P. (1977) *Private Security, Police and the Law in Canada.* Toronto: Centre of Criminology, University of Toronto.

Giddens, A. (1976) *New Rules of Sociological Method.* London: Hutchinson.

Helder, H. (1978) "Power Relationships and Proactive Police Searches." unpublished paper, Toronto: Centre for Criminology, University of Toronto.

Hosticka, C. (1979) "We Don't Care What Happened, We only Care About What Is Going to Happen: Lawyer-client Negotiations of Reality." *Social Problems* 26: 599–610.

Kaufman, F. (1974) *The Admissibility of Confessions.* Toronto: Carswell.

Kokis, R. (1977) "Domestic Violence: A Study of Police Non-Enforcement." M.A. Dissertation, Centre of Criminology, University of Toronto.

LaFave, W. (1965) *Arrest: The Decision to Take a Suspect into Custody.* Boston: Little Brown.

Law Reform Commission of Canada (1973) *Evidence: Compellability of the Accused and the Admissibility of his Statements.* Study Paper, 44 pp.

McBarnet, D. (1976) "Pre-trial Procedures and the Construction of Conviction" in P. Carlen (ed.) *The Sociology of Law.* Keele: Department of Sociology, University of Keele.

McBarnet, D. (1979) "Arrest: The Legal Context of Policing" in S. Holdaway (ed.) *The British Police.* London: Edward Arnold.

McDonald, L. (1976) *The Sociology of Law and Order.* London: Faber.

Manning, P. (1972) "Observing the Police Deviants, Respectables and the Law" in J. Douglas (ed.) *Research on Deviance.* New York: Random House.

Manning, P. (1977) *Police Work*. Cambridge, Mass.: MIT Press.

Manning, P. (1977a) "Rules in Organizational Context: Narcotics Law Enforcement in Two Settings." *The Sociological Quarterly* 18: 44–61.

Manning, P. (1979) "Organization and Environment: Influences on Police Work." Paper presented to the Cambridge Conference on Police Effectiveness, Cambridge, England, July 11–13.

Packer, H. (1968) *The Limits of the Criminal Sanction*. London: Oxford University Press.

Pepinsky, H. (1975) "Police Decision-Making" in D. Gottfredson (ed.) *Decision-Making in the Criminal Justice System: Reviews and Essays*. Rockville, Md.: NIMH.

Pepinsky, H. (1976) "Police Patrolmen's Offense-Reporting Behavior." *Journal of Research in Crime and Delinquency* 13(1): 33–47.

Reiss, A. and Bordua, D. (1967) "Environment and Organization: A Perspective on the Police" in D. Bordua (ed.) *The Police: Six Sociological Essays*. New York: Wiley.

Rubinstein, J. (1973) *City Police*. New York: Farrar, Strauss and Giroux.

Sanders, W. (1977) *Detective Work*. New York: Free Press.

Silverman, D. (1970) *The Theory of Organizations*. London: Heinemann.

Skogan, W. (1976) "Crime and Crime Rates" in W. Skogan (ed.) *Sample Surveys of Victims of Crimes*. Cambridge, Mass.: Ballinger Press.

Skolnick, J. (1966) *Justice Without Trial*. New York: Wiley.

Sparks, R. et al. (1977) *Surveying Victims: A Study of the Measurement of Criminal Victimization, Perception of Crime, and Attitudes to Criminal Justice*. London: Wiley.

Strauss, A. (1978) *Negotiations*. San Francisco: Jossey-Bass.

Sykes, R. and Clark, J. (1975) "A Theory of Deference Exchange in Police Civilian Encounters." *American Journal of Sociology* 81(3): 584–600.

Turk, A. (1973) "Review of *The New Criminology*" Mimeo., Toronto: Centre of Criminology, University of Toronto.

Turk, A. (1977) "Class, Conflict and Criminalization." *Sociological Focus*. 10: 209–220.

Weick, K. (1969) *The Social Psychology of Organizing*. Reading, Mass.: Addison-Wesley.

Wilson, J. (1968) *Varieties of Police Behavior*. Cambridge, Mass.: Harvard University Press.

Wilson, J. and Boland, B. (1979) "The Effect of Police on Crime." *Law and Society Review* 12: 367–390.

Zander, M. (1978) "The Right of Silence in the Police Station and the Caution" in P. Glazebrook (ed.) *Reshaping the Criminal Law*. London: Stevens.

59 The Administrative Revolution in the Canadian Office

Graham S. Lowe

GRAHAM S. LOWE teaches sociology at the University of Alberta, Edmonton. He has also taught at the University of Toronto and the Labour College of Canada. His research projects and publications span a range of topics in the sociology of work and industry. Recent articles have appeared in *On the Job*, edited by C. Heron and R. Storey, *The Canadian Journal of Sociology*; *The Canadian Review of Sociology and Anthropology* and *Work and Occupations*. Professor Lowe co-edited *Working Canadians* (with H. Krahn) and co-authored *Under Pressure: A Study of Job Stress* with H. Northcott. Issues raised in the excerpt below are explored in his book, *Women in the Administration Revolution: The Feminization of Clerical Work* (1987). Currently he is part of a research team studying the problems of youth employment, underemployment, and unemployment in three Canadian cities.

THE ADMINISTRATIVE REVOLUTION: MAJOR OCCUPATIONAL AND ORGANIZATIONAL DIMENSIONS

Not all offices, even within large organizations, experienced the full impact of the administrative revolution. We can nonetheless assert that by the Depression, five characteristics could be found in central offices of leading firms and major government departments across the country. Here, then, is what gave shape to the administrative revolution between 1911 and 1931: (a) a huge increase in the clerical sector of the labour force; (b) a dramatic shift in the clerical sex ratio toward female employees; (c) a concentration of new clerical jobs in the leading industries of corporate capitalism; (d) a relative decline in the socio-economic position of the clerk; and (e) the rationalization of office work by an emergent group of "scientifically oriented," efficiency-conscious office managers.

The Growth of Clerical Occupations

The proportion of clerical workers in a country's labour force is a good index of both the internal bureaucratization of enterprises and the general level of industrialization (Bendix, 1974:211). It is thus not surprising to find that rapid clerical growth paralleled the ascendancy of corporate capitalism in Canada after 1900. Table 1 shows that the number of clerks increased from 33,017 in 1891 to 1,310,910 in 1971. In other words, the proportion of the total labour force engaged in clerical occupations shot from 2 per cent to 15.2 per cent. Now the largest single occupational group in Canada, clerks have been at the forefront of the expansion of the white-collar labour force throughout the century.

The clerical growth rate peaked between 1911 and 1921. While this was followed by another decade of intensified expansion between 1941 and 1951, the earlier period is most significant because it demarcates the

611

Table 1
TOTAL LABOUR FORCE, CLERICAL WORKERS AND FEMALE CLERICAL WORKERS,
CANADA, 1891–1971*

	Total Labour Force	Total Clerical	Clerical Workers as a Percentage of Total Labour Force	Females as a Percentage of Total Clerical	Female Clerks as a Percentage of Total Female Labour Force
1891	1,659,335	33,017	2.0%	14.3%	2.3%
1901	1,782,832	57,231	3.2	22.1	5.3
1911	2,723,634	103,543	3.8	32.6	9.1
1921	3,164,348	216,691	6.8	41.8	18.5
1931	3,917,612	260,674	6.7	45.1	17.7
1941	4,195,951	303,655	7.2	50.1	18.3
1951	5,214,913	563,083	10.8	56.7	27.4
1961	6,342,289	818,912	12.9	61.5	28.6
1971	8,626,930	1,310,910	15.2	68.9	30.5

*Data adjusted to 1951 Census occupation classification.

Sources:
Canada D.B.S., Census Branch, *Occupational Trends in Canada, 1891–1931* (Ottawa, 1939), Table 5.
Meltz, *Manpower in Canada* (Ottawa: Queen's Printer, 1969), Section I, Tables A-1, A-2 and A-3.
1971 Census of Canada, Volume 3, Part 2, Table 2.

administrative revolution. The 1911 to 1921 boom in clerical jobs cannot be attributed to either population or labour force growth, both of which were much more pronounced during the preceding decade. The lag in clerical growth during the 1920s does not mean that the administrative revolution was losing its force. Rather, it was in this decade that the growing army of clerks was moulded into an efficient corps of administrative functionaries. Clerical procedures were increasingly rationalized and mechanized to consolidate and control the burgeoning office staffs. By the 1930s, the foundations of the modern office had thus been laid.

The Feminization of Clerical Work

Nowhere has the feminization trend in the labour force been more pronounced during this century than in clerical occupations. Strictly male-dominated at the turn of the century, by 1941 the majority of clerical jobs were held by women (see Table 1). The rate of feminization in the office was highest from 1891 to 1921. Increases exceeded 166 per cent in each decade, almost ten times that for the total female labour force (Lowe, 1980). There was an absolute increase in the number of female clerks over this period from 4,710 to 90,577, with the female share of clerical jobs reaching 22.1 per cent by 1921 (Table 1). This signals the emergence of a trend which resulted in the concentration of 30.5 per cent of all female workers in clerical occupations by 1971.

The segregation of women into a small number of relatively unrewarding occupations has remained fairly stable since 1900 (Armstrong and Armstrong, 1978: 20). This is especially true of clerical work, where the share of clerical jobs held by females steadily increased over this century. Segregation characterized certain key office jobs even in the early stages of the administrative revolution. In stenography and typing, for example, the "female" label became firmly affixed as the proportion of jobs held by women rose from 80 per cent to 95 per cent between 1901 and 1931 (Lowe, 1980)....

The Changing Industrial Distribution of Clerical Workers

There is a direct connection between shifts in the industrial employment patterns of clerks and the advance of corporate capitalism. In brief, clerks became concentrated in manufacturing and in major service industries. The most rapid expansion of clerical jobs between 1911 and 1931 occurred in manufacturing, the sector most directly connected with the entrenchment of corporate capitalism. Facilitating the creation of a manufacturing base in the economy was the development of a wide range of services, especially in trade, finance and transportation and communication. By combining these four sectors—manufacturing, transportation and communication, trade and finance—we can account for over 85 per cent of total clerical growth between 1911 and 1931. It was during this period that the most dramatic shifts in the industrial distribution of clerical employment occurred.

Most of the new clerical jobs created in manufacturing and service industries between 1911 and 1931 were fundamentally different from the craft-like bookkeeping jobs typical of the nineteenth-century office. Traditional clerical tasks were fragmented and routinized. Employers thus offered lower salaries, expecting less job commitment from workers. Women were considered more suitable for this new stratum of clerical jobs than men. Lower female wage rates, the higher career aspirations of male clerks and stereotypes of women as better able to perform monotonous, routine work underlay this shift in clerical labour demand. Consequently, we find that by 1931 manufacturing, trade and finance each accounted for over 20 per cent of all female clerical employment (Lowe, 1980). These three sectors had over 40 per cent of their positions occupied by women by 1931 (Lowe, 1979: 190). The most dramatic shift in sex composition occurred in the finance industry. Women were a rarity in banks, insurance companies and other financial institutions in 1900, yet within years they came to occupy almost 50 per cent of the clerical posts in such firms (Lowe, 1979: 184).

The Relative Decline of Clerical Earnings

Accompanying the rapid growth of clerical jobs was the erosion of the clerk's socio-economic position. This is to be expected, given the de-skilling of the clerical labour process and the influx of lower paid females into offices.... Wages entered into a steady decline after 1921, cutting below the labour force average wage by 1951.[1] Influencing this general trend was the rise in blue-collar wages over the century, and the expansion of the potential clerical supply through the spread of public education.

The feminization process created two fairly distinct clerical labour pools, one male and the other female. It is noteworthy, then, that the wages for both groups have declined relative to the total labour force since 1901. Male clerical wages dropped from 25 per cent above the labour force average in 1931 to 11 per cent below the average by 1971. Likewise, female clerks, while better off than women in other job ghettos, have been rapidly losing ground. From a wage advantage of between 48 per cent and 49 per cent from 1931 to 1941, female clerical salaries fell to only 6 per cent above the female labour force average by 1971. In making the comparisons between male and female clerical wage trends, we must bear in mind that female clerks earned 53 per cent of their male counterparts in 1901, inching up slightly to 58 per cent by 1971 (Lowe, 1980).[2] ...

... The advance of office rationalization, when combined with the general clerical wage trends, provides evidence of gradual clerical proletarianization. Indeed, the women who now operate modern office machines are considered the most proletarianized sector of the white-collar work force (*Work in America*, 1973: 38; Rinehart, 1975: 92; Glenn and Feldberg, 1977). Clearly, the roots of proletarianization can be traced back to the administrative revolution in the early decades of the twentieth century.

The Rationalization of the Office

The transition from nineteenth-century small-scale entrepreneurial capitalism to twentieth-century corporate capitalism involved a number of fundamental organizational changes. Foremost among these was the growing predominance of bureaucracy, for it was the form of work organization best suited to capitalism (see Weber, 1958; 1964). As Bendix (1974: 2) argues, industrialization is "the process by which large numbers of employees are concentrated in a single enterprise and become dependent upon the directing and co-ordinating activities of entrepreneurs and managers." Accompanying the rise of bureaucracy was the emergence of a new occupational group, the expert salaried manager. The growing size and complexity of enterprises compelled owners to delegate daily operating responsibility to hired managers. Administration thus became a specialized activity after 1900, as managers sought the most efficient ways to achieve organizational goals (see Chandler, 1978; Nelson, 1975). The major strategy utilized by managers was organizational rationalization. Consequently, rigid hierarchies with clear lines of authority were developed, new accounting procedures were implemented to control production and labour costs, traditional labour skills were broken down as the division of labour became more specialized, and workers' control over the productive process passed to management with increasing standardization and mechanization of tasks. Braverman (1974: 107) claims that the key to all modern management is "the control over work through the control over decisions that are

made in the course of work." This principle applied equally to office and factory.

When William H. Leffingwell (1917) published the first book on scientific office management in 1917, he found a receptive audience among many American and Canadian office managers. By the early 1920s, there is evidence that large offices were being rationalized according to the dictates of scientific management in order to increase administrative efficiency.[3] In fact, after 1910 major business publications such as the *Monetary Times*, *Industrial Canada* and the *Journal of the Canadian Bankers' Association* devoted increasing coverage to a variety of managerial reforms designed to rationalize work procedures. Even as early as 1905, Canadian manufacturers were cautioned to control rising office overhead (*Industrial Canada*, July 1905: 843). In the finance sector, the Bank of Nova Scotia pioneered a system for measuring the efficiency of branch staff (Bank of Nova Scotia Archives, n.d.). Not until 1910, however, did the new science of management really catch hold in Canadian industry. Canadian businessmen, as well as senior government administrators, were attracted to the ideology of efficiency inspired by F.W. Taylor's program of scientific factory management....

Mechanized clerical procedures were perhaps the most visible feature of office rationalization. As we have indicated above, tasks such as typing and operating other office machines were defined as "women's work" from their inception. The close interconnection between feminization and the mechanization of office work clearly demonstrates how the rationalization of the clerical labour process was fundamental to the administrative revolution. Interestingly, early stenographers performed craft-like jobs—evidenced by their consequently attained considerable socio-economic status (Lowe, 1980). However, by World War I, dictation and typing, the two core elements of the job, were being separated. Dictation machines facilitated the organization of central typing pools. Combining technical innovation with organizational rationalization, these pools gave rise to the "office machine age" (Mills, 1956: 195)....

ADMINISTRATIVE CONTROL AND THE TRANSFORMATION OF THE OFFICE

... We have argued that the modern office is the administrative centre of corporate capitalism. Through the office, managers attempt to exercise greater control and co-ordination over internal operations and employees as well as larger environmental factors affecting the organization. However, in order for the office to function effectively in this role, increasing control had to be exercised over office administration. The notion of administrative control thus has a dual meaning. In the first sense, control can help us explain the growth of clerical occupations. The second can account for the rationalization of the office and the clerical labour process. In short, we are suggesting that in order for administrative control to be exercised *through* the office, managers also had to apply the same principles of control *over* the office.

Let us set this argument out in more detail before exploring its theoretical underpinnings. The concept of administrative control encompasses the organizational, occupational and economic dimensions of the administrative revolution. But exactly how did these variables interact to transform the means of administration? On the economic plane, the rise of corporate capitalism after 1900 brought rapid expansion to Canada's manufacturing and service industries. It was in these industries, we have noted, that the escalating demands for the processing, analysis and storage of information created a boom in clerical employment. The central organizational feature of the administrative revolution was the rise of the office bureaucracy. Driven by the competitive forces of the marketplace, cap-

italists carried out mergers and consolidations. The resulting corporate entities had their equivalent in the public sector in the form of large government bureaucracies. Whether the organizations were public or private, or engaged in services or manufacturing, the office became the nerve centre of management. For it was through the office that the daily operations of large-scale organizations were run. This brings us to the main occupational dynamic underlying the administrative revolution. The modern corporation—and in a similar fashion, the public bureaucracy—delegates operating authority to expert salaried managers. This new semi-professional group became increasingly concerned over aspects of organizational design, the work process and other nontechnical factors which may have hindered the achievement of overall goals, be they profit maximization or efficient public service.

As the role of the office became enlarged to include co-ordination of internal activities and regulation of environmental factors impinging upon the organization's future, strains and inefficiencies resulted. In short, the office itself became stricken with bureaucratic maladies. Soaring clerical costs threatened to undermine profits or, in the case of public bureaucracies, cost efficiency. By the First World War, office managers were beginning to recognize the advantages of office rationalization. It was the managerial drive for higher efficiency in clerical operations and greater regimentation of the office labour force which underlay the rationalization of the clerk's job.

Two trends thus converged, precipitating a transformation in office work. First, more clerks were required to process the flood of information. Second, managers increasingly came to rely upon the office as the support system for their power and authority. The office was the key instrument in all managerial decision making. Together, these factors magnified the scope of office procedures. Inefficiencies in clerical routines—resulting from organizational weaknesses as well as from the underlying tensions of worker resistance to their subordination—were exacerbated. This launched a managerial drive for control over the clerical labour process. The result was a highly rationalized office in which de-skilled jobs were defined as suitable women's work. What this suggests is that three factors, linked by the concept of administrative control, underlay the administrative revolution: (a) the rapid growth of manufacturing and service industries; (b) the growing predominance of large-scale bureaucratic work organizations; and (c) the operation of these organizations by a cadre of salaried managers concerned with the efficient co-ordination of work activities and the regulation of workers. It is now useful for us to analyse how each of these factors contributed to the administrative revolution.

The Dynamics of Corporate Capitalism

There can be little doubt that the rise of corporate capitalism paralleled the changes we have already documented in administration between 1911 and 1931. Manufacturing, the cornerstone of an industrial economy, underwent tremendous expansion after 1900. Between 1880 and 1929, the number of manufacturing establishments was reduced from 50,000 to 22,000 through mergers and acquisitions (Firestone, 1953: 160). At the same time, the gross value of production soared from 700 million to 3,116 million (constant) dollars (Firestone, 1953: 160). The wheat boom in western Canada during the first decade of the twentieth century provided the primary stimulus for this rapid industrialization (Buckley, 1974: 4; Brown and Cook, 1976: 83–84). The First World War also was crucial, precipitating faster, more far-reaching expansion of industry than would have occurred under normal conditions. Much of the new industry established was accounted for by U.S. direct investment. The number of U.S. manufacturing branch plants

increased from 100 in 1900 to 1,350 by the end of 1934 (Marshall, et al., 1976: 18). By 1918, we find that "the foundation for a modern industrial economy had been laid" (Firestone, 1953: 1952). . . .

A direct measure of the growing demand for clerical workers in manufacturing is the changing ratio of administrative to production workers. As the economy expanded and factories grew, more office staff was required to administer the rising production. We thus find that the number of administrative employees (mainly clerical, but also including supervisory workers) for every one hundred workers in manufacturing increased from 8.6 in 1911 to 16.9 by 1931 (International Labour Office, 1937: 513). What this demonstrates is the direct connection between the advance of industrialization and the development of large central offices.

Service industries also underwent remarkable growth in response to the demands of an emerging industrial economy. Similarly, this sparked an enlargement of office staff. The development of white-collar bureaucracies was, in fact, most apparent in the service sector. For example, the insurance business grew by 850 per cent between 1909 and 1929, yet the number of companies only increased by one, to 41 (Poapst, 1950: 14). Sun Life Assurance began acquiring other insurance firms in 1890, when its head office staff numbered 20. Between 1910 and 1930, a total of 13 acquisitions was made, bringing the number of head office staff to 2,856 employees (see Neufeld, 1972; Sun Life Archives, Personnel File no. 2). . . .

In sum, the rise of manufacturing and service industries established a modern capitalist economy in Canada by the 1930s. Fundamental to this economic development was the concentration of employment into large bureaucracies. It is indeed significant that, during the period we are studying, there were two major waves of corporate mergers and acquisitions, one from 1909 to 1913 and another more pronounced wave from 1925 to 1929 (Weldon, 1966: 233). This combination of industrialization and bureaucratization set the stage for the rise of modern administration.

BUREAUCRACY AND THE MODERN OFFICE

... Neither the Marxian nor the Weberian view alone can fully address the question of how and why the administrative revolution took place. It is therefore useful to combine aspects of both. The Marxian perspective helps us to see how modern management largely entails the transfer of control over the productive process from workers to managers. The results, plainly evident in the twentieth-century office and factory, are devastating: job fragmentation, rigid hierarchies, and the coercive discipline and surveillance of workers—what Braverman (1974) refers to as the degradation of labour. But it is also reasonable to assert that inefficiency stemming from organizational problems often has sparked rationalization. How else would one explain the dramatic transformations in government offices, executed by foremost American scientific management experts, during the 1920s? The issue of organizational inefficiency suggests, then, that a modified Weberian view is also useful. The problems of large-scale organization reflect the tendency for co-ordination and integration to break down with increased division of labour and structural differentiation. These are organizational problems, although one could argue that the rise of modern bureaucracy was itself fundamentally a by-product of capitalist development. What this misses, however, is that against the background of capitalist development, managerial initiatives were also directed against problems resulting directly from the expansion of bureaucracy.

By combining the economic and class perspectives of Marxism with the organizational emphasis of the Weberian tradition, we can thus account for the growth of clerical jobs and the transformation of office procedures in both public and private bureaucracies. This is achieved by defining administrative control as encompassing strategies to deal with the economic forces of competition and capital accumulation, means of regulating labour and diminishing class conflict, and systems to improve the co-ordination and integration of organizational operations. To more fully understand how administrative control was exercised through the office, and its impact on clerical workers, we must consider the origins and functions of modern management.

Modern Management and the Office

The rise of modern management was a crucial aspect of the administrative revolution, for only through the actions of this new semi-professional group were changes brought about in the office. The office began to assume its contemporary functions in the closing decades of the nineteenth century. Litterer (1963) documents how specialized staff functions originated with the advent of cost clerks and production control clerks in factories (see Nelson, 1975). Cost accounting—toward which Canadian manufacturers turned their attention after the turn of the century—and other scientific approaches to factory management were the administrative sequel to mechanized production (Landes, 1969). The office thus began to dominate the factory, becoming the "visible hand" of management....

The most prominent managerial strategy for dealing with organizational problems and regulating workers' activities was Taylorism. Frederick W. Taylor's science of management, widely disseminated by the start of the First World War, involved three basic axioms: (a) the dissociation of the labour process from the skills of the workers; (b) the separation of the conception and execution of a task; and (c) the application of management's resulting knowledge of the labour process to control each step in production (see Braverman, 1974; Copley, 1923; Urwick, 1957; Nelson, 1975). The cumulative effect of these initiatives leads Rinehart (1978: 6) to observe that "today, most workers are locked into jobs that require little knowledge and skill and that are defined and controlled from the upper echelons of complex organizations."

Two points can be made regarding the impact of the managerial thrust for control of the office. First, especially in manufacturing we find a direct link between the extension of managerial control and clerical growth.... And second, as the scope of office operations expanded, managers in both manufacturing and service industries found it necessary to apply principles of rationalization, which originated in the factory, to clerical work.

"Management, the brain of the organization," to use a physiological analogy, "conveys its impulses through the clerical systems which constitute the nervous mechanism of the company" (Murdoch and Dale, 1961: 2). This underlines how clerical work furnished the means of integrating the components of an organization. Even in white-collar industries, such as insurance or banking, special departments were established to facilitate managerial control over administrative practices. As one insurance executive asserts, "office administration is not a job by itself. We are in the insurance business, and office administration, scientific office administration, is merely one of the tools to help us carry on the insurance business more efficiently" (Life Office Management Association, 1927: 188). By the First World War, office managers in both Canada and the U.S., already aware of the importance of systematic administration, were being told that Taylorism and other scientific factory management schemes could be easily adapted to the office (Hagedorn, 1955: 167; Leffingwell, 1917: 5). The logic of office rationalization is clearly expressed by the father of scientific management, W.H. Leffingwell (1917: 35, 111, 109):

> Effective management implies control. The terms are in a sense interchangeable, as management without control is inconceivable, and both terms imply the exercise of a directing influence.... The clerical function may then be correctly regarded as the linking or connecting function, which alone makes possible the efficient performance of hundreds of individual operations involved in the "sub-assembly" cycles of the business machine as a whole....

This statement encapsulates the essential nature of the modern office. Without clerical procedures as efficient, predictable and regimented as the factory assembly line, managerial control over external and internal factors affecting organizational goals would be diminished.

CONCLUSIONS

The purpose of this paper has been to analyse the administrative revolution which occurred in major Canadian offices between 1911 and 1931. By the onset of the Depression, the central features of the contemporary office were well in place. Increasingly, the typical clerk was a woman who performed a specialized job, often machine-paced, in a highly regimented bureaucratic setting. As in any kind of large-scale social change, the transition from the old nineteenth-century counting house to the modern twentieth-century office was not a smooth, all-encompassing process. The changes described above in the nature of clerical work as well as in office organization and management took place in a more or less halting, uneven fashion. Evidence suggests, though, that alterations in the means of administration were sufficiently sweeping and well rooted by the 1930s to characterize them as a "revolution."

Theoretically, our task has been to unite

into a comprehensive explanation the broad occupational, economic and organizational forces associated with the rise of modern administration. This has been achieved by using the concept of administrative control. We have shown that control was the central feature in both the growth of the office and its rationalization by management....

Notes

[1] This wage pattern seems to be standard in advanced capitalist societies. Research in the U.S. by Braverman (1974) and Burns (1954) and in Britain by Lockwood (1966) documents how the growth of the white-collar sector of the labour force has been marked by a relative decline in clerical wages.

[2] This is consistent with broad labour force trends. In 1971, the average income of women doing paid work was about half that of men (Armstrong and Armstrong, 1975: 371).

[3] While Taylorism was undoubtedly the label most commonly attached to attempts to rationalize the labour process, it was only one strategy in the broad "thrust for efficiency" which took root after 1900 (see Palmer, 1975). The term scientific management includes, then, a variety of systematic programs initiated by management to inject order and efficiency into the organization and execution of work.

References

Albrow, Martin (1970) *Bureaucracy*, London: Macmillan.

Armstrong, Hugh and Pat Armstrong (1975) "The Segregated Participation of Women in the Canadian Labour Force, 1941–71," *Canadian Review of Sociology and Anthropology* 12: 370–84.

———— (1978) *The Double Ghetto: Canadian Women and Their Segregated Work*. Toronto: McClelland and Stewart.

Bank of Montreal (1956) *The Service Industries*. Study No. 17, Royal Commission on Canada's Economic Prospects.

Bank of Nova Scotia Archives n.d. "The Bank of Nova Scotia, 1832–1932, One Hundredth Anniversary." Toronto.

Bendix, Reinhart (1974) *Work and Authority in Industry*. Berkeley: University of California Press.

Blau, Peter M. (1963) *The Dynamics of Bureaucracy*, revised ed. Chicago: University of Chicago Press.

Braverman, Harry (1974) *Labor and Monopoly Capital: the Degradation of Work in the Twentieth Century*. New York: Monthly Review Press.

Brown, Robert Craig and Ramsay Cook (1976) *Canada 1896–1921: A Nation Transformed.* Toronto: McClelland and Stewart.

Buckley, Kenneth (1974) *Capital Formation in Canada, 1896–1930*. Toronto: McClelland and Stewart.

Burns, Robert K. (1954) "The Comparative Economic Position of Manual and White-Collar Employees," in *Journal of Business* 27: 257–67.

Canada Censuses, 1891–1971 (published and un-published data).

———— (1907) Wage-Earners by Occupations. 1901 Census, Bulletin 1. Ottawa: King's Printer.

———— (1939) Occupational Trends in Canada, 1891–1931. Special Bulletin, D.B.S. Census Branch, Ottawa: King's Printer.

———— (1961) *Manufacturing Industries of Canada*. Ottawa: D.B.S.

———— (1973) *1971 Annual Census of Manufacturers, Summary Statistics, Preliminary*. Ottawa: Statistics Canada.

———— (1974) *Canada Year Book*. Ottawa: Information Canada.

Chandler, Alfred D., Jr. (1977) *The Visible Hand:*

The Managerial Revolution in American Business. Cambridge, Mass.: Harvard University Press.

Clement, Wallace (1975) *The Canadian Corporate Elite.* Toronto: McClelland and Stewart.

Copley, F.B. (1923) *Frederick W. Taylor, Father of Scientific Managemen,* 2 Vols. New York: Harper and Row.

Dreyfuss, Carl (1938) *Occupation and Ideology of the Salaried Employee,* 2 Vols. trans. Eva Abramovitch. New York: Works Progress Administration and the Department of Social Science, Columbia University.

Firestone, O.J. (1953) "Canada's Economic Development, 1867–1952," paper prepared for the Third Conference of the International Association for Research in Income and Wealth, Castelgandolfo, Italy.

Glenn, Evelyn Nakano and Roslyn L. Feldberg (1977) "Degraded and Deskilled: The Proletarianization of Clerical Work," in *Social Problems* 25: 52–64.

Gulick, Luther (1937) "Notes on the Theory of Organization," in *Papers on the Science of Administration.* Luther Gulick and L. Urwick (eds.) New York: Institute of Public Administration.

Haber, Samuel (1964) *Efficiency and Uplift: Scientific Management in the Progressive Era, 1890–1920.* Chicago: University of Chicago Press.

Hagedorn, Homer J. (1955) "The Management Consultant as Transmitter of Business Techniques," in *Explorations in Entrepreneurial History* 7: 164–173.

Hoos, Ida R. (1961) *Automation in the Office.* Washington: Public Affairs Press.

Industrial Canada

International Labour Office (1937) "The Use of Office Machinery and Its Influence on Conditions of Work for Staff," in *International Labour Review* 36: 486–516.

Journal of The Canadian Bankers' Association

Kaufman, Herbert (1968) "The Administrative Function," in *International Encyclopedia of the Social Sciences* Vol. 1, David Sills (ed.) New York: Macmillan Co. and the Free Press.

Landes, David (1969) *The Unbound Prometheus: Technological Change and Industrial Development in Western Europe from 1750 to the Present.* Cambridge: Cambridge University Press.

Lederer, Emil (1937) *The Problem of the Modern Salaried Employee: Its Theoretical and Statistical Basis.* Trans. E.E. Warburg. New York: State Department of Social Welfare and the Department of Social Science, Columbia University.

Leffingwell, William Henry (1917) *Scientific Office Management.* Chicago: A.W. Shaw.

Life Office Management Association: Proceedings of Annual Conferences.

Litterer, Joseph A. (1963) "Systematic Management: Design for Organizational Recoupling in American Manufacturing Firms," in *Business History Review* 37: 369–391.

Lockwood, David (1966) *The Blackcoated Workers.* London: Allen and Unwin.

Lowe, Graham S. (1979) "The Administrative Revolution: The Growth of Clerical Occupations and the Development of the Modern Office in Canada, 1911–1931." Unpublished Ph.D. thesis, University of Toronto, Toronto.

———— (1980) "Women, Work and the Office: The Feminization of Clerical Occupations in Canada", 1901–1931, in *Canadian Journal of Sociology* 5 (forthcoming).

Marglin, Stephen A. (1971) "What Do Bosses Do?: The Origins and Functions of Hierarchy in Capitalist Production." Harvard Institute of Economic Research, Discussion Paper No. 222.

Marshall, Herbert, F.A. Southard and K.W. Taylor. (1976) *Canadian-American Industry.* Toronto: McClelland and Stewart.

Melman, Stewart (1951) "The Rise of Administrative Overhead in the Manufacturing Industries of the United States, 1899–1947," in *Oxford Economic Papers,* New Series 3: 62–112.

Meltz, Noah M. (1969) *Manpower in Canada, 1931–1961.* Ottawa: Queen's Printer.

Merton, Robert K. (1952) "Bureaucratic Structure and Personality," in *Reader in Bureaucracy.* R.K. Merton et al. (eds.) New York: Free Press.

Mills, C. Wright (1956) *White Collar: The American*

Middle Classes. New York: Oxford University Press.

Monetary Times

Murdoch, Allan A. and J. Rodney Dale (1961) *The Clerical Function: A Survey of Modern Clerical Systems and Methods*. London: Sir Isaac Pitman and Sons.

Nelson, Daniel (1975) *Managers and Workers: Origins of the New Factory System in the United States, 1880–1920*. Madison: University of Wisconsin Press.

Neufeld, E.P. (1972) *The Financial System of Canada*. Toronto: Macmillan.

Palmer, Bryan (1975) "Class, Conception and Conflict: The Thrust for Efficiency, Managerial Views of Labour and the Working Class Rebellion, 1903–22," in *Radical Review of Political Economics* 7: 31–49.

Poapst, James (1950) "The Growth of the Life Insurance Industry in Canada, 1909–47." Unpublished M. Comm. thesis, McGill University, Montreal.

Rinehart, James W. (1975) *The Tyranny of Work*. Don Mills: Longman Canada.

———— (1978) "Contradictions of Work-Related Attitudes and Behaviour: An Interpretation," in *Canadian Review of Sociology and Anthropology* 15: 1–15.

Rountree, Meredith G. (1936) *The Railway Worker: A Study of the Employment and Unemployment Problems of the Canadian Railways*. Toronto: Oxford University Press.

Rushing, William A. (1967) "The Effects of Industry Size and Division of Labour on Administration," in *Administrative Science Quarterly* 12: 273–295.

Shepard, Jon M. (1971) *Automation and Alienation: A Study of Office and Factory Workers*. Cambridge, Mass.: M.I.T. Press.

Simon, Herbert A. (1952) "Decision-Making and Administrative Organization," in *Reader in Bureaucracy*. R.K. Merton et al. (eds.) New York: Free Press.

———— (1976) *Administrative Behaviour*, 3rd ed. New York: Free Press.

Sun Life Assurance Co. Archives, Montreal.

Urquhart, M.C. and K.A.H. Buckley (1965) *Historical Statistics of Canada*. Toronto: Macmillan.

Weber, Max (1958) *From Max Weber: Essays in Sociology*. Trans. and ed. H.H. Gerth and C.W. Mills. New York: Oxford University Press.

———— (1964) *The Theory of Social and Economic Organization*. New York: Free Press.

Weldon, J.C. (1966) "Consolidation in Canadian Industry, 1900–1948," in *Restrictive Trade Practices in Canada*, L.A. Skeoch. (ed.) Toronto: McClelland and Stewart.

Work in America (1973) Report of a Special Task Force to the U.S. Secretary of Health, Education and Welfare prepared by the W.E. Upjohn Institute for Employment Research. Cambridge, Mass.: M.I.T. Press.

Theodorson, George A. and Achilles G. Theodorson (1969) *A Modern Dictionary of Sociology*. New York: Thomas Y. Crowell.

Urwick, Lyndall P. (1957) *The Life and Work of Frederick Winslow Taylor*. London: Urwick, Orr and Partners.

60 Alienated Labour

James W. Rinehart

JAMES W. RINEHART, Professor of Sociology at the University of Western Ontario, specializes in the study of social class, industrial relations and the labour process. In addition to the book from which this excerpt is taken, *The Tyranny of Work: Alienation and the Labour Process* (1987), Professor Rinehart is the author of numerous articles including "Improving the quality of working life through job redesign" (1986); "Appropriating workers' knowledge: Quality control circles at a General Motors plant" (1984); "A research note on class and authoritarian perspectives in Canada" with Edward Grabb (1980); and "Contradictions of work-related attitudes and behaviour: An interpretation" (1978). He has presented many papers at scholarly meetings and has organized a number of conferences and conference sessions, most particularly in connection with blue collar workers.

. . . According to Marx, there are four aspects of alienated labour. First, this condition entails an estrangement of working people from the products of their labour. The product—the purpose for which it is created, how it is disposed of, its content, quality, and quantity—is not determined by those whose labour is responsible for its manufacture. Under industrial capitalism, workers are obliged to surrender their power to determine the product of labour via a wage contract which in effect gives this power over to employers, that is, the capitalist class. . . .

Because the products of labour are determined by employers rather than by workers, it is employers who reap most of the benefits of productive activity. Even when working people experience absolute gains in their standard of living, their position, relative to that of capitalists, deteriorates. Marx wrote: "It follows therefore that in proportion as capital accumulates, the lot of the labourer, be *his payments high or low*, must grow worse."[1] Because products are under the control of owners of the means of production, increases in labour output such as those resulting from scientific advances, technological innovations, and refinements in the social organization of the workplace, accrue to the benefit of the propertied class. "The increase in the quantity of objects," Marx observed, "is accompanied by an *extension* of the realm of alien powers to which man is subjected."[2] Intensified productivity, then, extends and deepens the alienated position of workers in the system of production; it simultaneously stretches out the class system by increasing the political and economic gulf which separates workers and capitalists.[3]

If working people are estranged from the products of labour, they must also be alienated from the work process itself, that is, from their own labour activity. As Marx wrote, "the external character of labour for the workers appears in the fact that it is not his own but someone else's, that it does not belong to him, but to another."[4] Just as workers must give up their power to control the product of their toil, they also cede their ability to determine the intensity and duration of work, to define the manner in which work is organized, divided, and allocated, and to determine the tools and machines used in the production process. Furthermore, it is the employer who decides whether or not work will be performed at all.

From the fact that working people are estranged from the process and product of labour, Marx deduced two more aspects of alienation. The first one, self-estrangement, is tied to his conception of the meaning and purpose of work, which he viewed as *the* medium for self-expression and self-development. Work, Marx said, was the activity in which people can most clearly manifest their unique qualities as human beings. Properly organized, work brings out and reflects distinctively human attributes, that is, those which differentiate humans from all other species. It is through labour that humans should be able to shape themselves and the society in which they live in accordance with their own needs, interests, and values. Under alienating circumstances, however, work becomes not an endeavour which embodies and personifies life, not a source of personal and social gratification, but simply a means for physical survival. Marx argues that working people come to feel most contented in those activities that they share with all other living species—in procreating, drinking, and eating—in a word, in the satisfaction of physiological needs, while in their peculiarly human activity—work—people feel debased. Accordingly, work takes on an instrumental meaning: it is regarded simply as a means to an end. Individuals, then, are estranged from themselves; they are alienated from their own humanity.

The final type of alienation deals with the relationship of individuals to one another. Marx believed that people who occupy dominant and subordinate positions at the workplace are alienated from each other. Their relationship is an antagonistic one and is based purely on pecuniary considerations. This asymmetry of workplace relationships creates the foundation for a class structure that entails sharp differences in power, privilege, and life chances, and that inhibits social intercourse across class lines. Marcuse argues that "the system of capitalism relates men to each other through the commodities they ex-change. The social standing of individuals, their standard of living, the satisfaction of their needs, their freedom, and their power are all determined by the value of their commodities."[5] Alienation obviously characterizes the relationship between classes, but it also penetrates the interaction of people in the same class. Capitalists are compelled to drive out their competitors, and workers must competitively sell their labour power—their skills, talents, and energies—in order to survive.[6] This necessity leads to or exacerbates divisions within the working class, most notably along the lines of sex, age, and ethnicity. . . .

Since Marx's time, the concept of alienation has been broadened to apply to a bewildering array of disadvantaged groups, deviant behaviours, and aberrant mental states. After examining the literature on the subject one writer concluded that the term "has been used in such a variety of ways that it comes close to being a shorthand expression for all the socially based psychological maladies of modern man."[7] Despite this melange, there are two ideas that are common to most usages of the concept. Alienation always entails a notion of human estrangement—from persons, objects, values, or from oneself. Second, the source of alienation is seen as residing in the social structure rather than in individual personalities; its causes are social rather than psychological. Our usage of alienation retains the notions of estrangement and social causation. At the same time, we follow Marx in viewing alienation as characteristic of a certain kind of organization of work, one whose source lies primarily in the special set of socio-economic circumstances that accompanied the development of industrial capitalism.

When we speak of alienation in this book we are referring to a condition in which individuals have little or no control over (a) the purposes and products of the labour process, (b) the overall organization of the workplace, and (c) the immediate work process itself.[8] Defined this way, alienation is objective or structural in the sense that it is built into human relationships at the workplace and exists independent of how individuals perceive and evaluate their jobs. Alienation, then, can be viewed broadly as a condition of objective powerlessness.[9] . . .

Structural alienation means that work is not organized in accordance with the needs and interests, talents and abilities of working people. However, a complex set of psychological, cultural, and social forces influence the degree to which individuals *recognize* the sources of alienation, *adapt* to alienating work, and *express*—verbally and behaviourally—their disenchantment with work. Obviously, not all working people are conscious of their alienated position in work organizations in the sense that they are able to locate and articulate the socio-economic factors responsible for it. But all workers in objectively powerless circumstances do possess an *alienated consciousness* in that they directly experience and are acutely aware of the *effects* of structural alienation, such as repetitive and insecure jobs, insufficient wages, and arbitrary work rules. The test of the existence of alienated mental states is to be found not so much in the ability of individuals to articulate the causes of alienation, but primarily in their verbal and behavioural reactions to work. . . .

SOURCES OF ALIENATION

We can single out three major sources of alienated labour—concentration of the means of production in the hands of a small but dominant class, markets in land, labour, and commodities, and an elaborate division of labour. . . . A brief explanation of each is required at this point.

The alienating impact of elite ownership of the means of production is direct and obvious. If relatively few individuals control the productive apparatus, they will operate it to their own advantage. The majority of people, who will be obliged to work for the few, will be excluded from determining the products and the labour process.[10] The relationship between wage labour and capital is also an *exploitative* one, in so far as employers extract unpaid labour from working people. A major source of business profits is the appropriation by employers of surplus value, which is the difference between the value of commodities and services produced or provided by workers and the wage cost of maintaining these workers. Workers are required to remain at work beyond the point when they have produced an amount equal to their wages. During these unpaid hours a surplus (surplus value) is produced. Employers appropriate this surplus and reinvest a portion of it in the business in order to further expand their profits. This relationship of alienation and exploitation establishes the basis for permanent antagonisms between wage labour and capital. In their drive to generate profits and expand capital, employers strive to keep wages low, introduce labour-replacing machinery, and speed up, routinize, and control work. For their part, workers seek job security, adequate wages, the reduction of work time, and control over the labour process.[11]

The term "market" refers to an economic arrangement in which the distribution and use of land, the production of goods and services, and the income and security of individuals are regulated by money and prices, operating through supply and demand and subject to the relative power of buyers and sellers, employers and employees, and creditors and debtors.[12] A market society places land, labour, and commodity production under the domain of prices. Prices and profits become the ultimate determinants of the means and ends of production, and people are compelled to make decisions based on calculations of pecuniary gain. Business firms must take whatever steps are necessary to accumulate capital or to simply stay afloat. Consequently, human considerations are secondary to those of profitability. From the point of view of the employer workers represent merely another cost of production and are evaluated as commodities like any other object that is bought and sold.

The division of labour also exerts an alienating impact on work. While there are a number of different types of the division of labour, the most important ones are specialization and the separation of mental and manual labour or, more accurately stated, the separation of the conception of work from its performance. Specialization is a twofold process which entails a fragmentation of work into minute tasks and the permanent assignment of these tasks to specific individuals. Performed under such conditions, work becomes repetitive and mindless and narrowly circumscribes the development of human capacities. Although the separation of the conception and performance of work is only one type of specialization, we discuss it separately because it is the most salient form of labour division in terms of its consequences for alienation. In this case, certain individuals are responsible for the organization, conceptualization, and design of work, while others are assigned to the role of carrying out the tasks.

The structure and consequences of the three sources of alienation can be analyzed separately, but what must be stressed is their interdependence. With the rise of industrial capitalism each one stimulated the development of the other two. While markets and the division of labour antedated the industrial revolution, industrial capitalists intensified the fragmentation of work and stimulated the expansion of domestic and international markets. In turn, the greater productivity and profits made possible by the extended division of labour and the growth of consumer demand, in conjunction with mergers and the bankruptcy of non-competitive firms, contributed to the concentration of the means of production in fewer and fewer hands.

TECHNOLOGY AND INDUSTRIALISM

All too often the three factors discussed above are ignored, and alienated labour in modern society, if recognized at all, is regarded either as a permanent feature of the human condition or as the inevitable price we pay for the benefits of industrial technology. One way of evaluating the first thesis—that alienation transcends socio-historical boundaries—is to review the anthropological materials on the subject of work. Even a cursory perusal of these data reveals situations that are completely different from our own. In peasant and primitive societies work is an integral and not unpleasant aspect of existence. Work is fused with the totality of activities carried out by the community; it is embedded in and permeated by family and community relationships and obligations. Instead of being viewed as an onerous necessity by those who perform it, work is often regarded as indistinguishable from play, sociability, and leisure.[13]

It may come as a surprise to some readers that technology, mechanization, or industrialism have not been included among the causes of alienated labour. Many scholars who acknowledge the presence of serious discontents with work in modern societies attribute the problem to sophisticated technology, which allegedly requires centralization of knowledge and authority and a detailed division of labour.... This position of technological determinism cannot be sustained. At a given level of technological development, wide variations in alienation still exist in relation to the different ways in which production is socially organized. Alienation is *created* not by the existing state of technology and productive capacity but, as Edwards and his associates realize, by "the power relations in society which, for example, dictate the ends of productive effort, the use to which technology is to be put, and the very criteria by which some technologies are methodically developed and others left dormant and undeveloped."[14] The primary causes of alienation, then, reside in the social relations of production and particularly in relations of domination and subordination which give to the few the ability to direct and shape production to their own ends.[15]

Under capitalism, the development and selection of technology are guided not only by the goals of productivity and profitability, but also by employers' and managers' determination to minimize workers' control over the labour process.[16] Braverman states: "The capacity of humans to control the labour process through machinery is seized upon by management from the beginning of capitalism as the *prime means whereby production may be controlled not by the direct producer but by the owners and representatives of capital*. Thus, in addition to its technical function of increasing the productivity of labour—which would be a mark of machinery under any social system—machinery also has in the capitalist system the function of divesting the mass of workers of their control over their own labour."[17]

That the social relations of production are the primary cause of alienation does not mean that technology has no effect on workers. Some forms of technology are certainly more onerous to workers than others. The point we wish to stress is that technology's role in contributing to alienated labour is a derivative and secondary one. . . .

POSSIBLE SOLUTIONS

A number of possible solutions to alienated labour were considered. Leisure is no answer because work dominates our waking hours and affects the way in which we spend our time away from the job. Advanced technology provides no solution because its character and uses are decided by individuals and organizations interested in profitability and the perpetuation of class relationships. The net result of developments in automated technology is to shift employment toward the least desirable end of the occupational spectrum. Moreover, the monitoring capabilities of new electronic equipment enable managers to tighten their control over the labour process. Workplace reforms introduced by practitioners of classical human relations and its contemporary QWL versions have the appearance of striking at the core of alienation. Ostensibly, these programs democratize the workplace and provide more challenging jobs. Once the progressive rhetoric is penetrated, however, these measures are exposed as schemes implemented to achieve management's purposes. Similarly, job redesign is undertaken not to create challenging jobs but to enhance profits by rationalizing the labour process. Both the human relations approach and its more sophisticated contemporary variant—participative management—are used to promote collaborative relationships between bosses and workers and to erode and ultimately destroy the collective power of workers and unions. Unions have improved workplace conditions and the terms on which employees are obliged to dispose of their labour power. At the same time, unions represent an institutionalization rather than a resolution of conflict; collective bargaining and the contract stabilize labour-management relations. Since unions operate within rather than challenging the essential boundaries of capitalist power, they are able to deal with some of the effects but not the causes of alienated labour.

We are left with one answer—workers' control. Recall that alienation in the first instance is a structural condition in which workers are detached from control of their labour and its products. The antithesis of alienated labour is workers' control—not just over their immediate jobs but over the entire work process and its objectives. Workers' control strikes at the fundamental sources of alienation; it would entail a transfer of power from elites to working people. Decisions about the purposes of work could thus be aligned with the interests, values, and needs of workers and their communities. Technology would be designed and deployed not to enhance profits and class power but to fulfill the needs of workers and the broader community. The specialization of labour could be attacked and jobs rotated and enlarged in accordance with the needs and dispositions of individuals. The gulf separating manual and intellectual labour could be bridged, in part by the act of conceptualizing and planning, which workers in control must do, and in part by mass education, which would arm ordinary working people with a knowledge of the processes of production and distribution. These goals cannot be reached through the medium of worker-owned enterprises operating in capitalist economies dominated by gain corporations. While worker-owned enterprises obviously relieve alienation, opportunities for beginning and successfully running such undertakings are limited. Moreover, the transforming potential of such enterprises is constrained by market forces and the necessity to generate profits. The only genuine solution to alienation involves a total restructuring of the workplace, the economy, and the state; that is, the establishing of a truly collective mode of production—a democratically planned economy and worker-managed enterprises. No less than such a radical change can overcome alienation. The most intransigent source of alienation is the market, which transcends national boundaries and exerts its centripetal pull over even the most reluctant nations. But the market is nothing more than a term which summarizes a very complicated set of human relationships. As such it is not a mysterious force and is amenable to change to the degree that the social relationships underlying it are transformed....

Notes

[1] Karl Marx, *Capital*, Vol. I, London: Lawrence and Wishart, 1974, p. 604. (Italics added.)

[2] Cited in Istvan Mészáros, *Marx's Theory of Alienation*, New York: Harper Torchbooks, 1972, p. 156.

[3] The magnitude of the disparity in wealth and power of working people and capitalists is staggering. A rough estimate of the discrepancy could be obtained by comparing the net holdings of the working class with those of the capitalist class, which in the case of the latter must include not only their personal net worth but the factories, utilities, financial institutions, military establishments, etc., that they control and that are used to further their interests. *Cf.* Martin Nicolaus, "The Unknown Marx," in Carl Oglesby, ed., *The New Left Reader*, New York: Grove Press, 1969, pp. 84–110.

[4] *Economic and Philosophic Manuscripts of 1844, op. cit.,* pp. 72–73.

[5] Herbert Marcuse, *Reason and Revolution,, Boston: Beacon Press, 1968, p. 279.*

[6] "Labour power" refers to the human capacity for labour and consists of the mental and physical capabilities we exercise in the production of useful goods and services. The term "labour process," which appears throughout...is defined as the process "by which raw materials are transformed by human labour, acting on the objects with tools and machinery: first into products for use and, under capitalism, into commodities to be exchanged on the market." See Paul Thompson, *The Nature of Work: An Introduction to Debates on the Labour Process*, London: Macmillan, 1983, p. xv.

[7] William A. Faunce, *Problems of an Industrial Society*, Second Edition, New York: McGraw Hill, 1981, p. 134.

[8] Alienation from the purposes and products of labour involves the question of whether the basic aim of production is profit or the

satisfaction of human needs, and as a related question, what will be produced and for whom. Alienation from the organization of production entails issues like the allocation of jobs, employment policy, work rules, organization of the flow of work, the purchase of machinery, etc. The referent of the final dimension is the worker's specific job. Relevant considerations here are the pace of work, freedom of movement about the workplace, the choice of work techniques, etc.

[9] While unequal power is at the root of alienation, for the most part power is neither sought nor maintained for its own sake. Under capitalism, for example, power enables those who hold it to extract economic surpluses from workers and to monopolize wealth and privilege.

[10] In Western societies the basis of elite control of the means of production is private property, which confers on owners the legal right to use property as they see fit. In the Soviet Union and Eastern Europe, the means and ends of production are controlled by the upper echelons of the Communist Party, *Cf.* Milovan Djilas, *The New Class*, New York: Frederick A. Praeger, 1957.

[11] Karl Marx, *Capital, op. cit.,* pp. 173–221.

[12] As Karl Polanyi notes, markets were never more than incidental to the economies of pre-capitalist societies. See his *The Great Transformation,* Boston: Beacon Press, 1957.

[13] *Cf.* George Dalton, ed., *Tribal and Peasant Economies*, Garden City: The Natural History Press, 1967; Marshall Sahlins, *Stone Age Economics*, New York: Aldine-Atherton, 1972.

[14] Richard C. Edwards, Michael Reich, and Thomas E. Weisskopf, eds., *The Capitalist System*, Englewood Cliffs: Prentice-Hall, 1972, p. 3. One illustration of the independence of alienated labour and technology is the transformation of Canadian Eskimo carving. In traditional Inuit society objects were carved for decoration, use in games, religious purposes, or self-amusement. However, over a long period of time the nature and functions of Eskimo carving were transformed through contact with white society. The change was accelerated around 1949 when the Cana-dian government began to encourage the development of a "carving industry" in order to provide a new income source for the Inuit. The result was a form of art which differed markedly from that which had prevailed in the remote past. The size, media, motif, and style of the carvings were shaped by government representatives so that the objects would appeal to the standards of taste of white society. From the point of view of our discussion of technology and alienation it is instructive to find out what happened to the modern Eskimo carver. In one study, 20 Inuit artists were interviewed. "With the exception of a seventeen year old boy who had made only three things in his life, and didn't mind it at all, all the others stated that they didn't like it, or that they hated carving. They went ahead at it in the realization that if they wanted money this was one of the few methods at hand for earning it. In this sense it happens to be a necessary occupation, but to the majority carving had become boring and mechanical." This study as well as a fascinating account of the development of Eskimo carving is contained in Charles A. Martijn, "Canadian Eskimo Carving in Historical Perspective," *Anthropos*, 59, 1964, pp. 546–596. The above quote is taken from page 570 of this article. We are grateful to Don Barr for bringing this case to our attention.

[15] The ideological implications of attributing alienation to technology per se or industrialism should be obvious. This common practice obscures and distorts the role of class relationships in creating and perpetuating alienation. It portrays technology as the villain and humans as helpless prisoners of the machine. Lewis Mumford writes: "It was because of certain traits of private capitalism that the machine—which was a neutral agent—has often served, and in fact has sometimes been, a malicious element in society, careless of human life, indifferent to human interest. The machine has suffered for the sins of capitalism; capitalism has often taken credit for the virtues of the machine." See *Technics and Civilization*, New York: Harcourt, Brace, 1934, p. 27.

[16] *Cf.* David F. Noble, *Forces of Production: A*

Social History of Industrial Automation, New York: Alfred A. Knopf, 1984.

[17] Harry Braverman, *Labor and Monopoly Capital: The Degradation of Work in the Twentieth Century,* New York: Monthly Review Press, 1974, p. 193.

61   The Danger of Off-Shore Oil Work

J. Douglas House

J. DOUGLAS HOUSE, Professor of Sociology and Research Director (Institute for Social and Economic Research) at Memorial University of Newfoundland, specializes in the sociology of work and occupations, and the sociology of economic and social development. His books include *Contemporary Entrepreneurs: The Sociology of Residential Real Estate Agents* (1977); *The Last of the Free Enterprisers: The Oilman in Calgary* (1980) and *The Challenge of Oil: Newfoundland's Quest for Controlled Development* (1985). Recent articles include "Premier Peckford, petroleum policy and the popular politics in Newfoundland and Labrador" (1982) and "The Don Quixote of Canadian politics? Power in and power over Newfoundland society" (1985). Professor House served as a consultant to the City of St. John's and to a variety of private organizations, and Chaired the Royal Commission on Employment and Unemployment for the Government of Newfoundland and Labrador, in connection with which he wrote several research reports.

I have been struck by the extraordinary parallels which can be drawn between the history of something as up-to-date as North Sea Safety and that of the earliest efforts to improve statutory control upon the operations of the 'dark satanic mills' of the nineteenth century.

W.G. Carson, *The Other Price of Britain's Oil*

If by "development" we mean improvement in the quality of life, then the conditions under which people spend their working lives are a crucial consideration. "First consideration" for training and employment opportunities must go to Newfoundland residents according to Section 51 of the Atlantic Accord. This should ensure that most of the jobs to be created offshore will go to Newfoundlanders. Drilling rigs, drill ships and production platforms are large industrial workplaces, similar in many respects to iron ore mines, pulp mills, and oil refineries in which thousands of Newfoundlanders have worked. There is one important difference, however: isolation from land-based social control. The operating and drilling companies have taken advantage of this situation to establish industrial relations and working conditions more akin to the nineteenth century than to modern, enlighened capitalism. Largely because of this, working offshore is more dangerous than working in almost any other industry. The deaths of 84 men aboard the Ocean Ranger in February, 1982, brought this home to Newfoundlanders. . . .

THE POLITICAL ECONOMY OF OFFSHORE SAFETY

The North Sea, too, has been beset by adminstrative wrangles between government departments that have had a negative impact upon safety. The emphasis was upon creating a regime in which the companies could get on with the job; safety considerations were all but overlooked.

In its panic to bring what it ingenuously called "law and order" to the British Continental Shelf, the Government produced a statute that must stand as a fairly damning indictment of a legislature which, as more than one speaker noted at the time, already had nearly 150 years' experience of safety legislation.[1]

The early regulatory vacuum in Britain has subsequently been filled in a *post hoc* fashion. As problems arose and accidents occurred, new legislation was introduced. Rules governing life-saving appliances and fire-fighting equipment on rigs and platforms were not introduced until 1977 and 1978, some 15 years after exploration had begun in the North Sea. A committee of inquiry (the Burgoyne Committee) into offshore safety was set up within the Department of Energy, but, under heavy lobbying from the oil industry and the department, the majority decision came down in favour of the following recommendation: "We conclude that there is a strong case for the single agency to be the Department of Energy and that the Department of Energy would be capable of performing the task."[2]

Much has been made by both British and Canadian commentators about the Norwegian government's approach to oil and gas development. Norwegian critics, however, have expressed doubts about their own government's performance, pointing to large discrepancies between the letter of the law and its enforcement. The inquiry into the Alexander L. Kielland disaster found that more regulations had been ignored than obeyed, With respect to eight rules governing lifeboat drills, for example, it concluded:

> It is clear that the requirements of the regulations have not been met on board Alexander L. Kielland on all of these points ... No instructions as to the use of liferafts has ever been given. The engines for the man-overboard drills were not started in connection with the lifeboat reporting. Neither was the boat launched and no information was given on how to use it.[3]

The main finding of the Alexander L. Kielland inquiry for present purposes is that the disaster was due to human and mechanical error and to inadequate safety provisions, rather than to anything inherent in the frontier technology of the offshore industry. The commission's findings read like specific instances of Perez' generalizations about the social causes of offshore accidents. Specifically, the commission attributed the tragedy to the following causes:

(1) A structural weakness, due to a faulty weld, during the construction of one of the platform columns which eventually caused it to collapse.

(2) Inadequate inspection procedures which meant that the fault was not discovered.

(3) Inadequate stability provisions governing the residual strength of the rig once it had been damaged; and inadequate regulations governing such provisions.

(4) Inadequate rescue boat, lifeboat, and survival suit provisions. The stand-by boat assigned to *Alexander L. Kielland* did not arrive on the scene until nearly an hour after the accident and failed to rescue anybody. The lifeboat hooks on three of the four lifeboats lowered could not be released, and they were blown against the platform and crashed.

Canada is in the enviable position, potentially at least, of being able to learn from the Gulf of Mexico and North Sea experiences. One might have thought that Canadian governments, in particular the Newfoundland government, which has made so much of its intention to control offshore oil development, would have learned from the experiences of others about offshore safety. Such, however, has not been the case.

Less than two months after the *Alexander L. Kielland* disaster, I discussed the issue of offshore safety with a senior official of the Newfoundland government. He said that he had been worried by the number of fatalities he had heard about in the North Sea, and he thought there had been "about five" fatalities off Newfoundland until that time (May 1980), "but there may have been more." He pointed to an overlap in inspections between the federal and provincial governments. The latter had been using mines inspectors from the Department of Mines and Energy, but intended to turn the responsibility over to the Department of Manpower and Labour. He pointed out that the rigs had to be approved for each project: however, "we rely on the reputation of the companies." A Manpower and Labour official was equally uncomfortable on the issue of safety and stated that it was an area his department intended to get around to later. A federal spokesman I interviewed around the same time was even more vague about the whole issue. It took the Ocean Ranger disaster (the reputation of the rig among oil workers was captured in its nickname, the "Ocean Danger") to make the Newfoundland and Canadian governments begin to give priority to offshore safety. Canada had to have its own disaster before it too learned that safety is too important an issue to be left to the oil companies.

SOCIAL CONTROL AND THE OCEAN RANGER DISASTER

The Royal Commission on the Ocean Ranger documents the following litany of neglect as the background conditions to the loss of the rig and its crew.[4]

(1) The rig was inadequately designed and constructed.

(2) It had been inadequately inspected.

(3) It had failed to meet the requirements specified for it in its last U.S. Coast Guard inspection.

(4) Canadian federal safety regulations and enforcement procedures were inadequate.

(5) Newfoundland provincial regulations were equally inadequate.

(6) The operating manual for the rig was deficient.

(7) The crew (Americans as well as Newfoundlanders and other Canadians), especially those responsible for ballast control, were poorly trained in operating procedures.

(8) The lifeboats and other lifesaving equipment on the rig were inadequate. There were, for example, no survival suits for the crew.

(9) The crew was poorly trained and drilled in lifesaving practices.

(10) The standby vessels and helicopters that service the rigs in the area were not provided with lifesaving equipment.

(11) The crew of the Ocean Ranger's standby vessel, the Seaforth Highlander, was not trained in lifesaving procedures.

(12) The too little, too late efforts of Canadian search and rescue offices lacked preparedness and displayed "no sense of urgency."

These were the proximate causes of the tragedy. It is clear, however, that the disaster should not be taken as an isolated incident. The general context in which it happened pervades the oil industry internationally. In an atmosphere of what Carson has called the "political economy of speed," the oil and drilling companies have been allowed to get away with labour practices offshore that would not have been permitted onshore.

A powerful coalition of financial interests between national governments and multinational corporations has dictated that safe working conditions for offshore workers be given low priority. The same constellation of interests has been at play in Canada, with the struggles among federal, provincial and corporate power-wielders overriding the less obvious conflict of interests between workers and managers in both industry and state. Sociologically, what is most striking about the Ocean Ranger disaster in Newfoundland is the way in which the official class has taken control of the aftermath of what was essentially a working-class tragedy.[5]

Marine disasters, in which thousands of working-class Newfoundlanders have lost their lives, have been common throughout the province's history. For the most part, these tragedies at sea are looked upon as a sad but inevitable feature of life for a people that wrests its living largely from the sea. The risk of death at sea has been accepted with a fatalistic resignation common to maritime cultures. Fatalism serves the psychological needs of the bereaved as well as the social need of the community, especially the official class, not to feel threatened in any way.

The advent of an offshore oil industry was seen by the official class as a great new opportunity, and the Peckford regime successfully convinced the majority of people of all social classes that its strident approach to resource control would be in their best interests. For the working class, oil promised jobs; and the success of the government's policy for hiring local offshore workers was seen as serving the needs of the working class. Offshore jobs, not offshore safety, was everybody's first priority.

When the Ocean Ranger sank, all 84 men on board died. Because of the success of the province's hiring policy, 53 of these men were Newfoundlanders. The tragedy sent shockwaves throughout the community of Newfoundland. Nearly everyone in St. John's seemed to know somebody who had died on the rig, or to know someone who knew someone who died. The province's initial romance with oil ended at one cruel blow. Popular reaction did not view the sinking of the Ocean Ranger as a fateful inevitability. Before the official class had time to control the situation, a former master and former weatherman with the Ranger who were interviewed by the national media spoke of the lax safety conditions on the rig and of a conflict in the chain of command between the master and the toolpusher.

In a CBC interview, the former captain claimed that he had been thwarted in his attempts to run safety drills by the rig's toolpusher, who prevented him from taking workers away from other tasks. "A toolpusher is not a marine man. You cannot put a hillbilly from Mississippi in charge of a ship. The most important thing for an oil company is to keep that bit turning. Never mind the safety of the people. Never mind if they get injured. Keep it turning."[6] The captain claimed that a U.S. Coast Guard inspection had found 200 deficiencies in the design, structure and maintenance of the rig. The Coast Guard denied this, but admitted that at the time of the sinking the Ranger did not have a valid certificate of inspection.

In the immediate aftermath of the accident, even the big oil companies were rattled. Mobil Oil, which had the rig under contract, put its community relations officer (a Newfoundland resident) on the firing line to face the media, but failed to provide her with the information she needed to deal convincingly with the questions levelled at her by unsympathetic reporters. As well as shock and sympathy for the bereaved families, the popular mood exhibited anger.

Caught initially unawares, official reaction by industry and government was at first upstaged by the media and a few maverick oilmen. But the officials rebounded quickly and bgan to institute mechanisms to normalize the situation, to gain control of the aftermath of the disaster. The Church, which had lost much of its secular power with Newfoundland society in recent years, was mobilized by the Petroleum Directorate to reassert its moral authority. The Church made the first painful contacts with the victims' families and called for an official inquiry into the tragedy. These steps alone helped to normalize the state of affairs, and a grateful provincial government was willing to comply. At first, the federal and provincial governments stated their intention to conduct separate inquiries; but, as this seemed too grave a matter for a new federal-provincial squabble, they eventually agreed upon a joint commission of inquiry. The scale of the inquiry, expected to cost from 10 to 15 million dollars, reflects the severity with which governments felt unsettled by the accident. ODECO, the rig owners, controlled directly by their head office in New Orleans, maintained a stony and unsympathetic silence. Mobil, which could hardly avoid the public eye, recovered from its initial shock to take on the guise of the concerned, sympathetic corporate citizen, willing to cooperate with the authorities in their inquiry. Behind the scenes, industry and government officials were scrambling to avoid any appearance of having been culpable for the disaster.

The striking feature about the reaction, in terms of Newfoundland society, is the way in which the aftermath of the tragedy has been co-opted by the official class. Neither the families of the workers who died, nor any working-class organization has had a significant part to play in subsequent events and procedures. The commissioners chosen for the inquiry epitomize official-class respectability. Chaired by a judge, they include a former lieutenant governor, a former president of Memorial University, a well-known lawyer, and two successful local engineers. No one with working-class experience or affiliation or with proven oil industry expertise is included.

Hopefully, the commission's recommendations will improve safety conditions offshore in the future. But I would emphasize that there is another, latent social function of the inquiry—helping the community reconcile itself to the disaster. And, as eminently respectable official-class representatives, the commissioners are handling the absoprtion of suffering for the working class as well as for themselves. In a small but symbolic way, this class dimension of the community's response was seen in the hierarchical seating arrangements at the Ocean Ranger hearings. The commissioners were seated in large, plush

armchairs arranged on a platform; government and industry representatives and their lawyers had smaller armchairs; members of the press had armless but padded chairs; and the members of the bereaved families and the general public had ordinary, unpadded chairs situated at the back of the new hall. The organization of the hearings was a microcosm of Newfoundland's social stratification system.

The Ocean Ranger disaster has also been a source of economic opportunity for several members of the official class. Not only were the commissioners of the inquiry and their staff handsomely rewarded for their services, but the legal wrangling that ensued was a bonanza for Newfoundland lawyers. Some represented the commission itself and the companies involved, notably Mobil. Others, led by the former minister of Mines and Energy, were retained by the families of the victims. The legal situation was highly complex:

> The legal outlook is entangled in the multi-national nature of the offshore drilling operation, the fact that the victims were employed by a dozen different companies, uncertainties in U.S. and Canadian law, and even the constitutional dispute between Ottawa and Newfoundland about jurisdiction over the continental shelf, where the rig went down.[7]

The lawyers representing the families of the victims attempting to sue ODECO would have preferred that their case be heard in the United States where settlements are generally higher than in Canada. But the U.S. court initially ruled that it did not have jurisdiction and that the case had to be heard in Canada. This put the families at a disadvantage. Not only would an American settlement have given them more for damages, but since ODECO had few assets in Canada there would have been nothing to be attached should the company have defaulted on whatever payments might have been prescribed by the Canadian courts. ODECO, in the meantime, played every legal trick in the book to try to disclaim responsibility for the accident. Not only did it bring suits against Mobil, Seaforth Nav (the operator of its standby vessel) and the builder of the rig, but it threatened to sue some of the families of the victims themselves. Such is the nature of ODECO's corporate citizenship.

By early 1984, most of the victims' families had agreed on an out-of-court settlement with Mobil and ODECO. The settlements are generous by Canadian standards. Mobil and ODECO had good reason to appear to be generous, the latter because it is anxious to return as a player in the Hibernia oil game. American and Newfoundland lawyers initially fought tooth and nail for the families' custom, but eventually reached an agreement that sees them take 30 percent of the settlements as their fees. The lawyers involved had a joyous celebration when the case was settled, and some are alleged to have collected six-figure fees. The spoils of the Ocean Ranger disaster have indeed been sweet for some members of Newfoundland's official class. The settlements have at least ensured that the victims' families will be spared financial difficulties in the long run.

As is common in the aftermath of marine disasters, many Newfoundlanders wanted to contribute to a disaster fund to aid the stricken families. Such a fund was set up by the St. John's *Evening Telegram*, and hundreds of people from all over the province and elsewhere in Canada contributed amounts ranging from a few dollars to $5,000. The total collected as of March 29, 1983, was $92,558.86. Rather than distribute the money to the victims' families, or hand it over to an organization set up to represent them, the *Evening Telegram* followed the usual Newfoundland practice of passing decision-making power over to a group of respected official-class representatives. A board of trustees was set up comprising the publisher of the *Telegram*, the chairman of the board of one of Newfoundland's oldest companies, the president of a local consulting firm, the regional manager of the Royal Bank of Canada, and the presidents of Newfoundland's three major institutions of higher learning.

The trustees wrote to all the families, and disbursed $24,050 directly to those who claimed to be in immediate need. Many of the families, who had received money from life insurance policies or the Workmen's Compensation Board, replied that they were not in need. The trustees then decided to set up a scholarship fund with the bulk of the money. Children of the victims will have the opportunity to apply for scholarships to either of the three institutions of higher learning. If there are not sufficient applications from this category "then other residents may apply and receive the scholarships or bursaries."[8] Many of the families are unhappy about this decision, particularly as the rights of other family members, including the widows of the lost men, are not specified, and there is a possibility that at least some of the money will go to people who had no connection at all with the disaster. The Ocean Ranger Families Foundation wrote to the trustees to say: "We do not support this idea and we are certain that it goes against the intent of many of the donors to the disaster fund who expected to help with immediate needs of the families."[9]

Whatever the rights or wrongs of the decision, it is again the official class, with official-class values and priorities, making decisions on behalf of the working-class people. The consequence of setting up a scholarship fund is that only those families who aspire to upward social mobility (into the official class) will be able to reap any benefits from the fund.

The difficulties experienced by the Ocean Ranger Families Foundation show the obverse side of the official absorption of disaster by the Newfoundland community. The Foundation was set up in April, 1982, with the support of local church groups and labour organizations, and included family members of the victims and some sympathetic outsiders on its board of directors. Its first priority was to contact all the families of the victims in order to offer moral support and to represent the families in dealing with other organizations. The contacts were made mainly by three women directors who had themselves lost their husbands in the disaster. Some of those contacted preferred to handle their grief alone in their own way, but the majority were grateful for group support, and over 60 families became formal members of the foundation.[10] The foundation can legitimately claim to represent the families of the victims, and it has been recognized in this light by the local media and, after some initial hesitation,

by the commissioners of the Ocean Ranger hearings. The foundation initially experienced financial difficulties, which were exacerbated by its dispute with the Evening Telegram Disaster Fund.

In Newfoundland, then, even the tragic sinking of the Ocean Ranger was quickly brought under control of the province's dominant class. The community was rocked but absorbed the disaster while remaining on the same social track that had been laid down through a long history of social differentiation and inequality.

Notes

[1] W.G. Carson, *The Other Price of Britain's Oil* (Oxford: Martin Robertson, 1982), p. 144.

[2] Quoted in Carson, p. 197.

[3] Norwegian Public Reports Nov. 1981:11, "The Alexander L. Kielland 'Accident,' " 1981, pp. 153–54.

[4] Royal Commission on the Ocean Ranger Marine Disaster, *Report One: The Loss of the Semisubmersible Drill Rig Ocean Ranger and its Crew* (Ottawa: Supply and Services Canada, 1984).

[5] For a descriptive model of Newfoundland's

stratification system, see J.D. House, *Newfoundland Society and Culture* (St. John's, Newfoundland: Memorial University of Newfoundland, 1978).

[6] Quoted in the *Evening Telegram*, February 18, 1982.

[7] *Evening Telegram*, February 20, 1982.

[8] *Evening Telegram*, April 9, 1983.

[9] Quoted in *ibid.*

[10] Ocean Ranger Families Foundation, annual presidential report, 1983.

Community and Region

Introduction

Many difficult problems we currently face in sociology are definitional. We saw that illustrated in the last section when we tried to define "work." The definitional problem is no less complicated when we come to study "community," the subject of this section. The problem of definition does not arise because we lack a common sense or first-hand understanding of the topic. On the contrary, we might be talking about too many different things. Plain talk, often a virtue, is sometimes a seedbed for misunderstanding.

When we say "community," do we mean a physical entity, with boundaries, a government and a name? A community like "Oakville" or "Lethbridge" or "Africville?" Making the comparison to "ethnic groups," is a "community" a group of people in close proximity to one another who are institutionally complete and practise exclusion?

Or is a "community" a set of people who interact meaningfully with one another, whether or not they are geographically proximate, have collective institutions, self-government and an identifying name? Is "community" a set of social networks

through which people communicate and exchange resources? Increasingly, dispersed racial or ethnic groups whose homeland has been usurped—Native Americans, Macedonians, Palestinians, or Ukranians, for example—constitute this kind of "community." But is this kind of community significantly different from deviant groups (e.g., Toronto gays; the international "jet set"; or European aristocracy) or special interest groups (e.g., international arms sellers or world-ranking genetics experts) whose members also share certain ways of thinking and behaving and try to stay in touch with one another?

Finally, is a community none of the above but, rather, a state of mind: a sub-culture, or common outlook on life, and a shared commitment to this way of life? For over a century, sociologists have discussed the ways small rural communities differ from urban communities. The concepts *gemeinschaft* and *gesellschaft* seem to capture not only the difference between rural and urban, but also between traditional and modern, warm and engrossing *versus* cold and narrowly self-interested, ways of life. Thus, for some a "community" is a set of people who share a *gemein-schaft* relationship.

They are also people heavily invested in a particular tradition, a particular small town and its particular families, jokes, traditions, gossip, grievances, and so on. Living in Smith Falls (population 3000) may be a lot like living in Jones Junction (population 3200) but it is not the *very* same, and similarity is not quite good enough. The particularity of a setting makes a community what it is.

Out of this particularity arises what people call "regionalism." Regionalism is a state of mind, or world view, leading people to attach value and sentiment to a particular region of the country. A collection of adjacent communities, a region often has a name, boundaries and political authority. Labrador, Quebec and the Prairies are all regions, but as this example shows, regions may also be part of provinces, entire provinces or collections of provinces. In all cases, they are made up of people in close proximity who try to govern themselves, have some institutional completeness, and are identifiable to others by a regional name.

People living within a region often satisfy the second criterion of community too: they interact with one another more often than with others outside their region. They tend to communicate, travel, and relocate within their own region. For example, someone leaving Alberta is far more likely to move to British Columbia than to Ontario: not only shorter distance but a sense of common "westernness" will motivate this behaviour. People and communities often flow north and south in North America within regions straddling the Canada/US border. This migration pattern has made Canadian unity hard to achieve, and outside Ontario the flow has nourished a strong sense of continentalism.

Because people within a region communicate with one another, they often share a world view. This was clear in Harry Hiller's paper on humour and political protest, in the earlier section on culture. A region is felt to have a particular way of life. Citizens will tell you that life in Newfoundland is not the same as life in New Brunswick; and life in the Maritimes is not the same as in Ontario, the Prairies or British Columbia. The difference is outlook. Partly because they perceive that ways of life vary a lot from one region to another, people in poorer regions of the country often want to stay and develop their regions economically, rather than leave for opportunities elsewhere.

A region is more than a community of communities, however. The article by Carl Cuneo shows that a region stands in a particular relationship of dominance or subordination to other regions. This relationship, in turn, arises from the flow of capital and resources in the Canadian economy. Capital flows out of Ontario to develop the "hinterlands." Out of the hinterlands flow raw materials to be exported for profit, or to be manufactured into goods in Ontario, then shipped back to the hinterland at a profit. This unequal interdependence strengthens the solidarity or cohesion among people living within a region, and weakens the feelings of common interest among people in different regions. As people become more attached to regions, nationalist sentiment, or attachment to the country as a whole, grows weaker.

Thus, a region is at least a community of communities, but, more than that, it is a set of communities in a hierarchical relationship to other regions. For this reason, regions "behave" like social groups (professions, ethnic groups, social classes) with more or less control over the access to desired resources. The processes of exclusion governing inequality also govern regions, as do the processes governing community formation and cohesion.

Appropriately, this section begins with a brief attempt to define community. John Jackson reminds us of the important research done on community organization in the tradition of rural sociology. Some early Canadian sociology, particularly in Quebec and Western Canada, contributes to this tradition. Volumes in the "Social Credit in Alberta Series" organized by S.D. Clark and containing work by Jean Burnet (*Next Year Country*, 1951) and W.E. Mann (*Sect, Cult and Church in Alberta*, 1955), as well as Clark's (1959) own contribution (*Movements of Political Protest in Canada, 1640–1840*) exemplify this fruitful approach, which was influenced both by Harold Innis's political economy outlook and the ecological approach of Carl Dawson.

In the next article, Barry Wellman and Barry Leighton examine communities from a network perspective. For them, the "community" in a modern society no longer requires geographical proximity. Many who surround us are people with whom we have no contact and share no point of view. Conversely, many others with whom we have frequent, significant contact, and share an identical world view, may live dozens or even hundreds of miles away. Today, distance breaks community ties less often than it did in the past. This fact raises the question, What constitutes a "community" in a world where distance is so unimportant? Or stating the question differently, What is the new relationship among those various elements that we have customarily thought made up a community: proximity, interaction, shared outlook, sentimental attachment, common life chance?

Having answered that question, we can hope to answer another that seems to keep cropping up in the twentieth century: Is "the community" dead? This question implies that, today, no one has meaningful or stable social relationships, or shares a way of thinking with anyone else. Stated otherwise, the questioner supposes that we are living in a mass society made up of millions of isolated, atomized individuals. This bleak point of view, essentially conservative, which is to say, anti-liberal and anti-modern, though not quite so prevalent today as in the 1950s, keeps resurfacing. Professors Wellman and Leighton give us reason to hope that Canadians are not, in fact, "a lonely crowd," to borrow David Riesman's (1950) compelling metaphor of three decades ago. Appropriately redefined, "community" is still useful for describing modern life.

Two kinds of community occupy our attention in the next part of this section. One is the community destroyed by urban redevelopment. The pluses and minuses of urban redevelopment occupied a great deal of sociological attention in the 1950s and 1960s. Then, urbanologists helped decision-makers think about ways to avoid destroying neighbourhoods while achieving urban renewal or expansion. How to assess the social, as well as economic and political, costs and benefits of different zoning, building and transportation strategies was much debated if, perhaps, never fully answered.

In their study of a small Black neighbourhood of Halifax destroyed by urban renewal, Donald Clairmont and Dennis Magill imply that Africville should have been preserved. This community, with a long and important history, had been allowed to run down. People in power had made no effort to keep Africville clean, economically viable, or law abiding. It became a "deviant service centre" for the city of Halifax. How much of this failure to act was due to simple racism? How much was due to the shortsightedness many city politicians showed towards old neighbourhoods only a few decades ago? Was some economic advantage to be gained by destroying this community and using its land for another purpose? These are all questions the authors try to answer, just like the authors of comparable studies in large American cities undergoing the same kinds of destruction.

So, from one standpoint, *Africville* is a Canadian contribution to the shelf of American books on the social harm done by urban redevelopment. But it is also a celebration of what had been a strong and healthy community before decay set in. Further, it recalls a piece of history unknown to most Canadians: the history of Blacks in Canada.

The other kind of community discussed in this section is the minetown, milltown, or railtown described so effectively by Rex Lucas. As Professor Lucas points out, our national history is a history of staple production which brings people together in previously uninhabited places to extract or ship raw resources. The communities formed for these purposes—complete with families, schools, churches and services— are extremely vulnerable, since they all rest on a single industry's success or failure. Indeed, they often rest on the fortunes of a single company. But the economic viability of these communities, however problematic, is not really Lucas's central interest. He is fascinated by the striking similarity of social forms one finds in travelling from one such community to another.

Single-industry communities are like social experiments. They are created out of nothing, often in quite a hurry, with a particular economic goal in mind. People are shipped in, houses built, and soon the community is up and running. But what will everyday life be like in such a community and how will it differ from life in other communities? What is the effect of everyone's complete dependence on a single industry or company? Of the community's lack of history and, conceivably, lack of a future? Of its lack of demographic variety? Of the somewhat rootless charac-

ter of people who come to work there? Of the lack of personal privacy? These kinds of questions interest Professor Lucas. If we were able to answer these questions completely, we would not only have learned everything important about single-industry communities, but a great deal about the dynamics of community life in general. Still, Professor Lucas goes even further. He thinks the single-industry community is Canada in microcosm. But how is Canada like an enormous single-industry community? And in what senses are all Canadians like the citizens of single-industry communities? Read Professor Lucas's article to find out.

The single-industry community is common in Northern Ontario but rare in Southern Ontario. It is, generally, commoner in the North and West—where valuable resources (minerals, oils, timber) are still extracted, than where either stable rural life (e.g., the single family farm or ranch) or stable urban life has taken root. The majority of Canadians do not now and never have lived in single-industry communities.

Yet the disproportionate share of such communities in some regions, the greater dependence of some regions than others on resource extraction and export, feeds the sense of regionalism and regional exploitation we discussed earlier. Carl Cuneo's article identifies "regionalism" as an economic and class (or power), rather than subcultural, phenomenon. Many students of regionalism focus on the subcultural differences: the sentiments and loyalties that people attach to particular regions. Professor Cuneo would argue that though such sentiments exist, they are the consequence, not the cause of regional differentiation. Ultimately the explanation of regionalism must be found in dominance and subordination, in unequal relations to the means of production.

Put community and inequality together,

and often you get social protest and social change. The articles in the next section will carry further many of the concerns we have discussed here, especially in relation to French Canadian nationalism.

References

Burnet, Jean. *Next-Year Country: A Study of Rural Social Organization in Alberta*. Toronto: University of Toronto Press, 1951.

Clark, S.D. *Movements of Political Protest, 1640–1840*. Toronto: University of Toronto Press, 1959.

Mann, William E. *Sect, Cult and Church in Alberta*. Toronto: University of Toronto Press, 1955.

Riesman, David, Nathan Glazer and Reuel Denny. *The Lonely Crowd*. New Haven: Yale University Press, 1973.

62   What Is a Community?

John D. Jackson

JOHN D. JACKSON, Professor of Sociology and Director of the Centre for Broadcasting Studies at Concordia University, Montreal, specializes in the sociology of literature and communications, and in community studies and urban sociology. His books and articles include *Community and Conflict: French-English Relations in Ontario* (1975); "The state of the art and new directions," Volume 1, *Sociology in Anglophone Canada* (1986); and "Toward a research strategy for the analysis of CBC English-language radio drama and Canadian social structure" with G. Neilsen (1984). At Concordia, he has served as Chairman of the Department of Sociology and Anthropology. Professor Jackson was Editor (sociology) of the *Canadian Review of Sociology and Anthropology* (1980–83), President of the Canadian Sociology and Anthropology Association (1986) and, since 1985, a member of the Board of Directors, Social Science Federation of Canada.

There are two basic ideas embedded in the concept of "community." One is concerned with order and consensus and the other with locale. The second report of the Task Force on Canadian Unity (1979) stated that "a community is a group of persons joined together by a consciousness of the characteristics they have in common ... and by a consciousness of the interests they share." Any given human group will exhibit such a consciousness to one degree or another, be it a local sports club, a group of scientists with a special interest, an ethnic group, or an age group. On the other hand, community studies as such usually focus on places—hamlets, villages, towns, cities—as the unit of analysis. Everett Hughes's *French Canada in Transition* (1939), John Bennett's *Northern Plainsmen* (1969) and John Jackson's *Community and Conflict* (1975), to name a few of the many studies of local settings in Canada, all deal with a particular locale. An American sociologist, Jessie Bernard, referred to these two concepts of community as "community" and "the community." The first denotes shared values, interests and a common sense of identity; the second denotes places and the activities therein, or locale. Indeed, it has been said that "the term settlement might serve as well as the term community."

Although the two concepts are easily distinguished from each other, a problem arises when the latter is defined in terms of the former. If "the community" is defined as shared values, interests and identity, as is often the case, then it would be difficult to find a locale or settlement that conformed to these criteria. Any given locale is as likely as not to exhibit within its boundaries harmony and disharmony, conflict and consensus, order and disorder as various social groupings struggle over resources. The idea of "community" is therefore better retained as an empirical question in relation to particular communities as locale, or to "the community." Westhues and Sinclair's *Village in Crisis* (1974), a study of conflict over development plans in an Ontario town, Gold's *St. Pascal*, a study of changing elites in a Québec town, and Clairmont and Magill's *Africville* (1974), a study of a land development crisis in Halifax, address the issue of conflict within a particular locale—conflicts which are rooted in differing, not common, values and interests.

The tendency to confuse the two ways of defining the concept has its origins in earlier sociological studies that stressed the broad historical changes occurring in Western societies as the growth of capitalism and its concomitant processes of rapid urbanization and industrialization gradually transformed human relations into commodity relations. The change from person-centred to commodity-centred human relations is part of the transformation of human labour into a commodity to be bought and sold in the marketplace. This transformation was a classic theme in 19th- and early 20th-century sociology. Exemplary among those who wrote on this theme was Ferdinand Tönnies. His 1887 essay, *Gemeinschaft (Community) and Gesellschaft (Association): A Treatise on Communism and Socialism as Empirical Forms of Culture*, drew attention to this shift in the quality of human relations. Tönnies was writing about communities in the sense of a particular quality of human relations which permeated all activities and social groups, a quality which was disintegrating in the wake of capitalism. The confusion arose when sociologists later reduced this general historical thesis to a definition of communities as settlements, thereby associating a particular quality of human relations, which may or may not be present in any given group, with human settlements as such.

For the most part the confusion has been resolved or, at worst, put aside. Over the past 20 years, Canadian community studies have followed one of two routes: network analysis or continuing studies of locale. Regarding the first, the Centre for Urban and Community Studies and the Sociology Department at the University of Toronto have developed network analysis into a highly sophisticated tool for describing and understanding human interaction at the local level by analysing the bonds among persons relative to the positions and roles they occupy in particular social settings. Their findings demonstrate that "community" is still very much part of the everyday experiences of people in urban centres.

In the continuing studies of locale, the emphasis is on the fate of particular settlements in relation to the political economy of regions and of Canada as a whole. M. Patricia Marchak's *Green Gold* (1983) studies the effects of decisions made by multinational corporations in BC's forest industry on the everyday lives of people in two resource-based settlements. Carle Zimmerman and Gary Moneo's *The Prairie Community System* (1970) examines different types of western settlements in relation to the overall organization of the West to meet the interests of central Canadian capital.

There is perhaps a third route, one that is as yet underdeveloped but is present in various studies. It is at the local level, in "the community," where most people live out their daily lives—go to school, raise families, work, join associations, attend religious ceremonies—forming networks with others based on common values and interests (communities in the first sense). In the formation of such networks, be they based on friendship, kinship or workplace, there exists a potential for collective action, for mounting resistance and opposition to the overwhelming forces of individualization. This kind of activity, which takes the form of self-determination and self-organization, is not new to Canadian life. Ralph Matthews considers this issue in his study of three settlements in Newfoundland, where he found resistance based on "community" to the plans of government policymakers. The potential to oppose the impositions of public and private corporations on local life has been referred to as "emancipatory practices" by Marcel Rioux, a University of Montréal sociologist. "The community" as a base for emancipatory practices is a relatively unexplored route in the field of community studies, but one which may be pursued.

63 Networks, Neighbourhoods and Communities

Barry Wellman   Barry Leighton

BARRY WELLMAN, Professor of Sociology at the University of Toronto, is the co-ordinator of the International Network for Social Network Analysis. He is the author of such works as "Networks, Neighborhoods and Communities" and "Network Analysis: Some Basic Principles"; and co-editor, with S.D. Berkowitz, of *Social Structures: A Network Approach*. Born in the Bronx in New York, he has enjoyed living his entire life in the heart of big cities.

BARRY LEIGHTON, Research Officer in the Federal Department of Justice, Ottawa, received his doctorate in sociology at the University of Toronto in 1986. His thesis was titled "Experiencing Personal Network Communities."

... Sociologists have been concerned with the community question, investigating the impact the massive industrial bureaucratic transformations of North America and Europe have had on primary ties in the home, the neighborhood, the workplace, with kin and friends, and among interest groups. Have such ties attenuated or flourished in contemporary societies? In what sort of networks are they organized? Have the contents of such ties remained as holistic as alleged to be in preindustrial societies or have they become narrowly specialized and instrumental? ...

We suggest that the *network analytic perspective* is a more appropriate response to the community question than the traditional focus on neighborhoods.[1] A network analysis of community takes as its starting point the search for social linkages and flows of resources. Only then does it enquire into the spatial distribution and solidary sentiments

Barry Wellman and Barry Leighton, "Networks, Neighborhoods and Communities, *"Urban Affairs Quarterly,* 14, 3 (March 1979), pp. 363–390. Copyright © 1979 by Sage Publications, Inc. Reprinted by permission of Sage Publications, Inc.

associated with the observed linkages. Such an approach largely frees the study of community from spatial and normative bases. It makes possible the discovery of network-based communities which are neither linked to a particular neighborhood nor to a set of solidary sentiments.

The network perspective is not inherently anti-neighborhood. By leaving the matter of spatial distributions initially open, this perspective makes it equally as possible to discover an "urban village" (Gans, 1962) as it is to discover a "community without propinquity" (Webber, 1963). A network analysis might also tell us that strong ties remain abundant and important, but that they are rarely located in the neighborhood. With this approach we are then better able to assess the position of neighborhood ties within the context of overall structures of social relationships.

The community question has been extensively debated by urban scholars. In this paper, we evaluate three competing scholarly arguments about the community question from a network perspective. The first two arguments to be discussed both focus on the neighborhood: the *community lost*, asserting the absence of local solidarities, and the *community saved* argument, asserting their persistence. The *community liberated* argument, in contrast, denies any neighborhood basis to community. . . .

COMMUNITY LOST

The community lost argument contends that the transformation of Western societies to centralized, industrial bureaucratic structures has gravely weakened primary ties and communities, making the individual more dependent on formal organizational resources for sustenance. The first attempts to deal with the community question (e.g., Tönnies, 1887) were, at the turn of the century, closely associated with broader sociological concerns about the impact of the Industrial Revolution on communal ties and normative integration (e.g., Durkheim, 1893; Simmel, 1908). . . .

Community lost imagery has had a good deal of scholarly impact, appealing to radical (e.g., Engels, 1845; Castells, 1976), liberal (e.g., Kornhauser, 1959; Stein, 1960; Slater, 1970), and conservative (e.g., Nisbet, 1962; Banfield, 1968; Grant, 1969) concerns. Lost scholars of all political persuasions have been concerned about the upheavals caused by the large-scale transformation of industrial bureaucratic societies and the social disorganization and depravity allegedly let loose by the weakening of traditional communal bonds. Running through many lost analyses has been the implicit assumption that human beings are fundamentally evil (or easily capable of being driven to evil by industrialism, bureaucraticism, or capitalism), and that where restraining communal structures have been destroyed by the Industrial Revolution, riot, robbery, and rape have swept the city.

The social disorganization theme has remained a popular one in North American

thought (for reviews, see White and White, 1962; Marx, 1964; Bender, 1978). Nostalgia for "the myth of the lost paradise" (Gusfield, 1975) has mingled with the identification of the contemporary city as the home of rootless masses in a continuing tradition from Jeffersonian pastoralism through Progressive reformism (e.g., Woodsworth, 1911) to such urban panic movies as "Death Wish" (1974). Affluent suburbs (see the review in Popenoe, 1977) as well as poor inner cities are despaired of as privatized, isolated, and alienated.

Lost Networks

The community lost argument makes a number of specific assertions about the kinds of primary ties, social networks, and community structures that will tend to be present under its assumptions. By casting the lost argument in network analytic terms, we shall be better able to evaluate it in comparison with the community saved and community liberated arguments:

(a) Rather than being a full member of a solidary community, urbanites are now *limited members* (in terms of amount, intensity, and commitment of interaction) of *several social networks*.

(b) Primary ties are *narrowly defined*; there are *fewer strands* in the relationship.

(c) The narrowly defined ties tend to be *weak in intensity*.

(d) Ties tend to be *fragmented* into isolated *two-person* relationships rather than being parts of extensive networks.

(e) Those networks that do exist tend to be *sparsely knit* (a low proportion of all potential links between members actually exists) rather than being densely knit (a high proportion of potential links exists).

(f) The networks are *loosely bounded*; there are few discrete clusters or primary groups.

(g) Sparse density, loose boundaries, and narrowly defined ties provide *little* structural basis for *solidary activities or sentiments.*

(h) The narrowly defined ties dispersed among a number of networks create *difficulties in mobilizing assistance* from network members.

Policy Implications

The community lost argument has significantly affected urban policy in North America and Western Europe. There have been extensive "community development" programs designed to end alienation and to grow urban roots, such as the putative War on Poverty. The desired community ideal in such programs has been the regeneration of the densely knit, tightly bounded, solidary neighborhood community. When, despite the programs, a return to the pastoral ideal has not seemed achievable, then despair about social disorganization has led to elaborate social control policies, designed to keep in check the supposedly alienated, irrational, violence-prone masses. When even the achievement of social control has not seemed feasible, policies of neglect—benign or otherwise—have developed. Administrators have removed services from inner-city neighborhoods, asserting their inability to cope with socially disorganized behavior and leaving the remaining inhabitants to fend for themselves. The residents of such inner-city American areas as Pruitt-Igoe and the South Bronx have come to be regarded as irredeemably "sinful" as they suffer the supposed war of all against all.

COMMUNITY SAVED

The community saved argument maintains that neighborhood communities have persisted in industrial bureaucratic social systems as important sources of support and sociability. It argues that the very formal, centralizing tendencies of bureaucratic institutions have paradoxically encouraged the maintenance of primary ties as more flexible sources of sociability and support. The saved argument contends that urbanites continue to organize safe communal havens, with neighborhood, kinship, and work solidarities mediating and coping with bureaucratic institutions.

Saved scholars have tended to regard human beings as fundamentally good and inherently gregarious. They are viewed as apt to organize self-regulating communities under all circumstances, even extreme conditions of poverty, oppression, or catastrophe.

Hence the saved argument has shared the neighborhood community ideal with the lost argument, but it has seen this ideal as attainable and often already existing. Neighborhood communities are valued precisely because they can provide small-scale loci of interaction and can effectively mediate urbanites' dealings with large-scale institutions. Densely knit, tightly bounded communities are valued as structures particularly suited to the tenacious conservation of their internal resources, the maintenance of local autonomy, and the social control of members (and intruders) in the face of powerful impinging external forces (e.g., Jacobs, 1961).

Saved Networks

The saved argument, cast into network analytic terms, is quite different from the lost argument:

(a) Urbanites tend to be *heavily involved members* of a *single neighborhood community,* although they may combine this with membership in other social networks.

(b) There are *multiple strands* of relationships between the members of these neighborhood communities.

(c) While network ties vary in intensity, many of them are *strong.*

(d) Neighborhood ties tend to be organized into *extensive networks.*

(e) Networks tend to be *densely knit.*

(f) Neighborhood networks are *tightly bounded*, with few external linkages. Ties tend to loop back into the same cluster of network members.

(g) High density, tight boundaries, and multistranded ties provide a structural basis for a good deal of *solidary activities and sentiments.*

(h) The multistranded strong ties clustered in densely knit networks *facilitate* the *mobilization* of assistance for dealing with routine and emergency matters.

Policy Implications

Public acceptance of the saved argument has greatly increased during the past two decades. Active neighborhood communities are now valued as antidotes to industrial bureaucratic societies' alleged impersonality, specialized relationships, and loss of comprehensible scale. "Streetcorner society" (Whyte, 1955), "the urban village" (Gans, 1962), and "Tally's Corner" (Liebow, 1967) have become exemplars of saved communities.

The neighborhood unit has been the twentieth-century planning ideal for new housing. Saved ideologues have also argued the necessity for preserving existing neighborhoods against the predations of ignorant and rapacious institutions. The saved argument has been the ideological foundation of the neighborhood movement which seeks to stop expressways, demolish developers, and renovate old areas (e.g., Powell, 1972). Some neighborhoods have been successfully rescued from "urban renewal," although Gans's West End in Boston (1962) and Clairmont and Magill's Africville in Halifax (1974) have been lost.

In political analyses, rioters, far from being socially disorganized, are now seen to be rooted, well-connected community members (see Feagin and Hahn, 1973; Tilly, 1973, 1978). Their motivations tend to be in defense of existing communal interests or claims to new ones, rather than the irrational, individualistic, psychologistic responses claimed by the lost argument. Indeed, the means by which urbanites get involved in a riot are very much associated with the competitions, coalitions, and solidary ties of their social networks.

Many saved social pathologists have encouraged the nurturance of densely knit, bounded communities as a structural salve for the stresses of poverty, ethnic segregation, and physical and mental diseases (see the review in Caplan and Killilea, 1976). Getting help informally through neighborhood communities is alleged to be more sensitive to peculiar local needs and protective of the individual against bureaucratic claims. . . .

Current Status

In the early nineteen-sixties the saved argument became the new orthodoxy in community studies with the publication of such works as Gans's *The Urban Villagers* (1962), Greer's (1962) synthesis of postwar survey research, and Jacob's (1961) assertion of the vitality of dense, diverse central cities. Such case studies as Young and Willmott's (1957) study of a working-class London neighborhood, Gans's (1967) account of middle-class, new suburban networks, and Liebow's (1967) portrayal of innercity Blacks' heavy reliance on network ties helped clinch the case.

The rebuttal of the lost argument's assertion of urban social disorganization has therefore been accomplished, theoretically and empirically, by studies emphasizing the persistence of neighborhood communities. In the process, though, the lost argument's useful starting point may have come to be neglected: that the industrial bureaucratic division of labor has strongly affected the structure primary ties. Saved scholars have tended to look only for—and at—the persistence of functioning neighborhood communities. Consequently we now know that neighborhood communities persist and often flourish, but we do not know the position of neighborhood-based ties within overall social networks.

Many recent saved analyses have recognized this difficulty by introducing the "community of limited liability" concept, which treats the neighborhood as just one of a series of communities among which urbanites divide their membership (see Greer, 1962; Suttles, 1972; Hunter, 1975; Warren, 1978). Hunter and Suttles (1972: 61), for example, portray such communities as a set of concentric zones radiating out from the block to "entire sectors of the city." However, while such analyses recognize the possibilities for urbanites to be members of diverse networks with limited involvement in each network, the "limited liability community" formulation is still predicated on the neighborhood concept, seeing urban ties as radiating out from a local, spatially defined base.

COMMUNITY LIBERATED

The liberated argument, like the other two arguments, begins with the concept of space. Yet where the other arguments see communities as resident in neighborhoods, the liberated argument confronts spatial restrictions only in order to transcend them. Although harkening back to some of the more optimistic writings of Georg Simmel about the liberating effect of urban life (e.g., 1902–1903: last portion; 1908: 121) and Robert Park (e.g., 1925b: 65 ff.), the argument has become prominent only in the past two decades following the proliferation of personal automotive and airplane travel and telecommunications in the Western world. It contends that there is now the possibility of "community without propinquity" (Webber, 1964) in which distance and travel time are minimal constraints.

The liberated argument is fundamentally optimistic about urban life. It is appreciative of urban diversity; imputations of social disorganization and pathology find little place within it. The argument's view of human behavior emphasizes its entrepreneurial and manipulative aspects. People are seen as having a propensity to form primary ties, not out of inherent good or evil, but in order to accomplish specific, utilitarian ends.

The liberated argument, as does the lost argument, minimizes the importance of neighborhood communities. But where the lost argument sees this as throwing the urbanite upon the resources of formal organizations, the liberated argument contends that sufficient primary ties are available in nonneighborhood networks to provide crucial social support and sociability. Furthermore, it argues that the diverse links between these networks organize the city as a "network of networks" (Craven and Wellman, 1973) to provide a flexible coordinating structure not possible through a lost formal, bureaucratic hierarchy or a saved agglomeration of neighborhoods.

The liberated argument recoils from the lost and saved arguments' village-like community norm. The argument celebrates the structural autonomy of being able to move among various social networks. It perceives solidary communities as fostering stifling social control and of causing isolation from outside contact and resources. Multiple social networks are valued because cross-cutting commitments and alternative escape routes limit the claims that any one community can make upon its members.

Liberated Networks

With its emphasis on aspatial communities, the liberated argument has been methodologically associated with network analytic techniques (e.g., Kadushin, 1966; Wellman, 1979). However, it must be emphasized that network analysis does not necessarily share the liberated argument's ideological bias and can be used to evaluate the existence of *all three* community patterns: lost, saved, and liberated.

In network terms, the liberated argument contends that:

(a) Urbanites now tend to be *limited members of several social networks*, possibly including one located in their neighborhood.
(b) There is *variation in the breadth of the strands* of relationships between network members; there are multistranded ties with some, single-stranded ties with many others, and relationships of intermediate breadth with the rest.
(c) The ties range in intensity: *some* of them are *strong*, while others are weak but nonetheless useful.
(d) An individual's ties tend to be organized into a *series of networks with few connections* between them.
(e) Networks tend to be *sparsely knit* although certain portions of the networks, such as those based on kinship, may be more densely knit.
(f) The networks are *loosely bounded, ramifying* structures, branching out extensively to form linkages to additional people and resources.
(g) Sparse density, loose boundaries, and narrowly defined ties provide *little structural basis for solidary activities and sentiments* in the overall networks of urbanites, although some solidary clusters of ties are often present.
(h) *Some network ties can be mobilized* for general-purpose or specific assistance in dealing with routine or emergency matters. The likelihood of mobilization depends more on the quality of the two-person tie than on the nature of the larger network structure.

Policy Implications

Liberated analysts have called for the reinforcement of other social networks in addition to the traditional ones of the neighborhood and the family. Whereas industrial power considerations have worked against the development of solidary networks in the workplace, much attention has been paid recently to fostering "helping networks" that would prevent or heal the stress of physical and mental diseases. No longer is the neighborhood community seen as the safe, supportive haven; no longer are formal institutions to be relied on for all healing attempts. Instead, networks are to be mobilized, and where they do not exist they can be constructed so that urbanites may find supportive places. However, the efficacy of such deliberately constructed "natural support systems" (to use current jargon) has not yet been adequately demonstrated.

The liberated argument has had an important impact on thinking about political phenomena, especially that related to collective disorders. Research by Charles Tilly (e.g., 1975, 1978) and associates, in particular, has shown such collective disorders to be integral parts of broader contentions for power by competing interest groups. In addition to the internal solidarity emphasized by the saved argument, a contending group's chances for success have been shown to be strongly associated with the capacity for making linkages in external coalitions that crosscutting ties between networks can provide (e.g., Gans, 1974a, 1974b; Granovetter, 1974b).

Recent British New Town planning (e.g., Milton Keynes) has been predicated on the high rates of personal automotive mobility foreseen by the liberated argument. However, the argument's contention that there are minimal costs to spatial separation has come up against the increase in the monetary costs of such separation associated with the significant rise in the price of oil within the last decade. One response has been to advocate increased reliance on telecommunications to maintain community ties over large distances. New developments in computer technology foreshadow major increases in telecommunications capabilities, such as "electronic mail" and "computer conferencing" (see Hiltz and Turoff, 1978). Yet the strength of the liberated argument does not necessarily depend on technological innovations. Recent research in preindustrial social systems has indicated that long-distance ties can be maintained without benefit of telephone or private automobiles, as long as such ties are structurally embedded in kinship systems or common local origins (e.g., Cohen, 1969; Laslett, 1971; Jacobson, 1973; Howard, 1974; Mayer and Mayer, 1974; Ross and Weisner, 1977; Bender, 1978).

Current Status

Contemporary studies making the liberated argument have proliferated in the past decade. They have examined the nature of membership in multiple social networks (e.g., Kadushin, 1966; Laumann, 1973; Breiger, 1976; Bell and Newby, 1976; Shulman, 1976), the use of network ties to obtain needed resources (e.g., Lee, 1969; Granovetter, 1974a; Jacobson, 1975), and the ways in which links between social networks can structure social systems (e.g., Granovetter, 1973; Wireman, 1978; Laumann, Galaskiewicz, and Marsden, 1978).

The strength of the liberated argument is that it can account for, and at the same time propose, socially close communities which stretch over large distances. "Community" need no longer necessarily be tied to "neighborhood." However, in propounding the virtues of nonlocal communities the liberated argument may have unduly neglected the usefulness of quick local accessibility and the advantages of the solidary behavior that can come with densely knit, tightly bounded, multistranded ties. . . .

COMMUNITIES: LOST, SAVED, OR LIBERATED?

Are communities lost, saved, or liberated? Too often, the three arguments have been presented as (a) competing alternative depictions of the "true" nature of Western industrial bureaucratic social systems, or (b) evolutionary successors, with pre-industrial saved communities giving way to industrial lost, only to be superseded by postindustrial liberated. In contrast, we believe that all three arguments have validity when stripped of their ideological paraphernalia down to basic network structures. . . .[3]

Saved Communities/ Dense Networks

In saved networks, densely knit ties and tight boundaries tend to occur together. This may be because network members have a finite lump of sociability, so that if they devote most of their energies to within-network ties, they do not have much scope for maintaining external linkages. Conversely, tight boundaries may also foster the creation of new ties within the community, as internal links become the individual's principal hope of gaining access to resources.

Such dense, bounded saved networks, be they neighborhood, kinship, or otherwise based, are apt to be solidary in sentiments and activities. They are well-structured for maintaining informal social control over members and intruders. The dense ties and communal solidarity should facilitate the ready mobilization of the community's resources for the aid of members in good standing. But because solidarity does not necessarily mean egalitarianism, not all of the community's resources may be gathered or distributed equally.

Community studies have shown the saved pattern to be quite prevalent in situations in which community members do not have many individual personal resources and where there are unfavorable conditions for forming external ties. Certain ethnic minority and working-class neighborhoods clearly follow this pattern (e.g., Liebow, 1967). In such situations, concerns about conserving, controlling and efficiently pooling those resources the beleaguered community possesses also resonate with its members' inability to acquire additional resources elsewhere. A heavy load consequently is placed on ties within the saved community.

Liberated Communities/ Ramified Networks

If saved network patterns are particularly suited to conditions of resource scarcity and conservation, liberated network patterns are particularly suited to conditions of resource abundance and acquisition. Such sparsely knit, loosely bounded networks are not structurally well-equipped for internal social control. Implicit assurance in the security of one's home base is necessary before one can reach out into new areas.

Loose boundaries and sparse density foster networks that extensively branch out to link up with new members. These ramifying liberated networks are well-structured for acquiring additional resources through a larger number of direct and indirect external connections. Their structure is apt to connect liberated network members with a more diverse array of resources than saved networks are apt to encounter, although the relative lack of solidarity in such liberated networks may well mean that a lower proportion of resources will be available to other network members.

It may well be that the liberated pattern is peculiarly suited to affluent sectors of contemporary Western societies. It places a premium on a base of individual security, entrepreneurial skills in moving between networks, and the ability to function without the security of membership in a solidary community. However, its appearance in other social contexts indicates that it reflects a more fundamental alternative to the saved community pattern.

Both the saved or liberated community patterns can appear as desirable alternatives to those enmeshed in the other pattern. To those unsatisfied with the uncertain multiplicities of liberated networks, holistic, solidary saved communities can appear as a welcome retreat. To those who feel trapped in all-embracing saved networks, the availability of alternative liberated primary networks may offer a welcome escape route. Much migration from rural areas may follow this tendency.

Lost Communities/ Sparse Networks

What of circumstances where no alternative network sources of escape or retreat are possible? It is in such situations that the lost pattern of direct affiliation with formal institutions can become attractive: the army, the church, the firm, and the university. However, the lost pattern may always be unstable for individuals and communities as formal institutional ties devolve into complex primary network webs. Therefore, as primary ties develop between or within organizations, we may expect to find networks taking on the patterns of saved or liberated communities.

Neighborhood and Community

Almost all of the people we studied have many strong ties and they are able to obtain assistance through a number of close relationships. Yet only a small proportion of these "intimate" ties are located in the same neighborhood (Wellman, 1979).

Neighborhood relationships persist but only as specialized components of the overall primary networks. The variety of ties in which an urbanite can be involved—with distant parents, intimate friends, less intimate friends, coworkers, and so on—and the variety of networks in which these are organized can provide flexible structural bases for dealing with routine and emergency matters.

In sum, we must be concerned with neighborhood *and* community rather than neighborhood *or* community. We have suggested that the two are separate concepts which may or may not be closely associated. In some situations we can observe the saved pattern of community as solidary neighborhood. In many other situations, if we go out and look for neighborhood-based networks, we are apt to find them. They can be heavily used for the advantages of quick accessibility. But if

we broaden our field of view to include other primary relations, then the apparent neighborhood solidarities may now be seen as clusters in the rather sparse, loosely bounded structures of urbanites' total networks.

Notes

[1] Network analysis is essentially a perspective which focuses on structured relationships between individuals and collectivities. As yet there is no commonly agreed definition. We believe that network analysis's salient characteristics are that it gives attention to: (a) structured patterns of relationships and not the aggregated characteristics of individual units, analyzed without reference to their inter-relationships; (b) complex network structures and not just dyadic ties; (c) the allocation of scarce resources through concrete systems of power, dependency, and coordination; (d) questions of network boundaries, clusters, and cross-linkages; (e) structures of reciprocal relationships and not just simple hierarchies. For summaries of the network perspective, see White (1965); Mitchell (1969, 1974); Barnes (1972); White, Boorman and Breiger (1976). See also the bibliographies of Wellman and Whitaker (1974); Freeman (1976); Klovdahl (1977).

[2] Our review of the saved literature has already indicated the abundant evidence for the presence of densely knit, tightly bounded communities in contemporary Western social systems (e.g., Whyte, 1955; Young and Willmott, 1957; Gans, 1962; Liebow, 1967). While only Bender (1978) has explicitly attempted

to argue the prevalence of liberated patterns in preindustrial social systems, historians have begun reporting nonsolidary aspects of pre-industrial Western Europe (e.g., Laslett, 1971; Scott and Tilly, 1975; Shorter, 1975; Tilly, 1975). We can look to studies of peer groups, interest groups, travel out of the local area, and complex households (masters, servants, laborers; multiple generations, with nonlocal marriages) having a variety of external ties as providing some basis for the existence of liberated patterns. The prevalence of long-distance, liberated ties in contemporary non-Western social systems has been more extensively documented (see review of the liberated literature).

[3] The data were collected in 1968 random-sample, closed-ended survey of 845 adult East Yorkers. East York (1971 population = 104,646) is an upper working-class, lower middle-class, predominantly British-Canadian inner-city suburb of Toronto. It has the reputation of being one of the most solidary areas of the city. Respondents were asked about "persons outside your home who you feel closest to" up to a maximum of six. See Wayne (1971), Shulman (1972, 1976), Wellman (1979), for findings.

References

Banfield, E. (1968) The Unheavenly City. Boston: Little, Brown.

Barnes, J.A. (1972) Social Networks. Reading, MA: Addison-Wesley.

Bell, C. and H. Newby (1976) "Community, communion, class and community action," pp. 189–

207 in D.T. Herbert and R.J. Johnson (eds.) Social Areas in Cities II: Spatial Perspectives on Problems and Policies. London: John Wiley.

Bender, T. (1978) Community and Social Change in America. New Brunswick, NJ: Rutgers University Press.

Breiger, R.L. (1976) "Career attributes and network structure: blockmodel study of a biomedical research specialty." American Sociological Review 41 (February): 117–135.

Caplan, G. and M. Killilea (1976) Support Systems and Mutual Aid. New York: Grune & Stratton.

Castells, M. (1976) The Urban Question. London: Edward Arnold.

Clairmont, D. and D. Magill (1974) Africville. Toronto: McClelland & Stewart.

Craven, P. and B. Wellman (1973) "The network city." Sociological Inquiry 43 (December): 57–88.

Crump, B. (1977) "The portability of urban ties." Paper presented at the Annual Meetings of the American Sociological Association, September, Chicago.

"Death Wish" (1974) Directed and Coproduced by Michael Winner. Written by Wendell Mayes. Produced by Hal Landers and Bobby Roberts. Starring Charles Bronson. A Dino DeLaurentis Production. From the novel by Brian Garfield.

Durkheim, E. (1893, 1933) The Division of Labor in Society. New York: Macmillan.

Engels, F. (1845, 1969) The Condition of the Working Class in England. St. Albans, Herts.: Panther Books.

Feagin, J.R. (1973) "Community disorganization: some critical notes." Sociological Inquiry 43 (December): 123–146.

_____ and H. Hahn (1973) Ghetto Revolt: The Politics of Violence in American Cities. New York: Macmillan.

Fischer, C.S. (1976) The Urban Experience. New York: Harcourt Brace Jovanovich.

Freeman, L.C. (1976) A Bibliography of Social Networks. Monticello, IL: Council of Planning Librarians, Exchange Bibliographies Nos. 1170–1171.

Gans, H.J. (1974a) "Gans on Granovetter's 'Strength of Weak Ties.' " American Journal of Sociology 80 (September): 524–527.

_____ (1974b) "Gans' response to Granovetter." American Journal of Sociology 80 (September): 529–531.

_____ (1967) The Levittowners. New York: Pantheon.

_____ (1962) The Urban Villagers. New York: Free Press.

Granovetter, M. (1974a) Getting a Job. Cambridge, MA: Harvard University Press.

_____ (1974b) "Granovetter replies to Gans." American Journal of Sociology 80 (September): 527–529.

_____ (1973) "The strength of weak ties." American Journal of Sociology 78 (May): 1360–1380.

Grant, G. (1969) "In defence of North America," pp. 15–40 in Technology and Empire. Toronto: Anansi.

Greer, S. (1962) The Emerging City. New York: Free Press.

Gusfield, J.R. (1975) Community: A Critical Response. New York: Harper and Row.

Hiltz, R.S. and M. Turoff (1978) The Network Nation: Human Communication via Computer. Reading, MA: Addison-Wesley.

Howard, L. (1974) "Industrialization and community in Chotanagpur." Ph.D. dissertation. Cambridge, MA: Harvard University.

Hunter, A. (1975) "The loss of community: an empirical test through replication." American Sociological Review 40 (October): 537–552.

_____ and G. Suttles (1972) "The expanding community of limited liability," pp. 44–81 in G. Suttles (ed.) The Social Construction of Communities. Chicago: University of Chicago Press.

Jacobs, J. (1961) The Death and Life of Great American Cities. New York: Random House.

Jacobson, D. (1975) "Fair-weather friend: label and context in middle-class friendships." Journal of Anthropological Research 31 (Autumn): 225–234.

_____ (1973) Itinerant Townsmen: Friendship and Social Order in Urban Uganda. Menlo Park, CA: Cummings.

Kadushin, C. (1966) "The friends and supporters of psychotherapy: on social circles in urban life." American Sociological Review 31 (December): 786–802.

Keller, S. (1968) The Urban Neighborhood. New York: Random House.

Klovdahl, A.S. (1977) "Social networks: selected references for course design and research planning." Mimeographed. Canberra: Department of Sociology, Australian National University.

Kornhauser, W. (1959) The Politics of Mass Society. New York: Free Press.

Lasch, C. (1977) Haven in a Heartless World: The Family Besieged, New York: Basic Books.

Laslett, P. (1971) The World We Have Lost. London: Methuen.

Laumann, E.O. (1973) Bonds of Pluralism. New York: John Wiley.

———— J. Galaskiewicz, and P. Marsden (1978) "Community structures as interorganizational linkages." Annual Review of Sociology 4: 455–84.

Lee, N.H. (1969) The Search for an Abortionist. Chicago: University of Chicago Press.

Liebow, E. (1967) Tally's Corner. Boston: Little, Brown.

Marx, L. (1964) The Machine in the Garden. New York: Oxford University Press.

Mayer, P. and I. Mayer (1974) Townsmen or Tribesmen. Capetown: Oxford University Press.

Mitchell, J.C. (1974) "Social networks." Annual Review of Anthropology 3: 279–299.

———— (1969) "The concept and use of social networks," pp. 1–50 in J.C. Mitchell (ed.) Social Networks in Urban Situations. Manchester: University of Manchester Press.

Nisbet, R. (1962) Community and Power. New York: Oxford University Press.

Park, R.E. (1936) "Human ecology." American Journal of Sociology 42 (July): 1–15.

———— (1925a) "The city: suggestions for the investigation of human behavior in the urban environment," pp. 1–46 in R.E. Park, E.W. Burgess, and R.D. McKenzie (eds.) The City. Chicago: University of Chicago Press.

———— (1925b) "The urban community as a spatial pattern and a moral order," pp. 55–68 in R.H. Turner (ed.) Robert E. Park on Social Control and Collective Behavior. Chicago: University of Chicago Press.

Popenoe, D. (1977) The Suburban Environment. Chicago: University of Chicago Press.

Powell, A. [ed.] (1972) The City: Attacking Modern Myths. Toronto: McClelland & Stewart.

Ross, M.H. and T.S. Weisner (1977) "The rural-urban migrant network in Kenya." American Ethnologist 4 (May): 359–375.

Scott, J. and L. Tilly (1975) "Women's work and the family in nineteenth century Europe." Comparative Studies in Society and History 17 (January): 36–64.

Sennett, R. (1970) Families Against the City. Cambridge, MA: Harvard University Press.

Shorter, E. (1975) The Making of the Modern Family. New York: Basic Books.

Shulman, N. (1976) "Network analysis: a new addition to an old bag of tricks." Acta Sociologica 19 (March): 307-323.

———— (1972) "Urban social networks." Unpublished Ph.D. dissertation, Department of Sociology, University of Toronto.

Simmel, G. (1908, 1971) "Group expansion and the development of individuality," pp. 251–293 in D.N. Levine (ed.) Georg Simmel: On Individuality and Social Forms. Chicago: University of Chicago Press.

———— (1902–1903, 1950) "The metropolis and mental life," pp. 409–424 in K. Wolff (ed.) The Sociology of Georg Simmel. Glencoe, IL: Free Press.

Slater, P.E. (1970) The Pursuit of Loneliness. Boston: Beacon.

Suttles, G.D. (1972) The Social Construction of Communities. Chicago: University of Chicago Press.

Tilly, C. (1978) From Mobilization to Revolution. Reading, MA: Addison-Wesley.

———— (1975) "Food supply and public order in Modern Europe," pp. 380–455 in C. Tilly (ed.) The Formation of National States in Western Europe. Princeton, NJ: Princeton University Press.

———— (1973) "Do communities act?" Sociological Inquiry 43 (December): 209–240.

Tonnies, F. (1887, 1955) Community and Association. London: Routledge & Kegan Paul.

Walker, G. (1977) "Social networks and territory in a commuter village, Bond Head, Ontario." Canadian Geographer 21 (Winter): 329–350.

Warren, D.I. and R.B. Warren (1976) "The helping role of neighbors; some empirical findings." Unpublished paper, Department of Sociology, Oakland University December.

Warren, R. (1978) The Community in America. Chicago: Rand McNally.

Wayne, J. (1971) "Networks of informal participation in a suburban context." Unpublished Ph.D. dissertation, Department of Sociology, University of Toronto.

Webber, M. (1964) "The urban place and the non-place urban realm," in M. Webber et al. (eds.) Exploration into Urban Structure. Philadelphia: University of Pennsylvania Press.

———— (1963) "Order in diversity: community without propinquity," pp. 23–54 in L. Wingo, Jr. (ed.) Cities and Space: The Future of Urban Land. Baltimore: Johns Hopkins.

Wellman, B. (1979) "The community question." American Journal of Sociology.

Wellman, B. and M. Whitaker (1974) Community—Network—Communication: An Annotated Bibliography. Toronto: Centre for Urban and Community Studies, Bibliographic Paper No. 4, University of Toronto.

White, H. (1965) "Notes on the constituents of social structure." Cambridge, MA: Department of Social Relations, Harvard University (mimeographed).

White, H.C., S.A. Boorman, and R.L. Breiger (1976) "Social structure from multiple networks I: blockmodels of roles and positions." American Journal of Sociology 81 (January): 730–780.

White, M. and L. White (1962) The Intellectual Versus the City. Cambridge, MA: Harvard University Press.

Whyte, W.F. (1955) Street Corner Society. Chicago: Univ. of Chicago Press.

Wireman, P. (1978) "Intimate secondary relations." Paper presented at the Ninth World Congress of Sociology, August, Uppsala, Sweden.

Wirth, L. (1938) "Urbanism as a way of life." American Journal of Sociology 44 (July): 3–24.

Woodsworth, J.S. (1911, 1972) My Neighbour, Toronto: University of Toronto Press.

Young, M. and P. Willmott (1957) Family and Kinship in East London. London: Routledge & Kegan Paul.

64 The Making of a "Problem" Community

Donald H. Clairmont   Dennis W. Magill

DONALD H. CLAIRMONT, Professor of Sociology at Dalhousie University in Halifax, Nova Scotia, specializes in social problems, the sociology of work and labour markets, and race and ethnic relations. His recent publications include "The segmentation perspective as a middle-range conceptualization in sociology" with R. Apostle and R. Kreckel (1983); "Segmentation and labour force strategies" with R. Apostle and L. Osberg (1985); "Segmentation and wage determination" with R. Apostle and L. Osberg (1985); "Economic segmentation and politics" with R. Apostle (1986); and "Job mobility, wage determination and market segmentation in the presence of sample selection bias" with L. Osberg and R.L. Mazany (1986). Currently Book Review Editor and Associate Editor of the *Canadian Review of Sociology and Anthropology,* Professor Clairmont has served as chairman of the Department of Sociology at Dalhousie University. He has recently received grants to study the quality of work life and community policing, and issues related to youth and drunk driving.

DENNIS W. MAGILL, Associate Professor of Sociology at the University of Toronto, specializes in the study of ethnicity, inequality, community, and the relation between gender and career paths. He has also taught at St. Francis Xavier University.

AFRICVILLE AS A SOCIAL PROBLEM

It was lovely, lovely. They talk about Peggy's Cove but I am going to tell you, it was the most beautiful sight you would want to see—Africville. You get on the hill, and look over the Bedford Basin in the fall of the year, say from October to around December, and that was a sight to see, especially at twilight when the sun is sinking over the hills at Bedford. . . . And another thing, during the War . . . when the convoys were in the Basin, there was another beautiful sight. It was one of the most beautiful spots I've been in, in Nova Scotia. *And the City didn't develop it.* Africville should have been developed years ago when labour was cheap. Africville would have been a pretty sight. *Why didn't they do it? There is only one meaning I can put to it. Because black people was living out there* (Italics added).

> —Tape-recorded interview with an Africville relocatee.

In the last quarter of the nineteenth century, Africville was referred to as a "community of intelligent young people, much is expected of them."[1] In 1957, a field representative of a national human rights group visited Nova Scotia's black communities: she referred to Africville as "the worst and most degenerate area I have ever seen." This chapter attempts to explain how such a dramatic change, discounting some overstatement in the 1957 characterization, took place with the result that Africville became "a social problem" and, consequently, "ripe for relocation." Basically, two processes account for the peculiar development of Africville. On the one hand there was an external process of encroachment by the various levels of government and by private economic interests which aborted Africville's possibilities as a potentially fine residential area. Railways, city disposal yards, and fertilizer plants were situated in and around the Africville community. One relocatee, reacting angrily to the mistaken but widely held idea that Africville residents were mostly squatters, pointed to these developments and observed: "They said the people in Africville encroached on the government, but I would say the government encroached on the people."

The other important process was an internal one that ate away at Africville's potential from the inside. . . .

In 1959, the Institute of Public Affairs, Dalhousie University, conducted a survey of socio-economic conditions among blacks in Halifax.* Data from this survey, recalculated and revised, point out clearly that underemployment and low earnings characterized the work world of Africville residents in the immediate pre-relocation period. Only about a third of Africville's labour force had regular work (that is, a scheduled work life); less than a third had full-time work. Except for the postmistress and the keepers of the two small stores, all the women who reported significant work during the year preceding the survey had worked as domestics in Halifax. Most men, employed as stevedores or labourers, worked well under fifty weeks a year even when they were regularly employed.

A handful of males were employed regularly as cleaners and a similar number had secure, semi-skilled dockyard jobs; people in this latter activity were referred to as "civil servants" by many of the other residents. A few males were tradesmen—all mechanics, and two whites living temporarily in the community were members of the armed forces.

Over 40 per cent of the work force earned less than $1000 in 1958. The severity of poverty in Africville is brought into sharp relief when we compare Africville data with the larger Halifax situation. Approximately 7 per cent of males and 13 per cent of females in the 1951 Halifax labour force reported an earned income in 1950 of less than $1000; nearly a decade later, 32 per cent of males and 60 per cent of females in Africville's labour force were earning less than $1000 a year. One Africville male who had a macabre sense of humour noted, "When I filed my income tax report for $125, they [tax officials] were amazed." The large households and boarders that some Africville residents took in was, at least from one point of view, a way of adjusting to this situation. Nevertheless, about one-third of the households reported a total earned income in 1958 of less than $1000; in half the sixteen households where the total earned income was $3000 or more there were multiple wage earners.

In addition to earned income, transfer payments were crucial to the survival of Africville residents. In 1959, some fifteen persons lived on pensions, and several households depended to a considerable extent on the meagre family allowance payments. Unemployment insurance was helpful, but a major problem was to continue in employment long enough to establish eligibility. Even so, surprisingly few Africville residents received welfare assistance. Economic prospects for Africville youth were not promising as indicated by the fact that half the unemployed in Africville in 1959 were in the 15–29 age category, and few of the employed worked a full fifty weeks. One older resident emphasized this problem, observing that "I know there are some here who are no good and they make it bad for the rest, but there are several around who are fine young men who want work."

Despite such a depressing employment and income situation in Africville, the 1959 survey indicated that most respondents were optimistic about the future for the children and reported the belief that things would be easier for new additions to the labour force. This belief may have reflected an underlying sentiment that things could hardly get worse. Several respondents pointed to a decline in racial discrimination as a major factor in their optimism; one male observed that "everything has changed," and a female noted that "you see coloured girls working downtown . . . if we'd only had that break." The majority of respondents did not refer to discrimination but, rather, they emphasized educational improvements as the reason for their optimism concerning the future.†

MAKING OUT EDUCATIONALLY

... Recalculated and revised data from the 1959 survey by the Institute of Public Affairs reveal that males and females who were out of school had similar educational attainment. For both categories, slightly more than 40 per cent obtained Grade 6 or less. Only four males and one female had reached Grade 10.‡ Perhaps what is more significant is evidence that out-of-school youth living at home had not obtained an education appreciably better than that of their parents. None of the former obtained more than a Grade 9 schooling and virtually all reached only Grade 7 or 8; fully 60 per cent reached Grade 7 or less. This pattern of stagnation and relative decline in contrast with developments in the broader society was common among blacks throughout Nova Scotia.[2]

While the out-of-school population in 1959 did not have significant educational achievement and while the prospects for the children still in school were dim, most respondents were optimistic about the future for their children. The authors of the Institute report did not share this optimism. They concluded their analysis of the 1959 educational data by observing that "the probability of Negro receptivity to increased education is very slim."

While the Institute report contended, reasonably under the circumstances, that education was not the answer to "Africville problems," respondents did not take this position. Being relatively powerless, lacking in resources, and often politically unaware as a result of historical neglect and deprivation, what solution other than education could they suggest? Education *had* to be the key to improvement—it was part of society's official morality to emphasize education; it was something that they, themselves, might perhaps be able to do something about, even if it were no more than telling children to "get it." Respondents did not think that their children were inherently inadequate and they knew facilities were available; small wonder that they experienced frustration and confusion. They still clung stubbornly to education as the key to a better life, but it was a hope, not a fact.

RELATIONSHIP WITH THE CITY

... Throughout Africville's one hundred and twenty-five years of existence, marginal and relatively powerless blacks often had to put up with conditions that residents elsewhere in the city would not tolerate. The night-soil deposit pits in 1858, the Trachoma Hospital in 1903, and the open city dump in the 1950s are all examples of undesirable institutions that were relocated in Africville.[3] In addition, Africville enjoyed so little in the way of public services, such as police protection, paved roads, or snow-plough services, that the residents felt they did not belong to the city.

It is common for areas facing relocation threats to undergo a cycle of deterioration. Africville residents, especially the oldliners and mainliners, often pointed to the City's lack of concern about Africville. They observed that, by not applying standard City ordinances to Africville, and by allowing some people, especially around the time of the Second World War, to squat on government property, the City allowed Africville to deteriorate into a slum and did nothing to change the impression that everyone in the settlement was a squatter. The City did little to facilitate orderly residential development, and, in fact, its policy attenuated the viability of the community and was a factor in the emigration of many of the more ambitious residents and in the immigration of opportunists.

Under these circumstances it is understandable that a sense of powerlessness and alienation developed in the Africville community . . . Residents lacked trust in City officials because, as one relocatee put it, "they had been stung so many times; the older people had a real memory for these things." Some residents struck back by not paying taxes, but this action appears not to have disturbed City Council; in fact it made it easier for City authorities to remain impervious to the history of negativism on the part of the City and perhaps, from the perspective of some officials, justified that policy. The relationship between the City and Africville can be stated in terms of three considerations—water and sewerage facilities, Africville's deviance service centre, and the dump.

WATER AND SEWERAGE

One of the more blatant examples of City neglect towards Africville is the fact that the area never obtained water and sewerage services. . . .

Lack of water and sewerage facilities had serious implications for the life and health of Africville residents. Contamination of wells was a constant problem and periodically newspaper headlines made the larger Halifax public aware of the fact. It is remarkable, in view of the water and sewerage situation, and also the presence of the nearby dump, that health was not a continuing crisis in Africville. An outbreak of three cases of Paratyphoid "B" occured in 1962[4] but, according to residents as well as the Director of Health Services for Halifax, on the whole health problems were kept in check.

A related hazard was fire. In 1948, when the extension of sewerage and water service to Africville was being discussed, the fire chief pointed out that the fire service was as nec-

essary as domestic services.[5] City firefighters not only had difficulty getting into the unpaved and unploughed Africville area but, once there, they could do little without equipment to draw water from the Basin, and the wooden homes burned quickly. Throughout the years, fires ravaged the settlement, causing many deaths and discouraging residents from improving the quality of housing.

THE DUMP

In the mid-1950s, City Council resolved that the open city dump be moved to the Africville area. This action illustrates well the negative exchange system that characterized the relationship between Africville and City authorities. Little consideration, if any, was given to the wishes or opinions of Africville residents. The latter, having learned what to expect from City authorities, did not protest the dump's relocation; they silently "accepted it" and some residents adjusted to it by taking advantage of the situation and illegally salvaging usable and salable materials. . . .

The authorities' winking at the salvaging and scavenging that did occur perhaps assuaged guilt feelings concerning the plight of the residents. The City's Department of Welfare, noted for its stringency in assisting the needy, applauded the stereotype of the resourceful Africville resident who, rather than seeking welfare, scrounged amidst the squalor of the dump. The Director of Halifax's Welfare Office, familiar with the Africville situation since 1947, expressed a high regard for the resourcefulness of the residents. Dependence upon this kind of resourcefulness unfortunately entailed risks to health as well as occasional legal action. There were several cases of families, unable or unwilling to obtain welfare assistance, which sometimes salvaged truck and car batteries for fuel in their stoves and were subsequently hospitalized as a result of lead poisoning caused by the burning batteries. . . .

DEVIANCE SERVICE CENTRE

Minority group members, if oppressed and discriminated against, often find a mode of adjusting to their situation by performing less desirable and sometimes illegal services for the majority group. Moreover, under these conditions, the minority group members often acquire a certain functional autonomy; that is, not sharing fairly in society's wealth, they are allowed a range of behaviour in their neighbourhoods by the authorities that would not be countenanced elsewhere. Such indulgence by the authorities reflects not liberality but rather the view that the minority people are "different" and a reluctance to expand sufficient resources to control the undesirable behaviour in these areas. This model applies aptly to Africville and to the reaction of Halifax authorities. . . .

The proximity of Africville to the dockyards and general port activity meant that a pattern was soon established whereby Africville became a deviance centre. . . .

Most Africville residents who complained of these changes identified the turning point from "acceptable" deviance service centre to potentially dangerous place as being around the Second World War, when Africville received a complement of migrants displaced from the mid-city area. White authorities with some intimate contact with Africville occasionally reiterated this observation concerning a drastic decline in Africville life-style and also occasionally linked this development with in-migrants during and after the Second World War. One alderman noted that "the class that settled [in Africville] after the War sort of ruined the area."

There is no doubt that the community changed during its last several decades, but it is too simplistic to explain this development in terms of the relatively small number of later in-migrants. It would be more realistic to see these people as opportunists who, having virtually nowhere else to go, gravitated towards a rapidly deteriorating Africville because of its possibilities for cheap housing, relative freedom and autonomy, and because of contacts established previously with its residents. Most of the outsiders who eventually settled in Africville had, for several years previously, been coming to Africville to drink and to party. Obviously they reinforced the drift of Africville towards a more blatant and hazardous deviance service centre. . . .

With the aftermath of the Second World War, a final pre-relocation equilibrium phase was reached within the community and between it and the broader society. Africville became regarded by outsiders as harbouring a risky deviance service centre and being a model of social disorganization. Blacks elsewhere in Halifax advised their children not to go near the community; middle-class whites advised their friends that Africville was an interesting but dangerous place to visit. Inside the community, according to outsiders and some Africville residents, there was a decline in morale; as one Halifax City Council alderman noted:

> The character of the area had gone down and the character of some of the people who lived there had changed too. Instead of being a good type of citizen as they were prior to the thirties, they seemed to deteriorate to an extent that they just didn't care; certain activities went on there that didn't lend anything to the area.

Yet it would be unwarranted to see the state of affairs in Africville as socially disorganized and to exaggerate the deviance that occurred. The official crime rate over the past forty years was not particularly high, and only a handful of Africville males were sentenced to terms in prison. The Director of Health Services in Halifax reported that, while veneral disease was not uncommon in Africville in the post-Second World War period, usually the same few people were the only residents involved. Moreover, outsiders continued, at little risk, to visit Africville for booze and conviviality right up to the time of relocation. One frequent black visitor observed: "Everybody had a good time. More bootleggers than you could shake a stick at. Girls available for a good time." A white visitor reported that he and his colleagues at the dockyard always went to the community on payday for "drinking and carousing" and that "it was rough, but if you weren't looking for trouble, it wasn't bad." Other black and white outsiders frequenting the community underlined this observation, indicating that the risks were no greater than one would expect from drinking and carousing anywhere. . . .

STIGMA

. . . While most Haligonians, black and white, rich and poor, *circa* 1960, appear to have believed that Africville was a slum, there was considerable ambivalence among the Africville people themselves. In post-relocation interviews approximately 40 per cent indicated that Africville had been a slum and 60 per cent disagreed; regardless of response, the majority of relocatees typically qualified their assessment. There was important variation according to social grouping; mainliners and marginals/transients were the least ambivalent. The large majority of mainliner respondents agreed that Africville was a slum, pointing to the stigma and the lack of facilities and often reflecting the sentiments expressed by one mainliner in 1959, prior to the relocation: "I'm ashamed of this place; the sewer is almost in my mouth." The re-

sourceless marginals/transients virtually all contended that Africville had not been a slum. While acknowledging the existence of poor housing, they were not bothered by the stigma or the presence of the dump; typically they shared the view expressed by one of their number prior to relocation: "Living in Africville is cheaper; you can pick up things such as kindling wood."

For reasons mentioned earlier, as the years passed, Africville became more and more a community of "refuge" and less and less viable. Most residents prior to relocation were eager to have improvements made in their community; this was the major alternative regularly proffered by Africville residents whenever City officials suggested relocation. Despite their fragmentation into cliques and distinct social groupings, they did have a sense of "solidarity in oppression" which was especially manifested in their post-relocation assessment of the friendliness and trustworthiness of their fellow residents. Despite the poverty and inadequate resources, the majority of residents prior to relocation indicated that they enjoyed living in Africville. They cited the privacy and freedom, the clean air, the beautiful view, the open spaces, and the "country style" of life. It is important to remember that people in their everyday life compare their status most frequently with others who are, broadly speaking, on the same socio-economic level. Africville blacks usually used mid-city blacks as their reference group on matters of housing and general lifestyle. Thus they could say that Africville "was better than in the city [*sic*], better than some of those slums downtown"; they could quite legitimately point out that many of the Africville homes on the inside were as good or better than those in the downtown area and the costs of accommodation substantially less. Finally, the Africville residents could and did say that whatever Africville was, it was theirs. . . .

Notes

The revised and recalculated data on Africville employment and income differ from those presented in the Institute report of 1962 *(The Condition of the Negroes)*. In the latter report, Africville boundaries were misread and non-Africville persons were included in the tables: moreover, a significant number of Africville residents, for one reason or other, were by-passed by the 1959 survey team. The tables reported in the present study depict accurately the pre-relocation socio-economic conditions.

†A few of the more upwardly mobile residents did not share in this general optimism. They believed that youth would find employment opportunities even more difficult to obtain

‡Data for 140 persons were available in the out-of-school category. A close examination of the cases for which no data existed indicators that the basic patterns remain valid.

1 P.E. MacKerrow, *A Brief History of the Coloured Baptists of Nova Scotia, 1832–1895* (Halifax, N.S.: Nova Scotia Printing Company, 1895). p. 65.

2 Donald H. Clairmont and Dennis W. Magill, *Nova Scotia Blacks: An Historical and Structural Overviews* (Halifax, N.S.: Institute of Public Affairs, Dalhojusie University, 1970), p. 24.

3 *Minutes of the Halifax City Council,* June 29, 1858; *ibid.*, November 5, 1903; *ibid.*, June 16, 1949.

4 Letter from Dr. Allan R. Morton to the Mayor of Halifax and Members of the City's Health Committee, August 9, 1962. The letter is in the Africville File, Social Planning Office, City Hall, Halifax, N.S.

5 *Minutes of the Halifax City Council*, February 4, 1948.

65   The One-Industry Community

Rex A. Lucas

REX A. LUCAS (1924–1978) was born in Bath, England. He was raised in Chapleau, Ontario and his early childhood years sparked his sociological interest in one-industry communities. During his academic career, he taught at Acadia University (1954–1960) and the University of Toronto (1963–1978). Professor Lucas wrote monographs on the nursing profession, the development of the arts in Montreal, and human consequences of the changing industrial environment. His two major book publications were *Men in Crisis: A Study of a Mine Disaster* (1969) and *Minetown, Milltown, Railtown: Life in Canadian Communities of Single Industry* (1971). He was a Programme and Documents Officer for H.R.H. The Duke of Edinburgh's Second Commonwealth Study Conference (1960–1962), and founding Secretary-Treasurer of the Canadian Sociology and Anthropology Association.

The community of single industry is significant to Canadian society for several reasons. In the first place a considerable proportion of the population lives in this type of community, and half lives in communities of 30,000 or less. Second, because of the nature of Canadian geography and the distribution of natural resources, there is little chance that the total number of such communities will decrease. At least one writer has suggested that the number of single-industry communities will increase.[1] The third reason is that many Canadians have been brought up in this type of community. Perhaps the majority of the citizens of the larger, more diverse communities of the nation have had their attitudes, expectations, and behavioural patterns moulded within the peculiar social structure of the single-industry community. Finally, this peculiar structure is common to both French and English Canada.

Communities of single industry seem to have a particular flavour. Patterns of life and expectations arise from the single occupational base and the absolute limitations imposed by the size and isolation of the community. If citizens have wants, defined as legitimate, but yet unattainable because of limitations inherent in the system, they often handle these conflicts by "putting up with things" or maintaining the fatalistic assumption that circumstances are beyond their control. We will return to some possible implications of this theme shortly. . . .

ISOLATION

The one-industry community exists to house the employees who exploit the area's natural resources; the location of the community, within a few miles, is predetermined by the location of the resource, the electric power necessary for the process, or the technical requirements imposed by the transportation system that moves the products. For this reason the communities are, almost without exception, found in the sparsely settled parts of the country. Indeed, if we trace them by province we find many communities of single industry in the rugged interior of Newfoundland, none in the farm-based communities of Prince Edward Island, a few in the more rugged parts of Nova Scotia, and far more in New Brunswick. There are a few south of the Saint Lawrence River and only one or two in

Southern Ontario—that are lying south of North Bay and Sudbury. The majority of these communities lie in northern Ontario and northern Quebec—the area characterized by the production of pulp and paper, gold, copper, nickel, and where the transcontinental railways pass through the Pre-Cambrian shield wilderness. Moving west, the communities of single industry hug the northern boundaries of the prairie provinces; the few to the south are located above the oil deposits and coal seams. A high proportion of the population centres of the Yukon and the Northwest Territories are communities of single industry and the remainder are found in the rugged terrain far from the fertile valleys of British Columbia.[2]

The peculiar location and isolation of these communities almost guarantee that they remain communities of single industry. The economic and technical factors that were instrumental in locating and developing communities of single industry are the same factors which rule out additional industry, diversification of the economic base, and expansion of population. In areas where the communities are close to a larger population and market they become diversified, expand, and so are no longer communities of single industry. One notable exception is the mining community where several competing companies work the same ore body; another is the community with an abundance of cheap electrical power fortuitously located where two basic resources such as minerals and forests can be exploited.

Communities of single enterprise are and remain isolated. Physical and geographical isolation, however, is a relative quality. At one end of the continuum there is the isolation of the community whose only contact with the outside is through infrequent air service; at the other end, is the community surrounded by 50 miles of scrub forests with the closest community 60 miles away by road. People living in a Northern Ontario railway community on the main line of one of the transcontinental railways, with dozens of passenger and freight trains daily pausing for service and change of crew, may feel, and in some senses are, isolated, and the same thing applies to individuals living in the community three hours' drive by first-class highway from a major city.

It is clear that these people are not talking about social isolation as it is usually defined in the social sciences. They are not talking about "failure of the individual through inability, preference or whatever to establish or maintain communications with those about him."[3] This isolation is not related to the interpersonal relationships *within* the community, but rather to the relationship between citizens of the community and others in outside communities. The preoccupation with this quality of life persists despite mass communication. McLuhan's global village is not meaningful to them in terms of interpersonal relationships or potential relationships with others. The isolation of the single-industry community seems to refer to the potential relationships of the individuals with other groups and communities outside their own. The phenomenon is probably quite close to the vicinal isolation, the physical separation which isolates and limits accessibility, as discussed by Becker; "nature presents man with his geographical location; culture provides his vicinal position."[4]

That these definitions of isolation are subtle is supported by the preliminary findings reported by Matthiasson. Residents of an isolated community of single industry ranked services and facilities that should be available in a typical resource community; the first four were: entertainment and recreation, income in relation to cost of living, housing and accommodation, and good access to cities in the south. The services in their own community which needed improvement were, in order of frequency of choice, access to cities in the south, communications, medical facilities, and entertainment and recreation. Yet, when given a check list of terms descriptive of northern living, "isolated" was ranked fourth, after "friendly," "expensive," and "challenging" ("gossipy" was fifth). The responses could be interpreted in a number of ways, and the author carefully points out that the findings are still preliminary and incomplete.[5]

In extreme isolation there seem to be geographical and measurable restrictions on the interrelationships possible with people of other communities. On the other hand, although there are few restrictions of this type imposed on an urban dweller, he seldom takes the opportunity of making contact with a neighbouring city or village. This suggests that isolation is a feeling, which, while based upon physical fact, has little relation to any absolute standard of geographical location. . . .

SINGLE INDUSTRY

We now turn our attention to a second variable, that of single industry. If we leave the population and the degree of isolation constant what happens if we add a second industry to our community? If the second industry has the same resource base, such as two mining companies working on one ore body, there are a series of implications. To begin with, there are two sets of management personnel moving in and out of the community. Inevitably one of the two industries is defined as a better industry to work for and stratification is affected by the greater prestige attached to the Smith Company than the Jones Company. At the same time, however, because there are two work structures and two bases for stratification, there is a more complex set of formal and informal patterns of association. Further, the level of observability is reduced considerably; despite the fact that the size of the community has remained constant there are many activities in the Smith Company which would not necessarily come to the attention of all who work in the Jones Company.

The interaction between people and the role of the two corporations in the community depends largely on the early history of responsibility undertaken by the corporation in the development of the community—the degree of support for local organizations, the support and subsidization of recreation facilities and so on. Corporate competitiveness is introduced by the second industry. The two corporations are vulnerable to polite blackmail by the citizens, their associations, and organizations; almost inevitably the corporations are forced to vie for the goodwill of employees and their community associations. This at least opens the possibility for citizens to feel that their social and political action could affect their lot in life. The addition of a second industry, then, provides a potential flexibility in social life.

All other variables held constant, the addition of a second industry does not affect the institutional and professional services available in the community. It does not increase the number of doctors and dentists or teachers or alternative streams in the school system; it does not affect the nature of the relationships with professional people; it does not affect the range of occupational choices open to the youth; it does not affect forced migration or the range of available marriage partners.

If, instead of two industries sharing the same resource base, an industry with a different base is introduced, more widespread ramifications are expected. If, for instance, a pulp and paper mill and a mine share the same community, the social differences are highly intensified. The two resource bases accentuate the differences in reputation of the two firms; the differences in the type of work have important ramifications for the prestige structure within the community. Because the two firms are unlike, different types of expectations are attached to their activities as well as an intensification of their competition. There is a wider variety of local jobs but the migration level from the community remains much the same. Further, the institutional and professional aspects of community life remain much the same regardless of the second industry.

FISHING, FARMING, AND COMMERCIAL COMMUNITIES

Social patterns and attitudes in a small industrial community are, however, quite different from those in a community built upon fishing and farming (and perhaps trapping), or in a centre based upon commercial and distribution services. The fishermen or farmers share occupations characterized by an indeterminacy and insecurity often classified as "acts of God." The return for work is ruled by changes in the weather, the season, and other variables not controlled by man. Men often cope with these unknowns by being fatalistic; if this is not a good year, next year may be, but in any event, there is nothing to be done about it. . . .

At the same time, the individual's position in the stratification structure is obscure because the symbols are far more varied and subtle than would appear from his pay cheque. The individual in a single-industrial hierarchy can spend his money in various ways, but everyone knows the amount he is paid; this knowledge, along with his occupation category, symbolizes his position in a stratification hierarchy. In a fishing, farming, or commercial community the returns are not clearly and definitely known in a monetary sense and the symbols of social status are indeterminate—in order to evaluate the status of a farmer, no one is sure whether to look at the barn, the house, the herd, the number of vacations, the number of paid employees, the clothes, the machinery, the type of car, or the amount of money borrowed. The symbols of position, then, can be highly specialized or very diverse; in this situation curiosity about the innuendo or the real story behind a particular set of symbols becomes

tremendously important; it is under these conditions that a high level of speculation and gossip is devoted to the evaluation of the position of the individual.

In contrast with the industrial town, this type of community is made up of many independent but interrelated capitalists. Each man starts with some capital investment, and together with his talents, judgment, and labour, he carries out his work operating under a general level of luck. Although he can blame fate and impersonal forces, he has no industry to blame. He has no industry to use; he knows that recreational facilities, the school, his church and other institutional facilities are a product of his own participation and that he cannot call upon any local industry to assist him to build and maintain them. Similarly his position in the hierarchy and his relation to his fellows is not dependent upon a corporate structure. His relationship with store owners differs because the farmer, fisherman, and store-keeper are all entrepreneurs. In contrast, the institutional complement of professional services is much the same as in the community of single industry; the professional services rendered by doctors, dentists, teachers, and clergy are subject to many of the variables discussed previously. The level of role observability is much lower than in the community of single industry. This is partly because each man has his "own domain" as insulation and partly because status attributes are not achieved within the single structure. Observability is low and the level of curiosity and gossip is high.

THE COMMUNITY OF DOMINANT INDUSTRY

Occasionally people refer to Oshawa, Hamilton, Sault Ste Marie, or even Ottawa as a one-industry town. This, of course, is a misnomer; they are not one-industry towns but rather communities with a dominant industry. Superficially, the community with a dominant industry has many characteristics of the one-industry town because the giant industry is seen as having an untoward effect upon the whole community. Executive decisions about how much, if anything, is to be contributed to a certain cause, changes in technology, when to lay off employees, raising employment qualifications—decisions in any area—have wide-spread implications for all citizens. . . .

It is clear, however, that the social stratification in a community of dominant industry is far more complex than that of a small community of single industry. . . .

COMMUNITY SIZE

We have considered the implications of holding all factors constant and varying first isolation and then the number and type of industries. Now, we vary a third factor, size. And as was noted earlier a very large community of single industry is a negation of terms; a large community involves major changes in allocated community responsibilities and concomitant credit and blame.

The level of observability of the individual and his family is reduced considerably, firstly by the diversification of industry and secondly by the size of the community, so that is it now no longer possible to keep track of all of the citizens of the community.

Once the community has a large population, the role of industry is not so crucial in the non-work facets of community life; the institutions of the community are more varied and larger in number, the recreational services are more diversified with many added participation groups; the range of and competition among the stores is increased; alternative educational streams are found; the quality and number of teachers is increased; the range of medical institutions, doctors, dentists and specialists in the medical and paramedical fields is enlarged. Medical aid is always available and the relationships be-

tween the patient and doctor are far less complex than in a small community; with any luck the patient may have a physician long enough that he is able to maintain a continuing medical history.

But although an increase in the size of the community seems to be crucial in changing the whole nature of the relationships between individuals, the assumptions held, the patterns of behaviour, and the distribution of responsibilities, this may be more apparent than real. If we consider, for instance, the metropolitan area, characterized by many industries, many stores, services, and a most complex institutional structure, we find that the round of life of most families is not very different from that of a one-industry community. Many families in the suburbs, in fact, go through the various stages of the development of their community, or their piece of community, as evidenced by the work of White and Clark.[6] Although the family shares a geographical base with a few hundred thousand other families, and potentially has at its service a thousand doctors and a thousand dentists and thousands of teachers and thousands of stores, schools, churches, and recreational outlets, life is restricted to a small segment of this potentiality.

PERSONAL RELATIONSHIPS

These repetitive contacts with friends and relatives have been confirmed in a number of studies, including Peter Pineo's study of Hamilton:

> . . . the people in the Hamilton neighbourhood were involved in primary relationships; and their frequency of contact with relatives outside their own households was roughly equivalent to that found in studies in the United States or England. Sixty-eight per cent reported at least weekly contact with some relative outside their own home.

These people were also in frequent contact with friends and neighbours. Their involvement with friends seemed as intense as their involvement with kin. While 68 per cent reported at least weekly contact with "their best friend in the neighbourhood," in fact, more (37 per cent) reported daily contact with the best friend than reported daily contact with some relative (21 per cent).[7]

Pineo goes on to say:

Age and number of years spent in the neighbourhood are closely related phenomena in the neighbourhood studied. A gradual accumulation of friends through neighbouring may have produced the larger friend networks among the older residents. When we asked the respondents how they made friends the largest proportion (40 per cent) said that initial contact had been made through neighbouring—they had simply run into them on the street, in the shops, through the children.

It would seem then, that one of the features of interpersonal relationships in the urban area that distinguishes it from the small town is neither the kinship relationships nor the primary relationships, but the lack of in-between civilities. The number of accumulating biographies and obligatory ritual exchanges is not as great. But, this is merely a matter of degree, for before long, the housewife finds out that the sister of the supermarket cashier is ill, and the cashier will enquire about the housewife's little girl who is not accompanying her. The breadwinner knows that his secretary is having "man trouble," or that his fellow-welder's wife has cancer. . . .

Within this area of kinship, neighbours, and friends there is a high level of role observability; but the urban family is able to carry on activities outside of this web of relationships and so achieve a certain level of privacy. The breadwinner of the family characteristically moves several miles to his work and it is unlikely that neighbouring families have breadwinners working in the same industry. Thus men's successes and failures at work are not common knowledge within the neighbourhood. But as White and others have pointed out, because neighbours are never sure of the social status of the individuals in the neighbourhood, court, or street, and as they are never sure which symbols should be accepted as indicative of what degree of success, the level of probing and curiosity is probably more extreme than it is in the community of single industry where the position of the individual at work, at home and in the community is well known to all.

COMMUNITY SERVICES

Although, the suburban housewife or the downtown family cannot be considered to be isolated from neighbouring communities, they seldom visit these communities. Within the urban community emergency medical and dental assistance is always available but, as we well know, the urban family tends to place its health requirements in the hands of one practitioner in much the same way that the citizen of the single-industry community does. Although, in theory, a wide range of medical generalists and specialists is available to the family, the choice of a doctor is made on irrational and non-specialist laymen's grounds, usually the recommendation of a friend or neighbour. The children go to the neighbouring school and the process by which they get their education is much the same as it is in small communities. Usually the teacher is not under the intense scrutiny of the parents because it is possible for him or her to live in another part of the city. If the child has difficulty in a particular school or with a particular teacher it is extraordinarily difficult to move him to a different school because of suburban and urban school jurisdictions. . . .

In other words, urban life is carried on basically within neighbourhoods and even when the occupational requirements take the husband outside the neighbourhood, it is within a very restricted area. There are many barriers—real and imaginary, involving money, time, and convenience—that restrict the social economic and work life of the urban family. One English-speaking family, who lived in the eastern part of Montreal, at the time of interview had not been downtown to the main stores or to the central core of the city for five years—it had not been necessary. . . .

In urban centres there are many potential marriage partners, but marriage can be consummated only when propinquity brings the two together. Although migration is not enforced by a job shortage, youth leaves the family home to set up its own establishments, often many miles physically and many more miles socially from parents.

On the other hand the wide range of competing institutions, organizations, and structures within the urban areas creates a diffuse level of responsibility for difficulties—labour blames management, management blames government, and the government blames the city. The municipality blames the provincial government, and smog, traffic problems, and school difficulties are all the responsibilities of people who are unnamed and unknown.

The city abounds with facilities and opportunities that are never utilized and for many, at least superficially, the life round of the suburban family is amazingly similar to that of the family in the single-industry community. The basic difference is that the urban resident has alternatives that are seldom used; the availability, whether used or not, affects social definitions which have a great importance to the individual and his attitudes. It is one thing to choose not to select certain alternatives and it is another not to be able to choose. . . .

THE COMMUNITY OF SINGLE INDUSTRY AND CANADA

. . . People who share a community tend to share an outlook toward it and the world outside. These attitudes become important because, as W.I. Thomas stated, "if men define situations as real they are real in their consequences."[8] We have noted the preoccupation with isolation on the part of many respondents, but another commonly expressed attitude is that "small towns are a great place to live." These respondents list the advantages—"great hunting and fishing," and "wonderful outdoors life, right on your doorstep"; it is very rewarding to "know everyone in town"—city life is too impersonal, too many people. The extent to which these types of attitudes are transmitted to the young is impressive; when a questionnaire, on the advantages and disadvantages of remaining in their community of single industry (Railtown), was administered to high school students, 90 per cent talked of healthy outdoor life and friendliness.

Other attitudes and behaviour deal with persistent problems or intrinsic limitations and restrictions. Interviews disclosed at least two ways of handling these limitations. Despite the complaints, and sometimes the unhappiness expressed by respondents, many talked with a sense of inevitability. Whether the respondent was living in a community of single industry by choice or by default, temporarily or permanently, the comments suggested that there was nothing that could be done about the difficulties because they were inherent in the nature of the community. Further, these problems were minor compared with the fear that technological and economic change might bring about the disappearance of their whole way of life.

A second method of coping with limitations was the lowering of the level of expectations, particularly noticeable when interviews from the four stages of community development are compared. At the recruitment stage, respondents are indignant about their housing, medical, and shopping services. In the stage of maturity, young people who have been born and brought up in the community view it with affection for it is the only world they know; their parents have adjusted expectations and behaviour to adapt to an inevitable situation. The rebels who were unable to live within the strictures have long since left.

When people have to share a community with neighbours, acquaintances, and work-mates, they find it useful not to antagonize their associates. When they do not have ab-solute faith in their doctor, they remember that he is the only person who stands be-tween them and illness. When conflict is con-sidered futile and damaging, the working out of problems and difficulty is constrained, cau-tious, and conservative. Resignation to events is common. . . .

Notes

[1] Ira M. Robinson, *New Industrial Towns on Canada's Resource Frontier*, University of Chi-cago, Department of Geography, Research Paper no. 73 (Chicago, 1962).

[2] Many of these communities lie within the so-called mid-Canada corridor. See Richard Rohmer, *The Green North* (Toronto, 1970).

[3] R.T. Lapiere, *A Theory of Social Control* (New York, 1954), p. 330.

[4] Howard Becker, "Current Sacred-Secular Theory and Its Development," in H. Becker and A. Boskoff, eds., *Modern Sociological Theory in Continuity and Change* (New York, 1957), pp. 164–5.

[5] J.S. Matthiasson, *Resident Perception of Quality of Life in Resource Frontier Communities*, Center for Settlement Studies, University of Manitoba (Winnipeg, 1970). Also see Center for Settlement Studies, University of Manitoba, *Proceedings—Symposium on Resource Fron-tier Communities, December 16, 1968* (Winni-peg, 1968).

[6] William H. White Jr., *The Organization Man* (New York, 1956); S.D. Clark, *The Suburban Community* (Toronto, 1966).

[7] Peter C. Pineo, "Social Consequences of Urbanization," in N.H. Lithwick and Gilles Paquet, eds., *Urban Studies: A Canadian Per-spective* (Toronto, 1968), p. 971. Similar trends were found among French Canadians in Montreal by Garigue: Philippe Garigue, "French Canadian Kinship and Urban Life," *American Anthropologist*, 58, no. 6 (Dec. 1956), pp. 1090–101. See also Scott Greer, "Urbanism Reconsidered: A Comparative Study of Local Areas in a Metropolis," *American Sociological Review*, 21 (Feb. 1956), pp. 19–25; Helgi Osterrich, "Geographical Mobility and the Ex-tended Family in Montreal," unpublished MA thesis (McGill University, 1964).

[8] W.I. Thomas and F. Znaniecki, *The Polish Peasant*, 2nd ed. (New York, 1958), p. 81. See also the discussion in R.K. Merton, *Social Theory and Social Structure, enl. ed. (Glencoe, 1968)*.

66 The Class Dimensions of Regionalism

Carl J. Cuneo

CARL J. CUNEO, Professor of Sociology at McMaster University, Hamilton, Ontario, specializes in the study of social stratification and political sociology. His recent publications include "Class in a classless model of nationalism" (1982); "Class struggle and measurement of the rate of surplus value" (1982); "Surplus labour in staple commodities during merchant and early industrial capitalism" (1982); "Has the traditional petite bourgeoisie persisted?" (1984) and "Have women become more proletarianized than men?" (1985). Professor Cuneo is currently engaged in writing a series of books, *Class Formations in Canada,* the first volume of which is *Nine to Five to Nine: Struggles over Women's Work.* He is on the editorial board of *Insurgent Sociologist,* and has reviewed manuscripts extensively for the *Canadian Journal of Sociology, Canadian Review of Sociology and Anthropology, and Studies in Political Economy.*

A CLASS MODEL OF REGIONALISM

The skeleton of our theoretical model of regionalism is presented in Figure 1. Although the details of this model must await the remaining sections of the paper, an overview of the model at this point will help the reader better understand the relationships of the different parts of the model as they are discussed throughout the paper. The interaction between a capitalist mode of production and the social class structure (a) produces a regional centralization and concentration in corporate business monopolies (b). Such corporate centralization and concentration, in turn, shapes the economic class struggle between unions and management (c). This struggle occurs most intensely between large unions and large corporations, resulting in higher wages and salaries. Large corporations, because of their oligopolistic and monopolistic position in markets, can pay higher wages by increasing the prices of the commodities they sell. Corporate concentration thus increases regional disparities in wealth through the economic class struggle (c and d). Interregional wage differences help to shape the way Canadians perceive regional differences in wealth and power (e). Such perceptions are one factor among many that influence the decision by Canadians to migrate to the wealthiest areas (f). This interprovincial migration, by supplying the labour power needed by the expanding corporations in the core (Ontario) and semi-peripheral areas (British Columbia, Alberta, and Quebec) allows their further growth in these regions (g) and further exacerbates interregional wage differences (h) by attracting the most highly paid and skilled personnel to the core and semi-peripheral regions. Corporations in the peripheral regions (Atlantic Canada, Manitoba, and Saskatchewan) are much smaller, are tied in a dependent manner to those in the Canadian and American core areas, have uncertain production runs and markets, and are unable to pay high wages

Figure 1
A CLASS MODEL OF REGIONALISM

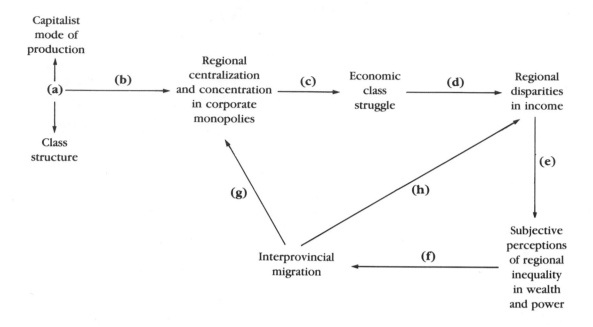

because of their subordinate position in commodity markets.

THE CAPITALIST MODE OF PRODUCTION IN A REGIONAL CONTEXT

By the third quarter of the twentieth century, an evolving monopoly capitalist system had become the predominant economic mode of production in Canada. This means essentially a combination of four conditions, the first three of which are characteristic of the capitalist mode of production in general and the last of which is characteristic of the monopoly capitalist mode of production in particular.

First, labour is free to be sold to different capitalists rather than being tied to specific employers for extended periods of time as in the slave and feudal modes of production.

Second, in the capitalist mode of production, labour is separated from control over

the means of production. The roots of this condition lie in the last century. Nineteenth-century Canada was essentially an agricultural, handicraft, and trading society. Small farmers had control over their land, livestock, rudimentary machinery, and crops; although they often were in debt to merchants. Small handicraftsmen owned their own businesses and made the products they sold in their stores. However, after 1880 the concentration and centralization of production into larger units began. Together with a revolution in the techniques of production, this consolidation movement destroyed the labourers' control over the means and pace of production in agriculture and urban handicrafts. In this way, a dependent labour population, with little control over the means of production and working for a wage as subsistence income, was created.[1] However, the introduction of mechanization by capitalists was not accepted without a struggle by workers. Skilled craftsmen in Toronto and Hamilton organized into unions to maintain control of the workshops under the onslaught of the technological revolution.[2]

Third, under capitalism capital is invested primarily to expand capital.[3] This was not always the case. Under precapitalist modes of production, capital was invested simply to reproduce the structure of the economy rather than to expand it. Two reasons for this were the underdeveloped world market and rudimentary techniques of production. Both of these conditions changed with the emergence of the capitalist mode of production. The development of almost unlimited world markets and the revolution in production technology gave capitalists the incentive to keep expanding their capital investments. With the emergence of transnational corporations and a surplus of labour, capitalists were able to invest with an eye toward the accumulation of capital. This brought financiers into closer contact with industrial capitalists and led to the rise of what is now currently known as "finance capitalism," or the merging of industrial and financial capital.[4]

Fourth, the capitalist economy today is dominated by oligopolistic and monopolistic forms of organizations. "Oligopoly" means market control of a product by several large corporations, while "monopoly", in the strictest sense, means market control by a single large corporation. The distinction is more apparent than real, since various formal and informal agreements among leading corporations in an oligopoly structure produce the same effects as monopolies—the removal of control of decision making over what is produced from small businesses and consumers.[5] Monopolies started to emerge in Canada in the last two decades of the nineteenth century. Their rise was rooted in a general world depression and a crisis of overproduction and underconsumption. Monopoly capitalism in Canada today is most highly developed in Ontario, followed by Quebec, British Columbia, and Alberta.

Within this broad contour of the Canadian economy, three caveats must be offered. First, there exists a "competitive" capitalist sector in which those who control their means of production may perform labour in the traditional sense of "working for themselves"—in which the units of economic organization are very small and the laws of supply and demand are somewhat more operative than in the monopoly sector. This competitive sector has survived mainly in agriculture and fishing, in small-scale manufacturing, and in retail trade. Yet the competitive sector is rapidly being taken over by the monopoly sector. For example, although production in agriculture still assumes many of the characteristics of competitive capitalism, large corporations are now beginning to consolidate agricultural enterprises into large corporate units and much of the distribution of agricultural products is controlled by a handful of wholesale and retail companies. Second, there is some petty or independent commodity production in which part of what is produced is sold in the marketplace and the other part is consumed by their producers.[6] This form of production and consumption has survived in agriculture and the isolated hinterland areas, such as rural New Brunswick, more than in secondary manufacturing and the urban metropolitan centres, such as Vancouver and Montreal. Third, the political state at the federal level increasingly participates in the economy as an employer of labour (e.g., the Post Office), as a consumer of commodities and services produced in the private sector (e.g., government office equipment), and as a direct owner and controller of the means of production (e.g., Petro Can). This introduces certain political elements in the economy that are lacking in the private sector. The state pays wages partly out of taxes while private corporations pay wages entirely out of their returns on investments. Furthermore, managers of state corporations are ultimately responsible to Parliament, which expects from them a social conscience in addition to their capital-gains conscience, while managers in the private sector are expected to be interested only in capital gains.

SOCIAL CLASS AND REGIONAL INEQUALITY

Sociologists have traditionally defined social class in a number of different ways, only one of which will be adopted here. At least in its economic aspects in the capitalist mode of production, social class is defined by the relation of the individual to the means of production, distribution, and financing (see the double arrow "a" in Figure 1).

One class, commonly called the *capitalist class,* owns or controls the major means of production and their supplementary trading and financial functions. The most powerful operating arm or "fraction" of this class is the "economic elite." This consists of the major owners and boards of directors of the dominant corporations in Canada. The capitalist class and the nerve-centre of its corporations are heavily concentrated in Toronto and Montreal (see arrow "b" in Figure 1). The head offices of 75 per cent of the "leading corporations" and 85 per cent of the "major financial institutions" in Canada are located in these two cities.[7] However, the "comprador" fraction of this class (that is, the boards of directors of foreign subsidiaries in Canada) must submit to the external control of foreign economic elites. The organizational counterpart of this external class linkage is reflected in the concentration of American manufacturing subsidiaries in particular areas of Canada linked to head offices in a few locations in the United States. These foreign links tend to flow primarily into Toronto and secondarily into Montreal. Thirty-eight per cent of American manufacturing subsidiaries in Canada are located in Toronto and 11 per cent in Montreal. The next two highest concentrations are Hamilton with 5 per cent and Vancouver with 3 per cent. This external class control has intense effects on regional inequality in Canada. Ray concludes that "regional economic development in Canada will tend to reflect the economic health of adjacent regions of the United States."[8] Given the great economic strength of the north-eastern and north-central parts of the United States, it is not surprising that the greatest economic strength in Canada has been located along a small belt stretching from Quebec City to Windsor, Ontario. A further consideration is the fact that "the distance a parent company penetrates into Canada to locate a branch plant is directly proportional to the distance of the parent company from Canada."[9] A cursory glance at a map will show how much southern Ontario "dips down into the United States." It is therefore not surprising that "Toronto provides the optimal market location for American subsidiaries and few subsidiaries locate beyond it."[10] This concentrates wealth in the Toronto area relative to more hinterland regions of Canada.

A second major class in Canadian society consists of people who neither own nor control corporations and who are thus forced to sell their ability to work to others in order to earn a livelihood. These people are commonly called the *working class,* consisting primarily of clerical and sales personnel, service workers, craftsmen, machine operatives, and unskilled labourers. Although there are numerous prestige and income distinctions among these types of workers, they all sell their potential for work to others in order to earn a living. As the capitalist mode of production in Canada advances, this class increases in size. In the 1965 Ethnic Relations survey of the Canadian population,[11] 30 per cent of the respondents born in 1905 or before had fathers in the working class. This percentage increases among younger respondents until we reach respondents born in 1941 or later, 59 per cent of whose fathers were members of the working class. This increase has produced a working class that today is not equally represented in all regions in Canada. Only 44 per cent of the heads of households on the Prairies are working class. Where industrial capitalism is least developed and agricultural production most enduring, as on the Prairies, we find the weakest development of the working class but the highest proportion of rural old middle class (21 per cent).

Various fractions within the working class can be distinguished. Two of the most important ones are: productive workers whose labour directly produces surplus value for the capitalist class; and unproductive workers whose labour is paid for out of the surplus value produced for capitalists elsewhere.[12] Surplus value is a central concept in Marxian sociology, although its meaning can only be briefly indicated here. The value of commodities produced in industry is the sum of constant capital, variable capital, and surplus value. Constant capital represents the investments of capitalists in the means of production, such as plant, equipment, machinery, buildings, and land. The value of this investment is simply transferred to the commodities produced by using such means of production. This value does not increase or expand. Therefore, it is called "constant." Variable capital represents the investments of capitalists in the labour of the workers. Marx divided their working day into "necessary labour," for which they are paid wages or variable capital, and "surplus labour," which represents the portion of the day the workers labour gratis for the capitalist for which they receive no wages. "Variable" capital receives its name from the fact that it expands in value to produce a surplus value. It is the source of the accumulation of the wealth of capitalists. Thus, surplus value represents the capital accumulation of the capitalist class based upon the labour of the working class. It is this wealth that is created by productive workers mainly in manufacturing, resource, and transportation industries. Part of this wealth is then distributed to the financial sector (e.g., the Royal Bank of Canada) and the mercantile sector (e.g., the Dominion Stores). Workers in these latter two sectors are unproductive in that they do not produce surplus value, but are paid wages out of the surplus value generated by productive workers in such industries as Stelco, Imperial Oil, and Massey-Ferguson.[13]

In Canada, productive workers have developed in two different sections of industrial capitalism. Productive workers in secondary manufacturing are concentrated in the urban centres of Ontario and Quebec. Because of a process known as "de-industrialization,"[14] or the stunted growth of Canadian manufacturing due to non-Canadian capitalist control, this section of the working class has not expanded as much as its counterpart in more autonomous western capitalist countries. By contrast, also because of foreign capitalist control, the other section of productive workers in the resource industries in the hinterland areas of Canada has expanded comparatively more than its counterparts in advanced autonomous capitalist countries. This means that class exploitation (the expropriation of surplus value by the capitalist class from the worker's labour) has a peculiar regional feature in Canada that is absent in most other advanced capitalist nations. Whereas in most advanced capitalist countries the core of the productive working class is concentrated in urban areas, in Canada this fraction of the working class has a significant representation in the resource industries of the hinterland areas. This increases the regional disparity in class exploitation, since the surplus value of the capitalist class in the eastern urban core and foreign metropolitan countries is very much dependent on the activity of productive workers in the hinterland. The other main fraction of the working class, the unproductive workers, has also experienced a comparatively great expansion in Canada because of the dominance of state, mercantile, and financial corporations in Canadian history.

Two other classes that are important are the managerial and professional personnel of the independent proprietors. The former, sometimes called the new middle class, are in an ambiguous position in that objectively they occupy the same position in the class structure as the working class (that is, they are hired for their work ability), but subjectively they may identify with the capitalist class. In addition, many managers act as capitalists in the hiring and firing of members of the working class.[15] From the late nineteenth century to about the middle of the twentieth century, this class doubled in size from 6 per cent to 12 per cent. By 1977, the new middle class reached 19 per cent of the Canadian labour force.[16] In 1965, it was most heavily represented in Ontario, comprising 21 per cent of the province's adult respondents, and least represented in the Atlantic provinces, comprising only 12 per cent of the adult population. It will later be seen why this is so. The other class, independent proprietors or the old middle class, consists of farm proprietors as well as independent businessmen in the towns and cities. Both share the common characteristic of owning their own means of production and, at the same time, working for themselves with little or no help from others (aside from their families). The old middle class is declining as a force in Canadian society, although the demise of the independent farmers is much further advanced than that of the small businessmen.

Two characteristics of the class structure and their interrelationships should be set out in order to grasp more fully the class forces behind interprovincial migration and regional inequality. These characteristics are economic class interest and class control.

Economic class interest indicates that each class tends to adopt a set of attitudes and actions that will advance the economic standard of living and power of its members. Although there are exceptions to this, it holds true in the long run. In the case of the capitalist class, this means that the board of directors of each corporation will attempt to increase its profits as much as possible and

within the limits imposed by the nature of its relations with other parts of the economy. Consistent with this will be attempts to expand markets, increase the size of the corporation, and establish intimate working relationships with other corporations closely related in function. The working class, on the other hand, is interested in raising as much as possible its average wage levels and other supplementary income. Some writers have argued that a further working-class interest is the direct taking over of control of the means of production.[17] Although there are dramatic examples of this in world history as well as in Canadian society (particularly in Quebec), this does not appear to be the general case yet.

Class interests are translated into reality if they are linked to efficacious class control, the second characteristic mentioned above. Class control exists to the degree that a particular class can determine the conditions under which it will pursue its own class interests, despite opposition from one or more other classes.[18] Obviously, where any one class is in such a favoured position, pursuit of its own class interests will have major effects on other aspects of Canadian society. In the long run, members of the capitalist class seem to attain this characterization of class control more than do members of the other three classes outlined above. However, this control is by no means absolute and must operate within a broad set of compromises, especially in relation to the more well-organized sections of the working class.

Implementation of the interests of the capitalist class in general or the economic elite in particular is possible because of the high degree of control they exercise from Montreal and Toronto across the various regions of the country. This results in a regional pattern of inequality or imbalance, as noted above. The structures through which this occurs are complicated, but the following seem to be central to their understanding.

First, the economic elite within the

capitalist class expands its corporations most in those regions which have the potential of either directly or indirectly sustaining or advancing its interests, especially those related to its profit-making activities (see arrow "b" in Figure 1). Thus, it expands its organizations in those areas where it has crucial contacts with other members of the same class (Montreal and Toronto), or where it is close to markets (southern Ontario and Quebec), or where it is close to natural resources (gas and petroleum in Alberta, and forestry and mineral resoures in British Columbia).

Second, the central corporations under the control of the economic elite are organizationally monopolistic and are technologically sophisticated. In view of the first point above, these two characteristics will thus predominate in Ontario and Quebec and, to a lesser extent, in British Columbia and Alberta. In 1978, the regional distribution of manufacturing corporations with 1,000 or more employees was: Ontario (58 per cent), Quebec (35 per cent), and British Columbia (7 per cent). Thus, these three provinces together accounted for 92 percent of the largest monopolies in manufacturing in spite of having only 75 per cent of Canada's total population.

Third, to undertake economic expansion in these geographical areas, the capitalist class requires highly skilled personnel for their organizations, especially highly educated and specialized managerial and professional personnel (the new middle class), as well as skilled manual workers (the aristocracy of the working class). This requirement flows from the technological content of these organizations. Two problems that immediately arise here are that such personnel are highly paid (which diminishes profit levels), and they are in relatively scarce supply.

The first problem is partly solved by the fact that monopolistic organizations are better able to pay high salaries and wages because they have greater control over the prices of their products. Prices can often be easily passed on by such organizations to the con-

sumer. The regional concentration of monopolies partly accounts for regional disparities in incomes (see arrows "c" and "d" in Figure 1). In a study conducted for the Royal Commission on Corporate Concentration, Murray and Dimick found in 1975 an average income of $11,827 in ten large companies and $10,108 in ten medium-sized companies. This difference was greatest for junior typists, senior secretaries, new production workers, key punch operators, stationary engineers, and first line supervisors.[19]

But why do larger corporations pay their employees higher wages? Their ability to pay through their market strength is only part of the reason. The other part has to do with the more intense economic class struggle in larger corporations. Large corporations and large unions go hand in hand. Workers employed by large corporations are more likely to be unionized than workers employed by small corporations. As the size of corporations increases, so does the size of unions. Between 1966 and 1981, the average number of workers per union in Canada increased from 10,028 to 15,605, or by 56 percent.[20] The average size of manufacturing corporations also increased, from 49 employees per establishment in 1966 to 55 in 1978, or by 12 percent.[21] This is also the case for non-manufacturing corporations. In 1966, only *one* Canadian union—the United Steelworkers of America—had a membership exceeding 100,000 (120,000). By 1981, *six* unions were in this category.

Terrence White has shown that large corporations go hand in hand with both larger unions and a high frequency of strikes.[22] Nowhere is this more evident than among state employees. The state at the federal, provincial and local levels is the largest employer in Canada. In 1981, 1.4 million or 12 per cent of the labour force was employed by the three levels of government.[23] No private corporation in Canada came close to being such a large employer. It is therefore not surprising that the public sector is the most unionized.

In the private sector, the economic class struggle between union and management has marked regional characteristics. It is most intense in the three provinces with the largest corporations—Ontario, British Columbia and Quebec. Alberta may be the one exception to this pattern. Labour-management conflict is less intense in other parts of Canada.[24] In 1979, the largest unions were in British Columbia which had an average 336 union members per local; this was followed in descending order by Ontario (269), Alberta (261) and Quebec (214). The smallest unions were in the other provinces with smaller corporations: Manitoba (196), Newfoundland (194), Nova Scotia (171), New Brunswick (143), Saskatchewan (140), and Prince Edward Island (100).[25] The provinces with the largest corporations are slightly over-represented in union members. In 1979, Ontario, Quebec and British Columbia accounted for 79 per cent of all union members but only 75 per cent of the national labour force. Alberta, although having moderately large corporations, has a fairly low rate of unionization. It accounted for 9 per cent of the national labour force, but only 6.4 per cent of all union members in Canada. Similarly, the Atlantic provinces, Saskatchewan, and Manitoba made up 16 per cent of the national labour force but only 14.6 per cent of all union members.[26]

The regional nature of this economic class struggle is to a great extent responsible for the income inequality among the provinces ("d" in Figure 1). With the exception of Alberta, the provinces with the largest corporations and most intense economic class struggle have the highest average incomes; the provinces with the smallest corporations and least intense economic class struggle have the lowest average incomes.

The problem of the relative scarcity of highly educated personnel needed by large corporations is solved partly through interregional migration of such personnel. Because of the demand for such personnel by corporate monopolies concentrated in the richer provinces, there is a net drain of the highly educated and skilled from the poor regions of Canada to the richer areas. This is assisted by a subjective perception of regional inequality among potential migrants (see the chain of arrows from "c" to "d" to "e" to "f" in Figure 1). This migration tends to reinforce even further the above noted regional disparities in corporate size (arrow "g") and income (arrow "h") by draining the poor regions of many of their high-income earners. In this chain of influences, the subjective perception of regional inequality of wealth and power will first be examined.

INTERPROVINCIAL MIGRATION

Generally speaking, people in Canada have migrated from areas with declining or small economic organizations to areas with expanding or large organizations.

Early in the twentieth century, especially between 1901 and 1921, many of the interprovincial migrants, as well as migrants from outside of Canada, flowed into Alberta, Saskatchewan, and Manitoba. This movement corresponded to the emergence of the wheat economy in the west and the existence of vast expanses of land as yet unsettled.[27] After the Second World War, however, with the growing movement toward consolidation and mechanization in wheat farming, the expulsion of labour from the Prairies, and the rise of monopolies in Ontario, Alberta, and British Columbia which offered high-paying jobs, this pattern was reversed somewhat. Saskatchewan and Manitoba began to suffer net losses in their populations, most of which migrated to British Columbia, Alberta, and Ontario. Throughout the entire twentieth century, British Columbia has always been a net gainer in population from interprovincial migration. When migration figures are considered in the context of those on the expansion of the capitalist mode of production presented above, we see that the labour force in Canada flows in the direction of the greatest expansion in monopolistic organizations controlled by the economic elite—with the possible exception of Quebec due to linguistic and other factors (see arrow "g" in Figure 1).

In order to determine what effects such migration has on the particular regions involved, we must compare especially the class and educational composition of the migrants with that of the nonmigrants. The new middle class and highly educated personnel have higher rates of migration over longer distances than do the working class and the less educated and less skilled.[28] Ontario and Quebec seem to benefit the most from such migration: 33 and 29 per cent, respectively, of their migrants from other provinces are new middle class. These figures drop to 21 per cent in the Atlantic provinces, 25 per cent on the Prairies, and 19 per cent in British Columbia. In terms of schooling, 47 per cent of the interprovincial male migrants in Canada in 1971 had grade twelve education or better, compared to only 32 per cent of the total male civilian labour force.[29] Analysis by province shows, for instance, that 20 per cent of the interprovincial male migrants who had settled in Ontario by 1971 had university education. The comparable figure for Quebec was 21 per cent. In all other provinces, these percentages varied from 14 per cent to 17 per cent, once again indicating that the centres of corporate power in Canada (Ontario and Quebec) attract the most "qualified" personnel. While some of these personnel certainly do come from other "have" provinces, such as British Columbia and Alberta, it seems that the poorest areas of Canada lose much of their most highly qualified labour to the richest provinces. This places a severe strain on the educational resources of the less well-to-do provinces. It must, of course, be remembered that much of the tax burden for educating these personnel falls on the residents of such poor provinces, the vast majority of whom are not rich. While it is the case that the poorer provinces do receive some highly educated personnel and new-middle-class members from the richer provinces, these are likely to have different characteristics from their counterparts migrating in the opposite direction. Many of the managerial and professional personnel sent from Toronto and Montreal to the outlying areas of Canada are placed in supervisory or high-status positions. This either increases and reinforces the dependency of peripheral regions on the central capitalist class and its economic elite, or reserves a disproportionate number of prestigious positions in the poor areas for "outsiders." Thus, the pattern of interprovincial migration supplies the needed qualified labour for the central expanding monopolies and, at the same time, drains the poorer regions of much of their needed skills and higher-income earners. This makes them even more dependent on the central regions of Canada. By this mechanism, regional inequality and dependency in the country are strengthened.

Notes

[1] Cf. Karl Marx, *Capital,* Vol. 1 (New York, 1967), VIII; and James W. Rinehart, *The Tyranny of Work* (Toronto, 1975), Chapters 2 and 3.

[2] Cf. Gregory Kealey, *Toronto Workers Respond to Industrial Capitalism, 1867–1892.* (Toronto, 1980); and, Bryan Palmer, *A Culture in Conflict: Skilled Workers and Industrial Capitalism in Hamilton, Ontario, 1860–1914.* (Montreal, 1979).

[3] Marx, *Capital,* Vol. 1, VII; Vol. 2, XVII and XXI.

[4] Ernest Mandel, *Late Capitalism.* (London, 1975).

[5] Paul Baran and Paul Sweezy, *Monopoly Capital.* (New York, 1966).

[6]See Leo A. Johnson, "The Political Economy of Ontario Women in the Nineteenth Century", in Janice Acton, Penny Goldsmith, and Bonnie Shepard (eds.), *Women at Work: Ontario, 1850–1930* (Toronto, 1974), pp. 22–27.

[7]Donald Kerr, "Metropolitan Dominance in Canada", in John Warkentin (ed.), *Canada: A Geographical Interpretation* (Toronto, 1968), p. 534.

[8]Ibid., p. 31.

[9]Ibid., p. 32.

[10]Ibid., p. 31.

[11]Details of this survey may be obtained from the Institute for Behavioural Research, York University.

[12]Cf. Ian Gough, "Marx's theory of productive and unproductive labour", *New Left Review,* 76 (1972), pp. 47–72; James O'Connor, "Productive and Unproductive Labour," *Politics and Society,* 5, 3 (1975), pp. 297–336; Nicos Poulantzas, "On Social Classes", *New Left Review,* 78 (1973), pp. 27–54; and Nicos Poulantzas, *Social Classes in Contemporary Capitalism* (London, 1975), especially pp. 209–23.

[13]Canadian applications of these ideas may be found in Carl Cuneo, "Class Exploitation in Canada", *Canadian Review of Sociology and Anthropology,* 15 (3), 1978, pp. 284–300; "Class Contradictions in Canada's International Setting", *Canadian Review of Sociology and Anthropology,* 16 (1), 1979, pp. 1–20; "Class, Stratification, and Mobility," Pp. 236–77 in Hagedorn, *Sociology;* "Class Struggle and Measurement of the Rate of Surplus Value", *Canadian Review of Sociology and Anthropology,* 19 (3), 1982; and, "A Marxist Approach," in J. Paul Grayson and Joanna Grant (eds.), *Introduction to Sociology: An Alternative Perspective,* (Toronto, 1983).

[14]See Jim Laxer, "Canadian Manufacturing and U.S. Trade Policy", in Robert M. Laxer (ed.), *(Canada Ltd.): The Political Economy of Dependency* (Toronto: 1973), pp. 127–52.

[15]See Braverman, *Labor and Monopoly Capital,* (New York, 1974), pp. 404–05.

[16]William Johnston, "Social Class, Social Life and Political Attitudes in Canada", Unpublished Ph.D. Dissertation, York University, 1981. Based on Carchedi's definition of class.

[17]Rinehart, *The Tyranny of Work,* pp. 156–65.

[18]See Poulantzas, *Political Power and Social Classes,* p. 104.

[19]Victor Murray and David Dimick, *Personnel Administration in Large and Middle-Sized Canadian Businesses.* Study No. 25. Royal Commission on Corporate Concentration. (Ottawa, 1977), pp. 40–41.

[20]Calculated from Canada, Department of Labour, *Labour Organizations in Canada.* (Ottawa, 1966), p. xiii; and, Labour Canada, *Directory of Labour Organizations in Canada.* (Hull, Quebec, 1981), p. 21.

[21]Calculated from Dominion Bureau of Statistics, *Manufacturing Industries of Canada. Section A-Summary for Canada, 1968.* (Ottawa, 1971), p. 22; and, *Canada Year Book,* 1980–81, p. 687.

[22]Terrence H. White, *Organization Size as a Factor Influencing Labour Relations.* Study No. 33. Royal Commission on Corporate Concentration. (Ottawa, 1977), pp. 25, 28–29.

[23]Calculated from Statistics Canada, *Federal Government Employment, October-December, 1981* (Ottawa, 1982), pp. 16; 48; *Provincial Government Employment October-December, 1981).* (Ottawa, 1982), pp. 10, 26; *Local Government Employment, October-December, 1981* (Ottawa, 1982), p. 18; Statistics Canada, *The Labour Force, December, 1981* (Ottawa, 1982), p. 28. Figures are for December, 1981. See also Hugh Armstrong, "The Labour Force and State Workers in Canada", Pp. 289–310 in Leo Panitch (ed.), *The Canadian State.* (Toronto, 1977).

[24]Pentland has argued that the union movement between 1897 and 1919 was most radical in Western Canada (especially in British Columbia) where larger monopolistic, resource-extraction companies paid little heed to the needs of workers. See H.C. Pentland, "The Western Canadian Labour Movement, 1897–1919", *Canadian Journal of Political and Social Theory,* 3 (2), 1979, pp. 53–78.

[25]Calculated from Statistics Canada, *Annual*

Report of the Minister of Supply and Services Canada Under the Corporations and Labour Unions Returns Oct. Part II - Labour Unions, 1979. (Ottawa, 1981), p. 36.

[26] Calculated from *ibid;* and from Statistics Canada, *Patterns of Full- and Part-year Employment and Unemployment: Results of the Annual Work Patterns Surveys, 1977 to 1980.* (Ottawa, 1982), p. 17. See also Canada, Department of Labour, *Union Growth in Canada, 1921–1967* (Ottawa, 1970); and, J.K. Eaton, *Union Growth in Canada in the Sixties* (Ottawa, 1976).

[27] See R. Marvin McInnis, "Provincial Migration and Differential Economic Opportunity", in Stone, *Migration in Canada,* pp. 134–38.

[28] For examples of readings in the voluminous literature which corroborates this statement, see Anthony H. Richmond, "Sociology of Migration in Industrial and Post-Industrial Societies", in J.A. Jackson (ed.), *Migration* (Cambridge, 1969), p. 247; Anderson, *Internal Migration in Canada,* p. 31; Jack Ladinsky, "Occupational Determinants of Geographical Mobility among Professional Workers", *American Sociological Review,* 32, 2 (1967), pp. 253–64; George, *Internal Migration in Canada,* pp. 11–13; and Marvin McInnis, "Age, Education and Occupation Differentials in Interregional Migration: Some Evidence for Canada", *Demography,* 8, 2 (1971), pp. 195–204.

[29] Calculated from Statistics Canada, *1971 Census of Canada,* 1, Part 5, Bulletin 1. 5–9 (Ottawa, 1975), Table 24.

Social Movements and Social Change

Introduction

The introduction of the last section ended by saying that if you put community and inequality together, you probably got social protest and social change. That cryptic comment, though largely true, is also somewhat misleading.

It is misleading because much social change occurs without inequality or social protest playing a part. Further, the combination of community and inequality does not always produce social protest and social change. Indeed, sociologists who study social movements try to discover the conditions under which community and inequality *will* give rise to radical change.

A great deal of social change occurs without plan, through the invention and dispersion of new technologies. No one knew beforehand all the ways the telephone, automobile and computer would transform our lives. Technological change often leads to unanticipated and largely uncontrolled change; and so does change generated outside our own society. Changes in the international balance of trade, world peace, or the availability of needed resources will all have major impacts on our social and economic lives. Canada, historically a staple-producing country, has always been particularly vulnerable to change in the demand for food and resources outside our borders. Such economic changes affect industrial and communal life, and through these, the private lives of individual Canadians.

Another kind of change studied by Talcott Parsons and other "functionalist" sociologists is evolutionary, a kind of change that does not break radically with tradition but extends it. Such change includes differentiation and integration. *Differentiation* (as for example, an increasing division of labour at work) adds to the complexity of the social order. *Integration* co-ordinates the complex social order more effectively. For example, the Canadian Charter of Rights integrates some legal principles that are already recognized, but never stated so explicitly, with others that are completely new. The new combination is, on the one hand, simpler, creating a coherent body of thinking about people's rights. On the other hand, the seemingly simple statement of rights masks an enormous complexity that will need spelling out in case law over the decades and centuries to come. Integration in this instance has not so much simplified the social order as cleared the way for another leap into greater complexity.

Thus, change by technological innovation, by external intervention, and by differentiation and integration are all important. They may not have any immediate or obvious connection to inequality or community, but they often do; and other kinds of change do much more usually.

Marx helped to found the study of social movements and social change. He theorized that all history was the playing out of class conflict: the continual struggle of subordinate and dominant classes, and the replacement of one social order by another. Naturally, in analyzing nineteenth century capitalism, Marx wanted to understand the current condition of the working class, or proletariat, and theorize about the conditions for a successful proletarian revolution. Accurately predicting the decline and overthrow of capitalism would rest on correctly understanding the working class and its mobilization.

Marx predicted a progressive immiseration of the working class in the countries where capitalism was most advanced— England and Germany, for example—followed by a mobilization and successful overthrow of the capitalist classes there. Yet, this is not what happened. Revolution did *not* occur in England, Germany, the United States or France—indeed, anywhere in the industrial world. It occurred in Russia and, ever since, in Third World countries. Nor was Marx correct in supposing that the working class would make the revolutions. In every instance, the urban intelligentsia, aided by farmers or peasants, and occasionally by small groups of workers or soldiers, have been the chief revolutionists.

Marx predicted wrongly because he focused primarily on inequality and community—on immiseration and class consciousness. Inequality and community are certainly important in the mobilization

for protest. But history shows that they are neither necessary nor sufficient. Neither objectively extreme inequality nor growing inequality will necessarily lead to protest. Conversely, some evidence suggests that declining inequality may lead to protest because of a "revolution in rising expectations." People are often outraged if conditions do not improve as fast as they would like, even though they are in fact improving. Reduced inequality also makes more "resources" available that facilitate protest: money, food, technology, expertise, free time, and so on. The extremely impoverished have fewer of these resources for protest than relatively affluent North American college students, for example.

Consider the electoral support for Social Credit in Quebec in the early 1960s. Maurice Pinard shows that, in general, there was a "strong linear and positive relationship between short-term changes for the worse in one's economic conditions and Social Credit support." Yet the poor were not particularly strong supporters of this party, which appealed to people discontented with the major parties. Why didn't the poor, especially vulnerable to economic setbacks, throw their weight behind Social Credit?

Pinard concludes that worry and hopelessness—fatalism about their condition— tended to reduce support by the poor; in many cases the poor abstain from politics and voting altogether. Poor people disproportionately lack information about political issues; and this lack of information also reduces their willingness to vote for Social Credit. Though exposed to Social Credit party propaganda as much as the other income groups, the poor are less influenced by it, perhaps because of their hopelessness. Finally, restricted social participation—social isolation—also more common among the poor, has a strong effect. Among the poor, people with limited social contacts are especially unlikely to vote for

Social Credit. This may reflect the importance of social integration for the diffusion of new ideas.

These findings, similar to the findings of other studies of the poor and unemployed, show that inequality and immiseration are not enough to produce support for a protest movement or anti-establishment political party.

Though Marx was wrong about the role of inequality, he was certainly right about the role of community. Social protest requires some communal, shared commitment to change: this in turn demands geographic proximity, interaction and communication, awareness of common experiences and problems, and a common world view. Bringing the oppressed together, whether in segregated parts of large cities, in factories or in factory towns, ought, therefore, to radicalize and mobilize them. And so it did, in nineteenth century England, and again in the 1960s, when American Blacks in northern cities mobilized to demand their rights. Similar mobilization hadn't happened, indeed couldn't have happened in the rural south: first, because of insufficient proximity and communication (i.e., no critical mass); second, because of the greater impoverishment of Blacks there; and third, because of the relatively closer control and more effective repression of Blacks down south. As well, northern urban Blacks were particularly outraged. They had believed the North would be different from the South: less racist and full of greater opportunity. To some degree the North was different, but not nearly different enough. Black incomes had risen and so had free time and freedom from repression; add to this the possibility for easier communication, and protest was virtually assured.

In looking at Black protest, we can see more variables operating than we started out with. But even these are not enough. Consider the French Canadian case: why did

significant protest occur in Quebec when it did, and not a decade, a generation or a century earlier? Let's tick off the conditions. First, there was never any shortage of "community" among French Canadians in Quebec (although, as we noted in the Pinard article, the poor were relatively unintegrated socially, hence less likely to protest their condition). A change in community cohesion cannot, by and large, account for the surge of nationalism, terrorism and separatist sentiment in the 1960s and 70s. Nor is it likely that immiseration explains it. Like the American Blacks, many French Canadians left the countryside and came to live in cities after the First World War. But there is no evidence the French Canadian economic condition got worse as a result.

In his classic work, *French Canada in Transition*, excerpted in this section, Everett Hughes documented the disruption of traditional ways of life and community. He felt this disruption accounted for the hostility of French Canadians towards English Canadians and Jews. The problem was not a revolution of rising expectations at that time, he felt; it was what we might call "culture shock," even "future shock."

The rise of Francophone pride and self-assertion in the 1960s began with the so-called "Quiet Revolution." By then, Quebec was well along into modern, industrial urban living, and Francophones were demanding the right to be "maîtres chez nous." But what is most striking about that fiery decade, 1966–1976, is not the change in community or inequality, but the importance of intellectuals and radical ideologies.

Marx, though himself an intellectual with an ideology, had surprisingly little to say about the social role of intellectuals and ideologies. He thought intellectuals stood outside social conflict—as being neither proletariat nor capitalist— as mere recorders of the truth. Marx thought of ideology as a smokescreen the capitalist class blows over the masses to keep them confused, disorganized and peaceful. This view kept Marx from anticipating the dominant reality of twentieth century social change: namely, that revolutionary change is led by intellectuals using ideology as a tool.

Intellectuals and ideologies are important to the foundation, maintenance and success of protest movements. People are more than walking bellies; as Weber knew, we also have hungry minds and hearts. Ideologies are food for hungry, despairing minds— they promise a better world, justify action, lower the mighty, and raise the fallen. Intellectuals are the craftsmen of ideology: they trade in ideas, words, imagery, imagination. Intellectuals are not the only people trading in ideologies: clergymen are versed in this as well. It is not accidental that much of political protest in Canadian history has often accompanied religious protest, or has been led by religious leaders (for example, J.S. Woodsworth of the CCF and William Aberhart of the Social Credit Party).

Intellectuals often have the skills, the time and the economic security to lead protests. Moreover, in this age of science and secularism, they have enough credibility as "people of knowledge" to be able to sell ideologies as "the truth." Religious leaders have more difficulty doing the same.

Not only are ideologies and intellectuals important, they also embody the interests and experiences of people who use them, a fact that lends itself to several interpretations. A cynical interpretation is that the ideologist never really meant what he was saying. However, as well as being ideological, people are also practical. Having worked to win social change, they will not give up on the change if it fails to conform exactly to what their ideology has prescribed. Only saints and fools do that. People will usually come to "understand"

new situations in ways that enable them to accept change even if it violates ideology.

Weber had another way of seeing this. He recognized that every social movement was made up of phases. There was the "charismatic phase" of powerful emotion, communal sentiment and blind willingness to follow a leader to the limit. Then came the "routinization of charisma," a period when people needed orderliness and established authority. In the routinization phase, typically after the charismatic leader had died, followers came to terms with the real world. They used the victories of the movement to meet the current needs of the movement members. Professor Sinclair shows this happened to the CCF after gaining power; and it usually happens when movements have been successful, says Weber.

Quebec offers a particularly interesting case of social change in Canada. Quebec has always seen itself as a nation within a nation. Through the nineteenth century, it was a laboratory for the study of relations between two different language/culture groups, one dominant in economic affairs and the other in cultural, religious and private affairs. In the first two thirds of the present century, Quebec was a laboratory for studying the industrialization of a peasant people largely untouched by nineteenth century progress. In the last two decades, Quebec has been a laboratory for the study of national self-assertion in a world where nationalism means less and less.

We have included three pieces on Quebec—by Hughes, Pinard and Guindon— in this section. The first piece, by Everett Hughes, was written about 40 years before the third, by Hubert Guindon; and the comparison is informative for several reasons. First, the two analyses differ dramatically in scholarly tone and explanatory style, telling us something about the evolution of sociology in Canada. Second, they both record times of tension in Quebec society. The first was written when both the spread of industry and the Depression were causing a great deal of anxiety, even scapegoating. The third article was written shortly after the PQ victory in Quebec and shortly before the Referendum, in which a majority of voters decided not to seek sovereignty-association with Canada. At that time, the air was crackling with suspense; charisma was not yet fully routinized. In his paper, Professor Guindon calls for renegotiation between Canada and Quebec, to find a legitimate basis for cooperation.

In the first period, the Church is still in charge of ideology. Forty years later, ideology is originating in the halls of academia and the provincial capital in Quebec City. The language of the first analysis is disinterested and perhaps a little patronizing. The third is radical, cynical; experiments in reform have been tried and failed, we are told; now is the time for more significant action.

We finish this book where we began: with S.D. Clark, Canada's premier historical sociologist, writing about changes in Canadian society since the Second World War. The writing is as even and dispassionate as it was 40 years earlier; and Clark's position is still liberal-democratic. Change has come about for many reasons, he tells us. There have been enormous demographic changes in the makeup of the country, largely due to immigration. But the baby boom, large-scale migration to cities, and interprovincial movements have also played a part. People released from their traditional communities are experiencing the challenge and opportunity of a new, relatively affluent life-style. New technology, a booming economy, and American imperialism have made Canadians (comparatively) rich.

In the midst of this new wealth comes a pressure for change. The old order of society no longer fits the greater complexity of society, its rapid changeability, and the substitution of individual for communal interests. People all around are questioning traditional authority relations; their legitimacy is in doubt.

A quiet revolution is taking place throughout Canada, Clark says. In this middle-class revolution, equal access to the "good things" is demanded: an access to university education, good jobs, decent housing. This middle-class revolution goes a long way toward erasing traditional regional differences. Far from breaking down the Establishment, everyone becomes part of it, according to Professor Clark.

Are Clark and Guindon describing the same society? Writing at the same time? Yes, they are, on both counts. The difference between them illustrates the variety of approaches in Canadian sociology and also the effects on sociological writing of ideological preferences. For Clark, significant change has occurred without violence; for Guindon, it hasn't. Part of the difference between them is definitional: what is "significant change?" Part of the problem is evidentiary: how would we prove that most Canadians are now part of the Establishment without distorting the original, exclusionary meaning of the term "Establishment"? What this disagreement shows is the complexity of social change as a topic for study and the difficulty of disentangling networks of causes and effects. Inequality, community, ideology, intellectuals, technology, demography, charisma—all of these and so many other factors shape our collective destiny.

In this book we have identified some key sociological variables and some important social issues. We have described compelling situations and heard tight arguments. Now the sociology can begin.

67 The Saskatchewan CCF Takes Power and Socialism Declines

Peter Sinclair

PETER SINCLAIR, Professor of Sociology at Memorial University of Newfoundland, St. John's, specializes in the study of social movements, rural organization and socioeconomic development. His books and articles include *Village in Crisis* with Kenneth Westhues (1974); *From Traps to Draggers: Domestic Commodity Production in Northwest Newfoundland* (1985); *A Question of Survival: The Fisheries and Newfoundland Society* (forthcoming); "Political powerlessness and sociodemographic status in Canada" (1976); and "The survival of small capital: State policy and the dragger fleet in northwest Newfoundland" (1986). Professor Sinclair has served as Director of Sociological Research at Memorial University's Institute for Social and Economic Research, and is currently Head of the Sociology Department.

In 1944 the Cooperative Commonwealth Federation [CCF] won a sweeping victory in the Saskatchewan provincial election, a victory which has often been hailed as the rise to power of North America's first socialist government.[1] This paper will review the development of the party up to 1944, paying particular attention to its relationship with other political organizations and to the transformation of its early socialist policy on land ownership.

The history of the CCF before 1944 is best understood by emphasizing that it was more a political party than a social movement....

The concept of social movement implies a diffuse, relatively unorganized support for fundamental social change. A political party is a formal organization committed to winning power, usually within the framework of existing electoral and governing institutions. Such a party may be the organized expression of a social movement, but it is the party character of the CCF which must be emphasized if we are to make sense of its development in Saskatchewan. Commitment to winning power by popular election led to a conservative compromise in its policy and pragmatic attempts to form coalitions with Social Credit.[2]

Elaboration of the above theme should begin with an account of the radical origin of the Saskatchewan CCF, which emerged early in the depression as a coalition of farmer and labour groups. Much earlier (1921) those farmers who were most interested in reform had established an independent Farmers' Union. A major concern of this group was political education, a task which they continued when the Farmers' Union merged with the Saskatchewan Grain Growers' Association to form the United Farmers of Canada [UFC]. By 1928 the left had two important successes. At the 1928 convention of the UFC a resolution was passed which favoured the compulsory marketing of wheat through the pool co-operative on condition that 75 per cent of farmers sign contracts with the existing voluntary organization. The few socialists in the organization had long been campaigning for a compulsory pool because they saw it as the only way to have some control over selling prices. In additon, George Williams, the leader of this group, was elected vice-president of the UFC.[3] This achievement was consolidated in 1929 when Williams became president and an unqualified resolution for compulsory co-operative marketing was passed.[4] The radical trend is evident in the speech of the retiring president, J.A. Stoneman, who commented, "We should stress more and more that we do support public ownership and control of not only railways but natural resources as well."[5] This was a very important statement because in asking for the public ownership of natural resources he could be interpreted to mean that farmers should give up *personal* ownership of land.

One result of the depression was increased pressure for direct political action. Addressing the 1930 UFC convention, E.A. Partridge demanded a form of Christian socialism to replace capitalist exploitation: "We must organize along class lines, we must realize that it is the same class, who exploits labour, who exploits the farmer, only in a different way, and that the propertyless farmer must join hands against the common enemy.... True co-operation has its final goal in socialism, which is the continual observance of the Golden Rule, the gospel the man Jesus Christ preached and practised, two thousand years ago.[6] Following this speech a motion to allow the UFC to undertake direct political action was narrowly defeated.[7] However, it was agreed that farmers should set up another organization 'for the purpose of more directly selecting and electing representatives to the legislature and the House of Commons, pledged to support the demands of organized agriculture."[8] As 1930 drew to a close, there was no sign of an end to the depression and the farmers were growing more bitter because many were facing foreclosure after years of working to build up their farms. They were in the best possible mood to agree with Partridge at the 1931 convention when he demanded a transition "from a system of production for profit to a system of production for use."[9] Now George Williams was able

to persuade the convention to support direct political action by the UFC.

This decision was taken in order to implement the UFC economic policy which had been established at the same convention. The policy appears confusing in that it combined requests for agricultural *reform* with a long-range objective of social ownership which was based on a critique of the total capitalist system.[10] Part of the economic policy demanded that " 'Use-Leases' be implemented, and that all land and resources now privately owned be nationalized, as rapidly as opportunity will permit."[11] This resolution passed despite opposition from those who wanted to retain title to their land. It marked the biggest policy victory for the left. However, it should not be thought that all the farmers in Saskatchewan were committed socialists, owners of well-thumbed copies of *Capital*. The policy was passed after heated debate in an organization which represented a minority of Saskatchewan farmers and was instrumental in the rejection of the CCF during the thirties. All other parts of the UFC platform were directed to patching up the existing system.[12]

By this time the socialist-inclined farmers had been co-operating with Saskatchewan's tiny Independent Labour Party (ILP) for some two years. In 1931 the UFC and ILP presented joint proposals for reform to the Conservative-led coalition government and, after all their demands had been rejected, a conference was held at which the two groups agreed to work together to build a co-operative commonwealth. Formal recognition was brought to the agrarian-urban coalition in 1932 by the founding of the Saskatchewan Farmer-Labour Group with M.J. Coldwell from the ILP as its leader. This year also saw the establishment of the national CCF to which the Farmer-Labour Group affiliated. Although it did not change its name until 1934, the Farmer-Labour Group was, de facto, the Saskatchewan CCF. By virtue of its affiliation, the

Saskatchewan organization was required to accept the national CCF policy, but the manifesto statement was sufficiently ambiguous to enable anyone to see what he wished in the document. The provincial sections had only to subscribe to the vague general principles of the manifesto and could construct their own specific policies in the provincial sphere. Therefore, one is justified, overall, in treating the Saskatchewan section as the unit of analysis in this paper.

The provincial election of 1934 was the first opportunity for the CCF to test its strength, which did not appear great. At the 1933 convention the secretary reported that little work could be done because there was no money available and voluntary workers were constantly out of pocket. Office staff rarely received full pay and several times the central office was on the brink of closing.[13]

The CCF fought from a socialist platform which included "the social ownership of *all* resources and the machinery of wealth production.[14] Such proposals agitated the established parties. Apart from the general assault on socialism as a threat to individual freedom, the most frequently criticized policy was the aim to socialize land. The opposition raised the spectre of Saskatchewan farmers being forced into state collectives, complained that under the proposed system the farmers would lose control of their land, that they would have no choice but to surrender their title, and that they would lose the value of improvements which they had made to their holdings.[15] There were also more general charges that the CCF was communist and supported violent revolution.[26]

Religion became a major issue in the campaign. M.J. Coldwell accused the Liberal party of spreading fear among the Roman Catholic population that the CCF would prevent them from practising their religion. The church itself denounced socialism and two students from Notre Dame College in Wilcox were forced to resign from the CCF. Later a letter from the archbishop of Regina to Coldwell,

assuring him of the political neutrality of the church, was published in the *Leader-Post*, but the damage to the left had already been done.[17] Even the United Church, strongly anti-capitalist in 1931, rejected socialization at a conference held just before the election.[18]

In these circumstances the CCF won 25 per cent of the popular vote and five seats, the Liberals taking all the rest (but with a minority of the popular vote). CCF leaders were distressed at the result, for some had expected to sweep the province, as the United Farmers of Alberta had done across the western border in 1921. Responding to the defeat, M.J. Coldwell described himself as "bitterly disappointed" and feeling "both tired and sick."[19] The resounding defeat in 1934 marked the end of the socialist phase for the CCF in Saskatchewan.

Why did a socialist appeal fail in Saskatchewan? Unfortunately, we have no record of how the public perceived the various parties. The ecological analysis of voting statistics does not in itself permit us to infer the motivation for political support, but Lipset's evidence that the CCF vote was lowest among poor farmers (those in areas of low tax assessment and high rates of tenancy) is supported by the observations of several CCF candidates.[20] Helmer Benson remembered that most of the down-and-out people voted Liberal: "It was like their religion."[21] George Hindley, who ran in Wilkie, said, "When you get people down so far they stop thinking. They lose their initiative, they lose their capacity to fight and they begin to accept things."[22] At this time people in the poorest areas did not support the CCF, perhaps because they saw their situation as hopeless.

Certainly socialism was the big issue of the election. A review of speeches at conventions, public statements, and letters in the farming journals suggests that those who supported the CCF saw socialism as Christian cooperation which would protect their way of life, while those in opposition tended to define socialism in terms of Soviet totalitarian rule, collective farms, and anti-religious at-titudes, that is, as a threat to the small capi-talist producer and the family farm. No party perceived in such a way could hope to win an election in a society whose people were committed to personal ownership of land. The history of co-operative action does not provide grounds for changing this assessment because producers' co-operatives are de-fence mechanisms best described as "the joint entrepreneurship of individuals. . . ."[23]

The initial socialist land policy called for farming to be carried on under a "Use-Lease," which would allow the individual farmer to carry on as before, except that he would lease the land from the state. The plan was devised to ensure security of tenure by stopping evic-tions caused by defaulting on mortgage pay-ments. Opponents were assured that there was no intention of introducing collective farms as in the Soviet Union. Both Liberals and Progressives rejected state ownership because they wanted to hold personal title to the land. For example, S.N. Horner, who had been elected to the legislature in 1929 as a Progressive, states that he did not go directly to the Farmer-Labour Group because "each should own his own home and the farmer's home is on his land. Therefore, if this land is leased, his home is leased."[24]

As early as 1932 opposition to land na-tionalization produced a change of wording. The policy became known as "Use-Hold" to emphasize the security-of-tenure aspect rather than state ownership. In July 1933 a motion was tabled by the political directive board that the land policy should be amended "so that occupants be granted the privilege of exchanging their 'Use-Lease' for clear title any time after their indebtedness had been paid in full."[25] A pamphlet from this period stated that the policy aims were to preserve free-dom, individual rights, and dignity of race. The policy was described in detail. All lands being opened for settlement would be held by the state and "Use-Hold" titles would be issued. Lands which had reverted to the mu-nicipalities because of tax arrears would be returned to the original occupant under a "Use-Hold" title after the government had settled with the municipality. Lands on which the occupant could not meet his debts would be made secure for the farmer on voluntary application for "Use-Hold" title. This would occur after debt adjustment and revaluation of the land by an arbitration board. Bonds would be issued on the equities agreed. Those who held a clear Torrens title (a deed of ownership) and were not embarrassed by creditors could carry on as before or apply for "Use-Hold" title.[26] A 1933 pamphlet stated that "despite criticism from the old parties it is not a system of government farming or collectivization . . . use hold title gives every power of the Torrens except that of mort-gage."[27] It could be willed and participation was voluntary. The alternative was perceived to be corporation farming by the finance companies. Thus, the earlier programme to nationalize *all* natural resources had been modified. By 1934 the official manifesto was advocating security of tenure but gave no details of the land policy. . . .

Since it was committed to winning power through the electoral machinery, defeat in the 1934 election accelerated the process of compromise in policy and also encouraged a co-operative attitude towards other reform-oriented parties, especially after the CCF had its first encounter with Social Credit in the 1935 federal election. Fresh from its triumph in Alberta, the Social Credit League began forming constituency associations through-out Saskatchewan with the aim of winning federal representation. Social Credit's mon-etary-reform policy had appeal for those who wanted reform but were frightened by vi-sions of totalitarian socialism under the CCF.

The CCF was campaigning on its imme-diate reform programme which was percep-tively described by the editor of the *Melville Canadian*: "The CCF program of action calls for nothing else but repairs to capitalism. . . . It is pointless to answer that there is a difference between the CCF's immediate action and the ultimate goal. Its proposed repairs to capitalism are not steps to socialism if that's what it wants. They are steps in the opposite direction, steps towards making capitalism more efficient and more satisfactory to the public."[28] Those leaders in Saskatchewan who still believed in socialism feared the compromise and ambiguity of this position. In January, George Williams told Coldwell that there was no place for the CCF as a reformist organization, since there were already two of these. Instead, he claimed:

> ... I do sincerely believe that by being outright Socialists, we will qualify ourselves for power when the Fascist experiment has run its course. It may be a long and weary road. My personal opinion is—the sooner we reconcile ourselves to out and out socialism and all the abuse that term means, the sooner we will be worthy of the crown of success. In this regard it might be wise to err on the side of being rather abrupt rather than err on the side of being too suave, and I feel that our immediate program adopted at our last Convention erred on the side of being too suave. However, that is past, and all we can do about it now is to go ahead and battle as out and outers, and in my humble opinion, this course will prove in the end to be far the wisest course.[29]

Others in the party (notably Coldwell, Hugh McLean, Clarence Fines, and Tommy Douglas) were more prepared to compromise and co-operate with Social Credit in order to prevent duplication of effort by the opposition parties.... Many people were prepared to co-operate with Social Credit because they wanted immediate action and tangible results. They saw little reason for conflict among organizations with reform goals. Hence, the pressure for a reform party to pursue pragmatic policies insofar as it needs the support of the people.

The trend to pragmatic party politics was stimulated further by the failure of the CCF in the election. In Saskatchewan, the Liberals took 16 of 21 seats, while Social Credit and the CCF both won two, the Conservatives taking the final constituency. For the CCF leaders this was the second severe defeat in little more than a year. It was followed by a further decline in the socialist part of the party programme.

At the provincial convention in 1936 a reform platform was adopted which made no reference to socialism and the policy of land nationalization was officially dropped.[30] In the budget debate of 1937 Williams did not mention "Use-Hold" but advocated protection of the Torrens title by limiting the power of the mortgage companies. For example, he suggested that no payments should be made in poor crop years and that the government should proclaim a moratorium on debt when necessary.[31] Thus, the CCF position in Saskatchewan had become similar to what the Social Credit government was actually doing in Alberta.

In 1936 the CCF constitution was also amended to allow for co-operation with any organization for the purpose of bettering the immediate interests of the common people.[32] Having removed the socialism there could be little objection on ideological grounds to co-operating with Social Credit, a course which George Williams and his supporters now advocated, in order to prevent all the reform parties running their own candidates in every constituency. It was felt that such a policy would stop the Liberals winning constituencies on a minority of the popular vote. Nothing more than temporary coalitions was intended by the party leaders, as Williams made clear later in the year: "When the CCF convention voted for cooperation, they just as emphatically turned down affiliation and made it quite clear that the CCF did not intend to sink their identity in a compromise party. They did not intend to give up any of their principles or platform nor do they suggest that other groups should do so.[33] Williams went on to reject Social Credit theory, but added that Social Crediters should not be obstructed too much in their attempt to get a new deal. In this presentation Williams was trying to strike a balance between retaining an image of the individual identity of the CCF and preparing the way for a united front of reform parties. . . .

In accordance with the 1936 resolution on co-operation, Williams and A.J. Macauley had visited William Aberhart, but no agreement was reached at that time. Williams had tried to prepare the ground by encouraging the leader of the CCF in Alberta to stop attacking Social Credit. It was clear to Williams that continued clashes in Alberta would make co-operation in Saskatchewan all the more difficult. However, William Irvine, leader of the Alberta CCF, was not prepared to compromise because he predicted an early end to the Social Credit experiment and did not want the CCF to be associated with such a failure.[34]

In September 1937 the Saskatchewan CCF executive decided to approach the Social Credit League at its autumn convention in Saskatoon with a request to discuss co-operation in the next election.[35] At that convention a motion to receive the CCF message was passed, but then Ernest Manning, visiting from Alberta, produced what seems to have been an instant rule that such a motion had to be unanimous. This determined opposition by Manning may be explained partly by his anger at the persistent attacks of CCF supporters in Alberta,[36] but it is also reasonable to suppose that the Social Crediters retained hopes of a sweeping victory in Saskatchewan after their relative success in 1935 when there was little time to organize. Therefore, the Alberta leaders may have felt that they had little to gain from an alliance with the CCF.

Following its rejection of CCF overtures in the fall of 1937, the Social Credit League announced that its aim was to have a candidate in every constituency for the election expected in 1938.[37] Despite this announcement many in the CCF continued to work for a coalition. Reponding to pressure in the constituencies for joint candidates, the CCF issued a press statement in which it was recognized that there was a popular demand for co-operation and that the CCF, as the best-organized group, was the logical centre for this. Where the CCF was strongest it should not be opposed by others, but where it had little hope of winning it was only reasonable for CCF supporters to find a candidate from another progressive group whom they could back without compromising their principles. The decision whether to nominate or not was to be made in a properly called CCF convention. There was to be no compromise, no fusion party, and no fusion candidates. In addition, the aim of the CCF was still to elect enough candidates to form a straight CCF government.[38] This proposal for limited "saw-off" arrangements could hardly satisfy Social Crediters, ambitious as they were for victory. William Aberhart again rebuffed the CCF's approach for united action. . . .[39]

Following the worst crop-failure year in the history of the province each party was claiming to be in the one which could handle the effects of the disaster. The CCF abandoned any reference to socialism and concentrated on social planning and the protection of the family farm by better debt adjustment legislation, crop insurance, and the like. But when the votes had been counted the Liberal party was once again in control. The CCF leaders were moderately satisfied with their performance. Compared with 1934, their share of the vote fell, a result of placing fewer candidates in the field and the intervention of Social Credit. CCF representation in the legislature was increased to ten,[40] most of which came from east-central Saskatchewan where recent crops had been better than in other regions. For Social Credit the election was a disaster, only two of its forty-one candidates being successful. There was encouragement only in the constituencies close to Alberta, especially Cutknife which was won from the sitting CCF member. . . .

Why did Social Credit fail in conditions so

similar to Alberta of 1935? Lacking data on voters' perceptions of Social Credit, any answer must be speculative. Several factors seem worthy of consideration. The Social Credit League was an imported organization which had to build up from scratch in areas where the CCF had been organizing for years. Also, the authoritarian method of having candidates selected by an outsider was distasteful to the people of Saskatchewan who had not experienced the failure of the United Farmers of Alberta in their attempt at constituency autonomy. Only those who lived close to the border with Alberta had been exposed over a long period to Aberhart's religious broadcasts and to the evangelists who poured over the countryside from his Bible Institute in Calgary. Perhaps most important of all, there was no evidence after three years in power that Aberhart was bringing the promised utopia to Alberta. . . .

While Social Credit received a mauling, the CCF emerged from the electoral conflict of 1938 as the undisputed challenger to Liberalism in Saskatchewan. The earlier rejection by Social Credit of CCF approaches and the party's increased strength relative to Social Credit encouraged a new anti-coalition attitude on the part of the pragmatic CCF leaders. It was now recognized that there was no need to combine with Social Credit in order to win, and so the CCF took a hard line towards further unity proposals, rejecting strong demands in several constituencies to sanction a united front under such labels as United Reform, United Progressive, and New Democracy.

It is important to recognize that this rejection of co-operation with other reform groups did not mean the adoption of a more socialist position by the CCF. The party continued to emphasize social planning and social security; social ownership was to be restricted to financial institutions, some natural resources, and public utilities (all of which was consistent with the agrarian populist tradition of North America). The few leaders

who were still prepared to discuss socialism were careful to define it pragmatically—for example, George Williams wrote a pamphlet in 1939 which begins: "This is not a treatise in Socialism according to Marx, Lenin, Stalin, Henderson, Bellamy or Engels. The writer does not pretend to be outlining a theoretical socialism. . . . The people of Canada are not interested in ascertaining whether a proposed economic system agrees with Marxism, or any other 'ism'; they want to be reasonably sure it will work."[41] In its next test of popular support, the federal election of 1940, the CCF exhibited its growing popularity by winning five of the twenty-one seats with an especially strong performance in the predominantly rural constituencies. Such support was heartening for the CCF members because the party organization had been weakened by the conflicting attitudes of neutralists and interventionists regarding Canadian participation in the war.

For the farmers war had brought only a small increase in the price of wheat, although their income increased since the crops were bigger. In 1941 the CCF supported the farmers in their demands for higher wheat prices. That year the Liberal federal government would only guarantee a price of 70 cents per bushel, while the farmers were demanding $1.00, which they backed up with a petition of 185,000 signatures. This pressure was enough to force the government guarantee up to 90 cents (still well below pre-depression prices).[42] As the only party to give complete support to the farmers in their struggle, the CCF benefitted by having its membership more than double during 1941–2.

The other major event of 1941 was the election of Tommy Duglas as president of the Saskatchewan CCF in preference to a candidate supported by George Williams (who had joined the army and was overseas). Apparently some party members felt that Williams had too much personal influence in the CCF, but the real significance of this event was that it consolidated the reformist pragmatic direction of the party and showed the influence of the urban middle class in the farmers' organization. (Douglas was a Baptist minister and early member of the ILP).

In 1942 a record crop permitted supporters to contribute more to the party treasury, which allowed more intensive organizational publicity. The CCF would probably have won any election called at this time, but had to wait until June 1944 because the Liberal government passed a special bill extending the life of the legislature. This probably added to the liabilities of a Liberal party already hurt by its identification with big business and the depression.[43]

In the critical area of land policy the CCF had changed little since the middle thirties. In 1944 the CCF promised to:

1. Protect the farmer from unjust foreclosure and eviction.

2. Protect from seizure that part of a farmer's crop that is needed to provide for his family.

3. Use, if necessary, the power of moratorium to compel reduction of debts to a figure at which they can reasonably be paid with prevailing prices of farm products.

4. Prevent the growth of debt by placing a crop failure clause in all mortgages and agreements of sale.[44]

Another pamphlet stated that "the CCF believes in the family farm as the basis of rural life" and that it would protect the family farm by increasing farm income through guaranteed minimum prices, encouraging the development of co-operatives, crop insurance, and pressing for the abolition of the Winnipeg Grain Exchange.[45] This was a "conventional" populist programme. Emphasizing this agricultural policy and social welfare measures, in 1944 the CCF took 53 per cent of the vote and all but five seats in the legislature. . . .

Notes

1. For example, S.M. Lipset, *Agrarian Socialism* (New York 1968); Dean E. McHenry, *The Third Force in Canada* (Berkeley and Los Angeles 1950), p. v; Gad Horowitz, *Canadian Labour in Politics* (Toronto 1968), p. 9; David E. Smith, "A Comparison of Prairie Political Developments in Saskatchewan and Alberta," *Journal of Canadian Studies*, 4, 1969, p. 17; Walter D. Young, *Democracy and Discontent* (Toronto 1969), p. 71.

2. Its relationship with the Communist party also demonstrates the party nature of the CCF. See Peter R. Sinclair, "The Saskatchewan CCF and the Communist Party in the 1930's," *Saskatchewan History*, XXVI, 1973, 1–10.

3. UFC (SS) Minutes, 1928, Archives of Saskatchewan [AS].

4. *Ibid.*, 1929. Supporters saw it as 100 per cent control, opponents as 100 per cent compulsion.

5. *Ibid.*

6. UFC (SS) Minutes, 1930, Address of the honorary president.

7. The minutes show that few of the speakers were against direct political action because they had faith in existing remedies or parties. Indeed, some opposed the motion because they wanted an *independent* political party which could unite farmers and workers.

8. UFC (SS) Minutes, 1930.

9. *Ibid.*, 1931.

10. *Organized Farmer and Labour Programme (Sask.)*, 1931. Farmer-Labour Group pamphlet, AS.

11. UFC (SS) Minutes, 1931

12. In addition to the "Use-Lease" policy the provincial government was asked to prevent any more foreclosures, evictions, and seizures; to give the farmer absolute safety on his

homestead quarter; to improve debt adjustment legislation; to undertake a plebiscite on the compulsory pool; and to see that no more new farms were set up in the province. It probably reflects the division in the UFC that much of this policy becomes redundant in view of the plan to nationalize land.

[13] Farmer-Labour Group Minutes, 1933, secretary's report, AS. See also secretary Eliason's personal hardship and commitment to the party in a letter to Coldwell, 2 June 1933, CCF Papers, file no. 32, pp. 3223–5, AS.

[14] *Handbook for Speakers*, 1933, CCF pamphlets, AS.

[15] *Regina Star*, 8 July 1933; and Lipset, *Agrarian Socialism*, p. 136.

[16] *Regina Star*, 6 July 1933; *Regina Leader-Post*, 3 Jan. 1934. George Williams was particularly subject to attack because he had visited the Soviet Union.

[17] *Regina Leader-Post*, 26 May 1934.

[18] *Ibid.*, 5 June 1934.

[19] Coldwell to Eliason, 20 June 1934, CCF Papers, file no. 20/3; Lipset, *Agrarian Socialism*, p. 138, states, "To the CCF leaders . . . the election was a great defeat. They had been sure that they would win. . . ."

[20] Lipset, *Agrarian Socialism, p. 202.*

[21] H.J. Benson, interview, 14 Sept. 1970, in AS, file no. X15/45.

[22] G. Hindley, interview, 21 Jan. 1971, in AS. File No. X15/60.

[23] J.W. Bennett and C. Krueger, "Agrarian Pragmatism and Radical Politics," in Lipset, *Agrarian Socialism, p. 351.*

[24] S.N. Horner, interview, 2 Jan. 1971, in AS, file no. X15/55.

[25] CCF Papers, Minutes, political directive board, 8 July 1933.

[26] *Agricultural Land Policy*, Saskatchewan Farmer-Labour Group (approx. 1932), CCF pamphlets.

[27] *Is your Home Safe?* CCF pamphlets.

[28] *Melville Canadian*, 8 Aug. 1934.

[29] Williams to Coldwell, 30 Jan. 1935, CCF papers, file no. 32, p. 3252.

[30] CCF Minutes, first annual convention, 1936.

[31] George Williams, *Budget Debate*, 1937, CCF pamphlets.

[32] CCF Minutes, first annual convention, 1936.

[33] George Williams, *Cooperation*, radio address, 9 Dec. 1936, CCF pamphlets.

[34] Williams to Irvine, 15 Dec. 1936 and 23 Dec. 1936; Irvine to Williams, 19 Dec. 1936, CCF Papers, file no. 287, pp. 29923–8.

[35] CCF Papers, Minutes, Executive meeting, 11/12 Sept. 1937.

[36] Lipset, *Agrarian Socialism*, p. 144, gives this interpretation, but fails to point out that a majority of Saskatchewan delegates wanted to hear the offer.

[37] *Moose Jaw Times-Herald*, 6 Jan. 1938.

[38] CCF Papers, Minutes, Executive meeting, 19/20 March 1938.

[39] CCF Papers, Minutes, Provincial Council, 16/17 April 1938.

[40] This was quickly increased to 11 when Joe Burton won the Humboldt by-election, an important victory for the CCF in that it showed that the CCF could win in German Catholic areas.

[41] George Williams, *Social Democracy in Canada*, 1939, p. 4, CCF pamphlets.

[42] Lipset, *Agrarian Socialism*, p. 149.

[43] Sanford Silverstein, "The Rise, Ascendency and Decline of the Cooperative Commonwealth Federation Party of Saskatchewan, Canada" (PhD thesis, Washington University, 1968), pp. 77–8.

[44] CCF *Land Policy*, 1944, CCF pamphlets.

[45] *The Farmer and the CCF*, 1944, CCF pamphlets.

68　Quebec Seeks a Villain

Everett Hughes

EVERETT HUGHES (1897–1983) was born in Beaver, Ohio, received his A.B. in Classics from Ohio Wesleyan and completed a Ph.D. at the University of Chicago. Upon graduation, he moved to Montreal where he taught with Carl Dawson in the fledgling Department of Sociology at McGill from 1927 to 1938. While there he wrote *French Canada in Transition* (1943), a classic analysis of the impact of foreign-controlled industrialization on a small Quebec town in the 1930s, which had a major long-term impact on Quebec sociology. In 1938, Hughes returned to Chicago where, save for brief appointments at Laval, Frankfurt/Main, Columbia, Radcliffe and Kansas, he taught until 1961. He finished his career with major appointments at Brandeis and Boston College, teaching briefly at McGill and the Université de Montréal. From 1952–60 he was editor of the *American Journal of Sociology*. Among the more than 50 articles and books he wrote—mostly in the areas of race relations and occupations—his most important works are *Where Peoples Meet* (1952); *Men and Their Work* (1958); *Boys in White* (1961) and *The Sociological Eye* (1971). In recognition of his contribution to Canadian sociology he was made Honorary Life President of the Canadian Sociology and Anthropology Association and awarded honorary degrees by Sir George Williams, Queen's, McGill and the Université de Montréal.

The numerous social and political movements of Quebec show, in a peculiar degree, the tendency to condemn the modern economic world while engaged in the very attempt to obtain a better place in it. Attack upon the foreign leaders of business and industry for their alleged discrimination against French Canadians is combined with hints that their own leaders have not adapted, as they presumably should have done, French-Canadian education to the demands of those same business and industrial authorities. Some account of the manifestations of discontent, drawn from newspaper accounts during the 1930's and from interviews and personal observation, will illustrate these points.

In the early days of the great depression French Canadians in and about Montreal were reported to have rioted and attacked foreign-born workmen engaged in public works. Throughout the decade they continued, occasionally by such action and constantly by word, to express strongly the notion that jobs belonged first to French Canadians. In Cantonville a labor agitator interpreted the "closed shop" to mean one closed to all but French Canadians as well as to nonunion workers.

During the latter part of the thirties the National Catholic Labor Syndicates, hitherto promoted without much success as an antidote to the few unions affiliated with the American Federation of Labor, spread rapidly into industries which had not been organized successfully in either the United States or Canada. This happened at the very moment of the upsurge of industrial unionism in the United States. Many strikes and some violence occurred. The American manager of a silk mill in a small town was kidnapped while playing golf, set across the not far distant United States border, and told to stay in his own country. The American manager of an asbestos mill was ridden out of town on a rail. An inkpot was thrown into the face of the English-Canadian president of Canada's largest textile manufacturing company when he visited a plant where the men were on strike. In Cantonville stones were thrown through the windows of the houses of some English executives during various strikes. In a neighboring town similar treatment was given the French-Canadian manager of a foundry.

Not all manifestations of the discontent of labor took these elemental forms. There were many well-organized strikes, conducted to the end of forcing the employers to negotiate with the syndicates. Even in such cases, the theme of conflict between French-Canadian worker and English employer appeared clearly.

The National Catholic Labor Syndicates, whose leaders co-ordinated, if they did not promote, the unrest and collective action of labor, preach the common interest of employer and workman and decry, in the terms of the papal encyclicals, the development of extreme forms of industrialization. The situation presented the contradiction of workmen striking under the aegis of organizations whose doctrine regards the strike as fundamentally dangerous.

The other important movement of industrial workers developed in this period is the Jeunesse ouvrière catholique. It is organized on the parish basis, with divisions for each sex, to which have lately been added sections for married workers and for pre-working youth. The principle of organization—by parish, age, sex, and marital condition—is not adapted to industrial conflict but to the exercise of piety, instruction, recreation, pilgrimages, and demonstrations. The public activities of the Jeunesse ouvrière catholique consist, in fact, of festive parades and demonstrations. The most notorious was the mass demonstration in which more than a hundred couples were married at once in a Montreal ball park before an audience of thousands of uniformed Jocistes from all over the province.

In this period numerous smaller movements attested the rise of a more passionate

nationalism among the middle classes of French Canadians. The nationalistic theme appeared in organizations nominally devoted to economic interests. Leagues of proprietors, chambers of commerce, junior chambers of commerce (a type of organization recently borrowed from the English-speaking world), and retail merchants' and professional associations flourished. Their resolutions, designed to promote action to relieve the depression, were often strongly anti-foreign in word and spirit. Political groups, dominated by students and young professional men, attacked, in the same breath, the evils of capitalism, British imperialists, Jewish plotters, and American and Canadian financiers, whom they held responsible for the troubles of French Canada. The villains among their own people were party politicians (*politicailleurs*) and wealthy people who allegedly had sold out to foreigners. Again the cry of discrimination in the economic world carried an undertone of criticism of their own elders for not having so adapted the educational system that young French Canadians could compete equally with English. On the positive side, these political movements proposed economic reorganization which would limit the power of financiers, put Quebec resources back into French hands, and develop small industries. Some talked of a corporative state.

A strong current of anti-Semitism ran through these movements. Chain stores, department stores, high finance, and the burden of mortgages, as well as communism, were blamed on the Jews. Anti-Semitic statements frequently occurred in conjunction with complaints concerning the English and American domination of business and industry. This connection appeared also in certain popular demonstrations, although not in all.

A good many street demonstrations occurred in the period. A group, alleged to be students of the French University of Montreal, marched upon and interrupted a dancing marathon said to be operated by a Jew.

Newspapers reported that students of Laval University in the city of Quebec raided houses of prostitution in an access of rage against the demoralizing influences of the modern age. On several occasions Montreal students were reported to have attacked the shops of Jewish news dealers and bookdealers, alleged to be distributors of communist literature and "American obscenity."

The anti-communist phase of these movements reached its peak during the Spanish Civil War. The church took an open stand against the Republicans. In vigorous sermons the people were warned that even minor criticisms of the church at home were the beginnings that might end in the heinous sins of burning churches and murdering priests. When a Spanish priest, alleged by French Canadians to be no longer in good standing, visited Montreal in support of the Republican cause, a crowd, again alleged to be students of the French university, marched to the hall where he was to address an audience of English students. In the resulting disturbances the meeting was called off by the police. For a day or two following, there were reports of street parades with some attacks upon Jewish newsstands and bookshops which were supposed to be communistic. The final act, which seemed to bring the excitement to an end, was the gathering of a crowd of young French men before the office of an English newspaper thought to represent the big businesses of Canada; there the crowd cried: "Down with the English!" "Down with imperialism!" . . .

It also happened, during this period, that two important Catholic churches in Montreal, a cathedral in a smaller town, and a Catholic boarding-school for boys in another small city were destroyed by fire. In the burning of the school some forty adolescent boys, sons of small-town, middle-class families, lost their lives. These distressing catastrophes gave rise to accusing rumors, in which the Jews and the communists were the villains. An openly Fascist weekly, *Le Patriote*, which bore

the swastika combined with the Christian cross, wondered why synagogues never burned. The school fire was laid, by rumor, first to Jews and communists, then to the slow arrival of the fire department, to the carelessness of the aged night watchman and janitor, and finally to the provincial fire-inspection authorities. A similar sequence of rumor followed the burning of the churches.

These smoldering antagonisms were fanned by the activity of a French-Canadian ex-priest who, as an Anglican missionary in charge of a small parish in a distinctly French section of Montreal, carried on a propaganda of bitter attack against what he alleged was exploitation of the Catholic masses by a wealthy church and clergy. This was simply the usual activity of a renegade priest; carried on in the French language and in a French district, it aroused strong feeling. The sectarian Jehovah's Witnesses added their quota by determined distribution of tracts condemning the church and state as ungodly. This, too, was done in the French language and by French Canadians. . . .

It is not surprising that French Canadians were unusually restless in a period of unemployment and world-wide turmoil and anxiety. Nor should it be concluded that this was a period of much disorder and violence; the French Canadians were, as usual, an orderly and peaceful people. Our interest is rather in the objects upon which the malcontents vented their anger.

The French-Canadian culture, like any other, has its traditional objects of aggression, some internal and some external. No culture can operate without pressure upon individuals, a pressure which leaves some feelings of restriction and resentment. They find expression in small complaints, guardedly stated, against even the more sacred rules and authorities. But it is perhaps commoner to vent feelings of frustration upon objects or persons outside the sacred "we-group."[1]

A minority people has constantly close at hand an alien group upon which to cast its troubles. Canada is doubly blessed by having both England and the United States to blame for her difficulties. French Canada has such blessings too numerous to mention. She has had the American continent into which to spill her excess and misfit people; thus she has not had to absorb her own toxic by-products, as must a completely isolated society. That is a fact of another order. On the psychological level, the booming, disorderly, polyglot American world is an all too convenient scapegoat upon which to cast the aberrations of her own people and culture. Upon the English majority of Canada, upon the imperialism of England, and upon the expanding English-American capitalistic industrial economy can be and are placed the blame for both the disturbance of the old order in Quebec and the inferior place of French Canadians in the new order. In addition, the immigration of a certain number of Continental Europeans and especially of Jews has provided an internal enemy and disturber completely outside the range of those things which are held dear or are at least respected. The French Canadians have a whole range of "outsiders" in their very midst. Given the mentality of defense against alien pressure and influence bred by a century and a half of minority existence, it is but natural that French-Canadian eyes should see the hand of cultural aliens in all their difficulties. Whether their eyes deceive them does not concern us in this discussion.

Physical attack of workmen upon the persons and property of managers and other executives is an elementary form of industrial conflict, not uncommon among people new to industrial work. It is relatively rare where union tactics have been developed over a long period. The significant point about these manifestations in Quebec is that the persons attacked were usually English. Of course, there were relatively few French managers to attack. But in the minds of the workers, the foreignness of their employers was more than an incident. This is obvious in the setting of one plant manager over the border. One strongly prevailing definition of labor's troubles has been that they are due to the fact that employing corporations and managers are cultural and sometimes political aliens.

The church has sponsored two movements to meet the problems of labor. They are the National Catholic Labor Syndicates and the Jeunesse ouvrière catholique. The active promoters of both are young priests and centrally appointed laymen; through them the church deals directly with the masses of working people without the mediation of those old allies of the church, the middle and upper classes. The latter, the people who are churchwardens and parish leaders, are a little apprehensive both of the emphasis on the laboring class and of the tendency of the church to by-pass the local, middle-class lay leaders.

Observation throughout the period leads me to conclude that the symbolic Jew receives the more bitter of the attacks which the French Canadians would like to make upon the English or perhaps even upon some of their own leaders and institutions. When French Canadians attack the English, they pull their punches. Long association on fairly good terms had led to a good deal of honest mutual respect between the French and English of Quebec. It is a rare nationalist speech which does not accord the English a rightful place in Canada. The two groups have shared the responsibility of government for a long time. Even though they do not celebrate the same holidays, they both have a strong body of sentiment for Canada. The English are also powerful. Against the Jew, however, attack may proceed without fear either of retaliation or of a bad conscience.

Whether or not this interpretation is correct, many of the accusations made against the Jew in Quebec—with the obvious exception of communist leanings—would be justified in some measure if made against the English. The department stores, chain stores, banks, and large industrial and utility corporations have been introduced and are controlled by Anglo-Saxons. In fact, the Jew in Quebec is the physically present small competitor rather than the hidden wirepuller of high finance and big business. The Jew operates and competes upon the French-Canadian businessman's own level; it is the English who have introduced the new forms of economic enterprise which threaten the French-Canadian way of living and working.

No problem of human behavior is more intriguing than that of discovering why people, when they feel the distress of uncertainty and frustration, lay blame upon one villain rather than another. It is common-enough knowledge that groups of discontented individuals seize upon one tentative explanation of their difficulties after another before they arrive at a stable definition of their situation. A fruitful suggestion is that, in such a case, aggression is displaced upon persons or symbols which lie outside the range of those persons and things which one has been taught to love and respect.[2] They seek in their environment objects which their consciences will allow them to attack and which may be effectively associated with the circumstances from which they think they suffer.

A considerable number of French Canadians have for the past decade or more been engaged in just such exploration. It is by no means certain that the eventual definition of their situation has yet emerged. Among the more severely attacked objects have been the Jew, capitalism, and communism. The symbols of democracy have come in for a more moderate drubbing, but one still severe enough to frighten some Canadians. One must remember that the fact of political democracy is much more important to the French Canadian than is the word. The word has belonged so definitely to Protestant countries, such as England and the United States, or to anticlerical countries, such as the French Republic, that it has a certain non-Catholic connotation. . . .

But whatever villains are blamed, the circumstances complained of remain mainly those which accompany the development of the modern industrial economy, including the American type of urban life and institutions; their threat to the old French economy, rural and town; and the unsatisfactory place of French Canadians in the newer economic system. . . .

Notes

[1] See John Dollard, "Hostility and Fear in Social Life," *Social Forces*, XVII (1938), 15–26.

[2] *See ibid.,* p. 18. for development of the conception of displaced aggression.

69 Poverty and Political Movements

Maurice Pinard

MAURICE PINARD, Professor of Sociology at McGill University, specializes in the study of social movements and political sociology. His books and articles include *Quatre elections provinciales au Quebec* with R. Boily, M. Chaloult, J. Hamelin, A. Garon and V. Lemieux (1969); *The Rise of a Third Party: A study in Crisis Politics* (1971, 1975); *The People and Politics of Quebec: From the Quiet Revolution to the Parti Québécois Victory* with Richard Hamilton (forthcoming) and "The motivational dimensions in a nationalist movement" with Richard Hamilton (1986). Presenter of many papers and lectures both inside and outside the academic community, Professor Pinard was elected a Fellow of the Royal Society of Canada, has received two Killam Senior Research Fellowships, and has served on the editorial boards of the *Canadian Review of Sociology and Anthropology, Political Behavior* and the ASA Rose Monograph Series.

The analysis of the rise of the Social Credit party in Quebec in the federal election of 1962 revealed that there is a stong linear and positive relationship between short-term changes for the worse in one's economic conditions and Social Credit support. Unemployment in the respondent's family, for instance, bears a strong positive relationship to the support for this political movement.[1] On the basis of this, one could be tempted to infer that ... the poor were the most likely supporters of the new party. Is this so? Were the poor particularly strong supporters of Social Credit? ...

It is the hypothesis of this paper that the poor, although they may come to form an important element in new political movements and even may come to be disproportionately represented in them, are not their first recruits.... We suggest that the poorer segments of the population are not the first joiners, but late joiners of mass movements. We are not, of course, the first to suggest this, though there is little sound empirical evidence on this question. The purpose of this paper is to present some such evidence and to try to interpret it.

The survey data have been obtained from a multi-stage stratified cluster sample of 998 Quebec residents nineteen years of age and over. The results presented in the paper are usually based on a lower N: this is generally due (except when otherwise indicated) to the fact that about 14 per cent reported not to have voted, and that another 22 per cent either refused to reveal their vote or did not remember. ...

That misery is not a sufficient condition for protest action has been suggested by many. Trotsky, for instance, wrote: "In reality, the mere existence of privations is not enough to cause an insurrection; if it were, the masses would always be in revolt".[2] Closer to us in time, Key wrote: "A factor of great significance in the setting off of political movements is an abrupt change for the worse in the status of one group relative to that of other groups in society. The economics of politics is by no means solely a matter of the poor against the rich; the rich and the poor may live together peaceably for decades, each accepting its status quietly".[3] Similarly Bell, discounting the importance of mass society in the rise of extremist movements, wrote:

"It is not poverty *per se* that leads people to revolt; poverty most often induces fatalism and despair, and a reliance, embodied in ritual and superstitious practices, on supernatural help. *Social tensions are an expression of unfulfilled expectations*".[4] Turner and Killian argued that "frustration by itself is never a guarantee of receptivity to movements. Long-continued frustration characteristically leads to hopelessness which mitigates against participation in the promotion of any reform. Frustration from *recent* losses or the experience of *improving* conditions is more likely to make receptive individuals than long-continued frustration. . . ."[5]

Let us try to document this general proposition by showing that the poor did not form the basis on which Social Credit grew in Quebec in 1962. . . .

THE POOR AND SOCIAL CREDIT

If poverty is defined as a net income of less than $3,500 a year,[6] the survey data clearly indicate that, unless there was unemployment in the family, that is, a change for the worse in people's economic conditions, the poor were not the strongest supporters of the new movement (Table 1). . . . Those above the poverty level, not those who live in poverty, were the first joiners in the Social Credit upsurge in Quebec, Notice, however, that this does not hold among those whose family had at least one person unemployed.[7] This would suggest that unemployment—and very likely any sudden economic reversal—is a sufficient condition to stir the low-income people out of their low tendency to protest. . . .

The hypothesis can also be documented in a different way for a subgroup in the population. Among farmers, those with medium-size farms were the most likely to have voted Social Credit. Among those who had large farms, the support was small, But those with very small farms were only slightly more favourable than the former.

The relationships observed at the individual level also obtain with aggregate data, thus providing independent tests of the hypothesis. We also found that *economic reverses* in a district—as indicated by the net out-migration rates—were a factor leading to the success of the new party. If we consider now the income *level* of the districts, we find the same curvilinear relationships as the ones just shown.

If the proportion of commercial farms, rather than the average family income, is taken as an indicator of the wealth of a district, similar results are obtained.

Again we found that *changes*—mainly a reduction—in the proportion of commercial farms in a district were related to the success of the Social Credit candidates. When the proportion of commercial farms in 1961 is now taken as an indicator of the *state* of the economy in that district, we find once more that the poorer as well as the richer districts resisted the Social Credit party drive.[8]

An obvious objection could be raised against our interpretation. One could say that Social Credit is a conservative party or, more properly, a party with populist appeals based on an ideology of the right,[9] and therefore it failed to recruit the most disinherited strata of the population, attracting instead some kind of middle-class support. In other words, the party's support would reflect the party's ideology.

We do not think that this interpretation is correct for a multiplicity of reasons. First in occupational terms, the party got the bulk of its support definitely not from the middle class, but from the working class and the farmers. The objection is further challenged if we now add that the party was particularly successful among workers who identify with the working class and not among those who identify with the middle class.

Indeed, in all three occupational groups—non-manual, manual, and farmers—the party got a disproportionate support from those who identify themselves with the working

Table 1

SOCIAL CREDIT SUPPORT BY INCOME LEVELS AND EMPLOYMENT SITUATION (PERCENTAGES)

	Income Groups of Respondents*		
	Low	Middle	High
Vote 1962:	No unemployment in the family		
Social Credit†	16	27	11
Progressive Conservative	40	29	25
Liberal	44	42	3
N.D.P.	1	2	3
N (Respondents) =	(140)	(176)	(150)
	Some unemployment in the family		
Social Credit†	36	32	21
Progressive Conservative	27	28	45
Liberal	32	38	34
N.D.P.	4	2	0
N (Respondents) =	(69)	(50)	(29)

*Low income—a yearly net income of less than $3,500; middle income—between $3,500 and $5,000; high income—$5,000 or more. Actually, in the above, as in the following tables, in order to increase the case base and to make income comparable, those who refused to give their income are classified according to the rent or property value of their home and farmers are always classified according to the size of their farms. The relationship presented in the above table holds of course without these modifications; among those with no unemployment, for instance, the proportion of Social Credit by income groups are: less than $3,000—18%; $3,000 to $3,499—16%; $3,500 to $3,999—28%; $4,000 to $4,999—24%; $5,000 or more—7% (Ns equal to 84, 64, 79, 76, and 81, respectively).

†The probability that this curvilinear relationship could have resulted from chance is smaller than .001. (This test follows A.E. Maxwell, *Analysing Qualitative Data* (London: Methuen, 1961), chapter 4, pp. 63–9.

class.[10] We also found that it got a disproportionate support among the unionized segments of the working class. One cannot, therefore, interpret the greater support of the middle-income group as resulting from a middle-class ideology. . . .

THE PSYCHOLOGICAL AND SOCIAL WORLD OF THE POOR

The literature suggests four clusters of factors that might account for the weak response of the poor. We shall discuss each of them and try to test whether they in fact account for the above findings.

Worry and Hopelessness

Poverty generates, it can be suggested, a high degree of worry about one's future, which detracts from any consideration of long-term solutions to one's problems. A worried person becomes a self-centred individual, for whom everything outside his immediate and urgent needs is of little relevance.[11]

Closely related to their worry is the hopelessness, the fatalism, and despair of the very poor that they will ever escape their miserable conditions. . . . Unless some event occurs that can reactivate their hope, they are not likely to turn to political action. They abstain from politics altogether and become chronically apathetic.[12] To put it in Smelser's conceptual frame, the poor are unable to develop the generalized belief necessary for the appearance of a social movement.[13] Are these some of the processes that actually account for the low support of Social Credit among the poor?

Surprisingly, no differences are found in the degree of worry of the low-and middle-income groups: 27 per cent of the first group as compared to 28 per cent of the second group[14] said that they were much worried "about how they would get along financially in the next year".[15] Nevertheless, the consideration of worry as an additional variable is interesting in that it specifies the curvilinear relationship in a suggestive way. The lower one's income, the less likely one is to be led to protest as a consequence of worry. Although "much worry" has some depressing effect in the middle-income group, the level of protest in that group is still higher in such a case than when there is no worry. On the contrary, much worry seems to lead to the lowest level of protest within the low-income group. In short, worry tends to enhance one's tendency to protest in higher-income groups, while it would tend to hamper it in the low-income group. This suggests that among the poor to worry means something different than among the other groups: for the poor to be in a permanent psychological state, while for people of the middle-and high-income groups, worry would stimulate them to protest rather than restrain them. . . .

It was also suggested that the poor's low ability to protest is due to their hopelessness and resignation. This is supported indirectly by some findings in *Agrarian Socialism*. When the C.C.F. party became successful in Saskatchewan, the poorer farmers and workers fled to it, while they had failed to do so previously. We suggest that their hopes were reawakened by the growing success of the movement.[16]

More convincingly still, Lipset shows that the weaker the Communist parties are in various countries, the less surely can they win the support of the poorer workers. Only where the Communists are the largest party on the left do they receive a strong support from the low-income groups. . . .

Let us document the effects of hopelessness more directly from our survey data. The respondents were asked whether they thought the Social Credit party would have some chances of winning the next *provincial* election, were they to present candidates at that level also. A negative answer can be considered as a rough indicator of hopelessness that the party can secure power and change things. Interestingly enough, the data indicate poor respondents were more likely to be hopeless than those of the middle-income group.

This may of course reflect the lower Social Credit vote in 1962 in the former group. But it is interesting to note the effect of this variation when the respondents' vote intention, rather than their 1962 vote, is considered. Among both those who are hopeful and those who are hopeless, the curvilinearity tends to disappear, indicating some effect of the Social Credit success in the low-income group.[17] So far, therefore, the data support the hypothesis that worry and hopelessness are at least some of the mechanisms that reduce the support for the new party among the poor people.

Sophistication

It has also been suggested that a lack of sophistication is one of the factors accounting for the inability of the poor to translate their grievances in political terms. With a low sophistication a voter is more likely to abstain[18] or follow a traditional path of protest.[19]

Does the lack of a certain degree of political information account for the low-income group's inability to protest? First, as one would expect, the data do indicate that one's political information is positively related to one's income level. For instance, when asked for the names of those occupying four cabinet posts (two provincial and two federal), 39 per cent of the respondents in the low-income group could not report any name correctly, as compared to 28 and 18 per cent in the middle-and high-income groups respectively.[20]

When the degree of the respondents' information is introduced to interpret the poor's low degree of protest, the degree of information again does not strictly speaking interpret the relationship: at equal degrees of information, the poor remain less likely to support the new movement than the middle-income group, although this is particularly true when the degree of information is low. However, the lack of information does reduce the ability to protest among the poor, while it does not among the other income groups....

Social Participation

A third cluster of factors that has been suggested as reducing the poor's ability to protest covers various aspects of social participation. Formal social participation, which permits the development of skills and means that are crucial to build a new political organization, is characteristically lower in the lower classes.... The degree of informal social participation is also more restricted in the lower classes. This may possibly contribute to the poor's inability to protest by making the world outside their immediate concern less meaningful. Furthermore, a social movement, like any other element in a culture, must be diffused, and in all likelihood through some of the same processes as other elements....

In the present data there is no difference between the two lowest-income groups in their amount of informal relations. From the low-to high-income groups, 20 per cent, 19 per cent, and 16 per cent, respectively, had a low degree of informal social contacts.[21] When this variable was introduced to interpret the low degree of Social Credit support among the poor, a relationship of the same type obtained.... The lack of social contacts would reduce the support of Social Credit among the poor, but not among those who are better off.

The same pattern of results obtains when participation in voluntary associations of various sorts is considered. However, a more specific type of participation, i.e., participation in labour and trade associations, seems to have different effects. The middle-income group is much more likely to participate in such organizations than the other two groups.... Participation in labour and trade organization fails to produce a higher degree of support in the low-income group, while it stimulates the middle-and high-income groups, which then exhibit a higher degree of support for Social Credit. Thus, here the low-income group fails to respond to a stimulating factor, and this accounts in part for their over-all lower support for the new movement.

Exposure to Political Propaganda

One might suggest that the low degree of Social Credit support among the poor might be related to their low degree of exposure to the new party's propaganda, either directly through the mass media, or indirectly through participation in different social contexts.

With regard to direct exposure to the Social Credit propaganda on television, the data do not reveal that the poor were less exposed than the middle-income group; if anything, it was the other way around. While only 52 per cent in the low-income group had a low degree of exposure, 57 per cent and 56 per cent in the middle-and high-income groups were as little exposed.[22] But when this variable is introduced as a test factor, a relationship quite similar to the previous one emerges. While all those not exposed to the propaganda were low in their Social Credit support, when people had been exposed the middle-income group was much more responsive than others. Thus the poor, while not less exposed to the party's propaganda, failed to be as much stimulated by it. . . .

The same type of relationship obtains when we look at the effect of social contacts. When the respondents' friends were from occupational groups[23] which were low in their support of the new movement, the respondents from all income groups were themselves low in that support too; but when the poor's friends were from occupational groups which were high in their support of Social Credit, the poor themselves were less responsive to this influence than the middle-income group.

SUMMARY

The data presented support the hypothesis that the Social Credit party in Quebec, as other political movements of both the left and the right, has usually failed to enlist the support of the poor, at least as long as the parties remain relatively weak. An apparent exception is when the poor are adversely affected by changes in their economic conditions. The data indicate that in that case— and in that case only—the poor are the most likely of all income groups to protest. . . .

Notes

[1] See Maurice Pinard, "One-Party Dominance and Third Parties", *Canadian Journal of Economics and Political Science*, XXXIII (August 1967), pp. 358–73.

[2] Quoted by Crane Brinton, *The Anatomy of Revolution* (New York: Vintage Books, 1960), p. 34.

[3] V.O. Key, Jr., *Politics, Parties, and Pressure Groups* (4th ed.; New York: Thomas Y. Crowell Company, 1958), p. 28.

[4] Daniel Bell, *The End of Ideology* (Rev. ed.; New York: Collier Books, 1962), p. 31. Italics in original.

[5] Ralph H. Turner and Lewis M. Killian, *Collective Behavior* (Englewood Cliffs: Prentice-Hall, 1957), p. 432. Italics in original.

[6] The Conference on Economic Progress has defined on the basis of studies by the U.S. Department of Labor that families in the U.S.A. with an income below $4,000 "live in poverty", while those with an income between $4,000 and $5,000 "live in deprivation". See Conference on Economic Progress, *Poverty and Deprivation in the United States: The Plight of Two-Fifths of a Nation* (Washington, 1962), especially chapter 3. It is interesting to note that the main break in the data is at a net income of $3,500, which is close to the above definition for the poverty level.

[7] In his analysis of Gallup Poll data, Alford reports that "the emerging Social Credit party took over the votes of the poorer Quebeckers". This divergent finding may be due to the loose definition of socio-economic status (interviewers' rating from A to D) and/or to the fact that he does not control for immediate strains in the respondents' families as we do. Robert R. Alford, "The Social Basis of Political Cleavage in 1962", this volume, V/15. However, using aggregate data, Irving reports a finding similar to ours (see Table 3). W.P. Irvine, "An Analysis of Voting Shifts in Quebec", in John Meisel (ed.), *Papers on the 1962 Election* (Toronto: University of Toronto Press, 1965), pp. 131–2

[8] It has been argued that the Gaspésie and Bas-du-Fleuve regions resisted the Social Credit tide because they had not been exposed to the Social Credit television propaganda. Since this is one of the poor regions, at least a part of the explanation would also be in their income level.

[9] Very much like Father Coughlin's movement in the United States during the thirties. See S.M. Lipset, "Three Decades of the Radical Right: Coughlinites, McCarthyites, and Birchers", in Daniel Bell (ed.), *The Radical Right* (Garden City: Anchor Books, 1964), pp. 374–446, especially pp. 374–91.

[10] The relationship is maintained if only those without unemployment in the family are considered.

[11] See James C. Davies, *op. cit.* In trying to explain why some workers in France and Italy are not Communist voters, Cantril wrote that many are too much concerned with their own daily personal problems and "just don't see any point in worrying about the political scene because their own private worries are so pressing". H. Cantril, *The Politics of Despair* (New York: Basic Books, 1958), pp. 119–20. See also S.M. Lipset, *Political Man*, pp. 150ff. and pp. 113 ff.; Genevieve Knupfer, "Portrait of the Underdog", in R. Bendix and S.M. Lipset, *Class, Status and Power* (Glencoe: Free Press, 1957), pp. 255 ff.; Donald R. Whyte, "Sociological Aspects of Poverty: A Conceptual Analysis", *The Canadian Review of Sociology and Anthropology* (1965), pp. 175–89; and R.E. Lane, *Political Life* (New York: Free Press of Glencoe, 1959), pp. 224–5

[12] Kahl, in his analysis of the values of the various classes, writes that "the lower-class persons . . . react to their [conditions] by becoming fatalistic, they feel that they are down and out, and that there is no point in trying to improve, for the odds are all against them. They may have some desires to better their positions, but cannot see how it can be done." Joseph A. Kahl, *The American Class Structure* (New York: Rinehart and Co., 1957), p. 211. See also Oscar Lewis, "The Culture of Poverty", *Scientific American* (October 1966), pp. 19–25, especially p. 23.

[13] Strictly speaking, they are unable to reach the positive stages of envisioning alternatives. They go through the negative steps of losing faith in a given normative set-up, but fail to develop the vision of a movement as an omnipotent cure. See Neil J. Smelser, *Theory of Collective Behavior* (New York: Free Press of Glencoe, 1963), especially chapter 5. See also H. Blumer, "Collective Behavior", in A. McClung Lee (ed.), *Principles of Sociology* (New York: Barnes and Noble, 1951), p. 199.

[14] Ns equal to 232 and 261 respectively; for the high-income group, the figure is 21 per cent (N equal to 223) (unemployed excluded).

[15] In these data, as in all those to be presented below, the "unemployed" group of Table 1 is excluded in order to provide a control, since, as we have seen, among the unemployed the curvilinear relationship does not hold.

[16] Lipset suggests however that their hopes were brought out by the uprising in the business cycle. S.M. Lipset, *Agrarian Socialism*, p. 167.

[17] The curvilinearity remains strong among the "don't knows", but we suspect this might be due to two different possible meanings of a don't know answer: "I have never thought about it" or "I am not sure if they have a chance or not." Since the proportion of don't knows is much higher in the middle-income group, we suspect more of the latter type are found among them.

[18] See Robert R. Lane, *op. cit.*, p. 232. He sees the lack of some of the "skills required for participation" as "largely concentrated in the lower ranges of the working class". Also. S.M. Lipset, *Political Man*, pp. 190 ff. Ideological sensitivity was also found to be an important factor of political participation in the International Typographical Union; see S.N. Lipset, Martin A. Trow, and James S. Coleman, *Union Democracy* (Glencoe: The Free Press, 1956), pp. 92–102 and 333–5.

[19] S.M. Lipset, *Political Man*, pp. 150–1; also pp. 122 ff.

[20] Ns equal to 235, 267, and 227 respectively. (Unemployed excluded).

[21] Ns equal to 233, 261, and 223 respectively. (Unemployed excluded.)

[22] Ns equal to 229, 259, and 220 respectively. (Unemployed excluded.) This index of exposure is based on questions asking respondents how often and for how long they had seen the Social Credit party television programmes.

[23] Based on data on the occupations of the respondents' three best friends.

Further Reading

Robert R. Alford, *Party and Society* (Berkeley: University of California Press, 1963). A comparative study of class support of political parties in several modern democracies, based on secondary analysis of public opinion polls.

S.D. Clark, *Movements of Political Protest in Canada, 1640–1840* (Toronto: University of Toronto Press, 1959).

Frederick C. Engelmann, "Membership Participation in Policy-Making in the C.C.F.", *Canadian Journal of Economics and Political Science*, XXII (May 1956), pp. 161–73. An examination of the extent to which Michel's "iron law of oligarchies" develops in a political party that upholds the principle of membership control.

L. Epstein, "A Comparative Study of Canadian Parties", *The American Political Science Review*, LVIII, No. 1 (March 1964).

G. Horowitz, "Conservatism, Liberalism and Socialism in Canada: An Interpretation", *The Canadian Journal of Economics and Political Science*, XXXII, No. 2 (May 1966).

John A. Irving, *The Social Credit Movement in Alberta* (Toronto: University of Toronto Press, 1959). Examines the origin and development of Social Credit as a social movement against the background of social chaos in Alberta in the 1930s. Contains illuminating material on William Aberhart.

S.M. Lipset, *Agrarian Socialism* (Berkeley: University of California Press, 1950). An outstanding sociological analysis of the origin, growth to electoral victory, and the first years of government of the Saskatchewan CCF. As well as being a study of one political party, it makes an important contribution to the literature on social movements.

————, *The First New Nation: the United States in Historical and Comparative Perspective* (New York: Basic Books, 1963). This study of the role of values in the political evolution of the United States is an important contribution to political sociology.

June H. Macneish, "Leadership among the Northern Athabascans", *Anthropologica*, II (1956), pp. 131–63. A study of a pre-literate group with a minimum of political organization.

C.B. Macpherson, *Democracy in Alberta* (Toronto: University of Toronto Press, 1953). A perceptive analysis of the social-class basis of the rise of the Social Credit party in Alberta. The November and December 1954 issues of *The Canadian Forum* contain an interesting review of the book by S.M. Lipset, and the January 1955 issue, a reply by Professor Macpherson.

John Meisel, *The Canadian General Election of 1957* (Toronto: University of Toronto Press, 1962). An explanation, based on a detailed analysis of a variety of factors, of the outcome of the election which ended the King-St. Laurent era.

————(ed.), *Papers on the 1962 General Election* (Toronto: University of Toronto Press, 1965).

Jean-Paul Montiminy, "Les Grands Thèmes de L'étude du pouvoir au Québec", (The Great Themes of the Study of Power in Quebec), *Recherches Sociographiques*, Vol. 7, No. 1–2 (Jan.–Aug. 1966), pp. 245–50, p. 68/67.

Michael Oliver, "Quebec and Canadian Democracy", *Canadian Journal of Economics and Political Science*, XXIII (November 1957), pp. 504–15. An analysis of the influence of French-Canadian nationalism on political ideology.

Marcel Rioux, "Sur l'évolution des idéologies au Québec" (On the Evolution of Ideologies in Quebec), *Revue de L'Institut de Sociologie*, Vol. 1 (1968), pp. 95–124.

P.E. Trudeau (ed.), *La Grève de L'Amiante* (Montreal: Editions Cité Libre, 1956). An important contribution to the sociology of French Canada. Although its main focus is the Asbestos strike of 1949, it throws much light on the structure of power in Quebec and the effect on Quebec institutions of the growth of industrialization.

Norman Ward, *The Canadian House of Commons: Representation* (Toronto: University of Toronto Press, 1950), chapter 7, "The Personnel of Parliament". Pre- and post-parliamentary career data of Members of Parliament from 1867 to 1945.

L. Zakuta, *A Protest Movement Becalmed: A Study of Change in the C.C.F.* (Toronto: University of Toronto Press, 1964).

70 The Modernization of Quebec and the Legitimacy of the Canadian State

Hubert Guindon

HUBERT GUINDON, Professor of Sociology at Concordia University, specializes in the study of political sociology and Quebec society. He has published numerous articles on those topics and has, in addition, co-edited (with D. Glenday and A. Turowetz) *Modernization and the Canadian State* (1978). He has taught at the University of Montreal and has served as Visiting Professor in the Institute of Canadian Studies at Carleton University. Honours include election to the presidency of the Canadian Sociology and Anthropology Association, the executive of the International Sociological Association and the Royal Society of Canada.

THE MODERNIZATION OF QUEBEC AND THE FEDERAL STATE

... The preliminary report of the Royal Commission on Bilingualism and Biculturalism (1965: 125) began by proclaiming a state of crisis in Canada. Deep cleavages were said to exist between the francophone and anglophone components of the country. This alarmist manifesto concluded with the urgency of defining a federal language policy for the Canadian state, its state agencies, and crown corporations that could become the basis to forge a new consensus for the two "societies" sharing a common state.

Some ten years later, in the summer of 1976, the defeat of the federal state's policy was publicly· consummated with the successful resistance of the Canadian Air Traffic Controllers (CATCA) and the Canadian Airline Pilots Association (CALPA) to the implementation of the official language policy.[1] For the first time in Canadian history, to my knowledge, a special interest group was able to dictate to the Crown a "free vote" in Parliament on matters that are not related to issues of personal conscience.[2] That this clause was not perceived as a direct threat to the very essence of British parliamentary democracy is quite revealing. Even more so, when one realizes that this policy had been endorsed by all political parties. Obstacles to democracy do not always come from Quebec.

Such a spectacular "crash" of federal state policy needs to be accounted for. CATCA and CALPA could not have succeeded were it not for the mobilized emotional support of English-speaking Canadians. The prime minister, in his usual somber manner, solemnly proclaimed this was a threat to national unity.[3] Other ministers of the Crown more mundanely stated that they had failed to do a good "selling job" of the official languages policy to English-speaking Canadians (Montreal *Star*, 25–8 June 1976). It might be the proper time to address oneself to the content of the policy, and to wonder whether the policy itself may have something to do with the problems it has generated for the state. Maybe it was doomed to fail.

A critique of the official languages policy might profitably start with a recall of the political and social context within which the

Royal Commission on Bilingualism and Bi-culturalism was instituted. It was established by Prime Minister Pearson after a series of editorials by André Laurendeau in *Le Devoir* (26 August 1961 to 24 July 1963; about 48 editorials in all). His lead editorial quoted from a momorandum written by a French-Canadian federal civil servant for the attention of his French-Canadian subordinates. This memorandum was leaked to the press and in part read as follows: "Since everyone in the Department is bilingual, all reports must be written in English" (*Le Devoir*, 26 August 1961). In this civil servant's mind, this was not a political act, but a suggestion to increase internal administrative efficiency. In the larger political context, such a memo meant, if not speak white, at least write white. In the broader political scene it underlined two things: the unilingualism of the public service, the fact that anglophones could enter the civil service and be unilingual, while French Canadians could only enter government service if they were fluently bilingual. Proceeding from this barrier to entry, it followed that French Canadians were highly underrepresented in the civil service, increasingly so as one moved up the bureaucratic hierarchies of the public service and crown corporations (RCBB, Book III: Chap. 9). The alienating effect of these features for the French-speaking population of Canada towards the federal state was underlined. The royal commission set as a major objective to resolve this contradiction. It therefore sought to define a policy that would increase the use of French in the federal civil service and increase the proportion of French Canadians within its ranks at all levels of its bureaucratic hierarchy (RCBB, Book III: Chaps. 9–10).

Another major objective of the royal commission was also a response to a leitmotif of French-Canadian nationalism of the fifties. This leitmotif concerned the treatment of minorities. Quebec was seen as a model of majority-minority relations, a model that contrasted sharply with the way French Canadians were treated in every other province in Canada. The other provinces, dating back to the Manitoba School Question and Ontario's "Rule XVII," had severely curtailed the legal status of French within their public school systems. In the previous dispensation, when most institutions were territorially integrated within communities, locally financed and administered by local citizens, the English-speaking population of Quebec did have local autonomy and full legal status within the public school system of the state. As a consequence, Quebec was seen as the model for French-English relations, and the commission set out to exhort provincial legislatures to effect changes that would bring the status of French Canadians outside Quebec more in line with the status of anglophones in Quebec, especially as regards the legal status of French in provincial school systems.

These two concerns—increasing the participation and the upward mobility of French Canadians within the federal state's bureaucracies and increasing the institutional support of French Canadians outside Quebec—became the major objectives of the commission's bilingual policy.

Given these objectives, the royal commission could not seriously consider a territorially based language policy (RCBB, Book I: Chap. 4). And without such a policy, it was doomed to become a political irritation in English Canada, and a political irrelevance in a modernizing French Quebec. Unfortunately, social scientists should not underestimate the state's capacity to commit itself to both.

The commissioners appointed to the Royal Commission on Bilingualism and Biculturalism were all fluently bilingual. While this may have ensured its basic commitment to bilingualism, and facilitated the efficiency of internal communication for its members, it certainly constituted a "rare event" rather untypical of what happens nationally at the level of professional associations, voluntary associations, corporations, and even federal-provincial summit conferences.

A sense of "noblesse oblige" can easily permeate a body of distinguished bilingual citizens gathering together to forge a national language policy after a proclaimed crisis in national unity. Having personally achieved the "noble" thing, such distinguished gentlemen are apt to forget that "noblesse oblige la noblesse," not the ordinary common mortal. . . .

While factually incorrect in terms of its report, as a psychological fact it is quite correct to state that the commission generated the impression in the public view that a good Canadian ought to be bilingual. This impression was further strengthened by the commission's recommendations seeking to facilitate bilingualism for federal civil servants. This cast the unilingual Canadian in a defensive moral posture he duly and rightfully resented.

No matter how lofty its ideals, the legacy of the political disaster created by the official language policy is there for anyone to see.

1/ It did not appreciably increase the francophone share of the federal state's bureaucracies (public service and crown corporations) (Posgate and McRoberts, 1976: 141–2) and yet it did give rise to the shibboleth "French power" that becomes the battle cry of the social groups who feel threatened by its implementation.

2/ It is not successful in arresting the accelerated assimilation of French Canadians outside Quebec, nor will it increase the viability of French communities outside the Sudbury-Moncton perimeter.

3/ It hinders rather than facilitates the changes needed as a consequence of the social modernization of the Québécois.

4/ It contributes to a climate of ambiguity for immigrants in Quebec and uncertainty for the large private corporate sector in Quebec.

It is a short list but a major indictment that needs some elaboration.

The language policy and the promotion of French Canadians in the civil service and crown corporations

While the promotion of French Canadians to higher executive positions was one of the major aims of the royal commission, its policies, after a decade, failed to bring about any substantial changes. The number of francophones in such posts increased from 13 per cent in 1966 to 14.4 per cent in 1971. Furthermore, within that increase, it is known that Québécois are highly underrepresented (Posgate and McRoberts, 1976: 141, 142). At that rate, it would take 50 years for the number of French Canadians in executive positions to match the statistical proportion of French-speaking Canadians in the total population. Furthermore, since most of that increase is recruited from French Canadians outside Quebec and, therefore, already bilingual, its political irrelevance for Quebec becomes even clearer.

The failure of the immersion programs to increase the French competence of anglophone civil servants was admitted by the former commissioner of official languages in one of his annual reports (1976).

In short, the number of French Canadians in executive positions is not increasing significantly and the English-speaking civil servants are not becoming significantly more bilingual. Rather than questioning the validity and the nature of the whole language policy, Keith Spicer insists on remaining within a dream world and recommends that the resources be directed towards teaching French to school children. Myths die hard, especially when they are noble ones.

Given the negligible increase in the francophone representation at the various levels of the federal bureaucracy and its crown corporations, one can only wonder what would have given rise to the shibboleth "French power" that underlies the anti-French backlash the official languages policy generated across English-speaking Canada, the backlash that peaked with the CATCA and CALPA strikes.

The backlash, in my opinion, is traceable to one of the basic principles emanating from the royal commission and incorporated in the Official Languages Act. That principle, which can be labelled the 10 per cent principle, specifies that when a French or English minority is sufficiently great (roughly 10 per cent of the population), government services, in such cases, should be made available in that minority's language, whether English or French (RCBB, Book I: Recommendations). When implemented, this principle has systematically brought about ethnic tensions....

The viability of French communities outside Quebec

Framed in response to the Québécois nationalism of the fifties whose grievances with the Canadian political system rested, in part, on the contrast between the treatment of French minorities outside Quebec and the status of the English minority in Quebec, the royal commission, after having documented this unequal treatment, set out as its objectives, not only to redress these historical inequalities, but to insure that Canada be a bilingual country in its geographical totality. Given this objective, it could not and did not conceive a bilingual policy for the country that would be territorially based. It therefore discarded, with strikingly unconvincing reasons, serious consideration of any territorially based language policy (RCBB, Book I: 88). It opted instead to try through exhortation of the appropriate jurisdictions (mainly the provincial governments), to initiate what is called "institutional bilingualism," whose main principle has already been outlined....

Institutional bilingualism: administrative idealism and the sociology of language

With ten years of hindsight, admittedly, it nonetheless somewhat stuns the average intelligence that the royal commission managed to develop a whole series of urgent language policies without any studies on the sociology of language. What the sociology of language involves, simply defined, is a study of language interaction in different kinds of social settings, at the community level, at the level of public space, at the level of voluntary organizations, at the level of institutions, etc. It raises such questions as who becomes bilingual, when, and why. How do bilingual people remain bilingual? When does language become an issue of community conflict? How do language conflicts get solved in minority/majority contexts? When and why do language conflicts become larger societal events and give rise to language movements and counter-movements? When and how do language frontiers shift? What are the consequences of such shifts on local institutions?

Since the royal commissin managed to avoid all such questions in its deliberations and commissioned research, and since it did make specific recommendatioins, one must therefore raise the issue of what were its assumptions about the sociology of language. It is precisely these assumptions that I have labelled "administrative idealism."...

... Its administrative "idealism" as regards its language policy is witnessed by its belief in "institutional bilingualism."

Committed to reinforce the billingual character of Canada, the commission decided on a policy of increasing francophone presence at all levels of the state bureaucracies and agencies. In this it failed as has already been shown. Acutely aware of the historical institutional deprivation of the French Canadians outside Quebec, it assumed that by increasing the institutional supports for francophone life outside Quebec, it would not only right an historical wrong but ensure the "bilingual" character of the country. Is this assumption warranted? This paper argues that it is not.

French communities have indeed managed to survive remarkably well until the recent past. Not surprisingly, the very processes that made this survival possible are becoming increasingly visible now that they are in a state of collapse. What were these processes and why are they collapsing?

The conditions that enabled the survival, indeed the growth, of French communities outside Quebec preceded the massive urbanization and industrialization that has restructured the political economy of Canada.[4] They could and did develop in a rural world of small-scale family farming, sometimes bordering on self-sufficient economies. The church was the pivotal institution of social life, around which small voluntary associations as well as elementary schools could be developed. The bilingual people in such a setting were those who dealt with the "outside" world. Those who lived most of their lives within the community lived it in French. . . .

The industrial setting under which very similar conditions could obtain is to be found at the level of the primary sector of the economy. Labour-intensive industries involved in the extraction process—mining, lumberjacking, or fishing—provided a similar basis for community survival. This Quebec demographic overflow gave rise to what Joy has called the Soo-Moncton belt (1972: chap. 4).

The days of marginal or self-subsistence farming and of labour-intensive extractive industries are over. As their relative importance in the political economy shrinks, so does the economic base of the communities they supported. The increasing productivity in farming has meant an increased need for capital, not farm-hands. Technological improvement in extractive industries equally contributes to a dwindling need for labour. In other words, economic development dooms these communities to stagnation. What made them viable, paradoxically enough, was economic underdevelopment. While one could live out one's whole life in French in St Isidore de Prescott, and many did, no one can live their whole lives in French in Cornwall. . . .

Within the urban context, French Canadians outside Quebec had to deal with an English world: the world of the market, the world of state institutions from the courts to city council, the world of higher education, as well as the world of public space. This required fluency in English. The only acknowledgment the royal commission made to the sociology of language was a casual reference to the fact that people became bilingual because of necessity (RCBB, Book I: 6). Having said this, they dropped the topic, to pursue their normative bureaucratic analysis. . . .

The political irrelevance of Canada's bilingual policy in a modern Quebec

It becomes apparent that language has been working as a sorting device in the allocation of people in English and French workplaces. The institutions dependent on the provincial state became French workplaces and the corporate world remained an English workplace. Both workplaces expanded bureaucratically in the postwar period. The French workplace gave rise to new elites in the public and parapublic sector. These elites were created by the provincial, not by the federal state. In fact, the federal state's own record within its own corporations *in Quebec* is not substantially better (definitely not in the case of airline pilots and air traffic controllers, to name two politically aggressive groups) than the corporate world itself. In both cases, perfect bilingualism is the required passport for upward mobility, when not for mere entry. Within such a context of a rapidly modernizing Quebec, the federal state's language policy was not only politically irrelevant but clearly reactionary. That it led to the progressive alienation of Québécois elites is a glaring fact. The consequence of prolonged and expanding elite alienation had its electoral outcome on 15 November, 1976. On 16 Novenber, though stunned, the federal establishment was convinced that the Québécois did not want independence but good government. Undoubtedly, but from which government?

The inertia of the federal state and its irrelevance, in my opinion, can be traced to the basic thrust of the official language policy. The royal commission's frame of reference precluded it from focusing on the structurally required changes to make the Québécois true partners in the Canadian political economy. Its objectives should have been concerned principally with the French majority in Quebec, not the French minorities outside Quebec. Secondly, it should have changed the language "rules" of the corporate game in Quebec, not imposed uneconomic French TV and radio stations on British Columbia. Its central concern should not have been to try to shore up the collapsing language frontiers upholding vanishing French communities outside Quebec, but to break down unacceptable language frontiers preventing the expanding Québécois elites from penetrating both the federal state's own corporations and the private corporate world in Quebec. Prophetic in its proclamation of an impending crisis in the legitimacy of the federal state, it provided the state with bad counsel when it cavalierly refused to give serious consideration to the forging of a bilingual Canada on a territorial basis. . . .

The royal commission's reasons for not considering a territorial definition of bilingualism for Canada are uncommonly ludicrous. In a nutshell, the commission would have us believe that as North Americans we have the unique cultural characteristic of being very mobile geographically. This, in contrast to Europeans. Mobility as a cultural trait made it impractical therefore to consider seriously territoriality as the organizing principle for

bilingualism. If mobility were a cultural trait, not a consequence of economic variables, why have Maritimers been going to Ontario but not vice versa? Is it that the culture of the Maritimes has this characteristic to a much higher degree than Ontario's? That distinguished Canadians should serve such gobbledegook to the Canadian public in order to dismiss a possible basis for forging a bilingual policy is quite bewildering. . . .

Canada's bilingual policy and the continuing ambiguities: the case of the corporate world and immigrants to Quebec

By refusing to adopt a territorial bilingual policy, the royal commission could not logically proclaim that the main objective of the federal state's language policy should be to make Quebec French in all societal functions, including the language of the workplace.

While the corporate world and multinational corporations may be faulted for many things, they cannot be faulted for not implementing what is not the official policy of the Canadian state. . . .

The American multinationals, in the particular instance we are concerned with, only followed the historical practice that had been initiated by the Anglo-Canadian and British corporate world years before the massive American entry in the Canadian corporate scene. The ratio of British ethnics in Quebec has been declining for more than a century (Joy, 1972: 91–109). If the anglophone proportion of the population in the greater metropolitan area of Montreal has been able to maintain itself, it was by the absorption and integration of immigrants (Joy, 1972: Tables 21 and 26, pp. 48, 59). . . .

The case of the immigrants: a structural analysis

If the federal state, not the multinational private corporate sector, can and must be faulted for refusing to define as a state policy that all sectors of societal life in Quebec should become French, much less can the immigrants in Quebec be faulted for integrating into the economic system and wanting to learn the language of that system. Here again, one sees clearly that the ambiguous situation of immigrants in Quebec is as much the consequence of the language policy of the federal government as the social and political pressures of the Québécois majority.

The thorny issue involving immigrants in Quebec revolves on the fact that roughly 80 per cent of them integrate into the English institutional system and insist on choosing the English school system (Joy, 1972: 57–63). Given the structure of the political economy of Quebec, that this choice is a rational one is not difficult to demonstrate....

The immigrant rationality

Immigrants in Quebec had no dilemma until language became a political issue. And language did not become a political issue in Quebec until the Québécois new middle class needed further outlets, outlets blocked by the language frontier.

While the political function of immigrants in the political economy of Quebec was to ensure the institutional autonomy and the economic hegemony of the English in Quebec, this was not, obviously, their conscious motive. Consciously, immigrants to Quebec, like everywhere else in the world, were seeking to better their economic opportunities. In the case of the postwar, skilled and professionally trained immigrants, the war-ravaged economies of Europe made it difficult or impossible for them to find the same opportunities in their countries as could be found in Canada. In the case of unskilled immigrants, a self-selected group from economically underdeveloped regions within their national homeland, they were immigrating to Canada, Quebec as elsewhere, in the hopes of avoiding the urban proletariat fate or *Lum-*

penproletariat fate awaiting them in Naples, Rome, Athens, or Lisbon. While these hopes were not to materialize for the majority, the hope that their children might escape the proletarian fate by education was kept alive.

In the case of skilled and professionally trained immigrants, integration in the English workplace, where they were needed, was smooth and instant. They came equipped with a working knowledge of English, and their children could proceed through the educational system from primary school to university without interruption. Their career fate was and is linked to the fate of the anglophone workplace and the anglophone parapublic institutional sector. This for two reasons: the first being that the corporate workplace needed external reinforcement to remain English; the second that the French public and parapublic sector was being built from scratch and was not short of manpower.

In the case of unskilled immigrants, choosing the English school system for their children is rationally imperative in order to secure a twofold objective: upward mobility for their children in Quebec and Canada in the corporate world or the anglophone institutional system on the one hand; and, failing that, geographical mobility, through acquired fluency in English, in order to have access without handicap to the whole Canadian labour market....

CONCLUSION: THE PRICE OF NATIONAL UNITY

This essay has argued that the political discontent of Quebec is rooted in and is a consequence of the modernization of Quebec. The provincial state created new elites in the public and parapublic domain of health, education, and welfare. The new middle classes that emerged as a consequence of this institution-building process are confined to the public sector and, because of language, practically unrepresented in the ranks of the large private corporate economy.

While the federal state, through the Royal Commission on Bilingualism and Biculturalism and the consequent Official Languages Act, proclaimed a state of crisis in national unity, it failed to address itself to the core of the issue: the economic underdevelopment of Quebec and the Québécois. Its recommendations, by refusing to consider seriously territoriality as a basis of its bilingual policies, came forth with an institutional bilingual policy, setting forth antiquated institutional arrangements in Quebec as the model for French-English relations in Canada. Concerned with attempting to shore up crumbling language frontiers for the French communities outside Quebec, it failed to address itself to the unacceptable language frontiers in the political economy of Quebec.

The federal state has, ever since, followed a language policy that can only be characterized as a political irritation to English Can-

ada and a political irrelevance to a modernizing Quebec.

There is a price for a new political consensus in Canada, and certain groups have to pay the price. The two unfortunate groups will have to be the French outside Quebec and the English in Quebec.

For Canada to survive, short of the use of military coercion, a new social contract will have to be negotiated. For this to happen, the unequal union, in Stanley Ryerson's apt characterization of the Act of Confederation, will have to be renegotiated. This renegotiation will have to lead to the full participation of the Québécois in their political economy. For this to happen, basic changes in the rules of the economic game as historically elaborated will have to be implemented. These basic alterations will probably have to deal, not only with Quebec, but with the regional underdevelopment of the Maritimes and the monopolization of economic growth in the "Golden triangle" to the detriment of western industrialization. . . .

Notes

[1] The CATCA strike vote was held 15 June 1976; the strike began 20 June 1976 and ended 28 June 1976 (Canadian News Facts, 1976).

[2] Otto Lang accepted "settlement" by air workers 28 June 1976 (Canadian News Facts, 1976).

[3] P.E. Trudeau in a television address 23 June 1976 (Canadian News Facts, 1976).

[4] Much of this section is based on the unheralded work of Joy, 1972.

References

L'Association des professeurs de l'Université de Montréal 1961 L'Université dit non aux Jesuites. Montreal:

Clement, Wallace 1975 The Canadian Corporate Elite. Toronto: McClelland and Stewart

Commissioner of Official Languages 1976 Annual Report for 1975. Ottawa: Information Canada

Dion, Gérard, and Louis O'Neill 1956 Deux Prêtres dénoncent l'immoralité politique dans la province de Québec. Montreal:

Drache, Daniel, ed. 1972 Quebec, Only the Beginning: The Manifestoes of the Common Front. Toronto: New Press

Group de travail sur l'urbanisation 1976 L'urbanisation au Québec. Quebec: Ministre des Affaires Muncipales et de l'Environment

Guindon, Hubert 1965 "Social unrest, social class, and Quebec's bureaucratic revolution." Queen's Quarterly LXXI (summer, 1964): 150–62

———— 1968 "Two cultures: an essay on

nationalism, class and ethnic tension." Pp. 56–9 in R. Leach, ed., Contemporary Canada. Toronto: University of Toronto Press

Jackson, John D. 1973 "Institutionalized conflict: the Franco-Ontarian case." in G. Gold and M.A. Tremblay, eds., Communities and Culture in French Canada, Toronto: Holt, Rinehart and Winston

Joy, Richard J. 1972 Languages in Conflict. Toronto: McClelland and Stewart

Keyfitz, Nathan 1963 "Canadians and Canadiens." Queen's Quarterly 70: 171–4

Porter, John 1965 The Vertical Mosaic. Toronto: University of Toronto Press

Posgate, Dale, and Kennneth McRoberts 1976 Quebec: Social Change and Political Crisis. Toronto: McClelland and Stewart

Rioux, Marcel 1971 Quebec in Question. Toronto: James Lewis and Samuel

Royal Commission on Bilingualism and Biculturalism (RCBB) 1965 Preliminary Report. Ottawa: Queen's Printer

———— 1969 Report. Ottawa: Information Canada

Ryerson, Stanley 1968 Unequal Union. Toronto: Progress

Taylor, Norman W. 1964 "The French-Canadian industrial entrepreneur and his social environment." Pp. 271–95 in M. Rioux and Y. Martin, eds., French-Canadian Society, Vol. I. Toronto: University of Toronto Press

Trudeau, Pierre Elliott 1968 Federalism and the French Canadians. Toronto: University of Toronto Press

———— 1974 The Asbestos Strike. Toronto: James Lewis and Samuel.

71 The Post-Second World War Canadian Society

S.D. Clark

S.D. CLARK, Professor Emeritus of Sociology at the University of Toronto, specializes in rural sociology, social movements and the study of social change. His publications include *The Canadian Manufacturers Association* (1939); *The Social Development of Canada* (1942); *Church and Sect in Canada* (1948); *Movements of Political Protest in Canada* (1959); *The Developing Canadian Community* (1963, 1968); *The Suburban Society* (1966); *Canadian Society in Historical Perspective* (1976) and *The New Urban Poor* (1978). In 1943–44 Professor Clark was Guggenheim Fellow at Columbia University, in 1958–59 he was President of the Canadian Political Science Association and in 1960 he was awarded the Tyrell Medal by the Royal Society of Canada for work in Canadian sociological history. Elected a Fellow of the Royal Society of Canada, in 1975 he became President of the Society. He has been elected a Foreign Honorary Member of the American Academy of Arts and Sciences, and appointed by the Governor General of Canada an Officer of the Order of Canada. Professor Clark has received honorary degrees from Calgary, Dalhousie University, the University of Western Ontario, the University of Manitoba, St. Mary's University and Lakehead University. He has held visiting professorships at the University of California (Berkeley), Dartmouth College, the University of Sussex (England), Dalhousie University, the University of Guelph, Lakehead University and Tsukuba University (Japan). In 1980–81 he was the Visiting Professor of Canadian Studies at the University of Edinburgh.

... It is with an explanation of what has happened to the Canadian society since the second world war that this paper is primarily concerned. It takes off from, and is intended to provide something of a background to, the ideas developed in an earlier paper (Clark, 1970). That paper fastened attention upon some of the consequences of the changes that had taken place in the Canadian society after the second world war and particularly in the decade of the sixties. Here the concern is with the character of these changes as such. Only by an understanding of the forces shaping the character of the Canadian society in the two centuries or more before the second world war can an understanding be gained of those forces shaping its character in the years since. ...

In the occupation of the North American continent and in the development of new forms of economic exploitation and of new modes of living, there emerged new opportunities for individual enterprise in the economic realm and in the political, social, cultural, religious, and moral realms as well. Thus the California gold fields of the 1850s could be viewed as a frontier, or the Toronto suburbs of the 1950s. Such a breaking through of established authority structures, however, was never complete, even in the case of such a wide-open society as that in the California gold fields. Powerful vested interests of an economic, political, social, and cultural sort sought to maintain or to extend their control of the economic, political, educational, religious, and other such markets. In this manner powerful financial institutions or church establishments, for instance, sought to reach out and secure conformity to those rules and regulations which secured their position in the market.

This play of forces between enterprise and bureaucracy, centralism and autonomy, was as characteristic of the development of the American society as of the Canadian; witness, for example, the federalist reaction to the revolutionary consequences of the American War of Independence. In the balance between this play of forces, however, was a very marked difference between the development of the two societies.

The resources of the part of the continent that now makes up the United States were easily accessible, resources that lent themselves to exploitation by individuals acting on their own or by small groups of individuals. . . . For the exploitation of such resources, large accumulations of capital, large-scale corporate forms of economic organization, or support of the state were not required. The United States possessed what H.A. Innis called a "soft" frontier. Empires could struggle to maintain control, whether centred in the Netherlands, Spain, Britain, or, later, in the Atlantic seaboard states, but their control was continuously challenged by powerful autonomous forces in those new expanding areas on the periphery of the established society.

In contrast, Canada, in Innis's terms, was a "hard" frontier. Canadian resources were generally hard to get at: the fisheries of the continental shelf, the fur trade receding ever farther into the interior, farm land limited to Prince Edward Island and the Annapolis, Saint John, and St Lawrence valleys until the peninsula of western Ontario was reached, and minerals hidden away in the precambrian shield or in the rock-bound interior of British Columbia. What was called for in the opening up of this northern half of the continent were massive accumulations of capital, large-scale forms of economic organization, long lines of communication and transportation, and extensive state support.

The development of this empire to the north clearly constituted a threat to the expanding society to the south. It was the fear of encirclement that led to the Iroquois uprising of the 1640s, what can be described as the first American war of independence, and it was this fear that lay behind the long drawn out struggle which followed between the English colonies and the colony of Canada. An economic-political order based upon routes of transportation and military establishments reaching down the Mississippi to the Gulf of Mexico and westward into the Saskatchewan region challenged the very existence of a society growing out from the Atlantic seaboard through rapid population increase and the exploitation of resources which, but for the claims of empires and native peoples, were within easy reach.

On the other hand, a society like that taking shape on the northern half of the continent, dependent as it was upon long lines of communication reaching into the interior, was inevitably highly vulnerable to attack from its powerful southern neighbour. The English colonies, or what became the United States, prospered by a rapid growth of population and the development of a rich home market. The resources of Canada that made people rich, however, were of a sort that encouraged no great population growth and thus no great development of a home market. Settlement interfered with rather than furthered the interests of the fisheries, the fur trade, and later the timber trade, mining, and the pulp and paper industry. What limited settlement of people on the land did take place resulted largely from the interest of authorities, business as well as political and ecclesiastical, who wished to strengthen the claims of empire to the northern half of the continent. Such certainly remained the case until the abolition of the British corn laws in 1846 opened up a market for wheat for the farm communities of western Ontario.

It was this play of forces on the continent that largely shaped the character of development of the American and Canadian societies, from the seventeenth through the nineteenth centuries. Canada had its frontier as did the United States, and out of the frontier experience there developed on the part of the Canadian people the same strong spirit of independence, impatience of authority, local autonomy, democracy, and egalitarianism that was characteristic of American people. But whereas in the United States, or earlier in the English colonies, the spirit of the frontier found expression in the war upon the claims of the native peoples and of empires intruding on the continent from the south and the north and thus furthered the manifest destiny interests of the state and business, in Canada the expression of this spirit threatened the separate political existence of the community and the monopolistic or semi-monopolistic interest of business, the church, and the ruling oligarchy. Thus can be explained the much tighter type of controls of frontier developments in Canada evident in the limitations upon processes of direct democracy, in the greater readiness of the state to intrude in economic affairs, in the very considerable amount of supervision in education exercised through the church or provincial departments of education, in the maintenance of a tradition of élitism in institutions of higher learning and in journalistic enterprises, in the rigorous enforcement of the law in the face of the danger of criminal elements in the population linking up with treasonable elements, and in the encouragement of the efforts of diverse ethnic peoples to cling to their cultural heritage where assimilation inevitably meant Americanization.

What developed in Canada was a very narrow middle class and, almost wholly isolated from the seats of power, both ecologically and socially, a large rural and working class population offered few opportunities for advancement. In the United States, almost every community in the country got itself a bank

and a college, and the credit provided by such a bank or the education provided by such a college afforded the individual an important means of rising into the middle class. Few routes for advancement, however, existed in the Canadian society. Not many persons could become the president of a bank, a railway company, or a university in a country where the number of such enterprises was sharply limited.

It was upon a precarious base that the Canadian society was built; demographic pressures led to an overcrowding of population not only at the rural and working class levels but at the middle class level as well. By the time these pressures made themselves seriously felt, however, the expanding republic to the south had come to provide an important outlet for Canada's excess population. From about 1850 until the 1930s, emigration to the United States made possible the maintenance of a reasonably stable balance between land in the rural areas and a population growing by means of a high birth rate, and unskilled jobs in urban areas and a population growing by means of overseas immigration. More crucial still, however, was the effect of emigration to the United States which drained off those members of the rising generation in the middle class who could not be absorbed within the narrowly based Canadian bureaucratic structure.

This was how, in the century before the second world war, Canada avoided anything like a middle class revolution. There were, of course, widespread movements of protest over the years by dissident farmer and labour groups in the country, and some of them developed a measure of support from marginal elements of the established middle class. And symptoms of unrest within middle class circles were not wholly lacking. It was before the turn of the century that a brash young student by the name of William Lyon Mackenzie King engaged in the first serious brush with university authorities.

Though subject to periodical strain,

however, the Canadian society remained much as John Porter (1965) portrayed it until the second world war. If one were to quarrel with the Porter analysis of this society as it was, it would be only on the score that by seeking to relate ethnic affiliation to the hierarchical structure he tended to obscure the underlying forces producing this hierarchical structure. Members of the British charter group were admittedly very much on the top, but they were on the very bottom as well, occupying marginal farm lands in eastern Nova Scotia, northeastern New Brunswick, and eastern and central Ontario, or engaged in a subsistence fishing industry in Newfoundland. The division of the country into French and English has led to viewing Canadian society too much from an ethnic standpoint. Thus one talks about the "old order" of French Canada as if the society of the past here was in some way inherently different from the society of the rest of the country. In truth, the rural and working class masses of French Canada were caught up in a social system denying them opportunities for advancement not essentially different from the social system in which the rural and working masses of English-speaking Canada were caught up.

The recognition of this fact gives new meaning, it seems to me, to those developments which have taken place in the years since the second world war in English-speaking and French-speaking Canada, events called, in French-speaking Canada, the "quiet revolution." What emerged after the war was a new Canadian society, one characterized by a widespread movement of people out of rural and unskilled working class levels of the population into middle class levels.

It was the war itself that initiated these far-reaching changes in the Canadian society. The first world war had been a gentleman's war. What it required were officers with the capacity to command and troops so unaware of what was occurring that they had no choice but to obey. But the second world war, as it progressed, challenged the technological skills

and inventive genius of the opposing sides. Canada's role in the war, with its emphasis upon the antisubmarine campaign in the Atlantic and the struggle in the air and its provision of massive supplies of war materials, called for the sudden creation of a large and highly trained labour and military force. What was involved was a transformation of the country's class structure almost overnight.

Had these forces of social change generated by the war died out with the war's end, the old order of Canadian society might have reestablished itself without experiencing too much strain. But the forces unleashed by the war, instead of dying out, gathered in strength in the twenty years that followed. Massive shifts of population from the country to the city and from the city to the suburbs, and large-scale immigration from Europe and from other overseas countries, increasing United States investment in Canada, the reversal of the trend of Canadians moving to the US to one of Americans moving to Canada, the emergence of new and expanding types of business enterprises such as household finance, construction, and housebuilding offering opportunities for rapid economic advancement to elements of the population hitherto unprivileged, the increased intrusion of women into the labour force, and the enormous expansion of facilities of higher education in the country were developments that did much more than simply reflect a growing state of economic expansion and prosperity. They brought about an enormous broadening of the base of the Canadian middle class. There were people left behind: impoverished farmers and fishermen in Atlantic Canada and other areas of the country who clung to a marginal form of economic production, the unskilled of the city driven into dead-end types of occupation, the native Indian and Eskimo. But the years 1945–60 witnessed nevertheless a great upward socioeconomic movement of Canadian people.

The new middle class produced by postwar economic growth had made it the hard way: the farm or working class boy who put himself through medical college by earnings from odd jobs, the Italian immigrant who, during the lunch break, learnt the trade of plasterer by working on the inside of the clothes closets in houses under construction and went on to become a successful dry wall contractor, the Jewish hawker of second hand goods who, by speculation in land or engaging in loan finance, made a small fortune and came to live in a smart suburb, the French Canadian migrant from the land who by the acquisition of a second-hand truck built up a transportation firm and branched out into the motel business, the German immigrant who started out building one house on speculation and ended up building whole subdivisions, and so on. There was no carping among people such as these about American investment in Canada, the irrelevance of what educational institutions had to offer, the arrogance of a government establishment, or the meaninglessness of the amenities of a middle class way of life. These were attributes of the society which made possible the good fortune enjoyed.

What was apparent in the years after the war was a vast widening of opportunities for individual enterprise and social advancement. Finance and trust companies now competed with the country's major banks, trucking firms drew traffic away from the two giant railway companies, housebuilding became one of the country's major industries and in it no large-scale corporation could exert a dominant control, new universities grew up to compete with the old and the old only succeeded in remaining in existence by opening their doors to vastly increased numbers.

At the same time, of course, there proceeded mergers and consolidations, the taking over of the small by the large in the social and cultural as well as in the economic realm, and out of these developments emerged the spectre of United States imperialism and the multinational corporation. The decade of the 1950s was one, however, in which few peo-

ple could become seriously concerned about such developments. The large inflow of American capital in Alberta, Quebec, and, indeed, all across the country meant conditions of economic, social, and cultural expansion which secured the upward movement of great masses of population into a middle class social world. For this population there could be no reason for waging war upon a social system that offered to it opportunities for advancement hitherto far beyond reach.

For those young people growing up after the war, however, the struggle for position in the postwar Canadian society assumed a very different guise. This generation, with the high birth rate that followed the war, came along in vast numbers, and however buoyant may have appeared the Canadian economy and however bountiful the opportunities for economic and social advancement, there seemed now no assured means of securing and maintaining an acceptable socioeconomic position in the society, and emigration to the United States no longer offered itself as a possible or inviting means of seeking a way up.

It was in the universities, vastly swelled in population, that the pressure on this new rising generation to "make it" were most fully felt. A generation which had made it into a middle class social world the hard way was determined that the socioeconomic status it had attained should not be lost by the generation coming after. In the sixties many thousands of young men and women were pushed into the universities to secure the qualifications required to maintain a middle class way of life.

The response to such pressures took many seemingly contradictory forms. One response, represented in its extreme form by the hippy movement, was simply to drop out, to refuse to qualify for a middle class way of life by means of vocational training, the acceptance of polite manners of speech and behaviour, and conventional morality. Another response was by raising the flag of revolution, determining to bring down the whole social system, beginning with the universities. Still another found expression in the effort to soften the demands made by the university and thus make less rigorous those qualifications required for a postuniversity career.

What was characteristic of all these various responses was the extent to which they developed out of the feelings of frustration of middle class youngsters seeking to make their way in a social world in which opportunities for advancement appeared to be severely limited. It was not the poor farm or working class boy who led the attack upon the social system, though if the demands made upon him by that system could be made more agreeable he not unwillingly joined in the attack. Couched in a language that appeared to make an appeal to the downtrodden and oppressed, the ideology that found expression in the gathering movements of protest of the sixties arose out of the fears and striving of a body of young people, vastly increased in numbers, which had been suddenly pitched into a middle class social world with no certain means in sight of being made fully a part of it.

Nowhere was this fact more apparent than in French Canada. Here the postwar economic upsurge had led to a widespread movement of French-speaking people out of marginal farming areas or unskilled forms of industrial employment into middle class types of work or business enterprise, but for the generation coming after, with large numbers being equipped in the universities with the kind of education that gave them a claim to a middle class way of life, the route into a middle class social world was largely blocked by an English-speaking establishment. In the mounting attack upon this establishment, language offered itself as the most effective instrument with which to press the claims of those who now wanted to be made a part of it.

Outside French Canada the lines of battle could not be so clearly drawn. There existed here as well, of course, something that could be called an establishment, and well before it figured prominently in the language of the university student its sinister associations had been masterfully exploited by Mr Diefenbaker in his attack upon the Liberal government in Ottawa. In English-speaking Canada, however, no attack upon such an establishment could be successfully mounted in ethnic terms, however much John Porter's analysis had sought to establish its close relationship to the British charter group.

Thus it was in English-speaking Canada that American imperialism and the multinational corporation were seized upon as the major representative of the establishment. For the French-speaking graduate of the Quebec university the claims of language could serve as a telling case for pushing out the English-speaking member of the establishment to make room for himself, but in English-speaking Canada any effort to take over the establishment had to be made in terms of the claims of nationalism.

Given this basis for the developing movement of Canadian nationalism, it is not too difficult to understand why some of its most vigorous exponents should seize upon a left-wing ideology as a means of realizing its ends. It was here, in the endorsement of such an ideology, that the nationalist movements of the sixties, in French-speaking and English-speaking Canada, came close to joining ranks and gaining a popular following. In English-speaking Canada the half-century development of powerful international trade unions had made labour leadership in that part of the country very much a part of the establishment, but in French-speaking Canada, where international trade unionism had gained only a weak foothold and the new movement of trade unionism secured much of its leadership from university graduate schools of industrial relations, nationalism imbedded in a left-wing political ideology could make a strong appeal. Ultimately, among that large body of labour in English-speaking Canada which was not reached by the international trade unions, there was fertile ground for the development of forms of trade union organization that linked a militantly nationalistic outlook to a left-wing ideology. It was to this element of Canadian labour that the Waffle wing of the New Democratic Party could make a strong appeal.

Thus, in English-speaking and French-speaking Canada, the developing movement of Canadian nationalism secured what can be described as grass roots support. But whether the constituency was composed of bodies of students gathered together in the Canadian universities, school teachers, nurses or other such professional groups, or workers in construction or service industries like the post office, what was clearly apparent was that the leadership of the Canadian nationalist movements of the sixties and into the seventies came from that generation of middle class youngsters who entered the Canadian scene in the sixties. It was the role played by these persons, seeking to make a place for themselves in the business, political, educational, and labour establishment, which gave to the movements of the sixties the character of a middle class revolution.

To say this is not to suggest that the movements of the sixties were motivated simply by selfish interests or that the ends they sought to achieve carried no benefits for the great mass of Canadian people. Rather, I would argue that they represented the second important stage of what can be called the quiet revolution in Canadian society. The first stage was marked by the great movement up of the Canadian people which came with the economic growth following the second world war. What was evident in this stage was the development outside of the establishment of a great number of new types of enterprise—business, educational, and so on. The elite that John Porter wrote about now found crowding into its ranks vast numbers of new people propelled upwards in the social hierarchy.

No society, however, can absorb an oncoming generation of middle class people unless it has the means to expand the career opportunities appropriate for such people, and, as a result of the high birth rate after the war, the problem of absorbing this rising generation was particularly acute in the sixties. Thus the second stage of the quiet revolution was marked, not by the development of new types of enterprise outside the establishment, but by a direct assault on the establishment itself. The consequence of such an assault, to the extent that it was successful, was a broadening still further of the base of the Canadian middle class.

It is here, in the broadening of the base of the middle class, that the real gains for the Canadian people at large are made. What in effect is wanted, if the end in sight is the much greater diffusion of wealth and power in the society, is not the breaking down of the establishment but its speading out to the point where virtually everyone is made a part of it. Whether that is brought about in the name of socialism or liberal democracy is of little consequence. . . .

Reference

Clark, S.D. 1970 "Movements of protest in post-war-Canadian society." Transactions of the Royal Society of Canada, Fourth Series, 8: 223–37

Davis, Arthur K. 1971 "Canadian society as hinterland versus metropolis." Pp 6–32 in Richard J. Ossenberg (ed.), Canadian Society: Pluralism, Change, and Conflict. Scarborough, Ont.: Prentice-Hall.

Horowitz, Irving Louis 1973 "The hemispheric connection: a critique and corrective to the enterpreneurial thesis of development with special emphasis on the Canadian case." Queen's Quarterly 80 (3): 327–59

Lipset, Seymour Martin 1970 Revolution and Counter-revolution: Change and Persistence in Social Structures. New York: Doubleday.

Porter, John 1965 The Vertical Mosaic. Toronto: University of Toronto Press.

P. 4. Robert Brym, "Foundations of Sociological Theory." Unpublished piece; by permission of the author.

P. 13. Courtesy, *The Canadian Encyclopedia*, s.v. "sociology."

P. 17. From *First Sociology* by Kenneth Westhues, (New York: McGraw-Hill, 1982) pp. 20, 21–23, 26–29. By permission of the McGraw-Hill Book Company.

P. 23. From S.D. Clark, *Canadian Society in Historical Perspective* (Toronto: McGraw-Hill Ryerson Ltd., 1976), pp. 5–14. By permission of the author.

P. 31. From "Approaches Toward a 'Canadian Society'" by Wallace Clement in *Alternate Routes: A Critical Review*, 1 (1977), pp. 1–37. By permission of Alternate Routes Collective and the author.

P. 46. Courtesy, *The Canadian Encyclopedia*, s.v. "culture."

P. 49. From Chapter 1 of M. Patricia Marchak's *Ideological Perspectives on Canada*, 3rd ed., (Toronto: McGraw-Hill Ryerson Ltd., 1988). By permission of the publisher.

P. 58. From "Historical Traditions and National Characteristics: Comparative Analyses of Canada and the United States" by S.M. Lipset in *Canadian Journal of Sociology*, 11, 2 (Spring 1986), pp. 113–155. By permission of the publisher.

P. 78. From "Novelty Items as Cultural Artifacts" by Harry Hiller in *Journal of Canadian Culture*, 1 (1984), pp. 110–118. By permission of the publisher.

P. 85. From A.R. Gillis, Madeline Richards and John Hagan,"Ethnic Susceptibility to Crowding" in *Environment and Behavior*, Vol. 18, No. 6 (November 1986), pp. 683–706. Copyright © 1987 by Sage Publications, Inc. Reprinted by permission of Sage Publications, Inc.

P. 98. From "Socialization: Changing Views of Child Rearing and Adolescence" by Marlene Mackie in *The Family: Changing Trends in Canada*, ed. Maureen Baker (Toronto: McGraw-Hill Ryerson Ltd., 1984) pp. 35–62. By permission of the publisher.

P. 111. From "Exchange, Cooperation and Competition" by Peter Archibald in his *Social Psychology as Political Economy* (Toronto: McGraw-Hill Ryerson, 1978), pp. 98–122. Reprinted by permission of the publisher.

P. 124. From "Perceptions of Social Inequality among Public School Children" by Bernd Baldus and Verna Tribe in *Canadian Review of Sociology and Anthropology*, 15, 1 (February 1978), pp. 50–60. By permission of the publisher.

P. 133. Edited from Chapter 9, *Crestwood Heights* by John R. Seeley, R. Alexander Sim and Elizabeth W. Loosley (New York: John Wiley and Sons, 1967). Omissions indicated by ellipses. Copyright © Canada, 1956 by the University of Toronto Press. By permission of the University of Toronto Press.

P. 139. From "The Professionalization of Medical Students" by Jack Hass and William Shaffir in *Symbolic Interaction*, 1 (Fall, 1977), pp. 77–88. Reproduced by permission of JAI Press Inc.

P. 154. From "Law, Conflict and Order: From Theorizing Toward Theories" by Austin Turk in *Canadian Review of Sociology and Anthropology*, 13, 3 (August 1976), pp. 282–294. By permission of the publisher.

P. 168. From John Hagan, *The Disreputable Pleasures: Crime and Deviance in Canada*, 2nd ed. (Toronto: McGraw-Hill Ryerson, 1984) pp. 46–55, 117–118, 147–149. By permission of the publisher.

P. 176. From "Public Deviance: An Experimental Study" by T. Gabor, J. Strean, G. Singh and D. Varis; reprinted by permission from the *Canadian Journal of Criminology*, 28, 1 (January 1986), pp. 17–29. Copyright by the Canadian Criminal Justice Association.

P. 183. Reprinted from E. Leyton, "A Social Profile of Sexual Mass Murderers" in T. Fleming and L.A. Visano, eds., *Deviant Designations: Crime, Law and Deviance in Canada* (Toronto: Butterworths, 1983), pp. 98–107. By permission of the publisher and the author.

P. 191. From Colin H. Goff and Charles H. Reasons, *Corporate Crime in Canada* (Scarborough: Prentice-Hall Canada Inc., 1978), pp. 2–15. By permission of the publisher.

P. 204. Reprinted from *Social Forces* (60, September 1981, pp. 188–210). "Secret Societies and Social Structure" by Bonnie Erickson. Copyright © 1981 by The University of North Carolina Press.

P. 213. From "Demographic Aspects of Career Mobility" by Lorne Tepperman in *Canadian Review of Sociology and Anthropology*, 12, 2 (May 1975), pp. 163–172. By permission of the publisher.

P. 224. From "Sociability and Social Interaction" by Marcel Rioux in G. Gold and M.A. Tremblay, eds., *Communities and Culture in French Canada* (Toronto: Holt, Rinehart and Winston, 1973), pp. 154–163. By permission of the author.

P. 232. From "Lowering 'the Walls of Oblivion'" by Brian Osborne and Robert Pike in *Canadian Papers in Rural History*, Vol. IV, Donald H. Akenson, ed. (Gananoque, Ontario: Langdale Press, 1984), pp. 200–225. By permission of the publisher.

P. 245. From Robert Prus, "Price Setting as Social Activity," in *Urban Life*, 14, 1 (April 1985), pp. 59–93. Copyright © 1985 by Sage Publications, Inc. Reprinted by permission of Sage Publications, Inc.

P. 262. From "Stratification and conflict between ethnolinguistic communities with different social structures" by Raymond Breton in *Canadian Review of Sociology and Anthropology*, 15, 2 (1978), pp. 148–157. By permission of the publisher.

P. 273. Paul Bernard and Jean Renaud, "Les nouveaux visages de l'inegalité," trans. Jack Veugelers, in *Le*

Devoir, 4 February 1982, p. 18. By permission of the publisher.

P. 277.   From "Teachers and the evolving structural context of economic and political attitudes in Quebec" by Raymond Murphy in *Canadian Review of Sociology and Anthropology*, 18, 2 (1981), pp. 279–295. By permission of the publisher.

P. 291.   From "Merchants against Industry" by R.J. Richardson in *Canadian Journal of Sociology*, 7, 3 (1982), pp. 279–295. By permission of the publisher.

P. 302.   Edited from "Mobility Deprivation through Education Deprivation" by John Porter in his *The Vertical Mosaic: An Analysis of Social Class and Power in Canada* (Toronto: University of Toronto Press, 1965), pp. 49–59. Omissions indicated by ellipses. By permission of the publisher.

P. 315.   From "Chinese immigrants on the Canadian prairie, 1910–47" by Peter S. Li in *Canadian Review of Sociology and Anthropology*, 19, 4 (1982), pp. 527–540. By permission of the publisher.

P. 324.   Published by permission of Transaction, Inc., from "The Ethnic Sub-Economy: Explication and Analysis of a Case Study of the Jews in Montreal" by Morton Weinfeld in *Contemporary Jewry*, vol. 6, no. 2 (1983), pp. 6–25. Copyright © 1983 by Transaction, Inc.

P. 334.   Reprinted from R.M. Bienvenue, "Colonial Status: The Case of Canadian Indians" in R.M. Bienvenue and J. Goldstein, *Ethnicity and Ethnic Relations in Canada*, 2nd ed. (Toronto: Butterworths, 1985), pp. 199–214.

P. 343.   From "Racial Attitudes of Canadians" by Ronald D. Lambert and James Curtis in *Past and Present*, February 1985, pp. 2–4. Copyright © 1985 by R.D. Lambert and J. Curtis. By permission of the authors.

P. 349.   From "Another Look at Ethnicity, Stratification and Social Mobility" by Gordon Darroch in *Canadian Journal of Sociology*, 4, 1 (Winter 1979), pp. 1–25. By permission of the publisher.

P. 365.   From "The Domestic Economy" by Martin Meissner in *Women's Worlds: From the New Scholarship*, edited by Marilyn Safir, Martha T. Mednick, Dafne Izrael and Jesse Bernard. Copyright © 1985 by Praeger Publishers. Reprinted and abridged by permission of Praeger Publishers.

P. 373.   From an unpublished paper; by permission of the author.

P. 385.   This is a slightly revised version of a paper presented to Bethune College Annual Conference, York University: "Unemployment: Causes, Consequences and Cures," Toronto, March 5–7, 1984. By permission of the author.

P. 394.   This article originally appeared in *Canadian Woman Studies/les cahiers de la femme*, Vol. 3, No. 4 (Summer 1982), pp. 13–17. By permission of publisher and author.

P. 400.   Excerpted from William Michelson, "The Daily Routines of Employed Spouses as a Public Affairs Agenda," *Public Affairs Report*, Vol. 26, August 1985, No. 4. (A publication of the Institute of Governmental Studies, University of California, Berkeley.)

P. 415.   From "Women, Class and Family" by Dorothy E. Smith. An unpublished paper, from original SSHRC collection; by permission of the author.

P. 427.   From "Models of the Family" by Margrit Eichler in *Canadian Journal of Sociology*, 6 (1981), pp. 367–388. By permission of the publisher.

P. 436.   From "Marital Satisfaction Over the Life Cycle" by Eugen Lupri and James Frideres in *Canadian Journal of Sociology*, 6 (1981), pp. 283–305. By permission of the publisher.

P. 449.   Edited from "On the Wholesomeness of Marriage" by Nathan Keyfitz. An unpublished paper; by permission of the author.

P. 463.   From "Demographic Change and the Family" by Roderic P. Beaujot and Kevin McQuillan in *Canadian Journal of Sociology*, 21, 1 (Spring 1986), pp. 57–69. By permission of the publisher.

P. 472.   From Jean E. Veevers, *Childless by Choice* (Toronto: Butterworths, 1980), pp. 155–169. By permission of the author.

P. 483.   From "Foreign ownership and the myths about Canadian development" by Gordon Laxer from *Canadian Review of Sociology and Anthropology*, 22, 3 (1985), pp. 311–344. By permission of the publisher.

P. 497.   From "The Canadian Multinationals" by Jorge Niosi in *Multinational Business*, 10, 2 (1982); The Economist Publications Ltd., 40 Duke Street, London W1A 1DW, UK.

P. 506.   From "Politics and Moral Causes in Canada and the United States" by Mildred A. Schwartz in *Comparative Social Research*, 4 (1981), pp. 65–90. By permission of JAI Press Inc.

P. 518.   From "Voter Motivation in Canada and the United Kingdom" by R. Ogmundson and M. Ng from *Canadian Journal of Sociology*, 7, 1 (Winter, 1982), pp. 41–59. By permission of the publisher.

P. 528.   From "The political ideology of the Canadian capitalist class" by Michael Ornstein in *Canadian Review of Sociology and Anthropology*, 23, 2 (1986), pp. 182–209. By permission of the publisher and the author.

P. 548.   From "Student Perception of Teachers' Pets and Class Victims" by Wilfred B. Martin in *Canadian Journal of Education*, 9, 1 (Winter 1984), pp. 89–99. By permission of the Canadian Society for the Study of Education.

P. 554.   From "Educational Reform in Quebec" by Pierre Belanger. An unpublished paper; by permission of the author.

P. 565.   From "Changing patterns of educational inequality in Canada" by N. Guppy, P.D. Mikicich and R. Pendakur in *Canadian Journal of Sociology*, 9, 4 (Fall 1984), pp. 319–331. By permission of the publisher.

P. 571. From "Changing Conceptions of Education and Social Mobility" by C. James Richardson in *Canadian Journal of Sociology*, 2, 4 (Fall 1977), pp. 417–433. By permission of the publisher.

P. 583. From "Post-industrialism and Postsecondary Education" by John Porter in *Canadian Public Administration*, 14 (Spring 1971), pp. 32–50. By permission of the Institute of Public Administration of Canada.

P. 595. From "'The Labour Force' is an Ideological Structure" by Lorna R. Marsden in *Atlantis*, 7, 1 (Fall 1981), pp. 57–64. By permission of the publisher.

P. 601. From R.V. Ericson, *Making Crime: A Study of Detective Work* (Toronto: Butterworths, 1981), pp. 1–22. By permission of the publisher and the author.

P. 611. Reprinted from G.S. Lowe, "The Administrative Revolution in the Canadian Office: An Overview" in K.L.P. Lundy and B. Warme (eds.), *Work in the Canadian Context: Continuity Despite Change*, 2nd ed. (Toronto: Butterworths, 1986), pp. 100–120. By permission of the publisher.

P. 622. James W. Rinehart, "Alienated Labour," from Chapter 2 and pp. 208–210 in his *The Tyranny of Work*, 2nd ed. Copyright © 1987 by Harcourt Brace Jovanovich Canada Inc. Reprinted by permission of the publisher.

P. 630. From Chapter 10, pp. 205–289 of J.D. House, *The Challenge of Oil: Newfoundland's Quest for Controlled Development*, Social and Economic Studies #30, Institute for Social and Economic Research, Memorial University, 1985.

P. 642. Courtesy, *The Canadian Encyclopedia*, s.v. "community."

P. 644. Barry Wellman and Barry Leighton, "Networks, Neighborhoods and Communities," *Urban Affairs Quarterly*, 14, 3 (March 1979), pp. 363–390. Copyright © 1979 by Sage Publications, Inc. Reprinted by permission of Sage Publications, Inc.

P. 656. From "The Making of a 'Problem Community'" by Donald H. Clairmont and Dennis W. Magill in Chapter 4 of their *Africville: The Life and Death of a Canadian Black Community* (Halifax: The Institute of Public Affairs, Dalhousie University, 1974). By permission of the authors.

P. 663. From Rex Lucas, *Minetown, Milltown, Railtown: Life in Canadian Communities of Single Industry* (Toronto: University of Toronto Press, 1971), pp. 390–408. Omissions indicated by ellipses. By permission of the publisher and the author.

P. 671. From "The Class Dimensions of Regionalism" by Carl J. Cuneo, Dept. of Sociology, McMaster University, Hamilton, Ont., L8S 4M4. By permission of the author.

P. 688. Edited from "The Saskatchewan CCF: Ascent to Power and the Decline of Socialism" by Peter R. Sinclair in *Canadian Historical Review*, 54, 4 (December 1973), pp. 419–433. Omissions indicated by ellipses. By permission of the University of Toronto Press and the author.

P. 697. From "Quebec Seeks a Villain" by Everett Hughes in Chapter 19 of his *French Canada in Transition* (Chicago: University of Chicago Press, 1943). By permission of the publisher and the author.

P. 702. Copyright © 1967 by The Society for the Study of Social Problems. Reprinted from *Social Problems*, Vol. 15, No. 2, Fall 1967, pp. 250–263, by permission.

P. 711. From "The Modernization of Quebec and the Legitimacy of the Canadian State" by Hubert Guindon in *Canadian Review of Sociology and Anthropology*, 15, 2 (1978), pp. 227–245. By permission of the publisher.

P. 720. From "The Post Second World War Canadian Society" by S.D. Clark in *Canadian Review of Sociology and Anthropology*, 12, 1 (1975), pp. 25–32. By permission of the publisher.